Critical acclaim for t

"[The Berkeley Guides are] brimming with useful information for the low-budget traveler—material delivered in a fresh, funny, and often irreverent way." —*The Philadelphia Inquirer*

"The [Berkeley Guides] are deservedly popular because of their extensive coverage, entertaining style of writing, and heavy emphasis on budget travel...If you are looking for tips on hostels, vegetarian food, and hitchhiking, there are no books finer." —*San Diego Union-Tribune*

"Straight dirt on everything from hostels to look for and beaches to avoid to museums least likely to attract your parents... they're fresher than Harvard's Let's Go series." —*Seventeen*

"The [Berkeley Guides] give a rare glimpse into the real cultures of Europe, Canada, Mexico, and the United States...with in-depth historical backgrounds on each place and a creative, often poetical style of prose." —*Eugene Weekly*

"More comprehensive, informative and witty than Let's Go." —*Glamour*

"The Berkeley Guides have more and better maps, and on average, the nuts and bolts descriptions of such things as hotels and restaurants tend to be more illuminating than the often terse and sometimes vague entries in the Let's Go guides." —*San Jose Mercury News*

"These well-organized guides list can't-miss sights, offbeat attractions and cheap thrills, such as festivals and walks. And they're fun to read." —*New York Newsday*

"Written for the young and young at heart...you'll find this thick, fact-filled guide makes entertaining reading." —*St. Louis Dispatch*

"Bright articulate guidebooks. The irreverent yet straight-forward prose is easy to read and offers a sense of the adventures awaiting travelers off the beaten path." —*Portland Oregonian*

On the Loose

On the Cheap

Off the Beaten Path

THE BERKELEY GUIDES

Fodor's BERKELEY budget guides

mexico '97

On the Loose
On the Cheap
Off the Beaten Path

WRITTEN BY BERKELEY STUDENTS IN COOPERATION WITH
THE ASSOCIATED STUDENTS OF THE UNIVERSITY OF CALIFORNIA

THE BERKELEY GUIDE TO MEXICO

Editors: Michele Back, Marisa Loeffen
Managing Editors: Tara Duggan, Kristina Malsberger, Sora Song
Executive Editor: Sharron S. Wood
Creative Director: Fabrizio La Rocca
Cartographer: David Lindroth; Eureka Cartography
Text Design: Tigist Getachew
Cover Design: Fabrizio La Rocca
Cover Art: Poul Lange (3-Dart), © Robert Frerck/Tony Stone (photo in frame), Paul D'Innocenzo (still life)

SPECIAL SALES

The Berkeley Guides and all Fodor's Travel Publications are available at special discounts for bulk purchases for sales promotions or premiums. Special editions, including personalized covers, excerpts of existing guides, and corporate imprints, can be created in large quantities for special needs. For more information, contact your local bookseller or write to Special Markets, Fodor's Travel Publications, 201 E. 50th Street, New York, NY 10022. Inquiries from Canada should be directed to your local Canadian bookseller or sent to Random House of Canada, Ltd., Marketing Department, 1265 Aerowood Drive, Mississauga, Ontario L4W 1B9. Inquiries from the United Kingdom should be sent to Fodor's Travel Publications, 20 Vauxhall Bridge Road, London, England SW1V 2SA.

PRINTED IN THE UNITED STATES OF AMERICA

10 9 8 7 6 5 4 3 2 1

Contents

· LEARN SPANISH ·

Cuauhnáhuac
Esc. C.I.C.L.C., S.C.

Spanish Language School since 1972 in Cuernavaca, México.

WHAT MAKES CUAUHNÁHUAC SPECIAL?

- Over twenty five years of teaching Spanish intensively.
- Classes begin every week at all levels, including courses designed to meet your particular needs.
- Six hours of classes daily.
- Small, intimate grammar classes, often one-on-one, but never more than four students to a class.
- Outstanding staff with many years of experience and extensive training in our own method of teaching Spanish intensively.
- Personal attention and flexibility in order to meet your individual needs. Special classes for people in different professions.
- University credit available.
- Convenient location with beautiful spacious grounds and a large swimming pool.
- Housing with a Mexican family who really cares about you and who will give you the opportunity for additional conversation practice.
- Interesting and varied excursions to historical sites and recreational areas.

"Northeastern Illinois University has been sending students to Cuauhnáhuac for 18 years. They improve their language skills and also broaden their knowledge of Mexican culture"

- Dr. Valeska Najera, Spanish prof., NIU

For more information, contact:
Marcia Snell
519 Park Drive
Kenilworth, IL 60043
Tel: 1-800-245-9335
Fax: (847) 256-9475
e-mail: lankysam@aol.com

What the Berkeley Guides Are All About

Five years ago, a motley bunch of U.C. Berkeley students launched a new series of guidebooks—*The Berkeley Guides.* Since then, we've been busy writing and editing 14 books to destinations across the globe, from California, Mexico, and Central America to Europe and Eastern Europe. Along the way our writers have weathered bus plunges, rabies, and guerrilla attacks, landed bush planes above the Arctic Circle, gotten lost in the woods (proverbially and literally), and broken bread with all sorts of peculiar characters—from Mafia dons and Hell's Angel bikers to indigenous families deep in the Oaxacan jungle.

Coordinating the efforts of 65 U.C. Berkeley writers back at the office is an equally daunting task (have you ever tried to track manuscript from Morocco?). But that's the whole point of *The Berkeley Guides*: to bring you the most up-to-date info on prices, the latest budget-travel trends, the newest restaurants and hostels, where to catch your next train—all written and edited by people who know what cheap travel is all about.

You see, it's one of life's weird truisms that the more cheaply you travel, the more you inevitably experience. If you're looking for five-star meals, air-conditioned tour buses, and reviews of the same old tourist traps, you're holding the wrong guidebook. Instead, *The Berkeley Guides* give you an in-depth look at local culture, detailed coverage of small towns and off-beat sights, bars, and cafés where tourists rarely tread, plus no-nonsense practical info that deals with the real problems of real people (where to get aspirin at 3 AM, where to launder those dirty socks).

Coming from a community as diverse as Berkeley, we also wanted our guides to be useful to everyone, so we tell you if a place is wheelchair accessible, if it provides resources for gay and lesbian travelers, and if it's safe for women traveling solo. Many of us are Californians, which means most of us like trees and mountain trails. It also means we emphasize the outdoors in every *Berkeley Guide* and include lots of info about hiking and tips on protecting the environment.

Most important, these guides are for travelers who want to see more than just the main sights. We find out what local people do for fun, where they go to eat, drink, or just be merry. Most guidebooks lead you down the tourist trail, ignoring important local issues, events, and culture. In *The Berkeley Guides* we give you the information you need to understand what's going on around you, whether it's the latest on the devaluation of the peso or the peace talks in Chiapas.

We've done our best to make sure the information in *The Berkeley Guides* is accurate, but time doesn't stand still: Prices change, places go out of business, currencies get devalued. Call ahead when it's really important, and try not to get too stressed out.

Thanks to You

Putting together a guidebook to Mexico is always an adventure. Our writers pressed on despite disappearing tearsheets, hurricanes, various gastrointestinal disorders, and the innumerable distractions that stood in the way of getting their manuscript back to Berkeley on time. Throughout Mexico our writers relied on helpful souls for their advice and encouragement, and we'd like to thank the following people—as well as the hundreds of others who our writers met in passing on the road. Drop a line—a postcard, a scrawled note on toilet paper, whatever—and we'll try our best to acknowledge your contribution. Our address is 515 Eshleman Hall, University of California, Berkeley, CA 94720.

Mexico City and **Veracruz**: Magalie and Fernando (Tlacoltálpan); Isis (Jalapa); Socorro and Felicidad (Xilitla); "trail guides" Augustin, Valerio, and Valentín (Xilitla); Katy and Malin (San Miguel de Allende); Victor Gonzales (San Francisco, CA). **Baja, North Central Mexico,** and **Sonora and Los Mochis**: Jorge Fischer (San Ignacio); Memo (Ensenada); Miguel, Ramón, and Gabriel (La Paz); Bill and Tom (The Traveling Willburys). **El Bajío, Central Highlands,** and **Northeastern**: Brunt "Sr. Grande" Rohan (Miami, FL); Katrina Muñoz (Morelia); Terry Ross (San Diego, CA); James Wishart (San Francisco, CA); Chase "El Vagabundo" Davis (somewhere on the trail to happiness); Sarah Murat and David Adams, "the hippies from Seattle"; Eric Thurnberg (Honduras); Jeff Levine, (Brooklyn, NY); Beth Facendini (Santa Rosa, CA); Roberto Oliveros, Irma Andrade, Betsabel Cárdenas, Erica Estrada (Guadalajara); the Weisenbergers (Guadalajara); Teresa Martínez and Juan-Jose Arroyo-Ramírez (Pozos); Yuriria Sofia Mendoza Quijano (Monterrey); Sue and Richard "my saviors" (London, UK); Edgar (San Miguel de Allende); Emilio "Angel Verde" Cervantes-Gutiérrez (Guadalajara). **The Pacific Coast** and **Central Cities**: Juan Bretón (Puebla); José Villanueva García (Cuernavaca); Lorena Ramos (Mazatlán); Kevin (Ixtapa); Mary (Cuernavaca); and Magui (Mazatlán). **Oaxaca, Chiapas, and Tabasco**: Mariana Emilia Arroyo y familia (Oaxaca); los maestros de CECAM (Tlahuitoltepec); Sylvia and Minnie Dahlberg (Puerto Escondido); Ana Márquez (Puerto Escondido); Hana Villar (Berkeley, CA); Checo, Carey, and Lourdes (Puerto Ángel); Beto (Puerto Ángel); John and Carlos (Mazunte); Ana Laura Flores Delgado (La Crucecita, Huatulco); Julín Contreras (Tehuantepec); Robert (San Cristóbal); Kippy and Maya (San Cristóbal); Dana at La Pared; Ambar and Andrés at Taller Leñateros (San Cristóbal); Jacobo "Gatos" Katz (Davis, CA); Paul (Santa Barbara, CA); Bladimir y familia (Tuxtla Gutiérrez); Nolberto (Chiapa de Corzo); Magui and Amelinda (Tapachula); Noelia Gómez Cupil (Villahermosa); Lloyd Denton (San Antonio, TX); William S. Burroughs; RIPE Communications. **The Yucatán Peninsula**: Andy and Laura (Chetumal, via New Zealand and Switzerland, respectively); David Ayala and Jorge from the doctor's office (Isla Mujeres); Don Toribio, Wilberth, Milka, and Tania (Ticul); Eduardo and Reina (Holpechén); Maestro William Chan (Dzibalchén; Kelli Harding and Sarah Heward (Reno, NV); Wilberth (Cancún).

The editors are especially grateful to the following people, who provided advice, information, and moral support: Linda Back McKay (Minneapolis, MN); Jonathan Leff and Sarah Parker (in our cubicle, CA); David Henschel and the Mexican Government Tourism Office (San Francisco, CA); Cecilia Rodriguez and Global Exchange (San Francisco, CA); Jamie O'Shea (Berkeley, CA); and Fran Tepper (Chicago, IL).

Berkeley Bios

Behind every restaurant blurb, lodging review, and introduction in this book lurks a student writer. You might recognize the type—they're the ones who couldn't hang out and drink with you that night in Oaxaca because they had stuff to do. Six Berkeley students spent the spring and summer scribbling their way through Mexico. Meanwhile, back at the ranch, two envious editors wished they were in the thick of things instead of at their all-too-stationary computers.

The Writers

After being asked, "¿Cuánto cuesta?" ("How much do you cost?") and getting flashed in broad daylight by a Mexican policeman—all in her first week on the job—**Olivia Barry** became quickly immune to the ethos of Latin lust. After making her rounds in the Central Cities, Olivia dashed to the Pacific Coast, where she soaked up sweltering sun rays and the mellow, good-natured attitude of the coastal villages. Currently, she's back at Cal for a fourth year, contemplating yet a third jaunt with the Guides. She won't be taking the History of Mexico class, however, since her trips to countless museums and ruins served as a firsthand crash course.

Rachael Courtier thought she had found respite from smoggy Mexico City in "sunny" Veracruz—until her hotel flooded in a tropical rainstorm. Alas, it was eating lots of mangos and Mexican *dulces* (sweets) that gave her the strength to go on. Rachael eventually found inner peace by having a *limpia* (spiritual cleaning) performed by a *brujo* (male witch), and by participating in pre-Columbian sweat lodge rituals in the tropical rain forest. A very, very clean Rachael is now back in San Francisco temping, substitute teaching, and pondering graduate school and teaching credential programs.

After living in Spain and Brazil and traveling to the most remote regions of South America, **Allison Eymil** was well prepared to tackle the Bajío, Central Highlands, and Northeastern regions of Mexico. Just days after the successful completion of her B.A.s in Mass Communications and Spanish and Portuguese, Allison found herself in the thralls of traveling, which she enjoyed immensely despite a minor kidnapping, Mexican machos, and 12-hour, second-class bus rides through the desert. Allison is currently taking a short respite in her home town of Hanford, California, before employing her survival skills once more in the jungles of New York City and graduate school.

While conducting a sociological study on the correlation between Western wear and machismo in Chihuahua, **Carrie McKellogg** found time to take some wild rides in the Copper Canyon, appreciate the wonders of modern technology (air-conditioning being at the top of her list in the blisteringly hot Sonoran desert), and even managed to tolerate El Fuerte's enormous mosquitoes, which she insists were genetically engineered to make her life miserable. After an extended hiatus on the Sea of Cortez, Carrie plans to contemplate her future from a very cold place.

On sabbatical from his formal education, **Andrew Dean Nystrom** found his divine inspiration in compromising positions: trapped in a cave by a driving hail storm, sandwiched between a sleeping mother and a rank bucket of fish in a chicken bus out of Puerto Ángel, and buried beneath bundles of aromatic herbs in a pitch-black Aztec *temazcal* sauna. He emerged from it all in fine fettle and spent the summer exploring the underbelly of Los Angeles for the Guides. Armed with a degree in human Geography from U.C. Berkeley, he plans to return to Montessori school as a teacher. His favorite word is still copacetic. You can e-mail him at: adean@uclink2.berkeley.edu.

Upon arrival in Cancún, **Marisa Plowden** began a fastidious eight-week attack on the most daunting creature in Mexico's animal kingdom—*la cucaracha*. When several drowning attempts failed and spraying 100% DEET repellent simply made the little devils run faster, Marisa resorted to crushing their hard-shelled bodies to smithereens with the end of a broomstick. The turning point in her ruthless massacre occurred at Mérida's bustling marketplace, where she realized she could actually sell cockroaches if she could somehow manage to glue fake jewels and gold chains to their backs. A recent graduate in Political Economy, Marisa is currently considering an offer to succeed Don Toribio as the next great snake healer of Ticul.

The Editors

Somewhere between shots of tequila and freebasing Earl Grey tea, **Michele Back,** former Mexico *and* Central America writer, managed to edit a book about Mexico, all the while proclaiming she had "nothing to do." You probably won't be hearing that complaint from the students in her high school Spanish class, where she'll wield a mighty pedagogical whip. Ever since a destined fortune cookie prophesied, "You will step on the soil of many countries," she's been scheming to sate a thwarted wanderlust. Of course, she'll also be expanding her women-focused travel newsletter, writing a sex guide, and scoping for the ultimate soul mate.

It was all good for **Marisa Loeffen,** who discovered halfway through the summer that painting her toenails was the ultimate way to soothe her jangled nerves. As she kept the staff in line with her snappy retorts, she demonstrated a keen and envied ability to concentrate in the chaos that is the Berkeley Guides office. While amusing her fellow editors with glossy bridal magazines and tales of her off-the-hook fiancé, Marisa brooded over the fact that she still had one more year of undergraduate work to tackle. Now she's plotting to conquer Mexico with her co-editor, where she will ingest vegetarian tacos at a shocking rate, explore the Chupacabras myth, and educate the masses on the correct usage of "hootchie momma."

Study Spanish in a small, internationally-acclaimed school emphasizing quality and individual attention.

SPANISH LANGUAGE INSTITUTE
of Cuernavaca, Morelos, Mexico

- All levels of Spanish in classes of five students maximum
- Family stays and full excursion program
- All adult ages (17 min.) and levels — college, professionals, retirees
- College credit available through U.S. university
- Begin on any Monday year-round, courses from 2-12 weeks

Call Language Link toll free at 800-552-2051 or visit our web site at http://www.langlink.com
It adds no additional cost to register through Language Link than directly with the school. We make it easy, convenient, and give you complimentary insurance. Programs also in Costa Rica, Ecuador, Peru, and Guatemala.

Introduction

By Michele Back and Marisa Loeffen

When you step into Mexico, you enter a landscape that lures from the depths of whispering *volcanes,* across high plateaus, through valleys of rustling cornstalks, and into the tugging seas. In a land so rich and varied, it's easy to lose yourself. And in a sense, that's what a visit to Mexico is about—wandering the twisted streets of colonial *barrios* (neighborhoods), stumbling upon ancient ruins in dense tropical jungle, or drifting aimlessly through the warm waters of the Caribbean. But while a trip to Mexico is about leaving the complications and stresses of home behind, it's also about finding and appreciating a way of life that has nothing to do with dreamy beachside reveries and adrenaline-driven adventure treks. Discovering the real Mexico isn't an effortless process though: To catch more than a glimpse of Mexican life, you need to travel to untouristed sites, take classes at the city's university, engage in conversation with the vendor at the local market, or volunteer for a nonprofit organization. Anywhere you go, if you make the effort to speak even a few words of Spanish, you will no doubt be greeted like an old friend, invited to share meals and perhaps even to spend the night. These encounters will allow you to discover a people that are as warm and open as the country itself. And hopefully, along with some regretfully tacky souvenirs and stunning photographs, you'll take home a solid understanding of what it means to live in Mexico today.

A rich conglomeration of cultures has been the foundation of many traditions and characteristics we view as typically Mexican: the jovial marimba music found in Veracruz, the Spanish-influenced jarabe tapatío (Mexican hat dance) of Guadalajara, and Puebla's mestizo culinary delicacy, mole poblano.

Home to some 85 million people, Mexico boasts a diverse population consisting of *mestizos* (those of mixed Spanish and Indian descent), *indígenas* (indigenous people; measured by those who speak one or more of the estimated 50 Indian languages), and a small number of Pan Africans and Asians. Despite the miscegenation evident in most Mexicans, a race- and class-based hierarchy still exists, with lighter-skinned mestizos at the top of the social scale and indígenas at the bottom. However, this stratification doesn't encompass all aspects of society; Catholicism, for example, plays a central role in the lives of most Mexicans, acting as a unifying force within the community. Since many folk religions and traditions were assimilated into the Catholic church during Spanish rule, a unique blend of Spanish and indigenous cultures flourishes today. This syncretism can be seen in nationwide *fiestas* such as the *Día de los Muertos* (Day of the Dead), created from the merging of All Souls Day (a Catholic holiday for remembering the dead) and an Aztec festival in honor of the glorious deaths of warriors and children.

Festivals may unite entire cities in a spirit of celebration, but once the music has died down and the fireworks are over, Mexico's grim economic, social, and political situation is all the more apparent: Corrugated tin shacks line the roads to luxury tourist resorts, indigenous children peddle trinkets for their families' only income, and eager laborers line the treacherous United States–Mexico border, plotting how to reach the other side. The presence of a cheap and available workforce on the border, combined with virtually nonexistent environmental restrictions, has resulted in an influx of foreign-owned factories, known as *maquiladoras*. These factories, most of which are associated with the garment industry, promise steady employment and above-average pay, but most workers only receive 30¢–$1.50 per hour and face appalling health conditions. Many laborers (mostly women) lose their jobs after six years, when eye strain prevents them from threading a needle, or when work-related dust fills their lungs, causing bronchial infections and permanent damage.

This sweatshop nightmare is largely a product of Mexico's faltering economy. In December 1994, following a period of chronic borrowing from the World Bank, erratic United States investment in Mexican bonds, and a general undercutting of national business, the Mexican government devalued the peso by 50%, sending the country's already depressed economy into a tailspin. The country's gross domestic product dropped by nearly 7%, causing two million people to lose their jobs and leaving nearly one in two Mexicans in poverty. At the present rate of population growth, nearly one million new jobs must be created each year to meet the demand. But with an enormously devalued peso, one of the lowest minimum wages in the world, and extremely limited technical means, it's highly unlikely that the much-needed jobs will ever develop. Sadly, concern for the country's poor has been pushed aside in the government's drive to meet First World standards of industry and modernization. This has meant increased borrowing and dependence on the United States and the World Bank for financial relief and restructuring. This frantic rush to increase industry and agroexports has also taken its toll on Mexico's valuable natural resources—air, water, land, and wildlife. Half of Mexico's land is eroded, forcing farmers to further deforest delicate land for a small plot of crops.

As industry grows in the north, it brings the kind of big-city problems endemic to Mexico City, such as heavy pollution and a lack of housing; Mexico has an estimated deficit of six million homes.

This economic crisis has also served to entangle the Mexican people in a web of political upheavals. Popular reaction began with the January 1, 1994 revolt by the Zapatista National Liberation Army (EZLN) in the southern state of Chiapas. Reacting to the initiation of the North American Free Trade Agreement (NAFTA), a group of poorly armed but well-organized *campesinos* (rural dwellers) attacked four Chiapan towns, demanding land redistribution, improved education and health care, and democratic reform for southern Mexico's indigenous population. The uprising led to a series of peace talks between the Zapatistas and the Mexican government, which have been progressing slowly due to alleged abuses by the government. Torture of indigenous leaders, ineffectual and fraudulent land redistribution, and persecution of foreign volunteers in Chiapas are just a few of the accusations to which current PRI (Institutional Revolutionary Party) president Ernesto Zedillo must respond.

Zedillo was narrowly elected president in August 1994 after the assassination of the would-be PRI candidate, Luis Donaldo Colosio. Although the fairness of the election was debatable, it was supposedly the cleanest in recent history. Zedillo's party, the monolithic, quasi-centrist PRI, has had a stranglehold on Mexican politics for the last six and a half decades, and now carries the burden of Mexico's social, political, and economic woes. The PRI's recent efforts to privatize formerly state-run services, such as the electric and telephone companies, have left much of the populace nervous and skeptical about the real beneficiaries of economic reform. The PRI has done little to assuage these fears: In March 1996, for example, 12,000 employees of Mexico's largest public bus company, Ruta 100, were expelled at gunpoint from the bus yards. This forceful attempt to divide Ruta 100 into 10 smaller private firms was also a convenient way for the PRI to bust the bus workers' union, SUTAUR-100, one of country's largest and most powerful.

In January and February 1996 the U.S. Border Patrol detained 146,000 illegal border crossers: an average of 400 arrests daily.

Mexico's complicated and contentious political landscape is nothing new, and the disparities of modern-day Mexican society have deep historical roots. Even a brief look at the country's past reveals a history of complex interdependencies, competing interests, and repeated patterns of loss and survival. The Olmecs, considered the "mother culture" of Mesoamerica, appeared around 1000 BC, becoming a flourishing society adept in artistry, technology, and agriculture. By 400 BC the Olmec civilization had essentially disappeared. During the next few centuries several sophisticated cultures emerged almost concurrently: the Zapotec and Mixtec of southern Mexico, the Huastec and Totonac of Veracruz, the Tarascans of Michoacán, the Maya of the Yucatán and northern Central America, and the nameless founders of Teotihuacán. Of all these early civilizations, the Maya were perhaps the most influential and advanced, constructing pyramids, keeping sophisticated and concise calendars, and developing a writing system that included over 300 glyphs. Despite these achievements, most Mayan cities were abandoned sometime in the 10th century, for reasons still unclear to archaeologists.

However one final pre-Columbian power waited in the wings. Claiming to come from Aztlán— either the present-day U.S. Southwest or a mystical heaven, depending on whom you ask—the Aztec people migrated to central Mexico in the 12th century, basing themselves in the ghost town of Teotihuacán and founding Tenochtitlán. Within a century, the Aztec earned a reputation for gruesome human sacrifice and all around ass-kicking, conquering nearly every Mesoamerican civilization in their rise to power. By the time the Spaniards arrived in 1519, the Aztec empire was roughly equivalent in size to modern-day France. The meeting between Hernan Cortés and Moctezuma, the Aztec *cacique* (chief), was friendly at first, but quickly escalated into a series of bloody wars. The Aztec had accumulated a number of enemies in their rise to prominence, and the politically savvy Cortés turned this to his advantage, forming alliances with disgruntled tribes eager to throw off the yoke of Aztec tyranny. In the end, the last great indigenous empire in Mexico was overthrown by the Spanish. Over the next 20 years, Mexico's indigenous population, wiped out by battle and European diseases, fell from 22 million to just 1.5 million. Those that survived faced lives of servitude to both their former lands and the imposing Catholic church. For three long centuries Spanish rule was the ultimate authority.

Although the indigenous people did not bear their fate without resistance, it was not until significant numbers of a disaffected middle class emerged that a widespread, coordinated effort to throw off Spanish rule began. The struggle for Mexican independence, however, was not limited to Spain, but also involved wars with other greedy foreign powers intent on gaining Mexico's vast resources. In 1848 Mexico suffered the tremendous loss of half its territory—comprising modern-day California, Arizona, New Mexico, and Texas—to the land-hungry United States. France also had its eye on Mexico, sending troops in 1861 to clear the way for a new emperor, Maximilian, Archduke of Austria. Even after the French army's defeat at Puebla in 1862, France did not completely withdraw from the country until five years later, when Maximilian was executed by firing squad in Querétaro.

By the turn of the 20th century, many of the problems that exist today were established: A few *hacendados* (landowners) and foreign investors owned all of Mexico's wealth; indigenous people had been dispossessed of their land and relocated; and a vast, complicated network of patronage—in which elite families were placed in positions of power—controlled government processes. When dictator Porfirio Díaz first took over, it appeared that Mexico was finally headed in the right direction, moving towards modernization with improved public services such as rail and telegraph lines. However, the costs far outweighed the gains: Rigged elections, a stifled press, and a deeply impoverished majority were among the pitfalls of the dictatorship. In 1910, these problems spurred the 10-year Mexican Revolution, a series of civil wars fought by Mexico's bourgeoisie for political reform. The movement against Díaz was led by Francisco I. Madero, the liberal son of a Chihuahua landowner, who called for "Elective Suffrage—No Reelection!" Madero was joined by a number of rebel armies, including those led by "Pancho" Villa to the north and Emiliano Zapata in central Mexico. Together they were successful in forcing Díaz's resignation, and Madero was the almost unanimous winner in the free elections that followed. As is so often the case with the high ideals of revolutions, however, many goals fell by the wayside during Madero's regime. For example, Emiliano Zapata's demands for land redistribution were not met until Lázaro Cárdenas's presidency in 1934.

Though the middle class and the elite were the real winners of the Mexican revolution, its populist legacy remains—both superficially in the PRI's rhetoric and more profoundly in contemporary leftist revolutionary movements. Mexico's tradition of strength in the face of adversity continues today, and contemporary examples of determination and hope abound: In the Lacandón jungle, the Zapatistas have joined forces with other indígenas, creating cooperative "centers of resistance" in communities that were destroyed by the Mexican army during the uprising. In Guerrero, months of protests by human rights groups over the police killings of at least 25 peasants led to the resignation in March 1996 of the state's governor, who had attempted to cover up the murders. The civic organization El Barzón, formed after the peso's devaluation in December 1994, now has 600,000 members and continues to fight for the rights of the newly impoverished middle class. All of these popular movements indicate that political change is reaching a wider segment of Mexico's people, and Mexicans are optimistic that their continued struggle will bring even greater results.

Despite these current crises, or perhaps because of them, Mexico continues to fascinate visitors. But a trip to Mexico is what you make of it, and those who never look any deeper into the country than the bottom of their margarita glass will come away with nothing more than a lot of sand in their luggage and hazy memories of bumping and grinding on a table in Cancún. Hedonistic indulgences set to a soundtrack of strumming mariachis and crashing waves is all fine and good, but those in search of more intelligent escapes should hop on the first second-class bus out of any given resort town. Though traveling through an unknown landscape may at first bring butterflies to your stomach (though admittedly, these may have something to do with the cuisine), you'll soon encounter places and people who can tell you wonders about the Mexican reality: The elderly woman sitting next to you on the bus may have had firsthand experience of the Revolution, or your hotel owner may be eager to engage you in a lengthy discussion about NAFTA. All you need to experience Mexico to its fullest is a little travel savvy, some basic conversational skills, and a desire to go somewhere that no glossy tourist brochure would dare mention. As you venture deep into the essence of Mexico, you'll find that getting lost in this country's land, history, and politics could quite possibly be the most rewarding thing you've ever done.

Mexico

CALIFORNIA

ARIZONA

NEW MEXICO

Tijuana
Mexicali
Ensenada

BAJA
CALIFORNIA
NORTE

Golfo

Nogales

Ciudad Juárez

Nuevo Casas Grandes

Hermosillo

SONORA

CHIHUAHUA

Chihuahua

Guerrero Negro

de

Santa Rosalía

Cuidad Obregón

BAJA
CALIFORNIA
SUR

California

Los Mochis

SINALOA

SIERRA MADRE OCCIDENTAL

COAHUILA

DURANGO

Saltillo

La Paz

Culiacán

Durango

Mazatlán

ZACATECAS

Zacatecas

Ru

Tepic

AGUASCALIENTES

Sa
Po

NAYARIT

Aguascalientes

Puerto Vallarta

Guadalajara

Guanajuato

So

JALISCO

GUANAJUATO

Querétaro

Manzanillo

Colima

Morelia

Toluc

COLIMA

MICHOACÁN

SIERRA MADRE

GUERRERO

Ixtapa/Zihuatanejo

Chilpancing
Acapulco

PACIFIC OCEAN

N

0 ——— 200 miles

0 ——— 300 km

Mexico

OKLAHOMA

ARKANSAS

TENN.

UNITED STATES

TEXAS

MISS.

ALA.

LOUISIANA

Rio Grande

Nuevo
Laredo

NUEVO
LEÓN

Ilo

Reynosa

Monterrey

Matamoros

TAMAULIPAS

Gulf of Mexico

Ciudad
Victoria

San Luis
Potosí

SAN LUIS
POTOSÍ

Tampico

San Miguel de Allende

QUERÉTARO

VERACRUZ

HIDALGO

México
City

Pachuca

D.F.

TLAXCALA

Veracruz

luca

Tlaxcala

Jalapa

ORELOS

Puebla

Cuernavaca

PUEBLA

MADRE DEL SUR

ingo

TABASCO

Villahermosa

Oaxaca

OAXACA

San Cristóbal
de las Casas

Tuxtla
Gutiérrez

CHIAPAS

Mérida

Cancún

YUCATÁN

Campeche

Cozumel

QUINTANA
ROO

CAMPECHE

Chetumal

BELIZE

Caribbean Sea

GUATEMALA

HONDURAS

BASICS

1

If you've ever traveled with anyone before, you know the two types of people in the world—the planners and the nonplanners. You also know that travel brings out the very worst in both groups: Left to their own devices, the planners will have you goose-stepping from attraction to attraction on a cultural blitzkrieg, while the nonplanners will invariably miss the flight, the bus, and the point. This Basics chapter offers you a middle ground, providing enough information to help plan your trip without saddling you with an itinerary or invasion plan. Keep in mind that companies go out of business, prices inevitably go up, and buses rarely arrive on time. If you wanted predictability, you should have stayed home.

Planning Your Trip

WHEN TO GO

The most popular vacation times in Mexico are Semana Santa (Holy Week, the week before Easter) and the period from Christmas through New Year's. During these holidays, hotels in most communities, even small ones, are usually booked well in advance, prices may be jacked up, and armies of tourists swarm popular attractions. Resorts popular with college students (i.e., any place with a beach) tend to fill up in the summer months, when schools are out. To avoid hordes of foreign and local tourists, heavy rains, and high prices, the best times to go are October and March–May.

CLIMATE Temperate is the word in central Mexico, where the high elevation keeps the area mild year-round. Northern Mexico and Baja are dry and scorching, while the south lapses into cool, stormy, and hot cycles. The coastal regions are graced by cool ocean breezes, which provide a welcome respite from simmering inland temperatures. As you meander through mountains and desert, beach and jungle, be ready for distinct climate changes. From December though February, the air tends to cool down and dry up; in inland northern Mexico, temperatures can approach freezing. Mexico's long rainy season extends from June until mid-October, so don't forget your rubbers.

HOLIDAYS On public holidays, expect lively celebrations that consume whole towns and close most businesses (especially offices). The following are some of the most important Mexico-wide holidays. Regional festivals are listed in individual chapters.

January 1: The **New Year** is celebrated with mariachi music, midnight church bells, and an early morning *misa de gallo* (rooster mass). Many agricultural and livestock fairs are also held around this date.

January 6: **El Día de los Reyes** (Feast of the Epiphany or Three Kings Day) is a traditional day of gift-giving.

February 5: **Día de la Constitución,** or Constitution Day, is a national holiday during which official speeches and ceremonies are conducted nationwide.

Late February or early March: "Eat, drink, and be merry, for tommorow we shall fast" is the idea behind the raucous **Carnaval**—the last chance to gorge on food and fun before the 40 somber days of Lent. It's primarily celebrated in Mazatlán and Veracruz.

March 21: **Natalicio de Benito Juárez** and **Día de la Primavera** celebrate the birthday of Mexico's reformist president, Benito Juárez, and also mark the date of the spring equinox.

March or April: **Semana Santa** (Holy Week) arrives the week preceding Easter. The holiday is basically an excuse for Mexican families to hit the beach for a week.

May 1: All businesses close for **Día del Trabajo** (Labor Day), which is celebrated with workers' parades and speeches.

May 5: **Cinco de Mayo** is a national holiday that tributes the Mexican defeat of the French at the Battle of Puebla in 1862.

September 15–16: **Día de la Independencia** (Independence Day) commemorates the speech, or *grito,* by Father Miguel Hidalgo that called for rebellion against the Spanish in 1810.

November 1–2: On **Día de los Muertos** (Day of the Dead), dead friends, relatives, and ancestors are honored. People visit the graves of the dearly departed, eat an honorary meal in a candlelit cemetery at midnight, and build altars in their homes with offerings of food, flowers, fruits, and sweets.

November 20: The **Aniversario de la Revolución** recalls the Mexican Revolution with parades, speeches, and patriotic events.

December 12: **Día de la Virgen de Guadalupe** (Day of the Virgin of Guadalupe) honors the patron saint of Mexico with religious rites, processions, and pilgrimages.

The Highs and the Lows

Average daily highs and lows stack up as follows:

City	January: High/Low	June: High/Low
Acapulco	88°F/72°F (31°C/22°C)	91°F/77°F (33°C/25°C)
Cozumel	82°F/68°F (28°C/20°C)	89°F/75°F (32°C/24°C)
Ensenada	64°F/45°F (18°C/7°C)	75°F/61°F (32°C/24°C)
Guadalajara	75°F/45°F (24°C/7°C)	79°F/59°F (25°C/15°C)
La Paz	72°F/57°F (22°C/14°C)	95°F/75°F (35°C/24°C)
Mexico City	70°F/41°F (21°C/5°C)	73°F/52°F (23°C/11°C)
Monterrey	68°F/48°F (20°C/9°C)	91°F/72°F (34°C/22°C)
Oaxaca	82°F/46°F (28°C/8°C)	84°F/60°F (29°C/16°C)
Veracruz	77°F/64°F (25°C/18°C)	87°F/77°F (31°C/25°C)

December 24–25: **Navidad** (Christmas) is a family celebration with dinner and midnight mass on Christmas Eve, followed by mass on Christmas Day.

TRAVEL RESOURCE ORGANIZATIONS

Global Exchange (2017 Mission St., suite 303, San Francisco, CA 94110, tel. 800/497–1994, globalexch@igc.apc.org) is a multifaceted organization that, among other things, arranges politically oriented "Reality Tours" throughout Mexico and Central America, sponsors public speakers, and brings long-term human rights volunteers into conflict zones. For more specific information on their work in Chiapas, see Chapter 13; you can also call or write for brochures and up-to-date info on the current political situations in Mexico and Central America.

The **North America Coordinating Center for Responsible Tourism** (2 Kensington Rd., San Anselmo, CA 94690–2905, tel. 415/258–6594) is a private, nonprofit organization that works on several levels to change the way that North Americans travel. The staff will gladly tell

Responsible Tourism

Tourism is one of Mexico's largest industries, so as a traveler it's important to recognize the influence you have on the country. Though tourism does inject much-needed hard currency into an economically challenged nation, the sudden influx of cash can also cause problems, and it rarely trickles down to those who need it. In addition, the industry must accommodate the masses, damaging delicate environmental and social frameworks in the industrializing process. Tourists, with their shiny new backpacks and stacks of traveler's checks, can alter locals' self-perceptions and accentuate the division between the haves and the have-nots. Mexicans, especially those in rural areas, may end up feeling inferior, denigrating themselves and their unique culture in an attempt to become "Westernized." Too often, tourism ends up damaging what it seeks to discover.

The Center for Responsible Tourism (see above) works with various organizations that promote mindful traveling. What follows are some excerpts from their Code of Ethics for Tourists:

- Travel in a spirit of humility and with a genuine desire to meet and talk with local people.

- Be aware of the feelings of the local people; prevent what might be offensive behavior. Photography, particularly, must respect persons.

- Realize that other people may have concepts of time and thought patterns which are different from yours—not inferior, only different.

- When shopping by bargaining, remember that the poorest merchant will give up a profit rather than give up her/his personal dignity.

- Make no promises to local people or to new friends that you cannot implement.

- Spend time each day reflecting on your experiences in order to deepen your understanding.

you how to travel in Mexico and other developing countries without having a negative impact on the country's economy or society. Aside from conducting workshops and seminars, they publish a quarterly newsletter called *Responsible Traveling,* which states their goals and gives info on workshops around the United States.

The **South American Explorers Club** offers a great deal of adventure-oriented info about Mexico (despite the fact that the country is nowhere near South America). Among other things, membership gets you the quarterly *South American Explorer* magazine, which covers all sorts of off-the-beaten-track activities; access to "Trip Reports" submitted by club members after their travels; and discounts club maps and brochures. Annual membership is $40. *126 Indian Creek Rd., Ithaca, NY 14850, tel. 607/277–0488, explorer@samexplo.org, http://www.samexplo.org.*

GOVERNMENT TOURIST OFFICES State and local tourist offices can answer general questions about travel in their area or refer you to other organizations for more info. Be as specific as possible when writing to request information or you may just end up with a stack of glossy brochures on expensive jungle expeditions. If you can get someone to answer specific questions over the phone, so much the better—the offices are often staffed by Mexican nationals.

➤ **IN THE UNITED STATES** • The **Mexican Government Tourism Office** at each of the following addresses can answer questions and provide maps and any travel information you may need: 405 Park Ave., Suite 1401, New York, NY 10022, tel. 212/755–7261, fax 212/980–2588; 1801 Century Plaza East, Los Angeles, CA 90067, tel. 310/203–8191, fax 310/203–8316; 5075 Westhammer St., Suite 975W, Houston, TX 77056, tel. 713/629–1611, fax 713/629–1837; 1911 Pennsylvania Ave. NW, Washington, D.C. 20036, tel. 202/728–1750, fax 202/728–1758; 2333 Ponce de Leon Blvd., Suite 710, Coral Gables, FL 33134, tel. 305/443–9160, fax 305/443–1186; 70 E. Lake St., Suite 1413, Chicago, IL 60601, tel. 312/606–9252, fax 312/606–9012.

Council Travel Offices in the United States

ARIZONA: Tempe (tel. 602/966–3544). **CALIFORNIA:** Berkeley (tel. 510/848–8604), Davis (tel. 916/752–2285), La Jolla (tel. 619/452–0630), Long Beach (tel. 310/598–3338), Los Angeles (tel. 310/208–3551), Palo Alto (tel. 415/325–3888), San Diego (tel. 619/270–6401), San Francisco (tel. 415/421–3473 or 415/566–6222), Santa Barbara (tel. 805/562–8080). **COLORADO:** Boulder (tel. 303/447–8101), Denver (tel. 303/571–0630). **CONNECTICUT:** New Haven (tel. 203/562–5335). **FLORIDA:** Miami (tel. 305/670–9261). **GEORGIA:** Atlanta (tel. 404/377–9997). **ILLINOIS:** Chicago (tel. 312/951–0585), Evanston (tel. 708/475–5070). **INDIANA:** Bloomington (tel. 812/330–1600). **LOUISIANA:** New Orleans (tel. 504/866–1767). **MASSACHUSETTS:** Amherst (tel. 413/256–1261), Boston (tel. 617/266–1926), Cambridge (tel. 617/497–1497 or 617/225–2555). **MICHIGAN:** Ann Arbor (tel. 313/998–0200). **MINNESOTA:** Minneapolis (tel. 612/379–2323). **NEW YORK:** New York (tel. 212/661–1450, 212/666–4177, or 212/254–2525). **NORTH CAROLINA:** Chapel Hill (tel. 919/942–2334). **OHIO:** Columbus (tel. 614/294–8696). **OREGON:** Portland (tel. 503/228–1900). **PENNSYLVANIA:** Philadelphia (tel. 215/382–0343), Pittsburgh (tel. 412/683–1881). **RHODE ISLAND:** Providence (tel. 401/331–5810). **TEXAS:** Austin (tel. 512/472–4931), Dallas (tel. 214/363–9941). **UTAH:** Salt Lake City (tel. 801/582–5840). **WASHINGTON:** Seattle (tel. 206/632–2448 or 206/329–4567). **WASHINGTON, D.C.** (tel. 202/337–6464). For U.S. cities not listed, call tel. 800/2–COUNCIL.

➤ **IN CANADA** • The **Mexican Government Tourism Office** provides travel information and maps at the following locations: 2 Bloor St. West, Suite 1801, Toronto, Ont. M4W 3E2, tel. 416/925–0704, fax 416/925–6061; 1 Place Ville Marie, Montreal, Suite 1526, Que. H3B 2B5, tel. 514/871–1052, fax 514/871–3825; 999 W. Hastings St., Suite 1610, Vancouver, BC V6C 2W2, tel. 604/669–2845, fax 604/669–3498.

➤ **IN THE UNITED KINGDOM** • The **Mexican Government Tourism Office** in London (6061 Trafalgar Sq., London, England WIX 1 PB, tel. 171/734–10–58) supplies maps and travel information.

BUDGET TRAVEL ORGANIZATIONS

Council on International Educational Exchange (**Council**) is a private, nonprofit organization that administers work, volunteer, academic, and professional programs worldwide. Its travel division, **Council Travel,** is a full-service travel agency specializing in student, youth, and budget travel. They offer discounted airfares, rail passes, accommodations, guidebooks, budget tours, and travel gear. They also issue the ISIC, GO25, and ITIC identity cards (*see* Student ID Cards, *below*). Forty-six Council Travel offices serve the budget traveler in the United States, and there are about a dozen overseas (including ones in Britain, France, and Germany). Council also puts out a variety of publications, including the free *Student Travels* magazine, a gold mine of travel tips (including information on work-, study-abroad, and international opportunities). *205 E. 42nd St., New York, NY 10017, tel. toll-free 888/COUNCIL.*

The **Educational Travel Center** (**ETC**) books low-cost flights to destinations within the continental United States and around the world. Their best deals are on flights leaving the Midwest, especially Chicago. For more details, request their free brochure, *Taking Off. 438 N. Frances St., Madison, WI 53703, tel. 608/256–5551.*

STA Travel, the world's largest travel organization catering to students and young people, has over 100 offices worldwide and offers low-price airfares to destinations around the globe, as well as rail passes, car rentals, tours, you name it. STA issues the ISIC and the GO25 youth cards (*see* Student ID Cards, *below*), both of which prove eligibility for student airfares and other travel discounts. Call 800/777–0122 or the nearest STA office for more information. You can also check out their web site (http://www.sta-travel.com/).

STA Offices

- *UNITED STATES. CALIFORNIA: Berkeley (tel. 510/642–3000), Los Angeles (tel. 213/934–8722), San Francisco (tel. 415/391–8407), Santa Monica (tel. 310/394–5126), Westwood (tel. 310/824–1574). FLORIDA: Miami (305/461–3444), University of Florida (tel. 352/338–0068). ILLINOIS: Chicago (tel. 312/786–9050). MASSACHUSETTS: Boston (tel. 617/266–6014), Cambridge (tel. 617/576–4623). NEW YORK: Columbia University (tel. 212/865–2700), West Village (tel. 212/627–3111). PENNSYLVANIA: Philadelphia (tel. 215/382–2928). WASHINGTON: Seattle (tel. 206/633–5000). WASHINGTON, D.C. (tel. 202/887–0912).*

- *INTERNATIONAL. AUSTRALIA: Adelaide (tel. 08/223–2426), Brisbane (tel. 07/221–9388), Cairns (tel. 070/314199), Darwin (tel. 089/412955), Melbourne (tel. 03/349–2411), Perth (tel. 09/227–7569), Sydney (tel. 02/212–1255). NEW ZEALAND: Auckland (tel. 09/309–9995), Christchurch (tel. 03/379–9098), Wellington (tel. 04/385–0561). UNITED KINGDOM: London (tel. 0171/937–9962).*

The World At a Discount

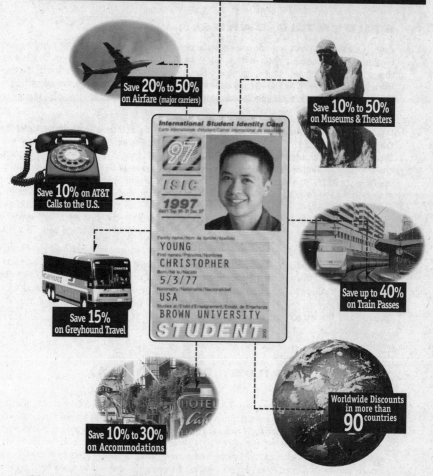

Save 20% to 50% on Airfare (major carriers)

Save 10% to 50% on Museums & Theaters

Save 10% on AT&T Calls to the U.S.

Save up to 40% on Train Passes

Save 15% on Greyhound Travel

Worldwide Discounts in more than 90 countries

Save 10% to 30% on Accommodations

International Student Identity Card
Carte internationale d'etudiant/Carnet internacional de estudiante

'97

ISIC

1997

Family name/Nom de famille/Apellido
YOUNG
First names/Prénoms/Nombres
CHRISTOPHER
Born/Né le/Nacido
5/3/77
Nationality/Nationalité/Nacionalidad
USA
Studies at/Etabl.d'Enseignement/Estab.de Enseñanza
BROWN UNIVERSITY

STUDENT

The International Student Identity Card
Your Passport to Discounts & Benefits

With the ISIC, you'll receive discounts on airfare, hotels, transportation, computer services, foreign currency exchange, phone calls, major attractions, and more. You'll also receive basic accident and sickness insurance coverage when traveling outside the U.S. and access to a 24-hour, toll-free Help Line. Call now to locate the issuing office nearest you (over 555 across the U.S.) at:

Free 40-page handbook with each card!

1-888-COUNCIL (toll-free)

For an application and complete discount list, you can also visit us at **http://www.ciee.org/**

Travel CUTS is a full-service travel agency that sells discounted airline tickets to Canadian students and issues the ISIC, GO25, ITIC, and HI cards. Their 25 offices are on or near college campuses. Call weekdays 9–5 for information and reservations. *187 College St., Toronto, Ont. M5T 1P7, tel. 416/979–2406.*

STUDENT ID CARDS

Foreign student ID cards are not universally accepted in Mexico; discounts for museum and theater admission usually apply exclusively to students at Mexican universities. Don't leave your student ID at home, though, because discounts are often left to the discretion of the person working the door. While an ID card issued by a home university or college may be sufficient to prove student status for admission discounts, the following cards have the extra feature of providing insurance in case of accident or other catastrophes:

If purchased in the United States, the $19 cost for the popular **International Student Identity Card (ISIC)** buys you $3,000 in emergency medical coverage; limited hospital coverage; and access to a 24-hour international, toll-free hotline for assistance in medical, legal, and financial emergencies. In the United States, apply to Council Travel or STA; in Canada, the ISIC is available for C$15 from Travel CUTS (*see* Budget Travel Organizations, *above*). In the United Kingdom, students with valid university IDs can purchase the ISIC at any student union or student travel company. Applicants must submit a photo as well as proof of current full-time student status, age, and nationality. Upon request, purchase of the ISIC card includes the *International Student Identity Card Handbook,* which details the discounts and benefits available to cardholders.

The **Go 25: International Youth Travel Card (GO25)** is issued to travelers (students and non-students) between the ages of 12 and 25 and provides services and benefits similar to those given by the ISIC card. The $19 card is available from the same organizations that sell the ISIC. When applying, bring a passport-size photo and your passport as proof of your age. The **International Teacher Identity Card (ITIC)** provides similar services and is issued to teachers of all age groups, from kindergarten to graduate school. This card is also $19 and available from Council Travel offices.

TOURIST CARDS, PASSPORTS, AND VISAS

All foreigners traveling for more than 72 hours in Mexico must obtain a tourist card (called an F.M.T.). Although adult U.S. and Canadian citizens technically need only a birth certificate and a photo ID to obtain one, a passport is sure to come in handy in case of a problem. Minors must present a notarized consent form signed by a parent and their passport or birth certificate. Legal permanent residents of the United States must have an alien registration card and a passport or driver's license to get a card. Western Europeans, Aussies, and Kiwis must present a passport; citizens of all other countries must obtain a visa at any Mexican consulate. U.S. and Canadian citizens only need a visa to work or study at a Mexican university.

TOURIST CARDS If you intend to visit border towns only, you can do so without a tourist card for up to 72 hours. Otherwise you must show proof of citizenship (either an original birth certificate and a photo ID, or a passport) and obtain a tourist card. Driver's licenses, credit cards, and military papers will not suffice. A naturalized citizen must carry at least one of the following documents: naturalization papers, a U.S. passport, or an affidavit of citizenship. F.M.T.s are available at Mexican government border offices at any port of entry, on flights into Mexico, and at any Mexican Ministry of Tourism or consulate in the United States. No matter where you get it, when crossing the border you must sign the card in the presence of the Mexican immigration official, who may also ask to see proof of citizenship. Be sure to hold on to your receipt, because you are required to fork it over on departure. If you lose it, expect to visit with the border officials for a while.

Tourist cards last up to six months, at which time you must go to the local **Delegación de Servicios Migratorios** to apply for a new one. When you hand in the completed application form upon entering Mexico, tell the immigration official you plan to stay for the full six months; if you estimate a shorter period of time and later decide to prolong your stay, you'll have to go through an incredible amount of administrative hassle to get your card extended. Upon leaving Mexico, your card is taken and a new one is issued if and when you return. If you lose your card, you must also go to the Delegación de Servicios Migratorios. To cut through at least a portion of the red tape involved, it's a good idea to make a photocopy of your card and keep it in a separate place. Carry the original with you at all times; it's required by law.

OBTAINING A PASSPORT

➤ **U.S. CITIZENS** • First-time applicants, travelers whose most recent passport was issued more than 12 years ago or before they were 18, travelers whose passports have been lost or stolen, and travelers between the ages of 13 and 17 (accompanied by a parent) must apply for a passport in person. Other renewals can be taken care of by mail. Apply at one of the 13 U.S. Passport Agency offices (Boston, Chicago, Honolulu, Houston, Los Angeles, Miami, New Orleans, New York, Philadelphia, San Francisco, Seattle, Stamford, and Washington, D.C.) a *minimum* of five weeks before your departure. For the fastest processing, apply between August and December. If you blow it, you can have a passport issued within five days of departure if you have your plane ticket in hand and pay the additional $30 fee to expedite processing. This method will probably work, but if there's one little glitch in the system, you're out of luck. Local county courthouses, many state and probate courts, and some post offices also accept passport applications. Have the following items ready when you go to get your passport: (1) A completed passport application (form DSP-11), available U.S. post offices, at federal or state courts, and at U.S. Passport Agencies; (2) Proof of citizenship (certified copy of birth certificate, naturalization papers, or previous passport issued in the past 12 years); (3) Proof of identity with your photograph and signature (for example, a valid driver's license, employee ID card, military ID, student ID); (4) Two recent, identical, two-inch photographs (black-and-white or color head shots); (5) A $55 application fee for a 10-year passport, $30 for those under 18 for a five-year passport. First-time applicants are also hit with a $10 surcharge. If you're paying cash, exact change is necessary; checks or money orders should be made out to Passport Services. For more information or an application, contact the **Department of State Office of Passport Services** (tel. 202/647–0518) and dial your way through their message maze.

Those lucky enough to be able to renew their passports by mail must send a completed form DSP-82 (available from a passport agency); two recent, identical passport photos; their current passport (less than 12 years old); and a check or money order for $55 ($30 if under 18). Send everything to the nearest passport agency. Renewals take three to four weeks.

➤ **CANADIAN CITIZENS** • Canadians should send a completed passport application (available at any post office, passport office, and many travel agencies) to the **Bureau of Passports** (Suite 215, West Tower, Guy Favreau Complex, 200 Rene Levesque Blvd. W., Montreal, Que. H2Z 1X4, tel. 514/283–2152). Include C$60; two recent, identical passport photographs; the signature of a guarantor (a Canadian citizen who has known you for at least two years and is a mayor, practicing lawyer, notary public, judge, magistrate, police officer, signing officer at a bank, medical doctor, or dentist); and proof of Canadian citizenship (original birth certificate or other official document as specified). You can also apply in person at regional passport offices in many locations, including Edmonton, Halifax, Montreal, Toronto, Vancouver, and Winnipeg. Passports have a shelf life of five years and are not renewable. Processing takes about two weeks by mail and five working days for in-person applications.

➤ **U.K. CITIZENS** • Passport applications are available through travel agencies, a main post office, or one of six regional passport offices (in London, Liverpool, Peterborough, Belfast, Glasgow, and Newport). The application must be countersigned by your bank manager or by a solicitor, barrister, doctor, clergyman, or justice of the peace who knows you personally. Send or drop off the completed form; two recent, identical passport photos; and a £25 fee to a regional passport office (address is on the form). Passports are valid for 10 years (five years for those under 16) and take about four weeks to process.

➤ **AUSTRALIAN CITIZENS** • Australians must visit a post office or passport office to complete the passport application process. A 10-year passport for those over 18 costs

AUS$81. The under-18 crowd can get a five-year passport for AUS$41. For more information, call toll-free in Australia 008/131–232 weekdays during regular business hours.

➤ **NEW ZEALAND CITIZENS** • Passport applications can be found at any post office or consulate. Completed applications must be accompanied by proof of citizenship and two passport-size photos. The fee is NZ$80 for a 10-year passport. Processing takes about 10 days.

LOST PASSPORTS If your passport is lost or stolen while traveling, you should immediately notify the local police and nearest embassy or consulate. A consular officer should be able to wade through some red tape and issue you a new one, or at least get you back into your country of origin without one. The process will be slowed up considerably if you don't have some other forms of identification on you, so you're advised to carry a driver's license, a copy of your birth certificate, or a student ID separate from your passport. You might also tuck a few photocopies of the front page of your passport in your luggage and your traveling companion's pockets.

A U.S. embassy or consulate will only issue a new passport in emergencies. In nonemergency situations, the staff will affirm your affidavit swearing to U.S. citizenship, and this paper will get you back to the United States. The British embassy or consulate requires a police report, any form of identification, and three passport-size photos. They will replace the passport in four working days. Canadian citizens face the same requirements as Brits. A replacement passport usually takes five working days. New Zealand officials ask for two passport-size photos, while the Australians require three, but both can usually replace a passport in 24 hours.

MONEY

"Nuevos pesos," or new peso notes, come in denominations of 10, 20, 50, and 100 pesos. Old bills still circulate in some areas; they come with three zeroes attached (i.e., 10,000 = 10; 50,000 = 50). *Do not* accept old pesos as change from anyone, as it will be impossible to spend them elsewhere. The "no change" dilemma will also confront you: Many shop and restaurant owners don't have change for your purchase even if the note you offer is valued as low as $3.50. In these situations, you'll just have to chill while they run next door to see if anyone else can make change. Enough of these encounters may compel you to request *billetes chicos* (small bills) when you exchange money. All prices in this book are quoted in dollars: Given the turbulent nature of the peso, it makes sense to give prices in a more stable currency. Prices quoted here are based on an exchange rate of 7.25 pesos to the dollar.

HOW MUCH IT WILL COST The past two years have been bad ones for the Mexican economy, but the peso remained relatively stable in 1996, and financial wizards predict no serious fluctuations in 1997. Still, devaluation plus steady inflation mean that the dollar (and most other foreign currencies) buys a lot more in Mexico than it does in Western Europe and the United States. Prices vary according to the universal rule, however—the more cosmopolitan the city, the more expensive the tortilla. Your travel to and from Mexico will probably be your biggest expense, followed by lodging and transport.

➤ **WHERE TO SLEEP** • Most travelers bed down in hotels, though camping is a safe option in designated spots. Hotel prices range from dirt cheap (about $5 per person) to stratospheric. In a typical city, expect to pay $8–$12 for a single, $10–$15 for a double, and a couple of bucks extra for an additional person or air-conditioning. Rooms with a double bed often cost a dollar or two less than those with two singles. Mexico's few hostels run less than $5 a night.

➤ **FOOD** • If you're willing to forgo tourist fare, you'll be able to spend very little money on food. One sure cost-cutting strategy is to buy fresh fruits and vegetables in the local market (every city, town, and village has one). Most markets also have small *fondas* (covered food stands) offering *comidas corridas* (fixed-price lunch specials) for less than $3. *Panaderías* (bakeries) sell cheap breads and pastries. More variety and more risk is involved when you buy from street vendors, who sell tacos, tamales, and the like for rock-bottom prices.

➤ **TRANSPORTATION** • Buses are widely used in Mexico, so fares remain very low. Buses range from antiquated second-class school buses to first-class coaches (*see* Getting

Around, *below*). Prices correlate less with the number of hours traveled than with the popularity of the route—heavily traveled routes are served by more classes of service at lower prices. Local city buses and transportation between rural towns cost less than 50¢, while a nine- to 12-hour ride on a first-class bus costs around $10. Trains (especially second class) are considerably cheaper than buses, but much slower and often less comfortable. During peak travel times such as Semana Santa, trains fill up with locals and their animals. Driving your own car in Mexico gives you flexibility, but toll fees and poor road conditions can make driving an expensive hassle. Domestic plane fares will flatten your wallet considerably (*see* Getting Around, *below*).

➤ **ENTERTAINMENT** • Entertainment costs can be very high in big cities, where getting a foot in the door of an average club means coughing up anywhere from $5 to $30. Drink prices at an average bar are comparable to those north of the border: Beers run $1–$2 at popular watering holes. Movie tickets, at least, are a reasonable $2–$3. In many cities, thanks to government subsidies, entrance to some theater, dance, and musical events is free (these bargains are usually cultural events featuring traditional music or dance). Most museums and historical sites charge a $1–$2 admission, and many in smaller towns are free. If your cash flow has dwindled to a drip, join the locals for traditional (and free) entertainment—an early evening stroll around the town's *zócalo* (main square). Or check out the swapmeet or *tianguis* (open-air market), where locals flock to bargain over housewares, clothes, food, and miscellaneous goods.

TRAVELING WITH MONEY Cash never goes out of style, but traveler's checks and a major credit card are usually the safest and most convenient way to pay for goods and services on the road. Depending on the length of your trip, strike a balance among these three forms of currency, and protect yourself by carrying cash in a money belt or "necklace" pouch (available at luggage or camping stores) or front pocket. Keep accurate records of traveler's checks' serial numbers, record credit card numbers along with an emergency number for reporting the cards' loss or theft, and keep this information separate from the checks and cards themselves. Credit cards are rarely accepted by budget establishments in Mexico, but they do come in handy at mid-range hotels and restaurants. Visa and MasterCard can also be used to obtain cash advances in banks or at ATM machines (*see* Cash Machines, *below*). An American Express card will allow you to cash personal checks and purchase traveler's checks at an American Express office (*see* Obtaining Money From Home, *below*), but AmEx is rarely hooked up to Mexican ATMs. Carrying at least some cash is wise, since most budget establishments will

Distributing funds about your person is a good idea that damp $50 in your sock may well get you out of a jam when some friendly fellow runs off with your backpack.

accept cash only, and changing traveler's checks may prove difficult outside of urban areas. Bring about $100 (in as many single bills as possible) in cash; changing U.S. dollars is usually easier than cashing traveler's checks.

CHANGING MONEY You can transform your cash or traveler's checks into pesos at most banks, or visit a private exchange office, called a *casa de cambio*. Most banks only change money on weekdays until 1 (though they stay open until 5), while casas de cambio generally stay open until 6 and often operate on weekends. Bank rates are regulated by the federal government and are therefore invariable, while casas de cambio have slightly more variable rates. Some hotels also exchange money, but they usually do it at extortionate rates. It helps to exchange money before the banks close, when everybody else's rates tend to worsen. You'll get a better deal buying pesos once you arrive in Mexico rather than at your bank before you leave. However, it's still a good idea to change $20–$50 into pesos before you leave, in case the exchange booth at the Mexican airport is closed or has an unbearably long line. When changing money, do not accept any partially torn or taped-together bills; they will not be accepted anywhere.

TRAVELER'S CHECKS Budget establishments in Mexico are extremely unlikely to accept traveler's checks of any sort. They are, however, accepted at most banks, casas de cambio, and some fancy hotels. Some banks and credit unions will issue checks free to established customers, but most charge a 1%–2% commission fee. Buy the bulk of your traveler's checks in small denominations (a pack of five $20 checks is the smallest), as many establishments won't accept large bills.

BASICS

If you don t have an AmEx gold card, you can still get American Express traveler s checks free with an AAA membership. Talk to the cashier at your local AAA office.

American Express cardmembers can order traveler's checks in U.S. dollars and six foreign currencies by phone, free of charge (with a gold card) or for a 1% commission (with your basic green card); up to $1,000 can be ordered in a seven-day period. In three to five business days you'll receive your checks. Checks can also be purchased through many banks, in which case both gold and green cardholders pay a 1% commission. AmEx also issues **Traveler's Cheques for Two,** checks that can be signed and used by either you or your traveling companion. At AmEx's Travel Services offices (about 1,500 around the world) you can usually buy and cash traveler's checks (most American Express offices in Mexico claim to change AmEx checks, but they don't always have enough cash), write a personal check in exchange for traveler's checks, report lost or stolen checks, exchange foreign currency, and pick up mail. Ask for the *American Express Traveler's Companion,* a handy little directory of their offices, to find out more about particular services at different locations. *Tel. 800/221–7282 in the U.S. and Canada.*

➤ **LOST AND STOLEN CHECKS** • If your traveler's checks are lost or stolen, they are replaceable as long as you produce the purchase agreement and a record of the checks' serial numbers; common sense dictates that you keep the purchase agreement separate from your checks. Better-safe-than-sorry types should also leave a copy of the agreement and the serial numbers with someone back home. It's also wise to record the toll-free or collect number for lost or stolen checks in several places. Most agents will promise to replace checks within 24 hours, but in remote places of Mexico, this is unlikely.

CREDIT CARDS You'll be hard-pressed to find a budget establishment that accepts credit cards in Mexico, but they can be lifesavers in financial emergencies, allowing you to rent a car, reserve a flight, or keep a roof over your head when your pockets are empty. Though you won't want to rely on the plastic too heavily while traveling (accrued interest on a wild night in Cancún could leave you a pauper), it never hurts to have a card tucked away somewhere on your person. You can also use your credit card to get cash at many banks (*see below*).

GETTING MONEY FROM HOME

Provided there is money at home to be had, there are at least six ways to get it:

- If you're an **American Express** cardholder, cash a personal check at an American Express office for up to $1,000 ($5,000 for gold cardholders) every 21 days; you'll be paid in U.S. traveler's checks or, in some instances, in foreign currency.

- The *MoneyGram*^{SM} can be a dream come true if you can convince someone back home to go to a MoneyGram agent and fill out the necessary forms. The sender pays up to $1,000 with

Making the Most of Your Parents Credit Card

Even if you have no job, no credit, no cards, and no respect, you can still tap into services offered by the Visa Assistance Center if one of your parents has a Visa Gold or Business card and you are a dependent of 22 years or less and at least 100 miles from home. Write down the card number in a safe, memorable place and call the center for emergency cash service, emergency ticket replacement, lost-luggage assistance, medical and legal assistance, and an emergency message service. Helpful, multilingual personnel await your call 24 hours a day, seven days a week. In the U.S. call 800/847–2911; from overseas call 410/581–3836 collect.

The best places to travel may be the best places to get hepatitis A.

You can pick up hepatitis A when traveling to high-risk areas outside of the United States. From raw shellfish or water you don't think is contaminated. Or from uncooked foods — like salad — prepared by people who don't know they're infected. At even the best places.

Symptoms of hepatitis A include jaundice, abdominal pain, fever, vomiting and diarrhea. And can cause discomfort, time away from work and memories you'd like to forget.

The U.S. Centers for Disease Control and Prevention (CDC) recommends immunization for travelers to high-risk areas. *Havrix*, available in over 45 countries, can protect you from hepatitis A. *Havrix* may cause some soreness in your arm or a slight headache.

Ask your physician about vaccination with *Havrix* at your next visit or at least 2 weeks before you travel. And have a great trip.

Please see important patient information adjacent to this ad.

**Havrix®
Hepatitis A Vaccine,
Inactivated**

The world's first hepatitis A vaccine

For more information on how to protect yourself against hepatitis A, call

1-800-HEP-A-VAX (1-800-437-2829)

Manufactured by
SmithKline Beecham Biologicals
Rixensart, Belgium

Distributed by
SmithKline Beecham Pharmaceuticals
Philadelphia, PA 19101

Hepatitis A Vaccine, Inactivated
Havrix®

See complete prescribing information in SmithKline Beecham Pharmaceuticals literature. The following is a brief summary.

INDICATIONS AND USAGE: *Havrix* is indicated for active immunization of persons ≥ 2 years of age against disease caused by hepatitis A virus (HAV).

CONTRAINDICATIONS: *Havrix* is contraindicated in people with known hypersensitivity to any component of the vaccine.

WARNINGS: Do not give additional injections to patients experiencing hypersensitivity reactions after a *Havrix* injection. (See CONTRAINDICATIONS.)

Hepatitis A has a relatively long incubation period. Hepatitis A vaccine may not prevent hepatitis A infection in those who have an unrecognized hepatitis A infection at the time of vaccination. Additionally, it may not prevent infection in those who do not achieve protective antibody titers (although the lowest titer needed to confer protection has not been determined).

PRECAUTIONS: As with any parenteral vaccine (1) keep epinephrine available for use in case of anaphylaxis or anaphylactoid reaction; (2) delay administration, if possible, in people with any febrile illness or active infection, except when the physican believes withholding vaccine entails the greater risk; (3) take all known precautions to prevent adverse reactions, including reviewing patients' history for hypersensitivity to this or similar vaccines.

Administer with caution to people with thrombocytopenia or a bleeding disorder, or people taking anticoagulants. Do not inject into a blood vessel. Use a separate, sterile needle or prefilled syringe for every patient. When giving concomitantly with other vaccines or IG, use separate needles and different injection sites.

As with any vaccine, if administered to immunosuppressed persons or persons receiving immunosuppressive therapy, the expected immune response may not be obtained.

Carcinogenesis, Mutagenesis, Impairment of Fertility: *Havrix* has not been evaluated for its carcinogenic potential, mutagenic potential or potential for impairment of fertility.

Pregnancy Category C: Animal reproduction studies have not been conducted with *Havrix*. It is also not known whether *Havrix* can cause fetal harm when administered to a pregnant woman or can affect reproduction capacity. Give *Havrix* to a pregnant woman only if clearly needed. It is not known whether *Havrix* is excreted in human milk. Because many drugs are excreted in human milk, use caution when administering *Havrix* to a nursing woman.

Havrix is well tolerated and highly immunogenic and effective in children.

Fully inform patients, parents or guardians of the benefits and risks of immunization with *Havrix*. For persons traveling to endemic or epidemic areas, consult current CDC advisories regarding specific locales. Travelers should take all necessary precautions to avoid contact with, or ingestion of, contaminated food or water. Duration of immunity following a complete vaccination schedule has not been established.

ADVERSE REACTIONS: *Havrix* has been generally well tolerated. As with all pharmaceuticals, however, it is possible that expanded commercial use of the vaccine could reveal rare adverse events.

The most frequently reported by volunteers in clinical trials was injection-site soreness (56% of adults; 21% of children); headache (14% of adults; less than 9% of children). Other solicited and unsolicited events are listed below:

Incidence 1% to 10% of Injections: Induration, redness, swelling; fatigue, fever (>37.5°C), malaise; anorexia, nausea.

Incidence <1% of Injections: Hematoma; pruritus, rash, urticaria; pharyngitis, other upper respiratory tract infections; abdominal pain, diarrhea, dysgeusia, vomiting; arthralgia, elevation of creatine phosphokinase, myalgia; lymphadenopathy; hypertonic episode, insomnia, photophobia, vertigo.

Additional safety data
Safety data were obtained from two additional sources in which large populations were vaccinated. In an outbreak setting in which 4,930 individuals were immunized with a single dose of either 720 EL.U. or 1440 EL.U. of *Havrix*, the vaccine was well-tolerated and no serious adverse events due to vaccination were reported. Overall, less than 10% of vaccinees reported solicited general adverse events following the vaccine. The most common solicited local adverse event was pain at the injection site, reported in 22.3% of subjects at 24 hours and decreasing to 2.4% by 72 hours.

In a field efficacy trial, 19,037 children received the 360 EL.U. dose of *Havrix*. The most commonly reported adverse events were injection-site pain (9.5%) and tenderness (8.1%), reported following first doses of *Havrix*. Other adverse events were infrequent and comparable to the control vaccine Engerix-B® (Hepatitis B Vaccine, Recombinant).

Postmarketing Reports: Rare voluntary reports of adverse events in people receiving *Havrix* since market introduction include the following: localized edema; anaphylaxis/anaphylactoid reactions, somnolence; syncope; jaundice, hepatitis; erythema multiforme, hyperhydrosis, angioedema; dyspnea; lymphadenopathy; convulsions, encephalopathy, dizziness, neuropathy, myelitis, paresthesia, Guillain-Barré syndrome, multiple sclerosis; congenital abnormality.

The U.S. Department of Health and Human Services has established the Vaccine Adverse Events Reporting System (VAERS) to accept reports of suspected adverse events after the administration of any vaccine, including, but not limited to, the reporting of events required by the National Childhood Vaccine Injury Act of 1986. The toll-free number for VAERS forms and information is 1-800-822-7967.

HOW SUPPLIED: 360 EL.U./0.5 mL: NDC 58160-836-01 Package of 1 single-dose vial.

720 EL.U./0.5 mL: NDC 58160-837-01 Package of 1 single-dose vial; NDC 58160-837-02 Package of 1 prefilled syringe.

1440 EL.U./mL: NDC 58160-835-01 Package of 1 single-dose vial; NDC 58160-835-02 Package of 1 prefilled syringe.

Manufactured by **SmithKline Beecham Biologicals**
Rixensart, Belgium
Distributed by **SmithKline Beecham Pharmaceuticals**
Philadelphia, PA 19101

BRS–HA:L5A

Havrix is a registered trademark of SmithKline Beecham.

a credit card or cash (and anything over that in cash) and, as quick as 10 minutes later, it's ready to be picked up. Fees vary according to the amount of money sent, but average about 3%–10%. You have to show ID when picking up the money. Be certain that whoever sends you money spells your name exactly as it appears on your ID—Mexican banks, especially Banamex, are very picky about such details. For locations of MoneyGram agents, call 800/926–9400.

- **MasterCard** and **Visa** cardholders can get cash advances from many banks, even in small towns, but keep in mind that most banks charge a commission for this handy-dandy service. If you get a four-digit PIN number for your card before you leave home, you can also withdraw cash at many ATM machines (*see* Cash Machines, *below*).

- **Western Union** offers two ways to feed your hungry wallet, both of them requiring a beneficent angel with deep pockets on the other side of the wire. Said angel can transfer funds from a MasterCard, Visa, or Discover card (up to the card's limit, or $10,000) by calling 800/325–6000. (Credit card transfers cannot be done at Western Union offices.) Alternately, your friend can trot some cash or a certified cashier's check over to the nearest office. The money will reach the requested destination in minutes but may not be available for several more hours or days, depending on the whim of the local authorities. Fees range from about 5% to 15%, depending on the amount sent.

- In extreme emergencies (arrest, hospitalization, or worse) there is one more way American citizens can receive money overseas: by setting up a **Department of State Trust Fund.** A friend or family member sends money to the Department of State, which then transfers the money to the U.S. embassy or consulate in the city in which you're stranded. Once this account is established, you can send and receive money through Western Union, bank wire, or mail, all payable to the Department of State. For information, talk to the Department of State's Overseas Citizens' Emergency Center (tel. 202/647–5225).

CASH MACHINES Virtually all U.S. banks belong to a network of **ATMs** (Automated Teller Machines), which gobble up bank cards and spit out cash 24 hours a day in cities throughout the world. The networks most commonly found in Mexico are **Cirrus** and **Plus.** Major banks and their handy ATMs are everywhere, except for the smaller, more remote towns. If your transaction cannot be completed—an annoyingly common occurrence—chances are that the computer lines are busy and you'll just have to try again later. Another problem is that some Mexican ATMs only accept PINs of four or fewer digits; if your PIN is longer, ask your bank about changing it. **Visa** and **MasterCard** work in many Mexican ATMs (*see* Getting Money From Home, *above*), but **American Express** does not. The ATMs at **Banamex,** one of the oldest and perhaps the strongest nationwide bank, tend to be the most reliable, and generally give you an excellent exchange rate. **Bancomer** is another bank with many *cajero automatico* (ATM) locations, but generally they don't accept Plus or Cirrus cards and you can receive money only with Visa or MasterCard. The newer **Serfín** banks have reliable ATMs that accept credit cards as well as Plus and Cirrus cards. That said, remember that your bank back home will charge you either a percentage of the withdrawal or a fixed fee for each withdrawal you make in Mexico. To find out if there are any cash machines in a given city in Mexico, call your bank's department of international banking. Or call **Cirrus** (tel. 800/424–7787) for a list of worldwide locations.

WHAT TO PACK

As little as possible. Besides the usual suspects—clothes, toiletries, camera, a Walkman— bring along a day pack or some type of smaller receptacle for stuff. It'll come in handy not only for day excursions but also for those places where you plan to stay for only one or two days. You can usually check cumbersome bags at the bus or train station and just carry the essentials with you while you're out and about.

Backpacks are the most manageable way to lug belongings around, but they instantly brand you a foreign tourist. Also, outside pockets on backpacks are especially vulnerable to pickpockets, so don't store any valuables there. If you want to blend in more with the local population, bring a duffel or a large shoulder bag. Like new shoes, fully packed luggage should be broken in: If you can't tote your bag all the way around the block at home, it's going to be worse than a ball and chain in Mexico. Leaving some room for gifts and souvenirs is also wise.

By distributing the weight of your luggage across your shoulders and hips, backpacks ease the burden of traveling. You can actually choose among three types of packs: external-frame packs (for longer travels or use on groomed trails), internal-frame packs (for longer travels across rougher terrain), and hybrid travel packs (that fit under an airline seat and travel well in cities or the back country). Although external frames achieve the best weight distribution and allow airspace between you and your goodies, they're more awkward and less flexible than packs with an internal frame. Hybrid packs are ideal for travel in and out of cities: They often provide an adjustable internal support system, and all the straps zip away out of sight so you can look respectable when necessary. Since any decent pack will run you $100–$300, be sure to have it fitted correctly when you buy it. Make sure that it's waterproof, or bring an extra waterproof poncho to throw over it in downpours. Straps, zippers, and seams are the most vulnerable points on a bag; straps should be wide, adjustable, and offer some padding; check the stitching on zippers (look for a wide one) and seams. Backpacks that can be locked don't hurt either.

CLOTHING Smart—and not terribly fashion-conscious—travelers will bring two outfits and learn to wash clothes by hand regularly. Packing light does not mean relying on a pair of cut-off shorts and a tank top to get you through any situation, though. Shorts, along with other skin-exposing vestments, will make you awfully conspicuous in small Mexican towns, and women wearing them will attract attention they could probably live without. At resorts and most beach areas, however, shorts are fairly common and locals have become accustomed to seeing lots of foreign flesh. In general, though, you'll find that Mexicans dress more formally than gringos, and Mexican women stay more covered than their northern compañeras.

For maximum comfort, bring about two pairs of cotton pants; these will also dry more quickly than jeans. Bring several T-shirts and one sweatshirt or sweater for cooler nights. Socks and undies don't take up too much room, so throw in a couple extra pairs. In jungle areas, you'll need to wear socks and long pants to prevent bug bites and scratches from possibly toxic plants. You'll probably want a swimsuit even if you're not headed for the beach—you never know when you'll stumble across a swimming hole, river, or public pool. Rain gear is a must if you're traveling during rainy season. If you sunburn easily—and you're going to burn more easily than you think in Mexico—definitely bring or buy a large-brimmed hat to keep the sun off your face and ears (baseball caps don't work).

Recommended footware: a sturdy pair of walking shoes or hiking boots (broken in before your trip), a spare pair of shoes (preferably sandals) to give your tootsies a rest, and plastic sandals or thongs to protect feet on shower floors and for camping or beach-hopping. Since many Mexican shoe stores don't carry sizes larger than seven for either men or women, you may be in

The Four Rules of Luggage

- *You must be able to carry it at least a mile in hot, steamy weather.*

- *You must be able to fit it into a conventional storage locker or be fully prepared to schlep it with you everywhere.*

- *Keep anything you cherish in the middle of your bag. Pack your heaviest stuff in the middle of a pack and whatever you need quick access to (maps, guidebooks, address book) in an outer pocket. Keep money and travel documents on your body if possible.*

- *Attach a clearly marked, water-resistant luggage tag to your bag or write directly on the luggage with indelible ink. Also put some identifying paper or tag inside.*

serious trouble if you have big feet and your shoes give out. Your only option may be to ask a marketplace artisan to customize a pair of leather sandals.

LAUNDRY *Lavanderías* (laundromats) exist in all parts of Mexico and usually charge about $1–$3 per kilo. Or do your own dirty work at your hotel room. A do-it-yourself laundry kit includes: a plastic bottle of liquid detergent or soap (powder doesn't break down as well), about six feet of clothesline (enough to tie to two stable objects), and some plastic clips (bobby pins or paper clips can substitute). Porch railings, shower-curtain rods, bathtubs, and faucets can all serve as wet-laundry hangers if you forget the clothesline. A universal sink plug will come in handy; lacking that, a sock or plastic bag in the drain will do the trick. All of these things are, of course, available in stores in Mexico.

TOILETRIES You can find almost any toiletry you might need in a Mexican pharmacy—probably even the brand you're used to—at a reasonable price. If you do bring your favorite brands of shampoo, soap, and other necessities, put them in small containers to avoid bulk and weight. Use a separate, waterproof bag (zip-type bags are ideal) for containers that seal tightly; the pressure on airplanes can cause lids to pop off and create instant moisturizer slicks inside your luggage. Contact lens wearers should bring all the paraphernalia they need to conduct chemical warfare on their lenses, though saline solution is available at pharmacies. Condoms and birth control are also important, especially if you don't know the Spanish word for "dental dam" (all right, it's *presa dental,* but they won't have any in Mexico, trust us). Finally, bring insect repellent, sunscreen, and lip balm from home. **Avon Skin So Soft** body moisturizer is the best bug repellent in the world, even if it's not marketed as such. Check the phone book under AVON and make an appointment with your friendly Avon representative. Another option is **Green Ban's** environmentally sound insect repellent: stinky, but reasonably effective.

CAMERAS AND FILM While traveling, keep film as cool as possible, away from direct sunlight or blazing campfires. If your camera is new, or new to you, shoot and develop a few rolls before leaving home to avoid spoiling travel footage with prominent thumb shots. Unless you're an artiste, the smaller and lighter the camera, the better, although consider splurging on a $15 skylight filter to protect your lens and reduce haze in your photos. Also pack some lens tissue and an extra battery for cameras with built-in light meters. For any photo-related questions, call the **Kodak Information Center** (tel. 800/242–2424). On a plane, unprocessed film is safest in your carry-on luggage—ask security to inspect it by hand (it helps to keep your film in a plastic bag, ready for quick inspection). The higher the film speed, the more susceptible it is to damage.

BEDDING If you're planning to stay in hotels, you won't need to bring any bedding. Depending on where you're headed and during what time of year, though, you may want to pack a sheet, a light sleeping bag, or a thermal bag for sleeping on the beach or in a hammock. If you have a backpack, consider a sleeping mat that can be rolled tightly and strapped onto the bottom of your pack; these make train and bus station floors a tad more comfy. Sleep sheets often come in handy to make up

THE SLEEP SHEET DEFINED

Take a big sheet. Fold it down the middle the long way. Sew one short side and the long, open side. Turn inside out. Get inside. Sleep.

for skimpy bedding: You may run into beds with no more than an undersheet, and sometimes even that is of dubious cleanliness and/or a home for insects.

CAMPING GEAR If you're set on the happy-camper experience, be sure to arrive prepared: Camping supplies are scarce in Mexico. Before packing loads of camping gear, however, seriously consider how much camping you will actually do versus how much trouble it will be to haul around your tent, sleeping bag, stove, and accoutrements. Even finding a place to store your gear can be difficult, as storage lockers tend to be small. Also consider climate in choosing what to bring; camping in dry Baja demands different equipment than camping in the tropical, humid Lacandón jungle.

Down sleeping bags are more expensive but much warmer than synthetic bags, and can be scrunched into a tiny sack, but they're useless when wet. For further protection against cold from the ground, pick up an Ensolite pad or other thin foam pad that can be rolled up and tied to your pack. High-tech sleeping pads like Therma-Rests are a bit expensive, but worth it if you're a serious camper.

Tents come in cotton or synthetic canvas. The synthetic variety is more water-resistant and shelters against wind. Test the weight of the tent and try to visualize yourself packing it around on your back. For camping in damp areas, make sure your tent has edges that can be turned up off the ground to prevent water from seeping in, or bring a plastic tarp along. Also check the tent's windows and front flaps for mosquito-proof netting, and make sure the front flap can be completely zipped shut during rain. Expect to pay about $100–$150 for an average two-person tent, much more for a fancy ultra-light model.

You can buy a white-gas–burning ministove that provides one amazingly powerful flame and folds up into a little bag, for about $35. A kerosene-burning lantern costs about $40. Other handy odds and ends include matches in a waterproof container, a Swiss-army knife, something for banging in tent pegs (your shoe can work if it's sturdy enough), mosquito repellant, a mess kit ($15), a water purifier ($35), and water-purification tablets or iodine crystals ($8).

MISCELLANEOUS Stuff you might not think to take but will be damn glad to have: (1) a flashlight, good for electricity failures, reading in the dark, and exploring caves; (2) a pocket knife for cutting fruit, spreading cheese, removing splinters, and opening bottles; (3) a water bottle; (4) sunglasses; (5) several large zip-type plastic bags, useful for wet swimsuits, towels, leaky bottles, and rancid socks; (6) travel alarm clock; (7) a needle and small spool of thread; (8) some good books (you can trade with other travelers on the road); (9) batteries; (10) an English-Spanish dictionary; (11) duct tape; (12) a Walkman; (13) daypack for valuables or short jaunts; (14) a sturdy padlock to secure your luggage in lockers; (15) first-aid kit (*see* Staying Healthy, *below*); and (16) photos of family and friends to show your new *amigos*.

PROTECTING YOUR VALUABLES When is it safe to take your valuables off your body? Hostels and even hotel rooms are not necessarily safe; don't leave anything valuable out in the open. When sleeping or if you leave your room, keep what you cherish on your body or. And it may go without saying, but *never* leave your pack unguarded or with a total stranger even if you're only planning to be gone for a minute—it's not worth the risk. If you're carrying a smaller bag with a strap (or a camera), sling it crosswise over your body and try to keep your arm down over the bag in front of you. Back pockets are fine for maps, but don't store a wallet there; you might get the wrong kind of admiring attention. The best way to avoid theft is to leave expensive jewelry and cameras at home. When packing, ask yourself if you can go on living if a given item is lost or stolen. If not, put that item right back where it belongs—safe at home. The U.S. Printing Office publishes a pamphlet called "Safe Trip Abroad" ($1), which includes very general information on travel abroad. Send a check and a S.A.S.E. to: Superintendent of Documents, U.S. Printing Office, Washington, D.C. 20402. You can also phone the office at 202/512–1800.

STAYING HEALTHY

For up-to-the-minute information about health risks and disease precautions in all parts of the world, you can call the U.S. Center for Disease Control's 24-hour **International Travelers' Hotline** (tel. 404/332–4559), or check out their travel info home page at http://www.cdc.gov/cdc.html. The **Department of State's Citizens' Emergency Center** (Bureau of Consular Affairs, Room 4811, N.S., U.S. Dept. of State, Washington, D.C. 20520, tel. 202/647–5225, or 202/647–3000 for return fax info) provides written and recorded travel advisories. The "return fax line" offers you several prompts and will return information immediately to your fax number.

BEFORE YOU GO Although Mexico does not require a vaccine certificate of its visitors, you may want to use your upcoming trip as an excuse to update routine immunizations. These include measles, mumps, rubella, diphtheria, tetanus, polio, and hepatitis B. Also consider updating your influenza and pneumococcal vaccines. Immune globulin (IG), or the longer-lasting Havrix Hepatitis A vaccine—both used to prevent Hepatitis A—are suggested if you are traveling to underdeveloped areas that may have dubious sanitation. Beyond that, the vaccines you should get are determined by your specific destination and a careful consideration of the vaccines' effectiveness and side effects. Check with your physician to be sure you get all of the shots you need before you go. If your doctor isn't familiar with the risks associated with travel in your destination, you might be better off at a travel clinic (sometimes located in international airports). Ask your doctor to suggest one.

Finally, compared to the risks of malaria and dengue fever, sunburn may not seem very important, but you're much more likely to suffer from a painful sunburn than any exotic disease. Even if you have a dark complexion, bring plenty of powerful sunscreen, and slather it on at every opportunity.

➤ **HEALTH AND ACCIDENT INSURANCE** • Some general health-insurance plans cover health expenses incurred while traveling, so review your existing health policies (or a parent's policy, if you're a dependent) before leaving home. Most university health-insurance plans stop and start with the school year, so don't count on school spirit to pull you through. Canadian travelers should check with their provincial ministry of health to see if their resident health-insurance plan covers them on the road.

Organizations such as STA and Council (*see* Budget Travel Organizations, *above*), as well as some credit card conglomerates, include health-and-accident coverage with the purchase of an ID or credit card. If you purchase an ISIC card, you're automatically insured for $100 a day for in-hospital sickness expenses, up to $3,000 for accident-related medical expenses, and $25,000 for emergency medical evacuation. For details, request a summary of coverage from Council (205 E. 42nd St., New York, NY 10017, tel. 888/COUNCIL, http://www.ciee.org). Council Travel and STA also offer short-term insurance coverage designed specifically for the budget traveler. Otherwise, several private companies offer coverage designed to supplement existing traveler's health insurance; for more details contact your favorite student travel organization or one of the agencies listed below:

Carefree Travel Insurance (100 Garden City Plaza, Box 9366, Garden City, NY 11530, tel. 800/323–3149) is pretty serious about providing coverage for emergency medical evacuation and accidental death or dismemberment, and also offers 24-hour medical phone advice. **International SOS Assistance** (Box 11568, Philadelphia, PA 19116, tel. 800/523–8930) offers insurance through Insure America, providing emergency evacuation services, medical reports on your destination, and referrals. **Travel Guard** (1145 Clark St., Stevens Point, WI 54481, tel. 800/782–5151) provides the usual services and is endorsed by the American Socity of Travel Agents. **Wallach & Company** (107 W. Federal St., Box 480, Middleburg, VA 20118, tel. 800/237–6615, fax 540/687–3172) covers hospitalization, surgery, office visits, prescriptions, and medical evacuation. All insurance companies offer a variety of plans, based on length of stay and your budget.

➤ **MEDICAL ASSISTANCE** • Mexico has socialized medicine that, happily, travelers can take advantage of. Nearly every city or town has a **Centro de Salud** (government health center) or **Cruz Roja** (Red Cross), where you can receive free emergency medical care. The surroundings may look less than sanitary, but the visit and any drugs you may need are free. English-speaking doctors are usually found only in larger cities; a list of them is generally available from your embassy, local tourist offices, or the phone book. Private hospitals and clinics offer more medical specialists and a nicer atmosphere, but they can be expensive. To better inform yourself before you go, get a copy of the ***Medical Guide for Third World Travelers*** (KW Publications; $17.95), a comprehensive self-care handbook by Bradford L. Dessery amd Marc R. Robin. It should be shelved at your locakl bookstore. The following organizations are also helpful.

International Association for Medical Assistance to Travelers (IAMAT) is a nonprofit travelers' health organization that provides a worldwide directory of English-speaking physicians who are on 24-hour call and who have agreed to a fixed-fee schedule. IAMAT also issues a series of regularly updated immunization charts, pamphlets on tropical diseases, and info on sanitary conditions in countries around the world. Membership is free; donations are appreciated. *United States: 417 Center St., Lewiston, NY 14092, tel. 716/754–4883. Canada: 40 Regal Rd., Guelph, Ont. N1K 1B5, tel. 519/836–0102. New Zealand: Box 5049, Christchurch 5.*

British travelers can join **Europe Assistance Worldwide Services** (252 High St., Croyden, Surrey CRO 1NF, tel. 0181/680–1234) to gain access to a 24-hour hotline that can help in a

BASICS

medical emergency. The American branch of this organization is **Worldwide Assistance Incorporated** (1133 15th St. NW, Suite 400, Washington, D.C. 20005, tel. 800/821–2828), which offers emergency evacuation services and 24-hour medical referrals. An individual membership costs $62 for up to 15 days, $164 for 60 days. Family memberships are also available.

Diabetic travelers should contact one of the following organizations for resources and medical referrals: **American Diabetes Association** (1660 Duke St., Alexandria, VA 22314, tel. 800/232–3472) or **Canadian Diabetes Association** (15 Toronto St., Suite 1001, Toronto, Ont. M5C 2E3, tel. 416/363–3373). *The Diabetic Traveler* (Box 8223, Stamford, CT 06905, tel. 203/327–5832), published quarterly, lists vacations geared toward diabetics and offers travel and medical advice. Subscriptions cost $18.95. An informative article entitled "Management of Diabetes During Intercontinental Travel" and an insulin adjustment card are available for free.

➢ **PRESCRIPTIONS** • Some drugs sold in the States by prescription only are sold over the counter in Mexico. Just to be on the safe side, however, bring as much as you need of any prescription drugs as well as your written prescription (packed separately). Ask your doctor to type the prescription and include the following information: dosage, the generic name, and the manufacturer's name. To avoid problems clearing customs, diabetic travelers carrying syringes should have handy a letter from their physician confirming their need for insulin injections. No matter where you're traveling, most Mexican cities have at least one all-night pharmacy, and many that don't actually stay open advertise *servicio nocturno* (night service), meaning that someone sleeps on-site and you can ring the doorbell and wake them up, should the need arise.

➢ **FIRST-AID KIT** • Packing a few first-aid items could save you physical and financial pain during your travels. Prepackaged kits are available, but you can pack your own from the following list: bandages, waterproof surgical tape and gauze pads, antiseptic, cortisone cream, tweezers, a thermometer in a sturdy case, an antacid such as Alka-Seltzer, something for diarrhea (Pepto-Bismol or Imodium), and, of course, aspirin. If you're prone to motion sickness, take along some Dramamine as well. Pack lots of sunscreen to protect against cancer-causing rays. Women: If you're prone to yeast infections, over-the-counter medication like Monistat or Femstat will save you prolonged grief on the road. However, self-medicating should only be relied on for short-term illnesses; seek professional help if any symptoms persist or worsen.

➢ **CONTRACEPTIVES AND SAFE SEX** • AIDS and other STDs (sexually transmitted diseases) do not respect national boundaries, and protection when you travel takes the same form as it does at home. If you are contemplating an exchange of bodily fluids, latex condoms and/or dental dams (oral condoms) are the best forms of protection against STDs. Women: If you're on the pill, be sure to fill your prescription before departure and bring enough to carry you through your trip; you may not be able to get the same dosage or type of pills in Mexico. Birth control in general can sometimes be a touchy subject in this still predominantly Catholic country, and while you can buy it, you're probably better off bringing your own. Pack condoms or diaphragms in a pouch or case where they will be kept cool and not become squashed or damaged. *Do not* carry condoms close to your body (this includes pockets) because body heat can damage them. Council Travel (*see* Budget Travel Organizations, *above*) distributes a free "AIDS and International Travel" brochure containing information on safe sex, HIV testing, and hotline numbers.

➢ **WOMEN'S MEDICAL AID** • Most towns have a medical center—and some larger ones have family planning centers—where gynecologists are on staff and most routine examinations can be performed, including pregnancy tests. In bigger cities, medical care is of higher quality, female doctors are more common, and doctors will often send you to a *clínica de análisis* (analysis clinic) for tests, which are generally inexpensive. Although abortions are practiced in private clinics and private hospitals, Mexico is not a safe place to get one. It's important to keep in mind that in addition to the fact that the doctor may not have appropriate or sanitary equipment, you're not insured should complications arise.

DISEASES FROM FOOD AND WATER

DIARRHEA For many people, traveling in Mexico means an extended case of the ever-unpopular Montezuma's revenge, a.k.a. *turista* (tourists' disease). Contaminated food and drink are the major causes. Diarrhea, sometimes accompanied by nausea, bloating, and general malaise, usually lasts a few days or up to a week. Unfamiliar foods and changes in climate and lifestyle can all contribute to diarrhea. The best treatment is rehydration (no dairy products, carbonated liquids, coffee, cocoa, or alcohol) plus rest. In severe cases, mix purified water with a few pinches of salt and a couple of teaspoons of sugar, and drink. If you're hungry, stick to small portions of dry toast, banana, and *caldo de pollo* (chicken broth); avoid greasy, spicy foods. The best cure for diarrhea is to let it pass out of your system, but if you are very uncomfortable or need to travel to your next location, ask a local doctor or pharmacist to treat you for turista. Drugs such as Bactrim and Septra (available in the States) may help shorten the time you suffer. Lomotil or Imodium may decrease the number of trips you make to the toilet; however, if you have a serious infection, these drugs can cause more serious complications. If you maintain a fever over 102°F, if you have persistent vomiting, if you cannot rehydrate, if your stool is bloody, or if your bout lasts longer than a week, seek immediate medical attention.

➤ **HOW TO AVOID IT** • To avoid turista, be sure to drink only boiled or chemically disinfected water. Don't even brush your teeth with water that hasn't been treated. You can purchase water disinfectants such as Globaline and Potable-Aqua in the States before you leave. If your boiled water seems flat and tasteless, add a pinch of salt to bring back some taste. It may seem self-evident, but do NOT add ice cubes to boiled water.

Also be cautious when selecting meals. Raw foods are often contaminated, so be wary of salads, uncooked produce, and milk products. Meats and shellfish are usually suspect as well. To be on the safe side, avoid cooked food that has sat out too long and cooled, and unpeeled raw fruits or vegetables (wash them in a solution of purified water and a bit of vinegar first). Many fish, such as reef fish, red snapper, amberjack, grouper, sea bass, barracuda, and puffer fish should be avoided at all times due to the high levels of toxins in the areas they inhabit. You may think it safe to consume suspect foods if you see people of the region doing so, but think twice. These folks may have developed immune systems to combat sicknesses you aren't prepared for, or they may live with chronic illness themselves. All that said, if you spend your whole trip consuming only what appears sterile, you'll cheat yourself out of some spectacular local cuisine. The best strategy is to give your immune system a little time to get used to the new challenges it faces by exercising restraint during the first week or so of your trip.

CHOLERA This distressing intestinal infection is caused by a bacterium carried in contaminated water or food. It's characterized by profuse diarrhea, vomiting, cramping, and dehydration. If you think you may have contracted cholera, seek medical attention right away. Most people recuperate with simple fluid and electrolyte-replacement treatment, such as the rehydration packet *suero oral,* sold at any pharmacy. Right now cholera is at epidemic proportions in some areas of Oaxaca, Chiapas, and the Yucatán Peninsula. Like diarrhea, cholera is best avoided by eating only cooked foods that are still warm, drinking only bottled, boiled, or chemically treated water, and peeling fresh fruits. Avoid seafood, food sold by street vendors, and ice. The vaccine, in the form of a series of injections, is only 50% effective, and the U.S. Centers for Disease Control (CDC) does not recommend it as a standard vaccine for all travelers.

TYPHOID FEVER Typhoid, a bacterial infection common in Mexico, is spread through contaminated food and water. Drinking out of a contaminated person's glass or sharing that person's food can also put you at risk. Fever, headaches, exhaustion, loss of appetite, and constipation all indicate an onslaught of typhoid. If you think you have contracted typhoid, seek medical attention right away. A typhoid vaccine is available in oral form taken over a week, or as a series of injections taken over a month. The vaccine is only about 70%–90% effective, so it is important to drink only bottled, boiled, or treated water and to eat foods that have been cooked thoroughly.

HEPATITIS A Hepatitis A is a viral infection that attacks the liver. It's transmitted through contaminated food and water or between people, and it causes exhaustion, fever, loss of appetite, queasiness, dark urine, jaundice, vomiting, light stools, and achiness. Although prevalent in rural areas of Mexico, there is no specific treatment available.

➤ **HOW TO AVOID IT** • Once again, be sure to drink only treated water and thoroughly cooked foods. It's also an excellent idea to receive a dose of immune globulin (formerly known as gamma globulin) before traveling. A single dose of immune globulin should protect you from contracting Hepatitis A for a three-month period. Check with your doctor regarding dosage requirements for the length of your stay. If you are a frequent traveler to at-risk areas, you should get the Hepititis A vaccine, Havrix, four weeks before you begin traveling. Make sure to get a second "booster" dose 6–12 months after the first. Protection lasts about 20 years and there are no side affects. Both Havrix and immune globulin have been proven to be extremely effective. While in Mexico, be aware that what is advertised as immune globulin may not be equal to what you would receive in the United States.

INSECT-BORNE DISEASES

Mexico—especially the southern states—is teeming with mosquitoes, flies, fleas, ticks, and lice, all just itching to give travelers a mélange of foul diseases. For starters, you should reduce your exposure to mosquitoes by using mosquito netting and wearing clothes that cover most of your body. Beyond that, *bring the strongest insect repellent you can find and use it.* The CDC recommends DEET, a particularly strong (toxic) ingredient found in most insect repellants, including **Off.** Due to its strength, you shoud avoid applying products with more than 35% DEET to your skin. You can also purchase spray repellents and Permethrin to shower on clothing and bedding. You'll still get nailed, but why surrender to the critters without a fight?

If all of this sounds a bit too much like chemical warfare to you, there are a few other options. Thanks to modern science, we know mosquitoes don't like the taste of vitamin B. By megadosing (using two to four times the recommended daily allowance) on B-complex vitamins daily for at least a month before your trip, you'll put enough of the stuff in your blood to make you a less delectable dish than your friends. It won't completely solve the problem, but most people who try it notice the difference. Be warned, though, that taking large doses of vitamin B (or any other vitamin) can have side effects and may not be good for you in the long run. Your pee will be bright orange, too. Another option is to apply Avon Skin So Soft Moisturizer (*see* What to Pack, *above*), which bugs can't stand. The stuff is so effective that thousands of gallons were shipped to American soldiers during the Gulf War.

MALARIA Malaria thrives in many areas of Mexico. According to the CDC, the states with the highest incidence of malaria (in decreasing order) are: Oaxaca, Chiapas, Guerrero, Campeche, and Quintana Roo. The disease is transmitted by the bite of anopheles mosquitoes, hungry from sundown to sunup. Malaria usually resembles a feverish flu at the onset, but can develop into chills, aches, and weariness. It can lead to anemia, kidney failure, coma, and death if neglected. If you experience any of these symptoms while traveling or up to a year after exposure, seek medical attention.

➤ **HOW TO AVOID IT** • If you are going to a risky area, chloroquine or melfoquine is the recommended deterrent. Although most travelers take chloroquine, melfoquine is preferred when visiting San Blas, since the mosquitoes there have become resistant to choloroquine. Both drug regimens begin a week before you enter the malarious zone. Be sure to consult your doctor about side effects before taking either of these treatments. Cloroquine and melfoquine are not 100% effective, but they're worth taking to lessen your risks of getting this very unpleasant disease.

DENGUE FEVER Dengue fever is at epidemic proportions in Mexico right now. The fever is transmitted by the aedes mosquito, which, unlike other mosquitoes, is most active during the day and around dawn and dusk. This mosquito is often found near human habitations. Dengue usually becomes a problem during and after rainy seasons. It's most common in urban areas, especially below an elevation of 4,000 feet, but is found in rural areas as well. Dengue suddenly manifests itself with flu-like characteristics, a high fever, severe headache, joint and muscle aches, nausea, and vomiting. About three or four days after the fever appears, a rash develops. Treatment is simple: rest, fluid intake, and over-the-counter fever-reducing medications, but you should avoid aspirin. Dengue lasts for up to 10 days, and full recovery may take up to a month. There are more intense and rare forms of dengue that are characterized by faintness, shock, and general bleeding. If you develop any of these symptoms during your trip or up to a month after your return, visit your doctor immediately. Since there is no vaccine, the best way to avoid dengue is to protect yourself from mosquito attacks: Wear clothes that don't leave you exposed, sleep under mosquito netting, and slather on insect repellant. Also try to avoid wearing perfumes and dark colors; this will make you less appealing to the agressive aedes.

OTHER DISEASES

PARASITES In addition to all the diseases and viruses Mexico has to offer, parasites abound. They are transmitted through contaminated food and water, directly through contact with infected water and soil, or by insect bites. Again, be sure to use precautions to avoid insect bites, drink and eat foods you know are safe, and be sure to wear shoes when walking outside.

RABIES Rabies is also a concern in Mexico for anyone traveling in rural regions or areas with large dog populations. Rabies is a viral infection, contracted by the bite of an infected animal, that attacks the central nervous system. A pre-exposure rabies vaccination series provides adequate initial protection, but, if you are bitten by a potentially rabid animal, you will need additional inoculations. Be safe, not sorry, and don't go near stray dogs, cats, or other mammals.

RESOURCES FOR WOMEN

Travel guides often refer to the chauvinism and sexual aggressiveness of Mexican men. And although this is largely a caricature, it's clear that Mexican *machismo* is not completely dismissable as a stereotype. Foreign women traveling alone in Mexico *do* tend to receive plenty of *piropos* (compliments) from total strangers, but there are few places in the world where they don't. The hard part is dealing with the persistence of Mexican men. What may have started out as a request for directions or a friendly conversation can suddenly become a springboard for something more. Polite excuses won't do any good: You can't meet them for a drink because you're changing your place ticket? No problem—they'll be glad to accompany you. The best strategy is a firm "No, gracias," or "Mi novio me está esperando en el hotel" (My boyfriend is waiting for me back at the hotel). In general, exercise the same caution you would traveling anywhere—be alert, be cautious about who you are alone with, appear confident—and you should minimize problems. If you are traveling alone, don't let your gender prevent you from adventuring, but think twice about hitchhiking or camping solo. Needless to say, you'll attract less attention if less of your skin is showing: The "good girl/bad girl, Madonna/whore" dichotomies still have a secure place in Mexico's consciousness.

ORGANIZATIONS **Movimiento Nacional Para Mujeres** (San Juan de Letrán 11-411, México, D.F., tel. 5/512–58–41) can put you in contact with women's organizations all over Mexico. **Women Welcome Women** (**WWW**) (contact Betty Sobel, U.S.A. Trustee, 10 Greenwood Lane, Westport, CT 06880, tel. 203/259–7832) is a nonprofit organization aimed at bringing together women of all nationalities, ages, and interests. WWW publishes a newsletter three times a year and can get you in touch with women around the globe who are interested in a variety of women's issues. **Woodswomen** (25 W. Diamond Lake Rd., Minneapolis, MN 55419, tel. 612/822–3809 or 800/279–0555, fax 612/822–3814) specializes in adventure travel for women of all ages. This nonprofit organization, which claims to be the largest and most extensive women's travel outfit in the world, organizes safe, educational, and environmental excursions for its members. Yearly membership donations start at $20.

PUBLICATIONS Along with the lesbian-oriented *Women's Traveler* (*see* Resources for Gays and Lesbians, *below*), travel publications for women include *Women Travel: Adventures, Advice, and Experience* (Prentice Hall; $12.95). Over 70 countries receive some sort of coverage in the form of journal entries and short articles. As far as practical travel information goes, it offers few details on prices, phone numbers, and addresses. The *Handbook for Women Travelers* ($14.95) by Maggie and Gemma Moss, published by Judy Piatkus, has good general info on women's health and personal safety while traveling. Mary Morris's *Nothing To Declare* is a fascinating autobiographical account of her experiences traveling and living alone in Mexico. This absorbing read also provides some helpful insights on the dynamics between Mexican machismo and the lone gringa.

Women Out of Bounds (contact M. Back, 2119 Essex St., Berkeley, CA 94705, WmOutOf-Bnd@aol.com) is a newsletter for women travelers that offers practical advice and lists of helpful organizations. *Maiden Voyages* is a literary magazine for women who travel, with an emphasis on women's solo travel. Subscriptions are $20 a year in the United States. *109 Minna St., Suite 240, San Francisco, CA 94105, tel. 800/528-8425, http://www.maidenvoyages.com.*

RESOURCES FOR PEOPLE OF COLOR

Mexico is both racially diverse and very stratified. Although exceptions certainly exist, in general the elite is almost entirely white, the middle class is *mestizo* (of mixed ancestry), and the substantial *indígena* (indigenous) population lives for the most part in rural poverty. This said, racism is not a significant problem for travelers. The "worst" thing one may encounter is curiosity: Those of African and Asian descent are rare enough in most parts of Mexico that they may receive some extra attention. Nicknames such as *negro* (black person) and *chino* (Chinese person, which all Asians will receive regardless of country of origin) are common, but it is important to realize that they are not pejorative in Mexican culture, and are simply based on physical appearances. What does cause substantial differences in treatment, however, is one's nationality. The wealthier your country, the stronger the fascination (as well as the disdain) you may sense from the people you meet. Like most places, money and power speak more strongly than color. In general, though, you'll rarely experience any hostility, as Mexicans are on the whole hospitable to all foreigners, regardless of race.

RESOURCES FOR GAYS AND LESBIANS

Gender roles in Mexico are pretty rigidly defined, especially in rural areas. Openly gay couples are a rare sight, and two people of the same gender sometimes have trouble getting a *cama matrimonial* (double bed) at hotels. This intolerance may seem strangely juxtaposed with the hugs and kisses you'll see exchanged by people of the same sex, but physical affection in Mexico only goes so far. Homophobia in the country may have something to do with the Catholic church, whose strict codes on "morality" are taken as law by most natives. Although this influence has limited the development of a gay community, gay activity is not nonexistent. Alternative lifestyles (whether they be homosexuality or any other bending of conventional roles) are more easily encountered and accepted in metropolitan centers such as Acapulco, Guadalajara, and Mexico City. However, all travelers, regardless of sexual orientation, should be extra cautious when frequenting gay-friendly venues, as police sometimes crash these clubs and assault whomever they please. The victims receive little sympathy from the public.

ORGANIZATIONS The International Lesbian and Gay Association (ILGA) (81 Rue Marche au Charbon, 1000 Brussels 1, Belgium, tel. 02/502-24-71) is an excellent source for info about conditions, specific resources, and trouble spots in dozens of countries. **Doin' It Right Travel** (Box 192212, San Francisco, CA 94119-2212, tel. and fax 800/936-DOIN or 415/621-3576) offers extensive information on gay-owned and gay-friendly accommodations in Mexico.

PUBLICATIONS The *Damron Address Book* ($14.95) is an excellent resource focusing on gay male travel in a variety of destinations including Mexico, the United States, Canada, and parts of Central America. Also published by Damron is the *'97 Women's Traveler* ($11.95), which offers vast coverage of lesbian tours, accommodations, and bars, as well as funkier aspects of travel such as spiritual groups and erotica. The folks at their office can also sell you a copy of *Spartacus* ($32.95), which bills itself as *the* guide for the gay/lesbian traveler, with practical tips and reviews of hotels and agencies in over 160 countries, including Mexico. *Box 422458, San Francisco, CA 94142, tel. 415/255-0404 or 800/462-6654, fax 415/103-9049, damronco@aol.com.*

The guidebook *Ferrari Guides' Gay Travel A to Z*, published by Ferrari, includes listings of accommodations and nightlife, as well as general articles about gay/lesbian culture in Mexico and elsewhere. To receive a copy, send a check or money order for $16. Ferrari also publishes two pocket guides, one for gay men and one for lesbians. *Box 37887, Phoenix, AZ, 85069, tel. 602/863–2408, fax 602/439–3952, ferrari@q-net.com.*

One of the better gay and lesbian travel newsletters is **Out and About**, which lists gay-friendly hotels and travel agencies, plus health cautions for travelers with HIV. Free of advertisements, the magazine is relatively unbiased. A 10-issue subscription costs $49; single issues cost $4.95. One percent of the proceeds goes to funds for HIV research. Ask for issues specific to your destination country; several articles on Mexico were published in 1996. *Tel. 800/929–2268 for subscriptions.*

RESOURCES FOR TRAVELERS WITH DISABILITIES

Mexico is poorly equipped for travelers with disabilities. Most hotels and restaurants have at least a few steps, and while rooms considered "wheelchair accessible" by hotel owners are usually on the ground floor, the doorways and bathroom may not be maneuverable. There are no special discounts or passes for disabled travelers in Mexico, nor is public transportation, including the Mexico City Metro, wheelchair accessible. Renting or bringing a car or van is your best bet. Roads and sidewalks are often crowded, in poor condition, and without ramps, and people on the street will not usually assist you unless expressly asked.

Whenever possible, reviews in this book will indicate whether establishments are wheelchair accessible. The best choice of accessible lodging is found in resorts like Acapulco and Mazatlán, as well as other tourist-frequented locations. It's a good idea to call ahead to find out what a hotel can offer. Keep in mind, though, that many hotel proprietors don't understand the notion of accessibility. Despite these barriers, Mexicans with disabilities manage to negotiate places that most travelers outside Mexico would not consider accessible.

ORGANIZATIONS **Directions Unlimited** (720 N. Bedford Rd., Bedford Hills, NY 10507, tel. 800/533–5343 or 914/241–1700 in NY) organizes individual and group tours for people with disabilities. **Mobility International USA** (**MIUSA**) (Box 10767, Eugene, OR 97440, tel. and TDD 503/343–1284, fax 503/343–6812, miusa@igc.apc.org) is a nonprofit organization that coordinates exchange programs for people with disabilities around the world. MIUSA also offers information on accommodations and organized study programs for members. Membership costs $25 annually; nonmembers may subscribe to the newsletter for $15. **Moss Rehabilitation Hospital's Travel Information Service** (tel. 215/456–9900, TDD 215/456–9602) provides free information by phone on tourist sights, transportation, accommodations, and accessibility in destinations around the world. **The Guided Tour** (7900 Old York Rd., Suite 1148, Elkins Park, PA 19027–2339, tel. 800/783–5841, gtour400@aol.com) organizes guided vacation programs for the developmentally and physically challenged in various areas of Mexico. Trips last 3–12 days and you must be 17 years or older.

PUBLICATIONS Twin Peaks Press specializes in books such as **Travel for the Disabled**, which offers helpful hints as well as a comprehensive list of guidebooks and facilities geared to the disabled. Their **Directory of Travel Agencies for the Disabled** lists more than 350 agencies throughout the world. Each book is $19.95 plus $3 ($4.50 for both) shipping and handling. Twin Peaks also offers a "Traveling Nurse's Network," which connects travelers with disabilities with registered nurses to aid and accompany them on their trip. Fees range from $30 to $125. *Box 129, Vancouver, WA 98666, tel. 360/694–2462 or 800/637–2256 for orders only.*

WORKING IN MEXICO

If you have sea legs and happen to be headed where the wind is blowing, head down to the marina and ask about crew jobs. Waterside resorts are also eager to put gringos into the "career of a lifetime"—time-shares. Demand also exists for English teachers and for English speakers to work in posh hotels. Advertisements for such positions appear in newspaper classified ads, especially the English-language newspapers; also try calling language schools or hotels directly. The legal requirements for work are stringent (*see below*).

LEGAL REQUIREMENTS By law, a foreigner may legally work in Mexico only if contracted in his or her native country before arriving in Mexico. A Brit, for example, would need a work permit sponsored by his or her employer in England; the employer's affiliate in Mexico would process the permit and pave the way for the newcomer in Mexico. The process is very bureaucratic, and the professions with the best chance of success are those that require specific skills, such as engineering.

ORGANIZATIONS IAESTE sends full-time students abroad to practice their engineering, mathematics, and computer skills in over 50 countries. You don't get paid much, though the program is designed to cover day-to-day expenses. Applications are due between September and December for travel the following summer. *10 Corporate Center, Suite 250, 10400 Little Patuxent Pkwy., Columbia, MD 21044, tel. 410/997–2200, fax 410/997–5186.*

The **YMCA** oversees a variety of international work exchanges in over 25 countries; the most popular is the **International Camp Counselor Program** (**ICCP**), which entails teaching English, building houses, hanging out with local kids, you name it. The program rarely lasts longer than a summer, and participants stay at local YMCAs or with families. Don't expect to make much money. Write for a detailed brochure. *71 W. 23rd St., Suite 1904, New York, NY 10010, tel. 212/727–8800.*

PUBLICATIONS Council (*see* Budget Travel Organizations, *above*) publishes two excellent resource books with complete details on work/travel opportunities. The most valuable is *Work, Study, Travel Abroad: The Whole World Handbook* ($13.95), which gives the lowdown on scholarships, grants, fellowships, study-abroad programs, and work exchanges. Also worthwhile is Council's *The High-School Student's Guide to Study, Travel, and Adventure Abroad* ($13.95). Both books can be shipped to you book rate ($1.50) or first class ($3).

Vacation Work Press publishes two first-rate guides to working abroad: *Directory of Overseas Summer Jobs* ($14.95) and Susan Griffith's *Work Your Way Around the World* ($27.95). The former lists over 45,000 jobs worldwide; the latter has fewer listings but makes a more interesting read. Look for them at bookstores, or contact the publisher directly. *Peterson's: 202 Carnegie Center, Princeton, NJ 05843.*

STUDYING IN MEXICO

Many Mexican universities are open to foreigners for Spanish-language programs and general enrollment. Language schools are listed in the Basics sections for the cities where they exist, but the most popular places to study (and consequently the most packed with English speakers) are Cuernavaca and San Miguel de Allende, as well as the more cosmopolitan Mexico City and Guadalajara.

The **Center for Global Education at Augsburg College** (2211 Riverside Ave., Minneapolis, MN 55454, tel. 612/330–1159, fax 612/330–1695, globaled@augsburg.edu) offers informative, alternative travel seminars in Mexico and elsewhere in Central America that bring travelers in direct contact with grassroots organizations in the developing world. Call for a copy of their newsletter, *Global News and Notes,* and brochures on current travel seminars.

For more information on options for study in Mexico, contact **The National Registration Center for Study Abroad** (823 N. 2nd St., Milwaukee, WI 53203, tel. 414/278–0631, ask@nrcsa.com) or Council's **College and University Programs Department** (205 E. 42nd St., New York, NY 10017, tel. 212/822–2600).

VOLUNTEERING

There are plenty of volunteer opportunities in Mexico, from teaching to working on an archaeological dig. However, many require the volunteer to pay some sort of fee and/or living expenses. For those who have saved up some extra time and money, volunteer positions provide a great opportunity to get to know Mexican culture from more than a tourist's perspective.

ENCUENTROS
SPANISH ▼ LANGUAGE

Meet Mexico

Meet the People • Meet the Culture

ENCUENTROS is a total-immersion Spanish language program in
Cuernavaca, Morelos, Mexico. We devote special attention to those
who need Spanish for practical purposes such as business, travel, or
professional use in the workplace. Each student's language program
is designed for his or her needs and is evaluated on a weekly basis.
Classes can accomodate beginning, intermediate, and advanced
students and can be scheduled by the week or month.

Meet the Language

- Programs begin every Monday throughout the year.
- Four students maximum in language practice classes.
- Schedule from 9:00 am to 2:30 pm includes three hours of
classroom learning complemented by 2 hours of discussion groups,
conferences, and "living" communication activities.
- 1/2 hour of assessment and study-help daily.
- Teachers are native Mexicans.
- "Communicative" approach emphasizes natural verbal interaction.

Street address:
Calle Morelos 36 (antes 140)
Colonia Acapantzingo CP 62440
Cuernavaca, Morelos, México.

(011 from US)
Tel / fax: (52 73) 12 5088
E-mail: encuent@infosel.net.mx
E-mail: encuent@microweb.com.mx

Mailing address:
Encuentros Comunicación y Cultura
Apartado Postal 2-71
CP 62158 Cuernavaca, Mor., México

ORGANIZATIONS Council's **Voluntary Services Department** (205 E. 42nd St., New York, NY 10017, tel. toll-free 888/COUNCIL, or 212/822–2695, http://www.ciee.org) offers two- to four-week environmental or community service projects in 22 countries around the globe. Participants must be 18 or older and pay a $195 placement fee. Council also publishes *Volunteer! The Comprehensive Guide to Voluntary Service in the U.S. and Abroad* ($13.95, plus $1.50 postage), which describes nearly 200 organizations around the world that offer volunteer positions.

At one time or another everyone considers joining the **Peace Corps** for two years of volunteer service abroad. You don't have to be an expert in your field, but you do need a college degree and a strong sense of commitment. Room and board is provided, along with a small monthly stipend. *1990 K St. NW, Washington, D.C. 20526, tel. 800/424–8580, http://www.peacecorps.gov.*

Volunteers for Peace (**VFP**) sponsors two- to three-week international work camps in the United States, Europe, Africa, Asia, and Latin America for around $175. Send for their *International Workcamp Directory* ($12); it lists over 800 volunteer opportunities. *43 Tiffany Rd., Belmont, VT 05730, tel. 802/259–2759, fax 802/259–2922.*

PUBLICATIONS Bill McMillon's *Volunteer Vacations* ($13.95) lists hundreds of organizations and volunteer opportunities in the United States and abroad. Look for it in your local bookstore. The Archaeological Institute of America annually publishes *Archaeological Fieldwork Opportunities*, a very detailed listing of field projects around the world. *656 Beacon St., Boston, MA 02215-2010, tel. 617/353–9361, fax 617/353–6550.*

Coming and Going

GETTING THE BEST DEALS

While your travel plans are still in the fantasy stage, start studying the travel sections of major Sunday newspapers: Courier companies, charter flights, and fare brokers often list incredibly cheap flights. Travel agents are another obvious resource, as they have access to computer networks that show the lowest fares before they're even advertised. However, budget travelers are the bane of travel agents, whose commission is based on ticket prices. That said, agencies on or near college campuses, such as STA or Council Travel (*see* Budget Travel Organizations, *above*) actually cater to this pariah class and can help you find cheap deals.

Flexibility is the key to getting a serious bargain on airfare. If you can play around with your departure date, destination, amount of luggage carried, and return date, you will probably save money. Options include charter flights, student discounts, courier flights, and APEX (Advanced Purchase Excursion) and Super APEX fares; read on to help get through this maze. Hot tips when making reservations: If the reservation clerk tells you that the least expensive seats are no longer available on a certain flight, ask to be put on a waiting list. If the airline doesn't keep waiting lists for the lowest fares, call them on subsequent mornings and ask about cancellations and last-minute openings—airlines trying to fill all their seats sometimes add additional cut-rate tickets at the last moment. When setting travel dates, remember that off-season fares can be as much as 50% lower. A useful resource is Michael McColl's *The Worldwide Guide to Cheap Airfares*, an in-depth account of how to find cheap tickets and generally beat the system. If you don't find it at your local bookstore, you can mail a check for $14.95 plus $2.50 for shipping and handling to Insider Publications (2124 Kittredge St., 3rd Floor, Berkeley, CA 94704), or call 800/782–6657 and order with a credit card.

STUDENT DISCOUNTS Student discounts on airline tickets are offered through **Council Travel,** the **Educational Travel Center, STA Travel,** and **Travel CUTS** (*see* Budget Travel Organizations, *above*). **Campus Connection** (1100 E. Marlton Pike, Cherry Hill, NJ 08032, tel. 800/428–3235), exclusively for students under 25, searches airline computer networks for the cheapest student fares to worldwide destinations. They don't always have the best price, but because they deal directly with the airlines you won't get stuck with a heavily restricted or fraudulent ticket. Keep in mind that most airlines will often *not* entitle you to frequent-flyer mileage for discounted student, youth, or teacher tickets. For discount tickets based on your

status as a student, youth, or teacher, have an ID that proves it when you check in: an International Student Identity Card (ISIC), GO25, or International Teacher Identity Card (ITIC).

CONSOLIDATORS AND BUCKET SHOPS Consolidator companies, also known as bucket shops, buy blocks of tickets at wholesale prices from airlines trying to fill flights. Check out any consolidator's reputation with the Better Business Bureau before starting; most are perfectly reliable, but better safe than sorry. If everything works as planned, you'll save 10%–40% on the published APEX fare. There are, however, some drawbacks to consolidator tickets: They're often nonrefundable, and the flights to choose from often feature indirect routes, long layovers in connecting cities, and undesirable seating assignments. If your flight is delayed or canceled, you'll also have a tough time switching airlines. As with charter flights, you risk taking a huge loss if you change your travel plans. If possible, pay with a credit card, so that if your ticket never arrives you don't have to pay. Bucket shops generally advertise in newspapers—be sure to check restrictions, refund possibilities, and payment conditions. One last suggestion: Confirm your reservation with the airline both before and after you buy a consolidated ticket. This not only decreases the chance of fraud, but also ensures that you won't be the first to get bumped if the airline overbooks. For more details, contact one of the following consolidators.

Mena Travel (2479 N. Clark St., Chicago, IL 60614, tel. 800/536–6362 or 312/472–5361, fax 312/472–2829) is a consolidator specializing in Latin American destinations. **Travel Network** (13240 Northup Way, Suite 4, Bellevue, WA 98005) will send you to anywhere in the world from anywhere in the world. **Buenaventura Travel** (595 Market St., 22nd Floor, San Francisco, CA 94105, tel. 800/286–8872 or 415/777–9777, fax 415/777–9871) has discount fares to many destinations in Mexico.

CHARTER FLIGHTS Charter flights have vastly different characteristics, depending on the company you're dealing with. Generally speaking, a charter company either buys a block of tickets on a regularly scheduled commercial flight and sells them at a discount (the prevalent form in the United States) or leases the whole plane and then offers relatively cheap fares to the public (most common in the United Kingdom). Summer charter flights fill up the quickest and should be booked a couple of months in advance. Despite a few potential drawbacks—among them infrequent flights, restrictive return-date requirements, lickety-split payment demands, frequent bankruptcies—charter companies often offer the cheapest tickets around, especially during high season when APEX fares are most expensive. Make sure you find out a company's policy on refunds should a flight be canceled by either yourself or the airline. You can minimize risks by checking the company's reputation with the Better Business Bureau and taking out enough trip-cancellation insurance to cover the operator's potential failure. The list below is far from exhaustive; check newspaper travel sections for more extensive listings. Council Travel and STA (*see* Budget Travel Organizations, *above*) also offer exclusively negotiated discount airfares on scheduled airlines.

SunTrips (SunTrips Building, 2350 Paragon Dr., San Jose, CA 95131, tel. 800/786–8747 or 408/432–1101) is a charter operator specializing in destinations in Europe, the United States, and Mexico. **Travel Time** (1 Halladie Plaza, Suite 406, San Francisco, CA 94102, tel.

Playing the Airfare Game

There are two kinds of regular-fare tickets in this world: Full-fare and APEX (advance purchase excursion). The APEX price is the lowest published fare for any ticket purchased at least 21 days in advance. APEX tickets are what pleasure travelers buy if they aren't to be bothered with seeking cut-rate fares. Regular full-fare tickets are for business travelers on corporate accounts and supermodels who have to jet to Paris tonight, darling. APEX fares are worth looking into, but real bargain hunters should focus on the three Cs: consolidators, charters, and couriers.

800/956–9327 or 415/677–0799, fax 415/391–1856) is a discount travel agency with access to charter fares worldwide.

COURIER FLIGHTS A few restrictions and inconveniences are the price you'll pay for the colossal savings on airfare offered to air couriers—travelers who accompany letters and packages between designated points. The way it works is simple. Courier companies list whatever flights are available for the next week or so. After you book the flight, you sign a contract with the company to act as a courier (some places make you pay a deposit, to be refunded after the successful completion of your assignment). On the day of departure, you arrive at the airport a few hours early, meet someone who hands you a ticket and customs forms, and off you go. After you land, you simply clear customs with the courier luggage and deliver it to a waiting agent.

The main restrictions are (1) flights can be booked only a week or two in advance, and often only a few days in advance, (2) you are often allowed carry-on luggage only, because the courier uses your checked-luggage allowance to transport the time-sensitive shipment, (3) you must return within one or two weeks, sometimes within 30 days, (4) most courier companies only issue tickets to travelers over the age of 18.

Both **Now Voyager** (74 Varick St., Suite 307, New York, NY 10013, tel. 212/431–1616) and **Air Facility** (153-40 Rockaway Blvd., Jamaica, NY 11434, tel. 718/712–1769, fax 718/712–1574) serve Mexico City and depart from New York. For other courier companies, check newspaper travel sections, the yellow pages of your phone directory, or mail away for a telephone directory that lists companies by the cities to which they fly. One of the better publications is *Air Courier Bulletin* (IAATC, 8 South J St., Box 1349, Lake Worth, FL 33460, tel. 407/582–8320), sent to IAATC members every two months once you pay the $35 annual fee. Another good resource is the newsletter published by **Travel Unlimited** (Box 1058, Allston, MA 02134), which costs $25 for 12 issues. Publications you can find in the bookstores include *Air Courier Bargains* ($14.95), published by The Intrepid Traveler, and *The Courier Air Travel Handbook* ($9.95), published by Thunderbird Press.

LAST-MINUTE DEALS Flying standby is almost a thing of the past. The idea is to purchase an open ticket and wait for the next available seat on the next available flight to your chosen destination. However, most airlines have dumped standby policies in favor of three-day-advance-purchase youth fares, which are open only to people under 25 and (as the name states) can only be purchased within three days of departure. Return flights must also be booked no more than three days prior to departure. If you meet the above criteria, expect 10%–50% savings on published APEX fares. If you're desperate to get to Mexico by Friday, try **Air-Tech Ltd.** (584 Broadway, Suite 1007, New York, NY 10012, tel. 212/219–7000, fax 212/219–0066, info@aerotech.com), which offers standby flights to coastal cities in Mexico leaving from West Coast, northeast, and Chicago airports only. **Last Minute Travel Club** (1249 Boylston St., Boston, MA 02215, tel. 800/527–8646) has access to a variety of fares, but has more East Coast than West Coast departures.

CUSTOMS AND DUTIES

ARRIVING IN MEXICO When going through customs, looking composed and presentable (wealthy and innocent doesn't hurt either) expedites the process. If you're bringing any foreign-made equipment, such as cameras or video gear, on your trip, it's wise to carry the original receipt or register it with customs before leaving the United States (ask for U.S. Customs Form 4457). Otherwise, you may end up paying duty on your return. To avoid problems, don't even think about drugs. Being cited for drug possession is no joke, and embassies and consulates often can't do much to persuade country officials to release accused drug traffickers/users (*see* Crime and Punishment, *below*). If you're bringing prescription drugs into Mexico, carry the doctor's signed prescription with you.

If you're arriving in Mexico City, you may be one of the one in 10 people whose luggage is searched. Before passing through customs you'll press a button in front of a small stoplight apparatus. If the resulting light is green, you can pass go; if it's red, officials search your baggage. You will be given a baggage-declaration form to itemize what you're bringing into the country. You're allowed to bring in 3 liters of spirits or wine for personal use, 400 cigarettes, two boxes of cigars, a reasonable amount of perfume for personal use, one movie camera and one regular camera, eight rolls of film for each, and gift items not to exceed a total of $120.

RETURNING HOME It's best to have all the souvenirs and gifts you're bringing home in an easily accessible place, just in case officials would like to have a peek.

➤ **U.S. CUSTOMS** • You're unlikely to have run-ins with U.S. customs as long as you *never* carry any illegal drugs in your luggage. When you return to the United States you have to declare all items you bought abroad, but you won't have to pay duty unless you come home with more than $400 worth of foreign goods, including items bought in duty-free stores. For purchases between $400 and $1,000 you have to pay a 10% duty. You also have to pay tax if you exceed your duty-free allowances: 1 liter of alcohol or wine (for those 21 and over), 100 non-Cuban cigars or 200 cigarettes, and one bottle of perfume. A good way to get around paying taxes at all is to send goods home via Mexican mail or a more reliable express mail service. The **U.S. Customs Service** (Box 7407, Washington, D.C. 20044, tel. 202/927–6724) provides a free leaflet, "Know Before You Go," about customs regulations and illegal souvenirs; call for your copy.

➤ **CANADIAN CUSTOMS** • Exemptions for returning Canadians range from C$20 to C$500, depending on how long you've been out of the country: For two days out, you're allowed to return with C$200 worth of goods; for one week out, you're allowed C$500 worth. Above these limits, you'll be taxed about 15%. Duty-free limits are: up to 50 cigars, 200 cigarettes, 400 grams of tobacco, and 1.14 liters of liquor—all of which must be declared in writing upon arrival at customs and must be with you or in your checked baggage. To mail back gifts, label the package: "Unsolicited Gift—Value under C$60." For more scintillating details, call the automated information line of the **Revenue Canada Customs, Excise and Taxation Department** (2265 St. Laurent Blvd. S., Ottawa, Ont., K1G 4K3, tel. 613/993–0534 or 613/991–3881), where you may request a copy of the Canadian customs brochure "I Declare/Je Déclare."

➤ **U.K. CUSTOMS** • Travelers age 17 or over who return to the United Kingdom may bring back the following duty-free goods: 200 cigarettes or 100 cigarillos or 50 cigars or 250 grams of tobacco; 1 liter of alcohol over 22% volume or 2 liters of alcohol under 22% volume, plus 2 liters of still table wine; 60 ml of perfume and 250 ml of toilet water; and other goods worth up to £136. For further information or a copy of "A Guide for Travelers," which details standard customs procedures as well as what you may bring into the United Kingdom from abroad, contact **HM Customs and Excise** (Dorset House, Stamford St., London SE1 9PY, tel. 0171/928–3344).

➤ **AUSTRALIAN CUSTOMS** • Australian travelers 18 and over may bring back, duty-free: 1 liter of alcohol; 250 grams of tobacco products (equivalent to one carton of cigarettes or cigars); and other articles worth up to AUS$400. If you're under 18, your duty-free allowance is AUS$200. To avoid paying duty on goods you mail back to Australia, mark the package: "Australian goods returned." For more rules and regulations, request the pamphlet "Customs Information for Travelers" from a local **Collector of Customs** (GPO Box 8, Sydney NSW 2001, tel. 029/213–2000).

➤ **NEW ZEALAND CUSTOMS** • Although greeted with a "*Haere Mai*" ("Welcome") or "*Kai Ora*" ("Hello"), homeward-bound travelers face a number of restrictions. Travelers over age 17 are allowed, duty-free: 200 cigarettes or 250 grams of tobacco or 50 cigars or a combo of all three up to 250 grams; 4.5 liters of wine or beer and one 1,125-ml bottle of spirits; and goods with a combined value of up to NZ$700. If you want more details, ask for the pamphlet "Customs Guide for Travelers" from the customs office (New Zealand Customs, Box 29, Auckland, New Zealand, tel. 09/397–3520.)

BY AIR

On your fateful departure day, remember that check-in time for international flights is a long two hours before the scheduled departure. When homeward bound, be prepared to pay a departure tax of $12 (payable in cash only) at the airport. Also note that flights lasting more than six hours are smoking flights. The fume abhorer should book short air-hops or ask for seats as far away from the smoking section as possible; if you love to light up, book long and straight.

FROM THE UNITED STATES Airlines serving Mexico with direct flights from major U.S. cities include **Aerocalifornia** (tel. 800/237–6225) from Los Angeles; **Aeroméxico** (tel. 800/237–6639) from Houston, Los Angeles, Miami, New York, and Tucson; **American** (tel. 800/433–7300) from Dallas/Fort Worth, Miami, and Raleigh/Durham; **Continental** (tel. 800/525–0280) from Houston and Newark; **Delta** (tel. 800/221–1212) from Atlanta, Dallas/Fort Worth, Los Angeles, and Orlando; **Mexicana** (tel. 800/531–7921) from Chicago, Denver, Los Angeles, Miami, Newark, San Antonio, San Francisco, and San Jose; **Northwest** (tel. 800/225–2525) from Detroit, Minneapolis, and Tampa; and **United** (tel. 800/241–6522) from Chicago, Washington/Dulles, Los Angeles, and San Francisco.

LUGGAGE You've heard it a million times. Now you'll hear it once again: Pack light. U.S. airlines allow passengers to check two pieces of luggage, neither of which can exceed 62 inches (length + width + height) or weigh more than 70 pounds. If your airline accepts excess baggage, it will probably charge you for it. Foreign-airline policies vary, so call or check with a travel agent before you show up at the airport with one bag too many. If you're traveling with a pack, tie all loose straps to each other or onto the pack itself, as they tend to get caught in luggage conveyer belts. Put valuables like cameras and important documents in the middle of your carry-on, wadded inside clothing, because outside pockets are extremely vulnerable to probing fingers.

Valuables and anything you'll need during the flight should be stowed in a carry-on bag. Foreign airlines have different policies but generally allow only one carry-on in tourist class, in addition to a handbag and a bag filled with duty-free goodies. The carry-on bag cannot exceed 45 inches (length + width + height) and must fit under your seat or in the overhead luggage compartment. Call for the airline's current policy. Passengers on U.S. airlines are limited to one carry-on bag, plus coat, camera, and handbag. Carry-on bags must fit under the seat in front of you; maximum dimensions are 9 x 45 x 22 inches. Hanging bags can have a maximum dimension of 4 x 23 x 45 inches; to fit in an overhead bin, bags can have a maximum dimension of 10 x 14 x 36 inches. If your bag is too porky for compartments, be prepared for the humiliation of rejection and last-minute baggage check.

BY CAR

Compared to bus and train ticket prices in Mexico, renting a car is outrageously expensive unless you share the cost with other travelers.

Bringing a car into Mexico has become seriously complicated. The owner of the vehicle must provide proof of ownership, state registration, and a valid driver's license issued outside Mexico. The owner must also provide a credit card number (American Express, Visa, Diner's Club, or MasterCard) or a bond as security against selling the car while in Mexico. All documents and credit cards must be in the name of the owner, who must be driving the car. All this information must be presented to Mexican customs officals as you enter Mexico. Usually, their office, often combined with the office that issues tourist cards, is adjacent to the border crossing. If your permit runs out or you are found without the proper documents, your car can be immediately confiscated. However, these restrictions only apply for

Bikes in Flight

Most airlines will ship bikes as luggage, provided they are dismantled and put into a box. Call to see if your airline sells bike boxes (around $10). International travelers can substitute a bike for their second piece of checked luggage at no extra charge; otherwise, it will cost $100 extra. Domestic airlines are less gracious and uniformly charge bike-toting travelers a $50 fee.

— see Chapter 4 for details.

a10 minutes. The border officials do not care if you buy any insurance or not, but a

chke traffic. Toll-road prices vary tremendously: From Tijuana to Ensenada you pay less than $5 total for 100 kilometers, whereas the toll roads around Mexico City can run $30 for the same distance. Two excellent road atlases published in Mexico are Pemex's *Atlas de Carreteras y Ciudades Turísticas* and another put out by Guía Roji. Both of these are widely available in bookstores and at newsstands.

RENTAL CARS If you want to rent in the United States and drive down to Mexico, you'll find rental companies less than obliging. You can rent a car from **Avis** (tel. 800/852–4617) in Yuma, Arizona, or San Diego, California, and drive it into Mexico, but only for a maximum of 714 kilometers (450 mi) one-way. **Dollar** (tel. 800/800–4000) will allow you to drive 241 kilometers (150 mi) into Mexico from San Diego or from McAllen, Texas, as far as Monterrey. Finally, **Thrifty** (tel. 800/367–2277) allows you to drive from San Diego into Mexico, but only for 80 kilometers (50 mi).

If your travel dates are fairly rigid, setting up a car rental through an agency in the United States is a cheaper alternative to renting south of the border. You will save at least $10 per day and will be assured of actually getting a car. Check with agencies to see if they have branches in the Mexican city you desire; **Avis** (tel. 800/331–2112), **Budget** (tel. 800/527–0700), **Dollar** (tel. 800/800–4000), **Hertz** (tel. 800/654– 3131), and **National** (tel. 800/227–3876) all rent cars in Mexico, and their prices are basically the same. Each of these companies requires you to purchase Mexican insurance (usually about $15–$20 per day), and all rental agencies add a 10% tax to the price. An average rate for a Volkswagen Beetle with stick shift, unlimited mileage, and basic insurance coverage is $50–$60 per day. Most agencies rent only to drivers 25 years old or over, but you need only be 21 years old at Avis and 22 at National (though you do need two major credit cards). Cash or credit cards are usually accepted as payment. These prices are constant throughout the year, but there is some variation between locations. The companies that rent for Baja have different prices and sometimes different rules than mainland Mexico.

BY BUS

Unless you're on a tour, such as those run by Green Tortoise (*see below*), there aren't many direct buses into Mexico. Usually, you must trundle down to the border, cross, and then change to a Mexican bus on the other side to continue your journey (*see* Getting Around, By Bus, *below*). At the El Paso–Ciudad Juárez border crossing, **Greyhound** (tel. 800/231–2222) has a bus (30 min, $5) that will take you from El Paso to the Ciudad Juárez bus terminal, stopping at border customs along the way. San Diego–Tijuana has a similar system, called **Mexi-Coach** (*see* Chapter 3), which runs from San Ysidro, on the U.S. side, to downtown Tijuana. Otherwise, Greyhound will get you to, but not across, the border; the company serves El Paso, Del Río, Laredo, McAllen, Eagle Pass, and Brownsville, Texas; Nogales, Arizona; and Calexico and San Diego, California.

Green Tortoise Adventure Travel (494 Broadway, San Francisco, CA 94133, tel. 415/956–7500, or 800/867–8647 outside CA) is the cheap alternative to humdrum bus travel. From November through April, Green Tortoise buses—equipped with sleeping pads, kitchens, and stereos—offer nine- and 14-day trips from the West Coast of the United States to Baja. In November and December, limited space is available for longer trips to Mexico City, Mérida, and Guatemala.

BY TRAIN

Amtrak (tel. 800/872–7245) will get you as far as San Diego, El Paso, or San Antonio. From San Antonio, you'll have to catch another bus to Laredo, on the border. From El Paso or Laredo, you'll be able to walk across the border. The wheelchair-accessible **San Diego Trolley** (tel. 619/231–8549) will get you from the train station to downtown San Diego, where another trolley departs every 15 minutes for the San Ysidro border crossing (*see* Tijuana, in Chapter 3).

Staying in Mexico

GETTING AROUND

BY PLANE Domestic plane travel will save you travel time, but it will cost about four times as much as a first-class bus. **Mexicana** (tel. 800/5–02–20) and **Aeroméxico** (tel. 800/9–09–99) are government-subsidized and offer similar fares. **Aerocalifornia** (tel. 800/6–05–79) flies between Baja California cities and some places in northwestern Mexico. **Aerolitoral** serves various destinations in northwest Mexico, including Los Mochis and La Paz. **Aerocaribe** (tel. 800/7–05–79) and **Aviacsa** (tel. 800/6–21–26) operate in southeast Mexico. All of the above phone numbers can only be dialed from Mexico.

Learning the Spanish names for the cardinal directions will help you find your way around most Mexican cities, which are usually laid out in a grid formation: Nte./Norte = North; Sur = South, Ote./Oriente = East; Pte./Poniente = West.

BY BUS Bus travel throughout Mexico is cheap and easy (*see* How Much It Will Cost, *above*). Buses are basically divided into first and second class, but in reality they run the gamut from dilapidated school buses with shrines to the Virgin of Guadalupe attached to the grill and blasting *ranchera* music, to luxury liners with air- conditioning, bathrooms, on-board movies, and free refreshments. Most of the time, however, second-class means a comfortable bus with no air-conditioning that makes a number of stops, while first-class service consists of a cleaner bus, chilled beyond reason, and (usually) a direct ride. Super-deluxe buses are usually designated *plus* or *especial*. The largest second-class bus line in Mexico is **Flecha Amarilla**; first-class lines include **Omnibús de Mexico, Futura, Transportes del Norte,** and **Élite.** Although **ETN** doesn't serve as many destinations, it is by far the best and well worth the extra expense.

BY TRAIN Of all the forms of transport in Mexico, trains have the worst reputation: notoriously run-down, slow, late, and a haven for thieves. Depending on the type of train and route, they can arrive absurdly late or leave absurdly early, but they are always slower than buses. Buying a ticket is also a uniquely frustrating experience, as ticket offices are often closed most of the day, generally until trains actually roll in; it's a good idea to call the train station in advance whenever possible. There are several classes of service, not all of which are available for any given route. Special first class usually has air-conditioning and functioning bathrooms with water. A limited number of expensive sleeper cars are available on some trains offering special first class. Advantages to train travel include great scenery, a certain romantic air, and a leisurely pace. If you're going to ride any train, your best bet is the **Chihuahua al Pacífico** (the Copper Canyon train), which is tourist-friendly and has an on-time, safe, and easily accessible first-class line.

BY CAR Go where you want to when you want to, roll the windows down, and pop in your favorite tape as you cruise down the highway. Sounds heavenly, but be ready for anything: Driving in a foreign country is always an adventure, and the quality of Mexican roads varies substantially. Drivers need a current license and registration, as well as a vehicle permit from border officials for cars not registered in Mexico. For the lowdown on permit procedures, *see* Coming and Going, By Car, *above*.

The maximum speed on most highways is 100 kilometers (62 mi) per hour (120 km on some expressways). On many state and local roads, however, you'll be lucky to do half that, as many roads, even those connecting major towns, are single-lane routes clogged with smoke-belching trucks. Trucks will often help you out by flashing their turn signals to let you know that it is safe to pass. Toll roads, or *autopistas,* connect some major cities, charging random prices at randomly dispersed toll booths. However, it may be worth the added expense: Emergency phones and water pumps are available about every 15 kilometers (9 mi), the fees keep traffic to a minimum, and road conditions are excellent. Driving at night is discouraged, as roads are often poorly marked and, in rural areas, animals wandering onto roadways can be a major hazard. If you have an acci-

For those who don t believe machismo has its good points: Mexican police officers are specifically told in their training not to fine women drivers, so women usually get off the hook for minor driving infractions.

dent, notify the police immediately; take pictures of all cars involved; and, collect information from the other driver (provided he or she hasn't driven away). Even if the accident wasn't your fault, the rule in Mexico is "guilty until proven innocent," and the police will not necessarily take your word as gospel if the other driver blames you. Photos will strengthen your case.

You are required to stop and show your personal and vehicle documents at *all* roadside customs checkpoints. You are also required to stop anytime a police officer waves you over, but be cautious: Travelers are prime targets for robbers who pose as police officers. Highways 1 and 15 in Sinaloa have become infamous for this sort of robbery. If you are pulled over, keep calm, look important (if possible), and be amicable. A 50–100 peso ($6–$13) *mordida* (bribe; literally, "bite") will usually speed the process along. However, don't volunteer this until it looks like there's no other option. As for fuel, all the gas you buy will be from Pemex, Mexico's state-owned oil monopoly. Quality is low, so you may hear some unfamiliar engine knocks. Pemex's unleaded *Magna Sin* gas should be safe for most vehicles requiring unleaded gasoline. Fill up when you see a station, since the next one may have a broken pump.

Roadside emergency service is available in much of the country from the **Ángeles Verdes** (Green Angels), a group of radio-dispatched, English-speaking mechanics. If you break down, pull over and pop your hood up; one will come cruising along if you wait long enough and pray hard enough. It's a good idea to keep their 24-hour toll-free emergency number on hand (tel. 800/90–39–200). Service is free. The **Asociación Mexicana Automovilística** (AMA), Mexico's motoring club, gives discounted services to AAA members. For a $50 registration fee, they'll provide roadside repairs, fuel and tire service, plus free towing (up to 10 km) in Mexico City, Puebla, and other central Mexican towns. *Orizaba 7, Col. Roma, Distrito Federal, CP 06700, México, tel. 5/511–62–85. Emergency tel. 5/588–70–40 or 5/761–60–22.*

BY MOTORCYCLE Motorcycling conditions in Mexico are not ideal. Roads are not always in the best condition, but there are plenty of long stretches to open up the bike and watch the land whiz by. Small dirt bikes are good for bouncing around the desert. For best results, bring your own bike, because rentals are quite expensive. You should know how to do your own repairs and bring plenty of supplies. As with any vehicle in Mexico, avoid driving at night. The same rules apply to bringing a motorcycle into Mexico as bringing a car in (*see* Coming and Going, By Car, *above*).

BY BIKE Bike travel in Mexico is for the hardy and experienced rider. Some roads have never seen a bicycle, and drivers are not used to bikers. In addition, most Mexican roads lack shoulders and are often pitted. Despite these drawbacks, traveling by bike in Mexico can be fun if you plan ahead. Bikes are especially useful for travel to places where there are only dirt roads or tracks, or where public transportation is scant. In the Yucatán, for example, bikes are a primary form of transportation for locals, and bike-repair shops are common even in smaller towns. When planning your trip, consult an up-to-date AAA, Pemex, or Guía Roji map. Be sure to carry plenty of water and everything you might need to repair your bike. Pack extra patch kits, as shards of glass often litter the roads. If you can take your bike apart and fold it up, buses will allow you to store it in the cargo space. Bikers in the Copper Canyon can transport their bikes on the trains.

Some adventurous cyclists have organized tours of Baja; write to **The Touring Exchange** (Box 265, Port Townsend, WA 98368) for details. **Backroads** (811 Cedar St., Berkeley, CA 94710–

1740, tel. 800/245–3874) offers trips around Baja and the Yucatán, and **Expedition Touring** (300 3rd Ave. W., Seattle, WA 98119, tel. 206/463–4081) can give you information on biking tours in Mexico. *Latin America by Bike* (The Mountaineers, 306 2nd Ave. W., Seattle, WA 98119, $14.95), by Walter Sienko, provides information on biking opportunities in Mexico as well as Central and South America. *Bicycling Mexico* (Hunter Publishing Inc., 300 Raritan Center Pkwy., Edison, NJ 08818, tel. 201/225–1900 fax 201/417–0482), by Ericka Weisbroth and Eric Ellman, is the bible of bicyclists, complete with maps, color photos, historical info, and a kilometer-by-kilometer breakdown of every route possible. If you go on your own and plan on pedaling only part of the way, Amtrak will transport your bike to the border. They provide the bike box, but require you to disassemble the bike.

HITCHING Hitching in Mexico is a risky business. Reports of robberies and violence come from all parts of the country, so keep your belongings and your wits close by, and don't hitch alone if you can possibly avoid it. Offer gas money and be somewhat flexible, but never accept a ride if you are unsure about the driver. Always be aware of your location and options. Don't hesitate to tell a driver to stop if you feel at all unsafe, and try not to sit in between people, so you're free to bolt if necessary.

PHONES

Like other public services in the country, Mexican phones are a crapshoot. Your experiences will vary with the phone, the place, the time, and perhaps the alignment of the heavens that particular day. Many different options for making phone calls exist, but none are completely reliable everywhere. Simply put: Calling out of Mexico can be a challenging, frustrating, and expensive experience.

The country code for Mexico is **52**. The city code for Mexico City is 5. Dial 02 for the domestic operator in Mexico; 09 for the international operator (who should speak English or be able to find someone who does); 04 for local information; and 01 for long-distance information. You can dial long-distance calls directly: to the United States, dial 95 + area code + number; direct to the rest of the world, dial 98 + country code + city code + number; direct to other parts of Mexico, dial 91 + number. Long-distance carriers in the United States often have direct numbers that you can dial to access an operator to place a collect or calling-card call. Ask your carrier if they have an access number *before* your departure. **AT&T**'s is 95 + 800/462–4240; **Sprint**'s is 95 + 800/877–8000.

CASETAS DE LARGA DISTANCIA For local or long-distance calls, one option is to find a *caseta de larga distancia,* a telephone service usually operated out of a store such as a *papelería* (stationery store), pharmacy, restaurant, or other small business; look for the phone symbol on the door. Casetas may cost more to use than pay phones, but you have a better chance of immediate success. To make a direct long-distance call, tell the person on duty the number you'd like to call, and he or she will give you a rate and dial for you. Rates seem to vary widely, so shop around. Sometimes you can make collect calls from casetas, and sometimes you cannot, depending on the individual operator and possibly your degree of visible desperation. Casetas will generally charge 50¢–$1.50 to place a collect call (some charge by the minute); it's usually better to call collect (*por cobrar*) from a pay phone.

Berkeley Guides writers have had budget-draining run-ins with the dangerously convenient (but outrageously expensive) Capitol Network Systems, Inc. (CNSI) phones. The orange phones, which read TO CALL THE U.S.A. COLLECT OR WITH A CREDIT CARD: SIMPLY DIAL ZERO, *can be found all over northern Mexico.*

PHONE CARDS In some areas, pay phones accept prepaid cards, called **Ladatel** cards, sold in 10-, 30-, or 50-peso denominations (approximately $1.75, $5, or $8.25) at newsstands or pharmacies. Many pay phones in Mexico only accept these cards; coin-only pay phones are usually broken. To use a Ladatel card, simply insert it in the slot of a silver **Multitarjetas** phone, dial 95 (for calls to the States), and the area code and number you're trying to reach. Credit is deleted from the card as you use it, and your balance is displayed on a small screen on the phone so you can keep tabs on how much you've got left.

COLLECT CALLS AND CALLING CARDS For an international collect or calling-card call, dial the long-distance operator (09), wait as long as 30 minutes for the bilingual long-distance operator to pick up the line, and give him or her the number you want to call and your name or card number, as appropriate. You can also use a Ladatel card (*see above*) to make an international call. Collect calls can also sometimes be placed from casetas de larga distancia (*see above*) for a fee.

MAIL

All cities and most towns have an *oficina de correos* (post office) that sells stamps and has *Lista de Correos* (poste restante) service (*see below*). Some post offices also offer telegram, fax, and express mail services.

SENDING MAIL HOME Mail to points beyond Mexico takes anywhere from one to six weeks to arrive, depending on your luck and the size of the city from which you mail the missive. If you're in a hurry, you can send a letter via registered mail, which takes about five to seven days, or by Mexpost, the fastest (about two days) and most expensive method. Mailing a package from Mexico isn't easy. It involves buying the necessary paper, tape, box, and string, then visiting the post office and the customs office. Go to the post office first for instructions, as the procedure varies from city to city. Do not attempt to pack up and wrap the goods yourself; the post office worker will rip everything apart, inspect the contents, and charge you to rewrap it Mexican-style. They will also charge you duty tax if your package contains anything of value. The person who receives the package will probably have to pay a tax as well. The whole process can take up to an hour, so be patient. Packages from Mexico can take a notoriously long time to leave the country.

Almost everything but restaurants closes between 2 and 4 PM for the lunchtime siesta. Expect to do what everyone else does: lounge in the z calo until the bank or bookstore reopens.

RECEIVING MAIL You can receive fan mail in Mexico via *Lista de Correos* (poste restante). Mail is held for up to 10 days, then returned to sender if you don't show up with a picture ID and fetch it. For the Lista de Correos address in any given town, look under the heading "Mail" for that town.

WHERE TO SLEEP

Mexico offers nearly every type of hotel imaginable, from spotless, sterile rooms, to cozy, colonial houses, to cubicles with bare concrete floors and saggy beds. In general the more you pay for a room, the better quality you'll receive, though this—like everything in Mexico—varies. Checkout time at most hotels is 1 PM, and you can usually leave your valuables behind the desk while you roam about during the day. Some places will watch your backpack for several days, usually at no charge. Hotel/motel chains are not in the budget range, and what most people understand as bed-and-breakfasts are very rare in Mexico, though some budget places will include breakfast in the price of a room. Mexico also has a network of about 16 youth hostels, called *villas juveniles.* No sort of membership card is necessary to stay in the hostels—you can leave that HI card you used in Europe at home. Though they usually cost less than $5 a night, hostels can be a major hassle to reach. The hotels featured in this book are generally the cheapest we could find, moderately priced ones with character, or more upscale places with budget deals. The price categories in this book typically refer to the cost of the least expensive double room available plus tax.

CAMPING A host of camping opportunities exist in Mexico, but don't expect the typical U.S.-style campground. Mexico's campgrounds are usually nothing more than trailer parks with running water, cooking areas, and room to pitch tents; sites can cost $1–$8. To enjoy more rustic surroundings, you can set up camp off the road or on the beach in relative safety, and save loads of money. Usually, you can camp at an *ejido* (farming community) or on someone's land for free as long as you ask permission; ask locals about the best spots. Do not camp, however, at archaeological sites or in marijuana-growing areas. For more detailed camping information and humorous camping anecdotes, look to *The People's Guide to Mexico* by Carl Franz ($19.95, published 1995).

ROUGHING IT Along Mexico's coasts, you can usually sleep on the beach for free; just ask a local to make sure it's permissible. Nine times out of 10 it will be just fine. Hammocks are another alternative; lots of beach communities have hammock hooks between trees or inside palapa huts where you can string a hammock for free or for a nominal fee. Within cities, it's hard to find a place to rough it without being picked up by police if you're alone. The only time you can really camp out in cities is by spending the night with strikers or other protestors in a town's zócalo. If you really don't want to pay for a hotel, you could always dance the night away at a disco. Some bus stations are open 24 hours, though you may be the sole bench occupant.

LODGING ALTERNATIVES Formed in the aftermath of World War II, **Servas** is a membership organization dedicated to promoting peace and understanding around the globe, and that enables you to arrange two-night stays with host families. Longer visits must be arranged privately with the family. Becoming a member makes you eligible to receive their host-list directory for any country you desire. Servas has 204 hosts scattered throughout Mexico, though some regions have only one or two per state. Servas is not for tourists or weekend travelers; peace-minded individuals who want more than a free bed can write or call for an application and an interview. You can arrange a stay with a Servas host or host family in advance or just try your luck when you reach the country. Membership is $55 per year, and a deposit of $25 is required for each five host lists you receive. *11 John St., Suite 407, New York, NY 10038, tel. 212/267–0252, http://www.crsy.it:80/~gavino/SERVAS/servas_eng.html. Call the New York number for referral to volunteer contacts in your country.*

FOOD

Mexican restaurant dining can be a disconcerting experience at first. When you sit down, a waiter brings you a menu, then returns after about 30 seconds to take your order. He or she expects you to be ready; if you need more time, you'll have to ask for it and you might get a look of surprise. This speediness is balanced by the length of time it takes to actually receive your food—sometimes decades. Choosing a dish gets even more complicated when you try to order and find out that maybe 5% of the items on the menu are actually available, as in this following traveler's experience: "Good morning! I'd like the mixed fruit plate, but could I have it without papaya?" "Of course. No papaya." "Uh, excuse me, but this plate has only papaya." "Oh, yes, it's the only kind of fruit we have right now." Standard practice in Mexico is to tip 10% or a bit higher at sit-down restaurants and bars—there's no need to tip at food stands.

The price categories used in this book are loosely based on the assumption that you are going to chow down a main course, a drink, and maybe a cup of coffee. Antacids are extra. For info about health risks from food, see Staying Healthy, above.

Mexicans make use of their natural resources, which means that corn and the tortillas made from them are plentiful. Other staple elements include chile peppers, refried pinto (or black) beans, grilled and stewed meats, rice, cheese, and salsa. *Desayuno* (breakfast) often consists of a slab of meat or spicy *huevos rancheros* (fried eggs with salsa, served on tortillas), tropical fruit salads, fresh-squeezed juices, and an array of sugary sweetbreads. Lunch, or *comida*, is the big meal of the day, served between 1 and 3. Getting a *comida corrida* is the best way to fill up inexpensively; these four-course, fixed-price lunch specials won't set you back more than $3. A lighter *cena* (dinner) is served between 6 and 8 PM.

Sincronizadas (grilled tortilla sandwiches, filled with cheese or ham) and *tortas* (Mexican sandwiches served in a roll) are especially popular at food stands. Other delectable delights include *pozole* (a corn stew with meat or vegetables), *mole* (a salsa made out of chocolate and chiles, served over meats), and *chiles rellenos* (chiles stuffed with cheese or meat, deep-fried, and served in a red sauce). Vegetarian restaurants are difficult to find, but with the abundance of

beans, fresh fruit, vegetables, and nuts, herbivores should do just fine. Be aware that lard is often used in the preparation of tortillas and refried beans.

LANGUAGE

Although Spanish is the official language of Mexico, 50 different Indian languages are spoken by more than 5 million people in Mexico. In fact, about 15% of the population does not speak Spanish. Different Mayan tongues are spoken as a first language in a few places, especially in the south, and variants of Nahuatl, the Aztec language, are also common. Knowing even a little Spanish, though, makes your trip more enjoyable, and Mexicans generally appreciate the fact that you're trying. Upper-class Mexicans commonly speak English and/or one or two other European languages, but in general, English is not commonly spoken or understood.

ARTS AND ENTERTAINMENT

Despite rapid industrialization since the Mexican Revolution, Mexico has still managed to maintain—and even improve upon—the *artesanía* (crafts), dance, and music that have existed since pre-colonial times. Unfortunately, the depressed economy has forced many artists to give up their craft and search elsewhere for better paying work. Others have compromised centuries-old traditional art for styles in demand by the tourist market. However, Mexico's artistic tradition continues to thrive, reflecting the resiliency of the Mexican people. As Diego Rivera once said, "Art is like ham. It nourishes people."

VISUAL ARTS Mexico's visual arts scene is probably most famous for the muralist movement instigated by Diego Rivera (1886–1957) shortly after the Mexican Revolution. Although seen as a 20th-century art form, murals have their roots in pre-Columbian tradition. The function of the mural was originally to educate a community on common myths. Similarly, Rivera used this medium to educate the post-revolutionary Mexican community and to instill pride in the Mexican mestizo heritage. The use of art as a political tool can also be seen in the cartoons of José Guadalupe Posada (1852–1913), who used the *calavera* (skull) motif of Mexican folk art to criticize the Eurocentric Porfirio Díaz regime. This political satire influenced the Marxist-themed work of muralist David Siqueiros (1896–1974). Although technically not murals, the wall-size yarn-and-bead paintings of the northern Huichol Indians also function as a narrative tool to keep their spiritual traditions alive.

Frida Kahlo (*see box* in Chapter 2), with her autobiographical portraits of personal suffering, is probably almost as famous now as Rivera was in his day, effectively demonstrating the maxim "The personal is political." This is also evident in the work of José Luis Cuevas, who broke with

What Did You Call Me?

Travelers who consider themselves well educated in the Spanish language often find themselves befuddled when trying to interpret Mexican slang. For example, if someone tells you, "No me mames" or "No mames," don't take it literally (Don't suck on me). You're actually being asked to lay off. The use of the words for mother and father often have nothing to do with the family. If something "no tiene madre" (has no mother) it's absolutely the coolest. "Que padre" (literally, how father) is equivalent to "how cool." "Pinche" (damn) is a word you will hear in every other sentence. "Pendejo" roughly translates as "ass" or "idiot." Other handy expressions include "híjole," an exclamation meaning anything from "wow" to "shit" to "uh-oh"; "andale," which means "hurry up," "really," or "go for it"; and "güero" or "güera," meaning, basically, "white boy" (or girl). For more banal expressions, see the glossary at the back of this book.

the muralist movement, feeling it had become too institutionalized. The opening of his exhibit of autobiographical, erotic paintings caused a huge controversy. Today, the revolution—artistically speaking—continues.

FOLK ART From a Mexican perspective, objects produced by hand are not "folk art"; they're just useful, everyday objects used to keep a household functioning. Regional specialties include Talavera pottery from Puebla, silver from Taxco, opals from Querétaro, blankets and rugs from Teotitlán del Valle (near Oaxaca city), wall hangings from Jalisco, and leather, found in the ranching regions of Zacatecas. When bargaining, it is important to remember that even though the exportation of Mexican artesanía is a profitable enterprise, the artisan generally sees little of that profit. Remember that you're already getting a low price for the amount of time that went into a quality piece of work.

MUSIC The most well-known form of Mexican music is **mariachi.** Mariachi bands were formed in the 18th century; the name comes from the French word "marriage," as they were often commissioned to play at weddings (*see* box in Chapter 8). **Música ranchera** is Mexico's "country music," right down to the common themes of love, betrayal, and murder. The genre dates back to Spanish chivalric ballads, which were known in Mexico as *corridos.* **Música tropical,** a fusion of African, Latin, and Mediterranean rhythms that first appeared in the Caribbean, is the most popular form of music in Veracruz city and Mexico City's *salones* (dance halls). With names like *eumbé, fango, rumba, habanera,* and *danzón,* the dances are almost as fun to pronounce as they are to learn the moves to. Recently growing in popularity is a derivative of the rumba called **rumba urbana,** with a faster rhythm and lyrics concerned with social and urban themes. Mexico's **peña** music, brought to the country by political refugees, has close ties to South America. Nowadays, these *canciones de protesta* (protest songs) criticize U.S. treatment of Mexican immigrants. Among Mexican youth, the **rock en español** movement continues to grow, a hybrid of young Mexicans' love for rock 'n' roll and a desire to understand and perform the music in the context of their native language and culture. Look out for groups like Café Tacuba and Fobia.

CRIME AND PUNISHMENT

Apart from drugs (*see* Drugs and Alcohol, *below*), police rarely hassle travelers unless they are excessively loud, drunk, or involved in a brawl, in which case the police can incarcerate you overnight in jail and take your money. Since you are not protected by the laws of your native land once you're on Mexican soil, your embassy can do little for you. If you do get into a scrape with the law, you can call the **Citizens' Emergency Center** (tel. 202/647–5225) in the United States, weekdays 8:15 AM–10 PM, Saturday 9 AM–3 PM, EST After hours and on Sundays, call the emergency duty officer (tel. 202/634–3600). In Mexico you can also call the English-speaking **Procuraduría de Protección al Turista** (Attorney General for the Protection of Tourists). The 24-hour hotline in Mexico City is 5/14–21–66 or 5/14–01–55.

DRUGS AND ALCOHOL The '60s and '70s were loose in Mexico, just as they were in its northern neighbor. Mushrooms, peyote, and alcohol were easily available, and you'd only get a few days in the *bote* (jail) if caught. In the past 10 years, however, the drug problem has proliferated, with heavy trafficking to the United States. Enforcement is now at an all-time high, and 20% of the world's foreign drug prosecutions are filed in Mexico. Travelers with just a third of an ounce of marijuana may be arrested and thrown in the can for two to nine years. Smuggling across the border warrants up to fifteen years, and your embassy can do little to help. It's rumored that car searches along the Pacific Coast may pick up again.

Drinking in Mexico is like eating—it's cheap and people are always doing it. Stay away from cantinas; their swinging doors give way to small, dark holes-in-the-wall frequented by seedy, guzzling men. Stick to clubs and cafés, which serve all ages (though technically, the drinking age is 18) in a more pleasant environment. Keep in mind that Mexico is a hard-drinking country, and you're likely to be pressed to drink more than your fill by your well-meaning Latin friends. Refusing a drink can be taken as an offense; a safe response is a firm "*No gracias. No tomo mucho*" (No thanks. I don't drink a lot) or "*Me hace daño*" (I get sick to my stomach).

FURTHER READING

HISTORY Good general reference books from pre-Columbian history to today include: *In The Shadow of the Mexican Revolution* (University of Texas Press, Austin, 1993); David Carrasco's *Moctezuma's Mexico* (University Press of Colorado, 1992); Michael D. Coe's *The Maya* (1987) and *Mexico* (1988), both published by Thames and Hudson, and *In the Land of the Olmec* (University of Texas Press, 1980) in collaboration with Richard A. Diehl; Hernán Cortés's *Letters From Mexico* (Yale University Press, 1986); Bernal Díaz de Castillo's *The Discovery and Conquest of Mexico* (De Capo Press, 1996); Bartólome de Las Casas's *The Devastation of the Indies* (Johns Hopkins University Press, 1992) and *In Defense of the Indians* (Northern Illinois University Press, 1992); Mary Miller and Karl Taube's *The Gods and Symbols of Ancient Mexico and the Maya* (Thames and Hudson, 1993); Elizabeth Salas's *Soldaderas in the Mexican Military: Myth and History* (University of Texas Press, 1990); Michael C. Meyer and William L. Sherman's *The Course of Mexican History* (Oxford University Press, 1995); and Hugh Thomas's *The Conquest of Mexico* (Simon & Schuster, 1994). If you want to read about the ancient Mexican civilizations in their own words, a few texts remain and have been translated. *The Destruction of the Jaguar: Poems from the Books of Chilam Balam,* (City Lights Books, 1987) and *Popol Vuh* (Simon & Schuster, 1985) are both based on ancient Mayan codices. A translation of the Aztec *Codex Chimalpopoca* (University of Arizona Press, 1992) is also available.

POLITICS AND CURRENT EVENTS Recommended works include: Tom Barry's *Mexico: A Country Guide* (The Inter-Hemispheric Education Resource Center, 1992); Ruth Behar's *Translated Woman* (Beacon Press, 1993); Robert D. Bruce and Victor Perera's *The Last Lords of Palenque: The Lacandón Mayas of the Mexican Rain Forest* (University of California Press, 1982); Roderic A. Camp's *Politics in Mexico* (Oxford University Press, 1993); Augusta Dwyer's *On the Line: Life on the U.S.–Mexican Border* (Latin American Bureau, 1994); David Frye's *Indians into Mexicans: History and Identity in a Mexican Town* (University of Texas Press, 1996); John M. Hart's *Revolutionary Mexico* (University of California Press, 1987); and John Ross's *Rebellion from the Roots: Indian Uprising in Chiapas* (Common Courage Press, 1995). Two anthologies have documented the strife of the Zapatistas: *Zapatistas! Documents of the New Mexican Revolution* (Autonomedia, 1994), and *First World, Ha Ha Ha! The Zapatista Challenge,* edited by Elaine Katzenberger (City Lights Books, 1995).

CULTURE For cultural awareness, check out the following: Ana Castillo's *The Mixquiahuala Letters* (Anchor, 1992); Mathew C. Gutman's *The Meanings of Macho and Being a Man in Mexico City* (University of California Press, 1996); Aldous Huxley's *Beyond the Mexique Bay* (Vintage Books, 1960); Alma M. Reed's *The Mexican Muralists* (Crown, 1960); Diego Rivera's autobiography *My Art, My Life* (Citadel Press, 1991); Chloe Sayer's *Arts and Crafts of Mexico* (Thames and Hudson, 1990); John L. Stephens's *Incidents of Travel in Central America, Chiapas and Yucatán* (Rutgers University Press, 1949); and Martha Zamora's *Frida Kahlo: The Brush of Anguish* (Chronicle Books, 1990).

LITERATURE IN TRANSLATION Mexican literature is obviously a vast and varied field, but the following works are highly recommended: Rosario Castellanos's *The Nine Guardians* (Readers International, 1992); Carlos Fuentes's *Where the Air is Clear* (Farrar, Straus, and Giroux, 1970) and *The Old Gringo* (Farrar, Straus, and Giroux, 1985); Elena Garro's *Recollections of Things to Come* (University of Texas Press, 1969); Octavio Paz's *The Labyrinth of Solitude* (Penguin Books, 1990) and *A Tree Within* (New Directions, 1988); Elena Poniatowska's *Massacre in Mexico* (Viking Press, 1975); Juan Rulfo's *The Burning Plain, and Other Stories* (University of Texas Press, 1990) and *Pedro Páramo* (Grove Press, 1994); and Alan Trueblood's *A Sor Juana Anthology* (Harvard University Press, 1988).

MEXICO CITY AND ENVIRONS

2

By Rachael Courtier

The first thing that strikes you about Mexico City is the sheer number of people. It's simply mind-boggling to think that so many human beings could possibly exist. To comprehend how the masses can share this city is an even greater challenge, especially given the statistics: Approximately 20% of Mexico's population lives on the 1% of Mexican land known as "El Distrito Federal," or Mexico City. But learning how to share the space crunched between the states of Mexico and Morelos has always been a fundamental part of living in Mexico City—a challenge that has shaped the city's character into a distinct blend of tenacity and vitality.

Overpopulation is only one of the factors that defines D. F. life; another is a tangible connection with the past, made possible by the fact that this site has served as a capital ever since the Aztec people founded the city of Tenochtitlán here in 1325. In 1519 Hernán Cortés began constructing what would become present-day Mexico, leveling most of the ancient Aztec city and building directly on top of the ruins. Today, the routine of cosmopolitan life takes place amidst the remnants of this ancient city, parts of which lay partially excavated several meters below the level of the modern D.F. Thus, historical space ceases to be a fenced-off site, becoming, instead, a familiar neighbor that lends a supportive hand to the present: Colonial churches share room with modern highrises, children roller-skate on Sundays past the ruins of the pre-colonial ceremonial center in the Plaza Tlatelolco, and street vendors hawk their wares in the shadow of the 400-year-old Templo Mayor.

This blending of cultures, ideas, and history is nothing new for Mexicans. A history of foreign intervention, colonization, rebellion, and strife has given chilangos, as Mexico City's residents are called, a decisive aura of resiliency that perpetuates vitality and hope. This resiliency stems partly from the chilango ability to keep elements of history firmly melded in everyday life: The recent popularity of self-appointed tour guides, the return to natural medicine, and the artesanía booths that beckon with handcrafted wares all demonstrate the drive to both preserve and capitalize on the past.

Expatriates, political exiles, immigrants, and visitors from around the world mix with Mexicans from every state in the country to form the chilango identity. Rural migrants pour into the city daily, looking for work and a better standard of living after resources from the countryside have dried up. Although Mexico has paid lip service to *lo indígeno* (the indigenous) since the Revolution, indigenous migrants—mostly from the Zapotec, Mixtec, and Otomí tribes—actually end up as the lowest classes in Mexico City, living in slums and selling chewing gum or shining shoes to survive. Residents call them *paracaidistas* (parachuters), because they come out of nowhere and seize any scrap of land available, from abandoned lots to the meager strips of land beside railroad tracks. Such poverty is well hidden from the delicate eyes of those who

Paseo de la Reforma

Vaso
Regulador
El Cristo

Av. Parque

CUATRO
CAMINOS

2

EL ROSARIO
6 7
Calz. del Rosario

Vía

MIGUEL HIDALGO

Av. Ejército Nacional

Av. Río San Joaquín

Calz. Legaria

Calz. México

Av. Marina Nacional

Av. Tacubaya

TACUBA

Eje 3 Nte.

Calz. de Camarones

ZONA
ROSA

Bosque de
Chapultepec

Paseo de la Reforma

AZCAPOTZALCO

Av. Cuitláhuac

Calz. Vallejo

Eje Central

Eje 5 Nte.

Eje 1 Pte.

Estación F.F.C.C.
Nacional
Buena Vista

Eje 1 Nte.

Circuito Interior

POLITÉCNICO

5

G. A.
MADERO

B

Central

8

GARIBALDI

CUAUHTEMOC

Eje 2 Nte.

Eje 3 Nte.

Eje 4 Nte.

Av. de los Insurgentes

3

INDIOS VERDES

Calz. Ticomán

Parque Nacional
"El Tepeyac"

TLALNE

Eje 1 Ote.

Fray Servando Teresa de Mier

Eje 3 Ote.

Eje 2 Ote.

4 6
MARTÍN CARRERA

Eduardo Molina

Oceanía

Circuito
Interior

Eje 1 Nte.

Bosque San Juan
de Aragón

GUSTAVO A.
MADERO

Eje 5 Nte.

Aeropuerto
Internacional
Benito Juárez

Av. 602

Under
Construction

B

PANTITLÁN

45

Within the country, Mexico City is known as México D.F. (Distrito Federal), or just "D.F." Unofficial nicknames include "Chilangolandia" (a fusion of "chilango" and "Disneylandia") and "DFectuoso," a pun on the defects of D.F. life.

occupy the more posh districts of town, such as Polanco, Lomas, and Coyoacán. Any meeting between the two classes reveals an unsettling and somewhat depressing contrast: Poor children peddle roses and put on street shows late at night for the crowds of trendy *fresas* (spoiled rich kids) who club-hop in their bright red Jettas.

Even the environment in Mexico City is experiencing turbulent changes. Famed for its clean mountain air at the beginning of the century, the city is now notorious for its smog—brought about by rapid industrialization and population growth. The problem is exacerbated by the uninterrupted range of volcanic mountains that encircles the city, trapping in the pollution. Smog isn't the capital's only problem: The soft soil upon which the city is built (the site was a lake, but has been gradually filled in by successive civilizations) has caused many buildings to sink several inches per year.

But despite all its environmental and economic problems, the oldest capital in the Americas continues to flourish with no sign of backing down. Excellent museums, layered ruins, fine arts, and great soccer games continue to beckon travelers from all over the world. Aficionados of Mexico City may even experience the same inexplicable and irrational passion that many feel for their first loves. So though you may be reluctant to embrace this unwieldly city of staggering pollution and obvious overcrowding, come with your arms open and your preconceptions in check. You'll soon find that the warmth and humility of Mexico City and its residents is overwhelmingly infectious.

Basics

AMERICAN EXPRESS This main branch replaces and sells traveler's checks, cashes cardholders' personal checks, and provides travel services. Avoid changing money here, since the rates are poor. Cardholders' mail will be held if sent to the following address: *Paseo de la Reforma 234, esq. Havre, Col. Juárez, México, D.F., CP 06600, México. Tel. 5/514–06–29 or 5/207–72–82. Open weekdays 9–6, Sat. 9–1. From Metro Insurgentes, take Génova north to Reforma, turn right and go 2 blocks. Hotel Nikko office: Campos Eliseos 204, tel. 5/282–21–47; Metro: Auditorio. Hotel Camino Real office: Mariano Escobedo 700, Col. Anzures, tel. 5/203–11–48; Metro: Chapultepec.*

BOOKSTORES In a city with more than 30,000 English-speaking expatriates, you'll have very little trouble locating English-language publications. Be on the lookout for *The Mexico City News*, available at most bookstores, which contains summaries of national and international news, entertainment, classifieds, and, most importantly, horoscopes and Ann Landers. *The Mexico City Daily Bulletin* is full of ads and handy sections like "Bible Digest" and "The World of Science." Published Tuesday–Sunday, it's available free at many hotels and at tourist offices. Look beyond the propaganda for helpful suggestions about hotels, restaurants, and places to shop; also cut out the great city map to carry around with you.

The American Bookstore offers a large selection of books and magazines in English, as well as the *Guía Roji* and the *Guía Pronto,* two good maps of Mexico City. *Madero 25, tel. 5/512–03–06. 4½ blocks west of Zócalo. Open Mon.–Sat. 9:30–7, Sun. 10–3.*

The Benjamin Franklin Library, in the U.S. Embassy, was designed to nurture understanding between the United States and Mexico. Even mutual understanding has its limits, however: Although anyone can peruse the shelfs, only Mexico City residents and foreigners who can prove they're working in Mexico can check out books. The library has a good reference section, numerous novels, and U.S. periodicals and magazines. On the second floor, the **English Language Program**'s office lists institutions looking for English teachers. *Londres 16, tel. 5/211–00–42. Open Mon. and Fri. 3–7:30 PM, Tues.–Thurs. 10–3.*

Gandhi, a coffeeshop/bookstore in San Ángel, supplies a noteworthy selection of Spanish tiles, supplemented by gorgeous art books and a handful of English books. For those who make a hobby of spotting famous literati, Mario Vargas Llosa has been known to browse here among the UNAM students. If you're in Coyoacán, **El Parnaso** (cnr of Carrillo Puerto and Jardín Centenario) features the same books as Gandhi, as well as the same hours of operation. *Gandhi: M. A. de Quevedo 134, tel. 5/662–06–00 or 5/661–09–11. ½ block west of Metro M. A. de Quevedo. Open weekdays 9 AM–11 PM, weekends 10–10.*

CASAS DE CAMBIO All banks offer the same government-set *tipo de cambio* (exchange rate), but they often change money only until noon or 1:30. Even worse, banks usually require you to run a lengthy bureaucratic obstacle course of signatures and receipts before the financial alchemists will turn your foreign currency into pesos. **Banamex** (tel. 5/709–98–85 or 5/542–42–61) is the most accessible bank, with branches on practically every block in the downtown area.

If time is more important than filthy lucre, you'll find several **casas de cambio** willing to do the job faster, later in the afternoon, and, if you're lucky, at better rates than banks. The best rates can usually be found in the Zona Rosa. **Casa de Cambio Consultoria Internacional** (Río Tíber 110, tel. 5/207–99–20) and **Casa de Cambio Ameres** (Ameres 40, tel. 5/207–05–97) are both open weekdays 8:30–5:30 and Saturdays until 2 PM.

DISCOUNT TRAVEL AGENCIES **Agencia de Viajes Tony Pérez** does a lot of business with the U.S. Embassy across the street and knows about the latest airline promotions. *Río Volga 1, at Río Danubio, tel. 5/533–11–48 or 5/533–11–49. Near Ángel de la Independencia monument, across from Zona Rosa. Open weekdays 8:30–6:30, Sat. 9–1.*

Turismo Mirey wins the prize for most honest travel agency in the D.F., and the staff goes out of their way to find you the best travel deals. They also offer great day trips from Mexico City: $27.50 per person will buy you a tour of the Teotihuacán pyramids, transportation included. *Londres 44, in Zona Rosa, tel. 5/514–57–93 or 5/514–47–72. Open weekdays 9:30–7, Sat. 11–2.*

EMBASSIES **Australia.** *9255 Rubén Darío 55, Col. Polanco, tel. 5/531–52–25 (information) or 5/905–407–1698 (emergencies). Metro: Polanco. Open Mon.–Wed. 8–2 and 3–5, Thurs. and Fri. 8–2.*

Canada. The embassy also has a lending library. *Schiller 529, at Tres Picos, Col. Polanco, tel. 5/724–79–00. Metro: Polanco. Open weekdays 9–1 and 2–5; library open weekdays 9–12:30. Closed Canadian and Mexican holidays.*

New Zealand. *José Luis Langrange 103, 10th floor, Col. Polanco. tel. 5/281–54–86, fax 5/281–52–12. Metro: Polanco. Open Mon.–Thurs. 8:30–2 and 3:30–5:30, Fri. 8:30–2. Closed Mexican holidays.*

United Kingdom. *Río Lerma 71, Col. Cuauhtémoc, tel. 5/207–24–49 or 5/207–20–89. Metro: Insurgentes. Open weekdays 8:30–3:30; weekdays 9–2 for visas and registration. Closed some Mexican and all British holidays.*

United States. *Paseo de la Reforma 305, Col. Cuauhtémoc, near Ángel de la Independencia monument, tel. 5/211–00–42, fax 5/511–99–80. Metro: Insurgentes. Open weekdays 8:30–5. Closed Mexican and U.S. holidays.*

EMERGENCIES The all-purpose number for emergencies is 08. Or call directly to the **fire department** (tel. 5/768–37–00), the **Cruz Roja** (Red Cross, tel. 5/557–57–57), or the **police** (tel. 5/588–51–00).

The **Procuraduría General de Justicia** (Public Prosecutor) offers emergency assistance to tourists in Mexico City. Police, lawyers, and a doctor staff the two offices 24 hours a day. If you lose your passport or are a victim of a serious crime, you can make a report in English and the staff will translate it into Spanish for you. *Zona Rosa: Florencia 20, tel. 5/625–70–20 or 5/625–87–61; Metro: Insurgentes. Centro: Argentina, at San Ildefonso, tel. 5/625–87–62; Metro: Zócalo.*

The government-funded AIDS awareness group, **CONASIDA**, provides crisis counseling, medical referrals, lab testing, and support groups. The organization also sponsors the AIDS hotline,

TELSIDA (tel. 5/207–40–77; phones open weekdays 9 AM–9:30 PM). All services are free and available in English. *Flora 8, Col. Roma, tel. 5/207–44–43. Metro: Cuahtémoc. Open weekdays 9–7 PM.*

CETATEL is a 24-hour rape and sexual abuse hotline provided by the **Centro de Terapia y Apoyo para Víctimas de Agresión Sexual** (Center for Therapy and Support for Victims of Sexual Violence), a government-sponsored agency that also offers one-on-one services. All services are free, and some are offered in English. *Pestalozze 1115, Col. Valle, tel. 5/575–54–61 from 9 to 5 and 5/625–80–52 evenings and holidays. Metro: Division Del Norte.*

The **Locatel** (tel. 5/658–11–11) information and referral service offers information and assistance for almost anything: lost persons or vehicles, medical emergencies, public transportation, and mental illness, among others.

LAUNDRY Laundromats are scarce in the center, which means you'll either have do the dirty work yourself or lug the load to another part of town. Your best bet is to find a hotel with laundry service. **Lavandería Edison** (Edison 91, near Monumento de la Revolución, no phone; open weekdays 10–7, Sat. until 6) is the (only) Laundromat near the hotels in the Metro Revolución area, though once you get a look at their prices, you'll realize your clothes aren't so dirty after all. Doing your own load costs $1.75 to wash or dry; letting someone else handle it (one-hour service) costs $6. From Metro Revolución, walk toward monument on Buenavista, and then turn right on Edison. At **Lavandería Kiko** (Misioneros 9, Local B, no phone; open Mon.–Sat. 10–6) 3 kilos of dirty laundry cost $2 to wash and dry if you do it yourself, or $3.25 if someone else does it. From Metro Pino Suárez, walk east 6 blocks on Misioneros.

LUGGAGE STORAGE If your hotel won't take your bags, the airport, train station, and all four bus stations have luggage storage (*see* Coming and Going, *below*). If you'll be gone more than a few days, use the service at the airport or at TAPO (the eastern bus station), where you can keep the key to your locker.

MAIL The **Dirección General de Correos** (main post office), in a neo-Renaissance building across from Bellas Artes, sells stamps at the ESTAMPILLAS windows and distributes mail at the LISTA Y POSTE RESTANTE window. Mail sent to you at the following address will be held for up to 10 days: Lista de Correos, Administración 1, Palacio Postal, México, D.F., CP 06002, México. Smaller branches are located at the Central Poniente and Central Sur bus stations, and at the UNAM campus next to the main library. *Main branch: Lázaro Cárdenas, at Tacuba, tel. 5/521–73–94. 1 block from Alameda Central. Open weekdays 9–5 (8–9 and 5–8, stamps only), Sat. 8–4, Sun. 8–1 PM.*

Wander around Mexico City for a day, and you can't help noticing a Sanborns. This restaurant/pharmacy/bookstore chain is rumored to have connections to Carlos Salinas de Gortari—many people believe that the former president is the real owner and that the chain was part of his many commercial ventures.

Cetel, located in the heart of the Zona Rosa, offers the best deal on faxes at $2 a page. *Liverpool 162-A, btw Florencia and Amberes, tel. and fax 5/533–64–21.*

MEDICAL AID Two private hospitals with English-speaking staff are: **Hospital Español** (Eje Nacional 613, Col. Granada, tel. 5/203–37–35) and **American British Cowdray Hospital (ABC)** (Sur 138, at Observatorio, tel. 5/230–80–00). To reach the latter from Metro Tacubaya, take pesero CUAJIMALTA or NAVIDAD to Colonia Las Américas.

If you need free or inexpensive medical care, the following hospitals also have some English-speaking staff: **Hospital General Balbuena (DDF)** (Cecilio Robelo y Sur 103, Col. Jardín Balbuena, tel. 5/764–03–39; Metro: Moctezuma) and **Hospital Santa Fé** (San Luis Potosí 103, tel. 5/574–10–11; Metro: Chilpancingo). **Hospital de la Mujer** (Díaz Mirón 375, Col. Santo Tomás, tel. 5/341–43–09 or 5/341–19–52; Metro: Colegio Militar) offers 24-hour emergency services for women, and a drop-in, low-cost gynecological clinic (about $3 for an office visit) weekdays, 8 AM–noon.

For late-night pharmaceuticals, **Sanborns** (open daily 7:30 AM–11 PM) is your best bet. The pharmacy chain **El Fénix** also has several stores throughout the city, including one at Madero

39 (tel. 5/521–98–02), open Monday–Saturday 8 AM–9 PM, Sunday 10–7. For 24-hour service, try **Vyb** (San Jerónimo 630, in Comercial San Jerónimo, near Periférico Sur, tel. 5/595–59–83 or 5/595–59–98). Each of the bus stations also has a 24-hour pharmacy.

PHONES Place local calls (20¢) at any orange public phone or from either the blue or gray **Ladatel Multitarjetas** phones; that is, if you can find a phone that works, identifiable by the long line of folks waiting to use it. If you'd rather avoid the wait, many establishments will let you use their phone, but at a higher cost. For local directory assistance, dial an operator at 04.

The easiest way to make a long-distance call is with a prepaid LADA card on a Ladatel phone. You can buy LADA phone cards at any newsstand, lottery booth, or Sanborns in 10-, 30-, or 50-peso denominations. A more expensive option is to place long-distance calls at a *caseta de larga distancia* (long-distance telephone office), generally marked with a large, blue sign. They're in all bus stations, the airport, and the train station; some (airport, Central Poniente, Tasqueña) are open 24 hours. At all casetas, you place the call and pay when you're done.

SCHOOLS The **Centro de Enseñanza para Extranjeros** (School for Foreign Students) at **UNAM** (Universidad Nacional Autónoma de México) offers classes for visitors. Intensive and regular semester courses covering Spanish, Chicano studies, art, history, and literature are open to anyone with a high school degree. Each intensive course is about $240; most classes are taught in Spanish. Registered students have access to the university's facilities, such as gyms, swimming pools, libraries, and the campus medical center. *Mailing address: CEPE, AP 70-391, C.U. Delegación Coyoacán, México, D.F., CP 04510, México, tel. 5/622–24–70, fax 5/616–26–72, racr@servidor.unam.mx or baum@servidor.dgsca.unam.mx.*

TOURS For inexpensive, city-sponsored tours, contact **Paseos Por Centro Historico** (tel. 5/12–10–12). For $3 you'll get to hop on a streetcar and cruise around downtown while a guide rambles on about the historical significance of each building or site. The only catch is that you can't get off at any of the sites. The 50-minute tours leave daily, every hour on the hour 10–5, from the Museo de la Ciudad de México and the Palacio de Bellas Artes (*see* Exploring Mexico, *below*). To reserve an English-speaking guide, you must have a group of at least 20 people and call a day in advance. For a more involved tour, contact **Paseos Culturales de INAH** (Instituto Nacional de Antropología e Historia; Frontera 53, Col. San Ángel, tel. 5/616–52–28) for a program of pre-scheduled thematic tours. These unique tours, usually taking place on the weekends, head for outlying historical areas, such as Teotihuacán and Meztitlán, or may cover the footsteps of important people like Sor Juana. Tours last from 8 to 8, cost $17, and leave from Córdoba 45, Colonia Roma, at 8 AM.

VISITOR INFORMATION Tourist offices in both the international and domestic terminals of the **airport** and in the **TAPO** (*see* Coming and Going, By Bus, *below*) offer help with directions and hotel reservations. The **Asociación Méxicana de Hoteles y Moteles** (tel. 5/203–04–66) also has offices at the airport, and will make reservations for you. They're located next to the baggage claims at the domestic and international terminals, before the immigration booths.

Dirección General de Turismo is centrally located in the Zona Rosa and provides information on shopping centers, museums, galleries, the Metro, and attractions in other cities and regions in the country. The staff is helpful but not as bilingual as one would hope, and their information tends to be a bit outdated. *Amberes 54, at Londres, tel. 5/525–93–80 or 5/525–93–82. Open weekdays 9–9, weekends 9–7.*

Tiempo Libre is a Spanish weekly that lists entertainment info on almost everything, including gay clubs and events. Pick one up at Sanborns or a kiosk for $1.

Another good source of information is the **Secretaría de Turismo** (SECTUR), whose competent and friendly English-speaking staff distributes brochures and maps, assists in trip planning, and makes hotel reservations anywhere in Mexico. Choose from their array of phone numbers: 5/250–01–23 for 24-hour complaints and emergencies, 5/250–01–51 for 24-hour multilingual tourist info, and toll-free 91–800/9–03–92 (from Mexico) or 800/482–9832 (from the U.S. and other countries) for general info. *Presidente Mazarik 172, Col. Polanco, tel. 5/250–85–55 ext. 168 or 5/255–22–95. From Metro Polanco, walk south on Horacio and 2 blocks west on Hegel. Open weekdays 8 AM–9 PM.*

COMING AND GOING

BY BUS Each of Mexico City's four main bus terminals is located at a different cardinal point of the city, and *generally* services the corresponding section of the country. If you're traveling during Christmas, Easter, or during the peak tourist months of July and August, buy your tickets well in advance and be prepared for a mob scene. Tickets for most buses go on sale about three weeks before the departure date. It's best to check your baggage about half an hour before departure and board 20 minutes in advance. Find out the departure point for your bus and stick close by; the boarding announcements are virtually unintelligible, even to Spanish-speakers. Unless otherwise noted, the prices listed below are the lowest available, generally on *clase económica* (2nd-class) buses.

If you plan to cross the United States–Mexico border by bus, you can purchase connecting tickets for U.S.-bound buses at **Greyhound** (Paseo de la Reforma 27, tel. 5/535–42–00 or 5/535–26–18). Another option is **Estrella Blanca** (Terminal Central del Norte, tel. 5/729–07–25), which lets you purchase Greyhound tickets for trips across the Texas and New Mexico borders.

➤ **TERMINAL CENTRAL DE AUTOBUSES DEL NORTE** • The northern terminal is a massive semicircular building across the street from Metro Autobuses del Norte. The bus station is huge and intimidating, but if you want to go anywhere north of Mexico City, you'll have to come here. Companies serving this station include: **Estrella Blanca** (tel. 5/729–07–62 or 5/729–07–25), with service to Guadalajara (7½ hrs, $18), Hermosillo (30 hrs, $59), Mazatlán (17 hrs, $34), Monterrey (12 hrs, $25), Nuevo Laredo (15 hrs, $33), Puerto Vallarta (14 hrs, $37 1st class), Querétaro (3 hrs, $6), and Tijuana (44 hrs, $63); **Flecha Amarilla** (tel. 5/567–80–33), which serves Aguascalientes (17 hrs, $14), Guadalajara (8 hrs, $18), Morelia (6 hrs, $10), and San Miguel de Allende (4 hrs, $7.50); **Omnibús de México** (tel. 5/368–74–02), which reaches Chihuahua (20 hrs, $53), Durango (12 hrs, $33), and Guanajuato (5 hrs, $13); and **Autobuses del Oriente (ADO)** (tel. 5/567–15–77), with buses to Jalapa ($10, 4 hrs). All long-distance buses have TV, air-conditioning, and cushy seats.

Autobuses del Norte is the biggest and best-equipped station in the city, furnished with a **casa de cambio** (open weekdays 8–8 and weekends 9–4), a Banamex **ATM**, a 24-hour **caseta de larga distancia,** and **luggage lockers** ($1.50–$2.50 for 24 hrs). A small booth marked HOTELES ASOCIADOS (tel. 5/587–85–51; open weekdays 2–9) offers free help with hotel reservations. *Av. de los 100 Metros 4907, tel. 5/587–59–67 or 5/587–59–73.*

There are no budget hotels near the terminal, but you can easily reach the centro by public transportation. For a pesero, go down into the Metro and cross under the street: The RUTA 1 BELLAS ARTES pesero runs to the Bellas Artes/Alameda Central area and the RUTA 88 METRO REVOLUCION goes to the hotels near Metro Revolución. If you're dying for that first Metro ride, jump on Line 5 toward Pantitlán, change at Metro La Raza to Line 3 towards Universidad (inconvenient if you have a lot of luggage, since the "Tunnel of Science" connecting the two lines is a million miles long), and get off at Metro Juárez or Metro Hidalgo, where many budget hotels are clustered. A regulated taxi to a hotel in the centro will cost you about $4; buy a ticket at the taxi booth next to the Banamex ATM. Collective taxis are about half that price, but you may have to wait for half an hour and tip whoever found the cab for you.

➤ **TERMINAL CENTRAL DEL SUR/TASQUENA** • Tasqueña, as this station is usually called, is easily reached from the Metro station of the same name on Line 2. This terminal is almost always a madhouse and serves mostly southern and southwestern Mexico. **Estrella de Oro** (tel. 5/549–85–20) serves Acapulco ($25 express; $15 with stops) and Ixtapa/Zihuatanejo ($35 express; $20 with stops). The first-class **Autopulman de Morelos** (tel. 5/549–35–05) line heads for Cuernavaca (1 hr, $3), Cuautla (1½ hrs, $3.50), and Tepoztlán (1 hr, $2.50). **Cristóbal Colón** (tel. 5/544–24–14), another first-class line, offers wheelchair-accessible buses to Oaxaca (6 hrs, $15), Huatulco (16 hrs, $24), Puebla (2 hrs, $4), and Puerto Escondido (18 hrs, $27). Tasqueña lacks a casa de cambio or ATM, but has a 24-hour **caseta de larga distancia** that accepts both Visa and MasterCard. The caseta also has a fax, photocopying machine, and doubles as a travel agency offering cheap packages to the beach. There's also a **pharmacy** and **luggage storage** (opposite door 3; $1.50–$2.50 per day), both open 24 hours. *Tasqueña 1320, tel. 5/544–21–01 or 5/689–97–95.*

The Metro is by far the cheapest transport from Tasqueña to the budget hotels in the centro: Hop on at Metro Tasqueña and take Line 2 toward Cuatro Caminos and get off at Metro Allende. Taxis provide a more comfortable alternative. The ticket system mandates a rate of about $5 to the downtown area and $6 to the airport; purchase tickets at the taxi booth in front of door 3.

➤ **TERMINAL AUTOBUSES DE PASAJEROS DE ORIENTE (TAPO)** • TAPO is in a working-class area just east of the city center and is easily reached from the adjacent San Lázaro Metro station (Line 1). Buses depart this large clean terminal for eastern destinations, although you can also catch a southbound bus from here. **ADO** (tel. 5/542–71–92 or 5/542–71–98) serves Cancún (21½ hrs, $44), Jalapa (5½ hrs, $10), Oaxaca (6 hrs, $15), and Veracruz (5 hrs, $14). The first-class **Cristóbal Colón** (tel. 5/542–72–63) line reaches Oaxaca de Juárez (6 hrs, $15), San Cristóbal de las Casas (16 hrs, $34), and Tuxtla Gutiérrez (15 hrs, $34). Luggage storage ($2.50 for 24 hrs), a **caseta de larga distancia** (open daily 7 AM–11 PM), a Banamex **ATM**, and the friendly bilingual staff at the **tourist information desk** (near the Metro exit; open daily 9–9) make this one of the more pleasant if not comical terminals to be stranded in. The boarding announcements at TAPO are audible but not necessarily intelligible, especially if you've fallen prey to the music videos played here on large monitors. *Zaragoza 200, tel. 5/762–59–77.*

There are several ways to reach the cheap hotels in the centro: The RUTA 22 ZOCALO/BELLAS ARTES pesero or the ALAMEDA bus will pick you up right in front of the terminal; or take the Metro toward Observatorio, get off at Balderas, change to Line 3, head toward Indios Verdes, and get off at Juárez. You can also take a taxi for $2.50 to the downtown area, $3.50 to the airport.

➤ **TERMINAL CENTRAL PONIENTE** • If hell were a bus station, this would be it. The terminal is huge and dark, and the roof leaks. Of course it's not all bad—there's 24-hour **luggage storage** in room E ($1 for 24 hrs), a 24-hour **caseta de larga distancia** from which you can call your loved ones and share your misery, and a **post office** (open weekdays 8 –7). Most destinations from this station are also served by the three other, more modern and convenient stations. **Tres Estrellas de Oro** (tel. 5/271–05–78) runs only from here, serving Tijuana (48 hrs, $64), Mazatlán (18 hrs, $34), and Guadalajara (8 hrs, $18). To reach the centro from the station, take Line 1 to Pino Suárez, switch to Line 2, and get off at Zócalo. Otherwise, purchase a regulated taxi ticket to the downtown area (about $5) in the station. *Cnr of Sur 122 and Río Tacubaya, tel. 5/271–00–38.*

BY TRAIN The train is slow, and it's not fun. Any illusions you may have had about rushing through the countryside by night (thereby saving money on hotels) should be quickly forgotten. Of course you can't ignore the fact that second-class train tickets are 60% (first-class 20%) cheaper than bus prices. **Estación Central Buenavista** is in a rather run-down area of the city— not the best place to lug your suitcase around late at night. To reach the budget lodging near Metro Revolución from here, walk south on Insurgentes Sur. To reach hotels south of the Alameda by minibus, take a RUTA 99 ALAMEDA/BELLAS ARTES pesero from Metro Revolución; to reach lodging near the Zócalo, take RUTA 99 TACUBA.

The friendly folks at the **information booth** (left of ticket window, tel. 5/547–65–93 or 5/547–10–84) field queries about rail travel daily 6:30 AM–9:30 PM. For help in English, stop by the **Oficina Comercial de Pasajeros** (next to caseta de larga distancia, tel. 5/547–86–55; open weekdays 10–3 and 5:30–8). **Luggage storage** (down ramp across from second-class ticket booth) costs 75¢ per hour per bag, but it's only open 6:30 AM–9:30 PM. There is no ATM near the station, but you can visit Banamex or Bancomer near Metro Revolución on Buenavista.

First-class and **sleeper-car** tickets can be purchased from any one of the BOLETOS windows. They're almost twice as expensive as second-class tickets, but at least you're guaranteed a seat and won't run the risk of having to stand for 36 hours. Likewise, if you're going on a long trip, the sleeper cars (available only on some routes) are indispensable and well worth the money. Trains are packed during the summer and Christmas season, so make reservations in advance if possible. **Second-class tickets** (same-day cash purchases only) are sold from a line of windows hidden in the back of the building: Go down the ramp at either side of the main building to find the second-class *taquillas* (ticket booths), open from 6 AM until the last train leaves. Seats are not reserved, so it's best to arrive at least 1–4 hours before departure; the earlier you get here, the better your chance of getting a seat.

The first-class **Tren División del Norte** leaves daily at 8 PM for Ciudad Juárez (27 hrs, $36), stopping along the way in Querétaro, Aguascalientes, Zacatecas, and Chihuahua, as well as many other cities. **Tren Tapatío** leaves daily at 8:30 PM for Guadalajara; first-class fare is $12, and $32 will get you a sleeping berth (only available on the weekends). **Tren Regiomontano** departs at 7 PM for Monterrey (13 hrs; 1st class $18, 2nd class $11, $48 for weekend-only sleeping berth) stopping in San Luis Potosí and Saltillo. To Oaxaca, take **Tren Oaxaqueño** (14 hrs; $11.50 1st class, $7 2nd class), which leaves daily at 7:10 PM and stops in Puebla and Tehuacán. The **Tren Jarocho** departs daily for Veracruz (10 hrs; $10 1st class, $6 2nd class, $24 for weekend-only sleeping berths) at 9:15 PM.

BY PLANE The **Aeropuerto Internacional de la Ciudad de México** is big but manageable and always buzzing with activity. The uncomfortable plastic chairs in the lounges are difficult to nest in, but you can spend a night slumped in one without being hassled. Most major carriers, including Mexicana, American, Delta, Air France, and Iberia, operate from this airport, which connects Mexico with just about every destination in the world.

At the airport, **Bancomer** (open daily 6 AM–10 PM) and **Banamex** (open daily 6 AM–8 PM) have the same exchange rates, and the latter has a 24-hour ATM that accepts Cirrus and Plus cards. **Storage lockers** ($3 for 24 hrs) in both the domestic and the international terminals are always open; the lockers are located in terminal E, right across from customs, and in terminal A, behind the stairs to the restaurants. There are two **tourist information offices** (tel. 5/762–67–63 or 5/762–67–73; open daily 9–9), one in domestic terminal A and the other in international terminal F. Their friendly and well-informed staff makes hotel reservations, provides directions and maps, and dispenses advice. The office of the **Asociación Mexicana de Hoteles y Moteles** (*see* Visitor Information, *above*), which can recommend accommodations for every budget, also has offices in terminals A and F, and purports to be open 24 hours a day. The **Caseta Pública** in terminal F is open 24 hours. You can call long distance and send faxes, but you cannot make collect calls. The airport also has a **pharmacy,** open daily 7 AM–10 PM.

➤ **AIRPORT TRANSIT • **The only realistic airport transportation for budget travelers is the **Metro.** It's a cheap but fairly time-consuming (1 hour to the centro) way to travel and probably not the safest after dark, especially since you'll have to make at least one line change to get to or from downtown. From the international exit at the airport, turn left, and walk for about a kilometer (think twice about doing this with heavy luggage). Get on Line 5 at the Terminal Aérea station and follow the signs for PANTITLÁN. When you reach Pantitlán, change to Line 9, and follow the signs for TACUBAYA. At the Chabacano stop, transfer to Line 2 and follow signs for CUATRO CAMINOS. You can get off at the Allende, Zócalo, or Bellas Artes stops for the budget hotels in the centro. Just remember that the Metro does not run past 12:30 AM. If you have a late flight, your only option is to take a taxi, or crash at the airport until 6 AM, when the metro starts running again. **Taxi** service from the airport is regulated and you must purchase a ticket at the office in the far end of the domestic terminal or at the international terminal next to the baggage claim, where prices are set according to destination and number of passengers. Rates for downtown-bound taxis run from about $3 for one or two people to $12 for three or four passengers. If you have an early flight or just plain want to make it there on time, a radio taxi is your best bet (*see* Getting Around, *below*), at about $8. If you want to rent a car, visit the few rental agencies located in Sala E.

BY CAR A quick count of the roadkill and the memorial crosses on the sides of the roads will help you understand why many Mexicans keep religious figurines on their dashboards or hanging from their rearview mirrors—no doubt you'll want to set up a similar shrine of your own. The main highways approaching Mexico City are 85 from the north, 136 and 150 from the east, 95 from the south, and 15 from the west. These main highways are generally well maintained; just be careful driving at night, as occasional steep shoulders and deep gutters can cause your car to roll over. Tolls for these roads are relatively inexpensive. However tolls for *super carreteras,* government-sponsored super highways with better road conditions, can be outrageous. If you ever need assistance, the **Auxilio Turístico Ángeles Verdes** ("Green Angels"; tel. 5/250–82–21 or 5/250–01–23) is a group of radio-dispatched mechanics.

GETTING AROUND

Mexico City's size serves to confuse and intimidate. The streets are not all neatly set out in a grid, and their names can change as often as five times as they pass through some of the 350 *colonias* (neighborhoods). You can orient yourself in the downtown area by using the two major arteries, **Paseo de la Reforma** and **Avenida Insurgentes,** as guides. Insurgentes runs north–south, intersecting Reforma in the busy downtown area and continuing south through the trendy Zona Rosa. Reforma passes through Chapultepec Park in the southwest of the city and continues north through the downtown, almost touching the Alameda Central. Here Reforma intersects another important street, **Avenida Juárez.** West of Reforma, Juárez ends in the Plaza de la República and the Monumento a la Revolución; east of Reforma, Juárez runs from the Alameda Central to the Zócalo, becoming Avenida Madero as it runs through the *centro histórico* (historic center) of the D.F.

It's a good idea to keep your backpack or personal belongings in front of you, especially around rush hour and at Metro transfer stations; thieves have been known to slit backpacks and purse straps before you can say "¡Socorro!"

An intricate web of public transportation connects the neighborhoods of this overwhelming city. While most points of interest are accessible on foot from centrally located Metro stops, exploring the entire city may require a mind-boggling combination of Metro trains, buses, taxis, and peseros. An *abono de transporte* (transport pass; about $2) is good for 15 days of unlimited travel both on buses and the Metro. It goes on sale twice a month, about three days before the first and then three days before the middle of the month, at Metro and lottery ticket booths. It's a worthwhile investment if you plan to explore the city on public transportation or if you're staying at least two weeks.

BY METRO The Metro is by far the fastest and cheapest way to explore Mexico City, and is simple to use: Each of the nine lines is color coded, and stations are named for major sights nearby. Route maps are posted throughout every station, and free *Red del Metro* maps are available at the information booths of the principal stations. To avoid accumulating a pocketful of change every time you buy a ticket (10¢), you can purchase 10 at a time; they don't expire. Tickets are sold at the windows labeled TAQUILLA, near the main entrances to the metro lines. Transfers don't cost extra, but make sure not to follow the crowds out of the station; once you pass through the *salida* (exit), you'll need a new ticket to reenter.

Large backpacks or luggage are technically not allowed on the Metro, though it's unlikely anyone will stop you. Because of crowds, however, it's actually difficult to fit into the Metro with a large bag during peak hours, when the trains become a claustrophobic's nightmare. When it's crowded, get close to the door well before your stop—the rush of incoming passengers gives you little time to exit. During rush hours (7–10 and 5–9), the first car on Lines 1, 2, and 3 is reserved for women and children, and guards posted at the gates strictly enforce the rule. Lines 1–9 run weekdays 5 AM–1 AM, Saturday 6 AM–2 AM, and Sunday 7 AM–1 AM.

BY BUS Every day, hundreds of thousands of passengers ride Mexico City's buses. Although the system serves the entire city (destinations are marked on the windshields), two routes are particularly useful and run all night long: RUTA 55, the principal route between the Zócalo and Chapultepec Park, along the Paseo de la Reforma, Juárez, and Madero; and RUTA 17, the route connecting Metro Indios Verdes to *Ciudad Universitaria* (University City, or UNAM), passing along Insurgentes through San Ángel. Most other buses run daily 5 AM–midnight. While service is generally reliable and always cheap (about 10¢), the lumbering vehicles absolutely crawl during rush hours (7–10 AM and 5–9 PM). Buses are also extremely crowded during these peak

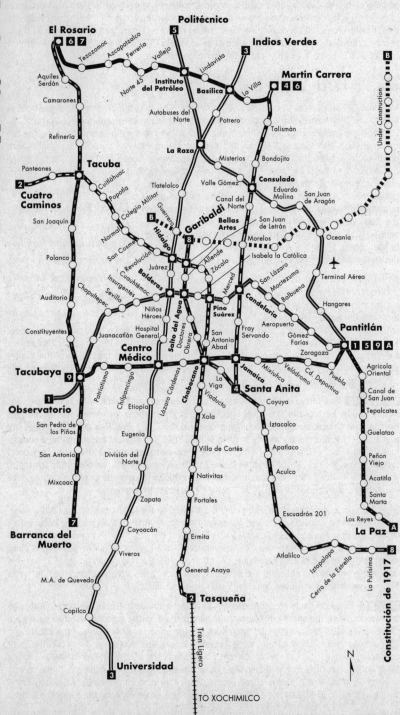

Mexico City Metro

El Rosario [6] [7]
Tezozomoc
Azcapotzalco
Ferrería
Aquiles Serdán
Norte 45
Camarones
Instituto del Petróleo
Refinería
Autobuses del Norte
Panteones
Tacuba
Cuatro Caminos
Cuitláhuac
Popotla
San Joaquín
Colegio Militar
Normal
San Cosme
Polanco
Cuauhtémoc
Auditorio
Chapultepec
Insurgentes
Sevilla
Constituyentes
Juanacatlán
Tacubaya [9]
Observatorio [1]
San Pedro de los Piños
San Antonio
Mixcoac
Patriotismo
Chilpancingo
Etiopía
Eugenia
División del Norte
Zapata
Coyoacán
Barranca del Muerto [7]
Viveros
M.A. de Quevedo
Copilco
Universidad [3]

Politécnico [5]
Vallejo
Lindavista
Indios Verdes [3]
Martín Carrera [4] [6]
Basílica
La Villa
Potrero
Talismán
La Raza
Misterios
Bondojito
Tlatelolco
Valle Gómez
Consulado
Canal del Norte
Eduardo Molina
San Juan de Aragón
Guerrero
Garibaldi
Bellas Artes
San Juan de Letrán
Oceanía
Hidalgo [B]
[8]
Allende
Morelos
Isabela la Católica
Revolución
Juárez
Zócalo
San Lázaro
Terminal Aérea
Balderas
Merced
Moctezuma
Balbuena
Niños Héroes
Pino Suárez
Candelaria
Hangares
Hospital General
San Antonio Abad
Fray Servando
Aeropuerto
Pantitlán [1] [5] [9] [A]
Salto del Agua
Doctores
Obrera
Gómez Farías
Centro Médico
Zaragoza
Agrícola Oriental
Lázaro Cárdenas
Chabacano
Jamaica
Mixiuhca
Cd. Deportiva
Puebla
Canal de San Juan
La Viga
Viaducto
Santa Anita [4]
Velódromo
Tepalcates
Xola
Coyuya
Guelatao
Villa de Cortés
Iztacalco
Peñón Viejo
Nativitas
Apatlaco
Acatitla
Portales
Aculco
Santa Marta
Ermita
Escuadrón 201
Los Reyes
La Paz [A]
General Anaya
Atlalilco
Iztapalapa
Cerro de la Estrella
La Purísima
Constitución de 1917 [8]
Tasqueña [2]
Tren Ligero
TO XOCHIMILCO
B
Under Construction

N

54

hours. If you can't make out the tangle of bus lines on your own, any of the friendly tourist agencies in the Zona Rosa will help you get where you're going.

BY PESERO Throughout the D.F., *peseros,* which include *combis* (old VW vans) and *micros* (a slightly larger version of the combi), squeeze through impossible spaces, turn left from the far right lane, go from full throttle to a dead stop in seconds, and manage to deliver people alive to thousands of street corners all over the city. Peseros cover general zones marked by a number, preceded by the words RUTA NO. painted on the side of the minibus. Individual routes within the zones vary, though, so it's a good idea to ignore the ruta numbers and concentrate on reading the destination posted in the window. Corners with stoplights and bus stops are the easiest places to catch peseros, but they generally stop wherever you hail them. Designated stops along Insurgentes and Reforma, however, are indicated by a white-and-green sign. The fare is based upon how far you go: about 15¢ for up to 5 kilometers, 25¢ for 5–12 kilometers, and 30¢ for 12 kilometers or more. For more information or to file a complaint, call 5/605–66–67 or 5/605–59–22 between 9 AM and 3 PM or between 6 PM and 8 PM.

The word "pesero" dates from the good old days when a ride actually cost one peso.

BY TAXI Taxis are easy to come by all over the D.F., especially in the downtown area. The big American sedans parked outside major hotels and museums (and all around the Zona Rosa), called *sitio* cabs, are tourist taxis whose English-speaking drivers will gladly take you on shopping tours or off to see the sites. Of course, at the end of your leisurely drive through the city they'll also charge you a small fortune—generally twice as much as the metered taxis. Your best bet is to stick to the "real" taxis—usually green VW Bugs and small sedans available when the sign on the dash says LIBRE. Plus, since these cabs only use unleaded gasoline, they're more environmentally sound. If the meter works, the driver will tell you, and the standard, non-negotiable rate will be used. However, if the meter is "broken," you'll have a chance to bargain for your ride before you get in. You'll be glad you did, when, after a series of convoluted circles and backtracking, you finally reach your hotel and the meter has skyrocketed. After all, the D.F. is a huge city, and most drivers only have a general idea of that museum or hotel's whereabouts. After 10 PM, fares go up by about one-third and drivers tend to be reluctant to venture very far out of the city. Also beware of crossing the line between the D.F. and the *Estado de México*. Although there is no visible difference between these two areas, taxi drivers automatically double their rates once they cross the border. Tipping is necessary only when the driver helps you with your bags, drives in a non-life-threatening manner, or otherwise goes out of his way to make your journey somewhat pleasurable.

Radio-dispatched taxis will fetch you wherever you are, although finding a cab downtown isn't a problem at any hour. If you've made an appointment the night before, it's best to call and remind them half an hour before they're supposed to arrive. Several companies are listed in the phone book under *Sitios de Automóviles,* or try **Taxi-Radio** (tel. 5/566–00–77 or 5/566–72–66), with free wake-up call service, or **Servicios Taxi-Mex** (tel. 5/538–49–66 or 5/538–99–37), with airport service only.

BY CAR Only the very brave or very foolish attempt to drive in Mexico City. Parking is nearly impossible to find, roads are confusing, traffic is hellish, and most other drivers are *totalmente locos.* Plus, all cars are prohibited from driving one to two days a week, depending on the pollution level. The days are determined either by a colored sticker on the car or the last digit of the vehicle's license plate number. This law does not apply to vehicles with foreign license plates nor to rental cars (your rental car *should* have a special plate that exempts it from the restriction). If you are driving, get a good street map like the *Guía Roji* or the *Guía Pronto* and try to drive like a chilango—fearlessly and with death as your backseat driver.

To rent a car you must have a credit card and a driver's license and be willing to shell out some moolah (the most affordable rental goes for about $45 a day, mileage and insurance included). Though the minimum age requirement differs from company to company, one thing remains constant: All companies charge a 15% government tax. Rental company offices at the airport are open 24 hours, and there are a slew of branches in the Zona Rosa. Major companies include **Avis** (tel. 5/588–88–88 or toll free 91–800/7–07–77), **Budget** (tel. 5/566–68–00), **Dollar** (tel. 5/207–38–38), and **National** (tel. 5/525–75–43 or toll free 91–800/9–01–86). **55**

Mexico City Bus Routes

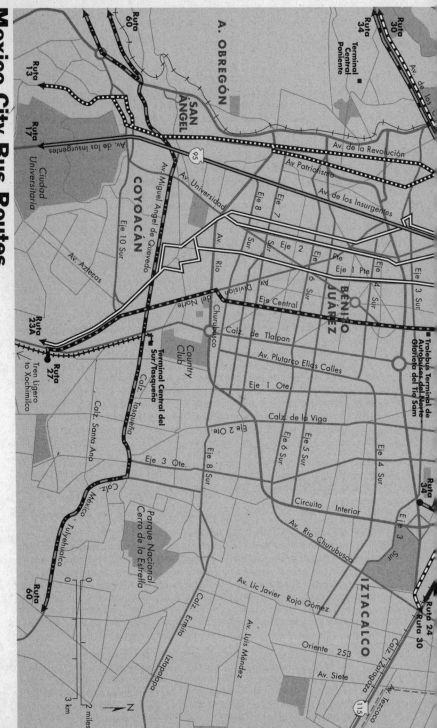

If you're in the pariah 18–25 age category, go with **Hertz** (tel. 5/592–60–82 or toll-free 91–800/7–00–16), which *will* rent to you.

Where to Sleep

Cheap hotels in Mexico City are filled with traveling families, Mexican business-men, and that faint but ever-present Carpet-Fresh scent. The budget hotel areas listed here are conveniently clustered around Metro stops Pino Suárez, Zócalo, Bellas Artes, and Revolución. Reservations are *always* a good idea, especially during major holidays and the summer months. If you don't make reservations, arrive close to check-out time (noon–2), when other guests will be vacating the rooms. Tax is included in the government-controlled price.

NEAR THE ZÓCALO

The huge colonial buildings in the area near the Zócalo have been divided over time to create a densely populated commercial and residential area. The busy downtown area is heavily traveled by day and virtually still by night. Be cautious when wandering the deserted streets, especially alone.

➤ **UNDER $10** • **Hotel Habana.** Sleekly decorated in Miami-Vice pastels, this is *the* place to pamper yourself for the fewest pesos. The room (and beds) are decadently over-sized, the bathrooms are clean and modern, and there's steaming hot water. With control switches for the TV and lights, you may find no good reason to leave your bed—many Mexican couples seem to agree. Singles and doubles with one bed are $8.25, doubles with two beds $11. *República de Cuba 77, btw Palma and República de Chile, tel. 5/518–15–89 or 5/518–15–90. 50 rooms, all with bath. Luggage storage, safe-deposit box, snack bar. Reservations advised.*

Hotel Isabel. True, you do hear a lot of German and the hotel's business card *does* proudly trump itself up as being "an ideal place for tourists." Nevertheless, the place is *gorgeous*. The theme here is the Spanish Inquisition meets modern comfort: Dangerous-looking iron relics and numerous portraits of "La Isabel" overlook a huge, but cozy, lobby perfect for socializing with other international travelers. Try for one of the quiet fourth floor rooms with outdoor patios facing away from the street. Singles or doubles with a clean communal bathroom cost $9; singles or doubles with bath cost $12 and $14 respectively. *Isabel la Católica 63, tel. 5/518–12–13, fax 5/521–12–33. 72 rooms, 63 with bath. Restaurant/bar. AE, MC, V.*

Hotel Juárez. Tucked away from bustling 5 de Mayo, this budget hotel is hard to find but worth the effort. The cool, trickling fountain in the Moorish-style lobby sets the tone, although the dim corridors make you wonder how much the management is trying to save on electricity. The paneled rooms, with TV, phone, and even piped-in Muzak, are a great deal at $8.25 for one bed, $11 for two. *Cerrada de 5 de Mayo 17, on a side street btw Isabel la Católica and Palma, tel. 5/512–69–29 or 5/518–47–18. From Metro Allende, 1 block south on Isabel la Católica, left on 5 de Mayo. 39 rooms, all with bath. Luggage storage. Reservations advised.*

Excuse Me, But Do You Have the Time?

If you find yourself on Calle Uruguay (just southwest of the Zócalo), look for number 90. It was the home of Count Juan Manuel Solórzano, an eccentric gentleman with the most disquieting of habits: After dark, he walked in front of his house and asked passersby for the time. If they knew (and were naive enough to tell him), Don Juan killed them on the spot. Legend has it that just before he committed his bloody deeds, he would heartily congratulate them for knowing—with exactitude—the hour of their death.

Hotel La Marina. The lobby, with a ship's steering wheel commanding the turquoise walls, is the only thing "marine" about this hotel. Rooms ($8.50 singles, $9 doubles) have valentine-red carpets and pink bedspreads that are comfortable, if worn. The bathrooms are clean and modern. *Allende 30, at Domínguez, tel. 5/518–24–45. 47 rooms, all with bath. Luggage storage. Reservations advised. Wheelchair access. AE, MC, V.*

Hotel Zamora. The clean, rectangular rooms here are spartan, with neither a picture nor a rug to smooth out their sharp edges. The señora who runs the place is easily rubbed the wrong way, but smile insistently, and she'll soften up. Singles cost $5 ($6.50 with bath) and doubles run $6.25 ($9 with bath). *5 de Mayo 50, tel. 5/512–82–45. 36 rooms, 18 with bath.*

➤ **UNDER $15 • Hotel Principal.** The management at this nunnery-turned-hotel has done wonders to liven up the place—plants and natural light make it look like a giant greenhouse. Clean and comfortable single rooms run $6.25 without bath, $11 with. Doubles with baths (soap and towels included) cost $13.25 for a *cama matrimonial* (double bed), or $15.25 for two beds. *Bolívar 29, btw 16 de Septiembre and Madero, tel. 5/521–13–33 or 5/521–20–32. 100 rooms, 60 with bath. Luggage storage, restaurant. Wheelchair access.*

Hotel San Antonio. This quiet hotel on a dead-end alley usually has vacancies even in the afternoon. Persevere until you find it (it's only a block from the Zócalo) and you'll be rewarded with goodies like a TV, phone, soap, and towels. The small, bright rooms, priced $9–$10 for a single, $11.50 for a double, and $15 for four people in a double, have green bedspreads and impeccably clean bathrooms with water that takes a while to get hot. Avoid the noisy rooms on the ground floor. *2o Callejón 5 de Mayo 29, tel. 5/512–99–06. From Zócalo, west on 5 de Mayo, left on Palma, right on Cerrada de 5 de Mayo until it turns into Callejón 5 de Mayo. 44 rooms, 40 with bath. Wheelchair access.*

➤ **UNDER $20 • Hotel Canadá.** This hotel tries to make you feel important from the moment you walk in. A uniformed bellboy greets you at the door, the reception staff is always on its best behavior, and the rooms, although small, possess all the amenities needed to pamper yourself. Singles go for $18, doubles with one bed $20 (two beds $22), and triples $28. *5 de Mayo 47, tel. 5/518–21–06, fax 5/512–93–10. 85 rooms, all with bath. Laundry, safety vaults, travel agency. Wheelchair access. MC, V.*

➤ **UNDER $30 • Hotel Catedral.** If you're feeling used and abused by the smog and traffic, spend a night or two in this very comfortable hotel. Rooms are decorated in soothing pastels, and the beds and mirrors are tastefully trimmed in oak. Singles cost $22, doubles $27–$30, and all rooms have TVs, phones, and huge closets. For a real splurge, get the junior suite with a Jacuzzi for $5 added to the price of your room. The large, clean bathrooms have huge showers and rivers of hot water. *Donceles 95, tel. 5/518–52–32, fax 5/512–43–44. 120 rooms, all with bath. Garage, laundry, luggage storage, restaurant, safe-deposit box, travel agency. Reservations advised. AE, MC, V.*

Hotel Gillow. A short walk from the Zócalo, this luxury hotel has huge rooms and all the accoutrements: room service, TVs, and phones. Bathrooms have a tub and a wood-trimmed mirror. Singles cost $22, doubles with one bed $26, two beds $30. *Isabel la Católica 17, btw Madero and 5 de Mayo, tel. 5/518–14–40. 103 rooms, all with bath. Laundry, luggage storage (for nonguests also), restaurant, safe-deposit box, travel agency. AE, MC, V.*

SOUTH OF THE ALAMEDA CENTRAL

The area just south of the Alameda Central is packed with hotels, cheap *taquería* chains, and stores selling all sorts of odds and ends. Most hotels are just a short walk from the Palacio de Bellas Artes and the Museo Mural de Diego Rivera. The small *barrio chino* (Chinatown) on Dolores is also nearby. Although the area is fairly safe and a bit more lively at night than the neighborhoods around the Zócalo, take normal precautions when out late.

➤ **UNDER $10 • Hotel Calvin.** This hotel is right across from the Metropolitano movie theater and its bright sign, making it a cinch to find at night. The peach-colored rooms ($9.50 for one bed, $12.50 for two beds) come equipped with TV and phone; for one with a Jacuzzi,

Mexico City Lodging

Casa de los
Amigos, **1**
Casa González, **9**
Gran Hotel Texas, **2**
Hotel Calvin, **11**
Hotel Canadá, **23**
Hotel Carlton, **7**

Hotel Catedral, **19**
Hotel del Valle, **13**
Hotel Edison, **3**
Hotel Fleming, **12**
Hotel Frimont, **8**
Hotel Gillow, **22**
Hotel Habana, **18**

Hotel Ibiza, **4**
Hotel Isabel, **25**
Hotel Juárez, **20**
Hotel La Marina, **17**
Hotel Latino, **28**
Hotel Marlowe, **14**

Hotel
Monte Carlo, **26**
Hotel Oxford, **6**
Hotel Parador
Washington, **10**
Hotel
Pennsylvania, **5**

Hotel Principal, **16**
Hotel Roble, **27**
Hotel
San Antonio, **24**
Hotel Toledo, **15**
Hotel Zamora, **21**

60

you'll shell out $16.50. Try to get a room facing away from the Metropolitano sign, especially if you plan on turning in early. The large bathrooms are shedding paint and some are missing toilet seats, but they're clean and have warm water. *Azueta 33, tel. 5/521–79–52. 29 rooms, all with bath. Laundry, luggage storage, restaurant. Reservations advised. AE, MC, V.*

Hotel del Valle. Don't be put off by the nondescript lobby or rooms. The location and price ($8.50 for one bed, $9.50 for two) are good, and the bathrooms are as clean as they come. Plus, each room is equipped with a phone and TV. The reliable but somewhat dilapidated elevator makes this hotel relatively wheelchair accessible (one step at front door). *Independencia 35, tel. 5/521–80–67. 50 rooms, all with bath. Laundry, luggage storage, restaurant. Reservations advised.*

Hotel Toledo. The lobby is cozy and welcoming despite the *telenovelas* (soap operas) flickering on the TV. A mint-green stairway winds up to spacious and airy rooms with worn carpet and thinning bedspreads. Street noise is minimal, unless you're in a room facing the street. The bathrooms are old, but clean and have reliable hot water. Singles are $8.50, doubles $10–$12, triples $14. *López 22, tel. 5/521–32–49, fax 5/518–56–31. From Metro Bellas Artes, south on Cárdenas (Eje Central), right on Independencia, left on López. 35 rooms, all with bath. Luggage storage, snack bar. Reservations advised.*

➢ **UNDER $30** • **Hotel Fleming.** Don't let the vinyl in the '50s-style lobby fool you—this is a posh hotel. Spacious rooms with plenty of mirrors and matching pastel curtains and comforters have TVs, phones, and other extras. Singles are $24, doubles $29. For 10 bucks more you can get a room with a Jacuzzi. *Revillagigedo 35, tel. 5/510–45–30. From Metro Juárez, 2 blocks east on Juárez, right on Revillagigedo. 75 rooms, all with bath. Laundry, luggage storage, parking, restaurant. Reserve at least 2 days in advance. AE, MC, V.*

Hotel Marlowe. The beautiful, fully carpeted rooms here have large desks, TVs, and touch-tone phones, while the impeccable bathrooms have so much hot water their full-length mirrors become steamy enough to write notes to the next occupant. If that's not enough, entertain yourself by playing with the switches on the headboard of the bed, which control the TV and lights. Singles cost $24, doubles $27–$28.50. *Independencia 17, btw López and Dolores, tel. 5/521–95–40. 107 rooms, all with bath. Garage, laundry, luggage storage, restaurant, travel agency. Wheelchair access. AE, MC, V.*

NEAR METRO REVOLUCIÓN

The budget hotels near the Metro Revolución cluster within a block of each other, as if they couldn't bear a meter's separation. Despite the peaceful atmosphere on the tree-lined streets, it's only a five-minute Metro ride to the hustle and bustle of the city center. The area is also bordered by major thoroughfares—Insurgentes Norte, Puente de Alvarado, and Reforma—which provide easy access to all points in the city.

➢ **UNDER $10** • **Casa de los Amigos.** The friendly, English-speaking staff at this Quaker house won't make you pass a test to stay here, but you must abide by some of the Casa's rules: No alcohol or drugs allowed, and smoking permitted only on the patio. In return you'll get the lowdown on volunteer opportunities and Spanish language classes in Mexico and Guatemala, as well as use of their library. The Casa serves huge, healthy breakfasts ($1.50) weekdays 8–9 AM, the perfect time to socialize with other young international travelers. Single-sex dorm beds are $5.50, private singles without bath $7.50, and private doubles $11 ($12.50 with bath). An apartment with a kitchen and bathroom costs $15, $17 for two, $18.50 for three, and $20 for four. Fax in a reservation to ensure your stay. *Ignacio Mariscal 132, tel. 5/705–06–46 or 5/705–05–21, fax 5/705–07–71. 24 dorm beds, 3 singles and 3 doubles without bath, 2 doubles with bath, 1 apartment. Kitchen, laundry, luggage storage.*

Hotel Ibiza. Okay, so this recently remodeled hotel looks like an outdoor bathroom struggling to be elegant with its pink and gray marble, but it's refurbished, clean, and has an elevator. Plus you get all the amenities that accompany modernity: a phone, TV, hot water, and piped-in music. Singles are $8, doubles $10. *Ponciano Arriaga 22, tel. 5/566–81–55. 29 rooms, 22 with bath. Limited luggage storage.*

Hotel Pennsylvania. The newly renovated "king-size" rooms (singles $8, doubles $11) are done in light peach and baby blue, while the older, cheaper, and mustier rooms (singles $7, doubles $8.50) tend to have a more motley decor. Showering should be considered a lesson in patience: The hot water will come, eventually. *Ignacio Mariscal 101, tel. 5/703–13–84. 80 rooms, all with bath.*

➢ **UNDER $15** • **Hotel Carlton.** Across the street from a tree-filled plaza, this hotel features spacious and clean rooms and bathrooms. The management fumigates the place once a month—the odor is unpleasant, but at least you can rest assured that nothing will slither, crawl, or otherwise find its way into your bed. Rooms come in two prices: nonrenovated ($8 singles, $10 doubles) and renovated ($11.50 doubles). *Ignacio Mariscal 32-B15, tel. 5/566– 29–11 or 5/566–29–14. From Metro Revolución, east on Puente de Alvarado to Ramos Arizpe and right 1 block. 41 rooms, all with bath. Luggage storage, restaurant, safe-deposit box. Reservations advised.*

Hotel Edison. The attractive outdoor courtyard with lush plants is an oasis of tranquility in this otherwise noisy little hotel. The large rooms come with a TV and phone and cost $12.50 singles, $14–$15 doubles, $18.50 triples, and $21.50 quads. Clean, tiled bathrooms provide plentiful hot water. *Edison 106, near Ponciano Arriaga, tel. 5/566–09–33 or 5/566–09–34. 45 rooms, all with bath. Garage.*

Hotel Oxford. With wood-paneled walls and gray marble floors, the hotel's entryway tries valiantly to live up to its British namesake. The rooms are huge, clean, and win the prize for clashing patterns; ask for one overlooking the plaza. Singles are $8, doubles $10–$11.50, triples $14.50, and quadruples $16.50. If you need a stiff drink, the bar next door offers room service from noon to midnight. *Ignacio Mariscal 67, tel. 5/566–05–00. 48 rooms, all with bath. Luggage storage, safe-deposit boxes.*

➢ **UNDER $20** • **Gran Hotel Texas.** Yet another hotel with an American name and a Spanish owner. The rooms aren't as nice as the graciousness of the lobby would have you believe, but they throw in a phone, cable TV, and purified drinking water. Singles cost $15, doubles $18. *Ignacio Mariscal 129, tel. 5/705–57–82, fax 5/566–97–24. 52 rooms, all with bath. Garage, laundry, luggage storage, safe deposit box.*

Hotel Frimont. Spacious rooms decked out in a light-brown color scheme come with TV and phones, and almost-scalding water steams out of the shower. There are also Ladatel phones in the lobby. Should you find yourself low on pesos, the friendly staff offers currency exchange. Many business travelers take advantage of the reasonable prices: singles $13, doubles $15–$17. *Jesús Terán 35, tel. 5/705–41–69. From Metro Revolución, east on Puente de Alvarado, right on Jesús Terán. 85 rooms, all with bath. Garage, laundry, luggage storage, restaurant, travel agency. Reservations advised. MC, V.*

NEAR METRO PINO SUÁREZ

The hotels here appeal to traveling salespeople and tourists willing to stay a bit out of the way. There isn't much to see in these few blocks south of the Zócalo, but the hotels are cheap, you're likely to find vacancies year-round, and getting to the major sights is a breeze, thanks to the Metro. During the day the streets are crowded with shoppers looking for bargains on everything from clothing to cashews. At night, however, it's obscenely quiet—great for sleeping, but a bit scary if you're out alone.

➢ **UNDER $10** • **Hotel Latino.** This modern, pastel-decor hotel has its advantages: TVs, cleanliness, great water pressure, and incredibly quiet rooms (perhaps because they have no windows). On the downside, you may have to wade through hordes of people waiting for the bus right in front of the hotel's only entrance. Singles and doubles set you back $8. *Netzahualcóyotl 201, tel. 5/522–36–47. 40 rooms, all with bath. Luggage storage. Reservations advised.*

Hotel Monte Carlo. This beautiful, quiet hotel is by far the nicest in its price range. A large, marble staircase rises from the lobby to the black-and-white-tiled second floor. The huge rooms, complete with kitschy decorations, phones, and French doors, are spotless, and the bathrooms have hot water. Singles cost $8.50 ($11.50 with bath), doubles $9 ($16 with bath). *República de Uruguay 69, tel. 5/518–14–18 or 5/521–25–59. 70 rooms, 35 with bath. Garage, luggage storage, money exchange. Reservations advised. Wheelchair access (1 step).*

➤ **UNDER $15** • **Hotel Roble.** The convenience of the excellent restaurant next door, combined with the clean and modern rooms puts this hotel on the A list for comfort. The gray carpets go quite charmingly with the pastel decor, and the water in the clean bathrooms gets hot if you give it time. Drop $11.50 for singles, $14–$15.50 for doubles. *República de Uruguay 109, tel. 5/522–78–30 or 5/522–80–83. 61 rooms, all with bath. Luggage storage, restaurant, room service. MC, V.*

ZONA ROSA

Hotels in the Zona Rosa are as posh and expensive as the bars and restaurants that surround them. Still, you can find comfortable and affordable lodging in the residential areas bordering the tourist zone. Insurgentes and Paseo de la Reforma run right through the area, and the greenery of Parque Chapultepec is a hop, skip, and a jump away.

➤ **UNDER $15** • **Hotel Parador Washington.** This sprawling pink building on a tree-lined plaza boasts Sevillian architecture, large but lived-in rooms, and one of the friendliest staffs around. If the manager happens to be in, he's always willing to offer free Spanish lessons, and will tell you all about his experiences with the KGB. Singles cost $10.50–$11.50, doubles $13–$14. *Dinamarca 42, at Londres, tel. 5/703–08–93. From Metro Insurgentes, 4 blocks east on Chapultepec, left on Dinamarca. 25 rooms, all with bath. Laundry, luggage storage.*

➤ **UNDER $30** • **Casa González.** This guest house is so secluded that you may feel like you've accidentally stumbled into a 19th-century home. You'll never feel like an intruder, however, since the tastefully decorated living room looks as if it has been anticipating your arrival. The cozy, old-fashioned rooms are immaculate, graced with wood furniture; the spotless bathrooms, complete with tubs, are lined with traditional *azulejos* (tiles). Singles cost $20–$23, doubles $27. Señor González, who speaks fluent English, cooks delicious, relatively inexpensive meals to order (breakfast $4.25, dinner $10), so let him know if you'll be home to eat. *Río Sena 69, tel. 5/514–33–02. From Metro Insurgentes, take Génova across Reforma and Río Lerma. 20 rooms, all with bath. Luggage storage.*

ROUGHING IT

If you're a thrill seeker or incredibly poor, there are always the bus stations. Crashing at any one of these for the night is pretty safe, but it's wise to stash your valuables in a luggage locker while you snooze. Sleeping on the extremely uncooperative plastic chairs in the airport lounges is another option. For a close-up experience in Mexican political activism, join the occasional hunger strikers on the Zócalo, who camp out under roughly constructed tents.

Food

You can spend plenty of pesos eating your way through Mexico City, which supplies a wide range of restaurants for any size wallet. All over the city, but particularly in the Zona Rosa, you can find just about anything to suit your tastes—from snazzy sushi bars to the ubiquitous Taco Bell.

It's possible to eat for very little money, but only if you're not scared by the myth that eating at tiny mom-and-pop operations or at street stands will send you running for the bathroom. The food at these places is usually cooked to order, so you can tell if it has been sitting out too long or hasn't been cooked well enough. If there's a crowd of local folk at a certain place, you can bet the food there is good. Another budget survival tactic is the *comida corrida* (pre-prepared lunch special), usually beans and rice with meat, plus coffee and sometimes soup or salad, usually for under $4. Try the restaurants along Isabel la Católica in the downtown area: They usually post their daily comida corrida conspicuously. If you don't mind standing, *puestecitos* (food stands) almost always surround Metro stations, selling everything from *tacos de cabeza* (head meat tacos) to *tamarindo* (tamarind) candy. Cheap fruits and vegetables as well as taco stands flourish at the markets (*see* Shopping, *below*), and for those with delicate tummies or sudden, uncontrollable hankerings for a hamburger, there is always **Sanborns** or **Vips,** chain restaurants serving a hybrid of American and Mexican cuisines. The supermarket closest to the downtown area is **Aurrera,** on Calle Tlulpán, near Metro Nativitas.

SOME HEALTHY STREET EATS:

- *Alegrías: large cookies made with amaranth (a whitish grain) and honey*
- *Cocktel de frutas: sliced mangos, papayas, watermelon, or jicama, with salt, lemon, and chile*
- *Licuados: milk blended with such fruits as banana, mamey, or papaya*

ZÓCALO/BELLAS ARTES

Plenty of restaurants crowd the center of the city, from humble *fondas* (food stands) to elegant tourist-oriented places. **Café El Popular** (5 de Mayo 52, tel. 5/518–60–81) dishes up the basics—everything from pancakes to tamales—24 hours a day. Satisfy your sugar cravings at **Dulcería Celaya** (5 de Mayo 39), still located in the same beautiful 19th-century building in which it was founded in 1874. Fans of *churros* (an elongated, sugar-coated donut) crowd into the 24-hour **Churrería El Moro** (Lázaro Cárdenas 42, tel. 5/512–08–96). **La Michoacana,** an ice cream and *agua fresca* (juice drink) chain, dots the city. Forgo the usual vanilla ice cream and go for more adventurous flavors such as guanábana, mamey, or alfalfa.

➢ **UNDER $5** • **Café Cinco de Mayo.** Come here to slurp delicious soup and soak in the lunch-counter atmosphere, complete with twirling stools. A full Mexican food menu is also featured, but the soups are the real draw; among the best are cream of mushroom and *caldo xochimilco* (chicken-rice stew with cilantro and avocado), both for $1.75. *5 de Mayo 57, tel. 5/510–19–95. 1 block west of Zócalo. Open daily 7 AM–11 PM. Wheelchair access.*

Le Rendez-Vous. The tile-and-mirror, ballroom-like ambience here makes this joint a special place for any meal. A decadently large plate of thick hotcakes or huevos rancheros, served with coffee and fresh orange juice, is a mere $2. A generous order of enchiladas (with mole or green sauce), with soup, coffee, and dessert is $3. *Madero 29, no phone. From Metro Allende, south on Isabel la Católica, right on Madero. Open daily 8 AM–10 PM. Wheelchair access. AE, MC, V.*

Super Soya. Everything in this bright little health food store and vegetarian restaurant is orange: the floor, counters, and even the waitresses' uniforms. At lunchtime you'll have to fight for a seat to enjoy your soyburger ($1) or veggie taco (40¢). A large fruit salad with yogurt is $2. If you crave ice cream, don't miss the fragrant, homemade waffle cones. *Tacuba 40, at Motolinia, no phone. Near Metro Allende. Open daily 9–9.*

Vegetariano y Dietético. You'll have to hunt carefully to find this hotbed of vegetarianism—it's up a long, narrow stairway squeezed between two jewelry shops. Look for the doormat in the entryway. From 1 to 7 PM, a filling veggie *menú del día* (daily special), including fruit or vegetable salad, hot or cold soup, two main dishes, dessert, and *agua fresca,* is served for only $2.75. À la carte dishes, such as mushrooms in *salsa verde* (green sauce), are $2. With any luck, you'll catch the occasional piano player, who'll liven up your meal with an off-tune version of *The William Tell Overture. Madero 56, 1st floor, tel. 5/521–68–80. 1 block west of Zócalo. Open Mon.–Sat. 9–7.*

➢ **UNDER $10** • **Café de Tacuba.** Founded in 1912, this expensive but lovely chandelier-lit restaurant is perfect for a splurge. If you can keep from laughing at the ridiculously huge bows stuck to the waitresses' heads, you'll enjoy the traditional spinach-topped *enchiladas tacuba* ($7) and the filling *pozole* (corn soup; $4.50). Lighter dishes, such as garlic soup, cost less than $2.25. The café usually gets pretty crowded for lunch and dinner, especially Thursday–Sunday 6–10 PM, when there's live music. *Tacuba 28, near Metro Allende, tel. 5/512–84–82. Open daily 8 AM–11:30 PM. Wheelchair access. AE, MC, V.*

La Ópera. Once a popular cantina, this restaurant/bar boasts a colorful history. Porfirio Díaz and his decadent crowd drank here, and Pancho Villa once stormed in and shot holes in the ceiling. Today the old fashioned, carved wood booths and gilded, ornate ceiling (complete with bullet holes) make this an elegant escape from the hectic rhythm of the Zócalo. Enjoy the delicious paella for $7 or the avocado stuffed with shrimp for $3.75. If you're feeling adventurous, ask for the *Pancho Villa* cocktail—tequila served in a hollowed cucumber, accompanied by *sangrita* (tomato juice) in a fresh tomato ($2.50–$3.75, depending on the tequila you select). *5 de Mayo 10, at Filomeno Mata, tel. 5/512–89–59. 5 blocks from Zócalo. Open Mon.–Sat. 1–midnight, Sun. 1–6. Wheelchair access. AE, MC, V.*

Restaurant Emir. If you're tired of the same old enchilada, dust off your taste buds and make them tingle again at this airy Lebanese restaurant. The *platón libanés* ($5.50), with spinach empanadas and lentil rice, is a delectable edible, as are the *tortitas de falafel* ($3.50) with a side of hummus. *República de Salvador 146, 1st floor, tel. 5/510–15–90. Btw Correo Mayor and Pino Suárez. Open daily 10–7.*

ZONA ROSA

The Zona Rosa brims with restaurants, bars, and nightspots—most of them beyond a budget traveler's means. Some streets are closed to vehicular traffic, and pedestrians leisurely stroll past street performers and beggars. Copenhague, a tiny block-long street just south of Paseo de la Reforma, supplies a great variety of restaurants and boutiques, but this area tends to be pricey. If your wallet is as empty as your belly, there are cheaper joints on Chapultepec near Amberes, right outside Metro Insurgentes. To eat away from the tourist zone, cross Reforma and continue beyond the U.S. Embassy to Río Lerma (or any other street whose name begins with Río), where you'll find small restaurants offering cheap but tasty comidas corridas.

➢ **UNDER $5** • **El Gallito Taquería.** This taquería serves a variety of hot, delicious snacks sure to satisfy most late-night cravings. The restaurant fills up by 3 AM, when the clubs in the Zona shut down but no one's ready to go home. A filling order of *tacos poblanos con queso* (tacos prepared with pork and cheese) is $3.50. Vegetarians can broaden their culinary horizons with the *nopal con queso* (diced cactus leaves and melted cheese) for $2.25. *Liverpool 115, tel. 5/511–14–36. ½ block north of Génova. Open Mon.–Thurs. 10 AM–5 AM, Fri. and Sat. 10 AM–6 AM, Sun. noon–2 AM.*

El Huarache Azteca. Though slightly grimy and yellowed with age, this small, nondescript restaurant lures hungry locals on their lunch break, causing the occasional wait. In the morning, typical Mexican breakfasts—eggs and rice, *huaraches* (long, stuffed tortillas), and juice— are served for $1.50. The $2.25 comida corrida will definitely fill you up. *Chapultepec 317, at Amberes, tel. 5/525–13–04. Open Mon.–Sat. 7:30–7:30. Wheelchair access.*

Kobá-Ich. This small, clean restaurant seems to attract a largely foreign clientele, perhaps because of the posted sign claiming to provide "All the flavor of Yucatán at your table." One taste of the *pollo pibil* (chicken baked in banana leaves; $2.75)—so tender it falls off the bone—will get you hooked. For the more adventurous, try *tacos de cazón* (baby shark tacos; $2.25). *Londres 136-A, btw Génova and Amberes, tel. 5/208–57–91. From Metro Insurgentes, take Génova to Londres and turn left. Open Mon.–Sat. 8 AM–10 PM.*

➢ **UNDER $10** • **Fonda El Refugio.** Gleaming white walls, shiny copper pots, and small wooden tables make this an elegant place to dine in. The *sopa de hongos* (mushroom soup; $3) and the *pescado a la veracruzana* (red snapper cooked with tomatoes, onions, capers, peppers, and herbs; $7.50) both go well with the $3 powerhouse margaritas. *Liverpool 166, at Génova, tel. 5/207–27–32. Open Mon.–Sat. 1–midnight, Sun. until 10.*

➢ **UNDER $15** • **Bellinghausen.** Don't let the German name deceive you—this posh restaurant in the center of Zona Rosa specializes in Mexican food. The wood-paneled interior and the outdoor garden create a cozy, upscale atmosphere, and the food is delicious and well worth the splurge. Try fried *huachinango* (fish) or the *filete chemita* (beef) for $10. Especially good are *chiles en nogada* (stuffed chiles topped with cream; $9.50), a Puebla specialty available only in September. *Londres 95, at Niza, tel. 5/207–49–78 or 5/207–40–49. Open daily 1–10:30. Wheelchair access. AE, MC, V.*

COYOACÁN

Although people come to Coyoacán from all over the D.F., the area manages to retain the atmosphere of a small neighborhood, where cozy family establishments and tiny taquerías cluster around plazas. About one and a half blocks south of the plazas on Carrillo Puerto is a particularly inviting collection of fondas and taquerías. Or walk four blocks north on Allende to the Mercado, where you can fill yourself up on fresh fruit and veggies or delicious chicken, shrimp, or beef tostadas for about $2.

Fonda El Morral. This bright, Spanish-style fonda is framed by beautiful wrought-iron windows and blue-and-white-tiled doorways. The comida corrida here is a reasonable $3, while a generous and sizzling *carne tampiqueña* (grilled meat) goes for $7. *Allende 2, tel. 5/554–02–98. From Metro Coyoacán, take pesero VILLA COAPA to Jardín Centenario. Open daily 8 AM–10 PM.*

Merendero "Las Lupitas." This restaurant lies on a narrow cobblestone street just off sleepy Plaza Santa Catarina. The dining area is suffused with natural light, earth-tone tiles cover the floor, and sturdy wooden beams support the ceiling. The food has a *norteño* (northern Mexican) influence, so flour rather than corn tortillas are used; try the *gorditas norteñas* (flour tortillas stuffed with potatos and chorizo) for $2.25. The lightly fried cheese or meat *empanadas* (turnovers) are practically greaseless and cost less than $3. *Jardín de Santa Catarina 4, at Francisco Sosa, tel. 5/554–33–53. From Jardín Centenario, west on Francisco Sosa for a few blocks. Open daily 9 AM–midnight.*

Taco Inn. As the name suggests, this clean and colorful *taquería* is gringo-pandering. The food, however, is as authentic as it gets. The beef tacos with cilantro and onions and the ignominiously named *gringas* (pork and cheese sandwiched between two flour tortillas) both go for $1.50. *Presidente Carranza 106, at Carrillo Puerto, tel. 5/659–88–62. From Jardín Centenario, left on Carrillo Puerto. Open Sun.–Thurs. 1 PM–1 AM, Fri. and Sat. until 3 AM. AE, MC, V.*

SAN ÁNGEL

Most visitors avoid the busy Avenidas Insurgentes and Revolución and head up to the quiet cobblestoned streets of Plaza San Jacinto to relax and enjoy the serenity of this small, colonial neighborhood. There's a good selection of restaurants along Madero, but even cheaper fare can be found on the side streets near the Pemex station at the base of the Plaza del Carmen. The intersection of Quevedo and Universidad (near Metro M. A. de Quevedo) is another great place to find fast, cheap food in small hectic restaurants or *puestecitos* (food stands).

La Casona del Elefante. Next to the Bazar Sábado (*see* Shopping, *below*), the entry to this sophisticated and relatively inexpensive Indian restaurant is hidden behind a group of tall potted plants. The reward for your little scavenger hunt is delicious food served by frenzied waiters in glittery Indian vests. A tray of spicy salsas arrives at your table before you know what to order, although service slows considerably after that. All of the meat curries ($6) are recommended, and the curried vegetables make a good meal for about $4. *Plaza San Jacinto 9, tel. 5/616–16–01 or 5/616–22–08. From Metro M. A. de Quevedo, west on Quevedo, left on La Paz; when it forks, take Madero to Plaza San Jacinto. Open Tues.–Thurs. 1–11, Fri. and Sat. 1–midnight, Sun. until 6.*

Fechoria. This Argentine restaurant has a huge upstairs window through which you can look down upon sweaty pedestrians—if only they knew you were relaxing in front of a plate of ricotta ravioli ($4) and a cool glass of wine ($1.50). Expect a youthful, hungry crowd on weekends. *La Paz 58-A, tel. 5/550–18–34. From Metro M. A. de Quevedo, west on Quevedo to La Paz. Open Mon.–Thurs. 1–11, Fri. and Sat. 1–midnight, Sun. until 7. AE, MC, V.*

Parrilla El Tecolote. This taquería stands out for its incredibly inexpensive food. The waiters are in a constant, frantic rush, and by 1 or 2 the place is packed. Keep cool in the dark interior with a bowl of *sopa de verduras con pollo* (vegetable soup with chicken) for 50¢, or the filling comida corrida ($1.50). The innocuous-looking light-green salsa will have you begging for a glass of water. *M. A. de Quevedo 75, no phone. 1½ blocks from Metro M. A. de Quevedo. Open daily 8 AM–11 PM.*

CAFÉS

½ Luna Café. This tiny café on the western tip of the Zona Rosa is a great place to escape from the hectic pace of the surrounding area. Its small wooden tables are perfect for writing letters, and the strong cappuccino is only $1. *Florencia 36, btw Londres and Hamburgo, tel. 5/511–27–77. Metro: Insurgentes. Open weekdays 8 AM–9 PM, Sat. 10–6.*

Café Gandhi. If you packed a beret, whip it out for a visit to this well-known gallery/bookstore/coffeehouse. Strong cappuccino can be ordered with Kahlua or Amaretto ($2) for an added kick. Service is about as slow as the chess players, who pass entire afternoons brooding over moves while their cigarettes burn low. Nonsmokers can rejoice, however; the enlightened management provides a tiny no-smoking section. *M. A. de Quevedo 128, tel. 5/550–25–24. Metro: M. A. de Quevedo. Open weekdays 9:30 AM–11 PM, weekends 10:30–10.*

El Parnaso Café. Bliss is sitting comfortably beneath the shady awnings of this popular café/bookstore in the eastern corner of Coyoacán's Jardín Centenario. Although it gets crowded on weekends, it's quite acceptable to share a table. The waiters are always on the run, so they don't pay much attention to you—but once you get your coffee (about $1), the afternoon is yours. *Carrillo Puerto 2, tel. 5/554–22–25. From Metro M. A. de Quevedo, take pesero VILLA COAPA to Jardín Centenario. Open daily 7:30 AM–11 PM. Wheelchair access.*

La Vienet Café. After a visit to the Kahlo museum, be sure to stop by this little café for some of the sweetest desserts around. Its balcony and beautiful wrought-iron chairs almost make you forget that the best of Barry Manilow is playing in the background. A bite of the delicious mocha cake ($1.50) may anesthetize you to "Copacabana." *Viena, at Abasolo, tel. 5/554–45–23. 2 blocks north and 1 block east of Frida Kahlo museum. Open Tues.–Sun. 8–8.*

Exploring Mexico City

Since you could live in Mexico City for years and still never see all there is to see, your best bet for tackling this overwhelming metropolis is to see the sights district by district. Keep in mind that each area has a distinct personality that goes beyond the tourist attractions; you'll understand life in Mexico City better by taking things one at a time than by storming through the sights on automatic pilot. Start your tour at the excavated site of the Templo Mayor, located on the northeast end of the **Zócalo.** A view from its museum gives a good introduction to Mexico City's multilayered history: Stare past the pre-Columbian ruin and colonial Catedral Metropolitana, to the modern high-rises in the **Zona Rosa.** Next, head for the **Alameda Central,** home to a cluster of excellent museums that allow you to submerge yourself in the country's dramatic art. Once bedroom communities for Mexico City's elite, **San Ángel** and **Coyoacán** brim with quaint cobblestone streets and colonial mansions. Also an easy metro ride from the centro is the **Basílica de Guadalupe,** fundamental in understanding the religious fervor surrounding the Virgin of Guadalupe. Finally, end up where it all began—at the ancient city of **Teotihuacán** (*see* Near Mexico City, *below*), where you can stand on top of the Pirámide del Sol as the Teotihuacán priests did, 500 years before the Aztec people arrived.

ZÓCALO

The spot presently occupied by Mexico City's Zócalo used to function as the center of Tenochtitlán, the Aztec capital. Sadly, hardly anything from this majestic era remains: Arrogant and anxious to secure a hold on the New World, the Spanish built directly on top of Aztec structures. Beginning in the 16th century, ornate churches and convents, fancy mansions, and other stately edifices were constructed around the plaza, sometimes incorporating the volcanic stone pilfered from Aztec buildings. Toward the end of the 19th century, the upper classes began moving out of the crowded downtown, leaving their mansions to be partitioned and occupied by the working class and the poor. Today the Zócalo, bordered by some of the most beautiful buildings of the colonial era, is a constant buzz of activity. Men in search of employment line up by the cathedral gate and busloads of school children on field trips periodically mob the plaza. The Zócalo is also the city's forum for political activity. Most protest marches end here, and many anti-PRI groups distribute flyers or sell newsletters on the plaza. This is also the place to stock up on Carlos Salinas de Gortari puppets or Subcomandante Marcos T-shirts.

LA CATEDRAL METROPOLITANA This enormous cathedral on the north side of the Zócalo was built between 1573 and 1813. The first large altar in the center of the cathedral, the **Altar de Perdón,** is a copy of the original that burned in a 1967 fire. Smaller chapels line both sides of the cathedral; all are beautiful, but a few deserve special attention. The first chapel on the left contains a display with sculpted flowers, each with four petals—an example of the indigenous influence on the church's architecture. The petals represent the Aztec view of the universe, each petal symbolizing one of the four principal gods. Toward the back of the church is the third chapel (also on the left), containing **El Señor del Cacoa,** an image of Christ fashioned from corn paste, human nails, and hair. The paintings in the seventh chapel are dedicated to Felipe de Jesús, a martyred saint, and illustrate the story of his journey to Mexico from the Philippines. Apparently his ship was blown off course and wrecked in Japan, where he was condemned to death by the emperor. Legend has it that before his execution he predicted that the city in which he died (Nagasaki) would go up in flames. The **Sagrario Municipal,** on the east side of the cathedral, was built in 1749 to hold the church's most sacred relics. The cathedral is a perfect example of the ultra-baroque architecture known as *Churrigueresque,* which was introduced in the Americas by Jose Churriguera. The cathedral's ornate columns actually don't support the ceiling at all—they were designed purely for decorative purposes.

For more information on the history and architecture of the cathedral, ask at the information booth for Martín Castellanos. For $10 this artist-turned-tour-guide will tell you (in English or Spanish) everything there is to know about La Catedral—or any other place in Mexico City for that matter. Official guides, sporting green "Secretaria del Turismo" badges, are also available for $3.50. *Zócalo, across from Palacio Nacional. Mass held daily at 9:30 AM.*

MUSEO DE LA CARICATURA Formerly the Colegio de Cristo (College of Christ), this beautiful building now houses the Latin American Cartoon Museum. The drawings run the gamut from sophisticated political commentary and satire to simple jokes that don't demand any knowledge of Spanish. During restoration of the building after the 1985 earthquake, pre-Columbian artifacts, including the sculpted head of a serpent, were unearthed here. The serpent's head was left as it was found and lies at the back of the museum. Next door is the **Salón de la Plástica Mexicana II** (tel. 5/789-19-57; open weekdays 10–5), hosting a small collection of politically-oriented 20th-century art and collage. Most works here protest the long-reigning PRI, often with the use of nontraditional materials. One installation in particular examplifies this trend: Titled "2 de Octubre 1968", it contains actual shoes and earth gathered from the student massacre at Plaza Tlatelolco (*see* Alameda Central, Plaza de las Tres Culturas, *below*). *Donceles 99-A, tel. 5/789-14-08. 2 blocks north of Zócalo. Admission: 75¢, 50¢ students. Open weekdays 10–6, weekends until 5.*

MUSEO JOSE LUIS CUEVAS Housed in a former convent, this museum caused quite a stir when it was opened in 1992 by the famous Mexican artist, José Luis Cuevas. The inauguration of Cuevas's "Sala de Erotica"—a permanent collection of paintings with erotic themes—

From Pedestal To Plaza

The Zócalo—officially called the Plaza de la Constitución—is the largest plaza in the Western Hemisphere. The word "Zócalo" actually means "pedestal." In the 19th century there were plans to build a monument to Mexican Independence in Mexico City's main plaza. For whatever reason, the monument was never built, and all that remains of those designs is the name for the base of the monument—the "pedestal"—that never came into being. The misnomer stuck and is now the term applied to the main plazas of most Mexican cities.

The Zócalo and the Alameda Central

featured a real live woman masturbating on a bed. The empty bed still sits in its place of honor in the corner of the room. Before entering the Sala, you can watch a video of Cuevas lying languidly on the bed and explaining his paintings, his sexuality, and the way the two . . . um . . . intertwine. Temporary exhibits (changing every six weeks) include contemporary Latin American artists. Performance art pieces (changing weekly) are held in the main room of the museum. *Academia 13, btw Moneda and República de Guatemala, tel. 5/542–89–59. Admission: 75¢; free for students and on Sun. Open Tues.–Sun. 10–6. Performance art held Sat. at noon, Sun. at noon, 2, and 6.*

PALACIO NACIONAL The National Palace was built under the direction of Hernán Cortés, on the site where Montezuma's Grand Palace once stood. In fact, the *tezontle* (volcanic rock) now in the facade was taken from the Grand Palace and incorporated into the Spanish design. It was in the courtyard of this impressive edifice that Cortés entertained guests with Mexico's first bullfights. Today the bell rung by Padre Hidalgo to proclaim Mexico's independence in 1810 hangs on the central facade; inside you'll find the offices of the president, the Federal Treasury, and the National Archive.

The second story of the Palace's main courtyard is covered with more than 1,200 square feet of murals that took Diego Rivera and his assistants more than 16 years to paint (1929–45). The series, called *Epic of the Mexican People in Their Struggle for Freedom and Independence,* portrays two millennia of Mexican history. The hero of the pre-Hispanic panels is the plumed serpent god of wind, Quetzalcoatl, whose prophesied return supposedly facilitated Cortés's conquest. Also prominent are a man offering a human arm for sale; Spanish soldiers arriving in the not-so-New World; bell-ringing Hidalgo; revolutionaries Zapata and Pancho Villa; and even Karl Marx, smiling amid scenes of class struggle. Today a visit to the Palacio speaks volumes about the country's political uneasiness: Heavily armed guards flank the door and patrol the interior. To get in, you have to leave an ID at the door. *East side of Zócalo, tel. 5/512–20–60. Admission free. Open daily 9–5.*

TEMPLO MAYOR The Templo Mayor (Great Temple) was the political and spiritual center of the Aztec empire. For more than 400 years it remained buried beneath the Zócalo until, in February 1978, electric-company workers struck a small section of stone that turned out to be a portion of an 8-ton carving of Coyolxauhqui, goddess of the moon.

The temple itself was a massive structure, improved and enlarged on at least five separate occasions. Each renovation was a symbolic affirmation of the reigning Aztec's supremacy in the conquered Valley of Mexico. While most temples are typically dedicated to one major deity, Templo Mayor was dedicated to both Huitzilopochtli (hummingbird god of the sun) and Tlaloc (god of rain and lightning). The Aztec sacrificed as many as 10,000 persons every year (most of them either human tithes from conquered tribes or rival warriors captured in ritual "flower wars," or staged battles) in an effort to appease the gods and scare the bejesus out of any tribes who dared defy Aztec hegemony. According to Aztec religion, without this sort of divine nourishment, the sun god would refuse to move across the sky and Tlaloc would withhold water.

Artifacts found during the excavation of Templo Mayor are displayed in the **Museo del Templo Mayor.** Exhibited items include ceramic warriors, stone knives, skulls of sacrificial victims, the massive stone disk of the moon goddess, and a miniature model of Tenochtitlán. Free tours are available in English and Spanish, but you must reserve two weeks in advance. Certified tourist office guides are available at the door and charge about $7 for a group tour. *Seminario 8, at República de Guatemala, tel. 5/542–06–06 or 5/542–47–84, fax 5/542–17–17. Admission: $2.25, free Sun. Open Tues.–Sun. 9–5.*

ALAMEDA CENTRAL

The Alameda Central was the site of a *tianguis* (open-air market) during the reign of the Aztec, and the spot where heretics were burned during the Inquisition. By the mid-19th century it had become a park where the rich strolled under the trees, while the poor (who were kept out) looked on. Now everybody meanders through the grounds, lounging during lunch hour, playing chess, sleeping on the grass, or smooching on the benches. The white marble semicircle on the

The Hospital de Jesús on Pino Suárez (the entrance is down the alleyway next to Gigo's Pizza) stands on the site where the Aztec emperor Montezuma II first stood face to face with Hernán Cortés. The hospital itself, the oldest in the Americas, was founded by Cortés in 1524.

south side of the park, opposite Metro Bellas Artes, is the **Monumento a Benito Juárez,** which commemorates one of Mexico's greatest presidents. On the eastern edge of the park, the baroque **Casa de Los Azulejos** (Madero 4, behind Bellas Artes) peeks out from behind the Palacio de Bellas Artes. Originally the residence of aristocrats, it became the elite Mexico City Jockey Club, and, during the revolutionary turmoil, served as the headquarters for anarchist groups. Today it houses an ever-popular Sanborns.

MUSEO FRANZ MAYER Originally built in the 16th century, and alternately used as a hospital, an orphanage, and a convent, this structure now serves as an art museum. The displays feature an impressive collection of 16th- to 19th-century Mexican ceramics, furniture, and paintings, amassed by Franz Mayer (a.k.a. Don Pancho), a German-born farmer who lived in Mexico nearly his entire life. The shady, colonial courtyard and fountain serve as a refreshing breather from the flurry of traffic on Avenida Hidalgo. *Hidalgo 45, in front of Metro Bellas Artes, tel. 5/518–22–66. Admission: $1.25, 25¢ students; ½ off admission Sun., free Tues. Tours: 50¢. Open Tues.–Sun. 10–5. Guided tours Tues.–Fri. at 10:30, 11:30, 12:30, 1:30, Sat. at 10:30, 11:30, and 12:30.*

MUSEO MURAL DE DIEGO RIVERA Diego Rivera's mural *Sueño de una Tarde Dominical en la Alameda Central* (Dream of a Sunday Afternoon in the Alameda Central) is showcased in its own museum. Despite its apparently uncontroversial subject matter, the work initially caused a stir when Rivera captioned it "Dios no existe" (God doesn't exist). After several incidents of vandalism, Rivera painted over the offending words with "Conferencia de Letrán, año de 1836," a reference to a speech given by the mid-19th century radical congressman Ignacio Ramírez, in which he declared God to be "nonexistent." Stroll through the Alameda Central afterward and notice the still-present vendors and other characters who are exposed in Rivera's work. Intriguing temporary exhibits of modern art and photography that showcase Mexican as well as international artists are also featured. *Plaza Solidaridad, tel. 5/510–23–29 or 5/512–07–54. From Metro Balderas, cross street to Plaza Solidarida. From Metro Juárez, north on Balderas to plaza. Admission: $1, free on Sun. and for students. Open Tues.–Sun. 10–6.*

MUSEO NACIONAL DE ARTE This imposing stone building, once home to the Palacio de Comunicación (Communications Palace), now houses an impressive collection of artwork on two floors, each open on alternate days of the week. The 20th-century exhibits on the first floor include some of the more famous works in post-revolutionary *indigenismo* (indigenous style). Indigenismo painters, including Rivera, Orozco, and Siqueiros, glorified rural life, the *indígena* (indigenous person), and the *campesino* (rural dweller), finding in these figures a new understanding of *lo mexicano* (Mexicanness) and a basis for a national, non-anglocentric style. Nineteenth-century works, like those of José María Velasco (famous for his innovative landscapes), are on the second floor, along with occasional temporary exhibits. *Tacuba 8, tel. 5/512–22-41. Admission: $1.50, free Sun. 1st floor open Wed., Fri., and Sun. 10–5:30; 2nd floor open Mon., Thurs., and Sat. 10–5:30.*

MUSEO NACIONAL DE LA REVOLUCION Housed in the basement of the **Monumento a la Revolución,** this museum is well worth a couple blocks detour from the Alameda. Newspapers, films, and dioramas carefully document more than half a century of Mexican history, from the presidency of Benito Juárez to the signing of the constitution in 1917. *Plaza de la República, tel. 5/546–21–15. From Alameda Central, west on Juárez. Admission free. Open Tues.–Sat. 9–5, Sun. until 3.*

PALACIO DE BELLAS ARTES The two attractions here are the amphitheater and museum. Construction of the neoclassical Palace of Fine Arts began in 1904 under President Porfirio Díaz. It was scheduled for completion in 1910, the centennial of Mexican independence, but neither Díaz nor Italian architect Adamo Boari took the area's porous subsoil into account (the building is still sinking today). Technical difficulties coupled with the upheaval of the Mexican Revolution delayed completion of the building until July 1932. By then architectural fads had changed, and the building was given an art deco interior by architect Federico Mariscal, who combined geometric shapes, straight lines, and traditional Mexican forms.

In the main amphitheater, breathtaking murals by Rivera and Siqueiros grace the walls. Also check out the chandelier, which majestically depicts the two volcanoes to the south of the D.F.; it was designed by Gerardo Murillo (a.k.a. Dr. Atl) and assembled by Tiffany's of New York City. The amphitheater is where the **Ballet Folklórico,** the **Compañía Nacional de Danza** (National Ballet), and the **Orquesta Sinfónica Nacional** (National Symphony Orchestra) perform. Tickets for performances (*see* After Dark, *below*) can be purchased at counters (open Mon.–Sat. 11–7 and Sun. 9–7) on the first floor of the palace, next to the main entrance.

The top floor of the palace houses the **Museo Nacional de Arquitectura** (National Architecture Museum); its permanent collection includes murals by Diego Rivera, Siqueiros, Orozco, and Tamayo, and includes the plans for the future construction of Bellas Artes. Temporary exhibits are also showcased here. For guided tours, call 5/510–13–88 in advance. *Lázaro Cárdenas, at Juárez, across from Alameda Central, tel. 5/512–25–93 ext. 227. Museum admission: $1.50, free on Sun. and for temporary exhibits. Museum open Tues.–Sun. 10–6. Wheelchair access.*

PLAZA DE LAS TRES CULTURAS/TLATELOLCO At the center of the Tlatelolco District, this plaza is best known for the events that took place here on October 2, 1968. On that fateful evening, about 5,000 people gathered on Plaza de las Tres Culturas in a peaceful demonstration to decry the government's failure to meet student demands. Discontent focused on President Díaz Ordaz's anti-activist laws, the use of a paramilitary riot squad (*grenaderos*) against students, and the huge expenses incurred by Mexico's preparations for hosting the 1968 summer Olympics. The protesters were met by army and police units in tanks and armored cars. The government claims to this day that snipers in surrounding apartment buildings then opened fire, which police returned. Others claim that the army shot first. At any rate, few today doubt that the death toll was well into the hundreds.

The plaza is named for its symbols of the three main cultures of Mexico—indigenous, Spanish, and mestizo. The indigenous is present in the massive ruins of a pre-Hispanic ceremonial center that surround **Iglesia de Santiago Tlatelolco.** The church is representative of the Spanish, and houses the baptismal font of Juan Diego, the Indian convert to whom the Virgin of Guadalupe appeared in 1531. A battle monument on the plaza translates as: "This was neither victory nor defeat. It was the sad birth of the mestizo people, who are Mexico today." It refers to the defeat of Tlatelolco's Aztec by Cortés. Mestizo culture is represented on the plaza by the ultramodern Ministry of Foreign Affairs. *From Metro Tlatelolco, east on Manuel González, right on Lázaro Cárdenas.*

TORRE LATINOAMERICANA This 44-story tower springs up amid the downtown colonial buildings. The view from the *mirador* (observation deck) will leave you breathless, especially if

The Man Without a Face

Despite Diego Rivera's outspoken opposition to capitalism, in 1933 the Rockefeller Foundation commissioned him to paint a mural, called "Man at the Crossing of the Ways," for the RCA Building in New York City. As the details of the painting began to take shape, the public, not to mention the Rockefellers, was shocked: What had looked like a faceless man helping a group of workers in the original sketches was transformed into Lenin in the mural. Although Diego's refusal to remove Lenin resulted in the mural's destruction, Rivera soon found a home for a reproduction of his masterpiece in the Palacio de Bellas Artes (see above).

you decide to forgo the elevator. If the line of voyeurs waiting to use the telescopes is too long, head to the **Fantástico Mundo del Mar** ("Fantastic World of the Sea"), the highest aquarium in the world, on the 38th floor. *Lázaro Cárdenas, 3 blocks from Metro Bellas Artes. Tower admission: $2.50; open daily 9 AM–11 PM. Aquarium admission $4; open daily 9 AM–10 PM.*

BOSQUE DE CHAPULTEPEC

Known simply as "Chapultepec," this park is a haven from all things urban for families, joggers, cyclists, and young lovers. Unfortunately, all these people usually want to escape city life together, making the park quite crowded on weekends. Guarding the entrance to the park is the **Monumento a los Niños Héroes,** which honors six young military cadets who died defending *la patria* (the fatherland) during the U.S. invasion in 1847. The invasion cost Mexico almost half its national territory, including what are now the states of Texas, California, Arizona, New Mexico, and Nevada. Tuesday–Sunday you can boat ($1.25 per hr for up to 5 people) on the bright green **Lago Chapultepec.** Any day of the week you can see how long that taco you had for lunch stays down on any of the rides in **La Feria** amusement park (admission $3). All museums are clustered along Paseo de la Reforma, so if you only have a few hours to spare, stick to this main thoroughfare. Metros Chapultepec and Auditorio are located inside the park, and buses and peseros to the park run west from the centro down Paseo de la Reforma.

CASTILLO DE CHAPULTEPEC The neoclassical Chapultepec Castle sits perched atop *Cerro Chapulín* (Grasshopper Hill), overlooking the entire Valley of Mexico. The oldest part of the castle still standing dates to 1785, when Viceroy Bernardo de Galvez built the first fort here. In 1841 the castle was converted into a military academy. Shortly after, at the end of the bloody battle for Mexico City during the U.S. invasion, a young cadet named Juan Escutia, realizing the battle was lost, climbed to the top of the northern tower, wrapped himself in the Mexican flag, and jumped to his glorious death. A tomb at the foot of the hill marks the place where he landed. Almost 20 years later, Emperor Maximilian, installed by the French, remodeled the castle and moved in. It remained the official residence of the head of state until 1944, when President Lázaro Cárdenas moved his headquarters to Los Pinos, the current presidential residence, and gave the castle to the Mexican people as the **Museo Nacional de Historia.** Using teacups, jewelry, and clothing from different social classes and various time periods, the museum is a fascinating illustration of Mexico's economic, cultural, and political history. The $2 admission to the museum also gets you a peek at the castle interior. Tours show some of the castle's rooms, preserved in their original state, including the bedroom of the fiery general (and future president) Porfirio Díaz. It's all complemented by murals by José Clemente Orozco and Diego Rivera. If you're not up to walking up to the castle, take a 60¢ train from Niños Héroes to the top of the hill. *Uphill, beyond Monumento a Los Niños Héroes, tel. 5/553–62–46. Admission: $2; free Sun., for students, and after 4 PM. Open Tues.–Sun. 9–5.*

MUSEO DE ARTE MODERNO Amid the greenery of Chapultepec Park, this museum is dedicated to modern painting, photography, and sculpture. The permanent collection includes works by Frida Kahlo, Dr. Atl, Rufino Tamayo, and Diego Rivera. The annex to the main building houses temporary exhibits of contemporary Mexican and international painting, lithography, sculpture, and photography. The surrounding gardens are sprinkled with sprawling sculptures that look like strange creatures nestled among the trees. *South side of Reforma, at Gandhi, tel. 5/553–62–33 or 5/211–83–31 Admission: $1.50, free Sun. and for students. Open Sun.–Fri. 10–5:30, Sat. until 9.*

MUSEO NACIONAL DE ANTROPOLOGIA Mexico's complex anthropological heritage demands a museum as grand as this one. It's by far the best in the country, with perhaps the finest archaeological collection in the world; each room displays artifacts from a different geographic region and/or culture. Pace yourself—if you try to cover it all at once, you'll end up hating the place. Make sure to check out stelae from Tula, a town north of Mexico City, with bas-reliefs carvings that indicate a heavy Mayan influence. The museum also houses the original *Piedra del Sol,* the famous Aztec calendar. Although private tours aren't officially sponsored by the museum, if you stick around Tuesday–Saturday 10–11 or 3–4, and ask politely, you may be able to get in on a tour with a school or some other group. **Cafeteria Museo,** located downstairs, offers an outdoor patio where you can relax, sip a cappucino, and eat for under $5.

Chapultepec and Zona Rosa

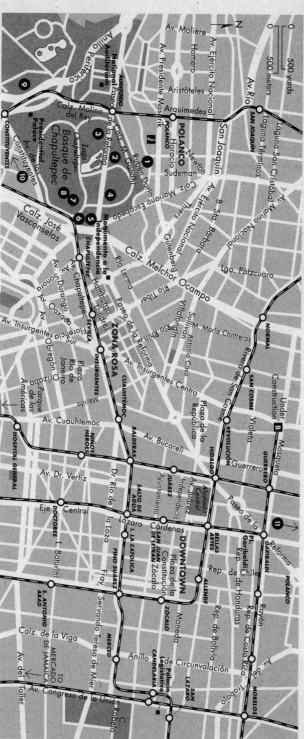

Paseo de la Reforma, at Gandhi, tel. 5/553–62–66 or 5/553–63–54. Admission: $2.25, free Sun. Open Tues.–Sat. 9–7, Sun. 10–6. Wheelchair access.

MUSEO TAMAYO DE ARTE CONTEMPORANEO INTERNACIONAL Finding this museum hidden within the dense foliage of Chapultepec Park may seem impossible. Don't give up—just look for the abstract fire-engine-red sculpture in front of the main entrance off Paseo de la Reforma. In 1981, artist Rufino Tamayo and his wife, Olga, donated their personal collection of paintings and sculpture to the people, establishing this sleek, granite museum. It contains pieces by Lilia Carillo, René Magritte, Joan Miró, and quite a few of Tamayo's own works. Check out the aquatic sculptures at the front of the museum, which were once immersed for months at a time in the Atlantic Ocean to become oxidized. *Reforma, at Gandhi, tel. 5/286–58–89. Admission: $1.50; free Sun. and for students. Open Tues.–Sun. 10–6.*

EL PAPALOTE/MUSEO DEL NINO Established in 1995 with money from the Mexican government and the Lotería Nacional (National Lottery), El Papalote is reminiscent of an indoor amusement park, with more than 360 interactive science demonstrations. If you're willing to subject your body to science, you can lounge on a bed of nails, experience momentum on a spinning machine, blow bubbles that encapsulate your whole body, or stomp out the Mexican national anthem on a musical carpet. *Constituyentes 268, at Periférico, tel. 5/224–12–59. Admission: $3.25. Open daily 9–1 and 2–6.*

SALA DE ARTE PUBLICO SIQUEIROS Just before his death, muralist David Alfaro Siqueiros (a supporter of Stalin who had been involved in an unsuccessful attempt to assassinate Trotsky) bequeathed his home and studio to the people of Mexico. The interior walls of his workshop are covered with murals, and the house is cluttered with paintings, photographs, and some of the sketches he made for his most famous works, such as *New Democracy,* currently on display in the Palacio de Bellas Artes (*see* Alameda Central, *above*). *Tres Picos 29, btw Schiller and Hegel, Col. Polanco, tel. 5/531–33–94 or 5/545–59–52. From Metro Auditorio, north on Arquimedes, right on Rubén Darío, left on Hegel, and right on Tres Picos. Admission: $1, free for students. Open Tues.–Sun. 10–6.*

ZOOLOGICO DE CHAPULTEPEC In its recent remodeling campaign, the zoo forsook cages and fences in an attempt to preserve wildlife in a setting similar to its natural habitat. The only inconvenience of this natural setting is that it's easier for certain animals to camouflage themselves; you may find yourself in front of a sign that says LIONS, wondering where the lions are. A glimpse of the panda bears, however, is well worth the trip: This is the zoo in which the panda has best survived in captivity. You can see the pandas 9–11 and 3–4. *Reforma, next to the lake, tel. 5/553–62–63, 5/553–62–29, or 5/256–41–04. First entrance to park from Metro Auditorio. Admission free. Open Tues.–Sun. 9–4:15.*

SAN ÁNGEL

The past 50 years have seen this *pueblito* (village) develop into an exclusive suburb for Mexico City's rich. The sprawl of the city, however, impinges upon San Ángel's tranquility: Avenidas Insurgentes and Revolución transect the suburb, bringing traffic, noise, and a lively nightlife. Still, this neighborhood has its share of quiet, cobblestoned streets and colonial architecture, with homes hidden behind high walls. In the center of San Ángel is **Plaza San Jacinto,** where artists peddle their wares on Saturdays during the **Bazar del Sábado** (open 10–8). Gawking tourists and wandering *fresas* (upper-class preppies) buy fashionable handicrafts from vendors that accept credit cards. Despite the commercialism, the market is well worth the visit. East of the plaza sits the **Convento e Iglesia del Carmen** (tel. 5/548–28–38 or 5/548–53–12; open Tues.–Sun. 10–5), now a museum that displays religious artifacts, a few mummified corpses, and rotating art exhibits. Admission is $2.50, but come on Sunday when it's free. West of Insurgentes, the **Monumento a Obregón,** in honor of the general of the Mexican Revolution, dominates the corner of La Paz and Insurgentes.

MUSEO CARRILLO GIL Álvaro Carrillo Gil, a doctor and pharmaceuticals producer, set up this spacious museum to house his art collection, which features works by Wolfgang Paalen, David Alfaro Siqueiros, Gunther Gerzso, and José Clemente Orozco. For muralist buffs, this is

Your vacation.

Your vacation after losing your hard-earned vacation money.

 Lose your cash and it's lost forever. Lose American Express®
Travelers Cheques and you can get them quickly replaced.
They can mean the difference between the vacation of
your dreams and your worst nightmare. And, they are
accepted virtually anywhere in the world. Available at participating banks, credit
unions, AAA offices and American Express Travel locations. *Don't take chances.
Take American Express Travelers Cheques.*

do more

**Travelers
Cheques**

All the best trips start with **Fodor's**.

San Ángel and Coyoacán

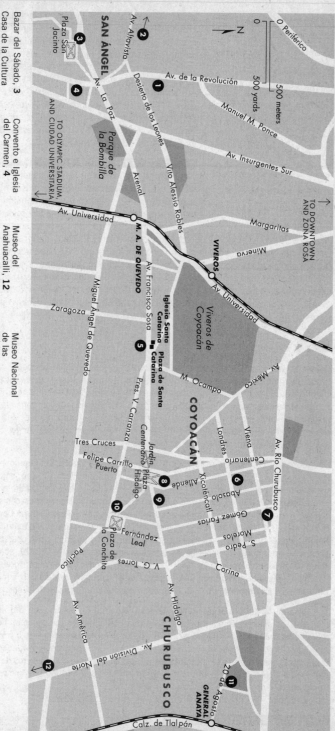

Plaza San Jacinto was the end of the line for about 50 Irish soldiers in 1847. They came to fight in the Mexican–American War on the American side, but later deserted and joined the Catholic Mexicans. Needless to say, the American soldiers who later caught them were none too pleased. Before executing them, they branded the Irish soldiers' foreheads with the letter "D" for deserter.

a chance to see many of the important, smaller paintings composed by Siqueiros and Orozco, aside from their better-known and more grandiose masterpieces. Dr. Gil liked slapping paint on the canvas as well, and some of his own creations hang on the gleaming white walls. The museum also hosts rotating exhibits by contemporary Mexican artists. *Revolución 1608, at Desierto de los Leones, tel. 5/550–12–54 or 5/550–39–83. From Metro Barranca del Muerto, catch a SAN ANGEL bus from Avenida Revolucín; get off at cnr of Altavista and Revolución. Admission: $1, 50¢ students; free Sun. Open Tues.–Sun. 10–6. Wheelchair access.*

MUSEO ESTUDIO DIEGO RIVERA Some of Diego's last paintings are still on easels, and his denim jacket and shoes sit on a wicker chair, waiting: The museum that once was home to Diego Rivera appears as if the muralist could return at any moment to continue work or share some tequila with his cronies Leon Trotsky, Lázaro Cárdenas, or John Dos Passos. Juan O'Gorman, a famous architect and close friend of Rivera's, designed the house in the spirit of functionalism, with an intent to economize space: Diego's bedroom also served as a place to store pigeon food and as a place and meal's changing room. Papier mâché skeletons hanging like jungle vines from the ceilings and the walls, suggest that Rivera shared the Mexican penchant for black humor. *Diego Rivera 2, at Altavista, tel. 5/616–09–96 or 5/550–11–89. Take RUTA 43 ALTAVISTA pesero from cnr of Revolución and La Paz (in front of Pemex station). Or walk 15 min along Altavista. Admission: $1.50, free Sun. Open Tues.–Sun. 10–6.*

COYOACÁN

Coyoacán was a rural village until the 1940s, when wealthy chilangos began moving out here to escape the urban madness of Mexico City. Now it's just half an hour by Metro from the center of town and has evolved into one of the many suburbs engulfed by the D.F.'s sprawl. Centuries-old homes, narrow cobblestoned streets, an abundance of bohemian markets and restaurants, and proximity to the Universidad Nacional Autónoma de México (*see below*) attract an affluent and academic elite. Although Coyoacán and San Ángel are often paired together, Coyoacán attracts a more artsy, politically conscious group.

On weekends, concerts and handicraft vendors dot the **Jardín Centenario** between Carrillo Puerto and Tres Cruces. Next door, families wander around **Plaza Hidalgo,** enjoying the karate demonstrations or exercise classes going on outside. The red building on the plaza's north side is the **Palacio de Cortés,** once the conquistador's home and now Coyoacán's administrative center. In the back portion of the palace are the offices of the **Foro Cultural Coyoacanense** (tel. 5/658–48–91), whose friendly staff provides loads of information (ask them to tell you about Cortés's secret tunnel), as well as the scoop on free concerts. For a crash course in political science, visit the **Museo Nacional de las Intervenciones** (tel. 5/604–06–09; admission $2, free students and Sun.; open Tues.–Sun. 9–6), which chronicles Mexico's foreign interventions through displays of guns, flags, documents, maps, and other artifacts. The museum is inside the beautiful **Ex-Convento de Churubusco,** on the corner of Agosto and General Anaya.

The **Casa de la Cultura Jesús Reyes Héroes** (Francisco Sosa 202, tel. 5/658–55–19) publishes an indispensable monthly calendar of cultural activities in Coyoacán. For a free guided tour of Coyoacán's main attractions, call the **Delegación de Coyoacán** (tel. 5/659–22–56). The tour leaves from the kiosk in Plaza Hidalgo at 10 AM on weekends and wanders through some of the most beautiful sections of Coyoacán: the beautiful tree-filled **Víveros de Coyoacán** park; part of the UNAM campus; and the **Plaza de la Concepción** (popularly known as Plaza de la Conchita), where you'll see the **Casa de la Malinche,** the house Cortés built for his Aztec translator and lover. *From Metro Coyoacán, take PLAZA VILLA COAPA pesero.*

MUSEO CASA DE LEON TROTSKY This lime-green house was the home of one of the most important figures of the Russian Revolution, and its history reads like a soap opera. In

1937, after being exiled from the Soviet Union, Leon Trotsky was granted asylum in Mexico by President Lázaro Cárdenas at the urging of muralist Diego Rivera, whom Trotsky had met in Paris. Upon their arrival, Trotsky and his wife moved to this anonymous and forbidding fortress. The first attempt to assassinate Trotsky left bullet holes that are still visible in Trotsky's bedroom. Unfortunately for Leon, the second attempt was successful. The study where Trotsky was fatally stabbed remains untouched: On the desk lies an article he was going over when Ramón Mercader, his secretary's boyfriend, stabbed him with an ice pick on August 29, 1940. If you speak Spanish, the guards will tell you, among other things, how Trotsky's teeth left a permanent scar on Mercader's hand; how he clung to life for 26 hours; what his last words were; and where his ashes are interred in the garden. *Río Churubusco 410, btw Gómez Farías and Morelos, tel. 5/658–87–32. From Plaza Hidalgo, north on Allende 6 blocks, then right. Admission: $1.50, 75¢ students. Open Tues.–Sun. 10–5.*

MUSEO DE CULTURAS POPULARES Rotating exhibits of folk art from Mexico and elsewhere are beautifully displayed here, accompanied by plentiful information (in Spanish). More than just a museum, this solid colonial building has become a center for community activities, hosting art and dance workshops. Stop by and check out the flyers posted on the door. The monthly newsletter *El Canario de Coyoacán* is distributed here, and provides the latest on music and dance shows in Coyoacán. *Hidalgo 289, btw Allende and Abasolo, tel. 5/658–12–65. From Metro Coyoacán, take PLAZA VILLA COAPA pesero to Jardín Centenario and walk a few blocks along Hidalgo. Admission free. Open Tues.–Fri. 9:30–6, weekends until 8.*

MUSEO DE FRIDA KAHLO This blue house in Coyoacán is where painter Frida Kahlo (*see box* Retrato de Frida, *above*) was born, grew up, and lived briefly with husband Diego Rivera until she died in 1954. Now a museum, the building is filled with colorful yet sad remnants of Kahlo's life: self-portraits; illustrated journals; love notes; pictures of Mao Tse-tung, Lenin, and Stalin; clunky clay jewelry; and the beautifully embroidered Tehuana skirts Kahlo favored. Life-size papier-maché statues and other folk art collected by Kahlo and Rivera adorn the house and lush garden. As a result of childhood polio and a bus accident when she was a teenager, Kahlo endured more than 30 difficult operations; her decorated body cast and her startling paintings convey both her intense emotional and physical suffering, as well as her pride in and passion

Retrato de Frida

Frida Kahlo, probably the most famous Mexican woman artist ever, was born and died in La Casa Azul in Coyoacán. Her image now adorns T-shirts and postcards all over the world, and she has become something of a feminist icon both in Mexico and abroad. Her paintings are as colorful and flamboyant as was their main subject—Frida herself. Born to a Hungarian Jewish father and a Mexican mother in 1907 (though she often claimed that her birth date was 1910, the year the Revolution began), she was almost killed in a bus accident when she was a teenager, which left her in almost constant pain for the rest of her life. She depicted that suffering in her paintings, which often represent her bleeding, cracked open, or torn apart and sewn back together. Other themes are political (she was a Communist and a revolutionary who, in spite of her devotion to Stalin, became involved with Leon Trotsky when he lived in Mexico), or concern aspects of her personal life, such as her stormy marriage to Diego Rivera. Her frank, unapologetic portrayal of her own pain, physical and emotional, illustrates her public refusal to be a "typical" Mexican woman, a sufrida (long-suffering woman) who bears her sorrow in silence. Her last painting, completed eight days before she died, shows juicy melons, cut open and waiting to be eaten. It is titled Viva la Vida (Live Life).

for Mexican culture. *Londres 247, at Allende, tel. 5/554–59–99. From Metro Coyoacán, take* PLAZA VILLA COAPA *pesero to the plaza, and walk 5 blocks north on Allende. Admission: $1.50, $1 students. Open Tues.–Sun. 10–6.*

MUSEO DEL ANAHUACALLI What *do* you do with all those pre-Columbian artifacts you've collected over the years? If you're Diego Rivera, you design your own museum. The huge black building that houses Rivera's collection was constructed in the 1960s from dark volcanic rock. Even if you're tired of archaeological treasures, visit the building just because it's so strange, like an aboveground tomb that promises (and delivers) echoing footfalls amid eerie silence. The third floor displays sketches for some of Rivera's murals, including *Man at the Crossroads*, now in the Palacio de Bellas Artes (*see box*, The Man Without a Face, *above*). *Calle del Museo 150, tel. 5/617–43–10 or 5/617–37–97. From Metro Tasqueña, take trolley to Xotepingo stop; exit to right at* CALLE DEL MUSEO *sign, backtrack to intersection, and turn left. Admission free. Open Tues.–Sun. 10–6.*

UNIVERSIDAD NACIONAL AUTÓNOMA DE MÉXICO (UNAM)

The National Autonomous University of Mexico, one of the oldest universities in the Americas, rests upon a lava bed in a residential district in the southern part of the city. Originally made up of various *facultades* (schools) scattered throughout the city, the UNAM was consolidated into one huge campus in the 1950s and now has more than 100,000 students. The campus is generally known as the *Ciudad Universitaria* (University City), or simply C.U., a name well deserved considering you have to take a bus just to cross campus.

A generation or two ago, a degree from the UNAM was a ticket into political circles and positions of power, but these days the political and business elite tend to come from private institutions. The UNAM is confronted by the same severe economic problems that plague most public universities: Professors skip classes when low incomes force them to take additional jobs, and overenrollment puts pressure on an already populous campus. Despite all its problems, however, the university retains its well-deserved reputation for academic excellence and continues to attract students from around the world.

Over the past three years the campus has served as a center of political activity. In sympathy with the Zapatista movement in Chiapas, students have staged several marches and hunger strikes in protest of the government. Many believe that while the government pretends to tolerate UNAM's high level of political activity, it does so only to identify its adversary. The massacre at Tlatelolco in 1968 (*see* Plaza de las Tres Cultures/Tlatelolco, *above*) brutally exemplifies the opposition between student and state.

UNAM tuition costs about as much as a pack of chiclets (about 20 centavos—not even one peso). Any attempts to raise it are met with angry protests by students.

The university's architects sought to incorporate the best of traditional and modern design and still harmonize with the natural landscape of cactus and black volcanic rock in designing the campus. They succeeded with the huge volcano-shaped **Estadio Olímpico** (Olympic Stadium), site of the 1968 Olympics. The outer ramps of the stadium are decorated with yet another Diego Rivera mural, this one titled *La Universidad, la familia mexicana, la paz y la juventud deportista* (University, Mexican Family, Peace, and Athletic Youth). Murals by Carlos Mérida, David Alfaro Siqueiros, and Juan O'Gorman are just about everywhere on the campus, from the **Torre de la Rectoría** (Tower of the Rectory) on the northwest side of campus to the **Vestíbulo de la Sala Nezahualcóyotl** in the south.

The **Espacio Escultórico** (Sculpture Space), an ecological reserve at the southern end of the campus, is home to numerous sculptures by Mexican artists. The reserve is easily accessible via a long, winding lava path, and is popular for climbing, picnics, or cutting class on a sunny afternoon. Just down the street, behind the **Biblioteca Nacional** (National Library; open weekdays 9–7) is the sculpture, *Las Serpientes del Pedregal,* which slithers around the library. The campus is full of free perks for broke student look-alikes, and there are often free concerts or lectures in the evenings. Check the flyers posted around campus for more info, or pick up a free copy of *Gazeta UNAM*. Transportation on campus is free, so exploring is easy if you can figure out the intricate web of peseros needed to cross the campus. *Take TLALPAN JOYA pesero south on Insurgentes to 3rd pedestrian overpass on campus; cross street, and head north past Biblioteca Nacional. Or from Metro Universidad, exit through Salida E and take ZONA CULTURAL pesero to Espacio Escultórico.*

LA VILLA DE GUADALUPE

La Villa, with two basilicas dedicated to the Virgen de Guadalupe, is the most revered Christian site in Mexico. To this day, millions flock to the site where the Virgen is said to have appeared to Juan Diego, an indigenous convert to Christianity, in 1531. Unlike the fair Mary of the Roman Catholic tradition, the Virgen de Guadalupe had a brown complexion and spoke Nahuatl, Diego's native tongue. The Virgen instructed Diego to gather a bunch of roses—an impossible task in winter—as a testament of the truthfulness of his vision. When Diego told his story to a priest, the father scoffed, calling him a heretic and claiming that the story was pure fantasy. Yet when Juan Diego opened his cloak, out fell the roses the Virgen had told him to gather, leaving an image of the Virgen imprinted on the inside of the cloak.

Now a museum, the baroque **Antigua Basílica** (dating to 1536) contains exhibits of European and Mexican colonial art. The long entryway is plastered from floor to ceiling with *retablos* that pilgrims have painted over the years. Recognized by Diego Rivera as a national art form, these small paintings give thanks to the virgin for everyday miracles, such as surviving an illness or a car accident. Nearby, the hulking, gray mass that is the **Basílica Nueva** operates as a full-service church. Here you can glide past Juan Diego's cloak on a moving sidewalk. If you're in need of some spiritual nourishment—or just plain thirsty—you can drink holy water out of Virgen de Guadalupe-shaped bottles sold at the stands outside. At the top of Tepeyac hill, inside the **Capilla del Posito,** pilgrims stand in line to file past a replica of Juan Diego, rub their hands on the glass that encloses him, and proceed to pass the holiness onto their clothes, their children, and their spouses. Coming down the steps from the Capilla, have your picture taken on a plastic burro in front of a shrine to the Virgen; they'll make it into a keychain for you. *Calzada de Guadalupe, btw Juan de Zumárraga and Hidalgo, near Metro La Villa. Basílica admission: 20¢. Open Tues.–Sun. 10–6.*

CHEAP THRILLS

In colonial times, when literacy rates were low, scribes would sit in the plazas and read or write letters for a nominal fee. Today the tradition continues (although in a slightly modernized form) on the **Plaza Santo Domingo.** Modern-day scribes can be found in the local plaza with their typewriters, transcribing everything from term papers to love letters; they'll even help you compose the latter if your passion doesn't transfer too gracefully to paper. In a row across from the typists are the printers, who churn out everything from business cards to wedding invitations. Both printers and typists work the plaza daily from about 9 to 6. *3 blocks north of Zócalo on Monte de Piedad, which becomes República de Brasil.*

Whether you're desperate to replenish your dwindling travel funds, or just woke up feeling really lucky, you can always give the **Lotería Nacional** (National Lottery) a whirl. For 50¢–$1 (depending on the game) you can close your eyes, cross your fingers, and wait for the winning numbers to be announced on Channel 13 or posted on lottery booths around town. Just walk to any lottery ticket booth in Mexico City, hand the ticket seller four pesos, and proudly announce, "Quiero ser millonario/a."

The following museums are free Sundays:

- *Convento e Iglesia del Carmen*
- *Museo Nacional de Arte*
- *Museo Carrillo Gil*
- *Museo Estudio Diego Rivera*
- *Museo de Culturas Populares*
- *Museo Nacional de la Revolución*

If you don't succeed in becoming a millionare, try your luck at a rather unorthodox *limpia* (spiritual cleansing) conducted by disgruntled magic practitioners, who stand outside of the metro stop near the foot of La Villa de Guadalupe (*see above*). Cups of boiling mud, a real snake, and disappearing business cards combine to help extract the negative thoughts of curious onlookers. Though the whole thing seems more like an infomercial than a spiritual purifier, at least you'll be treated to a prosperity candle for participating.

Rhythmic drummers and Aztec dancers grace the Zócalo daily, from about 10 to 5. Passively observe or join in if you have no shame and think you can follow the deceivingly simple-looking steps. On weekend evenings Coyoacán's Plaza Hidalgo and Jardín Centenario also see plenty of activity. These usually peaceful areas become packed with families and young couples milling around, listening to street performers and musicians. You can usually find anything from modern dance to clowns to traditional South American music. Grab a bag of warm churros from the vendors lining the street, and take advantage of the free culture.

FESTIVALS

Easter (late March/early April): Like everywhere else in Mexico, Semana Santa (Holy Week) is a die-hard cause for celebrations and religious processions throughout the city. In Iztapalapa, in the southeastern part of the city, devotees reenact the Stations of the Cross, complete with a dramatization of the crucifixion. If you're into mutilation or S&M, this is the place to go: The reenactments are often bloody. On a lighter note, on **Sábado de Gloria** (the Saturday before Easter Sunday), people often run around throwing water at each other. Although this act originally had religious significance, any such meaning is often lost amid the chaos.

September 15 and 16, Independence celebrations. Weeks ahead of time, the city is festooned in the national colors: red, green, and white. The celebrations commence on the evening of the 15th, when the president steps onto the balcony at the Palacio Nacional to read Hidalgo's "Grito de Dolores," the call for independence that provoked 10 years of struggle against the Spanish. The Zócalo is so packed with people that you could faint and still not hit the ground; confetti lies inches thick throughout the centro; and fireworks explode all night long. You can also get an adrenaline rush by dodging *los toritos*: Drunk with the spirit of rebellion, some revelers don bull masks and chase people while fireworks explode from the horns. Run for your life and try to not get burned.

October 2, Anniversary of the Massacre at Tlatelolco. People gather in the black-draped Plaza de las Tres Culturas (*see* Plaza de las Tres Culturas/Tlatelolco, *above*) in the early afternoon, and, at about 5 PM, begin marching through the city streets to the Zócalo. Because the commemoration is not supported by the government, the marchers' path is periodically blocked by the feared *grenaderos* (riot police). But, as the Mexicans say, "Perro que ladra no muerde" ("A dog that barks won't bite"), and the police usually only detain the crowd for about half an hour before allowing the marchers to continue. The event brings together relatives of the victims of the 1968 massacre, students of all ages, workers, and opposition sympathizers who carry banners and sing bawdy songs mocking the government.

December 12, Feast Day of the Virgin of Guadalupe: The celebration of the patron saint of Mexico fills the elaborately decorated city with processions and dances. On this day, pilgrims from all over the country head to the Basílica de Guadalupe (*see* La Villa de Guadalupe, *above*),

All Saints Have Their Day

For Mexican Catholics, your Saint's Day is a day on which you receive gifts and the well-wishing of friends and family: For example, if your name were Pedro, you would get lots of goodies on the Día de San Pedro (June 29). For most Mexicans, their Saint's Days are more important than their birthdays. Mexican towns also have patron saints (e.g., San Miguel de Allende's saint is San Miguel), and if you're in a particular town on its Saint's Day, expect some serious dancing, music, and libations.

many placing large cactuses on their backs and crawling on their knees in the final steps of the pilgrimage. Have someone teach you the words to "Las Mañanitas," the birthday song, or you'll feel left out when the entire city begins singing it in honor of "the birth" of the Virgin. If you have a son, dress him up like Juan Diego; this is the way legions of Mexican children pay homage to the indígena to whom the Virgin first appeared.

December 25, Christmas Day. The festivities begin about two weeks before *Navidad* (Christmas), with the entire city being draped in lights. Street processions reenact Mary and Joseph's search for an inn in Bethlehem (which may seem all too familiar after your own search for a vacancy during this holiday season). The processions conclude with festive *posadas*—traditional Christmas parties involving piñatas, plays, and *pastorelas* (religious comedies). Take a tour through the city's more residential neighborhoods to see *los nacimientos*: life-sized replicas of the nativity scene set up in people's gardens and yards. Made of wood or stone, these can get pretty elaborate—oftentimes including actual livestock.

Shopping

Everything can be purchased in Mexico City, from a Gucci bag to the silverwork and *artesanía* (crafts) for which the country is famous. Those heading out to the wilderness can even stock up on camping gear at **Deportes Martí** (Venustiano Carranza 19, Col. Centro, tel. 5/585–02–99). For cheap clothing, the area around Metro Pino Suárez, just south of the Zócalo, is the place to find a decent pair of fake Levi's for about $10. On the weekends in Coyoacán and the neighborhoods around Plaza Hidalgo, sidewalk sales offer an interesting selection of vintage jewelry and used clothing for low prices.

Handicrafts are generally more expensive in Mexico City than elsewhere in the country. During the height of tourist season (July and August), stalls with all sorts of goodies are set up on the Zócalo, just west of the cathedral. Even more expensive wares are sold year-round in the Zona Rosa on Génova, near Reforma.

Bazar de Velas. In a small shop, about a block away from the Museo de León Trotsky, Bazar de Velas specializes in candles of every sort. These ornate, baroque-looking, handcrafted candles are small works of art, and are primarily used during Navidad and other religious holidays. They are sculpted to look like small pillars or colored to resemble elaborately painted frescos. Others are carved to resemble flowers, waterfalls, bees, and dolls. Most cost $3.50–$6. They'll fit in your backpack; just make sure they don't get too hot and melt. *Río Churubusco 306, tel. 5/554–45–96. Open Mon.–Sat. 10–7. Metro: Coyoacán.*

La Ciudadela. Tucked away past a doorless iron entryway, this market consists of wall-to-wall handicraft stores. Mounds of beautiful silver jewelry from Taxco, bags and jackets from Chiapas, and even those "My parents went to Mexico City. . . " T-shirts can be found if you look hard enough. The merchants are tourist-wise—many accept credit cards, but bargaining is still expected. *Balderas, at Plaza La Ciudadela. 5 blocks south of Metro Juárez, or 1 long block north of Metro Balderas. Open daily 10–7.*

Fonart. High-quality, government-approved folk art is available in any one of the several Fonart (National Fund for the Promotion of Arts and Crafts) outlets in the city. The pieces come from all over Mexico, so you can get just about anything here, though it will probably cost you at least twice as much as it would in that remote highland village. Plus, only a small percentage of your purchase trickles down to the artisans themselves. *Juárez 89, tel. 5/521–01–71. Other locations: Londres 136, Zona Rosa, tel. 5/525–20–26; Patriotismo 691, Metro Mixcoac, tel. 5/563–40–60; Carranza 115, Coyoacán, tel. 5/254–62–70. All stores open Mon.–Sat. 10–7.*

La Lagunilla. Once known as the Thieves' Market, La Lugunilla consists of three main markets: The **Mercado de Ropa** (Eje 1 Norte, btw Allende and Chile) sells shimmery dresses à la *Saturday Night Fever,* while the **Mercado de Comestibles** (Eje 1 Norte, at Comonfort) sells fruit and vegetables. The **Mercado de Artesanía** (Allende, btw República de Honduras and Ecuador; open daily 9–7) overflows with furniture, coins, tacky paintings of the Last Supper, and a smattering of nice antiques. This market is at its liveliest on Sunday, when curio stalls are set up outside the main building.

Mercado de Jamaica. The odors of meat, onions, and tacos waft through the corridors of this market, where bananas, pineapples, papayas, and mangos sit in enormous heaps. But the market is mainly known for the rows of stalls selling huge bunches of roses, carnations, lilies, and birds of paradise. *Morelos (Eje 3 Sur), at H. Congreso. Metro: Jamaica. Open daily 8–6.*

Mercado San Juan. Officially the Mercado de Curiosidades Centro Artesanal, this conglomeration of tiny shops in a pink-and-white concrete building feels more like a shopping mall than a crafts market. However, good-quality artesanía, blankets, hammocks, silver, and mounds of tourist trinkets also pop up here. Don't expect too much leeway in the prices—anything short of throwing yourself on the market floor and weeping uncontrollably will probably not move the gringo-wise vendors. *Ayuntamiento, at Dolores, 4 blocks south of Metro Juárez and Alameda Central. Open Mon.–Sat. 9–7, Sun. 9–4.*

La Merced and **Sonora** are separate markets connected by a small side street, Cabaña. Edible goods are sold in the huge warehouse of La Merced, pervaded by the sweet smell of fresh fruits and vegetables. Also inside is the **Mercado de Dulces** (candy market), with more sweets than you've ever seen in your life. Outside you can buy just about any useful item: umbrellas, pots, pans, clothes, and even some toiletries. Sonora, just across the way, promises to cure what ails you: Here you'll find herbal potions that guarantee effectiveness against everything from evil spirits to impotence. At the very back, tropical birds, goats, puppies, and other sad caged animals are also for sale: some for pets, and some as food, no doubt. *Mercado de La Merced: Circunvalación, at San Pablo. Metro: Merced. Mercado Sonora: 2 blocks south of La Merced on Fray Servando Teresa de Mier. Both open daily 8 AM–7 PM.*

Tepito. Anything in the way of consumer goods can be purchased in this semidisreputable market, raided almost daily by police in search of illegal merchandise. The selection is overwhelming—you can find everything from electronics to athletic shoes. But much like a mall full of crazed grandmothers on the last day of a Macy's white sale, it's crowded and rough; leave your valuables at home and bring a *cuate* (buddy) to watch your back. *Eje 1 Nte, at Aztecas. From Metro Guerrero, take TEPITO pesero. Open daily 8–6, except after police raids.*

Having marital problems? Vendors at Mercado Sonora claim the answer lies in controlling your spouse. For one peso, buy a little sachet of magic with titles such as "Sígueme y obedéceme" (Follow and obey me) and "Yo domino a mi mujer" (I dominate my woman).

Tianguis del Libro. Here's your chance to stock up on a little Mexican popular culture: Videotapes of elusive Mexican films are an especially good bargain here. The complete, three-tape collection of María Félix (Mexico's most revered movie star of the '30s and '40s) is $17. Individual videotapes, featuring the popular comedian Cantínflas, or modern documentaries such as *Los Niños de Chiapas*, will run you about $5–$7. Jazz, blues, classical, rumba, salsa, and Mexican pop cassettes are $2 each. If you read Spanish, a wide selection of classic and modern Latin American and Spanish literature runs 75¢–$3. *128 M. A. Quevedo, near La Paz. Metro: M. A. Quevedo.*

Tianguis El Chopo. This punk-style swap meet is a change of pace from the fruits and trinkets of most of the city's markets—you'll find fliers, info on bands, T-shirts, and underground magazines. You may even come away sporting a new tattoo. *Sol, near train station. Metro: La Raza. Open Sat. 10–4.*

After Dark

El reventón (the party) starts late and keeps going until the early hours of the morning; even after the clubs close at 3 AM, people grab a taco and beer and wait until the more respectable hour of 4 to mosey off to bed. The most happening areas at night are the Zona Rosa and Insurgentes Sur in Colonia Juárez, where snazzy clubgoers in black evening wear, "cool" teenagers in ripped jeans, and camera-toting tourists all mingle till dawn. Clubs are the places to be, whether they play disco or *música tropical*—a mix of salsa, merengue, and cumbia. Dance club covers are usually quite high, but women often get in free or at a reduced price. Movies and cafés provide a cheaper alternative. If you'd rather let someone else have the spotlight while you relax and soak in the culture, there's always Mexico City's theater scene. A wide variety of performances, from musicals to works by Mexican and international playwrights, ensure something for everyone. Check listings in *Tiempo Libre* ($1 at most newsstands) for theater information and other entertaining hot spots.

Fair-skinned and/or blond women receive plenty of attention from D.F. men, usually in the form of catcalls, though sometimes as up close and personal as an ass-pinch. These unwelcome advances seldom lead to anything more serious, but follow standard precautions and watch your butt.

A favorite nightspot with locals and tourists alike, **Plaza Garibaldi** (Eje Central, at República de Perú) heats up with competing mariachi bands in full regalia, who sing of lost love and cheatin' women. Couples come to be serenaded, and foreigners come to experience "traditional" Mexico. Buying a song can be a bit pricey ($2.75–$4), but it's simple enough to walk around and listen in on other people's favorite mariachi tunes. Otherwise, you can always escape to one of the cantinas or dance clubs (many of which charge no cover) that line the square.

BARS **Bar Mata.** High up on the fourth floor of a colonial building in the centro, this bar is one of the hottest spots around for the under-30 crowd. The music is soft enough to carry on a conversation, and the atmosphere is conducive to mingling and flirting. Roam around on the open-air roof, where you can sip your beer ($1.50) and look out on the view of the Alameda. There's no cover or drink minimum. The place gets packed after 10:30. *Filomeno Mata 11, at 5 de Mayo, tel. 5/518–02–37. Metro: Bellas Artes. Open Tues.–Sat. 8 PM–3 AM.*

Bar Milan. With a young crowd and mellow music, this bar is among the most unpretentious around. Experience the comfort of having a beer ($2) without having to get dressed up. *Milán 18, tel. 5/592–00–31. Metro: Cuauhtémoc. No cover. Open Tues.–Sun. 9 PM–3 AM.*

La Casa del Inquisidor. This huge, two-story bar is decorated like an inquisitor's home: Start off by having a drink in the garden, and by the end of the evening you may end up partying in the bedroom. This is a hard place to leave, especially if you go for one of the bar's adventuresome drinks, such as *medias de seda* (silk stockings), *semen de burro* (donkey semen) or *orgasmo* (Do you really need a translation?). There's no cover charge, and drinks go for $2–$4. *Durango 181, 2 blocks from Metro Insurgentes, tel. 5/511–673–15. Open Tues.–Sun. 8 PM–2:30 AM. Wheelchair access. AE, MC, V.*

The five best tequilas, according to a bartender at La Guadalupana:

- *Herradura Blanco, Reposado*
- *Sauza, Generaciones*
- *Sauza, Conmemorativo*
- *Cuervo, 1800*
- *Sauza, Hornitos*

La Guadalupana. This Coyoacán cantina, dating from 1932, is heavy on atmosphere and local color and is always packed with regulars. Sit at the cloth-draped tables or stand at the bar while you deliberate on which of the eight tequilas to order. The crowd is overwhelmingly male, so unaccompanied women will be the target of quite a bit of friendly attention (and possibly free drinks). If you're harassed, the waiters will politely remove the offender from your area and, if necessary, from the establishment. *Higuera 14, tel. 5/554–62–53. From Metro Coyoacán, take VILLA COAPA pesero to Plaza Hidalgo. Open Mon.–Sat. noon–midnight, Sun. until 6.*

CINEMAS Most U.S. movies show in Mexico within a few months of their release, so finding a film in English is easy. They're listed in *Tiempo Libre* by title and theater. The films are sometimes in poor condition, full of scratches and squiggly lines, and the volume tends to be low, since most of the audience depends on the subtitles, but for $2 ($1 on Wednesdays) it's not so bad. Paseo de la Reforma in the Zona Rosa has quite a few big screens showing recent American and European films; look for **Diana** (Reforma 423, near Metro Sevilla, tel. 5/511–32–36), **Latino I** (Reforma 296, near Metro Insurgentes, tel. 5/525–87–57), **París** (Reforma 92, near Metro Hidalgo, tel. 5/535–32–71), and **Paseo** (Reforma 35, tel. 5/546–58–43). For artsier films, check out the government-run **Cineteca** (México-Coyoacán 389, near Metro Coyoacán, tel. 5/688–32–72).

DANCE The Ballet Folklórico de México, which performs in the Palacio de Bellas Artes (*see* Worth Seeing, *above*), is world-renowned for its stunning presentations of Mexican regional folk dances. Performances are held Wednesday evenings at 8:30 PM and Sundays at 9:30 AM and 8:30 PM. You can buy tickets ($16–$25) on the first floor of the Palacio (tel. 5/512–36–33; open Mon.–Sat. 11–7, Sun. 9–7) or through Ticketmaster (tel. 5/325–90–00). For the same stellar dancing, for half the price, the **Ballet Folklórico Nacional Aztlán** performs at Teatro de la Ciudad (Donceles 36, tel. 5/510–21–97, btw Bolívar and Chile). Purchase tickets through Ticketmaster or in the lobby for shows on Sunday at 9:30 AM and Tuesday at 8:30 PM.

GAY CLUBS The days when clubs were raided and homosexuals got beaten up are not a thing of the past. However, as one club worker stated, there usually aren't problems with the police as long as there isn't too much "display" (i.e., men making out outside the club). Still, once a year the Operativos de Seguridad will make a pre-announced visit to check out a place. This is supposedly a normal procedure, and done at all the discos. Nevertheless, be careful.

Bota's Bar. One of the most happening gay bars in the D.F., Bota's has enough mirrored walls and bright neon lights to snap you out of the deepest funk. The transvestite shows (Thurs.–Sat.) and frequent striptease competitions are extravagant, to say the least. The $5 cover includes two drinks. The gay bar is upstairs from a straight and unhip bar of the same name. *Niza 45, tel. 5/514–46–00. Metro: Insurgentes. Open Thurs.–Sun. 9 PM–4 AM.*

Butterfly. This techno club looks more like a bus terminal than a disco. With five bars, two snack shacks, about 50 tables, and a huge dance floor that's packed to capacity, it's by far the largest gay (and minutely lesbian) club in town. The two transvestite shows (11:30 PM and 2 AM) are rumored to be the best around. It's rather tricky to find since there is no sign, but it's a block and a half from Metro San Juan de Letrán. Cover is $5 and includes a drink. *Izazaga 9, tel. 5/761–18–61. Open daily 9:30 PM–5:30 AM.*

El Don. Despite the name, this casual discoteque does not cater to Spanish noblemen. To the contrary, it attracts jean-clad lesbians, who dance to everything from Elvis Presley to techno. The $7 cover includes a drink, and transvestite shows are held on Saturday nights at 1:30 AM. *Tonalá 79, Col. Roma, tel. 5/207–08–72. Metro: Insurgentes. Open Wed.–Sat. 9 PM–4 AM.*

Spartacus. Dim lights, throbbing techno-pop, and a drag show (at 10 PM) make this place especially popular with a diverse crowd of gay men. Cover is $2. *Cuauhtémoc 8, Ciudad Neza, tel. 5/558–49–59 or 5/792–44–70. Metro: Cuauhtémoc. Open Fri. and Sat. 8 PM–6 AM.*

El Taller. This club prides itself on its longevity (10 years and running), made possible by a low profile: There's no sign, and only a small, inconspicuous door marks the entrance to this popular gay bar in the Zona Rosa. Stairs lead down to a dark, grooving disco of *men only* (women are not allowed). The dress code is mostly black, leather, and chains. The $3 cover on weekends includes one drink; Monday–Thursday there's no cover. *Florencia 37, Zona Rosa, tel. 5/533–49–70. 1½ blocks from Ángel de la Independencia monument. Metro: Insurgentes. Open daily 9:30 PM–3:30 AM.*

El Vaquero. You'll have to search a bit for this inconspicuous bar; it's squeezed between a laundromat and a bookstore in a small commercial center. The music here is mostly Latin, and if you like to *cumbia,* this is the place to do it. The management is extremely concerned with keeping things hush-hush, so it may be difficult to get anyone on the phone. The atmosphere is similar to that at El Taller. Cover is $4. *Insurgentes Sur 1231, 3 blocks from Rockotitlán, tel. 5/598–25–95. Take SAN ANGEL pesero south on Insurgentes. Open Thurs.–Sat. 9 PM–2 AM.*

MUSIC AND DANCING   Mexico City's music scene has something for everyone—if you're a night person, that is. If you're not, you'll miss out on the *Rock en Español* (Rock in Spanish) movement, which is gaining strength. New bands abound, playing everything from mainstream pop to obscure punk. To find out about Mexico City's underground scene, ask patrons at El Antro or Rockotitlán. You can also check Tianguis El Chopo (*see* Shopping, *above*) for flyers.

➢ **JAZZ • La Mansión.** This upscale restaurant is a laid-back place to listen to classic jazz, with a lot of Glenn Miller and Nat King Cole. Bonuses include great margaritas ($2.50) and a nonexistent cover. *Taine 322, Col. Polanco, tel. 5/545–43–08. Metro: Polanco. Open Mon.–Sat. 1 PM–11:30 PM, Sun. 1–9.*

New Orleans. This restaurant/bar delivers the best jazz bands in Mexico City, with Ezequial Miranda performing his popular blend of Latin jazz on Friday and Saturday nights. Watch out: You'll be expected to order something, and the $3.50 cover charge will slyly be added to your bill before you leave. *Revolución 1655, San Ángel, tel. 5/550–19–08. Metro: M. A. de Quevedo. Open Tues.–Sat. 8:30 PM–2 AM, Sun. 7 PM–1:30 AM.*

➢ **ROCK, RAP, AND ALTERNATIVE MUSIC • El Antro.** The name translates directly as The Joint (the type you go to, not the type you smoke), and offers just what the name suggests: an obscure place to enjoy Mexico City's up-and-coming rock and alternative bands. Cover is $5, and drinks are reasonably cheap (about $1.50). *Carretera México–Xochimilco 14, in front of La Luna, tel. 5/655–10–84. Open Thurs.–Sat. 8:30 PM–2 AM. Wheelchair access.*

El Hijo del Cuervo. Young, hip students pack into this cool art deco bar for an interesting mix of rock and *nueva canción* and the occasional theater show. Check *Tiempo Libre* under "bares con variedad" for schedules. Cover varies (up to $5), depending on the show. *Jardín Centenario 17, Coyoacán, tel. 5/658–53–06. From Metro Coyoacán, take VILLA COAPA pesero to Jardín Centenario. Open daily 1 PM–midnight. Wheelchair access.*

Rockotitlán. After jamming nonstop for more than 10 years, this bar deserves a medal for longevity. Come listen to Mexico's best rock, alternative, and funk bands in an unpretentious setting that manages to look simultaneously like a garage and an outdoor terrace. Cover ranges from $5 to $15, depending on the band. Women usually pay less. *Insurgentes Sur 953, Col. Nápoles, tel. 5/687–78–93. Take SAN ANGEL pesero south on Insurgentes; it's on the 3rd floor of a small commercial building on a traffic circle. Open daily 9 PM–2 AM. Wheelchair access.*

Rockstock. This place is considered by many to be *the* club in Mexico City—arrive before 10:30 PM or you'll have to wait to get in. It doesn't hurt to make goo-goo eyes at the young bouncers who pick and choose among the mass of black-swathed bodies jamming the entry-way. Covers begin at $11.50 and rise to $17 as the weekend progresses; women get in for free on Saturdays. The crowd is young, not too dressed up, and there to party. *Reforma 260, Zona Rosa, tel. 5/533–09–06. From Metro Insurgentes, take Génova north to Reforma and turn right. Open Thurs.–Sat. 9 PM–3 AM.*

➢ **MÚSICA TROPICAL •** Música tropical refers mostly to the rumba, which has Cuban roots. During the past 20 years, a new style of rumba—rumba urbana or rumba chilanga—has emerged, with a faster, more aggressive rhythm and lyrics that touch on social and urban themes more often than romantic ones. Two rumba chilanga bands to keep an eye out for are "Caliente" and "La Nueva Familia."

Bar León. The live music at this swanky club lures the cool and goofy alike. Patrons are a mix of students, foreigners from the hotel upstairs, and regulars stepping to rumba chilanga. Cover is $4.25, with a one-drink minimum. *República de Brasil 5, Col. Centro, tel. 5/510–29–79. North of cathedral. Metro: Allende. Open Wed.–Sat. 9 PM–3 AM.*

Mocamboo. Ask a group of young Mexicanos where you should go to dance salsa and merengue and they'll say the Mocamboo "es padre!" (is cool). Three different orchestras play hour-long sets to a filled-to-capacity dance floor. It's so packed here you don't need to know how to dance salsa to look like a pro—just get in the middle, smile, and let the people around you do all the work. Cover ranges from $5 to $10 depending on the band, the day of the week, and your chromosomes. *Puebla 191, Col. Roma, tel. 5/533–64–64. From Metro Insurgentes, west to Chapultepec, right on Puebla. Open Mon.–Sat. 9 PM–4 AM.*

Salón Q. This huge salsa club is one of the more popular places to come and shake your booty. The crowd is young, the music loud, and the drinks are expensive but strong. A muppet (Hornitos tequila and grapefruit juice) will run you about $3. Cover is about $5.50. *Reforma 169, Col. Guerrero, tel. 5/529–34–95. Metro: Insurgentes. Open Fri. and Sat. 9 PM–4 AM.*

➤ **DANCE HALLS** • *Salones de baile* (dance halls) are the essence of working-class popular culture in Mexico City. The dance-hall craze, which began in the late 1920s, reached a peak during World War II, when live bands played mambo, swing, fox-trot, and the ever-popular *danzón* to crowds of eager young dancers. The youth of today prefer the downtown discos, and salones are slowly fading away. The two dance halls listed below attract a crowd of 20- to 80-year-olds whose common denominator is their love of dancing and dressing up.

Salón Colonia. Opened in 1922, Colonia is Mexico City's original dance hall and a favorite with the older crowd. The atmosphere is low key, and the folks on the dance floor are friendly—it's the perfect place to practice your moves. Cover is $3 for men, $1.50 for women. *Manuel M. Flores 33, Col. Obrera, tel. 5/578–06–19. 3½ blocks east of Metro San Antonio. Open Mon., Wed., and Sun. 6–11 PM.*

Salón Los Ángeles. This place attracts a younger crowd that moves to the sounds of salsa instead of the slower *danzón*. The 1930s decor looks as if it came right from an old Mexican movie, with a soda fountain and a huge, open dance floor. Internationally known musicians kick down about once a month. Cover for these groups ranges from $8 to $11; regular cover is $3 for men and $1.50 for women. *Lerdo 206, near Flores Magon, Col. Guerrero, tel. 5/597–51–81. Metro: Tlatelolco. Open weekdays and Sun. 6–11 PM.*

➤ **PEÑAS** • *Peñas* (musical gatherings) appeared in the mid-'60s, when leftists gathered to sing songs of revolution, using the music of rural Latin America then ignored by commercial radio. When dictatorships throughout the Americas imposed *apagones culturales* (cultural blackouts), artists were forced into exile, prompting thousands of Chileans, Uruguayans, and Brazilians, among others, to make their way to Mexico City. They brought with them *nueva canción,* the folk music that is still an important element of peña atmosphere. Although these days peñas are less ardently revolutionary, with a feel somewhere between a café and a bar, they function as cultural centers where people 18 and up relax, listen to music or poetry, or just spend time with friends.

El Condor Pasa. This classic peña with a comfortable, low-key atmosphere is a great place to hear live Latin American folk music. The cover is only about $2, and drinks are all well under $2.50. *Rafael Checa 1, Col. San Ángel, tel. 5/548–20–50. Take SAN ANGEL pesero to end of line, walk back 1 block on Insurgentes, left on small road btw Mercado de Discos and Mama's Pizza. Open Tues.–Sat. 7 PM–1 AM.*

If you just want a little agua, ask for "Un Monterrey en las rocas" (a Monterrey on the rocks). The expression springs from the people of Monterrey's ignominious reputation as the stingiest in the country.

Hostería El Trobador. Walk into this bar and you'll think you walked into an old ranch house from the northern territories of Cohahuila—a great atmosphere if you don't mind a dead antelope staring you down from the wall. El Trobador offers live Latin American folk music, nueva canción, and sappy romantic music six days a week with no cover charge or drink minimum. *Presidente Carranza 82, at 5 de Febrero, Col. Coyoacán, tel. 5/554–72–47. From Metro Coyoacán, take VILLA COAPA pesero to the Jardín Centenario; the peña is 3 blocks away. Peña performed 7 PM–1 AM.*

Mesón de la Guitarra. One look at the decked-out crowd at this fancy peña and it becomes obvious that this place is for having a good time, not planning revolutions. Under the same management, **Peña Gallos** (Revolución 736, near Metro Mixcoac, tel. 5/563–09–63) is larger, but identical in every other respect. Cover is $4 in both peñas, although women get in free on Thursdays, and everyone gets in free after midnight on Fridays and Saturdays. Reservations are a good idea if you plan to arrive after 9:30 PM. Beers run $1.50, mixed drinks $2.50. Music consists of Andean pipe music, traditional Mexican *ranchera* songs, indigenous music from Oaxaca, and tropical music from Veracruz. No American music allowed! *Félix Cuevas 332, btw Patricio Sands and Moratel, tel. 5/559–15–35 or 5/559–24–35. Take a bus down Insurgentes Sur to Félix Cuevas, and ask to be let off at the Liverpool department store; walk east 5 blocks. Open Thurs. 7 PM–1 AM, Fri. and Sat. 7 PM–3 AM.*

Outdoor Activities

Not surprisingly, outdoor activities are scarce for the budget traveler in this sprawling city. Besides jogging or an occasional pickup game, most activites end up being spectator sports that border on the theatrical. Bullfighting and *fútbol* (soccer) are the most popular and elaborately staged events. The *corrida* (bullfight) itself resembles a play, divided up into three acts called *tercios.* The objective is to kill the bull, which takes place in the third act, the act of death. The corrida mostly attracts groups of men, who look like they would feel equally at home at a *charreada* (rodeo) in their cowboy hats and boots. Fútbol matches tend to draw a more motley bunch, with college kids and grandmothers alike screaming in the stands. During *clásicos,* in which arch-rivals Las Águilas (Mexico City) and Las Chivas (Guadalajara) square off, groups of bare-chested young men resemble a rowdy Greek chorus. Each team's audience goads the other with chants and songs; they also don't hesitate to throw in a salty word or two. Other sport enthusiasts fuel the fast-paced betting that goes on at the jai alai games, while others bet more sedately at the racetracks.

SOCCER Fútbol is the passion of the country, and matches practically paralyze the entire city. The professional season lasts from September to June. Most games take place in the gigantic **Estadio Azteca,** in the southern part of the city, where the World Cup Finals were held in 1970 and 1986. Tickets for the games (sold at the taquillas outside) range $8–$15; you can buy them the day of the game, but arrive at least an hour before kickoff. From Metro Tasqueña, catch a *tren ligero* (a sort of trolley) or *trolebus* (electric bus) straight to the stadium.

Good places for pickup soccer games:
- *Parque Estadio, near Metro Hospital General*
- *General Parque Les Venadas, near Metro División del Norte*
- *Parque Pilares, Col. del Valle*

HORSE RACES AND RODEOS You can risk whatever money you have at the **Hipódromo de las Américas.** The entrance fee to the track is 15¢, and once you're inside, you only need 20¢ to gamble. The horses run Tuesday, Thursday, and Friday 5:30 PM–10:30 PM and weekends 2:45–8. *Industria Militar, tel. 5/557–41–00. From Metro Polanco, walk 2 blocks north to Av. Ejército Nacional to catch DEFENSA NACIONAL pesero.*

Charreadas (rodeos) are held Sunday at noon in two locations: **Lienzo Charro de la Villa** (Metro: Indios Verdes) and **Lienzo del Charro** (Constituyentes 500; take any pesero from Metro Chapultepec). A show usually costs about $1. Check in the newspaper *Ovaciones* for any announcements regarding prospective rodeos or call 5/277–87–06 or 5/277–87–10, weekdays 9–5.

BULLFIGHTING Brought to Mexico by Hernán Cortés, the tradition of bullfighting continues today. Although the very best matadors perform in the fall, an off-season *corrida* (bullfight) with a novice matador is still worth a trip to the arena, especially if you've never seen a corrida before. **Plaza México** is the largest bullfighting arena in the world, with a 50,000-person capacity, and corridas are held here Sundays at 4 PM. Ticket prices range from 75¢ to $8, with seats on the sunny side (*sol*) tending to be cheaper and rowdier than the seats on the shady side (*sombra*). The ticket window is open Thursday, Friday, and Saturday 9:30–1 and 3:30–7, and on Sunday (corrida day) from 9:30 until the third bull dies. Get there about an hour before the corrida. *Augusto Rodín 241, Ciudad de los Deportes, tel. 5/563–39–59. Take INSURGENTES SUR/SAN ANGEL pesero south on Insurgentes Sur.*

JAI ALAI The skill and coordination required to play *frontón* (jai alai), a lightning-fast Basque handball game (the fist-sized balls have been clocked at more than 110 mph), draws crowds of spectators. Of course, they aren't so awestruck that they forget to place bets, which—at about a dollar a match—are as innocuous as they come. You can check out the action at **Frontón México** (NW cnr of Plaza de la República) Monday–Thursday and Saturday from 6 PM to 1 AM. Women's matches are played at **Frontón Metropolitano** (Bahía de Todos los Santos 190) Monday–Saturday 4–10.

Near Mexico City

XOCHIMILCO

More than 700 years ago the Valley of Mexico was almost entirely underwater. This shortage of terra firma prompted the indigenous Xochimilco, the first tribe to inhabit the area, to build a series of *chinampas* (floating islands of mud, reeds, and grasses) and anchor them to the lake bed with long poles. As the natural grasses and reeds on the islands began to grow, their roots extended into the water, becoming permanently affixed to the lake bed. As more and more of these floating islands took root, the lake was slowly transformed into a maze of canals. The Xochimilco's vast agricultural knowledge—which enabled them to yield four harvests annually from the fertile chinampas—was picked up by the Aztecs 300 years later, providing a sound economical base for the empire. Even now, after six centuries of conquest, colonialism, and change, the floating gardens of Xochimilco, 21 kilometers south of Mexico City's Zócalo, remain a testament to this ingenious innovation.

As you drift through the canals on your lancha, you'll often hear the strains of "Las Mañanitas" (the birthday song); many Mexican families use the lancha as an inexpensive place to hold a fiesta. Lunch is spread out on the table that runs through the boat, and the mariachi band bellows robustly.

Xochimilco, with its central plaza and market, feels like a small village rather than a group of drifting islands. The gardens are a favorite picnic spot for middle-class families, but visitors are rare during the week. Sunday is the busiest day, when you'll be squashed by boats on all sides. Enterprising boat owners pick out tourists and try to persuade them to commit to their *lancha* (flat-bottom boat; $4–$7 per hr depending on size) before they've even seen the water. Although the government sets prices, you can usually negotiate. A ride in a more touristy *chalupa* (small canoe) lasts about two hours and costs around $5 for two or more people. You can bring your own lunch to Xochimilco, or buy warm tamales from the smaller lanchas that circulate on the lake. Xochimilco is open daily 7–7. For further information, call their tourist hotline at 5/676–88–79 or 5/676–08–10.

Many of the flowers grown on the Xochimilco floating gardens are sold at the **Mercado de Flores de Pedregal de San Ángel**, a 24-hour flower market in Mexico City. It costs $1 for a dozen long-stemmed red roses. *Av. Revolución, near Iglesia del Cármen, no phone. From Metro Tasqueña, take Line 2 toward Cuatro Caminos, get off at Pino Suárez and change to Line 1; head toward Observatoria and exit at Insurgentes. Take AVENIDA REVOLUCION pesero and get off near Iglesia del Carmen.*

COMING AND GOING The easiest way to reach Xochimilco is to take the Metro to Tasqueña, hop on the *tren ligero,* and get off at the last station. From here, walk south on Cuauhtémoc to Morelos, make a left, and you'll be in the town center. The trip to Xochimilco takes less than an hour. If you're driving, take highway Periférico Sur and get off at the Cuemalco/Xochimilco exit. From here, take Avenida Prologación División Del Norte until you reach the EMBARACADERO sign, then take the Manantiales exit, which will take you to the lancha docks.

TEOTIHUACÁN

By the 12th century, when the Aztec migrated to the Valley of Mexico, Teotihuacán had already been abandoned for more than 500 years. Awestruck by the massive stone temples jutting high above the lush, green valley floor, the Aztec named the mysterious ruins "Place of the Gods."

More than a millennium has passed since the Teotihuacán people inhabited the beautiful stone city, and information about the ancient civilization remains scant. Archaeologists have managed only to divide the history of the site into four distinct stages. What was to become the greatest city of Mesoamerica began in a rather humble way, as a few farming villages in the center of the Valle de Teotihuacán around 900 BC. Gradually the villages grew into larger settlements, increasing their wealth through mining and trading obsidian with neighboring towns. By 100 BC, Teotihuacán was a prosperous society controlled by an ecclesiastic oligarchy.

The powerful union of religious and political authorities made it possible to mobilize a labor force capable of building two massive pyramids: the **Pirámide del Sol** (Pyramid of the Sun) and the **Pirámide de la Luna** (Pyramid of the Moon). By around AD 300 Teotihuacán had reached the height of its power; its empire spread outward from the valley across Mesoamerica. The Teotihuacán's expansionist thirst was temporarily quenched, and they turned their attention to beautifying their capital city. It is from this period that the most impressive artwork dates. Around AD 650, the city began to wane, although no one is quite sure why. Buildings eroded and the city was slowly abandoned. Eventually, Teotihuacán was pillaged by outsiders, forcing the remaining residents to migrate elsewhere, leaving the once-great city to be enveloped by the surrounding vegetation.

Cleared of foliage, the ruins have been groomed for easy tourist access. After you enter the archaeological zone and cross the main thoroughfare, **Avenida de los Muertos** (Avenue of the Dead), you come to the **Ciudadela** (Citadel), a huge square with apartment complexes and temples. The detail and workmanship of the artwork here have led archaeologists to speculate that they were once the living quarters of ruling priests. At the far end of the citadel is the **Templo de Quetzalcoatl,** made up of two pyramids; the one on top is a reconstruction of the older pyramid below. The facade of the older one bears bas-reliefs of the plumed serpent Quetzalcoatl (with a lion's mane around his head) and the square-faced rain god Tlaloc. For a better view of the sculptures, go around to the walkway between the two buildings. Halfway down the Avenida de los Muertos is the enormous, unmistakable **Pirámide del Sol**; rising more than 65 meters high, it's the third-largest pyramid in the world. After 248 panting steps, the view of lush green mountains and white fluffy clouds is equally breathtaking. Discovered in 1962, the **Palacio de Quetzalpapálotl** was probably the home of a powerful Teotihuacán indígena, and is now almost fully reconstructed. Some of the butterflies carved into the columns still have their original beady obsidian eyes, which gaze, as they have for centuries, over the beautiful open plazas of the city. Just west of the palacio is the **Jaguar Palace,** with reconditioned red-and-green murals showing jaguars dressed in feathers and performing various human activities. These same brilliant reds and greens, as well as blacks and yellows, once covered much of the city. A thorough tour of the ruins would take an entire day, but you can see a lot, if not every pyramid, in three or four hours. *Admission: $2.50. Open Tues.–Sun. 8–5.*

With clear explanations in both Spanish and English, **Museo de Sitio de Teotihuacán** gives an excellent overview of the Teotihuacán empire. Through artifacts found on site, it details Teotihuacán's technological and religious development; particularly interesting are the mass burials of human "offerings" (the museum tastefully sidesteps the word "sacrifices") to the temple, with all their jewelry intact. The museum culminates in a huge scale model of the original city beneath a glass floor. *At Puerta 5, tel. 595/6–01–88. Open daily 8–6.*

If you're prone to sunburn, bring a hat and sunscreen to Teotihuacán. The hot sun beams down on the valley, and there isn't any smog to filter it. However, even during summer a chilly wind blows, so wear layers. A water bottle is also a good idea, because the climbing is hard work, especially at this altitude.

COMING AND GOING Autobuses Teotihuacán (tel. 5/587–05–01) departs from the far north end of the Autobuses del Norte terminal in Mexico City about every 20 minutes 6 AM–

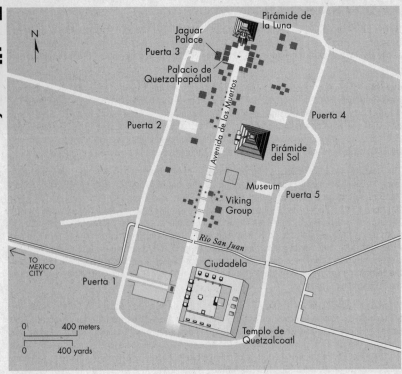

Teotihuacán

Pirámide de la Luna
Jaguar Palace
Puerta 3
Palacio de Quetzalpapálotl
Puerta 2
Avenida de los Muertos
Puerta 4
Pirámide del Sol
Museum
Puerta 5
Viking Group
Río San Juan
TO MEXICO CITY
Puerta 1
Ciudadela
Templo de Quetzalcoatl
0   400 meters
0   400 yards

3 PM. The bus (1 hr, $1.25) drops you off at the main entrance, Puerta 1. The last bus back to Mexico City leaves Teotihuacán at 6 PM.

FOOD Just outside Puerta 1, a series of fondas sell comida corrida for about $2, in addition to the usual tacos. Although no food or drink is officially permitted in the archaeological zone (except in the overpriced restaurant inside the complex), no one searches bags at the entrance, and the garbage cans on the site are filled with food wrappers and bottles. It's doubtful anyone will complain if you pull out your lunch, as long as you take your trash with you.

TULA

The small city of Tula, known in ancient times as Tollán, is a favorite retreat for day-trippers. If you decide to stay overnight, you'll escape the frenzy of Mexico City but not the air pollution, which is still present 70 or so kilometers north of the D.F. Tula's main attraction is the archaeological site displaying remnants of the Toltec civilization's capital city, complete with ball courts, pyramids, and a palace. Ancient Tula, thought to have been occupied from AD 900 to AD 1150, was inhabited by as many as 40,000 people at its height. The reigning symbols of the site are the Atlantes—imposing, 4-meter-high warriors, some of which were used as roof supports. Hundreds of these once brightly painted statues and reliefs are dedicated to Quetzalcoatl, the plumed serpent god. The site itself is on the outskirts of town (which consist mainly of electrical plants and oil refineries), some 3 kilometers from the bus station. It's best reached by taxi (about $2), but you can also catch a TEPETITLAN or ACTOPAN pesero. These leave from Tula's zócalo and zoom by the ruins, so make sure you tell the driver you'd like to be tossed out near Las Pirámides. *Admission: $2, free Sun. Open Tues.–Sun. 9:30–4:30.*

COMING AND GOING Autotransportes **Valle de Mezquital** departs Mexico City from the Autobuses del Norte terminal (Sala 8) for Tula (1½ hrs, $2.50) every 30 minutes from 5 AM to 10:30 PM.

WHERE TO SLEEP AND EAT Directly east of the bus station is **Motel Lizbeth** (Ocampo 200, tel. 773/2–00–45), a clean, modern, and expensive outfit; singles cost $12.50, doubles $16. They offer a filling breakfast of orange juice, *huevos al gusto*, bread, and coffee for $2.75. Downtown, opposite the cathedral, is **Hotel Cuellar** (5 de Mayo 23, tel. 773/2–04–42), a smaller hotel with singles for $9, doubles $11. If you tell the management at the **Hostería Cueva** restaurant (5 de Mayo, at Madero, no phone; open daily 8–8) that you're staying at Hotel Cuellar, you'll get a discount on dinner. Mexican dinner specials run about $6. For American food, visit the clean and colorful **Cafetería El Cisne** (at end of Juárez, tel. 5/773–201–33; open daily 9–9). A filling plate of fried chicken will run you about $1.50.

VALLE DE BRAVO

Valle de Bravo's popularity with upper-class *chilangos* has given it a split personality. During the week, the village sees little activity and locals go about their business. From Friday to Sunday, however, Valle becomes crowded with weekenders who come to hike, waterski, windsurf, and hang glide. Although these activities have given Valle de Bravo the image of a posh resort town, it's filled with plenty of thrills for the budget traveler. The village's red tile roofs and impeccable stone-paved streets are wonderfully maintained, and the designation of the nearby hills and **Lago Avándaro** as ecological reserves has kept the area clean and unpolluted.

If you're dying to spend a day on the lake, rent a *lancha rápida* (motorboat) for $34 per half day (equipment included; up to five people), or just take a leisurely boat ride for $2.50. To explore the village, rent a bike ($2.50 an hr) from the shop on 17 de Septiembre 200 (open daily 9–8). When it comes to hiking, the courageous attack the steep **Cerro de la Peña**, a half-hour walk northwest of town. You won't need rock-climbing equipment—just a lot of stamina to reach the cross on the top of the hill, where you'll be treated to a stunning view of the lake and the town. The less active can take a collective taxi from the center (50¢) to the nearby town of **Avándaro** and walk the 3-kilometer **Velo de Novia** trail, which borders a small cascade and follows the stream into the surrounding hills. The trailhead for Velo de Novia begins at the bridge on the river. If this still sounds like too much exertion, rent a horse ($6 an hour) from the stables on the corner of Avándaro and Glorieta.

BASICS **Centro de Cambio Valle** (Benito Juárez 103, at Porfirio Díaz, tel. 726/2–40–05) exchanges money daily 9–3. The **post office** (Joaquín Pagaza 200, tel. 726/2–03–73) is open weekdays 9–4 and Saturday 9–1. Ladatel phones abound, and the **caseta de larga distancia y fax** (Plaza de la Independencia 6, tel. 726/2–09–00) is open 7 AM–9 PM. The main plaza is lined with pharmacies, including **Farmacia y Perfumería Paty** (Villa Gran 200, tel. 726/2–01–62; open daily 9–3 and 4–9).

COMING AND GOING México–Zinacantepec buses depart Mexico City's Central Poniente for Valle de Bravo (3 hrs, $4.50) every 20 minutes 5 AM–7:30 PM. The last bus from Valle de Bravo back to Mexico City leaves at 7 PM from the Central Camionera (cnr of 16 de Septiembre and Zaragoza).

WHERE TO SLEEP AND EAT **Hotel Mary** (Jardín Central, facing the plaza, tel. 726/2–29–67) rents decent rooms at decent prices: $11 singles, $13.50 doubles. **Posada María Isabel** (Vergel 104, tel. 726/2–30–36) has a well-kept patio garden and medium-size rooms for $11.50 singles, $13 doubles. When the weather is good, your cheapest (free) option is to camp. From the plaza, walk down Joaquín Pagaza, turn right on Calle de la Cruz, and continue to the piers; from here take a colectivo boat ($2.50) across the lake to the campgrounds.

Filling your tummy can be expensive and difficult (especially if you come on a weekday when most places are closed), but we've found a few cheap eats: **El Bocaito** (Vergel 202, tel. 726/2–01–33; open Fri.–Sun. noon–2 AM) serves incredible homemade pizzas for about $4 and **La Cueva del León** (Plaza de la Independencia 2, tel. 726/2–40–62; open Mon.–Thurs. 11–9:30, Fri.–Sun. 8:30– midnight) has colorful tables overlooking the plaza. Try their grilled trout (fresh from Lake Avándaro) for about $4. You can also sample tacos at the main market (cnr of Hidalgo and Independencia).

BAJA CALIFORNIA 3

By Carrie McKellogg

The image of a tall, spiny saguaro cactus framed against the cool blue of the Pacific typifies the rugged landscape of Baja. Throw in sedate, out-of-the-way towns, beachside resorts, and bustling, northern cities renowned for wild nightlife and you'll have an idea of the peninsula's diversity. This variety attracts very different types of travelers—from sport enthusiasts who come for the windsurfing, fishing, and scuba diving to those who do nothing except fry their skin by day and their brain cells by night.

Only in recent years, with the influx of people from all over the country, has Baja become genuinely integrated into mainstream Mexican culture and consciousness. Before then, the peninsula was largely considered frontier territory. Although Hernán Cortés officially "discovered" Baja while looking for Amazon queens and pearls, Jesuit missionaries in the late 17th century were the first Europeans to settle the peninsula successfully. From their original outpost in Loreto, the Spaniards extended the Spanish frontier into what is now Northern California. However, with Mexico's independence and the demise of the missions, Baja withered, leaving a few scattered ranches and mining towns that stood untouched until tourism briefly boomed in the 1930s. It wasn't until the early 1970s, with the completion of the trans-peninsular highway (Highway 1), that Baja's isolation finally eroded and the region became a popular destination.

The peninsula's relative isolation from the mainland means that prices are often higher here than in other parts of Mexico.

Today, Baja California Norte (Northern Baja California) is characterized by border towns, where tourists (primarily American college students) come to take advantage of the lower drinking age, and beach towns, filled with similarly minded tourists who leave the city to frolic on the sand. Baja California Sur (Southern Baja California) is much more mellow, with a tourist industry centered around sailing, fishing, and whalewatching. If you've got access to a four-wheel-drive vehicle, you can also venture to the isolated Sierra la Gigante mountains. La Paz, the state capital, offers the same spectacular beaches as the rest of the peninsula, but the friendly city is unique in its authentic Mexican ambience and culture. At the southernmost tip of the peninsula is Los Cabos, a region famous for white sandy beaches and the vivid hue of its waters. Cabo San Lucas is the major resort town here, where self-indulgence reigns supreme and fishing ranks a close second. San José del Cabo, just to the east, is a quieter city that attracts a less obnoxious type of traveler. Although these and other towns are rapidly being built up, there are still miles of infrequently visited coastline and remote mountain hideaways in Baja. However, these isolated regions are nearly inaccessible to the budget traveler: If you're determined to get off the beaten path, bring a sturdy vehicle, be prepared to blow your life savings on taxi drivers and guides, or start exercising your thumb.

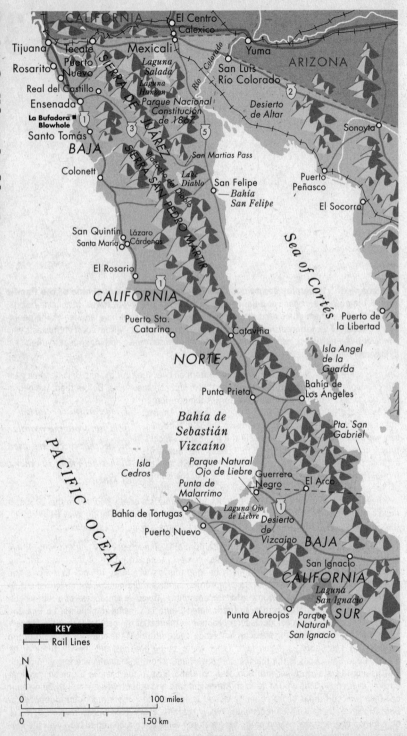

Baja California Norte

CALIFORNIA
El Centro
Calexico

Tijuana
Tecate
Mexicali
Rosarito
Puerto
Nuevo
San Luis
Río Colorado
Yuma
ARIZONA

Real del Castillo
Laguna
Salada
Colorado

Ensenada
Laguna
Hanson
Río
San Luis
Río Colorado

La Bufadora ■
Blowhole
Parque Nacional
Constitución
de 1867

Santo Tomás
3
5
Desierto
de Altar

BAJA
Sonoyta

Colonett
San Martias Pass

Lake
Diablo
San Felipe
— *Bahía
San Felipe*

Puerto
Peñasco

SIERRA DE JUÁREZ
SIERRA SAN PEDRO MÁRTIR

El Socorro

San Quintín
Santa María
Lázaro
Cárdenas

El Rosario

CALIFORNIA

Puerto Sta.
Catarina
Cataviña

Sea of Cortés

Puerto de
la Libertad

NORTE

*Isla Angel
de la
Guarda*

Punta Prieta
Bahía de
Los Angeles

*Bahía de
Sebastián
Vizcaíno*

Pta. San
Gabriel

PACIFIC

*Isla
Cedros*

Parque Natural
Ojo de Liebre
Guerrero
Negro
El Arco

Punta de
Malarrimo

OCEAN

Bahía de Tortugas
*Laguna Ojo
de Liebre*
Desierto
de
Vizcaíno

BAJA

Puerto Nuevo

San Ignacio

CALIFORNIA

*Laguna
San Ignacio*

SUR

Punta Abreojos
Parque
Natural
San Ignacio

KEY
Rail Lines

N

0   100 miles
0   150 km

Baja California Norte

Baja California Norte is a favorite with tourists, thousands of whom cross the border in search of exotica; most just end up buying trinkets and partying in Tijuana until they drop. Farther south, the beach towns of Rosarito, Ensenada, and San Felipe attract similar weekend crowds seeking daytime fun and nighttime parties. Because of the region's tawdry reputation, people interested in an authentic Mexican experience often skip Tijuana and its environs altogether. The perversities of tourism aside, those willing to wander off the tourist track and explore will see a more intriguing side of northern Baja. The rise of the *maquiladoras* (*see* box, *below*) has caused hordes of people, mostly from the poorer southern states, to infiltrate Tijuana looking for work; they bring with them the food, arts, and customs that make this region diverse.

Tijuana

Sprawling along what is reputed to be the most heavily crossed border in the world, Tijuana largely attracts tourists with a single objective: to party. Popular wisdom among foreigners and Mexicans contends that Tijuana is more an amalgamation of Mexican and gringo cultures than a "real" Mexican city, and a lawless den of hedonism at that. In certain respects, these impressions are accurate, and those shy of crowds of foreigners, made-for-export *artesanía* (crafts), dollar beers, and eyebrow-raising sex shows may want to avoid this city altogether. The main drag, Avenida Revolución, is by day a magnet for the middle-aged, trinket-buying crowd; by night it attracts U.S. partyers (most under 21) who come to drink and dance. Just one block west of Revolución, however, is Tijuana's principal commercial street, Avenida Constitución, bustling

> *"Poor Mexico, so far from God, so close to the United States."*–Porifirio Díaz

with hardware stores, pharmacies, microphone-wielding salesmen, and strolling families. Here you'll find restaurants and shops representing almost every state in Mexico—evidence of the diverse mix of Mexican cultures that exists here, inevitably influenced by the *gigante al norte* (giant to the north). As you would expect from a city saturated with residents from all over the country, Tijuana is also an important departure point for numerous destinations in Mexico.

BASICS

AMERICAN EXPRESS The AmEx office is in the **Viajes Carrousel** travel agency. In addition to the usual cardholder services, even nonmembers can change up to $100 in cash or traveler's checks or have their mail held at the following address: Blvd. Sánchez Taboada y Clemente Orozco, Edificio Husa, Zona Río, Tijuana, Baja California Norte, CP 22320, México. *Sánchez Taboada, at Clemente Orozco, tel. 66/34–36–60. Open weekdays 9–5, Sat. 9–1.*

AUTO PARTS/SERVICE **Serviautos** and **Servipartes** (Revolución 216, at Coahuila, tel. 66/85–97–22) can help you out Monday–Saturday 8:30–7:30. The **Green Angels** (tel. 66/24–83–93), a government service, offers free 24-hour assistance to drivers with car trouble, including gas and limited repair work. Call them and they'll come to you.

CASAS DE CAMBIO American dollars are accepted in Tijuana, Mexicali, Ensenada, and Rosarito, but you'll get a poor exchange rate. Money changers abound in Tijuana's tourist district, but only deal in cash. For changing pesos to dollars, you'll find the best rates from money changers on San Ysidro Boulevard in San Ysidro, just before you cross the border. To purchase or change traveler's checks, try the AmEx office (*see above*) or **Banamex** (La Juventud, just across pedestrian bridge, tel. 66/83–52–48). The latter is open for exchange weekdays 9–5. ATMs accepting Visa, MasterCard, Plus, and Cirrus cards can be found at most banks; try **Serfín** at Constitución and Calle 6.

CONSULATES **Canada.** Citizens of Australia can also find help at the Canadian consulate. *Germán Gedovius 10411–201, Zona Río, tel. 66/84–04–61. Open weekdays 9–1.*

United Kingdom. *Salinas 1500, tel. 66/86–53–20. Open weekdays 9–3.*

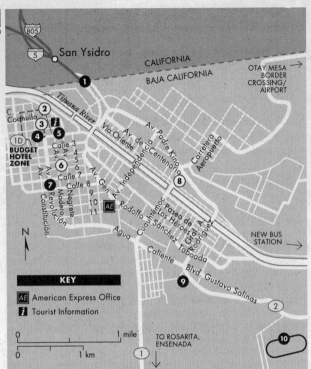

Sights ●

Caliente
Race Track, **10**

Central Viejo
Bus Station, **5**

El Toreo, **9**

Palacio Frontón, **7**

Plaza Revolución, **4**

San Ysidro Border
Crossing, **1**

Lodgings ○

Hotel y Baños
Enva, **3**

Hotel Catalina, **6**

Hotel
San Nicolás, **2**

Villa Juvenil, **8**

Map labels: San Ysidro, CALIFORNIA, BAJA CALIFORNIA, OTAY MESA BORDER CROSSING/AIRPORT, Tijuana River, C. Coahuila, BUDGET HOTEL ZONE, Via Oriente, Av. de la Centenaria, Av. Padre Kino, Carretera Aeropuerto, Calle 3, 4, 5, 6, 7, Calle 8, 9, 10, 11, Av. Negrete, Av. Madero, Av. Revolución, Av. Constitución, Av. Gen. A., Av. Independencia, Rodolfo Sánchez Taboada, Cuauhtémoc, Paseo de los Héroes, A. Rodríguez, Agua Caliente, Blvd. Gustavo Salinas, NEW BUS STATION, TO ROSARITA, ENSENADA

KEY

AE American Express Office

i Tourist Information

0 —— 1 mile
0 —— 1 km

N

Maquiladoras

Much coverage has been given in the past decade to maquilas, or maquiladoras—foreign-owned factories that take advantage of cheap labor and tariff-free zones to export cars, electronics, and other consumer goods from developing countries to the "First World." The rise of the maquilas in Mexico is a result of the Mexican government's Border Industrialization Program, which opened the northern border to labor-intensive export plants in 1965. After the 1982 Mexican peso devaluation, Mexican labor became some of the cheapest in the world, prompting multinational companies to set up plants in Tijuana, Mexicali, Nogales, Ciudad Juárez, and Matamoros. According to Tom Barry's "Mexico: A Country Guide" (The Interhemispheric Education Resource Center, 1992) there are now 3000 of these plants, employing more than 750,000 Mexican citizens. Though the maquilas have created jobs for the northern region, there has been no parallel development of housing, health services, or basic sanitation for these workers. Instead, maquila employees have erected communities of cardboard shacks, where residents suffer from diseases caused by malnutrition and unsanitary water supplies. In addition, the Mexican government's lax environmental laws allow toxic wastes from the maquilas to contaminate the groundwater that these communities use for bathing, drinking, and cooking.

United States. In an after-hours emergency, call the San Diego office at 619/585–2000 and an agent in Tijuana will be contacted. *Tapachula 96, Col. Hipódromo, tel. 66/81–74–00. Open weekdays 8–4:30.*

CROSSING THE BORDER U.S. and Canadian citizens don't need tourist cards to travel as far south as Ensenada, or farther down the mainland to Mazatlán. When entering or leaving Baja by land, a driver's license or birth certificate is sufficient identification, although it's a good idea to bring your passport if you plan to travel elsewhere in the country. For travel south of Ensenada, tourist cards are available from the **Oficina de Migración** (immigration office, tel. 65/82–49–47; open 24 hrs) just across the border, under the bridge that passes over the freeway. For more information on tourist cards, *see* Chapter 1.

EMERGENCIES In Tijuana, contact the **police** at 134; the **fire** department at 136; and the **Cruz Roja** (for an ambulance) at 132.

LAUNDRY Tijuana's laundromats are inconvenient, and you're probably better off rinsing your undies in the hotel sink. If you're desperate, try **Lavamática La Burbuja,** where washing and drying your own clothes costs about $2.50 and giving the honor to someone else is $3.50. *Calle 2 No. 1443, btw Calles F and G, Centro Tijuana. Open 24 hrs.*

MAIL It's cheaper and faster to send international mail from the United States than from Mexico. If that's impractical, Tijuana's **post office** is at Avenida Negrete and Calle 11. They'll hold mail for you at the following address for up to 10 days: Lista de Correos, Avenida Negrete y Calle 11, Tijuana, Baja California Norte, CP 22000, México. Head next door to **Telecomm** to send telegrams and faxes. *Post office tel. 66/84–79–50. Open weekdays 8–5, Sat. 9–1. Telecomm open weekdays 8–8, weekends 8–1.*

MEDICAL AID Dr. Manuel R. Laza at the **Centro Médico España** (Calle 2 No. 1844, near Constitución, tel. 66/85–24–50) speaks English and is available Monday–Saturday 8:30–8 and Sundays until 2 PM. Plenty of 24-hour pharmacies lie along Constitución, including **Farmacia Regis** (tel. 66/85–13–49), at the corner of Calle 5, where someone can usually help you in passable English.

PHONES Collect calls are easy to place from Tijuana's pay phones, but it's more expensive to make international calls from Mexico than from the United States. If you want to call from a *caseta de larga distancia* (long-distance telephone office), go to **Copias Rubi,** where calls to the States are discounted 50% weekdays after 8 PM, all day on Saturdays, and Sundays until 5 PM. *Calle 7 No. 1906, near Constitución, tel. 66/85–03–11. Open daily 9 AM–10 PM.*

VISITOR INFORMATION Tijuana has a number of tourist offices. The most centrally located, **CANACO** (Revolución, at Calle 1, tel. 66/88–16–85, fax 66/85–84–72; open daily 9–7), is run by Tijuana's chamber of commerce, and has an English-speaking staff and decent maps. A less busy bureau is the **Tourism and Convention Bureau** (tel. 66/83–14–05; open daily 9–7), just across the border past the taxi stand, in the small, white building shared with Smokin' Joe's liquor. The English-speaking staff here is very knowledgeable and friendly. They sell auto insurance, give directions to places in Baja, and provide maps of Tijuana, but despite the location, do not offer tequila shots.

For information on Tijuana's gay scene, check out **Café Emilio's** (Calle 3, btw Constitución and Niños Héroes, no phone). This café/club is also a resource center for gay groups and boasts a makeshift AIDS clinic, the newspaper *Frontera Gay*, and other resources. The center is fairly underground, so hours are sporadic.

COMING AND GOING

BY BUS Tijuana has two bus stations: The **Central Camionera,** which is served by major mainland companies, and the **Central Viejo,** for buses to Tecate. **Greyhound/Trailways** (tel. 66/21–29–48) buses to the United States depart from both stations, as well as from the station on the San Ysidro side of the border (799-E San Ysidro Blvd., tel. 619/428–1194). They leave every hour 5 AM–6 PM for San Diego (50 min, $5) and Los Angeles (3½ hrs, $18), and you can change in Los Angeles to continue on to San Francisco (12–13 hrs, $49). There are large, expensive lockers in San Ysidro's Greyhound bus station, but it's better to lug your gear next door to **UPS** (tel. 800/742–5877; open Mon.–Sat. 9–6, Sun. 10–2), which only charges $1 for 24 hours.

➤ **CENTRAL CAMIONERA** • Three bus companies share the Central Camionera (tel. 66/21–29–85) on the eastern edge of Tijuana, far from the budget-hotel area and most tourist activities. **Transportes Norte de Sonora** operates buses throughout the country, with frequent first- and second-class service to Guadalajara (36 hrs; $68 1st class, $63 2nd class) and Mexico City (48 hrs; $74 1st class, $71 2nd class). **Transportes Pacífico** (tel. 66/21–26–06) also has express buses down the mainland coast to Guadalajara and Mexico City. **Autotransportes de Baja California** (tel. 66/21–24–58 or 66/21–24–61) serves Baja with hourly first- and second-class buses 6 AM–8 PM to Mexicali (3 hrs, $7–$8), San Felipe (6 hrs, $14), and Ensenada (1½ hrs, $3–$4). La Paz (22 hrs, $42) is served only by first-class buses, with departures at 8 AM, noon, 6 PM, and 9 PM.

From downtown Tijuana, a taxi will take you down Revolución to the Central Camionera for $7–$10, but your best option is to catch a brown-and-white CENTRAL CAMIONERA *colectivo* (communal taxi; 15 min, $1.25) from the stop on Madero, between Calles 2 and 3. To get from the bus station to the budget-hotel area, find a bus marked CENTRO. The station offers luggage storage (open daily 6:30 AM–10:30 PM) for 65¢ an hour. You can also place long-distance calls (cash only) here from the **Sendetel** booth (tel. 66/21–23–04), open daily 4 AM–11 PM. Money exchange is available daily 6 AM–10 PM.

➤ **CENTRAL VIEJO** • Buses to Tecate (1½ hrs, $2) leave from the Central Viejo (Madero, at Calle 1, tel. 66/88–07–52) from 5:30 AM to 9 PM. The station is within walking distance of both the border and the budget-hotel area. To reach the station from the border, cross over the Río Tijuana pedestrian bridge and continue straight on Calle 1. To reach the budget-hotel area from the bus station, continue on Calle 1 to Coahuila.

BY TROLLEY The wheelchair-accessible **San Diego Trolley** (tel. 619/231–8549) runs from the America Plaza Transfer Station (C St., btw Kettner and India Sts.) in downtown San Diego to San Ysidro, stopping right at the border. Trolleys make the 45-minute trip about every 15 minutes 5 AM–12:15 AM, except on Saturday night, when hourly service continues from midnight until 5 AM Sunday. Many trolley stations along the line provide free parking, which can save you $6 in parking expenses at San Ysidro. Be sure to park in a guarded and well-lit parking lot.

BY CAR There are two border crossings in Tijuana. The San Ysidro–Tijuana crossing is the busiest; on weekends and holidays, the wait to enter the United States by car can be two hours. Lines are shorter at the less central Otay Mesa border (near Tijuana airport, 10 minutes east of San Diego), but it's only open 6 AM–10 PM. If you're in Mexico and want to check on border traffic, call 66/83–14–05 for information in English.

If you're going to TJ (as Tijuana is commonly called by gringos) and you opt not to take the trolley, you should park on the U.S. side at one of the many well-lit, 24-hour lots within walking distance of the border ($6 per 24 hours). If you want to rent a car, try **AVIS** (tel. 800/852–4617), which has an office in San Diego and will let you take a car 714 kilometers (450 mi) south into Baja for up to 30 days. For more details about the legal and financial formalities involved with taking a car into Mexico, *see* Chapter 1.

BY PLANE The airport is on the eastern edge of the city, by the Otay Mesa border crossing; from the San Ysidro border or downtown, a taxi out here costs $7–$10. The city bus marked AEROPUERTO (30–40 min, 30¢) also makes the trip to the airport—catch it at the traffic circle near the border. Domestic plane fares in Mexico are no bargain, but they're usually substantially cheaper than international flights into Mexico. If you're in Southern California, you're better off crossing into Tijuana and buying your ticket there. When you leave Mexico, don't forget the $12 departure tax, payable in dollars or pesos. The **Aerocalifornia** office (Plazería Commercial Center, across from Cultural Center, tel. 66/84–21–00 or 800/258–3311 in the U.S.) is open weekdays 8–7. They serve Los Angeles and Phoenix in the United States, and also fly daily to La Paz and four times per day to Mexico City ($190 one-way). **Aeroméxico** (Revolución, at Calle 8, tel. 66/85–44–01 or 800/237–6639 in the U.S.) and **Mexicana** (Paseo de los Héroes 112, tel. 66/83–28–50 or 800/531–7921 in the U.S.) both offer flights throughout Mexico at comparable prices.

GETTING AROUND

Tijuana, unlike most Mexican cities, lacks a definite center; there's no principal church or square by which to orient yourself. Avenidas Revolución and Constitución—the nightlife hubs—lie in the most "central" part of town. Bars, dance clubs, street vendors, and the jai alai arena are all located in this area, which is best explored on foot. To reach the outlying bullring or racetrack on Boulevard Agua Caliente, take a minibus from the stop on Madero, between Calles 2 and 4. Avenidas in Tijuana run north–south and calles run east–west. Address numbers were just changed in 1993, so many buildings have two numbers—the ones written in blue are current.

BY BUS Buses marked 5 or 10 CENTRO go down Boulevard Agua Caliente, but *peseros* (minibuses) are faster and come more frequently. Both cost less than $1. The peseros on the Agua Caliente route are red-and-black station wagons; catch them on Calle 2 near Avenida Revolución. Tan-and-white station wagons go to the Glorieta Cuauhtémoc and the shopping centers along the Río Tijuana; catch them on Calle 3. Buses to the airport and the bus station stop at the traffic circle across from the border crossing and on Calle 4 at Niños Héroes. The easiest way to reach the border from downtown is to catch a **Mexi-Coach** bus ($1), which leaves Revolución (btw Calles 6 and 7) every half hour 9–9, making stops along Revolución on the way.

BY TAXI Cabs don't have meters, so be sure to negotiate the fare before entering. A trip between the border and downtown should cost about $5, while a ride from the border or city center to the Central Camionera or airport should run $7–$10.

WHERE TO SLEEP

Tijuana's really cheap hotels are northwest of Revolución and around Coahuila. They're only a little darker, dingier, and noisier than those on or around Revolución, which cost $5–$10 more. Women, however, may find the attention they get in the red-light district bothersome and should think twice before staying here. All the hotels listed below have hot water 24 hours a day.

➢ **UNDER $10** • **Hotel y Baños Enva.** The small, dark rooms at this hotel face a newly painted courtyard, and though a bit worn, they each have a fairly clean private bathroom. Men who don't like the look of their shower can go to the baths next door and use the sauna, whirlpool, and steam baths for $3, but women are unwelcome at the facilities. Singles and doubles cost $9, with a $1.50 key deposit. *Artículo 123 (Calle 1) No. 1918, near Constitución, tel. 66/85–22–41. 38 rooms, all with bath. Luggage storage.*

➢ **UNDER $20** • **Hotel Catalina.** Clean, quiet, and comfortable, this is the best deal in the tourist area. Singles cost $12, doubles $16, more if you want a TV. All rooms have phones from which you can make free local or collect international calls. Reservations are recommended on weekends. *Calle 5, at Madero, tel. 66/85–97–48. 38 rooms, all with bath. Luggage storage. Reservations by mail: P.O. Box 3544, San Ysidro, CA 92073, U.S.A.*

Hotel San Nicolás. This quiet, safe hotel has a liveable lobby with couches, a TV, and local phones; singles here are $14, doubles $19. You can enjoy a picnic on the tables in the rear lot, or take advantage of the secure parking area. The front

Tijuana's budget hotels fill up quickly on weekends, so make reservations or come early on Friday to stake out your room.

desk also changes money, and long-distance collect calls can be made around the clock. The **Hotel Económico** next door (where sad, dark cubicles run $10 for a single, $14 for a double) has a decent restaurant. *Madero 538, btw Calles 1 and 2, tel. 66/88–05–29. 28 rooms, all with bath.*

HOSTELS **Villa Juvenil.** If by some odd chance you're in Tijuana to sleep and not to party, make the 10-minute drive from downtown to this hostel, where $5 ($4 students) will get you a bunk bed in a five-person room. The passable bathrooms are coed and there are no shower curtains, so keep that towel close at hand. You must check in before 7 PM, when the office closes. *Airport Hwy. and Via Oriente, Zona Río, tel. 66/34–30–89. Take colectivo marked EL POSTAL from Calle 3 and Revolución, and ask driver to stop at CREA. Curfew 10 PM.*

FOOD

Because people move here from all over Mexico, Tijuana is a great place to sample the diversity of Mexican cuisine. Food stalls at the **mercado municipal** (Niños Héroes, btw Calles 1 and 2) serve dishes from Jalisco, Guanajuato, Michoacán, Guaymas, and other areas for $3–$5. The market is open daily 8–7 but come during 1 and 2 PM for the best food selection. Along Calle 2, between Revolución and Constitución, there's a good selection of inexpensive eateries that cater primarily to a working-class clientele. Prices on Revolución tend to be higher than on surrounding streets, and even more expensive restaurants line Agua Caliente.

Café Pekín. This family-style Chinese restaurant is popular with locals and serves terrific $3–$5 lunch combos (consisting of an egg roll, almond veggies, two super-hot chiles, and either a huge pile of fried rice or pineapple chicken). Delicious dinners like shrimp curry also cost $3–$5, and you can get food to go. *Constitución 1435, at Calle 7, tel. 66/85–24–30. Open daily 11 AM–midnight. Wheelchair access.*

Restaurant Los Norteños. Tables outside this small restaurant are great for watching the action on Plaza Revolución. If you've hit taco overload, try the meat or veggie sandwiches ($2–$3). Breakfast costs less than $2. *Constitución 530, near Calle 2, tel. 66/85–68–55. Open daily 6 AM–2 AM.*

Tortas Ricardo's. Looking somewhat like a '50s diner, this 24-hour restaurant has an extensive menu and serves breakfasts ($1–$3) at all hours. They also have traditional Mexican food ($2–$3) and fish or meat dishes ($4–$6). *Cnr of Calle 7 and Madero, tel. 66/85–40–31. Open 24 hrs daily.*

La Vuelta. This fabulous place doubles as an all-hours nightclub, featuring live mariachi music (Mon.–Thurs. 8 PM, Sat. 8:30 PM, and Sun. 6:30 PM). The grilled meats ($7–$10) and *antojitos* (appetizers) are delicious. If you can't afford that, nurse a $2 beer or one of the two-for-one margaritas (available weekdays 7 AM–10 PM), and plunge into the free chips, salsa, and atmosphere. *Revolución No. 8210, at Calle 11, tel. 66/85–73–09, fax 66/85–73–09. At curve where Revolución changes to Agua Caliente. Open 24 hrs.*

AFTER DARK

Finding something to do at night is not a problem here. Barkers along Revolución (btw Calles 1 and 2) lure young, minimally clad revelers into neon-lit dance halls with offers of free tequila. If you feel like getting smashed and grooving to the latest American hits, the following places fit the bill. Happily, none charges a cover, so you can scope out each club until you find your niche or become too drunk to care. Typically, a margarita costs $3–$4, and beer is $2.50. If you plan on crossing back over the border at the end of your wild night, pretend you're sober: U.S. customs has been known to give M.U.I. (Minor Under the Influence) citations and fines for public drunkeness to those who are on the verge of *manejando la camioneta porcelana* (driving the porcelain bus).

Tilly's Fifth Avenue (Calle 5 No. 901, at Revolución, tel. 66/85–72–45) and **People's** (Calle 2, at Revolución, tel. 66/85–45–72) are both open Monday–Thursday 11 AM–2 AM and Friday–Sunday until dawn. Saturday nights are the most popular—so popular that they may charge men a $3–$5 cover on holiday weekends. Usually you can negotiate a deal for the cover charge if your party has a majority of women—let machismo work for you! **Red Square** (Revolución, near Calle 6, tel. 66/88–27–82) boasts a red spiral staircase leading up to a balcony where you can sip margaritas from noon until 3 AM while watching the commotion below.

If you're tired of dancing with the under-dressed and underage, try to keep up with the locals at the restaurant/nightclub **La Vuelta** (*see* Food, *above*). On Friday, Saturday, and Sunday nights, **Disco Salsa** (Revolución 751, btw Calles 1 and 2a; open 7 PM–3 AM) plays salsa and merengue, while **La Loa** (Revolución, at Calle 2; open 8 PM–2 AM) is the place to hear bands. **El Ranchero** (Plaza Santa Cecilia 769, tel. 66/85–28–00) is a no-games gay bar, frequented by both tourists and locals. Women are welcome but are an obvious minority. El Ranchero is open Sunday–Thursday 10 PM–3 AM, Friday and Saturday 10 PM–7 AM.

CLUBS **La Estrella.** Packed with locals, this is the place to dance to cumbia and an occasional salsa tune. Hard-working *tijuanenses* come here to let loose, and women without men in tow should be prepared to dance a lot. The $2 cover (for men only) includes a free Tecate, but those without an attitude may want to skip this club. La Estrella occasionally gets rough. *Calle 6, tel. 66/88–13–49. Just east of Revolución under star sign. Open daily 10 AM–5 AM.*

Most of the dancing in small bars and clubs on Coahuila is done by strippers. Women walking through the area may feel uncomfortable and should be cautious at night.

Mike's Disco. If you're looking for a way into the gay scene in Tijuana, this is a good place to start. Drag shows are the main draw at this alternative nightclub, with men dressed up like famous Mexican actresses singing torch songs. Performances happen every night at midnight and 3 AM. The cover on Friday and Saturday nights is $4—regardless of gender. You can also pick up the newspaper *Frontera Gay* here to get an idea of what else is going on around town. *Revolución 1220, near Calle 6, tel. 66/85–35–34. Open weekdays (except Wed.) 9 PM–3 AM, weekends until 7 AM.*

SPECTATOR SPORTS

BULLFIGHTING Tijuana has two bullrings: **El Toreo de Tijuana,** the downtown bullring on Agua Caliente, and the preferred beachside **Plaza de Toros Monumental,** the second-largest bullring in the world, known as the "Bullring by the Sea." Fights take place Sundays at 4 PM from May until late September. Tickets start at $7 for seats in the sun and $11.50 for seats in the shade. The bloodthirsty can purchase $50 seats that will put them close enough to get splattered. Buy tickets at the caseta on Revolución (btw Calles 3 and 4, tel. 66/85–22–10), open weekends 10 AM–7 PM, or at the ring (Highway 1-D, by the ocean); get there early to guarantee yourself a ticket. The easiest way to reach the Plaza de Toros is to take the Mexi-Coach bus (½ hr, $2) that leaves at 3:30 PM from Revolución (btw Calles 6 and 7). Otherwise, take a blue-and-white PLAYAS bus (40¢) from Calle 3 and Niños Héroes.

DOG RACES Yet another opportunity to lose your money awaits at the greyhound races at **Caliente Race Track.** Races are usually held at 8 PM, but there are matinees on weekends. *A few km east of town, where Agua Caliente becomes Díaz Ordaz, tel. 66/81–78–11. From Calle 2, take bus marked BLVD AGUA CALIENTE (10 min, 4¢).*

JAI ALAI This Basque game, known as *frontón* in Spanish, is played at **El Palacio Frontón** (Revolución, near Calle 8, tel. 66/38–43–07), a dramatic Moorish-style palace. Something like racquetball, the game is played with a curved, wicker basket, three walls, and a balsa-wood, goatskin-wrapped ball moving at about 110 miles per hour. Almost as fun as watching jai alai is betting on it. Next door, you can wager on football, baseball, and horse races. For game times call 66/85–25–24 or 66/38–43–08.

NEAR TIJUANA

ROSARITO About 45 kilometers from the border, Rosarito is one big, expensive beach party. This is the first popular beach south of Tijuana—not because it's so great, but because it's easy to get to—and you'll know you've reached a tourist trap when a fish taco costs nearly $1. Drunk American college students are abundant here, especially on weekends or during summer months; most can be found in **Papas and Beer on the Beach** (Coronado, at Eucalipto 400, tel. 661/2–04–44), a popular outside bar, volleyball court, and dance club. The cover charge is

$3–$10 (depending on how busy it is), and a margarita costs $4.50. Thursday is ladies' night—meaning no cover and two-for-one drink specials for the fairer sex. The best time to show up in Rosarito is May 14, when parades, traditional dances, and the crowning of an annually selected queen celebrate the founding of Rosarito. For info on this and other shindigs, stop by the **tourist office** (Benito Juárez 8, on the north end of town, tel. 661/2–02–00). The friendly, English-speaking staff gives out maps of Baja Monday–Saturday 9–7, Sunday 10–4.

Around 20 minutes south of Rosarito by car, **Puerto Nuevo,** (or Lobster Village, as it is commonly called) consists of a cluster of restaurants, each trying to sell you the lobster for which the town is famous. The town has become so popular that some restaurants now charge $15 for a plate of crustaceans—although you might luck out and get a lobster with fixin's and a margarita for $11. With better waves and fewer swimmers than Rosarito, Puerto Nuevo is also a great surf spot.

If you're too cheap to pay the $3 toll on the highway to Rosarito, or you want to get a glimpse of the real Baja, join low-riders and produce trucks on the pothole-filled carretera libre (free road). Be aware that traffic makes it take twice as long to get anywhere on the carretera.

➤ **COMING AND GOING** • Buses don't serve Rosarito; colectivos do. To reach Rosarito from downtown Tijuana (1 hr, 50¢), catch a yellow-and-white colectivo on Revolución—these run 24 hours a day. You can catch the colectivo back to Tijuana half a block north of the Rosarito Beach Hotel. To reach Puerto Nuevo from Rosarito (15 min, $1), take the white taxi with burgundy and blue stripes that runs from the Brisas del Mar Hotel (Benito Juárez 22), daily 5 AM–11 PM.

➤ **WHERE TO SLEEP** • The popularity of Rosarito beach, especially on weekends and holidays, makes it hard to find a cheap place to crash; you might be better off making this a day trip from TJ. Large, expensive, American-owned hotels and resorts have taken over, but **Villa Nueva** (Benito Juárez 97, no phone) still provides dingy rooms for about $20 (single or double), and the owner speaks some English. Another option is to rent a tiny cabin ($10 for up to two people) one block from the beach (cnr of Sánchez Taboada and Cárdenas, tel. 661/2–09–76). To get here, walk two blocks towards the beach from the red CALIMAX sign on Benito Juárez; the office is open Monday–Saturday only. Camping on the beach is the cheapest option, but is not recommended for people traveling alone.

TECATE If you want a break from the hectic pace of Tijuana, head one hour east by bus to Tecate. Set on the outskirts of the Sierra de Juárez, this small, elevated town lies right on the United States–Mexico border. No city sits across from Tecate on the American side, and the Mexican government has not developed the town for tourism, which accounts for its small-town, friendly feeling. There's not much to do in Tecate except enjoy the shady green plaza and pleasant atmosphere, but if you plan a couple of days in advance, you can take a free tour of the huge **Tecate Brewing Company** (Guerra 70, tel. 665/4–20–11 ext. 123 or 291). The brewery is open 8–noon and 1–5, and tours are given at varying times, depending on the production schedule. For samples, stop by the new beer garden, **Jardín de Cerveza** (Hidalgo, tel. 665/4–20–11 ext. 123), open Tuesday–Saturday 10–5, Sunday 10–4. For something a little more highbrow, head to the **Casa de Cultura** (next to the tourist office, tel. 665/4–14–83; open weekdays 9–6), where a gallery exhibits paintings and sculpture on a monthly rotating basis. People from surrounding ranches and northern Baja descend upon the town July 8–25 for a traditional *fiesta ranchera* (country fair), including food, crafts, music, and dancing.

➤ **BASICS** • Change cash and traveler's checks at **Bancomer** (Juárez, at Presidente Cárdenas, tel. 665/4–19–14) weekdays 9 AM–1:30 PM; it also has an ATM that accepts Plus and Cirrus cards. To make collect and credit card calls, try the **Computel** phone office (open daily 7 AM–9 PM) in the bus station on Juárez. For **medical aid,** the English-speaking Dr. Nestor López Arellano (Presidente E. Calles 56, tel. 665/4–07–39) is available weekdays 10–2 and 3–8, Saturday 7:30 AM–5 PM. **Farmacia San Carlos** (Juárez 106, tel. 665/4–12–06) is open 8 AM–10 PM daily. The **tourist office** (tel. 665/4–10–95) on the *zócalo* (main square) is open weekdays 8–7, weekends 10–3 and has lots of helpful maps and brochures.

➤ **COMING AND GOING** • Buses to Tecate ($2) leave every half hour 5:30 AM–9 PM from Tijuana's Central Viejo (*see above*). From Tecate, seven buses go to Ensenada (2 hrs, $3) daily 8 AM–10 PM. Buses also leave for Mexicali (2 hrs, $5.50) every hour 7 AM–10 PM. Tecate's **bus station** (tel. 665/4–12–20) is on Benito Juárez, toward the east side of town. As you leave the station, turn left on Juárez and walk one block to the zócalo.

➤ **WHERE TO SLEEP AND EAT** • The cheapest lodging in Tecate is at **Hotel Juárez** (Juárez 230, near bus station, tel. 665/4–15–04). Newly painted and semi-refurbished, this hotel has dinky little rooms with relatively clean bathrooms ($8.50 singles, $10 doubles). Call first, however, as it's sometimes closed. **Motel Paraíso** (Alderete 83, at Juárez, tel. 665/4–17–16) has comfortable, clean rooms, each with a fan and private bath; singles cost $10, doubles $13. To get here, walk about five blocks west of the zócalo on Juárez. The rooms are basically the same at **Hotel Tecate** (SW cnr of zócalo, at Libertad and Presidente Cárdenas, tel. 665/4–11–16). You pay a bit extra for the convenient location: Singles and doubles with private bath are $11, $14 with TV.

For good food served on a shady patio, try **Jardín Tecate** (south side of zócalo, tel. 665/4–34–53; open daily 7 AM–10 PM), with a menu featuring chef salads ($2.50), onion soup ($2), and garlic fish ($3). **Restaurant Íntimo** (Juárez 181, tel. 665/4–48–19) has picnic tables in the front garden and is a nice place for breakfast (omelets and hotcakes cost $2). They also serve *pescado veracruzano* (red snapper cooked in tomatoes, onions, capers, peppers, and herbs; $4) and a *comida corrida* (pre-prepared lunch special; $3).

Mexicali

Huge, poor, and urban, Mexicali is easily stereotyped in familiar border-town terms. The capital of Baja California Norte, Mexicali is similar in character to Tijuana, but because of its relative isolation (160 kilometers east of Tijuana), awful summer heat, and the absence of tourist diversions, it's much less frequently visited. Recently the city has made aggressive attempts to shed its tawdry image and recruit more respectable tourists and shoppers, as the downtown shopping center and the new **Centro Cívico-Comercial** (commercial and civic center) attest. Despite these improvements, most tourists still spend only as much time here as is necessary to fill the gas tank, but immigrants from rural Mexico flock here seeking work in the *maquiladoras* (*see* box, *above*), set up near the border.

Mexicali's most distinct feature is its large Chinese population, made up mostly of descendants of immigrants brought to Mexico to build the Imperial Canal to the north in 1902. The city has numerous Chinese restaurants and shops and a small Chinese-language newspaper. For more cultural diversions, Mexicali's free **Museo Regional de la Universidad de Baja California** (Reforma, at Calle L, tel. 65/54–19–77) includes exhibits on human evolution, geological photography, paleontology, and the colonial history of Baja California. At least one Sunday a month between October and May, Mexicali's **Plaza de Toros Calafia** hosts some of the best matadors and bulls in all of Mexico; the cheapest tickets, available at the Centro Cívico-Comercial (Calafia, at Av. de los Héroes, no phone), cost about $10. If you're in Mexicali during the beginning of October, check out the city's biggest bash, the 15-day **Fiesta del Sol** (Sun Festival), which features live music, drinking, dancing, cockfights, and cultural exhibits. The festival is held at the **Parque Vicente Guerrero** on López Mateos.

BASICS The **post office** (Madero 491, tel. 65/52–25–08; open weekdays 8–6:30, weekends 9–1) is a few blocks from the border, but it's much cheaper and quicker to send international mail from the United States: **Casa de Cambio Lin** (236 1st St., tel. 619/357–5304), on the same block as the Greyhound station in Calexico (*see below*), is a money exchange office that sells stamps and has mailboxes out front. Get those much-needed pesos at **Bancomer** (Madero, 1 block from border, tel. 65/54–26–00), which changes money weekdays 9–1 and has an ATM. You can make cash but not collect calls until around 7:30 PM from the **caseta** across from Hotel 16 de Septiembre (*see* Where to Sleep, *below*). If you have a health problem that needs immediate attention, **Dr. Juan David Molina Velasco** (Madero 420, Suite 102, tel. 65/52–65–60 or 65/65–32–67 after hours) provides 24-hour emergency service, although his office is only open weekdays 10–3 and 5–8, Saturday 10–3 (June–Sept., Mon.–Sat. 10–

3 only). **Farmacia Benavides** (Reforma, at José Azueta, tel. 65/52–29–18) is open daily 8 AM–10 PM and has a helpful staff for nonemergencies.

The **tourist office** (López Mateos, at Carmelia, about 2 km from border, tel. 65/57–23–76) is open weekdays 9–7, and has a cornucopia of maps, pamphlets, and newspapers in English. English-speaking employees are available all day, except 2–4 PM, when they're out to lunch. For border crossing information, *see* Tijuana, Crossing the Border, *above*. For more information on visas and tourist cards, as well as the formalities involved in bringing a car into Mexico, *see* Chapter 1.

COMING AND GOING

➢ **BY BUS** • The **Greyhound** bus station (tel. 619/357–1895) is located across the border from Mexicali in Calexico, directly in front of the pedestrian bridge. Hourly departures for San Diego (2 hrs, $15), Los Angeles (5 hrs, $25) and El Paso ($80) keep this station open 6 AM–midnight. Luggage storage costs $4 for 24 hours or $2 for six hours. Mexicali's **Central Camionera** is in the Centro Cívico-Comercial on Independencia. Four companies operate from this station and share the same phone number (tel. 65/57–27–57). The counters to your right as you enter the station sell first-class tickets, those on the left sell second-class ones. **Élite** offers first-class service to Baja and major cities on the mainland, with departures to destinations such as Guadalajara (32 hrs; $69 1st class, $59 2nd class) and Mazatlán (24 hrs; $55 1st class, $47 2nd class) every hour around the clock. Buses to Mexico City (42 hrs; $84 1st class, $72 2nd class) leave every two hours. **Autotransportes de Baja California** has both first- and second-class service throughout Baja. Hourly buses from Mexicali leave for Tijuana (2½ hrs; $7.50 1st class, $6 2nd class) and Ensenada (4 hrs; $10.50 1st class, $8 2nd class). Second-class buses depart for San Felipe (2½ hrs, $6) at 8 AM, noon, and 6 PM. First-class buses (2½ hrs, $6.50) leave at 4 PM and 8 PM. The station also has a 24-hour **Computel** office for long-distance calls; use a public phone to call collect. The budget-savvy can reach the station by catching the bus (40¢) that chugs down Altamirano, stopping a block west of the bus station. Otherwise, a cab to the station from the border or downtown costs $4.

➢ **BY CAR** • Driving to Mexicali from Tijuana or Ensenada is relatively easy on Highway 2, although tolls along the road will run you about $3. For $50–$60 per day, **Budget** (in the Hotel Araiza, tel. 65/66–48–40; open daily 8–8) rents cars that you can take all over Mexico with few restrictions. If your big Mexican road trip left you stranded in Mexicali, **Oasa** (López Mateos 850, tel. 65/52–82–15; open Mon.–Sat. 8–6, Sun. 9–2) sells auto parts and repairs cars.

➢ **BY TRAIN** • The train station is at the south end of Ulises Irigoyen, north of the intersection with López Mateos. To get here, catch a bus marked FERROCARRIL (40¢) from Calle F at Madero, in front of the park. One first-class and one second-class train depart daily for Guadalajara, with connections to Mexico City. Both trains stop at all major cities on the way (the second-class train makes many more stops); and you can transfer at Los Mochis for the Copper Canyon train. The first-class train takes about 36 hours to reach Guadalajara and costs $42 for a comfortable reserved seat (make reservations 15 days to a month in advance). The second-class train to Guadalajara takes about two days and costs only $23. Second-class seats are not reserved, however, so arrive about four hours early. For more information, contact **Ferrocarril Sonora-Baja California** (tel. 65/57–23–86).

GETTING AROUND
Mexicali has two downtown areas on opposite sides of town. The first, **La Frontera** (the border), a.k.a. *el mero centro* (the very center), is characterized by cheap hotels, taco stands, Chinese restaurants, and loads of street vendors. The **Centro Cívico-Comercial** (civic center) is home to government offices, the city hospital, the Calafia bullfighting arena, and the bus and train stations. Both areas are easily explored on foot, but to get from one to the other you'll need to take a city bus (40¢) down Boulevard López Mateos, the city's main thoroughfare. Buses to other parts of the city congregate near the border on the west side of Reforma, and on Altamirano near Madero. To reach the budget hotels in La Frontera from the bus terminal, cross the pedestrian bridge and wait directly on the other side for a bus marked CENTRO (40¢). Conveniently, their last stop is on Altamirano, near Hotel 16 de Septiembre and Hotel Altamirano. Taxis are not worth the expense ($5–$8) unless you have a carload or it's late at night. From the bus station, cab prices are preset, so don't bother bargaining.

WHERE TO SLEEP The cheapest hotels are in the Frontera area, and are accessible on foot from any of the local bus stops on Reforma or Altamirano. Most hotels on Reforma are seedy and unsanitary, but cheap. Accommodations near the Centro Cívico-Comercial are nicer but difficult to find and more expensive. At **Hotel 16 de Septiembre** (Altamirano 353, tel. 65/52–60–70), it's the bathrooms, rather than the rooms themselves, that make for a pleasant stay: The spacious, tiled shower stalls are among the cleanest in Mexicali. A single costs $6 ($10 with private bath and air-conditioning); doubles run $7–$12. **Hotel Altamirano** (Altamirano 378, tel. 65/52–83–94) has small rooms and a fairly sanitary communal bath; singles cost only $5, doubles $7. Air-conditioning and carpeting in each room make the wheelchair-accessible **Hotel Plaza** (Madero 366, 1 block from border, tel. 65/52–97–59) reasonably comfortable. A single costs $13, a double $15—more if you want a TV and phone.

FOOD The border area abounds with cheap places to eat, primarily taco stands and Chinese restaurants. At **Restaurant Buendía** (Altamirano 263, tel. 65/52–69–25; open daily 7 AM–9 PM), the Mexican-Chinese decor is complemented by the Mexican-Chinese menu. Heaping portions of chow mein or wonton go for $3.50, and Mexican dishes cost $2–$4. **El Nuevo Ken Seng** (Reforma 264, tel. 65/53–46–71; open daily 6–6) is a dingy downtown restaurant that serves some of the best Chinese food in Mexico ($2–$4). Unfortunately it's a hangout for cabbies and drunks; women may not want to linger here after dark. **Nevería Blanca Nieves** (Snow White's Ice Cream Shop; Reforma 503, tel. 65/52–94–85; open daily 8 AM–9:30 PM) is crowded with old Happys, Dopeys, and Sneezys downing malts ($1.50) and sundaes ($2) at the soda fountain. They've got a great breakfast menu ($2–$3) and salads and sandwiches for $2–$4.

Ensenada

Since the completion of the toll road between Tijuana and Ensenada in 1973, Ensenada has blossomed into one of Baja's most popular resorts. Cruise ships call regularly in the port here, and passengers tired of shuffleboard head for the fine beaches nearby. Surfers catch waves 20 kilometers north of the city at **Playa San Miguel,** while sport fishers pursue yellowtail and marlin. By night, Ensenada offers a miniaturized version of Tijuana-style nightlife, attracting crowds of hell-raising U.S. college students and Mexicans. But with a population of about 200,000, Ensenada is considerably smaller than Tijuana and its pace is less frenetic, although increased tourism has led to higher prices.

From May 15 to 19, Ensenada celebrates its foundation with musical performances, dance, and a traditional fair. August 2–11, the Vendimia (wine festival) comes to town; local wineries exhibit their famed wines and the newly crowned Queen of the Harvest heads a raucous parade along Boulevard Costero.

The missionaries who colonized much of Baja skipped Ensenada on their trek north because it lacked fresh water. The city's first major growth period came in the 1870s, after gold was discovered in Real de Castillo to the east. Following the discovery, Ensenada became the major supply center, seaport, and, for a while, even the capital of northern Baja. It also enjoyed a brief fling with the Hollywood jet set, serving as a playground for the Southern California elite during Prohibition. With the repeal of Prohibition and the Mexican government's decision to make gambling illegal, tourism in Ensenada dried up. More recently, the loosening of restrictions on foreign ownership of beachside property has spurred a dramatic increase in the number of visitors here. Today, the hills surrounding Ensenada are terraced with tar-paper shacks, home to the city's most recent migrants, who have come to look for work in northern Baja's booming construction industry.

BASICS

➢ **CASAS DE CAMBIO** • Dollars are accepted—and expected—everywhere in Ensenada. **Banco Mexicano** and **Serfín** (both on Ruíz, at Calle 3) change cash and traveler's checks weekdays 9–1:30 and give cash advances on Visa and MasterCard; Serfín has an ATM that accepts Plus and Cirrus cards. Change cash and traveler's checks at **Cambio de Cheques**

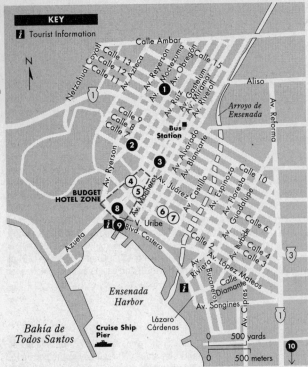

KEY

i Tourist Information

N

Calle Ambar

Netzahual Coyotl
Calle 13
Calle 12
Calle 11
Av. Azteca

Av. Reyerson
Av. Moctezuma
Av. Obregón
Av. Ruiz
Av. Gastelum
Av. Miramar
Av. Riveroll
Calle 15

Aliso

Arroyo de
Ensenada

Av. Reforma

Calle 9
Calle 8
Calle 7

**Bus
Station**

Av. Ryerson

Av. Alvarado
Av. Blancarte
Av. Juárez
Av. Castillo
Av. Espinoza
Av. Floresta
Av. Guadalupe

Calle 10

Calle 6

**BUDGET
HOTEL ZONE**

Av. Macheros

Av. Iturbide
Calle 4
Calle 3

i

V. Uribe
Blvd. Costero

Calle 2

Azueto

Av. Riviera
Av. Bucaneros

Av. López Mateos

Calle
Diamante

Calle 5

i

Av. Cipres

Av. Songines

3

1

*Ensenada
Harbor*

*Bahía de
Todos Santos*

**Cruise Ship
Pier**

Lázaro
Cárdenas

0   500 yards

0   500 meters

10

(López Mateos 1001-1, at Blancarte, tel. 617/8–14–59), open Sunday–Friday 9–7, Saturday 9:30–3:30. They'll also allow you to make long-distance calls, including international credit card and collect calls, for a 50¢ fee.

➤ **EMERGENCIES** • Dial 134 from any phone for the **police**; 136 for the **fire** department; or 132 for the **Cruz Roja** (ambulance).

➤ **LAUNDRY** • **El Lavandero** has automatic washers ($1 per load) and dryers (25¢ for 10 min). If you prefer to leave the dirty work to someone else, same-day service is available ($1 extra per load). *Obregón 664, btw Calles 6 and 7, tel. 617/8–27–37. Open Mon.–Sat. 7:30 AM–8 PM.*

➤ **MEDICAL AID** • For an English-speaking doctor, contact Dr. Antonio Orosco Soto (Riveroll 679, btw Calles 6 and 7, tel. 617/4–03–90), who has office hours daily 10–1 and 5–8. For 24-hour emergency service, call Dr. Orosco at home (tel. 617/6–42–29). You can pick up whatever he prescribes for you at **Farmacia Regia**. *Calle 28-B, at Miramar, tel. 617/4–05–57. Open Mon.–Sat. 8 AM–10 PM, Sun. 8 AM–9 PM.*

➤ **PHONES AND MAIL** • You can make collect calls from public phones along López Mateos or at the Cambio de Cheques (*see above*). The **post office,** near Hotel Riviera del Pacífico, will hold mail sent to you at the following address for up to 10 days: Lista de Correos, Administración 1, Avenida López Mateos, Ensenada, Baja California Norte, CP 22800, México. *López Mateos, at Floresta, tel. 617/6–10–88. Open weekdays 8–7, Sat. 9–1.*

➤ **SCHOOLS** • The **Colegio de Idiomas de Ensenada** (tel. 617/6–01–09, Blvd. Rodríguez 377) offers six-week, intensive Spanish courses throughout the year. Classes are held weekdays and cost $125 per week, plus a one-time registration fee of $125. Family stays are also available ($20 per day, meals included).

➤ **VISITOR INFORMATION** • The **tourist information booth** at the north end of the waterfront has a friendly, English-speaking staff and an ample supply of maps and pamphlets, but they don't know much about out-of-the-way places. *Costero, at Gastelum, tel. 617/8–24–11. Open weekdays 9–7, Sat. 10–4, Sun. 10–3.*

Baja's **Secretaría del Estado de Tourismo,** farther south, has fewer pamphlets about local merchants but a more knowledgable staff and better general info about Baja. *Centro de Gobierno, Costero 1477, at Las Rocas, tel. 617/2–30–22 ext. 3181 or 3182. Open weekdays 9–7, Sat. 10–3, Sun. 10–2.*

COMING AND GOING Transportes Norte de Sonora (TNS) and Autotransportes de Baja California (ABC) are housed in Ensenada's bus terminal (Riveroll, at Calle 10). TNS (tel. 617/8–67–70) has first-class departures for Guadalajara (36 hrs, $54) at 3 PM, 8:30 PM, and midnight. Buses for Mexico City (48 hrs, $78 1st class, $68 2nd class) leave at 11:30 AM and 4:30 PM. ABC (tel. 617/8–66–80) has frequent first-class buses bound for San Quintín (3 hrs, $5.50), La Paz (18–20 hrs, $42), and towns in between. Buses depart 5:30 AM–8 PM for Mexicali (3 hrs; $12 1st class, $10.50 2nd class); at 8 AM and 6 PM for San Felipe (3½ hrs, $10); and hourly for Tijuana (2 hrs, $3–$3.50). The station has 24-hour luggage storage (50¢ for 5 hrs) and a caseta de larga distancia (open daily 7:30 AM–10 PM) for cash calls only. To reach the budget-hotel area from the bus station, turn right as you leave the station and walk eight blocks. It's a seedy part of town, so be careful walking alone at night. Colectivos (50¢) also run to the center of town until midnight. Taxis to the center are $3.

GETTING AROUND Except for the beaches, which lie 10 kilometers south of town and beyond, Ensenada is easy to cover on foot. The waterfront (Boulevard Costero) and the parallel tourist drag (López Mateos, a.k.a. Calle 1) serve as the town's focal points. The old **Hotel Riviera del Pacífico** (*see* Worth Seeing, *below*), on López Mateos, serves as a good landmark. Avenida Juárez, about six blocks inland, is the main commercial street. To reach the **Estero** or **El Faro** beaches, flag down a yellow-and-white CHAPULTEPEC van from anywhere along the waterfront on Boulevard Costero; the vans stop within 3 kilometers of the beach. You can also take a red-and-white CHAPULTEPEC bus from the depot on Calle 6, at Ruíz, or from Avenida Juárez. Get off at the ESTERO sign, and walk the 2–3 kilometers to the beach. To reach **La Bufadora** (*see* Near Ensenada, *below*) take the yellow-and-white MANEADERO van ($2) all the way to Maneadero and change to a blue van ($1) for the remaining 16 miles. Vans and buses run daily 6 AM–10 PM. If you're in need of bike-related equipment, **Los Duran Bicicletas** (Riveroll 542, tel. 617/4–01–60) has parts and a knowledgeable staff.

WHERE TO SLEEP Ensenada has plenty of cheap rooms, but the low price is often the only thing they have going for them. The budget-hotel area is on Avenidas Miramar and Gastelum, between Calles 2 and 3. Miramar is a run-down street lined with bars, so if you arrive after dark, try Gastelum first. Rooms are usually clean but worn, and communal and private bathrooms are often in need of a good scrubbing. Another good place to look for cheap lodging is the area around López Mateos. If you're determined to sleep cheap and everything else is full, try **Hotel Río** (Miramar 231, tel. 617/8–37–33), which has 52 rooms, 10 of which are clean and reserved for tourists. These cost $7 for one or two people.

➤ **UNDER $10** • **Hotel El Pacífico No. 1.** El Pacífico is a popular stop for European cyclists on their way up or down the peninsula. Basic singles and doubles are the same price—$4.50 without bath and $7 with. The private baths are surprisingly clean, and the communal ones are nothing you can't deal with, but the thin walls make for a potentially noisy evening. If you ask nicely, the owners may let you use the kitchen facilities. *Gastelum 235, btw Calles 2 and 3, no phone. 30 rooms, 12 with bath. Luggage storage.*

Motel Perla del Pacífico. To compensate for the seedy location, they run a tight ship here, with no alcohol or visitors in the clean but dark rooms. Even the communal baths are up to *Good Housekeeping* standards, making the $6 singles and doubles with shared bath a great deal. A single or double with private bath costs $10. Prices rise $2–$5 during holiday weekends and other busy times of the year. *Miramar 229, tel. 617/8–30–51. 72 rooms, 41 with bath. Luggage storage, parking.*

➤ **UNDER $20** • **Hotel Cinderella.** Run by a family, this quiet, tidy motel is gated to ensure no unwanted visitors. The small but clean rooms with quirky bedspreads cost $10 (singles) and $15 (doubles). *Castillo 198, at Calle 2, tel. 617/8–11–94. 8 rooms, all with bath. Luggage storage.*

Motel Gris. Only two blocks southeast of López Mateos, this pleasant motel with friendly management attracts families and backpackers alike. Rooms with air-conditioning, TV, and big comfy beds cost $15 for one or two people. *Calle 2 No. 1180, btw Castillo and Mar, tel. 617/8–26–13. 25 rooms, all with bath. Luggage storage.*

➤ **CAMPING** • **Playa el Faro** has a nice stretch of white sand for camping if you don't mind being 10 kilometers from town. Facilities include toilets and showers. A site for a car with two people costs $7, motorcycles $2, and only 50¢ for people without a vehicle. Camping is also plentiful at La Bufadora (*see* Near Ensenada, *below*). You can also camp for free on any undeveloped beach between Ensenada and La Bufadora, but watch out for crazy truck and motorcycle drivers on the dunes. For directions to El Faro, *see* Getting Around, *above*.

FOOD Ensenada's specialty is fish tacos. You can find the best and cheapest at the many seafood stalls surrounding the **fish market** or in the pink **Plaza de Mariscos** (Costero, at Virgilio Uribe). Besides the mouthwatering tacos, piled high with cilantro, salsa, guacamole, onions, and tomatoes, you can also buy fresh seafood cocktails and *mariscos* (shellfish) prepared in a variety of ways. Cheap restaurants serving Mexican food that will fill your stomach without dazzling your palate can be found between Calles 2 and 3 and between Miramar and Gastelum. The **Gigante** (Gastelum 672, at López Mateos, tel. 617/8–26–44) supermarket is open daily 7 AM–10 PM, and they accept traveler's checks, Visa, or MasterCard.

El Charro. This log cabin—complete with a fireplace and a dark, smoky atmosphere—sits right in the heart of the tourist area. El Charro serves excellent spit-roasted chicken, dished up with tortillas and condiments; half a chicken costs $8. Complement your meal with wine from the Bodegas de Santo Tomás (*see* Worth Seeing, *below*). *López Mateos 475, near Gastelum, tel. 617/8–38–81. Open daily 11:30 AM–2 AM.*

Restaurant-Bar Corralito This 24-hour joint looks sketchy from the outside, but the great chow draws a large local crowd. Oddly decorated from floor to ceiling with old cigarette cartons, Corralito serves up a mean *huevos rancheros* with lots of beans and tortillas for only $2.25, as well as other traditional Mexican dishes. *López Mateos 627, tel. 617/8–23–70. Wheelchair access.*

Mariscos de Bahía de Ensenada. Mariscos is recommended by locals as the best place for fresh and inexpensive seafood (they catch their own). It's also great for a long, sit-down meal. The tortilla-maker in the window attracts some tourists, but Mexicans often outnumber foreigners. Anything that's not seafood is expensive, but shrimp ($5), squid ($4.50), and fresh fish ($4) are good deals. *Riveroll 109, at López Mateos, tel. 617/8–10–15. Open daily 10–10. MC, V.*

The fish market at the north end of Boulevard Costero displays the richness of northern Baja's coastal waters. Come early in the morning to see fishermen preparing for the day's work, or in the late afternoon when the pangas (fishing boats) bring in the latest catch.

➤ **CAFÉS** • **Café Café.** Get a dose of San Francisco at the hippest place in town, decorated with recycled furniture, the work of local artists, and a rack of vintage clothing. Here, you can play a game of backgammon, drink a cup of coffee flavored with molasses ($1), or chat with Memo (the owner) and his friends about Zapatista politics. (¡Que siga la lucha!) *López Mateos, near Gastelum, tel. 617/8–35–44. Open Mon., Wed., and Thurs. 10–5, Fri. whenever the owners wake up until 1 AM, Sat. 10 AM–1 AM, Sun. 10–10.*

Pueblo Café and Deli. Locals and tourists come here to enjoy the eclectic music, wine, beer, and California cuisine. It's a great place for breakfast, with omelets for $3 and french toast and eggs for $3.50. Vegetarians will be delighted by their salads—try the Oriental ($4). *Ruíz 96, btw Calle 1 and Virgilio Uribe, tel. 617/8–80–55. Open daily 8 AM–midnight.*

WORTH SEEING The remnants of Ensenada's "frontier" past are still visible in the older neighborhood in the northwest part of the city, especially along Avenida Reyerson. **Parque Revolución** (btw Calles 6 and 7 and Obregón and Moctezuma) is the place to park yourself on a bench in the shade. For a glimpse behind the scenes at Baja's oldest commercial winery, visit the **Bodegas de Santo Tomás** (Miramar 666, btw Calles 6 and 7, tel. 617/8–25–09; open daily 9–4), a legacy of the Dominican fathers of the Santo Tomás mission. Although the grapes are grown 50 kilometers south of the city, wine production was moved to this large warehouse in the middle of Ensenada in 1934. Half-hour bilingual guided tours of the warehouse end with rewarding wine tasting. Admission is $2, and tours are given daily at 11 AM, 1 PM, and 3 PM. The **Museo de Historia de Ensenada** (tel. 617/7–15–07; admission $1; open Tues.–Sun. 10–2 and 3–6), in the old **Hotel Riviera del Pacífico** on López Mateos, offers a glimpse of Baja's history; afterwards you can tour the gardens of the old resort hotel. A statue of **La Diosa Tara** sits peacefully on a hill looking over the city. This East Asian goddess, painted in vivid colors, was given to Ensenada by the Nepalese government a few years ago. Visiting her will not only bring you knowledge and compassion, but a great view of Ensenada.

OUTDOOR ACTIVITIES For cleanish sand and moderate waves without too many beachgoers, check out the beaches 10 kilometers south of town: **La Joya, El Faro,** and **Estero.** Rent a horse ($8–$10 per hr) right on the beach and gallop down an empty stretch of sand, or plow through the empty dunes in a four-wheel drive or ATV (*see below*). For directions to the beaches, *see* Getting Around, *above*.

➤ **WATER SPORTS** • Ensenada is an angler's town. Most sportfishing outfitters are located next to the fish market, just off Boulevard Costero, including **Gordo's Sport Fishing** (tel. 617/8–35–15; open 24 hrs), where they'll take you out to sea for $35 per day. If you prefer fish as swimming companions rather than entrées, try snorkeling or scuba diving at **El Faro** and **Estero** beaches, or off the **Banda Peninsula.** Here you can see surfperch, rockfish, barracuda, dolphins, and sharks, most of which do not eat people. In Maneadero, the area immediately south of Ensenada, well-used masks, snorkels, and fins are easy to come by ($6 a day), as several palapas on the beach serve as rental stores. Scuba equipment is available at Estero Beach, and you can dive at La Bufadora (*see Near Ensenada, below*).

The best surfing is north of Ensenada, but the waves crash on a rocky shore, which may prove dangerous for beginners. The waves aren't as vicious near El Faro and Estero beaches—a few places here rent old, trashed boards, and prices fluctuate with demand. **Sam's Beach Toy Rentals** (Estero Beach) rents boards for $10 a day. They also rent boogie boards ($5 a day) and sea kayaks ($20 a day). Sam's is 1½ kilometers from Highway 1 at the Estero Beach turnoff; to get in touch with them, you can harass someone at the Estero Beach Hotel (tel. 617/6–62–25).

➤ **THREE-WHEELIN'** • For those who would rather tear up Baja landscape and damage delicate ecosystems, the dunes south of Ensenada are prime terrain for off-road vehicles. Around El Faro Beach, Estero Beach, and Maneadero, you can rent ATVs for about $20; Sam's Toy Rentals (*see above*) has a sizable collection.

AFTER DARK Ensenada's nightlife centers around López Mateos, especially near the corner of Ruíz. Take your pick from a number of dark, neon-lit nightclubs that feature loud American music and crowds of college students from Southern California. The ever-popular **Papas and Beer** (López Mateos, at Ruíz, tel. 617/4–01–45) provides plenty of beer ($2.50), booze, and boogie daily 10 AM–3 AM. To mingle with the locals, head to **Bar Andaluz** (in Old Hotel Riviera del Pacífico, tel. 617/7–17–30; open Tues.–Sun. noon–2 AM), where you can dance to salsa, cumbia, and traditional Mexican favorites with Ensenada's more cultured residents. Another popular joint is **Hussong's Cantina** (Ruíz 113, at López Mateos, tel. 617/8–32–10), a historic establishment that retains its character despite its popularity with tourists. For an alternative to drinking and dancing, visit one of the **billiard halls** along Calle 2, between Gastelum and Miramar. Come during the day if you actually want to play billiards (each joint has a few pool tables); come at night to take in the scene. However, women are rare in these places after dark. **Coyote Club** (Costero 1000, near Diamante; open weekdays 2 PM–midnight, weekends until 3 AM) is the only gay bar in Ensenada.

NEAR ENSENADA

LA BUFADORA Although the surrounding coastal cliffs are spectacular in their own right, the main attraction here is the dramatic blowhole, La Bufadora, which sprays water and foam as high as 55 meters into the air. Local legend has it that the geyser's real source is a whale that ventured beneath the rocks as a calf and grew too big to escape. The blowhole is outside the town of **Punta Banda,** 45 minutes south of Ensenada, and is easy to reach via public transport (*see* Ensenada, Getting Around, *above*). If you're feeling particularly adventurous (and rich), **Dale's La Bufadora Dive** (Calle 10 No. 320, just off main road at La Bufadora, tel. 617/3–20–92) rents complete scuba equipment ($25) and offers boat dives into the depths of La Bufadora ($50 for one or two people, $20 per additional person). Dives begin at 9 AM and noon. You can also rent snorkel equipment for $15. Dale's is open weekdays 8–3, weekends 8–6.

Dale also rents out a mint-green house ($10 per person per night) that can sleep up to 15 people, located about 100 feet from the shop. Call him at 617/3–20–92 for inquiries about reservations or more info. Campsites without water or hook-ups at **Rancho La Bufadora** (Calle 10 No. 305, right across from Dale's, tel. 617/8–17–72) cost $5 per night for a carload of two; each additional person is 50¢ extra. You can also camp at nearby **La Jolla Beach Camp** (Carretera La Bufadora Km. 12.5, tel. 617/3–20–05, fax 617/3–20–04), which charges $6 for two people and $1.50 for each additional person. They also have showers and a mini-mart.

If you're sick of sea salt, Balneario Ramos, on the highway from Ensenada to La Bufadora at Kilometer 1300, offers a quiet swimming pool with shaded picnic tables. The facilities are open daily 9–7, and it costs $2 for use of the pool, waterslide, and surrounding grass area.

SIERRA DE JUAREZ The craggy mountain ranges of the Sierra de Juárez and the Sierra San Pedro Mártir run down the spine of northern Baja. The Sierra de Juárez begins south of the U.S. border and extends to meet the Sierra San Pedro Mártir where Highway 3 cuts across the peninsula. The Sierra de Juárez range is home to the **Parque Nacional Constitución de 1857,** a great place for some quiet camping. The park is on a plateau covered with ponderosa pines, and it surrounds Laguna Hanson, a clear, cold mountain lake. Hiking trails are rare or unmarked, so you'll need a compass and topographical maps, available through the Secretaría del Estado de Turismo (*see* Ensenada, Basics, *above*). There are few formal campsites, but finding a spot shouldn't be a problem except during *Semana Santa* (Holy Week—the week preceeding Easter), when the park fills up. No buses serve the dirt roads that access the park, so take your own vehicle. Hitching is not recommended, especially in summer when you'll fry to death waiting for a ride. The best way to get here is from Highway 3: Follow the highway toward San Felipe to Kilometer 55.2, where you'll see a sign reading LAGUNA HANSON. Follow the dirt road marked by the sign; the park is 35 kilometers (21 mi) farther. This can really be rustic, so be prepared; bring extra water, enough gas, and a spare tire.

Even fewer people visit the rugged, granite terrain of the **Parque Nacional Sierra San Pedro Mártir,** where Baja's highest point, **Piacacho del Diablo** (Devil's Peak) soars to 3,100 meters. Inside the park, you can hike along small mountain paths through *piñon* (nut pine) and oak trees, as well as the rare San Pedro Mártir cypress. The mountains are also home to mountain goats and puma. Rock climbers will find a number of challenging rocks, including the Class 3 ascent up Devil's Peak. Bring plenty of water, food, a repair kit, and enough gas for the round trip; supplies are scarce in these parts. Three routes penetrate these mountains, but you'll need a car that can take a beating. The easiest route to the park, but not to Devil's Peak, is the 24-kilometer dirt road off Highway 3 at San Matías. This leads to Mike's Sky Ranch at the northwestern base of the park. Otherwise, a dirt road 16 kilometers south of Colonet along Highway 1 heads 80 kilometers east through San Telmo to Devil's Peak. To reach the eastern base of the park from San Felipe, take the dirt road that runs to Rancho Santa Clara, near Laguna Diablo. For more information on the trails in this park, get a copy of *The Baja Adventure Book* by Walt Peterson (The Wilderness Press, 1992).

San Felipe

Those who love fishing, sailing, and off-roading flock to San Felipe, on the northern coast of the Sea of Cortez. Although the surrounding desert and extremely hot summers prevented any permanent settlement until the 1920s, this small beach town is not undiscovered. With the completion of Highway 5 from Mexicali in 1951, fishermen came to San Felipe and were soon followed by other sport lovers. Today, sailors from all over Mexico and the United States blow through in April and October to compete in Hobie Cat races. San Felipe is one big party during the annual **Carnaval** (Feb. 16–20), when the town comes to life with parades, dances, and sporting events; over Spring Break (late March to early April), college students from the States trek down here to test the limits of inebriation. On June 1, **Día de la Marina Nacional** is celebrated with colorfully decorated boats that parade through the water in front of the *malecón* (boardwalk). If you'd rather have the town to yourself, come in July and August, when temperatures averaging 37°C (100°F) drive most sane individuals away.

BASICS

➤ **CASAS DE CAMBIO** • **Prestaciones de Servicios Mitla** (cnr of Mar de Cortez and Chetumal, tel. 657/7–11–32) will change traveler's checks and cash daily 9–9. You can also stick your Visa in the ATM at **Bancomer** (Mar de Cortez 165, tel. 657/7–10–51) weekdays 8:30–2 PM.

➤ **MEDICAL AID** • Dr. Ubaldo Espinoza Ángel (Mar de Cortez 238, tel. 657/7–11–43) speaks English and is available for drop-ins Monday–Saturday 5 PM–8 PM. For emergencies, call Dr. Gerardo Olvera Duran at his office (Mar de Cortez 238, tel. 657/7–11–43) or at his home (tel. 657/7–15–84). Buy your drugs at **Farmacia San Ángel Inn**. *Chetumal, near Mar de Cortez, tel. 657/7–10–43. Open weekdays 9–9, weekends 9 AM–10 PM.*

➤ **PHONES AND MAIL** • The **post office** (Mar Blanco 187, tel. 657/7–13–30) is open weekdays 8–3 and Saturday 9–1. From Mar de Cortez, walk five blocks away from the beach along Chetumal and turn left at Mar Blanco. **Farmacia San Ángel Inn** (*see above*) charges $1 for collect and credit card calls to the U.S. and Canada, but you can also make regular long-distance calls.

➤ **VISITOR INFORMATION** • The staff here speaks some English and can tell you anything you want to know about San Felipe, but not much about the rest of Baja. *Mar de Cortez 300, at Manzanillo, tel. 657/7–11–55. Open weekdays 8–7, Sat. 9–3, Sun. 10–1.*

COMING AND GOING

The bus station is about a 10-minute walk from "downtown"—the strip along the water that contains all of the hotels, restaurants, and rental shops. **Autotransportes de Baja California (ABC)** buses leave San Felipe's terminal (Mar Caribe, btw Manzanillo and the Pemex gas station, tel. 657/7–15–16) daily at 8 AM and 6 PM for Ensenada (3½ hrs, $7.50), and at 6 AM and 7:30 PM for Tijuana (5 hrs, $13). Buses leave for Mexicali five times daily (2½ hrs, $7.50). None venture onto the dirt roads south of San Felipe, however, so your best bet is to rent an ATV.

WHERE TO SLEEP

Hotels are expensive, so camping is your best option. There are plenty of RV trailerparks along Mar de Cortez, including **Playa Laura RV** (Mar de Cortez 333, tel. 657/7–11–28), which rents spaces for cars ($13) or pedestrian campers ($5); the managers will usually watch your bags. However, pitching a tent along the beach north of the trailer parks won't cost anything, and toilets (50¢) and showers ($1) are nearby. If you're lucky, you'll find an empty room at **José's House** (Manzanillo 244, no phone), where clean, air-conditioned singles and doubles cost $20 (including use of the kitchen and a big front porch). Look for the pink neon sign behind the tourist office. The wheelchair-accessible **Pelicano's Motel** (Mar de Cortez No. 472, tel. 657/7–15–70) has clean, air-conditioned rooms for $25. It's a few blocks north of the center of town but worth the walk.

FOOD

It's no surprise that the meal of choice in this fishing town is seafood. Fish and shrimp tacos, ceviche, and clams are served from picnic tables along the malecón for 60¢–$5. At **Restaurant y Mariscos Puerto Padre** (Mar de Cortez 316, tel. 657/7–13–35; open daily 7 AM–10 PM), you can order breakfast ($2) or a seafood entrée ($6). If the sun gets too hot, the air-conditioned **Los Gemelos** (Mar de Cortez 136, near Chetumal, tel. 657/7–10–63) serves seafood and Mexican dishes ($4) daily 6 AM–11 PM.

OUTDOOR ACTIVITIES The sandy desert that borders San Felipe to the west and the dunes and dirt roads to the south are inviting landscapes for motorcyclists and ATV riders. Rent a vehicle at **Bahía ATV** (malecón 122, no phone) for $11 an hour, or haggle for a full-day deal. Riding on the beach is illegal, so unless you're willing to risk the $100 fine, don't try it. The calm surf and strong winds of the Sea of Cortez are perfect for windsurfing; launch your sailboard at any beach south of **Punta Estrella**. Boards can be rented from **Charters Mar de Cortez** (El Dorado Travel Center, on Airport Rd., tel. 657/7–17–78 or 657/7–12–77) for $20 an hour. The wide beach in town is also good for catching rays, playing Frisbee, and swimming.

➤ **WATER SPORTS** • Locals and their generations-old fishing boats head out to sea from San Felipe. If you're broke, try to finagle tackle and a boat ride with a local in exchange for beer. Otherwise, **Tommy Sport Fishing** (Costero 176, no phone) organizes sportfishing tours—the catch often includes white sea bass, corvina, dorado, yellowtail, and other sea creatures. Trips require at least four people (five maximum) and cost $25 per person.

New in town and specializing in exotic adventures is **Enchanted Island Excursions** (tel. 657/7–14–31), located just outside San Felipe—call if you want them to pick you up. In addition to Hobie Cats ($10 per hr), Skippers (small boats; $20 per hr), and kayaks ($5 per hr), they have a fishing panga for rent for $100 per day. If you're out of Dramamine, you can take an off-road dune buggy tour (2 hrs, $15) or explore Indian caves, fossil fields, and waterfalls (8 hrs, $50). These guys also rent a "Party House" that sleeps up to 18 people for $100 a night.

San Quintín and Lázaro Cárdenas

The twin towns of San Quintín and Lázaro Cárdenas parallel Highway 1 for several kilometers, their ugly cinderblock stores and restaurants doing nothing to attract tourists. Separated by a bridge and 3 kilometers of highway, both towns lie humble and windblown, although Lázaro Cárdenas has more markets and restaurants to choose from. The towns are major stopping points along Highway 1, and it's a hell of a long bus ride to Guerrero Negro or San Felipe if you don't stretch your legs here for a while. Once you're thoroughly bored and cold, catch a bus out to your final destination.

BASICS In Lázaro Cárdenas, **Banco Internacional** (Ignacio L. Alcérraga, north side of park, tel. 616/5–21–01 or 616/5–21–02) has an ATM that accepts most bank cards. The bank will also change cash or traveler's checks weekdays 8–5 and Saturdays 9–2:30. At the south end of San Quintín, **Lavamática M.A.C.** (Hwy. 1, tel. 616/5–25–83; open Sun.–Thurs. 7 AM–8 PM and Friday 7–4) has automatic washers and dryers ($1 each). Pay an extra $1.50 and the staff will do the job for you. North of the bus station in Lázaro Cárdenas, **Farmacia del Parque** (tel. 616/5–26–65) is open 24 hours and works with English-speaking **Dr. Ricardo Rojo Marín**. You can make long-distance calls to the States here for $1 per minute, or a five-minute collect call for 50¢. In Lázaro Cárdenas, the **post office** (Carretera Transpeninsular, no phone) is open weekdays 8–5, Saturday 9–noon. They'll hold mail sent to you at the following address for up to 10 days: Lista de Correos, Valle de San Quintín, Baja California Norte, CP 22930, México.

COMING AND GOING First-class buses stop in San Quintín and at the **Autotransportes de Baja California (ABC)** bus station (Carretera Transpeninsular, tel. 616/5–30–50), at the southern end of Lázaro Cárdenas. From here, three buses a day head south toward La Paz (19 hrs, $31) at 1 PM, 5 PM, and 10 PM, stopping in Guerrero Negro (7 hrs, $12). Seven buses go north to Tijuana (5 hrs, $9) at 6 AM, 9 AM, 10 AM, noon, 3 PM, 5 PM and 7 PM, and three buses destined for Mexicali (7 hrs, $15) leave at 7 AM, 1 PM, and 4 PM, stopping in Ensenada (3½ hrs, $5.50). They'll store your luggage for free at the station, but there's nothing formal or secure about the setup. **Autotransportes Aragón**, a smaller station farther north, has more frequent buses to Ensenada and Tijuana.

GETTING AROUND San Quintín is 5 kilometers from the shoreline, right where a small peninsula branches off from the rest of Baja. To travel between San Quintín and Lázaro Cárdenas, catch a blue-and-white microbus (or the wheelchair-accessible green-and-yellow microbus) from anywhere along the highway. Microbuses run every 15 minutes 6–6. The best beach in the area, **Playa Santa María,** is not that exciting, and local transportation drops you off a good 3 kilometers from the beach, at which point you'll have to schlep with your backpack or take a $10 taxi from the plaza in San Quintín. You could hitch a ride with local fishermen, but it'll be hard to distinguish between you and the catch of the day when you get off. If you're driving, look for the HOTEL LA PINTA sign along the highway; the hotel is near the beach.

WHERE TO SLEEP AND EAT As there's nothing of interest in San Quintín or Lázaro Cárdenas, and as they're both a few miles from the beach, staying in town is a dismal prospect. If you really want to stay here, your best bet for lodging is to camp for free along the stretch of open, isolated coast (there's little protection from the wind, however). **Playa Santa María** is the easiest to reach—pitch your tent around Hotel La Pinta and use their bathrooms at no charge. If you're not prepared to camp, **Motel Romo** (Hwy. 1, tel. 616/5–23–96) is close to the bus station and has nice rooms with spotless baths for $10 a single and $12 a double; they accept MasterCard and Visa. Their popular restaurant is open daily 7 AM–11 PM, but if you want to taste the huge chocolate clams (named for the brown coloring on their edges) that are San Quintín's specialty, head to **Palapa El Paraíso** (300 meters north of Pemex in San Quintín, no phone), which dishes up huge plates of the steamed critters for $2. Lázaro Cárdenas has several cheap restaurants: Near the bus station, fill up on gigantic bean burritos or fish tacos with cilantro, guacamole, tomatoes, and onions at **El Gran Triunfo,** a white shack on the north side of Hotel Romo, open 24 hours. Adjoining the bus station is **Restaurante Herradero** (open daily 7 AM–10 PM), which serves fish tacos ($2) and a comida corrida for $2–$3.

Baja California Sur

Southern Baja is a land for escapists. Thrills here include camping, fishing, and swimming, exploring the miles of lonely beaches, and whalewatching (January–March). Highway 1 runs through a number of small towns, which, except for the French mining town of Santa Rosalía, bear the imprint of the Spanish missionaries who founded them as outposts of "civilization": Today, adobe missions built with Indian labor still survive. Dirt roads crisscross the Sierra (the mountainous interior), connecting isolated hamlets, ranches, abandoned missions, and small fishing villages.

Guerrero Negro

The only sign of civilization on the nine-hour drive between San Quintín and San Ignacio is the wind-chilled town of Guerrero Negro. Located on the dividing line between northern and southern Baja, Guerrero Negro greets visitors with a giant, metallic eagle adorned with bird's nests, which marks the exact middle of Baja California. Cacti and coyote fill the desert on one side of Guerrero Negro and on the other, across the San José estuary, near-white sand dunes rest like an unstraightened tablecloth. Except for a brief deluge of whale-watching tourists during the winter months, Guerrero Negro lives off the world's largest solar-evaporated salt mine. If evaporative salt-production techniques don't turn you on, there's no reason to stop in this town outside of whale-watching season.

If you *are* here during the whale-watching season, you're in for a treat. The salty waters that hug Guerro Negro's shores provide a seasonal home for the more than 20,000 gray whales who migrate from the Bering Sea to Baja. They come to birth their calves in the warm, calm waters of Scammon's Lagoon (27 kilometers south of town). This lagoon, also known as **Laguna Ojo de Liebre** (Hare's Eye Lagoon), is within the bounds of **Parque Natural de Ballena Gris** (Gray Whale Natural Park), established to protect the whales from poachers. Bring binoculars to better admire the spouts of water shooting high into the air and the huge 4-meter-wide flukes thundering against the water. Farther south, in **Laguna de San Ignacio,** you can hire a boat from local fishermen to get a spectacularly close view—the whales sometimes swim so close to the boat that you can touch their barnacle-encrusted backs. During the first two weekends of

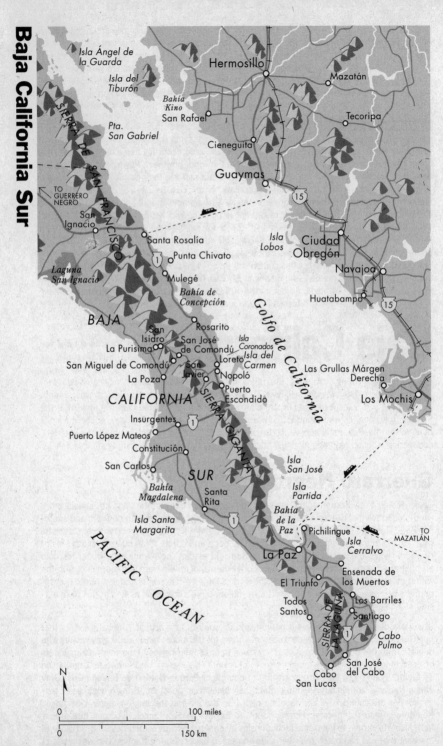

Baja California Sur

Isla Ángel de
la Guarda

Isla del
Tiburón

Bahía
Kino
San Rafael

Pta.
San Gabriel

Cieneguita

Hermosillo

Mazatán

Tecoripa

Guaymas

TO
GUERRERO
NEGRO

San
Ignacio

SIERRA DE SAN FRANCISCO

Santa Rosalía

Punta Chivato

Mulegé

Laguna
San Ignacio

Bahía de
Concepción

BAJA

San
Isidro

La Purisima

San Miguel de Comondú

La Poza

Rosarito

San José
de Comondú

San
Javier

Loreto

Nopoló

Puerto
Escondido

Isla
Coronados
Isla del
Carmen

CALIFORNIA

Insurgentes

Puerto López Mateos

Constitución

San Carlos

SIERRA GIGANTA

Isla
Lobos

Ciudad
Obregón

Navajoa

Huatabampo

15

Golfo de California

Las Grullas Márgen
Derecha

Los Mochis

SUR

Bahía
Magdalena

Santa
Rita

Isla Santa
Margarita

Isla
San José

Isla
Partida

Bahía
de la
Paz

Pichilingue

Isla
Cerralvo

TO
MAZATLÁN

La Paz

El Triunfo

Ensenada de
los Muertos

Todos
Santos

Los Barriles

Santiago

SIERRA DE LA LAGUNA

Cabo
Pulmo

San José
del Cabo

Cabo
San Lucas

PACIFIC OCEAN

N

0   100 miles

0   150 km

February the town honors these giants at the **Festival de Las Ballenas** (the Festival of the Whales), which features regional food, dances, and the selection of a local queen. In the plaza, you can see a 12-meter-long gray whale skeleton outside the **Biblioteca Pública**.

No public transportation goes to the Laguna de San Ignacio. If you want to hitchhike, look around the western part of town in the morning for tourists who can give you a ride back (you don't want to get stuck at the lagoon). You can also join an organized tour in town, although reservations are recommended, especially during January and February. **Cabañas Don Miguelito** (*see* Where to Sleep, *below*) runs day-long trips to the lagoon ($35 per person, including lunch) and to the hunting-oriented cave paintings ($60 per person) in the Sierra de San Francisco (*see* Near San Ignacio, *below*). Tours operate April–June and in October and November. **Tours Mario's** (inside Restaurant Mario's, tel. 115/7–08–88, fax 115/7–07–88) also organizes whale-watching trips and two-day tours to the cave paintings ($35 per person), both only available when the whales are around.

BASICS You can change money at **Banamex** (Av. Baja California, tel. 115/7–05–55; open weekdays 8:30–1), which also has an ATM that accepts Plus, Cirrus, Visa, and MasterCard. In case of emergency, try the 24-hour phone lines for **police** (tel. 115/7–16–15), **fire** (tel. 115/7–05–05), or **ambulance** (tel. 115/7–11–44). If you need medical attention, the **Clinica Hospital** (Zapata, tel. 115/7–04–33) is open 24 hours a day. Pick up prescriptions and do all of your long-distance chatting at **Farmacia San Martín** (Zapata, tel. 115/7–11–11; open Mon.–Sat. 8 AM–10 PM, Sun. 9–4), which charges $1 for collect calls and $2 per minute for calls to the States. Guerro's **post office** is on a sketchy, unnamed street—walk past the plaza and turn left at the Lion's Club. The office is open weekdays 8–3 and will hold mail for you for 10 days if sent to the following address: Lista de Correos, Guerrero Negro, Baja California Sur, CP 23940, México.

COMING AND GOING Autotransportes de Baja California (ABC) and **Águila** both serve the **Terminal de Autobuses** (near hwy. on motel strip, tel. 115/7–06–11). Six daily northbound buses pass through Guerrero Negro between 2:30 AM and 10 PM, stopping in San Quintín (7 hrs, $12.50), Ensenada (10 hrs, $19), and Tijuana (12 hrs, $22). Seven daily buses head south between 4 AM and 11 PM, stopping in San Ignacio (2 hrs, $5.50), Santa Rosalía (3 hrs, $7), Mulegé (4 hrs, $9), Loreto (6 hrs, $13), and La Paz (10–12 hrs, $24).

GETTING AROUND Guerrero Negro is divided into two very different halves: the old section around the square, and the new commercial and tourist strip on Zapata near the highway. A yellow minibus travels between the two every half hour, but it's only a 20- to 30-minute walk. Taxis are also an option, as is jumping in the back of some kind soul's truck. Dirt roads lead from town to Scammon's Lagoon and Bahía de Tortugas, but unless you're with a tour, you'll need your own transportation to reach either.

WHERE TO SLEEP Although the hotels near the bus station look cheap, only some are within the budget traveler's reach. All fill up December–March, so call ahead for reservations. In the new part of town, the more reasonable joints include **Hotel San Ignacio** (Zapata, tel. 115/7–02–70), with $13 singles and $14 doubles; **Motel Las Ballenas** (behind El Morro, tel. 115/7–01–16), where wheelchair-accessible singles cost $11 and doubles cost $13; and **Motel Brisa Salina** (Zapata, tel. 115/7–13–25), with $9 singles and $10 doubles. All of the rooms at these hotels have color TVs, but Motel Brisa Salina, with its well-kept courtyard, has the most charm of the three. On the right as you exit the bus station, look for **Malarrimo** (tel. 115/7–02–50 or 115/7–00–20), which has beautiful, quiet rooms in modern bungalows for $19 (singles) and $25 (doubles). Malarrimo is run by the same management as **Cabañas Don Miguelito**, an RV park that charges $10 per car space for two people (additional persons $3 each) and $4 for a tent space with two people. If the above hotels will break your budget, try **Motel Gámez** (Zapata, tel. 115/7–03–70), on the other side of town. The sheets and curtains droop forlornly, but singles and doubles with bath are just $7.

FOOD If you're passing through Guerrero Negro, you don't have to wander far from the bus terminal to eat well. Next door, **El Taco Feliz** (tel. 115/7–06–59; open daily 7 AM–11 PM) is recommended by locals and has great Mexican dishes ($2.50–$15). If you're lucky, the owner might even call up the local radio station and have them broadcast a *bienvenida* (welcome) for you. Around the first bend in Zapata there are a string of cheap eateries: **Café Alejandra** (just past the first Pemex station; open daily 7 AM–10 PM) sells $3 eggs and plain ol' $2 burgers. In the evenings, hot dog vendors hit the streets, selling dogs smothered in beans and chile for $1.

NEAR GUERRERO NEGRO

THE LONELY COAST About 35 kilometers southeast of Guerrero Negro is the hot, dry **Vizcaíno Desert,** which juts out into the Pacific Ocean. Although arid, this Biosphere Reserve is no barren wasteland: A few several-hundred-year-old plants, such as *tillandsia recurvata* (ball moss) and *datillo* (a.k.a. *yucca válida,* resembling the Joshua tree) manage to live in this harsh environment. Due to deep wells, the small farming community of **Ejido Vizcaíno** also thrives in the midst of the desert, producing crops such as tomatoes, onions, chiles, and grapes. At the peninsula's northern edge is a junk collector's dream come true: **Playa Malarrimo,** otherwise known as Scavenger's Beach. This shore lies perpendicular to the currents moving down Baja's Pacific coast, and acts as a junkyard for ocean debris. The southern side of the peninsula, from **Bahía de Tortugas** to **Punta Abreojos** (a prime surf spot) is an empty stretch of coastline. From January to mid-March, you can see whales calving in **Laguna Ojo de Liebre,** and sea turtles laying eggs in the small Bahía de Tortugas. In Guerrero Negro, **Mario's** (*see above*) gives tours to areas within the reserve, and the people at **Casa de la Fauna** (Domingo Carballo y Ruíz Cortínez, tel. and fax 115/7–17–77; open weekdays 8–4) have good maps and recommendations for exploring the area. To get here, take a bus towards San Ignacio and have the driver let you off at Ejido Vizcaíno. Ask around there for a guide; for a small fee, someone will undoubtedly show you around.

San Ignacio

The lush town of San Ignacio rests over an underground stream that brings the desert to life with birds, insects, flowers, and fruit trees. Date palms, introduced by Jesuit missionaries, dominate the landscape. This is a good departure point for whalewatching in **Laguna de San Ignacio** or exploring 300-year-old Rupestrian cave paintings in the **Sierra de San Francisco** and the **Sierra de Santa Marta.** If you arrive from northern Baja, San Ignacio is the first town you'll encounter laid out in traditional Mexican fashion, with a zócalo at the center of everything. Life for San Ignacio's residents revolves around this tree-shaded square and the adjacent **Misión San Ignacio de Loyola.** Jesuits began constructing the mission's 4-foot-thick walls out of volcanic rock in 1716, but the structure wasn't completed until the Dominicans took over and finished the job in 1786. A particularly beautiful mass is held here Sundays at 11 AM. Next door, the **Museo Local de San Ignacio** (admission free; open weekdays 9–4, Sat. 9–noon) has displays (in Spanish) on the cave paintings, including photographs and a small replica in the back.

Boojum Trees

Straight out of a Dr. Seuss book, this oddly shaped species has been described most accurately as an upside-down carrot. Outliving seven human generations and growing up to 27 meters tall, boojum trees tower over their neighbors: datillos, elephant trees, and giant cardon cacti. Boojums are endemic to a small region in Baja California, stretching from El Rosarío in the north to Las Tres Vírgenes near San Ignacio in the south, and they can be best seen from Highway 1 at Cataviña, one hour south of Guerrero Negro. A small colony also exists in the Sonoran desert. The boojum's common name, cirio, originated when Spanish missionaries noticed a resemblance between the slender candles used in church services (cirios) and the hanging yellow flowers of the tree.

Many of the buildings around the square, shaded by Indian laurel trees, are more than a century old, their adobe walls sometimes peeking through new layers of plaster and paint. If you're here in the fall, you can pick dates and grapes and make homemade wine, another legacy of the missionaries. Sample the local wine, goat cheese, and *cajeta* (a sweet made from goat's milk) from the nearby ranches at the markets on the plaza. Residents of San Ignacio used to live off the land, but the town is now primarily a supply center, and several residents have migrated to the coast to earn their living fishing. Many return by July 27, though, to get their fill of mariachi music and Tecate beer at San Ignacio's five-day fiesta.

BASICS You can get auto parts and 24-hour service at **Autopartes Cadena** (south side of highway, where the bus stops, no phone; open 24 hrs). The **Centro de Salud** (Independencia, at Valdina, no phone; open weekdays 8–2 and 4–6, Sat. 9–1) has an English-speaking doctor. Make long-distance phone calls at **Video Club Premiere** (on the plaza next to Jorge Fischer's store, tel. 115/4–03–97), where calls to the United States are $1.50 per minute (sorry, no collect or credit card calls). The **post office** (open weekdays 8–3) is directly across the plaza from the video club. For information about the town and the surrounding area, ask Jorge Fischer at his grocery store/**tourist information center** on the plaza (tel. 115/4–01–50; open daily 8–7). You can make reservations for his cave-painting and whale-watching tours (a good idea if you plan to be in the area Jan.–Mar.) by writing to him at: Domicilio Conocido, San Ignacio, Baja California Sur, CP 23930, México.

COMING AND GOING The bus station consists of two shaded benches on the highway, 3 kilometers outside town. The one next to the Pemex station is the stop for buses going north; cross the street for southbound buses. Seven buses go south to La Paz (6 hrs, $19) every day between 6 AM and 1 AM. Buses headed north to Tijuana (14 hrs, $17) and Ensenada (12 hrs, $15) pass through town five times a day. The staff at the store next to the Pemex station can tell you about changes in schedule, but you have to buy your ticket on the bus. The Pemex station is also an easy place to hitch a ride. The only way to ride from the bus stop into town is by taxi ($2), but the walk is pleasant, if sweaty. To return to the station, find one of the taxis that hover around the plaza day and night. If you're traveling by car, the road from Highway 1 to San Ignacio is easy, safe, and relatively well marked. The only thing you have to watch out for is tailgating, kamikaze bus drivers.

WHERE TO SLEEP San Ignacio may be restful, but unless you're prepared to camp, it's not a cheap place to spend the night. Running water is often sporadic, so check the sink before you sign in. **Motel Posada** (Carranza, tel. 115/4–03–13) offers clean rooms with the most reliable water supply in town (singles and doubles $20). To get here, follow the curving road that runs from the front of the mission. If you prefer to stay in a local home, **Restaurant Chalita** (*see* Food, *below*) has two small, stuffy rooms ($11 singles or doubles). Although there's a private entrance, the friendly family encourages you to walk through their kitchen and backyard gardens. They also serve the best meals in town.

➢ **CAMPING** • San Ignacio has several fairly cheap campgrounds, although most have backbreakingly hard ground or are infested with insects. The best is **Las Candelarias,** a few hundred meters down the dirt road. Here you can camp for $2 in a well-maintained grove of date palms, but the bathrooms are simple outhouses without showers. The best swimming hole around is also here, which is free whether or not you're a guest. Right next door, **Trailer Park El Padrino** (1½ kilometers south of Hwy. 1, near Hotel La Pinta, tel. 115/4–00–89) provides campgrounds, toilets, and showers ($7 per car), and their on-site restaurant serves cold beer and margaritas ($1.50).

FOOD There are only a few restaurants in town, the best of which is **Restaurant Chalita** (Hidalgo 9, west side of zócalo, tel. 115/4–00–82), where the elderly owners have turned their living room into a restaurant. The comida corrida costs $3, while the Mexican à la carte menu is $2–$4. **Rene's Restaurant/Bar** (Hidalgo 39, no phone) has a thatched roof, a variety of breakfasts (including french toast; $2), and two evening dinners of fish ($5) or shrimp ($7). Jorge Fischer's

Artículos de Segunda Mano, a shack on the only road behind the mission, sells used furniture and trinkets; if nobody is there, just hop the fence and walk through the field to take a peek.

CONASUP grocery store (Hidalgo, on the plaza, tel. 115/4–01–90) has fresh fruits and veggies, as well as supermarket stuff.

NEAR SAN IGNACIO

Gray whales stop in **Laguna de San Ignacio** between January and March as they migrate from Alaska to Baja. The lagoon is two hours southwest of San Ignacio, 74 kilometers (46 mi) along rough dirt roads, so you'll need to drive a sturdy car, hitch (and expect to be stranded for a while), or hire a guide (*see below*). Once there, hire a local fisherman to take you out in his boat (about $20). A little south of the lagoon is **Punta Abreojos,** a local surf spot with no amenities. To reach these places, follow Highway 1 south and watch for signs leading you to the dirt roads.

To reach the **cave paintings** in Sierra de San Francisco and Sierra de Santa Marta from San Ignacio, you'll need to make a mule-back trek through Baja's high desert mountains. The trip is spectacular in its own right, and the caves are one of Baja's most incredible experiences. The now-faded, multicolored paintings depict giant men, fish, deer, hunting scenes, and religious rituals. When the missions in the area declined, many indigenous Baja Californians fled to the Sierra de San Francisco, where their descendants remain today, living off their gardens, goats, and, more recently, fees from guiding visitors to the caves. If you're entering the caves on your own you must first register with the INAH (Institutio Nacional de Antropolgía e Historia) in Hermosillo or let your guide do it for you. To reach the trailhead, you'll need to drive or hitch; finding a guide at the caves is no problem, however—they foist themselves on visitors. Admission to the caves, including guide, is $10; mules to get you from cave to cave cost another $10 per day, and the trip to Sierra de San Francisco takes two to three days.

If you don't have your own transportation and don't want to hitch, talk to Oscar Fischer of San Ignacio's Motel Posada (*see* Where to Sleep, *above*), or his nephew, Jorge Fischer (*see* Basics, *above*). Both take up to six people on day-long trips to the caves for $120 (price includes guide and transportation by both car and mule). Jorge Fischer will drive you to Rancho San Francisco or Rancho Santa Marta, where you head out on mules to explore the caves. If you don't want to go back to San Ignacio immediately, you can camp at the caves, where the guides from the ranch cook dinner. Oscar also runs tours to the Laguna San Ignacio ($45 per person), a two-hour drive and two-hour boat ride. Jorge will do it for $20–$120 per person, depending on the number of people and type of boat. Whalewatching is better and cheaper from Guerrero Negro (*see above*).

Santa Rosalía

Traveling south down Highway 1, Santa Rosalía is the first town on the Sea of Cortez. Founded by a French copper-mining company in the mid-1800s, Santa Rosalía looks unlike any other town in Mexico: French-style buildings constructed with imported European wood have long, sloping roofs hanging over small, fenced porches. *Mecedoras* (rocking chairs) also seem to be an obligatory addition to every house. Santa Rosalía was laid out in a regimented fashion, with rows of identical houses corresponding to various ranks within the company, and the old residences of French mining officials sit high above the canyon where the town lies. Some locals have blond hair or East Indian features, testament to the varied ancestry of the town's original workers, which included native Californian, French, East Indian, and Chinese people.

Santa Rosalía is home to the Iglesia Santa Bárbara, a prefabricated iron church designed by Alexandre Gustave Eiffel (of Tower fame) and imported from Europe by the mining company that founded the town.

When the mining company left in the early 1950s, Santa Rosalía's economy hit a slump and never recovered. Today, most residents make their living from the sea or by working in plaster mines on nearby Isla de San Marcos. Santa Rosalía is one of Baja's poorer towns, with an unkempt central square and houses in need of repainting. But while lodgings in this town may be a little sketchy, locals are kind to strangers—in two days you'll recognize everyone and everyone will recognize you. There are no good beaches in Santa Rosalía proper; explorers must go 3 kilometers north of town to rocky **Playa Santa María** for surf and chocolate-clam digging. Unsociable beachgoers can travel a little further to the more isolated shoreline near the fishing village of **Punta Chivato.**

BASICS **Autopartes Plaza** (Constitución, tel. 115/2–12–34; open daily 8 AM–9 PM) has a helpful, English-speaking staff and almost any car part you could need. You can change cash and traveler's checks weekdays 8:30–2 at **Bancomer** (tel. 115/2–02–65) and **Banamex** (tel. 115/2–09–84), both on Obregón, at Altamirano. They also give cash advances on Visa and MasterCard. There are new, working Ladatel **phones** on the plaza and around town. You can make collect calls by dialing 09 from the pay phone outside the ferry terminal (*see below*). The **post office** (Constitución, btw Calle 2 and Altamirano, tel. 115/2–03–44) is open weekdays 8–3, Saturday 8–noon. They'll hold mail sent to the following address for 10 days: Lista de Correos, Avenida Constitución, Santa Rosalía, Baja California Sur, CP 23920, México.

The **police** can be reached at 115/2–02–90 or 115/2–05–05; the **fire department** can be reached at 115/2–01–88, and the number for the **Cruz Roja** is 115/2–06–40. For less urgent medical attention, try **Farmacia Central** (Obregón, at Plaza, tel. 115/2–20–70, fax 115/2–22–70), where the English-speaking Dr. Eduardo Antonio Chang Tam can help with general medical problems. The pharmacy, open Monday–Saturday 9 AM–10 PM and Sunday 9–1 and 7–10, also has fax service and a caseta de larga distancia, but calls must be paid for in cash.

COMING AND GOING

➢ **BY BUS** • **Autobuses de Baja California (ABC)** (tel. 115/2–01–50) buses run from the terminal south of town on Highway 1, a quick taxi ride ($1.50) or 10-minute walk from downtown. Seven buses head south daily between 8 AM and 2 AM, stopping in Mulegé (1 hr, $2.50), Loreto (3 hrs, $6), and La Paz (8 hrs, $15). Five buses a day go north to Mexicali (16 hrs, $34), stopping in Guerrero Negro (3 hrs, $7) and Tijuana (14 hrs, $28). To reach the beach at Punta Chivato, hop on any southbound bus and ask the driver to let you off. You can also try to catch a ride at the Pemex station, located on Highway 1 before the bus terminal.

➢ **BY FERRY** • **Sematur,** off Highway 1 and a 5-minute walk from the center of town, offers biweekly ferry service from Santa Rosalía to Guaymas, in the state of Sonora. Ferries to Guaymas (7 hrs) leave Wednesday and Sunday at 8 AM; seats cost $13.50 and a bed in a four-person cabin costs $47. To bring a car to the mainland, get a car permit from the **Delegación de Servicios Migratorios** offices, located next to the ferry office (for more information, *see* Chapter 1). The office is open sporadically; the best time to catch them is around 3 PM on Tuesdays and Fridays, when the ferry arrives from Guaymas. *Pier south of town, tel. 115/2–00–13 or 115/2–00–14.*

WHERE TO SLEEP The huge front porch of the 110-year-old **Hotel Francés** (Jean Mitchel Cousteau, tel. 115/2–20–52) is an excellent place to sip a margarita ($2) while enjoying fresh seafood ($7–$10) and a view of the sea. The wood-furnished rooms with showers and bathtubs ($26 singles and doubles) include use of the pool and are a worthwhile splurge. Newly painted to cover up cosmetic defects, the **Hotel Minos** (Obregón, at Calle 10, tel. 115/2–10–60) charges $17 for singles or doubles with air-conditioning and TVs. A cheaper option is the clean and centrally located **Hotel Olvera** (Plaza 14, tel. 115/2–00–57). A single room with a TV costs $9, doubles are $11 ($13 with air-conditioning). The closest place to camp is **RV Park San Lucas Cove,** on the beach 14 kilometers south of Santa Rosalía, off Highway 1. They charge $6 a night per vehicle, and have 20 campsites with new flush toilets and hot showers.

FOOD Santa Rosalía has a few decent restaurants, but the stands selling fresh fish tacos during the day and beef tacos or quesadillas at night are the way to eat well. Be sure to get your snacks before 10 PM, however, as nothing stays open later. For a sit-down meal, **Steak House Don Ramón** (Constitución, at Plaza, no phone; open Mon.–Sat. 8:30 AM–10 PM) serves breakfasts of chimichangas ($2) or cheese omelets ($2.50), and charges $2.50–$3 for most Mexican entrées. Be sure to stop by **Panadería El Boleo** (Revolución, at Calle 4a; open daily 8–7:30), a bakery founded by the French mining company to supply the town with baguettes. If you're up before 8 AM, peek through the side doors and watch the bakers loading dough into brick wood-burning ovens.

OUTDOOR ACTIVITIES Other than poking around the rusty locomotives and copperworks (officially closed to the public) near the harbor breakwater, there's not much to do here but read in the shade, sweat in the sun, or fish. If the latter sounds fun, talk to English-speaking Ángel Jesús Rodríguez (tel. 115/2–00–11), who works at the **Santa Rosalía Marina** (on the water where Americans anchor their yachts) Monday–Saturday 8–3. His friends take tourist groups on fishing trips ($20 per person, $100 minumum): a five- to six-hour trip in a boat that fits five people. Landlubbers can take a walk up the hill to the Hotel Francés (*see* Where to Sleep, *above*)—a good place to admire the large houses in *La colonia francesa* (the French neighborhood) and spectacular views.

Mulegé

The Santa Rosalía River courses through Mulegé, watering the small forest of date palms and creating a seaside desert oasis just 18 kilometers north of the spectacular beaches of **Bahía de Concepción.** The calm, warm waters here, in a wide spectrum of blues, contrast sharply with the surrounding semidesert landscape. Mulegé's own rocky beach lies at the mouth of the river, 2 kilometers east of town along the main road; although the beach is not as white-sand spectacular as those farther south, it's a pleasant place to walk and okay for swimming. Best of all, camping here is free. Mulegé is also a popular departure point for trips to the Cochimi Indian cave paintings in the surrounding area (*see* Tours and Guides, *below*).

Although everything from T-shirt and curio shops to recently paved roads caters to the town's tourist industry, Mulegé hasn't completely lost its small-town charm, and still harbors remnants of its traditional past. One such relic is the **Misión Santa Rosalía de Mulegé,** built in 1766 and reconstructed in the early 1970s. To reach the mission, follow Calle Zaragoza south from the plaza and turn right after you pass under the bridge. Follow the road up the hill to the mission and you'll be rewarded with views of the town and a sea of date palms. The free **Museo Mulegé** (open daily 9–1) is housed in a building overlooking the town on the north bank of the hill on the far north side of town. The structure functioned as a prison from 1906 to 1975, and now houses artifacts from the original mission, old mining lamps from Santa Rosalía, and arrowheads that were dug up in the area. To reach the museum, take Calle Principal to the dirt path at the base of the hill and start walking up.

BASICS For auto parts and service, talk to the folks at **Refaccionaria Mulegé** (Gral. Martínez, at Zaragoza, tel. 115/3–00–41; open Mon.–Sat. 8–1 and 3–7). Mulegé doesn't have a bank, but if you have to change money, **El Peso de Oro** (Moctezuma 7, no phone; open Mon.–Sat. 9–1 and 3–7) will change cash and traveler's checks. You can wash clothes at **Lavamática Claudia** (Moctezuma, tel. 115/3–00–57; open Mon.–Sat. 8–6). Free collect calls can be placed at the **Minisuper Padillo** (Zaragoza and Martínez, tel. 115/3–01–90; open Mon.–Sat. 8 AM–9 PM), which also serves as a supply center for your drug needs.

➤ **TOURS AND GUIDES** • The tourist office is run by Javier, the owner of **Hotel and Restaurant Las Casitas** (Madero 50, tel. 115/3–00–19). He can provide you with information on kayaking tours, fishing expeditions, and trips to see the Cochimi Indian cave paintings in Trinidad, San Borjitas, and Piedras Pintas. These cave paintings depict traditional hunting and religious rituals and are said to be more than 14,000 years old. To reach the paintings, you need to go with a guide; the best in town is **Kerry Otterstrom,** who has written a book on the area, *Mulegé–Baja California Sur: the Complete Tourism, Souvenir and Historical Guide of Mulegé,* available at **Mulegé Divers** (*see* Outdoor Activities, *below*). Unfortunately, he has no phone number and is difficult to reach; you can try to hunt him down at the restaurant **El Candil** (cnr of Zaragoza and Madero) daily between 4 and 6 PM. Otherwise, **Ramón Monroy** leads tours to San Borjitas—look for him at his restaurant (Plaza Márquez de León, at Col. Benavides, tel. 115/3–02–23), distinguished by a 6-foot chicken painted on the door. The day-long tours cost $55 per person, but Ramón is willing to negotiate.

COMING AND GOING Mulegé is small and easy to navigate. If you don't have a car, it's a 30-minute walk or a five-minute bus ride to Mulegé's beach. The better beaches of Bahía de

Concepción are too far away to reach on foot, but it's easy to hitchhike. You can also catch a southbound bus from town to the beach; flag down one heading north to return to Mulegé.

At the entrance to town (the "Y") is a shaded bench that functions as the bus station. You can buy tickets for the bus at the terminal that doubles as a restaurant just behind the bench. Seven northbound buses pass through, with stops in Santa Rosalía (1 hr, $2) and Tijuana (15 hrs, $31). Eight buses per day go south to Loreto (2 hrs, $4) and La Paz (7 hrs, $15). You can ask at the terminal when the buses are expected to pass, but you should arrive a half hour early and be prepared to wait—schedules are rarely kept. Buy your tickets a day before traveling to guarantee yourself a seat.

WHERE TO SLEEP Most beds for rent in Mulegé start at $15, but three guest houses offer cheaper, simpler rooms. At **Casa de Huéspedes Manuelita's** (Moctezuma, tel. 115/3–01–75) the facilities are spartan, but the private baths are fairly clean, and you pay only $5.50 for a single, $7 for a double. At **Casa de Huéspedes Canett** (Francisco, at Madero, tel. 115/3–02–72), singles with rickety beds and acceptable baths cost $3.50 (doubles $7). **Hotel Suites Rosita** (Madero 2, no phone) is a deal if you're traveling with friends. The huge apartment-style rooms come complete with kitchenette, living room, and air-conditioning, and cost $17 for up to four people.

➤ **CAMPING** • Camping is free on Mulegé's beach (the southern end is less rocky) 3 kilometers east of town, but it's not as safe or as peaceful as the beaches farther south. **Orchard RV Park Resort** (south side of river, tel. 115/3–03–00), a ½kilometer walk from town, is the closest and most deluxe campground, with clean, white-tiled bathrooms, a volleyball court, bonfire pit, and shady fruit trees. One person in a tent costs $6, two people $7, and space for an RV costs $15. Farther up the road is **Villa María Isabel** (tel. 115/3–02–21), a smaller RV park with laundry service, a pool, and a delicious bakery (bakery open Oct.–June). Tent camping costs $5 per person with use of all on-site facilities.

FOOD Restaurants in Mulegé are not cheap, but they're worth the extra money. The most inexpensive ones are near the bus stop on Highway 1: Join the crowds waiting for great guacamole at **Taquería Doney's** (righthand side of Moctezuma, 1 block west of the bus station; open Thurs.–Tues. noon–10 PM). Directly across from the bus station, **La Cabaña** (Moctezuma, no phone; open daily 8–8) serves an egg-and-tortilla breakfast for $2, as well as Mexican lunch and dinner plates for $2.50–$4. On Fridays from October to June, head for **Las Casitas** (Madero 50, tel. 115/3–00–19) for the "mariachi buffet" ($5), a huge Mexican dinner accompanied by live mariachi music. Mexican and seafood dishes of all kinds are served for $6–$10. The restaurant is open daily 7 AM–10 PM, except on the weekends when they open up the place as a disco (open 7 PM–2 AM). If you get a sudden craving for chocolate-chip cookies (60¢), try the bakery at Villa María Isabel (see Camping, above).

OUTDOOR ACTIVITIES **Baja Tropicales** at Hotel Las Casitas (Madero 50, tel. 115/3–00–19) rents kayaks ($25–$35 per day) so you can paddle along the river among the date palms. Roy and Becky of **Mexico Adventures** (Palapa 17, in front of Ana's Restaurant on Playa Santispac, tel. 115/3–04–09) charges $25 per day for a kayak, $30 with drinks. They also rent snorkeling gear for $5 per day. Tours of Bahía de Concepción with a knowledgeable, English-speaking guide can also be arranged for $39, which includes a lunch of clams that you collect yourself. For fishing trips, the best in town is Mario Yee at **Captain's Sport Fishing** (fax 115/3–02–69), who has day-long expeditions for $150. The folks at Las Casitas (see Food, above) know where to find him.

The warm, plankton-rich waters here usually offer good visibility and teem with colorful aquatic life. The best diving spots are off the Santa Inez Islands and are accessible only by boat. Miguel and Claudia at **Mulegé Divers** offer snorkeling trips for $20 ($25 with gear; $10 for gear only) and scuba-diving forays, which run $40–$50 per person, depending on how much equipment you rent. They also rent bikes at $10 for four hours (minimum) and $2 per hour after that. *Gral. Martínez, tel. 115/3–00–59. Open Mon.–Sat. 9–1 and 3–6.*

NEAR MULEGÉ

BAHIA DE CONCEPCION The most beautiful bays in Baja lie along Highway 1, 32 kilometers (20 mi) south of Mulegé. The highway runs along 40 curvy kilometers of coastline, where hidden coves open onto white-sand beaches and electric-blue water—excellent for snorkeling, scuba diving, kayaking, swimming, and windsurfing. The first beach you'll hit heading south is **Playa Punta Arena** (20 km south of Mulegé on Highway 1), popular among sailboarders. **Playa Santispac**, 24 kilometers (15 mi) south of Mulegé, can turn into RV-camper hell overnight, but for the most part it's a mellow stretch of sand with good facilities. Local entrepreneurs provide tourists with palapas ($5 per night), showers ($1), and fairly inexpensive restaurants. Sign up with **Baja Tropicales** (next to Playa Posada Concepción, fax 115/3–01–90) for a $39 kayaking excursion, complete with a guide knowledgeable about the birds, fish, and shells of the area. Snorkeling gear is an affordable $5. A few kilometers to the south, the beautiful beaches of **Playa Escondida, Playa Los Cocos, Bahía Los Burros,** and **El Coyote** remain unexplored, and have more modest facilities (i.e., pit toilets and scattered palapas). **Playa Requesón,** 14 kilometers (8 mi) south of El Coyote, surrounds a bay so shallow that you can walk across the sand bar to a small volcanic island. To reach any of these places, catch a southbound bus from Mulegé and ask the driver to drop you off on the highway in front of any of the beaches.

Loreto

Life in Loreto revolves around fishing and not much else. For many years, this town was only accessible to the wealthy or adventurous who flew in on private planes or arrived by yacht. Today it plays host to fishermen from all over, who cast for dolphin fish, marlin, and sailfish. The beaches in Loreto are small and grungy; a more popular diversion is the reefs around **Isla del Carmen, Isla Coronada,** and **Isla Danzante,** which offer good diving and snorkeling. However, both Mexican and gringo residents don't exactly welcome newcomers with open arms, so you'll probably want to make your stay here a short one.

If you do stop here, two sights in Loreto are worth your time. The **Misión de Nuestra Señora de Loreto,** built in the late 1600s in the shape of a Greek cross, was the first of Baja's missions and is still the town's social and religious center. Beautifully restored in the early 1970s, the chapel is impressive for its masonry, wood ceiling beams, and gilded altar bearing the figure of the **Virgen de Loreto**—famous throughout Baja for her miraculous powers. Every September 8, the statue is paraded down from her mountain shrine to Loreto, where a fiesta with music, dancing, eating, and drinking is held in her honor. Next to the church is the **Museo de las Misiones** (tel. 113/5–04–41; admission $1.50; open daily 10–5), which features relics from missions throughout Mexico.

Stingrays are known to lurk in the sand off Loreto's beaches; as you walk though the water, shuffle your feet to scare them off. Their bites hurt for 3–5 hours and should be cleaned thoroughly with boiling water to prevent infection.

BASICS You can change money at **Bancomer** (Salvatierra, at Madero, tel. 113/5–03–15; open weekdays 8–2:30) and let the people at **Lavandería El Remojón** (Salvatierra 79, no phone; open Mon.–Sat. 8–8, Sun. 8–2) do your duds, although they aren't always around. For medical attention, look for the English-speaking Dr. Moreno at the **Centro de Salud** (Salvatierra 71, near Hotel Salvatierra, tel. 113/5–00–39; open 24 hrs). Pick up prescriptions and supplies from **Farmacia de la California** (Salvatierra 66, tel. 113/5–03–41; open daily 8 AM–10 PM). Make long-distance phone calls at **Caseta Soledad** (Salvatierra, tel. 113/5–03–50; open Mon.–Sat. 8–1 and 3–9, Sun. 8–1), where collect and credit card calls are $1.50. Send mom a postcard from the **post office** (Deportiva, tel. 113/5–06–47; open weekdays 8–3, Sat. 9–1). For visitor info, the **tourist office** (Palacio del Gobierno, on Madero, tel. 113/5–04–11) is open weekdays 8–5.

COMING AND GOING The bus station (tel. 113/5–07–67), served by **Autotransportes de Baja California (ABC)** and **Águila,** is at the beginning of Salvatierra and Paseo Tamará, a 10-minute walk east of the town center. Five buses a day travel south to La Paz (5 hrs, $10) between 8 AM and midnight. Northbound buses to Tijuana (18 hrs, $35) leave at 3 PM and 9 PM; two others bound for Santa Rosalía (3 hrs, $6) leave at 2 PM and 5 PM. Morning buses heading in either direction are often very crowded, but after a stop or two, there's more room.

WHERE TO SLEEP Most hotels in Loreto are geared toward anglers who have a larger lodging allowance than the average budget traveler. If you can forgo the facilities, camp for free on Loreto's beaches. Camping at **Loremar** (Zaragoza and Green, 1 km south of town) or **El Moro RV Park** (closer to the center, on Rosendo Robles) is also cheap; Loremar is nicer, though, and offers camping for three people, toilets, and showers for $10.

Although **Hotel Salvatierra** (Salvatierra 123, tel. 113/5–00–21) is not the cheapest hotel in town or the closest to the water, its rooms are clean and air-conditioned, and both singles ($11) and doubles ($15) have great bathrooms. It's only a five- or 10-minute walk to the town plaza from here, and the bus station is almost next door. **Hotel San Martín** (Juárez 4, at Davis, tel. 113/4–04–42) caters to young travelers from all over the world in this less-than-backpacker-friendly town. Singles and doubles with fans are $7 and $9 (respectively), but the hotel might be closed during the off-season (July and August).

FOOD The cheapest restaurants in Loreto are on Hidalgo, at the fork in Salvatierra. Of these, **Restaurant Acapulco** (open daily 6:30 AM–8 PM) takes the cake with its enormous comidas corridas ($2) and friendly clientele. Sit at a sunny table outside **Café Olé** (Madero, near zócalo, tel. 113/3–04–96; open daily 7 AM–10 PM) and enjoy oatmeal and fruit salad ($2) for breakfast and banana splits ($2.50) for dessert. For seafood, follow the fisherfolk to **Embarcadero** (Calle de la Playa, up from Hotel La Misión, tel. 113/5–01–65). Steamed clams are $4, and a fish dinner is $5 (slightly cheaper if you bring your own fish). They're open Thursday–Tuesday 7 AM–9 PM.

OUTDOOR ACTIVITIES Prices for fishing trips vary, so shop around: Ask the fishermen coming into the marina in the afternoon, or befriend a tourist with a private boat. **Alfredo's Sport Fishing** (Calle de la Playa, tel. 113/5–01–32) offers excursions costing a hefty $100 for two people (negotiable during the low season; boat and fishing licenses included), plus $8 per rod. Alfredo's also rents cars for $56 per day or 25¢ per kilometer. To rent a car for the trip to San Javier (*see* Near Loreto, *below*), they charge $57. **Diamond Eden Loreto** (6½ km south of town, tel. 113/3–03–77) rents equipment and arranges fishing ($120 for 2 people) and kayaking excursions for an equally hefty sum.

Islas del Carmen, Coronado, and Danzante are the best places for scuba divers to see dorado, yellowtail, sailfish, roosterfish, and even sea lions. Snorkeling is also popular in the shallow water surrounding Nopoló and Puerto Escondido. **Deportes Blazer** (Hidalgo 23, tel. 113/5–09–11; open Mon.–Sat. 9–1 and 3–7) rents scuba equipment for $27 and snorkeling gear for $8. You can also just rent tanks ($7). Guided underwater tours aren't offered, but the staff has good advice for those doing it on their own.

NEAR LORETO

SAN JAVIER The one-street village of San Javier is in the mountains, 32 kilometers southwest of Loreto. The main reason to make the one-hour trek from Loreto is to see the beautiful **Misión de San Javier,** a well-preserved mission built in Moorish style, with domes and exquisitely detailed stone carvings. Construction on the mission began in 1699, but was abandoned two years afterwards due to Indian attacks. The mission was finally finished in 1759. The town and surrounding ranches are more modest than the mission—most people here grow their own food and herd goats. Their houses consist of large palapas with a small adobe building for cooking and storing belongings. Days in this mountain desert are hot and the sunlight is punishing, but the evenings are quiet and beautiful. If you're in the area December 1–3, don't miss the big **Fiesta de San Javier,** which resounds with music, dancing, drinking, and horse races. The road from Loreto to San Javier is rough, and while taxis do make the trip for a large sum ($50), it's best driven in a high-clearance car or jeep; from Loreto's center, head east into the mountains, following the road marked with an arrow off Highway 1. You can camp for free in San Javier near the dam, or rent a room from Doña Elena; ask around. Bring your own bottled water, as it's not sold up here.

La Paz

Although beautiful desert beaches are only 15 minutes away by bus, La Paz is not a beach town. Rather, this capital of southern Baja is a sophisticated city with a university and a good museum. If you're coming from the backroads of Baja, the size of La Paz may come as a shock, but the city maintains an intimate and friendly atmosphere; in a matter of hours you'll be able to navigate between the downtown area and the malecón, stopping to greet people along the way. Tourists do come here, but the new airport outside Los Cabos is causing many to bypass La Paz altogether. Mainland-bound travelers are most likely to pass through on their way to pick up the ferry to Mazatlán or Los Mochis. Those who don't stop miss out: The ocean surrounding La Paz contains spectacular rocky reefs, a black coral forest, and an enormous variety of marine life. Visitors here can also enjoy excellent scuba diving, snorkeling, and kayaking.

Forget the crowded, overpriced gringoville of Cabo San Lucas and get your rest 'n' relaxation in La Paz, a big city with excellent beaches and the most culture on the peninsula.

La Paz was founded by Hernán Cortés in 1535 during his search for pearls (pearl diving continued until the 1940s) and was developed by Jesuit missionaries. The town's social life is split between the zócalo and the malecón, which is lined with restaurants and bars. On weekend evenings, after older residents have finished their promenade along the water, the malecón transforms into a hangout spot for local youth.

BASICS

AMERICAN EXPRESS The travel agency **Turismo La Paz** provides AmEx services, including personal check–cashing for cardholders; they'll hold letters (not packages) for up to one month. *Esquerro 1679, La Paz, Baja California Sur, CP 23000, México, tel. 112/2–76–76 or 112/2–83–00. Behind Hotel Perla. Open weekdays 9–2 and 4–6, Sat. 9–2.*

CASAS DE CAMBIO **Banco Mexicano** (Arreola, at Esquerro, tel. 112/2–31–55) has shorter lines than AmEx (across the street) and changes cash and traveler's checks weekdays 8:30–1:30. However, AmEx has a 24-hour ATM that accepts Visa, MasterCard, Cirrus, and Plus.

EMERGENCIES You can dial 06 from any phone in La Paz to reach the **police, fire** department, or an **ambulance.**

MAIL The post office is one block from the main plaza. They'll hold mail sent to you at the following address for up to 10 days: Lista de Correos, Centro La Paz, Baja California Sur, CP 23000, México. *Revolución, at Constitución, tel. 112/2–03–88. Open weekdays 8–7, Sat. 9–1.*

MEDICAL AID For serious medical attention, the **Centro de Salud,** on the corner of Altamirano and 5 de Mayo, is open weekdays 8–8. The **Cruz Roja** (Domínguez, between Bravo and Ocampo, tel. 112/2–11–11) is open 24 hours. Less urgent problems can be solved at the **Farmacia Baja California** (Madero, on plaza, tel. 112/2–02–40), open Monday–Saturday 7 AM–11 PM, Sunday 8 AM–10 PM.

PHONES You can make collect calls from any pay phone by dialing 09. **Librería Contempo** (Arreola 25-A, at Obregón, tel. 112/2–78–75) has long-distance phones ($1.50 a minute to the U.S.) and is a good place for a private conversation. *Open weekdays 10–3:30 and 5–9:30, Sat. 10–9:30, Sun. 9–5.*

VISITOR INFORMATION The staff at the tourist office is knowledgeable and speaks English, but be prepared to ask lots of questions, because they don't offer information voluntarily (they may also not be open when they're supposed to be). Pick up maps and southern Baja's free English paper, *Los Cabos News,* here. *Obregón, at 16 de Septiembre, tel. 112/2–59–39. Open weekdays 8–8.*

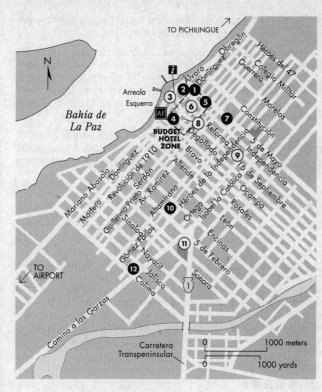

Sights ●
Biblioteca de las
Californias, **1**
Bus Station, **12**
Cathedral, **5**
Mercado
Municipal, **4**
Museo de
Antropología, **7**
Teatro de la Cuidad
(Unidad
Cultural), **10**
Terminal Malecón, **2**

Lodging ○
Hotel Yeneka, **6**
Pensión
California, **8**
Posada
San Miguel, **9**
Suites Misión, **3**
Villa Juvenil, **11**

COMING AND GOING

BY BUS ABC and Águila buses stop at the **main bus station** (Jalisco, at Héroes de la Independencia, tel. 112/2–42–70), a 30-minute walk or a $2.50 taxi ride from downtown. Down-
town city buses marked IMSS will also let you off three blocks from the terminal. To get
downtown from the terminal, take any city bus and get off at the municipal market (Revolución, at Degollado). First-class buses for Tijuana (22 hrs, $46) and destinations en route
depart La Paz four times daily. Eight buses depart daily for Cabo San Lucas and San José del
Cabo ($5). The Pacific route through Todos Santos (1 hr, $2.50) takes 2½ hours to Los Cabos—
an hour less than the route via Los Barriles (2 hrs, $3.50). Águila buses also depart from the
more convenient **Terminal Malecón** (Obregón, near tourist office, tel. 112/2–78–98), with
more frequent service to Cabo San Lucas at the same price. Eight buses depart daily for Los
Cabos (via Todos Santos), and seven run via Los Barriles. The bus to the beaches and the ferry
terminal in Pichilingue (10 per day, 20 min, $1) also leaves from Terminal Malecón. On week-
ends buses continue past Pichilingue as far as El Tecolote. The last bus back to La Paz departs
Pichilingue at 6 PM.

BY FERRY **Sematur** offers passenger and vehicle service from Pichilingue to Topolobampo
(near Los Mochis) and Mazatlán, but buying tickets is a huge hassle if you don't plan ahead.
Boats for Topolobampo depart Pichilingue Monday–Saturday at 11 AM, arriving at 7 PM that
evening. On Tuesdays, however, the ship carries "dangerous cargo" and—get this—women are
forbidden on board. The ride costs $13 for a seat. The boat to Mazatlán (18 hrs) leaves daily
at 3 PM; it costs $22 for a seat and $40 for a bunk (not available Wednesdays). Ferry tickets
can be purchased one day ahead of time from the **Sematur** office (5 de Mayo, at Guillermo Prieto, tel. 112/5–38–33), which is open weekdays 8–1 and 4–6, and weekends 8–1. If you
want to leave on a day when beds are available, it's easier to buy tickets in advance from **Agencia de Viajes Yurimar** (5 de Mayo, near Domínguez, tel. 112/2–86–00; open weekdays 9–7,

Sat. 9–2). To reach the Sematur ferry station, go half an hour south of La Paz to Pichilingue (*see* By Bus, *above*). Arrive at the station an hour before departure.

If you want to take a vehicle to the mainland, brush up on your Spanish and get a car permit from the **Oficina de Banjército,** or the *váscula* (weighing station; next to ferry station; open weekdays 8–1) in Pichilingue. Bring your passport, driver's license, and registration or ownership papers. With permit in hand, go to the Sematur office (*see above*) to reserve a place. Price varies according to the size of the vehicle, but an average car costs about $100. Try to arrive at the ferry terminal four hours prior to departure.

BY PLANE From La Paz, **Aerocalifornia** (tel. 112/5–10–23) and **Aeroméxico** (tel. 112/2–00–91) serve Mazatlán ($77 one-way), Mexico City ($153 one-way), and Los Angeles ($300 round-trip). The airport is 8 kilometers north of town and taxis are the only transportation from town to the airport—a monopoly that is reflected in the price ($7).

GETTING AROUND

The downtown area doesn't follow the rest of the city's grid pattern, but most sights in La Paz are here, within easy walking distance of each other. Get your bearings from the cathedral and market (both on Revolución), which mark the limits of the downtown area. Obregón (the boardwalk, or *malecón*) runs along the water and is also a major reference point. To reach the main bus station, youth hostel, or theater and cultural center, catch a bus at the municipal market, on Revolución at Degollado. The Pichilingue beach and Sematur ferry terminal are south of La Paz, and are easily reached by bus (½ hr) from Terminal Malecón (*see* Coming and Going, *above*). From the ferry terminal, walk south for five minutes to Pichilingue beach. To reach any of the three beaches south of Pichilingue (Puerto Balandra, Playa el Tecolote, and Playa el Coyote), take the bus to Pichilingue, then hitch or catch a cab ($3). On the weekends, buses from Terminal Malecón run as far as Playa el Tecolote.

WHERE TO SLEEP

La Paz boasts a number of inexpensive lodgings with tons of character, especially in the downtown area. If you're traveling with several people, **Suites Misión** (Obregón 220, near Arreola, tel. 112/2–00–14) offers small, $25 suites that have a living room, kitchen, balcony with a sea view, and a bedroom with two double beds; reservations are necessary. The office is open 9–2 and 4–7:30; if it's closed, head next door to **Curios Mary** (tel. 112/2–08–15), the owner's jewelry and picture-frame store. **Posada San Miguel** (16 de Septiembre, at Independencia, tel. 112/2–18–02) is a tiny, popular hotel with an inner courtyard and Spanish tile. Singles cost $9, doubles $11, but you must arrive around 1 PM to get a room. Camping in La Paz isn't worth it, considering the number of decent hotels in the city center for the same price. Campsites are abundant 2 kilometers southwest of town and cost about $10 for two people with an automobile. Cheaper rates may be offered to walk-in tent campers.

Hotel Yeneka. There are cheaper places around, but this is the funkiest hotel you'll find, with large, well-furnished rooms, a restaurant, and a resident monkey. The lobby resembles an artfully tended junkyard, with a rusty Model-A and other discarded machinery. Singles cost $15, doubles $18, and all have clean bathrooms. The owner is opening a dormitory in the back of the hotel and plans to charge $12 per bed, including breakfast and dinner. *Madero 1520, btw 16 de Septiembre and Independencia, tel. 112/5–46–88. 20 rooms, all with bath. Laundry ($2.50), luggage storage. Wheelchair access.*

Pensión California. This classic budget traveler's abode offers nothing but a mattress on a cement bed, a ceiling fan, buzzing fluorescent lights, and a primitive bathroom. You can use the communal stove and laundry, although unattended bras have been known to disappear. Singles cost $7, doubles $10. *Degollado 209, ½ block from market, tel. 112/2–28–96. 25 rooms, all with bath. Luggage storage. Wheelchair access.*

HOSTELS **Villa Juvenil (CREA).** In a sports complex outside the center of town, this hostel offers standard bunks ($4) in excessively air-conditioned single-sex dorms. The communal baths are well kept and there's a laundromat and grocery store nearby, but this place is rather inconvenient from downtown. Tell the staff if you'll be staggering in after 11 PM so they can leave the gate open. *5 de Febrero, at Carretera al Sur (Hwy. 1S), tel. 112/2–46–15. From bus station, walk down Jalisco and turn left on Camino a las Garzas. Or take bus marked CREA or 5 DE FEBRERO. 70 beds. Reception open 7 AM–11 PM. Luggage storage. No alcohol.*

FOOD

The nicest places to eat in La Paz overlook the water. Apart from sidewalk vendors, however, eateries along the malecón are usually pricey. **El Camarón Feliz** (Obregón, at Bravo, tel. 112/2–90–11; open daily noon–midnight) is a reasonably priced restaurant on the malecón, serving fish ($5), stuffed crab au gratin ($5), and shrimp ($11). The thrifty should stick with Mexican dishes or come for happy hour (daily 6 PM–8 PM), when all national drinks are two for one. Cheaper eats lie downtown, especially at the **market** (Revolución, at Degollado; open daily 6–6), where *loncherías* (snack bars) serve comidas corridas for $3. As you enter, the cooks yell out their offerings to draw your attention; try **Conchería Colonial** (inside the market) for a $3 seafood feast.

El Quinto Sol. La Paz's vegetarian restaurant and health food store sells granola, wheat germ, vitamins, and other healthy items. Mexican dishes ($3–$5) are made with tofu or wheat gluten as a substitute for meat. For breakfast, try a bowl of yogurt, fresh fruit, and granola ($2.50). *Belisario Domínguez 12, at Independencia, tel. 112/2–16–92. 1 block from plaza. Open Mon.–Sat. 8 AM–9:30 PM.*

Café Expresso. With patio tables overlooking the malecón, this is the place for hip locals to see and be seen. Scope out the crowd while munching on one of their deli-style sandwiches ($4.50) or sipping a cappuccino ($2). *Obregón, at 16 de Septiembre, tel. 112/3–43–73. Open daily noon–midnight.*

El Íntimo (Esquerro 60; open Mon.–Sat. 7 PM–3 AM), one of La Paz's most popular bars, features live music every Monday, Friday, and Saturday night. While you're here, try a shot of Damiana ($1.50), a sweet liquor from a local desert plant that's thought to be an aphrodisiac.

WORTH SEEING

La Paz is the place to stock up on culture, especially if you've been trudging through the Baja backroads, where putting mainland-made salsa on a taco counts as a cultural activity. The modern **Teatro de la Cuidad** (Navarro, at Gómez Farías, tel. 112/5–03–76) presents folkloric dance, music, and theater performances. Check the box office when you arrive in town, because some excellent acts pass through La Paz and tickets are cheap ($10 for the best seats). Buy tickets weekdays 10–1 and 4–8 in front of the theater. The theater is part of the **Unidad Cultural Jesús Agundez,** a complex that includes an art gallery and several monuments to heros of La Paz. **Biblioteca de las Californias** (across from cathedral, in old Municipal Palace, tel. 112/5–37–67) is a unique library with an extensive collection of material on Baja in both English and Spanish. They also have a free permanent exhibit of art depicting the missions of Baja and the colonial period. The library is open late May–September, daily 8–3 (October–early May, daily 8–8). The small **Museo de Antropología** (5 de Mayo, at Altamirano; open weekdays 8–6, Sat. 9–2) provides information on the history and people of the peninsula, and has an English-speaking docent to help you out. The museum has over 1200 artifacts, as well as a botanical garden outside. A donation is requested; so leave a few pesos to be polite.

OUTDOOR ACTIVITIES

The beaches in town are small and skanky, making swimming pretty hazardous to your health. A better bet is to head to the beautiful, secluded beaches only minutes away from town to the north and south. Northwest of town lie **Playas Hamacas** and **Comitán**; in the opposite direction are gorgeous sands and free camping opportunities at playas **Palmira, El Coromuel, Caimancito, Punta Colorada, Tesoro,** and **Pichilingue.** The last is just a five-minute walk from the ferry terminal. To reach the others, take a bus toward Pichilingue and ask the driver to let you off. The best beaches, **Balandra, El Tecolote,** and **El Coyote** lie beyond Pichilingue and can be reached by bus (weekends only), by cab ($10), or by thumb. El Tecolote is popular, with a restaurant, bar, and rest rooms. Puerto Balandra, a beautiful cove with white sandy beaches, shady palapas, and few gringos, was once a pirate's refuge.

The waters around La Paz also offer prime scuba diving. The most popular sites are around **Espíritu Santo** island, where clear waters provide excellent visibility almost year-round. For $96 per person, the English-speaking folks at **Viajes Palmira** (Obregón, btw Rosales and Allende, tel. 112/2–40–30 or 112/5–72–78) offer a two-tank dive including equipment, guides, lunch, and a boat ride. Viajes Palmira does it all; they offer dive classes ($350 for a two-day course) and snorkeling trips to the island ($40), rent bicycles ($11 per day) and horses ($30 per day), and will take you on sunset tours of the bay ($15, including champagne— whee!). Full-day fishing trips including rods, licenses, a boat, and a guide are also available ($170 for two people), and whale-watching trips cost $80 per person in season (Jan.–Mar.). **Baja Diving Service** (Obregón 1665, near 16 de Septiembre, tel. 112/2–18–26, fax 112/2–86–44) offers an all-day scuba tour ($77), a one-tank night excursion ($45), and snorkeling ($40). They also rent kayaks ($50) and mountain bikes ($11 for 24 hrs), and sell fishing tackle and rods. If you're not keen on a package deal, rent scuba equipment here for $15. They also have PADI certification courses (four days of dives) for $400, including equipment. About 30 minutes southwest of town, the calm, reef-protected water is perfect for kayaking. Ask at **Hotel Yeneka** (see Where to Sleep, *above*) for guided boat rentals ($42 per person per day).

Los Cabos

In 1982 the Mexican government decided to propel Los Cabos into tourist consciousness and began a promotional blitz. Their efforts were largely successful: Today San José del Cabo, Cabo San Lucas, and the stretch of beach between them make up the peninsula's primary tourist destination. Unfortunately this popularity has turned Cabo San Lucas into a hotel hell, overwhelmed by resorts and the gringos who love them. For now San José del Cabo has managed to avoid this fate, and retains a certain modicum of charm and local identity. Even if you are normally turned off by places that receive this kind of hoopla, the beauty of Los Cabos's smooth, sandy beaches and high desert cliffs justifies the attention. If that fails to float your boat, you can retreat back up the peninsula to the quiet town of Todos Santos or hang out with windsurfers in Los Barriles or Buenavista. People come to this region in droves to enjoy kilometers of white beaches and warm, turquoise waters that swell into good surfing waves. But you'd better hurry—time is running out for the few gorgeous and isolated spots that remain.

San José del Cabo

Until recently, San José del Cabo dominated the tip of the peninsula. Jesuits founded the town in the 1700s, taking advantage of an underground stream that surfaces nearby and creates a large natural estuary. The mission, zócalo, and other buildings erected during this period give San José del Cabo a sense of history—it feels more like a real Mexican town than a tourist trap, despite the gringos wandering aimlessly about. The gazebo on the square is perfect for people watching, while the 18th-century **Palacio Municipal** (Mijares, at Castro) is worth a peek for the cave-painting motif in its courtyard. About 46 kilometers (28 mi) northeast of San José del Cabo, **Cabo Pulmo** has the peninsula's only coral reef, and hundreds of brightly colored fish are visible in the clear water offshore.

BASICS The best rates (and longest lines) for cashing traveler's checks are at **Bancomer** (Zaragoza, at Morelos, tel. 114/2–00–40), open weekdays 8:30–1:30. Rates at the exchange booth (tel. 114/2–00–40) farther up Zaragoza are not as good, but they're open Monday–Saturday 8 AM–9 PM and Sundays until 5. Almost all the restaurants, hotels, and shops in San José accept Visa, MasterCard, and AmEx, as well as traveler's checks. **Casitas y Casitas** (cnr of Obregón and Hidalgo, tel. 114/2–24–64) has long-distance telephone service 8 AM–9 PM daily and charges $1 to make a collect call. Don't use the more upscale telephone office down the

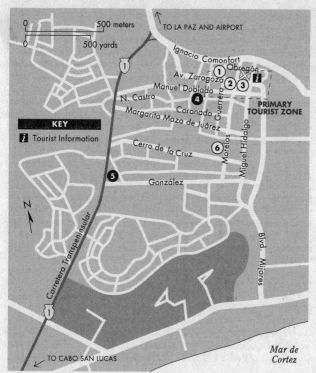

Sights ●
Mercado
Municipal, **4**
Bus Station, **5**

Lodging ○
Hotel Ceci, **2**
Hotel Colli, **3**
Hotel Consuelo, **6**
Hotel San José, **1**

Mar de Cortez

street near Zaragoza unless you want to pay twice as much for direct calls. The **post office** (Mijares, at Margarita Maza de Juárez, tel. 114/2–09–11) will hold mail sent to you at the following address for up to 10 days: Lista de Correos, Blvd. Mijares, San José del Cabo, Baja California Sur, CP 23400, México. You can pick up and send mail weekdays 8–7, Saturday 9–1.

The phone number for the **police** is 114/2–03–61 or 114/2–30–61; for the **Cruz Roja** (ambulance), it's 114/2–03–16. **Lavandería VERA** (González, east of bus station; open Mon.–Sat. 8–8) sells suds and has self-serve washers for $1.50; dryers are $2. Next to the zócalo, the **tourist office** (Zaragoza, at Mijares, tel. 114/2–04–46; open weekdays 9–3) carries mostly resort brochures and doles out a tiny little map. The staff's English isn't great, but they're eager to help.

COMING AND GOING The bus station (tel. 114/2–11–00) is on González, near Highway 1, on the southwest edge of town. From here, it's a 30-minute walk or $1.50 cab ride east down González and north up Mijares to the town center. Fourteen first-class buses leave daily for La Paz (3 hrs, $5), half traveling via Los Barriles (1 hr, $2) and the other half via Todos Santos (1½ hrs, $3.50). Ten first-class buses head to Cabo San Lucas (30 min, $1) and one leaves daily at 4 PM for Tijuana (26 hrs, $43); for more frequent departures to other destinations, transfer in La Paz. Another, more centrally located terminal is **Terminal Enlaces Terrestres** (Vicente Ibarra, at Doblado, no phone), about five blocks west of downtown. They have eight first-class buses daily to Cabo San Lucas (30 min, $1) that continue on to La Paz (2½ hrs, $7).

➤ **BY PLANE** • The **Aeropuerto Internacional Los Cabos** is served by **Aerocalifornia** (tel. 114/3–08–48), **Mexicana** (tel. 114/3–04–12), **Alaska** (tel. 114/2–10–15), and **United** (tel. 95–800/00–30–07 or 114/2–28–81). **Yellow Taxi** colectivos shuttle people between the airport and Los Cabos ($9). They have a booth at the arrival gate and most of their yellow-and-black vans are air-conditioned. A bus heading toward La Paz will drop you on the highway near the airport (15 min, $1), but you'll have to walk an easy 1½ kilometers from there.

WHERE TO SLEEP If you've got camping gear, use it here—hotels are expensive and beautiful beach sites are plentiful along the coast. Otherwise, rest your head on a freshly washed Star Wars pillowcase and eat in the small restaurant at **Hotel Consuelo** (Morelos, above Cerro de la Cruz, tel. 114/2–06–43). It's one of the cheapest places in town ($7 a single and $9 a double), only a 10-minute walk from the center. Clean, well-ventilated **Hotel Ceci** (Zaragoza 22, near church, no phone) is smack dab in the center of the tourist zone; singles or doubles are $9 with a fan, $10 with air-conditioning. **Hotel Colli** (Hidalgo, near Zaragoza, tel. 114/2–07–25) offers quiet, secure singles for $13 and doubles for $16, all with private bath. Rooms cost $4 more with air-conditioning, and prices rise during tourist season. **Hotel San José** (Obregón, at Guerrero, in front of Banco Serfín, tel. 114/2–24–64) has rooms with private bath ($7 singles, $8 doubles), and also offers laundry service and a long-distance caseta.

➤ **CAMPING** • You can pitch your tent anywhere along the beach near town (though it's best to avoid the big hotels or the mosquito-ridden estuary), as long as you set up camp late, don't build a fire, and leave in the morning. A few kilometers down the road toward Cabo San Lucas you can set up at a more permanent surfer camp next to the **Costa Azul Hotel.** Scamming a shower is a virtual impossibility; you can use the resort's outdoor showers on the beach to rinse off, but soaping up may get you some strange looks. Two trailer parks, **Brisas del Mar** and **Montanes de Palmillas,** outside town on the highway toward Cabo San Lucas, charge $15 for two people in a tent. They're expensive, but both have showers, flush toilets, a pool, laundry, and a restaurant.

FOOD Food stalls at the **mercado municipal** (Castro, at Vicente Ibarra) serve seasonal fare and $2.50 comidas corridas—get here early, though, because food runs out by 4 PM. For a cup of coffee (and plenty of gringos), **El Café Fiesta** (Mijares 14, at Zaragoza, tel. 114/2–28–08; open daily 7 AM–10 PM) has endless refills and a patio from which to watch passersby. Their extensive vegetarian menu ranges from lentil soup ($2) to tofu fajitas ($3.50). **Café Rosy** (Zaragoza, at Green, no phone) is a more traditional Mexican restaurant with more traditional Mexican prices. Burrito and taco plates ($1–$3) are served weekdays 9 AM–10 PM.

OUTDOOR ACTIVITIES The water in front of most of San José's beach hotels conceals strong currents, and swimming can be dangerous; both residents and tourists head instead to Hotel Palmilla's **Playa Palmilla,** 7 kilometers west of town. Surfboards ($15 a day), boogie boards ($8 a day), snorkel gear ($8 a day), fish tackle ($10 a day), and bicycles ($11 day) are available from **Killer Hook Surfshop** (Hidalgo, near Zaragoza, tel. 114/2–24–30; open Mon.–Sat. 9–8). The owner, Rafael, can fill you in on the best surf spots, as well as answer general questions about the surrounding beaches. For other choice local surf spots, *see box, above.* You can rent ATVs and tear around the beach for $10 per hour ($40 for 9 hrs) at **Baja's Sports** (parking lot of Hotel Presidente, tel. 114/2–01–00).

AFTER DARK For real disco action, head to Cabo San Lucas, a half-hour drive or $15 taxi ride away. If you can't get motivated, the **Eclipse** (Mijares, near Coronado; open Thurs.–Sun.) is the local downtown disco. Beers are $1 during happy hour (6 PM–10 PM), but this doesn't make up for the blaring TVs, obnoxious karaoke, and the louses who pay the $5 weekend cover (no charge Thurs.) to hang out here and bother women. **Bones** (Mijares, next to Hotel Presidente, tel. 114/2–02–11; open Tues.–Sun. 9 PM–2 AM) is a disco specializing in noisy explo-

Secret Surfing Spots

Surfers will find treasures around Los Cabos that don't appear on maps: Nine Palms is the spot for long-boarders, Punto Perfecto has Hawaii-size waves, and La Bocana is a walk-in freshwater estuary that features giant tubes, created when heavy rains open up the river mouth. For consistently gut-wrenching waves, Playa Acapulguitos, Playa Monumentos, and Costa Azul are the beaches of choice for gringo and local surfers. Once you're in the vicinity, ask anybody with long hair and a tan to point you in the right direction.

sions and fancy lightworks. Cover is $3 except Wednesdays, when women get in free; drinks cost $1.50–$5.

Cabo San Lucas

Cabo San Lucas was originally a small fishing village where a few hardy or rich sportfishermen boated or flew in to go after huge marlin and sailfish. Over the past decade, however, spectacular growth has turned Cabo into a tourist nightmare. The small town is congested, claustrophobic, and expensive, although overdevelopment does mean all sorts of water-sport equipment is available (for a small mound of cash). The beaches, happily, are still free of charge. On the street, English is the lingua franca, U.S. dollars are expected, and the major hotels water the desert green. Stray a few blocks north of the tourist track to the dirt roads and taco stands, however, and you'll discover Cabo as it existed before the landscape architects arrived.

BASICS Money changers line Lázaro Cárdenas between Hidalgo and Matamoros, but U.S. dollars are preferred in most places, and credit cards and traveler's checks are widely accepted. If you do need pesos, **Bancomer** (Cárdenas, btw Hidalgo and Guerrero, tel. 114/3–19–24) is open for money exchange weekdays 8:30–noon, and the **Serfín** branch (Cárdenas, at Morelos, tel. 114/3–01–91) in the Plaza Shopping Center has an ATM that accepts Visa, Plus, and Cirrus. The Cabo San Lucas **post office** (Lázaro Cárdenas, at 16 de Septiembre, tel. 114/3–00–48; open weekdays 9–6, Sat. 9–1) will hold mail sent to you at the following address for up to 10 days: Lista de Correos, Av. Lázaro Cárdenas, Cabo San Lucas, Baja California Sur, CP 23410, México. Public phones are common downtown, but you can place calls from most resort hotels in the area. For cash calls, the **Casa de Larga Distancia** (Lázaro Cárdenas, at San Lucas, tel. 114/3–00–80) is your best bet, but they charge a $1 connection fee if you call collect. There's no extra charge for local calls at the phones next to the elevators in **Plaza Las Glorias**—just dial 0 first. You can make collect calls from pay phones by dialing 09 for the Mexican operator; don't use the blue phones that say DIAL 0 or you'll go bankrupt.

The phone number for the **police** is 114/3–00–57; for the **Cruz Roja** (ambulance service), it's 114/3–33–00. **Farmacia Rincón** (Blvd. Marina, in front of Plaza Las Glorias Hotel, tel. 114/3–07–95) is open 24 hours and has an English-speaking employee who can recommend a good hangover regimen or refer you to a doctor. **Libros** (Plaza Bonita, on Marina, tel. 114/3–31–71), open daily 9–9, has an adequate supply of best-sellers in English, as well as a selection of magazines and newspapers in both English and Spanish. The local **lavandería** (San Lucas, btw 5 de Mayo and Constitución, tel. 114/3–20–25) is open Monday–Saturday 8–8. They charge $2 for you to wash and dry your own clothes, or they'll do it for you for $3.50. There are several booths around town that claim to be tourist information centers, but they generally can't offer more than a map and a smile. For thorough advice in English, seek the people behind the information desk at **Hotel Plaza Las Glorias.**

COMING AND GOING

➤ **BY BUS** • The **bus station** (Zaragoza, at 16 de Septiembre, tel. 114/3–04–00), two blocks north of downtown and 10 blocks from the hostel, is served by the ABC and Águila bus lines. Frequent buses leave daily for La Paz (3 hrs, $6), San José del Cabo (½ hr, $1), and Todos Santos (1 hr, $2). For other destinations, travel to La Paz and transfer.

➤ **BY PLANE** • There is one airport for both Cabos (see San José del Cabo, above). The cheapest way to reach the airport from Cabo San Lucas is on a bus headed to La Paz via San José del Cabo, which will drop you off near the airport on Highway 1 (1 hr, $2). If there are no taxis waiting to drive you the remaining kilometer, the walk is easy.

WHERE TO SLEEP Lodging here is generally expensive, so camping is your best option. Hotel owners don't like you to crash on the beaches near town, so head a few kilometers away to Migriño or Playa los Cerritos—they're gorgeous, secluded, and the way to go if you've got gear and are not traveling alone. Both beaches are close to the highway, so catch a bus for San José del Cabo ($1) and ask the driver to let you off on an open stretch of beach. For something more organized, **Club Cabo** (tel. 114/3–33–48) charges $6 for two people in a tent, $18 in an RV, and $40 for a little house. Ask the driver to let you off at Club Cascades and walk down to the beach, where you'll see signs pointing you in the right direction. **Vagabundos** (tel. 114/3–02–90) is visible from the highway and charges $18 for two people, regardless of whether you're in a 50-foot Winnebago or a 4-foot tent.

If you're not into doing the back-to-nature thing, **Villas Juveniles (CREA)** (Av. de la Juventud, 3 blocks east of Morelos, tel. 114/3–01–48) is the cheapest indoor place to stay in Cabo San Lucas, though you may have to ask the folks at the hostel to turn on the water and electricity for you. The inconvenient walk up Morelos from the center of town (a $2 taxi ride) is compensated for by the lack of curfew or check-in time and the low prices: A night in a single-sex dorm costs $5, a private room with your own bath costs $8 ($5 per person if you share it with the mate of your choice). Bring your own toilet paper. If you want to splurge, do it at the wheelchair-accessible **Hotel Mar de Cortez** (Lázaro Cárdenas 11, at Guerrero, tel. 114/3–00–32), where a basic, well-maintained room with one bed and air-conditioning costs $39 for one person and $44 for two. A third person costs $4.50 extra. Perks include the tropical courtyard and inviting swimming pool. Be sure to ask for a room in the old section, otherwise the prices are $51 and $56.

FOOD Surprisingly, Cabo San Lucas has several decently priced restaurants, mostly on or north of Niños Héroes. Along Morelos (perpendicular to Lázaro Cárdenas) you'll find a number of authentic Mexican restaurants frequented by the locals. **Café Cabo** (Morelos, near Lázaro Cárdenas, no phone; open daily 7 AM–9 PM) has a cheery staff and serves big breakfasts for $3, as well as sandwiches ($2), hamburgers ($2.50), and fajitas ($3.50) in the afternoon. For neo-hippie California culture or cuisine, **Mama's Royal Café** (cnr of Hidalgo and Zapata, tel. 114/3–42–90; open daily 7 AM–10 PM) delivers on both counts. Omelets, salads, and sandwiches here all cost $5.50. **Mariscos Mocambo** (Morelos, at 20 de Noviembre, tel. 114/3–21–22; open daily 9–9) is the undisputed favorite among locals, who spend their afternoons over red snapper (sold by weight), crab in garlic sauce ($6), or seafood soup ($5.50). The fresh-squeezed king-size lemonade ($1) is also good. At **Hippo's Fish 'N Chips** (Plaza de los Mariachis, on Blvd. Marina, no phone; open daily 7 AM–midnight), a plate of crispy, English-style fish and chips will put you out $5. For a mango shake, add another $3.

SHOPPING Cabo San Lucas has attractions for those who aren't enthralled by gasoline-smelling water and boat traffic. Due to the number of cruise ships and tourists in the area, Cabo has several outdoor markets that sell artesanía and crafts from all over Mexico to eager shopaholics. Just past the marina on Boulevard Marina, one market (open daily 8–5) has the best prices on silver from Oaxaca, ceramics from Morelia, and cheesy Baja souvenirs. Another market (open daily 10–9), consisting of shady palapas, lies across from the Supermercado Plaza on Niños Héroes, but if you wander around near the zócalo you'll find some out-of-the-way places with even better deals.

OUTDOOR ACTIVITIES Cabo San Lucas's waters are ideal for any water sport—you can rent everything from waterbikes and catamarans to Windsurfers and wave runners. Try **Plaza Las Glorias Beach Club,** open daily 7–7, for these toys. Travelers with tight budgets may want to rent more economical equipment, such as snorkel gear ($10 per day), surfboards ($15–$20 per day), or boogie boards ($5 per day) at **Cabo Sports Center** (Madero, near Guerrero, tel. 114/3–07–32; open daily 9–9). The best swimming beach is **Playa El Medano,** but for snorkeling try **Playa Santa María** and **Los Barriles**—*tranquilo* (mellow) spots east of town. For the very daring, **Baja Bungee** sends people attached to a big rubber band off a 27-meter tower ($45 per jump); contact Alex Darquea at Siesta Suites (tel. 114/3–27–73). You can get a $10 discount on your jump if you buy it with a $30 parasail at **The Activity Center** (by Las Palmas Restaurant on Medano Beach, tel. 114/3–30–93), which serves as a ticket outlet for all of Cabo San Lucas's water sports and activities.

Los Arcos and **Lover's Beach** sit south of town, at the tip of the rocky peninsula. Here the Pacific Ocean and the Sea of Cortez meet, the waves sculpting formations and tunnels in the offshore rocks. Many locals will try to lure you onto their boats for trips to Lover's Beach, but the 30-minute hike is easy and offers spectacular views. Another option is to take a $7 ride in the glass-bottom boat that leaves periodically from behind **Plaza Las Glorias Beach Club,** daily

10 AM–6 PM. Currents in the water here send a cascade of sand
30 meters. You can view the top of the sand waterfall with sn
the full effect, and to enjoy the diversity of the marine life he
Cabo Acuadeportes (a.k.a. Water Sports Center at Hotel
Bonito, or Chileno Beach, tel. 114/3–01–17) arranges
Rock, Los Arcos, and Cabo Pulmo (Baja's only coral reef
a place you want to miss, and if you aren't certified, it'
for certified divers (if you don't have your PADI card
ber). Diving certification courses cost $400, and resort cou
Adventures (Plaza Bonita, tel. 114/3–26–30) and **Cabo Diving**
Plaza Las Glorias, tel. 114/3–01–50) both have similar prices and tri
ing where you'd like to dive and then calling to see who's going there that

AFTER DARK Cabo San Lucas is *the* center for nightlife in southern Baja, whic
necessarily mean you'll have a quality outing. The crowd drinks $1 margaritas at **Río Grill**
9 PM, then makes its way to the **Giggling Marlin** (tel. 114/3–11–82). The last stop is at **El
Squid Roe** (tel. 114/3–11–69), where the sufficiently inebriated dance themselves silly to
pop hits of the '80s and the waiters perform a nightly pelvic thrust that somewhat resembles a
dance; food and beer are served, but tequila shots are more popular. All these bars are on
Boulevard Marina (the main drag), which turns into Lázaro Cárdenas; none of them charge a
cover. Just off the main drag lies the infamous **Cabo Wabo** (Guerrero, near Lázaro Cárdenas,
tel. 114/3–11–88), owned by members of Van Halen. Well-known acts often play here on
weekends, and any fool who's got $15 burning a hole in his pocket (and that's just the cover)
can come here to look for aging rock stars.

NEAR LOS CABOS

TODOS SANTOS Good (but sometimes dangerous) surf, free camping, and the absence of
obtrusive hotels make Todos Santos the perfect place to retire at 20. Founded by Jesuit missionaries in 1734, and subsequently abandoned due to resistance from the local Pericú people, Todos Santos was finally permanently settled by sugar-planting mestizos in the 19th
century. When the sugarcane industry collapsed, the newly unemployed began growing chiles
and raising cattle for beef. Today Todos Santos remains a small town that revolves slowly
around its shady zócalo. Despite the slow pace, adventurous visitors will find kayaking, sailing,
sailboarding, and cruises easily accessible.

➤ **BASICS** • There's no bank in Todos Santos, but **Baja Money Exchange** (1 block from
post office on Colegio Militar, no phone) will hook you up with some pesos Monday–Saturday
9–6. The **post office** (Colegio Militar, near Marqués de León, no phone; open weekdays 8–1
and 3–5) is on the same block. **Farmacia Todos Santos** on Juárez is open daily 7 AM–10 PM,
but you can knock at the door at any hour for emergency help. Otherwise, the **Centro de Salud**
(Juárez, btw Zaragoza and Degollado, tel. 114/5–00–95) is open 24 hours and Dr. Servín
speaks English. Also on Juárez, **El Tecolote** English bookstore doubles as the hub of the resident gringos' social network. They can tell you where the best beaches are, as well as trade
used books (two for one) daily 9:30–5. Next door is **The Message Center** (open Mon.–Sat. 8–
5), where you can make direct international calls, call collect, use a calling card, receive phone
messages (at 114/5–00–03), send a fax, or receive one (at 114/5–02–88). This also serves
as the town's travel agency.

➤ **COMING AND GOING** • Buses depart from **Pilar's O.G. Fish Tacos** (Colegio Militar,
tel. 114/5–01–46) for Cabo San Lucas (1 hr, $2) every couple of hours 8 AM–9 PM; those con-
tinuing on to San José del Cabo leave four times daily (1½ hrs, $2.50). Frequent buses also
leave for La Paz (1 hr, $2). You can store a few bags for free at Pilar's. From the bus stop, the
zócalo is three blocks up the hill (towards La Paz) and one block west. Everything else of note
is in between.

➤ **WHERE TO SLEEP** • The sandy stretch of beach 2 kilometers south of town is great
for camping, but a dangerous place to swim. Buses headed for Cabo San Lucas will drop you
off along the highway, but it's still a 2- to 3-kilometer walk; although easy, hitching is not rec-

lone travelers. If you want a room, try the clean and affordable **Hotel Miramar** , at Pedrajo, tel. 114/5–03–41). This tranquil retreat at the town's edge is wheel-sible and has parking, a Laundromat next door, and a swimming pool; single rooms doubles $10. Clean, centrally located, and pool-blessed is **Motel Guluarte** (cnr of and Morelos, no phone); the air-conditioned singles and doubles here cost $15 ($11 fan), and rooms upstairs have shared balconies with rocking chairs.

FOOD • **Caffé Todos Santos** (cnr of Centenario and Topete, no phone; open Tues.–Sun. 7 AM–8 PM) has all-you-can-eat blueberry or banana pancakes ($4), bagels and cream cheese ($1.50), and real coffee for breakfast. Later in the day they serve sandwiches and salads. If you don't mind the not-so-friendly staff, the food is pretty good. **Restaurant Las Fuentes** (Delgado, at Colegio Militar, tel. 114/5–02–57; open daily 7 AM–9 PM) has patio tables and a varied menu—most meals cost $3–$6. **Lonchería Karla** (Colegio Militar, opposite park, tel. 114/5–02–93; open daily 6:30 AM–5 PM) has $2.50 plates of tacos, tamales, and other *antojitos* (appetizers).

➤ **WORTH SEEING** • The annual **art festival**, held around the third weekend in January, offers displays of local artists in the plaza and special exhibitions in all of the town's galleries. On October 12, the town celebrates its foundation with the **Día de la Virgen del Pilar.** Art exhibits, traditional food, and *baile folklórico* (folkloric dance) are all part of the celebration. You can find out about other events that take place throughout the year through Professor Agundez at the **Casa de la Cultura** (Gral. Topete, tel. 114/5–90–59; open Mon.–Sat. 8–6), which also has a library and displays artifacts, paintings, and children's art. The yellow **Misión de Nuestra Señora de Pilar,** built in 1733, is your typical mission; nevertheless, it offers a spectacular view of the Valle del Pilar and the ocean from its overlook. One block west of the mission towards the water is the fabled **Hotel California** of Eagles fame.

SONORA AND LOS MOCHIS

4

By Carrie McKellogg

Sonora has always resisted visitors. The indigenous people of this region—the Yaqui, Seri, Guarijio, Mayo, and Papago—adapted to the region's sweltering deserts, but were as fierce as the harsh soils they walked upon. When European settlers arrived, they were thwarted by blistering summers and long battles with native tribes. Although the indigenous people achieved a few successful rebellions, their traditions and rituals were eventually smothered by dammed rivers and chemical fertilizers. Agriculture became Sonora's buried treasure, rendering it the second-richest and second-largest state in Mexico. Today, Sonora's proximity to Arizona has attracted an irritating swarm of money-eyed Tucson tourists, not to mention numerous *maquiladoras* (foreign-owned factories), where U.S. companies continue to benefit from the cheap cost of Mexican labor. It's no wonder Sonorans ask tourists in an ambiguous tone if they are from "*el otro lado*" ("the other side").

The Sonoran Yaqui people are reknowned for their perpetual resistance to outside domination. Porfirio Díaz set the army against them in the 1890s when they objected to his selling their land to private investors; thousands of prisoners were then sent to work building railroads in southern Mexico. Even so, the Yaqui were not fully "subdued" (that is, kept from killing settlers) until the late 1920s.

Travelers without reptilian blood may be tempted to bypass Sonora during summer months, when the 37°C (100°F) heat can be almost unbearable. A few visitor-friendly areas exist, however. Nogales caters to day-tripping souvenir seekers, offering colorful markets full of woven blankets, wrought-iron furniture, and handmade crafts from all over the country. The barely sullied beaches of San Carlos, Bahía Kino, and Puerto Peñasco are the best spots to cool off in the Sea of Cortés, and the sleepy, colonial town of Alamos hearkens back to its mining-town days with narrow cobblestone streets and elegantly restored haciendas. Hermosillo, the bustling state capital, offers museums, parks, and a unique ecology center to keep you entertained. Although it's not particularly pretty, you'll inevitably visit Los Mochis: The city is a transportation hub and essential stop if you plan to take a ferry to Baja or the train through the Copper Canyon (*see* Chapter 5).

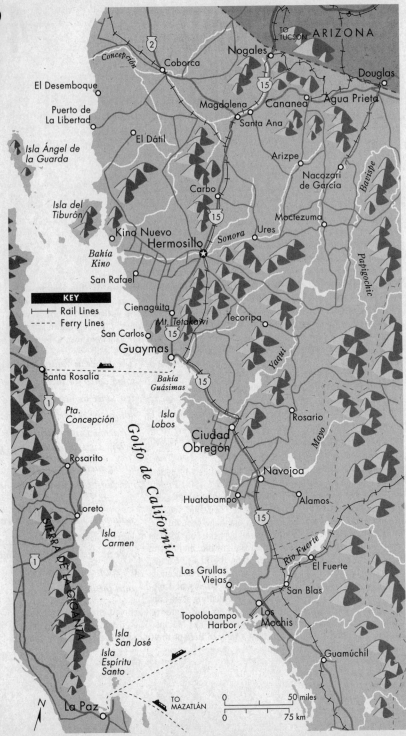

Sonora

Nogales

The nondescript town of Nogales, Mexico, crowds against the border across from Nogales, Arizona. Like Tijuana to the west (but on a much smaller scale), Nogales is famous for its shopping and attracts hordes of Arizonans bargaining for tacky knickknacks. This is the place to find that stuffed armadillo that's been eluding you elsewhere. Blue glass from Guadalajara, silver from Zacatecas, and burnished pottery from Oaxaca also fill the stores, although you'll find these wares for lower prices farther south. The main shopping district lies just across the border, along the five blocks of alleyways that line Calle Ochoa between López Mateos and Obregón. After a tough day of bargaining, you can kick back with an overpriced margarita and pulsating techno music in one of the many bars overlooking Obregón. Nogales also boasts a decent bullfighting arena—an especially hot spot during **Cinco de Mayo.** This festival, composed of bullfights, cockfights, horse races, and *artesanía* (crafts) exhibitions, celebrates Mexico's defeat of the French in the Battle of Puebla and lasts from the end of April until May 5.

Nogales serves as a major export depot for Sonora's rich agricultural produce but, like many of its border cousins, has also been affected by major economic changes over the past decade. Foreign (mostly U.S.) companies take advantage of cheap Mexican labor by setting up an increasing number of industrial parks and *maquiladoras,* or *maquilas,* in special duty-free zones outside the city (*see* box, Maquiladoras, in Chapter 2). Though these factories employ the bulk of Nogales's residents, the town lacks the slimy criminal element found in other maquila-influenced border towns, such as Ciudad Juárez and Tijuana. The most negative impact of the maquilas in Nogales is environmental: The surrounding desert takes a great deal of toxic-waste abuse, resulting in a depressing lack of wildlife and flora.

BASICS

CASAS DE CAMBIO Banks on the U.S. side don't change dollars into pesos, but you'll find money changers there on Grand Avenue, one block from the border. Or, try **Casa de Cambio Gaby** (Morelos 18, near Ochoa, tel. 631/2–19–09) in Nogales, open weekdays 8–7 and Saturday 8–noon. **Bancomer** (López Mateos, 5 blocks south of border crossing, tel. 631/2–10–48) has an ATM that accepts Visa cards. The ATM at **Banamex** (cnr of Ochoa and Obregón), about two blocks from the border, accepts Plus System cards. Unfortunately, ATMs in Mexico are often broken or out of cash, so you'll probably want to cross the pedestrian bridge back to the States and follow the lower ramp, which runs into Grand Avenue: One block down on the right-hand side, **Bank of America** (tel. 520/287–6553; open weekdays 9–6, Sat. 9–2) has a reliable ATM that accepts Plus cards.

CROSSING THE BORDER Both the U.S. and Mexican customs offices at Nogales are open 24 hours a day. U.S. citizens and Canadians planning to stay in Mexico longer than 72 hours or traveling south of the border towns need tourist cards. To get one, present proof of citizenship at the **Mexican Government Border Office** (tel. 631/2–17–55; open 24 hrs), immediately to the right when you cross the border. Allow yourself extra time at border crossings because there can be backups due to staff shortages. If you've had a long, lascivious stay in Mexico, try to clean up (e.g., shave and get rid of the hangover) before going through customs or they may detain you for questioning, especially if you're under 21.

EMERGENCIES Bilingual operators staff the emergency telephone service (tel. 91/525–001–23 or 91/525–001–51) 24 hours a day. Or call the **police** (tel. 631/6–15–64 or 631/2–17–67) or **fire** and **ambulance** services (tel. 631/4–07–69) directly.

MAIL Your mail has a better chance of reaching its destination if you send it from the United States. The post office in Nogales, Arizona (300 N. Morley Ave., tel. 520/287–9246), six blocks from the border, is open weekdays 9–5. The *oficina de correos* (post office) on the Mexican side will hold mail sent to you at the following address for up to 10 days: Lista de Correos, Benito Juárez y Calle Campillo, Nogales, Sonora, CP 84000, México. *Benito Juárez, at Campillo, tel. 631/2–12–47. 2 blocks from border crossing. Open weekdays 8–7, Sat. 8–noon.*

MEDICAL AID Several reputable, English-speaking doctors have offices on the first few blocks of Obregón. Try **Roberto Belches Vásquez, MD** (tel. 631/2–37–21) and **Rene Romo De Vivar, DDS** (Obregón 263, tel. 631/2–05–00). For less-urgent medical attention, **Farmacia San Xavier** (Campillo 73, 2 blocks from border crossing, tel. 631/2–55–03) is open 24 hours daily and the staff speaks English.

PHONES Working **Ladatel** pay phones can be found along major streets, and there is a *caseta de larga distancia* (long-distance telephone office) in the bus terminal. **Nabila** (tel. 631/2–01–42; open daily 8–6), a small bric-a-brac shop a few blocks down Obregón on the left-hand side, charges $1.50 to make a collect call and $1.50 per minute to dial direct.

VISITOR INFORMATION The English-speaking tourist office, on the right just across the border, provides general information on accommodations and transportation and hands out a bite-size city map. Fortunately, Nogales is easy to navigate. *López Mateos, at Internacional, tel. 631/2–06–66. Open daily 8–6.*

COMING AND GOING

Almost everything you could need or want to see is near the border-crossing area and easily accessible on foot. Local buses run to other parts of town from López Mateos, the main drag. Foot traffic stomps around Ochoa and Obregón. Taxis will charge you roughly $1 per kilometer, but be sure to set a price before getting in.

BY BUS The bus station in Nogales is actually 6 kilometers from the center of town on Highway 15—you can get here on one of the local CENTRAL CAMIONERA buses (40¢) that run along López Mateos. Three bus companies use the station: **Transportes Norte de Sonora** (tel. 631/3–17–00) and **Élite** (tel. 631/3–02–33) serve Baja as well as mainland Mexico, while **Transportes del Pacífico** (tel. 631/3–16–06) serves the western mainland. Four buses go daily to Mexico City (1½ days; $75 1st class, $65 2nd class). Elite and Transportes Norte de Sonora each have an evening departure for Mexicali (9 hrs; $18 1st class, $16 2nd class). Another option is to take any bus headed south to Santa Ana (2½ hours, $3.50 1st class, $3 2nd class) and transfer there to a Mexicali-bound bus. Buses also leave Nogales for Tijuana (12 hrs; $26 1st class, $20 2nd class), Hermosillo (5 hrs; $10 1st class, $7.50 2nd class), Guaymas (7 hrs; $12 1st class, $11 2nd class), Los Mochis (12 hrs; $23 1st class, $11 2nd class), Mazatlán (17 hrs; $40 1st class, $33 2nd class), and Guadalajara (31 hrs; $56 1st class, $48 2nd class). The terminal has phones, luggage storage (50¢ per bag per hr), and a money-exchange booth.

On the Arizona side of the border, **Grey Line** (tel. 520/287–5628; open daily 7 AM–9 PM) has frequent, direct service to Tucson (1½ hrs, $6.50) and other destinations throughout the States, and will let you cram your luggage in a locker ($1 per day). Collective taxi/vans go directly to the airport in Tucson from the Grey Line station for $11 per person. The station is to your left just off the ramp as you cross the border.

BY CAR If you're driving less than 21 kilometers (13 mi) across the border, no special rules apply; bringing a car farther into Mexico is not complicated if you're properly prepared. U.S. rental cars are not permitted past the 21-kilometer mark, but everyone else is allowed a permit for up to 6 months. The state of Sonora has renovated its highway system, with a smooth, four-lane highway and well-maintained toll roads. A new program, called **Only Sonora** (tel. 800/4–SONORA from the U.S. or 800/6–25–55 in Mexico), registers those traveling by car within the state. An office located on the 21st kilometer of Highway 15 at Aguazarca issues tourist cards and registers vehicles. After you sign a promissory note to bring your car back across the border, an identifying hologram sticker gets slapped on the car's windshield. The only catch is that you must leave Mexico by Highway 15 to stop by the same office on your way out of the country. It's a good idea to purchase Mexican auto insurance ($8) from the **Puerta de México Edificio Banderas** (government border office; tel. 800/446–8277; open Mon.–Sat. 7 AM–10 PM, Sun. 7–1), just over the border in Nogales. Bring registration in your name, your driver's license, and your passport, plus a photocopy of each.

BY TRAIN The train station (tel. 631/3–02–05 or 631/3–10–91) is across from the bus station, 6 kilometers outside town (off Highway 15), and can be reached via any local bus marked CENTRAL CAMIONERA or FERROCARRIL (40¢) or by taxi ($4 from the center). Daily first- and second-class trains leave here for Benjamin Hill ($3 1st class, $1.75 2nd class), Hermosillo ($5 1st class, $3 2nd class), Sufragio (transfer point for the Copper Canyon; $14 1st class, $7.50 2nd class), Mazatlán ($21 1st class, $12 2nd class), and Guadalajara ($23 1st class, $17 2nd class). For Mexico City, change trains in Guadalajara; for Mexicali, change in Benjamin Hill. The first-class train leaves at 4:30 PM; the second-class train at 7 AM. The main difference is the lack of air-conditioning in second class, not to mention the slower service. Purchase tickets at the station, and be sure to arrive at least 30 minutes prior to departure.

WHERE TO SLEEP AND EAT

If you're meandering farther into Mexico, you might be better off avoiding Nogales's overpriced hotels and taking an overnight bus straight out of town. If you do decide to stay, the wheelchair-accessible **Hotel Yolanda** (Morelos, on a walkway just off Campillo, no phone) is the cheapest in town. The decent rooms with private bathrooms and hot water are worth the price ($9 singles, $14 doubles), if you can tolerate the saggy beds and lack of ventilation. **Hotel Orizaba** (Juárez 29, near Campillo, tel. 631/2–58–55) provides similar conditions and prices ($10 singles, $12.50 doubles), except here you'll get your own fan instead of your own bathroom. The communal baths get nasty when the place is full, but they do have hot water. Across the street, **Hotel San Carlos** (Juárez 22, tel. 631/2–13–46) is pleasant, with air-conditioning, TVs, and clean bathrooms in each room, but you'll pay the price: Singles cost $17, doubles $20.

There are no supermarkets in the downtown area, and the Nogales restaurant scene is pricey unless you get off the main boulevard. The taquerías and pushcart vendors crowding almost every corner are an inexpensive alternative at $2–$3 a meal, and cheap eateries cluster along Ochoa. Of these, **Restaurant Café Río Sonora** (Ochoa, near Hidalgo, tel. 631/2–03–89) serves the best and cheapest multicourse *comida corrida* (pre-prepared lunch special; $2). They're open 24 hours Tuesday–Sunday. **Café Olga** (Juárez, at Campillo, tel. 631/2–16–41; open daily 6 AM–3 AM) is a popular breakfast spot, with hotcakes and eggs for just $3. **La Fábula Pizza** (López Mateos, near Vásquez, tel. 631/2–20–48) serves up good Chicago-style pizza ($6 for a small, $9 for a large) daily noon–11 PM. You can also get your pizza *a domicilio* (delivered).

AFTER DARK

Except for weekends, when Arizonans cross the border to whoop it up, Nogales's nightlife is pretty mellow. Tons of gringo bars line Avenida Obregón, all of which serve up expensive drinks, $2 beers, and American music. About 1 kilometer from the border is **Mr. Don** (Obregón 1036, tel. 631/3–19–07; open Fri. and Sat. 9 PM–3 AM), a huge disco that plays everything from salsa to rap. On Fridays there's no cover, and the $8 cover on Saturdays includes an open bar. The popular **Epidaurus** (Privada Becerril and Corinto, just off Obregón, tel. 631/3–26–13; cover $9) attracts a bevy of locals and tourists with its mix of rap, techno, and traditional Mexican and rock favorites. The bar is open Tuesday–Sunday 5 PM–1 AM, and the adjoining disco is open Friday and Saturday until 3 AM. **Harlow's Discotheque** (Elías 21, no phone; cover $5), open Thursday–Sunday 8 PM–2 AM, offers all the latest in lasers, lights, and hip-hop music.

Near Nogales

PUERTO PEÑASCO

Founded as a fishing village in 1927, this quiet town sits on the northern coast of the Sea of Cortez. The town is hugged by the stifling **Desierto de Altar,** where the temperature often soars to more than 37°C (100°F) in summer. The best time of year to visit the area is late spring, when temperatures are milder and the cholla, saguaro, organ pipe, and barrel cacti bloom into red, yellow, and white flowers. Vacationing Arizonans in search of the sea congregate on the southern side of town, at **Miramar** and **Hermosa Bonita** beaches, armed with RVs, dune buggies, and Jet Skis. Besides heading to the beach, there is little to do or see here, except during festivals such as **Navy Day** (June 1st), when Puerto Peñasco celebrates with mariachi

Jesuit Father Eusebio Kino, who established a number of missions in northwestern Mexico in the late 17th century, reportedly drew a parallel between the Desierto de Altar and his vision of Hell.

music, boat parades, and beauty pageants. In mid-June there's an annual **fishing tournament,** when you can eat enough seafood to just about grow fins yourself.

COMING AND GOING To reach Puerto Peñasco from Nogales, take an **Élite** bus to Caborca (4 hrs, $9) and transfer there to a Puerto Peñasco–bound bus (2 hrs, $2). Trains also run from Puerto Peñasco to Mexicali (4 hrs, $4.50), Caborca (2 hrs, $2), Hermosillo (6 hrs, $4), and Ciudad Obregón (9 hrs, $6).

WHERE TO SLEEP AND EAT Unfortunately the rich have a monopoly over most beachfront hotels, but **Motel Davis** (Emiliano Zapata 100, near Calle 13, tel. 638/3–43–14), only three blocks from the beach, offers well-maintained, air-conditioned singles and doubles for $10–$15. If you're broke, try camping on peaceful **Playa Sandy** for $3. Pay at the booth located at the entrance to the Cholla Bay private road. **Restaurant Los Arcos** (Eusebio Kino, at Tamaulipas, tel. 638/3–35–97) has breakfast specials for $2 and is open daily 7:30 AM–10 PM. You can also head for one of the many seafood stands near the end of Boulevard Kino, where fish tacos cost about 50¢. **La Cita Café** (Paseo Victor Estrella 72, tel. 638/3–22–70; open daily 7 AM–9:30 PM), located in the old part of town, has served diner-style Mexican and American food since 1957. Breakfasts cost $3, hamburgers $2.50, and milkshakes $2. **Manny's Beach Club** (Playa Miramar, tel. 638/3–36–05) has a raging happy hour nightly 6–8 PM, when beers are $1 and Jimmy Buffett's "Margaritaville" is played over and over for the amusement of drunk gringos. Fortunately, they also have live music on weekends.

PARQUE NACIONAL EL PINACATE

On the road to Sonoita (Highway 8), 48 kilometers (30 mi) north of Puerto Peñasco, lies Parque Nacional El Pinacate. The huge park—about 2,000 square kilometers (1,240 sq mi)—was declared a UN biosphere reserve in 1993, which put its 500 plant and animal species under protection. Because of its similarity to the moon's surface, the park's craters, sand dunes, and lava fields were used by NASA to train astronauts for moon walks. The most popular spots within the park, largely due to their accessibility to Highway 8, are Volcán Elegante and Volcán Colorado, but there are more than 600 other volcanic craters, as well as archaeological sites that date back almost 30,000 years. Because of temperature extremes in the summer and winter, visiting the park is recommended only between October and April. Going with a guide is strongly advised: The best is **Señor Munro** (tel. 638/3–32–09), Puerto Peñasco's town historian, who runs a photo studio in the commercial district. Day-long tours run about $50 per person, but you can get a group together and negotiate. The park is still largely underdeveloped, so unless you're with a guide don't expect anything but vast spaces for independent exploration. If you want to go alone, you really need a truck or a car with four-wheel drive. You can camp in the park for free or at a neighboring *ejido* (farming community) for a few dollars: The latter is the safer option. When entering the park, you must register at the entrance booth off Highway 8 so that they can track down your dehydrated body if you get lost.

Hermosillo

Bustling and on the verge of modernization, the prosperous capital of Sonora boasts a state university and a population of almost a half million. Five-star hotels and American fast-food restaurants blend into colonial plazas and narrow alleys, giving the city a distinct feel. Like other large Mexican cities, Hermosillo is plagued by the growing pains of crime and poverty, but the university community imbues the city with a scholarly dignity. Although you probably won't spend much time here, you could easily pass a day touring the city's sights, and another day at the impressive **Centro Ecológico** (*see* Worth Seeing, *below*). Special events include **La Fiesta de la Vendimia** (The Grape Harvest Celebration) in mid-July, and Yaqui Indian dances, held during **Semana Santa** (Holy Week, the week before Easter). When you've had your fill of city life, head south with the rest of the *güeros* (white folks) to beach resorts such as Bahía Kino and Mazatlán.

BASICS

AMERICAN EXPRESS The AmEx office in **Hermex Travel** sells traveler's checks, insurance, and plane tickets, and cashes personal checks for cardholders. *Rosales, at Monterrey, tel. 62/13–44–15. Open weekdays 9–1 and 3–6, Sat. 9–noon. Mailing address: Edif. Lupita, Hermosillo, Sonora, CP 83000, México.*

CASAS DE CAMBIO A number of banks line Rosales (in the downtown area) and Eusebio Kino, in the northwest corner of town. **Bancomer** (Sonora, at Matamoros, tel. 62/12–13–62) changes traveler's checks weekdays 9–1 and has a *caja permanente* (ATM) that takes Visa. More ATMs can be found downtown, on Serdán between Juárez and Jesús García.

CONSULATES United States. The consulate has an answering machine that is checked after hours. *Monterrey 141, behind Hotel Calinda, tel. 62/17–23–75. Open weekdays 8–4:30.*

EMERGENCIES Dial 08 for emergencies, or call the **police** (tel. 62/13–40–46); **fire** (tel. 62/12–01–97); or **ambulance** (tel. 62/4–07–69). The **Ángeles Verdes** (Green Angels) provide emergency repair service and assistance if you have car trouble. *Calle Caridad 85, btw Blvd. Kino and Lampazos, tel. 62/58–00–44 or 800/6–25–55.*

LAUNDRY Lavandería Automática de Hermosillo lets you wash and dry a load of your dirty duds for $3. *Cnr of Sonora and Yáñez, tel. 62/7–55–01. Open Mon.–Sat. 8–8, Sun. 8–1.*

MAIL The post office downtown will hold mail sent to you at the following address for 10 days: Lista de Correos, Blvd. Rosales, Hermosillo, Sonora, CP 83000, México. You can send or receive telegrams and faxes at the office next door. *Post office: Serdán, at Rosales, tel. 62/12–00–11. Open weekdays 8–7, Sat. 8–noon.*

MEDICAL AID Clínica del Noroeste (Plaza Juárez, at L. D. Colosio and Juárez, tel. 62/12–18–90) provides 24-hour emergency service and some English-speaking doctors. Nonemergencies are handled weekdays 8–8, Saturdays 8–1. For simpler problems, **Farmacia Margarita** (Morelia 93, at Guerrero, tel. 62/13–15–90) is open 24 hours.

PHONES Pay phones dot the streets downtown, but finding one that works could take you all day. It's quicker to head to **Hotel Monte Carlo** (*see* Where to Sleep, *below*), which has working phones. Long-distance calls and faxes can be placed at **Farmacia Margarita**'s caseta (*see above*; tel. 62/12–05–06), which charges $1.50 for a collect call and $2 per minute for direct calls to the United States. Look to the bus station's caseta for free collect calls.

VISITOR INFORMATION The **Secretaría al Fomento de Turismo** (Secretary of Tourism), in the Centro del Gobierno Edifico Estatal usually has someone on hand who speaks English, but anyone here can eagerly load you down with brochures and maps. *Blvd. Paseo Canal and Comonfort, 3rd floor, tel. 62/17–00–76. Open weekdays 8–4 and 5–9, Sat. 10–1.*

COMING AND GOING

With several hills to orient you, it's difficult to get lost in Hermosillo. The most prominent hill downtown is **Cerro de la Campana.** Highway 15 runs through Hermosillo and on to Nogales to the north. Boulevard Transversal transects the city northwest–southeast. Local buses are cheap (40¢ or less) and dependable, if not always fast. Taxis charge roughly $1 per kilometer, but it may cost two or three times as much at night or from the bus station.

BY BUS Three main bus companies serve Hermosillo's bus station (Blvd. Transversal 400): **Transportes Norte de Sonora** (tel. 62/13–24–16), **Transportes del Pacífico** (tel. 62/17–05–80), and **Élite** (tel. 62/13–24–16). To reach the station from downtown, take any bus marked CIRCUITO NORTE, PERIFERICO, or TRANSVERSAL (40¢). Taxis charge $3.50 from the station to downtown, but you can pay less (about $3) if you walk away from the station and flag one down. Buses run north to Tijuana (12 hrs, $31), stopping in Nogales (3½ hrs, $7) and Mexicali (10 hrs, $23); and south to Mexico City (31 hrs, $79), stopping in Guaymas (2 hrs, $3.50), Los Mochis (7 hrs, $14), Mazatlán (12 hrs, $35), and Guadalajara (26 hrs, $55). Luggage storage (30¢ per hour) and money exchange are available at the terminal.

BY TRAIN The train station (tel. 62/15–35–77 or 62/10–34–57) is 3 kilometers north of town, just off Highway 15. First-class trains leave for Mexicali (10 hrs, $13) and Nogales (4 hrs, $5) daily at 1 PM. Second-class service to these same destinations leaves at 5 PM, takes somewhat longer, and costs about one-third of the price of first class. First-class trains for Guadalajara (24 hrs, $30) leave daily at 8 PM; second-class trains (at least 27 hrs, $13) leave daily at noon. If you're bound for Mexico City, you'll need to change trains in Guadalajara. Buses marked EST. FERR. will take you from the market in central Hermosillo to the station; a cab from the center costs $4.

WHERE TO SLEEP

Since a government antiprostitution sweep closed many of the flophouses in the budget lodging area, the area around Plaza Juárez has improved, but it's still unsafe for women alone, and all travelers should avoid the area after dark. Spared from the sweep was the best of the worst, **Casa de Huéspedes Hotel Carmelita** (Sonora, btw Revolución and Gonzáles, tel. 62/13–13–96), where a decrepit room with bath costs $8.50 and singles and doubles without bath are $6.50. Ignore the drunks hanging around outside **Hotel Monte Carlo** (Juárez, at Sonora, on Plaza Juárez, tel. 62/12–08–53), because inside you'll find clean private bathrooms and good air-conditioning. Singles cost $14, doubles $16, quads $20. Hermosillo may not be the place for a big splurge, but the travel-weary can head to **Hotel San Andrés** (Oaxaca 14, near Plaza Juárez, tel. 62/17–30–99) for security and relative opulence. The big rooms—some of them wheelchair accessible—have TVs, phones, and air-conditioning. The hotel also has a restaurant, bar, and shaded outdoor patio. Singles cost $25, doubles $27.

FOOD

The downtown area is loaded with cheap taquerías and street vendors selling everything from fruit to hot dogs. Here, you can go to dinner with $5 in your pocket and come back with a full belly and some change. Those oh-so-fresh fruits and vegetables are also sold at the **mercado municipal** (Matamoros, at Roberto Elías Calles) daily 7–7. The baseball paraphernalia covering the walls of **Café Monte Carlo** (In Hotel Monte Carlo, Juárez, at Sonora, tel. 62/12–22–59), open Monday–Saturday 7 AM–10 PM, adds ambience to this eclectic place. Try a tongue omelet ($2) with pineapple juice ($1) for breakfast. The extensive dinner menu includes chicken in green sauce ($3) and liver and onions ($2.50). The wholesome fare at **Jung** (Niños Héroes 75, near Matamoros, tel. 62/13–28–82) includes salads, sandwiches, and entrées, all fashioned from fresh fruits, vegetables, and whole-wheat breads ($2–$5). With new age music and an adjoining health food store that sells homemade granola bars ($1), this restaurant gives vegetarians a welcome respite from *frijoles refritos*. Jung is open Monday–Saturday 8–8.

WORTH SEEING

Hermosillo's old section, located near Plaza Juárez and the budget lodging, has a certain charm, with its decaying buildings and cramped alleyways. Even in the "newer" part of town, you can see traces of colonial history in the **Catedral de la Asunción** and the **Palacio de Gobierno,** located on the central Plaza Zaragoza. At the eastern base of Cerro de la Campana, the free **Museo de Sonora** (tel. 62/13–12–34) holds a fine collection of pre-Columbian artifacts and is open Wednesday–Saturday 10–5, Sundays 9–4. Nearby, the **Capilla del Carmen** occasionally holds a "mariachi mass"—a loud, colorful trumpet- and guitar-accompanied Sunday mass worth getting out of bed to attend. In **Parque Madero** (Jesús García, btw P. Elías and Norwalk), jungle gyms, long slides, merry-go-rounds, and swings drive the local kiddies wild—you might as well play too. Watch out for children who jump into the fountain, emerge dripping and jubilant, and embrace anyone not quick enough to get out of the way.

CENTRO ECOLOGICO DE SONORA With over 400 plant species and 240 animals, including wolves, hippos, and condors, this government reserve is focused on education and preservation. In addition to the plant and animal exhibits, there is a library, a botanical garden, and a theater that shows documentaries on endangered species. The center also leads groups to a nearby observatory on Friday nights 7:30–10:30 to observe the sky through a high-powered telescope. Call 62/50–12–25 one week in advance for reservations. *Carretera a Guaymas Km. 2.5, tel. 62/50–11–37, fax 62/50–12–36, http://yaqui.cideson.mx. From Plaza Juárez, take a LUIS ORSCI bus (15 min, 20¢) and ask driver to let you off at centro ecológico; walk down paved road about 10 min to entrance. Admission: $1, 75¢ students. Open June–Sept., Wed.–Sun. 8–6, Oct.–May until 5.*

AFTER DARK

Downtown Hermosillo (especially the area surrounding Plaza Juárez) is filled with men looking for trouble at night. Single women shouldn't even bother with the bar scene—it's dangerous and you'll get harassed 10 times more often than you would during the day. All travelers should avoid walking the streets at night; buses and taxis are easy enough to find. For diehard partyers, there's **Blocky'O** (Rodríguez, at Juárez, tel. 62/15–18–88), a huge disco that plays Mexican and American rock and offers frequent bar specials. A little farther south, just off Rodríguez, you'll find **Nova Olimpia** (Frontera, at C. L. de Soria, tel. 62/17–30–13), where the music alternates nightly between cumbia, salsa, and disco. Both clubs charge a $5 cover for men and $3 for women. A few blocks farther south, **Marco 'n' Charlie's** (Blvd. Rodríguez 78, tel. 62/15–30–61; open Mon.–Sat. 1 PM–2 AM) is a popular, cover-free bar and grill for young, middle-class locals and the few gringos in town.

Near Hermosillo

BAHÍA KINO

The two towns of Kino Viejo and Kino Nuevo share the Bahía Kino on the Sea of Cortez, and both are blessed with pristine beaches, warm, clear waters, and a sizeable population of manta rays and pelicans. Although both towns are easily explored from Hermosillo (about 120 kilometers away), they couldn't have less in common. The poor, sleepy fishing village of **Kino Viejo** was established in the 1700s by the Jesuit priest Eusebio Kino as a mission for Seri Indians; today it consists of a few stores, restaurants, and fishermen's houses strung along a dusty road. The charm of this town lies in its friendly atmosphere (sometimes a little too friendly for women traveling alone), cheap fresh seafood, and colorful sunsets. **Kino Nuevo**, about five minutes away from Kino Viejo by bus, is a haven for American retirees—their well-tailored houses blend into the desert landscape but seem out of place next to run-down shacks and coconut stands. The small, free **Museo de los Seris** (Mar de Cortés, at Calle Progresso; open daily 10–1 and 3–6) in Kino Nuevo gives out historical and cultural information on the indigenous Seris, who you may see selling the ironwood sculptures for which they are known. Local hustlers may try to persuade you to visit the **Isla del Tiburón** (Shark Island), home to the Seri Indians until they were forcibly resettled in the '50s. The island is now a fragile wildlife refuge for tortoises, rams, coyotes, and birds; please don't visit.

COMING AND GOING Ten buses (1½ hrs, $3.50) run from Hermosillo to the Kinos daily 5:40 AM–5:30 PM. Buses depart from the old **Transportes Norte de Sonora** station (Sonora, btw Revolución and González) in Hermosillo, not the main bus station. These buses pass through both Kinos every one or two hours, but walking and hitching between towns is easy. To return to Hermosillo, catch the bus on the main road in either Kino between 6 AM and 5:30 PM.

WHERE TO SLEEP Although you can do the Kinos in a day, you might regret missing the fiery sunset over the Sea of Cortez. Of the two Kinos, Kino Nuevo has the only hotels, the cheapest of which is **Hotel Saro** (midway down Kino Nuevo's main road, tel. 624/2–00–07), where clean singles are $27, doubles $30, and you can pay by MasterCard or Visa. In the off-season, various RV parks in both Kinos rent tent spaces for $5–$10, which includes use of their bathroom and shower facilities. In Kino Nuevo, try **Trailer Park Kino Bay** (tel. 624/2–02–16) at the end of the main road, or **Islandia Marina** (tel. 624/2–00–81), on the water near Puerto Peñasco and Guerrero. The latter has beach bungalows with kitchen facilities ($22 for four) right on the water. You can also string up a hammock or plop your tent under one of the many *palapas* (thatched huts) along the 18-kilometer beach in Kino Nuevo for free. Camping here is generally safe, but you need to watch your stuff. Avoid camping on the beach in Kino Viejo; there's a lot of foot traffic here at night.

FOOD Kino Viejo has a few good restaurants, and a number of fish and taco stands. **Restaurant Dorita** (no phone; open daily 7–7), just opposite the police station/post office/Red Cross building on the main drag, serves good, cheap lunches (about $5) to fussing children and their exasperated parents. In Kino Nuevo, you can enjoy a shrimp cocktail ($4) accompanied by fresh lemonade ($1) while taking in the sea view at **La Palapa** (midway down main road, tel. 624/2–02–10; open daily 8 AM–10 PM).

LA PINTADA

The archaeological site at La Pintada, 60 kilometers (37 mi) south of Hermosillo off Highway 15, was once a refuge for Pima, Yaqui, and Seri Indians fleeing the Spanish. The site's main feature is **La Pintada cave,** located in one of the canyons just off Highway 15. Inside the cave are vibrantly colored Rupestrian-era rock paintings dating to 9000 BC. These paintings depict deer, reptiles, and birds, as well as hunting rituals; the impressions of hands and feet around the paintings are supposedly the continent's oldest. To reach La Pintada, catch a **TNS** (Transportes Norte de Sonora) bus from Hermosillo heading toward Guaymas (1 hr, $3) and ask the driver to let you off at La Pintada. From here, follow the dirt road 3 kilometers back to the site. La Pintada is open Monday–Saturday until dusk and admission is free.

Guaymas
The port city of Guaymas is hot, humid, and smells like decaying fish. An extensive shrimp- and sardine-fishing fleet operates from these docks, and seafood processing is one of the main local industries—check out the town's **Monumento al Pescador,** an enormous statue of a fisherman battling a huge fish. All this makes Guaymas a memorable olfactory experience and little else, but if you're too broke to stay in San Carlos (*see* Near Guaymas, *below*), wandering along Guaymas's docks watching the fishing boats is one way to kill a few hours before or after frying on the nearby beaches. Another reason to visit is strictly practical: There is twice-weekly ferry service from Guaymas to Santa Rosalía on the Baja Peninsula.

BASICS

If your clothes are beginning to smell like fish too, **Guaymas Superlava** (García López 884, 1½ km west of bus station, tel. 622/2–54–00; open Mon.–Sat. 8–7:30) has automatic washers for $1.35 and dryers for $2.50. Fans of self-medication should try **Farmacia Sonora Centro** (Serdán, at Calle 18, tel. 622/2–30–44), open 24 hours. For more urgent medical attention, see **Dr. David Robles Rendón** (Serdán, at Calle 17, tel. 622/2–83–13 or 622/2–16–69; open weekdays 9–1 and 4–8, Sat. 9–1), a general practitioner who doesn't speak English.

If you're low on pesos, change cash and traveler's checks at **Bancomer** (Serdán, at Calle 18) weekdays 8:30 AM–12:30 PM or head to the **Banamex** ATM (Serdán, at Calle 20), which accepts Plus and Cirrus. The public **phones** along the streets often don't work: Make local, long-distance, and international calls from the caseta at **Farmacia Eco San Alberto** (Calle 19, 1 block south of Serdán, tel. 622/4–20–44), which charges 20¢ to call collect daily 8 AM–9 PM. The **post office** (Av. 10, at Calle 20. tel. 622/2–07–57; open weekdays 8–7, Sat. 8–noon) has all the usual services and will hold mail sent to you at the following address for up to 10 days: Lista de Correos, Avenida 10, Guaymas, Sonora, CP 85400, México.

COMING AND GOING

In Guaymas, Highway 15 becomes García López. Avenida Serdán, which splits off from García López on the east side of town, is central to everything but the beaches and is served by rickety but well-marked local buses. Buses marked SAN CARLOS (40¢) make the 15-minute trip out to San Carlos from in front of the Comex building on Serdán, near Calle 16.

BY BUS Buses here are more convenient than trains since they run more frequently and the station is centrally located. Three bus lines, **Transportes Norte de Sonora** (tel. 622/2–12–71), **Transportes del Pacífico** (tel. 622/2–30–19), and **Élite** (tel. 622/2–12–71), operate from terminals across the street from one another on Rodríguez, near Calle 13, two blocks south of Serdán. Buses depart hourly, heading south to Mexico City (29 hrs; $75 1st class, $65 2nd class), with stops in Los Mochis (5 hrs; $10 1st class, $9 2nd class), Mazatlán (10 hrs; $32 1st class, $27 2nd class), and Guadalajara (24 hrs; $54 1st class, $44 2nd class); and north to Tijuana (17 hrs; $36 1st class, $31 2nd class), stopping in Hermosillo (1½ hrs, $3), Nogales (5 hrs, $14), and Mexicali (15 hrs; $28 1st class, $24 2nd class). Transportes del Pacífico leaves frequently for Navojoa (3 hrs, $6), the transfer point for Alamos.

BY TRAIN The train station (tel. 622/3–10–65) is 10 kilometers south of Guaymas in a town called Empalme. To get here, take a red-and-white Transportes Norte de Sonora bus (50¢) marked EMPALME from any bus stop on Serdán or from the bus station; a taxi costs $5. If you're coming from the south, buses stop in Empalme on the way to Guaymas, but the bus stop is 1 kilometer from the station. Northbound trains run to Mexicali (12 hrs, $16 1st class; 15 hrs, $9 2nd class), Nogales (6 hrs, $8 1st class; 8 hrs, $4 2nd class), and Hermosillo (1½ hrs, $3 1st class; 2 hrs, $1.50 2nd class). Southbound trains depart for Guadalajara, the transfer point for Mexico City (24 hrs, $26 1st class; 26 hrs, $15 2nd class).

BY FERRY The **Sematur** ferry terminal (tel. 622/2–23–24) is at the east end of town, just off Serdán. Ferries to Santa Rosalía, on the eastern Baja coast, run on Tuesday and Friday at 8 AM (7 hrs; $13.50 regular class, $27 tourist class, which includes a cabin). You can put a car on the ferry as well, but it's expensive—they charge by size, and the smallest car costs $100. You can buy tickets at the ferry terminal Mondays and Thursdays 8–3 or the morning of departure 6 AM–7:30 AM.

WHERE TO SLEEP

There are plenty of clean, quiet, reasonably priced hotels on and near Serdán. **Casa de Huéspedes Lupita** (Calle 15 No. 125, tel. 622/2–84–09) is only a few blocks from Serdán and the bus terminals. Singles with bath cost $7, doubles $9. Without bath the prices drop to $5 and $7 (respectively) and you might as well save your dough—the communal baths are pleasant, and the lukewarm water doesn't get any warmer in the pricier rooms. The same owner has recently opened **Casa de Huéspedes Marta** (Calle 13 and Av. 9, 3 blocks from Lupita, tel. 622/2–83–32), which offers wheelchair-accessible rooms with bath for $6 a single, $8 a double. Rooms with air-conditioning go for $8 (singles) and $12 (doubles). **Hotel Santa Rita** (Serdán, at Meza, tel. 622/4–14–64, fax 622/2–81–00), a short walk from the center of town, offers small rooms with TV and air-conditioning for $15 (singles) and $18 (doubles). They take traveler's checks, AmEx, and Visa, and have some wheelchair-accessible rooms. A motel with the same name but higher prices lies less than a block away at Calle 9; don't let the taxi take you there.

FOOD

Serdán is lined with reasonably priced restaurants, bars, *loncherías* (snack bars), and *taquerías* serving fresh local seafood and typical Mexican dishes. Buy your fruits and veggies at the **mercado municipal** (open daily 7–7), in a long building one block south of Serdán, near the intersection with Yáñez. If you want to splurge, **Del Mar** (Calle 17, at Serdán, tel. 622/4–02–25) serves excellent fresh seafood dishes, such as shrimp flambé ($7) and lobster burritos ($6) in a cool, dark refuge from the sun. Del Mar is open daily noon–midnight, but the bar stays open until 2 AM. For a traditional Mexican breakfast, **Restaurant Las Cazuelas** (Av. 12, at Calle 15, tel. 622/2–65–96) serves eggs, rice, and beans ($2), as well as a tasty comida corrida ($3) in the afternoon. They're open Tuesday–Saturday 8 AM–9 PM, and Sundays until 3 PM. **Restaurant Todos Comen** (Serdán, at Calle 15, tel. 622/2–11–00; open daily 7 AM–midnight) has a selection of breakfast dishes, most under $3. Later on, they serve fish fillets ($3) and a huge Mexican combo plate with tacos, *flautas* (fried tacos), tostadas, and enchiladas for $3.50.

Near Guaymas

SAN CARLOS

The desert escapes into the azure waves of the Sea of Cortez at San Carlos, where Mt. Teta Kawi dominates the shoreline. More and more diving enthusiasts from the United States call this town home, and you'll find them putting on the golf courses and schmoozing at nearby Club Med. If you have the cash, it's easy to participate in a number of water sports here, including sailing, kayaking, jet skiing, and—for a slower pace—fishing. San Carlos hosts an international fishing tournament in July and a multilevel sailing competition called **Cristóbal Colón** (Christopher Columbus) around October 12.

Club Med chose San Carlos for its white sand beaches and turquoise waters. A 40¢ bus ride from Guaymas will give you the same thing for a lot less.

COMING AND GOING Buses marked SAN CARLOS (30 min, 60¢) leave from Serdán in Guaymas every half hour, starting at 6 AM. The last bus returns to Guaymas from San Carlos at 9 PM. If you don't have a car, taxis provide the only means of transportation from San Carlos to the less-populated beaches. A taxi to **Frenchie's Cove** or **Lalo Cove** (both about 7 km from town) will cost $7; it's $8–$10 to **Catch 22** beach (a.k.a. **Playa Los Algodones**), 8 kilometers away, and $7 to **Las Mangas** (16 km away).

WHERE TO SLEEP Unless you've got a tent, you'll probably want to make San Carlos a day trip. **Hotel Fiesta** (at entrance to town, 1½ km down main road, tel. 622/6–02–29) and **Motel Crestón** (tel. 622/6–00–20) are the cheapest hotels, but both charge more than $30 for double rooms. Both have a pool, long-distance phone service, and accept Visa and MasterCard, but Hotel Fiesta has a private beach and a restaurant. The more reasonably priced **Departamentos Ferrer** (1 block from beach on Bajada del Comedor, tel. 622/6–04–67) has apartments with air-conditioning and kitchenettes that fit up to four people ($22). Make reservations at least two weeks in advance, as the place is full even in the summer months.

For $7 a night you can camp at **Teta Kawi Trailer Park** (behind Best Western, tel. 622/6–02–20, fax 622/6–02–48), just outside town toward Guaymas, or next door at **Totonaka Trailer Park** (tel. 622/6–04–81 or 622/6–03–23) and take advantage of the swimming pools and nearby laundry ($1.50). Beach camping is legal, but watch your stuff. The best places to camp are **Playa San Francisco** (just before entrance to town from Guaymas), **Lalo Cove,** and **Playa Los Algodones** (in front of Howard Johnson's).

FOOD Food stands along the Carretera Turístico (the highway that runs through town) are the cheapest way to fill your belly. However, if you want to have a real sit-down meal, try **Rosa Cantina** (tel. 622/6–10–00; open daily 6:30 AM–9:30 PM) on the main drag, which has a long list of breakfast items ($3), a salad bar ($2.50), and pork chops ($5.50). The **San Carlos Grill** (Plaza Comercial San Carlos No. 1, at turnoff to marina, tel. 622/6–06–09; open daily 1–10) specializes in Lingo Gringo (beef fillet; $5) accompanied by a frosty margarita ($1.50).

OUTDOOR ACTIVITIES Finding budget outdoor activities in San Carlos is, unfortunately, about as difficult as catching a chill in Sonora. If you like to sweat, you can rent a bike ($5 for 3 hrs) at **El Mar Diving Center** (263 Creston, tel. 622/6–04–04), but make sure you have plenty of water or you'll dehydrate and pass out from the heat. Another cheap option is to rent scuba masks and fins for $3 per day at **Gary's** (near El Mar, on main road). Gary's also organizes fishing trips and has a 2½-hour snorkeling trip ($33) to the Aquarium Cove, one of the nearby attractions. If you have money to blow, you've come to the right place—everything from windsurfing equipment ($20 per hr), to Jet Skis ($55 per hr), to banana boat rides where you're pulled behind a boat on a rubber float ($5.50 per hr) is available.

➢ **SCUBA DIVING** • Divers and snorkelers are drawn to San Carlos for its accessibility and the clear waters that reach Jacuzzi-like temperatures in the summer. Gary's (*see above*) has four-day certification courses for $414 that include five open-water dives and all gear. His prices are competitive with those at **Cortés Explorations** (near the marina, tel. 622/6–08–08) and **El Mar Diving Center** (*see above*). If you're already certi-
fied, a two-tank dive to sites off nearby islands goes for $60 (add another $30 if you need equipment).

Aguamalos (jellyfish) are abundant on the beaches of San Carlos. You'll notice thousands of the bright-blue bodies with long tails on the sand and in the water. If you get stung, put fresh lemon juice on the wound to stop the burning. It'll hurt like hell, but you'll live.

ALAMOS

This small city, 256 kilometers (158 mi) southeast of Guay-mas, is one of the oldest in northern Mexico. Once the land of the indigenous Guarijio people, Alamos was converted into a silver-mining town by European businessmen seeking their fortune. It may be a bit complicated to reach, but once you get here, the narrow cobblestone streets, ranchers on horseback, and secluded haciendas with elegant inner courtyards may charm you into staying longer than you had planned.

Entertainment in Alamos comes in the form of exploring the crumbling adobe buildings. The **Iglesia de la Purísima Concepción** has a towering three-tier bell tower and impressive Spanish colonial architecture, while the beautiful **Hotel Mansión de la Condesa Magdalena** (Obregón, tel. 642/8–02–21) is worth peeking into, even though you probably can't afford to stay. The **Plaza de las Armas** is a beautiful park that livens up with kids, couples, and people-watchers as soon as the sun dips below the horizon. At the north end of the plaza, the **Museo Costumbrista de Sonora** (admission 50¢) merits a visit for its displays on Sonora's history. It's open Wednesday–Sunday 9–1 and 3–6. If you'd like an oral version of Alamos's history, **Pepe** at the Hotel Casa de los Tesoros (*see* Where to Sleep, *below*) gives a two-hour walking tour of the city ($7). Alamos is also famous for its *brincadores* ("Mexican jumping beans"; in reality butterfly larva), which are found in the hills surrounding the city. September is the best time to catch the little guys, but they're usually hopping year-round.

BASICS You can change cash or traveler's checks 8:30–1 at the **Bancomer** (tel. 642/8–03–25) at the south end of Plaza de las Armas, but there are no ATMs anywhere in the city. The **post office** is next to the police station on Madero. There are no public phones on the streets, but **Polo's Restaurant** (tel. 642/8–00–01), at the far end of Zaragoza, has a small caseta that charges $1.50 for collect and credit-card calls. The **tourist office** (tel. 642/8–04–50), below Hotel Los Portales, is open weekdays 9–2 and 4–7, Saturday 9–2. You can rent **bicycles** ($1 an hr) on Plaza de las Armas next to Bancomer Monday–Saturday 8–1 and 3–6, but it will be a bumpy ride along the cobblestone streets.

COMING AND GOING Alamos is only accessible by car, or by local bus from the town of Navojoa. After the **Transportes del Pacífico** bus from Guaymas lets you off at the corner of Revolución and Guerrero in Navojoa, walk 10 minutes down Guerrero (toward the town center) to the small **Los Mayitos** terminal, at the corner of Rincón. Buses leave here for Alamos (1 hr, $1) every 40 minutes 6:30 AM–midnight. From Alamos, hourly buses (last bus 6:30 PM) make the return trip to Navojoa from the station on Morelos, at Plaza Alameda. If you're coming by car, head south on Highway 15 from Guaymas and look for the turnoff for Alamos in Navojoa.

WHERE TO SLEEP Rooms in Alamos are not cheap. The short walk to **Motel Somar** (Madero 110, tel. 642/8–01–95) from the center of town is more than compensated for by the reasonable prices ($14 singles, $17 with air-conditioning; $16 doubles, $19 with air-conditioning), comfortable, wheelchair-accessible rooms with fans, and fairly clean, private bathrooms. If you know you'll be staying here, ask the bus driver to drop you off when you see the MOTEL SOMAR sign on your left as you enter town. Next door, **Dolisa Motel** (Madero 72, tel. and fax 642/8–01–31) has singles ($18) and doubles ($20) with TV, air-conditioning, and possibly a fridge (depending on the room). The wheelchair-accessible **Hotel Casa de los Tesoros** (Obregón 10, behind cathedral, tel. 642/8–00–10), a former convent, has been beautifully restored and offers air-conditioning, fireplaces, an inner courtyard with a pool, lots of elderly gringos in the winter months, and a restaurant serving Mexican and Puerto Rican food. Singles are $35, and doubles cost $40 in the summer months; in winter the same rooms cost $75.

➤ **CAMPING** • The Dolisa Motel (*see* Where to Sleep, *above*) has a big dirt lot where you can pitch a tent ($5 for 2 people) or park an RV ($12). The owner of Motel Somar will also let camp in the back and charges whatever you can afford. There are a few RV parks where less than $10 will get you a tent site for two with showers and a swimming pool; try **Trailer Park Acosta Ranch** (tel. 642/8–02–46), just over a kilometer from town near the cemetery, or **Los Alamos Trailer Park** (tel. 642/8–03–32), at the entrance to town on the highway.

FOOD The vendors clustered around Plaza Alameda serve tacos and such for about $1. The **mercado municipal** (east end of plaza) has inexpensive meats, cheeses, and locally grown fruits and vegetables, but you can eat almost as cheaply at some local restaurants. **Taquería Blanquita** (Antonio Rosales, next to market) is packed with locals 6 AM–11 PM. Long, get-to-know-your-neighbor tables are generously stocked with chile and guacamole to dress the $2 comida corrida. The air-conditioned **Restaurant Bar María Bonita** (Rosales 36, tel. 642/8–04–92) overlooks a garden and serves terrific, reasonably priced food. Breakfasts are $3, plates of tostadas or enchiladas are $4, and fish or shrimp with rice, beans, and salad is $7. **Antojitos Laura** (Rosales, just behind Plaza Alameda, no phone) serves to-die-for tostadas ($2) and guards their family recipe under lock and key. Right now they're only open for dinner daily 6–10 PM, but that'll change *muy pronto*.

Los Mochis

Just over the Sonora–Sinaloa border on Highway 15, the agricultural boomtown of Los Mochis is surrounded by farmland. The city was founded in 1893 by Benjamin Johnston, who managed to buy huge quantities of land during Porfirio Díaz's massive land grab (just before the turn of the century). During this time almost a fifth of the entire Republic was turned over to Díaz's friends and foreign investors. Díaz developed sugar production in this area, and brought the Chihuahua al Pacífico railroad across the Sierra Madre Occidental to Los Mochis. Today, most tourists pass through only to catch the train for the famous Copper Canyon ride, or to board a Baja-bound ferry. Aside from this, Los Mochis and its environs boast few points of local interest, apart from the town's lively Sunday morning market, or the remains of Johnston's opulent estate, with its pleasant botanical garden. But even this normally *tranquilo* (mellow) town rocks out on a few occasions. Around the second week of February, **Carnaval** comes to town with musical groups and dancing parades, and May 31 is the **Día del Marino** (Day of the Sailor), which begins with a procession of boats in Topolobampo and ends with the election of a *reina* (queen) in Los Mochis.

BASICS

AMERICAN EXPRESS The AmEx representative in **Viajes Araceli** changes traveler's checks and provides the usual cardholder services. The travel agency (open Mon.–Sat. 8:30–6:30, Sun. 10–1) also sells first-class plane, bus, and train tickets. *Álvaro Obregón 471-A Pte., Los Mochis, Sinaloa, CP 81200, México. Tel. 681/2–20–84 or 681/2–41–39. Open weekdays 8:30–1 and 3–6:30, Sat. 8:30–2.*

BOOKSTORES **Librería Los Mochis** has a wide selection of literature in Spanish, as well as an occasional English newspaper. *Madero 402, at Leyva, tel. 681/5–72–42. Open daily 8 AM–10 PM.*

CASAS DE CAMBIO A number of banks and several casas de cambio line Calle Leyva downtown. **Servicio de Cambio** (Leyva 271 Sur, near Juárez, tel. 681/2–56–66) changes cash and traveler's checks weekdays 8–7:30, and Saturdays until 7 PM. If you get going early, you can get much better rates at **Bancomer** (Leyva, at Juárez, tel. 681/5–80–01): The exchange window is open until 1 PM, but try to be in line by noon. **Banamex** has three 24-hour ATMs in the downtown area; the most centrally located (Prieto and Hidalgo) accepts Visa, MasterCard, Cirrus, and Plus cards.

EMERGENCIES You can reach the **police, fire department,** or **ambulance** service by dialing 06 from any public phone.

LAUNDRY The self-serve **Lavarama** is around the corner from the bus terminals. Automatic washers cost $2, dryers $2, soap 50¢, and they'll do it all for you for another 75¢ per load. *Juárez 225, tel. 681/2–81–20. Open daily 8–7.*

MAIL The post office will hold mail sent to you at the following address for up to 10 days: Lista de Correos, Los Mochis, Sinaloa, CP 81281, México. *226 Ordóñez Pte., tel. 681/2–08– 23. Open weekdays 8–6:30, Sat. 9–1.*

MEDICAL AID **Farmacia San Jorge** (Flores and Independencia, tel. 681/5–74–74) is open 24 hours. For more urgent medical attention, the 24-hour **Centro Médico de Los Mochis** has some English-speaking doctors, as well as a 24-hour pharmacy. *Rosendo G. Castro, btw Allende and Guillermo Prieto, tel. 681/2–74–26 or 681/2–01–98.*

PHONES There are brand-new **TelMex** pay phones all over downtown from which you can make local or long-distance calls. At the quiet, air-conditioned **Fax Tel** (Leyva, btw Hidalgo and Obregón, tel. and fax 681/8–10–20), you can make local or long-distance cash calls (as well as free collect calls and credit-card calls) and use the fax machine 8 AM–10 PM daily.

VISITOR INFORMATION Camping supplies for the Copper Canyon abound at **Equipos y Deportes** (Leyva, at Juárez), open daily 9–7. The small tourist office in the **Unidad Administrativa** building is intimidatingly disguised as a private office behind dark, reflective windows. Don't be deterred: The English-speaking staff is happy to help you. *Allende, at Cuauhtémoc, tel. 681/2–66–40. Open weekdays 8–3 and 5–8.*

COMING AND GOING

BY BUS Unless you're heading straight to Chihuahua via the Copper Canyon, traveling by bus is the easiest way to leave Los Mochis. The **Élite** (tel. 681/2–17–57) and **Transportes Norte de Sonora** (tel. 681/8–49–67) terminal is on Juárez between Allende and Prieto. The **Transportes del Pacífico** (tel. 681/2–03–41) terminal is a few blocks north of downtown, on José María Morelos, between Leyva and Zaragoza. Both stations are open 24 hours, but none has luggage storage. The terminal on Juárez is the newest and busiest and offers first- and second-class service to Mazatlán (6 hrs, $16–$18), Guadalajara (11 hrs, $33–$38), Mexico City (24 hrs, $38–$50), Nogales (10 hrs, $19–$22), Mexicali (22 hrs, $26–$41), Tijuana (24 hrs, $29–$32), and Navojoa (3 hrs, $4–$5).

BY TRAIN The railroad station (tel. 681/2–93–85), 2 kilometers from downtown on the southeastern outskirts of town, is the southwestern terminus of the famous **Chihuahua al Pacífico** iron horse, which winds its way through the Copper Canyon region (*see* Chapter 5). If you only take one train ride in Mexico, this should be it. Two trains depart from Los Mochis: The first-class *Vista* departs at 6 AM, with stops in the Copper Canyon towns of Bahuichivo (6½ hrs; $13 1st class, $4 2nd class), Divisadero (7½ hrs; $15 1st class, $3 2nd class), and Creel (9½ hrs; $18.50 1st class, $3 2nd class), arriving in Chihuahua ($33 1st class, $7 2nd class) some 12 hours later. The second-class *Mixto* (also called *pollero* or *burro*) train departs at 7 AM, and takes a whole lot longer to arrive at any given destination. Buy tickets a day in advance if you can; travel agencies and most hotels sell tickets for the Vista train, but Mixto tickets are only available at the train station the morning of departure starting at 6 AM. During Semana Santa you'll have to fight everybody and their *abuelita* (grandmother) for tickets. To reach the station from town, look for taxis ($5) in front of Hotel Santa Rita on Leyva and Hidalgo; buses marked COL. FERR. go to the train station but don't operate in the early morning and are therefore useless to most travelers, since this is precisely when the trains leave.

Travelers heading north to Mexicali ($21 1st class, $7 2nd class) or south to Guadalajara ($23 1st class, $7 2nd class) depart from the Sufragio station on the **Ferrocarril del Pacífico** line (tel. 681/4–01–28). To reach Sufragio, take a bus headed for El Fuerte from Calle Cuauhté-moc and Zaragoza (50 min, $2) and ask the driver to let you off at the Sufragio station.

BY FERRY You can buy tickets for a **Sematur** ferry to La Paz (on the Baja Peninsula) at **Viajes Paotam** (Serapio Rendón 517 Pte., tel. 681/5–19–14) in Los Mochis Monday–Saturday 8–1 and 4–6, Sunday 10–noon. Tourist class (a cushy seat) costs $13, and a cabin costs $27. Be sure to buy tickets at least 24 hours in advance if you're determined to leave on a specific day. Tickets are also on sale at the ferry dock weekdays 8 AM–11 AM. Ferries leave from the dock in Topolobampo, 25 kilometers west of Los Mochis, at 9 PM, and the trip takes about nine hours. Buses marked TOPOLOBAMPO (50¢) leave from the corner of Cuauhtémoc and Prieto every 15 minutes 6 AM–8 PM, stopping along Boulevard Rosendo G. Castro on the way out of town.

BY PLANE The Los Mochis airport, 20 kilometers south of town, is served primarily by **Aerocalifornia** (tel. 681/5–21–30 or 681/5–22–50) and **Aeroméxico** (tel. 681/5–25–70), which provide limited one-way service to major Mexican cities such as Guadalajara ($106) and Mazatlán ($95), and to U.S. destinations such as Tucson ($60). To get here, either take a taxi ($12) or take the TOPOLABAMPO bus to the main crossroads (it should be marked by an AEROPUERTO 5 sign) and either walk the 5 kilometers to the airport or hitch a ride.

GETTING AROUND

Los Mochis is easily navigated, and everything but the train station, airport, and ferry terminal is accessible by foot. Calles Allende, Guillermo Prieto, Zaragoza, and Leyva run parallel to one another, with hotels, drugstores, restaurants, and just about anything else you could need enclosed by Boulevard Castro and Avenida Madero. Budget lodging can be found close to Independencia on the west and Leyva on the north. City buses (20¢) are easily hailed all around town, and many originate at the **mercado,** on the corner of Guillermo Prieto and Cuauhtémoc.

WHERE TO SLEEP

Most budget accommodations in the downtown area need a good scrubbing but are fairly comfortable and centrally located. The interior of **Hotel del Parque** (Obregón 600, tel. 681/2–02–60) is better than the exterior would lead you to believe, but not by much. This wheelchair-accessible hotel, close to the refreshingly verdant Plazuela del 27 de Septiembre, offers basic rooms with fans for $9 (singles) and $12 (doubles), but there's no hot water. **Hotel del Valle** (Guillermo Prieto, at Independencia, tel. 681/2–01–05) is fairly modern, and those with cash-flow problems will be happy to find that Visa and MasterCard are accepted here. The shabby but comfortable rooms have fans and bathrooms with hot water that comes when it feels like it. Singles start at $10, doubles at $12 (with TV and phone, $13 and $15 respectively). The colonial-style **Hotel Montecarlo** (Ángel Flores 322 Sur, at Independencia, tel. 681/2–18–18) is tucked between a restaurant and a noisy bar in the downtown area, not far from the cathedral. Rooms on the second story have small balconies, while doubles on the first floor are wheelchair accessible. All rooms have air-conditioning, TV, a phone, and clean bathrooms with hot water. Singles are $13, doubles $19.

CAMPING **Los Mochis Trailer Park** (1 km west of Hwy. 15, tel. 681/2–68–17) charges $10 for a tent for two people and $12 for an RV. In addition to the communal bath facilities, there are coin-op laundry machines and a recreation room. The trailer park is almost 2 kilometers out of town: Follow the TOPOLOBAMPO/ AEROPUERTO signs from downtown.

FOOD

The downtown area teems with taco, fish, and fruit stands. The **mercado municipal** (Guillermo Prieto, at Cuauhtémoc Pte.; open daily 5–5) has raw edibles, a huge fish and meat market, and several decent *comedores* (sit-down food stands). **Restaurant Chic's** (Plaza Fiesta, at Rosales, at Obregón, tel. 681/5–47–09), a few blocks west of downtown, seems characterless, but once the families start strolling in after mass it's a good place to people-watch. Try the $4 breakfast of tamales, *chorizo* (spicy sausage), and beans, or the fresh fruit plate ($3). Chic's is open daily 6:30 AM–midnight. **El Taquito** (Leyva, btw Hidalgo and Independencia, tel. 681/2–81–19) not only looks like Denny's and tastes like Denny's, but it's open 24 hours for late-night binges and it's wheelchair accessible, just like Denny's. Mushroom omelets and french toast (both $3) are served for breakfast, and hamburgers and fries are on the menu for lunch ($3). **El Farallón** (Obregón, at Ángel Flores, tel. 681/2–14–28; open daily 7 AM–11 PM), specializing in fresh, spicy seafood, is a favorite of Los Mochis businessmen. Dishes such as calamari ($10) and ceviche ($5) come with tortillas and beans. **Jugos Chapala** (Independencia 366; open daily 7 AM–10:30 PM) pours fresh carrot, strawberry, and papaya juices (to name a few) for $1–$2.

WORTH SEEING

If you happen to be here on Sunday around 11 AM, be sure to visit the *tianguis* (open-air market), in the downtown shopping area (on Leyva, just across Rendon), where you can stock up on that oh-so-necessary Tupperware before heading to more remote areas of Mexico. The city's locals flock here once church services are over, and the shops and stalls are packed with hagglers. Come early, though—everything closes down by 2 PM. If you're in a more intellectual frame of mind, the **Escuela Vocacional de Artes** (Rosales, past shopping center, tel. 681/15–15–11) offers workshops and classes in traditional arts, crafts, and dance. They even have classes in the indigenous Nahuatl language. Call for more info.

PARQUE ECOLOGICO DE SINALOA This unassuming park occupies the grounds of sugar baron and town founder Benjamin Johnston's former estate, and is home to trees imported from around the world, including towering palms from Cuba and fuzzy cypress from Arizona. Near the entrance, a giant tree bears Indian carvings of an eagle, bear, snake, deer, and that ultimate animal, Mr. Johnston himself. There's also a children's playground right in front of the gardens, where, if you're lucky, you can join an impromptu soccer game. *On Rosales, behind Woolworth shopping center, no phone. Open daily 8–7.*

MUSEO REGIONAL DEL VALLE DEL FUERTE Ensconced in a colonial-style house, this museum consists of a photography exposition and archaeological exhibits depicting the history and culture of the region. Be sure to check out the oh-so-P.C. description of the indígenas' evangelization. Traditional theater and *baile folklórico* (folk dancing) productions are also staged here throughout the month. Stop by for a calendar of events. *Obregón, just east of Rosales, no phone. Open daily 10–1 and 4–7. Admission 75¢.*

Near Los Mochis

Buses headed for the towns of Topolobampo and El Fuerte depart Los Mochis from Cuauhtémoc, between Prieto and Zaragoza. Buses to Topolobampo (50 min, 50¢) leave daily about every half hour 7 AM–8 PM. If you're heading for La Paz, don't get off at the first bus station in Topolobampo—the bus will continue on to the ferry dock. Buses to El Fuerte (1½ hrs, $2) depart a little less often, 7 AM–6 PM.

TOPOLOBAMPO

About 25 kilometers west of Los Mochis is the town of Topolobampo, founded at the end of the 19th century by a bunch of Americans looking to set up a socialist utopia. This dream was soon squashed when the colonists began fighting amongst themselves and Los Mochis sugar baron Benjamin Johnston managed to scoop up the water rights to the area and evict everybody. Today the harbor town is largely dependent on shrimping and industry, and sea lions frolic in the deep bay, using Isla El Farallón, just off the coast, as a breeding ground. You are most likely to come here only to get on or off the ferry, but if you do stay a day or two you can take advantage of the spectacular natural surroundings of this less-than-spectacular town.

Although the harbor itself lacks swimming or sunning beaches, shell collectors will have a ball here. Boat rides to the five islands in the bay near Topolobampo can be arranged through Teodolfo Cital at the **Sociedad Cooperativa de Servicios Turísticos** (next to the customs building, on the water), which looks like a vacant, unfinished house. Teodolfo takes groups of eight people to the pristine **Playa Copas** ($30 a person), **Isla Santa María** ($45 a person), the duck sanctuary at **Isla Santuario** ($15 a person), or **Isla El Farallón,** where the sea lions play ($115 a person). He'll also take you on shorter fishing trips around the bay (45 min, $15), and bargaining on all of these trips is always an option. In September, *camarones* (shrimp) are practically spilling out of the ocean, and you can arrange a boat ride to watch the fishing boats take up their nets.

Most lodging in Topolobampo is expensive, and camping is unsafe. The best options are a $4 bunk dorm bed or a $9 single ($11 doubles) at **Pensión Paotám** (at the ferry dock). However, neither of these options includes a private bath or air-conditioning. A little farther away, but much more comfortable is **El Yacht** (tel. 681/2–66–01), about a half kilometer south of town on the highway. Here you can get a room that fits five people for about $15, including air-conditioning and TV. The hotel also has a private beach, a bar, and a restaurant built like a yacht, with a panoramic view of the bay and islands.

EL FUERTE

If your previous experiences of colonial architecture in northwestern Mexico have left you ambivalent, come to El Fuerte. Cobblestone streets, gracefully aging buildings, and newly remodeled haciendas with lush green patios provide a scenic backdrop for this slow-paced town. El Fuerte was originally founded in 1564 as a gateway to the northern Indian territories of Sonora, Arizona, and California. It was not easily won land for the Spanish, however, and they spent the next 50 years fending off the fierce Tehueco, Sinaloa, and Zuaque Indians. In 1610 a fort was built here, and the following three centuries saw the area around El Fuerte grow into one of the most important commercial and agricultural centers in northwestern Mexico.

Today this small colonial city, 75 kilometers (47 mi) east of Los Mochis, attracts fishermen to nearby **Lake Hidalgo** (11 kilometers north), **Lake Domínguez** (19 kilometers west), and the **Fuerte River** (a 10-minute walk west from the plaza), all known for their largemouth bass. If you didn't bring your fishing gear, you can swim in the lakes or the river, or take in the architecture. **La Iglesia del Sagrado Corazón de Jesús** (Church of the Sacred Heart of Jesus), built in 1854, the **Palacio Municipal,** and **La Casa de la Cultura** (admission free; open daily 10–7), surround the shaded **Plaza de Armas** at Degollado and Rosales. This plaza was voted the second most beautiful in the state of Sinaloa by the state's residents, and has a graceful white gazebo surrounded by palm trees, rose bushes, and lush ferns. Perhaps the best reason to visit El Fuerte is to splurge on a room at **Posada Hidalgo** (Hidalgo, just off plaza, tel. 681/5–70–46), a former colonial mansion. At $55 for two people, it has exotic gardens, outdoor patios, a swimming pool, and hammocks. The staff is also more than willing to provide you with information on the city's attractions, whether or not you're a guest. The adjoining **Disco Palace** (open Fri. and Sat. until 1 AM) attracts all the locals, who rock out to ranchero and mariachi music in their tightest Spandex. Stop by **Restaurant Supremo** (cnr of Rosales and Constitución) for fresh bass ($5) or a ham-and-egg breakfast ($3) daily 7 AM–11 PM.

NORTH CENTRAL MEXICO AND THE COPPER CANYON

5

By Carrie McKellogg, with Allison Eymil

The north central states of Chihuahua and Durango are characterized by their vast deserts, which circle the magnificent Sierra Madre Occidental mountain range. Regal cacti and run-down *ranchitos* (small farms) freckle the landscape, and when farmers aren't working the tomato, green pepper, and corn fields, they can be heard wailing *ranchero* songs in the local bars. These farmers have been struggling with financial hardship for five years, thanks to a persistent drought, but the recent rains are expected to bring relief to the withered crops and dying livestock. Adversity is not uncommon to north central Mexico, though, and the people have a history of digging in their heals and fighting back: Two founding fathers of contemporary Mexico, Miguel Hidalgo and Pancho Villa, called this region home, and today north central Mexico remains at the forefront of popular dissent—Chihuahua being a long-standing bastion of support for the PAN (Mexico's leading opposition party; *see* box, *below*).

"Throughout the ages the inhabitants of Chihuahua, whether miners, farmers, or priests, have always been warriors—because their environment has demanded of them more than their best efforts" (from a Mexican history textbook in the Paquimé Museum).

The highlights of this region begin to reveal themselves after you pass the overpopulated, drug-infested border town of Ciudad Juárez. The state of Chihuahua (which means "dry, sandy place" in the indigenous Tarahumara language) is most known for its natural beauty. The Sierra Madre Occidental comprises five large canyons sewn together by massive waterfalls, rivers, and hot springs. The most famous of these is **Las Barrancas del Cobre** (The Copper Canyon), which has been inhabited for centuries by the Tarahumara people. While many have been displaced due to the mining and lumber industries, 50,000 still uphold traditional customs on their original lands. The Chihuahua al Pacífico railway weaves 670 kilometers (415 mi) through the canyon, conveniently stopping at popular jumping-off points for hiking and camping, such as Creel, Batopilas, and Bahuichivo. Many tourists are also attracted to the enigmatic pre-Columbian ruins of Paquimé and the lively, historic city of Chihuahua.

The dusty landscape around the capital city of the state of Durango is what many people picture when they think of Mexico—probably because it's been used as the setting for a number of Hollywood westerns. The city itself is more a stopover point for travelers than anything else; however, once you get past the urban sprawl of the outskirts, you'll find a friendly colonial city perfect for a day or so of aimless wandering.

ARIZONA

NEW MEXICO

25

El Paso

Douglas

Ciudad Juárez

TEXAS

20

2

Agua
Prieta

2

45

10

90

67

10

67

90

Nuevo
Casas Grandes

Paquimé

Casas
Grandes

Gallego

SONORA

23

CHIHUAHUA

Río

Grande

COAHUILA

Basaseachi

La Junta

Chihuahua

Cuauhtémoc

Meoqui
Delicias

Divisadero

Creel

Saucillo

Sierra

Bahuichivo

Parque Natural
Barranca del
Cobre

Cd. Camargo

Cerocahui

Navojoa

15

Urique

Batopilas

Hidalgo
del Parral

Jiménez

30

San Pedro
de las
Colonias

Los
Mochis

Madre

49

Guasave

TO
LA PAZ

SINALOA

24

45

Gómez
Palacio

Cd. Lerdo

40

Torreón

DURANGO

Cuencamé

Miguel
Ausa

Culiacán

15

Occidental

Durango

49

40

Sombrerete

45

PACIFIC
OCEAN

Mazatlán

Fresnillo

ZACATECAS

Zacatecas

KEY

Rail Lines

Ferry Lines

N

Acaponeta

Aguascalientes

NAYARIT

Tlaltenango

54

0   150 miles

Tepic

0   200 km

15

Guadalajara

Puerta
Vallarta

JALISCO

Ciudad Juárez

If you find yourself in Ciudad Juárez, leave fast. Only hang around if: (1) you're jonesing for an inexpensive root canal; (2) you need a cheesy wedding dress; or (3) you are wanted by the law on both sides of the border and need to hop jurisdictions easily. This sprawling city on the northern edge of Chihuahua state exhibits the worst of both Mexico and the United States. The passage of NAFTA (the North American Free Trade Agreement) in 1994 increased the number of *maquiladoras*, or *maquilas* (foreign-owned factories in duty-free zones) in and around Juárez, creating an unfavorable societal and environmental impact. The majority of Juárez's population is currently employed in the maquilas, and the cardboard settlements that have sprouted to house these people lack basic sanitation and are polluted by toxic waste.

Juárez, though a good example of emerging border culture, is an uninspiring tourist spot. However, if you're stuck here for a day, try to catch a bullfight at the **Plaza de Toros Monumental** (Paseo Triunfo de la República and López Mateos) or a rodeo at **López Mateos Charro** (Av. del Charro). Museum buffs can visit the **Museo de Historia** in the **Antigua Aduana** building (16 de Septiembre, at Juárez, tel. 16/12–47–07; open Tues.–Sun. 10–6). Unless Juárez's year-round sleazy bar scene and sex trade appeal to you, the best time to catch a positive glimpse of the city is during festivals. The **Festival de la Raza,** celebrated during the first week of May, culminates in a **Cinco De Mayo** parade along Avenida Juárez. During the last two weeks of June, the **Feria Juárez** fills the city with dancing and theater, as well as arts-and-crafts displays.

BASICS

AMERICAN EXPRESS The AmEx representatives at **Sun Travel,** in El Paso, can help with lost or stolen checks, insurance, and transportation arrangements. The office also sells traveler's checks, offers MoneyGram service, and holds mail for cardholders. The AmEx office in Juárez only offers travel services. *3200 North Mesa, Suite B, El Paso, Texas 79902, U.S.A, tel. 915/532–8900, fax 915/533–6887 Open weekdays 7:30–5:30. In Juárez: Av. Lincoln 1320, Local (suite) 175, tel. 16/29–27–40. Open weekdays 9–6, Sat. 9-1.*

El Partido Acción Nacional

The PAN (Partido Acción Nacional) is the most powerful opposition party in Mexican politics today, and its stronghold is in the northern, agricultural states of Sonora and Chihuahua, as well as in the state of Durango. Considered to be ideologically right-of-center, the party was founded in 1939 in protest of PRI (Partido Revolucionario Institucional) reforms. Today the PAN is more commonly linked to agricultural interests in the north. Outlining welfare programs for the region's poor is one of the PAN's priorities, but the party mostly caters to middle- and working-class citizens. Along with a moral economic policy, the PAN promises to stop fraudulent elections and political manipulation by Mexico's ruling party, the PRI. It appears that the PAN's message is being met with approval: In 1992, Chihuahua elected its first PAN governor.

PAN's influence is most visible in the smaller towns of northern Mexico: In Casas Grandes, Chihuahua, a town consisting of one square block, the PAN office occupies half the block. You'll also see the PAN logo emblazoned on cardboard shacks along the roadsides. The norteños need something to believe in during drought and economic hardship—maybe the PAN is it.

CASAS DE CAMBIO Many money-exchange places line Avenida Juárez near the bridge. **Cambios Juárez,** just meters away from the bridge's entrance, is open daily 9–9, but most are only open until 5. After business hours, try **Banamex's** 24-hour *cajas permanentes* (ATMs), on the corner of Avenidas Juárez and 16 de Septiembre.

CONSULATES **United States.** *López Mateos Nte. 924, tel. 16/13–40–48, after hours in El Paso tel. 915/525–6066. Open weekdays 9–5.*

CROSSING THE BORDER When entering Mexico, pick up a tourist card at the **Mexican Consulate** (E. San Antonio St., tel. 915/533–3644; open weekdays 9–1) in El Paso or at the immigration office (open 24 hours daily) near the Stanton Street Bridge. The bridge is eight blocks south of downtown El Paso on Santa Fe Street, and there's a 25¢ toll at the entrance and a 30¢ toll to return. If you travel farther than 32 kilometers from the border or stay in Mexico more than 72 hours, you may be asked to show the card at checkpoints. Bringing a car into Mexico is complicated but possible (*see* Coming and Going, *below*). For more information, *see* Passports, Visas, and Tourist Cards in Chapter 1, or call the customs office at the border (tel. 16/16–08–25).

EMERGENCIES For emergency assistance (including ambulance service) call the Ciudad Juárez **police** (tel. 16/15–15–98), or dial 911 from any phone on the U.S. side of the border.

LAUNDRY **Lavandería Express** (Hernán Baldez, just behind Mercado Juárez, no phone) will wash and dry your clothes for about $1 per kilo. Be prepared to wait two hours for the service.

MAIL The slightly chaotic and inconspicuous **post office** is located downstairs on Francisco Villa, at Calle de la Peña just south of 16 de Septiembre. It's open weekdays 9–7, Saturday 9–5, Sunday 9–noon. They'll hold mail for you for up to 10 days at the following address: Lista de Correos, Administración 1, Ciudad Juárez, Chihuahua, CP 32001, México.

MEDICAL AID Hospitals in Mexico are notoriously sketchy: Unless it's an emergency, it's a good idea to make the short trip to El Paso. **Hospital General** (Paseo Triunfo de la República 2401, tel. 16/13–15–71) offers emergency care but no English-speaking physicians. **Farmacia Iris** (16 de Septiembre, at Corona, tel. 16/14–89–90, fax 16/12–30–76) is small but has decent hours: Monday–Saturday 9 AM–10 PM.

PHONES Public phones here are dependable for cash, credit card (Visa, MasterCard, and calling cards accepted), and even collect calls. For Mexican long distance, dial 02; to call El Paso, dial 95; for other international calls, dial 09 or your long-distance carrier's access number. **Teléfonos Publicos** (Juárez 315-B Nte., tel. 16/15–21–28; open daily 9–5) charges about 80¢ per minute to anywhere in the United States. They also have fax service, FedEx, and U.S. priority mail, as well as luggage storage (30¢ per hr).

VISITOR INFORMATION The tourist office inside the **El Paso–Juárez Trolley Co.** (1 Civic Center Plaza, El Paso, tel. 915/544–0061; open daily 8–5) provides information for travelers crossing into Mexico. Ciudad Juárez's **tourist office** is on the ground floor of the Palacio Municipal, just west of the Stanton Street Bridge. The friendly staff speaks English. *Colegio Militar, btw Juárez and Lerdo, tel. 16/14–01–23. Open weekdays 8–8, weeekends 8–noon.*

VOLUNTEERING The **Partido Verde Ecologista** campaigns to involve Mexico's youth in ecological projects such as water conservation and toxic waste prevention. In Juárez, the group has an "eco-bus" that distributes literature and teaches poor communities about waste removal and clean water. People on both sides of the border are welcome to pitch in and volunteer. For more information write: Partido Verde Ecologista de México, Attn. Diego Cobo, Coordinador Nacional de la Juventud Ecologista, Callejón del Beso 235-C, FRACC Valle Verde, Ciudad Juárez, Chihuahua, México.

COMING AND GOING

BY BUS The best way to reach Ciudad Juárez from El Paso is to catch a Greyhound bus (30 min, $5), which leaves every half hour from El Paso's Greyhound station (next to the convention center) and takes you right to Juárez's bus station. The bus terminal (tel. 16/10–64–14) is way out of Juárez, at the junction of Highways 2 and 45. The monstrous building is stocked with two long-distance telephone offices, a money-changing booth, a pharmacy, cafeterias, and 24-hour luggage storage (30¢ per hr). **Estrella Blanca** (tel. 16/29–22–29) provides hourly service to Chihuahua (4½ hrs, $10), Nuevo Casas Grandes (4 hrs, $7), Mazatlán (21 hrs, $45), Durango (14 hrs, $40), and Zacatecas (15 hrs, $34). Four buses also depart daily to Mexico City (26 hrs, $49). **Transportes Chihuahuenses** (tel. 16/10–69–68) serves the same routes, and **Turistar, Omnibus,** and **Futura** charge a few dollars more for *especial* first-class buses with air-conditioning, bathrooms, and movies. **Greyhound** bus tickets can be purchased at the **Omnibus** counter (tel. 16/10–62–97) for trips to Los Angeles ($35), Albuquerque ($20), and Denver ($40), as well as other U.S. destinations. To reach the bus station from downtown Juárez, take a bus marked CENTRAL CAMIONERA (20¢) and allow at least an hour. A taxi from Juárez will cost you about $7.

BY TRAIN The train station (Juan Gabriel, tel. 16/12–31–88) is 12 long blocks down the tracks from the Stanton Street Bridge. Two trains leave Ciudad Juárez daily, heading south to Mexico City (12 hrs, $35 1st class; many hrs, $20 2nd class), with stops in Chihuahua ($7 1st class, $3 2nd class), Zacatecas ($23 1st class, $13 2nd class), and Aguascalientes ($25 1st class, $14 2nd class). Tickets for the 10 PM first-class departure should be purchased in advance Monday–Saturday 9 AM–noon. They usually sell out, so plan ahead. The second-class train leaves at 7 AM, and tickets go on sale at 6 AM. If you're looking for a taxi from the station, it's better to walk a block or two toward downtown and hail one there, where prices are less likely to be inflated.

BY CAR You can bring a car into Mexico for up to 90 days. To cross the border with your car, present the title (in your name), a current driver's license, your passport, and photocopies of all three documents. You also have to provide a guarantee (like your credit-card number) that you'll bring the car back across once your permit expires; if you don't, you'll be charged a fine. Those without a credit card will have to buy a bond of 1%–2% of the car's value from one of the bond sellers close to the border. Customs officials don't care if you buy Mexican insurance or not, but a policeman farther south (or the "other party" in case of an accident) might. Insurance is available from a number of companies near the border. All offer similar coverage—a basic 24-hour liability/collision policy costs $10–$20.

BY PLANE The airport is far from the center of town, just off Highway 45. **Aeroméxico** (tel. 16/13–80–89 or 800/237–6639 from the U.S.) is the main carrier, with daily flights to Chihuahua ($98 one-way), Mexico City ($144 one-way), and Mazatlán ($142 one-way). A taxi from downtown to the terminal costs $10, but it's cheaper to grab a CENTRAL CAMIONERA bus (20¢), get off at the bus station, and take a taxi the rest of the way.

GETTING AROUND

Juárez is spread out, and transport terminals are all far from each other. Fortunately, budget accommodations and restaurants cluster along Avenida Juárez, between the Stanton Street Bridge and Avenida 16 de Septiembre. Unfortunately, finding local buses that travel to outlying points can be confusing because of the number of one-way streets. Buses generally arrive and depart from Avenida Vicente Guerrero, one block south of Avenida 16 de Septiembre. Buses run until midnight and tickets (20¢) can be purchased from the driver. Taxis are plentiful, though not cheap—settle on a price before you get in, and don't hesitate to negotiate. Fares should run $1–$2 a kilometer. If you want your own wheels, try **Hertz** (Paseo Triunfo de la República 2408-2, tel. 16/13–80–60), which rents cars for about $30 per day.

WHERE TO SLEEP

Most tourists stay in El Paso rather than Juárez, so lodging options are limited. The real cheapies are run-down and often charge by the hour, but there are several reasonable places on or near Avenida Juárez. This area is *not* safe after dark. If you happen to arrive in Juárez's bus terminal at night, your best bet is to stay put: The station is brightly lit and sleeping here is probably safer than taking a bus to the sketchy downtown area. If you simply must reach a hotel before morning, call 16/12–00–17 for a taxi, as they aren't available at the bus station.

elchair-accessible **Hotel Génova** (Moctezuma 569 Nte., off Colón and Lerdo, ...–43) is off the beaten path—about six blocks from Avenida Juárez—but at least ...e kept awake by noise from the downtown discos. The friendly staff will turn on the ...oning in your room at no extra charge, and patience will bring hot water to your ...The $5.50 singles and $7 doubles all come with bath. **Bombín Café Bary Hotel** (Colón, ...k east of Juárez, tel. 16/14–23–20) is hot and dank, but the rooms ($6 singles, $11.50 ...les) are pretty decent, and each has a private bathroom with hot water. On the east side o. Juárez, **Hotel Morán** (Juárez 264 Nte., tel. 16/15–08–12) is a favorite with families. The small but comfortable rooms feature pink bedspreads and baths with cranky plumbing. Singles and doubles are $15, with cable TV in every room.

FOOD

Restaurants and taco stands line Avenida Juárez, and the lively **mercado municipal** on Avenida 16 de Septiembre offers fresh fruit, vegetables, and cheeses daily 8:30–8. **Antojitos La Herradura** (González 184, tel. 16/12–09–32) serves a $5 *comida corrida* (pre-prepared lunch special) daily noon–10 that'll satisfy even the hungriest traveler. For late-night cravings, the 24-hour **El Coyote Inválido** (Av. Lerdo, at Paisaje Continental, tel. 16/14–25–71) is basic and economical. The $5 comida corrida and *pollo en mole* (chicken in chile and chocolate sauce; $3.50) are the most popular dishes. Juárez's most tradition-steeped eatery, **Restaurant La Sevillana** (González 140 Pte., tel. 16/12–05–58; open daily 8–6), behind the old bullring, has been churning out the same dishes for 40 years. Try the pancakes and coffee ($3) or the *picadillo con chile verde* (shredded beef with green chile sauce; $5).

AFTER DARK

Every storefront on Avenida Juárez not open during the day magically transforms into a disco or bar after dark, as teenagers from both sides of the border throw themselves into mass alcohol consumption. Most places charge a $3–$8 cover, but if you come before 10 PM or on a slow night, you can often get in free. If you're a woman traveling alone, stay on your toes—the streets can be dangerous at night. Heavy-metal fans will like **Spanky's** (Juárez 887; open Thurs.–Sun. 8 PM–4 AM), where beer is served in *yardas* (yards). **Alive** (Juárez, ½ block from Stanton Street Bridge; open Thurs.–Sat. 8 PM–3 AM) is a popular dance spot where a $3 cover gives you access to the latest hip-hop played in a cave-like den. To avoid this scene and enjoy a well-crafted mixed drink, head to **Kentucky Club** (Juárez 629, tel. 16/14–99–90; open daily 10 AM–midnight), a haven of Naugahyde couches and decades-old sports memorabilia. You can also listen to strolling musicians at the **Plaza del Mariachi,** farther south on the east side of Avenida Juárez.

Nuevo Casas Grandes and Paquimé

Some 260 kilometers (161 mi) southwest of Ciudad Juárez lie the twin towns of Nuevo Casas Grandes and Casas Grandes. Nuevo Casas Grandes is a two-horse town with the only hotels and most of the restaurants in the area—most visitors pass a night or two here on their way to either Ciudad Juárez or Chihuahua, visiting the **Paquimé ruins** (*see* Worth Seeing, *below*) in nearby Casas Grandes as a day excursion. With wide, dusty streets and sauntering residents in full cowboy gear (including proudly displayed pistols), Nuevo Casas Grandes goes about its business, barely noticing the presence of a tourist or two. Believe it or not, Casas Grandes, just 8 kilometers away, is even sleepier— the whole town consist of about one square block.

BASICS

Two casas de cambio, **Serfín** (open weekdays 9–1:30) and **Inverlat** (open weekdays 9–noon) have ATMs and change cash and traveler's checks. Both are located across the street from each other on 5 de Mayo at Constitución. For medical aid, English-speaking **Dr. Amaro Prieto Saldovar** can be reached weekdays 12:30–3:30 at the **Farmacia de la Clínica** (5 de Mayo 404, tel. 169/4–07–70; open daily 9 AM–11 PM). The full-service **post office** (16 de Septiembre, 1 block east of Obregón, tel. 169/4–20–16; open weekdays 8–6, Sat. 8–1) is one block from **Geydi Teléfono Larga Distancia** (Obregón, near 5 de Mayo, tel. 169/4–12–71; open Mon.–Sat. 9 AM–10 PM), which has long-distance phones and fax machines.

COMING AND GOING

BY BUS Nuevo Casas Grandes has two adjacent terminals: first-class **Omnibus** (tel. 169/4–05–02) and second-class **Estrella Blanca** (tel. 169/4–07–80), both on Obregón at 5 de Mayo, in the middle of downtown. Both send several buses daily to Ciudad Juárez (4 hrs, $7) and Chihuahua (5½ hrs, $9). Neither station offers luggage storage. To reach Casas Grandes and Paquimé from Nuevo Casas Grandes, hop a blue-and-gold bus marked CASAS GRANDES (30¢) on the corner of Constitución and 16 de Septiembre; after a 15-minute ride you'll be deposited at the zócalo in Casas Grandes. To reach Paquime from here, follow the PAQUIME sign on Constitución; the 10-minute walk past the park will take you to the ruins. The last bus returns to Nuevo Casas Grandes at 8:30 PM.

WHERE TO SLEEP AND EAT

The few hotels in Nuevo Casas Grandes are rather expensive. Your best option is the comfortable and friendly **Hotel Juárez** (Obregón 110, next to Estrella Blanca, tel. 169/4–02–33), where clean singles cost $6, doubles $8. There's also a room that holds up to five people for $12. **Motel Piñón** (Juárez 605, tel. 169/4–01–66) has a swimming pool and a private collection of *ollas* (clay pots) from Paquimé. Singles are $18, doubles $20. Credit cards are accepted both here and at the wheelchair-accessible **Hotel Paquimé** (Juárez 401, tel. 169/4–13–20). The Paquimé has two categories of rooms to choose from: newly renovated (singles $18, doubles $21) or nonrenovated (singles $15, doubles $16). All include air-conditioning, cable TV, and phone. There is no lodging in Casas Grandes, but plans are in the works for a hotel just off the zócalo.

Taquerías and restaurants are plentiful in Nuevo Casas Grandes near the bus station or along Juárez. For a good sit-down meal, try **Denni's** (Juárez 412, at Urueta, tel. 169/4–10–75; open daily 8 AM–10 PM), which bears no relation to the cheesy U.S. chain. Big breakfast specials will set you back about $2. **Restaurante Constantino** (Juárez, across from Hotel Paquimé, tel. 169/4–13–74; open daily 8–8) makes great enchiladas ($3) and tacos ($3) and offers a full breakfast menu. The staff is friendly, the menu has English translations, and you can pay in dollars; if you threw in a 7% tax, it would be just like home! **Nevería Chuchy** (Constitución 202, tel. 169/4–07–09; open Mon.–Sat. 11–11) is a fun soda fountain with sandwiches ($1), burgers ($1.50), and ice-cream cones (50¢)—all the kids in town wind up here at some point during the day. In Casas Grandes, **El Pueblo** (off Juárez, tel. 169/2–41–22; open daily noon–1 AM) draws residents from Nuevo Casas Grandes with great food, a full bar, and TVs showing American movies. House specialties include shrimp and steak ($6) and spicy chicken wings ($2.50). For a shot of culture, try the *bebida nacional* (tequila; $1.50).

El Bandido (Juárez and Del Prado, tel. 169/4–03–29; open daily 1–1) fills up on weekends with regulars in tight jeans and cowboy hats shakin' it to '80s hits. You might feel like you've stumbled into a Pace Picante commercial, where anyone from north of the border is met with suspicion.

WORTH SEEING

If you're wandering around Casas Grandes, check out the **Museo del Siglo XIX** (Independencia, ½ block from Pueblo Viejo, no phone). This 19th-century stone house, now converted into a museum, features period paintings and furniture, as well as a room dedicated to the Mexican Revolution. Entrance to the museum is free, and it's open Tuesday–Sunday 10–5.

PAQUIME RUINS Located near the aspen-lined Casas Grandes River and sheltered by the burnt sienna peaks of the Sierra Madre Occidental, Paquimé was inhabited by Pima, Concho, and Tolima peoples between AD 700 and AD 1500, and served as a center for trade with the Pueblo civilizations of the southwestern United States. Paquimé was a cosmopolitan settlement, whose residents raised fowl and manufactured jewelry; today, you can still see evidence of this worldliness, from the recently restored heat-shielding walls to the intricate indoor plumbing systems. Note the unique mixture of architectural styles: T-shaped doors (similar to those of Pueblo dwellings) coexist with Mesoamerican masonry techniques. The new high-tech museum on the site houses Paquimé artifacts and ceramics, displays a to-scale replica of the ruins, and offers descriptions in Spanish and English of the cultural, religious, and economic practices of the tribe. A small movie theater shows documentaries, and interactive touch-activated computers are scattered throughout the museum. Both the museum and the ruins are free and open Tuesday–Sunday 10–5.

Chihuahua

The city of Chihuahua, capital of Chihuahua state, lies on a high hilly plain some 375 kilometers south of Ciudad Juárez. Agriculture and lumber are the primary moneymakers here, so you won't get the feeling that you are a big, walking peso, as you may in its much poorer and more tourism-dependent neighbor to the north. Chihuahua has long played a leading role in Mexican history: Founded in 1709, it witnessed the execution of Independence leaders Padre Miguel Hidalgo and Ignacio Allende. In 1847 it fell to U.S. forces, and was occupied by Pancho Villa's army during the Mexican Revolution. The days of invading hordes are long over, however, and the primary reason that travelers visit today is to hop on the Copper Canyon train. There's no reason to leave quickly, however—a day or two can be spent contentedly exploring the city's cathedral and historical museums.

Touring the city allows you to get a good overview of Chihuahua state's diverse population. Most notable are the indigenous Tarahumara, whose multilayered, brightly colored clothing foreshadows the sights of Guatemala's highlands. Continued invasions by timber and mining interests have forced the Tarahumara deeper into the mountains, but desperate families still come to town for money and medical services. You may also see an occasional Mennonite in somber dress. These generally reclusive people live in the community of Cuauhtémoc, a short train ride from Chihuahua, and are best known for their famous Mennonite or Chihuahua cheese. A proliferation of Western-wear stores on Chihuahua's main streets, however, will confirm that the bulk of Chihuahua's residents favor cowboy hats and boots over any other garb.

BASICS

AMERICAN EXPRESS The AmEx representative in the **Rojo y Casavantes** travel agency sells traveler's checks, holds cardholders' mail, replaces lost or stolen checks and AmEx cards, and offers MoneyGram service. However, the agency doesn't exchange traveler's checks or cash personal checks. *Guerrero 1207, Chihuahua, Chihuahua, CP 31000, México, tel. 14/15-58-58. Open weekdays 9–6, Sat. 9–noon.*

CASAS DE CAMBIO Most banks change money weekdays 9:30–noon, but several on Avenida Independencia have ATMs. **Serfín**'s ATM (Independencia, at Juárez) accepts Visa, MasterCard, Cirrus, and Plus. **Bancomer** (Av. Libertad, facing the cathedral, tel. 14/10-35-35; open weekdays 9–2) changes traveler's checks and has 24-hour ATM machines, but be prepared to wait in line while a digital monitor displays the wait time in minutes. The best rates for cash (and the shortest lines) are at **Centro de Cambio Rachasa** (Independencia 401, at Victoria, tel.

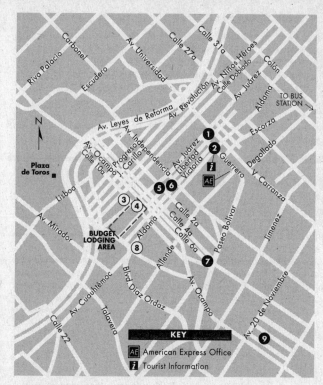

Sights ●

Catedral
Metropolitana
(Plaza de la
Constitución), **5**

Museo de la
Revolución
Mexicana, **9**

Palacio Federal, **1**

Palacio del
Gobierno, **2**

Plaza de Armas, **6**

Quinta Gameros, **7**

Lodgings ○

Hotel Carmen **4**

Hotel
Santa María, **8**

Posada Aida, **3**

KEY

AE American Express Office

i Tourist Information

14/15–14–14; open Mon.–Sat. 8–8.) They don't charge commission on traveler's checks, cash, or money orders but their exchange rates are a few pesos lower than at the banks.

EMERGENCIES You can dial 911 from any phone here for emergency assistance.

MAIL The **post office** is in the Palacio Federal, just opposite the old Palacio del Gobierno. They offer all the usual services and will hold mail sent to you at the following address for up to 10 days: Lista de Correos, Administración 1, Chihuahua, Chihuahua, CP 31000, México. *Libertad, btw Carranza and Guerrero, tel. 14/15–14–17. Open weekdays 8–7, Sat. 9–1.*

MEDICAL AID **Clínica del Parque** (Calle de la Llave, at Calle 12a, tel. 14/15–74–11) offers 24-hour emergency service and has some English-speaking doctors, as well as a 24-hour pharmacy. For a dentist, try **Central Médico Dental** (Niños Héroes 606, tel. 14/16–18–80), open Monday–Saturday 9–1 and 4–8. About three blocks from the Palacio del Gobierno is the 24-hour **Farmacia Mendoza** (Aldama 1901, tel. 14/16–44–14).

PHONES You'll find **Ladatel** public phones on the main square. Some take coins, while others take Ladatel phone cards, which can be purchased at the nearest kiosk or store that advertises Ladatel in the window. For cash calls, the Central Camionera (*see* Coming and Going, *below*) has a caseta de larga distancia, but it doesn't allow collect or credit-card calls. Downtown, the staff of the **Servicio de Larga Distancia** (Independencia 808, near Morelos, tel. 14/10–24–00; open Mon.–Sat. 8–8) operates out of a pharmacy where collect calls cost $1.50 for 15 minutes and calls to the U.S. are $2 per minute.

VISITOR INFORMATION Topographical maps of the Copper Canyon are available though Chihuahua's **SECTUR** office (tel. 800/9–03–92 in Mexico). The **state tourism office** is in the Palacio de Gobierno. There's usually someone on duty who speaks English, and maps and brochures are plentiful. *Calle 11a, at Libertad, tel. 14/10–10–77. Open Mon.–Sat. 9–7, Sun. 9–2.*

COMING AND GOING

BY BUS Chihuahua is a hub for bus transportation, and the companies serving its **Central Camionera** run routes all over Mexico. The modern terminal contains a phone office, 24-hour luggage storage (50¢ per hr), a video arcade, and a 24-hour cafeteria. Frequent first-class service is available to Creel (4½ hrs, $9), Ciudad Juárez (4½ hrs, $12), Mexico City (18 hrs, $47), Guadalajara (16 hrs, $39), Monterrey (12 hrs, $26), Zacatecas (15 hrs, $31), Aguascalientes (20 hrs, $53), and Nuevo Casas Grandes (3½ hrs, $9). To get here from downtown, take a city bus marked CENTRAL CAMIONERA (20¢) from the corner of Ocampo and Juárez. If you arrive in town at night, your only choice is to take a taxi from the station to downtown: Don't let the driver charge you more than $5.

BY TRAIN If you're on your way to Creel, the ride on the **Chihuahua al Pacífico** (Méndez, at Calle 24a, tel. 14/20–70–47), the famous Copper Canyon train, is much more scenic than traveling by bus. Two trains run daily to Los Mochis (13 hrs; $33 1st class, $7 2nd class), stopping in Creel (5 hrs; $15 1st class, $3 2nd class), Divisadero (6½ hrs; $18 1st class, $3 2nd class), and Bahuichivo (8½ hrs; $20 1st class, $4 2nd class). Leaving at 7 AM, the first-class *Vista* train passes through Creel around 12:30 PM and arrives in Los Mochis at 9 PM. The second-class *Mixto* train leaves Chihuahua at 8 AM and arrives in Los Mochis anytime between midnight and 5 AM. As a rule, second-class trains always lollygag and arrive late, but all in all they aren't that bad: The windows open (they don't on first-class trains) and the crowd includes food vendors, musicians, and other colorful characters. To be certain of a first-class seat during Semana Santa and the first week in July (when schools get out), you have to shell out extra

The Footrunners

The name "Tarahumara" is a Spanish rendition of the natives' original word for themselves—Rarámuri, or "footrunners." More than 15,000 years ago, these people arrived from Asia, making their home in a 32,000-square-kilometer stretch of the Sierra Madre Occidental, now known as the Sierra Tarahumara. Since that time, indigenous settlements have remained largely untouched by modern civilization, despite numerous attempts by outsiders to convert them to Christianity or enslave them as laborers in precious-metal mines. Although the Tarahumara resisted Jesuit influence by hiding in the mountains or by organizing violent rebellions, many aspects of Christianity have become part of their traditional religious ceremonies and rituals. The Virgin of Guadalupe festival (December 12) and Semana Santa (Holy Week) are both celebrated with elaborate costumes and dancing, and the sun is honored as the symbol of God, or Onorúame, who is both the father and mother of the people.

Today, many Tarahumara are visible selling crafts to tourists in small mountain towns such as Creel or Divisadero. Deforestation from excessive logging, as well as the five-year drought, have decimated the Tarahumara's traditional farming lands, resulting in tuberculosis and malnutrition among the people and forcing many of them into Chihuahua city to beg. Those who remain deep in the canyons are also threatened by the expanding lumber and tourist industries. When traveling in the Copper Canyon, remember to be respectful of the land and its residents. Although entering the inhabited cliffside caves and photographing the colorfully clothed women may seem appealing, it is important to ask for permission first, and comply if the request is denied.

dough to buy your ticket in advance from **Mexico by Train** (tel. 800/321–1699 in the U.S.). To reach the terminal, take a bus marked COL. ROSALIA or STA. ROSA (20¢) down Ocampo.

The station (tel. 14/1–05–14) for the **Juárez–Chihuahua–México** route is at the north entrance to town, just off Avenida Tecnológico. From here you can catch slow second-class trains to Ciudad Juárez (10 hrs, $4) and Mexico City (30 hrs, $13). To get here, hop on a COLON (20¢) bus from downtown.

GETTING AROUND

The downtown area, roughly 10 blocks by three, contains virtually all of the town's points of interest, including the **Plaza de la Constitución** (Chihuahua's zócalo) and the cathedral, as well as budget lodging and eateries. Odd-numbered streets lie north of Independencia, the core of the downtown area, and even-numbered streets are to the south. Buses for points all around the city leave from the corner of Ocampo and Juárez until about 8 PM. Tickets are 20¢ and can be bought from the driver. Taxis (usually consisting of a sorry-looking Subaru with a helpful driver) are relatively cheap, and, unless you're headed to the airport or have just stepped out of an expensive hotel, you can get practically anywhere for a few dollars.

WHERE TO SLEEP

Chihuahua's hotels cluster southwest of the Plaza de la Constitución, and most are well maintained and clean. Those listed here are the best of the cheapies, and all have air-conditioning and hot water, though the latter is often limited in the evenings. **Hotel Carmen** (Juárez, at Calle 10a, tel. 14/15–70–96) is centrally located, clean, and comfortable, and each of its small rooms come with a spotless bathroom. Singles are $6, doubles $7. Close to downtown, **Posada Aida** (Calle 10a No. 105, btw Juárez and Doblado, tel. 14/15–38–30) is the best deal in Chihuahua. The sheets are fresh, the bathrooms clean, and the pleasant Spanish-style courtyard is a good place to unwind if you're prepared to chat and play with the owner's dogs—Chihuahuas, of course. You'll pay $4 for a single and $5 for a double, both with private bath. **Hotel Santa Maria** (1212 Aldama, tel. 14/10–35–37) has 29 rooms built around an indoor courtyard. Single rooms are $7, doubles are $7.50, and all have TVs and tidy bathrooms.

FOOD

Seafood stalls and hot dog stands sprout from almost every corner in downtown Chihuahua, and fresh fruits, vegetables, meats, and cheeses are always available at the **mercado popular** (just north of Calle 4a, btw Niños Héroes and Juárez; open daily 10–8). The excellent **Restaurant Los Olivos** (Calle de la Llave 202, btw Calles 2a and 4a, tel. 14/10–01–61) serves organic fruits and vegetables, veggie burgers, and egg dishes in a smoke-free environment polluted only by New Age Muzak. Whole-wheat pancakes are about $2 and a fruit plate smothered with yogurt, granola, and honey is $2.50. Los Olivos is open weekdays 8–5, Saturdays 11–5. Late-night noshers sit in chrome and beige-vinyl booths in the wheelchair-accessible **Café Merino** (Ocampo, at Juárez, tel. 14/10–29–44; open Wed.–Mon. 24 hrs), downing standard diner grub: eggs, sausage, toast, pancakes . . . you get the idea. Breakfast costs about $4; the $1.50 hamburgers and $5 *enchiladas de pollo en mole* (chicken enchiladas in a chile and chocolate sauce) are popular lunch items. **Ah Chiles** (Aldama, at Guerrero, tel. 16/37–89–77; open daily 10–10) attracts a crowd at any time of the day. With five-for-$2 taco specials accompanied by a *refresco* (soft drink), this bright-red restaurant specializes in fast, cheap Mexican food and keeps the locals happy.

WORTH SEEING

In addition to the shaded plazas and cobblestone streets, there's a good deal of culture and history to be absorbed here, much of it free. If you're interested in seeing where Padre Miguel Hidalgo joined the choir invisible via firing squad, walk over to the **Palacio del Gobierno** (Juárez, btw Guerrero and Carranza), where a plaque on the inner courtyard wall marks the spot. The Palacio also houses murals by Aarón Piña Mora, depicting historic events from the 16th century up to the Mexican Revolution. The **Palacio Federal** across the street contains the tower in which Hidalgo was held prisoner before being executed. Although visitors can no longer climb the tower, the entrance has been turned into the **Calabozo de Hidalgo**—a small museum/cell containing Hidalgo's Bible, crucifix, and pistol. Efrén García Díaz, the museum's caretaker, will share relevant history for the 50¢ admission price Tuesday–Sunday 9–7. The **Centro Cultural de Chihuahua** (Ocampo, at Aldama, tel. 14/16–12–30) showcases art, theater, and dance throughout the year and posts listings of these events at its office, an old mansion three blocks from the cathedral (*see below*).

CATEDRAL METROPOLITANA DE CHIHUAHUA This 19th-century baroque-style cathedral is dedicated to St. Francis of Assisi, and its exterior is adorned with statues of Francis and the 12 Apostles. Inside, the **Museo de Arte Sacro** (tel. 14/10–38–77) houses a collection of 18th-century religious art. Admission to the museum is 50¢, and it's open weekdays 10–2 and 4–6. *On Plaza de la Constitución, btw Calle 2 and Independencia, at Libertad.*

MUSEO DE LA REVOLUCION MEXICANA **Quinta Luz,** as the former home of legendary Francisco "Pancho" Villa is sometimes called, is Chihuahua's biggest attraction. One of his many wives, Luz Corral, gave personal tours of the building until her death in 1982, when the house was turned into a museum. The mansion was built by Pancho himself and is now dedicated to relating the history of the Mexican Revolution through photographs, treaties, maps, and artifacts—including weapons and the bullet-riddled 1922 Dodge Villa he was driving when he was assassinated. Most Chihuahuans are familiar with the museum; don't hesitate to ask for directions. *Calle 10a No. 3010, about 1½ km from downtown, tel. 14/16–29–58. Take bus marked* COL. DALES *or* OCAMPO *south on Ocampo. Admission: 75¢. Open daily 9–1 and 3–7.*

QUINTA GAMEROS This turn-of-the-century manor was built in French Nouveau style by one Manuel Gameros to impress his fiancée, who nevertheless turned her affection to another. It is now home to a museum displaying the mansion's original furniture, gilt-framed paintings, and ornate chandeliers, as well as the works of local artists and art students and several rotating exhibits. Look for the reclining, headless nude on the outside upper reaches of the building, as well as the Little Red Riding Hood motif in the child's room, complete with a snarling wolf on the headboard of the bed. *Paseo Bolívar 401, at Calle 4a, tel. 14/16–66–84. Admission: $1.25. Open Tues.–Sun. 10–2 and 4–7.*

FESTIVALS

Chihuahuans like to consider themselves particularly spirited because of the historic role that the city has played in Mexican history. Three important annual festivals jump-start the city. The **Feria de Santa Rita,** held during the last two weeks in May, is when Chihuahuans pay homage to their patron saint with food, music, and regional crafts at the fairgrounds on the Carretera al Aeropuerto. People call Santa Rita "The Governor's Fair," because it has evolved into a bureaucratic, expensive event that excludes the poor. Locals prefer the **Expoban,** a livestock competition and county fair held the second week of October at the Unión Banadera (just outside of town). On September 15, people come from all over the state to participate in **Mexican Independence Day** celebrations. There are fireworks displays at the Palacio del Gobierno and traditional *teatro del pueblo* (outdoor theater) put on by the Chihuahua Cultural Center.

AFTER DARK

Chihuahua is not a big party town, and movies are one of the more popular evening diversions. **Sala 2001** (Guerrero, at Escorza, tel. 14/16–50–00) and **Cinema Revolución** (J. Neri Santos 700, just west of Palacio Federal, tel. 14/10–49–00) both show Hollywood films with Spanish subtitles and the occasional Latin American or Spanish flick for about $1.50. The disco **Robin Hood** (Cuauhtémoc 2207) charges $3 at the door and is the only dance place around where gay couples are tolerated: Public displays of affection remain an exclusively heterosexual privilege in these parts. Although some hip-hop and rock dance music is played, most of what you'll hear is in the ranchero vein. **Alameda Corona** (Juárez, behind Club de los Parados; open daily until midnight) is an outdoor bar where cheap beer and cheesy mariachi music provide a refreshing break from Chihuahua's smoke-filled bars. Don't look for the signs, though; there aren't any. Just ask around for *la cervecería* (the brewery).

The Copper Canyon

With majestic 3600-meter-high peaks and dramatic gorges dropping over a kilometer into raging waters, the region known as *Las Barrancas del Cobre* (the Copper Canyon) humbles anyone in the presence of its beauty. In the late spring and early summer, protruding brown rocks absorb the sun's intense heat, while the Apache pines and Chihuahua ash trees hold their breath until the first gray clouds appear. By September, after the heavy rains, the canyons are thick with green layers of vegetation that provide food for roaming skunks and salamanders.

A treasure for nature lovers, the five canyons and four main rivers in this area offer plenty of opportunities for hiking, mountain biking, and horseback riding. Guides are almost always recommended, not only because trails are rough and not clearly marked, but because of the illegal marijuana fields in the area, which are extremely dangerous to stumble upon. Creel, about halfway between Chihuahua and Los Mochis, is the most convenient take-off point for camping and hiking trips, and has become a favorite among backpackers. The most popular times to visit are September and October, when the waterfalls are at their best, or during the week-long festival of Semana Santa (Holy Week, the week before Easter).

The Copper Canyon only became accessible to the public in 1961, with the completion of the Chihuahua al Pacífico railroad. It took nearly 100 years to complete and boasts some 87 tunnels and 37 bridges. Long before the canyon was discovered by miners and tourists, however, the area was home to indigenous Tarahumara people (*see* box, *above*). The 50,000 Tarahumara that remain tenaciously maintain one of the most traditional indigenous cultures in North America. They continue to live in and around the canyons, farming and weaving pine-needle baskets, the majority of which are sold to tourists.

Ride the Chihuahua al Pacífico train while it's still cheap: The Mexican government has put the public railway up for sale, and once it's privatized, fares will be significantly higher.

GETTING AROUND

BY TRAIN Two trains run daily between Chihuahua and Los Mochis in each direction: the first-class *Vista* and the second-class *Mixto*. Both stop in most small towns in between, including Cuauhtémoc, Creel, Divisadero, and Bahuichivo. The Vista is faster and more comfortable, with climate control, a snack bar, and bathrooms, but at $33 for the journey, it's almost four times the price of a second-class ride. The first-class train is popular during the summer and Semana Santa, so try to book ahead if you're traveling then. Bring toilet paper and, for the mountainous areas, warm clothing; in first class you'll probably need a sweater even in the lowlands, as the air-conditioning is over-enthusiastically used. Tickets for the *Mixto* are only available the morning of departure, so be prepared to fight tooth and nail for both tickets and seats during Semana Santa and July.

It is possible to make up to two 24-hour stops at stations other than your final destination. You need to ask for an *escala* (stopover)—a 15% surcharge added to the price of your ticket. The escala must be purchased in either Chihuahua or Los Mochis at the beginning of your trip, and it's only worth your while during Semana Santa and the first week in July, when you need to make reservations and plan all of your stops. At any other time during the year, you can hop on and off the train at any stop in the Copper Canyon without being charged extra. For specific information on prices and departures, *see* Coming and Going, in Chihuahua, *above*; Creel, *below*; and Los

The second-class train has an unpredictable schedule and no reserved seating, but it provides the best opportunity to meet local campesinos (rural dwellers) and their poultry.

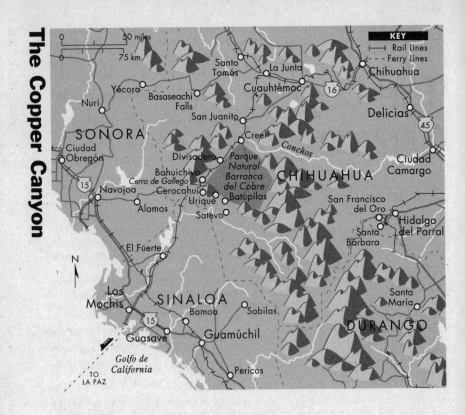

Mochis in Chapter 7. Starting your trip in Los Mochis is recommended, especially since the *Mixto* leaving from Chihuahua will probably pass the Copper Canyon in the dark. If you're heading out of Chihuahua, the best view is on the right until you pass Creel and on your left from Creel to Los Mochis.

BY BUS Trains are the primary mode of transportation through the canyons, but you can shorten the train ride in either direction by taking an **Estrella Blanca** bus. Eight daily buses run between Creel and Chihuahua (4 hrs direct, 5 hrs indirect; $8 for both). If you attempt this, board at either Chihuahua or Creel, as boarding at intermediate points may leave you standing for many leg-numbing hours due to lack of seats.

HITCHING Barring walking for days, hitchhiking is the only way to reach some points off the rail line. In rural areas it's fairly safe and common, but traveling in groups is always best. Some days you'll wait so long you can feel yourself getting older, especially on Sundays, when nobody's off to work. Trucks may charge a few dollars, depending on the length of the journey.

HIKING Extreme temperatures, lack of resupply points, and a wide range of altitudes make hiking in the Copper Canyon a challenge. However, if you know where you're going and have the proper equipment, overnight trips are undoubtedly the best way to see the canyons. Pick up hiking supplies in Los Mochis or Chihuahua. In Chihuahua, **Sears** (Libertad 106, tel. 14/16–52–72; open Mon.–Sat. 10–9, Sun. 11–7) is the most convenient place to purchase camping or hiking gear, and even tents and sleeping bags. Detailed topographical maps of the region are available through SECTUR, the state tourism office (tel. 14/16–21–06 in Chihuahua, or 800/90–03–02 throughout Mexico). The best book on the region, *Mexico's Copper Canyon Country*, by M. John Fayhee, is supposedly available in Creel but is often out of stock, so it's better to order it directly from the publisher at: Cordillera Press Inc., P.O. Box 3699, Evergreen, CO, 80439 U.S.A (tel. 303/670–3010). Within the canyons, the best jumping-off points for hikes are Creel and Batopilas, and it's easy to find a guide in these places. Use your head though—

holdups have been reported by tourists. Get someone moderately trustworthy (i.e., a hotel owner, rather than the guy hanging out on the corner) to refer you to a guide.

Creel

Set in a shallow valley high in the Sierra Madre (about halfway between Los Mochis and Chihuahua), the growing town of Creel is a favorite stop on the Chihuahua al Pacífico line for travelers who want to explore the Barrancas without too much hassle. The best way to enjoy the surrounding area, with its stunning green pine trees and jagged mountain peaks, is on bike, horse, or foot. Popular destinations include **Cusárare**, a waterfall 22 kilometers (13 mi) away; **Rekohuata,** a group of hot springs 17 kilometers (10 mi) south of Creel; **Lake Arareco,** 7 kilometers south of Creel; and **San Ignacio,** 4 kilometers south, past the town cemetery and a few Tarahumara caves. Even if you don't join a group tour from one of the hotels, it's a good idea to ask around for tips on trails. The nearby attractions of **Batopilas** and **Basaseachic Falls** provide more opportunities for amusement: To get to either place, hitch a ride from *la carretera* (Creel's main road) or ask the men with trucks and vans loitering around the train station about organizing a ride.

BASICS

CASAS DE CAMBIO **Serfín** (tel. 145/6–00–60), just east of the tracks, changes money weekdays 9–1:30, will give you credit-card cash advances, and charges a "flexible" commission (you shouldn't have to pay more than 2%) on traveler's checks.

LAUNDRY **Lavandería Santa María** belongs to the resort-like Pension Creel. One load costs $1.50 to wash and dry; pay an additional 20¢ and someone will do the dirty work for you. *López Mateos 61, tel. 145/6–00–71. Open weekdays 9–2 and 3–6, Sat. 9–2.*

MEDICAL AID There are a few English-speaking doctors at **La Clínica Santa Teresita** (Parroquia, behind Margarita's, tel. 145/6–01–05), open weekdays 10–1 and 3–5, Saturday 10–noon. The clinic offers a variety of services, including dental and emergency care. For pharmaceuticals and advice about minor medical problems, look for **Farmacia Rodríguez** (López Mateos 43, tel. 145/6–00–52; open Mon.–Sat. 9–1 and 3–7).

PHONES AND MAIL **Papelería de Todo** (López Mateos 30, tel. 145/6–01–22), open Monday–Saturday 9–9 and Sunday 9–6, charges $1.50 for collect calls. It also has a pay phone and a fax machine (fax 145/6–02–22). The **post office** (Enrique Creel 4, tel. 145/6–02–58; open weekdays 9–4) is in the Presidencia Municipal, south of the zócalo. They'll hold mail sent to you at the following address for up to 10 days: Lista de Correos, Presidencia Municipal, Creel, Chihuahua, CP 33200, México.

VISITOR INFORMATION The **Complejo Turístico Arareco** (tel. 145/6–01–26; open Mon.–Sat. 9–6) on López Mateos has a rough map of the area and provides information on tours. They arrange rowboat rentals for Lake Arareco ($3 per hr for up to 6 people) and rent bicycles ($1.50 an hr). Information in English is available at **Artesanías Misión** (tel. 145/6–00–97; open Mon.–Sat. 9:30–1 and 5–8, Sun. 9:30–1), next to Serfín. You'll also find topographical maps and many books on the Copper Canyon and the Tarahumara.

COMING AND GOING

BY BUS The **Estrella Blanca** terminal (tel. 145/6–00–73) is directly across the tracks from the train station. Eight buses depart Creel every 1½ hours between 7 AM and 5:30 PM for Chihuahua (4 hrs, $8), stopping at most of the towns along the way. Tickets for Batopilas (7 hrs, $8) can be bought at **Artesanías Raramuri** (tel. 145/6–02–79), across from Restaurant Lupita (*see* Food, *below*) on López Mateos.

BY TRAIN The train tracks run along the west edge of town, and the station is very close to food and lodging. First-class trains to Chihuahua leave Creel at about 12:30 PM (6 hrs, $15), second-class at 5:30 PM ($3.50). First- and second-class trains heading to Los Mochis leave Creel at about 3:15 PM ($18.50) and 2 PM ($4), respectively. The first-class trains are rarely late; the second-class trains show up when they feel like it, so be prepared to wait. You can buy tickets on the train.

WHERE TO SLEEP

As soon as you step off the train you will be assailed by a passel of children beckoning you to **Margarita's** (Mateos 11, tel. 145/6–00–45). Make the kids happy and jump on the hotel's courtesy shuttle. Margarita provides whatever type of accommodation you can afford, from a $2 mattress on the floor to a $4 bunk in a communal dorm room to a $14 double room with private bath (although the toilets are occasionally out of order). Meals (breakfast 7:30–9:30 AM, dinner 6:30–8 PM) are included in the price. Margarita has also recently opened another place with more upscale rooms, so be careful not to let the driver take you there. When there's demand, the hotel staff leads guided tours (about $5 per person) to Cusárare Falls, Recohuata, La Bufa and Tarahumara caves, and Divisadero. If you prefer to avoid the highly social scene at Margarita's, **Casa Valenzuela** (López Mateos 68, tel. 145/6–01–04) is usually semi-vacant, and the proprietor will accommodate your needs and budget. The communal bathroom is tiny and fairly clean, although sometimes without water, but the ceiling sags. Well, okay, the beds sag, too. Singles are $8.50, doubles $17, and five of the 13 rooms have baths. Although **New Pensión Creel** (López Mateos 61, tel. 145/6–00–71) is 1 kilometer out of town, it's worth the trek for the clean and cozy two- to four-person rooms ($7.50 per person, including breakfast). The B&B has a spacious patio, kitchen, common area, and laundry, and tours of the canyon can be arranged with the staff for about $10 (half-day trip). To get here, walk south down López Mateos and turn left after Calle La Terminal. Look for the tin roof with PENSION CREEL in red letters.

CAMPING There is a campground next to Lake Arareco that costs $1.50 per person per night. The entrance is at the white house on the way to the lake. The only thing to prevent you from camping anywhere else for free is lack of a flat spot and the occasional scorpion.

FOOD

Restaurante Jorge (open daily 10–10), located just behind the tracks, has fast food and a few friendly gringos. A burrito chock-full of goodies will set you back 75¢. **Mi Café** (López Mateos 21) has only one table and feels more like a home than a restaurant. Chicken tostadas and *ceviche* (fish pickled in lime juice) both cost $1 and are served daily 9 AM–9:30 PM. **Restaurant Lupita,** also on López Mateos, serves morning hotcakes for $1.50. Later, try the *bistec ranchero* (steak cooked with tomatoes and onions) or fish fillet, both $3, served until 10 PM. With green velour swivel-chairs and ESPN on color TVs, **Laylo's Lounge** (López Mateos 25, tel. 145/6–01–36) is a gringo-friendly bar that pours beer and mixed drinks nightly until 1 AM.

OUTDOOR ACTIVITIES

Creel is a convenient base from which to explore the natural beauty of the canyons and the rivers that tumble through them. While river-rafting is strictly for those adventurers who bring their own equipment (including rain), you can rent mountain bikes or take off on hikes that last between one hour and several days. Remember to take it easy for a while and let your body get used to changes in altitude. Guided tours are available to almost any place in the area: Try Complejo Turístico Arareco (*see* Visitor Information, *above*), join a group from Margarita's, or arrange your own tour by asking around at the main plaza; many knowledgeable residents own trucks and will take you anywhere if the price is right.

Topographical maps of the region are available at Artesanías Misión (*see* Visitor Information, *above*) for $5, but they're little help if you don't know how to read them. A live guide is often a better idea—ask at Margarita's or the adjacent **Expediciones Umárike** (Apartado Postal 61, fax 145/6–02–12). This new company, run by gringos, rents mountain bikes and bike gear for an exorbitant $65 per day, $40 per half day; guided tours are an additional $50 per day. Creel is the base for long treks to Basaseachic Falls and Batopilas (*see* Near Creel, *below*), but those with less time or less ambition may prefer to meander over to the statue of Jesus in the hills 15 minutes west of town, where you'll find a nice picnic spot. For an easy 1½-hour hike (this one along clearly marked trails), head to the nearby **Valle de las Monjas** (Valley of the Monks), so named for the rocks said to resemble a huddle of monks. Also close by is the **Valle de los Hongos** (Valley of the Mushrooms), where a few rock formations resemble overgrown toadstools (1 hr round-trip hike). While most of the Tarahumara caves in the area are abandoned, **Cueva Sebastián,** a few kilometers south of Creel at San Ignacio, is still inhabited and accessible by foot. The Tarahumara do not welcome visitors inside their homes, but there are tours available that have been given permission to enter the caves. To reach any of these places, ask directions from anyone in Creel.

NEAR CREEL

BASASEACHIC FALLS A four-hour drive northwest from Creel are the magnificent Basaseachic Falls, which plunge 250 meters into a pool below. This area is most magnificent after the rainy season (July and August)—if it rains, that is. Tours can be arranged in Creel for groups of four or more (the ones from Margarita's are $15 a person), or you can hitch from the town of **La Junta,** on the Pacífico rail line. If you do hitch, plan to stay overnight in the park— good (free) camping spots abound. Hiking trails are a dime a dozen, and there's an excellent swimming hole at the waterfall's edge. There are no shops here, so bring your own supplies.

DIVISADERO Only from Divisadero can you see the three canyons—Tararecua, Urique, and Cobre—merge, their never-ending peaks woven together by the meandering rivers below. Divisadero is on the Chihuahua al Pacífico line roughly one hour away from Creel; the train stops here for 15 minutes in the afternoon so tourists can snap pictures, buy baskets, and gawk over the canyon rim. If you want to stop and hike, you can catch a later train for a small surcharge. If you decide to spend the night, your best bet is to either hike away from town and camp (ask permission before pitching a tent on someone's land) or rent a room from a local family (up to $10 a night). Food and craft stands—selling cheap burritos and ridiculously high-priced Tarahumara crafts—provide info on either option. Even if you're not one of the privileged guests at **Hotel Divisadero Barrancas,** you can rent horses here for $8 a half day or join a tour of the canyons for the same price. You can also hire a guide yourself for overnight trips down to the **Río Urique.** Less formidable is the 2-kilometer hike from the north side of the hotel to an abandoned Tarahumara cliff dwelling.

Batopilas

When the Batopilas mines were in full operation, they produced chunks of silver as big as basketballs—the profits of which were used, in part, to throw lavish high-society parties in the town's grand haciendas.

About 140 kilometers (87 mi) south of Creel, in the heart of the canyon region, is the small mining town of Batopilas. Located beside the river of the same name, this untouristed town is hard to reach, but provides great access to the canyons. The tiny town of **Satevo,** which has a spooky abandoned mission worth exploring, is an easy 4-kilometer hike south; about 6 kilometers north is **La Bufa,** a forgotten gold mine. Both of these trails are marked, but a guide is recommended. A less adventurous trip allows you to explore the ruined mill (admission $1.50) across the river bed from town. Heavy drinkers beware: Batopilas has a *ley seca* (dry law), so you'd better bring your own beer and swig it secretly.

COMING AND GOING The cheapest bus to Batopilas departs Creel at 7 AM on Tuesdays, Thursdays, and Saturdays (7 hrs, $8); a smaller but faster bus (4 hrs, $11) runs every Monday, Wednesday, and Friday at 11 AM. Both leave from Artesanías Raramuri (*see* Creel, Food, *above*). The return bus departs Batopilas at 5 AM (yes, AM) on Mondays, Wednesdays, and Fridays, and the trip takes six hours, arriving in Creel in time for the first-class Los Mochis train. The road out here has been called the best and worst in North America: The scenery is magnificent, but riding a rickety bus on a dirt road with no guardrail above 500-foot cliffs can be a little nerve-racking, especially on the switchbacks.

WHERE TO SLEEP AND EAT To avoid Batopilas's steep prices, bring all necessary camping supplies with you (including food). You can swim and camp by the river, but it's not advised in the summer months, when the creepy-crawlies are out in legion. Deforestation upstream has also made dangerous flash floods frequent, so exercise caution near the river. The best indoor place to stay is **Hotel Palmera** (tel. 145/6–06–33), about a half mile out of town along the river. The seven cool rooms with spotless bathrooms ($10) are a great place to nap after a feast at the adjacent restaurant. Gerardo, the hotel and restaurant manager, prepares aguas frescas from the hotel's mango trees and whips up salads ($2) made from the fresh vegetables in his garden; sometimes there's even *carne asada* (grilled meat; $3) barbecued out on the patio. If the Palmera is full, swagger over to the sweltering rooms ($5) at the **Hotel Batopilas** (across plaza from church). **Quinto Patio** (1 block from church, overlooking river) serves warm Cokes and typical Mexican chow for under $2 daily 10–1 and 3–10.

Bahuichivo

Brick and mud houses and a few wandering chickens are about all you'll see along the winding dirt roads of this *muy tranquilo* (very mellow) small town. Bahuichivo hugs the railroad tracks 260 kilometers (160 mi) north of Los Mochis, and is the only departure point for exploring nearby Cerocahui and Urique. If you need some food before taking a bus or van the hell out of here, head to **La Amistad** (100 meters uphill from the train station, tel. 145/2–00–64). Newly remodeled with sturdy wooden furniture and pleasant round tables that inspire conversation, this place serves whatever local fare is available for about $2. For $3.50 per person, simple, clean rooms can be found next door at **Hotel Viajero**, but better digs await you out of town. Aside from a few small markets, there is no place in town to buy supplies, so stock up in Creel before you arrive. For medical help, see the reputable Dr. Leyva—his office is labeled FAR-MACIA ADRIANA and is near **Abarrotes Gabby**, a small grocery store.

COMING AND GOING Since Bahuichivo is a stop on the Chihuahua al Pacífico railway, it's the best place from which to set out for Cerocahui and Urique (*see below*). The first-class train stops here at 3:30 PM from Chihuahua, while the Los Mochis train gets in at about 12:30 PM. The second-class trains arrive whenever they feel like it. To reach Urique (2½ hrs, $4) from Bahuichivo, hop on the new bus or the white van, both marked TRANSPORTES CAÑON URIQUE, which meet the first-class trains. The vehicles occasionally wait for the second-class train, finally departing Bahuichivo at 6 PM. Both pass through Cerocahui (1 hr, $2) on their way to Urique. It's also possible to hitch between Cerocahui and Bahuichivo. Both **Hotel La Misión** and **Paraiso del Oso** in Cerocahui have gringo shuttles to and from the first-class trains, and they'll give you a free ride if they aren't already full of tour groups.

NEAR BAHUICHIVO

CEROCAHUI At only 1½ kilometers above sea level, Cerocahuis's twisting, no-name streets are nestled deep in one of the Sierra Madre's gorges. This isolated village offers perhaps the most spectacular stargazing in Mexico; when the electricity goes out after 10 PM, you're left standing amidst thick oak and pine trees under a pantheon of stars. If you're fortunate enough to be here during Semana Santa, be sure to catch the *matachines* (Tarahumara dances) at the old **Jesuit mission.** Founded in 1680 and restored in 1940, the mission still operates a boarding school for Tarahumara children. Services are held in the school's *iglesia* (church) weekday nights at 7:30 (if the padre is in town) and Sundays at 8 AM and noon. On June 24, locals douse each other with water in homage to John the Baptist.

Overlooking Cerocahui, Cerro de Gallego (Gallego Hill) was named at the end of the 19th century after Father Gallego, a padre from Urique who was found dead, still wearing his priestly garb, in a nearby cave.

From July to August, water is also abundant in the nearby waterfalls (a 2-kilometer hike from town). You can also explore the abandoned **Sangre de Cristo** gold mines (3 km from town). Each marked trail is short, and can be maneuvered on horseback or foot—ask at **Hotel La Misión** (off the central plaza) for specific directions. You can also set out from Cerocahui on a two- to three-day trek/horseback ride to Batopilas (*see above*), but you'll need a guide. Information is available in broken English from the knowledgeable Eduardo Muños, at the small artesanía shop on the way out of town (towards the waterfall). He gladly leads hikes to anywhere (including Batopilas) for a negotiable price, and he (or someone at Hotel Misión) can also get you a horse to rent ($4 per hr).

➤ **WHERE TO SLEEP AND EAT** • Rooms with private baths and hot water are available at **El Raramuri** (tel. 145/6–05–99) for $7 (singles) and $10 (doubles). It's the white house on the way out of town towards the waterfall. **Paraíso del Oso** (3 km north of Cerocahui, tel. 158/6–06–19) offers everything from $6 bunk beds to $125 luxury pads, and the bilingual staff leads morning hikes into the canyons ($3.50). If you want to camp, pick a spot and ask permission from the landowner—it shouldn't be a problem, although they may charge a small fee. The restaurant in the El Raramuri hotel serves up decent local fare for $2. The only other restaurant in town is diagonally across from the plaza; the menu changes daily, but meals are always less than $5.

URIQUE Thirty-eight kilometers (24 mi) southeast of Cerocahui, the village of Urique features fantastic views of sharp canyon peaks falling into the green hills. The gushing **Río Urique** runs a refreshing border around the scenery, making Urique one of the most visually pleasing towns in the Copper Canyon. You can take day hikes along the river, or walk down the dirt road at the edge of town to explore **Chiflón**, an abandoned mine near the foot of a 1-meter-wide, 110-meter-long hanging footbridge. To reach Chiflón, follow Urique's main street north, then follow the GUADALUPE C sign to the banks of the river; it's about a 20-minute walk. Although belly flops off the bridge are *not* advised, this is a great spot for a swim as long as the water isn't raging from heavy rains. It's also a good idea to avoid Urique in early summer, as the river will be nearly dry and temperatures reach 37° C (100° F).

➤ **COMING AND GOING** • One bus or one van (2½ hrs, $4) leaves Urique at 8:30 AM each day from the main drag to meet the trains in Bauhichivo, returning to Urique sometime after 8 PM. If you're prone to carsickness, pray that the newer bus comes to meet the train instead of the van, as the descent into Urique is worse than the switchbacks en route to Batopilas. A more expensive way to get here is to arrange a ride ($16 a person) through the Hotel Misión in Cerocahui; or try your luck at hitching.

➤ **WHERE TO SLEEP AND EAT** • Urique boasts three hotels, but your best bet is **Hotel Cañón Urique,** on the main drag beneath the huge ceiba tree. Singles with private bath are $5, doubles $10, and the rooms in the rear buffer the cries of farm animals. If you've brought camping equipment, ask for **Tom and Keith**'s house. These friendly expatriates from the States have got a great camping area under the mesquite trees by the river—watch out for small, biting chiggers during the rainy season. A $1 donation is requested for use of the squat toilet and fresh water. The best eats in town are found at **Restaurant Plaza,** down the street from Hotel Cañón Urique. The owner is nice and the patio out back is perfect for a late meal, when cool breezes come off the river. Ask for the $3 daily special 6 AM–11 PM. Travelers have complained about the town's other main restaurant, the **Zulema,** so don't risk it.

Durango
Resting in the Valle del Guadiana, the modern, industrialized city of Durango offers a hilly downtown area that retains some superb colonial architecture. If the dusty downtown landscape and exceptionally clear light you see on the bus ride into town strike a familiar chord, you're not crazy. You probably *have* seen the place before, as the area has been used in a number of Hollywood productions, most of them westerns. The most recent movie filmed here was *Wagons East,* the last film to star Canadian comedian John Candy. Proud of its contributions to the film industry, the tourist office often organizes weekend trips to two "western" towns used as film sets. Of these, **Villa del Oeste** (Village of the West) is the only one still used for moviemaking. Another set is known as **Chupaderos,** and although it's been forgotten by film, it has become a refuge for destitute people, who live in the sets.

If you happen to pass through Durango in July, you can take part in the city's main festivals. Durango wraps two weeks of **Feria Nacional** around two significant dates: July 8, the anniversary of Durango's 1563 founding by Francisco de Ibarra, and July 22, the day of the Virgen del

Refugio. The festival has taken on national status, and people come from all around to bet on cockfights, bid on cows, and enjoy the music, food, and rides.

BASICS

AMERICAN EXPRESS AmEx services are provided by friendly, English-speaking representatives in the travel agency **Touris Viajes**, a few long blocks west of the Plaza de Armas. You can buy or change traveler's checks here and have lost or stolen traveler's checks or AmEx cards replaced. Cardholders can also have their mail held or cash a personal check here. *20 de Noviembre 810 Ote., Durango, Durango, CP 34000, México, tel. 18/17–00–83, fax 18/ 17–01–43. Take blue-and-white bus marked TECNO from cnr of Victoria and 20 de Noviembre. Open weekdays 9–7, Sat. 10–5.*

CASAS DE CAMBIO Serfín (20 de Noviembre 400 Ote., tel. 18/1–15–03) changes traveler's checks weekdays 9–1:30. There are several casas de cambio on 20 de Noviembre near the Soriana supermarket, just east of the Plaza de Armas. **Mundinero** (20 de Noviembre 806 Ote., tel. 18/18–86–24), next door to the AmEx office, changes both cash and traveler's checks and has decent hours; unfortunately, the rates here are lousy. Mundinero is open weekdays 9:30–2 and 4–6:30, Saturday 10–2.

EMERGENCIES In case of trouble, call the **police** (cnr of Prolongación Felipe Pescador and Independencia, tel. 18/17–54–06). For an ambulance, call the **Cruz Roja** (cnr of 5 de Febrero and Trabajo, tel. 18/17–34–44).

LAUNDRY The friendly guys at **Lavandería Automática Ale** will wash, dry, fold, and even deliver 3 kilos of your clothes for $2.75. *Lázaro Cárdenas 232 Nte., tel. 18/17–22–20. Take blue-and-white bus marked TECNO from cnr of Victoria and 20 de Noviembre; get off at Helados Bing (cnr of Negrete and Libertad) and walk north 2½ blocks. Open Mon.–Sat. 9–7.*

MAIL The full-service post office will hold mail sent to you at the following address for up to 10 days: Lista de Correos, Administración No. 1, 20 de Noviembre 500-B Ote., Durango, Durango, CP 34001, México. *20 de Noviembre, btw Cuauhtémoc and Roncal, tel. 18/ 11–41–05. Open weekdays 8–7, Sat. 9–1.*

MEDICAL AID Two 24-hour clinics are: **Hospital San Jorge** (Libertad 249, tel. 18/17–22–10) and **Hospital de La Paz** (5 de Febrero 903, tel. 18/18–95–41). For 24-hour service, go to **Farmacia del Ahorro** (20 de Noviembre 100 Ote., no phone).

PHONES Several casetas de larga distancia line 5 de Febrero, and some Ladatel phones dot the Plaza de Armas. For cash calls, walk three blocks south of the plaza to the caseta at Bruno Martínez 206 Sur (tel. 18/13–30–01; open Mon.–Sat. 8 AM–9:30 PM, Sun. 8–3).

VISITOR INFORMATION The staff of the state tourism office is multilingual, friendly, and helpful, but unfortunately has a limited supply of written info. *Hidalgo 408 Sur, tel. 18/11–21–39. West of plaza on 20 de Noviembre, left on Hidalgo. Open weekdays 9:30–3 and 5–7, Sat. 11–2, Sun. 11–1:30.*

COMING AND GOING

BY BUS The **Central Camionera** is 4 kilometers east of the town center, but regular city buses and cheap taxis (about $2 to the central plaza) make it accessible. The station is served by a number of national lines, including **Omnibús de México** (tel. 18/18–33–61), **Transportes del Norte** (tel. 18/18–33–04), **Estrella Blanca, Futura,** and **Transportes Chihuahuenses.** The latter three all share the same phone number: 18/18–37–21. First-class buses run daily to points all over Mexico, including Chihuahua city (9 hrs, $20), Ciudad Juárez (12 hrs, $33), Mazatlán (7 hrs, $10), Mexico City (12 hrs, $31), Monterrey (9 hrs, $21), and Saltillo (7½ hrs, $17). A small pharmacy, long-distance telephone service, and luggage storage (20¢ per hr) are available at the station.

BY TRAIN Durango's train station (tel. 18/11–22–94) is right below the Cerro del Mercado, off Prolongación Felipe Pescador, about nine blocks north of the plaza. To get to most destinations (except Monterrey), you must change at another train station in some random town along the way and wait at least 4–6 hours for the next train. A first-class train to Mexico City (15 hrs, $20) departs at 6 AM. Another train departs for Ciudad Juárez (11 hrs, $22) at 7 AM, stopping in Chihuahua (8 hrs, $16) on the way. Other destinations include Monterrey (11 hrs, $7), Saltillo (9 hrs, $7.50), and Zacatecas (16 hrs, $5). The ticket office is only open 5 AM–noon. To get here, catch a blue bus marked BRUNO MARTINEZ at 20 de Noviembre and Bruno Martínez, or walk 20 minutes south on Bruno Martínez from downtown.

GETTING AROUND

The main thoroughfare, **20 de Noviembre,** runs east–west. Victoria, Constitución, and Juárez are the main streets that intersect 20 de Noviembre in the heart of the downtown area. Parallel to 20 de Noviembre are Pino Suárez and 5 de Febrero on the south side, Negrete and Aquiles Serdán on the north side. The main square, called the **Plaza de Armas,** is off 20 de Noviembre, between Juárez and Constitución. Addresses contain cardinal directions—Nte. for north, Sur for south, Ote. for east, and Pte. for west—which indicate where they are in relation to the plaza. City buses (35¢) congregate near the plaza, and taxis charge 40¢ a kilometer.

WHERE TO SLEEP

There are a few decent, central places, but budget hotels in Durango tend to be bottom-of-the-barrel. Around festival time (the first two weeks in July), either make reservations or expect to stay far from downtown, pay a lot, and get little. At **Hotel Gallo** (5 de Febrero 117, tel. 18/11–52–90), rooms are sunny, spacious, and all have private baths. However, the low price (singles $4.50, doubles $5.50) tends to attract a less than attractive crowd. **Hotel María del Pilar** (Pino Suárez 410 Pte., tel. 18/11–54–71) has wheelchair-accessible rooms that are clean and relatively comfy, if a bit drab. The spotless bathrooms with copious hot water may help you forgive the peeling paint. Singles cost $9, doubles $10. The **Hotel Posada Durán** (20 de Noviembre 506 Pte., at Juárez, tel. 18/11–24–12), next to the cathedral, is everybody's favorite—and they take credit cards. Large wooden doors, a bar, and a fountain-graced courtyard lead to impeccable rooms with hardwood floors, some with big glass doors that open onto balconies; spotless bathrooms provide plenty of scalding water. Singles cost $12.50, doubles $15, and it's a good idea to make reservations.

FOOD

There are almost no outstanding budget eateries downtown: A few small places serve comidas corridas, but not many distinguish themselves, unless you consider hot dogs a culinary novelty. The **mercado** on 20 de Noviembre is a good place to get fresh fruits and vegetables; *fondas* (covered food stands) toward the back serve standard meals for about $1.50.

The state of Durango is famous for its huge desert scorpions, but probably the only scorpion you'll encounter is a caramel one, sold at candy and souvenir shops.

Café Opera. This chic little place serves excellent Italian cuisine; the scent of garlic wafting from the doorway will instantly hypnotize your taste buds. Of the numerous pasta dishes, the *El mero barbero de Sevilla en Francia* (The Very Barber of Seville in France; trout in a creamy almond sauce served with pasta; $4) is highly recommended. For lighter fare, try the huge green salad doused in a garlic vinaigrette ($2). *Negrete 1005, at Independencia, tel. 18/25–15–00. Open Tues.–Sun. 2–midnight. Wheelchair access. AE, MC, V.*

La Casa de la Monja. Despite the name (the nun's house), this colonial building has a rustic elegance. Sit beside the interior garden and fountain and enjoy the $6 specialty *puntas de filete a la monja* (nun-style beef . . . hmm) or the $3 *comida del día* (daily menu). *Negrete 308 Pte., at Madero, tel. 18/11–71–62. Open daily 8 AM–11 PM. Wheelchair access.*

Sloan's. This small restaurant/bar is almost always full of young people and music, as well as a bizarre clutter of plane propellers, drum sets, and other random junk. Delicious crepes and hamburgers go for about $2; a monster-size piña colada is $2.50. *Negrete 1003 Pte., tel. 18/12–21–99. Open daily 6 PM–midnight. Wheelchair access. AE, MC, V.*

WORTH SEEING

Fortunately, most of Durango's interesting sights are well within walking distance of the main **Plaza de Armas**; facing the plaza is the huge, baroque **Catedral Basílica Menor,** Durango's main church. The best of the outlying sights is the **Parque Guadiana** (on Carretera Durango–Mazatlán). Fourteen long blocks from the main plaza, this park is a favorite spot for sports-minded locals: Miles of dirt paths makes it ideal for runners and bicyclists alike, and the huge public swimming pool is a great place to beat the afternoon heat. Free aerobics classes are held daily at 7 AM in the little clearing behind the pool. Just across the highway is the **Zoológico Sahuatoba** (tel. 18/12–44–57; open Tues.–Sun. 10–6), where you can gawk at the lions, panthers, hippos, and snakes free of charge. To get here, take a blue bus marked TIERRA Y LIBERTAD from the corner of Aquiles Serdán and Victoria.

MUSEO DE LAS CULTURAS POPULARES This museum has a small but interesting display of artesanía from the Huichol, Tepehuano, and Tarahumara indigenous peoples. The friendly staff will walk you through the exhibit and explain everything to you (in Spanish), or you can meander on your own. You can purchase some of these crafts for a moderate price in the museum's small store, or try making your own in the workshop facilities. A mere $2.75 allots you all the supplies you need to create pottery, papier mâché masks, or even paintings. *Juárez 302 Nte. and Gabino Barrera, no phone. 4 blocks north of Plaza de Armas. Open Tues.–Sun. 10–6.*

MUSEO REGIONAL DE DURANGO Built in the second half of the 19th century by architect Stanislaus Slonecky, the Regional Museum of Durango was originally a residence. Today the two-story building houses fossilized remains dating to the Paleozoic era. A mummified set of child-size human remains is also on display; its discovery in nearby El Mezquital has led some archaeologists to believe that a colony of pygmies once lived in Durango. The museum also houses paintings, textiles, and sculptures. *Victoria 100 Sur, tel. 12–56–05. Admission: 50¢. Open Tues.–Sat. 9–4, Sun. 10–3.*

PALACIO DE GOBIERNO This impressive 18th-century baroque palace houses the offices of state officials, including that of Durango's governor. The reason to visit, however, is the impressive murals on the top floor, which depict Durango's indigenous population's struggle for survival (a continuing battle for many in the southernmost portion of the state). On the ground floor you'll find an unfinished mural abandoned by painter Manuel Guerrero Lourdes in 1936. The state of Durango never got around to paying the master his salary. In protest, he refused to finish the painting. *5 de Febrero, at Zaragoza. From Plaza, head 4 blocks west. Admission free. Open daily 8–7.*

AFTER DARK

Nightlife isn't exactly hip-hoppin' in Durango, but things liven up on weekends. Hang out with local youth at **Club 100** (Piñón Blanco 101, tel. 18/11–05–52; open Thurs.–Sun. 11 PM–3:30 AM), on the highway to Mazatlán. Here, techno and rock music keep people dancing, and a "canta-bar" upstairs lets you try out your karaoke skills. To get here, catch a TIERRA Y LIBERTAD bus at Aquiles Serdán and Victoria; you'll have to get a taxi back into town when you're done. **Fiesta Estampida Rodeo** (tel. 18/25–33–77) is the weekend hot spot, especially on Fridays. The former factory was converted into a ranch-style nightclub complete with an electric bull and a midnight rodeo show. All types of music are played, but in keeping with the decor, country is the most popular. The club is located 5 kilometers from the town center, in El Pueblito; taxis ($2.50) are the only way to get here. If you're too tuckered out to two-step, **Buchagas Pool and Snack Bar** (20 de Noviembre 310 Ote., tel. 18/12–40–64) is a respectable place to play eight ball (tables are $4 per hour) and down a few pricey beers. They stay open into the wee hours, but do not admit patrons after 10 PM.

NORTHEASTERN MEXICO

6

By Allison Eymil, with Rachael Courtier

Stretching southward across the border from the dry, abandoned ranches of southern Texas, Mexico's increasingly industrial northeastern region offers a sobering reminder of the country's dependence on foreign industry and weekend tourism to bolster its unstable economy. In December 1994, one year after NAFTA was put into effect, foreign investors pulled out of Mexico, leaving border towns like Nuevo Laredo, Matamoros, and Reynosa glutted with disillusioned job seekers from all over the country. Stricter immigration policies have further exacerbated the situation, resulting in a large labor pool for the region's *maquiladoras* (*see* box Maquiladoras, in Chapter 3). These foreign-owned factories in duty-free zones have been present for decades, but in recent times more and more smaller corporations, especially computer and fiber-optic firms, have joined their big conglomerate brothers south of the border.

Despite suffering a repeated pattern of economic boom and bust, northeasterners somehow manage to strike a balance between modern materialism and the preservation of age-old traditions. In border towns like Reynosa, vendors from all over Mexico sell handmade crafts in open markets, while fresh red crab and baby shrimp are sold by the kilo in port towns like Tampico. In Saltillo, the slow-paced capital of Coahuila state and the original residence of revolutionary leader-turned-governor Venustiano Carranza, serape makers still produce the magnificently colored vests and blankets of their Tlaxcalan ancestors. Just 230 kilometers (142 mi) south of the U.S. border is Mexico's third largest city, Monterrey, home to a number of excellent museums and one of Latin America's finest universities.

Although the northeastern landscape tends to be mostly dry and unbearably hot in the summer months, this does little to deter scores of U.S. day-trippers who cross the border in search of ethnic kitsch and cheap tequila shots. The coastal town of Tampico offers a verdant escape from this souvenir hell; its extensive stretches of beach provide refreshing relief from the city heat. If you're a serious nature lover, the Parque Nacional Cumbres de Monterrey, an hour from Monterrey, offers dozens of hiking, spelunking, and camping opportunities.

Matamoros

Matamoros is the easternmost border crossing between the United States and Mexico, connected to Brownsville, Texas, by a 100-meter bridge. Located in the state of Tamaulipas, the city hugs the Río Bravo (or Rio Grande, as it's known in the States) 38 kilometers (24 mi) west of the Gulf Coast, and is home to close to a half million people. Although most of the city's inhabitants are employed in the ever-present maquiladoras, the devaluation of the peso over the past year has left many jobless and desperate. The ratio of men to women seems to be five to one on the streets, making it unpleasant for females to explore the city alone—although it's doubtful they'd even want to.

Still, if you're stranded here, some relics of Matamoros's preindustrial history and a few small galleries and theaters merit your perusal. The **Casamata** (Guatemala, at Santos Degollado, tel. 88/13–59–29; open Tues.–Sat. 9:30–5:30, Sun. 9:30–1:30) was established in 1845 to defend the city against an anticipated U.S. invasion. It wasn't completed in time, however, and U.S. troops under Zachary Taylor were able to capture Matamoros easily in 1846. The fortress is now a free museum housing photos and artifacts, mainly from the Mexican Revolution. The city's last remaining art gallery is housed in the slightly yellowing but regal **Teatro Reforma** (Calle 6, at Abasolo, tel. 88/12–51–20), where local artists exhibit their work. Admission to the gallery is free, and it's open Tuesday–Saturday 9–2 and 5–7. The theater also hosts regional and local dance and drama; check *Tu-Guía Matamoros,* a monthly publication of events in Spanish, available at the tourist information center (*see below*). Nearby **Calle Abasolo** is closed to traffic, making it an ideal spot to grab a seat and watch the river of pedestrians ebb and flow through the shops. Matamoros explodes with dance, theater, and art during the huge **Festival Internacional de Otoño,** which starts the second week of October. During the last week of Feburary, Matamoros's **Fiesta Mexicana** promotes U.S.–Mexican relations and kicks off with parades and outdoor concerts.

BASICS

AMERICAN EXPRESS Viajes Axial is affiliated with American Express but doesn't offer most AmEx services. The office only replaces lost cards and holds members' mail. *Morelos 94–107, Centro, Matamoros, Tamaulipas, CP 87300, México, tel. 88/13–69–69. Open weekdays 8–6, Sat. 9–1.*

CASAS DE CAMBIO Banamex changes cash and traveler's checks weekdays 9–3. It also has an ATM that accepts Plus, Cirrus, MasterCard, Visa, and, surprisingly, American Express. *Calle 7, at Morelos, tel. 88/13–60–35.*

CONSULATES The **American Consulate** is a madhouse. To avoid standing in line, show the guard your passport. *Calle 1 No. 2002, at Azaleas, tel. 88/12–44–02. Take yellow PRIMERA POPULAR/PUENTE pesera (minibus) from bus station. Open weekdays 8–5.*

CROSSING THE BORDER If you're only staying in Matamoros a couple of days, simply show the scowling border guard your passport or any other picture ID. If you plan to travel more than 22 kilometers (13 mi) into Mexico, get a tourist card (*see* Passports, Visas, and Tourist Cards, in Chapter 1) at the crossing. Most of the yellow *maxitaxis* (buses) just over the bridge in Matamoros will take you to the downtown area.

EMERGENCIES In an emergency, call the **police** (Luis Caballero, at R. F. García, tel. 88/17–22–05) or the **fire** department (tel. 88/12–00–03). For an ambulance, call the **Cruz Roja** (Luis Caballero, at Durango, tel. 88/12–00–44). Free emergency care is available at the **Centro de Salud** (Calle 6, at Querétaro, tel. 88/17–49–30 or 88/17–19–16) 24 hours daily.

MEDICAL AID Bótica Monterrey is a 24-hour pharmacy. *Calle 6, at Nafarrete, tel. 88/17–09–48.*

PHONES AND MAIL The main **post office** will hold your mail at the following address for up to 10 days: Lista de Correos, Calle 6 No. 214, Matamoros, Tamaulipas, CP 87300, México. There's also a branch at the Matamoros bus depot open daily 9–noon and 3–8. For faster delivery, mail your letters from the Brownsville post office (1001 E. Elizabeth St., 5 blocks west of international bridge, tel. 210/546–9462), open weekdays 9–5. You can make collect and credit-card international calls from the **Ladatel** pay phones (not the overpriced orange ones) in Plaza Hidalgo, Plaza Allende, and the bus and train stations.

VISITOR INFORMATION The small, white **Centro de Información Turístico** (Hidalgo 50, btw Calles 5 and 6, tel. 88/13–90–45; open weekdays 9–1 and 3–7) offers maps, brochures, and information about surrounding areas. Ignore the little green shack next door—they'll tell you anything to make a buck. The **Brownsville Chamber of Commerce** has excellent street maps of Brownsville and Matamoros. *Cnr of Taylor and Elizabeth Sts., Brownsville, tel. 210/542–4341. 1 block east of international bridge. Open weekdays 9–5.*

COMING AND GOING

For a city of its size, Matamoros is easily navigable. All north–south streets are numbered, and their cross streets form a neat grid. The city center is bordered by **Plaza Hidalgo** to the south and the **Mercado Juárez** to the north. The **puente internacional** (international bridge) connects Matamoros and Brownsville eight blocks north of downtown Matamoros. Walking is the easiest and fastest way to cross the border (25¢ each way); drivers pay $1.50. *Peseros* (minivans) run every 10 minutes to the bridge, bus station, and American Consulate.

BY BUS The Central de Autobuses (Calle 1, at Canales) is 25 blocks south of the international bridge. To get here, flag down a CENTRAL pesero at the international bridge or in Plaza Hidalgo. First-class **Autobuses del Orietne (ADO)** (tel. 88/12–01–81) serves Veracruz twice daily (16 hrs, $38). **Omnibús de México** (tel. 88/13–76–93) sends several daily buses to Monterrey (5 hrs, $10 1st class), Reynosa (2 hrs; $3 1st class, $2 2nd class), and Nuevo Laredo (6 hrs, $9 1st class). **Transportes del Norte** (tel. 88/12–27–77) has one bus daily to Guadalajara (18 hrs, $36) and Zacatecas (12 hrs, $25) and four buses to Mexico City (15 hrs,

$36). Inside the terminal you'll find a post office, plenty of Ladatel phones, a 24-hour cafeteria, and luggage lockers ($3 per day).

BY CAR As with every border town, be sure to have your papers in order and your hologram sticker firmly stuck to the driver's side of the front windshield. For more details on bringing a car into Mexico, *see* Chapter 1. Traveling to **Tampico** (501 km, 7 hrs) is a long, dry drive on Federal 180 south. To reach **Monterrey** (338 km, 4 hrs), head out on Federal 2 west toward Reynosa (104 km, 1 hr); at Río Bravo, just before Reynosa, get on the smoothly paved toll road (tolls $3). This conveniently connects with Autopista 40 southeast, which takes you directly into Monterrey (tolls $11). To reach **Mexico City** (990 km, 10 hrs), take Federal 180 south towards Tampico to Federal 70 west. This will hook up with Federal 105 south, which will take you to Autopista 130 south at Pachuca (tolls $5).

BY TRAIN El Tamaulipeco, offering both first- and second-class service, crawls from Matamoros to Monterrey via Reynosa in six hours. There's one daily departure at 9:20 AM, and tickets ($6 1st class, $4 2nd class) are sold 8–9 AM only, so get there early. *Hidalgo, btw Calles 9 and 10, tel. 88/16–67–06.*

BY PLANE Both **Aeroméxico** (tel. 88/12–24–60) and **Aerocalifornia** (tel. 88/12–22–20) offer daily flights to Mexico City and other destinations. The airport is 17 kilometers (10 mi) south of town, toward Ciudad Victoria. The frequent blue PEREÑO pesero from Plaza Allende (Independencia, at Calle 10) drops you off 250 meters from the gates. A taxi costs about $5.

WHERE TO SLEEP

Rooms in Matamoros are expensive by Mexican standards, but they're half the price of those in Brownsville. Budget hotels, virtually indistinguishable from one another, are clustered on and near Calle Abasolo. Keep in mind that Matamoros isn't the safest city in Mexico, and the cheaper hotels tend to attract a sketchier clientele. The air-conditioned rooms (singles $5, doubles $10) at **Casa de Huéspedes Margarita** (Calle 4 No. 79, btw Abasolo and Matamoros, tel. 88/13–72–78) have plenty of hot water and always seem to be full. The family that runs the place is always there, making it the safest budget option in town. **Hotel México** (Abasolo 123, btw Calles 8 and 9, tel. 88/13–36–80) has 23 fan-cooled rooms for those willing to put up with cockroaches in exchange for bargain-basement prices (doubles $8). At $8 for a single and $9.50 for a double, the wheelchair-accessible **Hotel Alameda** (Victoria 91, btw Calles 10 and 11, tel. 88/16–77–90) won't break the bank. The immaculate rooms are deliciously cool, and the snacks in the lobby rival those in any American movie theater. Parking is also available. For all this, you'll gladly put up with the pervasive smell of air freshener.

FOOD

Head to the Mercado Juárez for tacos, *tortas* (sandwiches), and other cheap eats. The heat may be excruciating in the summer months, but if you're on a tight budget, remember the direct correlation between air-conditioning and high prices. The huge, sticky, and run-down **Café El Económico** (Calle 10 No. 1003, btw González and Abasolo, tel. 88/12–14–58; open daily 6 AM–11 PM) is actually a mecca for starving travelers. A delicious meal consisting of a *guisado* (stew) of your choice, rice, beans, and tortillas is only 75¢. It's only 25¢ for a soda and $1–$1.50 for a helping of *gorditas* (fried tortillas filled with vegetables, beans, or meat). Local kids crowd around the orange Formica tables at the Howard Johnson–esque **La Canasta** (Abasolo 706, btw Calles 7 and 8, tel. 88/12–29–00; open daily 9–7), gobbling down the famous double burger with cheese ($1.75). The 75¢ burritos and 50¢ tacos with cheese are as cheap as they come. The air-conditioned **Las Dos Repúblicas** (Calle 9, at Matamoros, tel. 88/16–68–94; open daily 9–8) offers $4 for six *flautas* (fried, meat-filled tortillas with beans, chips, guacamole, and sour cream) or quesadillas (tortillas with white Chihuahua cheese and hot sauce). Wash it all down with an 18-ounce margarita—it may be a whopping six bucks, but you won't need another. All three restaurants are wheelchair accessible.

CHEAP THRILLS

The swarms of U.S. tourists testify to Matamoros's main draw—shopping. Loudly colored serapes, bullwhips, ceramics, glass, and mounds of silver jewelry are sold at **Mercado Juárez** (Matamoros, at Calle 10) and at Matamoros's old market, **Pasaje Juárez** (Calle 8, across from Hotel Roma). When you get consumer overload, head for the swimming pool at the **Centro Deportivo Eduardo Chávez** (Guatemala, near Laura Villar, tel. 88/16–28–37), across from Casamata (*see above*). This clean 50-meter pool is filled with madly splashing local kids by midday, so get your laps done early. There are dressing rooms and showers, but you must bring your own towel. The pool is open late March to mid-September, daily 8–6; admission is $1.50, $1 students. On Sundays, avid soccer players flock to the patchy field behind the old **Museo de Maíz** (cnr of Calle 5 and Constitución) for a serious pickup game.

AFTER DARK

Like other border towns, Matamoros attracts throngs of tourists for a night of unbridled indulgence. During the U.S. Spring Break, bars pop up all along Avenida Obregón, hosting students in various stages of alcoholic madness. A popular place year-round for eating and dancing to contemporary pop is the restaurant/disco **Blanca White** (Álvaro Obregón 49, at Gardenias, tel. 88/12–18–59; open Mon.–Sat. 1–1, Sun. noon–6). The clientele, as the bilingual name suggests, is divided between Mexicans and Americans. Cover is $5. A mellower crowd frequents the video-bar **La Tequila** (Álvaro Obregón 42, tel. 88/16–75–22), the best spot if you really want to dance (as opposed to standing around and gawking). The club is open until 2 or 3 AM, with a $3 cover Friday and Saturday ($2 Thurs. and Sun.).

Near Matamoros

PLAYA BAGDAD During the U.S. Civil War, Playa Bagdad was the Confederacy's only open harbor. Freighters skirting the Union naval blockade unloaded their war supplies here and loaded up with Confederate cotton destined for Europe. Today, *palapas* (thatched huts) run the length of the shore, and dozens of restaurants offer fresh seafood at reasonable prices. Showers and bathrooms are free, but drivers pay $2 to park. Camping is perfectly free and legal, but be careful—the beach is deserted at night and far from civilization. During *Semana Santa* (Holy Week, the week before Easter) the beach comes alive with parades, coronations, and partying in the waves. On Good Friday there is a re-enactment of the Passion of Christ. To get here from Matamoros, take a blue pesero marked PLAYA (45 min, $1.25) from Lauro Villar and Calle 1. The last pesero back to town leaves at 6 PM.

Reynosa
Because of Mexico's plummeting economy, Reynosa has become a destination for opportunity-seeking Mexicans and Americans hoping to take advantage of favorable exchange rates. Across the border from McAllen, Texas, Reynosa is a convenient starting point if you're bound for Mexico City, Monterrey, or El Bajío, yet it's still a border town of limited charm. Reynosa is one of Mexico's most industrial cities, with over 60 maquiladoras. Nonetheless, the city is not without its long-held traditions; agricultural goods are brought in weekly from as far as San Luis Potosí, Veracruz, and Sinaloa to be sold at Reynosa's spectacular open-air market, along with regional crops like okra, wheat, and corn. The **market** (Colón, btw Hidalgo and Morelos) stretches for two blocks, and on a typical day the smells of fruit, sweat, leather, and tamales intertwine as they waft through the crowded streets. At night, tourists from nearby McAllen, Texas, stop shopping and flock to the *Zona Rosa* for the raucous nightlife.

BASICS

AMERICAN EXPRESS Erika Viajes, eight blocks north of the plaza, provides limited AmEx services: The staff won't cash personal checks, but they do replace lost traveler's checks and

181

sell new ones. *Ávila Camacho 1325, at Ortíz Rubio, tel. 89/22–60–16. Open weekdays 9–6, Sat. 8:30–12:30.*

CASAS DE CAMBIO You'll pass several casas de cambio on Zaragoza heading downtown from the international border, most of which don't cash traveler's checks. **Banamex** (Juárez 650, at Guerrero, tel. 89/22–22-18; open weekdays 9–3) will cash them for you for good rates. It also has an ATM. **Casa de Cambio Sogo** has similar rates for changing traveler's checks, but the manager has to approve the transaction. *Juárez 610 Nte., near P. J. Méndez, tel. 89/22–11–04. Open weekdays 9–6, Sat. 9–2.*

CROSSING THE BORDER You can stay in Reynosa up to 72 hours without getting a tourist card, but if you plan to stay longer or venture more than 22 kilometers into Mexico, get one at the border crossing (*see* Passports, Visas, and Tourist Cards, in Chapter 1). The border crossing over the Río Bravo costs 25¢ if you're walking and $1.50 to cross by car.

EMERGENCIES You can call the **police** (Morelos, at Argentina, tel. 89/22–00–08); **fire** department (tel. 89/24–93–99); or **Cruz Roja** (tel. 89/22–13–14) for an **ambulance.**

MEDICAL AID **Farmacia López** is open 24 hours. *Aldama 101, at Hidalgo, tel. 89/22–84–84 or 89/22–96–67.*

PHONES AND MAIL The only public phone within two blocks of the bus station is at **7-Eleven,** across the street from the east side of the station. There's a cluster of **pay phones** in the plaza, where you'll also find a **Computel** office that's open daily 8 AM–10 PM. The main **post office** (cnr of Díaz and Colón, near the train station) is open weekdays 8–7 and Saturday 9–1. They'll hold your mail at the following address for up to 10 days: Lista de Correos, Reynosa, Tamaulipas, CP 88620, México.

VISITOR INFORMATION At the puente internacional (international bridge), you'll find the white, dusty **Delegación Estatal de Turismo.** The staff can only give you a few pamphlets and then send you on your way. *Tel. 89/22–11–89. Open weekdays 8–8.*

COMING AND GOING

A bridge over the Río Bravo connects Reynosa and McAllen, Texas. Reynosa is small: Its downtown area, laid out in a grid, can be crossed in less than 15 minutes. **Hidalgo** is the principal north–south axis, and **Morelos** the main east–west axis. Microbuses (25¢) run from the bridge to the plaza, the train station, and the bus depot at least every 15 minutes.

BY BUS The **Central Camionera** (Colón 1001, tel. 89/22–84–08) is behind the Gigante supermarket, five blocks south and 10 blocks east of the main plaza. To get here, catch a c. CAMIONERA/OBRERO microbus (30¢) from the bridge or the center of town. There have been a few thefts in and around the station, so be extra careful, especially at night. There's frequent service to Matamoros (2 hrs, $2.75) and Río Bravo (½ hr, $1). Three first-class buses also leave daily for Monterrey (3 hrs, $4). First-class **Omnibús de México** (tel. 89/22–33–07) sends buses west to Chihuahua (15 hrs, $31) and south to Mexico City (13 hrs, $34). **Transportes del Norte** (tel. 89/22–04–92) goes daily to Guadalajara (18 hrs, $34) and Mexico City (15 hrs, $33). **ADO** (tel. 89/22–87–13) has first-class buses to Tampico (3 per day, 6½ hrs, $13), Tuxpán (3 per day, 10 hrs, $17), and Veracruz city (daily, 16 hrs, $36). The station and its *caseta de larga distancia* (long-distance telephone office) are open 24 hours; luggage storage is available 6 AM–9 PM (25¢ per hr, $1 per day).

BY CAR Travel to Monterrey (224 km, 2 hrs) is easy sailing on the Autopista 40-D southwest (the toll is $8). Continue another hour past Monterrey on to Federal 40 to reach Saltillo. Travelers to Tampico (511 km, 5 hrs) should take Federal 97 south to Federal 180 south.

BY TRAIN The train station (tel. 89/22–00–85) is south of the plaza, at the end of Hidalgo. The special first-class **El Tamaulipeco** departs at 12:30 PM daily for Monterrey (4½ hrs; $5 1st class, $2.75 2nd class). The train to Matamoros (2½ hrs, $2) leaves at 3 PM. Tickets are sold from 10:30 AM until they're gone or until Margarita, the cashier, gets tired of sitting around.

The C. CAMIONERA/OBRERO and COLON microbuses run from the bridge and bus depot down Calle Colón; from here, get off at Hidalgo and walk south a short block to the tracks.

WHERE TO SLEEP

Hotels in the Zona Rosa and around the central plaza cater to businesspeople and vacationers, and are priced accordingly. For a budget room, head toward the train station; the cheapest rooms are found just north of the tracks. The seductively frosty air-conditioning makes the immaculate little **Hotel Avenida** (Zaragoza 885 Ote., at Canales, tel. 89/22–05–92) a hard option to turn down; at $12 for a single and $14 for a double, it's an affordable luxury. A plant-filled patio borders spotless, wheelchair-accessible rooms with clean carpets and TVs. The **Hotel Estación** (Hidalgo 305, tel. 89/22–73–02), just across the tracks from the train depot and a few blocks south of downtown, couldn't be more convenient. If you're tired enough, you won't even hear the roar of passing trains. Small but relatively clean singles and doubles go for $8 with air-conditioning—avoid the stuffy rooms with fans. If you've ever wanted to spend the night in an old ranch house, the **Hotel Nuevo León** (P. Díaz 580, tel. 89/22–13–10) is your big chance. Tiled stairs with wood banisters lead to low-ceilinged rooms complete with squeaky dressers and miniature double beds. The bathrooms are on the dirty side but at least there's hot water. Singles cost $7.50, doubles $8.75.

FOOD

Cheap taco stands and carts selling *elote* (grilled corn on the cob) can be found on almost every corner, and the piles of fresh fruit at the open market provide some of the cheapest snacks around. For sit-down meals, cruise the **peatonal** (pedestrian-only street) on Hidalgo from the main plaza to the train station, which leads to even more elegant eateries around the main plaza.

The mirror-lined **Café París** (Hidalgo 815, tel. 89/22–55–35) is always full, so you may have to loom in the doorway until someone vacates one of the paisley-cushioned booths. The delicious *comida corrida* (pre-prepared lunch special), served between 11–3, is a steal at $1.75; a filling breakfast omelet is $1.75. **La Fogata** (Matamoros 750, tel. 89/12–47–72), an elegant, air-conditioned restaurant/piano bar, is the place for a splurge. *Cabrito* (grilled baby goat) is $7, and beers are just $1. Vegetarians won't find much here besides the *queso flameado* (cheese broiled in a smoky oven) for $3. Enjoy the live music daily 11 AM–noon and 2–midnight.

CHEAP THRILLS

On weekends, maquiladora workers escape the relentless Reynosa heat and head out to **Bocatoma,** where the Río Bravo separates Reynosa from Mission, Texas. Plenty of aquaphiles can be found splashing around the tree-lined shore at the southeast edge of the river. You can also join one of the haphazard kickball games in the center of the park or just kick back and take in the cool breeze. The river can get pretty trashed by the end of the day, so come early. To reach "the Boca," take Bus 22 or a MAGNIPARK bus from the corner of Porfirio Díaz and Colón. After the 25-minute ride, you'll be let off a 15-minute walk from the park's entrance. Walk north for about five minutes to the SEYMOUR sign on the right-hand side of the road, turn left, and take the center dirt road toward the BIENVENIDOS sign all the way to the park. If you're in a car, take the road to Nuevo Laredo until you see the MAGNIPARK sign on the right. Turn right and follow the walking directions above.

AFTER DARK

At night, Reynosa gets overwhelmingly rowdy and seedy. Fortunately, most of the serious drug trafficking, prostitution, and violence is relegated to the city's *Zona Roja* (red-light district), located a good 10 blocks west of the city center. A little easier to swallow is the Zona Rosa, a five-block section of streets bordering the international bridge that becomes flooded with 18-year-olds blasting techno from their cars. If you're jonesing for some country, ranchera, and norteña music, head to the cover-free **El Rodeo** (Allende 890, just south of the bridge, tel. 89/22–95–33), where the gaping mouth of an enormous plaster bull serves as the entrance. The large circular dance floor is suitable for any number of honky-tonk moves. **Fiesta Mexicana** (Ocampo 1140, at Allende, tel. 89/22–01–11) has a mellower atmosphere and an older crowd. The house band plays everything from *baladas* (ballads) to salsa, Friday–Sunday 8 PM–3 AM. The $4 cover on Friday and Satruday nights allows you to drink all the alcohol you want.

Nuevo Laredo

Of all the eastern border towns, Nuevo Laredo, just over the international bridge from Laredo, Texas, gets the largest onslaught of American souvenir-seekers. Shopping is the primary pursuit here, and you'll find a warren of stalls and shops concentrated on Avenida Guerrero in a seven-block stretch from the international bridge to the main plaza. In addition to the standard border-town schlock, Nuevo Laredo's shops stock a good selection of high-quality handicrafts imported from all over Mexico, available at somewhat inflated prices. Wander a few blocks off the main drag in any direction for better prices and smaller crowds. There's also a large crafts market on the east side of Guerrero, just north of the plaza.

Nuevo Laredo's vibrant commercialism takes the form of street vendors parading meter-high stacks of straw hats while little kids stand against shaded walls with photos of the latest lucha libre (wrestling) heroes.

Nuevo Laredo was founded after the Treaty of Guadalupe Hidalgo in 1848, which ended the Mexican-American War. The treaty established the Río Bravo (or Rio Grande) as the border between the two countries, and forced Mexico to give up a substantial amount of territory. Many of Laredo's Mexican residents, suddenly finding themselves living in the United States, crossed the river and founded Nuevo Laredo on what had been the outskirts of town. Today, Nuevo Laredo's economy depends largely on gringos who head south for a few days of drunken revelry, returning home with suitcases full of souvenirs, a bottle of tequila, and a mean hangover. As with most border towns, Mexican men roam the streets aimlessly, hissing at every lone gringa—especially at night.

BASICS

AMERICAN EXPRESS You can buy and replace AmEx traveler's checks, change traveler's checks, cash personal checks, and receive mail at **Lozano Viajes Internacionales.** *Paseo Reforma 3311, Col. Jardín, Nuevo Laredo, Tamaulipas, CP 88260, México, tel. 87/15–44–55. Open weekdays 9–5:30.*

CASAS DE CAMBIO Change cash at one of several casas de cambio on Guerrero, just below the international bridge. To change traveler's checks, try **Lozano Viajes Internacionales** (*see above*) or **Divisas Terminal** (open Mon.–Sat. 6 AM–10 PM, Sun. 6 AM–8 PM) in the bus station. **Banamex** (Guerrero, btw Canales and Madero, tel. 87/12–30–01) has an ATM that accepts Cirrus, Plus, Visa, and MasterCard.

CROSSING THE BORDER Although it's unlikely anyone will stop you from sauntering past the customs guards and making your way into Mexico, it's best to have a passport or other photo ID. If you plan on traveling farther south (22 kilometers or more) or will be staying in Mexico longer than 72 hours, cross the parking lot west of the international bridge and ask the immigration office for a tourist card (*see* Passports, Visas, and Tourist Cards, in Chapter 1).

EMERGENCIES In an emergency, dial **06.** You can also call the **police** (tel. 87/12–21–46); **fire** department (87/12–21–24); or **Cruz Roja** (tel. 87/12–09–49) for an **ambulance.**

MEDICAL AID The **Cruz Roja** (Independencia 1619, at San Antonio, tel. 87/12–09–49) offers emergency and routine medical care. There are a number of well-stocked **Benavides**

pharmacies throughout town. Try the one on Guerrero 702 (at Padre Mier, tel. 87/12–21–60; open daily 8 AM–10 PM). For 24-hour service, head next door to **Farmacia Calderón** (Guerrero 704, tel. 87/12–55–63).

PHONES AND MAIL It's quickest and cheapest to drop foreign mail at the U.S. post office, about six blocks north of the border. Nuevo Laredo's main **post office** (cnr of Reynosa and Dr. Mier, tel. 87/12–20–90), behind the Palacio Municipal, is open weekdays 8–7 and Saturday 9–12:30. They'll hold your mail at the following address for up to 10 days: Lista de Correos, Nuevo Laredo, Tamaulipas, CP 88000, México. The same building boasts a telegram and fax service (both for sending only), open weekdays 9–7, weekends 9–noon. **Ladatel** pay phones can be found on Plaza Hidalgo, but it's cheaper to place international calls from the States; pay phones are across the international bridge, just past U.S. customs.

VISITOR INFORMATION The **tourist office** is housed in a large, dusty booth on the west sidewalk of the international bridge. An official secretary is available Monday–Saturday 8–2, but from 2 to 8 PM a more helpful staff occupies the office; they'll dig up tourist pamphlets and often supply free maps of Nuevo Laredo and other border towns. *Puente Internacional No. 1, tel. 87/12–01–04.*

COMING AND GOING

Nuevo Laredo is split down the middle by Avenida Guerrero, which runs north–south from the **international bridge** to Avenida Reforma (which connects with the highway to Monterrey). The city's two main squares, **Plaza Juárez** and **Plaza Hidalgo,** are also located on Guerrero, at the edges of the six-block area that makes up the central market. Buses marked PUENTE/CENTRAL and CAMIONERA/CARRETERA (50¢) run down Guerrero to the bus station; green-and-white COLONIAS 5 buses run from Plaza Hidalgo east to the train station.

BY BUS The **Terminal Central Maclovio Herrera** (J. R. Romo 3800) is a 25-minute bus ride south of the bridge. Take a PUENTE/CENTRAL or CAMIONERA/CARRETERA bus from the corner of Juárez and Victoria or from Galeano on the east side of the plaza. The 10-minute taxi ride costs $2. **Transportes Frontera** (tel. 87/14–09–88) runs buses every three hours to Mexico City (15 hrs, $42 1st class; 15 hrs, $36 2nd class). Buses also leave hourly for Saltillo (4 hrs, $9 1st class; 5 hrs, $8 2nd class), San Luis Potosí (12 hrs, $25 1st class), and Monterrey (3 hrs, $7 1st class). First-class **Omnibús de México** (tel. 87/14–06–17) serves nearby cities as well as Zacatecas (8 hrs, $24) and Guadalajara (14 hrs, $36). The caseta de larga distancia is open 24 hours a day, and the casa de cambio (open weekdays 6 AM–10 PM, Sun. 6 AM–8 PM) changes traveler's checks. Luggage storage is available Monday–Saturday 7 AM–10 PM, Sunday 7–5.

BY CAR For those headed to Monterrey (224 km, 2 hrs), the Autopista 80-D south is as quick and direct as they come (tolls $14). Traveling to Mexico City (1151 km, 12 hrs) involves taking Autopista 85 south through Monterrey to Federal 105 south to Autopista 130 south at Pachuca. The grand toll total is around $23.

BY TRAIN The **train station** (tel. 87/12–21–29) is on López de Lara, at Gutiérrez, about a dozen short blocks west of the main plaza. It's a 15-minute walk from the border to the station; or take an ARTEGA GONZALEZ bus from Juárez and Victoria. The first-class train to Mexico City (25 hrs, $22) leaves daily at 6:55 PM, with stops in Monterrey (3½ hrs; $4 1st class, $2.75 2nd class), Saltillo (7½ hrs) $8 1st class, $6 2nd class), San Luis Potosí (15½ hrs; $9 1st class, $5 2nd class), San Miguel de Allende (18½ hrs; $15 1st class, $12.50 2nd class), and Querétaro (19½ hrs; $18 1st class, $15 2nd class), among others. First-class buses to Mexico City, San Luis Potosí, San Miguel de Allende, and Querétaro come with air-conditioning. All tickets go on sale daily at 5:30 PM.

BY PLANE **Mexicana** (tel. 87/12–22–11) flies to Guadalajara and Mexico City. The airport is 15 kilometers (9 mi) south of town, and there's no public transportation there. A taxi costs about $3. Hitchhiking is a possibility, but for the most part you'll be ignored.

WHERE TO SLEEP

Hotels tend to be either too expensive or dreadfully run-down; your best bet for something in between is the area around Avenida Guerrero, between the bridge and central square. The streets stay lit until 9 or 10 PM, and Guerrero is almost always busy. Nevertheless, be careful of the many thieves who target tourists.

Hidden among the casas de cambio near the bridge, **Los Dos Laredos** (Matamoros 108, at 15 de Junio, tel. 87/12–24–19) is fairly clean and friendly, with fluffy towels that make up for the wimpy water pressure. The throb of nearby discos can be heard late into the night, but you can't beat the $8 singles and $11.50 doubles. On weekends, check in before 6 PM, as this place tends to fill up. Large, comfy rooms with air-conditioning and color TVs are standard at the **Hotel La Finca** (Reynosa 811, tel. 87/12–88–83), where the hot water runs day and night. Singles cost $14, doubles $13. But by far the cleanest, most reliable hotel in town is the wheelchair-accessible **Hotel Romanos** (Dr. Mier 2402, tel. 87/12–23–91), where pearly white bedcovers and spotless bathrooms are complemented by blissfully cool air-conditioning and plenty of hot water. Singles and doubles cost only $10, $11.50 with color TV.

FOOD

The dining scene here includes everything from cheap taco stands and fast-food joints to over-priced eateries that cater to touring Texans. For moderately priced restaurants, explore the side streets south of the main plaza. After a long day of shopping (or a long night at the discos), come to the wheelchair-accessible **Cafetería Modelo** (Dr. Mier, at Ocampo, tel. 87/12–15–66; open daily 7 AM–3 AM) for huge all-day breakfasts and a mellow atmosphere. Try the huevos rancheros with orange juice ($2), or fill up on the *plato mexicano,* which includes two flautas, one burrito, one tamale, and beans ($2). While the glowing photos, mirrors, and fluorescent lighting create a hospital-like ambience at **El Principal** (Guerrero 624, tel. 87/12–13–01; open daily 8 AM–11:30 PM), the meal-sized *botanas* (appetizers) are a real bargain. Try the *queso panela de cabra* (goat cheese broiled in a smoky oven; $2) accompanied by a stack of piping-hot tortillas. The 24-hour **Restaurant Hotel Reforma** (Guerrero 806, btw González and Canales, tel. 87/12–34–88) isn't much to look at, but it's always packed at lunchtime with hotel guests and local families. They come for one of the best comida corridas around—including salad, soup, dessert, and your choice of chicken or breaded beef, all for $4.

AFTER DARK

Nuevo Laredo's nighttime activities are every bit as frenzied as its daytime shopping. The most touristy and expensive discos are located on the south end of Guerrero, but local crowds head one block south of 15 de Mayo to **OK Tequila** (Victoria, at Matamoros, tel. 87/12–07–76), which plays everything from '70s hits to salsa and *nueva canción* (Latin American folk music). On Saturday nights, an $8 cover enables you to invent an unlimited amount of alcoholic stews at the open bar; Thursday and Friday nights, cover is only $1 for women, $2 for men. Solitary night owls should seek out **Pepper's Haus** (cnr of Perú and Ocampo, no phone). This drive-through cocktail and botana joint is packed early at night, but empties out when the discos open, making it the perfect place to sit under the trees and sip a cool beer ($1).

Monterrey

In this metropolis of three million people, decadence and absolute poverty coexist side by side, a jarring reminder that Monterrey is the country's unchallenged industrial giant. In juxtaposition to the city's grand buildings and luxurious suburbs is the ring of squalid huts and smoke-belching factories known as the *cinturón de miseria* (belt of misery). Pollution is a serious problem in this state capital, and unless you confine yourself to Monterrey's sprawling but manageable center, it's likely you'll end up with a serious case of the urban-industrial blues.

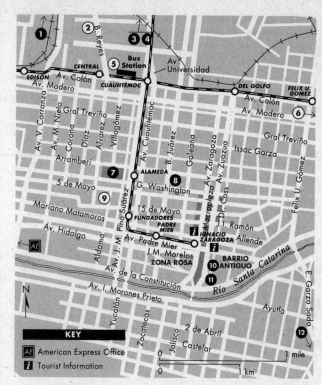

Sights ●
Catedral, **10**
Cervecería
Cuauhtémoc, **3**
Instituto
Tecnológico de
Monterrey, **12**
Mercado Juárez, **8**
Museo de Arte
Contemporáneo
(MARCO), **11**
Parque Alameda, **7**
Parque de los Niños
Héroes, **4**
Train Station, **1**

Lodging ○
Hotel Estación, **2**
Hotel Posada de
Los Reyes, **9**
Hotel Victoria, **5**
Villa Deportiva
Juvenil, **6**

KEY

AE American Express Office

i Tourist Information

After founding Monterrey in the late 1500s, the Spanish encouraged settlement in the region by granting vast tracts of land to a handful of families. The success of these sheep ranchers quickly created a small, wealthy elite, who, following the construction of a railroad in the 1880s, decided to invest in industry. The powerful Garza Sada family refined the art of mass-produced beer, and religiously reinvested the profits. They established glass factories and cardboard mills, and even produced their own barrels and delivery wagons. To ensure proper training for the future leaders of this vast industrial empire, the Garza Sadas founded the **Instituto Tecnológico de Monterrey,** now considered one of the best universities in Latin America.

Life in Monterrey, also known as "the Pittsburgh of Mexico," is hectic, and staying here can be quite expensive. Even so, those who take the time to wander the busy streets will encounter the region's best museums, good examples of colonial and modern civic architecture, and a spectacular central plaza that provides great views of the Sierra Madre, lush mountain peaks that form a semicircle around the southern edge of town. These pine-forested mountains are home to the **Parque Nacional Cumbres de Monterrey,** a national park known for several beautiful caves and waterfalls, as well as **La Silla** (The Chair), a saddle-shaped rock formation that you'll see on postcards everywhere.

BASICS

AMERICAN EXPRESS The AmEx office appears disorganized, but the staff is patient and friendly. They cash personal checks, replace lost or stolen traveler's checks, and hold card-members' mail indefinitely at: San Pedro 215 Nte., Colonia de Valle, San Pedro Garza García, Nuevo León, CP 64220, México. *Pino Suárez 214, at Isaac Garza, tel. 8/318–33–85. Open weekdays 9–6, Sat. 9–noon. From Zona Rosa, take* RUTA *39 bus north on Pino Suárez; get off at Isaac Garza.*

BOOKSTORES The **American Bookstore** has a great selection of English books. *Garza Sada 2404-A, near Pemex station, tel. 8/387–08–38. Open weekdays 9–7, Sat. 10–7, Sun. 10–3.*

CASAS DE CAMBIO **Base Internacional** (Pino Suárez 1217 Nte., tel. 8/372–86–22), just north of Colón and the Cuauhtémoc Metro stop, changes traveler's checks weekdays 9–6, Saturday 9–1. **Banamex** (Pino Suárez 933 Nte.) also cashes traveler's checks for decent rates and has an ATM that accepts Cirrus, Plus, MasterCard, and Visa.

CONSULATES **United States.** This office will replace birth certificates and lost passports, provide tax information and a notary public, and will help in emergency situations. *Constitución 411 Pte., tel. 8/345–21–20. Open weekdays 8–2.*

EMERGENCIES In an emergency, dial 06 or contact the **police** (Venustiano Carranza 215 Nte., tel. 8/370–00–48) or the **fire** department (tel. 8/342–00–53). For an **ambulance,** call the **Cruz Roja** (tel. 8/342–12–12).

LAUNDRY At **Lavandería Automática,** you can get 4 kilos of clothes washed for $3.50, or you can wash it yourself for 75¢ a load; drying costs 15¢ a minute. *Padre Mier 1102 Ote., at Antillón, tel. 8/42–11–88. Open weekdays 8–7, Sat. 8–5.*

MEDICAL AID For nonemergency consultations, try the **Cruz Roja** clinic (Alfonso Reyes 2503, Col. del Prado, tel. 8/342–12–12), near the Plaza de Toros. **Benavides** pharmacy (Morales 499, at Escobedo, tel. 8/345–91–91) is open daily 7 AM–10 PM. For 24-hour service, try **Farmacia Medix** (Pino Suárez 510 Sur, in front of Hospital Zoria, tel. 8/342–90–02).

PHONES AND MAIL The main **post office** is in the basement of the Palacio Federal building, at the north end of the Macroplaza. They'll hold your mail at the following address for up to 10 days: Lista de Correos, Administración 1, Monterrey, Nuevo León, CP 64000, México. *Washington, at Zaragoza, tel. 8/342–40–03. Open weekdays 8–7, Sat. 9–1.*

Phone calls from casetas are unjustifiably expensive here, so it's best to use one of the many **Latadel** phones scattered throughout the city. You can buy Latadel cards in 20- or 50-peso units at most supermarkets, drugstores, or 7-Elevens (look for the LATADEL sign in the store window).

VISITOR INFORMATION Call the **tourist information line** (tel. 8/40–07–07) for up-to-the-minute information on current events as well as directions to major sights. **Infotour** stocks great brochures and maps and has a friendly English-speaking staff. Ask for a copy of *Enjoy Monterrey* to find out about museum exhibits, cultural events, and concerts. *Padre Mier, at Dr. Cross, tel. 8/345–08–70. Open Tues.–Sun. 10–5.*

COMING AND GOING

BY BUS The huge **Central de Autobuses** (Colón, near Cuauhtémoc, in the NW part of the city) is an impressive transport hub serving virtually the entire country. Frequent first-class buses leave Nuevo Laredo (2½ hrs, $7 1st class), Reynosa (3½ hrs, $7 1st class), Matamoros (3 hrs, $8 1st class), Tampico (8 hrs, $17), Saltillo (1½ hrs, $2), and Mexico City (13 hrs, $30). Major first-class bus lines include **Omnibús de México** (tel. 8/374–07–16), which serves Chihuahua (12 hrs, $25) and Ciudad Juárez (18 hrs, $38) and **Transportes del Norte** (tel. 8/318–37–45), which, in conjunction with **Greyhound,** goes to San Antonio (7 hrs, $28), Dallas (12 hrs, $49), and Houston, Texas (10 hrs, $41). For other destinations, try **Transportes Zua Zua** (tel. 8/374–04–20) or **Tres Estrellas de Oro** (tel. 83/74–24–10). The terminal has a post office, 24-hour pharmacy, luggage lockers ($3 a day), Ladatel phones, and a medical center. Well-policed departure gates and plenty of traffic make this place perfectly safe to hang out in, but sleeping might be a little uncomfortable.

The easiest way to get here is to take the Line 1 Metro to the Central stop. From downtown, catch the RUTA 39 bus, which runs from the Macroplaza north along Juárez to the bus station. From the bus station to downtown, catch the RUTA 45 bus at Bernardo Reyes and Colón or a RUTA 206 PERIFERICO bus on Suárez.

BY TRAIN Three trains pass through Monterrey's station (tel. 8/375–46–04) daily. The first-class **El Regiomontano,** with sleeping berths, runs from Monterrey to Saltillo (2 hrs, $2) and San Luis Potosí (10 hrs, $8). The 14-hour trip to Mexico City costs $18 ($45 for a sleeping berth), and the train leaves at 7:50 PM. The first-class **El Tamaulipeco** travels to Matamoros via Reynosa (6½ hrs, $6). The Mexico City–Monterrey train is also first-class only, stopping in Saltillo (3 hrs, $13), San Luis Potosí (10 hrs, $8), and Querétaro en route to Mexico City (17 hrs, $18). There is also a direct train to Nuevo Laredo (5 hrs, $5). Tickets are only sold the day of departure at the TAQUILLA window between 8:30 and 12:30 and 4 and 8.

The train depot is six blocks northwest of the bus station and the Central Metro stop. To reach downtown, cross Venustiano Carranza in front of the train station, head east two blocks on Calzada Victoria to Bernardo Reyes, and take a RUTA 39 or RUTA 45 bus. To reach the bus station, get off at Colón; otherwise both buses will let you off at the Macroplaza. Your other option is to hoof it to the bus station and catch a bus there (*see above*).

BY PLANE The **Aeropuerto Internacional Mariano Escobedo** (tel. 8/345–44–32), equipped with luggage storage ($3 for 6 hrs) and a money-exchange booth, is 6 kilometers northeast of downtown. The only way to get here is by taxi, which will cost about $8. **Aeroméxico** (tel. 8/344–77–30) and **Mexicana** (tel. 8/344–77–10) serve most domestic destinations.

GETTING AROUND

Monterrey is a sprawling monstrosity, and very few places are within walking distance of one another. Luckily, the extensive public transit system makes it easy to get around. If you're traveling by car, avoid rush hours (noon–2 and 4–7) and stay alert. Several moderately priced parking garages dot downtown, so you may want to leave your car there while you explore the city. Downtown, also called the **Zona Rosa,** the city's luxury hotel and shopping area, is bordered on the east by the **Macroplaza** and on the west by **Juárez.** The intersection of Juárez and Arramberi marks the official center of town, and addresses to the west of this intersection are followed by "Poniente" (Pte.); to the east by "Oriente" (Ote.); to the north by "Norte" (Nte.); and to the south by "Sur." Street numbers become larger the farther you move from the intersection.

BY METRO The Monterrey Metro is a modern and efficient system that runs across the city both underground and along elevated tracks. Line 1 runs east–west from Exposición to the city's westernmost perimeter, and Line 2 runs roughly north–south from the Cuauhtémoc Brewery to the Macroplaza. Purchase tickets from station vending machines in units of one, two, four, or eight rides; each ride costs less than 30¢. The Metro runs daily 4:45 AM–11:45 PM.

BY BUS Monterrey's loud, rickety, smoke-belching buses (20¢) go everywhere. The buses on each route are color coded, and the names of major stops are often painted across the windshield—sometimes they're even legible. There are a few fixed bus stops, marked by blue PARADA signs, but buses will stop anywhere; just wave madly at the driver. Most buses run until midnight, except the 24-hour RUTA 1 bus, which travels from Ciudad Universitario and Pino Suárez to the Technológico, then up Juárez to Universidad every 20 minutes. The tourist office (*see above*) offers all the bus info you may need to help make sense of the chaos.

WHERE TO SLEEP

Monterrey's relative wealth, combined with a steady flow of business travelers, keeps hotel prices high. Most budget lodging is clustered by the obnoxiously loud bus station.

Hotel Estación. The hotel's stern management keeps things clean and quiet and charges $11 (single or double) for spartan rooms with fans. Its location (close to the train station) and reasonable rates attract a mixed crowd, including some backpacking travelers. The bathrooms are small but decent, and the hot water flows readily. Rooms fill fast, so come early. *Victoria 1450, tel. 8/375–07–55. From train station, cross Nieto and turn right. 25 rooms, all with bath. Luggage storage, parking. Wheelchair access.*

Hotel Posada de Los Reyes. Conveniently located two blocks from Pino Suárez in the Zona Rosa, this hotel is admittedly a popular *hotel de paso,* so don't be surprised when well-groomed, smiling couples without suitcases pass through the doors. Despite all the activity, the cordial staff and guards create a secure and welcoming environment. Tiles cover rooms big enough to dance in, and vigorous air-conditioning seems to keep the cockroaches and mosquitoes at bay. Singles and doubles cost $12.50. *Aldama 446 Sur, btw 5 de Mayo and 15 de Mayo, tel. 8/343-18-80. 23 rooms, all with bath.*

Hotel Victoria. Although this hotel's proximity to the bus station is convenient and the manager tries to keep it a decent for families, the exhaust-filled air has made for a slightly yellowed interior. Still, the rooms (singles $9, doubles $14) are spacious and well-kept, and the water here is sizzling—just wait patiently for its grudging arrival. *Bernardo Reyes 1205 Nte., tel. 8/375-45-42. 1 block NW of bus depot. 75 rooms, all with bath. Luggage storage.*

HOSTELS **Villa Deportiva Juvenil.** This enormous gymlike dormitory sits above a small school on the eastern side of the city in the Parque Fundadora. It's easily accessible by Metro, and the central patio is a beautiful place to breathe in some fresh air and look at the stars. A bed costs $5, but you may have to share it with an incalculable number of people, as the seven single-sex rooms have at least 20 beds in them. The bathrooms are kept clean and there's air-conditioning and even a TV in every room. The hostel also offers meals for less than $2 in the cafeteria. Free camping on the grassy outdoor patio is also an option, though giggling throngs of curious schoolchildren appear in the morning. If you need to call here, do so before 7 PM. If you plan on partying most of the night, make arrangements with whoever's in charge to let you in, since lockout is midnight–6 AM. *Madero 418 Ote., at Parque Fundidor, tel. 8/355-73-80. Take Metro Line 1 (direction: Exposición) to Y Griega; walk 1 block west on Colón, turn left on Preciliano Elizondo, and head south 1 block. 220 beds. Luggage storage, parking, showers.*

FOOD

Food stands in the major markets offer the best meal deals in town—grilled meats and rice-and-beans platters are less than $2. Come early, as popular dishes usually run out by 2 or 3 PM. The fast-food chain **El Pollo Loco** (open daily 10 AM–11 PM) has several branches that serve large chicken combination plates for $3. Most of Monterrey's moderately priced restaurants can be found in the Zona Rosa, especially around the Macroplaza.

➤ **UNDER $5** • **Café Sevilla.** For that late-night snack, this somewhat grungy 24-hour coffee shop serves taco plates, burgers, tasty enchiladas ($2), and surprisingly good coffee ($1). It's a favorite with bus drivers—always an encouraging sign. *Colón, at Villagran, no phone. Just west of bus depot.*

La Casa del Maiz. Vegetarians will rejoice at this hip bohemian eatery—everything can be ordered meatless. Typical Mexican appetizers are large enough to eat as a meal, and the owners/chefs have added their unique touch to every dish. Try the *molletes,* thick tortillas covered with black beans, cheese, and *huitlacoche* (corn fungus), for $2.50. The walls are decorated with local art and the candlelit tables attract an artsy crowd at night. *Abasolo 870-B, btw Diego de Montemayor and Dr. Cross, Barrio Antiguo, tel. 8/340-43-34. Open Mon.–Thurs. 9 AM–11 PM, Fri. and Sat. 9 AM–3 AM.*

Los Girasoles. Another haven of meat-free delights awaits you here. The comida corrida ($2.75) changes daily but always features vegetable combinations like hot broccoli, spinach, and potato soup, or vegetarian "pescado" (grilled filet of potato and shredded cheese). If you're not up for the full five-course menu, individual items cost 75¢. Still, you may want to stick around for one of the fruit, yogurt, and granola desserts. *Ocampo 961, at Cuauhtémoc, tel. 8/343-70-00. Open Mon.–Sat. 7:30 AM–8:30 PM.*

Las Monjitas. If you can stop laughing at the waitresses' nun outfits long enough to eat, you'll enjoy the tasty food at this taquería chain. Try the house specialty: bite-size pieces of steak sautéed with peppers, onions, mushrooms, sausage, and bacon, served with a huge platter of tortillas for about $3. Live xylophone music accompanies the meal—yeah! *Morelos 240 Ote., at Galeana, tel. 8/342-85-37. Open daily 8 AM–10:30 PM.*

WORTH SEEING

Architecturally distinguished buildings—some colonial, some modern—make a walk around town interesting in itself, but there are also a number of museums worth visiting. The many parks and plazas are great for relaxing, but if you just want to check out the scene, head to the Zona Rosa and the Macroplaza.

CENTRO CULTURAL ALFA This five-story complex resembles buildings from the "forbidden land" of *Planet of the Apes*; it was commissioned by an industrial megacompany to promote science and technology through interactive exhibits, art, and scientific experiments. The result is an educational madhouse, popular with schoolkids but a blast for all ages. The impressive **Multiteatro** planetarium doubles as an Omnimax theater, presenting Spanish-dubbed films on everything from astronomy to history. The middle two floors are packed with hands-on contraptions that will surprise your senses, test your perceptions, and tweak your reasoning. Science-themed modern art exhibits are displayed on two other floors, and the top floor features a collection of pre-Columbian and Mesoamerican artifacts. Also on the grounds are gardens, an aviary, a theater, and a playground with hands-on, gravity-defying equipment. Don't miss Rufino Tamayo's *El Universo*, a huge, stained-glass mural housed just outside the main complex in the airplane hangar–like *Pabellón* (Pavilion). *Gómez Morin 1100, Col. del Valle, tel. 8/378–58–19. Catch a free navy-blue bus marked* DELFIN, *which leaves hourly from Parque Alameda (G. Washington, btw Pino Suárez and Carranza). Admission: $2. Wheelchair access.*

CERVECERIA CUAUHTEMOC Named after the famous Aztec ruler, the Cuauhtémoc Brewery is the heart of an industrial empire producing a number of brands of beer. Brewery tours are offered Monday–Saturday at 10:30 AM. One of the old cervecerías next to the Cuauhtémoc Brewery has been converted into a collection of hodgepodge museums, but the free brew in the tree-lined **beer garden** (open Tues.–Sun. 10–3:30) is the biggest draw and definitely makes the trip worthwhile. Two huge, copper brewing tanks descend from the ceiling of the **Museo de Monterrey** (tel. 8/328–60–60; open Tues.–Sat. 11–8), housed within the walls of the original brewery. The museum also exhibits a collection of etchings, lithographs, and oil paintings. The **Salón de la Fama** (Hall of Fame), just south of the present brewery, provides a dizzying array of memorabilia from Mexico's baseball legends. The adjacent **Museo Deportivo** (Sports Museum) contains exhibits on Mexican boxing, bullfighting, and American college football. *Universidad 2202, about 10 blocks north of bus station. Take* RUTA *1 bus to Cuauhtémoc, at Anaya; cross street and head south ½ block. Admission free. Open Tues.–Sun. 10–6.*

MACROPLAZA At the heart of Monterrey is one of the world's largest public squares. Extending over 40 acres, the plaza begins on Washington, runs past the **Palacio del Gobierno** (city hall), and ends at the Santa Catarina riverbank. The southernmost boundary is marked by a beautiful Rufino Tamayo sculpture entitled *Homenaje al sol* (Homage to the Sun). The sound of gushing fountains and the pleasant aromas from the blossoming trees in the square's gardens offer a needed respite from the deafening roar of Monterrey's traffic. Stop in at Infotour (*see* Visitor Information, *above*) for a detailed guide to this central plaza.

MUSEO DE ARTE CONTEMPORANEO (MARCO) A huge black sculpture of a bird by artist Juan Soriano welcomes you into the air-conditioned halls of this architecturally daring art center. The museum contains 11 exhibit halls featuring modern artists from around the world. A posh little café offers weekly poetry readings. *Zuazua, at Ocampo, next to cathedral, tel. 8/342–48–20. Admission: $1.50, 75¢ students; free Wed. Open Tues. and Thurs.–Sat. 11–7, Wed. and Sun. 11–9.*

MUSEO DE HISTORIA MEXICANA Monterrey's finest new addition to the museum scene sits just off the Macroplaza, at the end of a huge canal-encircled patio. The second-floor exhibits trace the history of Mexico—from the creation of the earth to present-day, industrial Monterrey—with colorful, eye-jolting displays. On the ground floor you'll find a pricey restaurant and gift shop, as well as a room dedicated to rotating exhibits of famous Mexican artists, including Frida Kahlo and Pedro Coronel. *Dr. Cross 445 Sur (Paseo Santa Lucía), tel. 8/345–98–98. Open Tues.–Sat. 11–7, Sun. 11–8. Admission: $1.50, 75¢ students; free Wed. Wheelchair access.*

EL OBISPADO Droves of couples start climbing the long winding road to this tiny baptistry in the late afternoon, giving themselves plenty of time to catch their breath before watching the sunset illuminate all four of the city's cardinal points. Constructed in 1788, the baptistry served as a fort during the Mexican-American War and the French Intervention. Today it houses a number of artifacts, including branding irons and serapes from as early as the late 1600s. *Far west end of Padre Mier, tel. 8/346–04–04. From Macroplaza, RUTA 15 pesero to Calle El Gollado; walk 15 min up hill. Admission: $1.50. Open Tues.–Sun. 10–5.*

PARQUE DE LOS NIÑOS HEROES This extensive stretch of green encompasses meandering paths, lovely gardens, and a small man-made lake where people rent rowboats. Several excellent museums and a guano-filled aviary also provide interesting stopping points within the park. Auto enthusiasts will be thoroughly impressed by the more than 20 cars on display at the **Museo del Automóvil.** At the **Museo de la Fauna,** a pantheon of stuffed wildlife inhabits the dimly lit rooms, including a 6-foot-tall polar bear and ivory-tusked elephant head. In the **Museo de la Pinacoteca,** an exhibit of beautiful bronze and wood sculptures, including Fidias Elizondo's famous *La Ola* (The Wave), is surrounded by a collection of paintings by artists from the state of Nuevo León. The 50¢ park admission includes everything but rowboat rental and a $1 donation for animal care. Make sure to get a map at the office to the north of the main entrance. *From Padre Mier, catch a RUTA 17 bus and get off across from park entrance. To return to town, take RUTA 18 bus to Juárez or Ocampo. Open Tues.–Sun. 10–6.*

In the Museo de Pinacoteca, stand to the left of the painting "El Nacionalista," by Carlos Saenz, and notice how the subject's body—feet, shoulders, and even eyes—seems to be oriented to your left. Then slowly move to your right, noting how the gentleman's fixed stare shifts magically as you move. This technique, mastered by Saenz, is the same that Leonardo da Vinci used for his smirking Mona Lisa.

AFTER DARK

The government recently revamped the **Barrio Antiguo,** located just southeast of the Macroplaza, and dozens of hip new bars and restaurants now line the cobblestone streets. It's dead during the day but hopping at night, especially on weekends when the streets are blocked off; tables and chairs take the place of cars here, attracting throngs of students and artists. Other bars are located west of the Zona Rosa: **Koko Loco** (Pino Suárez, at Padre Mier) is the most convenient place for techno addicts to get their nightly fix. The club is open Thursday–Saturday 9:30 PM–2 AM, and the cover is $3. Around the corner at **Pachanga** (Pino Suárez 849 Sur, tel. 8/340–45–23), you can do the cumbia Fridays 7 PM–2 AM for no cover. On Saturday, women get in for $1 (men $2); Sunday everyone pays $2. If you're willing to splurge for some serious people-watching and one of the best transvestite and cabaret shows around, head to **Antonio's Le Club** (Constitución 1471, at Carranza, no phone), where the $8.50 cover is well worth it. The show starts at 10:30, but if you get here early you can head to the bar next door for drinks and zebra-skin decor. To reach Antonio's, take a RUTA 126 or RUTA 130 bus to Carranza on Constitución, and walk one west block. To get back into town before midnight, take the CENTRO bus from Hidalgo, one block north of Carranza. After midnight, take a taxi ($2). Antonio's is open Monday–Saturday 7:30 PM–2 AM.

Near Monterrey

LA CASCADA COLA DE CABALLO

An hour northwest of Monterrey, in the Sierra Madre mountains just off Highway 85, is the **Parque Nacional Cumbres de Monterrey.** One of the highlights of a trip here is a view of **La Cascada Cola de Caballo** (Horse Tail Falls), a dramatic waterfall that tumbles down from the pine-forested heights. From the pool at the foot of the falls, you can follow one of two short hiking paths that lead upstream and cross small wooden bridges laid haphazardly over the gurgling water. The waterfall is about 1 kilometer from the park entrance, up a cobblestone road.

You can rent a docile horse from the local kids who hang out by the ticket booth for about $3, or hop on a horse-drawn carriage for $2.50; entrance to the falls (open daily 8–7) will set you back $1.50.

COMING AND GOING Horse Tail Falls lies 6 kilometers up a winding road from the small town of **El Cercado.** From Monterrey's Central de Autobuses, **Autobuses Amarillos** buses run here every 15 minutes between 5 AM and 11 PM (45 min, $2). From the stop in El Cercado, walk two blocks to the town plaza and take a blue or orange *pesero* (van) to the foot of the falls; the fare ($1 partway, $5 to the entrance) is higher on weekends. The last pesero heads back to the plaza at 7:15 PM sharp; otherwise it's a long, mosquito-ridden walk back to town. A cheaper but more time-consuming option is to take a yellow-and-white bus marked MON-TERREY–ALAMO–VILLA DE SANTIAGO (1½ hrs, $1.25), which leaves Monterrey every 15 minutes 6 AM–9 PM from Félix U. Gómez, between Madero and Constitución, and drops you off in front of the park's main gates.

CAMPING You can pitch your tent upstream from the falls, 1 kilometer up the road from the turquoise entrance gate. The best sites are located on the north bank of the stream, where the ground is flat and the area more private. There are toilets and sinks with nonpotable water near the entrance to the falls. Use of the grounds and facilities is free. Although you probably won't get hassled, it's recommended that you obtain a *permiso para acampar* (camping permit) from the **Presidencia Municipal** (tel. 8/285–00–05), located in El Cercado's plaza.

GRUTAS DE GARCÍA

The awe-inspiring subterranean caverns of García have, sadly, been transformed into an over-done tourist attraction, the sort of place where stalagmites carry names such as Christmas Tree and the Hand of Death. But don't run screaming, because the impressive natural beauty of the caves overshadows the thick crowds and glittering signs. For $5 you can ride a tram to the cave entrance; it leaves every 10 minutes 10–4 and fills up quickly. The more rugged alternative is to make the steep, 20-minute hike up the gorgeous mountain path from Villa de García. Bring water and maybe even a small picnic; if you don't feel like hauling food, there is a small restaurant here. A one-hour guided tour of the caves is included in the entrance fee.

COMING AND GOING The Grutas de García are just outside Villa de García. From Monter-rey, catch one of the frequent MONTERREY–VILLA DE GARCIA buses (1 hr, $1.25) from the corner of Colón and B. Reyes, opposite the Hotel Victoria (*see* Where to Sleep, *above*). To return to Mon-terrey, take the MONTERREY–VILLA DE GARCIA bus, which leaves every 15 minutes across from where you were dropped off.

Saltillo

Set 1,600 meters up in the mountains, the capital of Coahuila state is a great place to take a deep breath and relax after the pollution and bustle of Monterrey. Saltillo's industrial complexes, including Chrysler and GM plants, are relegated to the suburbs, leaving the down-town plazas and parks clean and tranquil. The town is somewhat sleepy on the weekends, but during the week the streets overflow with people from all walks of life.

Saltillo developed around the **Plaza de Armas,** bordered by the elegant **Palacio del Gobierno** (government palace) and the **Catedral de Santiago,** with an elaborately carved stone facade that's considered one of the finest in Mexico. For a great view of the city, walk from the cathe-dral south along Hidalgo to the **Plaza de México.** If you're in town mid-July through early August, head to the fairgrounds to watch the entire town celebrate the **Feria Anual** (Annual Fair), with games, dancing, regional foods, roller coasters, crafts, and bloody *palenques* (cock-fights). You'll always find colorful handicrafts and cheap, filling meals at the **Mercado Juárez,** Saltillo's vibrant marketplace.

BASICS

Change your cash and traveler's checks at **Serfín** (cnr of Allende and Lerdo de Tejada, tel. 84/14–90–97) weekdays 9:30–1. The bank also has a 24-hour ATM that accepts Cirrus, Plus, MasterCard, and Visa. **Operadora de Cambios** (Manuel Atuña 167, at Allende, tel. 8/14–12–96; open weekdays 9–1:30 and 3:30–6, Sat. 9–1) has better hours but worse rates. For medical emergencies, call the **Cruz Roja** (84/14–33–33 ext. 25); dial 06 for all other emergencies, or call the **police** round-the-clock at 84/12–40–00. You can phone home from the small cluster of Ladatel **phones** in Plaza Acuña, near the Mercado Juárez, or make international cash calls (no collect calls) from Café Victoria (*see* Food, *below*) for $1.50 per minute. Get your epistolary fix at the main **post office** (tel. 84/14–90–97; open weekdays 7–7, Sat. 9–1), which will hold mail at the following address for up to 10 days: Lista de Correos, Victoria 453, Saltillo, Coahuila, CP 25001, México.

Don't expect much from Saltillo's **tourist office** (Periférico Echeverría 1560, 5th floor, tel. 84/15–17–14; open Mon.–Thurs. 9–3 and 5–8, Fri. 9–3 and 5–6); they can give you a decent free map, but that's about it. The office is located in the irritatingly hard-to-reach **Torre de Saltillo**; to get here, take Combi 9 north from Aldama and Hidalgo, get off at Gigante Supermarket on Periférico Echeverría, and walk three blocks east.

COMING AND GOING

BY BUS Saltillo's **Central de Autobuses** is about 2 kilometers southwest of the centro. Most smaller second-class lines provide service to obscure destinations, but the major **Transportes Frontera** (tel. 84/17–00–76) has frequent service to Monterrey (2 hrs, $2), Ciudad Juárez (18 hrs, $23), and Mexico City (12 hrs, $26). Six first-class lines, among them the ubiquitous **Omnibús de México** (tel. 84/17–03–15) and **Transportes del Norte** (tel. 84/17–09–02), offer frequent service to Guadalajara (10 hrs, $25), Mazatlán (16 hrs, $30), Ciudad Juárez (15 hrs, $37), and Matamoros (5 hrs, $14). **Greyhound** tickets to destinations in the United States and Canada via Texas are sold by **Autobuses Americanos**. The station has a 24-hour long-distance and fax office and Ladatel phones that accept credit cards and coins. Luggage storage is available 6 AM–9 PM (20¢ per hr). To reach downtown, catch a bus marked CENTRO. To reach the station from downtown, catch the RUTA 9 bus on Aldama and Hidalgo.

BY TRAIN The **Estación de Ferrocarril** (tel. 84/14–95–84) is a large, impressive building a few blocks southwest of Parque Zaragoza on Emilio Carranza. To get here catch Bus 1B anywhere on Pérez Treviño, two blocks over from the plaza. To get back catch Bus 3 on Cristóbal Colón. Three trains a day connect Saltillo to eight other cities in the republic. The first-class **Regiomontano** heads south to San Luis Potosí (6 hrs $7.50 1st class, $20 sleeper car) and Mexico City (12 hrs $33 1st class, $42 sleeper car). The first-class **México–Monterrey–Nuevo Laredo** train heads south to Mexico City (16 hrs, $15.50) and north to Nuevo Laredo (12 hrs, $4), stopping in Monterrey (3 hrs, $1.25). The **Coahuilense** runs to Piedras Negras ($6 2nd class, $10 reserved seat).

WHERE TO SLEEP AND EAT

Saltillo was overlooked when it came to supplying the budget travelers of the world with a comfy place to spend the night. The cheap hotels that do exist are in the city center, near Plaza Acuña. The **Hotel Bristol** (Aldama 405 Pte., tel. 84/10–43–37) is by far the best option, with mosquito-free rooms and clean bathrooms. Singles are $8.50, doubles $9. Even cheaper is **Hotel Ávila** (Padre Flores 211, tel. 84/12–59–16), although you may have to contend with a steady stream of fleas or ants sharing the hotel facilities. Rooms (singles $7, doubles $8; $1 extra for TV) are spacious and the water pressure is strong enough to wash your hair and clothes.

Saltillo doesn't offer fabulous cuisine, but you can grab a taco or slurp down some homemade soup at the *fondas* (covered food stands) in the Mercado Juárez in Plaza Acuña. Locals pack into **Taquería El Pastor** (Aldama 340 Pte., tel. 84/12–21–12) to wolf down corn tortillas filled with carne asada and *carne al pastor* (marinated pork). The taquería is open Sunday–Thursday

8 AM–midnight, Friday and Saturday 8 AM–1 AM. The unofficial house specialty at **Café Victoria** (Padre Flores 221, tel. 84/14–98–00; open daily 7 AM–11 PM) is the *palomas con aguacate* (flour tortillas filled with shredded beef and avocado; $2.50). A good comida corrida is available daily 11:30–4.

WORTH SEEING

Saltillo's winding streets may be colonial and quaint, but they're also confusing. Fortunately, most sights are within walking distance of the **Plaza de Armas** (Hidalgo, at Juárez), where the graceful **Catedral** shines in the strong Saltillo sun. Opposite the cathedral is the **Palacio del Gobierno**, a squat, rose-colored building that houses government offices and beautiful murals illustrating the political history of Coahuila, painted by Salvador Almaraz y Tarazona.

CULTURAL CENTERS/GALLERIES Though many of Saltillo's artists have packed up and moved to Monterrey, a few galleries are still going strong. The free **Centro de Arte Contemporáneo** (behind cathedral, tel. 84/10–09–32; open weekdays 10–1 and 4–7, Sat. 10–1) houses everything from paintings to sculpture. The pleasantly cool **Instituto Coahuilense de Cultura** (Juárez, at Hidalgo, tel. 84/14–22–45; open Tues.–Sun. 9–7) exhibits sculpture, *artesanía* (crafts), painting, woodwork, and photography by artists from the state of Coahuila.

EL SERAPE DE SALTILLO A small, rusting yellow sign swinging rhythmically in the afternoon breeze is the only marker for this fabulous serape factory-cum-store. Everything from silver earrings and chocolate beaters to teacups and cured tree bark is for sale in the tiny store, but the real draw is watching nimble-fingered craftspeople make the serapes. The store is open Monday–Saturday 9–1 and 3–7, but the serape makers only work during the week. *Hidalgo 305 Sur, no phone.*

OUTDOOR ACTIVITIES

Ciudad Deportiva (Sports City) offers tennis and basketball courts, as well as fishing in the man-made lake. To get here, take the ZAPALINOME bus from Pérez Treviño and Xicoténcatl to Ciudad Deportiva. For a pleasant change of scene, take a leisurely stroll through the quaint and far more lush town of **Arteaga**, a half-hour ride from Saltillo on the ARTEAGA bus from Pérez Treviño and Xicoténcatl. If you're set on hitting the hills, continue 20 minutes farther on the same bus to **Bella Unión** and a dusty parking lot. From here you can climb up two separate plateaus and take in the relentless, mountainous landscape while the hot desert air blows in your hair. Dip your feet in the river before heading back to the parking lot to catch the bus to Saltillo; the last bus leaves at 9 PM.

AFTER DARK

Saltillo doesn't have a lot to offer anyone over 15 years of age, and the streets are pretty empty by 11 PM. University students desperate to let off a little steam head to **Sahara** (Blvd. Fundidores Km. 3.5, tel. 84/30–25–25), a hopping techno disco also frequented by tourists from nearby expensive hotels. Cover Thursdays–Saturdays is $4, but all other nights are free (except Sundays, when it's closed). To get here, take the ZARAGOZA bus from Padre Treviño and Xicoténcatl. An eclectic variety of music and $1 beers attract a more diverse crowd to **El Zaguán** (Ocampo 338, tel. 84/14–76–67; open daily noon–1 AM), where small wooden tables and candlelight augment the overdone colonial atmosphere. If you're into laying low you can stroll around the **Plaza Acuña** or head to the patio behind the **Palacio del Gobierno** to watch blossoming adolescents overcome the thrill of their first romantic encounters.

Tampico

Lush mango trees and endless white-sand beaches make Tampico one of the more enjoyable places to visit in the northeast. Originally serving as a refuge for Huastecan tribes escaping the mosquito-ridden basin of the nearby Río Panuco, Tampico is now a grimy but bustling port town of 600,000, with a large open market and a traffic-filled central plaza (Plaza de la Libertad). Although the humid, salty air has taken a toll on the city's older buildings, some well-preserved structures still line the plaza and the sand-dusted streets. During the month-long **Feria de Abril** (April Fair), celebrating the anniversary of the Mexican Republic, the plaza is home to live concerts, theater, and historical presentations. Die-hard indigenous culture buffs should check out the **Museo de la Cultura Huasteca** (1 de Mayo, at Sor Juana Inés de la Cruz, inside Instituto Tecnológico de Cd. Madero, tel. 12/10–22–17; open Mon.–Sat. 10–5), which offers a varied display of Huastecan culture and artifacts. The nearby **Pirámide de las Flores,** a pyramid dating from the 12th century, receives a lot of hype for being the closest Huastecan ruin to Tampico, but it's rather unspectacular. If you're interested, take a bus marked BELLA-VISTA from the corner of 20 de Noviembre and Madero, two blocks southwest of the plaza, and tell the bus driver to let you off at the Pirámide. However, the main reason to come to Tampico is the glistening shoreline—surprisingly clean and pleasant given the run-down character of Tampico itself. Bordered by the Gulf of Mexico to the east, the Río Panuco to the south, and the Río Tamesi lagoons to the west, Tampico's beaches offer the chance to laze the day away in the tropical heat.

BASICS

AMERICAN EXPRESS The AmEx office is in **Viajes Pozos,** a travel agency about 10 minutes from downtown. The staff begrudgingly cashes personal checks, holds client mail, and sells and replaces traveler's checks. *Zapote 206, Colonia Águila, Tampico, Tamaulipas, CP 89220, México, tel. 12/13–72–00 or 12/17–14–76. Open weekdays 9–2 and 4–6, Sat. 10–1. From Plaza de Armas, take CHEDRAUE ECHAVERRIA bus from in front of Tres Hermanos shoe store to Zapote, and walk ½ block towards Hidalgo.*

CASAS DE CAMBIO Central Divisa (Benito Juárez 215 Sur, tel. 13/12–90–00) changes both cash and traveler's checks at decent rates weekdays 9–6, Saturdays 9–1. **Bancrecer** (Díaz Mirón 407, at López de Lara) has an ATM that accepts Visa and Cirrus cards.

EMERGENCIES Dial 12/12–10–32 for the **police**; 12/12–12–22 for the **fire department**; or 12/12–13–33 for the **Cruz Roja** or an **ambulance**.

MEDICAL AID Benavides is a large, well-equipped pharmacy right off the Plaza de Armas. *Olmos, at Carranza, tel. 12/19–25–25. Open Mon.–Sat. 8 AM–11 PM, Sun. 8 AM–10 PM.*

PHONES AND MAIL The **post office** (3 blocks SE of Plaza de Armas, tel. 12/12–19–27) will hold mail sent to you at the following address for up to 10 days: Lista de Correos, Madero 309, Tampico, Tamaulipas, CP 89000, México. Clusters of Ladatel **phones** can be found on the Plaza de Armas. Purchase Ladatel cards at **Refresquería La Victoria** on the plaza.

VISITOR INFORMATION The **tourist office** has a cheerful staff that will go out of their way to help you, but they seem to think "tourism" is equivalent to pricey group tours. Don't succumb if you don't want to—just take the maps and be on your merry way. *20 de Noviembre, tel. 12/12–26–68 or 12/12–00–07. Open weekdays 8–7, Sat. 9–2. From Plaza de Armas, walk north on Olmos, turn left on Obregón, left on 20 de Noviembre.*

COMING AND GOING

Downtown Tampico is easily managed on foot, with the beach just a painless colectivo or bus ride away. Downtown is centered on the **Plaza de Armas,** with the cathedral on the northside. **Carranza** runs along the plaza's northern border, with **Díaz Mirón** hugging its southern end. Numerous colectivos (25¢) and buses (25¢) marked PLAYA can be caught on the corner of Díaz Mirón and López de Lara heading towards the beach. Buses run 6 AM–midnight; colectivo service is 24 hours.

BY BUS Tampico's **Central de Autobuses** has both first- and second-class terminals divided by a small verdant courtyard, making comparing ticket prices a breeze. **ADO** (tel. 12/13–43–39) and **Transportes Futura/Transportes del Norte** (tel. 12/13–46–55) are major first-class carriers with service to Matamoros (6 hrs, $16), Mexico City (9 hrs, $18.50), and Poza Rica (4 hrs, $11). Second-class lines include **Transportes Frontera** (tel. 12/13–42–35), **Blancos** (tel. 12/13–42–35), and **Oriente Golfo** (tel. 12/13–45–47). Destinations include Monterrey (8 hrs, $18), Reynosa (8 hrs, $16), and Mexico City (10 hrs, $18.50). Each terminal is equipped with Ladatel phones and casetas de larga distancia. Lockers in the first-class terminal swallow your gear for $4 a day. To get downtown, catch a *micro* (minibus) marked CENTRAL CAMIONERA PERIMETRAL in front of the station; to reach the terminal, take the same micro from the corner of Madero and Colón.

BY CAR Highway 80 runs through Tampico from Veracruz state. The highway continues north, where it connects to Highway 180, which leads to Matamoros and the Texas border. Highway 70 runs west from Tampico to San Luis Potosí. All three highways are toll-free and have four lanes. Car rental agencies in Tampico include **Budget** (tel. 12/28–05–56 or 12/27–18–80).

BY TRAIN Once a bustling doorway to the northeast, the **Estación de Ferrocarriles de Tampico** has been all but forgotten. Three lonely trains a day still lumber to San Luis Potosí (10 hrs, $5), Ciudad Victoria (4 hrs, $3), and Monterrey (10 hrs, $4.50). Tickets are sold 6–8 AM only. *Aduana and Héroes de Nacozari, tel. 12/12–19–83.*

BY PLANE The **Aeropuerto Francisco Javier Mina** (Universidad 700, tel. 12/28–21–95) is a small airport in the northwest corner of town. **Mexicana** (tel. 12/13–97–59) and **Aerolitoral** (tel. 12/28–08–57) serve both domestic and international destinations. To get downtown, catch an AVIACION POR BULEVAR micro to Carranza and walk four blocks to the Plaza de Armas.

WHERE TO SLEEP

Rooms here tend to be mediocre and extremely overpriced. There are a few hotels with more reasonable rates a few blocks from the Plaza de Armas, but the neighborhood tends to be unsafe and poorly lit late at night. The aging but tidy **Hotel Imperial** (López de Lara 101, at Carranza, tel. 12/14–13–10) is the cheapest budget hotel near the plaza. Dingy carpeting in every room provides a dusty-attic ambience, and the air conditioners—standard in every room—shudder and wheeze so hard you almost feel sorry for them. Singles cost $13, doubles $14, and all have phones and TVs. Downtown, you'll find the **Hotel Posada Don Francisco** (Díaz Mirón 710, tel. 12/19–25–34), one of your cleaner budget options. The cramped, worn-in rooms don't live up to the promise of the hotel's charming lobby, but at $10 for a single or a double, it's your best bargain. All the rooms have phones, TVs, and plenty of hot water. If you want to splurge, the **Hotel Mundo** (Díaz Mirón 413, tel. 12/12–03–60) offers spacious, clean, and air-conditioned rooms with modern bathrooms, cable TVs, and telephones. Singles cost $20, doubles $24.

Hotels along the beach tend to be pricey and a tad run-down. The bright red-and-white **Hotel Orinoco** (NW of beach entrance, off Casero, no phone) fills up fast, so get here early in the day to stake your claim. Rooms are carpeted and cooled by a noisy but relatively effective floor fan. Singles and doubles cost $15, and six people can crash here for less than $5 each. If the great outdoors calls you, pitch a tent for free on **Playa Miramar,** where bathrooms and showers cost less than a taco in the nearby hotels and eateries.

FOOD

Like almost everything else in Tampico, food is overpriced. It's possible to eat cheaply, but only if you're not paranoid that eating at street stands will send you running for the bathroom. The food at the **mercado** on Juárez is cheap, cooked to order, and delicious. Try the *milanesa* (thinly sliced, breaded beef) with tortillas, beans, rice, salad, and a soft drink for $3. Most people come downtown to the **Restaurant y Cafetería Emir** (Olmos 207, tel. 12/12–51–39; open daily 6 AM–midnight) for the delicious $3 *filete de sol,* two deceivingly fishlike slabs of shrimp held together by a fine layer of egg and salted bread crumbs. Factor in the beans, home fries, salad, and fresh bread that are included, and it's clear why almost no one finishes the dish. Just around the corner, the **Restaurante/Refresquería Élite** (Díaz Mirón 211 Ote., tel. 12/12–03–64) is also a good place for local fish dishes, as well as the $1.25 piping hot *sopa xochitl*, a chicken soup with an exotic combination of tomato, avocado, onion, and cilantro.

OUTDOOR ACTIVITIES

Ten kilometers of white sand and blue-green waters make **Playa Miramar** a popular stretch of the Gulf of Mexico. The beach is divided into four sections; going from north to south you'll hit **Playa Parío, Playa Tampico, Playa Bañario**, and, finally, **Playa Escollera.** Beautiful views of the extensive shoreline can be had from the high-cliffed entrance to Playa Escollera, at the southeast end of the city. Bring a picnic and hang out at the pleasantly cool, grassy spots just west of the cliff's edge. The best place for swimming and lounging is Playa Tampico. You'll have to bring your own towels, but showers are only 25¢ a pop at any of the hotels along the beach, and you can rent beach chairs for $3 at the small straw huts near the beach entrance. There are currently no businesses on the beachfront for the water-sport set, but the tourist office (*see* Basics, *above*) can arrange parasailing and boogie board rentals for you. When the scorching sun settles below the waves, shoot some hoops at the basketball court behind Hotel Orinoco (*see* Where To Sleep, *above*). To reach any of the beaches, catch a PLAYA micro or colectivo (both 25¢) from in front of Hotel Mundo on Díaz Mirón. Micros run about every five minutes during the day and every 20 minutes after 7:30 PM; the last bus from the beach leaves around 11 PM. Colectivos run later, but are extremely sporadic and should not be relied upon.

If you're tired of sand in unmentionable places, the two Olympic-size pools at Tampico's sports center, **Unidad Deportiva Tampico** (López Mateos) provide an excellent alternative to the beach. The sports center is open Monday–Saturday 9–6, and it costs $3 to get in. To get here, take the MADERO micro from the plaza and tell the driver to drop you off at the *alberca* (pool).

AFTER DARK

Avenida Universidad, the long winding street that borders the university (La Universidad Autónoma de Tamaulipas), is the best place to start the evening. Most clubs luring the student population don't have a cover before 11 PM, and beers run about $2.50. To shake your booty to techno, head to **Eclipse** (Universidad 2004, tel. 12/13–14–95). The cover is $3 on Fridays, $4 on Saturdays, and it's open daily 9 PM–3 AM. The cheesy ranch-style facade of **Restaurante/Bar Santa Fe 1900** (cnr of Universidad and Francita) may be daunting, but it's surprisingly cozy inside, and the free live music (7 PM–closing) runs the gamut from mariachi to country-western. To reach the university-zone clubs, walk to the corner of Colón and Tamaulipas (3 blocks north of Plaza de Armas) and catch a bus marked UNIVERSIDAD. This will pass through Universidad and Francita, where the clubs are located. If you want to stay in the city center, try **El Globito** (north side of Plaza de Armas, no phone), a juice bar/soda fountain with a jukebox that attracts a lively crowd. The delicious smoothies and milk shakes ($1.50) are pretty expensive, but they're enormous. El Globito is open 24 hours a day and stays happening late into the night.

EL BAJÍO

7

By Allison Eymil, with Rachael Courtier

Encompassing the states of Querétaro, Guanajuato, Michoacán, and San Luis Potosí, the Bajío is a spectacular mix of fertile valleys, dry hills sprinkled with strange cacti, town centers with tranquil plazas, and busy industrial zones. The name Bajío (lowlands) is actually a misnomer—these fertile, mountain-ringed tablelands stand a good 1,675–2,135 meters above sea level. But it's more than altitude that distinguishes the Bajío from Mexico's crowded beach towns: In the Bajío's vibrant cities you'll find a rich colonial history and baroque architecture lacking in the coast's disco-dotted resorts.

Rich in both agricultural and mineral resources, the Bajío has long been exploited for its abundant natural wealth. Archaeologists believe that even before the Spanish arrived, the region had nearly 750 active mines, which were probably worked by slave labor. The Spanish were lured here by silver lust, eventually finding incredibly lucrative veins throughout the region. During the 17th and 18th centuries, Guanajuato alone was responsible for 30%–40% of the world's silver production. In addition to mineral wealth, the Spanish also "discovered" the richness of the volcanic soil. Grand *encomiendas* (plantations) were established, producing a variety of Old World and New World crops, including corn, wheat, squash, grapes, and pears. Franciscan friars also colonized the region; by 1740, Father Junipero Serra, who later established the mission system along the California coast, had overseen the construction of five baroque churches in the remote highlands of Querétaro.

By the early 19th century, the newly wealthy conquerors had founded an exploitative economic system in the Bajío; untold numbers of indigenous laborers died building opulent churches and enormous mansions for those of Spanish descent. It is therefore not surprising that the battle for Mexican independence began in Querétaro and the small town of Dolores Hidalgo (in Guanajuato state), where leaders Ignacio Allende, Miguel Hidalgo, and Doña Josefa Ortiz began their revolutionary exploits. Towns throughout the Bajío are fiercely proud of these leaders' accomplishments, which earned the region the nickname "The Cradle of Independence."

Today, international agricultural and automotive companies have invaded the area, but thankfully the region is not an industrial wasteland—many colonial cities have been preserved as national landmarks. As a result, the Bajío sustains a vibrant sense of history, made visible in its well-maintained baroque churches, narrow cobblestone streets, and excellent museums. Staunch traditionalism and progressive ideals coexist here in a strange harmony, resulting in a region rich in folklore and legends, as well as innovative cultural and artistic activity. Both Querétaro and Guanajuato boast thriving cultural centers, with active populations of artists, musicians, and students. The cities of Michoacán state have also preserved *artesanía* (handicraft) craftsmanship, stunning examples of which flourish in Pátzcuaro. San Miguel de

TO AGUASCALIENTES, ZACATECAS

Ojuelos de Jalisco

N

TO SAN LUIS POTOSÍ

Santa María del Río

Villa de Reyes

JALISCO

Ocampo

80

Lagos de Moreno

51

57

San Luis de la Paz

Dolores Hidalgo

110

Pozos

León

SIERRA DE GUANAJUATO

San Miguel de Allende

45

Guanajuato

111

Silao

GUANAJUATO

51

57

Manuel Doblado

Irapuato

45
D

Querétaro

57
D

Salamanca

Celaya

57
D

TO MEXICO CITY

La Piedad de Cabadas

Lago Yuriria

Lerma

51

Acámbaro

Moroleón

43

Lago de Cuitzeo

TO ZAMORA, GUADALAJARA

15

Ciudad Hidalgo

Quiroga

Morelia

Angahuán

Lake Pátzcuaro

15

51

Uruapan

14

Pátzcuaro

Zitacuaro

Parque Nacional Eduardo Ruíz

120

MICHOACÁN

Tuzantla

Nueva Italia

La Huacana

Nocupétaro

Bejucos

134

Presa del Infiernillo

Balsas

Huetamo

Allende, well-known for its expatriate American population, is so laid-back that you may want to stay a few years. The more vigorous visitor can indulge in the natural parks, waterfalls, caves, and *balnearios* (swimming areas) of San Luis Potosí and Uruapan.

San Luis Potosí

At first glance, the capital of San Luis Potosí state might seem as sterile as a big U.S. Midwestern town. Broom-wielding shopkeepers keep the sidewalks immaculate, and the town's skyscrapers and the occasional Burger King may remind you more of Ohio than Mexico. But look beyond the recent development and you'll see numerous central plazas dotted with fine examples of baroque and neoclassical architecture—elegant reminders of the city's heyday as a colonial capital whose domain once encompassed most of northern Mexico, Texas, *and* Louisiana. Today the plazas, especially **Plaza de Armas,** serve as meeting places where well-dressed families stroll after mass, entertained by roving clowns and musicians. At the same time, protesters from opposition groups like El Barzón and the Zapatistas draw their own attention, while guards at the Palacio Municipal idly chat with one another.

Silver was discovered in the nearby hills of San Pedro in the 16th century, and "Minas del Potosí" was temporarily adopted as the city's name in the hope that the mines here would yield wealth equal to that found in Potosí, Bolivia. But the silver was soon depleted, and other minerals and a burgeoning dairy industry are now the basis of the city's economy. The mines in the San Pedro hills still function, but they are basically just tourist attractions. San Luis Potosí also generates its share of high culture, with abundant theatrical performances, concerts, and conferences—the majority of which are free.

Though there's plenty to see and do in San Luis, don't cheat yourself out of the beautiful, untouristed landscape just beyond the city. **Santa María del Río,** a town specializing in the production of *rebozos* (silk shawls), is only a short day trip away, and campers or hikers can head to the caves and waterfalls of **Río Verde** and **Ciudad Valles.** The **Querétaro Missions** and the castle ruins of **Xilitla** are enthralling for anyone with the slightest interest in architecture. The ghost town of **Real de Catorce** also merits a visit—take the train for the full 19th-century effect.

BASICS

AMERICAN EXPRESS The AmEx office in the **Agencia de Grandes Viajes** will deliver MoneyGrams, exchange traveler's checks, and replace lost checks for cardmembers and noncardmembers alike. The staff will also hold mail for you for up to 15 days at the following address: Carranza 1077, San Luis Potosí, San Luis Potosí, CP 78250, México. *10 blocks west of Plaza de Armas, tel. 48/17–60–04, fax 48/11–11–66. Open weekdays 9–2 and 4–6, Sat. 10–1.*

BOOKSTORES Librería Cristal (Carranza 765, tel. 48/12–80–15) supplies a large and varied selection of books in Spanish. **Librería Española** (Othón 170, tel. 48/12–57–81) and **Librería Universitaria** (Álvaro Obregón 450, tel. 48/12–67–49) are both smaller than Cristal, but they sometimes stock books in English. All are open Monday–Saturday 9–2 and 4–7.

CASAS DE CAMBIO Banamex (Allende, at Obregón 355, tel. 48/12–16–56) changes currency and cashes traveler's checks weekdays 9–noon and also has a 24-hour ATM. Next to Café Pacifico, **Casa de Cambio** (Constitución 220, tel. 48/12–42–93) has good rates and long hours: Monday–Saturday 8:30 AM–9 PM, Sunday 9–5.

CONSULATES United States. *Carranza 1430, tel. 48/12–64–44 or 48/17–25–57. Inside Instituto Mexicano-Norteamericano. Open weekdays 9 AM–noon.*

EMERGENCIES For the **police** call 48/12–10–36; for an **ambulance** dial 48/15–33–32.

LAUNDRY Lavanderías Automáticas Superwash will clean 3 kilos of laundry for $1.75, or you can do the washing and drying yourself for 75¢ per load. If you drop your clothes off in the early morning, they should be clean by the evening. *Carranza 1093, tel. 48/13–93–22. 10 blocks west of Plaza de Armas. Open Mon.–Sat. 8–8, Sun. 9–2.*

MAIL The **post office** offers all the usual services and will hold mail sent to you at the following address for up to 10 days: Lista de Correos, Morelos 235, San Luis Potosí, San Luis Potosí, CP 78000, México. *Morelos 235, tel. 48/12–27–40. 2 blocks north and 1 block east of Plaza de Armas. Open weekdays 8–6, Sat. 9–1.*

MEDICAL AID The **Beneficiencia Española** (Carranza 1090, tel. 48/11–56–96) and the **Cruz Roja** (Juárez 540, tel. 48/15–33–32) provide 24-hour medical service. **Farmacia La Perla** (Escobedo, at Los Bravo, tel. 48/12–59–22) is open 24 hours.

PHONES Computel (Carranza 360, tel. 48/12–01–13; open Mon.–Sat. 7 AM–9 PM), three blocks west of Plaza de Armas, offers high-tech long-distance service and charges $1.50 for a 10-minute international collect call; you can also make cash calls here. Several **Ladatel** phones are clustered along Obregón and Escobedo, near the Banamex.

SCHOOLS The **Centro de Idiomas** (Zaragoza 410, tel. 48/12–49–55), associated with the Universidad Autónoma de San Luis Potosí, offers semester-long Spanish classes for about $70. For registration information contact: Lic. Angélica Jager, Canvillo, Centro de Idiomas, Universidad Autónoma de San Luis Potosí, Zaragoza 410, San Luis Potosí, San Luis Potosí, CP 78000, México.

VISITOR INFORMATION The staff at the **Centro de Turismo** will earnestly try to answer questions and weigh you down with maps and brochures. They can also provide guided tours of the city's historical center for $2.75. *Álvaro Obregón 520, tel. 48/12–99–06. ½ block west of Plaza de los Fundadores. Open weekdays 8–8, Sat. until 1.*

COMING AND GOING

BY BUS The **Central Camionera** lies a few kilometers east of the central plaza. To get downtown from the terminal, turn left as you exit, walk two blocks to Avenida de las Torres, and catch the ALAMEDA bus across from Hotel Central. **Flecha Amarilla** (tel. 48/18–29–23) provides frequent service to Mexico City (6 hrs, $12) and Guanajuato (4 hrs, $7). **Estrella Blanca** (tel. 48/18–29–63) serves Aguascalientes (3 hrs, $6) and Zacatecas (3 hrs, $5). **Omnibús de Oriente** (tel. 48/18–29–41) travels to Guadalajara (6 hrs, $12) and Ciudad Victoria (5 hrs, $11) every hour round-the-clock, as well as to intra-state destinations such as Río Verde (2 hrs, $4.50). **Omnibús de México** (tel. 48/18–29–85) sends three buses a day to Tampico (7 hrs, $12.50). Luggage storage is available for about 25¢ an hour. There is also a caseta de larga distancia and a 24-hour pharmacy in the station.

BY CAR To reach Zacatecas, take Highway Federal 49 northwest for 186 kilometers. For Mexico City (453 km), take Federal 57 south through Querétaro (200 km) and continue to the capital. To reach Tampico (400 km), take Federal 70 east through Ciudad Valles.

BY TRAIN The train station (Othón, at 20 de Noviembre, tel. 48/12–21–23) is north of the Alameda. From here, trains to Mexico City depart daily at 3:45 AM (6 hrs, $10 1st class) and 10:30 AM (9 hrs, $5 2nd class). Second-class trains leave for Aguascalientes (6 hrs, $2) at noon and for Real de Catorce (3 hrs, $2.50) and Nuevo Laredo (12 hrs, $12) at 5:30 PM. The ticket office is open daily 45 minutes prior to departure, but get in line at least 1½ hours before departure to buy a ticket. From the station, buses run east to the Central Camionera and the youth hostel; ask the driver to drop you off at your destination.

GETTING AROUND

San Luis Potosí is laden with plazas in the central area and most attractions are within walking distance of **Plaza de Armas,** also known as **Jardín Hidalgo.** On the plaza, the **cathedral**'s two bright-blue neon crosses form a shining nighttime reference point. Four main streets stem from Plaza de Armas: Venustiano Carranza runs west–east, changing into Los Bravo as it flanks the north side of the Plaza; Othón runs east–west and becomes Madero as it flanks the south side of the Plaza; Hidalgo/Zaragoza borders the east side of the plaza as it travels south; 5 de Mayo/Allende borders the west side as it runs north. East of the Plaza rests the **Alameda** (near the cheap restaurants, hotels, and the train station). City buses, which are rarely necessary, run 6 AM–11 PM and cost about 25¢.

WHERE TO SLEEP

The cheapest place to crash is the youth hostel, near the bus station. But don't stay here unless you're looking for a quick place to rest before catching the next bus out—the turf is sleazy and far removed from the action. The areas around Plaza de Armas and the Alameda offer reasonably priced rooms and more convenience. Travelers on the verge of bankruptcy can squeeze into one of the tiny, cramped, not-so-clean rooms at **Hotel Ma Elena** (Jiménez 243, ½ block west of the train station, tel. 48/12–47–52), where bathless singles and doubles cost $3.50 and $4.50 respectively.

Hotel Alameda. This is the cheapest place to stay without having to sacrifice too many comforts—rooms are small and dark but fairly clean, and the management is friendly enough. If you plan to use your bed for sleeping, the nonstop cumbia tunes from the bar next door may make it difficult. Singles cost $4, doubles $5. *La Perla 3, tel. 48/18–65–58. Just off Othón, behind Pemex. 13 rooms, all with bath. Luggage storage. Wheelchair access.*

Hotel Jardín Potosí. Sunny hallways welcome you to spacious rooms (singles $8, doubles $10) with well-scrubbed bathrooms. Not all the rooms are as sunny as the courtyard, so ask to see a couple before you decide. The restaurant on the first floor is cheap and clean. *Los Bravo 530, tel. 48/12–31–52. From the Alameda, 1 block north on 20 de Noviembre and left on Los Bravo. 57 rooms, all with bath. Wheelchair access.*

Hotel Plaza. Although this hotel is well past its prime, its central location and the balconies overlooking the plaza make it worthwhile. Large, carpeted rooms hint at the hotel's former glory, and the staff is extremely friendly and accommodating. For those who don't want to miss their favorite telenovela, there are two TV viewing areas with lots of vinyl seating. Singles cost $8, doubles $9, and rooms with balconies and space for up to five people cost $11. *Jardín Hidalgo 22, on Plaza de Armas, tel. 48/12–46–31. 27 rooms, 25 with bath. Luggage storage.*

Hotel Progreso. A wood-paneled foyer brimming with plants is the perfect prelude to clean, spacious rooms with wood floors, raised ceilings, and large spotless bathrooms. Singles go for $9, doubles $10, and rooms with TV's run $11.50. *Aldama 415, ½ block north of Plaza de San Fransisco, tel. 48/12–03–66. 50 rooms, all with bath. Luggage storage.*

HOSTELS **Villa Juvenil San Luis Potosí/CREA.** This state-run hostel packs 'em in eight to a single-sex room, but at $2 a pop, who can complain? There are baseball and soccer fields and over a dozen basketball courts at your disposal here, but the pool is off limits. Lack of publicity means that the place is never full. Unfortunately, there aren't any lockers. *Diagonal Sur, tel. 48/18–16–17. 1 block from bus station, opposite traffic circle. 72 beds.*

FOOD

San Luis Potosí boasts a number of regional specialties, including *enchiladas potosinas* (small, fan-shaped enchiladas with cheese and red sauce) and *zahacuil* (Huastecan pork tamales). The food may be creative, but the ambience at most restaurants is not—the popular ones resemble diners, complete with vinyl booths and fake plants. Food stands on the plazas are few, but several hole-in-the-wall spots along Carranza and Othón offer cheap, standard Mexican fare. Start the day at **Panificadora La Noria** (Carranza 333, tel. 48/12–56–92), which sells pastries and fresh breads beginning at 6:30 AM.

El Bocolito. This place benefits a cooperative for indigenous students, and its humble decor gives it a down-home feel. Unique specialties include *sarapes* (sautéed onions, peppers, ham, sausage, and cheese; $3) and *bocolitos* (thick tortilla-style bread stuffed with cheese, cilantro, and refried beans; $2). *Guerrero 2, at Aldama, tel. 48/12–76–94. Open Mon.–Sat. 8:30 AM–10:30 PM, Sun. noon–10:30.*

Café Pacífico. Within a two-block radius, you'll find three of these cheap and convenient San Luis "chain" diners. The one nearest the budget lodging area is open 24 hours. Enchiladas, *chilaquiles* (tortilla strips doused with salsa and sour cream), or *enchiladas potosinas* are available for less than $4. Breakfasts cost $2–$3. *Constitución 200, at Los Bravo, tel. 48/12–54–14. 4 blocks east of Plaza de Armas.*

La Corriente. This restaurant pleases with stone- and tile-decorated walls and lots of greenery. Try Mexican specialties like *chamorro pibil* (pork in sweet mole sauce wrapped in banana leaf) for $4, or a sampler of eight different dishes for $3.75. Breakfast is served 8 AM–11:30 AM, *comida corrida* (pre-prepared lunch specials) and a buffet are served 1–5, and *antojitos* (appetizers) and cocktails are served after 7 PM. *Carranza 700, tel. 48/12–93–04. 6½ blocks west of Plaza de Armas. Open Mon.–Sat. 8 AM–midnight, Sun. 8–6.*

Tropicana. Come to this semi-vegetarian restaurant with counter seating for huge fresh fruit drinks (50¢–$1) with goofy names like "Tú y Yo" (You and I) and "Sensual," made with everything from strawberries and papaya to alfalfa and egg. Yogurt with honey and granola is just 75¢. The comida corrida runs $1.50. *Othón 355-B, tel. 48/12–81–69. On NE cnr of Plaza del Carmen. Open Mon.–Sat. 8:30 AM–10 PM, Sun. 3:30–9:30.*

WORTH SEEING

All of the sights below are within easy walking distance of the Plaza de Armas. Sunday is the best sightseeing day—museums and churches are open, and the numerous plazas often have free daytime theater or early evening concerts. Both the **Casa de la Cultura** (Carranza 1815, tel. 48/13–22–47; open weekdays 10–2 and 4–6, Sat. 10–2 and 6–9, Sun. 10–2) and the **Centro de Difusión Cultural** (Universidad, at Negrete, tel. 48/16–05–25; open Tues.–Sat. 10–2 and 4–7, Sun. 10–2) double as museums and cultural centers, showcasing local art and free films. Pick up the monthly *Guiarte* from the tourist office for a schedule of these and other events around town. Upcoming concerts, plays, and literary events are also announced on the billboard outside the **Casa de Artesanías** (Plaza de San Francisco, tel. 48/12–75–21), a government-run store with a good selection of high-priced crafts from all over Mexico.

CHURCHES San Luis Potosí is divided into seven barrios, and the center of each neighborhood's social activities is its church. Among the most notable is the **Catedral** (Othón 105) in Plaza de Armas. Built in 1670, the cathedral's baroque facade features Italian marble statues of the 12 Apostles. Although some baroque paintings still remain, the interior has been remodeled with neoclassical altars. The hippest additions, however, are the two 1950s neon blue crosses. Another major church is the **Templo de San Francisco** (Universidad 180), in the Plaza de San Francisco, which flaunts a pink limestone baroque facade. It was built in 1686 to honor St. Francis of Assisi, and several paintings and stone carvings in the church depict scenes from his life. The strange artwork in the church—including a chandelier shaped like a boat and a toy truck in the hands of a statue of Sebastián de Aparicio—symbolizes St. Francis's evangelical travels. Construction began in 1749 on the **Templo del Carmen** (Villerías 105), which sits in the Plaza del Carmen. This temple flaunts a *Churrigueresque* (ultra-baroque) facade and neoclassical structures in back. The interior contains an astonishing amount of gold leaf, most notably on the gold-covered altar of the Chapel of the Virgin. Mass times are posted in church entryways, but you can drop in anytime 8 AM–9 PM.

MUSEO NACIONAL DE LA MASCARA This museum holds a collection of more than 1,000 ceremonial and decorative masks from all over Mexico. The written explanations in Spanish describe in detail the history and significance of the Mesoamerican masks and the festivals in which they are used. Not to be missed are the eerie exhibits of devil masks or the impressive *gigantes* (giants) of San Luis—eight huge puppets (about 3 meters tall) used in the festival of Corpus Christi. These represent royal couples from the four parts of the world known to Columbus—Asia, Africa, the Americas, and Europe. *Villerías 2, tel. 48/12–30–25. From Plaza de Armas, walk 2 blocks east on Othón, then right 2 blocks on Escobedo. Admission: 15¢. Open Tues.–Fri. 10–2 and 4–6, weekends 10–2.*

MUSEO REGIONAL POTOSINO This museum, housed in a former Franciscan monastery, exhibits one of the largest collections of artifacts from San Luis's Huasteca region, including a reproduction of a famous statue said to represent the young Quetzalcoatl. The lower floor also features a small mineral exhibit and an interesting series of early 20th-century photographs of the streets of San Luis, alongside current photographs of the same areas. Upstairs is the restored chamber of the Virgin de Aranzanzú, as well as a few 19th-century religious paintings. *Galeana 450, behind Templo de San Francisco. Admission free. Open Tues.–Fri. 10–1 and 3– 6, Sat. 10–noon, Sun. 10–2.*

PALACIO DE GOBIERNO The neoclassic, *cantera rosa* (pinkish stone) facade of this block-long edifice stands out as soon as you reach the Plaza de Armas. Construction was completed in 1825; in 1950 the building was restored to house the state government offices. Santa Ana and Benito Juárez are a few of the illustrious Mexican leaders who reigned from here. Upstairs, on your left, is the **Sala Juárez,** where you can't help but notice the wax figures of a kneeling "Princess Salm Salm" (Empress Carlota) and a mighty Juárez. As Juárez looks down at her, the princess begs for the life of her husband, Emperor Maximilian (Mexico's puppet ruler, installed by Napolean III in 1864), who had been sentenced to death. The other rooms are filled with small photos of other Mexican presidents and furniture supposedly used by Juárez himself. *East side of Plaza de Armas. Open weekdays 9–5.*

CHEAP THRILLS

The **Parque Tangamanga,** a few kilometers southwest of Plaza de Armas, consists of 411 hectares of lakes, trees, sports fields, and gardens—the best place to escape the smog and traffic of San Luis Potosí. Leg-powered buggies are available at $1.50 an hour for your exploring convenience. The free **Museo de Arte Popular** (tel. 48/12–15–85), inside the park, displays regional artesanía and a selection of pre-Columbian artifacts. There's also a **planetarium** and a huge open-air **Teatro de la Cuidad** (City Theater). Both the museum and planetarium are free and open Tuesday–Saturday 10–1:45 and 4–5:45, Sunday 10–2:45. The park itself is open daily 6–6. To get here, catch the PERIMETRAL or RUTA 32 bus from Constitución near the Alameda; get off at Avenida Nacho, near the park's main entrance. To get back to town, walk four long blocks to Diagonal Sur and catch the bus heading back to the Alameda.

FESTIVALS San Luis Potosí is one of the oldest cities in central Mexico and therefore maintains a rich tradition of religious festivals and fairs. In mid-January, pilgrims come to the shrine of **San Sebastián,** in the *barrio* (neighborhood) of the same name, bearing artwork and offerings for the church. The city really fills up during **Semana Santa** and on Good Friday, when the Passion of Christ is reenacted. It's followed by the Procession of Silence, in which men in hooded robes carry a model of Christ's body through the streets, mourning his death. In May, the 10-day **Festival de las Artes** features music, theater, and dance—much of it free to the public. In July, contemporary dance troupes come to town for the **Festival de la Danza.** On August 25th, the city celebrates its patron saint, **San Luis Rey,** with a parade and fiesta. The second half of August is also the time of the **Feria Nacional Potosina** (National Fair), celebrated with bullfights, cockfights, parades, and concerts.

AFTER DARK

Nightlife in San Luis Potosí is dead Sunday through Wednesday and explosive Thursday through Saturday. One of the more popular bars in town is **Nuff!** (Carranza 1145, tel. 48/13–65–53), where Lionel Ritchie, R&B, and rap tunes fill the air. Downstairs, the disco (open Fri. and Sat. 8 PM–2 AM) plays techno and Mexican and U.S. pop tunes. The cover is $3, but it's easily waived if you take advantage of the nightly two-for-one specials offered 6 PM—midnight at the bar. The newly remodeled **Staff** (Carranza 423, tel. 48/14–60–34) charges a $4 cover and attracts a large, young crowd with its disco and pop music. **Oasis** (Carretera a México Km. 417, tel. 48/22–18–82; cover $8.50), in the Hotel María Dolores, is a popular out-of-the-way club for rich kids looking for love. The gay scene in San Luis is pretty lively, at least by Mexican standards; meeting areas include the arches at the Plaza de Armas in the early evening and in the plaza itself later on. **Disco Sheik** (347 Prolongación a Zacatecas, behind the gas station, tel. 48/12–64–57; open weekends 11 PM–dawn) is a popular, surprisingly modern disco/bar that hosts nightly transvestite shows after midnight. **Chey's** (Mar Mediterraneo, behind Hotel

In the evenings, mariachi bands practice in the Jardín Escontría on Los Bravo, turning the otherwise unattractive plaza into a romantic spot for an early evening stroll.

Río) is a gay disco open on weekends. It's best reached by taxi, as it's quite a distance from the central plaza.

Near San Luis Potosí

SANTA MARIA DEL RIO Perfect as a day trip, this sleepy, unassuming town is famous for handcrafted cotton and silk *rebozos* (shawls) that take a month to make. The shawls are made with techniques that originated in Asia, were passed on to Spain during the Moorish invasion, and then brought to Mexico with the conquistadores. Today you can see how the patterned shawls are woven and purchase one for about $50 in the **Escuela de Artesanía** (Jardín Hidalgo 5, tel. 485/3–05–68). To reach Santa María, take a Flecha Amarilla or Autobuses Potosínos bus from the Central Camionera; buses (2 hrs, $1.50) leave every 15 minutes 6 AM–11:45 PM.

REAL DE CATORCE Perched among the high, desolate peaks of the northern *altiplano* (highlands), Real de Catorce is a dusty ghost town straight out of a B-grade western. Established in 1778 as a mining town, its glory days were in the 19th century. In the early 20th century, when the price of silver dropped, so did the population: from 144,000 to 2,700. Today, the town's residents number near 1,000, making exploration of the abandoned mines, baroque churches, and stone amphitheaters (once used for bull- and cockfights) a somewhat lonely experience—although the town's recent popularity with tourists has caused some souvenir shops to sprout up. Huichol Indians from Nayarit and Jalisco visit Real de Catorce every autumn to harvest peyote in the nearby hills.

After trekking around town you can relax at one of the restaurants around **Plaza Hidalgo**. An economic option for sleeping is the simple **Casa de Huespedes La Provincia** (Lanza Gorta, up from the Parroquia, no phone), where singles and doubles go for $4 a night. To reach Real de Catorce, you'll traverse through the 2 kilometer–long Ogarrio Tunnel, the only passage into town. From San Luis, Estrella Blanca offers one direct bus per day to Real de Catorce (2½ hrs, $6) at 3:30 PM; alternately, catch a more frequently departing bus bound for Matehuala (2 hrs, $4.50) and then transfer to a minibus for the rest of the journey.

RIO VERDE Surrounded by acres of orange trees and fields of corn and chiles, the little town of Río Verde lives up to its name—even the zócalo is awash in green. In the lush countryside around town you'll find ample opportunities for swimming, camping, and hiking. The largest and most developed swimming area lies about 14 kilometers from town, off Highway 70, at **Laguna de la Media Luna**. This sparkling clear lake is popular with scuba divers and snorkelers for its varied aquatic plants and underwater fossilized trees. It was a pre-Columbian cultural center until it was abandoned for unknown reasons in the 12th century. You can camp here for $1 and a few little restaurants rent inner tubes. To rent scuba gear, make arrangements at the restaurant/bar/disco/store **La Cabaña** (Carretera San Luis–Río Verde Km. 127.5, tel. 487/2–06–25). The guys here are also happy to tell you about other points of interest.

Less developed, but popular with locals, are the double swimming holes, **Los Anteojitos** (Little Eyeglasses), 2 kilometers south of town. You can usually camp in the nearby tree-filled area for free, but a caretaker may appear and charge you a dollar or two. A desert-like beauty surrounds the ponds of **El Charco Azul** and **Laguna El Coyote**, located 18 kilometers southeast of town. Both are very rustic, but camping is free and, according to locals, safe. Farther from town, spelunkers can explore the caves at **Las Grutas de Catedral** and **Las Grutas de Ángel**, where rock formations look vaguely like angels, altars, and pipe organs. The caves can be reached by a 3-kilometer trail that leads out of the community of Los Alamitos; it's recommended that you hire guides to take you in. Bring food, water, good trekking clothes, and a flashlight.

You'll have to make friends with someone who owns a car, or else hire a taxi to get to these areas—buses don't run on these backcountry dirt roads. Most journeys should cost $6–$10. Friendly *taxista* Salvador Hernández Castro is willing to drive just about anywhere; ask for him around the bus station, or call him at home (tel. 487/2–23–07). Get a map of the area from the **Cámara Nacional de Comercio, Servicios, y Turismo Río Verde** (Jardín de San Antonio "F", tel. 487/2–08–02), which is open weekdays 9:30–2 and 4:30–7, Saturdays 9:30–noon.

➤ **COMING AND GOING** • **Omnibús de Oriente** (tel. 48/18–29–41) sends buses hourly from San Luis Potosí to Río Verde (2 hrs, $4). The last bus back to San Luis Potosí leaves at 10:15 PM. From Río Verde, **Omnibús de Oriente** (tel. 487/2–01–12) and **Sistema** (tel. 487/2–12–88) make hourly runs to Ciudad Valles (2 hrs, $4).

➤ **WHERE TO SLEEP AND EAT** • **Hotel Morelos** (Morelos 216, no phone) is the best deal in town; it's clean, close to the plaza, and cheap—bathless singles cost $4, doubles $5. It's a 15-minute walk from the bus station: Go left on the San Luis Potosí–Río Verde highway, and then right on Morelos. Food in Río Verde is hearty, if uninspired. Try the busy 24-hour **Restaurant Rivera** (Plaza Constitución "B," tel. 487/2–01–03), right on the zócalo, where you'll spend less than $4 on generous portions of tacos, enchiladas, and antojitos.

CIUDAD VALLES The only reason to come to Ciudad Valles is to arrange excursions into the vast, untouristed countryside beyond the city limits—a region full of pristine rivers, waterfalls, and caves. The city itself has little to offer, unless you enjoy long blocks choked by cinderblock buildings and speeding cars. The Valles **tourist office** (Carranza 53 Sur, tel. 138/2–01–44; open weekdays 9–1:30 and 4–7:30, Sat. 9–1) hands out free maps on the rare occasions when they're in stock. Groups of four or more can arrange excursions into the outlying tropical rain forest (*see* Outdoor Activities, *below*) with Ana Maria Musa or Martha Santos at **Antani Viajes**, in the lobby of **Hotel Don Antonio** (Blvd. México-Laredo 15, tel. 138/1–19–16). They speak some English and understand budget travel, so they won't push you into some expensive deal. The main bus line in Ciudad Valles is **Vencedor** (tel. 138/2–37–55); buses run hourly to Río Verde (2 hrs, $4), San Luis Potosí (5½ hrs, $7), and Tampico (2½ hrs, $4).

➤ **WHERE TO SLEEP AND EAT** • Hotels here aren't particularly cheap, but try **Hotel Boulevard** (Blvd. México-Laredo 19, tel. 138/2–01–28), on the main road. Clean rooms with fans run $7. Otherwise you can camp right in the city for $5 on the extensive grounds of **Hotel Valles** (Blvd. México-Laredo 36 Nte., tel. 138/2–00–50). You'll have access to showers, bathrooms, and the large, inviting, blue-tile pool (if you want to splurge on a room, singles are $33, doubles $37). If you can afford it, **Hotel San Fernando** (Blvd. México-Laredo 5, tel. 138/2–01–84) offers comfortable, air-conditioned rooms at $17.50 singles, $18.50 doubles; the hotel also sells maps of the region. Inside the hotel, the clean and airy **Restaurant Bonanza** is open 24 hours and serves *enchiladas huastecas* ($5), a spicy regional dish, and a tasty *pollo con mole* (chicken in a chocolate-chile sauce; $3.50). Otherwise, dining options are pretty undistinguished here; lots of cheap food stands line Juárez, near Boulevard México-Laredo.

➤ **OUTDOOR ACTIVITIES** • The dense tropical rain forest around Ciudad Valles is ripe for exploration, but there's little tourist infrastructure here—be prepared to hike, haggle with taxistas, and hire the occasional guide to get you to where you want to go. The following places can all be reached from Highway 70 and lie between Ciudad Valles and Río Verde. **Las Cascadas de Micos,** a series of cascades and swimming holes, lies 18 kilometers north of Highway 70, just east of Valles. There's also a no-frills campsite here that locals consider pretty safe. Bring plenty of drinking water and food. Farther east, midway to Río Verde, is **La Cascada Tamasopo,** where a confluence of mountain rivers and streams form several high falls that crash into swimmable pools. You'll pass the town of Tamasopo on the way, so stock up on food and water there. If you decide to stay the night, Tamasopo also has campgrounds (with bathrooms). Just 2 kilometers away are more pools at **El Trampolín,** which boasts a natural limestone bridge. One **Vencedor** bus (tel. 138/2–32–81) leaves the central station in Ciudad Valles for Tamasopo (2 hrs, $2) at 2:30 AM (yes, AM) daily. Alternately, you can take one of the more frequent Vencedor buses to Río Verde (1½ hrs, $2); get off at the Tamasopo *crucero* (intersection), and walk 8 kilometers north to the falls. You can also hire a taxi from the crucero for $5.50.

A bit more remote is the **Cascada de Tamul,** a spectacular 11-meter-high waterfall. From Ciudad Valles, take a Vencedor bus headed for San Luis Potosí and ask the driver to drop you off at the crucero for Santa Anita on Highway 70; then hire a taxi or hitch south down the dirt road to the small town of Tanchachín. Here you can hire a guide (and his boat) to take you upriver to the falls. Ask for Don Catarino; he has the lowest prices. All in all, it'll take a good three hours to get here (the boat ride alone takes two hours).

If you're on your way to Xilitla (*see below*) from Ciudad Valles, and you're tired of splashing around, head to the **Sótano de las Golondrinas** (near the town of Aquismón, off Highway 85), a 375-meter shaft in the earth. It's home to hundreds of swallows, who swoosh out of the ground at sunrise and at dusk. Vencedor buses run regularly from Ciudad Valles to Aquismón (5 min, $1); at Aquismón's main plaza you can arrange transport to the *sótano* (literally, basement). Don't pay more than $7 per person for the ride. The truck will let you off after about an hour in front of the 2-kilometer trailhead to the sótano. Camping or staying here after dark is discouraged by locals.

XILITLA   Located on the slopes of the Sierra Gorda, Xilitla overlooks the deep green gorges cut by the Tahculín River. An Augustine church and convent were built here early in the Spanish Conquest (about 1557); their thick walls were designed to ward off Huastec attacks. About 3 kilometers northwest from the main plaza, the ruins of a mansion/castle lie moldering in the jungle. Built by Sir Edward James, the illegitimate son of King Edward VII of England, the house and gardens were designed to mimic the surrounding vegetation in a style James claimed "integrated architecture into nature." Take a look at the giant concrete mushrooms and blue metal snakes to see if he succeeded. Just outside the garden walls, you'll find **Las Pozas,** a series of waterfalls that plunge into several inviting pools. To reach the mansion you can take a taxi ($3), which leaves from the storefront of La Joyita, two blocks southwest of the plaza on Jardín Hidalgo. Or, make the easy 30-minute walk: From the plaza, walk north on Melchón Ocampo, turn right where it dead-ends, and follow the rocky path all the way down (east) until you reach the freeway; from here, turn left, take the first dirt road to your left, and follow the LAS POZAS signs all the way to the mansion ruins and the falls (it's really not that difficult). Entrance to the ruins is $1.

For another adventure, experience the enormous saltpeter stalactites in the **Cueva de Salitre.** To get here, take a taxi ($2) from La Joyita or walk a leisurely 1 kilometer: Follow Melchón Ocampo north, turn right (east) on the second street, follow it to the highway, and take the fork to the left. The cave is behind a *taller* (small auto parts workshop); the entrance is through the first hut on the left after the Pemex station. There are no official guides nor an entrance fee at the cave. However, one of the worker's children will gladly guide you down the steep, rocky hill to where the cave is hidden for a couple of pesos.

➤ **COMING AND GOING** • From Río Verde, one **Sistema** bus (tel. 487/2–12–88) leaves at 6:45 PM for Xilitla (5 hrs, $6). **Vencedor** (tel. 138/2–37–55) buses also run hourly from Ciudad Valles to Xilitla (1½ hrs, $2).

QUERETARO MISSIONS   Nestled among the rugged hills of the Sierra Gorda is a series of five small missions, constructed in the mid–18th century under the evangelical gaze of Father Junipero Serra. The elaborate facade of each church is carved in a baroque style, and displays both indigenous and Catholic iconography: Life-size saints do battle with demons and dragons, while flowers and grapes bloom peacefully beside them. The architecture, far from being simply decorative, was didactic, and supposed to "create a dialogue with God." Symbols were integrated into the woodwork to help facilitate the conversion process of the indigena: Look for moons, stars, and the pagan mermaid—all symbols of the Virgin Mary. The largest of the five mission towns, **Jalpan,** has the most places to stay, and is a good base for day trips to the other missions. The fancy **Mesón de Fray Junipero Serro** (Carretera Río Verde, tel. 429/6–01–64) charges $21 for a single or a double. The more modest **Camino Viejo** (Carretera Río Verde, 100 meters north of bus terminal, tel. 429/6–01–85) charges $10 for a single and $12 for a double. Jalpan also features the **Museo Histórico de la Sierra Gorda** (admission $1; open Mon.–Sat. 10–3, Sun. 9–1), which exhibits drawings, dioramas, and historical synopses of the culture and history of the Sierra Gorda region and its inhabitants. The other four Querétaro missions (Landa, Tancogol, Tilaco, and Concá) are small and remote and may be best explored as a day trip from Jalpan. If you'd rather spend the day soaking in soothing water, head for Concá, where locals can point you to the thermal springs, near the hotel Mesón de San Nícolas. Conveniently, Concá is a stopping point for buses between Jalpan and both Río Verde and Ciudad Valles.

➤ **COMING AND GOING** • The fastest and most direct way to reach the Querétaro missions is by bus from Río Verde or Ciudad Valles. From Río Verde, **Omnibús de Oriente** (tel. 487/2–01–12) runs hourly buses through Concá to Jalpan (2 hrs, $3). **Vencedor** (tel. 138/2–37–55) also runs this route hourly from Ciudad Valles (3½ hrs, $4).

Querétaro

Downtown Querétaro is a great example of the juxtaposition of past and present so common in Mexican cities: Centuries-old buildings now house electronic appliances and women's lingerie shops, and fast-food joints adjoin national monuments. The heart of Querétaro is an exquisite stretch of tree-shaded cobblestone streets lined with colonial mansions and punctuated by quiet plazas and well-kept gardens. Always an important center for the surrounding agricultural and cattle-raising country, this bustling state capital now has a population of more than one million people—but is still worlds away from the pollution and chaos of Mexico City. Women can walk alone at night on well-lit streets with a sense of security, and the universities attract young students and bohemian types, who can be seen playing chess in cafés. And, like other university cities, Querétaro has an active central square and a rocking nightlife.

As the city's numerous historic landmarks indicate, some of the most important events in Mexican history took place in Querétaro. The signing of the 1917 constitution and the formation of the PRI (Institutional Revolutionary Party), Mexico's ruling party, both took place in Querétaro. The Treaty of Guadalupe Hidalgo, under which Mexico ceded Texas, New Mexico, and the California territories to the United States, was also signed here. Mexico's struggle for independence received a push from Querétaro resident Doña Josefa Ortiz, who aided in the infamous "Grito de Dolores." Ortiz, also known as La Corregidora, was later executed for her subversive activities; her heroism is commemorated in the **Plaza de la Corregidora** and **La Tumba de Doña Josefa.** Other historical landmarks include the **Convento de la Santa Cruz**—the site of Emperor Maximilian's imprisonment before his execution on the **Cerro de las Campanas** (Hill of the Church Bells), just north of town.

BASICS

AMERICAN EXPRESS **Turismo Beverly** is a travel agency that provides all American Express services, including emergency check cashing, traveler's check sales, and card replacement. Cardholders' mail will be held for up to 10 days if sent to the following address: Tecnológico 118, Local 1, Querétaro, Querétaro, CP 76030, México. *Tel. 42/16–12–60. From Alameda, take any bus west along Constituyentes to Tecnológico; walk south 1½ blocks. Open weekdays 9–2 and 4–6, Sat. 9–noon.*

BOOKSTORES **Unidad Cultural del Centro** (16 de Septiembre 1, tel. 42/24–24–61; open Mon.–Sat. 9–8:30, Sun. noon–8) sells newspapers and tons of books (in Spanish) on Mexican history, literature, art, and film. The bookstore inside **Fonart** (Angela Peralta 20, btw Corregidora and Pasteur, tel. 42/12–26–48; open Mon.–Sat. 10–2 and 5–9), the government-sponsored artesenía store, sells books in English and the bi-monthly magazine *Arte de Mexico,* which features photographs and essays on Mexican cinema, arts, and crafts.

CASAS DE CAMBIO Both **Banamex** (16 de Septiembre 1, tel. 42/12–01–39) and **Bancomer** (Juárez 15, tel. 42/12–06–77) cash traveler's checks and exchange currency weekdays 8:30–3. You can also get cash advances on Visa or MasterCard from their 24-hour ATMs. Better rates can occasionally be found at **Cambio La Pasada** (Allende 2, no phone), which is open Monday–Saturday 9–6.

EMERGENCIES You can reach the **police** at 42/12–02–06, 42/14–11–49, or 42/12–30–03. For an **ambulance,** call 42/13–28–04 or 42/13–28–28.

LAUNDRY Laundromats are scarce near the center of town, but **Lavandería Verónica** lies six short city blocks west of the zócalo. It'll cost $4 to clean 3 kilos of clothes. *Hidalgo 153, btw Regules and Ignacio Pérez, tel. 42/16–61–68. Open weekdays 9–2:30, 4:30–8, Sat. 9–3.*

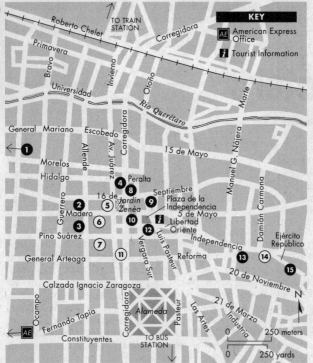

Sights ●

Artesan Libertad, **12**

Calzada de los Arcos, **15**

Cerro de las Campanas, **1**

Convento de la Santa Cruz, **13**

Museo de Arte de Querétaro, **3**

Museo Regional, **10**

Palacio del Gobierno Federal, **9**

Plaza de la Corregidora, **8**

Teatro de la República, **4**

Templo de Santa Clara, **2**

Lodging ○

Hotel Hidalgo, **6**

Hotel Plaza, **5**

Hotel San Francisco, **11**

Posada Academia, **7**

Villa Juvenil, **14**

MAIL The **post office** will hold mail addressed to you for up to 10 days if sent to the following address: Lista de Correos, Administración 1, Arteaga 7, Querétaro, Querétaro, CP 76000, México. *Tel. 42/12–01–12. From Jardín Zenéa, walk 2 blocks south on Juárez and turn right on Arteaga. Open weekdays 8–7, Sat. 9–1.*

MEDICAL AID **Grupo Médico Zaragoza** (Zaragoza 39, tel. 42/16–76–38) is a large, centrally located medical center that provides most medical services 24 hours a day. Doctors Enriquez Espinosa, Hector Húgo Encorrada, and Antonio Solís all speak English. **Farmacia Querétaro** (Constituyentes 17, at Ignacio de las Casas, tel. 42/12–44–23) is also open 24 hours.

PHONES **Ladatel** pay phones grace both the Jardín Zenéa and Plaza de la Independencia. Ladatel phone cards are sold in most kiosks or businesses displaying the LADATEL sign. The small kiosk, *Libros y Revistas,* on the corner of Juárez and Madero, always has an abundant supply of them, and also functions as a **caseta de larga distancia** (tel. 42/12–79–55, fax 42/14–39–17; open daily 9–9). It costs $1.75 per minute for long-distance calls to the United States.

SCHOOLS The **Universidad Autónoma de Querétaro** offers four- to six-week summer and winter courses in all levels of Spanish. For more information, write to: Escuela de Idiomas, Centro Universitario, Cerro de las Campanas, Querétaro, Querétaro, CP 76000, México. *In Centro Universitario, Hidalgo, tel. 42/16–74–66. From Jardín Zenéa, take* RUTA R *bus to the university.*

VISITOR INFORMATION For maps and detailed information, visit the **Secretaría de Turismo** (Luis Pasteur 4, at 5 de Mayo, tel. 42/12–14–12). Ask for Luis Alejandro Bustamante—he understands budget travel and won't try to coax you into an expensive hotel. The office is open weekdays 9–2 and 5–8.

COMING AND GOING

BY BUS Querétaro recently opened a fancy bus station about 6 kilometers south of the zócalo, composed of two separate buildings. Sala A sees mostly first-class bus lines, like **Omnibús de México** (tel. 42/29–03–29), which provides service to Aguascalientes (5 hrs, $12). Sala B deals with second-class bus lines such as **Estrella Blanca** (tel. 42/29–02–02), which goes to Zacatecas (5 hrs, $13), San Luis Potosí (3 hrs, $5), and Mexico City (3 hrs, $7); **Herradura de Plata** (tel. 42/29–02–45), which rumbles to San Miguel de Allende (1 hr, $2) every 40 minutes; and **Flecha Amarilla** (tel. 42/11–40–01), which sends five buses a day to Guanajuato (2½ hrs, $5). Each building has restaurants, phones, and luggage storage. Taxis wait at both salas; you need to buy a taxi ticket ($1.50 to the zócalo) from the kiosk near the exit. You can also take an *urbano* (local city bus) for about 50¢; walk to the end of Sala B and take the RUTA 8 minibus to the center. *Bernardo Quintano Sur, at Autopista México, tel. 42/29–00–61 or 42/29–00–62.*

BY CAR With major highways connecting it to the north, the Pacific Coast, and the Gulf Coast, Querétaro is fairly easy to reach. The six-lane Federal 57 runs north to San Luis Potosí and southeast to Mexico City. Driving around within the city is easier than in most Mexican cities, but since everything is within walking distance you don't really need a car. If you want a vehicle for day excursions beyond the city, try **Budget** (Constituyentes 73, tel. 42/13–44–98), **Hertz** (Constituyentes 132, tel. 42/15–58–50), or the Mexican-owned **Larios** (Constituyentes 134–13, tel. 42/15–11–03), which is reliable and more economical.

BY TRAIN The small, second-class train station lies 3 kilometers north of the historic center. Trains to Mexico City ($3) leave twice daily at 4 AM and 4 PM. The train for Ciudad Juárez ($17) departs daily at 2 PM, and the train to Guadalajara ($4) leaves at 12:30 AM. No one in a responsible position is willing to hazard a guess as to how long these trips take, which may be an indication of the reliability of the service. To reach downtown, take the RUTA 8 minibus. *Héroe de Nacozar, at Invierno, tel. 42/12–17–03. Ticket sales daily 9–11 and noon–5.*

GETTING AROUND

Most sights, lodging, and restaurants are tightly compressed in the *centro histórico* and revolve around **Jardín Zenéa**, also known as Jardín Obregón. The two main north–south drags near Jardín Zenéa—Juárez to the west and Corregidora to the east—stem from the **Alameda**. The Jardín is bordered on the north by 16 de Septiembre, and the south by Madero. Many of the city's cobblestone streets, called *andadores,* are closed to cars. On the few occasions that you may need a lift, white minibuses travel all over the city (destinations are painted on the front windshield) from 5 AM to 11 PM and cost about 30¢.

WHERE TO SLEEP

If you have the money, it's a good idea to stay in a moderately priced place—most of Querétaro's bargain hotels are near the noisy Jardín Zenéa. The more expensive hotels near the old bus station aren't much better, and the cheapest hotels are only semiclean and usually attract couples looking for a place to consummate their newfound affection. During December, hotels are booked solid for the Exposición Ganadera (*see* Cheap Thrills, *below*); to play it safe, you may want to reserve a month or so in advance.

➤ **UNDER $10** • **Hotel Hidalgo.** Huge wooden doors open onto this hotel's sunny courtyard. Rooms are furnished with TVs and clean bathrooms, and some have balconies overlooking the cobblestone street. The friendly proprietors speak English, but they aren't around very often. Singles cost $7, doubles $8.50. *Madero Pte. 11, tel. 42/12–00–81. 40 rooms, all with bath. Luggage storage. Wheelchair access.*

Hotel San Francisco. On the bustling Avenida Corregidora, this dark and spartan hotel attracts mostly Mexican families and businessmen. Rooms are clean—if the overpowering smell of disinfectant is any indication—and there's always hot water. For a more peaceful stay, ask for a room away from the street. Singles run $6.50, doubles with a matrimonial bed cost $8.50, and doubles with two beds are $9. *Corregidora 144, tel. 42/12–08–58. 58 rooms, all with bath. Luggage storage, TV. Reservations advised. Wheelchair access.*

Posada Academia. Rooms here are dark but relatively clean, and include TVs and plentiful hot water. The old woman who runs the place is cheerful and chatty, and she casts a blind eye to all the sex going on in the hotel. Singles are $4.50, doubles $7. *Pino Suárez 3, no phone. 18 rooms, all with bath.*

➤ **UNDER $15** • **Hotel Plaza.** Rooms here are clean, bright, and come equipped with TVs and phones. It's right on the noisy central square, so ask for a room away from the street. Singles run $10, doubles $13.50. *Juárez 23, tel. 42/12–11–38. 29 rooms, all with bath. MC, V.*

HOSTELS **Villa Juvenil (CREA).** If you don't mind the 10-minute walk to the center of town or the busloads of high school students traipsing in at all hours of the night, this is a good place to crash. It's clean and cheerful, and dorm beds go for $3 per person. You'll even be able to eat for under $1.75. There's just one catch: The Villa locks its doors at 10 PM, just when the nightlife gets rolling. If you're hopelessly nocturnal, so can always go out, stay until they open their doors again at 7 AM, and sleep all day. Sometimes the hostel is filled with student groups, so call ahead if you don't want to take your chances. *Ejército Republicano, tel. 42/23–11–20. PM. From Jardín Zenéa, south 1 block on Corregidora, then left on Independencia for 6 blocks; veer right at fork to Ejército Republicano and continue to crest of hill, right behind Convento de la Santa Cruz. Reception open daily 7 AM–10 PM. Luggage storage.*

FOOD

There are so many good, cheap things to eat in Querétaro that it's hard to know where to begin. By eating at food stands on the street, you can spend less than $5 on breakfast, lunch, *and*

Sola? Solita?

After revealing that they are traveling alone, tourists, especially female ones, often encounter incredulous responses from Mexicans. The double request for confirmation— "Sola? Solita?" ("Alone? All by your little self?"), asked by everyone from the grandma at the hotel desk to the university student sitting in a café—may momentarily give you cause for concern. You needn't worry though—it's a cultural difference. Most Mexicans react this way not only because they are concerned about your safety, but also because of the close familial bonds that exist in their own culture. Mexican youth travel with family and friends, and, as one female university student explained, "My parents would worry if I traveled by myself."

The influence of family is strong here, especially since most people live with their parents until they get married. Bragging about your studio apartment back home usually results not in envy but pity: For many Mexicans, living and traveling alone implies that your family doesn't care much for you. The extended family is a source of economic and emotional support, and any relative, no matter how distant, is welcome to show up looking for a meal, a job, or a place to stay. Typical outings, whether a month-long vacation at the beach or a Sunday afternoon in the park, almost always involve the entire family. The bonus of all this group activity is that the solo traveler is rarely at a loss for company: Many Mexicans are perfectly willing to expand the family temporarily to include a lone gringo for the day.

dinner (yes, all three combined). In the morning, vendors work the Jardín Zenéa and the streets surrounding the Alameda, selling 30¢ tamales and *atole* (a sweet, corn-based drink similar to hot chocolate). At lunchtime, stands sell fresh fruit cups doused with lime and chiles (75¢) and tacos (25¢). In the evening, you'll undoubtedly smell the aroma of freshly grilled corn on the cob (25¢) wafting from the *puestecitos* (food stands). Also be on the lookout for Queretaro specialties like *enchiladas queretanas*—tortillas drenched in red chili sauce, fried in oil, then filled with cheese and onions and eaten like a taco. *Las carnitas,* prepared by boiling strips of pork in their own fat for about three hours, marinating them in salt water, and serving them with tortillas and vinegar, is also a favorite.

➢ **UNDER $5** • **Café del Fondo.** This popular café may have lost some of its architectural charm in a recent move, but it's certainly retained its devoted bohemian following. The entry-way displays posters for current concerts and art exhibitions, and artsy types lounge in the simple white-washed rooms, dawdling for hours over $2 *cafés exóticos* (cinnamon- or alcohol-spiked coffees). Cheap, filling breakfast ($1.25) and lunch ($2) specials are also available. *Pino Suárez 9, tel. 42/12–09–05. Open daily 7:30 AM–10 PM. Wheelchair access.*

Comedor Vegetariano Natura. The decor is decidedly *Brady Bunch* rec room, complete with wood paneling and wall-sized forest posters, but the food is good. Try the mushroom and cheese soy burgers ($1.50), soy enchiladas ($1.75), or a fruit and yogurt shake. If you're suffering from a gastrointestinal disorder, the restaurant also sells natural remedies, including horsehair tea for dysentery. *Vergara 7, tel. 42/14–10–88. From Jardín Zenéa, 2 blocks east on 5 de Mayo, then right on Vergara. Open Mon.–Sat. 8 AM–9 PM.*

La Mariposa. This popular café/ice-cream parlor has been around for more than 50 years, and its original peacock-blue decor is kept lovingly clean. Delicious milkshakes are $1.50 and sandwiches are $1.25. Check out the tempting sweets at the back counter. *Peralta 7, tel. 42/12–11–66. 2 blocks north of Jardín Zenéa. Open daily 8 AM–9:30 PM.*

Restaurant Punto y Coma. This place is filled with students at midday, so conversation is pretty easy to come by. Your choice from the *menú del día* (daily menu) will cost $2 or $3 and includes soup, tortillas, rice, an entrée, and dessert. Meat lovers should try the *hígado en cebollado* (liver and onions) when it's available; vegetarians will appreciate the terrific lentil soup. Tortillas are made fresh in the front of the restaurant. *16 de Septiembre 27, 1 block east of Jardín Zenéa, tel. 42/14–16–66. Open daily 8–6.*

➢ **UNDER $10** • **Café Tulipe.** Mexican and international students frequent this pleasant restaurant at night. Diners can amuse themselves by checking out the art prints on the wall and the prominently displayed dessert cart. Try the *crema conde* ($1.50), a soup made of black beans, cream, oregano, and *epazote* (an herb particular to Mexico). Other dishes include chicken in orange sauce ($4) and fondue for two ($7). *Calzada de los Arcos 3, tel. 42/13–63–91. Walk 1½ blocks west of base of Ejército Republicano. Open Sun.–Wed. 8 AM–10 PM, Thurs.–Sat. 8 AM–11 PM.*

WORTH SEEING

Though Querétaro is large and ever-expanding, most sights are in the compact centro histórico, within walking distance of the Jardín Zenéa. The tourist office (*see* Visitor Information, *above*) offers extensive and informative walking tours of the city, conducted in Spanish or (if you prearrange) English. Tours begin daily at 10:30 AM and 6 PM and last for two hours. They're a good way to get a sense of the city's history and cost just $1.50 (plus any museum entrance fees). Tours meet in the tourist office.

CONVENTO DE LA SANTA CRUZ This still-functioning 16th-century convent is home to about 40 monks who serenely go about their business while tourists traipse through the building. Original furnishings and paintings are on display in several rooms, including the cell where Emperor Maximilian awaited his execution. The branches of the famous **Árbol de las Espinas** (Thorn Tree), in one of the convent's many patios, are filled with cross-shaped thorns. According to legend, the tree grows where a friar named Margil de Jesús buried his cane. Guides will take you on a 15-minute tour of the convent (in Spanish or English) and always ask for a small tip for their services. Near the convent is the city's emblem, the **Calzada de los Arcos,** Querétaro's huge, pink, 18th-century stone aqueduct. Though the calzada no longer carries water, it is one of the largest aqueducts ever constructed in the Americas. *From Jardín Zenéa, 1 block south on Corregidora, left on Independencia for 6 blocks. Small donation requested. Open Mon.–Sat. 9–2 and 4–6, Sun. 9–4:30. Wheelchair access.*

MUSEO DE ARTE DE QUERETARO This 18th-century building, once an Augustine monastery, was recently renovated and now houses a varied art collection. Most works date from the 16th, 17th, and 18th centuries, but several rooms on the ground floor are devoted to contemporary Mexican artists and photographers, with works by students from the University of Querétaro. *Allende 14, near Pino Suárez, tel. 42/12–23–57. Admission: $1.50; free for students and on Tues. Open Tues.–Sun. 11–7. Wheelchair access.*

MUSEO REGIONAL This regional museum is housed in an ornate building (formerly a Franciscan convent) that dates from the 16th century. The collection includes pre-Columbian artifacts from Querétaro state and items of historical import, including early copies of the first Mexican constitution and the coffin used to bring Emperor Maximilian's body to its final resting place. Films and other cultural events take place here after the museum has closed; check the entryway billboard for details. *Corregidora 3, SE cnr of Jardín Zenéa, tel. 42/12–20–31. Admission: $2, free Sun. and Tues. Open Tues.–Sun. 10:30–4:30. Wheelchair access.*

PALACIO DEL GOBIERNO FEDERAL Also called the Palacio Municipal or the Casa de la Corregidora, this enormous, neoclassical, 18th-century building was once the home of Querétaro's mayor-magistrate (El Corregidor) and his wife, Doña Josefa Ortiz de Domínguez (La Corregidora). The large room over the main entrance was where Doña Josefa was held under house arrest during the first rumblings of the War of Independence; it's now used as the governor's conference room and is not accesible to the public. As legend has it, Doña Josefa managed to warn Juan de Aldama and Ignacio Allende that their plot to declare independence from Spain had been discovered. Allende rushed to tell Padre Miguel Hidalgo, who then gave his famous call for liberty in the nearby town of Dolores Hidalgo that same night; this speech, the "Grito de Dolores," became the spark that ignited public support for independence. Today, with its arched walkways and gracious courtyards, the palacio brightens the bureaucratic lives of municipal administrators, whose offices are housed here. The guards will let you wander the building; if you want the full tour, ask if Isadora Salvala is around. *5 de Mayo, at Pasteur, tel. 42/12–91–00. Open weekdays 8 AM–9 PM, Sat. 9–2. Wheelchair access.*

TEATRO DE LA REPUBLICA This imposing neoclassical building was the site of some of the most important events in Mexican history, including the sentencing of Emperor Maximilian to death in 1867 and the drafting of the new constitution in 1917. Although you probably won't witness anything nearly so momentous, you can catch one of the theater's occasional plays or concerts. Check at the box office to find out what's going on. *Angela Peralta 22, tel. 42/14–29–53. Viewing hours: weekdays 10–2 and 5–8, Sat. 9–noon. Wheelchair access.*

Santiago de Querétaro

On July 25, 1531, a bare-hands battle between the indigenous Otomí and the land-hungry Spanish was fought on the site where the Convento de la Santa Cruz (see above) now stands. According to legend, the sun was completely eclipsed, the stars started to burn fiercely, and a rose-colored cross of light appeared in the sky. The apostle Santiago—who just so happened to be the patron saint of Spain—appeared in the sky on a white horse, "deciding" the battle in favor of the Spanish conquistadors. The city of "Santiago de Querétaro" was founded soon after, and the white horse of the apostle now graces Querétaro's coat of arms.

TEMPLO DE SANTA CLARA This 17th-century church sits in the tree-filled Jardín Madero. Exquisite baroque artwork and several gilded altar pieces grace the interior. Next to the church stands the **Fuente de Neptuno** (Neptune's Fountain), designed by renowned architect and Bajío native Eduardo Tresguerra. The fountain originally belonged to the monks of San Antonio, who sold it (along with part of their land) during tight economic times. *Madero, at Allende. Wheelchair access.*

CHEAP THRILLS

The huge, resplendent **Parque Alameda** (south of Jardín Zenéa; open daily 6 AM–8 PM) is the best place in town to rest your aching feet. It's also rumored to be a favorite cruising place for gay men. The nearby **El Molino** bakery (Juárez, at Zaragoza) sells goodies you can eat on the grass or feed to the ducks in the pond. This tranquillity is only slightly disturbed by the **tianguis** (open-air market) outside the park, where you can pick up a new belt or the latest Gloria Trevi tape. If you're tough enough to hang with mariachi bands (lone women might want to think twice about this), head to the corner of Universidad and Invierno (4 blocks north of Jardín Zenéa), where the musicians loiter and strum their instruments while waiting to get hired.

Some of the best fighting bulls come from the Bajío—if a bull is a real champion, his sperm is frozen and saved to produce powerful future generations.

A good place to wind down is in the 25,000 square meters of recreational park known as the **Parque Recreativo Querétaro 2000** (Bernardo Quintana, tel. 42/20–68–10, 42/20–68–13, or 42/20–68–14; open daily 7 AM–7:30 PM). For $3, you can rent a bicycle built for two (or four) at the entrance and explore the premises, which include the **Casa Ecológica,** a solar-run house; to learn more about the Casa's virtues, take a look at the informative video. While you're here, you can catch a performance in the outdoor theater, shoot a few hoops, or join in on a volleyball game at the gym.

FESTIVALS Querétaro explodes in music, dancing, and general revelry during all of its festivals. A full-scale *pamplonada* (running of the bulls) occurs on July 26 as part of the **Fiesta de Santa Ana**—a celebration of one of the two patron saints of the city. A sip of the potent *ponche* (a delicious concoction made of cinnamon water, sugar cane liquor, raisins, and guayaba that can be spiked with either red wine or rum) may make you think twice about

Maximilian of Hapsburg

French forces overtook Mexico City in 1863, and shortly thereafter Napoleon III sent Maximilian, an Austrian archduke, and his wife Carlota to serve as stand-in emperor and empress. Mexican president Benito Juárez was ousted and the couple moved into Chapultepec Castle (see Worth Seeing, Bosque de Chapultepec, Chapter 2), engendering public resentment with their luxurious lifestyle. Although more of a puppet emperor to Napoleon III, Maximilian nevertheless had a well-developed sense of entitlement: Even after Napoleon withdrew French troops in 1866 and ordered Maximilian to abdicate, the emporer refused to give up his throne. Without France's support, Maximilian was soon captured by Juárez's forces and executed by firing squad on June 19, 1867, on the site now known as the Parque Cerro de las Campanas (Gómez Farías, tel. 42/15–20–75; open daily 6–6). The park harbors a chapel (a gift from Austria); a 20-meter-tall statue of Benito Juárez that marks the spot where Maximilian met his death; and a small museum chronicling the events of the emporer's execution. An ardent aficionado of his adopted country, Maximilian's last words were "¡Viva México!" (Long live Mexico!)

joining the stampede. During the first two weeks of December, the city holds the **Exposición Ganadera,** a huge agricultural fair that includes more bullfighting and rodeos, along with carnival rides, music, and a lot of food. The usual holidays (Holy Week, Day of the Dead, Independence Day) are also celebrated here with style. The night before Easter Sunday, folks burn a model of Judas in effigy.

SHOPPING

You don't have to wander very far to go shopping in Querétaro: The andadores in the centro are chock-full of outdoor vendors beckoning you to their wares. Stores and stands lining Pasteur and Libertad are devoted to artesanía; fun, cheap trinkets like guitar-shaped wallets and beaded jewerly are also easy to come by. Queretaro is famed for its gemstones and opal jewelry; for quality goods at fair prices, navigate your way to **La Luna** (Pasteur 1213, tel. 42/24–20–25; open daily 10:30–9). If you can't make it to Puebla, and want the authentic Talavera pottery the city is known for, head to **Artesanía Libertad** (Libertad 42, no phone; open Sun.–Thurs. 10–9, Fri. and Sat. 10–10); the selection is good, and prices are rock-bottom. A good all-purpose place to purchase everything from a blanket to a picture frame is the huge **Feria de las Artesanías** (Juárez 49, tel. 42/14–11–98; open daily 9–9). Pick up a whimsical, hand-painted piggy bank ($1.50) for all those pennies you've saved budget traveling. The Feria also offers the best selection of inexpensive ceramic dishware and colored glassware.

AFTER DARK

At night, Querétaro's historical center is taken over by a nocturnal animal—the lounge lizard. By 9:30 almost every café and restaurant around Plaza Corregidora boasts a singer with synthesizer accompaniment; the soulful crooning echoes across the plaza until the wee hours of the morning. Club-hoppers usually head for the bars and discos lining Boulevard Bernardo Quintana, on the east side of town. Things begin to rock just before midnight and continue until dawn or when everyone decides they're done—whichever comes first. For a quieter evening, head for Café Tulipe or Café del Fondo (see Food, above), both of which serve coffee and dessert until 10 PM. High culture is also active, with plays, music, dance concerts, and art-film screenings happening in various theaters around the city.

BARS Students with money to burn hang out at **J.B.J. O'Brien's** (Bernardo Quintana 109, tel. 42/13–72–13), which boasts pool tables and karaoke, and is next to a popular disco of the same name. A similar crowd is attracted to the bar/restaurant chain **Freedom** (Constituyentes 119 Ote., tel. 42/23–32–12) and **Carlos 'N Charlie's** (Bernardo Quintana 160, tel. 42/13–90–36), both of which feature live music Thursday through Saturday.

CLUBS The enormous excess of glitter and lights called **Qiu** (Monte Sinai 103, tel. 42/13–04–21; open Thurs.–Sun.) is a disco that plays mostly pop and charges a $6 cover. On weekends, the disco inside the Hotel Santa Maria, **La Iguana** (Universidad, no phone), attracts the largest gay crowd in town. You'll have to take a taxi to either one of these discos; the drivers know where they are and will charge you about $2–$3 to get you there from Jardín Zenéa. Stumble along or find a slick partner to teach you some salsa moves at **Los Infiernos** (Bernardo Quintana 177, no phone; open Wed.–Sun.), where the atmosphere is laid-back enough to tolerate both amateurs and the John Travoltas-of-salsa. Cover is $3. For those searching for an alternative to the disco scene, **Quadros** (5 de Mayo 16, tel. 42/12–04–45), housed in a former mansion three blocks from the Jardín Zenéa, harbors three rooms draped with works by local painters and photographers. Jazz and folk concerts and occasional poetry readings attract students and artists; when it gets late, they push away the tables and dance in the courtyard.

If you're in town during Dia de Los Muertos (Nov. 1) or in December, head for the Casa del Faldón (Primavera 43, no phone), a 17th-century mansion that showcases holiday culture and traditions. All events are open to the public and include traditionally decorated rooms, art, and performances.

THEATERS AND CULTURAL CENTERS Theaters in Querétaro offer performances to suit every type of artistic sensibility. Due to the city's large, penny-pinching student population, enriching one's cultural life doesn't have to mean becoming a pauper. The university-affiliated **Cómicos de la Legua** (Guillermo Prieto 7, tel. 42/12–49–11 or 42/12–51–82) specializes in classic European plays written in the 17th and 18th centuries. At the **Corral de Comedias** (Venustiano Carranza 39, tel. 42/12–01–65 or 42/12–07–65), nibble on bread and cheese and sip wine while seeing your favorite musicals, farces, and comedies performed in Spanish. For cutting-edge Mexican theater, check out the small independent theater group **CUR,** which performs regularly at the Jesuit college-turned-cultural-center **El Patio Barroco** (16 de Septiembre 63, tel. 42/12–51–92). The theater group is under the direction of the renowned Rodolfo Obregón, and tickets are a steal at $3 a piece. If you don't understand Spanish, much less its artistic abstractions, relax and listen to the "universal language": instrumental music. The **Orquestra Filarmónica de Querétaro** (tel. 42/23–16–92) performs Friday nights at 8 PM in the **Auditorio Josefa Ortíz de Domínguez** (Constituyentes, at Zimapán, tel. 42/13–03–34). Tickets can be bought at the auditorio the night of the show.

Near Querétaro

SAN JUAN DEL RÍO

Some 54 kilometers southeast of Querétaro, the town of San Juan del Río boasts wide tile sidewalks, shady central streets, and well-maintained colonial churches. A particularly interesting church is the 17th-century **Parroquia de Santo Domingo** (Zaragoza, at Juárez); its most striking feature is the statue over the main altar—a Christ figure with African features. Also worth checking out is the **Museo de la Santa Veracruz** (2 de Abril, no phone; open weekdays 9:30–2 and 4–6, weekends 10:30–4), which houses local pre-Columbian artifacts. The pleasant *portales* (porches) on Avenida Juárez are good places to purchase the handwoven items, such as baskets and blankets, that Querétaro state is famous for. Querétaro state is also known for its opals; visit **La Guadalupana** (16 de Septiembre 16, tel. 427/2–09–13), where the gemstones are cut and polished on site.

Eighteen kilometers northeast of San Juan del Río is the town of Tequisquiapan, where you can gorge yourself on the delectable wines and cheeses that the town is known for.

During the week of June 15, San Juan hosts an enormous festival in honor of its patron saint, San Juan Bautista. Bullfights, cockfights, bicycle races, and beauty contests ("Mister y Miss" San Juan) mesh with plays, concerts, and dance performances. Contact the friendly **tourist office** (Juárez 30, at Oriente, tel. 427/2–08–84) for details. If you plan to stay the night, **Hotel Layseca** (Juárez 9, tel. 467/20–01–10) offers large rooms ($10 singles, $14 doubles) around a gracious courtyard.

COMING AND GOING Clase Premier buses depart for San Juan del Río (40 min, $1.25) every 10 minutes from Sala A in Querétaro's Central de Autobuses; when you arrive at San Juan's bus terminal, just head out the front door and catch a bus marked CENTRO. The principal intersection in the downtown area is Juárez and Hidalgo. The last bus back to Querétaro leaves at 9:30 PM.

SAN JOAQUÍN

About three hours northwest of Querétaro, in the high mountainous region called the Sierra Gorda, lies the tiny town of San Joaquín. Apart from the visitors who stop here on their way to the nearby ruins of **Toluquilla** and **Ranas,** this quiet rural settlement is the type of place where the bickering of backyard roosters and hens drowns out the noise from infrequent trucks. The zócalo looks more like a wide sidewalk, but the many freshly painted houses give an air of prosperity. There's even a "luxury" hotel here: **Hotel Mesón de San Joaquín** (Guadalupe Victoria 4, tel. 429/2–53–19 ext. 118), which supplies slightly upscale versions of the basic cinderblock special (singles $11, doubles $12). The manager, Mario Torres Camacho, is happy to answer questions about the town. You can also try your luck at staying with a family ($5 is a polite amount to offer for their trouble); ask around at the Flecha Amarilla bus stop. If you'd rather camp, do it for free at **Campo Alegro,** a small stretch of pine forest at the top of a hill overlooking the town. According to locals, it's a safe place to pitch your tent. To reach the camp, walk up Guadalupe Victoria from either the Flecha Amarilla or Flecha Azul bus stop; once you reach the central church, follow the blue signs with pictures of pine trees on them. If you're hungry, stop at one of the *loncherías* (lunch counters) near the church, or **Café Fonda** (Insurgentes, at Flecha Amarilla bus stop, no phone) for drinks and yogurt. There is also a restaurant in the Hotel Mesón, which has a bar and provides pretty much the only nighttime entertainment in town.

COMING AND GOING Both **Flecha Azul** and **Flecha Amarilla** send buses between Querétaro and San Joaquín (3 hrs, $2.50); the last Flecha Azul bus leaves San Joaquín at 3:30 PM, and Flecha Amarilla's final bus leaves at 4:45 PM.

RUINS

➤ **RANAS** • Strategically located on a high slope, these modest ruins are thought to have served simultaneous functions—as ceremonial center, trading post, and defensive structure. Built between the 7th and 8th centuries, this small city is divided into two parts. The ceremonial center, made up of several pyramids, covers the top of a steep hill. On the flatlands below are a provincial-sized ball court and the remains of what may have been military structures. From ceramic shards found here, archaeologists believe that the original inhabitants had extensive contact with the larger cities of El Tajín (*see* Chapter 11) and Teotihuacán (near Mexico City). The city was abandoned after the 11th century, and taken over by the Chichimeca people sometime in the 16th century. Ranas won't overwhelm you with architectural splendor (its buildings resemble huge party hats), but it will allow you to experience ruins as ruins—not as a touristy reconstructed version of Mexico's indigenous past. To get here from San Joaquín,

"Chichimeca"—the generic name for the nomadic bands who inhabited the northern Bajío—means "lineage of the dog." Actually the term was a compliment, and many Aztec dynasties proudly claimed this heritage.

walk straight up Calle Insurgentes from the Flecha Amarilla bus stop and follow the signs at the top of the small hill; the ruins lie about 3 kilometers from town. You can also hitch rides from the *camioneta* pickup trucks that pass by the Flecha Amarilla stop. Guides are available at the site for tours; they are not paid, so a small donation is appreciated. *Admission: $1.25, 50¢ students. Open daily 9–5.*

➤ **TOLUQUILLA** • Smaller and slightly more remote than Ranas, Toluquilla is similar in its history and architectural style. The ruins here include two ball courts that stretch in succession along the crest of the mountain top, as well as walls and foundations that are thought to have been military fortifications. As at Ranas, the term "lowly workers" was taken literally here—those who cultivated the fields and worked in the mines probably lived below the city. Although the ruins themselves aren't much, the elevation—even higher than at Ranas—provides a glorious view of the Sierra Gorda's blue peaks. It's a tempting campsite, but the guards are not impressed with the idea, and will give you a scary talk about the snakes that live among the ancient structures. To get here, your best bet is to take a camioneta pickup from San Joaquín's Flecha Amarilla station—just tell the driver you want to get off at Toluquilla. Walking will take a good 2½ hours, but if you so desire, walk back out of town along the main road, turn left at the blue sign with the picture of a pyramid on it, and follow the skinny highway. *Admission free. Open daily 10–4.*

San Miguel de Allende

The modest *pueblo* (town) of San Miguel de Allende, in Guanajuato state, seduces newcomers within a matter of days, and it's difficult to explain why. Ask any non-native resident why artists, troubadours, and tourists are drawn to this city and the expatriate is usually at a loss for words. Other towns in Mexico, they will assure you, are more picturesque, have better nightlife, and exhibit a more liberal attitude. Nevertheless, this is a place where people set down roots, whether to study Spanish at one of the language schools; to paint, sculpt, or dance at the Bellas Artes; or simply to live their version of the good life.

Neal Cassady, protagonist of Jack Kerouac's "On The Road," died in San Miguel in 1968 while walking on the railroad tracks.

San Miguel's popularity with foreigners supposedly started after WWII, when the GI Bill offered many Americans the financial means to travel abroad; although all of Mexico was economically appealing, many were specifically drawn to San Miguel by the Instituto Allende, which offered Spanish language and Mexican culture classes. Today the gringo population of San Miguel is one of the largest in Mexico, a fact that causes many travelers to ignore the town in search of "authenticity." This is unfortunate, as not all the expatriates are boorish tourists, disrespectful of Mexican culture; many play crucial roles in San Miguel society, whether by helping maintain the historical integrity of the town or performing social service work. Moreover, the Mexican residents still have a strong hold on local custom, as demonstrated during the many *días de fiesta*. The only negative side effect of the large gringo population is San Miguel's high prices. Otherwise this is the kind of place where a two-day stay can easily stretch into a few weeks, a few months, or even a lifetime.

BASICS

AMERICAN EXPRESS The AmEx representative, **Viajes Vertiz,** won't cash traveler's checks, but emergency check cashing is available. Mail for cardholders will be held if sent to: Hidalgo 1, AP 486, San Miguel de Allende, Guanajuato, CP 37700, México. *½ block north of Plaza Principal, tel. 415/2-18-56. Open weekdays 9-2 and 4-6:30, Sat. 10-2.*

BOOKSTORES **El Colibrí** (Diez de Sollano 30, 1 block east of Plaza Principal, tel. 415/2-07-51; open Mon.–Sat. 10-2 and 4-7), in business for 35 years, supplies an extensive selection of English-language paperbacks and magazines, as well as art supplies. You can also peruse the shelves at **El Tecolote** (Jesus 11, inside Café de la Parroquia, no phone) Monday–Wednesday, Friday, and Saturday 10-5, Sunday 10-2.

CASAS DE CAMBIO Although the Plaza Principal is surrounded by several banks, **Casa de Cambio Deal** (Correo 15, no phone; open weekdays 9-6, Sat. 9-1:45) is your best bet because it doesn't charge a commission and is open longer. **Banamex** (cnr of Canal and Hidalgo) changes cash and traveler's checks and has an ATM.

CONSULATES Canada: *Mesones 3, tel. 415/2-30-25. Open weekdays 10-2.* **United Sates:** *Macías 72, tel. 415/2-23-57, or 415/2-00-68 for emergencies. Open Mon. and Wed. 9-1 and 4-7, Tues. and Thurs. 4-7, or by appointment.*

EMERGENCIES Contact the **police** at 415/2-00-22; for an **ambulance,** call 415/2-16-16.

LAUNDRY **Lava Mágico** will clean a load of clothes for $3. If you drop off your clothes before noon, you'll get them back the same day. *Pila Seca 5, tel. 415/2-08-99. Open daily 8-8.*

MAIL The full-service **post office** will hold mail for up to 10 days if it's sent to you at the following address: Lista de Correos, Correo 18, San Miguel de Allende, Guanajuato, CP 37700, México. *2 blocks east of Plaza Principal, tel. 415/2-00-89. Open weekdays 8-7, Sat. 9-1.*

MEDICAL AID You'll have no trouble finding a pharmacy in San Miguel, but the English-speaking staff at **Botica Agundis** (Canal 26, tel. 415/2-11-98; open daily 10 AM–midnight) is particularly helpful. For more urgent medical assistance, **Hospital de la Fé** (Libramiento a

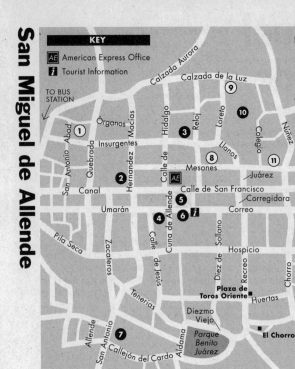

San Miguel de Allende

KEY

AE American Express Office

i Tourist Information

TO BUS STATION

Calzada Aurora

Calzada de la Luz

Órganos

Insurgentes

Hidalgo

Reloj

Loreto

Colegio

Núñez

Cuesta de San Jose

Atascadero

Macías

Hernández

Quebrada

San Antonio Abad

Canal

Umarán

Mesones

Calle de

Juárez

Calle de San Francisco

Corregidora

Correo

Pila Seca

Zacateros

Calle

Cuna de Allende

de Jesús

Tenerías

Diez de Sollano

Recreo

Hospicio

Pedro Vargas

Chorro

Plaza de Toros Oriente

Huertas

Diezmo Viejo

Parque Benito Juárez

El Chorro

Allende

San Antonio

Callejón del Cardo

Aldama

N

Sights ●
Bellas Artes, **2**
Biblioteca Pública, **3**
Instituto Allende, **7**
Jardín Botánico, **12**
Mercado Internacional Ramírez, **10**
El Mirador, **14**
Museo Histórico, **4**
Parroquia de San Miguel Arcángel, **6**
Plaza Principal (El Jardín), **5**

Lodging ○
Casa de Huéspedes, **8**
Hostal Internacional, **1**
Hotel La Huerta, **13**
Hotel Parador de San Sebastián, **11**
Quinta Loreto, **9**

Dolores Hidalgo 43, tel. 415/2–22–33) provides 24-hour medical treatment and can refer you to an English-speaking physician.

PHONES The pay phones in San Miguel are in sad shape, but a couple of **Ladatel** phones cluster around the Plaza Principal. Make long-distance calls from the phones in the **Central de Autobuses** (*see* Coming and Going, *below*). In the center of town, **Caseta de Pepe** (Sollano 4, tel. 415/2–60–61, fax 415/2–62–55; open daily 8 AM–9:30 PM) charges about $1.50 per minute for international calls, but nothing to place a collect call.

SCHOOLS Although people from all over the world descend upon San Miguel for the language and fine arts classes, they often end up speaking more English than Spanish. By studying during the school year instead of the summer, you'll avoid the crowds of English speakers. Schools tend to offer courses in continuous four-week sessions, but most are very willing to structure private lessons according to individual need. If you don't want to commit to an entire course, Spanish classes are also offered at the Hostal Internacional (*see* Where to Sleep, *below*). San Miguel is also the place to learn traditional jewelry making, pottery, and sculpture from local artisans, or to receive lessons in traditional dance.

Academia Hispano Americano (Mesones 4, tel. 415/2–03–49, fax 415/2–23–33, academia@mail.intermex.com.mx) offers Spanish and literature classes, from beginning to advanced levels. Scholarships and homestays are also available. **Bellas Artes/Centro Cultural El Nigromante** (Macías 75, tel. and fax 415/2–02–89) is a fine arts school offering classes in dance, art, and music. For more info, contact Director Carmen Masip de Hawkins at: Macías 75, San Miguel de Allende, Guanajuato, CP 37700, México. **Centro Mexicano de Lengua y Cultura de San Miguel** (Orizaba 15, tel. 415/2–07–63) offers individual or group instruction in Spanish, English, French, or Italian. Write to Josefina Hernandez: Orizaba 15, Col. San Antonio, San Miguel de Allende, Guanajuato, CP 37700, México. **Instituto Allende** (Ancha de San

Antonio 20, tel. 415/2–01–90 or 800/319–3624 from the U.S., ferr@abasolo.ugto.mx) is an internationally recognized fine arts school, but is rumored to be resting on its laurels.

VISITOR INFORMATION Pick up a copy of the local English-language newspaper, *Atención San Miguel* (50¢), for listings of events, religious services, literary discussion groups, and apartment rentals. You can also visit the **tourist office** (south side of Plaza Principal, tel. 415/2–17–47; open weekdays 10–3 and 5–7, weekends 10–2); some of the staff members speak English, and they'll load you down with maps, brochures, and hotel listings.

COMING AND GOING

BY BUS San Miguel de Allende's **Central de Autobuses** lies about 10 minutes from the center of town. The main bus lines here are **Flecha Amarilla** (tel. 415/2–00–84) and **Autotransportes Herradura de Plata** (tel. 415/2–07–25). Both lines provide frequent bus service to Mexico City (3½ hrs, $8), Querétaro (1 hr, $2), Guanajuato (1½ hrs, $2), Dolores Hidalgo (½ hr, $1.25), and San Luis Potosí (6 hrs, $4). The station offers long-distance telephone service (7 AM–11 PM) and luggage storage (7 AM–10 PM) for 50¢ per bag per eight hours. To reach downtown from the station, catch a local bus marked CENTRO.

BY CAR To reach Mexico City (256 km), head east on Highway 111 to the Federal 57 south through Querétaro (69 km) and continue southwest on Highway 57-D. To Guadalajara (376 km), take Federal 51 south to Highway 57-D east, then head east on Federal 110, and then farther east on Federal 90. To San Luis Potosí (160 km), take Federal 57 north.

BY TRAIN Trains are generally slower than buses and less reliable. They leave at 1 PM for Mexico City ($6 1st class, $3 2nd class) and Querétaro ($1.50 1st class, 75/ 2nd class), and to Monterrey at 2:30 PM ($12 1st class, $7 2nd class). The bus marked CENTRO will take you from the train station to the center of town. *Calzada de la Estación, tel. 415/2–00–07. Open for ticket sales daily 1:30–3 PM.*

GETTING AROUND

San Miguel is a small town, and most attractions are easily accessible on foot. Though picturesque, the cobblestone streets are impossibly bumpy and at times very steep—travelers in wheelchairs will have great difficulty here. The central **Plaza Principal** is surrounded by a neat grid of streets, around which all street names change. Bordering the plaza's northern edge is Canal to the west, San Francisco to the east; the southern side is flanked by Umarán to the west and Correo to the east. The only buses you're likely to need are those that run up and down Canal to the bus and train stations; buses run from 7 AM to 10 PM and cost 30¢.

In 1926, the Mexican government declared San Miguel a national monument, rendering it next to impossible to alter anything here (you can thank the government every time you trip over an uneven cobblestone).

WHERE TO SLEEP

Hotels abound within walking distance of the Plaza Principal, with rooms ranging from the impossibly expensive to reasonable. Your best bet, however, is the **Hostal Internacional** (*see* Hostels, *below*). If you're planning an extended stay, check with the tourist office (*see* Visitor Information, *above*) and the bulletin boards in stores and restaurants around town for rental lists. Or check with **Arrentadora San Miguel** (Ancha de San Antonio 21, tel. 415/2–16–38), which lists apartments for rent from $200 to more than $1000 per month. Discounts for prepayment and long-term stays are often available. Homestays are another option (*see* Schools, *above*). The prices listed here apply in the low season. During high season (Oct.–Jan.) hotel prices are jacked up by as much as 100%.

➢ **UNDER $10 • Hotel La Huerta.** Inexpensive rooms ($6 singles, $8.50 doubles) and peace and quiet make up for the 10-minute walk you'll have to make from the Plaza Principal. Rooms are clean and airy and open onto communal sitting rooms. *Cerrada de Becerra, tel.*

415/2–08–81. *From Plaza Principal, 1 block north on Reloj, right on Mesones 5 blocks, right on Atascadero, right on Cerrada de Becerra. 15 rooms, all with bath.*

➤ **UNDER $15** • **Casa de Huéspedes.** The tiled, plant-filled courtyard lends some exoticism to this tiny, friendly guest house. Rooms are large and well-lit, with balconies opening onto the street. The staff is amiable, and there's hot water 24 hours a day. Singles run $6.50, doubles $13. *Mesones 27, tel. 415/2–13–78. 6 rooms, all with bath.*

Hotel Parador de San Sebastián. This family-run establishment is a friendly place to come home to—and the owners have the most lovable dogs. Every room is clean and quaint with antique oak furnishings, and some boast a small kitchen, complete with utensils. Singles cost $8.25, doubles $14. *Mesones 7, no phone. 24 rooms, all with bath. Parking.*

➤ **UNDER $20** • **Quinta Loreto.** Spacious, clean rooms with patios, a large garden, and free use of the pool and tennis court make the Quinta Loreto worth the extra bucks. Upstairs rooms ($14 singles, $16 doubles) have better views, but are hotter than those downstairs. Most guests are foreign tourists. *Loreto 15, tel. 415/2–00–42. 38 rooms, all with bath. AE, MC, V.*

HOSTELS **Hostal Internacional.** This hostel gives you so much for your money, there's no reason *not* to stay here. For $4–$5 (it's cheaper with a hostel card or student ID) you sleep in single-sex dorm rooms and wake up to a free breakfast (there's also coffee and tea all day long), *and* you can use the kitchen facilities. On top of that, there's no curfew. One minuscule detail is that every guest is required to spend about 15 minutes at a chore of their choice. Rooms and bathrooms are cleaner than those in some hotels, and the friendly manager, Michael, gets rave reviews from his guests. He also pays a local teacher to give Spanish lessons (Mon.–Thurs. 4:30 PM–6:30 PM); you can join in for about $6 an hour. Two private rooms are available for $8–$10. *Órganos 34, tel. 415/2–06–74. From Plaza Principal, 1 block west on Canal, right on Macías 3 blocks, and left on Órganos for 3 blocks. Laundry.*

FOOD

One result of the influx of foreigners in San Miguel is the presence of an extraordinary number of restaurants that cater to a wide range of tastes and budgets. Wandering around the downtown area, you'll find just about anything you want, from standard tacos and *tortas* (sandwiches) to Lebanese or Italian food. You can get cheap and tasty baked goods at **Panadería La Espiga** (Insurgentes 9, tel. 415/2–15–80). The **Mercado Ignacio Ramírez** (Av. Colegio, tel. 415/2–28–44) provides *comedores* (sit-down food stands), where you can watch the town's culinary masters prepare staple Mexican fare. Prices are very reasonable and the food stands are generally open until dusk.

➤ **UNDER $5** • **Las Palomas.** Tacos, tostadas, and quesadillas with chicken mole, *nopales* (grilled cactus), or spicy pork fillings are super cheap here—three tacos and a drink come to less than $2. The seating is arranged around the small kitchen so you can watch your food being prepared. *Correo 9, off of Diez de Sollano, no phone. Open Mon., Tues., and Thurs.–Sat. 10–8, Wed. 10–5, Sun. 10–7.*

La Piñata. This unassuming corner diner serves up mountains of cheap food. Scrambled-egg breakfasts, including toast and fresh-squeezed juice, are $1.50; tostadas and burritos cost less than 75¢. Try the sugarcane, grapefruit, or carrot juice for another 75¢. *Jesús 1, tel. 415/2–30–60. 1 block west of Plaza Principal. Open Wed.–Mon. 9–9. Wheelchair access.*

El Ten-ten Pie. This restaurant serves up tacos and burritos (some of them vegetarian) in a relaxing space filled with works by local artisans. The manager guarantees the meat for the 50¢ tacos is fresh and the vegetables are washed in purified water. Try the excellent flan ($1). You can also while away the hours playing chess, dominos, or backgammon. *Cuna de Allende 21, tel. 415/2–71–89. Open daily noon–midnight. Wheelchair access.*

El Tomate. This small, clean eatery has a wonderful all-vegetarian menu; try the *hamburgesa de espinaca* (spinach hamburger) for $3 and you'll never want to eat elsewhere. A huge sign hanging from the kitchen counter assures customers that all vegetables have been sanitized. *Mesones 60, btw Hidalgo and Macías, tel. 415/2–03–25. Open Wed.–Mon. 9–9.*

➤ **UNDER $10** • **Mama Mía.** This open-air patio restaurant filled with huge trees and paper lanterns primarily serves Italian entrées, although some Mexican dish is always available. Small pizzas with tons of cheese are $4.75; pasta dishes run $3–$7. Live Andean or flamenco guitar music starts at 8 PM, making this a great place to eat and sip red wine. Have an after-dinner drink at one of their three bars (*see* After Dark, *below*). *Umarán 8, ½ block west of Plaza Principal, tel. 415/2–20–63. Open Sun.–Thurs. 8 AM–midnight, Fri. and Sat. 8 AM–2 AM.*

CAFÉS Cafés in San Miguel de Allende are mostly gringo hangouts where tourists and expats drink cappuccino. **El Buen Café** (Jesús 23, at Cuadrante, tel. 415/2–58–07; open Mon.–Sat. 9 AM–8 PM) pours excellent coffee for about $1, and prepares sandwiches and crepes for under $5. At **Café de la Parroquia** (Jesús 11, tel. 415/2–31–61; open Mon.–Wed., Fri., and Sat. 7:30 AM–4 PM, Sun. 7:30 AM–2 PM), you can enjoy a scrumptious breakfast of hot cakes or french toast for $1.50. Huge cappuccinos are only $1 and seating is available indoors or out.

WORTH SEEING

BELLAS ARTES/CENTRO CULTURAL EL NIGROMANTE Built in 1765, this former convent now houses a school of fine arts. A peaceful central courtyard and fountain are surrounded by two floors of art workshops and music rooms. Murals by David Siqueiros (contemporary of Diego Rivera) adorn the interior walls, and a small gallery on the first floor exhibits work by local artists. *Macías 75, tel. 415/2–02–89. 1½ blocks west of Plaza Principal. Admission free. Open Mon.–Sat. 9–8, Sun. 10–3.*

On Tuesdays, locals set up La Plazita, a market that stretches for four blocks. Pirated cassette tapes, spangly hair baubles, and nylon underwear share space with pastries and fresh fruit. To get here from the Plaza Principal, walk three blocks west on Canal and turn right on San Antonio Abad.

BIBLIOTECA PUBLICA San Miguel's public library has a great collection of books in both Spanish and English and is a good place to find out what's going on in town. A bulletin board in the foyer announces upcoming events, and the town's English-language newspaper, *Atención San Miguel*, is sold at the front desk, along with some English-language books and current Mexican newspapers and magazines. On Tuesday and Thursday afternoons, people meet in the library's sun-filled courtyard from 5 to 7 for a free, informal English–Spanish exchange. To borrow books, you must plunk down a refundable $30 deposit and supply two passport pictures. Sundays at noon the library sponsors 1½-hour tours of local homes for about $3. *Insurgentes 25, tel. 415/2–02–93. Open weekdays 10–2 and 4–7, Sat. 10–2.*

MUSEO HISTORICO DE SAN MIGUEL DE ALLENDE This former mansion is the birthplace of Ignacio Allende, one of the key figures in Mexico's fight for independence. It's now a museum that exhibits Allende's clothing and personal effects, as well as pre-Columbian artifacts from Guanajuato state. The placards and posters will tell you more than you ever wanted to know about the history of San Miguel. *Cuna de Allende 1, tel. 415/2–24–99. SW cnr of Plaza Principal. Admission free. Open Tues.–Sun. 10–4.*

PARROQUIA DE SAN MIGUEL ARCANGEL Not only is this church worth seeing, but you'd have to be blind *not* to see it. In the 18th century, the parish priest commissioned a stone carver, Cerefino Gutiérrez, to replace the original two-towered facade. Gutiérrez was an indigenous local with no formal training, and so he drew his plans in the sand every day with a stick. The resulting pseudo-Gothic exterior contrasts sharply with the *mudéjar* (Moorish-influenced) interior. *South side of Plaza Principal. Open daily 7 AM–10 PM.*

CHEAP THRILLS

El Mirador (the lookout), up a steep hill and away from the center of town, is a popular place to view the sunset; ask a local to set you in the right direction. The **Parque Juárez** is particularly beautiful, teeming with plants, flowers, and birds. This is also the place to join in a pick-up basketball game. The walk here from the center of town is a pretty one: Facing the church on the zócalo, walk down Diez de Sollano—the street that runs along the left side of the church; after three short blocks, you'll walk right into the park's front gate. Turn left on Calle Tenerías (which passes in front of the park) and walk two blocks uphill to reach **El Chorro,** a series of underground springs enclosed by a colonial building. Peer inside what looks like an old mansion to see the wells that once supplied the town with water. Today, these natural springs function as a "public laundry," where locals gather during the day to wash clothes and occasionally each other. Strolling around the **Mercado Ignacio Ramirez,** behind Plaza Cívica, is definitely a test in sensory overload: Squealing pigs and squawking chickens drown out blaring pop music, while the neon colors of cheap clothing compete with the glowing tones of tomatoes and melons.

For a really cheap thrill, visit the Posada San Francisco (NW cnr of Plaza Principal) and ask to see "El Loco" (if you're a man) or "La Loca" (if you're a woman). The chuckling staff will show you to the darkroom for a hair-raising surprise.

FESTIVALS The birth of the town's namesake, Ignacio Allende, is celebrated January 21 with a military parade. A procession featuring people in comical costumes takes place during the **Fiesta de San Antonio de Padua** (around June 12), which commemorates one of the town's patron saints. The first half of August brings San Miguel's **Festival de Música,** which features classical and jazz musicians from around the world. September 16 is the **Día de la Independencia,** celebrated with a marathon race and a reenactment of Father Hidalgo's "Grito de Dolores" (which signaled the beginning of the Mexican Revolution). The third Saturday in September is **Sanmiguelada,** marked by a wild *corrida de toros* (running of the bulls). On the Friday closest to September 29th, a feast called "La Alborada" is held in honor of **San Miguel Arcángel,** the town's patron saint. The day is celebrated with a parade of *xóchiles* (huge decorations of flowers, plants, and corn) and *concheros* (shell dancers)—cultural remnants of San Miguel's indigenous past.

AFTER DARK

San Miguel's bars and discos will not disappoint those wanting to party; most rock on until about 6 AM. Despite the large gay and lesbian population, conservative state laws prohibit "gay" bars from getting a license. **Villa Jacaranda Cine Bar** (Aldama 53, tel. 415/2–10–15) is a happening club that shows movies in English for about $5 (this price includes one drink). **Laberinto's** (Ancha de San Antonio 7, tel. 415/2–03–62; open Tues.–Sun. 10 PM–3 AM) plays a mix of Latin and American dance music and is always crowded with locals on weekends. Cover charge is $2.50, except on Thursdays and Sundays, when it's free. The coverless **Mama Mia's** (*see* Food, *above*) feaures three full-swing bars every night; stay to the right for a more happening atmosphere of live classic rock, R&B, reggae, and Beatles songs, or party on the roof. The discotheque **El Ring** (Hidalgo 25, 1 block from Plaza Principal; open Tues.–Sun. 9 PM–3 AM) is one of the most popular nightspots in town, complete with flashing laser lights and pulsating music. There's no cover charge for couples, so singles in the know avoid the $3.50 charge by entering into instant relationships at the door.

Cinema Gemelos (Plaza Real de Conde, tel. 415/2–64–08) shows first-run Hollywood movies and has two-for-one nights on Tuesdays and Wednesdays.

OUTDOOR ACTIVITIES

One of the best-kept secrets of San Miguel is the **Jardín Botanico el Charco del Ingenio** (Diez de Sollano 21, tel. 415/2–29–90). This 47-hectare area is located in and around a canyon that offers hours of hiking and climbing opportunities. The newly preserved garden itself features cacti and other succulents, along with other flora typical of the region. You'll also find the ruins of a colonial mill and an aqueduct. To reach the garden, catch a GIGANTE bus from the corner of Colegio and Mesones and get off at the Gigante shopping center. From here, walk west 20 minutes, following the poorly marked signs to the main entrance. Travelers should stick to the sidewalks in order to reach the Jardín rather than trekking through the hills at the end of Calzada de La Luz; several muggings have occurred in the hills. Admission is $1.50.

Eight kilometers outside of San Miguel, on the road to Dolores Hidalgo, lies **La Gruta Balneario** (tel. 415/2–25–30 ext. 145), a local escape for over 30 years. Here, three stone-enclosed mineral pools, each a different temperature, are connected by shallow canals. If you wade into the dark cavern off the middle pool, you'll reach the hot, sensual source—an experience unmatched elsewhere. The cost is a mere $3 and you can rent the whole, candlelit place at night for $30. Open hours are generally 10 AM–1 AM but are negotiable, so call first to make a reservation. The easiest way to get here is by taxi ($13). Or take a bus from the Central de Autobuses toward Dolores or Atotnilco and ask the driver to let you off at the balneario. To get back, wave frantically at any bus going back to San Miguel. The last bus passes the pools around 11:15 PM.

Guanajuato

If you visit only one city in the Bajío, make sure it's Guanajuato—Mexico's colonial jewel. Surrounded by green hills on all sides, the capital city of Guanajuato state seduces travelers with Churrigueresque churches, quiet parks, ornate theaters, colonial mansions, a university, and a flourishing arts tradition— all remnants of a prosperous mining industry. Guanajuato was established as a World Heritage Site in 1988 and today it continues to host a vital culture of resident dancers, musicians, and university students. The city's winding streets and subterranean roadways (built by miners in 1960) may make it easy to get lost, but you probably won't be in any hurry to leave.

The Festival Internacional Cervantino, held in mid-October, is an event NOT to be missed. Guanajuato erupts into one sprawling stage, where artists, musicians, and dance troupes from around the world gather to honor former resident Miguel de Cervantes, author of Don Quixote.

Besides Guanajuato city's significance as a major silver-mining town, it was also the scene of the first major military confrontation between rebel forces and royalist troops on September 28, 1810; monuments to the city's revolutionary heroes are everywhere. The town of **Dolores Hidalgo,** where Padre Miguel Hidalgo issued the famous "Grito de Dolores" is only an hour away, as is Pozos, an abandoned mining town ripe for exploration. In addition to the city's historical importance, Guanajuato is distinguished by a number of unusual points of interest, including the **Museo de las Momias,** a bizarre museum exhibiting well-preserved human corpses, and the home in which artist Diego Rivera was born.

BASICS

AMERICAN EXPRESS This office provides standard cardholder services and will cash AmEx traveler's checks. Cardholder mail should be sent to: Viajes Georama, Plaza de la Paz 34, Guanajuato, Guanajuato, CP 36000, México. *Across from Plaza de la Paz, tel. 473/2–51–01 or 473/2–51–02. Open weekdays 9–2 and 5–7, Sat. 10–1.*

BOOKSTORES Though there are no English-language bookstores in Guanajuato, the chain store **Librería de Cristal** supplies a great selection of literature, textbooks, and music in Spanish. *Plaza Agora del Baratillo 4, tel. 473/2–24–48. NW side of Jardín de la Unión. Open Mon.–Sat. 10–9, Sun. noon–8.*

CASAS DE CAMBIO **Banamex** (Plaza de los Ángeles, tel. 473/2–08–00) cashes traveler's checks and provides currency exchange weekdays 9–1:30. Its ATM accepts Visa, Cirrus, Plus, and MasterCard. **Centro Cambiario** (Plaza de la Compañía 2, in front of post ofice, tel. 473/2–50–91) has similar rates but better hours: weekdays 9–5, Saturday 9–1.

EMERGENCIES The phone number of the **police** station is 473/2–02–66; the **Cruz Roja** (ambulance service) is 473/2–04–87.

LAUNDRY **Lavandería del Centro** will wash, dry, and fold 3 kilos of laundry for $3. *Sopeña 26, near Museo Iconográfico del Quijote, tel. 473/2–06–80. From Jardín de la Unión, head west on Juárez. Open weekdays 9–8:45, Sat. 9–4.*

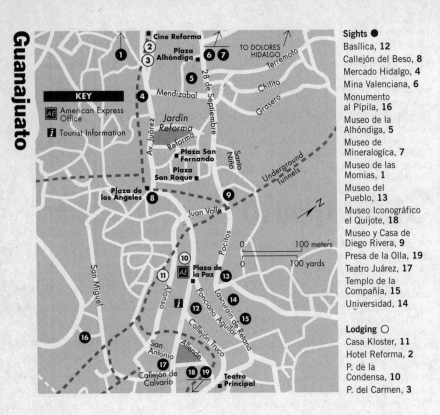

Sights ●

Basílica, **12**
Callejón del Beso, **8**
Mercado Hidalgo, **4**
Mina Valenciana, **6**
Monumento
al Pípila, **16**
Museo de la
Alhóndiga, **5**
Museo de
Mineralogíca, **7**
Museo de las
Momias, **1**
Museo del
Pueblo, **13**
Museo Iconográfico
el Quijote, **18**
Museo y Casa de
Diego Rivera, **9**
Presa de la Olla, **19**
Teatro Juárez, **17**
Templo de la
Compañía, **15**
Universidad, **14**

Lodging ○

Casa Kloster, **11**
Hotel Reforma, **2**
P. de la
Condensa, **10**
P. del Carmen, **3**

MAIL The city's post office is near the University of Guanajuato. Mail will be held for you for up to 10 days if sent to the following address: Lista de Correos, Guanajuato, Guanajuato, CP 36000, México. *Ayuntamiento 25, tel. 473/2–03–85. Open weekdays 8–7, Sat. 9–1.*

MEDICAL AID **Hospital Regional de Guanajuato** (Carretera Guanajuato Cilao, tel. 473/3–15–73 or 473/3–15–76) provides 24-hour medical service and a few English-speaking doctors. Pharmacies rotate the 24-hour shift, so check with the tourist office (*see* Visitor Information, *below*) for current listings, or ask any pharmacist. **Farmacia Santa Fé** (Plaza de la Paz 52, tel. 473/2–01–70) gives discounts on prescriptions.

PHONES **Ladatel** phones are sprinkled all along Juárez and on the northeast side of the Jardín de la Unión. International collect calls at **Caseta Selene Miscelanea** (Juárez 110; open Mon.–Sat. 10 AM–11 PM) cost $2.

SCHOOLS The **University of Guanajuato** (tel. 473/2–72–53) has an exchange program with several American universities, but you don't have to be affiliated with any of them to take Spanish-language and literature classes at its **Centro de Idiomas.** Programs are in semester units and run July–December and January–June, although you can start up at any time. Four-week intensive Spanish-language summer sessions are also available: The registration fee is $110 and courses cost a whopping $400. Homestays with local families can be arranged. For registration information, contact: Lic. Patricia Begne, Centro de Idiomas, Universidad de Guanajuato, Lascurain de Retana 5, Guanajuato, Guanajuato, CP 36000, México.

The **Instituto Falcón** (tel. 473/2–36–94) is highly recommended by former attendees. All levels of Spanish language classes are offered, in addition to courses on Mexican culture and history. The registration fee is $75 and weekly tuition ranges $50–$150 for one-on-one instruction (depending on number of sessions per day) but prices drop considerably for small groups. Homestays are also available. For information, write to Jorge Barroso, Registrar, Instituto Falcón A.C., Callejón de la Mara 158, Guanajuato, Guanajuato, CP 36000, México.

VISITOR INFORMATION The staff at the **tourist information office** (Plaza de la Paz 14, near Basílica, tel. 473/2–88–75 or 473/2–15–74) is happy to answer questions and hand you a free map. The office is open weekdays 8–8, weekends 10–2.

COMING AND GOING

BY BUS The **Central de Autobuses** (Carretera Guanajuato Cilao Km. 8, tel. 473/2–71–45) is served by four main lines: **Omnibús de México** (tel. 473/3–13–56), **Flecha Amarilla** (tel. 473/3–13–33), **Estrella Blanca** (tel. 473/3–13–44), and **Primera Plus** (tel. 473/3–13–33). Buses to Mexico City (4½ hrs, $10) leave seven times daily. Buses also leave frequently for León (1 hr, $1), San Miguel de Allende (1½ hrs, $2.50), Dolores Hidalgo (1½ hrs, $1), and San Luis Potosí (5 hrs, $5.25). From mid-morning to mid-afternoon, buses leave for Querétaro (3 hrs, $4.50), Guadalajara (5 hrs, $7), and Morelia (4 hrs, $5). Luggage storage (50¢ per hr) is available 7 AM–9:30 PM. The bus station is 6 kilometers west of the city; to get here from downtown, catch a bus marked CENTRAL on Juárez in front of Plaza de la Paz. To reach the center of town from the station, take a bus marked CENTRO.

BY CAR To reach Mexico City (374 km), take Federal 110 south to Highway 45-D east towards Querétaro (136 km); just outside Querétaro, catch Highway 57-D straight to the capital. Tolls run a total of $20. To Guadalajara (294 km), take Federal 110 south and then Federal 90 west till you hit the city.

GETTING AROUND

Whoever planned—or rather, didn't plan—this city was playing a mischievous joke on the uptight proponents of the simple grid system. You're gonna get lost. The most important street to remember is **Avenida Juárez,** the main thoroughfare. As you head east from Jardín Reforma, Juárez turns into Obregón and then Sopeña near the main plaza, **Jardín de la Unión.** Most directions to Guanajuato's sites use the Jardín as a reference point. City buses run 6 AM–10 PM and cost 30¢.

In keeping with the illogical layout of the city, Guanajuato's main square, Jardín de la Unión, is actually a triangle and is therefore also known as the "slice of cheese."

WHERE TO SLEEP

Most budget hotels are located along Avenida Juárez, between the train station and the Cine Reforma. Conveniently, this area is also near many of the city's attractions and much of the action. As you continue east along Juárez toward the Jardín de la Unión, accommodations become more attractive and more expensive. If you're planning to come in September or mid-October, when the Cervantes Festival is raging, you must make reservations 4–6 months in advance. When hotels are packed, the tourist office will provide information on families who will house travelers for low prices.

Casa Kloster. If you can live with a few house rules, this wholesome hotel is your best option. Run by the hospitable Pérez family, it features clean rooms, spotless communal bathrooms, and an interior courtyard filled with plants and chirping birds. Couples must be discreet (what Grandma doesn't know won't hurt her) and nighttime silence is strictly enforced. Nevertheless, this place is always full of backpack-toting gringos, so be sure to call ahead. Rooms are $6.50 per person. *Alonso 32, tel. 473/2–00–88. 18 rooms, 1 with bath.*

Hotel Reforma. This a true budget hotel, with saggy beds and makeshift showers, but the staff is pleasant and the rooms are clean. Singles go for $4, doubles $8. For $3 more, you can have a room with a TV. *Juárez 113, no phone. 30 rooms, all with bath. Luggage storage.*

Posada de la Condesa. This posada is much cheaper than most of its neighbors in this area. Rooms are cramped but clean, and all have private baths; the hot water takes awhile. Singles and doubles cost $5.50. *Plaza de la Paz 60, tel. 473/2–14–62. 22 rooms, all with bath.*

Posada del Carmen. Run by a friendly, professional staff, this clean and cheerful place even does laundry at just $1.50 per kilo. Off-season prices are $6.50 for a single, $12 for a double; prices go up during the Cervantes festival. *Juárez 111-A, tel. 473/2–93–30. 17 rooms, all with bath. Wheelchair access.*

FOOD

Restaurants cluster along Avenida Juárez and the surrounding streets. A number of cheap food stands serve up cheap grub at **Mercado Hidalgo** (Juárez, btw Cine Reforma and Jardín Reforma), in the ornate former train station. For a strange sweet treat, try *momias*—a hard, mummy-shaped sugarcane candy that is sold both at the **Museo de las Momias** (*see* Worth Seeing, *below*) and stores around town. Close to the Jardín de la Unión is **Pastelería de la Paz** (Plaza de la Paz 53, tel. 473/2–18–69), which sells scrumptious baked treats as early as 6:30 AM. For you coffee addicts who are wilting from that instant Nescafé stuff, **café dadá** (Hidalgo 6, no phone; open Mon.–Sat. 8:30 AM–10 PM, Sun. noon–11) is your revival spot. Fifty-cent coffees made from freshly roasted coffee beans are the best around. This place is also great for hearing about recent U.S. news, since the owner and many patrons are American.

El Café Galería. Multicolored walls, ceilings decorated with Mexican artesanía, and vibrant paintings create a comfortable environment. Yogurt with fruit and granola runs $1.50, while hamburgers and most appetizers, including *tortilla española* go for $2. *Sopeña 10, tel. 473/2–25–66. Open daily 8:30 AM–10:30 PM.*

El Chahuistle. Start the night out at this hole in the wall, which serves 14 different types of tacos for 25¢ a pop and filling pozole for $1.50. *Constancia 6, behind Teatro Juárez, no phone. Open Mon.–Sat. 7 PM–midnight.*

Restaurant El Agora del Baratillo. This restaurant near Jardín de la Unión offers patio dining complete with wrought-iron tables covered with checkered tablecloths. The comida corrida ($5.50) is more expensive than any entrée on the menu, but that's because it also includes a glass of wine. Breakfast chilaquiles also come with fruit, yogurt, and coffee—all for $2. *Jardín de la Unión 4, tel. 473/2–33–00. Near Hotel Posada San José. Open daily 8 AM–9 PM. Kitchen closes at 5:30 PM.*

Tasca de los Santos. This candlelit restaurant near the basilica features tasty Spanish food and attentive waiters. The *pollo al vino blanco* (chicken in white wine; $5) and the $3 *tapas* (Spanish appetizers) come recommended. *Plaza de la Paz 28, off Juárez, tel. 473/2–23–20. Open daily 8:30 AM–11:30 PM.*

WORTH SEEING

Getting lost in Guanajuato is, strangely enough, one of the more enjoyable things to do in the city. Most sights are near the center of town and are easy to see in a few days on foot. The maze of twisting *callejones* (alleyways) provides exciting opportunities to see the less-explored parts of the city.

Guanajuato's name comes from the Tarascan name "Quanas-huato," roughly meaning "place of many frogs."

BASILICA The baroque facade of the **Basílica Colegiata de Nuestra Señora de Guanajuato** is painted a buttery yellow and resembles one of the pastries sold at the nearby Pastelería de la Paz (*see* Food, *above*). Constructed in 1693, the basilica is illuminated by sparkling crystal chandeliers, and houses a bejeweled wooden statue of the Virgin, said to be the oldest existing Christian statue in Mexico. *Plaza de la Paz, near Juárez. Open daily 8–8.*

MINA VALENCIANA AND TEMPLO LA VALENCIA Founded in 1557, this prosperous mine used to produce 20% of the world's silver and a fair share of other minerals. Although its yield isn't as extravagant today, each of the 48 miners that work the cooperative mine dig up 7,257–18,143 kilograms (8–20 tons) of silver a day—proving that it is still Mexico's top producer. Tour guides proudly explain the architecture and history of the mine (for $1.50), but you won't get to go into it. The mine is open for visitors 8–7 and admission is 30¢. On the way here, you'll pass the **Templo La Valenciana** (also called Templo de San Cayetano), a product of all the wealth accumulated from the mine. Legend has it that a Spanish owner of the mine had promised St. Cayetano that he would build a church to honor the saint if the mine proved profitable. Another version claims that the construction of the church was motivated by guilt for all the indigenous people who died working the mine. The templo's Churrigueresque exterior is nothing compared to the five gold-leafed altars waiting inside; open hours are Tuesday–Sunday 9–7. *Catch a* VALENCIANA *bus from Plaza Alhóndiga, on 5 de Mayo. Buses leave every ½ hr.*

MUSEO DE LA ALHONDIGA DE GRANADITAS In the 18th century, grain was stored in this massive stone building. During the first major battle of the War of Independence, supporters of Spanish rule hid here, hoping to hold out until Royalist forces arrived. The strategy backfired when a miner known as *El Pípila,* ordered by Padre Miguel Hidalgo, set the granary's door ablaze, allowing the rebel fighters to swarm in and massacre almost all of the loyalists. When several rebel leaders (including Allende and Hidalgo) were later captured and decapitated, their heads were displayed on large hooks that are still visible on the building's exterior. Later, under Emperor Maximilian, the building became a jail. Today it's a museum that houses several excellent exhibits on Guanajuato's history. Contemporary art is displayed on the lower level, and huge, colorful murals by José Chávez Morado grace the stairwells. The collection of pre-Columbian clay stamps and seals is also interesting and may give you some ideas for that tattoo you've been thinking of getting. *28 de Septiembre 7, tel. 473/2–11–12. Admission: $1.50; free for students and on Sun. Open Tues.–Sat. 10–2 and 4–6, Sun. 10–2:30. Free guided tours in Spanish Tues.–Fri.*

MUSEO DE LAS MOMIAS About a century ago, greedy bureaucrats decided to dig up the city's graveyards, leaving only those whose descendants paid burial-plot fees—apparently the dead just weren't paying their fair share of taxes. As it turned out, special properties of Guanajuato's soil have a preservative effect, and the recovered bodies remained in excellent con-

El Callejón del Beso

For a few coins, the young men lingering around the "Alley of the Kiss" will tell you the following legend: A young woman named Doña Carmen, the only child of a violent father, fell in love with a man named Don Luis. When her father found out about the courtship, he threatened to marry her off to a rich, old Spaniard. The alleyway that separated Doña Carmen's house from the one across the way was so narrow that the houses almost touched, so Don Luis arranged to buy the neighboring house for a steep price. One starry night, as Doña Carmen went out onto her balcony, she was pleasantly surprised by the nearness of her lover. The enraged voice of Doña Carmen's father surprised them, however, and the father proceeded to plunge a dagger into his daughter's heart. Don Luis was only able to lean over and leave a kiss on her lifeless hand. Then, distraught with grief, he took his own life. Current tradition holds that if you kiss your loved one on the third step up to the balcony on which Don Luis died, you'll enjoy seven years of good luck. Lone females need not fear, however—one of the men standing by will undoubtedly offer to stand in as a temporary romantic interest. To reach the alley from the Jardín de la Unión, walk west on Juárez to Plaza de los Ángeles, go up Callejón del Patrocinio, and take a left on Callejón del Beso.

Like food from street vendors, a visit to the mummy museum is a pleasure for strong stomachs.

dition. The cadavers, complete with remnants of hair and skin (feeling queasy yet?), were judged fit for display in a local museum, which now has 108 mummified bodies in various states of undress. If you speak Spanish, be sure to take the guided tour to find out which mummy died from an attempted C-section, which one was hung, and which one was buried alive. *Esplanada del Panteón, tel. 473/2–06–39. Take* MOMIAS *bus to end of line. Admission: $2.50, $1.50 students; small donation for tour. Open Tues.–Sun. 9–6.*

MUSEO DE MINERALOGIA An exquisite array of over 20,000 different minerals awaits you at this impressive museum. The collection of rare minerals, including some found only in Guanajuato, will bedazzle any rock-lover. *Ex-Hacienda de San Matías, tel. 473/2–38–64. Catch* PRESA–SAN JAVIER *bus from cnr of 5 de Mayo and 28 de Septiembre and get off at Escuela de Minas campus. Open weekdays 9–1 and 4:30–7.*

MUSEO ICONOGRAFICO DEL QUIJOTE This shrine to Cervantes features hundreds of depictions of scenes from *Don Quixote* by a variety of artists, including Dalí and José Chávez Morada. *Manuel Doblado 1, tel. 473/2–67–21. From Jardín de la Unión, 1½ blocks up Sopeña. Admission free. Open Tues.–Sat. 10–6:30, Sun. 10–3.*

MUSEO Y CASA DE DIEGO RIVERA Muralist Diego Rivera was born in this redbrick house and lived here until he was six. Now beautifully restored, the museum displays some original furnishings, including the bed in which Rivera and his twin brother (who died in infancy) were born. The upper floors contain an excellent selection of Rivera's art, including work from various periods of his life. You can also see temporary exhibits of Mexican crafts; films (mostly in Spanish) are shown for free Tuesdays and Saturdays. *Calle de los Pocitos 47, near Plaza de la Paz, tel. 473/2–11–97. Admission: 75¢. Open Tues.–Sat. 10–1:30 and 4–6:30, Sun. 10–2:30. Free tours in Spanish Tues.–Fri.*

TEATRO JUAREZ The late 19th-century Juárez Theater is one of the most impressive buildings in Guanajuato. The neoclassical exterior features Doric columns, bronze lions, and giant statues of the muses. Inside, opulent decorations and walls hung with red and gold velvet exhibit Moorish and French influences. The theater now serves as the principal venue of the annual Cervantes Festival. Classical music concerts are held here Thursdays at 8:30 PM for $1–$3. Outside the theater, university students gather to gossip and flirt on the steps in the early evening. *Jardín de la Unión, tel. 473/2–01–83. Open Tues.–Sun. 9–1:45 and 5–7:45, later during performances.*

UNIVERSIDAD DE GUANAJUATO Founded as a Jesuit seminary in 1732, this institution became a state university in 1945 and serves as a good place to find out about the most current goings-on. Notices advertising lectures, films, art exhibits, and concerts are posted on bulletin boards everywhere, and on the right side of the entrance is a small, free gallery with temporary exhibits of contemporary art. *Lascurain de Retana 5, near Basílica, tel. 473/2–01–74. Closed weekends.*

Next to the University is the **Templo de la Compañía** (Lascurain de Retana; open daily 8 AM–6 PM), an elaborate baroque cathedral left over from the university's Jesuit days. Inside you'll find lots of scary religious art—check out the flayed and bloodied Jesus (complete with burned feet) housed in a glass box near the entrance. On the opposite side of the university is the **Museo del Pueblo** (Calle de Los Pocitos 7, tel. 473/2–29–90; open Tues.–Sat. 10–2 and 4–7, Sun. 10–3), which displays contemporary art on the first floor and has a small collection of colonial art upstairs. Admission is 50¢.

CHEAP THRILLS

If hiking around town has proved less than stimulating, the hills surrounding Guanajuato will get your heart rate up in no time. The hills behind **La Presa de la Olla** can make for a spiritual, if not desolate, experience. Getting here by foot takes about 30 minutes, but the hike is half the fun. From Jardín de la Unión, walk left on Sopeña to Sostens Rocha, which curves left and passes the ultra-shady **Jardín Embajadores**. Then follow Paseo Madero south as it curves into

Paseo de la Presa, an area lined by elegant colonial mansions. Follow Paseo de la Presa past the well-groomed **Parque Florencio Antillon** and the Presa de San Renovato until, at last, you hit Presa de la Olla—whew! A couple of food stands and restaurants at the top serve as filling stations where you can stock up on water and other necessities for more vigorous trekking. Camping, however, is not advised—thieves and Chupacabras (a mythical goat-sucking alien) are known to stalk the area. A much shorter but nevertheless exhausting hike leads up San Miguel hill to the **Monumento al Pípila,** which honors the miner responsible for setting fire to the door of the Alhóndiga de Granaditas (*see* Worth Seeing, *above*). After conquering the steep, 10-minute climb up the steps you'll be rewarded with a stupendous view of the city. For 30¢, you can climb to the top of the monument from the inside. From Jardín de la Unión, walk left on Sopeña about 1½ blocks, and turn right on Callejón del Calvario; look for the SUBITA AL PIP-ILA sign. The monument is open daily 9–8. If you still hunger for more rugged terrain, talk to some of the regulars at café dadá (*see* Food, *above*); they'll be more than happy to provide details on lesser-known paths.

AFTER DARK

Guanajuato is a lively place at night, when crowds fill the streets, pushing, laughing, cavorting, and flirting. On weekends at Jardín de la Unión, locals of all ages gather on the steps of the Teatro Juárez to see the student group *Las Estudiantinas* perform. The group dresses in troubador garb and strums traditional instruments; the audience sings along at the top of their lungs and then follows the Estudiantinas as they make their way through the streets. To catch an international film, try the Teatro Juárez or the **Teatro Principal** (Hidalgo, near Allende, tel. 473/2–15–23), which regularly runs international films. If a peña is more your speed, head to **El Rincón del Beso** (Alonso 21-A, tel. 473/2–59–12; open Mon.–Sat. 7 PM–4 AM), a dimly lit, intimate bar that features live Latin folk music. Before, during, and after the show, the crowd is encouraged to sing along and even display their own musical or poetic talents. Occasionally, musicians playing for high prices at theaters around town stop in for a spontaneous post-show concert. Music usually starts at 10, but show up earlier if you want to get a good seat. **El Retiro** (Sopeña 12, tel. 473/2–06–22; open Mon.–Sat. 1 PM–midnight) is a mellow place most party-hoppers hit sometime during the night. The crowd is predominantly Mexican, with a smattering of American students.

For a mellow evening of people-watching and free local music, grab a beer and head for the Jardín de la Unión on Thursday and Sunday evenings around 7 PM.

BARS AND CLUBS With big, comfortable wooden tables, excellent background music, and good cappuccino, **Café Truco 7** (Callejón del Truco 7, tel. 473/2–83–74; open daily 8:30 AM–11:30 PM) is a comfortable joint popular with university students. Though the atmosphere is best at night, you can also grab breakfast or a light lunch here for under $5. At **La Dama de las Camelias** (Sopeña 32, east of Jardín de la Unión, no phone), the walls are adorned with women's dresses and shoes from the first half of the century. Be sure to ask the owner about the history of the colonial window in the corner—it's his pride and joy. Drinks are $1–$2, and the bar is open Monday–Saturday 8 PM–dawn. Crowds of amorous students fill the **Guanajuato Grill** (Alonso 4, tel. 473/2–02–87; open daily 8 PM–3 AM). The thumping Mexican and American pop music pretty much precludes conversation, but that's hardly the point. Beers are about $2, and by night's end the crowd is usually singing and dancing on the tables. From Jardín de la Unión, south on San Antonio, then right on Alonso.

Near Guanajuato

DOLORES HIDALGO

The town of Dolores Hidalgo's principal claim to faim is the "Grito de Dolores," the speech given by Padre Miguel Hidalgo in front of the town's main church on September 16, 1810. Shortly before this, the Spanish had been tipped off to Ignacio Allende's plans to overthrow the government. Fortunately, Doña Josefa Ortíz, the magistrate's wife in Querétaro and sympathizer to Allende's cause, managed to notify Juan de Aldama, a fellow conspirator of Allende before Spain could take action. Aldama then ran to the town of Dolores and gave word to Padre Miguel Hidalgo. That night, Hidalgo rang the church bell, gathered his parishoners together on the steps of the town's main church, and gave the famous "Grito de Dolores," a speech powerful enough to ignite the armed struggle for Mexico's independence from Spain. The "Grito" was

Helados Torres, on Dolores Hidalgo's Plaza Principal, offers Corona, avocado, and even chicharrón (pork rind) ice cream for about $1.50 a cone.

sounded at the **Parroquia de Nuestra Señora de los Dolores** (on the Plaza Principal; open daily 7–2 and 4–8), which flaunts a lovely Churrigueresque facade that contrasts with the plain interior. Hidalgo's former house, the **Casa de Don Miguel Hidalgo** (Morelos, near Hidalgo; admission $1.75) is now a museum exhibiting documents from the independence movement, including the order for Hidalgo's excommunication from the church. The **Museo de la Independencia** (Zacatecas 6; admission 75¢) houses a series of impressive paintings depicting the struggle for independence. Both museums are open Tuesday–Saturday 10–5:45 and are free for students and on Tuesdays. This town is also a center for ceramic ware, making it a good place to go bargain hunting for tiles. Dolores is best visited as a day trip from either San Miguel de Allende (40 km away) or Guanajuato (50 km away). Flecha Amarilla buses leave every 20 minutes from the Central de Autobuses in each city.

LEÓN

When you think León, think shoes. Think leather goods, such as purses, belts, and jackets, and then start thinking about shoes again. León is a huge, fast-paced, smoggy, and industrial city. The most attractive part of this metropolis is the **Zona Peatonal**, where centuries-old buildings, like the **Palacio del Gobierno** and the **Parroquia del Sagrario**, sit side by side with modern high-rises and, yes, the omnipresent shoe stores. In this city, rarely frequented by tourists, you may find yourself the object of some incredulous stares, but León is definitely the place to find fantastic bargains. Flecha Amarilla buses leave from Guanajuato's and San Miguel's Central de Autobuses roughly every 10 minutes. The trip takes about 2½ hours ($1).

POZOS

Established as a mining camp in 1576, Pozos suffered a drop in population from 10,000 to 500 in the 19th century, when the mines were abandoned. Pozos is now something of a ghost town, a mystical, rustic place with buildings overrun by cacti. The opportunity to explore these deserted structures, coupled with the fresh crisp air, is the principal reason to visit. The **museum** on Ocampo, one block up from the **Plaza Principal,** is staffed by friendly folks who

Pozos is named for the craters found at the outskirts of town. Drop a rock into one, and it will be seven or eight long seconds before you hear it hit the bottom.

like to talk about Pozos's famed reproductions of pre-Columbian instruments; these include the *palo de lluvia* (rain stick), a decorative snake-shaped instrument filled with beads that make a gushing sound when turned upside down. The sticks represent the feathered serpent god Quetzalcoatl.

In an attempt to preserve Pozos's colonial remnants, Teresa Martínez and Juan José Arroyo (the unofficial resident historians) have opened two hotels: the luxurious **Hotel Casa Mexicana** (tel. 468/8–25–98 ext. 119), which charges a whopping $40 per person, and the **Hidalgo Bed and Breakfast** (Hidalgo 15, 2 blocks from Plaza Principal, tel. 468/8–25–98 ext. 116), which offers five spacious rooms and a communal bathroom for $12 per person (breakfast included). You can camp camp in town for about $1–$2. Talk to Teresa or Juan José to arrange camping, hiking, or horseback riding. To reach Pozos, take a Flecha Amarilla bus from either Guanajuato or San Miguel de Allende to San Luis de La Paz (1½ hrs, $4). From there, hop on a city bus, take a taxi, or call Teresa or Juan José for the 10-minute ride into Pozos.

Morelia

The capital of Michoacán state, Morelia is a product of its colonial past. From the gracefully arching walkways to the blocks and blocks of beige stone buildings with shady, foliage-studded courtyards, this expanding city (with a population near one million) manages to maintain dignity despite the crowds, traffic, and multitudes of street vendors. Although much of Morelia's architecture evokes the past, the city lives jubilantly in the present, and plaza-side cafés and a progressive arts scene lend Morelia a cultured air. On the streets, longhaired youths wearing their requisite Metallica T-shirts mingle with *campesinos* (rural dwellers) from surrounding villages, creating an unmistakable contrast. You'll also see relatively few foreign tourists: Although it's a popular vacation spot for Mexicans, the city remains largely unknown to the rest of the world.

Every year during Carnaval (late February or early March), a group of Morelian musicians and dancers perform a bullfight reenactment called the "toritos de petate," with a fake bull and a man in drag.

Founded in 1541 by the Spanish, who named it Valladolid, the city became the provincial capital in 1580. The city's name was changed to Morelia in 1828, in honor of José María Morelos y Pavón, born here in 1765. Unlike previous revolutionaries who were of the middle class, Morelos was a mestizo serf, thereby garnering unprecedented support from the Mexcian people. Although his personal fight for Mexico's independence ended when Morelos died, his aspirations were faithfully carried out until his dream materialized. Monuments, streets, and museums commemorate the city's independence-minded namesake and make for a good crash course in early 19th-century Mexican history. Special events include Morelos's birthday on September 30 and **Aniversario de Morelia** on May 18, both of which entail parades and fireworks. **Feria Regional de Morelia,** during the first two weeks in May, has little directly to do with Morelos, but it's a great time to check out a bullfight or a regional dance.

BASICS

AMERICAN EXPRESS **Gran Turismo Viajes** provides all services for cardholders, including emergency check cashing and holding mail if sent to the following address: Carmelinas 3233, Las Américas, Morelia, Michoacán, CP 58270, México. *1st floor of Bancomer building, across from Gigante shopping center, tel. 43/24–04–84. From downtown, take RUTA ROJA 1 combi west. Open weekdays 9–2 and 4–6, Sat. 10–2.*

BOOKSTORES **Bazar Ocampo** is a dusty bookstore with a decent collection of used English books. Don't despair: Somewhere between *The Sensuous Woman* and *The Sensuous Man* are hidden a few intellectually stimulating paperbacks. Pay $1 for paperbacks or exchange yours at a two-for-one rate. *Melchor Ocampo 242, no phone. From Plaza de Armas, 1 block north on Juárez, left on Melchor Ocampo. Open daily 9–8; sometimes closed 2–4 on weekends.*

CASAS DE CAMBIO Banks that change traveler's checks and cash are plentiful near the cathedral. **Banamex** (Madero Ote. 63, tel. 43/12–27–70) changes cash and traveler's checks weekdays 9–5 and has an ATM that accepts Cirrus and Plus cards. For similar rates and less of a wait, visit **Casa de Cambio Majapara** (166 Pino Suárez, at 20 de Noviembre, tel. 43/13–23–46), open weekdays 8:30–6:30, Saturdays 8:30–2.

EMERGENCIES Contact the **police** (Revolución, at 20 de Noviembre) at 43/12–22–22. For an ambulance, call the **Cruz Roja** (Ventura Puente 270) at 43/14–51–51.

MAIL The full-service main post office will hold mail sent to you at the following address for up to 10 days: Lista de Correos, Morelia, Michoacán, CP 58000, México. *Madero Ote. 369, tel. 43/12–05–17. 3 blocks east of Plaza de Armas. Open weekdays 8–7, Sat. 9–1.*

The **Universidad Michoacána** (*see* Schools, *below*) offers Internet services for about $10 a month. Ask for Enrique. *Sala de Computo, Edificio M, top floor, no phone. Open weekdays 10–3 and 5–8.*

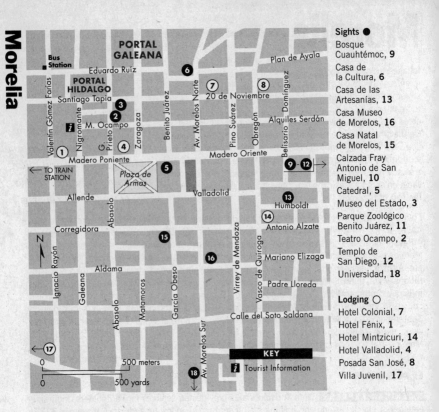

Bus Station

PORTAL GALEANA

Eduardo Ruíz

PORTAL HILDALGO

Santiago Tapia

Valentín Gómez Farías

Nigromante

M. Ocampo

G. Prieto

Zaragoza

Benito Juárez

Av. Morelos Norte

20 de Noviembre

Pino Suárez

Obregón

Belisario Domínguez

Plan de Ayala

Alquiles Serdán

Madero Oriente

Madero Poniente

← TO TRAIN STATION

Plaza de Armas

Valladolid

Allende

Abasolo

Corregidora

Ignacio Rayón

Galeana

Aldama

Abasolo

Matamoros

García Obeso

Virrey de Mendoza

Vasco de Quiroga

Humboldt

Antonio Alzate

Mariano Elizaga

Padre Lloreda

Calle del Soto Saldana

Av. Morelos Sur

N

⑥ ⑦ ⑧ ③ ② ① ④ ⑤ ⑨ ⑫ ⑬ ⑭ ⑮ ⑯ ⑰ ⑱

0   500 meters
0   500 yards

KEY

ℹ Tourist Information

Sights ●

Bosque Cuauhtémoc, **9**

Casa de la Cultura, **6**

Casa de las Artesanías, **13**

Casa Museo de Morelos, **16**

Casa Natal de Morelos, **15**

Calzada Fray Antonio de San Miguel, **10**

Catedral, **5**

Museo del Estado, **3**

Parque Zoológico Benito Juárez, **11**

Teatro Ocampo, **2**

Templo de San Diego, **12**

Universidad, **18**

Lodging ○

Hotel Colonial, **7**

Hotel Fénix, **1**

Hotel Mintzicuri, **14**

Hotel Valladolid, **4**

Posada San José, **8**

Villa Juvenil, **17**

MEDICAL AID   **Hospital Civil** (Isidro Huarte, at Fray de Margil, tel. 43/12–22–16), near the Bosque Cuauhtémoc, is open 24 hours a day. **Farmacia Central** (tel. 43/13–67–94), located at the west end of the bus station (*see* Coming and Going, *below*), is open around the clock.

PHONES   Make long-distance collect calls and send and receive faxes at either of **Computel**'s two central locations: one in the bus station (fax 43/13–92–81) and the other across the street from the cathedral (Portal Galeana 156, fax 43/13–62–56; open Mon.–Sat. 7 AM–10 PM). **Ladatel** phones are hard to come by, but there are a few in working order at the post office (*see* Mail, *above*). Make collect calls at any phone by dialing 09 for the international operator.

SCHOOLS   At the **Departamento de Idiomas** of Universidad Michoacána de San Nicolás de Hidalgo, short-term Spanish language classes begin on the first day of every month. Fees are $100 for one month but become cheaper depending on enrollment. Semester-long courses in Purépecha (the indigenous regional language), Mexican literature, history, and philosophy are also offered. You don't have to be affiliated with the university to take advantage of their classes. For more details, contact Dr. Miguel García Silva at the Departamento de Idiomas, UMSANH, Santiago Tapia 403, Col. Centro, Morelia, Michoacán, CP 58000, México, or call 43/16–71–01 between 8 AM and 2 PM.

VISITOR INFORMATION   **Secretaría Estatal del Turismo** is located on the south side of Palacio Clavijero. Here you'll find a friendly staff ready to answer questions and dish out maps and information about upcoming cultural events. *Nigromante 79, tel. 43/12–80–81 or 800/4–50–23. Open weekdays 9–2 and 4–8, weekends 8–3 and 4–8.*

COMING AND GOING

BY BUS   Several bus lines pass through the busy **Central de Autobuses** station. **Flecha Amarilla** (tel. 43/12–57–15) takes the prize for most frequent departures and cheapest fares. Their buses travel to Guadalajara (6 hrs, $6), Guanajuato (3½ hrs, $5), Mexico City (6 hrs, $8), Pátzcuaro (1 hr, $1.50), and Uruapan (2 hrs, $4). For a cushier traveling experience, try **ETN** (tel. 43/13–41–37), with hourly service to Mexico City (4½ hrs, $16) as well as frequent departures for Guadalajara (5 hrs, $15). To reach Plaza de Armas from the station, go left on Ruíz, then right (south) two blocks on Gómez Farías, and left on Madero. A taxi to downtown costs about $1.50. *Eduardo Ruíz 526, tel. 43/12–56–64. 4 blocks NW of Plaza de Armas. Long-distance telephone service, luggage storage (24 hrs, 50¢), pharmacy (24 hrs), post office.*

BY CAR If you're traveling to Mexico City via Super Carretera 15-D (304 km, 3½ hrs), the five randomly priced toll booths will cost you $9–$11 total. It's well worth it: Road conditions are excellent and there is little to no traffic. An alternative is the free Highway 15, which is very weathered, heavy with traffic, and two hours longer. It is the "scenic route," though, and winds you through little villages and hills. To reach Guadalajara (367 km, 4 hrs), take Highway 43 north for 27 kilometers and then head west on 15-D. West on Highway 14 will take you to Pátzcurao and Uruapan.

BY TRAIN Morelia's train station rests 2 kilometers west of town. The most comfortable way to get to or from the station is by taxi ($1.50), but a RUTA AZUL pesero is also convenient. Two trains reach Mexico City (10 hrs; $8 1st class, $3.50 2nd class) twice daily. The train to Uruapan (4 hrs; $3 1st class, $1.75 2nd class) leaves daily at 5:30 AM, with a second-class-only train at 5:30 PM. *Av. del Periodismo, tel. 43/16–39–12 or 43/16–39–65. Ticket office open daily 5–6 AM, 10–11 AM, and 10–11 PM.*

GETTING AROUND

Most of Morelia's points of interest lie within a six-block radius of **Plaza de Armas** and the **Catedral.** Both are bordered on the north by the main avenue, **Madero,** called Madero Poniente to the west of the plaza, and Madero Oriente to the east. Street names also change north and south of Madero, and occasionally elsewhere without warning. Of the couple nameplates posted on every street corner, the dark blue one usually corresponds to the name on your map.

BY BUS You can catch 20¢ combis at the designated blue-and-white parada (bus stops)— or any street corner for that matter—by waving your hand at the driver. Even though the colored strips on the VW bus indicate its destination, it's always wise to double-check with the driver.

BY CAR Although downtown is usually thick with traffic, Morelia is fairly easy to navigate by car. As always, be alert for pedestrians and watch for narrow one-way streets that may (or may not) be marked by a black-and-white arrow. To rent a car, try Dollar (Av. del Campestre 676, tel. 43/15-30-48) or Budget Rent-A-Car (Camelinas 2938, tel. 43/14-70-07).

WHERE TO SLEEP

If you've traveled to Morelia by bus and can't wait another minute to crash, you'll find a cluster of cheap hotels of dubious quality in front of the bus station. The best options are worth the four- to eight-block walk to Plaza de Armas. The tourist office provides a list of inexpensive hotels, but many of those are *hoteles de paso* (hotels that rent rooms by the hour). You're better off at any of the places listed below.

➤ **UNDER $10** • **Hotel Colonial.** Basic rooms with TVs are made more pleasant by their cleanliness, the friendly staff, and the immaculate enclosed courtyard. Ask for a room away from the street; cars and buses go by at all hours. Singles cost $5.50, doubles $7.50. *20 de Noviembre 15, tel. 43/12–18–97. 25 rooms, all with bath. Luggage storage. Reservations advised. MC, V.*

Hotel Fénix. This hotel is popular with older Mexicans who leave their doors open to socialize. The rooms are not exactly loaded with amenities, but they're clean, cheap, and the location is a plus. Street traffic can be annoying if your room is near the front. Singles without bath are a steal at $3.50 ($5 with bath); doubles are $4 ($6.50 with bath). Hot water runs all day, and cheap breakfasts ($1) and lunches are served. *Madero Pte. 537, tel. 43/12–05–12. 30 rooms, 20 with bath. Wheelchair access.*

Posada San José. A friendly management and huge rooms filled with Brady-era furniture characterize this hotel. The plant-filled courtyard is a good place to spend the day with your favorite novel. Negotiable prices are $3.50 for a single ($5.50 with bath) and $5 for a double ($8 with bath). You'll need to ring the bell to get in, as the door is always locked. *Obregón 226, tel. 43/12–09–79. 20 rooms, 5 with bath.*

➤ **UNDER $15** • **Hotel Mintzicuri.** The two main attractions here are the spectacular murals in the lobby and the sauna baths. Rooms are smallish but clean and have TVs, phones, carpeting, and private baths. Singles go for $10.75, doubles $14. This is the most luxury you'll get in Morelia for this price. *Vasco de Quiroga 227, tel. 43/12–05–90. 36 rooms, all with bath. Laundry, luggage storage, parking. Reservations advised.*

Hotel Valladolid. This hotel is immaculate, and most rooms have stone walls and curtained balconies. It's surprisingly quiet despite its stellar location on Plaza de Armas, and the staff is so friendly you might not want to leave. Singles cost $13.50, doubles $15.25. *Portal Hidalgo 245, tel. 43/12–46–63. 22 rooms, all with bath. Luggage storage.*

HOSTELS **Villa Juvenil.** Serious budget travelers will like the low prices ($1.50 per person), but you have to sleep four to a single-sex room, be in by 11 PM, and walk about 2 kilometers or take the RUTA AMARILLA combi to reach most of the attractions in town. The place is clean, the managers are young and hip, and there's a pool out front. Breakfast, lunch, and dinner are dished up for about $2. Sheets and towels are provided, and you get a 25% discount with a hostel card. *Chiapas 180, tel. 43/13–31–77. Inside Instituto Michoacáno de la Juventud y el Deporte. Take Madero Pte. west to Cuautla, left 5 blocks to Oaxaca, right 4 blocks to Chiapas. 76 beds. Wheelchair access.*

FOOD

Morelia teems with hole-in-the-wall restaurants offering decent fare; most reside within a couple blocks of Plaza de Armas. The farther you stray from the plaza, though, the cheaper the food. Stands on Gómez Farías, just outside the bus station, serve up the cheapest eats in town, with comidas corridas for just over a buck. Several restaurants serve rich *sopa tarasca* (tomato and bean soup with tortillas, cheese, cream, and dried peppers), as well as other regional specialties. Sweet-toothed travelers should make a beeline for **Mercado de Dulces** (Sweet Market), where you'll find *cocada* (coconut candy); the popular *morelianas*—condensed milk paste between two *obleas* (wafers); and *ate,* a thick candy of guava, fig, or pear paste.

➤ **UNDER $5** • **Los Comensales.** Here you can eat indoors or around an open-air, interior courtyard filled with plants, flowers, and caged chirping birds. Tasty specialties include *pollo con mole* (chicken in chile and chocolate sauce) for $4, and *paella* (saffron-flavored rice with seafood, sausage, and chicken) for $4.50. The $3.50 comida corrida includes soup, pasta or rice, beans, an entrée, coffee or tea, and dessert. *Zaragoza 148, tel. 43/12–93–61. 2 blocks north of Plaza de Armas. Open daily 8 AM–10 PM.*

Restaurant Las Palmas. The TV dictates the atmosphere here, but service is friendly, and the typical Mexican fare is as good as it gets for the price. The excellent and spicy egg *chilaquiles* (tortilla strips doused with salsa and sour cream) accompanied by juice, coffee, and refried beans make a filling breakfast for $2. Afternoon comidas corridas are also $2. *Melchor Ocampo 215, btw Zaragoza and Prieto, no phone. 1 block north of Plaza de Armas. Open daily 9 AM–9:30 PM.*

Restaurant Vegetariano. The food is as original as the name, and the service is slow and indifferent, but the interior courtyard setting is fresh and airy, and the price is right. Comidas corridas go for $2 and an *energético* (fruit, yogurt, and granola) is 50¢. *Hidalgo 75, at La Concordia, tel. 43/12–31–81. Open daily 8:30–5:30. Wheelchair access.*

El Rey Tacamba. This small restaurant near the cathedral serves only Michoacán specialties. The *pollo moreliano* (roasted chicken with red chile and cheese) comes with three enchiladas for $5.25. Also good are *medallones en salsa chipotle* (beef filet in chile sauce; $5). *Portal Galeana 157, tel. 43/12–20–44. Open daily 8:30 AM–11:45 PM. Wheelchair access.*

CAFÉS Families and hipsters converge at **Café Catedral** (Portal Hidalgo, next to Hotel Casino, tel. 43/12–32–89; open daily 8 AM–10:30 PM) to converse over the delicious $1.25 breakfast. Coffee and a variety of teas, from hibiscus to chamomile, are also served. On the second floor of the Teatro Ocampo, **Café del Teatro** (Melchor Ocampo, at Prieto, no phone; open weekdays 8–3 and 5–10, Sat. 10–3 and 5–10, Sun. 5–10) is the best spot in town for a cup of coffee and the most popular among the twenty- and thirtysomething crowd. Wood-beamed ceilings and red velvet curtains make you feel like you forgot your opera glasses. Grab a seat near the balcony overlooking the street and enjoy a cappuccino ($1) or dessert ($1.50).

WORTH SEEING

You don't have to look hard to find Morelia's center of activity: Cars and pedestrians whip through streets cluttered with imposter designer clothes and accessories as soon as you reach the downtown area. For the buzz on the latest craze, head to any newsstand for a copy of the Spanish newspapers *La Voz* and *El Sol de Morelia,* both of which publish a thorough cultural section listing upcoming events.

BOSQUE CUAUHTEMOC Framed by the arch of an 18th-century aqueduct, Morelia's largest park provides a pleasant setting for a picnic. At the edge of the park lies the free **Museo de Arte Contemporáneo** (Acueducto 342, tel. 43/12–55–04), with rotating exhibits of contemporary art from all over Latin America, including works by Chilean painters and female graphic artists. If you have time to spare, visit the **Museo de la Historia Natural** (Ventura Puente 23, tel. 43/12–00–44). It's not too thrilling, but on the top floor there is a room filled with jars of pickled animal (and human) fetuses.

CASA DE LAS ARTESANIAS This former Franciscan monastery houses a wide variety of handicrafts from all over Michoacán. The collection—from guitars to copper dishes—is varied, well-explained, and for sale. The casa also provides workshops where you can watch artisans practicing their crafts. **Museo de las Mascaras,** also located here, contains over 150 masks from throughout the state. *Vasco de Quiroga, at Humboldt, behind marketplace, tel. 43/12–17–48. Admission free. Open weekdays 10–8, weekends 10–6.*

CASA MUSEO DE MORELOS City namesake José María Morelos once owned this home, and abandoned it to join the fight for independence. His life story is interesting, but unless you can read Spanish the displays featuring his reading glasses and family tree won't do much for you. One look at the *"Dying is nothing when you die for the Fatherland."—José María Morelos (who did).* beautiful yet butt-flattening 19th-century carriages in the courtyard will make you vow never to complain about buses again. *Morelos Sur 323, tel. 43/13–26–51. Admission: $1.50, free Sun. Open Mon.–Sat. 9–2 and 4–7, Sun. 9–2.*

CATEDRAL This 17th-century architectural marvel took more than 100 years to build. Some 61 meters high, its bell towers are taller than those of any other church in Mexico. The cathedral's baroque exterior, however, gives way to a somewhat disappointing neoclassical interior, brightened only by warm rose- and gold-colored ornamentation. Works of particular interest include a sculpture of Christ made from cane paste and a fantastic Churrigueresque (ultra-baroque) organ. *Open daily dawn–dusk.*

MUSEO DEL ESTADO The Purépecha once dominated almost all of Michoacán, as chronicled here via pre-Columbian artifacts. The Purépecha still populate the area, producing a wide range of handicrafts, some of which you can see here along with rotating regional contemporary art exhibitions and artifacts from the independence movement. Especially worth a look is the section on Lake Pátzcuaro's fishing tradition. Explanations are in Spanish. *Prieto 176, tel. 43/13–06–29. Admission free. Open weekdays 9–2 and 4–7, Sat. 9–2 and 4–7.*

MUSEO REGIONAL MICHOACANO This museum traces the development of Michoacán from the beginning of the earth's creation to the present, meshing a hodge-podge of geological, archeological and artistic relics. In the end, it serves as a crash-course on Michoacán history and proves to be one of Morelia's more interesting museums. *Allende 305, near Abasalo. Admission free. Open Tues.–Sat. 9–2 and 4–6, Sun. 9–2:30.*

PARQUE ZOOLOGICO BENITO JUAREZ Morelia's spacious zoo is one of the best in Mexico, with picnic areas, a playground, a train, and a lake where you can rent boats. Rust-colored, eucalyptus-shaded trails guide you past 89 animal species, most of which are being taunted by hordes of devious school kids. *Calzada Juárez, tel. 43/14–04–88. Take combi RUTA 1 and ask to be dropped off at the zoológico. Admission: 50¢. Open daily 10–5:30.*

CHEAP THRILLS

A great way to spend a quiet afternoon is to head to the aqueduct, a 15-minute walk down Madero Oriente from Plaza de Armas. Along the way you'll notice the famous **Tarascan Fountain**—a sculpture of robust bare-breasted women dutifully supporting a huge basket of fruit above their heads. The sculpture is actually a replica of the original, which mysteriously disappeared one night in 1940 and is rumored to currently reside in Spain. Continue your walk just beyond the aqueduct to **Calzada Fray Antonio de San Miguel.** This lovely tree-lined, stone-paved promenade is surrounded by small schools and homes. At the end of the Calzada, on Avenida Tata Vasco, you'll encounter one of Morelia's most beautiful churches—the **Templo de San Juan Diego.** This is *the* place to get married, and on Saturdays the church overflows with ceremonies. Inside, the walls are adorned with murals depicting the missionaries' arrival and the beginning of the Catholic conversion process. At the altar, San Juan Diego is faithfully kneeling, with his cloak of roses, to the Virgen de Guadalupe.

At **Casa Natal de Morelos,** you can ooh and aah over the leader's signature and see the eternally lit torch in the spot where, as legend has it, Juana Pavon suddenly found herself in labor and gave birth to baby Morelos. The real reason to come here, however, is to meet the students studying and hanging out in the sunny garden. The **Cine Club** sponsors foreign films (10¢) here several times a week, as well as cultural events, such as poetry readings. For more info, check the bulletin board in the entranceway. *Corregidora 113, at García Obeso, tel. 43/12–27–93. Admission free. Open weekdays 9–2 and 6–8, Sat. 10–2 and 4–7, Sun. 10–2.*

AFTER DARK

BARS AND DANCING Morelia will not disappoint those who prefer mindless drinking and shaking. Most bars are open daily, but Thursday–Saturday nights are the liveliest. Highly recommended is **Siglo XVIII** (García de León, at Turismo 20, tel. 43/24–07–47), a bar decorated in the baroque style, complete with a water-spitting angel fountain. This is *the* hot spot in Morelia, so arrive before 10 PM to avoid waiting in line. There's a $10 cover Friday and Saturday, but women get in for half that. **Antigua's** (Camelinas 514, tel. 43/15–90–47), a bar versatile enough to let you cavort comfortably on the dance floor or have a quiet conversation on the terrace, has an $8 cover on Saturdays (the same fee includes drinks Thursdays and Fridays). Penny-pinchers should seek out **Carlos 'n Charlie's** (Camelinas 3340, tel. 43/24–37–42), packed with Morelia's preppy youth and American students. Beers are $1.

MUSIC AND THEATER Morelia's Orquesta Sinfónica performs frequently in the **Teatro Ocampo** (cnr of Melchor Ocampo and Prieto, tel. 43/12–37–34). The performance schedules change seasonally and prices range $2–$7. They also feature ballet folklórico performances, as well as classic and contemporary dance. Contact the **Instituto Michoacáno de Cultura** (tel. 43/13–13–20 or 43/12–37–34) for info. A student ID will get you a discount.

If you're looking for a little nourishment with your culture, the **Cantera Jardín** (Aldama 343, tel. 43/12–15–78) restaurant puts on dinner shows Thursday–Saturday at 9 PM. Programs and cover charges vary. For a fun and funny night, that is if you understand enough Spanish to get the jokes, check out **Corral de la Comedia** (Melchor Ocampo 239, tel. 43/12–13–74), which stages comedies Thursday–Saturday at 8:30 PM and Sunday at 7 PM. Cover is usually $3.50.

Pátzcuaro

This cool rainy city of 70,000 is the jewel of Michoacán state; bordered by a huge lake and green hills, it's a welcome sight for any traveler— as evidenced over the centuries. Pátzcuaro's first inhabitants were the Purépecha, who justly named the area "Place of Stones." Much later, a string of Spaniards sojourned here, beginning with the unscrupulous Nuño de Guzmán. Part of Cortés's crew, Guzmán created so much havoc that in 1536 Spain commissioned Don Vasco de Quiroga to repair the damage. Don Vasco ended the enslavement of the *indigenas* (indigenous people), chartered programs to educate them, and created industries that allowed the Purépecha to be self-sufficient; these deeds quickly earned him the endearing nickname "Tata Vasco." Encouraged by Don Vasco, each village in Michoacán soon developed expertise in a specialized skill; the craftmanship continues today and many fine goods can be found in the artesanía shops lining the streets of the city.

Hand-chiseled wooden furniture, primarily made of pine, is abundandant in the Pátzcuaro lake region. You can get great deals on these and other Michoacán crafts at the Tianguis Artesanal crafts festival the first week of November.

The city itself has somehow avoided becoming an overpopulated tourist attraction, and few 20th-century intrusions mar the quaint colonial setting. In keeping with an 18th-century ambience, most hotels enforce evening curfews and, with a few exceptions, the town settles in for the night by 10 PM. However the primary reason to visit Pátzcuaro isn't for nightlife, but the surrounding lake region, about 3 kilometers from the town center. Here you'll find **Lake Pátzcuaro** and the island of **Janitzio** (*see* Near Pátzcuaro, *below*), where people of Purépechan descent still live.

BASICS

CASAS DE CAMBIO Banamex (Portal Juárez 32, tel. 434/2–10–31) on Plaza Bocanegra changes cash and traveler's checks weekday mornings for good rates, which may explain the line. Half a block from the bank at Mendoza 16 is an ATM that accepts Cirrus, Plus, Visa, and MasterCard. **Casa de Cambio Multidivisas** (Padre Lloreda, at Buena Vista, tel. 434/2–3–83) changes cash and traveler's checks weekdays 9–6, Saturdays 9–1.

EMERGENCIES Call the **police** (Ibarra, 3 blocks from center, tel. 434/2–00–04).

LAUNDRY Lavandería Automática will wash, dry, and fold your clothes ($2 for 3 kilos). Get here as soon as the place opens if you want same-day service. *Terán 16, tel. 434/2–39–39. 1½ blocks west of Plaza Quiroga. Open Mon.–Sat. 9–8.*

MAIL The full-service post office will hold mail sent to you at the following address for up to 10 days: Lista de Correos, Administración de Correos, Pátzcuaro, Michoacán, CP 61600, México. *Álvaro Obregón 13, tel. 434/2–01–28. 1 block north of Plaza Bocanegra. Open weekdays 9–7, Sat. 9–1.*

MEDICAL AID The **ISSSTE hospital** (tel. 434/2–08–06), a half block west of Plaza Vasco de Quiroga, provides 24-hour service. **Farmacia del Carmen** (cnr of Romero and Navarrete, tel. 434/2–26–52) is also open around the clock. Other pharmacies take turns doing the night shift: Check the billboard under Portal Hidalgo 1, on the west side of Plaza Quiroga, for current information.

PHONES Pátzcuaro's two main plazas are surrounded by several casetas de larga distancia. **Hotel San Agustín** (*see* Where to Sleep, *below*) allows you to make collect calls daily 8:30 AM–10 PM for a 75¢ fee. Your party can call you back for the same price. A couple **Ladatel** phones are located in Plaza Vasco de Quiroga.

VISITOR INFORMATION The staff at **Delegación Regional de Turismo** will provide you with maps and tries (usually in vain) to answer your questions. Ask to speak with Gerardo—he's a fountain of info. *Ibarra 2, tel. 434/2–12–14. A few doors west of Plaza Quiroga. Open Mon.–Sat. 9–3 and 4–7, Sun. 9–3.*

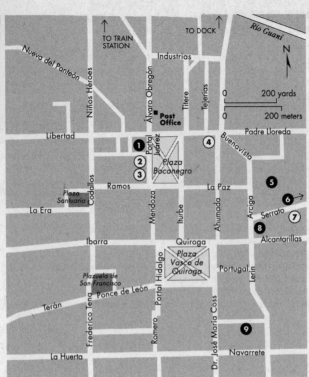

Sights ●

Basílica de
Nuestra Señora, **5**

Casa de los
Once Patios, **9**

El Humilladero, **6**

Mercado, **1**

Museo de Artes
Populares, **8**

Lodging ○

Posada de
la Rosa, **3**

Posada de
la Salud, **7**

Hotel
San Agustín, **2**

Hotel Valmen, **4**

COMING AND GOING

BY BUS **Central de Autobuses Pátzcuaro** (Libramiento Ignacio Zaragoza, tel. 434/2–16–18) sits 1½ kilometers south of the town center. City buses (15¢) and vans (20¢) labeled CEN-TRO leave the station every five minutes or so for the town center and budget lodging areas. **Autobuses del Occidente** (tel. 434/2–00–52) serves Guadalajara (5 hrs, $7) daily at noon; Mexico City (5 hrs, $13) at 9:45 AM and 11:45 AM; and Morelia (1 hr, $1.75) on the hour. **Autotransportes Galeana** (tel. 434/2–08–08) sends buses to Morelia (1 hr, $1.75) and Urua-pan (1 hr, $1.75) every 15 minutes 5:30 AM–9 PM. The station also has luggage storage (75¢), open 6 AM–10 PM, plus long-distance phone services (a caseta de larga distancia and Compu-tel), both open daily 7 AM–8:45 PM.

BY CAR In town, traffic is minimal and street parking is relatively safe and abundant. The wary driver can pay $1.50 to park overnight at **Taurus**, a parking garage on Ahumada, a half block from Padre Floreda. Leaving Pátzcuaro via Highway 14 brings you west to Morelia (56 km) or east to Uruapan (62 km). The four-lane road to Morelia is in excellent condition; to Uru-apan it's much worse.

BY TRAIN The train station lies 3 kilometers from the town center, near the Janitzio boat docks. Trains to Uruapan (2 hrs; $1.50 1st class, 75¢ 2nd class) leave twice daily. The train to Mexico City (11 hrs; $8 1st class, $4.50 2nd class) leaves at 8:40 AM. Only second-class service is available to Morelia (1½ hrs, 75¢), leaving at 9:05 AM. *Paseo Lázaro Cárdenas, tel. 434/2–08–03. Ticket window opens ½ hr before every departure.*

GETTING AROUND

You may have trouble finding street signs in Pátzcuaro—they're either high up on buildings or in some equally improbable place—but the central area is easily maneuverable. Minibuses

(15¢) and vans (20¢) are quickly mastered—just ask people on the street where you can catch them. Most points of interest are within walking distance of the two main plazas: the small and busy **Plaza Bocanegra** (also called Plaza Chica) and **Plaza Vasco de Quiroga,** one block south. Streets change names at both plazas, and to add to the confusion, most businesses around Plaza Quiroga use *portal* (walkway) names instead of street names. Several blocks north of Plaza Bocanegra you'll find the train station, a few bars, the dock for boats to Janitzio, and good seafood restaurants.

WHERE TO SLEEP

Prices for clean rooms are reasonable, and hot water is usually available. Ritzier hotels line Plaza Vasco de Quiroga, while the slightly noisier Plaza Bocanegra hosts many budget options. Campsites are available on nearby **Yunuen** island (*see* Janitzio, *below*), as well as cabins starting at $8 a person, meals included. You can also camp on **Pacanda** island by contacting **Instituto Nacional Indigena** (tel. 434/2–10–72) first. The organization provides free transportation to the campsite and opens restaurants and latrines with an advance reservation.

Hotel San Agustín. Although this establishment lacks charm and can be a bit noisy, it has some pluses: tidy spartan rooms and bathrooms, a bright courtyard, a great location, no curfew, and low prices. Singles cost $4, doubles with two beds $8. *Portal Juárez 27, on Plaza Bocanegra, tel. 434/2–04–42. 22 rooms, all with bath.*

Hotel Valmen. An extremely friendly owner and a courtyard filled with plants and chirping birds are the main attractions at this modest hotel. Rooms are large, and you have your choice of green or pink walls. It's the best of the bargain hotels, but there's a silly 10 PM curfew. Singles run around $5, doubles $10. *Padre Lloreda 34, at Ahumada, tel. 434/2–11–61. 16 rooms, all with bath. Luggage storage.*

Posada de la Rosa. Only two doors down from Hotel San Agustín, this hotel is as quiet as it gets on Plaza Bocanegra. The clean rooms ($5, $6.75 with bath), some with amazingly mismatched bedcovers, aren't great, but they'll do. The only drawbacks are the 11 PM curfew and the walk to the communal bathrooms. Bring your own toilet paper and towel. *Portal Juárez 29, tel. 434/2–08–11. 12 rooms, 3 with bath.*

Posada de la Salud. This cheerful establishment is priced a notch higher than the other budget hotels and has a 10 PM curfew, but it's as sweet, quiet, and proper as the lady who owns it. Built in traditional Mexican style with a tiled patio and a well-tended garden, it offers pleasant rooms with carved wooden furniture and large, clean bathrooms. Singles cost $7, doubles $11. *Serrato 9, tel. 434/2–00–58. 12 rooms, all with bath. Luggage storage.*

FOOD

Among local specialties worth trying are *pescado blanco* (whitefish); *charales,* tiny fried fish served with lemon and chile; and *sopa tarasca.* The best of the many fish restaurants are found near the lakefront. A huge open-air **market** operates daily on the west side of Plaza Bocanegra, with food stands open around the clock. Stop by **Chocolate Joaquinita** (Enseñanza 38, tel. 434/2–45–14) to buy a huge pack of gritty but delicious homemade chocolate for $2.

Those with a sweet tooth must try the helado de pasta, a custardlike ice cream made from milk. You'll find it at the stands lining Plaza Vasco de Quiroga.

Comedor T'Irekua. Set outside in an enclosed patio, this cheerful bohemian/artist/U.S. expatriate hangout serves some of the best meals for your money. Try the fruit salad, yogurt, honey, and granola combo ($1.50) or the traditional beans, eggs, and salsa ($1.50). Rocio, the proprietor, whips up a filling, regional comida corrida ($2) that changes daily. *Plaza Quiroga 29, no phone. Open daily 8–7.*

Los Equipales. This tiny, down-home taquería is always full in the evenings. At 15¢, quesadillas and tacos with beef, sausage, or tripe are ridiculously cheap. *Portal Allende 57, no phone. North side of Plaza Quiroga. Open daily 5 PM–10 PM.*

241

Hamburguesas y Tortas el Viejo Sam. If you can't handle tiny fish with eyeballs staring up blankly from your plate, you'll be glad to know there's a humble hamburger joint in town. Get 'em topped with cheese or ham for under 75¢. Add french fries for 50¢. *Mendoza 15, no phone. ½ block south of Plaza Bocanegra. Open daily 10 AM–11 PM.*

Restaurante Hotel Posada La Basílica. The enormous windows here open onto an incredible view of Pátzcuaro and the lake. The menú del día ($3.50) includes soup, rice, blue-corn tortillas, and breaded trout or beef prepared with tomatoes and onions. *Caldo de pescado*, a tomato-based fish consommé, is a lighter choice for $2.50. Be prepared for a leisurely meal—service is slow. *Arciga 6, tel. 434/2–11–08. From Plaza Bocanegra, east on Padre Lloreda, right on Buena Vista to Arciga. Open Wed.–Mon. 8–4.*

CAFÉS **Café de Flore.** Named after its renowned Parisian counterpart, and especially popular with American and European tourists, this charming Franco-Mexican enterprise serves warm pizzas ($1.50) and quiches (70¢). The amiable owner slaves over her pastries—and gets great results. *Portal Rayón 26, in front of the Basílica, tel. 434/2–19–46. Open Tues.–Sun. 11 AM–10 PM. Wheelchair access.*

WORTH SEEING

The bustling *tianguis* (open-air market) is a good place to get a sense of Pátzcuaro's character. It begins on the west side of Plaza Bocanegra and continues for several blocks. Here you'll find all kinds of fresh food, as well as vendors trafficking local handicrafts and cheap plastic watches and toys. You can also get some good deals on handmade woolens, including sweaters, blankets, and serapes. The area is a mass of humanity, so don't expect to go anywhere fast.

BIBLIOTECA GERTRUDIS BOCANEGRA On the back wall of this 16th-century church is a phenomenal mural by Juan O'Gorman illustrating the history of Mexico from pre-Columbian times to the Mexican revolution of 1910. An impressive collection of English books are available for check-out. *North side of Plaza Bocanegra. Open weekdays 9–2 and 4–6.*

LA CASA DE LOS ONCE PATIOS Built in the 18th and 19th centuries by Dominican monks, this former convent was broken up to make way for streets, leaving only five of the original 11 garden patios. Now it houses several craft shops. Prices here are reasonable, but better deals are found in the markets. The Casa's main appeal is watching artisans in action and learning about their work. *Madrigal de las Altas Torres, 2 blocks from Plaza Quiroga. Open daily 9–7.*

MUSEO DE ARTES POPULARES This dilapidated edifice, which housed Colegio de San Nicolás in the 16th century, now functions as Pátzcuaro's crafts museum. On display is a wide variety of local wares, including ceramic dishes, intricately painted masks, and lacquered goods. In the back garden sits a traditional Tarascan hut set on a 12th-century stone platform,

Purépecha or Tarasco?

Before the Spanish arrived in the 1500s, the people of Michoacán had developed a highly advanced society. This group was known by the first Spanish explorers as the Purépecha—a word borrowed from Nahuatl. In order to appease the Spanish, the Purépecha reportedly married off the tribe's female members. However, this did very little to hinder the Spaniards' efforts to establish supremacy. Frustrated with the unyielding Purépecha, the Spanish eventually began to call the indigenous people the Tarasco—a corruption of a derogatory Nahuatl word loosely meaning "son-in-law." Today the words Purépecha and Tarasco are used interchangably when discussing descendants of the Purépecha.

the last remnant of the indigenous ceremonial center over which the basilica was erected. *Enseñanza, at Alcantarillas, tel. 434/2-10-29. 1 block east of Plaza Quiroga. Admission: $1.75, free Sun. Open Tues.-Sat. 9-7, Sun. 9-3.*

CHURCHES Pátzcuaro was the episcopal seat of Michoacán until that honor was moved to Morelia in 1508, and its impressive colonial churches reflect the city's ecclesiastical importance. Two blocks east of Plaza Vasco de Quiroga is the **Basílica de Nuestra Señora de la Salud,** built atop a sacred Purépechan site by order of Don Vasco de Quiroga, who is entombed near the entrance. The most interesting piece here is the **Virgen de la Salud** (Virgin of Health) made from cornhusk paste and orchid nectar. At that time, dressing holy images in cloth was prohibited—ostensibly to keep the indígenas from hiding their own idols within the Catholic vestments and continuing to worship as before. Walk behind the altar and you'll see a collection of *ex-votos,* or *milagros,* tiny silver charms representing parts of the body and offered either in trust to become healed or in gratitude for a successful healing. The basilica is open daily until dusk, and the mass schedule is posted at the main entrance.

El Humilladero (The Place of Humiliation) is so named because it is where the Purépecha surrendered peacefully to the Spanish. Inside this plateresque church is a stone cross with a 1553 carving of Christ. The church lies 3 kilometers east of downtown on Calle Serato. Either make the 30-minute walk or catch a bus or van marked CRISTO from Plaza Bocanegra; they run 6 AM–9 PM and cost 50¢.

CHEAP THRILLS

Volcán del Estribo Grande, about 4 kilometers west of the town center, makes for an easy, one-hour hike, with phenomenal views of both Pátzcuaro and the nearby lake and islands. The walk takes you along cobblestone streets lined with centuries-old homes and trees. To reach the lookout, head west on Ponce de León from the southwest corner of Plaza Vasco de Quiroga. Ponce de León turns into Terán, which turns into Calle Paseo, finally becoming Cerro del Estribo. The route can be dangerous: be alert and don't travel alone or at night.

If you'd rather ride than stride, rent a bike from the hotel/restaurant **Mansión Iturbide** (Portal Morelos 59, tel. 434/2-03-68) for $3.50 an hour, $8 a day. Ignore the sign that says the bikes are for hotel guests only, since the management does. Pátzcuaro's cobblestone streets make for a bumpy ride, but it's a great way to explore the town's quieter residential areas.

FESTIVALS Pátzcuaro's colonial charm is especially brilliant during festival time. If you find yourself here on **Día de los Muertos** (Day of the Dead, November 2), you'll see the town come alive with all-night fiestas. **Semana Santa** (Holy Week) is also a lively occasion, both in Pátzcuaro and in nearby Tzintzuntzan (*see* Near Pátzcuaro, *below*). On Good Friday, locals reenact the Stations of the Cross, and on Holy Saturday they mourn Jesus's death with a silent candlelight procession. **Día de Nuestra Señora de la Salud** (Day of Our Lady of Health, December 8) honors the Virgin Mary with traditional Purépechan dances, including the Baile de Los Viejitos (dance of the old men).

AFTER DARK

Strolling the plaza until about 9 PM or cruising the streets with bored 17-year-olds may seem like your only nightlife options, but the friendly **El Campanario Video-Bar** (Portal Aldama 12, on Plaza Vasco de Quiroga, tel. 434/2-13-13) is actually a good place to relax and chat with other travelers. Don't be surprised when at 10 PM this seemingly reputable establishment turns off the music videos for an hour of cheesy U.S. pornos—no one seems to notice. For action of a slightly different sort, head to **Nevada Disco** (no phone; open Fri.-Sun. 8 PM–1 AM), *the* disco in town. For the cover price of $2.50 you can join an under-20 crowd who sings loudly and dances incessantly to popular Mexican and American dance tunes. To get here, head toward Morelia on Lázaro Cárdenas for about a kilometer; it's on the lefthand side.

Near Pátzcuaro

JANITZIO

The local Purépecha, who are practically the only inhabitants of the largest of Lake Pátzcuaro's five islands, call their isle Xanichu. The meaning of the name is disputed: Some claim it means "ear of corn," others say "where it rains," and still others "cornflower." During the summer rainy season there's no doubt which interpretation is most probable. The Purépecha here still speak, write, and study in their native tongue. The islanders' income derives from some fishing, but primarily from handicrafts imported to the island for the tourist industry; fittingly, the main reason to come here is to shop. Crowning the top of the island is a huge, if grotesque, statue of José María Morelos. You can climb inside it to the *mirador* (viewpoint) for an amazing view of the lake and countryside. **Tecuena, Pacanda,** and **Yunuen** are other islands on the lake that make worthwhile excursions. They're much less popular with tourists than Janitzio, lending them a completely different atmosphere. **Yunuen** and **Pacanda** are the only ones with overnight accommodations and camping (*see* Where to Sleep, *below*).

If you're near Janitzio on the first of November, don't miss the Día de los Muertos (Day of the Dead) celebration held here. The festival is renowned in Mexico for its fantastic dances and candlelight processions to the graveyards.

COMING AND GOING Boats to and from Janitzio run daily 8–5:30 and take 20 minutes. Tickets can be purchased at the *taquilla* (ticket window) among the shops at Pátzcuaro's lakeside dock. Round-trip tickets cost $2 for Janitzio, $3 for the other islands. Boats leave whenever they're full, so plan on taking your time. To reach the lakefront from downtown, go to the corner of Portal Juárez and Ramos (which border Plaza Bocanegra) and catch a northbound bus or van marked LAGO. The last boat leaves the island around 5:30. Don't miss it: There are no hotels on the island.

TZINTZUNTZAN

This small village, called "Place of Hummingbirds" in Purépechan, lies 18 kilometers northeast of Pátzcuaro. While here you have a choice of shopping, admiring the churches, or visiting the ruins, all of which you can accomplish in one afternoon. In the center of town, next to the crafts market, is the 17th-century **Templo de San Francisco,** another of Vasco de Quiroga's legacies, with a newly redone (and consequently somewhat sterile) interior. The olive trees in the front courtyard, planted by Quiroga himself, still bear fruit. The **Templo de la Soledad** next door is damp, but its original facade and elaborately clothed statues give it character.

The Purépechan deities were mostly female; important ones included Xaratanga, the goddess of fertility, and Cuerarapeni, the goddess of the sky and mother of all gods and goddesses.

Roughly a kilometer outside Tzintzuntzan are the crumbling remains of what used to be the Purépechan kingdom's religious and administrative capital, where Vasco de Quiroga based his evangelical mission. The huge ceremonial platform is topped with circular stone structures known as *yácatas,* which served as religious temples. There are no guides but a small museum offers information in Spanish about the Purépecha. To reach the ruins, walk back on the road to Pátzcuaro and turn left on a side road. You can't miss the ruins—they look alarmingly like larger-than-life beehives. If in doubt, ask for directions to the yácatas. *Museum admission: $1.50, free Sun. Open daily 10–5.*

COMING AND GOING **Autotransportes Galeana** buses marked QUIROGA (½ hr, 50¢) leave every 15 minutes 6 AM–8:30 PM from Pátzcuaro's main bus terminal. Tell the driver to let you off at Tzintzuntzan's plaza. Return buses depart from the same plaza; be sure to leave by 8:30 PM or you'll be hitching a ride back to Pátzcuaro.

Uruapan

Roughly situated in the center of Michoacán state, Uruapan is an unpleasant surprise for those expecting a picturesque town filled with well-preserved colonial architecture. With few exceptions, Uruapan—distinguished by blocks of dull modern buildings alongside older, unkempt colonial edifices—is difficult to appreciate. The city's true lure is the rich, natural setting and temperate climate. **Parque Nacional Eduardo Ruíz,** just blocks from the center of town, offers a fresh, quiet retreat from city life. Other highlights include an excursion to the **Tzararacua** waterfall and a horseback ride to the inactive (keep your fingers crossed) **Volcán Paricutín.**

Otomí and Chontal people took advantage of Uruapan's rich vegetation and free-flowing waters long before the Spanish arrived. When Father Juan de San Miguel showed up in 1531, he established a feudal *encomienda* system, reducing the indigenous peoples to serfs upon whose backs agrarian Uruapan grew and prospered. Today the town is known for its flower production and for being the world's avocado capital, producing five different varieties of the divine fruit. Every November, the city trembles with excitement during the week-long **Feria del Aguacate** (Avocado Fair). In fact, Uruapan finds some reason to break out the avocados and *charanda* (a local liquor) almost monthly. The biggest events include **Fiesta de San Pedro** (June 30), honoring the apostle Peter with a parade, band, indigenous dances, and lots of booze; **Fiesta de Santa María de Magdalena** (July 23), venerating the biblical prostitute-turned-saint with processions and dance performances reenacting battles between Moors and Christians; and **El Día de San Francisco** (October 4), commemorating Uruapan's patron saint with a dance by Purépechan women.

BASICS

CASAS DE CAMBIO **Banamex** (Morelos, at Cupatitzio, tel. 452/3–92–90) changes traveler's checks and cash weekdays 9–2 and has an ATM that accepts Cirrus and Plus cards. You can also change money and cash traveler's checks at **Divisas Tariacuri** (Portal Degollado 15, tel. 452/4–35–25) on the east end of Jardín Morelos; it's open weekdays 9–6, Saturday 9–2.

EMERGENCIES For an **ambulance,** call the **police** at 452/4–06–20.

LAUNDRY **Auto Servicio de Lavandería** will wash, dry, and fold your laundry ($3 for 3 kilos). For same day service, bring your clothes when they open. *Emiliano Carranza 47, at Jesús García, tel. 452/3–26–69. 6 blocks west of Jardín Morelos. Open Mon.–Sat. 9–2:30 and 4–8.*

MAIL The full-service post office will hold mail sent to you at the following address for up to 10 days: Lista de Correos, Uruapan, Michoacán, CP 60001, México. *Reforma 13, tel. 452/3–56–30. From Jardín Morelos, walk 3 blocks south on Cupatitzio, left on Reforma. Open weekdays 8–7, Sat. 9–1.*

MEDICAL AID **Hospital Civil** (La Quinta 6, tel. 452/3–46–60), in front of Parque Nacional, provides emergency service and a 24-hour pharmacy. Other pharmacies in town rotate night hours on a monthly basis—ask any pharmacist or call **Salubridad** at 452/4–01–56 to find out who's on duty.

PHONES The caseta de larga distancia at **Restaurant Las Palmas** (Donato Guerra 2, tel. 452/4–65–45) charges a $1 connection fee for a collect call. **Ladatel** phones are a rare find, but there are some in working order south of the plaza, on the corner of Melchor Ocampo and Emiliano Carranza. Ladatel cards can be purchased at **Kodak Photo 30** (Portal Carrillo 14).

VISITOR INFORMATION The tourist office provides maps and info on what to see and how to get there. *Ocampo 64, downstairs in Hotel Plaza, tel. 452/3–61–72. Open Mon.–Sat. 9–2 and 4–8, Sun. 9–2.*

COMING AND GOING

BY BUS Several bus lines frequent the **Central de Autobuses de Uruapan.** Flecha Amarilla (tel. 452/4–39–82), one of the cheaper lines, sends buses to Guadalajara (5 per day, 6 hrs,

$8.50), Mexico City (5 per day, 8 hrs, $12), Querétaro (2 per day, 6 hrs, $11), and San Luis Potosí (2 per day, 9 hrs, $17). The cushy **ETN** (tel. 452/3–86–08) line takes passengers to Guadalajara (7 per day, 4½ hrs, $13), Mexico City (6 per day, 6 hrs, $20), and Morelia (4 per day, 2 hrs, $8). For short distances try **Ruta Paraíso** (tel. 452/4–41–54) or **Autotransportes Galeana** (tel. 452/4–33–50), both of which have service to Pátzcuaro every 15 minutes. To get downtown, take any bus marked CENTRO; on the return take a CENTRAL bus. A taxi to the center is $1.25. *Carretera Pátzcuaro Km. 1, tel. 452/3–44–05. 3 km NE of Jardín Morelos. Caseta de larga distancia, food, luggage storage ($1.50 a day), pharmacy, post office.*

BY CAR The smoothest way to reach Guadalajara from Uruapan is via the two-lane Highway 37 north to Super Carretera 15-D; just follow the signs. On 15-D you'll encounter four toll booths totaling $9 for the 159-kilometer, two-hour drive. Traveling on the toll-free Highway 14 west will bring you first to Patzcuaro, then Morelia, and, if you drive until you hit the 15-D and continue west, you'll reach Mexico City.

BY TRAIN The station lies 11 blocks from the center of town, and is easily accessible by the FERR bus or taxi. Trains to Mexico City (12 hrs) leave at 6:30 AM ($5.50, 2nd class) and 7:10 PM ($9, 1st class), making stops in Pátzcuaro, Morelia, and other cities. *Paseo Lázaro Cárdenas, at end of Av. Américas, tel. 452/4–09–81. Ticket office open daily 6 AM–7 PM.*

GETTING AROUND

Although Uruapan is fairly large, your visit will most likely center around three main areas—the bus station, **Jardín Morelos** (also known simply as the plaza), and the strip of bars on Paseo Lázaro Cárdenas. Street names change as they cross the plaza, which makes finding things without a map confusing. To add to the chaos, streets immediately surrounding the Jardín often go by second *portal* (walkway) names. The main street, bordering the plaza's southern side, is called Emiliano Carranza to the west and Álvaro Obregón to the east. Most buses pass Jardín Morelos with routes or destinations written on their windshield. You'll have to take a taxi to sample the nightlife on Lázaro Cárdenas, since buses (20¢) only run 6 AM–9 PM. Taxi fare is usually $1.50.

WHERE TO SLEEP

Most hotels bordering Jardín Morelos have seen better days or are out of budget range. Fortunately, there are decent, inexpensive hotels within a short walk of the plaza. Tourism isn't big in Uruapan, so you shouldn't have trouble getting a room unless a festival is in full swing; in this case, reservations are advised. Crashing in Jardín Morelos may be conceivable, but after a night of cold and rain you'll be heading staight for a hotel. Camping is available at nearby Angahuan (*see* Near Uruapan, *below*).

Hotel del Parque. The plain, medium-size rooms are clean and airy. The couches and TV in the lobby invite you to hang out with the families who stay here. If you don't mind a seven-block walk to the center, you'll appreciate the proximity to Parque Nacional. Singles cost $5.50, doubles $8.50. *Independencia 164, tel. 452/4–38–45. 14 rooms, all with bath. Parking.*

Hotel Mi Solar. If spacious rooms, an indoor patio, and clean bathrooms with hot water do it for you, stay here. This establishment is popular with foreign travelers, so chances are you'll hear someone singing Dylan next door. Singles cost $4.50, doubles $6.50. *Juan Delgado 10, tel. 452/2–09–12. 2 blocks north of Jardín Morelos. 20 rooms, all with bath. Wheelchair access.*

Hotel Regis. Nestled between busy storefronts, this hotel has a surprisingly mellow air to it. All rooms ($10.50 singles, $14 doubles) have either tiled or wood floors and the doors have decorative labels—from women's names to unidentifiable Tarascan nouns. A sunroof, chirping birds, and comfortable couches outside the rooms make this a bright and cheery place. *Portal Carrillo 10, near southern end of Jardín Morelos, tel. 452/3–58–44. 43 rooms, all with bath.*

FOOD

At **Mercado de Antojitos,** inside the open-air market off the northeast side of Jardín Morelos, you'll have the opportunity to sample a variety of local dishes, including *churipos,* a hearty stew with chicken, pork, beef, veggies, and red chile. Stands selling fruits, vegetables, tamales, fresh cheese, and grilled meats are open 24 hours and won't set you back more than $2.

Antojitos Yucatecos Cox-Hanal. If you're hankering for Yucatecan cuisine, you can get your fill here for under $2. Try the *sopa de lima* (lime soup) or one of the many varieties of taquitos and chase it down with a cold Montejo beer. *Emiliano Carranza 37, no phone. 5 blocks west of Jardín Morelos. Open Tues.–Fri. 5:30 PM–11 PM, weekends 1–11.*

Boca del Río. Facing Plaza La Ranita, this tiny joint serves a *sopa de mariscos* (seafood soup; $4) that is famous throughout the city. You can also sample *tostadas de ceviche* (crisp tortilla covered with lemon-marinated fish) for 50¢. *Juan Delgado 2, 1 block north of Jardín Morelos, tel. 452/3–02–03. Open daily 10–5. Wheelchair access.*

Comedor Vegetariano. Although not much to look at, this is the only vegetarian restaurant near the center that serves comidas corridas ($2). The 50¢ tortas are delicious. *Cnr of Morelos and Aldama, no phone. 2 blocks south and 1 block east of Jardín Morelos. Open daily 8–5. Wheelchair access.*

CAFÉS Café La Lucha. A popular afternoon hangout for older men, this comfortable café invites you to do some serious lounging. Musicians often stop by to croon a few pesos out of you. *Café de olla* (coffee flavored with chocolate and cinnamon), espresso, and hot chocolate all cost $1, as do tasty pies and pastries. *García Ortiz 22, tel. 452/4–03–75. ½ block north of Jardín Morelos. Open daily 9–9.*

Café Tradicional de Uruapan. This place has a menu of more than 20 teas and coffees, which you can liven up with everything from ice cream ($2) or a stiff shot of brandy ($2). A plain old *café con leche* costs 60¢. The menu also includes egg breakfasts ($2.50), and a variety of 50¢ tamales for dinner. *Carranza 5-B, no phone. ½ block west of Jardín Morelos. Open daily 8:30 AM–10 PM.*

WORTH SEEING

The best place to get a sense of Uruapan's bustling activity is in **Jardín Morelos.** Though it's aesthetically uninspiring, the ice-cream vendors and children infuse the garden with liveliness. At the open-air market off the northeast end of the plaza, you'll find bargains on everything from juice presses to jewelry to leather sandals. The market's open daily from dawn to dusk.

DESTILADORA EL TARASCO This distillery gives free tours in Spanish for those who want to know more about *charanda,* the local firewater. Here you can see the whole process, from the fermentation of sugarcane juice to distilling and bottling. Tours end with samples of charanda. Call beforehand to ensure that there will be someone readily available to guide you. *Carretera Terétan Km. 26, tel. 452/8–20–78. Catch a CALZONZIN pesero from cnr of Obregón and Miguel Silva. Open weekdays 9–2 and 4–7, Sat. 9–2.*

LA HUATAPERA This large colonial structure, established as a hospital by Fray Juan de San Miguel, now functions as the **Museo Regional de Arte Popular.** You'll find every type of artesanal work from throughout the state displayed here. The patio out front serves as a hangout for families and couples, who toss coins into the wishing well or sit and chat on the moss-covered steps. Directly east, adjoining the museum, rests the **Templo de la Imaculada Concepción;** half a block west sits the **Templo de San Francisco.** Both have gorgeous *cantera* (pinkish stone) and plateresque exteriors but fairly dull, modern interiors. *North side of Jardín Morelos. Admission free. Museum open Tues.–Sun. 9:30–1:30 and 3:30–6. Churches open dawn–dusk.*

PARQUE NACIONAL EDUARDO RUIZ Perhaps the best reason to visit Uruapan, this park allows you to lose yourself in the semitropical flora of Michoacán without stepping outside city limits. Rich vegetation encroaches upon the stone paths that wind their way among streams,

If you're able to shake off that hangover on Sunday morning, visit the domingo saludable (healthy Sunday) held in Parque Nacional, consisting of free martial arts, yoga, aerobics, and ecology classes. The fun begins at 8 AM.

fountains, and waterfalls. The west side of the park offers the best scenery. English-speaking guides will divulge the legends of various fountains for $1.50; for the same price you can purchase the book (Spanish only) at the ticket window and read by a creek. *Calzada La Quinta, at end of Independencia, 7 blocks west of Jardín Morelos. Admission: 20¢. Open daily 8–6.*

AFTER DARK

Uruapan's nightlife and cultural activities are nothing to write home about. Information on current diversions, including film and theater, is provided by **Casa de la Cultura** (García Ortiz 1, tel. 452/4–76–13). Paseo Lázaro Cárdenas is lined with several bars that fill up on weekends with crowds who want to dance and scam (though not necessarily in that order). **Euforia's** (Madrid 10, off Lázaro Cárdenas, tel. 452/4–12–86) is a video bar with all-you-can-swill Thursday nights ($1.50 for women, $7 for men) and a $2 cover on the weekend. **La Scala** (Madrid 12, tel. 452/3–02–74) slings $2–$3 drinks, blares rock and techno music, and has an unfortunate tendency to attract high school students. Cover is $3 for men, $2 for women.

Near Uruapan

SAN JUAN PARANGARICUTIRO

The small village of **Angahuan,** northwest of Uruapan off of Highway 37, is situated in the midst of a green mountainous area. The town sees dozens of tourists daily in high season (Semana Santa and June–August), but with its small wooden houses, dirt roads, and reserved residents, it's far from being a tourist trap. The **Paradero Turístico de Angahuan** (opposite edge of town from bus stop, tel. 452/5–03–83) serves as a post for destinations farther afield. It rents cabins for $4 a person and offers free camping facilities on site. It also rents horses ($4) for the 5-kilometer trek to **San Juan Parangaricutiro,** a town buried by lava when Volcán Paricutín erupted in 1943. If you're feeling particularly active or adventurous, you can also hike the trail—though you'll have to start off at dawn to return before sunset. Be sure to bring hiking essentials: water, food, and an extra pair of legs.

In 1943 the Paricutín volcano burst from the middle of an unlucky farmer's cornfield. Lava spouted for 11 years straight until the volcano suddenly fell dormant. The mysterious beast has been quiet ever since—though you never know.

Once you arrive, you'll have to clamber over twisted moss- and plant-speckled lava to see the top of a church and other remnants of the buried town. From the church you'll get a great view

Paracho

A small indigenous town, Paracho is renowned for its handcrafted guitars; those hanging in Michoacán shops all come from here. The town itself is of no particular interest—the "downtown" area basically consists of shops selling wooden crafts—but if you're in a shopping mood, Paracho merits a visit. If you're a guitar enthusiast, be sure not to miss the town's Feria Artesanal de la Guitarra, which attracts folkloric dance groups, luthiers (guitar makers), and the most talented guitarists from around Mexico. The festival lasts one week and is usually held in late August; the tourist office in Uruapan (see Visitor Information, above) should have the exact date. Buses to Paracho (45 min, $1.50) leave from Uruapan's Central de Autobuses almost every half hour.

of the Volcán Paricutín. If you're interested in a longer trip, you can also rent horses to take you to the source of the destruction: Paricutín itself. Horses come with a guide, and the six-hour round-trip trek should cost near $9 a head. Whatever you choose to do, start out early from Uruapan, pack food and water, and don't worry about finding a guide—he'll find you. From Uruapan's bus station, **Autotransportes Galeana** buses leave for Angahuan (1 hr, 50¢) every half hour. The last bus back to Uruapan leaves around 6 PM. If you decide to stay, local families rent rooms in their homes; any guide should be able to point you in the right direction.

TZARARACUA

Ten kilometers south of Uruapan, on Highway 31, is the **Centro Turistico de Tzararacua**—the trailhead for a 2½-kilometer trek through a ravine to Tzararacua, a torrential 43-meter blanket of water that emerges from the dense, tropical vegetation, creating a swimming hole below. At the Centro you can rent horses ($3 roundtrip) for the trip to the waterfall, or hike down the long, rustic staircase. This is definitely one of the best day trips from Uruapan, though its popularity has taken a toll on the site in the form of litter and other icky human residue on the edges of the trail. **La Tzararacuita,** only 1 kilometer away from the main waterfall, is smaller and cleaner. Bring food, water, and a guide if you plan on jaunting to La Tzararacuita; you may get lost if unfamiliar with the area. To reach the Centro, catch a TZARARACUA bus (50¢) from the south side of Jardín Morelos. Buses generally run every half hour, and the ride takes about 30 minutes. The last bus back leaves at 5:30 PM—don't miss it.

THE CENTRAL HIGHLANDS

8

By Allison Eymil

The area encompassing the states of Jalisco, Zacatecas, and Aguascalientes main- tains a rich colonial setting, marked by winding cobblestone streets, classic zócalos, and restored century-old mansions. This sense of a proud preserved history is also evident in the large indigenous population that thrives in the region. Despite this emphasis on the past, old ways are quickly meshing with the new as local farmers and miners vie for service at the fax machine, and children watch MTV after a lesson in traditional dance. This strong sense of community and family extends to the visitor, especially international travelers, who seldom visit many parts of this fascinating territory. Rest assured that you'll always be welcomed with honest, open hospitality.

The Central Highland's historical significance and architectural splendor aren't its only attractions; its cities tend to be exuberant, with a distinct university feel (complete with lively, youthful students), and an unmistakeable artistic presense. Looming out of a dry and nearly unpopulated terrain like an oasis, Zacatecas city is home to the works of painter Francisco Goitia and the extensive art collections of the Coronel brothers. Art assumes a more hands-on role in Aguascalientes city, a school-saturated town that's the perfect place to take a lesson in language, sculpture, or folklorico dance; visitors are consistently greeted with a warm, almost-like-home friendliness. Finally, Guadalajara, Mexico's second-largest city, offers a cosmopolitan alternative to the more reserved and isolated towns in the region. Known as a bastion of traditional Mexican life, Guadalajara offers plenty of opportunities to enjoy mariachi music, dancing, and tequila.

Zacatecas

Perched in hilly desert land at an altitude of about 2,700 meters, the capital city of Zacatecas state derives its charm from chaotic *adoquín* (paving stone) streets and alleyways, beautiful colonial buildings, and a history made rich by nearby silver mines. The art museums here are fantastic, and the presence of a state university makes for lively weekend nights. Despite all these attractions, relatively few foreign tourists visit the city.

Although indigenous people knew of the mineral riches of the area long before the conquistadors arrived, it was not until the Spanish forced the mining of local hills that the city of Zacatecas was founded. The first operations began in the mid-16th century, and by 1728 local mines were producing one-fifth of the country's silver—a prosperity attested to by the extravagant mansions that line Zacatecas's streets. Silver mining tapered off during the fight for independence and declined even further during the Revolution, as political control of the area was hotly contested. Benito Juárez and his troops fought a decisive battle against local insurgents here in 1871, and Zacatecas was again the site of fighting in 1914, when Pancho Villa and his ragtag army routed 12,000 Huerta loyalists.

Amid the mining and fighting, Zacatecas remained a haven for intellectuals and artists, among them renowned artists Francisco Goitia and Pedro Coronel, whose namesake museums are world famous. Other Zacatecan cultural treasures have remained relatively untouched, including a stone aqueduct, colonial churches and haciendas, and one of the finest examples of colonial baroque architecture in all of Mexico—the **Catedral Basílica Menor.** Though currently home to a population of over 600,000, Zacatecas maintains a traditional, small-town attitude: Don't expect to do much here between 2 and 5 in the afternoon, when all the downtown businesses shut down for lunch. Straw hats and cowboy boots are almost mandatory gear for men of all ages, and solo women tend to disappear from the streets after 9 PM, while the young student population plagues the cafés and plazas around the city.

BASICS

AMERICAN EXPRESS **Viajes Mazzocco,** the AmEx representative, offers the usual services for cardholders, including emergency check-cashing and mail holding (Enlace 115, Colonia Sierra de Alicia, Zacatecas, Zacatecas, CP 98001, México) *Tel. 492/2–08–59. From cathedral, west on Hidalgo (which becomes Ortega), right on Enrique Estrada just before aqueduct, left on Enlace after Museo Goitia. Open weekdays 9–7, Sat. 9–noon.*

CASAS DE CAMBIO **Banamex** (Hidalgo 132, tel. 492/2–58–02) changes traveler's checks and cash weekdays 9–noon and has an ATM that accepts Cirrus, Plus, Visa, and MasterCard. **San Luis Divisa** (Independencia 82, in front of Jardín Independencia, tel. 492/4–33–24; open weekdays 9–7, Sat. 9–3) has better rates than the banks and also changes traveler's checks.

EMERGENCIES In an emergency, call the police (tel. 492/2–01–80) or the **Cruz Roja** (tel. 492/2–30–05). For medical or legal help, call the toll-free tourist line (tel. 91–800/9–03–92).

LAUNDRY **Lavandería Indio Triste,** north of the zócalo, will dry and fold 1 kilo of clothes for 75¢. Bring your load in before noon to get it back the same day. *Juan de Tolosa 826, tel. 492/2–07–38. Open Mon.–Sat. 9–3 and 4–9.*

MAIL AND PHONES The **post office** (Allende 111, tel. 492/2–01–96; open weekdays 8–7, Sat. 9–1) will hold mail sent to you at the following address for up to 10 days: Lista de Correos, Zacatecas, Zacatecas, CP 98001, México. For collect calls, use the **Ladatel** phones near the cathedral. You can also make international calls from the *caseta de larga distancia* (long-distance telephone office; Callejón de Cuevas 103) in the centro. It's open weekdays 9–9, Saturday 9–2 and 4–8.

MEDICAL AID **Farmacia Issstezac** (Dr. Hierro 512, tel. 492/2–88–89) is open round the clock. **Clínica Hospital Santa Elena** (Guerrero 143, tel. 492/2–68–61) is open 24 hours and has English-speaking doctors. **Clínica Dental Zacatecas** (Salazar 338, tel. 492/2–68–03; open weekdays 9:30–2 and 4–8, Sat. 9:30–2) gives free dental exams.

VISITOR INFORMATION The **Módulo de Información de Turismo** (Hidalgo 93, no phone; open Mon.–Sat. 9–8, Sun. 10–5) has an English-speaking staff, plenty of brochures, a great street map, and even computers that spit out info. They can also give you a copy of *Tips,* a brochure that lists monthly cultural events and activities. For tourist information over the phone, call their head office at 492/4–05–52.

COMING AND GOING

BY BUS The **Central Camionera** (Terrenos de la Isabélica 1) is on the western edge of town, and the RUTA 8 bus runs from here to downtown and back until about 9:30 PM. A taxi ride to the downtown area costs about $1.50. **Estrella Blanca** (tel. 492/2–06–84) travels to Aguascalientes (2½ hrs, $3.50), Durango (5 hrs, $8), Guadalajara (6 hrs, $10.50), Mexico City (8 hrs, $16), and San Luis Potosí (3½ hrs, $4.50) almost every hour. **Omnibús de México** (tel. 492/2–54–95) serves the above destinations and has one bus per day to Guanajuato (6 hrs, $10), leaving at 5:30 AM. Luggage storage is available (50¢ for 3 hrs) 7 AM–10 PM and they have a caseta de larga distancia.

BY CAR Head north on Highway Federal 54 to reach Monterrey (457 km), south to reach Guadalajara (1386 km). To reach Mexico City (616 km), take Federal 49 east through San Luis Potosí (191 km) and continue south on Autopista 57, which passes Querétaro (397 km) en route to Mexico City.

BY TRAIN The **train station** (tel. 492/2–02–95) is just off González Ortega, south of downtown. Buses marked FERR stop near the terminal, but a taxi ride costs only $1 from downtown. The ticket office is open about one hour before departure. Two daily southbound trains leave at around 4:55 AM (2nd class; buy tickets on the train) and 8:15 PM (1st class) for Aguascalientes (3 hrs; $2 1st class, 85¢ 2nd class), León (7 hrs; $4 1st class, $2 2nd class), and Mexico City (13 hrs, $8 1st class only). A northbound, first-class train to Chihuahua (16 hrs, $11) and Ciudad Juárez (22 hrs, $15) leaves at 9:55 AM.

GETTING AROUND

Although everything you could want to see is in or near downtown, it's easy to get lost here. The pattern of the streets is dictated by topography, and there are many side streets, *callejones* (alleyways), and winding thoroughfares. From the north, the main thoroughfare, Juan de Tolosa, branches into Hidalgo and passes the **Catedral Basílica Menor**—the heart of the town and an easily visible landmark. As it continues south, the street turns into González Ortega, which passes the **aqueduct**. Just to the east and almost parallel to the main drag is another busy street, Tacuba, lined with shops and restaurants. Avenida López Mateos, filled with *talleres* (mechanic shops) and some budget lodging, carves into the southeast corner of Zacatecas, several blocks from the center.

WHERE TO SLEEP

The hotel strip, López Mateos, is an entertaining five-minute walk from downtown—watch out for speeding buses and candy vendors who take up most of the narrow sidewalk space. To reach López Mateos from the center, walk south on Tacuba (it'll turn into Aldama), and turn left on Ventura Salazar. If you're low on funds, the safe but uncomfortable seats in the bus station will do.

➢ **UNDER $10** • **Hotel Conde de Villareal.** Because this hole-in-the-wall is closer to town, they charge more than what the rooms are worth. Nevertheless, it's still budget-friendly and clean, if you don't mind green paint, the pervasive smell of mildew, and the mostly single men who stay here. Singles cost $6, doubles $8. *Zamora 303, tel. 492/2–12–00. From pedestrian bridge on López Mateos, go ½ block west, right on Salazar until it becomes Zamora. 28 rooms, all with bath.*

Hotel Río Grande. Rooms in this three-story hotel overlook either a central courtyard or the city. Medium-size rooms are immaculate, with tiled floors, big comfy beds, and 24-hour hot water. The place is popular with backpackers and traveling families, all attracted by the great rates: Singles run $4.50, doubles $7. *Calzada de la Paz 513, tel. 492/2–53–49. From pedestrian bridge on Mateos at Salazar, walk right on Calzada de la Paz; a HOTEL sign directs you up the hill. 64 rooms, all with bath.*

➢ **UNDER $15** • **La Condesa.** A spacious, pastel-colored entranceway and a smiling staff greet you, while large carpeted rooms with clean bathrooms and comfy beds await upstairs. Most rooms open to a collective patio, and though it may seem peaceful, the many Mexican families here can create quite a racket. The central location is a plus. Singles cost $11, doubles $12. *Juárez 5, near Plaza Independencia, tel. 492/2–11–60. 61 rooms, all with bath. Laundry, parking. MC, V.*

Hotel Gami. This fairly new, three-story hotel is a great place to meet traveling students, probably because the management makes special deals with student groups. The large rooms have new red carpeting, a TV, and small, clean bathrooms. Singles run $8, doubles $11. *López Mateos 309, tel. 492/2–80–05. 3 blocks east of pedestrian bridge. 60 rooms, all with bath. Parking. MC, V.*

HOSTELS The **Turismo Juvenil Villas** is nestled in a rural, almost woodsy, setting a few kilometers east of downtown. A bed (towel and sheets included) in a single-sex dorm room runs a mere $3.50 per night. Soccer, basketball, and volleyball courts (and a pool, if you catch the manager in a good mood) are available. Lockout hours are midnight–7 AM, but talk to whoever is in charge for permission to stay out later. *End of Calle La Encartada, tel. 492/2–18–91 ext. 10. Catch RUTA 8 bus on López Mateos or from bus station; get off at Celaya and walk past the big orange-and-yellow building (you can't miss it) until you see a parklike area. 70 beds.*

FOOD

Zacatecan restaurants cater to a wide variety of tastes, offering everything from Greek to Italian to Chinese cuisine. Regional specialties are primarily in the dessert family: Among these are *queso de tuna* (a hard, dark-brown candy made from the *tuna* (prickly pear), available primarily July and August), *dulce de leche* (a candy made from milk that's so sweet it hurts your teeth), and *capirotada* (a sort of bread pudding with raisins and cinnamon, available around Easter). At **Las Norteñitas Auténticas-Gorditas de Nata,** a small mom-and-pop place wedged in between two stores on Salazar, about five doors up from López Mateos, the owner will serve you up a bag of hot *gorditas* (thick flour tortillas made with sweet milk) for 50¢. It's easy to miss, but just follow the sweet aroma in the air and you'll undoubtedly find it.

➤ **UNDER $5** • **Restaurant Camino Real.** This nondescript little eatery has all the ingredients for a good meal—it's clean, cheap, the food is great, and the service is efficient. The smiling owner will kindly bring you a filling $1.75 comida corrida, or his specialty *carne becerra* (pork meat boiled, fried, and then sautéed in tomato, chile, and garlic sauce; $2). Breakfasts go for $1.75. *López Mateos 420, ½ block south of pedestrian bridge, tel. 492/ 2–06–91. Open daily 8 AM–11 PM.*

Taquería y Rosticería La Única. The walk past roasting chickens and meat to the clean, wood-paneled dining area here will make you hungry for the meal to come. A big plate of roasted chicken with refried beans, salad, homemade potato chips, tortillas, and all the salsa and *rajas* (chile strips) you want is a steal at $1.75. Tacos are about 20¢ each and come in all types, from carne asada to *sesos* (brains) and *lengua* (tongue). *Aldama 245, tel. 492/2–57–75. From cathedral, SW on Hidalgo, left on Juárez to Aldama (also known as Zamora). Open daily 7 AM–1 AM. Wheelchair access.*

➤ **UNDER $10** • **La Cantera Musical.** Local families and tourists come here for the good food, excellent *ranchera* music, and the amusing mini-reproduction of the *teleférico* (tram) strung across the ceiling. The biggest seller is the *asado de Boda Jerezano* (pork with chiles, orange, and laurel, served with rice) for $4.50, but also try the *platillo ranchero,* a selection of appetizers such as quesadillas, *chicharrón* (pork rind), and guacamole ($5) for two people. *Tacuba 16, tel. 492/2–88–28. Underneath Mercado González Ortega. Open daily 8 AM–11 PM.*

El Dragón de Oro. Come here for something other than the same old tacos. If you're lucky, the stereo will be playing old American country and jazz to accompany your Chinese dinner. The *pollo almendrado* (almond chicken) is about $5, while the wonton soup and *sopa fu chuc* (a tofu and noodle soup in a miso-like broth) are perfect light choices for $2.50. Vegetarians will rejoice over the overflowing plate of chop suey for $5, which could easily fill two. *González Ortega, at Rayón, tel. 492/4–09–90. From cathedral, SW on Hidalgo (which becomes Ortega), 2 blocks past aqueduct. Open daily 2–10.*

WORTH SEEING

There's no way to see all of Zacatecas in one day; think about exploring one cluster of sights each day. Suggested areas for exploration include all points southwest (the aqueduct, Enrique

Estrada park, and the Goitia museum); hilltop sights (the Mina el Edén, Cerro de la Bufa, and teleférico); and the center of town (the two Coronel museums, the cathedral, and the Palacio del Gobierno). Check the weekly cultural paper *Tips* for a listing of upcoming shows, concerts, and exhibits—it's available free at the tourist office and around town.

ACUEDUCTO DEL CUBO This colonial aqueduct, constructed entirely of magnificent cantera rosa sandstone formed into 39 high arches, is a strange and beautiful sight in the middle of the city. Just behind the aqueduct is the old **Plaza de Toros,** which has been refashioned into an incredible luxury hotel, worth a look inside. Across the street is **Parque Enrique Estrada** (not to be confused with the hunk from *CHiPs*), a gorgeous, lush park with fountains, a waterfall, and romantic couples. *From cathedral, SW on Hidalgo (which becomes Ortega) for 6 blocks.*

CATEDRAL BASILICA MENOR This cathedral, on the corner of Hidalgo and Aguascalientes next to the Plaza de Armas, is without a doubt the most imposing structure in Zacatecas. The cathedral was built between 1612 and 1752, but the more recently refurbished interior is as powerful in its neoclassical simplicity as the exterior is in its complexity. The cathedral is open daily 8–2 and 4–9. Adjacent to the cathedral is the 1727 **Palacio de Gobierno** (Hidalgo 602; open weekdays 8–3:30 and 6–9), originally the mansion of a local silver baron. Inside you'll find a brilliant mural of Zacatecas's history by the noted Zacatecan artist Antonio Pintor Rodríguez. Just down the street is the state-operated **Teatro Calderón** (Hidalgo 501, tel. 492/2–86–20). Built in the late 19th century, the theater flaunts beautiful stained-glass windows and is the venue for national and international ballets, operas, and plays. Check *Tips* for schedules. Tickets run $2–$10, and the box office is open daily 4–8 PM.

CERRO DE LA BUFA Thought to resemble a *bufa* (wineskin) by the thirsty Spaniards, this mountain offers a magnificent view of Zacatecas and the surrounding countryside. You can hike a strenuous half-hour or take the teleférico to the top ($1.50 one-way) and explore the **Museo de la Toma de Zacatecas,** a museum dedicated to Pancho Villa's 1914 victory here, with photographs, diagrams, a cannon, and some weapons. Beside the museum is an 18th-century chapel honoring the patroness of Zacatecas, called **La Capilla de la Virgen del Patrocinio.** Just in back of the chapel is the **Mausoleo a los Hombres Ilustres de Zacatecas.** Both are free and open daily 9–6. *SW on Hidalgo to Callejón Luis Moya, right on Calle de la Mantequilla, then left and up, up, and up, across road to path. Museum admission: $1, 50¢ students. Museum open Tues.–Sun. 10–5.*

MINA EL EDEN A healthy 20-minute walk straight up Juárez, past the huge red IMSS hospital, takes you to another of Zacatecas's star attractions. The worthwhile tour of this mine is conducted in Spanish and begins with a ride on a miniature train into the middle level of the mine. In the mid-1500s, when the mine was at its peak, an average of eight slaves, responsible for carrying heavy loads through the wet darkness, died here each day. Conditions changed somewhat after independence and again with the Revolution, but mining continued (without electricity) until 1964, when incorrectly placed explosives caused the lower levels to flood. Interestingly enough, the mine is now home to a disco (*see* After Dark, *below*) and a couple of souvenir shops. Bring a sweater for the tour, as it gets pretty chilly down here. *Mina el Edén, tel. 492/2–30–02. From cathedral, SW on Hidalgo 4 blocks, right on Juárez (which becomes Torreón), and turn right after hospital. Admission: $2.50. Open daily 11–6.*

MUSEO FRANCISCO GOITIA This French-style mansion was built in 1948 for the governor, but now houses mainly works by the Zacatecan artist Francisco Goitia, a 20th-century painter most famous for his *Tata Jesucristo.* A copy of it is on display here (the original is in Mexico City), along with works by Pedro Coronal and his brother Rafael Coronal, among other modern artists. The grounds are beautiful, overflowing with well-tended flower beds and fountains. *Enrique Estrada 102, tel. 492/12–02–11. From cathedral, walk 6 blocks on Hidalgo, right on Miguel M. Ponce; the museum is just past the park. Admission: $1.50. Open Tues.–Sun. 10–1:30 and 5–7.*

MUSEO PEDRO CORONEL Two blocks northeast of the cathedral is a museum dedicated to Zacatecas's favorite son, artist Pedro Coronel. Coronel was a prolific collector (in fact, a much better collector than artist), and the masterpieces on display here include works by Goya, Miró, Cocteau, Kandinsky, Motherwell, Picasso, Chagall, and Dalí; ancient Greek pottery and statues; Indian, Chinese, Tibetan, and Japanese art; and a large collection of African and Latin American masks. Allow yourself plenty of time to take it all in. *Plaza de Santo Domingo, tel. 492/2–80–21. From cathedral, walk up steps next to visitor info. Admission: $1.50, 75¢ students. Open Mon.–Wed., Fri. and, Sat. 10–2 and 4–7, Sun. 10–5.*

MUSEO RAFAEL CORONEL Named for Pedro Coronel's brother, this museum is housed in the former Convento y Templo de San Francisco, and is best known by locals as Museo de las Máscaras (Museum of the Masks)—one of the best in Mexico. The grounds are beautiful enough in their own right, while the collection of character masks used in regional festivals is so enormous that you'll have a problem deciding where to look first. Detailed explanations in Spanish give historical and cultural background for the masks, and videos provides more information. The museum also contains a collection of 19th-century puppets. *Ex-Convento de San Francisco, tel. 492/2–81–16. From cathedral, NE on Hidalgo (which becomes Juan de Tolosa) and left at fountain along Abasolo. Admission: $1.50, 75¢ students. Open Mon. and Tues. 10–2 and 4–7, Thurs.–Sat. 10–2 and 4–7, Sun. 10–5.*

TELEFERICO This Swiss-made tram offers unparalleled views of Zacatecas. The ride is best combined with the Mina el Edén tour, since at the end of the tour you have the option of taking the elevator to the top of the Cerro del Grillo (Cricket Hill). Otherwise, you'll have to struggle up the exhausting flight of stairs next to the mine entrance, or hike up the Cerro de la Bufa to take a short ride on the tram (10 min each way). *Fare: $1.50 one-way. Tram runs Tues.–Sun. 10–6, weather permitting. From the center, walk east on Villalpando (which changes to Genaro Codina) and west on Callejón de García Rojas.*

AFTER DARK

You'll be at a loss for things to do at night during the week, but Zacatecas does pick up on the weekends. One bar that is open on weekdays is **La Otra España** (Tacuba 209, across from Plazuela Goitia; open Tues.–Sun. 6 PM–1 AM), popular with students. Two discos pump out the latest dance mixes and some disco favorites: **El Elefante Blanco** (Paseo Díaz Ordaz 2, tel. 492/2–71–04; open Thurs.–Sat.), near the teleférico station atop Cerro del Grillo, offers great views of nighttime Zacatecas for the steep cover charge of $5; **La Marcha** (Dr. Hierro 409, tel. 492/2–03–89; open Wed.–Sat. 10 PM–2 AM) is popular with wealthy youth. The cover here is usually $5 but it varies. Another disco is **El Melacante** (tel. 492/2–30–02; open Thurs.–Sun. 9:30 PM–3 AM), also known as La Mina, appropriately situated deep in the Mina El Edén. The cover is $5 (more than most miners earned in a year back in their day), and it's primarily a tourist trap. Drinks here run $1.50–$2. Highly recommended is the oddly named **Mr. Coyote** (José López Partillo 609-A, tel. 492/2–85–34) in the Hotel El Convento. For about $2.50 Fridays and Saturdays, you'll get to hang out with the Zacatecan collegiate crowd, amid loud disco music and pool tables. For movies, try **Biblioteca Mauricio Magdaleno,** across from Plaza Independencia, where a video center shows excellent free Mexican films and dubbed or subtitled foreign films nightly at 5:30. At the entrance is a bulletin board announcing upcoming local events, or look in *Tips* for more info.

For a night of inexpensive fun, hang out in the Plazuela Goitia (on Hidalgo, ½ block before the cathedral), where bands play on weekends. If you're lucky, you'll run into a private fiesta, known as a "callejonada," with music and a donkey with gallons of mezcal on its back.

Aguascalientes

A large and expanding industrial city, Aguascalientes, capital of the state of the same name, may disappoint those expecting the conspicuous historical charm of other highland destinations. The occasional colonial building lifts its weary head from the sprawl, but the city is mostly a tangle of pastel-colored modern buildings and neon. But although the city rates low on the aesthetic scale, and the *aguas calientes* (thermal waters) that originally attracted colonists to the region are no longer very thrilling (or even hot, for that matter), the city has never lost its appeal as a fine arts stronghold.

The main reason to come to Aguascalientes is to visit the art museums displaying works by famous locals Saturnino Herrán, Jesús Contreras, and Enrique Díaz de León. In keeping with the city's artistic legacy, there are at least a dozen art, music, and dance schools that offer a wide variety of classes. These schools, along with the state university, mean you'll find plenty of young, sociable students, most of whom are extremely friendly and curious about visitors. In fact, Aguascalientes is so devoid of tourists that people bend over backwards to lend a hand—a welcoming reception for the weary traveler. Be prepared to do some serious celebrating during the **Feria de San Marcos,** a month-long bash that attracts over one million people, including Mexican and international artists, musicians, actors, dancers, and poets. Grandiose parades, cockfights, bullfights, concerts, and earnest partying in the streets peak on April 25th, the saint's day itself. However, the celebration continues for another one to three weeks.

The Spanish dubbed Aguascalientes "ciudad perforada" (perforated city) because of the catacombs and tunnels that indigenous peoples built beneath it before the conquest.

BASICS

AMERICAN EXPRESS All cardmember services are provided here, and they'll hold cardmember mail sent to: Avenida Independencia 2351, Centro Commercial Galerías, Local 5556, Aguascalientes, Aguascalientes, CP 20130, México. *Next to Walmart, tel. 49/12–43–36. Catch Bus 5 or 6 on 5 de Mayo; alight at shopping center.*

CASAS DE CAMBIO Banamex (Plaza de la Patria, at 5 de Mayo, tel. 49/16–65–70) changes currency weekdays 9–5 and has an ATM that accepts Cirrus, Plus, Visa, and Master-Card. For longer hours but lower rates, visit **Operadora Internacional** (Juan de Monotoro 120, tel. 49/15–79–79), open weekdays 9–3 and 4–6:30, Saturday 9–4, Sunday 9–2.

EMERGENCIES Call the **police** (tel. 49/14–30–43 or 49/14–20–50) or **Cruz Roja** (tel. 49/15–20–55) for ambulance service.

LAUNDRY For $1, **Lavamatic** will wash a kilo of your clothes or let you wash 3 kilos yourself. *Montoro 418-B, 4 blocks east of Plaza de la Patria, tel. 49/16–41–81. Open weekdays 9–2 and 4–8, Sat. 9–8.*

MAIL AND PHONES Ladatel phones, along with coin-operated phones, are located in Plaza de la Patria. At the large, pink post office (Hospitalidad 108, tel. 49/15–21–18; open weekdays 8–7, Sat. 9–1), mail will be held for you for up to 10 days if sent to the following address: Lista de Correos, Aguascalientes, Aguascalientes, CP 20000, México. *From Plaza de la Patria, walk one block east on Madero, one block north on Morelos, and right on Hospitalidad.*

MEDICAL AID **Hospital Hidalgo** (Galeana 161, south of Plaza de la Patria, tel. 49/15–31–42) is open 24 hours and has some English-speaking doctors. **Farmacia Sánchez** (Madero 215, east of Plaza de la Patria, tel. 49/15–66–10) is open 24 hours.

SCHOOLS Dance schools, music schools, and even museums around the city offer courses in various subjects. The **Casa de la Cultura** (*see* Worth Seeing, *below*) offers dance, ceramics, music composition, and poetry summer classes for $5–$10 a month. Longer courses are available during the year. The **Centro Cultural Los Arquitos** (Alameda, at Héroe de Nacozari, tel. 49/17–00–23) offers similar classes at similar prices.

VISITOR INFORMATION The **Dirección General de Turismo** doesn't offer much, except a city map and friendly conversation. Some of the staff speaks English. *South of Plaza de la Patria, next to Palacio del Gobierno, tel. 49/16–03–47 or 49/15–11–55. Open weekdays 8:30–3 and 5–7, Sat. 10–1.*

COMING AND GOING

BY BUS The **Central Camionera,** open 24 hours, is on the southern edge of town, just off Avenida de la Convención. Numerous bus lines rumble through here, including **Omnibús de**

México (tel. 49/78–27–70) and Estrella Blanca's first-class line, **Futura** (tel. 49/78–20–54). Both zip to Guadalajara (3 hrs, $8), Mexico City (6½ hrs, $13), and Zacatecas (2½ hrs, $3.50), among other destinations. The bus station has a high-tech long-distance phone service and luggage storage (20¢ per hr). Taxis to downtown should cost $1.50, or you can take one of the many local buses lined up near the front entrance. Lines 3, 4, 9, 12 and 13 head to the center.

BY CAR To reach Cuidad Juárez, take Highway 45 Federal north past Zacatecas for a 1,300-kilometer ride—ugh! To Mexico City (500 km), take the 45 Federal south, then transfer to the 45-D at Celaya (tolls on this road total $10). This is the scenic route and winds through several well-known towns, such as León and Querétaro. To reach Guadalajara (260 km), drive east on the 70 Federal and continue south on the 54 Federal. All federal highways are free.

BY TRAIN The train station (tel. 49/15–21–51) lies on the eastern edge of town, some 5 kilometers from downtown. First-class trains depart daily for Ciudad Juárez (24 hrs, $14) at 7 PM, stopping in Zacatecas and Chihuahua along the way, and to Mexico City (11 hrs, $8) at 10:55 PM, stopping in Querétaro.

GETTING AROUND

Perhaps as a tribute to abstract art and *cubísmo* (cubism), the randomly placed streets in the center form more triangular and trapezoidal figures than actual "blocks." To add to the confusion, streets change names as they cross the **Plaza de la Patria** (the main square). From the north, Juárez and 5 de Mayo change into Colón and José María Chávez, respectively, south of the plaza. From the east, Madero transforms into Carranza west of the plaza. The one street that doesn't change names is López Mateos, two blocks south of the plaza, where many bars and nightclubs coexist. Luckily, almost everything you'll need is within walking distance.

WHERE TO SLEEP

Downtown is the place for budget travelers to be. What the hotels listed below lack in sophistication, they make up in convenience by putting you right in the middle of things. Definitely make reservations if you plan to stay here during the Feria de San Marcos—everything fills up.

Hotel Imperial. Wrought-iron staircases, an inner courtyard, and clean, large rooms (a few with balconies, TV, and phone) are what you'll find here. The management is so eager to please that you'll often be offered a discount if you stay for more than one night. Singles and doubles cost $11; rooms with a view run $15. *5 de Mayo 106, north side of plaza, tel. 49/15–16–50. 66 rooms, all with bath. Laundry, luggage storage.*

Hotel Rosales. This hotel looks like something from an M.C. Escher painting: An endless succession of halls leads to a number of inner courtyards, dizzying tile patterns adorn the floor, and spiral staircases lead to single rooms at odd levels. The woman who manages the place, despite her sweetness, seems to have been affected by the strange surroundings. Singles are $6, doubles $9.75. *Victoria 104, tel. 49/15–21–65. ½ block north of Plaza de la Patria. 40 rooms, all with bath. Luggage storage. Wheelchair access.*

Hotel Señorial. Rooms ($9 singles, $11.50 doubles) here have less character than those at Hotel Rosales, but they're also less worn and much quieter. The management is extremely accommodating. *Colón 104, tel. 49/15–16–30. SE cnr of Plaza de la Patria. 32 rooms, all with bath. Phone, TV. Wheelchair access.*

HOSTELS **Villa Juvenil Aguascalientes.** This hostel offers the cheapest place to stay, with eight people per small, single-sex room. The communal bathrooms are large and clean, the staff is pleasant, and if you ask nicely, they may even let you use the pool, normally open only to Villa Juvenil members. Beds cost $4 each, plus a $2.50 bedding deposit. *Av. de la Convención, at Jaime Nuño, no phone. From central López Mateos, catch Bus 22, 23, 24, or 25. From bus station, take Bus 20 to Pemex station; walk 2 blocks further in the same direction. Lockout 11 PM–8 AM.*

Eateries in Augascalientes cater to a wide variety of tastes and budgets. If you want to hang with students, head to the wheelchair-accessible **Jugos Acapulco** (Allende 106, 1 block north of Plaza de la Patria, tel. 49/18–15–20), where the afternoon comida corrida is $2.50 and a hamburger with fries costs $1.25. They also serve delicious all-natural *cerveza de raíz* (root beer; 75¢) daily 7 AM–9 PM.

Lonchería Max. If you have the late-night munchies, this taquería holds vampire hours: 8 PM–4 AM or so. Max himself reads minds and will usually have another taco (30¢) prepared for you just when you want one. The place is packed on weekends with drunks, families, and nighthawks. Sandwiches are 75¢. *331 Madero, 3 blocks east of Plaza de la Patria, tel. 49/15–45–65. Wheelchair access.*

Restaurant Mitla. The classiest bargain in town not only has service with a smile, but in dress whites and ties, no less. Try the *tampiqueña tradicional* (beef in salsa with tortillas) for $4.50, the *molletes* (a roll covered with beans and cheese) for $1.25, or any of their filling breakfasts ($2–$3). *Madero 220, tel. 49/16–36–79. East of Plaza de la Patria. Open daily 7 AM–midnight. Wheelchair access.*

Resturant Vegetariano "Devanand." Despite the name, this is not just a vegetarian restaurant—it's vegan! The all-you-can eat buffet ($3) features rotating dishes like brown rice, carrot and raisin patties, coconut ceviche, and tofu stew. Breakfast ($2.50) usually includes soy yogurt, granola, honey, juice, and some wonderful tofu dish. Meals taste best when eaten in the outdoor patio, complete with a fountain and a statue of Swami Guru Devanand. *Emiliano Zapata 201, at Libertad, tel. 49/18–27–21. 5 blocks from plaza, same side as cathedral. Open daily 9–noon and 1:30–5:30.*

WORTH SEEING

Plaza de la Patria is the heart of downtown and the site of political demonstrations and concerts; it's partially shaded, full of fountains, and an overall good place to just hang out. Here you'll find **Exedra,** a monument to King Carlos IV built in 1807 and later capped with the eagle-and-serpent symbol of revolutionary Mexico. You'll also find the **Palacio del Gobierno** (open daily 7 AM–8:30 PM), a fantastic example of colonial architecture with a deep-red hue created from sandstone and *tezontle* stones. Inside, 111 arches open onto two inner courtyards. The real highlight of the building, however, is the massive, colorful, and forceful murals by Chilean painter Osvaldo Barra, detailing the history of Aguascalientes. Barra, whose mentor was none other than Diego Rivera, worked on these murals in 1961–62, 1989, and 1991. Three blocks west of the plaza is the ever-green **Jardín San Marcos,** a family affair by day, and a make-out scene by night. Adjacent to the Jardín is the huge **Plaza San Marcos,** which livens up every year during the Feria de San Marcos with casinos, performers, and craft stands.

If you're at the Plaza de la Patria at 6 PM, you'll witness the Ceremonía de la Bandera (flag ceremony), when a group of prancing, uncoordinated soldiers march the flag into the Palacio de Gobierno for the night.

BASILICA DE NUESTRA SEÑORA DE LA ASUNCION This beloved cathedral has had a few facelifts since its inception in 1575, the most recent involving the two towers. The north one (the one with the clock) wasn't completed until 1946, which accounts for the difference in color. The neoclassic cantera rosa facade opens to a white interior laminated with gold and marble. In a side room, the *pinacoteca* (painting room) displays art by Miguel de Cabrera including oil paintings of the 12 apostles. You'll have to catch a priest—when he's not giving mass—and kindly ask him to let you in the pinacoteca. *East end of Plaza de la Patria. Mass held every 1½ hrs daily 7–7.*

CASA DE LA CULTURA Just behind the cathedral, the Casa is the artistic and social headquarters of Aguascalientes. Built in 1625 as a hacienda for a prominent Spanish family, the building has also been used as a monastery, seminary, and correctional school. Today it hosts rotating art exhibits, films, recitals, and classes of all kinds: dance, music, theater, pottery, and language. Something's always happening here, so be sure to ask about upcoming events. *Carranza 101, tel. 49/15–00–97. West of Plaza de la Patria. Admission to exhibits free. Open weekdays 7–2 and 5–9, weekends 11–8.*

MUSEO DE AGUASCALIENTES Self-taught architect J. Refugio Reyes Rivas undertook the construction of this bright orange building at the turn of the 20th century, creating an edifice in the neoclassical style with a few random details from his other favorite styles thrown in for good measure. Works by the famous local artist Saturnino Herrán are paired with appropriate quotes from Ramón López Velarde, a famous local poet and friend of the painter. Other rooms showcase changing exhibits by contemporary artists. *Zaragoza 505, tel. 49/15–90–43. Admission: 50¢, 25¢ students; free Sun. Open Tues.–Sun. 11–6. From Plaza de la Patria, walk 3 blocks east on Madero, left on Zaragoza.*

Across the street from the museum is the **Templo de San Antonio,** a bizarre structure with some neoclassical elements and a tall, domed bell tower. The interior is an explosion of colorful murals depicting events in the life of Saint Anthony, who is the patron saint of lost causes.

MUSEO DE ARTE CONTEMPORANEO This small but exquisite museum concentrates on local and national artists of the abstract, surreal, and *arte fantástico* (which blends common elements of everyday life into fantasy) movements. Exhibits rotate every two months, and each year the city hosts an art contest in honor of San Marcos. Some of the winning pieces are on display. *Montoro 222, tel. 49/18–69–01. 1½ blocks east of Plaza de la Patria. Admission: 50¢, free for students. Open Tues.–Sun. 10–6.*

MUSEO DE JOSE GUADALUPE POSADA This small museum is dedicated to the artist and journalist whose political caricatures and prints helped stir dissent against Porfirio Díaz during the Revolution. The museum exhibits Posada's art, contains a public library, and offers printing and painting classes. *North side of Jardín del Encino, tel. 49/15–45–56. From Plaza de la Patria, south on José María Chávez, 4 blocks left on Pimentel. Admission: 50¢, 25¢ students. Open Tues.–Sun. 10–6.*

Next door is the **Parroquia del Encino,** a baroque church with a black statue of Christ, as well as huge 19th-century oil paintings depicting the Stations of the Cross. *Open daily 6–1 and 4–9. Mass schedule posted at entryway.*

AFTER DARK

Aguascalientes's hip bars and nightclubs are a $2 taxi ride from the center. For closer-to-home fun, there are a number of working-class joints blaring the latest *quebradita* and *ranchera* music along López Mateos. If you prefer techno and pop, the place to be is **The Station** (Carretera al Campestre 129, tel. 49/12–09–91), which is crowded Fridays and Saturdays with beautiful people and those who want them. There's no cover and beers are $2. **IOZ** (Av. Miguel de la Madrid, no phone) is another good bar with the same people and the same music. For dancing, **El Cabus** (Hotel Las Trojes, Carretera al Campestre, tel. 49/73–00–06) packs in up to 400 people and dominates the music scene, with a $2 cover Thursday and Friday and a $4 cover Saturday. A quieter early evening scene prevails at **Café Parroquia** (Hidalgo, just before López Velarde, no phone), where bohemians spend hours over cappuccino and cigarettes. It's open until 9 PM, and coffee is about $1. **La Querencia** (Alarcón 105, near Emiliano Zapata, tel. 49/18–06–57; open Tues.–Sat. 7 PM–2 AM), a bar with a café atmosphere, attracts a hip, artsy crowd with nightly live music. For concerts ranging from ballet folklórico to classical music and theater, inquire at **Teatro de Aguascalientes** (Av. Aguascalientes, at Chávez, tel. 49/78–55–56 or 49/78–54–14) or **Teatro Morelos** (Plaza de la Republica, next to Basílica, tel. 49/15–19–41), both of which host frequent performances.

Guadalajara

Despite smog-spewing buses and over three million inhabitants, Guadalajara has retained a traditional atmosphere that can usually only be seen in smaller Mexican towns. This proud refusal to abandon a rich heritage isn't surprising, coming from the city that's considered the birthplace of several things typically Mexican: the woeful love songs of mariachi bands, the flirtatious *jarabe tapatío* (known to gringos as the Mexican hat dance), and heart-pumping *charreadas* (rodeos). These traditions are an important element of what makes Guadalajara a happening spot for tourists, and the city has taken steps to preserve the cultures and practices of the "typical" (some would say "stereotypical") Mexican.

The anonymity of modern urban life hasn't taken hold in Guadalajara: Introduce one Guadalajaran (or "tapatío," as they call themselves) to another and inevitably they will realize they have a friend or associate in common.

Elements of tradition are also evident in Guadalajara's politics. Within the last few decades, the city has often been characterized as politically conservative, mostly because of the strong influence the PAN (Partido de Acción Nacional; *see* box in Chapter 4) has here. But the PAN's and, consequently, Guadalajara's conservative air is an understandable response to the city's problems. Children are occasionally seen sleeping on the sidewalks, and, as in Mexico City, pollution worsens as the city absorbs surrounding suburbs. Guadalajara's dubious reputation as a playground for rich drug lords has also given the PAN cause for concern, and despite their best efforts to combat drug trafficking and increase police patrols, Guadalajara is no doubt still on the DEA's top 10 list.

These problems rarely touch the average traveler, however, and if you never leave the downtown area, it is easy to believe that you are in one of Mexico's finest cities. The beauty of clean, well-organized cobblestone streets and *calzadas* (walkways) and immaculately preserved colonial edifices combines with the convenience of plentiful taxis, a well-organized bus station, and enormous mercados to make Guadalajara an easily accessible and aesthetically pleasing city. A simple stroll around the *centro histórico* (historic center) will provide you with plenty of sensory overload, but there's a great deal more to see and do in Guadalajara. The huge number of students at the public Universidad de Guadalajara ensure that the city is constantly infused with new blood, and the gay population here is as "out" as is possible in Mexico: The presence of both groups ensures a diverse amount of activities, from lively peñas to transvestite shows.

The suburbs and nearby towns also offer adventure and excitement for travelers. In the towns of Tlaquepaque and Tonalá, you'll find plenty of local handicrafts, while Zapopan's basilica draws religious pilgrims from around the country. Close to the city is Lake Chapala, a favorite getaway for tapatíos and retired Americans. In the nearby town of Tequila, you can partake in the potent potable by touring distilleries and drinking your fill of free shots.

BASICS

AMERICAN EXPRESS Services provided by this AmEx office include: traveler's check exchange, personal-check cashing, and held mail for cardholders. Mail should be sent to: Vallarta 2440, Guadalajara, Jalisco, CP 44100, México. *In Plaza los Arcos, tel. 3/615–89–10. From downtown on Juárez, take PAR VIAL or Bus 500 west. Open weekdays 9–6, Sat. 9–1.*

BOOKSTORES Both **Librería México** (Plaza del Sol, tel. 3/821–01–14; open daily 8:30 AM–9:30 PM) and **Sandi's** (Tepeyac 718, tel. 3/121–08–63; open weekdays 9–6, Sat. 10–6) supply a huge selection of popular magazines and some paperbacks in English. **El Libro Antiguo** (Pino Suárez 86, Col. Centro, no phone; open Mon.–Sat. 9–8) lies 1½ blocks north of Plaza de la Liberación and swaps used books and sells English paperbacks, though most of the books they carry have titles like *Impatient Virgin* and *Lovers and Libertines*. Still, a few cheap treasures can be found, and if you read Spanish, there are plenty of choices.

CASAS DE CAMBIO **Banamex** (Juárez 237, at Corona, tel. 3/679–32–52) changes traveler's checks and cash weekdays 9–3 and has an ATM that accepts Cirrus and Plus cards. Banamex also gives cash advances on MasterCard or Visa. For better hours, try any of the

Guadalajara

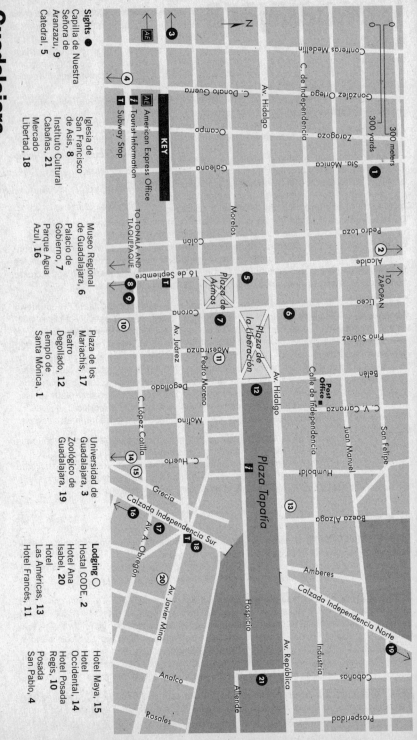

Sights ●

Capilla de Nuestra
Señora de
Aranzazú, 9
Catedral, 5

Iglesia de
San Francisco
de Asís, 8
Instituto Cultural
Cabañas, 21
Mercado
Libertad, 18

Museo Regional
de Guadalajara, 6
Palacio de
Gobierno, 7
Teatro
Degollado, 12
Templo de
Santa Mónica, 1

Plaza de los
Mariachis, 17
Plaza de
Armas
Plaza de
la Liberación
Plaza Tapatía
Parque Agua
Azul, 16

Universidad de
Guadalajara, 3
Zoológico de
Guadalajara, 19

Lodging ○

Hostal CODE, 2
Hotel Ana
Isabel, 20
Hotel
Las Américas, 13
Hotel Francés, 11

Hotel Maya, 15
Hotel
Occidental, 14
Hotel Posada
Regis, 10
Posada
San Pablo, 4

KEY

AE American Express Office
i Tourist Information
T Subway Stop

Post Office ■

TO TONALÁ AND
TLAQUEPAQUE

TO ZAPOPAN

money-changers cluttering López Cotilla between Corona and Maestranza; **Multidivisas Delta** (López Cotilla 224, tel. 3/613–16–37; open Mon.–Sat. 9–7) has good rates.

CONSULATES For countries not listed below, call the **Consular Association** at 3/616–06–29. **Canada:** Hotel Fiesta Americana, Aurelio Aceves 225, Local 30, tel. 3/615–62–15. *Near Glorieta Minerva. Open weekdays 9:30–5.* **United Kingdom:** M. A. de Quevedo 601, btw Parra and Acuña, tel. 3/616–06–29. *Open weekdays 10–1.* **United States:** Progreso 175, Col. Centro, tel. 3/825–72–00 or 3/625–55–53. *Open weekdays 8–noon.*

DISCOUNT TRAVEL AGENCIES Faculty and students make up most of the clientele at **Agencia de Viajes Universidad de Guadalajara** (Vallarta 976, in basement, tel. 3/625–85–52), so the staff knows about the cheapest plane fares and vacation packages. To get here, take the PAR VIAL or Bus 500 from downtown on Juárez. For a totally hassle-free reservation, visit **Mapamundi** (Hidalgo 2009, tel. 3/616–37–97), with a friendly, English-speaking staff that's hip to international travel. Take the PAR VIAL bus from Independencia to Hidalgo.

LAUNDRY At **Lavandería Lavarami** you can get 3½ kilos of your clothes washed, dried, and folded for $3.75. They'll also pick up and deliver if you call them. Doing your own clothes costs $1.25 per load. *Juárez 1520, tel. 3/657–16–83. Open Mon.–Sat. 9–8, Sun. 10–2.*

MAIL The full-service post office will hold mail sent to you at the following address for up to 10 days: Lista de Correos, Administración de Correo 1, Guadalajara, Jalisco, CP 44100, México. *Independencia, at Carranza, tel. 3/614–74–25. 3 blocks north of Plaza Tapatía. Open weekdays 8–7, Sat. 9–1.*

MEDICAL AID Both **Hospital del Carmen** (Tarasco 1, tel. 3/813–00–42) and **Hospital Regional ISSSTE** (at end of Av. de las Américas, tel. 3/633–02–48 or 3/633–02–52) are open 24 hours. The first has English-speaking doctors; the second is closer to downtown. **Farmacia Guadalajara** (Javier Mina 221, 2 blocks east of San Juan de Dios, tel. 3/617–85–55) has 24-hour service. Call for other locations within the city.

PHONES You can make collect or phone-card calls at any working **Ladatel** phone in Plaza Tapatía or Plaza de la Liberación. **Caseta Telefónica** (Morelos 417, at Colón, tel. 3/614–76–84) charges 60¢ for a three-minute collect call Monday–Saturday 8 AM–9 PM. You can also pay for direct-dialed calls here, but rates are higher than with a Ladatel card.

SCHOOLS The **University of Guadalajara** provides five-week Spanish language courses, as well as classes on Mexican culture, literature, and history. Contact the **Centro de Estudios Para Extranjeros** weekdays between 9 and 4 for more information or write to: Lic. Jocelyn Gacel, CEPE, AP 1, Guillón 1362, Guadalajara, Jalisco, CP 44100, México. *Guillón 1362, tel. 3/616–43–99, mercedes@corp.udg.mx.*

The **Departamento Escolar** at the **Instituto Cultural Cabañas** (*see* Worth Seeing, *below*) offers classes in Nahuatl (the Aztec language) and Mayan. You can also study Latin American literature, art, theater, folklórico dance, and music. Most classes last a semester, with a few offered during summer. For a schedule of classes and prices, stop by or write to: Dirección Escolar de la Secretaría de la Cultura, Instituto Cultural Cabañas, Cabañas 8, Plaza Tapatía, Guadalajara, Jalisco, CP 44100, México. *East end of Plaza Tapatía, tel. 3/619–36–11. Open Tues.–Sat. 10–6.*

VISITOR INFORMATION The helpful, English-speaking staff at the **Secretaría de Turismo de Jalisco** gives out complete maps of the city and information about upcoming cultural events. Several tourist information centers dot the main plazas, but you'll find the most info at the main office. *Paseo Degollado 105, Plaza Tapatía, tel. 3/658–22–22 or 3/614–86–86, toll free 91–800/3–63–22. Open weekdays 9–8, weekends 9–1.*

COMING AND GOING

BY BUS The **Central Camionera Nueva,** the main bus station, is on the Carretera Libre a Zapotlanejo (free road to Zapotlanejo) between Tlaquepaque and Tonalá, about half an hour southeast of downtown. Buses arrive here from destinations over 100 kilometers away. The huge, horseshoe-shaped structure is divided into seven terminals, each with its own group of bus lines. Each terminal has Ladatel phones, restaurants, and luggage storage—the storage in Terminal 1 is open 24 hours. Although you can always puchase bus tickets at the *taquilla* (ticket counter) from each line, tickets are also available for a number of first-class lines from **Global Travel** (Calz. Independencia Nte. 254, under Plaza Tapatía, tel. 3/617–33–30) for no extra charge. They're open weekdays 9–6:30, Saturday 9–4:30. The cheapest (20¢) way to get downtown is via Buses 275, 275-A, or 275-B, which run the length of Avenida 16 de Septiembre. Taxis to downtown cost about $3, but you have to buy your ticket at the terminal booth.

Leaving Guadalajara should be a breeze, as hundreds of buses depart daily. However, the problem lies in deciding which line to take, since they're spread out over seven terminals stretching for almost a kilometer. Running around to all of them is not a wise idea, so call several lines beforehand. If you're not one to plan ahead, go to **Flecha Amarilla** (tel. 3/600–05–26) in the first terminal for the cheapest fares and slowest buses. Destinations include Morelia (every 2 hrs, 6 hrs, $11) and Mexico City (15 per day, 9 hrs, $22). Other lines include **Autobuses del Occidente** (tel. 3/600–00–55), with buses to Morelia (6 hrs, $9.50), and **Rojo de los Altos** (tel. 3/679–04–55), with service to Ciudad Juárez (24 hrs, $40) and Zacatecas (5½ hrs, $8). **ETN** (tel. 3/600–04–72) is a good but somewhat pricey first-class line with frequent departures to Aguascalientes (3 hrs, $11), Manzanillo (5 hrs, $15), and Mexico City (8 hrs, $29).

The **Antigua Central Camionera,** the old bus station on 5 de Febrero, serves destinations within 100 kilometers of Guadalajara. **Autotransportes Guadalajara Chapala** (tel. 3/619–56–75) leaves every half hour 6 AM–9:40 PM for cities around Lake Chapala ($1.50). **Rojo de los Altos** (tel. 3/619–23–09) leaves for Tequila ($1.25) every 15 minutes 6 AM–9 PM. Luggage storage is available 7 AM–8 PM. From downtown, take Bus 110 south on 16 de Septiembre.

BY CAR To reach Mexico City (511 km), take Highway 15-D southeast and be ready to fork over $30 in tolls. You could also take the free 15 Federal, but road conditions are less safe, and you'll be driving an extra 129 kilometers. For Puerto Vallarta (366 km), take the 15-D west and pay $11 in tolls.

BY TRAIN The **train station** lies two blocks from Parque Agua Azul. The train to Mexico City leaves daily at 9 PM and takes 12 hours. Sleepers with two beds are available Friday and Saturday and cost about $28, but seats are a steal at $11 first-class, $6 second-class. The first-class train to Mexicali (36 hrs, $38) leaves daily at 9:30 AM, with stops in Mazatlán (10 hrs, $11) and Sufragio (16 hrs, $19). Much cheaper and slower is the second-class train to Mexicali (2 days, $22), which leaves daily at noon. All train tickets should be purchased prior to the day of departure to ensure availability. There is a long-distance telephone office as well as several stores selling food in the station. *South of downtown, tel. 3/650–08–26. Open daily 7 AM–9 PM. Tickets sold weekdays 9–1, Sat. 9 AM–11 PM, and Sun. before the train leaves. Take Bus 62 south on Calz. Independencia or Bus 54 south on 16 de Septiembre.*

BY PLANE Guadalajara's **airport** (tel. 3/688–57–20) lies 30 kilometers from downtown off the Carretera a Chapala. It's served by **Aerocalifornia** (tel. 3/826–19–62), **Aeroméxico** (tel. 3/669–02–02), **American** (tel. 3/616–40–90), **Continental** (tel. 3/647–46–05), **Delta** (tel. 3/630–31–30), and **Mexicana** (tel. 3/647–22–22).

If you've just arrived, the cheapest (70¢) way to the center of town is via a **Transportaciones Terrestres** (tel. 3/812–42–78) bus, which leaves from the front of the airport roughly every 20 minutes. If you need to reach the airport from the center, catch Bus 954 from the corner of Enrique Díaz de León and España. Taxis to the center of town cost $6, but, inexplicably, the ride in the other direction is $7. If you go to the taxi office inside the airport (tel. 3/688–52–48), you can get a better rate—as low as $5. In either case, you should call a day ahead to reserve a taxi.

GETTING AROUND

Although Guadalajara is the second largest city in Mexico, it's easy to get around if you stick to the centro historico. Downtown, things revolve around three connecting plazas—**Plaza Tapatía,**

Plaza de la Liberación, and **Plaza de Armas.** The plazas are bordered by Hidalgo and Avenida República to the north, Morelos and Hospicio to the south, Avenida 16 de Septiembre and Alcalde to the west, and Calzada Independencia Sur and Calzada Independencia Norte (not to be confused with Calle Independencia, a smaller street) to the east. Avenida Juárez heads west from downtown into the university area, crossing the wide, jam-packed Federalismo; after that it becomes Vallarta, crossing Chapultepec and Avenida de las Américas, and ends at a round-about called **Glorieta Minerva.** If you plan to enjoy the nightlife, you'll get to know López Mateos, which takes you south of Minerva to the huge shopping mall, **Plaza del Sol,** and the dozens of bars and clubs nearby. Get a complete street map from the tourist office (*see above*) or outside of the cathedral for $1.

BY SUBWAY Guadalajara's *tren lígero* (light-rail train), albeit a bit dodgy, is the fastest way to travel long distances. It runs both above and below ground, traveling the length of Federalismo between the Periférico Sur and the Periférico Norte stations, as well as east–west along the entire length of Javier Mina, Juárez, and part of Vallarta. Light green T signs indicate subway stations; the downtown stations are located at Juárez near Federalismo, Juárez near 16 de Septiembre, and Javier Mina at Calzada Independecia. *Fichas* (coins), which you'll need to board, should be purchased from machines located within the stations. Have exact change, as the machines will eat your money unmercifully. Trains run 6 AM–11 PM, and fare is 30¢.

BY BUS Hundreds of buses and minibuses (20¢) run all over Guadalajara daily 5 AM–11 PM. To reach Plaza del Sol and the all-important nightlife on López Mateos, take Bus 258 from Calzada Independencia Sur heading south. For destinations along Calzada Independencia Sur, such as Parque Agua Azul and the train station, hop on Bus 62 or 60. The PAR VIAL, which runs west on Juárez/Vallarta to the Minerva and east on Hidalgo to downtown, passes the university and the American Express office. Blue **Tur** buses offer air-conditioned comfort and cost 70¢. The 707 runs west on Juárez/Vallarta, while the 706 goes from 16 de Septiembre to Tlaquepaque and Tonalá. The tourist office (*see above*) can map out the bus routes for you if need be.

BY CAR Traffic in Guadalajara is not as bad as you might think, except during rush hours when things get cramped. Roads are well-maintained and parking is available on the street, but it's safest to keep your car in a hotel parking lot overnight. The parking garage **Mulbar** (tel. 3/614–89–40) on Corona, next to Hotel Posada Regis, costs $3 a day. To rent a car, choose from several companies clustered near 16 de Septiembre and Niños Héreos; **Flash** (16 de Septiembre 742, tel. 3/614–71–20) and **Dollar** (Federalismo Sur 540-A, tel. 3/826–79–59) are reputable agencies.

BY TAXI Taxis are plentiful and the only way to get around late at night. Cabs line up in front of expensive hotels, but these charge higher rates than those you hail on the street. A ride from the bar/club area around Plaza del Sol to the center of town should cost about $2. As night wears on, taxis jack up their rates by $1 or more.

WHERE TO SLEEP

The best reason to stay downtown is the proximity to sights in the center as well as to the bus lines that will take you elsewhere. The neighborhoods southeast of Plaza Tapatía have cheap accommodations, but you might not feel safe walking alone here at night. Directly northeast you'll find a similar situation, but as long as you stay within a five-block radius of the plaza, you shouldn't encounter anything too scary. The drawback to nearly all budget hotels in Guadalajara is the noise from street traffic, but you can often avoid it by requesting a room facing away from the street. If you plan to stay a while, *casas de huéspedes* (rooming houses) rent rooms by the month for a little more than $100. Ask for a list from the Universidad de Guadalajara's center for foreign students, or at the state tourist office (*see above*). If all the hotels below are booked, try the wheelchair-accessible **Hotel Maya** (López Cotilla 39, tel. 3/614–54–54), with clean singles for $9 and doubles for $11.50, both with bath.

➤ **UNDER $10** • **Hotel Las Américas.** This hotel, conveniently located across from Plaza Tapatía, provides bright, clean, carpeted rooms with TVs and phones. The area is pretty safe, but traffic can be a bit much, so get a room on the top floor (with sun roofs and plant-filled breezeways) or in the back. Singles cost $9, one-bed doubles $10, and two-bed rooms $12.50. *Hidalgo 76, tel. 3/613–96–22. 3 blocks east of Teatro Degollado. 49 rooms, all with bath. Luggage storage. Wheelchair access.*

Hotel Occidental. The hotel is clean and the staff young, raucous, and friendly—you won't have trouble making friends here, especially if you're female. It's situated on a grungy side street, but the brightly painted halls and rooms are sure to cheer you up once you're inside . . . if the smell of disinfectant doesn't knock you out first. The *matrimonial* (double) beds were made with a very slim couple in mind. Singles run $5.75, one-bed doubles $6.50, and rooms with two beds cost $9.50. *Villa Gómez 17, btw Molina and Huerto, tel. 3/613–84–06. 3 blocks south of Plaza Tapatía. 51 rooms, all with bath. Free parking.*

Posada San Pablo. This immaculate hotel offers the most amenities for your money: a sunny courtyard, a reading room stocked with books in English, a kitchen, and a back patio complete with a BBQ. The owner, Lilly, and her family are so successful in making guests feel at home that you won't want to leave. Singles cost $6.50 ($8 with bath), doubles $8 ($9.50 with bath). *Madero 429, btw Ocampo and C. Donato Guerra, tel. 3/614–28–11. 18 rooms, 12 with bath. Laundry, free parking. Reservations advised.*

➣ **UNDER $15** • **Hotel Ana Isabel.** Despite the dodgy nighttime surroundings and an apathetic staff, this hotel is a good economical choice. A long plant-filled hallway leads to peaceful rooms with ceiling fans, large bathrooms, and black-and-white TVs—one of the reasons why it's so popular with Mexican families. Singles cost $9, doubles $11. You can also get free coffee all day long. *Javier Mina 164, tel. 3/617–79–20. 42 rooms, all with bath.*

➣ **UNDER $20** • **Hotel Posada Regis.** This establishment offers small, carpeted rooms and a relaxing, if somewhat dilapidated, elegance. It's the place to stay if you are short on cash and need to exercise your plastic. Carmen and Lolita, the proprietors, will do all they can to ensure your stay is a pleasant one. Singles run $13, doubles $16, but the prices go down if you stay a week or longer. *Corona 171, at López Cotilla, tel. 3/613–30–26. 18 rooms, all with bath. Laundry, luggage storage. Pay parking next door with discounts for hotel guests. MC, V.*

➣ **UNDER $25** • **Hotel Francés.** After a weary day of traveling, treat yourself to a great night's stay here—your body will thank you if your wallet doesn't. Built in 1610 as Guadalajara's first hotel and trading post, this place is elegant, to say the least. Rooms ($23) are huge, with wood or tile floors, ceiling fans, and clean bathrooms (and tubs). On weekends, mariachi bands march into the lobby and entertain guests all night. The young, peppy staff will do anything to please you, especially Robert. *Maestranza 35, tel. 3/613–11–90. Behind Palacio del Gobierno. 67 rooms, all with bath. Luggage storage, parking, phones, TV. Wheelchair access.*

HOSTELS **CODE.** This youth hostel, affiliated with a sports complex, has four dorm rooms, each stuffed with 20 bunk beds. The communal bathrooms (with showers) are clean, well-maintained, and have toilet paper (a real luxury). Doors close at 10 PM, so if you miss the curfew, prepare to stay out until 6 AM. Beds (including sheets) cost $2. *Alcalde 1360, near the roundabout, tel. 853–00–11. From downtown, Bus 231 up Alcalde; get off ½ block after Instituto de la Artesanía Jaliciense. 80 beds, none with bath. Check-in 8–2 and 3–9. Luggage storage. Closed Christmas and Easter.*

FOOD

Though Guadalajara is a big city, the cuisine isn't as international as you might expect. Instead, foreigners and Mexicans alike come here for that "authentic" Mexican experience, so be prepared to dig into those tamales *con mucho gusto*. Regional specialties include *tortas ahogadas* (literally "drowned sandwiches," generously bathed in a tomato-based sauce). Also popular is *jericalla*, a rich, sweet custard. You'll find both at the stands in Mercado Libertad.

DOWNTOWN The city center doesn't cater to people searching for a fine dining experience, but you'll find lots of cheap fast food here, particularly *tortas* (sandwiches). During the afternoon on Moreno (1 block north of Juárez), tons of small shops offer specials, such as five tacos or three tostadas for less than a dollar. Mercado Libertad (*see* Worth Seeing, *below*) swarms with food stalls selling the cheapest meals in town, but one jocose resident ominously called those meals *platillos de cólera* (plates of cholera), so watch out. For an inexpensive breakfast, **Croissants Alfredo** (Morelos 229, across from Plaza de la Liberación; open daily 8 AM–9:30 PM) sells baked goodies for about 20¢ apiece.

La Chata. In business for over half a century, this cheerful restaurant serves excellent traditional food at decent prices. Though you can get cheaper dishes like *sopes* (fried tortillas topped with beans, salsa, and meat or cheese) for less than $2, you'll probably want to try a specialty such as the *platillo jalisciense* (one-quarter of a chicken, french fries, a sope, one enchilada, and one flauta; $3.50). Breakfasts run $1.75. *Corona 126, tel. 3/613–05–88. 2 blocks south of Plaza Tapatía. Open daily 8 AM–11:30 PM.*

Gorditas Estilo Durango. Students short on cash come here for *gorditas* (thick corn tortillas) stuffed with sausage, cheese, or shredded beef for less than $1 each. The menú del día (soup, refried beans, an entrée, and a drink) is a filling meal for $2. *Moreno 552, at Díaz de León, tel. 3/626–47–23. Open Mon.–Sat. 8–6.*

Krishna Prasadam. The peacock feathers, pictures of Hindu deities, and Indian music might give the impression that you took a wrong turn somewhere and left Mexico. The delicious comida corrida ($2), which includes soup, tofu and peppers in tomato sauce, breaded vegetables, copious amounts of salad loaded with veggies, whole-wheat tortillas, fruit, and a yogurt drink, will do nothing to dispel that impression. *Madero 694, at Federalismo, tel. 3/626–18–22. Open Mon.–Sat. 10–6.*

Restaurant Panamerican. Though the atmosphere here leaves a bit to be desired, the chicken mole ($2.25) more than makes up for it. The egg or chicken chilaquiles are the best breakfast deal in town at $1. *Plaza de los Mariachis 47, no phone. Open daily 8 AM–1 AM.*

Restaurant Sandy's. Despite its generic name, this restaurant delivers an out-of-the-ordinary menu. An overflowing platter of vegetables with shrimp, or a burger with mushrooms runs $2.50. The view of the shady Plaza de la Rotonda from the terrace is a good accompaniment to any meal. *Independencia, at Alcalde, upstairs, tel. 3/614–42–36. Open daily 8 AM–10 PM.*

Taco Cabana. This economic eatery is always packed with friendly families. Mexican music blares from the jukebox and the two-for-one beer specials add to the jovial environment. Breakfasts run less than $1.25, or choose from a variety of 30¢ tacos. *Pedro Moreno 248, at Maestranza, tel. 3/613–11–90 ext. 19. Open daily 9 AM–10 PM.*

AVENIDA CHAPULTEPEC/AVENIDA AMERICAS Restaurants get more upscale the farther west you go, as the area between Avenidas Chapultepec and Américas attests. Nevertheless, many restaurants are accessible to the budget traveler, and the peaceful, residential neighborhood is a welcome break from the topsy-turvy bustle of downtown. To get here, catch a PAR VIAL bus or take a leisurely walk (25 minutes) from downtown.

Los Itacates. The Mexican equivalent of the power-lunch meeting place, this restaurant specializes in traditional dishes such as *coachal* (shredded chicken and pork with corn) and *pollo itacates* (one-quarter of a chicken with cheese enchiladas, potatoes, and rice). Both dishes run about $2.75 and the breakfast buffet is only $2.50. *Chapultepec Nte. 110, tel. 3/825–11–06. 4 blocks north of Vallarta. Open Mon.–Sat. 8 AM–11 PM, Sun. 8–7.*

Las Margaritas. A friendly, English-speaking staff and unique vegetarian entrées make this small restaurant a perfect place for lunch al fresco. The lentil salad includes cottage cheese, tomato, and onions, served with bread, for $4. The owner is extremely proud of his *cacerola margarita*, a veggie casserole with mushrooms, olives, and soybeans, topped with cheese. Breakfasts cost $2–$3, and the comida corrida includes soup, bread, vegetables, an entrée, dessert, and coffee for about $3. *López Cotilla 1477, at Chapultepec, tel. 3/616–89–06. Open Mon.–Sat. 9–9, Sun. 10–6.*

PLAZA DEL SOL Plaza del Sol is a massive open-air shopping mall popular with Guadalajara's nouveaux riches. The neon lights, pulsing rock music, and not-so-subliminal messages to shop till you drop will soon have you longing for the taco stands and grittier life of downtown. On the plus side, the food around here is excellent, if a bit expensive.

Dainzú. In the middle of an upper-class residential neighborhood, this small restaurant introduced Oaxacan cuisine to Guadalajara in 1986. The $2 soups are a fantastic prelude to classic Oaxacan entrées such as *tlayuda con tasajo* ($6), a large corn tortilla cooked with black beans and cheese and a huge slab of marinated meat on the side. *Diamante 2598-A, tel. 3/647–50–86. From Mariano Otero, east past Expo, right on Av. Faro, then right on Diamante. Open Tues.–Sat. 1–10:30, Sun. 1–8.*

CAFÉS If you're going to take in a movie at the Videosala (*see* After Dark, *below*), the adjacent **El Café** (Hidalgo 1292, no phone; open Mon.–Sat. 9 AM–10 PM) offers outdoor tables on a lush patio and a bizarre, quasi-Victorian atmosphere indoors, complete with velvet. Coffee drinks run $1–$2, and light sandwiches and desserts cost $2–$3. Every night of the week something is stirring at **Café La Paloma** (López Cotilla 1855, 1 block west of Av. de las Américas, tel. 3/630–01–95; open daily 9 AM–10 PM). A few bohemian types are scattered among the Guadalajaran youth, all smoking and looking cool. The house specialty, *Santa Perico* (Kahlua, Rompope, vodka, and pineapple juice) will jolt you back to life for $2.

WORTH SEEING

Most of Guadalajara's sights are nestled on or around the Plaza Tapatía, in what is known as the centro histórico. To tour this area, grab a map of the centro from the tourist office and hoof it. Although Guadalajara's three important suburbs (Tlaquepaque, Tonalá, and Zapopan) are officially separate from the city, they have been engulfed by the metropolis and are easily reached by city bus.

CENTRO HISTORICO

➤ **CATEDRAL** • Completed in 1618 after 57 years of work, Guadalajara's religious centerpiece has undergone numerous modifications over the centuries, culminating in an eclectic combination of baroque, Renaissance, Moorish, and neo-Gothic styles. Its twin yellow spires were added in 1854, after an earthquake destroyed the original towers. The cathedral contains an excellent collection of religious art–relics of Guadalajara's colonial-era wealth and importance. King Fernando VII of Spain gave the city 10 silver-and-gilt altars in gratitude for financial aid during the Napoleonic Wars. Carved from a single piece of balsa, the altar and statue dedicated to Our Lady of the Rose was a gift from King Carlos V in the 16th century. To the right of the main altar are the remains of St. Innocence, brought here from the catacombs in Rome. The schedule for mass is posted at the entryway; the service is especially beautiful and solemn— don't wander around gawking during the ceremony, as some tourists have been known to do. *Hidalgo, at Alcalde. Open daily 7 AM–9 PM.*

Those unashamed of being tourists can take a ride on one of the numerous calandrias (horse-drawn carriages) that crowd the center. A 45-minute scenic tour costs $10, but it sure beats walking.

➤ **CHURCHES** • The baroque **Iglesia de San Francisco de Asis** is one of Guadalajara's first churches. Columns with vine-like ornamentation in the entryway lead into the plateresque interior. Note the Santo Niño de Atocha and Santo Ninó de la Misericordia to the right of the main altar who are happily showered with toys by visiting children. Mass schedules are posted at the door. *16 de Septiembre, at Prisciliano Sánchez.*

The **Capilla de Nuestra Señora de Aranzazu** is the only remaining chapel of the five that once surrounded the Iglesia de San Francisco; the others have been demolished. The chapel is unique among Guadalajara's churches because of its three richly detailed and gold-embellished wooden *Churrigueresque* (ultra-baroque) altarpieces, considered among the finest in the world. Their physical size and presence overpower the small interior of the church for a fascinating effect. *16 de Septiembre, at Prisciliano Sánchez.*

The **Templo de Santa Mónica** was built in 1773 for the Augustinian nuns who lived next door. With its ornate gold interior, the church is an excellent example of baroque architecture. In the northwest corner of the building is an interesting statue of St. Christopher with mestizo features. Sit among the tapatíos during mass (held every hour daily 7:30 AM–9:30 PM) and admire the beauty. *Santa Mónica, at San Felipe.*

➤ **INSTITUTO CULTURAL CABANAS** • Built between 1805 and 1810, this building served as an orphanage until 1979, when it was transformed into the city's cultural center. An important example of neoclassical architecture, the building is home to 23 wonderful courtyards, several art exhibits, a small theater, and a cafeteria. In the late 1930s, José Clemente Orozco painted a series of murals on the ceiling and walls of the building's main chapel, including what is considered his finest work, *The Man of Fire.* Also displayed here are some of Orozco's lithographs and paintings. Excellent tours are given in both Spanish and English. Guides work on a volunteer basis and should be tipped $1.50. *Hospicio 8, tel. 3/617–45–02. Admission: $1.50, 50¢ students; free Sun. Open Tues.–Sat. 10–6, Sun. 10–3.*

➤ **MERCADO LIBERTAD (SAN JUAN DE DIOS)** • Heavily promoted by the tourism department, this market is just a larger version of markets found all over Mexico. The existing market was built in the 1950s (which explains the architecture), but people have been buying and selling here for over 400 years. Three stories of jam-packed stalls sell everything from artesanía goods, like leather *huaraches* (sandals) and Mexican blankets, to *fayuaca,* the inexpensive electronic merchandise sold without warranties, instructions, or even packaging. Even the pickiest shopper or cultural anthropologist will leave satisfied. *Javier Mina, at Calz. Independencia Sur. Open daily 6 AM–8 PM.*

➤ **MUSEO REGIONAL DE GUADALAJARA** • The displays of pre-Columbian artifacts here are impressive, and the exhibit tracing Jalisco's history is interesting if you read Spanish. There's also a collection of colonial paintings, the most impressive of which is the newly restored *Alegoría del Paraíso de las Monjas Carmelitas.* In this 17th-century painting, a crucified Jesus's spurting blood turns into a field of flowers, plants, and trees at his feet, while a group of Carmelite nuns looks on approvingly. *Liceo 60, tel. 3/614–99–57. Admission: $1.75, free Sun. and holidays. Open weekdays 9–6:30, Sun. 9–3.*

➤ **PALACIO DE GOBIERNO** • The governor of New Galicia had this stately Churrigueresque mansion built in 1643. It was here that independence fighter Miguel Hidalgo decreed the abolition of slavery in 1810, and where Benito Juárez was almost assassinated by his enemies in 1858, before Don Guillermo Prieto stopped the would-be killers with the now-famous phrase, "*Los valientes no asesinan*" ("The brave do not kill"). All of these revolutionaries have been captured in bronze in the **Sala Jalisco** (open Tues.–Sun. 9–3 and 6–9), where

The $20,000 Cock

If you're interested in learning more about Mexican culture—and the Mexican psyche— drop by Veterinaria Gallero, a store that specializes in fighting cocks. Those for sale are on display, and for the bargain price of $70, you too could be the proud owner of a (cheap) fighting cock. Mexican cocks fight with various types of weapons attached to their feet, from the inch-long "arma de filo" (blade) to the shorter "navaja corta" (razor). There are about 60–70 different types of cocks, but those of Asian origin are favored, as are those with shorter spurs. The friendly vet will happily answer your questions about the contests and tell you where to find one. The most popular place is Palenque la Tapatía (tel. 3/635–29–37), at Revolución 2120. Normal wagers for cockfights are about $10–$20, though they can climb as high as $20,000. Losses like this can be a double bummer, for not only are you suddenly destitute, but your favored cock is a heap of dead feathers. Calz. Independencia Sur 500, tel. 3/658–18–40. Open weekdays 9:30–2 and 4–7, Sat. 9:30–2:30.

you'll also see portraits of Jalisco's past governors scattered across the walls. However, the main attraction is definitely Orozco's dramatic *Social Struggle* in the stairwell on the right. It features a huge portrait of a white-haired Hidalgo jumping out from the chaos of war, fascism, communism, and ecclesiastical oppression. *Corona, btw Morelos and Pedro Moreno. Admission free. Open daily 9–9.*

Across the street is the **Plaza de Armas.** France donated the wrought-iron kiosk, decorated with half-naked women, in 1910. Today the bright green structure is surrounded by eerie contrasts—small children run around feeding flocks of pigeons, while others are begging for money. Occaisonally, political protestors congregate in the plaza as well. Stick around for free concerts Thursday and Sunday at 7 PM.

➤ **TEATRO DEGOLLADO** • One of Guadalajara's most cherished possessions is this neoclassical opera house, modeled after Milan's La Scala and opened in 1866. Above the Corinthian columns grandly marking the theater's entrance is a relief depicting Apollo and the nine Muses. The interior was exquisitely restored in 1988, and if you don't attend a performance here, be sure to take a look when it's open to the public. The university's renowned **Ballet Folklórico** performs here every Sunday at 10 AM. Tickets range from $2 to $5.50. The city's **Ballet Folklórico de Guadalajara** kicks down Fridays at 8:30 PM for the same price (half price for students). *Belén, at Hidalgo, tel. 3/614–47–73. Box office open daily 10–1 and 4–7. Theater open to public Mon.–Sat. 10–2.*

➤ **UNIVERSIDAD DE GUADALAJARA** • The university's administrative offices rest in a beautiful turn-of-the-century building. Two famous Orozco murals are on view at the auditorium, one on the dome and another behind the stage. Across the street, take the elevator to the top floor of the university's main building (a big cement block) for a good view of southeastern Guadalajara. Or, take the elevator to the basement to watch movies at **Cine Foro** (*see* After Dark, *below*). One block south of the university is the **Templo Expiatorio** (Madero, at Escorza), a pseudo-Gothic cathedral that's just been completed after nearly 100 years of construction. It's so dark and imposing that you almost expect to hear Gregorian chants ascending from the choir. *Vallarta, at Enrique Díaz de León. Take Bus PAR VIAL west on Juárez and ask to be let off at the university.*

➤ **ZOOLOGICO DE GUADALAJARA** • With 32 hectares (79 acres) to cover and nearly 2,000 animal species to gawk at, you'll need a whole lot of energy and probably the entire afternoon to see the entire zoo. Luckily, there is a 50¢ train that traverses the circumference of the park, stopping mid-way at the *Barranca de Huentán,* where you can see part of the canyon that borders the city. *Paseo del Zoológic 600, tel. 3/674–44–88 or 3/674–43–60. Admission: $1.75. Take Bus 60-A north on Calz. Independencia (Norte or Sur) and get off at the main entrance. Open weekdays 10–5, weekends until 5:30.*

SOUTH OF THE CENTRO HISTORICO Guadalajara's premier getaway is the **Parque Agua Azul.** Nine hectares of eucalyptus, pine, and jacaranda entice you onto shady paths, benches, and grassy spots. There's also a small orchid greenhouse, a butterfly house, and a huge aviary where you can get up close and personal with parrots, peacocks, and other exotic birds. *Calz. Independencia Sur, south of Niños Héroes, tel. 3/619–03–28. Take Bus 62 south on Independencia and ask to be let off at Niños Héroes. Admission: 50¢, 25¢ students. Open Tues.–Sun. 7–6.*

At the northern end of the park is the **Casa de Artesanías de Jalisco,** a fabulous government-run crafts store, laid out like a museum, with examples of crafts from various regions in Mexico. Prices here are generally too high for mere mortals, but it's a good place to check out quality items before buying from street vendors. *Calz. Gallo 20, tel. 3/619–46–64. Open weekdays 10–7, Sat. 11–5, Sun. 11–3.*

The **Teatro Experimental de Jalisco,** next to the park's main entrance, performs everything from Shakespeare to Mexican avant-garde. Check the bulletin board near the park entrance, take a glance at "Tentaciones" (*see* After Dark, *below*), or call 3/619–37–70 for more information.

The **Museo de Arqueología del Occidente** is small, well-organized, and packed with pottery made by indigenous peoples of western Mexico. Inside the lobby, the museum store sells some

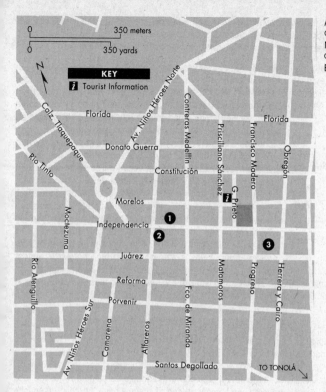

display items at slightly elevated prices. *Calz. Independencia Sur, at Calz. Campesino, across from park. Admission: 20¢. Open Tues.–Sun. 10–2 and 4–7.*

TLAQUEPAQUE Guadalajara's elite made Tlaquepaque a country retreat, but Guadalajara's automobiles and city sprawl later impinged on its rustic appeal. The town's spacious country homes fell into disrepair and continued to deteriorate until the 1960s, when artists converted the buildings into studios. Today, Tlaquepaque's center is a lively and colorful pedestrian zone lined with gallery after gallery of often overpriced handmade crafts and rustic furniture. Browsing is perfectly acceptable, and, as always, the vendors on the street offer a better deal and often a better selection on most items.

The main drag in Tlaquepaque is Independencia, a pedestrian-only street. **Artmex la Rosa de Cristal** (Independencia 232, tel. 3/639–71–80), a glass manufacturer, opens its studio to the public Monday–Saturday 10–6; witness the ancient craft of glassblowing and then browse through the shop. The free **Museo Regional de la Cerámica** (Independencia 237, no phone), housed in an old country estate, exhibits the work of expert potters and operates a small gift shop. Independencia ends in the lively **El Parián** plaza (Independencia, at Madero). Named after the Chinese section of Manila, the plaza is a great place to grab a beer and refuse the advances of mariachi bands and portrait artists. Several bars are situated on the outer part of the plaza, while the gazebo in the center features local bands on weekends. For maps, information on festivals, or any other tidbits, head to the **tourist office** (tel. 3/659–02–38; open daily 9–6) at Sánchez 74, right next to the post office. *To Tlaquepaque, take Bus 275 or 275-A south on 16 de Septiembre; after traveling about ½ hr down Revolución, get off at roundabout just after passing under brick arches, and walk NW to Independencia.*

Nearly all restaurants here are overpriced, so if you want a sit-down meal, go where it's worth the extra pesos. **Restaurante Sin Nombre** (Madero 80, tel. 3/695–45–20; open daily 8 AM– 9 PM) prepares excellent food, served on a beautiful outdoor patio. The waiter will recite the menu in English or Spanish as peacocks crow in the background. Soups and salads run $2, main dishes cost $4.50. At **Birriería El Sope** (C. Donato Guerra 142, tel. 3/635–65–38; open daily 9–8), meat lovers can sample a $3 plate of *birria* (roasted goat or pork stew).

TONALÁ This smaller, humbler version of Tlaquepaque is also a famous crafts center. In fact, many of the ceramics and other crafts sold in Tlaquepaque are made here, so prices tend to be cheaper. The town's simple adobe houses and down-to-earth feel draw those tired of the tourist track (although plenty of full-on tourists come

Tonalá was governed by a woman, Cihualpilli Tzapotzintli, when the Spaniards arrived in 1530. She decided to welcome the newcomers peacefully, despite the opposition of her male advisors. So much for women's intuition.

here as well). The small **tourist information booth,** right on the Plaza Principal, hands out maps and entertaining brochures, and the staff is quite friendly. Every Thursday and Sunday 8–4, there is a *tianguis* (open-air market), where vendors sell everything from local wares to trinkets from Hong Kong. The free **Museo Nacional de la Cerámica** (Constitución 110, tel. 3/683–04–94; open Tues.–Sun. 9–1 and 4–6) displays pottery from different states and eras and has a workshop and small store. The **Santuario del Sagrado Corazón,** with its brightly painted interior and Sacred Heart sculptures, is worth a visit. Behind the altar is a striking representation of Jesus Christ rising from the earth amidst huge, gray clouds. Also, don't miss the chance to witness a *charreada* (rodeo) complete with lassoes and wild-horse taming; **Lienzo Charro González Valle** stages rodeos every Saturday at 4 PM; tickets are $2. *To reach Tonalá, take Bus 275 or 275-A south on 16 de Septiembre, past Tlaquepaque.*

ZAPOPAN Another victim of Guadalajara's voracious appetite is Zapopan, about 11 kilometers north of Guadalajara's center. Zapopan boasts the **Basílica de Zapopan,** an 18th-century structure with an ornate baroque facade and a tiled dome, home to the **Virgen de Zapopan.** This 10-inch figurine is supposedly one of Mexico's strongest miracle workers, having first achieved fame in 1541, when a Franciscan monk and protector of the indígenas came up with the idea to dress the statue in bright colors and gems. When the sun shone on the Virgen she "glowed"—brightly enough to frighten the ignorant Spanish from further attacks on the struggling indigenous people. Today, veneration of the virgin culminates in a pilgrimage every October 12, when over one million faithful tapatíos honor the figurine's return to the basilica after her annual tour of every church in her diocese. The small **Museo Huichol,** at the east end of the basilica, is run by Franciscan monks who proselytize among the Huichol people (*see* box, *below*). The museum exhibits colorful clothing, beadwork, and the unique, elaborate renditions of Huichol myths "painted" entirely with yarn. Most items are for sale; proceeds benefit the Huichol people. For more information, visit Zapopan's **visitor information** center in the **Casa de Cultura** (Vicente Guerrero 233, tel. 3/633–05–71; open Mon.–Sat. 10–1 and 4–7). *To Zapopan, take Bus 275 north on 16 de Septiembre.*

CHEAP THRILLS

On the northeastern edge of Guadalajara, Calzada Independencia Norte comes to an abrupt end at the **Barranca de Oblatos,** a 630-meter-deep canyon. On weekends, the canyon park lures families with its numerous jungle gyms, spectacular views, and varied vegetation. To get here, take Bus 60 north on Calzada Independencia Norte and exit at the last stop. Admission is 20¢ and it's open daily 7–7. You need to take a different bus to reach the **Cola de Caballo** (Horsetail) waterfall, which shoots out into the depths of the canyon. Although you won't be able to swim here, you will be able to kick back and relax. To reach the waterfall, take Bus 54 on 16 de Septiembre to Glorieta la Normal; transfer to LOS CAMACHOS bus to Parque Dr. Atle (20–30 min total). The park is open Tuesday–Sunday 10–6, and admission is 75¢.

A full Sunday, and them some, could be spent browsing the rows of stands in **El Baratillo,** Mexico's second-largest outdoor market. Stretching primarily along Javier Mina (several blocks down from the San Juan de Dios market, after Belisario Domínguez), the market forms a huge maze covering some 30–40 city blocks. Just when you think you've seen it all—shoelaces, cassettes, vegetables, new and used clothes, a new drill press, live pigs and goats—something else pops up. *Take PAR VIAL bus east on Hidalgo until you see market. Open Sun. 8 AM–4 PM.*

If you haven't worn out your dancing shoes yet, head out to the small town of **Santa María Tequepexpan,** where a *tardeada* (afternoon dance) is held at the bullfighting arena after the sporting events on Sundays. Cowboy culture appears in all its glory, with men in Western-wear swinging their partners to *ranchera* music. Admission is $1 (women can usually get in free), and the fun lasts from about 5 to 10 PM. Check with the tourist office to make sure there's a bullfight that Sunday. *Take tren lígero south to Periférico Sur. Stop and ask someone to point you toward Santa María Tequepexpan; it's a 10-min walk.*

FESTIVALS

Lake Chapala (*see* Near Guadalajara, *below*) is the place to be for **Carnaval** (late February or early March). The **Fiestas de Junio,** from mid-June to early July, celebrate the artesanía of Tlaquepaque with music, dancing, cockfights, and loads of food and drink. The **Fiesta de Santiago Apostol** (July 25) is an all-day fair that takes place in Tonalá, culminating in the *Danza de los Tastoanes,* an indigenous dance reenacting the Spanish conquest. The **Fiestas de Octubre** is Guadalajara's month-long commercial and cultural fair. If you're not interested in exhibits demonstrating the richness of Jalisco's agriculture and industry, then pottery demonstrations, cheese and wine tastings, and musical performances—from folk to experimental—should keep you busy. Smack in the middle of the Fiestas de Octubre, on October 12th, Guadalajara also celebrates the **Día de la Virgen de Zapopan** (*see* Worth Seeing, *above*), when pilgrims walk the 7 kilometers between Guadalajara's cathedral and Zapopan's basilica.

AFTER DARK

Guadalajara once rivaled Mexico City in good times till dawn, but now ordinances require all fun to stop at 1 AM. Of course, it doesn't. Plenty of discos and bars have special contracts with

The Struggle of the Huichol

Most Huichol Indians live in northern Jalisco and southern Nayarit, in a 240,000-hectare (592,800-acre) reservation granted them in 1953. The reservation is primarily accessible by plane, although rocky dirt roads are beginning to cut their way to the reservation. Often the Huichol will travel for five days to bring their handicrafts to the museum in Zapopan. Although the Catholic Church, specifically the Franciscan order, has made a slight dent in the Huichol's religious beliefs, their primary spiritual leaders are shamans, who have a great deal of political influence in the Huichol community. The people insist on maintaining their traditions, as well as their land, resulting in an ongoing conflict with local landowners. The ownership and exact territorial boundaries of 22 hectares that the Huichol had rented out to farmers and cattle breeders are currently in dispute. There have also been allegations of human rights violations perpetrated by Nayarit police as well as the current "tenants." The government's Human Rights Comission (CEDH) has been investigating the violations since 1993 and has granted some financial and political support to the Huichol. In fact, a constitutional amendment recently passed, recognizing the autonomy of the Huichol and other indigenous communities within Mexico. Yet, even with these advances, ownership of the land continues to be a heated issue.

the city government to keep things churning after hours, but since buses stop at around 11 PM, taxis ($2–$3) are your only option back to the budget lodging area.

The old standbys—bars and discos—are clustered around Avenidas Chapultepec and Vallarta, though you'll need plenty of money and connections for the guy at the door to decide you're cool enough to get in. The alternative scene is also alive and well. Raves, or *dancerías,* complete with ecstasy and other Alice-in-Wonderland digestibles, are currently outlawed, but they continue underground. For information on the alternative scene, check with the guys at **El Quinto Poder** music shop (Madero 210, tel. 3/614–05–42) or at **Centro Cultural Roxy** (*see* Music, *below*). Plenty of happening gay and lesbian clubs are scattered throughout the city, though most concentrate on or near Obregón and Calles 50–60. For a mellow evening, scout newsstands or the tourist office for the free *Siglo 21,* a daily paper that lists movies, theaters, galleries, music, and dance. The Friday entertainment section, called "Tentaciones," has the most expansive information. The Sunday edition of *El Informador* also provides a listing of upcoming events.

The three quasi-plazas, **Plaza de Armas, Plaza de la Liberación,** and **Plaza Tapatía** buzz with frolicking people of all ages during the evening, especially on weekends. Caricaturists and marimba players call out to passersby, while mimes, puppet shows, and musicians enthrall small crowds. In the bandstand of Plaza de Armas, the Jalisco State Band gives free concerts (the sounds of which are piped into Plaza de la Liberación) Thursday and Sunday at 7 PM.

Next to the Iglesia San Juan de Dios and Mercado Libertad, the **Plaza de los Mariachis** (*see box below*) is actually a large alley lined with tables and worked by strolling musicians. Songs cost about $5 apiece, but you can usually listen in on someone else's. Sit at the first set of tables near the entrance, grab a $1 beer, and weep loudly as the music tugs your heartstrings.

BARS **Black Beards.** This bar is a Guadalajara institution, with live jazz and blues Thursdays and Saturdays. Other nights, the music varies. The $2.50 cover includes two drinks. *Justo Sierra 2194, no phone. Open Wed. noon–11, Thurs.–Sun. noon–3 AM. Wheelchair access.*

La Cripta. Dimly lit corridors with morbid decor will make you believe that you've arrived in the underworld. Loud music from the Smiths to the Cranberries attracts Guadalajara's wealthiest alternative crowd. Beers cost less than $1 and 2-liter pitchers are available for $4. *Tepeyac 4038, at Niño Obrero, tel. 3/647–62–07.*

La Maestranza. This rustic tavern, complete with sawdust-covered floors, also doubles as a *museo taurino* (bullfighting museum). Bullfighting memorabilia blankets the walls and the leather tables and chairs make a cozy perch for the young, partying crowd. Tequila and beer on tap ($1.50), appetizers ($1–$2), and free *botanas* (snacks) will fill you up in no time. *Maestranza 579, btw López Cotilla and Madero, tel. 3/613–58–78. Open daily 8 AM–2 AM.*

Subterraneo. Guadalajara's number-one alternative hangout is a long, dim bar with tables on the back patio. Patrons average at least five (visible) piercings. Live rock is the musical offering Fridays, and Saturday is the only day with a cover, when you're required to down $2 worth of drinks. The dark beer is so good that it won't feel like much of a sacrifice. *Vallarta 1480, at Chapultepec, no phone. Open Tues.–Sun. 8 PM–1 AM.*

CINEMAS Dozens of theaters around the city show fairly recent, undubbed American and international films. Current listings are in the daily paper *Siglo 21.* The **Cine Foro** (tel. 3/825–57–23), at the Universidad de Guadalajara, and the **Cine Teatro Cabañas** (tel. 3/617–43–22), at the Instituto Cultural Cabañas (*see* Worth Seeing, *above*), are good places for quality movies. Tickets are usually around $1. **Videosala** (Hidalgo 1296, tel. 3/825–57–23), also at the university, shows national and international art films weekdays for $2, and features everything from video art to TV docudramas. Its monthly program guide is available on site, or at the info booth in the university building on Vallarta.

DANCING Guadalajara has its share of big, flashy, and rather expensive discos. If you're among the (literally) "chosen" few, you can hang out with the city's hip, upper-middle-class youth and dance to the latest disco sounds. Among the in and trendy, **Lado B** (Vallarta 2451, tel. 3/616–82–97), with a wacky setting and unoriginal music and crowd, competes with **La**

Marcha (Vallarta 2648, tel. 3/615–89–99), a baroque-style disco, and El Preludio (Vallarta 1920, tel. 3/615–23–25), done up in heavy-on-the-angels neoclassic decor. All three offer all-you-can-drink open bars on Wednesday nights in exchange for $12 if you're male, nothing if your female. Free transportation via limousine or calandria is available between each disco. On Fridays and Saturdays, drink specials vary and the cover is $6 for women and $10 for men.

Of the *salones* (dance halls) that host live *bandas* playing traditional Mexican music, Salón Corona (López Mateos 2380, tel. 3/647–08–82) is one of the best. Women get in free Monday–Thursday (men pay $2). Also renowned is Copacabana (López Mateos, tel. 3/631–45–96), which plays live salsa and merengue. Casino Veracruz (Manzano 486, at Av. del Campesino, tel. 3/613–44–22) has tropical and salsa music. The last two salones are open Tuesday–Sunday around 8 PM, depending on the event, and charge $2.

GAY BARS AND CLUBS The place to be during the week is the coverless Máscaras (Maestranzas 238, at P. Sánchez, tel. 3/614–81–03). At this bar, masks adorn peach-colored walls while contemporary Mexican and American pop blares from the jukebox. On weekends, three main discos heat up: Mónica's (Obregón 1713, near Calle 64) is mostly for gay men while La Malinche (Obregón 1230, near Calle 48) attracts transvestites and lesbians. S.O.S. (Av. de la Paz 1413, at Federalismo) is the hottest club for both gays and lesbians. All three charge a $2.50 cover, play endless techno, and feature transvestite shows.

MUSIC The Centro Cultural Roxy (Mezquitan 80, at Hidalgo, tel. 3/658–00–53), in a converted art-deco movie theater, is *the* hip urban/underground hangout in Guadalajara. The art gallery Galería Margaritte is in front, while dance, theater, performance art, movies, and live music (everything from rock to reggae) are put on in the gutted theater. Come here to sample Mexico's best (usually) underground bands. Shows are normally Thursday–Sunday, but call beforehand or check "Tentaciones" in *Siglo 21*.

El Mariachi

Mariachi music has been around since the 16th century, when Mexican bands started playing the "son," a type of music from Galicia in northern Spain. At first the bands simply accompanied groups performing popular dances such as the jarabe, but by the 19th century they were gaining popularity and performing without the dancers. It wasn't until the modern age that the insistent trumpets now dominating the mariachi sound were added—commercial radio stations decided that raising the decibel level would make the music more popular. Mariachi bands today generally consist of two or more guitars, violins, trumpets, and the occasional harp. A guitar thumps in the background while the other instruments hum along at a rip-roaring pace or slow down to jerk tears from listeners. The songs generally concern heartbreak, heavy drinking, and love for the fatherland, and are punctuated by yells and yodels.

Outside Mexico, mariachi music is probably the best known—and least respected—Mexican popular music. The musicians' mournful "ay-ay-ay" and their often-garish costumes lead many foreigners to condemn the genre as tacky. Although high-society Mexicans usually describe mariachi as "de pueblo" (lower-class), most of them nevertheless know all the tunes by heart and end up singing along after a few shots of tequila. Sure enough, the music sells, not only in the record stores, but also live, in places like Guadalajara's Plaza de los Mariachis, where listeners shell out up to $5 for a song.

Peña Cuicacalli (Niños Héroes 1988, intersection of Glorieta Niños Héroes and Chapultepec, tel. 3/825−46−90) is Guadalajara's most popular *casa del canto*. The large, dim *peña* (musical gathering) attracts a mixed, enthusiastic audience. Music ranges from folk to salsa to nueva canción and rock. It's open Tuesday–Sunday beginning at 8 PM, and cover runs $2–$4. **La Peñita Teccizli** (Vallarta 1110, tel. 3/625−58−53; open daily noon–midnight) is a friendly restaurant with nightly live music similar to that found at Cuicacalli. Sundays are free nights; other nights you pay about $2–$5 to hear jazz, Afro-Antillean, blues, and Latin American music. The music usually starts at 9 PM (7 PM on Sundays). The tourist office provides monthly performance schedules.

Near Guadalajara

LAKE CHAPALA

Mexico's largest lake, bordered by green, almost tropical mountains, is a pleasant place to spend the weekend. Although the lake itself is plagued by severe ecological problems—the water from the Río Lerma is severely polluted, and huge pipelines pump water daily toward Guadalajara—the area offers a pleasant environment to relax in. The town of Chapala is a popular retirement community for Mexicans, Canadians, and Americans, and during the week English is frequently heard in the town's restaurants. On weekends, families from Guadalajara take over the boardwalk, and the air is festive with the sounds of vendors hawking ice cream and fried fish. For a more remote location, take the expensive $11 boat ride to Isla de los Alacrones (Scorpion Island).

COMING AND GOING Buses leave from the old bus station (*see* Coming and Going, in Guadalajara, *above*) every half hour 7 AM–8 PM (45 min, $1). Buses to Guadalajara depart every half hour until 9 PM from the bus station on Madero in Chapala.

WHERE TO SLEEP AND EAT The only cheap place to stay in Chapala is the **Casa de Huéspedes Las Palmitas** (Juárez 531, behind market, tel. 376/5−30−70). Basic rooms in this old converted house cost $9 singles, $12 doubles. A number of fairly decent restaurants hug the lakeshore, and they're not too outrageously priced. **La Playita** (Acapulquito Local 4, tel. 376/5−41−40) serves up big plates of fish and shrimp *al ajo* (with garlic) for $4, but you can get cheaper fare like chiles rellenos for $2. On the boardwalk, vendors also sell candy, nuts, and drinks that you can fill up on. Grab a bag of pistachios ($1 for ¼ kilo), sit on a nearby bench, and watch a slow Sunday afternoon go by. The English-speaking staff at the **tourist office** (Aquiles Serdán 26, behind Hotel Nido, tel. 376/5−31−41; open weekdays 9–7, weekends 9–noon) is eager to give out information.

TEQUILA

As the name suggests, this is the home of Mexico's national drink. Nearly everyone here works in the *agave* (the cactus from which tequila is made) fields or in one of the town's 10 tequila distilleries that ship the firewater to over 90 countries around the world. Cuervo, Sauza, and other companies produce their stuff here, and many offer tours in the late morning. **José Cuervo** (24 de Enero 73, 3 blocks from bus station, tel. 374/2−00−11) gives tours Monday–Saturday 10–1, ending with free samples. Groups of more than five people should make an appointment. If you really like tequila, visit the **Herradura** distillery in the nearby town of Amatitlán, which makes Mexico's best. You need to make an appointment to take the free tour; call the Herradura office (tel. 374/5−00−11 or 374/5−01−99) in Guadalajara and ask to speak to Salvador Huerta.

COMING AND GOING Buses (1½ hrs, $2.50) leave from the old bus station (*see* Coming and Going, *above*) in Guadalajara every 20 minutes 6 AM–9 PM. If you want to spend the night, Tequila has plenty of cheap places to stay, most catering to migrant workers.

THE PACIFIC COAST   9

By Olivia Barry

Journeying along the Pacific Coast, you'll never stray far from its essence: the ocean. Aquamarine swells provide a scenic backdrop to beachside *palapas* (thatched-roof huts) and palm trees; rolling waves offer a playground for boogie boarders, Jet Skiers, and surfers; and the salty waters offer up a smorgasbord of fresh seafood that is sliced, diced, and spiced into tasty regional dishes. Many cities regularly celebrate the ocean as their source of livelihood: San Blas blesses the sea in a joyous festival, Manzanillo holds world-renowned sailfish tournaments, and Mexcaltitán kicks off the opening of its shrimping season with fireworks and a fiesta. With all this going for it, it's not surprising that the Pacific Coast has been a haven for beach-seeking tourists since the 1950s, when the region was targeted by the Mexican department of tourism as a means of luring foreign currency to boost the flagging economy.

If you're looking for action, you've come to the right place. Cities such as Ixtapa/Zihuatanejo, Puerto Vallarta, and Acapulco boast myriad water sports and flashy discos guaranteed to keep you entertained day and night. The open attitude of these beach towns also draws many vacationing gays and lesbians—Acapulco is the traditional gay mecca, though it's soon to be replaced by Puerto Vallarta and San Blas, the latest queer hot spots. Though tourists and their freely spent pesos keep the coast's fishermen and hotel owners in business, the influx of foreigners has resulted in a pervasive "Americanization," with traditional Mexican cuisine, dress, and customs relegated to the poorer parts of the region's towns. But don't despair. Much of the Pacific Coast remains relatively underdeveloped, and beach towns such as Barra de Navidad, Pie de la Cuesta, and San Blas still offer peace and quiet in a traditional Mexican context.

However, those who think the Pacific Coast is all sun and surf will be surprised by the states of Sinaloa, Nayarit, Jalisco, Colima, and Guerrero. Farmland, volcanoes, and mountains extend the natural setting of the Pacific Coast past the water, and the towering Sierra Madre Occidental and Sierra Madre Sur mountain ranges attract hikers and shelter native people. Booming, westernized metropolises are only a bus ride away from quiet, inland towns that are home to *indígenas* (indigenous people); Huichols and Coras in colorful handmade apparel sell embroidered paintings in towns such as Tepic and Santiago Ixcuintla, profiting from the tourist industry enough to ensure their cultural (and financial) survival. But whether you choose to visit mountain villages, hit the powerful surf, maneuver through a tropical jungle, or hike an active volcano, do it in the tourist off-season (June–Sept.), when the crowded cities empty out and prices drop significantly.

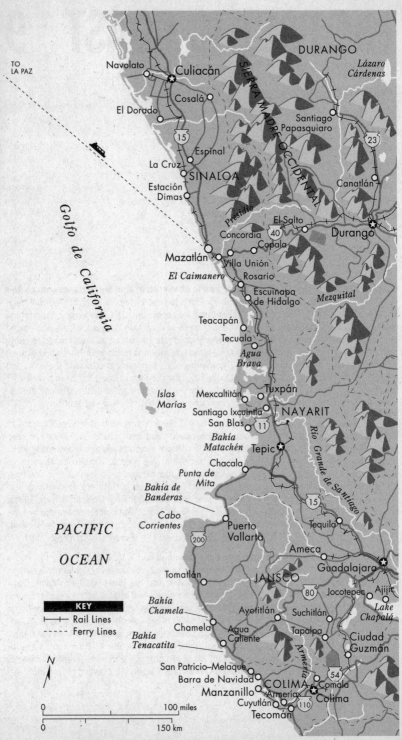

The Pacific Coast

TO LA PAZ

Navolato
Culiacán
Cosalá
El Dorado
Espinal
La Cruz
SINALOA
Estación Dimas
Concordia
Mazatlán
Villa Unión
El Caimanero
Rosario
Escuinapa de Hidalgo
Teacapán
Tecuala
Agua Brava
Islas Marías
Mexcaltitán
Tuxpán
Santiago Ixcuintla
San Blas
NAYARIT
Bahía Matachén
Tepic
Chacala
Punta de Mita
Bahía de Banderas
Cabo Corrientes
Puerto Vallarta
Ameca
Guadalajara
Tomatlán
JALISCO
Jocotepec
Ajijic
Lake Chapalá
Bahía Chamela
Ayotitlán
Suchitlán
Tapalpa
Chamela
Agua Caliente
Tapalpa
Ciudad Guzmán
Bahía Tenacatita
San Patricio–Melaque
Barra de Navidad
COLIMA
Comala
Manzanillo
Armería
Colima
Cuyutlán
Tecomán

DURANGO
Lázaro Cárdenas
SIERRA MADRE OCCIDENTAL
Santiago Papasquiaro
Canatlán
Presidio
El Salto
Copala
Durango
Mezquital
Río Grande de Santiago
Tequila
Armería

Golfo de California

PACIFIC

OCEAN

KEY
Rail Lines
Ferry Lines

N

0   100 miles
0   150 km

278

Mazatlán

Mazatlán, with a population of 450,000, offers a glimpse of the Pacific Coast's opposing identities. While the new **Zona Dorada** (Golden Zone) bursts with trendy time-shares, perpetually expanding resorts, and over one million tourists a year, **Mazatlán Viejo** (Old Mazatlán) continues its role as a flourishing seaport, a shrimp-packing city, and a sport-fishing haven. Between the two, Mazatlán has something for the merrymaker and the mellow alike: While party-crazed travelers bask in the amusement park atmosphere on the beaches and check out the city's happening discos, a resort-weary soul can wander through Mazatlán Viejo and see folk dance, art, and colorful colonial-style buildings. Mazatlán has always satisfied the needs of a variety of people—from the pre-Spanish conquest pirates who rested at their "Island of Mazatlán," to gold-driven miners in search of riches, to today's tourists.

Mazatlán's party atmosphere really kicks in during **Carnaval**, the city's biggest fiesta, celebrated just before Lent (usually February). Thousands of tourists, both domestic and foreign, descend on the town for six days and nights to enjoy music, dancing, fireworks, parades, drinking, and hormonal revelry. **Semana Santa** (Holy Week, the week before Easter) is a smaller festival that draws party-ready Mexicans with its religious reenactments, parades, and music. The changing seasons also bring different kinds of visitors to Mazatlán. During summer, the resort town becomes the humid playground of American students and Mexican tourists. When the mercury drops from the scorching 90s to the comfortable 70s, Mazatlán hits its winter high season, and older visitors from the United States and Canada flock to the expensive hotels.

BASICS

AMERICAN EXPRESS This office delivers MoneyGrams and changes traveler's checks at a decent rate. In addition, cardholders can cash personal checks and have mail held at the following address: T. Diagonal H, Av. Camarón Sábalo, Plaza Balboa, Local 4, Mazatlán, Sinaloa, CP 82000, México. *Camarón Sábalo, tel. 69/13–06–00. 1 block north of Dairy Queen. Open weekdays 9–6, Sat. 9–noon.*

CASAS DE CAMBIO The Zona Dorada teems with *casas de cambio* (money-changing offices). **Banamex** (Flores, at Juárez, tel. 69/82–77–33) exchanges cash and traveler's checks weekdays 8:30–noon at the best rates in town. They charge no commission and also have ATMs that accept Cirrus and Plus cards. Places to change money are scarcer downtown; try the **Casa de Cambio Camiga** in Plaza Concordia. The rates here aren't great, but there's no commission on traveler's checks. *Belisario Domínguez 2, at Flores, tel. 69/85–00–03. Open Mon.–Sat. 9–1:30 and 3:30–7.*

CONSULATES Mazatlán doesn't have an actual **United States** consulate, but you can visit Geri Nelson (Loaiza 202, in Zona Dorada, tel. and fax 69/16–58–89), the consular representative. Geri's office, open weekdays 9–1:30, is in front of Hotel Playa Mazatlán. In an after-hours emergency, call 62/17–23–75 for the Hermosillo consulate. **Canada's** representative, Fernanda B. Romero, works right next to Geri's office at Loaiza 203 (tel. 69/13–73–20, fax 69/14–65–55) weekdays 9–1. Citizens from other countries should try the tourist office at Olas Altas 1300 for information on consulates in Mexico City.

LAUNDRY For about $2 a load, **Lavandería Romy** will wash, dry, and fold your duds in as little as three hours. *120 Hidalgo, near 5 de Mayo, tel. 69/82–80–42. Open 24 hrs daily.*

MAIL The post office will hold mail sent to you at the following address for up to 10 days: Lista de Correos, Administración Postal No. 1, Centro, Benito Juárez y 21 de Marzo, Mazatlán, Sinaloa, CP 82000, México. You can send or receive telegrams at the office next door. *Juárez, at 21 de Marzo, tel. 69/81–21–21. Open weekdays 8–7, Sat. 8–1.*

MEDICAL AID Miguel Ángel Guzmán Elizondo (Nelson 1808, tel. 69/81–25–87, or 69/81–51–17 after hours) is a locally respected, English-speaking doctor. He sees patients weekdays 10–2 and 5–8, Saturday 10–1; consultations cost $14–$21. Any minor problems or prescriptions can be dealt with at the 24-hour **Farmacia Cruz Verde** (Gutiérrez Najera 901, at Obregón, tel. 69/81–22–25). Dial 06 for all **emergencies.**

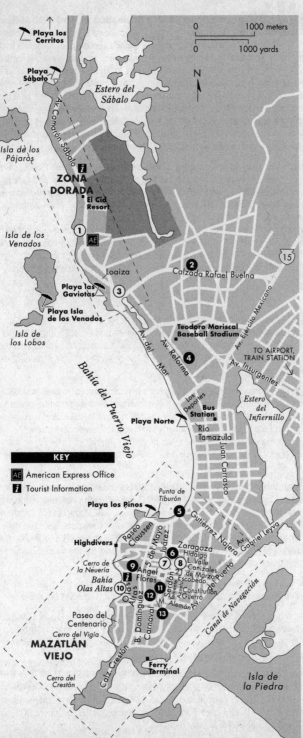

Mazatlán

Playa los Cerritos

Playa Sábalo

Estero del Sábalo

Isla de los Pájaros

Av. Camarón Sábalo

ZONA DORADA

El Cid Resort

Isla de los Venados

① **AE**

Loaiza

③

Playa las Gaviotas

Playa Isla de los Venados

Isla de los Lobos

② **Calzada Rafael Buelna**

15

Bahía del Puerto Viejo

Teodoro Mariscal Baseball Stadium

Av. del Mar

Av. Reforma

④

Av. Ejército Mexicano

TO AIRPORT, TRAIN STATION

Av. Insurgentes

Los Deportes

Bus Station

Playa Norte

Río Tamazula

Estero del Infiernillo

Juan Carrasco

KEY

AE American Express Office

i Tourist Information

Punta de Tiburón

Playa los Pinos

⑤

Paseo Claussen

Highdivers

Gutiérrez Nájera

Av. Gabriel Leyva

Zaragoza

⑥ Hidalgo

Cerro de la Nevería

⑨ ⑦ ⑧ L. Valle

Canizales

de Marzo

Escobedo

Ángel Flores

Bahía Olas Altas

⑩ ⑪ ⑫

5 de Mayo

Juárez

Serdán

Constitución

A. Guerro

M. Alemán

Av. del Puerto

⑬

Paseo del Centenario

Cerro del Vigía

Olas Altas

B. Domínguez

Carnaval

Canal de Navegación

MAZATLÁN VIEJO

Calz. Crestón

Ferry Terminal

Cerro del Crestón

Isla de la Piedra

Sights ●

Acuario Mazatlán, **4**

Mercado Central, **6**

Monumento al Pescador, **5**

Museo Arqueológico, **9**

Plaza de Toros, **2**

Plaza Machado, **12**

Plaza Revolución and Basílica, **11**

Teatro Ángel Peralta, **13**

Lodging ○

Casa de Huéspedes El Castillo, **8**

Hotel Belmar, **10**

Hotel Bugambilias, **1**

Hotel del Centro, **7**

Hotel San Diego, **3**

0   1000 meters

0   1000 yards

N

PHONES You'll find pay phones on almost every other block throughout the Zona Dorada and Mazatlán Viejo. To place cash calls, make free collect calls, or send faxes, **Computel** (Serdán 1512, btw Valle and Canizalez, tel. and fax 69/85–01–08) stays open 24 hours a day.

SCHOOLS The **Centro de Idiomas** in Mazatlán Viejo offers Spanish instruction at all levels. Twenty hours of instruction per week in small classes costs $130, plus a $30 registration fee. *Belisario Domínguez 1908, Mazatlán, Sinaloa, México, CP 82000, tel. 69/82–20–53, fax 69/85–56–06.*

VISITOR INFORMATION The huge federal tourist office has a helpful staff, some of whom speak English. You'll be sure to leave with an armful of pamphlets and maps. *Camarón Sábalo, at Tiburón, tel. 69/16–51–60, fax 69/16–51–66. 4th floor of Banrural building, across from Holiday Inn. Open weekdays 8:30–2 and 5–7:30 (open Sat. 9–1 for phone calls only).*

COMING AND GOING

BY BUS The amphitheaterlike **Central Camionera** (Calle Río Tamazula, near Av. Ejército Mexicano, tel. 69/81–76–25) is divided into two sections. One is devoted to first-class buses, and the other to second-class buses that serve nearby towns. First-class buses offer air-conditioned comfort; second-class buses are cheap and roomy. Second-class **Transportes Norte de Sonora** (tel. 69/81–38–46) buses stop in Mazatlán hourly on their way to Guadalajara (9 hrs, $16.50), Mexico City (19 hrs, $37), Tijuana (29 hrs, $52), and Nogales (18 hrs, $15). **Transportes Pacífico** (tel. 69/82–05–77) offers first-class service to Mexico City (16 hrs, $43), Guadalajara (7 hrs, $19), and Tijuana (26 hrs, $60). **Estrella Blanca** (tel. 69/81–53–81) runs second-class buses six times a day to Durango (7 hrs, $8). From Durango, you can transfer to a Monterrey-bound bus (17 hrs, $40). At 9:45 PM, **Élite** (tel. 69/81–36–80) sends a daily first-class bus to Acapulco (25 hrs, $54), with stops in Puerto Vallarta (8 hrs, $16.50) and Manzanillo (12 hrs, $27); buses to Tepic (4½ hrs, $10) leave every hour. Luggage storage is available at the station ($1 per 4 hrs), and there's a **Computel** phone office (tel. and fax 69/85–39–31) where you can make cash calls. To get downtown or to the market from the bus station, catch any bus marked INSURGENTES on Avenida Ejército Mexicano; or walk to the *malecón* (boardwalk) and take a southbound CAMARON SABALO bus. The same bus going in the opposite direction goes to the Zona Dorada.

BY TRAIN Mazatlán lies on the Pacific rail line, an efficient route compared to lines farther southeast. The train station (tel. 69/84–67–10) is northeast of Mazatlán Viejo, on Avenida Ferrocarril in the Colonia Esperanza. It's a bit far from town, so hail a bus labeled ESPERANZA from Olas Altas. Two trains run north to Mexicali (26 hrs, $30 1st class; 35 hrs, $16 2nd class), stopping in Culiacán (4 hrs, $5 1st class; 5 hrs, $2.50 2nd class), Sufragio (9 hrs, $10 1st class; 12 hrs, $5 2nd class) and Nogales (18 hrs, $23.50 1st class; 24 hrs, $13 2nd class). Southbound trains stop in Tepic (5 hrs, $6 1st class; 6 hrs, $3.50 2nd class) en route to Guadalajara (10 hrs, $14 1st class; 12 hrs, $6 2nd class). The first-class northbound train leaves daily at 7 PM; the second-class train leaves at 2 PM. Southbound trains leave daily at 3 PM (1st class) and 5 AM (2nd class). First-class trains fill up quickly, so reserve seats the morning of departure.

BY PLANE Mazatlán's airport (tel. 69/82–20–88) is a 40-minute drive from town. Taxis make the trip for around $18, and *pulmonías* (golf cart–like vehicles) charge $10. Cheaper still are Volkswagen *colectivos* (communal taxis), which charge roughly $4 between the airport and Mazatlán's major hotels. At the airport, numerous booths provide information on hotels and transportation. There are a few international phones, but no luggage storage area. Carriers that serve Mazatlán from the United States include **Aeroméxico** (Camarón Sábalo 310, tel. 69/14–11–11), **Alaska Airlines** (in airport, tel. 69/85–27–30), and **Mexicana** (Paseo Claussen 101-B, tel. 69/82–77–22). Domestic carriers include **Aerocalifornia** (tel. 69/13–20–42) and **Aviación del Noroeste** (tel. 69/14–38–55), both with offices in the El Cid Hotel on Camarón Sábalo.

BY FERRY **Sematur** makes the 18-hour ferry crossing to La Paz on the Baja peninsula at 3 PM, every day except Thursday and Saturday. An uncomfortable reclining seat costs $19, and a berth in a four-person cabin is $40. A two-person cabin with a bathroom is $58 a head. Vehicles can be ferried as well, but price varies according to size. You can reserve and buy ferry tickets in the office at the ferry landing on Playa Sur (Prolongación Carnaval, tel. 69/81–70–21), which is open weekdays 8–3:30, Saturday 9–1. You'll find the same ticket prices at the travel agency **Turismo Coral** (5 de Mayo 1705, tel. 69/81–32–90), open weekdays 8–2 and 3–7, Saturday 8–2. Make reservations a few days in advance (even earlier during Easter holidays), and arrive an hour before the boat departs. To reach the ferry terminal, take the PLAYA SUR bus from the market. The terminal has luggage storage ($1.50 per day), but no nearby markets, so stock up on edibles and water before you arrive. The boat has a high-priced restaurant and a snack bar on board.

GETTING AROUND

Mazatlán has two primary neighborhoods: Mazatlán Viejo, at the southern end of the city, and the Zona Dorada. Mazatlán Viejo is the civic and commercial center and includes the malecón and Playa Norte. This easily walkable area centers around **Plaza Revolución** (the *zócalo,* or main square) and the **Basílica de la Inmaculada Concepción,** Mazatlán's main church, on Avenida Benito Juárez. **Olas Altas,** a relatively quiet strip of beach, lies along the waterfront in Mazatlán Viejo, about seven blocks east of the basilica. Avenida del Mar connects Old and New Mazatlán, running north along Playa Norte to Valentino's disco, where its name changes to Camarón Sábalo. The Zona Dorada, with its resort hotels, overpopulated beaches, and timeshare condos, begins here.

The Zona is so stretched out that walking can be time-consuming. Fortunately, buses run from the central market to just about anywhere in town; purchase the 20¢ ticket on board. Bus stops are rare, so wave your hands to flag a bus down. The SABALO-BASILICA bus travels from the downtown market to the Zona Dorada and runs 5 AM–10 PM. Otherwise, pulmonías driven by maniacs cruise the streets of Mazatlán and are your cheapest option. Arrange the fare (and say your prayers) before boarding. If you're feeling even more adventurous, rent a scooter (and helmet) for $5.50 an hour or $18 per day at one of the rental shacks on the south end of the Zona Dorada. Try **Hot Wheels Moto Rent** (Camarón Sábalo 35, tel. 69/86–56–21), across from Hotel Rivera Mazatlán, open daily 10–7.

WHERE TO SLEEP

For a popular resort town, Mazatlán has a surprising number of decent, cheap hotels. You'll find budget digs downtown behind the Monumento al Pescador and in the area east of the basilica; there are even a few pockets of sanity within the Zona Dorada. Prices listed below are for the low season—if you're in town around Carnaval, Semana Santa, or the Christmas and New Year holidays, expect to pay more. If you're only in town for a night, the best of the hotels near the bus station is the **Hotel Emperador** (Río Panuco, tel. 69/82–67–24), where each room has a color TV. Singles cost $7, doubles $8; air-conditioning is $3 extra.

MAZATLAN VIEJO **Casa de Huéspedes El Castillo.** The collage of cute colorful stones outside gives way to spacious, country-kitsch rooms that boast rocking chairs, fans, soft mattresses, and quirky dressers. The year-round price is a mere $4.50 for one person and $6 for two. However, the nine rooms share two bathrooms, and a cockroach or two may be skittering about. *Teniente José Azueta 1612 Nte., btw Canizales and 21 de Marzo, tel. 69/81–58–97. Luggage storage.*

Hotel Belmar. With the beach in front and a gigantic pool in the back, you'll feel like you've discovered budget paradise. Elegant rooms come with either fans and ocean views ($9.50 singles, $11 doubles) or air-conditioning and no view ($11 singles, $12.50 doubles). All rooms have balconies and TVs. Stay away during Easter week and Carnaval, when prices triple. *Olas Altas 166 Sur, tel. 69/85–11–11. 100 rooms, all with bath. Luggage storage. Wheelchair access. AE, MC, V.*

Hotel del Centro. The ageing rooms here are small and slightly run-down, but blessedly air-conditioned. Each floor has a small lobby with potted plants and rocking chairs. Singles cost $8, plus $1.50 for each additional person or for a TV. Prices are constant year-round. *Canizales*

705 Pte., ½ block from Basílica, tel. 69/81–26–73. 19 rooms, all with bath. Luggage storage. Wheelchair access.

ZONA DORADA **Hotel Bugambilias.** Hidden in the heart of Zona Dorada, this charming hotel has 10 clean, medium-size rooms for $12 (singles) and $14 (doubles)—all with bath. There are also 11 apartments with kitchenettes that run $20 for two people and an extra $7 for each additional person. The top level has a sun-tanning area and great ocean views. *Camarón Sábalo, at Costa Azul, tel. 69/14–00–29. Luggage storage. AE, MC, V.*

Hotel San Diego. These medium-sized rooms flaunt newly tiled floors, ornate bedspreads, TVs, and large bathrooms. Each floor has a deck with ocean views. Many of the Zona Dorada's discos are conveniently located across the street, so you can stagger home in relative safety. Rooms with one bed and a fan cost $8.50 ($11 with air-conditioning). All rooms with two beds are air-conditioned and go for $16.50. Prices rise about $3 during Easter week. *Rafael Buelna, at Av. del Mar, tel. 69/83–57–03. 63 rooms. Luggage storage. Wheelchair access.*

CAMPING The Zona Dorada has a few expensive trailer parks ($10–$14 per night for a tent space). The best is **Mar Rosa** (Camarón Sábalo 702, near Holiday Inn, tel. and fax 69/13–61–87), with showers, 24-hour guards, and a waterfront location. Pay $10 for two people in your tent ($2 for each additional camper). You can also camp on the **Isla de la Piedra** beach (*see* Outdoor Activites, *below*). If you try to camp on any other beach, the local police will not-so-politely ask you to relocate.

FOOD

Like cheap hotels, inexpensive eateries are scattered throughout town. The **mercado municipal** (city market; open daily 5 AM–6 PM), at Avenidas Serdán and Melchor Ocampo, is your cheapest option. For an afternoon meal of delicious, cheap seafood, head for one of the palapas on Playa Norte, where a whole fried fish costs just $2. Mazatlán is known for its *mariscos* (shellfish) and *camarones* (shrimp); shrimp soup and shrimp with bacon and cheese are both popular dishes.

MAZATLAN VIEJO **Cenaduría Conchita.** Decked out in red and white, this small, simple restaurant is a local favorite. Traditional Mexican food is hearty and cheap. A ham-and-egg breakfast costs $1.50, and the $2 *comida corrida* (lunch) includes steak or chicken, fresh fruit, soup, beans, a fruit drink, and dessert. *Canazales 603, at Nelson, no phone. Open Mon.–Sat. 8 AM–9 PM.*

Panamá Restaurant y Pastelería. These bakery/restaurants can be found all over town, swarming with jolly crowds, but this branch is the largest. For breakfast, try the *huevos divorciados* (divorced eggs; one with green sauce, the other with red, separated by beans) for $2. Later in the day, savor anything from beef tenderloin fajitas ($3.50) to chef salad ($1.75). *Juárez, at Valle, tel. 69/85–18–53. Open daily 7 AM–10 PM.*

Royal Dutch. Originaly an in-home bakery, this place is now also a café with intimate courtyard dining, nightly live music (8 PM–10 PM), and an expansive menu. Two eggs, hash browns, and toast will cost you $2, soups cost $2, and sandwiches cost $2–$4. Breads and desserts are still made on the premises. *Juárez 1307, at Constitución, tel. 69/81–20–07. Open Mon.–Sat. 8 AM–11 PM.*

ZONA DORADA **Jungle Juice Restaurant and Bar.** The cheesy name says it all: This joint has a great selection of juice drinks ($2), and the bar is a popular hangout for locals and foreigners alike. They also serve a $4 soyburger platter with fries, beans, and rice, and a hearty $1.75 egg, potato, and toast breakfast. Try the shrimp-stuffed avocado or fresh fruit salad with yogurt ($4 each). *Calle de Las Garzas 101, btw Loaiza and Camarón Sábalo, tel. 69/13–33–15. Open daily 7 AM–11 PM; bar open until 1 AM.*

Restaurant Bar La Costa Marinera. Seafood here is a little expensive, but the ocean views, live mariachi music, and gourmet cuisine make for an enchanting experience. For $7.50, try the chef's specialities: fish soup, grilled shrimp, and *flan* (caramel custard). *Camarón Sábalo, btw Hotels Ocean Palace and Luna Palace, tel. 69/14–19–28. Open daily 11–9.*

WORTH SEEING

The best way to see Mazatlán Viejo, with its mix of crumbling old mansions and smaller homes, is on foot. The center of town is the **Plaza Revolución,** from which the blue-and-gold spires of the adjacent basilica rise above the downtown buildings. A few blocks away, **Plaza Machado** (Constitución and Carnaval) is surrounded by elegant colonial-style buildings that have been turned into cafés and restaurants with outdoor seating. As Avenida del Mar meanders north toward the Zona Dorada, you'll pass the unusual **Monumento al Pescador** (Fisherman's Monument): an enormous statue of a voluptuous nude woman reclining on an anchor, her hand extended toward a fisherman, also naked, hauling his nets.

ACUARIO MAZATLÁN Halfway between the Zona Dorada and Mazatlán Viejo is this aquarium/zoo, offering an aviary swarming with chirping birds and close-up views of tropical fish, turtles, and crocodiles. Visitors can observe fish in a feeding frenzy four times daily, followed by a sea lion show and a shark film half an hour later. Although the film is in Spanish, Anglophones won't have a hard time understanding what the sharks are doing to the smaller fish. *Av. de los Deportes 111, 2 blocks off Av. del Mar, tel. 69/81–78–17. Admission: $3. Open daily 9:30–6:30.*

MUSEO ARQUEOLOGICO One of the few nods to pre-Columbian Mexico you'll encounter here, this large museum features a fascinating permanent display of local artifacts, including war objects, burial ornaments, and pictures of women with cranial and dental deformation, a beauty custom still practiced in some parts of Mexico. Intriguing temporary exhibits display works by international painters, sculptors, and ceramicists, and the museum also houses the **Casa de la Cultura,** a good place to find out about cultural events. *Sixto Osuna 76, 1 block east of beach. Admission: $1, 50¢ students. Open Tues.–Sun. 10–1 and 4–7.*

PLAZA DE TOROS Bullfights are held here most Sundays between December and April. You can buy tickets in advance at Valentino's disco or most big hotels on the strip, as well as at the bullring the day of the fight. The cheapest seats are about $10 and fights start at 4 PM. *Rafael Buelna, near Zona Dorada, tel. 69/84–16–66.*

TEATRO ANGELA PERALTA Built in 1860, this striking neoclassical opera house was styled after an Italian design and complemented with Mexican flair. Its ornate interior is a sight in itself, and a powerful sound system and climate control make it the best theater in the city. It was declared a historic monument in 1990 and, after a two-year restoration, now hosts the music and dance performances of Mazatlán's active arts community. Details on what's playing can be found at the office, to the right of the entrance. It's 50¢ to tour the theater, $7–$10 for a ticket to see a choral group, opera, or play (all in Spanish). The theater also offers workshops in drama, painting, music, sculpture, and other artistic activities. *Sixto Osuna, at Carnaval, tel. 69/82–44–47. Box office open daily 8:30–2 and 4–7.*

`Ol !

Is bullfighting a bloodthirsty sport in which an unsuspecting animal ends up dead, or a fair challenge between an artist dressed in his "suit of light" and a thoroughbred bull? Mexicans consider "La Corrida de los Toros" more of an art than a sport, but you can decide for yourself at a number of bullfighting arenas along the Pacific Coast. The dramatic fight was brought to Mexico by the Spaniards, and now visitors regularly cheer the proud matador and his assistants through the three-act event. After an opening parade, each corrida consists of three matadors and six bulls, and the matador has 16 minutes to triumph over each bull. A quick death brings applause and roses; a slow process results in a sea of boos. Audience members cheering for the bull will also attract an unpopular response.

CHEAP THRILLS

On Sundays, locals of all ages gather in front of the cathedral near the Palacio Municipal to hear *bandas* (bands). The tourist office and the Casa de la Cultura (*see* Museo Arqueológico, *above*) offers calendars of these and other cultural events. If you'd rather stretch your sunburned limbs, take one of the following three hikes, which will reward you with awesome views: The walk to the **Cerro de la Nevería** (Icebox Hill), located in Mazatlán Viejo, off the malecón along Paseo Claussen, takes you past beautiful homes and various lookout points. Just south of Olas Altas, about halfway down the peninsula, is **Cerro de la Vigia** (Lookout Hill). It was originally used by the Spanish to keep watch for pirates—hence the rusty cannon here today. It's a steep climb up the Paseo del Centenario to the top, but there are vista points along the way where you can catch your breath while pretending to take in the view. Farther down the peninsula from Olas Altas is the **Cerro del Crestón**, which offers the best panoramic views. It's a 30-minute hike to the *faro* (lighthouse) at the top, where you can marvel at the sea and the city.

OUTDOOR ACTIVITIES

Playa Sábalo and **Playa Las Gaviotas** are worked by vendors that rent boogie boards and Jet Skis, or offer five-minute parasail rides. **Playa Norte,** populated by palapa restaurants, is more popular among locals; **Olas Altas,** farther south in Mazatlán Viejo, has dangerous surf but is the place to be at sunset. To avoid the crowds, head to the quieter beaches north of the Zona Dorada, such as **Playa Bruja** and **Playa Cerritos.** To reach these, take a CERRITOS bus from the Zona Dorada and hop off when you see the signs.

You can rent almost any kind of water sport equipment in Mazatlán, provided you're willing to pay through the nose for it. Vendors on the beach near Valentino's disco rent surf- and boogie boards for $5 an hour. At the **Aqua Sports Center** (tel. 69/13-33-33), next to El Cid, you can rent a Hobie Cat ($25 per hr), a boogie board ($3 per hr) or snorkeling gear ($8 for 6 hrs), or parasail for $20. The prettiest reefs are at **Isla de los Venados** (15 minutes away by boat), and Aqua Sports will transport you there for scuba diving. One-tank dives for certified divers ($50) include equipment and transportation. Uncertified divers can participate if they first take a $10 resort course. You can also go in a boat to the island to snorkel, sun, and eat for $9—snorkeling equipment and round-trip transportation included. People also come here to fish for mahimahi, red snapper, saltfish, and marlin. Eight-hour sportfishing trips for five or six people that include boat, guide, and all equipment ($200) are available.

To escape the gringo-laden beaches, check out **Isla de la Piedra,** where a line of palapas runs along a stretch of white sand beaches sheltered by palm trees. Here you'll find volleyball nets, boogie boards ($2 an hr), horseback riding ($6 an hr), and banana boat rides ($3 for 10 min). You can camp wherever you please, though facilities are nonexistent. Surfers can head over to the underdeveloped end of the beach, where waves are rougher. To reach the island, take a boat (10 min, 50¢) from the dock at the corner of Avenida Playa Sur and Calle Barranza, just past the ferry terminal. Frequent boats run daily 6–6.

AFTER DARK

Most of Mazatlán's nightclubs are in the Zona Dorada. Frequented by rowdy twentysomething gringos and done-up Mexican tourists, they aren't exactly cutting edge. Most have a cover charge, but it's often possible to take advantage of the mayhem at beach clubs and slip in through a back entrance. **Señor Frog's** (Av. del Mar, tel. 69/85-11-10) serves food daily noon–midnight but turns into a multiroom disco 11 PM–3 AM. There's no cover but be prepared to wait in line to get in. Music includes some techno and a lot of rock 'n roll. For more cheesy techno, the castle-like **Valentino's** (Punta del Malecón, tel. 69/ 86-49-49) has a disco overlooking the sea, a room where romantic music plays, and a *canta bar* (karaoke room) that gets everybody laughing. Cover is $3, and the club is open daily until 3 AM, when everybody heads next door to **Bora Bora** (tel. 69/84-16-66). This gringo-ized outdoor disco plays more rap than the clubs above; drunk people dancing seductively on the tables clinches the meat market image. **808 Café** (Launa, at Gargas, no phone) is cover-free and open daily 7 PM–3 AM, but only attracts a sizeable crowd on weekends. MTV, rock music, and an industrial decor make 808 the bar of choice with the rich kids. The bar **Café Pacífico** (Constitución 501, tel. 69/81–39–72) attracts an older, quieter crowd, while gay nightlife centers around **Pepe El Toro** (Av. de las Garzas 18, tel. 69/84–41–76).

Near Mazatlán

CONCORDIA

Located in the foothills east of Mazatlán, Concordia makes for a picturesque getaway from Mazatlán's commercialism. This small pueblo was founded in 1565 and is known for its beautiful wooden furniture and brown clay pottery, which can be found in shops along the highway. Church-goers, smooching couples, and rambunctious kids gather at the zócalo, which is the heart of this mining village. Overlooking the zócalo, the 18th-century **Iglesia de San Sebastián** is considered the only truly baroque church in Sinaloa. Also worth checking out are the four warm **thermal baths** that lie 10 minutes from town—spoiled only by the distasteful algae growth covering the bottom. If someone is watching over them, admission is 15¢; otherwise the baths are free and open 24 hours. To reach the baths, cross the bridge on the highway towards Mazatlán, make an immediate left on the dirt road, and continue for five minutes. There's no sign, but you'll see a big dirt parking area on your left, which leads straight to the baths. Second-class buses to Concordia (1 hr, $1.25) leave from Mazatlán's main bus station every 15 minutes 6 AM–8 PM. The last bus back from Concordia leaves at 7 PM. If you want to stay the night, spend $11 at the **Hotel Rancho Viejo** (El Vado Carretera Mazatlán–Durango, tel. 69/68–02–90).

COSALÁ

This former mining town in the mountains boasts lush, unspoiled flora and fauna that makes camping, swimming, and even the three-hour bus ride seem like a return to Mother Nature. However, if you decide to come here, set aside a few days; it's worlds away from the beaten track, and transportation and facilities are scarce. Within Cosalá itself, you can visit the free **Museo de Minería e Historia** (tel. 696/5–00–01) on the main plaza. It's open Tuesday–Friday 9–7 and weekends 10–3 and hosts a display of various stones mined in the area, as well as a collection of elephant and camel bones.

The best attractions, though, are outside of town: Just 15 minutes away is the **Balneario de Vado Hondo,** where you can swim in a cool pond surrounded by three waterfalls. It's located 3 kilometers from the highway leading into town; any Mazatlán- or Culicán-bound bus can get you to the crossroads. You can also visit the unchartered **Gruta México,** a dark cave with pre-Columbian hieroglyphics. Be sure to bring your own flashlight. To reach the cave, catch the 1 PM bus to Canzal (15 min, $1) and walk two hours to the cave. The same bus goes to the **Presa del Comedero** (1 hr, $3), a large lake ideal for fishing but a bit dirty for swimming. There are no facilities, but you can bargain with local fishermen to spend the day with them on their boat. Before visiting any of these sights, first stop by the **Palacio Municipal** (next to museum, tel. 696/5–00–01), where they'll assist with transportation. You can camp near the falls or the lake, but be sure to buy all your food and drinking water beforehand. The best place to stay in town is the modern, air-conditioned **Hotel Ray Cuatro Hermanos** (on the plaza, tel. 696/5–03–03), where rooms cost $11 for one or two people.

COMING AND GOING A bus for Cosalá (3 hrs, $4.50) leaves the main bus station in Mazatlán daily at 10 AM, returning at 1 PM. You can also take any Culiacán-bound bus to Espinal (1½ hrs, $3.50), where Cosalá-bound buses pass by every hour or so. Buses headed for Espinal from Cosalá (1½ hrs, $2.50) leave at 5:45, 7, and 10 AM and 2 and 3:30 PM.

San Blas

Between Mazatlán and Puerto Vallarta, this relatively underdeveloped town on the Nayarit coast is a place of rustic houses and intense sunshine. The flourishing wildlife and tropical jungles make it a perfect stop for the semirugged traveler or the dabbling naturalist. After overcoming the endemic and relentlessly biting jejene insects and mosquitoes, either type of wayfarer will be rewarded by iridescent waterfalls, river canals, and tangled vegetation. Egrets, ibises, and woodpeckers are among the 300 different bird species native to this region, and even if you don't see them, you will certainly hear their calls.

San Blas is the place to ponder the chemical reaction between suntan lotion and insect repellant: Will they neutralize each other, leaving me unprotected, or will I simply burst into flame?

San Blas wasn't always the epitome of tropical lethargy. From the 1500s to the 1800s it was an important Pacific port with a peak population of over 30,000. However it was soon eclipsed by Mazatlán and Manzanillo, leaving only the ruins of an old stone cathedral, fort, and accounting house as testaments to its former glory. Today, the town of 8,000 proud inhabitants is sometimes called the *puerto olvidado* (forgotten port), referring both to the dearth of tourism and government funds. One plausible reason for San Blas's decline is the vicious biting insects that plague it during the rainy season, from mid-June through October. The logs kept by Spanish explorers remark on the number of mosquitoes and jejenes, and describe how local people took cover at dusk. The bugs' persistence still keeps San Blas unpopulated, and other than a handful of surfers and hippies, you will probably have the beach to yourself.

BASICS

CASAS DE CAMBIO **Banamex** (Juárez 26, off zócalo, tel. 328/5–00–30) changes cash and traveler's checks weekdays 8:30 AM–11 AM, but lines are often long and the bank sometimes charges unwarranted commissions or runs out of cash altogether. Fortunately, the adjoining ATM accepts Cirrus and Plus cards. Across the street is the **Agencia de Cambio** (Juárez 21, no phone), which changes money Monday–Saturday 8–2 and 4–8.

EMERGENCIES The **police station** (cnr of Sinaloa and Canalizo, tel. 328/5–00–28) is open 24 hours.

MAIL The post office will hold mail sent to you at the following address for up to 10 days: Lista de Correos, San Blas, Nayarit, CP 63740, México. **Casa de María** (*see* Where to Sleep, *below*) also sells stamps. *Sonora, at Echevarría, 1 block NE of bus station, tel. 328/5–02–95. Open weekdays 8–1 and 3–5, Sat. 8–noon.*

MEDICAL AID The **Centro de Salud** (Batallón, at Campeche, tel. 328/5–02–32) is six blocks west of the zócalo. **Farmacia Botica Mexicana** (Juárez 7, at Batallón, tel. 328/5–01–22), open daily 8:30–1:30 and 5–9, has an English-speaking owner and lots of mosquito repellant.

PHONES There is a public **Ladatel** phone in the Palacio Municipal on the zócalo. From the *caseta de larga distancia* (long-distance telephone office; Juárez 3, tel. and fax 328/32–06–11) on the zócalo, you can place cash calls or pay 75¢ for five minutes of long-distance collect or credit-card calls. The office is open daily 8 AM–10:30 PM.

VISITOR INFORMATION Federico at **Posada Portola** (*see* Where to Sleep, *below*) is friendly and very knowledgable about the area. Although open hours (usually daily 9–noon and 8–9) fluctuate at the **Delegación de Turismo Municipal,** across from McDonald's restaurant (*see* Food, *below*), the staff offers up-to-date info and hands out brochures and maps. *Juárez 60, tel. 328/5–02–67.*

COMING AND GOING

The **bus station** (tel. 328/5–00–43) is on the corner of Sinaloa and Canalizo, just off the zócalo. One bus leaves for Guadalajara (5 hrs, $10) at 9 AM, and four buses depart daily to Santiago Ixcuintla (1½ hrs, $2) and Las Varas (1½ hrs, $2). Buses to Santa Cruz (30 min, 75¢) leave on the hour 6 AM–5 PM from the bus station; they also leave from the corner of Sinaloa and Paredes at 8:20 AM, 10:30 AM, 12:30 PM, and 2:30 PM. Santa Cruz buses stop at several tiny beach towns en route. The 3½-hour trip to Puerto Vallarta costs $6, and buses leave at 7 AM and 10:30 AM. Buses to Tepic (1½ hrs, $2.50) leave almost every hour between 6 AM and 5 PM. At 5 PM, a bus chugs to Mazatlán (5 hrs, $8.50).

WHERE TO SLEEP

If you arrive in San Blas by bus, you will likely be greeted by a hotel owner trying to get your business for the night. Be sure to check out the competition before agreeing to anything. Strangely enough, María at **Casa de María** (*see below*) will guard your luggage for free as you check out other places. Wherever you stay, if you're here between June and October, inspect the windows, screens, and doors for any possible entryways, lest you get sucked dry by voracious mosquitoes. Hotel prices vary depending on the season; the prices listed below apply during summer and fall, but expect to pay a few dollars more in winter and around Easter.

➤ **UNDER $15** • **Casa de María.** María, sometimes called Mamá by travelers, will take care of you if you fall sick and make sure you're not in trouble if you don't return one night. Her daughter, also called María, runs a similar casa across the street. In both, you'll find kitchen facilities and free laundry service. Basic, clean doubles are $11 with bath, $8 without. *Batallón 102 and 108, at Michoacán, tel. 328/5–06–32. 2 blocks south of zócalo. 12 rooms, 8 with bath. Laundry, luggage storage. Wheelchair access.*

Hotel Bucanero. Right across from the tourist office, this place is a hotel and entertainment center all in one. You can take a dip in the swimming pool, poke the stuffed alligator, inspect retired cannons, or shoot a game of pool. Singles cost $10.50, doubles $14. *Juárez 75, tel. 328/5–01–01. 2 blocks west of zócalo. 30 rooms, all with bath. Luggage storage. Wheelchair access.*

➤ **UNDER $25** • **Posada Portola.** Each of the bungalows here is graced with a large kitchen and living/dining room separated from a good-size bedroom. The gregarious owner, Federico, will gladly rent you a bike or car, wash a load of laundry for 35¢ per piece, or even make your plane reservations. Singles cost $17, doubles $24. Peso pinchers should ask for the cheaper apartments—one has no deck and costs $15, the other has one bed and goes for $6. *Paredes 118, just past Yucatán, tel. and fax 328/5–03–86. From church, 1 block west, then a few blocks north. 8 bungalows, all with bath. Laundry, luggage storage. Wheelchair access. AE, MC, V.*

CAMPING Camping is fine here, but be sure to have good screens and lots of repellant. The summer months bring torrential rains and tides so high that beach camping is out of the question. In winter, however, the palapa restaurants on the beach will often let you use their facilities to string up a hammock after closing. Prices range from free to $4, depending on how much money you spent at the restaurant and the proprietor's mood. On Playa Borrego, **Restaurante de Federico y Lucia** is a good bet, as the owners live there and will keep an eye on you. You can pitch a tent or borrow one of their three hammocks for the night. For camping with all the facilities, try the reasonably priced **Trailer Park Coco Loco** (Teniente Azueta, down Batallón toward the beach, tel. 328/5–00–55), conveniently near the beach. Facilities include decent bathrooms with hot water and an overpriced bar. Whether you're in an RV or a tent, the fee is $4 per person. There are 100 sites, and the park is wheelchair accessible.

FOOD

San Blas is a fishing town, so the seafood is fresh and not too expensive; a lunch of fried fish at a beach restaurant costs about $4. San Blas is also proud of its *pan de plátano* (banana bread). A group of local surfers called Team Banana supports its competitive surfing by selling some of the best in town. Juán, the founder of the Team and self-proclaimed creator of the town's recipe, sells the sweet-smelling loaves for $1.50 at **Tumba de Yaco** (Batallón 219, tel. 328/5–04–62). If you're in the mood to whip up your own meal, swing by the market on the corner of Batallón and Sinaloa, open daily between 4 AM and 3 PM.

Yellow stucco walls, Huichol paintings, and stuffed crocodiles decorate the snazzy **Restaurante y Bar Cocodrilo** (Juárez, at Canalizo, on the zócalo, tel. 328/5–06–10), open daily 5 AM–10:30 PM. Specialties include the spaghetti in Italian sauce ($3) and filet mignon ($3.50), but they also serve tacos and enchiladas. **McDonald's** (Juárez 36, ½ block west of zócalo, tel. 328/5–01–27; open daily 7 AM–10 PM) offers a fruit platter or *huevos rancheros* for $1.25, and the dinner specials (such as grilled chicken with enchiladas, french fries, beans, chips, salad, and tortillas) will immobilize you for $3. As they say in San Blas, this is the *Mexican* Micky D's, without a golden arch in sight. With its elegant atmosphere, **La Hacienda** (Juárez 41, tel. 321/5–07–72) is the talk of the town. The food at this traditional restaurant is delicious; try their $5 specialty, *pescado gaviota* (shrimp-stuffed fillet of sea bass in a cheese sauce). La Hacienda is open Wednesday–Monday 2 PM–10 PM (bar open until midnight). All three restaurants are wheelchair accessible.

CHEAP THRILLS

Just off the coast, the dusty **Isla del Rey** (Island of the King) sports a lighthouse and an empty beach, and is the place to go if you're suddenly seized by a severe case of misanthropy. To get here, take a boat (40 min, 50¢) from the dock next to the customs house anytime from dawn till dusk. For a historical look at San Blas and a fantastic view of the area, make the 15-minute hike from town to **Nuestra Señora del Rosario**, a fort built in 1769, now garrisoned only by sun-loving iguanas. After San Blas's decline as a port town, the hill itself was used by pirates to hide the riches they seized. To get here, follow the main road out of town; before the bridge, veer right past the restaurants and follow the stone road up the hill on your right.

FESTIVALS The residents of San Blas are a jovial group known to look for any reason to throw a party. On January 31, the anniversary of the death of revolutionary José María Mercado is celebrated with *cerveza* (beer), food, and fireworks. Mercado, who resided in San Blas in the early 1800s, was said to have covertly helped Miguel Hidalgo accumulate war supplies, and leapt to his death to escape capture by the Spaniards. Three days later, on February 3rd, San Blas enters a state of festive upheaval on the **Día de San Blas.** Mariachi bands and inebriated locals sing and dance in the center square, and the celebration migrates down to the beach as the day progresses.

OUTDOOR ACTIVITIES

At **Playa Borrego** (San Blas's main beach—1 kilometer from the town center), you'll find tangled vegetation, pelicans, and carnivorous summer insects. Quieter beaches lie to the south, at the **Bahía de Matanchén.** Bike rentals are available at **Posada Portola** (*see* Where to Sleep, *above*) for $5 a day, even if you're not a paying guest. You can also ask here for Toño Palma, who will be happy to take you out on a boat to watch whales or to fish for tuna and red snapper. His fees vary according to the season, and perhaps how much he likes the look of you. For $10, Lucio from the tourist office will lead you on a four-hour nature trip/hike through waterfalls, streams, and canyons—a great way to count the 300 bird sounds known to San Blas. He also offers $10 road trips to nearby coffee plantations, where you can learn about coffee harvesting and purchase the freshly roasted beans. Both tours leave at 8 AM and must be reserved a day in advance with the tourist office (*see* Basics, *above*).

LA TOVARA San Blas's famous jungle boat ride takes you through a labyrinth of thick mangrove swamps to this freshwater spring. Keep your eyes open for camera-shy crocodiles, exotic birds, and schools of turtles—you'll even pass by the fake huts used in the film *Cabeza de Vaca.* Boats embark on the three-hour tour down the Río San Cristóbal from the bridge just outside of San Blas; the trek costs $17.50 for up to four people. For a shorter tour ($15 for four people), take the SANTA CRUZ bus to Matanchén (10 min, $1) and leave from the embarcadero where the bus drops you off. This boat fits more people, but the price increases with additional passengers. Boats run until sundown, with no set schedule; if you take one of the first tours before 8 AM you'll have some time to swim before the bulk of tourists arrive. In the spring if you don't want to pay for a boat trip, or are feeling masochistic, you can hike to La Tovara during the dry season (November–early June), but it takes two hours and the rocks are slippery. Two kids will competently guide any size group for half of what the boats charge. Ask for them at Posada Portola (*see* Where to Sleep, *above*). Be sure to follow them out of the jungle again, though—camping here is dangerous and off-limits.

AFTER DARK

Compared to the heady high season (December–May), the summer months offer some very mellow nightlife. Keep an eye out for signs announcing shows by Los Bucaneros, a local band that plays salsa, merengue, and other tropical sounds. Fridays and Saturdays are the nights to go out dancing: The best option is **Disco La Fancy** (Yucatán, at Canalizo, no phone), where you can shake it until 3 AM for a $2 cover. The smaller and less modern **Disco La Fitte,** a block down from McDonald's (*see* Food, *above*) is open until 2 AM and charges a $1.50 cover for a pool-playing, kick-up-your-heels kind of night. Both discos play a mixture of rock, techno, salsa, merengue, and romantic music. **Restaurant y Bar Cocodrilo** (*see* Food, *above*) sports a large bar with dim lights and *rock en español*. The gay scene in San Blas is close knit and relatively large. On the second and fourth Saturdays of the month, **Mike's Bar** (above McDonald's) hosts a transvestite show. All week long, romantic songs can be heard blasting from the bar and Mike himself sings for couples of all persuasions Thursday–Sunday. **La Hacienda** (Juárez 41, tel. 328/5–07–72; open Wed.–Mon. until midnight) is a restaurant and bar popular with gay men.

Near San Blas

In addition to the nearby towns of Santiago Ixcuintla and Mexcaltitán (*see below*), there are a number of beaches worth visiting along the **Bahía Matanchén,** just south of San Blas. The first and best is **Playa Las Islitas** (also called Stoner's Beach), which is famous for the kilometer-long wave that occasionally appears in summer or fall, depending on some fortuitous conjunction of equinoctial and lunar forces. Juán at Tumba de Yaco (*see* Food, *above*) rents surfboards and boogie boards for $2 and $1.50 per hour respectively. He also gives surf lessons for all levels ($4.50 per hour, less for avid learners). Farther south along the bay, the beaches are rockier but less infested with mosquitoes. The oyster-harvesting town of **Aticama** has a small beach that runs into **Playa los Cocos,** a beautiful spot with lots of coconut trees. Here you can find a few seafood stands that serve Aticama oysters; but watch out—high tide basically envelops the entire beach. The trailer park here is difficult to miss, and although it isn't attractive, it does offer cheap, secure tent camping for about $5. From the corner of Sinaloa and Paredes in San Blas, buses run along the bay to Las Islitas (10 min, 25¢), Aticama (20 min, 55¢), and Playa Los Cocos (25 min, 65¢) at 5:20 AM, 8:20 AM, 10:30 AM, 12:30 PM, and 2:30 PM. Buses also leave on the hour from the main bus station 6 AM–5 PM. The last returning bus passes through Playa Los Cocos at 4:35 PM, so be sure to keep an eye on the time.

SANTIAGO IXCUINTLA

This midsize city is in the center of Nayarit's ranches, 40 kilometers northeast of San Blas. Far off the tourist track, it's the departure point for boats to Mexcaltitán. Santiago's main attraction, besides the rural atmosphere, is the **Centro Cultural Huichol** (*see box, below*), located 10 blocks east of the plaza on Calle Zaragoza; one of the center's founders, Susana, is a veritable fountain of knowledge about the region. On a hot afternoon, wander down Calle Hidalgo Sur to the **Río Lerma,** a great place to take a dip and count camouflaged lizards and iguanas. Cheap hotels surround Santiago's plaza and the central market: Try the reasonably priced **Hotel Santiago** (Ocampo y Arteaga, tel. 323/5–06–37), where most of the rooms have TVs. Singles cost $8, doubles $8.50, and air-conditioning is an additional $3.50. Buses for Santiago Ixcuintla leave regularly from Tepic (1 hr) and Tuxpán (1 hr), and four times daily from San Blas. **Transportes Norte de Sonora** (tel. 323/5–04–17) sends second-class buses from Santiago's **bus station** (Primera Correjidora, north side of pueblo) to Tepic (every 30 min, 1 hr, $2.50) and Acaponeta (daily at 9 AM, 2 hrs, $2.50). Buses to San Blas (1½ hrs, $2.50) leave at 8:30 AM, 9:30 AM, and 2:30 PM. Buses to Mazatlán (4 hrs, $7) leave four times a day. Half a block away, **Transportes**

del Pacífico (tel. 323/5–12–12) sends buses to the dock for Mexcaltitán (1 hr, $1.25) at 5, 7, noon, 3, 5 ,and 7:30.

MEXCALTITÁN

The village of Mexcaltitán, believed to be the mythical first city of the Aztecs, sits on an island in the middle of a saltwater lagoon. The town's name means "the place of the temple of the moon" in Nahuatl, and legend describes how an eagle with a serpent in its beak landed here, indicating where the Aztec capital should be built. The arrival of the Spaniards, however, scared the eagle into flight and its next landing spot was Tenochtitlán (present-day Mexico City), which became the alternate Aztec capital. You can see the ancient stone figure of the eagle and serpent and learn about Mesoamerican culture at the **Museo del Origen** (tel. 323/2–02–11; open Tues.–Sun. 10–2 and 3–5), on the main plaza. Opened in 1989, the museum houses indigenous art, maps, and costumes that tell the story of ancient Aztec culture, aided by TV monitors and recorded music. For a tour of the lagoon, find José or Edy at the Embarcadero Tuxpán on the east edge of the island. They'll charge you $4.50 per boat (it fits up to four folks), and you'll see lots of birds and fish during the relaxing ride. On

It s not surprising Mexcaltit n s 1,300 inhabitants are a tight-knit group: From September through January, heavy rains raise the water level around the island over 3 meters. Helicopters must fly in food, and those with intact homes house those who were not so lucky.

June 29, the villagers (plus a few thousand visitors) celebrate the opening of the shrimping season and honor the patron saints of the city, Pedro and Pablo. The annual fiesta features all-night dancing, lively bands, and lots of home-cooked seafood.

Centro Cultural Huichol

Susana and Mariano Valadez, an American anthropologist and a Huichol artist (respectively), founded this nonprofit center in Santiago Ixcuintla to provide local Huichol people with an alternative to working in chemical-ridden tobacco fields. The center provides medical care, shelter, legal aid, and training in art and farming techniques, and serves as a place where the Huichol can stay while working on the coast. The center helps indigenous people become economically self-sufficient through practicing sustainable agriculture and traditional art forms. Huichol artisans supposedly tap into the metaphysical world and then translate the acquired knowledge into meticulous beadwork, embroidery, yarn paintings, and weaving. Although the prices for the artesanía (handicrafts) aren't always lower here than in Tepic's stores, the work is often of higher quality, and proceeds go back into the project and community. Fridays until 3 PM, artists and musicians gather at the center for a morning of festivities. There is also a small, free, on-site museum and a breeding center for the unusual and endangered hairless Ixcuintla dogs, which are held sacred by the Huichol. People who are committed to learning about and participating in this social venture, especially those with valuable skills to share (such as doctors or carpenters) are welcome to stay for a while in exchange for labor. If you're interested, call 323/5–11–71 or fax 323/5–10–06 for more information; or try the U.S. office in Seattle (tel. 260/622–4067, fax 206/622–0646). Avenida 20 de Noviembre 452, at Constitución. Open daily 10 AM–6 PM.

You can reach Mexcaltitán by taking a bus from Santiago Ixcuintla (*see above*) to Embarcadero Batango, and then jumping on a boat (15 min, 50¢) to the village. Boat departures are coordinated with the arrival of combis and buses; boats return to the embarcadero at 8, 10:30, 12:45, 3:45, 5:15, and 6 (1 hr, $1.25). If you miss the boat, **Hotel La Ruta Azteca** (Venecia 5, south of the plaza, tel. 323/2–02–11 ext. 128) is seldom full and offers air-conditioned rooms ($10) for one or two people. For fresh shrimp or shellfish, try either **La Alberca** (tel. 323/2–02–11 ext. 134), on the west edge of the island, or **Restaurante Lomochina**, on a small island a free, three-minute boat ride from the dock. Both restaurants fill up with locals, tourists, and mariachi musicians in the afternoons. Open daily 9–9, both serve fresh fish ($4), but shrimp ($4) is the specialty of the island. Try the Aztec dish *taxtihuilli,* consisting of shrimp in a cornmeal sauce with herbs and spices.

Tepic

The capital of the agricultural state of Nayarit, Tepic is not a city to linger in if you're short on time or have the beach and an ice-cold coconut drink on your mind. However, the city's bus station is a hub for transportation throughout western Mexico, so your travels between Puerto Vallarta and San Blas or Los Mochis might make Tepic a required stop. The gray buildings of the city stand in marked contrast to the colorful Huichol embroidery and yarn paintings sold in the town's many markets. Tepic is a center of commerce for residents of the nearby hills: The indigenous Huichol and Aztec come down from the hills to buy supplies, and nearby ranchers and tobacco farmers, their faces darkened and wrinkled from labor in the sun, can be found chatting on street corners and shopping in small stores that sell leather goods, tools, ammunition, and chemical fertilizers.

If you're going to be in the city for more than a few hours, head for the free **Museo Regional de Antropología e Historia** (México 91, at Zapata, tel. 32/12–19–00), near the zócalo, where you'll find a fine collection of pre-Columbian clay figurines. The museum is open weekdays 9–7 and Saturday 9–3. Two blocks northeast is the small **Museo de los Cuatro Pueblos** (Hidalgo 60 Ote., tel. 32/12–17–05), open weekdays 9–2 and 4–7, Saturday 10–2. Also known as the Museo de Artes Populares, the museum hosts a five-room collection of Huichol clothing, wood and leather work, and sculpture. The **Ex-Convento de la Cruz de Zacate** (México, at Calzada del Ejército) was built to guard a grass cross that, legend has it, miraculously appeared nearby in 1540. The building now houses a ballet academy, an art store, and a progressive theater group, the latter of which offers acting and music lessons. To escape Tepic's noise and general drabness, take a stroll through **Paseo La Loma** (Insurgentes, at Colegio Militar), a large park with pine and eucalyptus trees and a miniature train—hop aboard for a ride reminiscent of "The Little Engine That Could."

BASICS

Banamex (Av. México, at Zapata, tel. 32/12–02–42) has an ATM that accepts Cirrus and Plus cards and changes traveler's checks weekdays 8–2. **Agencia de Cambio Serna** (México 139 Nte., at Zapata, tel. 32/16–55–30) gives slightly better rates but charges a commission; it's open Monday–Saturday 8–8. Mail your cheesy postcards at the **main post office** (Durango 33 Nte., tel. 32/12–01–30), open weekdays 8–7, Saturday 8–noon. The best place to make long-distance phone calls is the bus station, where you can place collect or credit-card calls for 75¢. It's open daily 7 AM–9 PM. You can get advice about minor medical problems and basic first aid near the zócalo at **Farmacia Benavides** (Hidalgo 6, at México, tel. 32/12–08–33), open daily 7–10; the **Cruz Roja** (tel. 32/13–11–60) can get you an ambulance in more dire situations. One block south of the cathedral, the **tourist office** (México 178-A Nte., tel. 32/12–19–05; open weekdays 9–2 and 3–8, Sat. 9–7) provides maps of Tepic and the state, as well as handfuls of tourist brochures, most of which are in Spanish. The knowledgable staff speaks some English.

COMING AND GOING

Central Tepic is walkable, with casas de cambio, restaurants, hotels, and most of Tepic's points of interest lying along Avenida México (the main commercial street), between Avenida Insurgentes and Avenida Victoria. Near Avenida Insurgentes is the Palacio Municipal and the Plaza de los Constituyentes; the basilica lies closer to Avenida Victoria. The main street crossing Avenida México is Avenida Insurgentes. Buses (15¢) traverse all these main thoroughfares.

BY BUS Tepic's bus terminal is on Avenida Insurgentes, about six blocks east of Avenida México. If you're flat broke, store your luggage ($1 for 7 hrs) and throw your sleeping bag down here. **Transportes del Pacífico** (tel. 32/13–23–20) sends second-class buses to Mazatlán (4 hrs, $7.50), Guadalajara (4 hrs, $8.50), Los Mochis (12 hrs, $24), Mexicali (30 hrs, $55), and Tijuana (32 hrs, $56.50). Service to Puerto Vallarta (3½ hrs, $6) leaves on the half hour 3 AM–8 PM; if you ask the driver, he will let you off at Rincón de Guayabitos or other beaches en route. Buses to San Blas (1½ hrs, $2.50) leave on the hour; those to Santiago Ixcuintla (1½ hrs, $2.50) leave every 45 minutes. **Transportes Norte de Sonora** (tel. 32/13–23–15) serves Acaponeta (2½ hrs, $4), and **Omnibús de México** (tel. 32/13–13–23), with first-class service only, has hourly buses to Guadalajara (3½ hrs, $10), evening service to Mexico City (11 hrs, $30), and one daily bus at 6 PM to Cuidad Juárez (28 hrs, $58). To get downtown from the station, take an ESTACION FRESNOS bus.

BY TRAIN To reach the train station, hop on a ESTACION FRESNOS bus, which passes the train station on its way to the bus station. Trains travel north from Tepic to Mexicali (32 hrs, $36.50 1st class; 38 hrs, $20.50 2nd class), with stops in Culiacán (8 hrs, $10 1st class; 10 hrs, $7 2nd class), Sufragio (10 hrs, $15 1st class; 12 hrs, $9 2nd class), and Nogales (23 hrs, $38 1st class; 28 hrs, $17 2nd class). The northbound train leaves daily at 1:15 PM (1st class) and 5:15 PM (2nd class). The southbound train leaves at noon (2nd class) and 8 PM (1st class), traveling as far as Guadalajara (5 hrs, $6 1st class; 6 hrs, $3 2nd class). Times may vary from season to season—call ahead to check. Tickets go on sale an hour before departure. *Tel. 32/13–48–61. Ticket office open 10 AM–about midnight.*

WHERE TO SLEEP

Tepic has a few inexpensive hotels right by the bus station—convenient for weary travelers but a 10-minute bus ride from downtown. Turn left out of the bus station, make another immediate left, and walk one block to **Hotel Nayar** (Martínez 430, tel. 32/13–23–22). The bathrooms are clean and have hot water, and it's not a bad choice considering the price: Singles are $5, doubles $6.50. **Hotel Sarita** (Bravo 112 Pte., tel. 32/12–13–33) is close to the basilica and has colonial-style furniture and clean, fan-cooled rooms. Rooms with one bed cost $7, $9.50 with two beds. A few rooms are wheelchair accessible. **Hotel Altamirano** (Mina 19, tel. 32/12–10–31), just off the zócalo and behind the Palacio Municipal, is quiet and wheelchair accessible. Singles cost $10 and doubles are $11.50. There is no campground in town, so those with a tent should head for the Laguna de Santa María del Oro (*see* Near Tepic, *below*).

FOOD

Food is generally cheaper in Tepic than in the seaside resorts, and better than you might expect. Fresh seafood comes straight from San Blas, and vegetarian restaurants pop up with surprising frequency. Grill joints stretch along Avenida Insurgentes below the park, and super-cheap grub is also sold near the bus station on Avenida Victoria, close to México. If you're in the mood for fruit and snacks, you'll find a market on the corner of Puebla and Zaragoza.

For tasty vegetarian food in a great location, try **Girasol** (tel. 32/13–42–93; open daily 8 AM–10 PM), in Paseo La Loma park. Soyburgers here are $1 and veggie *pozole* (corn soup) overflowing with mushrooms is about $2. The owner's brother runs the similar **Restaurant Vegetariano Quetzalcoatl** (León 224 Nte., at Lerdo, tel. 32/12–22–84), open Monday–Saturday 8:30–8:30, on the northern fringe of downtown. Carnivores can head for **Restaurant Altamirano** (México 109 Sur, near Palacio Municipal, tel. 321/2–13–77; open daily 7–1 and 3–11), where high ceilings, stone walls, and the sound of frying tortillas create an "authentic" atmosphere. *Lengua en salsa* (beef tongue in salsa) or *pollo en mole* (chicken in chile and chocolate sauce) will cost you $3. To get a feel for the student life in this university town, grab a coffee or beer ($1) at **Café Juventud** (Zacatecas, btw Hidalgo and Zapata, tel. 32/16–41–72), open daily until 11 PM.

Near Tepic

LAGUNA DE SANTA MARÍA DEL ORO

About an hour's drive on a curvy mountain road will bring you to the **Laguna de Santa María del Oro,** a stunning turquoise lake. Situated in the crater of an extinct volcano, the laguna is frequented by families from Tepic who come for swimming, shaded lakeshore food huts, and hidden campsites. Locals claim the 1985 quake killed off all the lake's fish, but the aquatic life now seems to be replenished, and the lake is popular for fishing. Sample the local specialty, *cuachala* (pork and chicken roasted with rice, vegetables, and spices) for $4 at **Restaurante El Viejo Aztlán** or **Restaurante Los Tules,** both on the south side of the lake. **Bungalows Koala** (tel. 32/14–05–09) has five bungalows that fit up to four people ($19 a night), a grassy field where you can camp ($5), and a swimming pool. You can also rent tents for $1.50 a night at El Viejo Aztlán and camp right on the warm sand. To reach Laguna de Santa Maria, take a 6 AM, 10 AM, or 2 PM bus ($1.25) from the Terminal Centro (Av. Victoria, at México) in Tepic. The last bus returns to Tepic at 4 PM.

Puerto Vallarta

Puerto Vallarta is famous for beaches, cobblestone streets, and the whitewashed, red-roofed buildings stacked along its precipitous hillsides. Unfortunately, many of the latter are condos and timeshares. Like most of the resorts on the Pacific Coast, the city has a gringo-ized hotel zone (the *Zona Hotelera*) separate from the "Mexican" part of town—staying here would be like living at your local shopping mall. The downtown area around the Río Cuale is more residential, with pleasant cafés and good restaurants. The biggest draw, however, is Puerto Vallarta's natural setting. Nestled between lush tropical hills and spectacular coastline, the resort gives way to a tropical jungle full of birds and natural caves.

Some credit for transforming Puerto Vallarta from a farming and fishing village to a popular destination belongs to *The Love Boat* and John Huston's *The Night of the Iguana*. Mexicana also had a hand in Puerto Vallarta's promotion—the airline "discovered," developed, and marketed the resort town in the early 1950s to combat Aeroméxico's monopoly on flights to Acapulco. Although the result is a big, often characterless resort, the rustic architecture of old Vallarta, the green waves of the Pacific, and the palm-fringed beaches frequented by strolling mariachis may make a visit here worthwhile.

BASICS

AMERICAN EXPRESS The office sells traveler's checks and changes them at a good rate. Cardholders can cash personal checks and have their mail held here. *Morelos 660, at Abasolo, Col. Centro Puerto Vallarta, Jalisco, CP 48300, México, tel. 322/3–29–55. Open weekdays 9–6, Sat. 9–1.*

CASAS DE CAMBIO Puerto Vallarta has many casas de cambio, usually in tiny storefront booths with caged-in employees. All of them change cash and traveler's checks at average rates. **Cambio de Moneda** (Libertad 349, tel. 332/2–09–13), near the mercado, is open Monday–Saturday 9–9 and Sunday 10–9. Across the street is the bank **Bital** (Miramar, at Libertad, tel. 322/2–02–27), open weekdays 8–7 and Saturday 9–2:30. They have an ATM that accepts Plus, Cirrus, Visa, and MasterCard.

CONSULATES Canada's **consulate** (tel. 322/2–53–98), open weekdays 9–5, and the **U.S. consulate** (tel. 322/2–00–69), open weekdays 10–2, are both located at Zaragoza 160 in the Palacio Municipal.

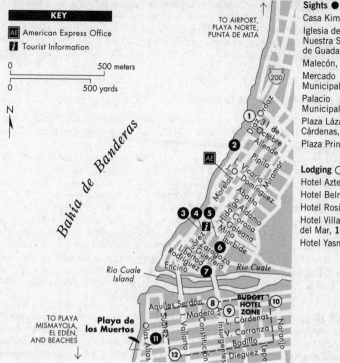

KEY

AE American Express Office

i Tourist Information

0 ——————————— 500 meters

0 ——————————— 500 yards

N

TO AIRPORT,
PLAYA NORTE,
PUNTA DE MITA

Bahía de Banderas

Río Cuale Island

TO PLAYA
MISMAYOLA,
EL EDÉN,
AND BEACHES

Playa de
los Muertos

Río Cuale

BUDGET
HOTEL
ZONE

Sights ●
Casa Kimberly, **6**
Iglesia de
Nuestra Señora
de Guadalupe, **5**
Malecón, **2**
Mercado
Municipal, **7**
Palacio
Municipal, **4**
Plaza Lázaro
Cárdenas, **11**
Plaza Principal, **3**

Lodging ○
Hotel Azteca, **9**
Hotel Belmar, **8**
Hotel Rosita, **1**
Hotel Villa
del Mar, **10**
Hotel Yasmin, **12**

EMERGENCIES The number for the **police** is 322/2–08–04. To reach the **Cruz Roja** (for ambulance service), call 322/2–15–33.

LAUNDRY **Lavandería Acuamatic** will wash, dry, and fold 3 kilos of clothes for $2. *Constitución 279, south of Río Cuale, tel. 322/1–64–90. Other location: Madero 289, north of Río Cuale. Open daily 9–2 and 4–8.*

MAIL The **post office** is a half block from the malecón, at Juárez. They offer the usual services and will hold mail sent to you at the following address for up to 10 days: Lista de Correos, Juárez 128, Puerto Vallarta, Jalisco, CP 48300, México. *Juárez 128, tel. 322/2–18–88. Open weekdays 8–7:30, Sat. 9–1.*

MEDICAL AID The **CMQ** clinic (Badillo 365, ½ block east of Insurgentes, tel. 322/3–19–19) attends patients 24 hours a day; English-speaking doctors are available daily 5–8 PM. Prices start at $20 for an appointment, and walk-in emergency care is also available. Next door, **Farmacia CMQ** (tel. 322/2–29–41) is also open 24 hours.

PHONES Both the **Transportes del Pacífico** (Insurgentes 282, tel. 322/2–10–15) and **Élite** (Carranza 322, tel. 322/3–27–70) bus stations have casetas de larga distancia, open 7 AM–10 PM. Both charge a flat $2 for collect calls. Save your precious pesos by calling from a pay phone—the Plaza Principal and the malecón are lined with them.

SCHOOLS The **University of Guadalajara**'s branch in Puerto Vallarta offers Spanish-language courses for credit (3 credits per 40 hrs). Weekly rates are $75 for two hours of instruction per day, $140 for four hours, and individual tutoring costs $15.50 per hour. There is also a $30 nonrefundable registration fee. Lodging and language exchange with a local Mexican student can be arranged upon request. For more info, write: UDG-Centro Internacional, Parían del Puente, Libertad y Miramar No. 43, Col. Central, CP 48300, Puerto Vallarta, Jalisco, México. *Tel. 322/3–20–82, fax 322/3–29–82, cipv@clxvta.udg.mx.*

VISITOR INFORMATION The Delegación Regional de Turismo is the central office for the state of Jalisco and has all the brochures, maps, and information you'd ever need. The branch office is closer to town in the Palacio Municipal (tel. 322/2–02–42) and is open weekdays 9– 9. Both offices have friendly, English-speaking staff. *Central office: Blvd. Fco. Medina Ascencio 1712, across from the Sheraton, tel. 322/3–08–44, fax 322/2–02–43. Open weekdays 9–7, Sat. 9–1.*

COMING AND GOING

BY BUS Puerto Vallarta does not have a central bus station. Instead, each bus line operates out of individual buildings, all of which are south of the Río Cuale, clustered on or near Avenida Insurgentes. **Élite** (Badillo 11, at Insurgentes, tel. 322/3–11–17) leaves for Hermosillo (24 hrs, $50) at 3 PM, with stops in Tepic (3 hrs, $7) and Mazatlán (8 hrs, $16.50). Buses leave for Manzanillo (5 hrs, $9.50) at 7 AM and 1 PM; the 1 PM bus continues on to Acapulco (18 hrs, $35). They also send four first-class buses every evening to Mexico City (14 hrs, $31), and an even more plush bus leaves at 8:30 PM ($44). **Transportes del Pacífico** (Insurgentes 282, tel. 322/2–10–15) sends buses to Guadalajara (6 hrs, $16) every hour between 7 AM and 1 AM. Traveling second class costs $2.50 less, but there's no air-conditioning. Tepic-bound buses (3½ hrs, $6.50) leave every half hour from 4:15 AM to 8 PM. **Transportes Norte de Sonora** (Carranza 322, btw Insurgentes and Constitución, tel. 322/2–66–66) has second-class service to San Blas (3 hrs, $6) and Mazatlán (8 hrs, $14). Luggage storage is available at this depot. **Transportes Cihuatlán** (Madero 296, at Constitución, tel. 332/2–34–36) has first-class service at 11:30 AM and 4:30 PM to Manzanillo (5 hrs, $9.50) and to intermediate points such as Bahía Chamela (3½ hrs, $4) and Barra de Navidad (4 hrs, $8.50).

BY PLANE Puerto Vallarta's international airport is 6 kilometers north of town, near the major resorts. **Aeroméxico** (Plaza Genovesa, tel. 322/4–27–77) and **Mexicana** (Centro Comercial Villas Vallarta, in the Zona Hotelera, tel. 322/4–89–00) have daily flights to Guadalajara ($68 one-way) and Mexico City ($100 one-way) and serve some U.S. cities. **Alaska, American, Continental,** and **Delta** also serve Puerto Vallarta. From downtown, city buses (25¢) marked AEROPUERTO, IXTAPA, or JUNTA will drop you off on the highway, a hop, skip, and jump from the terminals. You can also take an airport taxi from the town center for $6.

GETTING AROUND

Puerto Vallarta is divided into three parts: the northern Zona Hotelera (a long stretch of hotels, shopping centers, and overpriced restaurants); the pedestrian-friendly downtown (*Viejo Vallarta*, or "Old Vallarta"), which runs along the banks of the Río Cuale; and, to the south, **Playa de los Muertos,** the most popular beach in Puerto Vallarta proper. The **malecón** begins at Díaz Ordaz and runs south along the bay past the **Plaza Principal** (also called the Plaza de Armas).

To reach the Zona Hotelera from the downtown area, hop a HOTELES, AEROPUERTO, or MARINAS VALLARTA bus (25¢) on Insurgentes or Juárez. Buses return along Morelos and, south of the Río Cuale, along Insurgentes. Buses run 5 AM–11 PM. You can also take one of the many taxis roaming Vallarta—the aggressive drivers will flag *you* down for a ride. Due to inattentive bus drivers and numerous one-way unpaved streets, renting bikes or scooters may be hazardous. If you decide to take the risk, **Bike Mex** (Guerrero 361, 1 block north of market, tel. 322/3–16–80), open Monday–Saturday 8:30–2 and 4–8, rents cruiser bikes. **Moto Gallo** (Badillo 324, tel. 322/2–16–72) rents Honda scooters ($7 per hr, $35 per day) daily 9–3 and 4–7.

WHERE TO SLEEP

Almost all budget hotels lie just south of the Río Cuale along Madero, close to the bus stations and 4–7 short blocks from the beach. Remember that hotel prices jump as much as 30% between November and April.

➤ **UNDER $10 • Hotel Azteca.** With special rates for families, this cheap hotel fills with loud children and working locals. The good news is that there's an airy courtyard and the owners are particularly friendly. Singles cost $6, doubles $8, rooms with kitchenettes are $11, and the prices hold year-round. *Madero 473, tel. 322/2–27–50. 47 rooms, all with bath. Luggage storage. Wheelchair access.*

Hotel Villa del Mar. This spacious hotel, decorated with posters of James Dean and Brooke Shields, is a steal during summer, when the clean exterior rooms with balconies and fancy beds cost $7.50 for a single ($6.50 for an interior room), $9 for a double ($8 interior). For $12 you can have an apartment-style room for two with a kitchenette. *Madero 440, 3 blocks east of Insurgentes, tel. 322/2–07–85. 49 rooms, all with bath. Luggage storage. Wheelchair access. MC, V.*

➤ **UNDER $20** • **Hotel Belmar.** The nicest of the cheaper hotels, the Belmar has freshly painted walls, tile floors, creative artwork, and brightly striped bedcovers. The bathrooms are clean, and rooms ($11 singles, $16.50 doubles; $3 extra in the high season) open either onto a balcony over the street or onto the courtyard hallway. Ask for a room with TV—it's the same price. *Insurgentes 161, at Serdán, tel. 322/2–05–72. 29 rooms, all with bath.*

Hotel Yasmin. A lush courtyard, clean rooms, and a fine location one block from Playa de los Muertos make this place worth the extra cash. It's right in old Puerto Vallarta, upstairs from the Café de Olla (*see* Food, *below*). In summer, singles cost about $12.50, doubles $14, but prices are hiked during the winter season. *Badillo 168, tel. 322/2–00–87. 27 rooms, all with bath. Luggage storage. Wheelchair access.*

➤ **UNDER $25** • **Hotel Rosita.** You'll pay a bit more here, but you'll be where the action is (near the beach and malecón), and have a good view and access to the pool. In the low season, a small single costs $14.50, a larger one $22; double occupancy costs $22 regardless of the size of the room. If Puerto Vallarta has put you in the mood to splurge, go for a "suite"—a high-ceilinged room with brick walls, air-conditioning, a beautiful tiled bathroom, and a comfy king-size bed that will fit up to three of your favorite people ($30). *Díaz Ordaz 901 (north end of malécon), tel. 322/3–20–00, fax 332/3–21–51. 112 rooms, all with bath. Luggage storage. AE, MC, V.*

CAMPING There is no real campground here, and the hotels and the police don't look favorably upon (and sometimes even hassle) people sleeping on hotel beaches. If you're set on beach camping, it's better to crash at the south end of **Playa de los Muertos,** where campers are not bothered as frequently, or go to the beaches outside of Puerto Vallarta proper (*see* Near Puerto Vallarta, *below*). During Semana Santa, temporary campgrounds are set up in Puerto Vallarta to accommodate the crowds.

FOOD

There's a huge variety of food here, including many French and Italian restaurants, but prices are often exorbitant. Good $3 comidas corridas can be found at Puerto Vallarta's **market,** open daily 8–8, just north of the Río Cuale. Cheap eats are also available along Insurgentes, on the other side of the river. Fresh juice ($1.50) or a quick espresso (75¢) can be had at **Jugos y Café Malibu** (Morelos, at Guerrero, tel. 332/2–29–44; open daily 7 AM–11 PM).

➤ **UNDER $5** • **Café de Olla** has delicious $1.50 tamales and $4 chiles rellenos that come with rice, beans, tortillas, and tons of cheese. The *café de olla* (coffee flavored with chocolate and cinnamon) is good, too. The place swarms with gringos, but service is surprisingly efficient. *Badillo 168, btw Olas Altas and Pino Suárez, tel. 322/2–00–87. Open Wed.–Mon. 8 AM–midnight.*

Cenaduría el Campanario. This family-run restaurant is usually packed with locals and travel-smart tourists sampling the excellent $2 pozole and 50¢ tamales. *Hidalgo 339, at Independencia, tel. 322/3–15–09. Open Mon.–Sat. 7 PM–11 PM. Closed first 2 weeks of Aug. Wheelchair access.*

➤ **UNDER $10** • **Archie's Wok.** Founded by Archie Alpenia, formerly John Huston's private chef, this restaurant dishes out the best, most varied Asian food around. Choose from Hoisin ribs ($6.50) and Thai coconut fish ($7.50), or get your fix of stir-fried vegetables ($4). *Rodríguez 130, tel. 322/2–04–11. Near pier at Playa de los Muertos. Open Mon.–Sat. 2–11.* **297**

La Dolce Vita. If you've been craving pizza, indulge yourself with one of the oven-baked pies ($6.50) here. They are nothing like the pale imitations served in most Mexican "Italian" restaurants, and one feeds two hungry people. The $5 pasta is great too. *Díaz Ordaz 674, north end of malecón. tel. 322/2–38–52. Open Mon.–Sat. noon–2 AM, Sun. 6 PM–midnight.*

CAFES **Café San Cristóbal.** This Euro-style coffee shop has an underground feel and supplies its fresh-roasted beans to restaurants around the city. The café also has cheese, bread, and fruit plates ($2) to prelude coffee and dessert. Espresso and hot chocolate cost $1, or you can get your caffeine and chocolate fix together in a mocha ($1.25). *Corona 172, btw Juárez and Morelos, tel. 322/3–25–51. Open Mon.–Sat. 8 AM–10 PM.*

A Page in the Sun. Come here to sip a café latte ($1), buy used books in English, and even get a tarot card reading ($7). Inside, classic paintings fill the walls, while the outside tables catch the breeze from the beach a block away. *Olas Altas 399, 1 block from Playa de los Muertos, no phone. Open Mon.–Sat. 8 AM–10 PM.*

OUTDOOR ACTIVITIES

Most of the things to do in Puerto Vallarta involve getting wet. If you want to get sweaty before playing in the waves, **Bike Mex** (*see* Getting Around, *above*) organizes mountain-biking trips, which are divided into beginner, intermediate, and advanced levels, and range from four-hour excursions ($30) to week-long adventure tours ($800). All equipment and food is included. Horseback riding along Río Cuale is another option. Horses can be rented ($7 per hr) near Olas Altas, at the end of Carranza, daily 9–6.

BEACHES **Playa de los Muertos** is the most popular beach in Puerto Vallarta, and gets packed with tourists and vendors on sunny days. The gloomy name (Beach of the Dead) was derived from a battle with the Spanish that took place here. At sunset, people congregate to watch the bloodshot sun slip behind the bay. Parasailing at the beach costs $30, banana boat rides $6, inner tubes 50¢, and boogies $3 per hour. Snorkel gear ($10 for 24 hrs) or guided snorkel or dive trips ($22 and $49 respectively) are available through **Chico's Dive Shop** (Díaz Ordaz 772-5, tel. 322/2–18–95). They also offer more advanced, expensive trips, as well as a $200 certification course.

The underwater **Parque Nacional Los Arcos** is a set of large rocks under which caves have been formed by wave erosion. Chico's and other dive shops will take you scuba diving in these protected waters filled with tropical fish, sea turtles, and moray eels. Night diving, recommended for experienced, certified divers only, reveals rarely seen neon fish darting about. To save big bucks, however, rent some snorkel gear and take a RUTA 2 combi (20 min, 25¢) from Plaza Lázaro Cárdenas (cnr of Vallarta and Badillo) to **Playa Mismaloya.** Get off at the Arcos Hotel, walk down to the rocky beach, and swim out yourself. Playa Mismaloya is also a good sunning and swimming beach. If you walk inland 2 kilometers from Playa Mismaloya along the dirt road, you'll find the restaurant **Chino's Paradise,** where the cinematic masterpiece *Caveman,* starring Ringo Starr, was filmed. Five kilometers farther is **El Edén,** a restaurant near where *Predator* was filmed. If this movie tour isn't thrilling you, you'll still be rewarded for your 90-minute uphill walk by Puerto Vallarta's largest waterfall, where you can swim, slide down rocks, or play Tarzan by swinging on ropes into the water. You can also ride a horse to and from the falls for $20; contact Victor from **Rancho Manolo** (tel. 322/2–36–94).

The beaches of **Las Animas, Quimixto,** and **Yelapa** are on the southern side of the **Bahía de Banderas,** past Playa Mismaloya, and are best reached by boat. Yelapa offers pricey cabañas and a small colony of expatriate gringos who pretend they never left home. Las Animas has a white sand beach and choice waters for parasailing and waterskiing. The 200-family beach community of Quimixto recently installed its first "road"—a cobblestone walkway leading to a large waterfall 15 minutes inland. You can camp for free on any of these three beaches. The cheapest way to get here is by water shuttle (45 min, $11 round-trip), which leaves daily at 11 AM from the pier at Playa de los Muertos and returns at 4 PM. Larger cruises with meals and snorkeling equipment start at $25.

CHEAP THRILLS

Although the beaches are the main attraction here, a few downtown sights are worth checking out. **Casa Kimberly** (Zaragoza 445, behind the Guadalupe church, tel. 332/2–13–36) is connected by a bridge to the **Casa Bursus.** The first was given to Elizabeth Taylor by Richard Burton in the '60s; the second received its name from Burton and his third wife Susy. Tours are given daily 9–6; come and be enthralled by opulent furnishings and various theories about Dick and Liz's love lives. Numerous art galleries have sprouted up around town: **Galería Uno** (501 Morelos, tel. 322/2–09–08) has long been the center of the artistic community in Vallarta and features various Latin American artists, while **Galería Javier Niño** (Plaza Marina C-4, tel. 322/2–36–28) features psychedelic, Huichol-inspired paintings done in a singular style known as "Vallarta Art." Get information about cultural events from the owners of **Gallería Vallarta** (Juárez 263, tel. 322/2–02–90), where you'll find indigenous art and bronze sculptures.

FESTIVALS The **Christmas** holidays are a festive time in Puerto Vallarta, beginning as early as November 22 with the **Fiesta de Santa Cecilia,** patron saint of musicians. Musicians start parading through town as early as 5 AM to wish her a happy birthday. At 7 PM everyone heads to the malecón for a mass; the beer starts to flow soon afterward. December 1–12 sees daily parades for the Virgin Mary that include mariachis and dancing in traditional costumes. The town is beautifully decorated December 15–24, and daily dancing and piñata parties liven things up. By the time Christmas hits and the city is crammed with tourists, Puerto Vallarta's residents are ready to relax.

AFTER DARK

There are a million discos in Puerto Vallarta, but most either extort an outrageous cover or charge scandalous prices for drinks. Fortunately, you can sometimes get free or discounted passes by playing up to the oh-so-friendly timeshare people; once you're inside a club, you can often get free passes to return. Most of the Americanized bars/dance spots are on the north end of the malecón. Juaréz and Vallarta also host a collection of chic clubs, and the Zona Hotelera is more expensive still. To avoid the dance scene altogether, walk over the bridge from Insurgentes to **Le Bistro** (Río Cuale island 16-A, tel. 322/2–02–83; open daily 9 AM–midnight), one of the sleekest restaurant/bars in town. Sit at the black-and-white bar or in the dinner lounge and listen to the gurgling of the Río Cuale while a DJ spins your favorite jazz tunes. Sunday nights around sundown, there's usually a free dance or theater performance on the malecón.

DISCOS The **Zoo** (Díaz Ordaz 630, tel. 322/2–49–45) and **Carlos O'Brien's** (Díaz Ordaz 86, tel. 322/2–14–44) are considered the hip malecón hangouts, but have an unfortunate tendency to attract American high school groups. You're better off heading to the classier discos dominated by young locals. The only one in Viejo Vallarta is **Cactus** (Vallarta 399, tel. 322/2–60–77), a self-proclaimed "Disco Club and New Age Bar." It's open nightly 9 PM–6 AM; cover is $4.50. Wednesday nights bring a $10 cover and an open bar. The other discos lie near the resorts, 15–20 minutes north of town, and can be reached via any AEROPUERTO bus or by taxi ($3–$5). In the Hotel Krystal is **Christine's** (tel. 322/4–69–90), which plays rock, salsa, and techno nightly 9:30 PM–4 AM; cover is $5.50. The best disco in town is the gigantic **Collage** (Marina Vallarta, tel. 322/1–05–05), which plays techno and rock music nightly 11 PM–5 AM. The $7 cover also gives you access to pool tables and video games. If you prefer live salsa and *música tropical* and want to mingle with some more down-to-earth Mexicans, jump on a bus to the Zona Hotelera and get off at **Le Carrusel** (in front of Seguro Social building, tel. 322/4–94–40).

GAY/LESBIAN BARS AND DISCOS The downtown **Zótano** (Morelos 101, no phone) means "basement" in Spanish and has an appropriately underground feel, attracting a mixed straight and gay clientele. **Los Balcones Bar** (Juárez 182, 1 block south of Plaza Principal, tel. 322/2–46–71), open nightly 9:30 PM–4 AM, is a popular gay tourist hangout, with balcony tables that overlook the street. The large **Club Paco Paco** (Vallarta 266, btw Carranza and Ardenas, tel. 322/2–18–99) attracts a mixed local/tourist lesbian and gay crowd to its downstairs dance floor and upstairs pool table and video games. The newest gay disco in town, **Studio 33** (Juárez 728, at Vicario, tel. 322/3–11–65), features the area's best strip and drag shows at 1 AM Friday–Sunday.

Near Puerto Vallarta

PUNTA DE MITA

On the northern tip of the Bahía de Banderas, Punta de Mita and its nearby beaches offer glassy water and high-breaking waves perfect for swimming and surfing (respectively), although the rocky ocean floor demands some caution. The landscape here is drier than what you'll find along most of the Pacific coastline, and the view of the bay and mountains is fantastic. The beach is often crowded, especially around the restaurants and **Playa El Anclote,** but a short walk along the coast in either direction brings you to solitary stretches of sand. Next to the pier, English-speaking Chuy at **Sol y Arena** (no phone) makes boat trips (half an hour each way) to **Isla Marietas,** home to many seabirds; if you want to camp on the island, arrange a pickup time with the boat captain. Round-trip transport for up to five people is $44. Chuy also makes boat trips to other "hidden beaches" ($22 per hour for up to five people) and will rent you surfboards ($14 a day) and snorkel gear ($4 for 3 hrs). If you've got your own board, head straight to Punta de Mita, a 15-minute walk from Playa El Anclote. For beautiful, isolated, and oftentimes nude beaches, get off the bus to or from Punta de Mita at **Playa Destiladores, Cruz de Huanacaxtle,** or **Arena Blanca.** If you want to spend the night, you can camp anywhere along Playa El Anclote, or head uphill to the brand-new **Hotel Punta de Mita** (Hidalgo 5, no phone), where a beautifully furnished room five minutes from the beach is $15 a night for one or two people. Head back down to the beach to **Restaurante Rocio** for BBQ fish ($7) and lobster ($10). They'll even whip up a vegetarian dish, and all meals include a free drink of your choice.

COMING AND GOING Transportes Medina (Guatemala 264, at Brasil, tel. 322/2–69–43) in Puerto Vallarta has service to Punta de Mita (1 hr, $1.50) every half hour 6:30 AM–9 PM. To reach the bus terminal from downtown, take any CENTRO bus (15 min, 25¢), which will let you off two blocks south of the station. When thinking about bus schedules, keep in mind that 2 PM in Punta de Mita is 3 PM in Puerto Vallarta.

RINCÓN DE GUAYABITOS

Located 70 kilometers (43 mi) northwest of Puerto Vallarta, this beach town offers similar tourist services but without the jacked up-prices. The area around Guayabitos is virgin forest, and colorful tropical flowers and lush foliage line the town streets. Protected by the cove of Jaltemba, the golden beach has calm, clean waters perfect for banana boat rides ($3 per person)

Surfin on the Pacific Coast

Once one of the Pacific Coast's surfing hot spots, Punta de Mita may soon see the last of its wave-riding beach bums. Japanese investors bought the land at the point and intend to build a Four Seasons resort hotel on the virgin beaches. Already, the road out to the point—the best spot for swells—is totally blocked off to cars and buses, and an obtrusive cement wall along the road reminds you that access to the beach is limited. However, avid surfers still endure the 15-minute trek along the sand, board in hand, to the point. Others venture to up-and-coming surfing spots like La Bahía, Punta Pura, or La Lancha. All of these can be reached by catching a bus heading toward Vallarta from the main road in Punta de Mita (10 min). If you're itching to catch a wave, Sol y Arena (see, Punta de Mita, above) rents boards; during the high surfing season (January to March), you can try to hitch a ride with anyone who has a board on his or her roof.

and jet skiing ($25 an hr). You can also go sportfishing ($16 per hr) and take glass-bottom boat tours around the nearby island; walk to the southern end of the beach for rentals and information on all of these things. If you're up for a little sunning, walk past the boat docks and around the rocks to the small, quiet **Playa Los Ayala**. For surfing, hop in a taxi ($1) and head 10 minutes south to **Playa Lo de Marcos**.

COMING AND GOING From Puerto Vallarta, hop on one of **Transportes del Pacífico**'s Tepic-bound buses and get off at the crossroads for Guayabitos (1½ hrs, $3.50). To return to Puerto Vallarta, take a combi from Avenida Sol Nuevo to La Peñita de Jaltemba (10 min, 25¢), where there's a Pacífico bus terminal.

Each year during the first few days of November, Rinc n de Guayabitos hosts a Fly-In, in which more than 100 airplanes put on air shows for an audience representing over 300 countries. For more information, contact the town s tourist office (next to the church, tel. 327/4-06-94).

WHERE TO SLEEP AND EAT Guayabitos is the choice vacation spot for many Mexican families, and its bungalows fill up around Christmas, Easter, and during July. Between November and March, an onslaught of travelers from Canada and the United States visit, causing prices to rise. The fact that accommodations are mostly bungalows with kitchenettes and space for six people means lodging can be especially pricey for solo travelers. **Bungalows Zapotlanijo** (Sol Nuevo 18, tel. 327/4-00-02) is slightly run down but cheap: A bungalow for up to four people costs $11 ($17.50 in the high season). For beautiful, modern bungalows right on the beach, **Bungalows El Paraíso** (Tabachines 5, tel. 327/4-02-99) has prices ranging from $16.50 for two people to $35 for six. Camping is allowed along the beach, but pitch your tent between the hotels. Right on the beach, **Restaurante Toñita II** (in Hotel Costa Alegre, tel. 327/4-02-42) serves delicious shrimp ($3) and a giant Mexican plate ($4.50) that comes with a chile relleno, tacos, enchiladas, rice, beans, and the meat of your choice. It's open daily 7 AM–11 PM high season, until 6 during the low season. Guayabito's lush vegetation means you'll also find vendors on the streets and at the beach selling mangoes and fresh pineapple juice.

Bahía de Navidad

If simple living and soft, sandy beaches entice you, look no farther than the Bahía de Navidad. Two towns have sprouted around this tranquil bay, located in the southern corner of the state of Jalisco: **San Patricio-Melaque** and **Barra de Navidad**. In 1989, the government gave these beaches and those extending north through Puerto Vallarta the name *Costalegre* (Happy Coast), designating the area as a tourist zone. Many who knew these towns 10 years ago lament that increasing tourism has marred the beaches' natural beauty, but locals welcome the business. Significant cash inflow came in 1996, when *McHale's Navy*

Bah a de Navidad was the epicenter of a 7.8 earthquake in October 1995, and you can still see rubble throughout the towns here.

was filmed here. However, neither Hollywood films nor a few extra tourists has disturbed these beach-bum paradises; the sandy shores are still clean, the prices reasonable, and the pace decidedly laid back.

Melaque is popular with vacationers from Guadalajara, many of whom own beach homes that sit idle most of the year. People from the States and Canada roost here during winter months, but in general, Melaque has fewer gringo tourists than Barra does, making it more accessible to the budget traveler. Melaque also feels more like a Mexican town, especially in the evening, when people gather in the square under the neon glow of the church cross. As in Barra, the best and only pastime here is sunning on the grainy, golden sand and cooling off in the rolling waves. San Patricio-Melaque's patron saint is, of course, San Patricio, and the merrymaking in his honor begins on March 10, ending on his feast day, March 17. During this time, there is a week-long party, which includes a solemn mass and blessing of the fleet, folk dancing, and cake-eating contests.

Six kilometers down the beach from Melaque, **Barra de Navidad** boasts cool, hair-whipping winds that make for choppy afternoon waves. Most action happens at the hotels and restaurants along the small peninsula that stretches toward Isla de Navidad; Avenida Veracruz, where locals and tourists mingle, is a pleasant place for a stroll at any time of day. The unfinished **Iglesia de Cristo** is separated from the town square, leaving the Barra somewhat centerless. In the church, note that Christ's hands are by his side instead of attached to the cross: Local myth describes how Christ's hands fell from the cross to push the water away and save Barra during the 1973 hurricane. Despite this act of heroism, Christ takes a back seat during Barra's annual **Fiesta de San Antonio de Padua** (June 5–13), which honors the town's patron saint. Don't count on sleeping a wink during the unremitting fireworks and resonating tuba tunes.

BASICS

BOOKSTORES **Beer Bob's Book Exchange.** Leave your wallet in your hotel room and bring a book to trade instead. Bob has a fascinating collection of bestsellers and novels that will provide intellectual stimulation on Barra's mellow beaches. *Mazatlán 61, in Barra, no phone. Open weekdays 1–4.*

CASAS DE CAMBIO There's a casa de cambio in the **Centro Commercial Melaque** (Gómez Farías 27-A, behind Farmacia Nueva, tel. and fax 335/5–53–43). The casa will exchange traveler's checks and cash at no commission. In Barra, you can change money at the nameless casa de cambio (Veracruz 212-C, tel. 335/5–61–77) on the main strip. Both places are open Monday–Saturday 9–2 and 4–7, Sunday 9–2.

EMERGENCIES The number for the **police** in Melaque is 335/5–50–80; in Barra, the number is 335/5–53–99.

LAUNDRY In Barra, **Lavandería Jardín** (Jalisco 70, tel. 335/5–61–35), open weekdays 9–2 and 4–7 and Saturday 9–noon, charges $2 for 3 kilos.

MAIL Postal service for Barra and Melaque is conducted through Melaque's post office. They'll hold mail sent to you at the following address for up to 10 days: Lista de Correos, Melaque, Jalisco, CP 48980, México. *Clemente Orozco 13, at Gómez Farías, tel. 335/5–52–30. Open weekdays 8–3, Sat. 8–noon.*

MEDICAL AID If you need a doctor while you're in the Bahía, Melaque's **Centro de Salud** (tel. 335/5–62–26) is at the corner of Corona and Gómez Farías; for minor problems, stop by the **Farmacia Nueva** (Gómez Farías 27, near bus station, tel. 335/5–51–01), open daily 8 AM–10 AM. In Barra, **Farmacia Rubio** (Veracruz 332, by the bus station, tel. 335/5–54–12) is open daily 9–2 and 4–9.

PHONES Pay phones line Gómez Farías in Melaque and Avenida Veracruz in Barra. You can make cash calls and use the fax machine in Melaque at the Centro Comercial Melaque, in the casa de cambio listed above. **TelMex** (Jalisco 16, tel. and fax 335/5–52–37) in Barra has long-distance service and is open daily 9 AM–10 PM.

VISITOR INFORMATION Barra is home to the sole tourist office in the Bahía, with a helpful staff that doesn't speak English. The brochures, laden with lovely pictures, lack substance, but the maps are accurate. *Veracruz 81, tel. 335/5–51–00. Open weekdays 9–8.*

COMING AND GOING

The bus station in Melaque (tel. 335/5–50–03) is on the corner of Gómez Farías and Carranza, and comes equipped with a restaurant and rock-hard benches. From here, **Autocamiones Cihuatlán** (tel. 335/5–50–03), also known as Autocamiones del Pacífico, sends second-class buses to Guadalajara (6½ hrs, $9) and Puerto Vallarta (3½ hrs, $8.50). However it's definitely worth laying out an extra couple of bucks to take a faster *plus* bus, with videos and chilling air-conditioning. *Plus* buses leave five times daily to Guadalajara and Puerto Vallarta, stopping in Barra de Navidad at Avenida Veracruz, between Avenidas Pilipinas and 21 de Noviembre. There's no formal bus station here, but **Autocamiones Cihuatlán** (Veracruz 228, tel. 335/5–52–75) and **Flecha Amarilla** (Veracruz 269, tel. 335/5–69–11) both have offices where the buses stop. The latter company serves Manzanillo (1½ hrs, $2), with second-class buses leaving every hour.

GETTING AROUND

Barra de Navidad is more like one big neighborhood than a town. Avenida Veracruz, two blocks east of the beach, is the main commercial street. The farther south you go, the more restaurants and hotels you'll find clustered near the malecón, which runs along a piece of land that divides the lagoon from the sea. Melaque has a longer strip of hotels and restaurants that curve around the northern part of the crescent bay. The budget hotel zone is conveniently located in the few blocks between the bus station and the beach, near Avenida Carranza. Many services and restaurants, including the mercado, are also located near the bus station. Green-and-white minibuses (10 min, 25¢) constantly shuttle between the two towns. In Barra, you can flag down buses to Melaque on Veracruz; in Melaque, local buses run along Juárez.

WHERE TO SLEEP

Expect prices at all hotels to rise December–April, especially around the Christmas and Easter holidays. If everything below is full, try Melaque's **Hotel Hidalgo** (Hidalgo 7, tel. 335/5–50–45), a quiet and well-maintained hotel facing the beach. Singles run $5, doubles $7.50.

MELAQUE **Bungalows Villa Mar.** For the price of a standard hotel room, two people can kick it in a bungalow that fits up to eight people. During the high season, units with a kitchenette and bathroom cost $20 for two people and $12 for one person ($5 extra per additional person); low season prices are a few bucks less. The owner speaks English and is very accommodating. *Hidalgo 1, at Gómez Farías, tel. 335/5–50–05. 5 units, all with bath. Laundry ($3 a load), luggage storage. Wheelchair access.*

Posada Clemens. The 14 teal-and-yellow rooms here come equipped with clean but run-down bathrooms. Singles cost $5.50, doubles $8. Speak loudly if you want any response from the elderly woman who works the desk. *Gómez Farías 357, at Guzmán, tel. 335/5–51–79. Wheelchair access.*

Posada Pablo de Tarso. The elegant rooms in this two-story hotel near the beach surround an alluring garden and swimming pool. Air-conditioned rooms with refurnished wooden furniture, velvet-like bedspreads, and TVs cost $11 for one person, $18 for two. Bungalows with kitchenettes, fans, and a TV-equipped sitting room range from $25 for three people to $42 for six. *Gómez Farías 408, btw Guzmán and Orozco, tel. 335/5–51–17. 27 rooms, all with bath. Wheelchair access.*

BARRA DE NAVIDAD **Hotel Delfín.** Here you'll get immaculate rooms, managerial efficiency, and prices to match. Large rooms open onto a shared balcony, and guests (many of them German) have access to a pool, makeshift fitness room, and breakfast buffet. Singles are $20 and doubles $25, but there's a 20% discount in the low season. Reservations are advised in the winter. *Morelos 23, tel. 335/5–50–68. 24 rooms, all with bath. Luggage storage. AE, MC, V.*

Posada Pacífico. Veteran travelers consider this the best budget hotel in town. Each room is different, reflecting the owner's intent to treat every guest like a member of the family. His son, Ernesto, is into ecology, and if you ask, he'll show you pictures of an untouched Barra de Navidad from 10 years ago. Singles cost $7, doubles $8, and prices jump $2–$5 in high season. *Mazatlán 136, at Michoacán, tel. 335/5–53–59. 1 block from both beach and bus station. 22 rooms, all with bath. Laundry, luggage storage. Wheelchair access.*

CAMPING It's possible to crash almost anywhere on the beach, but the tourist office suggests camping on the underdeveloped section between Barra and Melaque to avoid getting shooed away by hoteliers. In Melaque, join the RV folk on a vacant-lot-turned-makeshift-campsite, located right on the beach north of the palapas. You can pay for bathroom and shower services here, too. If you prefer not to take your chances on the beach, try **Trailer Park La Playa**, a well-maintained parking lot/campground in Melaque that's crowded with RVs in winter. Tent spaces cost $7.50, and if you're camping elsewhere,*you can use the bathrooms (15¢) and showers ($1). *Gómez Farías 250, tel. 335/5–50–65. 1 block from bus station. 45 sites. Wheelchair access.*

FOOD

For cheap eats in Melaque, the **market** on López Mateos, near the zócalo, is a good place to start. The beach, sprinkled with palapas that serve seafood at moderate prices, is another option. In Barra, Avenida Veracruz is lined with inexpensive food stands and restaurants. Only some of these amiable restaurants are open during the day, but those that are serve full breakfasts for about $2. The more expensive seafood restaurants on the south end of the bay provide a prime spot to watch the setting sun and spend all of your money.

If you're loco for coconuts, try an atole de coco, a sweet, corn-based drink with coconut water. It's sold at stalls on Avenida Veracruz in Barra.

MELAQUE **César and Charly.** This seafood place has a patio that spills out onto the beach, and although it's a little more expensive than Los Pelícanos and has less character, you can get a delicious meal here without having to walk as far. Grilled fish costs about $4. *Gómez Farías 27-A, tel. 335/5–56–99. Past Centro Comercial Melaque towards water. Open daily 7 AM–10 PM.*

Los Pelícanos. The best of Melaque's palapas is run with motherly care by Italian-born ex-New Yorker Philomena "Phil" García. Her ham and eggs would make Dr. Seuss green with envy, and rumor has it that Robert Redford flies in for breaded octopus ($4). Sit at one of the customer-decorated booths, if you can get one, and don't leave without trying one of their icy margaritas ($3). *5th palapa from end of beach. Open daily 9 AM–10 PM.*

BARRA DE NAVIDAD **Restaurante Velero's.** Overlooking the lagoon, this restaurant enjoys a cooling breeze all day long. Views of the bay provide entertainment for your eyes, as do the psychedelic tablecloths and chairs. Both the ceviche ($4) and shrimp salad ($3) are delicious. *Veracruz 64, no phone. Open daily noon–11.*

Restaurant y Café Crepes Ámbar. Run by a French-Mexican couple, this romantic second-story restaurant serves savory French wine and a large variety of delicious seafood, veggie, and dessert crepes ($2–$6). Flamenco music plays throughout the night. *Veracruz 101-A, no phone. Open daily 3–11.*

OUTDOOR ACTIVITIES

The main diversions here (apart from bayside margarita-sipping) are swimming, surfing, splashing, or surveying the sunset. Barra's beaches are a little rougher than Melaque's, and Melaque offers better views of the rocky peninsula, local lagoon, and distant mountains. Sometimes called "Colimilla," the **Isla de Navidad** is another peninsula that begins near the Manzanillo airport. For $5, somebody from Barra's **tourist-boat cooperative** (Veracruz 40, look for red boats, no phone) will ferry you to Isla de Navidad and its first-rate beachfront restaurants. Another option in the Bahía is fishing: The Barra cooperative charges $16 per hour for up to eight people, equipment included, to troll the coastal waters for marlin, tuna, and sailfish. Unlike most outfits, they don't set a minimum number of hours for a trip, so you can give it a shot without breaking the bank. For surfing, trek 1 kilometer around the bend past Melaque to the pristine beach on the other side of the crescent bay.

AFTER DARK

This area is known for quiet beach towns, not high-energy night scenes. Even on weekends, the main social activity after 10:30 PM consists of men drinking in front of liquor stores. Locals and tourists looking to bust a move head to **Disco La Tanga** (Gómez Farías, at Av. La Primavera, tel. 335/5–50–01) in Melaque. The lively disco and techno beats blast out Thursday–Sunday 10–3, and there's a $3 cover. In Barra, **El Galeón** (Morelos 24, in Hotel Sands, tel. 335/5–50–18) plays salsa, merengue, and disco for a $1.50 cover. If you want to make your own music, take a shot at the karaoke set-up at **Bar Terraza Jardín** (Jalisco 71, tel. 335/5–65–31). The bar is open nightly 7 PM–2 AM, and the karaoke bar gets going at 9 PM.

Near Bahía de Navidad

BAHÍA CHAMELA

South of Puerto Vallarta, Highway 200 turns inland and doesn't meet the coast again for 150 kilometers (93 mi), until it touches Bahía Chamela. This bay is isolation with a capital "I"—one long stretch of unsullied beaches developed only in patches, such as the self-contained Lu Bay Village and Club Med's Playa Blanca resorts. You'll find an older RV crowd from the States here in winter, while Mexican holidays (August, Christmas, and Easter) herald the arrival of Guadalajaran families. For the rest of the year, you can expect relative seclusion (along with fewer open hotels and restaurants) in this dry, breezy coastal area. Thatched-hut restaurants and campgrounds are the primary services along most of the bay.

At the far northern end of Bahía Chamela is the rocky **Punta Perula,** from which you can take a short boat trip to **Isla La Pajerera,** a small island designated as an ecological sanctuary and home to many migrating tropical birds. The fishermen on the beach give rides to and from the island ($5 round-trip). South of Punta Perula lies a sweeping crescent of sand that includes beaches such as **Playa Fortuna** and **Playa Chamela,** as well as myriad exotic birds. At the south end of the bay, camping opportunities abound, and there's a small store where you can pick up supplies. For more civilized lodging, **Villas Polinesia Camping Club** (Carretera 200 Km. 72, tel. 328/5–52–47) is located 5 kilometers outside of the small town of Chamela. Polynesian-style two-story huts with bathrooms cost $16 for two people and $35 for 3–4 people. They also have barbecue pits and campgrounds ($5 per person), but these are poorly kept up during the off-season. Since the only restaurant is a 15-minute walk back to the highway from the villas, the accommodating staff will cook for you with advance notice (winter only).

COMING AND GOING To reach Bahía Chamela, take one of the hourly second-class buses traveling from Barra de Navidad (1½ hrs, $2.50) or Melaque (1 hr, $2.50) toward Puerto Vallarta; they'll drop you off at the crossroads leading to Chamela. For the 4-kilometer trek inland to the beach, you can try to snag a taxi from the highway, but you'll probably have better luck either hitchhiking or, if you can handle it, walking an hour in the sweltering heat.

Manzanillo

Manzanillo, with a population of just 110,000, encompasses the crescent-shaped Manzanillo and Santiago bays, which are home to 20 beaches and the busiest Pacific seaport in Mexico. The name Manzanillo comes from the *manzanilla* (chamomile) tree, whose exportation was significantly increased with the start of the shipping industry. Today, the port's industrial structures look like menacing Transformers staging an invasion, and oil and debris have spoiled the beaches in Manzanillo proper. Don't be scared away though; Manzanillo has much to offer the budget traveler and there are several outlying beaches where you won't have to scrape tar off your feet after a dip.

Manzanillo is known for its annual sailfishing tournaments in February and November; supposedly, tournament participants set a world record in 1957, catching over 300 sailfish within three days.

In spite of the oil contamination, the fish in the area flourish: Manzanillo claims to be the *pez vela* (sailfish) capital of the world, and marlin and red snapper are regularly reeled in as well. Manzanillo is large and spread out, so expect to spend some time on the bus, gazing out at the white buildings, cobblestone streets, fountains, and giant sculptures that reflect Manzanillo's Mediterranean, Moorish, and Spanish architectural influences. Foreigners receive a genuinely hospitable welcome here, and if you stay away from the resorts, you'll only see a gringo here and there. Mexican tourists abound though, especially wealthy Guadalajarans; expect prices to rise everywhere during Christmas and Easter.

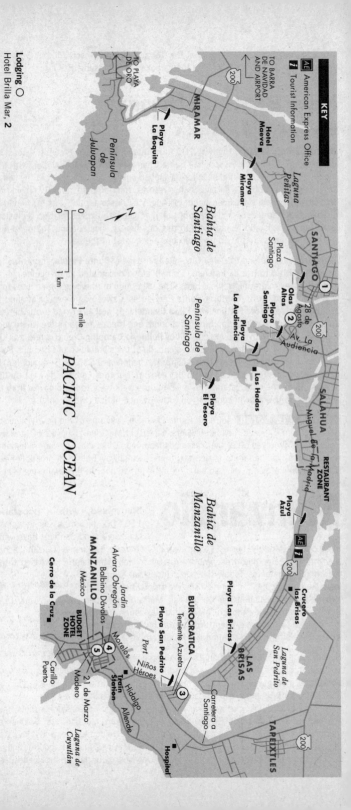

Manzanillo

Lodging ○
Hotel Brilla Mar, **2**
Hotel Colonial, **5**
Hotel María
Cristina, **1**
Hotel Miramar, **4**
Hotel San Pedrito, **3**

BASICS

AMERICAN EXPRESS The AmEx office here is in the travel agency **Bahías Gemelas** in the Salahua neighborhood. The staff cashes personal checks and holds mail for cardholders. You can also receive MoneyGrams here. *Blvd. Costero Miguel de la Madrid 1556, Manzanillo, Colima, CP 28200, México, tel. 333/3–10–00. Near IMSS building. Open weekdays 9–2 and 4–7, Sat. 9–2.*

CASAS DE CAMBIO Banamex (México 136, in Manzanillo, tel. 333/2–01–15) changes money weekdays 9–1 and has ATMs that accept Plus, Cirrus, MasterCard, and Visa. There's another branch in the Commercial Manzanillo on Boulevard Costero, in the Salahua neighborhood. The **Farmacia Americana** (México 224, tel. 333/2–37–55; open daily 9 AM–10 PM) also changes money.

EMERGENCIES The number for the **police** is 333/2–10–04. For **Cruz Roja** (Red Cross), call 333/2–51–69. For any kind of emergency assistance, dial 06.

LAUNDRY **Lavandería Casablanca** charges $1.25 per piece or $4 for 9 kilos of laundry. *Across from bus station, tel. 333/2–16–54. Open Mon.–Sat. 10–2 and 4–7.*

MAIL The post office in Manzanillo proper will hold mail sent to you at the following address for up to 10 days: Lista de Correos, Manzanillo, Colima, CP 28200, México. *Juárez, at 5 de Mayo, tel. 333/2–14–61. Open Mon.–Sat. 9–2 and 4–8.*

MEDICAL AID **Hospital Civil** (Calle Hospital, Col. San Pedrito, tel. 333/2–19–03), off the Carretera a Santiago as you leave Manzanillo proper, charges on a sliding scale. **Hospital Naval** (tel. 333/3–27–40), on the naval base in Colonia San Pedrito, has better facilities, but is more expensive. You can get all the drugs you need at **Farmacia Americana** (*see* Casas de Cambio, *above*).

PHONES Computel offers phone and fax services daily 7 AM–10 PM. Calls to the States cost $1 for two minutes, but on Sundays there's a 33% discount. *Morelos 144, ½ block from Jardín Obregón.*

VISITOR INFORMATION The **tourist office** has lots of brochures on Manzanillo, but is not very helpful with nearby towns. The staff is friendly, but their English is limited. Information is also available from hotels and the local AmEx agent (*see above*). *Blvd. Costero Miguel de la Madrid 4960, 2 blocks north of Hotel Fiesta Mexicana, tel. 333/3–22–77. Open weekdays 8:30–3 and 6–8.*

COMING AND GOING

BY BUS The **Central Camionera** is a long walk east of town and only taxis will take you straight to the city center. Luggage storage here costs $1 per 24 hours. **Autotransportes del Sur de Jalisco** (tel. 333/2–10–03) serves Tecomán and Armería, the jumping-off points for El Paraíso, Cuyutlán, and Boca de Pascuales (*see* Near Manzanillo, *below*); buses leave every 15 minutes (30 min, 50¢). Buses also depart for Colima (1½ hrs, $1) every half hour 2 AM–9:30 PM. **Élite** (tel. 333/2–01–35) buses leave for Acapulco (11 hrs, $23) at 12:30 PM and 5 PM, passing through Zihuatanejo (6 hrs, $16) en route. **Autotransportes Cihuatlán** (tel. 333/2–02–15) has first- ($11.50) and second-class ($10) buses to Guadalajara (4¼ hrs) every 90 minutes, 4 AM–10 PM, and a midnight bus to Puerto Vallarta (5 hrs, $10). **Auto-Caminos del Pacífico** (tel. 333/2–05–15) sends hourly buses to Barra de Navidad (1 hr, $2). Local buses leave frequently from the back of the station, all the way to the left, for Colonias San Pedrito, Las Brisas, and Santiago.

GETTING AROUND

Manzanillo's zócalo, known better as the **Jardín Obregón,** is bordered on its north side by the waterfront and Avenida Morelos. Calle México, the main commercial street, extends south from the Jardín and leads to budget hotels and banks. Manzanillo's beaches all lie north of town, in two sheltered bays divided by **La Punta** peninsula, where many resort hotels are clustered. Moving northeast from town, the Bahía de Manzanillo includes playas **San Pedrito** (1 km away; the first decent option), **Brisas, Azul, Salahua, Las Hadas,** and **El Tesoro.** In the Bahía de Santiago lie the more beautiful beaches: **La Audiencia, Santiago, Olas Altas, Miramar,** and the calm **La Boquita.** Each beach has its own corresponding neighborhood. Buses (20¢–45¢) marked SANTIAGO and LAS HADAS leave frequently from the bus station and the bus stop half a block east of the Jardín on Morelos, winding their way all the way around the bays. They take 15–45 minutes, depending on your beach of choice, and operate daily 7 AM–11 PM, after which you have to taxi around. It's about $4.50 to taxi from Santiago to the center of town.

WHERE TO SLEEP

Cheap hotels are concentrated in Manzanillo proper, near the pleasant activity of the Jardín Obregón. They're a bus ride away from the good beaches, but staying near the water is expensive, especially in the Santiago neighborhood and on La Punta peninsula. If you're feeling wealthy, stay at Santiago's wheelchair-accessible **Hotel María Cristina** (28 de Agosto 36, btw Morelos and Hidalgo, tel. 333/3–09–66), which offers $13 singles, $18 doubles, and a fish-shaped pool. As a last resort in Manzanillo proper, try the frenzied **Hotel Emperador** (Balbino Dávalos 69, tel. 333/2–23–74), where a single costs $5.50 and doubles cost $7 for one bed, $9.50 for two. Remember that hotel prices jump during Christmas and Easter.

MANZANILLO **Hotel Colonial.** Situated around a spiral staircase and pleasant restaurant, this hotel is reminiscent of an 18th-century mansion. Large, TV-equipped rooms for one or two ($11) come with a fan, but they're still pretty hot and humid. Pay the $14 for air-conditioning. *Bocanegra 28, at México, tel. 333/2–10–80. 36 rooms, all with bath. Laundry, luggage storage. Wheelchair access.*

Hotel Miramar. The odd staircases here will lure you onto huge balconies with tiles and doors straight out of *Alice in Wonderland*. Snag a top-floor room for a cooling breeze. Singles cost $4.50, doubles $9.50. *Juárez 122, ½ block from Jardín, tel. 333/2–10–08. Look for FANTA sign. 38 rooms, all with bath. Luggage storage.*

SAN PEDRITO **Hotel San Pedrito.** Although being near the port might not be appealing, a pool (with a mini-slide), tennis courts, and a picnic area may convince you to stay in this dumpy part of town. Being right next to the beach helps too. It's $8 for a single, $11 for a double. *Teniente Azueta 3, tel. 333/2–05–35. Laundry (25¢ per piece), luggage storage. Wheelchair access. AE, MC.*

SANTIAGO **Hotel Brilla Mar.** This is a great place to stay if you're traveling in a group. Impressive remodeled bungalows each have a modern kitchenette, TV, air-conditioning, a large bedroom, and breathtaking views of the Santiago bay. Six-person bungalows cost $48 ($54 during the high season). The four shabby double rooms with TV and air-conditioning cost $17.50 a night. *Bahía de Santiago, tel. 333/4–11–88. Take a SANTIAGO bus (35 min, 40¢) from the bus station or the zócalo and get off just before Jardín Santiago; it's a 10-min walk or 50¢ taxi ride west to the hotel. 20 bungalows, 4 rooms, all with bath. Wheelchair access.*

CAMPING Camping is only allowed during the high season (around Christmas and Easter), when the free trailer park on Playa Miramar next to Hotel Maeva (tel. 333/5–05–95) opens. Latrines and showers are also available during high season free of charge.

FOOD

Manzanillo has restaurants for all budgets. The cheapest place to eat in town is the **market** (Cuauhtémoc, at Madero), preferably at lunchtime, when the food is fresh. Budget restaurants in town are located around the Jardín, and there are a few seafood restaurants and pizza joints on Boulevard Costero, near the American Express office in Salahua, and around the Jardín Santiago.

LA BOQUITA **Ramada Tanilo's.** Although this popular waterfront restaurant is filled with Mexican tourists and the strains of live mariachi music, the sound of gentle waves keeps the atmosphere tranquil. Try the shrimp in garlic sauce ($4), or even better, the aphrodisiac *almejas vivas* (live clams; $4). *Playa La Boquita, no phone. Take SANTIAGO bus to Playa Miramar and walk 15 min north on beach, or ask bus driver to drop you off at La Boquita and taxi ($1) the rest of the way. Open daily 8–6.*

MANZANILLO **Chantilly.** Of the restaurants that surround the Jardín, this is the most popular. The food at this cafeteria-style spot is typically Mexican—tacos, enchiladas, quesadillas, etc.—and service is usually efficient. Chicken costs about $3, fish or shrimp about $5. *Juárez 60, at Madero, tel. 333/2–01–94. Open Sun.–Fri. 7 AM–10 PM. Wheelchair access.*

Plaza La Perlita. Live music (Thursday–Saturday) attracts an amorous clientele to the wrought-iron tables outside this seafood restaurant. The rest of the week the radio competes with the sounds of chirping birds and passing trains from the nearby train station. A regular shrimp cocktail costs $2, a huge one $3. A fish fillet, cooked to your liking, is $4. *Morelos, tel. 333/2–27–70. Open daily 10 AM–midnight. Wheelchair access.*

Restaurant Roca del Mar. This bargain joint, decorated with indigenous art and overlooking a garden, serves a filling, satisfying $3 comida corrida consisting of soup, rice, an entrée, and tortillas. Vegetarian soups are $1, and an order of meat or vegetarian quesadillas with guacamole is $2. *21 de Marzo 204, tel. 333/2–03–02. Open daily 7 AM–10:30 PM.*

OUTDOOR ACTIVITIES

Manzanillo's biggest attraction is its beaches, with waters much cooler and a bit murkier than its southern neighbors. Because of the port, many beaches in Manzanillo proper are dirty and dominated by fishermen casting their nets. A 20-minute bus ride away, the best beach closest to Manzanillo is **Las Brisas,** a dirty-gold beach shielded from traffic by hotels, restaurants, and homes. The waves here are known to be a little rough, but not dangerous. Near the fantastical Las Hadas resort—the setting for the Bo Derek flesh fantasy *10*—is the peaceful **Playa La Audiencia,** backed by green hills. **Agua Mundo** (tel. 333/4–20–00, ext. 759), inside the Las Hadas resort, rents windsurf boards ($16.50 for ½ hr), kayaks ($9.50–$12.50 per hr), and snorkeling equipment ($9.50 for 6 hrs). They also offer sunset tours, which debark at 5 PM daily from Las Hadas; the two-hour cruise costs $14 and includes two drinks. To get here, take a bus to the Las Brisas *crucero* (crossroads) and transfer to a LAS HADAS or AUDIENCIA bus.

For surfing and boogie boarding, head for the appropriately named **Olas Altas** (high waves), near Santiago. All the way at the end of the strip of beaches, about 35 minutes by bus from Manzanillo is **Playa La Boquita,** a sheltered beach popular with local families and tourists staying at nearby resorts. Here you can rent boogie boards ($1 per hr) and horses ($5 per hr), take a banana boat ride ($5 for 10 min), and enjoy wonderful seafood right on the beach (*see Food, above*). Nearby is the **Hotel Maeva** (tel. 333/3–20–00), where you can rent mopeds for as little as $11 per hour.

AFTER DARK

Manzanillo's nightlife centers around one area, Salahua, which can be reached by taking a MIRAMAR or SANTIAGO bus. The largest happening disco, **Vog** (Blvd. Costero, tel. 333/3–08–75), is open nightly during the high season but only Friday and Saturday during the off-season. Cover is $4 for women, $8 for men, and the disco closes at 4 AM. There's no cover at the adjacent **Bar de Félix** (tel. 333/3–08–75), where the atmosphere is a little more mellow, but the music and movies play almost all night long. On Playa Miramar, a small disco called **Boom Boom** (in Hotel Maeva, tel. 333/5–05–95) fills up on Fridays and Saturdays; for the same cover as the Vog, you get to gawk at strippers during the *piernas* (legs) shows. **El Navegante** (Blvd. Costero Km. 6.5), next to the oh-so-gringo Carlos 'n' Charlie's, is decorated like a ship, with mermaid statues and colorful murals. The bar gets people dancing on the tables, even on Sunday nights, and stays open until the last person leaves.

Near Manzanillo

South of Manzanillo is a stretch of coast dotted with golden beaches only slightly blemished by ash from Colima's volcanoes. Hotels exist in the area, but beach camping is free and encouraged. If you've got a hammock, most beachfront restaurants will let you string it up for a couple of bucks. To reach Cuyutlán or El Paraíso from Manzanillo, first catch a TECOMAN bus to **Armería** (40 min, $1.25), which leaves every half hour from the bus station. Buses leave Armería for Cuyutlán and El Paraíso (½ hr, 50¢) every 40 minutes 6 AM–8 PM from the mercado, three blocks behind and to the right of the Manzanillo–Armería bus stop.

CUYUTLÁN

Entering Cuyutlán through lush banana plantations and towering palms, you'll feel like you've discovered a tropical paradise. Beware, however: The crashing waves and powerful currents can turn a dip in the sea into a serious struggle. The most developed of the three beach resorts outside Manzanillo, Cuyutlán fills up with Mexican vacationers during August, Christmas, and Easter. The rest of the year the town is ghostly: The rainbow-hued umbrellas fold up, and the beach takes on the lonely, run-down feel of Coney Island in the winter.

Cuyutlán is best known as the home of the *ola verde* (green wave). No one agrees on what ola verde is, but they certainly talk about it a lot: Some swear it was a tidal wave that wiped out the entire town of Cuyutlán in 1942, while a tourist brochure claims that the ola verde happens every April and May, when the sun shines on the waves at a certain angle, making them look green. Still others believe it's just a local name for the phosphorescent algae that glows sparkly green in the water. If you'd rather not bother with all this hullabaloo, head to the barn-like **Museo Bodega del Sal** (follow green signs ½ block from zócalo, no phone), where you can learn all about where salt comes from daily 8–6:30. The museum's intricate model of salt refinement shows how locals strain salt from the nearby lagoon and crush it into crystals by hand for domestic use. Donations are encouraged.

WHERE TO SLEEP AND EAT You can pitch a tent for free on Cuyutlán's sandy beaches, except during Christmas and Easter week, when it's $3 a night. The helpful staff at the **Junta Municipal** (Hidalgo 144, tel. 332/6–40–14) suggests that women camping alone should keep close to the hotels for safety reasons. The same office has tourist brochures and is open 24 hours daily. Cuyutlán also has a good selection of affordable beachfront hotels, though prices double in the high season. Located at the northern end of the boardwalk, **Hotel Tlaquepaque** (Veracruz 30, tel. 332/6–40–11) has plain rooms and a long hall cooled by sea breezes. Sin-

Land of the Kamikaze Surfers

Boca de Pascuales is famous for huge, aggressive waves, making it a year-round hot spot for surfos—kamikaze surfers who ride the waves for hours and live on only a few dollars a day. Indeed, the only people who will want to visit Boca de Pascuales are surfers, admirers of surfers, or those looking for an inexpensive, isolated beach upon which to do nothing. The Manzanillo tourist office has virtually no information on conditions here, so snag a surfer and beg him or her to advise you, or call one of the town's two phone numbers (332/9–13–32 or 332/4–21–56) for more info. You can camp anywhere along the beach in Boca de Pascuales, but if you're not in the mood to rough it, a few hotels offer basic rooms. To reach Boca de Pacuales, take a bus to Tecomán (1 hr, $1.50) from Manzanillo. The depot for transfer buses (20 min, 50¢) is one block to the right as you leave Tecomán's main bus terminal.

gles are $4 and doubles are $7, but you can negotiate with the owner if you plan to stay a while. Five of the rooms at **Hotel Morelos** (Hidalgo 165, 2 blocks off zócalo toward water, tel. 332/6–40–13) come with a kitchen/dining room at no extra cost. Prices are the same as at the Tlaquepaque, although during the high season, $12 per person gets you a room and dinner. The hotel also serves decent, filling meals to nonguests for $2.50. Otherwise, try the adjacent **Hotel Fénix** (Hidalgo 201, tel. 332/6–400–52; open daily 8 AM–10 PM), which specializes in seafood and has a happy hour with two-for-one drinks.

EL PARAÍSO

Smaller and less developed than Cuyutlán, El Paraíso has one short road, Avenida de la Juventud, that runs the length of the town, passing hotels and restaurants overlooking the ocean. The surf here isn't too strong, making it a better place to take a dip than neighboring Boca de Pascuales (*see* box, *below*) and Cuyutlán. The town is wondrously small, and the beaches are more often than not yours and yours alone, but don't expect to find diversions apart from the waves.

WHERE TO SLEEP AND EAT Camping here is a breeze: No permit, no set sites—just plop your stuff on the beach and head to **Hotel Paraíso** (tel. 332/9–13–31) for 25¢ showers. For less rugged travelers, the Paraíso has the nicest rooms around ($16.50 for one or two people), and also has a restaurant and pool. **Hotel Equipales** (across from bus stop, tel. 332/4–60–26) has clean but dark rooms ($8.50) with lumpy beds and tiny showers. Pick a restaurant, any restaurant, in El Paraíso—they all serve fresh fish for around $3.

Colima

The easygoing capital of Colima state, Colima is a gleamingly clean city of well-maintained colonial buildings and safe, tidy streets. Although the towering volcanic peaks that surround Colima are impressive, a visit here is really about history and culture. Colima was the third city founded by the Spaniards in Mexico, but its history reaches much farther back: Archaeologists have discovered tombs filled with ceramic figurines that point to the existence of Nahuatl culture here. Many of the animal figurines are on display in Colima's museums, except for some titillating phallic ones that were whisked away to museums in Mexico City. In addition to the numerous museums, events such as poetry readings and performance art pieces are frequent and easily accessible. Signs for these events are posted all around town, at the tourist office, and the appropriately gigantic **Casa de la Cultura** (*see* Worth Seeing, *below*). Colima also boasts a thriving literary scene that centers around the University of Colima, which puts out 10 local newspapers and is constantly publishing new books of poetry and prose. Despite the potential for highbrow snobbery, Colima's friendly, politically progressive residents will make Mexican and international travelers alike feel welcome.

If you're in the mood to wax prosaic about Aristotelian theory, Colima's table of philosophers the Mesa de Despelleje meets nightly at 9 PM in Los Naranjos Restaurant (Gabino Barreda 34, tel. 331/2–00–29).

BASICS

BOOKSTORES **Galería Universitaria** (Torres Quintero 62, tel. 331/2–44–00; open daily 4:30–9), just off the Jardín Principal, carries books in Spanish about Mexican art and culture, including those published by the university. **Las Palmeras** (Portal Medellín 16, tel. 331/4–35–06; open daily 8 AM–11 PM) is a small magazine store next to Hotel Ceballos on the Jardín Principal. In the evenings, crowd in with the locals to browse through *Time, Newsweek,* and *National Geographic,* as well as many Mexican magazines.

CASAS DE CAMBIO Several banks on Madero have ATMs, but most only accept Visa and MasterCard. The ATM at **Bital** (Madero 183, right of Jardín Nuñez, tel. 331/2–36–24) also accepts Plus and Cirrus cards, and the bank itself changes cash and traveler's checks weekdays 8–7 and Saturday 9–2:30. **Casa de Cambio Majaparas** offers better rates for cash, but not for traveler's checks, which they change into U.S. dollars only. *Morelos 200, at Juárez, tel. 331/4–89–98. Open weekdays 9–2 and 4:30–7, Sat. 9–2.*

EMERGENCIES For assistance, call the **police** (tel. 331/2–18–01) or **fire** department (tel. 331/2–58–58).

MAIL The full-service **post office,** on the northeast corner of Parque Núñez, will hold mail sent to you at the following address for up to 10 days: Lista de Correos, Col. Núñez, Colima, Colima, CP 28001, México. *Madero, at Núñez, tel. 331/2–00–33. Open weekdays 8–7, Sat. 8–noon.*

MEDICAL AID The **Hospital Civil** (San Fernando, at Ignacio Sandoral, tel. 331/2–02–27) is open 24 hours daily. For minor problems, try the 24-hour **Farmacia Sangre de Cristo.** *Obregón 16, at Madero, tel. 331/4–74–74.*

PHONES There are public phones on all four corners of the Jardín Principal. You can place cash calls at **Farmacia Colima,** also on the Jardín. The connection fee for collect calls here is 50¢. *Madero 1, at Constitución, tel. 331/2–00–31. Open Mon.-Sat. 8:30 AM–9 PM, Sun. 9–2.*

VISITOR INFORMATION If you speak Spanish, ask about upcoming events at **Livornos Pizza** (*see* Food, *below*). For official information about Colima, city or state, talk to the immensely helpful staff at the air-conditioned **tourist office.** *Portal Hidalgo 20, west side of Jardín Principal, tel. 331/2–83–60. Open weekdays 9–3 and 5–9, weekends 10–1.*

COMING AND GOING

BY BUS The **Central de Autobuses de Colima** (tel. 331/2–58–99) is at the northeastern edge of town. To get downtown, catch any 4 CENTRO bus or take a taxi (about $1). The major bus lines are **Tres Estrellas de Oro** (tel. 331/2–84–99) and **Omnibús de México** (tel. 331/4–71–90). First-class buses leave for Guadalajara (3 hrs, $7.50) and Manzanillo (1½ hrs, $3) every two hours 4 AM–11 PM. Buses to Mexico City (12 hrs, $23) leave four times a day. Like the rest of Colima, the station is clean and well-stocked, with cheap eateries, pharmacies, and luggage storage. If you need to, you can camp out on the plastic chairs unmolested.

The **Central de Autobuses Sub-Urbana** (Carretera Colima–Coquimatlán, tel. 331/4–47–50) sends second-class buses to smaller, in-state destinations. Buses bound for Armería (50 min, $1), Manzanillo (1½ hrs, $1.50), and Tecomán (45 min, $1) depart every 15 minutes 4 AM–10:30 PM. To reach Zihuatanejo, first take a bus to Tecomán (1 hr, $1) and transfer to Zihuatanejo (3 hrs, $11). Buses for nearby towns and villages such as Suchitlán (50¢) and San Antonio/Laguna La María ($1) leave frequently during the day. The bus station is a 20-minute walk southwest on Cuautéhmoc from the Jardín Principal. RUTA 2 combis (10 min, 20¢) leave frequently from Morelos between Medellín and Ocampo, dropping you right at the station. Taxi rides to the station cost $1.

BY CAR Colima is easily accessible, lying on the freeway connecting Guadalajara to Manzanillo. To get from Colima to the nearby volcanoes, take Highway 16 north for 7 kilometers, then cut northeast for 11 kilometers to San Antonio and then another 2 kilometers northeast to Laguna La María.

GETTING AROUND

On a clear day, you can orient yourself by the volcanoes to the north of Colima. When it's cloudy, the parks along Avenida Madero are landmarks that make downtown Colima easy to navigate. The **Jardín Libertad** (also known as the zócalo or the Jardín Principal) is at the corner of Avenidas Madero and Reforma. This is the center of town, where families and friends gather in the evening. Four blocks east of here is the massive **Parque Núñez.** Colima has a modern fleet of microbuses that cost about 25¢ to ride; most stop at the corner of Reforma and Díaz, on Medellín along the Jardín Quintero, or on Avenida Rey Colimán, near the southwest corner of Parque Núñez. From Parque Núñez, RUTA 1 combis leave frequently for the **Universi-**

dad de Colima, located 10 minutes northwest of town on Boulevard Camino Real. A taxi ride anywhere in the city shouldn't be more than $2–$3.

WHERE TO SLEEP

Colima doesn't boast a huge selection of hotels, but the dearth of tourists here makes finding a room pretty easy. All budget hotels are near the center of town and attract Mexican businessmen. If the hotels below are full, try the sophisticated but noisy **Gran Hotel Flamingos** (Rey Colimán 18, tel. 331/2–25–25), with modern singles ($8) and doubles ($10) near the Jardín Núñez.

➤ **UNDER $10** • **Casa de Huéspedes Familiar.** Slightly worn but clean rooms sit above the house of the friendly manager, Señora Saucedo, and her lush garden. Singles cost $5.50 and doubles $8, but you may be able to talk the señora into giving you a better deal. *Morelos 265, near the Pemex station, tel. 331/2–34–67. 10 rooms, 8 with bath. Luggage storage.*

Hotel Núñez. Rooms in this converted colonial house surround a courtyard shaded by a gigantic mango tree. The rooms are small and lack personality, but the communal baths are spic and span. Singles or doubles without bath are $3.50, $6 with private bath. You can't find a better place for the price and people know it: Arrive early, especially if you want a room with a TV ($1.50 extra). *Juárez 88, on Jardín Núñez, tel. 331/2–70–30. 32 rooms, 16 with bath. Luggage storage. Wheelchair access.*

Hotel San Lorenzo. Though it's just a few blocks from the zócalo, this hotel sits in a quiet *barrio* (neighborhood), and not many travelers take advantage of the bargain rooms. The blue-and-white sitting area branches off to spacious rooms with fans and large closets. The floral bedspreads add a much needed homey feel. Rooms cost $6 for one person, $8 for two. *Cuauhtémoc 149, at Independencia, tel. 31/2–20–00. 3 blocks west of zócalo. 17 rooms, all with bath. Wheelchair access.*

FOOD

Colima prides itself on its *antojitos* (appetizers), such as enchiladas with sweet sauce, *ceviche* (diced fish, tomato, and onion), and *pozole blanco*. Restaurants are scattered throughout the city, but there are tons of cheap ones near the Jardín Principal.

Ah Qué Nanishe. For a change of pace, try the Oaxacan specialties at this downtown eatery (the name means "Oh, how delicious!" in Zapotec). Chicken tamales with Oaxacan *mole* (chile and chocolate sauce) are $3 each, and a *huarache* (corn-fungus turnover) is $1.50. They also have an assortment of soup specialties ranging from 75¢ to $1.50. Sweet tamales are 50¢. *5 de Mayo 267, 4 blocks west of Jardín Principal, tel. 331/4–21–97. Open daily 1:30–midnight.*

Livornos Pizza. At this publike pizzeria, $4 gets you a small meat or veggie pizza plus a drink. Have a beer and strike up a conversation with the manager for information about cultural events and the causes of the *ilusión óptica* (*see* Cheap Thrills, *below*). You can also catch CNN on their TV. *Constitución 10, near cathedral, tel. 331/4–50–30. Open daily 11–11.*

Restaurante Samadhi. Tables here are surrounded by indigenous paintings and ceramics, and overlook the sunny, palm-laden courtyard. Try the tasty soyburger ($1.50) or the unique *sangría*, a mix of pineapple, celery, radish, and orange juices ($1). The $2.50 buffet breakfast comes with yogurt, fruit, eggs, crepes, juice, and coffee. *Medina 125, 3 blocks north of Parque Núñez, tel. 331/3–24–98. Open Fri.–Wed. 8–8, Thurs. 8–5.*

WORTH SEEING

The **Jardín Principal** has been the center of Colima city since the city's founding, and is a good place to begin exploring. On the south side of the Jardín is the free **Museo Regional de Historia de Colima** (Morelos 1, at Reforma, tel. 331/2–92–28), where you'll find a few exhibits of pre-Columbian pottery and local crafts, as well as an occasional university art exposition. On the east side of the Jardín is the 19th-century, neoclassical **Santa Iglesia Cathedral** (Reforma 21, tel. 331/2–02–00), with a plain white exterior that gives way to a lavish interior. Next door is the beautiful **Palacio de Gobierno** (tel. 331/2–04–31), built at the turn of the century. Its mural portraying the history of Mexico was painted by Coliman artist Jorge Chávez Carrillo in honor of Independence leader Padre Miguel Hidalgo.

Cultural events are hosted at the Museo Regional, the Casa de la Cultura, and at the highly respected **Universidad de Colima,** home to the **Museo de Culturas Populares** (*see below*) and the artsy bookstore **Galería Universitaria** (*see Basics, above*). It also has a huge sports facility, the **Polideportivo,** which is free and open to the public; here you'll find swimming pools and fields used for casual soccer and football games. To reach the university, take a RUTA 1 bus (15 min, 25¢) from Jardín Núñez. The Polideportivo is the huge building on your left, about five minutes outside of downtown.

The Parque de la Piedra Lisa (Park of the Smooth Stone) is near the university. Legend has it that if you slide down this big rock, you will soon be wed.

LA CAMPANA RUINS Just opened to the public in 1996, these ruins date all the way back to 1500 BC, and were used by the Capacha tribe until AD 700–900. When the Spaniards arrived in the 16th century, Franciscan monks built churches around some of the ruins, but the majority of the ancient structures are intact. Most of the site's 50 hectares (123.5 acres) are still under exploration, and new sites will open to the public in the future. Currently you can observe magnificient tombs, an administrative-religious center, a vast drainage system, and living quarters. Look carefully at the stones in the structures and you'll see hieroglyphics and engraved maps. *Av. Tecnológico, Col. Villa de Alvarez, tel. 331/2–26–21. From Jardín Núñez, take RUTA 1 combi (15 min, 25¢). Open Tues.–Sun. 9–6. Admission: $1, students free.*

At La Campana, people were sacrificed for their blood, which was used to feed the lava of the volcano god and the red fire of the sun god.

CASA DE LA CULTURA The Casa de la Cultura shows a permanent collection of works by Coliman artists, as well as rotating exhibitions. The gallery is open Tuesday–Sunday 8 AM–8:30 PM, and admission is free. The Casa also gives free classes in arts and crafts, music, and regional dance, and shows foreign and national art films (75¢). Check the postings on the theater door for current films and showtimes. The playhouse showcases local theatrical productions weekends at 8 PM ($1.50, 95¢ students). **Café Dalí,** located within the Casa, is a good place to stop for a drink and to listen to live music, featured nightly 9–11 PM. *Galván Norte, at Ejército Nacional, tel. 331/2–84–31.*

MUSEO DE LAS CULTURAS DEL OCCIDENTE Next to the Casa de la Cultura, this excellent museum is dedicated exclusively to pre-Hispanic ceramicware from the Colima area. On display are a collection of figurines, among them the famous Coliman dogs, supposedly the product of a culture in which dogs were believed to mirror human personalities (and were a source of food as well). *Galván Nte., at Ejército Nacional, tel. 331/2–31–55. From Jardín Núñez, take RUTA 1 combi toward the university. Admission free. Open Tues.–Sun. 9–7.*

MUSEO UNIVERSITARIO DE CULTURAS POPULARES This university crafts museum is not particularly impressive, but it has a wonderful gift shop. Outside the museum, under a giant banyan tree, an artisan makes reproductions of pre-Columbian ceramics Monday–Saturday 9–3. Go to Room 30 in the museum building to find out about cultural events at the university. *Gallardo, at 27 de Septiembre, tel. 331/2–68–69. Admission free. Open Tues.–Sat. 9–2 and 4–7.*

CHEAP THRILLS

If you've got a car or access to one, you can experience a strange phenomenon on the road from San Antonio, just past Restaurante Los Pinos. Some say it's caused by an optical illusion (they call it *la ilusión óptica*), others say it's a magnetic field. Whatever the cause, move slowly where the road is level, just before the hill. Hold a bottle of water at the window and slowly pour it onto the highway. As you drive up the hill, the water will appear to be moving up the hill with you, instead of downhill. To reach the site of the *illusión óptica,* head towards Comala; just outside of Comala, look for Restaurante Los Pinos. You can also entertain yourself at the **Parque Regional Metropolitano** (Degollado, at 20 de Noviembre, tel. 331/4–16–76; open daily 10–

5), where 75¢ will get you a water slide, a mini-zoo, and a man-made lake. Another option is to join a game of *fútbol* (soccer) at the university's **Polideportivo** (*see* Worth Seeing, *above*). To meet the players (or at least their fans), stop by the field near the entrance to the "Uni."

AFTER DARK

Café Colima (Jardín Corregidora, tel. 331/2–80–93) is Colima's version of a *peña*, with spectators singing along with local musicians during Sunday performances (9 PM–midnight). The seats are outdoors in the Jardín Corregidora, under an awning where patrons eat pricey food and sip beer, wine, and a variety of coffees. To get here, take a RUTA 9 bus from Medellín, at Jardín Quintero. Students hang out at any one of a handful of party bars and restaurants on Avenida Felipe Sevilla del Río, a few blocks from the university. Especially good are **Atrium** (Felipe Sevilla del Río 574, tel. 331/3–04–77) and the nearby **Grillos** (in front of Plaza Country, tel. 331/4–88–44). Both start serving food and alcohol around 5 PM, but don't really get going until 8 PM. If you're in the mood for technopop, **Cheer's** (Zaragoza 521, tel. 331/4–47–00; cover $3) is *the* disco. Things get going around 10:30 PM and the party lasts until 4 AM. Cheer's is only open three nights a week: Wednesday is ladies' night (men pay a $5 cover), with a *barra libre* (open bar) for all. Friday and Saturday everyone pays $2.50. RUTA 1 combis run to these last three spots, but they stop running at 9 PM. Taxis from the zócalo only cost 75¢.

Near Colima

VOLCANES DE COLIMA

Just north of Colima in the Parque Nacional Nevado de Colima, are two volcanoes known as the Volcanes de Colima—despite the fact that one of them is actually just across the Jalisco state line. The taller one, at 4,335 meters, is the **Volcán de Fuego** (Fire Volcano). Nine kilometers away, the **Volcán Nevado de Colima** (also called the Volcán de Nieve, or Snow Volcano) rises 3,900 meters. The former has been living up to its name, belching out smoke and a small amount of lava in July of 1994. It's dangerous to visit the volcano, and there are no buses to the trails or facilities. If you're still determined to climb the fire-breathing beast, you'll need to catch an indirect bus heading for Guadalajara from the Central de Autobuses in Colima; get off in the town of Atenquique and get permission from the military there to embark on the 17-kilometer (10.5-mile) hike. Ask at the tourist office in Colima about hiking trails and current safety conditions. The forest at the base of the Volcán de Fuego is a good place to camp.

The Volcán Nevado, on the other hand, is a hiker's paradise. About two-thirds of the way up the volcano is a shelter called **La Joya,** where you can stay for free in a cabaña—a no-frills hostel that fits at least 20 people. The cabaña has a fireplace and nothing else, so bring food, drink,

In Case of an Eruption . . .

(1) Stay calm. (2) Click your heel together three times and say, "There's no place like Colima." (3) Sacrifice your annoying travel companion to appease the volcano god. Then maybe, just maybe, the Volcán de Fuego will return to its fitful slumber for another couple of years. Mexican and American geologists continue to predict that the impressive and constantly active volcano will soon explode into clouds of fire and lava. They say that such an eruption would not only destroy the vegetation of pines and evergreens in the fertile valley below, but the burning rocks and sulfur vapors would reach Colima's inland and coastal towns, causing destructive earthquakes and seismic waves. For Colimans, fear of the Volcán de Fuego, which has erupted five times this century, is a way of life.

and gear. Also bring layers of clothes to keep you warm at night and cool during the day. From La Joya it's a three- or four-hour hike to the snowy peak of the volcano. To reach Volcán Nevado from Colima, take a Guadalajara-bound bus from the Central de Autobuses de Colima, get off in Ciudad Guzmán (40 min, $4), and transfer to a bus to the town of Fresnito, at the base of the volcano. From here, you'll need to either find someone willing to drive you to La Joya (it's about 37 kilometers, or 23 miles) for a fee, or hitch a ride; because of the number of hikers who make this trip, the latter shouldn't be too difficult. Either way, plan on at least a three-day trip: It will probably take you the better part of a day to reach La Joya, another to climb and descend, and a third to return to Colima. If this sounds too ambitious for you, there are a number of small towns nearby, including **Laguna La María** (*see below*) and **San Antonio,** both at the base of the Parque Nacional Nevado de Colima, where you can see the volcanoes without having to expend much energy or time. Both of these towns can be reached by hopping a bus from the Sub-Urbana bus station in Colima.

LAGUNA LA MARÍA

Laguna La María is a vacation retreat for Colimans at the edge of the Parque Nacional Nevado de Colima. The verdant, isolated lakeshore is not an easy trek from Colima, but once you're here the lake offers great camping, swimming, and fishing—although frequent afternoon rains force visitors to take refuge under the *casitas* (covered picnic tables). Pay 25¢ at the park entrance for day use, or $1.50 to camp anywhere along the shore. Public bathrooms (without showers) are accessible to campers, but the lack of restaurants means you'll be packing in your food. You can also stay at **Cabaña La María** (right by the lake), which has clean $20 singles and $30 doubles with small kitchens and bathrooms. It's wise to make reservations—get in touch with the tourist office in Colima and they'll do it for you. From the Central de Autobuses Sub-Urbana in Colima, SAN ANTONIO buses leave for Laguna La María at 7 AM, 1:20 PM, 2:30 PM, and 5 PM. From the bus stop it's a 15-minute walk to the lake. Buses return at 9 AM, 3 PM, and 3:50 PM. If you miss the bus back to Colima, you can try to hitchhike from the main road, although cars going to Colima are infrequent.

Ixtapa/ Zihuatanejo

If only one resort on the Pacific Coast is worth visiting, it's Ixtapa/Zihuatanejo. A four-hour drive up the coast from Acapulco, this twin-town resort is less expensive and less frenetic than its big brother to the south. Only 4 miles apart and with a combined population of just 20,000, the towns of **Zihuatanejo** and **Ixtapa** have distinct personalities—the former is a sleepy fishing village and the latter is a happening tourist-ridden resort. Yet a common natural setting of green, house-freckled hills and beautiful, white-sand beaches bond the cities together as if they were siblings.

Despite its active fishing industry and mellow beachside tourist zone, Zihuatenejo has maintained the typical set-up of towns in Mexico, with a bustling mercado and side streets closed to traffic and open to evening strolls. It offers a good base for budget travelers, who'll get to experience Mexican culture before zipping off to Ixtapa's prettier but tourist-laden beaches 15 minutes away.

Hollywood hasn t passed Ixtapa by: When a Man Loves a Woman, starring Meg Ryan and Andy Garcia, was filmed at the extravagant La Casa Que Canta hotel.

Zihuatanejo also has local craft shops, inexpensive seafood restaurants, and affordable hotels and guest homes right on the waterfront. Near town, **Playas La Ropa** and **Las Gatas** on Zihuatanejo Bay are two of the most serene beaches in the area, attracting scuba divers and snorkelers alike.

In contrast, Ixtapa is one long strip of hot pavement, perfectly manicured lawns, and clunky buildings lining the white beach. Just 20 years ago, the area was blanketed by coconut and banana plantations, but all that changed once Ixtapa was targeted for development by Fonatur (the federal tourism department). Today you'll find plenty of luxury hotels, pricey shops, and air-conditioned minimalls, but you'll also get some of the prettiest beaches on the coast, free of the fishing boats and pollution that plague Zihuatanejo.

There's also a thriving night scene, which is quickly adopting a party-till-you-drop attitude. With these two cities you get the best of both worlds—dip into Ixtapa's liveliness and clear waters, then beat a retreat to peaceful and affordable Zihuatanejo.

BASICS

AMERICAN EXPRESS Cardholders can receive mail and cash personal checks at this office, which caters to upper-class travelers. *Area Comercial, Blvd. Ixtapa, Ixtapa/Zihuatenejo, Guerrero, CP 40880, México, tel. 755/3–08–53. Next to Hotel Kristal. Open Mon.–Sat. 9–6, Sun. 9–2.*

CASAS DE CAMBIO Banks seem to be on every streetcorner in Zihuatanejo. There are ATMs at **Banamex** (Cuauhtémoc 4, near Nicolás Bravo, tel. 755/4–21–96), which changes traveler's checks weekdays 9–noon. In Ixtapa, **Bital** (Blvd. Ixtapa, tel. 755/3–06–41) changes traveler's checks and money weekdays 8–7 and Saturday 9–2:30. Casas de cambio don't have the greatest exchange rates, but they do have better hours than the banks. In Zihuatanejo, try **Central de Cambio** (Galeana 6, tel. 755/4–28–00), open Monday–Saturday 8 AM–9 PM, Sunday 9–9.

EMERGENCIES **Fire department** (tel. 755/3–25–51); **police** (tel. 755/4–20–40).

LAUNDRY **Lavandería Super Clean,** in central Zihuatanejo, charges $1 per kilo, with a 3-kilo minimum. *González 11, at Galeana, tel. 755/4–23–47. Open Mon.–Sat. 8–8.*

Tourism 101: A Crash Course in Resort-Town Economics

In the 1960s, the Mexican government decided that tourism was the ticket out of Debt City. Tourism means an influx of foreign currency, and for Mexico that was supposed to translate into a painless way of repaying foreign debt. A department of tourism, Fonatur, was formed, and after careful consideration, five sites were singled out to become mega-resorts: Acapulco, Cancún, Ixtapa, Los Cabos, and the Bahías de Huatulco. These billion-dollar babies have enjoyed varying success: Cancún, a paradise carved out of the Yucatecan landscape, reigns supreme, while Huatulco, in Oaxaca, is still in the development stages.

No one can argue with the fact that increased tourism has ushered in a flood of foreign dollars, but just how much of this remains in the country? Construction money stays, since the law states Mexican labor must be used to build megaresorts. Fees for water and electricity remain, as does money spent by tourists in Mexican-owned businesses—and, of course, there are always taxes. However, Hyatt and Sheraton chains— conspicuously foreign corporations—are now flowering along the coast. There's also this unpleasant statistic to deal with: More than half of all the profit made on tourism in developing countries manages to find its way back to the rich north, and what does go to the Mexican government largely gets swallowed up by corrupt politicians. These massive resorts and tourist traps also result in radical environmental and cultural degradation. It's said that Fonatur, backed by enormous private investment dollars, is responsible for hacking down coconut and banana plantations in Ixtapa, as well as destroying entire neighborhoods to construct gringo paradise playgrounds.

MAIL The **post office** in Zihuatanejo is hard to find. Walk up Guerrero away from the water, turn right onto Morelos, and then turn right again onto a dirt road two blocks past the Pollo Feliz restaurant—the white TELECOM building will be in front of you. The office will hold mail sent to you at the following address for up to 10 days: Lista de Correos, Domicilio Centro SCT, Zihuatanejo, Guerrero, CP 40880, México. You can also just drop your letters in a *buzón* (mailbox), found all over town. There is no post office in Ixtapa. *Tel. 755/4–21–92. Open weekdays 8–7, Sat. 9–1.*

MEDICAL AID In Zihuatanejo, the **Centro de Salud,** a.k.a. Hospital General (Paseo de la Boquita, at Paseo del Palmar, tel. 755/4–20–88) charges $1.50 for a consultation. There are no 24-hour pharmacies in town, but **Farmacia del Centro** (Cuauhtémoc 20, at Nicolás Bravo, tel. 755/4–20–77) is open daily 7 AM–9 PM.

PHONES There are two pay phones in front of Zihuatanejo's Palacio Municipal on Álvarez, or you can try the **Central de Cambio,** which charges a 75¢ connection fee for a collect call. You can also pay cash here for long-distance calls. *Galeana 6, tel. 755/4–28–00. Open Mon.–Sat. 8 AM–9 PM, Sun. 9–9.*

VISITOR INFORMATION Don't be misled by the booths advertising tourist information— they are really fronts for time-shares and offer next to no info. The real tourist office is next door to Zihuatanejo's Palacio Municipal. *Álvarez, near Cuauhtémoc, tel. 755/4–20–01 ext. 120. Open weekdays 9–3 and 6–8, Sat. 9–2.*

COMING AND GOING

BY BUS The new bus station is on the highway on the outskirts of Zihuatanejo. To reach downtown Zihuatanejo from here, take any bus or VW combi marked ZIHUATANEJO or CENTRO (10 min, 25¢). You'll be let off on either Juárez or Morelos, both just a few blocks from most of the cheaper hotels in town. To return to the station, head to the corner of Juárez and Ejido and board a combi marked CORREO. Ixtapa doesn't have a bus station of its own; to get here, you have to take a local bus (15 min, 30¢) from the intersection of Morelos and Juárez in Zihuatanejo.

Estrella Blanca (tel. 755/4–34–77) is the main bus line that operates out of the Zihuatanejo station. Direct buses to Acapulco (4 hrs, $6.50) run on the hour daily 6–6. The bus to Huatulco (13 hrs, $20) leaves at 7:45 PM and stops in Puerto Escondido along the way. Two buses a day (10 AM and noon) also head for Mazatlán (20 hrs, $34), stopping in Manzanillo (9 hrs, $12) and Puerto Vallarta (12 hrs, $21). Buses to Mexico City (10 hrs, $26) leave four times daily. The above are all first-class buses. You can travel second class to Acapulco and Mexico City, but the longer travel times and lack of air-conditioning makes it not worth saving a couple bucks.

BY PLANE The international airport (tel. 755/4–22–37 or 755/4–26–34) is 11 kilometers east of Zihuatanejo on the Carretera Costera (Hwy. 200). **Aeroméxico** (tel. 755/4–20–18), **Mexicana** (tel. 755/4–22–27), and some U.S. carriers serve the airport. A one-way ticket to Mexico City is about $95. Only a taxi will whisk you away to the airport; a ride to or from Zihuatanejo costs $6 ($7.50 to or from Ixtapa).

GETTING AROUND

Zihuatanejo is easily walkable, with budget hotels, restaurants, shops, and the beach all near the center. This area is marked by Álvarez and the beach to the south, Juárez to the east, 5 de Mayo to the west, and Morelos to the north. Ixtapa has one main thoroughfare, the Paseo de Ixtapa—essentially a 3-kilometer strip of hotels and malls. To reach Ixtapa from Zihuatanejo (15 min, 15¢), catch one of the blue-and-white buses from Morelos at Juárez. If you feel like walking, head east on Morelos and follow the signs to Ixtapa—the 7-kilometer walk should take about an hour (unless the heat knocks you out). You can catch a bus back to Zihuatanejo anywhere along Ixtapa's Paseo de Ixtapa. Buses run daily 6 AM–10 PM.

WHERE TO SLEEP

Downtown Zihuatanejo is packed with fairly inexpensive hotels, many of which are near the waterfront. Unfortunately, budget hotels in Zihuatanejo are generally reluctant to let lots of people pack into a room for low rates, so groups may have a harder time getting a break. Staying in Ixtapa is pretty much out of the question—there are no nonresort hotels in sight, and the cheapest single will set you back $70. The prices listed below apply in Zihuatanejo's low season. Expect to pay a bit more from the middle of November to April.

➤ **UNDER $10** • **Casa Elvira.** The sweet, elderly proprietress at this hotel keeps the rooms clean, and the mirrors, calendars, and flowered curtains will make you feel right at home (until you step into the run-down bathroom). She charges $4 for a single and $7 for a double during low season, and $1 more for each during high season. *Álvarez 52, near 5 de Mayo, tel. 755/4– 20–61. 6 rooms, 4 with bath. Luggage storage. Wheelchair access.*

Hotel Casa Aurora. The narrow entryway of this hotel is hidden by souvenir shops and grocery stores, but wade through them and you'll find a tiled interior patio with sprawling plants. Most of the clean rooms have stone walls and floors, and second-floor rooms have huge, shaded decks with comfortable lounge chairs. Rooms are $5.50 per person low season and $6.50 high season. Air-conditioning costs an additional $5. *Nicolás Bravo 27, near Juárez, tel. 755/4– 30–46. 15 rooms, all with bath.*

➤ **UNDER $15** • **Hotel Raúl Tres Marías.** This hotel overlooks Zihuatanejo Bay and is the best in its price range. Each floor has a communal deck with tables, chairs, and a great view. The cement rooms ($11 singles, $14 doubles) are ample, clean, and have ceiling fans. The same management runs a slightly pricier ($16.50 singles, $20.50 doubles) hotel by the same name on La Noria, but there's no hot water there. Expect a 15-percent increase in rates during the high season. *Álvarez 52, tel. and fax 755/4–29–77. 1 block from beach. 17 rooms, all with bath. Luggage storage. MC, V.*

Hotel Rosimar. This clean, breezy hotel has sitting areas on every floor, each overlooking the street. The rooms have remodeled tiled bathrooms, floral comforters, and their very own TVs. Singles cost $9.50, doubles $11. *Ejido 12, btw Galeana and Guerrero, tel. 755/4–21–39. 13 rooms, all with bath. Laundry. luggage storage. Wheelchair access.*

HOSTELS **Villa Juvenil.** This friendly, crowded place is just outside town, less than a mile from the waterfront, and unfortunately borders the foul-smelling marina. Facilities are rudimentary but clean, and it's a good place to meet other travelers. A bed in one of the single-sex dorms costs $4. Breakfast costs about $2, and lunch and dinner are each $2.50. Be careful if you're going out at night—the doors lock at 11 PM, after which you have to enter through a side door. *Paseo de las Salinas, tel. 755/4–46–62. West on Morelos until it becomes Paseo de las Salinas, left at fork. 64 beds. Reception open 7 AM–10:30 PM. Luggage storage.*

CAMPING You can pitch a tent at the hostel (*see above*) and use their bathrooms and showers for $2.50 a night. Camping on the beach is also allowed at **Playa La Ropa,** south of Playa La Madera in Zihuatanejo, but at any other spot you'll have to ask the hotel fronting the beach for permission.

FOOD

The restaurants in Ixtapa tend to be fancy and overpriced, but some small restaurants serving *comida típica* (typical Mexican food) can be found a few blocks inland from the resort-laden beach strip. Zihuatanejo, however, has a good selection of serene seafood eateries, many of which are right on the beach. For quick snacks, try **Panadería Francesa** (González 15, tel. 755/4–27–42; open daily 7 AM–9 PM), a warehouse-size bakery with a wide selection of *pan dulce* (sweet rolls) and breads. All of the restaurants listed below are in Zihuatanejo.

Mamacita's El Chiringuito. This funky restaurant/bar, decorated with guitars, ponchos, and skinny, tinsel Day of the Dead skeletons, offers scrumptious food; try their specialty, Chiringuito shrimp ($6.50). Mamacita's serves up some of the best guacamole around, and three fish tacos cost just $2. The bar serves cold $1 beers and has an international selection of wines. *Cnr of Alvarez and 5 de Mayo, no phone. Open daily noon–midnight.*

Restaurant Bar Tata's. This is a happening spot with great food and lots of atmosphere. Super-hip waiters bop to your beachside tables to the beat of Top 40 pumping from the loudspeakers. Breaded red snapper with rice and tortillas costs about $6.50, as does the *filete a la tampiqueña*, a steak served with enchiladas, beans, and rice. They run a two-for-one special during happy hour (5–7 PM). *Paseo del Pescador, at Guerrero, tel. 755/4–20–10. Open daily 2–9.*

La Sirena Gorda. Seafood tacos are the specialty at this waterfront restaurant. The name means "the fat mermaid," and ceramic mermaids and other knickknacks adorn the tables and the busy wooden bar. Two tasty smoked-fish tacos are $3; octopus tacos cost $4. *Paseo del Pescador 20-A, near pier, tel. 755/4–26–87. Open Thurs.–Tues. 7 AM–10 PM. Wheelchair access. MC, V.*

Tamales Atoles Any. This fun and lively place specializes in tamales of all varieties, including sweet ones. They also have soups, *queso fundido* (melted cheese), and vegetarian selections. A meal will run you $2–$3. *Ejido, at Guerrero, tel. 755/4–73–73. Open daily 8 AM–midnight. Wheelchair access.*

WORTH SEEING

With maps, figurines, paintings, and photographs, the seven rooms of the **Museo Arqueológico de la Costa Grande** trace human settlement in America, particularly the Costa Grande, which extends from the mouth of the Balsas River to Acapulco. The museum displays ceramic objects and primitive carvings from the Zaputecas—the original settlers here—as well as representations of the *cihuateteos,* Amazon goddeses who received the sun each afternoon and welcomed it into the earth. *Plaza Olof Palme, right on the beach in Zihuatanejo, tel. 755/4–75–52. Admission: 60¢, 30¢ students. Open Tues.–Sun. 10–6.*

OUTDOOR ACTIVITIES

The beaches at Las Gatas and Isla Ixtapa are well-known scuba-diving spots, and shops along the waterfront in Zihuatanejo, Playa Las Gatas, and Isla Ixtapa rent diving equipment. The NAUI-certified **Zihuatanejo Scuba Center** (Cuauhtémoc 3, near Álvarez, tel. 755/4–21–47) has an English-speaking staff; for $70, beginners get pool lessons and one dive, while certified divers get an all-day trip. Deep-sea fishing is also popular, but it will cost you an arm and a leg. The **Cooperativa de Pescadores** (Paseo del Pescador, at 5 de Mayo, tel. 755/4–20–56) rents charter boats ($120–$200 a day), but your best bet is to go straight to the pier in Zihuatanejo and haggle with the fishermen—you can cut the boat price in half this way. For good snorkeling and an abundance of water sports, check out Playa Ixtapa, where each megaresort has equipment for rent. All resorts charge similar prices for boogie boards ($4 per hr), banana boats ($5 for a 10-min ride), parasailing ($20 for an 8-min flight), wave runners ($30 per half hour), and snorkeling ($20 for 4 hrs). Try **Hotel Fontán** (on Playa Ixtapa, tel. 755/4–20–56) for good service.

ZIHUATANEJO **Playa La Madera,** a pretty stretch of sand with inviting water, is a 10-minute walk away from Zihua proper. To get here, follow Álvarez east for half a mile until you reach a set of stairs leading over a canal; cross over and continue following the water. When you hear surf, cut to the right, past one of the big hotels. A 25-minute walk from Zihuatanejo leads you to **Playa La Ropa,** with clean, calm waters perfect for swimming or waterskiing. Make the sweltering trek from downtown on foot, or take a taxi ($1–$2). If you're walking, follow the route to Playa La Madera; keep to the right on the main road (the Paseo Costera); always heading up. As the road descends and the ocean comes into view, cut through the nearest hotel, or follow the road until it winds to the beach. You can also get here by walking 15 minutes north from Playa Las Gatas (*see below*).

Legend says an ancient Tarascan king ensured calm waters for his maidens by building a barrier of rocks at Playa Las Gatas.

The last beach off the Paseo Costera is the protected **Playa Las Gatas,** with calm water perfect for swimming. Unfortunately, the inviting waters hide a rocky bottom that is hard on bare toes, so keep paddling. Las Gatas is, however, perfect for snorkeling, as flippers will protect your feet. Colloquially named for the sharks that used to frequent the waters, Las Gatas now only attracts a few marlin and yellowfin sailfish. Also expect to be face-to-face with parrotfish and needlefish. To get here from Playa La Ropa, walk south along the beach for 15 minutes; or take a pleasant 10-minute boat ride ($2 per person round-trip) from the *muelle* (pier) in Zihuatanejo. Boats run daily 8:30–5.

IXTAPA **Playa del Palmar** is a long, sandy stretch bordering the Ixtapa hotels, ideal for swimming, snorkeling, and boogie boarding. The hotels all rent equipment (*see above*), so you can engage in your water sport of choice. To the northwest are several more pristine beaches, including **Playa Quieta, Playa Linda,** and Ixtapa's **Club Med** (near Playa Linda, tel. 755/2–00–44), where equipment and instruction for innumerable sports, as well as a gargantuan buffet lunch, is yours for $40. To reach Playa del Palmar from Zihuatanejo, take a minibus to Ixtapa from the intersection of Morelos and Juárez. Get off at any of the towering hotels and cut through to the beach. **Isla Ixtapa,** off the shore of Playa Quieta, has two good swimming and sunbathing beaches, and one that is better for divers. Snorkeling is popular too, and it's allowed on all three beaches. There are a few restaurants on the island, but no place to stay. The best thing about Isla Ixtapa is the hour-long boat trip from the pier in Zihuatanejo ($5 per person round-trip). Boats leave at 11:30 AM and return at 4 PM. They also leave every 15 minutes 8–5 from Playa Quieta ($2 per person round-trip).

AFTER DARK

You may not party as hard in Ixtapa/Zihuatanejo as in hedonistic Acapulco, but don't get ready for bed yet. Most of the action is where the dollars are: Ixtapa. If you crave a pulsating beat, try the local branch of the ubiquitous **Carlos 'n' Charlie's** (Paseo del Palmar, tel. 753/3–00–85), which sits at the northwest end of the hotel strip. Cover is $5 for guys, $2.50 for girls, and the disco draws locals and tourists, who shake it until 3 AM. Also open until 3, **Señor Frog's** (Centro Comercial Ixtapa, tel. 755/3–02–72) is the place to go if dancing on the table is your thing or if you want to have a few icy tropical drinks. Consider yourself warned: These two spots are gringo magnets. Next to the Hotel Kristal in Ixtapa is **Christine's** (tel. 755/3–03–33; open daily 10:30–3), which caters to a rich and sophisticated crowd consisting mainly of vacationing Mexicans from Mexico City. Cover is $6, except for Monday, when you can boogie for free. Ladies night is Wednesday. Over in Zihuatanejo, the only night club/disco is the tourist-free **Roca Rock** (5 de Mayo, at Nicolás Bravo, tel. 755/4–33–24), which pulls in the city's gays and lesbians and features a nightly drag show. It's open Thursday nights and weekends 10 PM–6 AM. Near the main bus station, the small **Bar Bohemio** is also popular with locals and sometimes hosts live guitar music. The happy hour at **Restaurant Bar Tata's** (*see* Food, *above*) is also pretty happenin' among locals. For a more sedate evening, catch a flick at the only moviehouse around, Zihuatanejo's **Cinema Paraíso** (Cuauhtémoc, near Nicolás Bravo, tel. 755/4–23–18), which shows American movies with Spanish subtitles on its enormous screen.

Sunday nights around 9 PM, the basketball court on Playa Principal fills up with locals who ve come to watch their friends and family perform traditional dances and music.

Near Ixtapa/Zihuatanejo

BARRA DE POTOSÍ

If even mellow Zihuatanejo is too touristy for you, make a midweek trip to the slow-paced seaside village of Barra de Potosí, a half-hour bus ride southeast of Zihuatanejo. During the week, there's absolutely nothing to do in Barra de Potosí but relax, swim, enjoy the fine weather and food, and chat with the locals. If you manage to roll out of your hammock, you can hike about on the rugged *morros* (cliffs), which offer breathtaking views of the Pacific Coast. Weekends, however, are a different story: The beaches fill up with teenagers whose boomboxes pound as the kids hit volleyballs around the sand courts. Each Sunday night, a *norteño* band strums traditional tunes around town.

Barra is also a good place to score cheap seafood. Here, red snapper with rice and tortillas will set you back about $3 (much less than in Ixtapa/Zihuatanejo). Try **Palapa Bacanona** (two palapas in from the end of the beach), where you'll be served $1 quesadillas and any *refresco* (soft drink) you want. Visitors are welcome to take a siesta or spend the night free of charge in the hammocks slung beneath the restaurant's eaves. If a bright-pink, unfinished hotel sounds better, try **Hotel Barra de Potosí** (tel. 755/4–82–90). Charming rooms (singles $14, doubles $20.50) overlook a pool, restaurant, and, of course, the beach.

COMING AND GOING To reach Barra from Zihuatanejo, catch a VW combi or one of the white minibuses that run along Juárez (heading away from the water), first verifying that the driver is stopping at the town of Los Achotes (30 min, 25¢). These minibuses run 9–8. From Los Achotes, *camionetas* (small flatbed trucks) run to Barra de Potosí every half hour 9–5. The trip through tropical countryside and a small pueblo takes 10 minutes.

Acapulco

Acapulco is, to steal a phrase from Dorothy Parker, not a city to be tossed aside lightly. It should be thrown aside with great force. The air hangs thick with grime, the smells of the ocean and freshly grilled fish compete with heavy exhaust fumes and open sewers, and the water is not as pristine as it used to be. Once the crowning star of the Pacific Coast, this city is now in many ways a fortyish bachelor, still partying the night away but desperately pushing his thinning hair back to conceal an ever-growing bald spot. In the luxury-hotel zone, which has existed in all its tacky brilliance for 40 years, tourists cruise the strip, shopping, supping, and spending. Acapulco Viejo, at the other end of the bay, is a maze of run-down streets swarming with buses and handicraft vendors. But Acapulco's main draw continues to be its discos, which are expensive, crowded, and rock through the night with special effects to rival Jurassic Park. If you need to get away from this "Mexico City with a beach" (as one Mexican woman put it), head to the quieter towns of Pie de la Cuesta, 45 minutes from the center of town, and Chilpancingo, one hour north of Acapulco.

BASICS

AMERICAN EXPRESS The main office is in the heart of the luxury-hotel strip. They deliver MoneyGrams, replace lost or stolen AmEx cards and checks, and change traveler's checks at rates comparable to those at the banks in Acapulco Viejo. Cardholders can cash personal checks or receive mail here as well. *789 La Gran Plaza, Acapulco, Guerrero, CP 39670, México, tel. 74/69–11–00. Open Mon.–Sat. 10–7.*

CASAS DE CAMBIO There are tons of casas de cambio on the luxury-hotel strip. Near the zócalo in Acapulco Viejo, **Banamex** (Costera Miguel Alemán 211, tel. 74/82–57–50) changes money weekdays 9–3 and has an ATM that accepts Plus and Cirrus cards. For later hours, try **Consultoria International** (Costera Miguel Alemán 48-3, Centro Comerical La Piluda, tel. 74/84–31–08), open daily 9–9.

CONSULATES In the Club del Sol Hotel (Costera Miguel Alemán, tel. 74/85–66–00), you'll find the **United States** consulate (tel. 74/85–72–07), open weekdays 10–2, and the **Canadian** consulate (tel. 74/85–66–21), open weekdays 9–1. The **United Kingdom** consulate is at Las Brisas Hotel (Carretera Escénica, tel. 74/84–66–05) and is open weekdays 10–2 and 5–6:30.

EMERGENCIES The number for the **police** is 74/85–06–50; they can get you an **ambulance.** The **fire department** can be reached at 74/84–41–22.

LAUNDRY At **Lavandería Coral,** you pay $1 per kilo to get your grimy clothes washed, dried, and folded. Same-day services are available if you drop off your load before noon. *Juárez 12, tel. 74/80–07–35, 1 block west of zócalo. Open daily 9–2 and 4–7.*

Sights ●

Mercado Municipal, **5**

Parque Acuático Cici, **1**

Parque Papagayo, **4**

Plaza de Toros Caletilla, **10**

La Quebrada, **9**

Zócalo, **6**

Lodging ○

Casa Mama Helene, **7**

Hotel Lupita, **2**

Hotel Misión, **8**

Hotel Playa Suave, **3**

KEY

AE American Express Office

ℹ Tourist Information

0 ———— 880 yards
0 ———— 800 meters

N

Cortines

Ruiz

Av.

Av. Cuauhtémoc

Av. W. Massieu

AE

Playa Hornitos

J. S. Elcano

Av. Durango

Av. Constituyentes

Av. Ejido

Niños Héroes

18 de Marzo

Av. Cuauhtémoc

Costera Miguel Alemán

Playa Hornos

Pro. D. H. de Mendoza

Av. Cuauhtémoc

Av. 5 de Mayo

Cuesta

Calz. Pie de la

Av. V. Guerrero

Morelos

Bahía de Acapulco

ACAPULCO VIEJO

Juárez

La Quebrada

BUDGET HOTEL ZONE

Av. L. Mateos

Tte. Azueta

Cpal. M. Alemán

Malecón

Av. Poza   del Rey

TO AIRPORT AND PUERTO MÁRQUEZ →

Península de las Playas

← TO PIE DE LA CUESTA

A C A P U L C O

Av. López Mateos

Gran Vía Tropical

Playa Caleta

Playa Caletilla

Playa Roqueta

PACIFIC OCEAN

Isla la Roqueta

MAIL The huge main **post office** is on the Costera, a few blocks east of the zócalo. The office will hold mail for you for up to 10 days if sent to the following address: Lista de Correos, Costera Miguel Alemán 215, Acapulco, Guerrero, CP 39300, México. *Tel. 74/82–20–83. Open Mon.– Sat. 8–8, Sun. 9–noon.*

MEDICAL AID For an English-speaking doctor, call **Servicio Médico Especialista** (in Hotel Club del Sol, opposite Plaza Bahía, tel. 74/85–80–66) 24 hours a day; Dr. Luís Roberto García Ruízf charges $30 for a consultation and makes hotel calls anywhere in Acapulco for $15 extra. In an emergency, try the **Cruz Roja** on Ruíz Cortínez (tel. 74/85–41–00) or the adjacent **Hospital General** (tel. 74/85–17–30). To reach either from the zócalo, follow Constituyentes north until it becomes Ruíz Cortínez—the hospital and clinic are on the 600 block. For less urgent medical attention, head for the 24-hour **Farmacia Emy** (Costera Miguel Alemán 176-C, tel. 74/84–53–33).

PHONES There are pay phones on the zócalo, and calls can be placed from the convenient **Caseta Telefonica,** near the post office. It costs $2.50 a minute to call the United States, and collect calls cost $1.50. *Costera Miguel Alemán 215, tel. and fax 74/82–87–19. Open Mon.– Sat. 8–8.*

VISITOR INFORMATION The streets here are patrolled by **tourist police** dressed in white— they'll answer any questions and come to the rescue if you have a problem. The main **tourist office** (Costera Miguel Alemán 187, a few blocks west of the Ritz, tel. 74/86–91–67) has an extremely helpful staff that will send you away with an armful of reading material, much of it in English. The tourist office is open weekdays 9–2 and 4–7, but someone is usually around 2–4 as well. The **tourist assistance bureau** (Costera Miguel Alemán 4455, tel. 74/84–44–16; open daily 8 AM–10 PM), in the luxury hotel area, offers equally informative advice.

COMING AND GOING

BY BUS The **Central de Autobuses Líneas Unidas del Sur** (Ejido, btw Calles 6 and 7, tel. 74/ 86–80–29), commonly called Estrella Blanca, is in Colonia La Fábrica and can be reached from the zócalo on any bus marked EJIDO or CENTRAL. Buses labeled CALETA or CENTRO make the trip in the opposite direction. The Estrella Blanca bus company has its own taxi company (tel. 74/83–30–70), which will take you to the zócalo for $2; you can call them from anywhere in the city between 7 AM and 10 PM. A number of companies serve the bus station, but **Estrella Blanca** (tel. 74/69–20–30) has both first-class and *ejecutivo* (deluxe) service to most destinations. First-class buses to Mexico City (7 hrs, $14) leave every hour between 6 AM and 2 AM, usually stopping in Chilpancingo (2 hrs, $5), Taxco (4 hrs, $9), and Cuernavaca (5 hrs, $11.50). Direct, luxury buses to Mexico City (5 hrs, $17.50) leave on the same schedule. First-class buses also run to Zihuatanejo (4 hrs, $6.50) and Huatulco (9 hrs, $14), with a stop in Puerto Escondido (7 hrs, $12). You can catch buses from a number of other companies to far-flung destinations like Guadalajara, Monterrey, and Tampico. Luggage storage costs 25¢ per hour, and you can sleep, albeit uncomfortably, at the station.

BY PLANE Acapulco's airport is 30 kilometers east of the city on Highway 200. There's no public transportation to the airport, and taxis cost $7–$10. If you're alone, a cheaper alternative is **Shuttle Aeropuerto Acapulco** (Blvd. de las Naciones Unidas, at Barra Vieja, tel. 74/62– 10–95). The shuttle costs $5 per person, and if you call 24 hours in advance, they'll pick you up at your hotel. You can call them daily 7 AM–10 PM. **Continental** (Andres Bello 45-18, tel. 91–800/9–00–50) has international flights only. For domestic flights, try **AeroMexicana** (Costera Miguel Alemán 286, tel. 74/85–16–00).

GETTING AROUND

Acapulco can be divided roughly into three sections: the city itself, known as Acapulco Viejo (Old Acapulco); the Zona Dorada, a.k.a. the strip, where all the fancy hotels are; and the Zona de Amantes, where the ritziest hotels and flashiest clubs congregate. Most of the budget hotels in Acapulco are in Acapulco Viejo, around the zócalo (also called **Plaza Álvarez**). On the zócalo you'll also find the city's cathedral, which is built over an unfinished movie theater. Bordering the zócalo to the south is the Costera Miguel Alemán, an 8-kilometer thoroughfare that runs along the bay through each section of the city. As you move east along the Costera, away from the zócalo, you'll encounter the **Parque Papagayo**, several beaches, the **Fuente Diana** traffic circle, and finally the Zona Dorada. The Zona Dorada stretches from the tunnel on the Costera to the naval base, and includes the decadent **Parque Acuático CiCi**. The walk from the zócalo to CiCi takes just over an hour.

Buses are by far the cheapest way to get around, with fares averaging 25¢. Buses marked LA BASE and HORNOS run in both directions along the Costera 6 AM–10 PM. Taxis are more expensive, and don't have meters. The nicer, larger cars are more expensive—stick to the white VW bugs for the cheapest rates. Don't be afraid to haggle—remember that if the first *taxista* (cabbie) won't lower his price, another bug will be along in 30 seconds.

WHERE TO SLEEP

Don't even think about staying on the strip unless someone just died and left you a sizeable inheritance. You needn't lose heart, however: Budget lodging is easy to find nearby, and competition keeps prices down—although couples may be frustrated by the common policy of charging by the person, rather than by room or bed. Hot water is available everywhere, 24 hours a day, but it's so hot here that you'll hardly need it. The best lodgings are clustered around the zócalo in Acapulco Viejo. This area is generally safe, but as always you should be alert walking at night. There are even a few budget options closer to the strip, several blocks past the Fuerte de San Diego and within binocular-view of the ritzy part of town. Wherever you stay, expect prices to jump substantially in the high season (December–April).

NEAR THE ZOCALO Casa Mama Helene. This slightly worn hotel is Mama Helene's house—as evidenced by the Ping-Pong table, bookshelves, aquarium, plants, and Mama Helene sitting around with her friends. Singles are $7 ($8 high season), doubles $14 ($20.50 high season). *Juárez 12, 3 blocks west of zócalo, tel. 74/82–23–96. 30 rooms, all with bath. Luggage storage. Wheelchair access.*

Hotel Misión. This place has the most charm of any budget hotel in Acapulco. The atrium is filled with philodendrons, mango trees, and wicker rocking chairs, and the rooms are decorated with assorted artwork and classy wood furniture. Powerful fans keep the rooms cool, and each has a dimly lit bathroom. Singles cost $10, doubles $14. *Felipe Valle 12, 3 blocks west of zócalo, tel. 74/82–36–43. 24 rooms. Luggage storage. Wheelchair access.*

NEAR THE STRIP Hotel Lupita. Statues of naked babies and mermaids surround the hotel's entrance and small pool. Narrow hallways open to spacious rooms, some of which can hold larger groups. Singles cost $7, doubles $9.50 (except during high season, when prices jump up). The hotel is located across the street from Parque Papagayo and a block from the beach. *Gómez Espinoza, right off the Costera, tel. 74/85–94–12. 16 rooms, all with bath. Wheelchair access.*

Hotel Playa Suave. This is a reasonable place to stay if you want to be as close to the beach as possible. The 30 rooms are dark but clean, and each has a bathroom. A breezy but noisy hallway leads to a restaurant, a swimming pool, and parking. Singles are $11, doubles $14, and air-conditioning costs an extra $4. *Costera Miguel Alemán 253, just west of Hotel de Brasil, tel. 74/85–12–56. Luggage storage. Wheelchair access.*

CAMPING Pitching a tent or even walking on the beach late at night is not a good idea—Acapulco has a high crime rate. Women especially should stay off the beaches and out of sparsely populated areas past dark. During high season, camping is allowed on the patrolled beach at Puerto Marqués (*see* Outdoor Activities, *below*). The **Playa Suave Trailer Park** (Costera Miguel Alemán 276, tel. 74/85–14–64) is right between Acapulco Viejo and the strip, a block away from the beach. For $7.50, one or two persons can comfortably and safely pitch a tent here and have access to private bathrooms, showers, and drinking water.

FOOD

The best meal deals are around the west side of the zócalo in Acapulco Viejo, especially on Juárez, where you'll find literally hundreds of small, clean establishments frequented by locals. For about $2 you can eat at one of the *fondas* (covered food stands) in the mercado—try **Fonda Christie** or **Fonda Doña Lupe**. To reach the market, take a HOSPITAL bus going inland from the zócalo. If you want to stock up on snacks for the beach, three warehouse-size grocery stores on the Costera, between Acapulco Viejo and the strip, sell cheap yogurt, fruit, deli meats, and freshly baked bread.

NEAR THE ZÓCALO Restaurante Ricardos (Juárez 9, tel. 74/82–11–40), near the zócalo, attracts a continuous flow of hungry locals looking for traditional food. For $2, chow down on soup, beans, an entrée, and dessert. Tucked in a secluded, shaded corner of the zócalo, the outdoor **Cafetería Astoria** (Plaza Álvarez, tel. 74/82–29–44; open daily 8 AM–11 PM) is the spot to sit and relax for hours with a cappuccino ($1) and some pan dulce. Also served are *chilaquiles rojos* (tortilla strips and chicken in red sauce; $1.50), meat enchiladas ($3), and club sandwiches ($1.50). **El Amigo Miguel** (Juárez 31, at José Azueta, tel. 74/83–69–81; open daily 10:30–8) has the freshest seafood and a second-floor balcony overlooking Acapulco Bay. There are two branches across the street from one another; the nicest, remodeled one lies farther off the beach. Fish soups are $2, and a fillet of sole ($2.50) comes with vegetables, rice, and warm bread. Lobster costs $9.

ON THE STRIP Don't come to the strip to find a budget meal—come to see what's happening. Acapulco's biggest health-food chain, **100% Natural** (Costera Miguel Alemán 200, tel. 74/85–39–82; open 24 hrs), just west of Parque Papagayo, has several outlets that serve green salads, steamed vegetable dishes, and soyburgers. (Warning: The branch on the zócalo is an imitation and not worth your time). Main dishes run $3–$4, and the restaurant is wheelchair accessible. In the afternoons, large crowds of young people flock to **El Zorrito** (Costera Miguel Alemán, just east of the Ritz, tel. 74/86–98–00; open daily 24 hrs). The food is good and not too expensive—hearty eaters should try the $7 *filete a la tampiqueña,* steak served with a chicken taco, chicken enchilada, guacamole, and beans. The menu also includes hamburgers ($3.50), onion rings ($1.50), and fried chicken ($4).

CAFÉS Cafetería Astoria (*see above*), on the northeast corner of the zócalo, is where most coffee-sippers relax for the afternoon, reading the newspaper or playing dominoes. Clusters of middle-aged men and women occupy the tables, tamely chatting among themselves. It's $1 for a cappuccino, best accompanied by one of their tasty desserts. **Café Los Amigos** (La Paz 10, no phone), on the west side of the zócalo, serves ice cream, fresh juice drinks, and a mean cappuccino (75¢). A younger crowd gathers at these outdoor tables, creating a slightly livelier scene. Both cafés are open daily 8 AM–11 PM and serve good breakfasts (about $1.50) and comidas corridas (about $3.50).

WORTH SEEING

Most points of interest lie within a Frisbee's throw of the Costera. Check out the **mercado municipal** (near Cuauhtémoc and Mendoza), where you'll find all kinds of food, painted ceramic statues, shell earrings, and Guatemalan vests and backpacks. Head to the zócalo or Parque Papagayo on Sundays—local bands play at both places around sunset. If you're in town in May, check out the **Festival de Acapulco,** an affordable music celebration that features singers and bands from around the world. Also in May is the **Festival de Gastronomía,** a huge food fest that encompasses the **Feria de Paella** held in the Hotel Acapulco Plaza. Call the hotel (tel. 74/85–90–50) for more information on the latter festival.

PARQUE ACUÁTICO CICI Swarming with waterlogged tourists of every age, this gigantic park on Costera Miguel Alemán features dolphin shows, water rides in an artificial lake, waterslides with names like "Kamikaze," and access to the beach. It's Acapulco's ultimate amusement park. The nearby **Casa de la Cultura** (tel. 74/84–38–14) displays pre-Columbian art and houses a small theater. *Tel. 74/84–19–70. From Acapulco Viejo, take a LA BASE or HORNOS bus; the park is on righthand side past the convention center. Admission: $5.50. Open daily 10–6.*

PARQUE PAPAGAYO This huge amusement park on the Costera—complete with a roller rink, tobaggans, an aviary, and bumper boats in two artifical lakes—is primarily a hangout for local youth and, on weekends, families. Located right across the street from the beach, it also makes a nice break from the sand and the sea. Admission is free, but the rides cost up to $1.25 each. *Costera Miguel Alemán, at Manuel Morin, tel. 74/85–62–09. Open weekdays 3:30–10:30, weekends 3–11.*

PLAZA DE TOROS CALETILLA Bullfights take place almost every Sunday between Christmas and Easter at this bullring, just a few minutes' walk northwest of Playa Caletilla (*see* Outdoor Activities, *below*). Fights start at 5:30 PM and the cheapest tickets, available at the bullring, are $5. *López Mateos, Península de las Playas, tel. 74/82–11–82.*

LA QUEBRADA A 10-minute walk northwest of the zócalo, these beautiful cliffs offer breathtaking views of the ocean and surrounding landscape. Acapulco's famous divers, the **Clavadistas** (tel. 74/83–14–00), risk their lives daily, plummeting 60 meters into the rock-filled waters below. This being Acapulco, you have to pay a $1.50 admission charge to join the crowds of tourists vying for the best viewing spots. The divers also accept/expect small gratuities. Dives take place daily at 12:45 PM and once an hour 7:30 PM–10:30 PM; the last two feature divers flinging themselves into the water bearing flaming torches. You can also get a spectacular view of the divers from the classy **La Perla** restaurant (Plazvela La Quebrada, tel. 74/83–11–05): All you have to do is buy a drink ($3). To reach the cliffs, walk straight up La Quebrada, the street that begins directly behind the zócalo's main church.

OUTDOOR ACTIVITIES

The beaches lining Acapulco Bay are deceptively beautiful: Remember that the bay is quite polluted, mostly with sewage. Cleaner and prettier than the beaches lining Acapulco Bay are those near Acapulco Viejo. Playas **Caleta** and **Caletilla** have big waves that crash in, tossing banana-hauling speedboats, paddling tourists, boogie boarders, and swimmers like a big, wet, dirty salad. Formerly Acapulco's hot spots, Caleta and Caletilla were left in the dust by the strip, and now cater more to Mexican tourists than to foreigners. Across the bay you can see **Isla Roqueta,** which is accessible from either beach by boat. The island has beautiful calm waters and a spectacular view from the lighthouse, and the boat ride there (10 min, $2.50 round-trip) is pleasant. Buy a ticket from the offices marked ISLA ROQUETA (near the wharf, tel. 74/83–00–66), or from a roaming ticket seller on the beach. To reach the dock, board a bus marked CALETA heading west along Costera.

Acapulco's cleanest beaches lie on the **Bahía de Puerto Marqués,** east of the city near the airport freeway. The water here is also less polluted than in Acapulco Bay, making the spot popular with waterskiers and skin divers. You can also snorkel, boogie board, and waterski. On weekends the more developed **Playa de Puerto Marqués** usually fills up with Mexican tourists. Buses marked PUERTO MARQUES (30 min, 15¢) leave from the Costera 5 de Mayo. Farther along is the pristine **Princess Beach,** named for the hotel that looms over it. The waves are big here, and swimmers should be very careful. To reach Princess Beach, take a cab ($1) or hitch a ride from the street that runs along Playa de Puerto Marqués. Another alternative is to sneak into a hotel pool: **Club del Sol** (Costera Miguel Alemán, tel. 74/85–66–00) might not notice if you take a dip.

Lots of water sports are popular here, though you might want to choose one that requires the least amount of contact between you and the water. Deep-sea fishing is a good bet: **Divers de Mexico/Fishing Factory** (Costera Miguel Alemán 100, a few blocks west of the zócalo, tel. 74/82–13–98) charges $50 per person (plus $8 for a fishing permit) for seven hours of marlin-, sailfish-, and tuna-fishing. All equipment and an English-speaking captain are included.

AFTER DARK

Acapulco's legendary disco scene is mind-boggling in its excess of mirrored walls, strobe lights, disco music, and laser beams; however, it does slow down during the low season (December through April). Covers average $15–$20 year-round, and in many cases drinks are as high as

$5. Women are in luck, though, as many discos offer cover-free nights for the superior sex. The deal to look for, assuming you are male and lack a company expense account, is a *barra libre* (free bar). This means there's a hefty cover, but all drinks are included in the price. If you want to go all out, there are even discos on ships that cruise Acapulco Bay, such as **Bonanza Cruise** (Costera Miguel Alemán, a few blocks west of the zócalo, tel. 74/83–18–03), which leaves daily at 11 AM, 4:30 PM, and 10:30 PM from the pier at Caleta Beach; $15 tickets include the three-hour trip, snacks, and an open bar. If you're into a calmer evening, check out **Los Amigos** (in front of Hotel Condesa) or **La Plaza de Mariachi** (Costera Miguel Alemán, at Mendoza) for a game of pool. There is also a handful of new, sparkling movie theaters that line the Costera in the Zona Dorada: Try **Cinepolis** (Costera Miguel Alemán, at Massieu, tel. 74/86–43–56) in La Gran Plaza.

BARS There are almost as many bars along the strip as there are fast-food places. **Carlos 'n' Charlie's** (Costera Miguel Alemán 999, tel. 74/84–00–39), open daily 6:30 PM–midnight, is usually a guaranteed rockin' good time; get there early or you'll wait in line. **The Hard Rock Café** (Costera Miguel Alemán 37, tel. 74/84–00–47) has live music and the standard funky paraphernalia, but is only open until 2 AM, which is pretty early by Acapulco standards.

DISCOS The latest hot spot for young locals and Americans is **The Palladium** (Carretera Escénica Las Brisas, tel. 74/81–03–00), open nightly 10:30 PM–6 AM. Sister clubs in San Francisco, New York, and L.A. explain the mini Statue of Liberty on one wall and the ghetto graffiti on the rest. It's packed throughout the week even though the cover is $22 for men and $17.50 for women: Tuesdays and Thursdays it's free before 12:30 AM for girls. Down the hill is **Extravanganza** (tel. 74/84–71–54), open nightly 10:30–6. Monday and Wednesday are open bar nights and covers range from zip to $22, depending on the night and your gender.

A mellow mix of salsa and rock plays at Acapulco's discos until around midnight, when the dance floor officially opens. (Don't be alarmed if everyone starts singing the national anthem.) From then on, it's pulsating techno.

Both of the above discos are not the type you'd want to walk into right off the beach—swimsuits and flip flops are a bit *gauche*. **Baby O** (Costera Miguel Alemán, near Nelson, tel. 74/84–74–74) is another popular spot with the 18–30 crowd, and is packed almost every night of the week during high season. The jungle decor seems to bring out the animals, and there's little chance of going home alone unless you're determined. There's no cover for women, but men pay $7 weeknights, $14 weekends. The bar inside is free, and the doors open at 10:30 PM. At **B&B** (Gran Vía Tropical 5, tel. 74/83–04–41), you'll hear American music from the '60s and '70s on the first floor and romantic Mexican pop on the second. B&B opens at 7 PM, the cover is $5, and drinks are $2–$3. This club is a distance from the zócalo, so you're better off taking a cab. **Disco Beach** (Costera Miguel Alemán, tel. 74/84–70–64) is a free (yes, free) outdoor disco in the middle of the strip overlooking the ocean. Expect lots of young muscle men, bleach blonds, and occasional $1 drink nights.

GAY/LESBIAN BARS AND DISCOS The gay bars in Acapulco are as active and seedy as the rest of the clubs. Most are conveniently clustered near Condensa Plaza, across the street from the Fiesta America Condensa. **Disco Demás** (Privada Piedra Picuda, tel. 74/84–13–70) is the best dance club, but it doesn't heat up until about 1 AM. Another happening dance spot, though smaller, is **Relax** (Lomas del Mar 4, tel. 74/84–04–21), open nightly 10–4 with a $4 cover. When you can't shake it anymore, descend to the bar, accentuated with erotic videos. **Open House Bar** (Plaza Condensa, tel. 74/84–72–85) has a small disco without cover, but it's more of a meet-up spot before heading off to the discos mentioned above. **Bar La Malinche** (Privada Piedra Picuda, tel. 74/81–11–47) also has a small cover-free disco, but is more of a bar scene. All of the above feature strippers at midnight, and Demas and Relax have drag shows. La Malinche gets hands-on—you can shower with the strippers for everyone's entertainment.

LIVE MUSIC Nina's (Costera Miguel Alemán 41, tel. 74/84–24–00), a dance place with live tropical and salsa music, is one of the few alternatives to disco hell. They open nightly at 10 PM, and the $12 cover includes drinks. **Cats** (Juan de la Cosa 32, tel. 74/84–72–35) is a similar salsa saloon that charges an $11 cover which includes all the alcohol you can drink. Cats opens nightly at 10 PM, there's a drag show at 1 AM, and the bar closes at 4 AM. The city's best after-bar, **Faces,** open nightly 4 AM–4 PM, picks up where Cats left off (and it's right next door).

Near Acapulco

PIE DE LA CUESTA

This stretch of sand is only 15 kilometers northwest of Acapulco. Residents don't swim here at all though, due to the incredibly forceful current and riptide: Two or three people, usually for-eigners, are killed each year. However, **Laguna de Coyuca,** just on the other side of the street, is a lake of *agua dulce*—sweet, fresh water. Although the area around the lagoon is not safe at night, during the day locals and tourists take advantage of its calm waters for swimming, waterskiing, and just plain escaping Acapulco. At **Tres Marías** (Fuerza Aerea Mexicana 375, tel. 74/60–00–11), an hour of waterskiing costs $28. For a less exhausting excursion on the laguna, take a boat tour (4½ hrs, $4) to the *barra* (sandbar), a beautiful swimming area. Boats take you through a swamp of thick mangrove trees and past **Isla de los Pájaros**—a bird sanctuary inhabited by peli-cans, flamingos, and storks. Boats leave daily at 11 AM from **Club de Ski Chuy** (Fuerza Aerea Mex-icana, tel. 74/60–11–04). To reach Pie de la Cuesta from Acapulco, catch an eastbound PIE DE LA CUESTA bus (½ hr, 15¢) on Costera, across the street from the post office.

WHERE TO SLEEP Pitching tents randomly along the beach is not safe—your stuff will get stolen. Women especially should be cautious around the beach and the laguna. The **Acapulco Trailer Park** (Fuerza Aerea Mexicana 381, tel. 74/60–00–10) is right on the beach and charges $5 for one or two people. Bring your own tent, and the park will provide water, bath-rooms, showers, and security. If you'd rather not camp, try **Villa Nirvana** (Playa Pie de la Cuesta 302, tel. 74/60–16–31), just steps away from the ocean, where clean, airy rooms with fans and terraces cost $16 (singles) and $25 (doubles). Discounts are available for stays of three or more nights during the low season, and owners Rosanna and Stan are friendly, helpful, and speak English. **Bungalows María Cristina** (Fuerza Aerea Mexicana 351, tel. 74/60–02–62, fax 74/60–30–33) offers homey bungalows directly on the beach and across the street from the tranquil lagoon. Rates are $21 for one or two people in the high season, $17.50 in the low sea-son. Year-round, it costs $4 for each extra person, and $42 for the whole bungalow.

FOOD Restaurants in Pie de la Cuesta are famous for their fresh seafood. The main strip, Fuerza Aerea Mexicana, is lined with small hotels, most of which sport their own beachfront restaurant. During low season, the wheelchair-accessible **El Zanate** (Fuerza Aerea Mexicana 693, tel. 74/60–17–09; open daily 6 AM–11 PM) has a $1.50 comida corrida. In the high sea-son, referred to by owner Berta as "the time of the gringos," they have a wide selection of fresh fish and "whatever else the gringos want." **Tres Marías** (*see above*; open daily 7 AM–8 PM) is popular with locals for its cordial service. There are two locations: a remodeled, more popular branch by the lagoon and another across the street on the beach. The specialty is the fried fish fillet ($9), but tacos are three for $2.

CHILPANCINGO

If you've partied a little too heartily in Acapulco's world-famous discos, then spend a day or two in Chilpancingo. Neither as glamorous as its infamous beach neighbor nor as ridden with shopaholics as Taxco to the north, Guerrero's state capital is an agricultural center and univer-sity town that may give you that needed break from the well-trodden tourist circuit. Little of historical importance has happened here since the Mexican Declaration of Independence was signed here in 1813, and the result is a place where you can enjoy a few *cervezas,* gaze out at the green hills, and shoot the breeze with regular folks.

BASICS Banamex (Zapata, on NW cnr of zócalo, at Morelos, tel. 747/2–20–20; open week-days 9–3) changes cash and traveler's checks; its ATM accepts Cirrus and Plus cards. You can make collect calls from the public **phones** on the zócalo, but for fax and other long-distance calls, go to **Caseta Auxiliar** (Ignacio Ramirez 9, 1 block east of zócalo, tel. and fax 747/2–94–

10), open daily 8 AM–10:30PM. Bring your mail to the tiny **post office** (Hidalgo 9, tel. 747/2–22–75; open weekdays 8–6, Sat. 9–1), two blocks west of the zócalo.

COMING AND GOING Estrella Blanca (21 de Marzo, tel. 747/2–06–34) sends direct buses hourly to Mexico City (3½ hrs, $12), every half hour to Acapulco (1 hr, $4.50), and three times daily to Taxco (3 hrs, $4.50). To reach the center of town from the station, turn right as you exit and walk two blocks to Juárez, where you can catch a red-and-white bus to the zócalo (10 min, 25¢). To return to the bus station from the zócalo, catch a bus on Guerrero, which runs parallel to Juárez.

WHERE TO SLEEP While part of Chilpancingo's charm is its unaffected atmosphere, when it comes to lodging, you'll wish the city was equipped to deal with tourists. **Hotel Cardeña** (Madero 13, no phone), in a former mansion one block off the zócalo, has rooms that open onto a courtyard. A smaller courtyard has a few stone washbasins in which you're welcome to scrub your clothes. Rooms are plain, and the bathrooms are only as frightening as the occasional cockroach. Singles cost $4 ($6 with bath); doubles are $5.50 ($10 with bath). The wheelchair-accessible **Hotel Roble** (Cuauhtémoc 5, 3 blocks west of the zócalo, tel. 747/2–53–23) is a slightly better choice, with remodeled rooms and an owner who's a fun, easygoing kind of guy. The price is just $7 for one or two people; TV costs $1.50 extra.

FOOD Cheap restaurants and cafés crammed with students are common on the zócalo and the streets surrounding it. Here, competition and student budgets keep the quality high and the prices low. In the student center on the zócalo, **Restaurante and Cafetería Casino del Estudiante** (Guerrero, at Madero, no phone), serves up hearty food at rock-bottom prices. The comida corrida includes soup, an entrée, and beans, all for $1.50. **El Portal** (NW side of the zócalo, near Madero and Guerrero, tel. 747/2–46–68) is an open-air café that serves big $2 breakfasts with coffee, fruit, and your choice of eggs or pancakes. They also have delicious $1 *aguas preparadas* (juice drinks). **Ton's Que** (Portales Also Centro, tel. 747/2–12–32), on the zócalo near Guerrero and Madero, is a restaurant and bar where local college students kick it. A beer is $1 and their speciality pizza will stuff two people for $4. For inexpensive fruits, vegetables, bread, meat, and cheese, head to the huge market on Guerrero near the bus station.

WORTH SEEING Chilpancingo is untouristed, and students of the Universidad de Guerrero fill the city's zócalo. The student center, **Casino del Estudiante** (Guerrero, at Madero, no phone) is a great place to hang out: It's full of people, Ping-Pong tables, and bulletin boards advertising upcoming dances, concerts, and movies. Although the university itself is a concrete atrocity, it's worth visiting to check out the event notices in the hallways. If you can't kick your museum habit, the **Instituto Guerrerense de la Cultura** is right on the zócalo and contains some impressive murals depicting local and national historical events. The **Museo Regional de Guerrero** (tel. 747/2–80–88; open Sun.–Fri. 11–6) is housed within the Instituto, and has a small but interesting collection of pre-Columbian artifacts, as well as relics from the colonial period. Admission is free. If you didn't get enough shopping done in Taxco or Acapulco, you can buy local crafts at **La Casa de Artesanías** (open weekdays 9–9). To get here, take the URBANOS or JACARANDA combi from Avenida Insurgentes in front of the market.

CENTRAL CITIES   10

By Olivia Barry, with Andrew Dean Nystrom

While traveling through the central cities of Mexico, you'll likely be asked, "Have you visited Mexico before?" Answering "Yes, I've been to Tijuana" will evoke the castigating response: "No, no. That's not Mexico. *This* is Mexico." Although American culture has saturated the country's border towns and beach communities, the central region of Mexico, consisting of the states of Tlaxcala, Puebla, Morelos, and part of Guerrero, has managed to hold on to traditional Mexican culture. In spite of the Woolworth's and McDonald's that have gradually invaded and set up permanent camp, the Mexican people here haven't forgotten who they are, and mariachis, *artesanía* (handicrafts), and Mexican-owned businesses continue to prevail over U.S. pop music, imported goods, and foreign conglomerates.

As you travel throughout this region, you'll notice that the struggle to resist outside influences isn't just a recent phenomenon. Almost all of the area's early civilizations—the Toltec, Mixtec, Zapotec, Tlahuica, and Xilanca tribes—reflect some Mayan influence, and were subject to several Aztec attacks. However, none of these tribes were fully overthrown until the Spaniards arrived; the numerous colonial churches built on or near indigenous pyramids testify to the Spaniards' religious and cultural dominance. This dominance, however, was not met passively: One of the most dramatic battles ever fought against the Spanish, the War of Independence, took place in Cuautla. In 1862, the region once again wrenched free of foreign control when Puebla won a decisive battle against French invaders, commemorated annually on Cinco de Mayo. In another act of resistance, Emiliano Zapata issued his call for land reform in Ayala in 1910. You'll see memorials to the turbulent War of Independence and the Revolution of 1910 in the imposing stone fortresses and bullet-riddled palaces throughout the region.

Landmarks of the central cities' pre-Columbian and colonial past are what draw Mexican tourists here, in spite of the chaos of expanding cities. After bum rushing the numerous museums, ruins, and gardens throughout the region, be sure to get that *true* Mexican experience: Sample the curative waters in Tlaxcala, feast on Puebla's renowned *mole,* learn to speak Nahuatl from the Tlahuican healers in Tepoztlán, and attend mass in Taxco's Catedral de Santa Prisca.

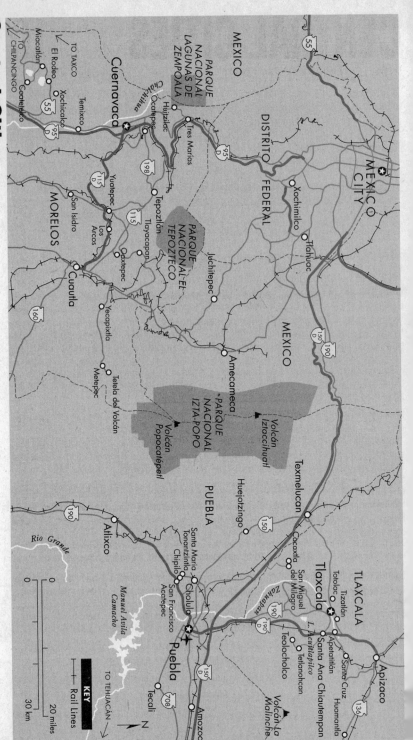

Tlaxcala

Tlaxcala, meaning "the land of corn" in Nahuatl, is a tiny state, only two and a half times the size of Mexico City. It's also among Mexico's poorest states: Most of its inhabitants rely on their *milpas* (small plots of land on which corn is grown) for subsistence. Tlaxcala city, the state's capital, lies only two hours east of hectic Mexico City but has remained relatively small—touting a population of 8,000—and unaffected by urban chaos. Like other central cities, Tlaxcala remains a reserved and conservative town whose friendly residents won't hesitate to introduce themselves to visitors. Though Tlaxcalans remain proud of both their indigenous heritage and the fact that their town was the first Catholic diocese in Mexico, residents are not without a sense of irony about this fusion of cultures: Today, the official name of the city is "Tlaxcala de Xicohténcatl," in honor of the only Tlaxcalan chieftain who opposed an alliance with Hernán Cortés (*see* Tizatlán, Worth Seeing, *below*).

The delicate arches surrounding the zócalo and the terraces overlooking the streets are just two traits that characterize Tlaxcala city as inviting and tranquil. The close proximity of the numerous historical sites provides a chance to see everything at a leisurely pace. But don't limit yourself: Exploring the **Cacaxtla** archaeological ruins, hiking the **Volcán La Malintzi,** and sampling the curative waters supposedly brought by the Virgin Mary only involve short trips beyond the city.

BASICS

CASAS DE CAMBIO Change dollars or traveler's checks weekdays 9–3 at **Banamex** (Plaza Xicohténcatl, 50 meters east of Independencia, tel. 246/2–25–36). The ATMs here accept MasterCard, Visa, and Plus and Cirrus system cards. You can also change cash and traveler's checks weekdays 9–4 at the **Casa de Cambio** (Independencia 3, at Morelos, tel. 246/2–90–85).

EMERGENCIES In an emergency call the **police** (tel. 246/2–07–35); for the **Cruz Roja** (ambulance service) call 246/2–09–20.

LAUNDRY **Lavandería San Felipe** charges $3 to wash 3 kilos of laundry. *Guridi y Alcocer 30, btw Juárez and Lira y Ortega, no phone. Open weekdays 8–7, Sat. 8:30–2.*

MAIL The full-service post office on the zócalo will hold mail sent to you at the following address for up to 10 days: Lista de Correos, Tlaxcala, Tlaxcala, CP 90000, México. *Plaza de la Constitución 20, at Morelos, tel. 246/2–00–04. Open weekdays 8–8.*

MEDICAL AID **Central Médico** (Guridi y Alcocer 40-A, btw Juárez and Lira y Ortega, tel. 246/2–58–51) provides medical services 24 hours a day and has an English-speaking doctor. For less serious medical problems, **Farmacia Mora** (Guerrero 10, at Independencia, no phone) is open 24 hours.

PHONES To make a collect call, use one of the many pay phones around town. On the main plaza, **Ladatel** phones allow long-distance calls, but first you'll have to buy a card at the **telephone office** (Guridi y Alcocer 7; open weekdays 8–4), or at the **Gómez-Esparza Papelería y Fotografía** (main address: Julian Carrillo, at Lira y Ortega, tel. 246/2–34–57; open Mon.–Sat. 9–8) chain. For cash calls and faxes, try the *caseta de larga distancia* (long-distance telephone office; Independencia, on west side of Plaza Xicohténcatl, fax 246/2–56–72), which is open Monday–Saturday 9–8:30.

VISITOR INFORMATION The **Secretary of Tourism**'s information desk is staffed by eager young people who distribute numerous flyers and can arrange for guided tours of the nearby attractions with a week's notice. *Juárez, at Lardizábal, tel. 246/2–00–27. Open weekdays 9– 7, weekends 10–6.*

COMING AND GOING

BY BUS The **Central Camionera** (tel. 246/2–03–62) is eight blocks west of the zócalo. From here, **ATAH** (tel. 246/2–02–17) runs buses to Mexico City (2 hrs, $4.50) every 15 minutes 4:30 AM–11:30 PM. **Flecha Azul** (tel. 246/2–33–92) sends buses to Puebla (45 min,

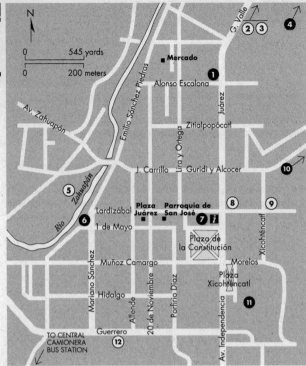

Tlaxcala

N

0 — 545 yards
0 — 200 meters

■ Mercado

Alonso Escalona

Av. Zahuapán

Emilio Sánchez Piedras

Zitlalpopócatl

Lira y Ortega

Juárez

G. Valle

② ③   **4**

1

J. Carrillo   Guridi y Alcocer

10

Río Zahuapán

5

6

Lardizábal   **Plaza Juárez** ■   **Parroquia de San José** ■

8   **9**

7 🛈

1 de Mayo

Muñoz Camargo

Mariana Sánchez

Hidalgo

Allende

20 de Noviembre

Porfirio Díaz

Plaza de la Constitución

Morelos

Plaza Xicohténcatl

Xicohténcatl

Av. Independencia

11

Guerrero

12

TO CENTRAL
CAMIONERA
BUS STATION

70¢) every eight minutes 5:30 AM–9 PM. To reach the zócalo from the bus station, take any CEN-TRO or SANTA ANA colectivo. Those marked CENTRAL head to the bus station from the corner of Lira y Ortega and Lardizábal.

BY CAR Having your own car makes travel to the many attractions just outside Tlaxcala city much easier. From Tlaxcala, it's an easy two-hour (120-km) drive to Mexico City on highway Puebla–Mexico. Three toll stops, totaling a whopping $13.50, keep this highway in good shape. Carretera de Cuatro Carriles, via Santa Ana, takes you on a smooth ride to Puebla (1 hr) with no toll fees.

GETTING AROUND

Tlaxcala is a walkable city. The main street running roughly north–south is called Independencia on the south side of Plaza de la Constitución (the zócalo), becoming Juárez, then Guillermo Valle, and finally Boulevard Revolución as you proceed north. Most anything of interest lies near or along Independencia/Juárez in the downtown area.

Colectivos—both *combis* (VW van look-alikes) and small buses—travel up and down the main drag, as well as to neighboring towns and the Central Camionera. Those heading north leave from the stop in front of Plaza Xicohténcatl on Independencia; those heading south, west, and to the Central Camionera depart from the northwest corner of the intersection of Lira y Ortega and Lardizábal. Colectivos cost 20¢ within town and to nearby cities and stop running at about 10 PM. Taxi stands are situated in front of the southern porch of the zócalo and Parroquia de San José. Within Tlaxcala, taxi fares should stay under $2, and a ride to nearby Santa Ana is $3.50. Unless you have heavy luggage, you probably won't even need a taxi.

WHERE TO SLEEP

Hotels here reflect the fact that Tlaxcala's visitors are few and far between. With no business to compete for, many hotel owners tend to veg out in front of the TV and forget they have a place to run. Reservations are only required during the fairs in October and May, and during the first week of July, when summer sessions start at the university. If the places below are full, your only alternative is a luxury hotel. The most affordable of these is **Hotel Jeroc's** (Revolución 4, tel. 246/2–15–77), which charges $30 for a single and $43 for a double.

➤ **UNDER $10** • **Hotel Zahuapán.** This hotel borders the river (meaning a slightly nasty odor from the water) and is a little tricky to find, especially at night. Once you get here though, you'll be greeted by a bubblegum-pink or aquamarine bedroom, a bathroom with hot water, and a tiny TV. Patrons come and go in silence, so you'll get some peace and quiet. It's $5.50 for one or two people. *Río Zahuapán 1, tel. 246/2–59–86. From center, take Guridi y Alcocer until it becomes J. Carillo, cross bridge, and walk down driveway on left where hotel's name is posted. 20 rooms, all with bath. Luggage storage. Reservations advised in summer.*

Posada Mary. This establishment, smack in the center of town, is cheap—just $5.50 for one or two people—and you get your own bath, access to a casual restaurant, and a young, friendly manager at your service. The rooms are small and unspectacular, however, with no amenities. *Xicohténcatl 19, at Lardizábal, no phone. 10 rooms, all with bath. Laundry, luggage storage. Wheelchair access.*

➤ **UNDER $15** • **Hotel Mansión de Xicohténcatl.** Not exactly the mansion it claims to be, this place is smack-dab in the middle of town. Rooms are clean but drab, and a few have small balconies. If you're a woman traveling alone, you might get some unwanted attention, but if you can ignore it, you'll find the hot showers and great location worth your while. Knock at the front door if you arrive after midnight. Singles cost $7.50, doubles $8.50. *Juárez 15, tel. 246/2–19–00. 1 block north of zócalo. 18 rooms, all with bath.*

Hotel Plaza-Tlaxcala. Next door to Hotel Jeroc's sits this quiet but popular hotel, complete with a gigantic garden, an underused playground, and a restaurant. Remodeled rooms have white-and-blue decor and color TVs with cable. It's pretty far from the center of town, but rooms are a bargain at $11 for a single, $12 for a double. *Revolución 6, tel. 246/2–78–52. From center or bus station, take a SANTA ANA combi; you'll see Hotel Jeroc's sign on left. 12 rooms, all with bath. Luggage storage.*

➤ **UNDER $20** • **Albergue de La Loma.** Perched atop a hill overlooking Tlaxcala, this hotel is nonetheless only four blocks from the center. Come here if you want to pamper yourself—the clean rooms are large and airy and equipped with phones, TVs, carpet, a panoramic view of Tlaxcala, and a restaurant. Singles cost $16.50, doubles $20. *Guerrero 58, at Allende, tel. 246/2–04–24. 24 rooms, all with bath. Luggage storage. MC, V.*

FOOD

Most of Tlaxcala's restaurants cluster around the zócalo and Plaza Xicohténcatl. People here seem to favor anything that isn't Mexican, but you'll also find plenty of regional specialties, including *pollo tocotlán* (chicken in maguey salsa, cooked in a thin paper bag). For the cheapest food in town, try the taco stands off 20 de Noviembre, near Plaza Juárez, which stay open late. Drinks are room temperature, the salsa is searing, and you'll probably have to eat standing up, but tacos are 20¢ each. Another option is the *rosticerías* (restaurants specializing in roasted chicken) where a whole chicken with a side of tortillas, beans, *rajas* (chile strips), and salsa costs $2. Several are located near the market, which extends from Emilio Sánchez Piedras to Lira y Ortega along Alonso Escalona. Try **El Pollo Rey,** open daily 8 AM–9 PM: You can't miss it—there's a string of dead chickens for sale at the entrance.

➤ **UNDER $5** • **La Fonda del Convento.** On the cobblestone path that runs between the Ex-Convento and Plaza Xicohténcatl, this popular restaurant is small, quiet, and enclosed. The *carne fonda del convento* (steak served with an enchilada, rice, fries, beans, and guacamole) costs $3.50. *Calzada de San Francisco 1, tel. 246/2–07–65. Open Mon.–Sat. 10–8.*

Los Portales. Squeezed between the multitudes of restaurants on the zócalo, this place is popular for its $2 breakfasts (enchiladas or ham and eggs, served with fresh-squeezed orange juice, melon, coffee, and all the bread and jam you can eat). Other options include the traditional $3 *pollo en pipián* (chicken in chile and pumpkinseed sauce), a variety of $4 steaks, and exotic hamburgers. There's al fresco dining on the porch, and salsa and merengue music highlight Friday and Saturday nights. *Independencia 8, on west side of zócalo, tel. 246/2–54–19. Open Sun.–Thurs. 7 AM–midnight, Fri. and Sat. 24 hrs. Wheelchair access.*

El Quinto Sol. Vegans will rejoice at the presence of soy milk on the breakfast menu—it's served hot and tastes suspiciously like *atole* (a sweet, corn-based drink). Add bread, fruit, yogurt, and some excellent granola, and you have breakfast for $1. The lunch menu varies, offering creative dishes such as soy steak. *Juárez 15, at Lardizábal, tel. 246/2–49–28. Next to Hotel Mansión de Xicohténcatl. Open weekdays 8–7, Sat. 8–6.*

➢ **UNDER $10** • **El Mesón Taurino.** This place is next to Plaza de Toros, and its ambience is marred only by the severed bull heads staring down at you as you eat—try dining in the patio room or outdoors in the garden. Although it's open for breakfast, this restaurant's forte is dinner, when pasta dishes cost $3–$4. For just a bit more you can have filet mignon in mushroom sauce ($5.50) or *filete Cacaxtla* ($6), steak topped with *huitlacoche* (a fungus grown on corn) and chile strips. *Independencia 12, at Guerrero, tel. 246/2–43–66. Open weekdays 7 AM–8 PM, weekends 11–8.*

WORTH SEEING

Tlaxcala's main points of interest all lie within walking distance of the zócalo and can be seen in a day or two. **Plaza de la Constitución** is quieter than most Mexican zócalos; goods are only sold here during fairs and weekend markets. Along the western edge of the plaza sits **Casa de Piedra,** a colonial-era house with a distinctive stone facade. Legend has it that the doctor who lived here asked his poor patients to pay with a stone of a certain size. In this manner, he went about building his house, stone by stone. Dominating the adjacent **Plaza Xicohténcatl** is a monument to the *cacique* (chieftain) of that name, who was hanged by the Spaniards after the successful assault on Tenochtitlán for refusing to participate in the slaughter of the Aztec people. From here, walk along the **Paseo de la Amistad** (Friendship Walkway), where amorous couples, kids on bikes, and elderly folks alike enjoy the sunshine.

Music lovers should check out Avenida Muñoz Camargo, between Díaz and Allende: Several mariachi bands have small shops here, and in the afternoon they suit up and practice before hitting the lunch and dinner crowds. The interested should not be shy— the musicians are generally more than happy to answer questions about their art.

BASILICA DE OCOTLAN This hillside shrine is one of Mexico's national treasures, and is considered the region's best example of the ornate Churrigueresque (ultra-baroque) style. The basilica's gleaming white plaster facade is carved with intricate figures and flanked by two 33-meter-high towers. These are symbolically tiled in red and sky blue; red and white are the colors of the flag of the ancient kingdom Tlaxcallan, and blue symbolizes the Virgin, in whose honor the shrine was built in 1640. According to church history, the Virgin appeared to a pious *indígena* (indigenous person) here in answer to his prayers for water during a drought.

Upon entering the basilica, you'll be bedazzled by the glittering **Chamber of the Virgin,** where a statue of **Our Lady of Ocotlán** is housed. It took sculptor Francisco Miguel Tlayoltehuamintzin 25 years to complete, and every single inch is gold plated and glimmering. Opposite the entrance to the basilica is a small alley leading to a papier mâché miniature of the basilica and the hillside. A sign overhead reads "Así se apareció la Virgen de Ocotlán" ("Thus appeared the Virgin of Ocotlán"). To sample the curative waters that the Virgin brought to the hillside, walk 10 minutes down the steep cobblestone road to **Capilla del Pocito de Agua Milagrosa,** a tiny, round chapel housing a well of the sweet, fresh water. The chapel walls are brightly decorated with a series of murals depicting biblical themes related to water, designed by Desiderio Hernández Xochitiotzin (*see* Palacio de Gobierno, *below*). Although the Virgin is quoted overhead as saying that the smallest drop of the water will bring perfect health, locals and tourists alike take bucketfuls away with them. Bring an empty water bottle or buy one of the brightly colored jugs for sale along the way. *From zócalo, north on Juárez, right at Guridi y Alcocer, left at Calzada de los Misterios, and uphill 2 km. Or take OCOTLAN combi from bus station and get off at basilica. Admission free. Open daily until dusk.*

EX-CONVENTO DE SAN FRANCISCO More than just a religious site, this former convent was witness to some key moments in Mexico's history: Services were held here before Cortés marched on to Tenochtitlán (present-day Mexico City). One of the oldest parts of the structure, the **Capilla Abierta** (Open Chapel), is thought to be the earliest 16th-century construction of its type in New Spain. Up the stairs and across the courtyard is the **Catedral de Nuestra Señora de la Asunción** and a beautiful view of Tlaxcala city. Built in 1526 after Tlaxcala was declared the first diocese in New Spain, the cathedral is known for its cedar ceiling, carved in the geometric mosarabe style. Here the four *caciques* (chiefs) of Tlaxcala were converted at the baptismal font, with Cortés and Alvarado acting as godfathers. The small **Museo Regional de Tlaxcala** (admission $1; open daily 10–5), next to the convent, specializes in Tlaxcalan archeology and paintings, tracing the history of the conquest through both mediums. *From zócalo, walk 1 block south past Plaza Xicohténcatl and turn left at Calzada de Capilla Abierta. Mass held daily at 6 PM.*

The atrium of the Ex-Convento is known to locals as "el jardín del pulpo" (octopus garden) because of all the groping that goes on here in the late evening.

JARDIN BOTANICO TIZATLAN This conservation garden sprouts flora characteristic of the *altiplano* (highland) region. Plants are labeled with both scientific and common names, and some have descriptions of their medicinal and practical uses. The Jardín is a good place for picnics or trysts, so bring a lunch or a lover. Tours are available weekdays in Spanish only; call 246/2–39–96 for reservations. Also in the garden, the **Sala Miguel Lira** theater (tel. 246/2–46–85) shows cultural films from around the world Tuesday–Sunday. Call to ask what's showing and when. *From zócalo, take SANTA ANA combi, get off just before aqueduct at Camino Real and bear to left 100 meters. Admission free. Open daily 9–5.*

MUSEO DE ARTES Y TRADICIONES DE TLAXCALA This living history museum is an unusually active and fun experience. In the first room, filled with paintings and ancient artifacts, videotapes explain the early history of Tlaxcala. Outside is an orginal stone steam bath used by the Otomí for bathing and healing. Two Otomí women take a break from weaving to guide you through the replica of a typical rural house. There's also an area dedicated to the process of making *pulque* (alcohol made from maguey). Ask permission before taking photographs. *Emilio Sánchez Piedras 1, at 1 de Mayo, tel. 246/2–23–37. Admission: $1, 50¢ students; free Tues. Open Tues.–Sun. 10–6.*

PALACIO DE GOBIERNO Now the municipal headquarters, this palace was built for Hernán Cortés around 1550. The interior walls are covered with spectacular, colorful murals painted by Desiderio Hernández Xochitiotzin, who had close ties to Diego Rivera. The murals depict symbolic and prophetic figures; the stairwell, for example, illustrates the heavens overrun by fantastic creatures, as gods plunge headfirst to the earth. You can wander around for as long as you like, so long as you steer clear of the government offices. Spanish-speaking guides from the tourist office provide a better background on the murals than the explanations painted on the walls. *North side of zócalo, tel. 246/2–00–06. Admission free. Open daily 8–8.*

PALACIO DE LA CULTURA This sprawling building, surrounded by an immaculate garden, houses Tlaxcala's cultural center. The first floor contains a **Sala de Cultura** with temporary exhibits by Tlaxcalan and national artists. Check the bulletin at the entrance for upcoming musical events. *Juárez, at Alonso Escalona, tel. 246/2–27–29. Admission free. Open Mon.–Sat. 9–8.*

FESTIVALS

Late February: The best festival in Tlaxcala is **Carnaval**, celebrated the week prior to Ash Wednesday. The event is characterized by bullfights and street parades in which people dance around wearing masks and costumes. Each village uses a specific color or design for its masks.

July 6: In 1591 a group of 400 Christianized Tlaxcalan families left Tlaxcala under orders from King Philip II of Spain and Pope Gregory XIV to colonize the north of "New Spain." An impressive reenactment of their departure takes place at the ruins of the **Convento de Nuestra Señora de las Nieves** in the town of **Totolac** (half a kilometer from Tlaxcala, on the road to San Martín Texmelucan) during the **Celebración de las Cuatrocientas Familias** (Celebration of the 400 Families). The highlight is a candlelight procession down from the hills.

August 15: The **Fiesta de la Asunción** in Huamantla (*see* Near Tlaxcala, *below*), about a half hour east of Tlaxcala, is a two-week festival celebrating the Assumption and the Virgin of Charity. The highlight is when a figure of the Virgin is paraded through the streets, which are carpeted with flowers arranged in symbolic designs. The procession ends when the sun rises, and the running of the bulls, à la Pamplona, begins. To reach Huamantla, catch a bus ($1) from the station in Tlaxcala.

October 8–13: The **Fería del Pan** in the town of Totolac is a typical Tlaxcalan festival with dancing and fireworks. The bread baked for the festival, Pan de Fiesta, is famous throughout Tlaxcala state, and can be purchased year-round in the pueblitos of San Juan de Dolac and San Juan de Huactzinco. The fruit-filled breads are only sold in private homes; ask around or look for signs posted on houses.

Late October: The **Tlaxcala Fair** features bullfights, *charreadas* (rodeos), cockfights, indigenous dances, carnival rides, and exhibitions of local handicrafts. The fair lasts two weeks, usually until early November.

AFTER DARK

Though the cafés on the zócalo are crowded in the evenings, Tlaxcalans generally retire early. During festivals and in July and August, students from Mexico City descend on Tlaxcala, causing things to pick up a bit. As for the rest of the year, if you go out after 10 PM, you've missed whatever action there was. If you just can't stay in, hook up with someone with a car to *dar una vuelta* (drive around aimlessly to see who else is also driving around), the activity of choice among local teenagers. Or, you can always catch a movie: Both **Cinema Tlaxcala** (tel. 246/2–19–62), on the south side of the zócalo, and **Cinemas 1 y 2** (G. Valle 113, tel. 246/2–35–44), 6½ blocks north of the center, show fairly recent Hollywood films with Spanish subtitles, as well as Mexican films. Shows cost $1.50.

"Alebrijes" are colorful, mythical creatures that look like flying iguanas or snakes; they were created out of delirium by a Mexican artist during a severe fever. Don't miss the chance to see them looming over the bar and tables at La Casa de los Alebrijes.

BARS AND MUSIC Several bars play music; most others are seedy cantinas where women are unwelcome. The best bar in town is **La Casa de los Alebrijes** (1 de Mayo 9, btw Allende and Sánchez, no phone) where a DJ mixes rock music Monday–Saturday 6 PM–2 AM, except Thursdays when there's *música protesta* (protest music)—slow and romantic despite its name. On weekends, live bands play alternative rock in English and Spanish. **Bar Tendido 7** (Plaza de la Constitución 19, at Porfirio Díaz, tel. 246/2–86–87) is open daily noon–midnight, with live music Thursday–Saturday. Don't be scared away by songs like "Bad Medicine" blaring in the tiny **Café Rock-Ola Fox** (tel. 246/2–80–62), downstairs from Bar Tendido 7. The café features live rock music ($3 cover) twice a month and the crowd is, according to the owner, 100% *jóvenes* (young people). Beers go for about $1 at all three places.

DANCING Most dancing occurs at weddings, *quinceañeras* (girls' 15th-birthday parties), and festivals. If you haven't been invited to any of these, you don't have much else to choose from. **Century** (20 de Novembre, at Hidalgo, tel. 246/2–78–33), close to the center of town, plays American and Mexican techno hits, and draws a young student crowd. It's open Wednesday–Sunday 5 PM–midnight and until 3 AM on weekends with a $2 cover. You can also shake it at **Armando's** (Independencia 60-B, tel. 246/2–49–88; open Thurs.–Sun. 9 PM–3 AM), where cheesy techno, endless mirrors, and Madonna posters dominate the scene. **Royal Adler's** (Revolución 4, tel. 246/2–15–77), in Hotel Jeroc's, is the most decent and popular disco at present. DJs mix techno with Latin hits, and locals cram the dance floor on weekends. The attire is dressy, cover is $1.50, drinks run $2, and it's open Wednesday–Saturday 9 PM–4 AM.

Near Tlaxcala

The preserved colonial town of **Huamantla,** 45 kilometers west of Tlaxcala city, was founded in 1534, and provides enough sights for a good day's explorations. If you're dying to see a bullfight, most occur here June–August and are well publicized. The baroque **Convento de San Luis Obispo** is across the street from the free **Museo Taurino** (Allende Nte. 203; open Wed.–Sun. 9–4), which features posters, costumes, swords, and photographs of bullfighting. The nearby **Museo Nacional del Títere** (National Museum of the Puppets; open Tues.–Sun. 10–2 and 5–7) showcases various puppets and marionettes. It costs $1.50 to enter. There's also a popular disco in town called **Fantasy** (Morelos Pte. 105, tel. 247/2–02–57). To reach Huamantla, take an ATAH bus (1 hr, $1) from the Central Camionera in Tlaxcala.

If you've seen enough churches and museums, take a break at **Centro Vacacional La Trinidad,** 15 kilometers northwest of Tlaxcala city in **Santa Cruz.** This resort lies on the banks of the Río Tequixquiatl, and you can swim in the cool water, go boating, and, on the weekends, ride horses. Rooms in the ajoining **Hotel Balneario** (tel. 246/1–03–33) are $24 for a double, or you can camp on the hotel grounds for $3. Toilets, showers, and a water cistern are available in the tree-shaded camping area. Colectivos (70¢) run from the Central Camionera in Tlaxcala to directly in front of Hotel Balneario. Another place for swimming, boating, and horseback riding is **Centro Turístico Efidal de Atlangatepec,** a dammed lake 41 kilometers (1½ hrs) north of Tlaxcala city. Nearby are an Apache fort and an Indian village. To get here, take a bus from Tlaxcala's Central Camionera to Apizaco and transfer to Atlangatepec.

PARQUE NACIONAL LA MALINTZI

At 4,461 meters, **Parque Nacional La Malintzi** comprises the highest region in Tlaxcala. The park is most well known for the beautiful volcano of the same name that rests quietly within its boundaries. Guides for the three-hour trek to the summit of La Malintzi aren't necessary, but they're usually available on weekends and charge $5–$7 per person. Hiking within the forest here is also great, except during the rainy season (July–September), when it's most dangerous.

La Malintzi volcano was named after the woman who was the translator and mistress of Hernán Cortés.

The Parque Nacional lies 43 kilometers southeast of Tlaxcala city, and can be reached by bus in 1½ hours. From the Central Camionera or the market in Tlaxcala, take a bus to Huamantla; from there catch another bus to **Centro Vacacional La Malintzi** (tel. 246/2–40–98), a government-run resort. You can camp here for $3 per person, or rent one of the six-person cabins for $35 a night. There's a restaurant here, but it's pricey, so bring food and water for the hike.

CACAXTLA

Cacaxtla, 19 kilometers southwest of Tlaxcala city, consists of a group of pyramids covering a space the size of four football fields, each with an amazing view of the endless cornfields from their respective summits—a sure sign of the strategic importance of these temples in pre-Columbian times. In 1975 a series of vivid polychrome murals was discovered here—one of the most important Mesoamerican archaeological finds in the past 50 years. Today you can still see these astonishingly well-preserved works, which are unique in their realistic style and detail.

The current theory holds that the murals were painted by the Xicalanca, a group of warrior merchants who arrived in the Tlaxcala Valley in AD 100 and were never conquered by the Aztec. The Xicalanca were descendants of the Maya, which explains why their murals contain elements more commonly found in southern Mexico. The murals date back to AD 600 and consist of five colors—white, red, yellow, blue, and black—produced from nopal cactus juice mixed with ground yellow ochre, ground charcoal, and red hematite. The figures adorned with blue body paint represent sacrificial victims, and the five-pointed stars are symbols of the goddess of fertility. Cacaxtla means "place where the water dies in the earth," and you'll see repeated representations of water and of Tlaloc, a rain god to whom human sacrifices were offered. The murals appear to have been deliberately preserved by the Indians: Archaeologists have discovered a layer of fine sand protecting the murals and a heavier filler added before each new part of the buildings was constructed. Modern protective coverings include an ugly, towering metal dome that you'll see from the entrance.

The Xicalanca, like the Maya, believed that human beings were made of corn.

The first set of murals, painted on columns flanking the entrance to a small room, depicts barefoot blue dancers. Archaeologists refer to this room as the **Star Chamber,** because the dancers are surrounded by five-pointed stars. It may have been here that captives were prepared for sacrifice. The next mural to the right represents water, fertility, and trade. Note that the ears of corn are actually human faces. The **Red Temple** is identifiable by the bands of red paint that run along the bottom of the walls, like a sea of blood. Unfortunately, the general public is not allowed inside the Red Temple: Murals depicting prisoners are painted on the floor of the temple and cannot be walked on.

The **battle mural** for which Cacaxtla is most renowned is found just beyond the Red Temple. The 48 victors wear jaguar pelts, and the vanquished wear bird headdresses. One interpretation is that the mural depicts the aftermath of a real-life battle; others speculate that it only symbolizes a confrontation between the two ethnic groups, whose union eventually gave rise to the Olmec-Xicalanca people. A final set of murals is located in **Building A,** to the right of the battle mural. The murals here line up with the two small pyramids on the east and west sides of the structure. The date on the **north mural** (denoted by the eye of a reptile in indigenous glyphs) corresponds with the supposed incarnation of the wind god Enecatl by Quetzalcoatl. Bordering these murals are pictures of various sea creatures, reflections of the Olmec-Xicalanca origins on the Gulf of Mexico. Spanish-speaking guides are available for one-hour tours that cost $5.50 per group.

Although the ruins of Cacaxtla are no longer undergoing excavation, another temple, built around AD 200, lies below the visible structures, and it's possible that yet another is buried farther down. In January of 1993 excavation began at **Xochitecal** (known as Pyramid of the Flowers) on the hill opposite Cacaxtla. The 2-kilometer climb through the fields from the pyramid of Cacaxtla is a hot and sweaty one, but definitely worth it. The site consists of three civic-religious temples, which you can enter. Human remains and close to 5,000 clay figures, mostly representing women, have been discovered here. Although female images dominate this site, archaeologists have yet to confirm whether this indicates a matriarchy, or what the link is between this temple and nearby Cacaxtla. You'll also find three monolithic baptismal fonts and four anthropomorphic monuments of engraved basalt stone. *Admission for both sites: $2. Open Tues.–Sun. 10–4:30.*

If you make the trek out to Cacaxtla, you might as well visit **San Miguel del Milagro,** down a cobblestone pathway just before the entrance to the pyramids. The archangel Michael supposeldy appeared here in 1630, asking Diego Lázaro de San Francisco, a local Indian boy, to tell the townspeople of a curative well. When he did not follow the order, the boy was struck with illness, only to be cured with the waters that the angel brought him. As in Ocotlán (*see* Worth Seeing, Basílica de Ocotlán, *above*) a fountain of healing water bubbled forth, and to this day the **Santuario de San Miguel** is a destination for pilgrims. You can take some of the water from the **Pocito de Santa Agua** (Well of Holy Water), in the courtyard outside the church, during one of its sporadic distributions. In the event that the gate is locked, ask someone in the church when the next distribution will be. The church itself is filled with 17th- and 18th-century paintings depicting angels, biblical stories, and the origin of St. Michael's curative water. At the lacquered **Chinese Pulpit** and **Cuarto de Exvotos,** to the right of the church, you'll find offerings—photographs, pairs of crutches, and handwritten notes—that healed pilgrims have left in gratitude.

COMING AND GOING From Tlaxcala, take a TEXOLOC bus from the Central Camionera, and ask to be let off at the *calzada* (30 min, 70¢). You'll be dropped off at a crossroads where combis wait to take people to San Miguel and Cacaxtla (about five minutes away). You'll then be dropped at the entrance to the ruins. From Puebla, catch a SAN MARTIN bus (1 hr, 90¢) from the CAPU terminal; you'll also be dropped off at the crossroads.

Puebla
Located 125 kilometers (78 mi) south of Mexico City, Puebla city may appear overwhelming at first. Music stores blast the latest Mexican hits onto crowded sidewalks as taxis and buses weave crazily down narrow cobblestone streets while traffic cops calmly eat ice cream from a safe distance. Although your first instinct may be to run and hide, this cosmopolitan state capital will soon seem less chaotic once you get to know the friendly residents and the infectious rhythm that dictates their daily lives.

Historically, Puebla is most known for the infamous battle on May 5, 1862, where 2,000 Mexicans defeated 6,000 French troops. The victory spurred the nationally recognized Cinco de Mayo holiday. Today, Puebla is a vibrant city best explored on foot; as you walk through the streets you'll discover a stunning blend of Spanish and indigenous architecture, exquisite Talavera tiles, and enough incredible cuisine to keep your mouth watering and your belly full. Puebla is the home of the famous *mole* (*see box* Holy Mole, *below*) and almost anything you eat here, whether prepared on a makeshift brazier on the street or in a fancy restaurant, is wonderful. In fact, this is the only Mexican city where a kitchen—**La Cocina de Santa Rosa**—is considered a tourist attraction. In the event that Puebla's two million teeming residents make you yearn for a breath of rustic simplicity, check out the nearby town of Cholula, where cathedrals and ancient ruins provide opportunities for exploration.

BASICS

AMERICAN EXPRESS The AmEx office in the Plaza Dorada shopping center is a five-minute bus ride from downtown. The staff will exchange, replace, and sell traveler's checks, and deliver MoneyGrams. Cardholders can also cash personal checks, replace lost cards, and have their mail held at the following address: Plaza Dorada 2, Local 21–22, Puebla, Puebla, CP 72530, México. *Tel. 22/37–55–58. From 13 Ote. and 2 Sur, take PLAZA DORADA bus. Open weekdays 9–6, Sat. 9–1.*

BOOKSTORES Librerías de Cristal has an enormous selection of books, magazines, videos, and compact discs, and a small selection of English books. *Reforma 511, btw 5 Nte. and 7 Nte., tel. 22/42–44–20. Open Mon.–Sat. 9:30–8:30.*

CASAS DE CAMBIO Exchange traveler's checks at **Bancomer** (3 Pte. 116, tel. 22/32–00–22) weekdays 8:30–2:30. Many of the banks along Reforma supply ATMs that accept Plus and Cirrus system cards, but those at **Banamex** (Reforma 135, tel. 91–800/9–03–83) are the most reliable. If you're set on changing cash later in the day, you'll have to go a bit out of the way: **Casa de Cambio Puebla** (5 de Mayo, tel. 22/37–74–73; open Mon.–Sat. 9–1:30 and 4:30–6) is four blocks from the Plaza Dorada shopping center.

EMERGENCIES Dial 06 from any public phone in Puebla for **police, fire,** or **ambulance.**

LAUNDRY Lavandería Roly charges $3 to wash and dry 3 kilos of laundry and $1 for self-service. *7 Nte. 404, at 4 Pte., tel. 22/32–93–07. Open Mon.–Sat. 8 AM–9 PM, Sun. 8–2.*

MAIL The main post office is two blocks south of the zócalo. Mail will be held for up to 10 days if sent to you at: Lista de Correos, 5 Oriente y 16 de Septiembre, Sur C, Puebla, Puebla,

CP 72000, México. *Tel. 22/42–64–48. Open weekdays 8–8, Sat. 9–1. Other location: 2 Ote. 411, btw 6 Nte. and 4 Nte. To send mail to this branch, write "Adm. 1" before "Sur C."*

MEDICAL AID Hospital Universitario (13 Sur, at 25 Pte., tel. 22/43–12–77) provides 24-hour emergency service (some English spoken). For 24-hour pharmacy service and free delivery to your hotel, try **Drogería Medina** (4 Pte. 107, tel. 22/32–37–89, fax 22/42–09–52).

PHONES Puebla probably has the highest percentage of functioning pay phones in Mexico. Casetas de larga distancia are also pretty abundant: Just look for a blue picture of a telephone and the word LADA hanging in store windows. **Printaform** (2 Sur 104, tel. 22/46–68–14; open weekdays 9–2 and 4–8, Sat. 10–2) is right on the zócalo and lets you make cash calls. **Helados Holanda** (16 de Septiembre 303, tel. 22/42–61–55), open daily 9–9, has long-distance service and a fax machine, but you can't make collect calls.

VISITOR INFORMATION Oddly enough, there are two tourist offices in Puebla. The **Oficina de Información Turística** (5 Ote. 3, tel. 22/46–12–85; open Mon.–Sat. 9–8:30, Sun. 9–2) is the state office, staffed by a helpful crew that provides good maps of the city and the state. With 30 years of experience and a great sense of humor, George Estrada is the person you want to ask for. He speaks English and leads tours to Cholula and the pyramids of Canton for $11 per person, including transportation. The nearby **municipal office** (Portal Hidalgo 14, tel. 22/46–10–93; open weekdays 9–8) can also give you tons of info.

COMING AND GOING

BY BUS Puebla's main bus terminal, **CAPU** (Blvd. Nte. 4222, tel. 22/30–19–03), is served by a number of bus lines. **Autobuses Unidos (AU)** (tel. 22/49–74–05) runs frequent buses to Mexico City (2 hrs, $4) and Veracruz (5 hrs, $9.50), and sends three buses to Oaxaca (8 hrs, $10) at 8:30 AM, 7:30 PM, and 11:30 PM. **Estrella Blanca** (tel. 22/49–75–61) serves Acapulco (7 hrs, $23) every two hours until 11:30 PM. **Cristóbal Colón** (tel. 22/49–73–27) buses depart for Salina Cruz (10 hrs, $24) twice daily. Besides serving many of the destinations listed above, **Autobuses del Oriente (ADO)** (tel. 22/49–70–42) sends buses daily at 9 PM to Mérida (21 hrs, $41) and at 11:45 AM to Cancún (24 hrs, $48). Several local companies, such as **Flecha Azul**, cruise to nearby towns like Tehuacán and Tlaxcala for about $1. The terminal has luggage storage (25¢ per hour; open daily 7 AM–10:30 PM), a tourist information booth, a police station, and a bank that changes money daily 9 AM–noon. Several cafeterias, a pharmacy, and nearby shops ensure that you'll be occupied as you wait for your bus. The terminal is big and always bustling, so if you want to crash here, go ahead—you'll be uncomfortable but safe.

Unfortunately the bus terminal is nowhere near downtown Puebla. To get here you have to take either a combi or a cab. Authorized taxis (prepay the fare at the booth inside the terminal) charge $1.25 to the zócalo, where most of the budget hotels are. The RUTA 48 combi (20 min, 30¢) will get you closest to the zócalo—about five blocks from the zócalo.

BY CAR The new Oaxaca–Veracruz highway makes traveling by car fast (3½ hours to either destination) and easy, but not cheap: Tolls to Oaxaca total $11.50, and to Veracruz, a whopping $25. To reach Mexico City, take the Puebla–Mexico freeway and pay $5.75 for two hours of easy driving.

GETTING AROUND

Puebla's streets are confusing at first, but they can be mastered with the help of the free maps provided by the tourist office (*see* Visitor Information, *above*). Streets are organized by number, in relation to the zócalo, and according to cardinal directions: norte (north; nte.), sur (south), oriente (east; ote.), and poniente (west; pte.). Two exceptions to the rule are 5 de Mayo, which becomes 16 de Septiembre south of the zócalo, and Avenida Reforma, which becomes Avenida Ávila Camacho after passing the zócalo east–west. Even-numbered sur and norte *calles* are east of the zócalo, odd-numbered streets are west of it. Even-numbered oriente and poniente *avenidas* are north of the zócalo, odd-numbered ones south. Puebla's streets are surprisingly safe for a city its size, and even solo women can walk around alone hassle-free. Areas to avoid at night, however, are 6 Poniente, but only between 7 Norte and 11 Norte and the area north-west of 20 Poniente and 3 Sur.

BY BUS Puebla's extensive system of colectivos (20¢) run 6 AM–11 PM. However, in order to preserve the historic buildings and control the noise, colectivos and combis don't travel the streets nearest the zócalo; the closest they come is 11 Poniente, about five blocks away.

BY CAR Driving within Puebla can be a harrying experience. The cobblestone roads are one-way in downtown and are crowded with honking cars, pedestrians, and policemen with obnoxiously loud whistles. Parking can be hard to find on the street, but if you've got a foreign license plate, you're exempt from parking citations. Parking lots are also an easy option. Car rental offices in the city include **Budget** (Juárez 2927-8, tel. 91–800/7–00–17) and **National** (Juárez 2318-M, tel. 22/48–50–48). Both rent sedans at around $30 a day, and you'll need to be at least 23 years old and in possession of a driver's license, credit card, and passport.

WHERE TO SLEEP

All of the hotels described below are within a few blocks of the zócalo, in the colonial **Centro Histórico** (historical center) of the city. The only hotel anywhere near the CAPU bus station is the quiet and modern **Hotel Terminal de Puebla** (Carmen Serdán 5101, tel. 22/32–79–80). Wheelchair-accessible rooms cost $13.50 for one, $16.50 for two. Solo travelers may not want to look for lodging west of Calle 7 Norte. The numerous brothels here make for a seedy atmosphere, and even a brief walk in the area can be uncomfortable.

➤ **UNDER $5** • **Hotel Avenida.** For $3 you get a single or a double room ($7 with bath) and friendly service that borders on motherly. The rooms are spacious, but muggy and bare, and you should bring your own towel, soap, and toilet paper. Hot water runs 6–10 AM and 7:30–11 PM. *5 Pte. 336, tel. 22/32–21–04. 1½ blocks west of cathedral. 52 rooms, 20 with bath. Luggage storage. Wheelchair access.*

Hotel Venecia. Established in 1897, Hotel Venecia isn't much to look at, but it's clean, and the clientele consists of friendly Mexican families. None of the rooms have private baths, but there's hot water all the time and a TV room downstairs. Singles cost $3.50, doubles $4. *4 Pte. 716, tel. 22/32–24–69. 2 blocks north and 3 blocks west of zócalo. 36 rooms, none with bath.*

➤ **UNDER $15** • **Hotel Imperial.** Go out of your way to stay at this hotel. The owner gives anyone carrying this book a 30% discount, putting the ordinarily pricey rooms in the budget traveler's range ($10 for a single, $14.50 for a deluxe double). From the busy pool table and restaurant on the first floor to the remodeled split-level rooms complete with TVs, phones, and filtered tap water, you'll feel like you've died and gone to backpackers' heaven. There are also safes for your valuables and a complimentary breakfast (7:30–10:30). The owner, Juan José Bretón Avalos (*el Licenciado*), is one of the most helpful guides in all Puebla. *4 Ote. 212, btw 2 Nte. and 4 Nte., tel. 22/42–49–81. 65 rooms, all with bath. Free laundry (bring soap) and luggage storage. Wheelchair access. MC, V.*

➤ **UNDER $20** • **Hotel Santander.** Entering this hotel's huge enclosed courtyard sur-rounded by opulent terraces will make you feel as if you arrived in a mansion. The very clean and quaint rooms come with endless hot water, TVs, and if you're willing to pay, phones and private bathrooms. Singles and doubles run $8.50–$20, depending on the amenities. The hotel fills up with Mexican and foreign travelers, so it's a good idea to reserve ahead of time if you want a cheaper room. *5 Pte. 111, tel. 22/46–31–75. 1 block west of cathedral. 33 rooms, 13 with bath. Luggage storage. Wheelchair access.*

➤ **UNDER $30** • **Hotel Colonial.** This place is a favorite of American and European stu-dents taking courses at the university across the street. Fittingly, the entire place is done up in colonial style, with the requisite statues, dark wood, and arches. Rooms are spacious, tiled, clean, and fairly quiet. There's also cable TV, room service, a library, money exchange, and a popular restaurant. Many exchange students stay for the whole summer, so hang out here if you're thirsting for some non-Spanish-speaking company. You'll have to cough up $20 for a single, $25 for a double. *4 Sur 105, tel. 22/46–46–12. 1 block east of zócalo. 70 rooms, all with bath. Laundry ($2.50), luggage storage. Reservations advised. MC, V.*

FOOD

Puebla's nuns had a special gift for culinary creation; *mole poblano* (*see box* Holy Mole, *below*) and *chiles en nogada* (chiles stuffed with beef and covered in a walnut sauce and pomegranate seeds) were both invented in convent kitchens here. For a particularly filling and original lunch, try the 50¢ *tacos árabes* (Arabian tacos, with seasoned beef and a yogurty sauce, rolled in pita bread) at **Taquería La Oriental** (Portal Juárez 107; open daily 8 AM–midnight) on the west side of the zócalo. Oddly enough, these tacos can only be found in Puebla. You can pick out the hole-in-the-wall places where they're sold by the rotisserie stands out front. Sugar addicts should stroll down **Calle de los Dulces** (6 Ote., btw 5 de Mayo and 4 Nte.), past numerous shops selling Puebla's famous fruit candies. Specialties include *camote* (candied yam) and a meringue concoction called *beso del ángel* (angel's kiss). **Super Churrería** (2 Sur, at 5 Ote., tel. 22/35–01–15) serves chocolate ($1) and traditional *churros* (15¢). The twisted, sugary pastries dipped into hot chocolate will send you floating away into ecstasy.

La Pasita (3 Sur 504, at 5 Pte.) is the only place in the world where you'll find a drink of the same name, a liqueur made from raisins. They serve $1 shots of La Pasita and other regional liqueurs daily noon–5:30.

➤ **UNDER $5** • **La Concordia.** Though the TV and stereo compete for attention in this small, colorful joint, the volume is low enough for a relaxed atmosphere. Come for the $2 breakfast, which includes juice, coffee, eggs, and *chilaquiles* (tortilla strips doused with salsa and sour cream). At lunch, choose from two types of comida corrida—regular ($2) and *ejecutivo* (executive; $2.50). Dinners are pricey, so stick to the $4 enchiladas. *2 Ote. 205-A, at 2 Nte., tel. 22/46–68–27. 1 block north of zócalo. Open daily 8 AM–10 PM. Wheelchair access.*

San Francisco el Alto Mercado (Garibaldi). What used to be a market has now been turned into this enclosed setting for about 15 fondas. In this lively atmosphere you'll find traditional poblano food, such as a $3.50 plate of chicken mole, rice, beans, and *chiles en nogada* (in

Holy Mole

Rumor has it mole was invented by the Aztec as a topping for that tastiest of meats, human flesh, but the more plausible explanation is as follows: Sor Andrea de la Asunción, an 18th-century nun in the Santa Rosa convent, was given the task of creating a special dish for the Archbishop of Puebla. Wanting to combine the best of Mexican and Spanish cuisine, she began with four types of chiles—mulato, ancho, pasilla, and chipotle—for the Mexican element, and almonds as a symbol of Spain. Believing the sauce was too spicy, Sor Andrea added raisins, plantains, and chocolate to sweeten the kick. Sesame seeds and peanuts were thrown in to thicken the sauce, clove and cinnamon for flavor, and anise to make it all go down easily. The finished product included 18 ingredients, and quickly became a standard of Mexican cuisine.

The word mole may be a garbled version of muele ("grind," which was what Sor Andrea did with all those ingredients), or the Nahuatl word mollí, which means "hot chile." Today there are as many different moles as there are cooks, but Pueblan restaurants keep a tight hold on what they claim is the original recipe. The Puebla mole festival, when poblanos compete to create the best recipe, is held every weekend of June.

season July–Sept.). On weekend nights mariachis play for the working-class crowd (upper-crust poblanos snub the place), and the market ends up resembling a rowdy bar. *14 Ote., at 14 Nte., no phone. 5 blocks north and 6 blocks east of zócalo. Open 24 hrs.*

Super Soya. This joint resembles a fun house but is a haven for die-hard vegetarians, health freaks, and ice cream fanatics. The yogurt/ice cream bar in front offers creative, nutritious concoctions in waffle cones that smell better than they taste. A health food store and restaurant serving mouthwatering *platos del día* for just $2 crowd the back of the building. *5 de Mayo 506, tel. 22/46–22–39. 3 blocks north of zócalo. Open Mon.–Sat. 9–9, Sun. 11–8:30.*

> **UNDER $10** • **Fonda de Santa Clara.** Typical comida poblana is served in this famous restaurant, decorated with *papel picado* (traditional Mexican cut paper) and *lupe muñecas* (papier-mâché dolls). Although it caters to tourists and the food isn't cheap, you'd be hard pressed to find their seasonal specials anywhere else. The menu features *gusanos de maguey con salsa borracha* (maguey worms in tequila sauce; $10) in April and May, and *chapulines* (grasshoppers; $6) during October and November. The *café de olla* (coffee flavored with cinnamon and chocolate; $1) will wake you from your post-meal coma. *3 Pte. 307, 2 blocks west of zócalo, tel. 22/42–26–59. Open daily noon–10. Wheelchair access. Other location: 3 Pte. 920. Open Mon.–Sat. 8:30 AM–11 PM. Both accept AE, MC, V.*

Restaurant Hotel Colonial. This place is packed for lunch, and the clientele includes regulars who come for the food, and exchange students who come to socialize. The menú del día ($4), served 1:30–5, is enough food to immobilize you for several days: It includes soup, rice with fried plantains, a vegetable dish, an entrée with black beans on the side, dessert, and coffee. *4 Sur 105, tel. 22/46–46–12. 1 block east of zócalo. Open daily 7 AM–10 PM.*

Villa del Mar. People wait in line to lunch at this terrace seafood restaurant. Try the shrimp, octopus, and oyster cocktails ($5), seasoned with cilantro, onion, avocado, chili, and sugar. Another good bet is the shrimp brochette with onion, bacon, and tomatoes ($5). *Juárez 1920, in Zona Esmeralda, tel. 22/42–31–04. Take RUTA 7 combi from 11 Ote. and 16 de Septiembre. Or walk 8 blocks west from zócalo, then 3 blocks south to Juárez. Open daily 10–5:30.*

CAFES **Café Aroma.** This romantic little place with brass lanterns and intimate tables, pours coffee for less than $1 ($1.50 with alcohol), and serves appetizers such as *chalupas* (fried tortillas). It also sells coffee beans from the nearby town of Villa Juárez for $3 per kilo. *3 Pte. 520-A, btw 5 and 7 Sur, tel. 22/32–60–77. Open daily 8 AM–9 PM.*

Café del Artista. Perched atop the Plazuela del Torno, this small café/bar offers a dim, candelit setting and live guitar music nightly at 7. Order a killer cappuccino for $1.25. *8 Nte. 410, at 6 Ote., tel. 22/42–15–27. Open Mon.–Wed. 4 PM–midnight, Thurs.–Sat. 4 PM–2 AM.*

Teorema. This dimly lit café/bookstore has the feel of a literary salon: If the resident professors and international students aren't discussing the latest literary trend, they sure put up a good front. Live music begins nightly at 9:30, varying from blues to rock to traditional guitar. The menu, complete with a poem, includes coffees (try the *Ira bien,* with five liquors and cream, for $2.50), desserts ($2), and beer and wine ($1.50). *Reforma, at 7 Nte., tel. 22/42–10–14. Open daily 9:30–2:30 and 4:30–midnight.*

WORTH SEEING

Student travelers are in luck in Puebla: Most sights reduce admission with any student ID. Almost all museums are free on Tuesdays and closed Mondays, with the exception of the **Museo Amparo,** which is free Mondays and open daily. La China Poblana restaurant (6 Nte. 1, no phone) is a must-see for a dose of folkloric overload. Everywhere you look there is *papel picado* (decorative paper cut-outs), tiles, painted wood, and other assorted kitsch, topped off by the life-size mannequin dressed in a flashy China Poblana costume (*see box* La China Poblana, *below*) in the front room.

AFRICAM SAFARI This zoo, on the outskirts of Puebla, is considered by many to be the best in the country. Founded in 1972, the wild animal reserve lets animals wander around freely—but don't worry, you get to visit from the safety of a car or bus. More than 3,000 animals and approximately 250 species dwell here. Africam Safari buses ($1.75) leave every hour 10–4 from Puebla's CAPU. Admission is $4. For more information, call 22/30–09–75.

CASA DE ALFENIQUE Known as the wedding-cake house, this 17th-century mansion is now the state museum. Second-floor exhibits focus on Puebla's history and archaeology. The third floor is a re-creation of a colonial-era residence and a small chapel. One highlight here is the original dress of the legendary China Poblana (*see box* La China Poblana, *below*). *4 Ote. 416, tel. 22/41–42–96. 2 blocks north and 1 block east of zócalo. Museum admission: 70¢, 25¢ students. Open Tues.–Sun. 10–5.*

CASA DE LA CULTURA This grand, two-story building was once the residence of Juan de Palafox y Mendoza, the Archbishop of Puebla, and later served as a convent and then a civic building. It now houses the Casa de la Cultura, complete with a concert and lecture hall, a movie theater (*see* Cinemas and Theaters, *below*), a playhouse, and art exhibits. Sharing the second floor is the luxurious **Biblioteca Palafoxiana,** a library that dates back to 1646. Monks used to study on the uncomfortable-looking pull-out benches on the walls. Next door to the library is the newly opened **Sala del Tesoro Bibliográfico,** with rotating displays of antique books. The oldest book in the collection is a 1493 history of the world from the beginning of time to the date of publication. Miguel Ramírez Meya, the guy in charge, is hard of hearing and very protective of *his* library and books, but he's more than willing to lecture you on anything to do with the library and knows a lot of interesting tidbits. *5 Ote. 5, tel. 22/46–19–66. Across from cathedral. Admission free; $1 for the library. Open Tues.–Sun. 10–5.*

CATEDRAL DE LA CONCEPCIÓN INMACULADA Construction on the cathedral began in 1575, and it's clear why it took almost 75 years to complete: This is one of the largest cathedrals in Mexico, with 14 chapels and the highest bell towers in the country. One tower is bell-less; according to one legend, the extra weight would have caused the tower to sink into an underground stream below. Another version claims that the builders simply ran out of money. The massive, gray-blue stone building is an example of the *mudéjar* (Moorish-influenced) style and boasts marble floors and a beautiful altar carved from gray onyx, as well as 300-year-old paintings. The altar at the center also functions as a crypt: The bishops of Puebla are buried here, and every November 2 (Day of the Dead) the crypt is opened to the public. On the north side of the church is a bell tower that you can climb daily 11–2 for a beautiful view of Puebla. *On zócalo. Admission free, 70¢ for bell tower. Open daily 10:30–noon and 4–7.*

CONVENTO SECRETO DE SANTA MONICA This convent opened in 1688 to women who chose to dedicate their lives to the church, as well as to young girls whose wealthy parents chose an ecclesiastical life for them. In 1897, after the constitutional reform separated church from state, the convent and two others in Puebla were banned for practices of involuntary servitude. Nevertheless, the convent continued to function until 1934, requiring the nuns to completely withdraw from the outside world; sympathizers brought them food through secret

La China Poblana

Pueblans still speak of Mirrah, the China Poblana (Chinese Woman of Puebla). Legend claims that she was a Mongol princess, captured by pirates from Acapulco and sold as a slave to the viceroy of Mexico. Somehow, she fell into the hands of a Pueblan merchant and his wife, who adopted and raised her. La China adapted her native dress to that of Mexico using the three colors of the Mexican flag: green, red, and white. According to the legend, the resulting costume was so beautiful and unusual that local women began to imitate her, and Mirrah kindly taught them to sew Chinese style. A modern version of her dress, elaborately embroidered and sequined, is worn by dancers performing the jarabe tapatío (hat dance). Mirrah died at 80 years of age in 1668 and is buried in the Iglesia de la Compañía de Jesús, one block east of the zócalo.

compartments. Today, Spanish-speaking guides show visitors the peepholes through which the nuns watched mass next door, and the underground crypt where they were buried. The heart of the convent's founder, some 130 years old, is kept on gruesome display here, and religious art fills the twisting hallways. The velvet paintings from the 1850s are startling; as you move from one side of the painting to the other, the faces and feet of the subjects seem to change position, and landscapes shift to the other side of the canvas. *18 Pte., near 5 de Mayo, tel. 22/32– 01–78. 9 blocks north of zócalo. Admission: $1. Open Tues.–Sun. 10–5. Mass twice on weeknights, 4 times on Sun.*

Around the corner is **Señor de las Maravillas,** a much-visited statue of Christ that is believed to perform miracles. The figure is said to be made from corn paste, but it looks remarkably similar to plaster. According to legend, the statue was fashioned by a fugitive carpenter hiding out in the convent. He and the Mother Superior both dreamed of the Señor on the same night, after which she ordered him to create this figure or be turned over to the police.

EX-CONVENTO DE SANTA ROSA The centerpiece of this remodeled convent is a huge, tiled kitchen—the birthplace of mole poblano. Most of the building is now devoted to the **Museo de Artesanías,** featuring folk art from Puebla state's seven regions. From 1697 to 1861, the building was a convent, after which it became a private psychiatric hospital. After serving a lengthy stint as an apartment building, it was remodeled and opened as a museum in 1972. Free tours are offered in Spanish only. *14 Pte. 301, tel. 22/46–45–26. 1 block west and 6 blocks north of zócalo. Admission: 70¢. Open Tues.–Sun. 10–5.*

FUERTES DE LORETO Y GUADALUPE A popular destination for both poblanos and tourists, these forts are the main attraction of a hilltop park complex. **Fuerte de Loreto** is dedicated to the Battle of Puebla (May 5, 1862), and the original cannons used to defeat the French army now guard the grave of victorious General Zaragoza. Other aspects of the battle are exhibited in the **Museo de Historia** within the fort, but don't make a special trip just to see the museum. Across the plaza is the **Fuerte de Guadalupe,** which is not as well preserved. The complex features a cluster of museums: the **Museo de Antropología Regional,** exhibiting artifacts from the early Puebla Valley cultures; the **Museo de Historia Natural,** with realistic wildlife scenes; and the excellent **planetario** (planetarium), featuring shows for stargazers hourly noon–6 PM. Admission prices are separate for each museum, ranging from 70¢ to $1.25, but it's all free on Sunday. *Take FUERTES combi from 8 Nte., at 10 Ote, or RUTA 72 combi from anywhere on 5 de Mayo after 8 Pte., and get off at Monumento Zaragoza; museums are to the east. Open Tues.–Sun. 10–4:30.*

IGLESIA DE SAN FRANCISCO Built in the 18th century, this church houses the preserved body of Franciscan Friar Sebastián de Aparicio, who is credited with convincing the Indians to stop carrying heavy loads on their backs and let oxen do the work instead. His skeleton is covered with a monk's robe, and there's a mask on his face because so many people have picked pieces from it. As a result, you can only tell he's a mummy by looking at his feet: His decomposed toes peek out from below his robe. Above the friar's body hangs the famous Conquistadora—Hernán Cortés's personal statue of the Virgin Mary. Her bloodstained gown is enough to make you shudder. Both the friar and the Conquistadora are at the front of the church, to the left of the altar. *8 Nte., at 5 de Mayo. 3 blocks east and 5 blocks north of zócalo. Admission free. Open daily 9–7:30.*

IGLESIA DE SANTO DOMINGO This church dates from 1659 and acquired its fame because of the **Capilla del Rosario** (Chapel of the Rosary), a baroque chapel with a surfeit of gold leaf and glitter that took 40 years to build. Notice the tiny dog at the feet of St. Domingo, a symbol of the Dominicans' loyalty to God. Free and interesting eight-minute tours are offered in Spanish 9:30–12:30 and 4–6. Three doors north of the church lies **Museo Bello Zetina** (tel. 22/32–47–20), the preserved home of the wealthy José Luis Bello family. The ornate home displays paintings and ceramics from around the world and includes a living room decorated in the French style during the reign of Napoleon III. *5 de Mayo 407, 1 block north of zócalo. Admission free. Open daily 7 AM–8 PM (museum closed Mon.).*

MUSEO AMPARO The airy, terra-cotta-colored building used to function as a hospital. Now it serves as a huge museum specializing in both *virreinal* (viceregal) and Mesoamerican art, with beautiful examples of Mayan, Olmec, and other artifacts on display. Interactive computers inform visitors about selected pieces in the museum. Signs in English and Spanish guide you through the exhibits or you can listen to a recorded audio tour (70¢ plus $1 deposit). Guides are available for tours in Spanish for $7 per hour (there's a free tour Sunday at noon). *2 Sur 708, at 9 Ote., tel. 22/46–46–46. 2½ blocks south of zócalo. Admission: $1.25, 70¢ students; free Mon. Open daily 10–6. Wheelchair access.*

MUSEO DE LA REVOLUCIÓN Known as **Casa de los Hermanos Serdán,** the house of Aquiles Serdán and his sister Carmen now honors these two heroes and a group of revolutionaries who perished here in 1910 after 14 hours of gunfight with the police and 500 federal army soldiers who were sent to arrest them on conspiracy charges. The building's facade was left intact, but bears the violent marks of the fight. In the parlor, pierced mirrors still hang on bullet-riddled walls, and broadsheets calling for revolution, published by the Serdán family, are on display. The assassination of Aquiles Serdán and his followers is believed by many to be the event that launched the Revolution of 1910. *6 Ote. 206, tel. 22/42–10–76. 3 blocks north of zócalo. Admission: 70¢, free Tues. Open Tues.–Sun. 10–4:30.*

CHEAP THRILLS

Those interested in Catholic paraphernalia will find plenty in Puebla's stores, including incense, rosaries, and electric "candles" with lights that flicker (for those opposed to the shameless consumption of wax). At **Librería Mariana** (Calles 2 Sur and 3 Ote., across from zócalo) you can buy prayer cards (20¢ each) identifying all those saints you've seen in churches around the city. The sports-minded traveler will enjoy the **Don Bosco** field (17 Pte., at 5 Sur), where you can join local soccer games, or just watch, from 4:30 PM on. At **Agua Azul** (11 Sur, at Circuito Interior, on the outskirts of town, tel. 22/43–13–30) you can wade or swim laps in the indoor pool or relax in the steam baths. It's open daily 7–5:30 and costs $3.50. One of the nicer areas in town for a leisurely stroll is the fashionable **Plaza de los Sapos**, where shops sell typical Pueblan wares, restaurants beckon with their rich aromas, and fountains provide the soothing sounds of running water.

FESTIVALS Every year on Mardi Gras (six weeks before Easter), the residents of Huejotzingo (*see* Near Puebla, *below*) reenact the kidnapping of the daughter of a *corregidor* (magistrate) against the backdrop of the Mexican triumph against the French. The costumes and masks of **Carnaval de Huejotzingo** are elaborate, and the festival is noisy and sometimes dangerous—the tradition of shooting colored gunpowder at celebrants often results in injuries. The **Feria Regional de Puebla,** held April 26 through May 20, celebrates the diversity of Puebla, combining agricultural and livestock expositions, industrial and mechanical productions, cultural and sporting events, and the best of *cocina poblana* and *artesanía*. On May 5 the city commemorates the 1862 Battle of Puebla, in which the Mexican army defeated French invaders, known as **Cinco de Mayo.** The city center is transformed for a day as fireworks, a military parade, sporting events, and traditional music take over. During the **Festival de San Agustín,** Pueblans celebrate with music, dancing, and fireworks during most of August. On the 26th (St. Augustine's feast day) it is customary to prepare chiles en nogada (*see* Food, *above*). The annual **Fiesta de San Francisco de Asis-Cuetzalán,** on the 4th of October, is the excuse for two weeks of indigenous dances, a *tianguis* (open-air market), and general merrymaking in the tiny town of Cuetzalán (*see* Near Puebla, *below*). Dancers wear traditional white robes and *tocas de lana* (large, turbanlike hats almost 40 centimeters high).

SHOPPING

The *majólica* techniques developed in Talavera de la Reina, Spain are used for making tiles and other ceramicware in Puebla. You can learn about the process at **Uriarte** (4 Pte. 911, tel. 22/32–15–98), a factory and shop devoted exclusively to beautiful Talavera ceramics. Free tours in English and Spanish take place daily 9–6. If the workers aren't too busy, they may even let you sit at the potter's wheel and make your own version. You'll find more Talavera pieces, including dishes and vases, at **El Parián** (6 Nte., btw 4 Ote. and 2 Ote.), a market that's been around since 1796. Nowadays the more artistic pieces are mixed in with a lot of cheap souvenirs, but it's a fun place to poke around and haggle. Across the street is the **Barrio del Artista** (8 Nte., at 6 Ote.), where painters and sculptors open their studios to visitors. On 5 Oriente and 6 Norte you'll find an upscale antique market known as **Mercado de Los Sapos,** popular with students and wealthy locals.

If you're interested in intricate silver work visit **Amozoc,** 16 kilometers east of Puebla. This town is famous for *charrería* (tack for rodeos). As a result, an abundance of spur-theme souvenirs is available. The Sunday mercado here is a gastronomic feast, known for its fish, avocado, and *pulque* (an alcohol made from pulque). A second-class AMOZOC bus leaves from the corner of 14 Oriente and 18 Norte in Puebla ($1). Ask to be let off near the zócalo; the town is very small, so you'll have no trouble finding your way around. The last bus to Puebla leaves at 6 PM from Amozoc's main plaza.

Originally an ancient Nahuatl settlement on a low mountain range, Amozoc means "where there is no mud" in Nahuatl.

Tecali, under an hour's drive from Puebla, is home to numerous onyx craftsmen, their workshops, and onyx items. **Casatellez,** located near the town center, is a store specializing in the local artesanía. From Puebla's CAPU, catch an Autobuses Unidos bus to Tepeaca and transfer there to Tecali; or take an 80¢ combi from the corner of 10 Poniente and 13 Norte in Puebla.

AFTER DARK

Pueblans tend to hit the sack around 10:30 on weeknights, but on weekends everyone is out for some sort of adventure, usually involving tequila. In any case, the scene here is amiable; strike up a conversation and you'll be sure to make some new friends.

BARS Just a five-minute walk southeast of the zócalo, **Plaza de los Sapos** offers a mellow scene. Enter the Western style **La Bóveda** (6 Sur 503-C, tel. 22/46–55–90), complete with a sawdust-covered floor, for a romantic atmosphere and a bohemian, lyrical guitarist. It's open Monday–Saturday until 2 AM, Sundays until 11 PM. Closing a bit earlier, the next-door **D'Pasadita** is decorated with unique items—from the antique cash register to the clocks on the walls. Speakers blast Mexican and U.S. rock across the gregarious crowd. **Los Alambiques** (6 Sur 504, tel. 22/46–35–65) sports a lively gay scene on weekends, while an older gay crowd heads to **El Ceroso** (6 Sur 506-F, tel. 22/32–42–89). Both bars are open until 1 AM.

DANCE CLUBS The best clubs in the area are located in **Cholula** (*see* Near Puebla, *below*), home of the respected Universidad de las Américas. If the half-hour commute turns you off, try **News** (Atlixco 3102, tel. 22/31–13–30), open Thursday–Saturday 10 PM–4 AM to those 18 and over. Young locals and tourists shake it here under a constellation of tiny lights to the beat of techno and pop. The underground house scene heats up by 11:30 PM at **Discotheque Nazty** (11 Sur 1509, at 15 Pte., tel. 22/37–36–45), open Friday–Sunday 9:30 PM–3 AM. Expect to be the only tourist in the club, which fills up with friendly teenage boys dressed in futuristic attire. A slightly older crowd lines up for **Freedom** (Circuito Interior 2907, tel. 22/37–74–07), with rock music and occasional live bands Tuesday–Sunday 6 PM–3 AM. For the greatest variety, head to **Zona Esmeralda,** also called **La Juárez,** on Juárez west of 18 Sur. Most places here charge a $2 cover, and none are close to the center of town—taxis ($1.50) are your best bet.

CINEMAS AND THEATERS New releases from the U.S., either dubbed in Spanish or with Spanish subtitles, are shown at **EcoCinema** (4 Ote. 210, tel. 22/32–19–55). At the Casa de la Cultura (*see* Worth Seeing, *above*), **Cinemática Luis Buñuel** shows $1.25 international and cultural films Wednesday–Sunday at 5 PM and 7:30 PM and free weekend matinees. Call for more information. Both **Teatro Espacio 1900** (2 Ote. 412, tel. 22/46–17–30) and **Teatro Hermanos Soler** (Hotel Camino Real, tel. 22/46–98–15) put on live theater and concerts on the weekends. Tickets cost about $4, and events are posted at their respective addresses.

Near Puebla

CHOLULA

Only 20 minutes east of Puebla by bus, the town of Cholula is gringo friendly, with signs and menus in English, and has plenty of restaurants that accept credit cards. Best of all, the 65,000 Cholulan residents are extremely helpful and much less harried than their Pueblan neighbors. The women of this town are much more open to conversation than in many other places, an aspect of life here that will put female travelers at ease. The center of town is small and quiet, with many restaurants and artesanía stores catering to the multitude of tourists passing through to see the **Great Pyramid** (*see* Worth Seeing, *below*).

> *Pueblans say that Cholulans counter the excessive religious devotion of their town by having the same number of bars as churches. That way they can strike the perfect balance between faith and sin.*

Before the Conquest, Cholula reportedly erected hundreds of temples and rivaled Teotihuacán as a cultural and ceremonial center. The *mercado-santuario* (market-sanctuary) system was developed here in AD 1200, whereby satellite cities of Cholula exchanged cultural ideas and began trading with the Gulf region and Oaxaca. When Cortés arrived, colonialism and Catholicism were strictly enforced; according to legend, conquering Spaniards built a church for each day of the year atop the ruins of Cholulan temples. Although the number is exaggerated, there are approximately 130 churches in Cholula and the surrounding areas today.

COMING AND GOING In Puebla, catch a PUEBLA/CHOLULA combi (30¢) from the bus stop on the corner of 11 Norte and 14 Poniente or an Estrella de Oro or Estrella Roja bus from CAPU (*see* Puebla, Coming and Going, *above*). These buses leave about every 10 minutes and cost 50¢. The bus stop in Cholula is at the corner of 5 de Mayo and 5 Poniente; to reach the zócalo from here, walk south on 5 de Mayo for three blocks. To reach Cholula by car, take the Puebla–Cholula highway ($2.50 toll).

WHERE TO SLEEP Perhaps because of its proximity to Puebla, Cholula is short on affordable hotels. The oldest hotel in Cholula, **Hotel Reforma** (4 Sur 101, tel. 22/47–01–49) is run by a friendly, talkative señora. Rooms go for $7–$9.50 for a single or double with bath. The 70-room **Hotel Las Américas** (14 Ote. 6, tel. 22/47–22–75) charges $7 for a single and $8.50 for a double, with private bath. It's close to the nightclub zone, but a 10-minute hike from the zócalo and most bus stops. Both hotels are wheelchair accessible. Campsites are available at the invitingly named **Trailer Park Las Américas** (30 Ote. 602, tel. 22/47–01–34), a five-minute bus ride west of Cholula. Pitching a two-person tent costs $5. Hot showers and swimming facilities are available, but it's not the most scenic spot.

FOOD Several restaurants serving Italian food are clustered on the zócalo, under the portal: At **Los Jarrones** (tel. 22/47–02–92) good pizza is served with salad, spaghetti, and a drink for $2, or huge burgers for under $2. **Güero's** (Hidalgo 101, tel. 22/47–21–88), en route to the pyramid, is the most popular joint in town, with locals taking in mouthfuls of nachos, pizza, and *comida típica* for $4 a meal. Two traditional restaurants near the pyramid, **La Lunita** (Morelos, at 6 Nte., tel. 22/47–00–11) and **La Pirámide** (Morelos 416, tel. 22/47–02–54) are popular with locals and serve mole, pipián, and *filete milanesa* (breaded steak) for $3.

WORTH SEEING

➢ **CHIPILO** • A five-minute bus ride past the villages of Santa María Tonantzintla and Acatepec, this trippy town of blond, blue-eyed Italian immigrants was founded in 1882 when Porfirio Díaz imported a group of white, Catholic Venetians in an attempt to "save the nation." The inhabitants adamantly proclaim themselves *Mexicanos* who just happen to uphold Italian traditions and speak an Italian dialect. Besides this unique blend of cultures, Chipilo's excellent sausage, cheese, and dairy products—which make their markets and Italian restaurants famous throughout the region—are an excellent reason to come here. **El Correo Español** (tel. 22/83–05–29), on the road to Chipilo, serves excellent Spanish and Italian food for less than $10. **Centro Artesanal** (tel. 22/83–07–82), open daily 10–7, sells beautiful arts and crafts as well as tariff-free wooden furniture. To reach Chipilo from Cholula, take a CHIPILO bus (15 min, 30¢) from 5 de Mayo and 6 Poniente and tell the driver where you're headed. From the bus you'll see a lone sign for the town across from the Central Artesanal.

➢ **GREAT PYRAMID** • Cholula's Great Pyramid actually consists of three pyramids built on top of one another. The final pyramid would have been the largest in the world if it had been finished; its base is 4,500 square meters. Construction began by the Cholulteca, a mix of people from several regions of Mexico, but was ended around AD 650 when they were attacked and conquered by warriors from nearby Cacaxtla. The view from atop the Great Pyramid reveals a panorama of steeples and spires. For $2 (free Fridays) visitors can also explore the pyramid's underground tunnels daily 10–5. Guides, available at the tunnel entrance, charge $4.50 per person ($5 for the English version) for an interesting one-hour tour. A museum across the road from the pyramid explains what you'll see in the caverns. If you're not totally exhausted, hike up the hill just past the exit of the pyramid to the small **Iglesia Nuestra Señora de los Remedios,** built in 1666. Adjacent to the Iglesia is the **Capilla** where people leave offerings to the Virgin Mary, such as charms, long braids of hair, baby clothes, and letters. To reach the Great Pyramid from the zócalo, walk east (away from the volcanoes) along Morelos for three blocks.

➢ **SANTA MARIA TONANTZINTLA/SAN FRANCISCO ACATEPEC** • Separated by a five-minute bus ride, these villages, 3 kilometers south of Cholula, are home to a pair of unique churches. Santa María Tonantzintla's **Iglesia de Tonantzintla** took almost 300 years to build, and is the only church in the area designed and built exclusively by Indians. The interior is a curious mix of baroque and indigenous aesthetics—an explosion of bright colors and gilt. Note that the angels and cherubs have Indian features (as does the Jesus on the cross to the left of the altar) and that the statue of the Virgin is framed in neon—wow. The graves of children taken by an early death are marked by the stones in the path leading up to the church.

The village of **Acatepec** boasts a 16th-century church, decorated on the outside with blue, yellow, and green Talavera tiles and twisting columns on the bell towers. Inside, the newly remodeled interior (the original was destroyed in a fire) rivals that of Santa María Tonantzintla's church in amount of gilt per square inch. You can visit the churches daily 10–6. Red-and-white CHIPILO buses leave from the corner of 5 de Mayo and 6 Poniente in Cholula; ask the driver to let you off at either church. The buses run frequently, so hopping on another to reach the second church is easy.

➢ **ZOCALO** • Down the hill, seven blocks east of the Great Pyramid, is Cholula's zócalo, which supposedly has the longest *portal* (porch) in Latin America. Along the portal are several shops, boutiques, and restaurants. Try to visit the zócalo on Sunday (market day), or a saint's day celebration (considering the number of churches in the area, each celebrating at least 10 feast days annually, finding one shouldn't be difficult). Facing the zócalo is the mustard-yellow **Convento Franciscano,** resembling a medieval castle. It was built in 1549 on the site of a temple dedicated to Quetzalcoatl; Cortés's troops and their Tlaxcaltecan allies massacred thousands of Cholulans here. The **Capilla Real** (Royal Chapel) inside the convent is unique in that it has 49 domes, inspired by the Great Mosque of Córdoba, Spain.

AFTER DARK With the Universidad de las Américas on the east side of town, Cholula is enough of a happening place that even Pueblans come here for a change of scene. **Keops** (14 Ote., at 5 de Mayo) is a bright purple building that houses the area's only gay disco. The place to go Thursday—Saturday nights is **Wilo** (tel. 22/47–21–06), with no cover charge and $1 beers. The place is jammed by 11, but the owner, best known as "*el chofo*," says he'll give a 30% discount on drinks if you bring this book. For those drunken hunger pangs, **Cielito Lindo** next door offers free *botanas* (snacks: tacos, quesadillas) as long as you consume their beer.

TEHUACÁN

If you end up visiting Tehuacán, it'll probably be through no fault of your own. Rather, an empty stomach or gas tank will force you to make a stop here en route to Oaxaca from Mexico City or vice versa. If you want to stretch your legs, take a stroll along the shaded zócalo and check out the murals on the circling roof of the Ayuntamiento/Municipio building. Depicting the hinterlands of Tehuacán, the murals include a psychedelic creation scene and a futuristic projection into the cosmic realm. Other sights include the **Ex-Convento del Carmen** (Reforma, at 2 Ote., tel. 238/2–40–45), which houses the **Museo del Valle de Tehuacán.** Though there are some interesting pre-Columbian artifacts, the displays consist mostly of stones, husks, and pods, and aren't worth the $1.25 admission. The **Iglesia del Carmen** and the massive baroque **cathedral,** both across the street from the zócalo, testify to the symbolic significance of the feminine in Mexican Catholicism. Altars and walls feature paintings and statues of the Virgin Mary and several female saints. Diagonally across from the cathedral is the **Casa del Gobierno,** a baroque building covered with Talavera tiles. The Casa contains murals that were the collaborative efforts of several artists, including Desiderio Xochitiotzín of Tlaxcala.

North of Tehuacán lies **Balneario San Lorenzo** park (admission $1.50; open weekdays 6–6) in the town of San Lorenzo. Locals visit this park to swim "where the water is born" in several natural spring-water pools, picnic, and fill up on sparkling mineral water. To get here, catch a SAN LORENZO bus (25¢) heading north from any bus stop along Calle 3.

COMING AND GOING Tehuacán's main streets are Independencia and Reforma, within walking distance of almost everything. The bus station (Independencia Nte. 119, tel. 238/2–19–36) lies two blocks from the zócalo; from here buses run to Mexico City (3½ hrs, $7.50), Oaxaca (3 hrs, $7), and Veracruz (4 hrs, $7). From Puebla's CAPU, **ADO** buses leave for Tehuacán (2 hrs, $3.50) every 20 minutes 6 AM–9 PM.

WHERE TO SLEEP AND EAT Hotels are numerous in Tehuacán, and several bargains are available. The rooms at **Hotel Madrid** (3 Sur 105, tel. 238/3–15–24) are a steal at $3 for singles ($5.50 with bath), $4 for doubles ($6.50 with bath). The restaurant/hotel **Casa de Huéspedes** (Reforma Nte. 213, tel. 238/2–02–20) is hard to notice under the large Corona sign, but it has a friendlier staff and similar prices. Food here is as exciting as the hotels are, except, perhaps, the regional specialty *mole de cadera,* a goat-meat stew only available in November (the goats have to be fed a special diet for six months beforehand). Try the dish in the patio of the apartment complex next to **Mercería el Botón** (2 Pte. 221, at Carmen Serdán). A meal here costs $10—not bad when you compare it to the $17 most restaurants charge. Cheaper food is available year-round at the family-owned **Restaurant Mary** (Independencia Nte. 130, no phone), across the street from the bus station. They sell filling breakfasts for $2, or comida corrida (including soup, rice, an entrée, and dessert) for $2.50.

VOLCÁN POPOCATÉPETL

Many people travel to Puebla with the sole purpose of attacking the 5½-kilometer-tall **Volcán Popocatépetl,** known simply as El Popo. Officially you need to be a registered hiker to climb Popo. Moreover, it's a hassle to reach without a car. But if you're determined, take a bus from Puebla's CAPU to Chalco, where you'll grab a bus headed for Amecameca, and then another to Tlamacas; the whole trip takes about 3½ hours and costs less than $4. In Tlamacas there's a hostel serving mostly climbers that charges $3 a night for a dorm bed. It's best to reach the hostel in the early evening the day before you plan to climb. Bring food for a couple of days. However, with the latest frenzy of unpredictable spewing, it's unlikely that you'll be able to hike at all. For an update on conditions call the **Legión Alpina de Puebla** (tel. 22/32–39–00).

El Popo has been increasingly active since its latest eruption in 1994. Since then, it's been shrouded by a cloud of gray ash and occasionally spits stones. Five hikers who attempted to reach the top, despite warnings, were killed when a sudden, small explosion wiped them out in April 1996.

CUETZALÁN

Although this town is four hours north of Puebla, it's worth visiting, as the indigenous population has preserved many of its traditional customs. The best day to visit is Sunday, market day, when the Totonac and Nahua peoples come down from the *cerro* (hill)—the men dressed in striking *huipiles* (embroidered tunics), and the women in elaborate, towering headdresses. Most people attend a Catholic mass given in Totonac, the local language, after which there's traditional dancing in the zócalo. On October 4, the feast day of St. Francis is celebrated (*see* Puebla, Festivals, *above*). The place to stay is **Hotel Posada Viky** (Guadalupe Victoria 16, tel. 233/1–02–72), which charges $7 per person. There is also a **tourist office** (Miguel Hidalgo, tel. 233/1–00–04) in Cuetzalán, although the office in Puebla (*see* Puebla, Visitor Information, *above*) provides info as well. From Puebla's CAPU terminal, **VIA** buses depart daily 6:20 AM–7:15 PM for Cuetzalán ($1).

Yohualichán lies 7 kilometers from Cuetzalán and boasts an L-shaped pyramid, home to the Totonac tribe who lived there 800 years ago.

Cuernavaca

Watched over by the great Popocatépetl volcano, Cuernavaca spreads down onto the rich agricultural plateau of Morelos state. Despite growing problems with poverty and pollution as the population approaches 2 million, Morelos's prosperous state capital attracts a steady stream of visitors. Travelers come from all over the world to study in the city's numerous language schools, to visit historical sites, or to simply hang out in the plazas amidst flowerering trees and fountains.

Mexicans make up the largest tourist group and many wealthy and famous *chilangos* (residents of Mexico City) buy second homes in Cuernavaca. But students and vacationers are only the most recent groups to shape Cuernavaca's character. At the ancient ruins of nearby Xochicalco, bas-relief sculptures suggest that this once-powerful religious center was influenced by the Maya, who dwelled south of Morelos. In the 1300s, the indigenous Tlahuica struggled against the Aztec, who attempted to enforce their supremacy by building new structures around existing Tlahuican pyramids. Ruins of these imposing structures can still be found in Cuernavaca and neighboring Tepoztlán. However, it wasn't until Cortés's brutal devastation of most native cities a century later that Tlahuican rule crumbled.

If you're here in April, witness the two-week Feria de la Primavera, established by horticulturists in 1865 to promote the local flower industry.

Despite this history of foreign domination, *cuernavaquenses* (Cuernavaca residents) aren't easily pushed around. The state of Morelos, where revolutionary leader Emiliano Zapata and his movement for agrarian reform were born, led the southern front of the Mexican Revolution in the early 1900s. Today, however, things are slightly less aggressive. The hustle of the city doesn't extend past the swerving taxicabs; people here take it slow and easy, often pausing to practice English with anyone willing.

BASICS

AMERICAN EXPRESS The AmEx office is nestled in the **Marin travel agency,** in Las Plazas shopping center. Exchange traveler's checks, cash personal checks, or have your mail held at the following address: Edificio Las Plazas, Local 13, Gutemberg 101, Col. Centro, Cuernavaca, Morelos, CP 62000, México. *Across from zócalo, tel. 73/14–22–66. AmEx service available weekdays 9–2 and 4–6, Sat. 10–1.*

BOOKSTORES A unique **bookstore** with a small selection of English books is located in Jardín Borda (*see* Worth Seeing, *below*). For a variety of Spanish books, visit the large **Libería Cristal** (Gutemberg 3, Edificio de las Plazas, Local 38, tel. 73/12–70–00) Monday–Saturday 10–9. They also sell tapes, videos, posters, and greeting cards.

CASAS DE CAMBIO Several casas de cambio cluster along Dwight Morrow, near the budget lodging area. The most reputable are **Gesta** (Lerdo de Tejada 2, tel. 73/18–22–87) and **Master Dollar** (Dwight Morrow 7-B, tel. 73/12–93–71), both open weekdays 9–6, Saturday 9–2. **Banamex** (Matamoros 6, at Arteaga, tel. 73/18–17–35) will change money weekdays 9–5, and has ATMs that accept Visa and MasterCard.

EMERGENCIES Dial 06 for **police, fire,** or **ambulance** service.

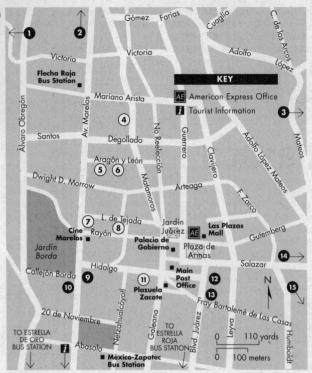

Sights ●

Ayuntamiento de Cuernavaca, **10**

Balneario Temixco, **2**

Casa de Maximiliano, **15**

Catedral de la Asunción, **9**

Jardín de Arte Luis Betanzos, **13**

Jungla Mágica, **14**

Palacio de Cortés, **12**

Pirámide de Teopanzolco, **3**

San Antón Falls, **1**

Lodging ○

Casa de Huéspedes la China Poblana, **6**

Hotel Colonial, **5**

Hotel España, **7**

Hotel Iberia, **8**

Hotel Las Hortensias, **11**

Hotel Roma, **4**

LAUNDRY Only two blocks from the budget hotel area, **Tintorería y Lavandería Morelos** charges $3 to clean 3½ kilos of laundry and will return it the same day if you drop it off before 10 AM. Bring your questions about Cuernavaca with your dirty clothes—the staff is friendly and helpful. *Matamoros 406, tel. 73/10–05–10. Open Mon.–Sat. 9–8.*

MAIL The **post office** will hold your mail and faxes at the following address for up to 10 days: Lista de Correos, Administración 1, Cuernavaca, Morelos, CP 62001, México. Faxes, telexes, and telegrams can be sent and received at the **telecommunications office** (tel. 73/14–31–81, fax 73/18–00–77) in the same building. *SW cnr of Plaza de Armas, tel. 73/12–43–79, fax 73/12–14–42. Open weekdays 8–7, Sat. until 1.*

MEDICAL AID Some of the staff at **Hospital Civil** (Domingo Diez, at Guadalajara, tel. 73/11–22–09) speak English. Next door is the 24-hour **Farmacia Cuernavaca** (Dr. Gómez Azcarte 200, Col. Lomas de la Selva, tel. 73/11–41–11, fax 73/17–47–59).

PHONES Cuernavaca's zócalo is graced with several **Ladatel** phones. Cash calls can be made from **Caseta Morelos,** which charges $1.50 per minute to the U.S. Collect calls are allowed at 25¢ per minute. *Pasaje Galeana 4, tel. 73/18–30–31. In a minimall across from Plaza de Armas. Open daily 8 AM–9 PM.*

SCHOOLS Cuernavaca is home to dozens of language schools offering language and cultural classes, including **Encuentros** (Mailing address: Encuentros Comunicación y Cultura, AP 2-71, CP 62158, Cuernavaca, Morelos, México; tel. 73/14–07–78) and the **Spanish Language Institute,** which is run by **Language Link** (Box 3006, Peoria, IL, tel. 800/552–2051, fax 309/692–2926, info@langlink.com).

Classes at **Cuauhnáhuac Escuela Cuernavaca** permit up to eight students per Spanish class. Registration is $70, and week-long classes cost $180 ($600 for a month). *Morelos Sur 123,*

Col. Chipitlán, tel. 73/12–36–73 or 73/18–92–75. Mailing address: AP 5-26, Cuernavaca, Morelos, CP 62051, México. U.S. contact: Marcia Snell, tel. 800/245–9335.

The other highly respected school in Cuernavaca is the **Center of Bilingual Multicultural Studies** (tel. 73/17–06–94, fax 73/17–05–33). Placement is into one of four levels, and grammar classes are tiny at five students. Cost of instruction runs $175 per week. Stop by or write to: San Jerónimo 304, Col. Tlaltenango, AP 1520, Cuernavaca, Morelos, CP 62000, México.

VISITOR INFORMATION Although partially English-speaking, friendly, and eager to help, the staff at the **state tourist office** is coping with severe budget cuts. Spanish information on language schools and various sights will be photocopied for you, but the free map is less than useful—significant streets are covered by advertising logos. Better maps can be found in most papelerías (stationery stores) for $5. For tourist information in English, your best bet is to chat with Joel and Alex at **Tintorería Morelos** (*see* Laundry, *above*). At least one of them is usually around, and they are authorities on local day trips and nightspots. *Morelos Sur 187, tel. 73/14–37–90. Take RUTA 4 combi down Galeana to Himno Nacional, then walk 1 block west. Open Mon.–Sat. 8 AM–9 PM.*

VOLUNTEERING **Desarrollo Integral de la Familia (DIF)** provides health care, education, and counseling to communities in Morelos. If you plan to be in the area for two weeks or longer and are interested in volunteering, contact Alejandro Vera Jiménez. *Chapultepec 25, tel. 73/15–51–68. Take a RUTA 11 combi from cnr of Las Casas and Leyva.*

COMING AND GOING

BY BUS Those traveling by bus will find themselves at one of Cuernavaca's four bus stations. The largest is **Flecha Roja** (Morelos 503, at Arista), two blocks from the budget lodging area. It houses the **Estrella Blanca** line (tel. 73/12–81–90), which sends hourly buses to Mexico City (1 hr, $3). First-class *directo* (direct) buses to Acapulco (3½ hrs, $12) leave every two hours; air-conditioning and a TV bump the price up to $16. Hourly *ordinario* (indirect) buses to Acapulco (5 hrs, $16.50) stop in Chilpancingo (3 hrs, $10). Buses to Taxco (2½ hrs, $2) depart every three hours until 10:30 PM. Luggage storage is available (75¢ for 5 hrs, 20¢ each hr after that). The station is clean and well lit, but not a good place to crash.

A 10-minute walk from the zócalo, the dark and dingy **Estrella Roja** station (Galeana 401, at Cuauhtémotzin, tel. 73/18–59–34) serves Cuautla (1 hr, $2) every 30 minutes 6:15 AM–10:15 PM; transfer in Cuautla for Oaxaca city. Buses to Puebla (3½ hrs, $7) leave every hour 5 AM–7 PM. The budget hotels are seven blocks from the station—take any CENTRO combi down Morelos to Aragón y León.

The remaining two bus stations are less significant. You'll probably only visit **México-Zacatepec Autos Pullman de Morelos** (Abasolo 12, at Netzahualcóyotl, tel. 73/14–36–50) only to reach Xochicalco (*see* Near Cuernavaca, *below*); buses to Coatlán or Miocatlán will drop you off at the Xochicalco crossroads. On the outskirts of the city center, **Estrella de Oro** (Morelos Sur 900, tel. 73/12–30–55) is a *de paso* station, which means buses only stop here en route to somewhere else—departure times are sketchy.

BY CAR The new Mexico–Acapulco freeway intersecting Cuernavaca is in excellent condition. Tolls total $5.50 to Mexico City and $48 to Acapulco. To reach Puebla, drive on the Cuernavaca–Cuatla highway until you see the sign for Cuatla–Puebla.

BY PLANE Cuernevaca doesn't have its own airport, but Mexico City's International Airport is only an hour's drive away. **Aerotransporte Terrestre** (tel. 73/18–91–87) van service makes the trip Monday–Saturday every half hour 7 AM–11 PM for $6. If you're arriving in Mexico City and need transportation to Cuernavaca, look for the ticket kiosk in the main concourse beneath the giant "A."

GETTING AROUND

Exploring Cuernavaca is not difficult; the budget hotel zone, major sights, and main bus stations are within walking distance of one another. The zócalo, at the center of town, is actually made up of two plazas: **Jardín Juárez** and **Plaza de Armas.** The main streets in Cuernavaca are

The scrolled ironwork on the bandstand in the center of Jardín Juárez may look strangely familiar—it was designed by Gustave Eiffel, of Eiffel Tower fame.

Morelos, with northbound traffic, and Obregón and Matamoros/Galeana, on either side of Morelos, both of which allow only southbound traffic. Colectivos, also called *rutas* or *combis,* are the major means of daytime travel within Cuernavaca (besides walking, of course). Drivers of these white, squared-off minibuses cram in as many passengers as possible, and the 25¢ fare will get you almost anywhere. The name of the final destination is scrawled in whitewash on the front window of the combi, but routes vary, so double-check before boarding. You'll have to travel by taxi if you plan to sample Cuernavaca's nightlife, as combis stop running after 10 PM. Taxis don't have meters, so fares should be negotiated *before* you get in. Generally the fare within the *centro* (downtown) is $1.50, and about $1.25 more for outlying neighborhoods. Fares can shoot up to $5 late at night. A reliable cab service is **Radio Taxi Ejecutivo** (tel. 73/22–12–02).

WHERE TO SLEEP

Cuernavaca is popular on Fridays and weekends, so be sure to make reservations. You may want to shop around during the high season (June–Aug. and Dec.–Feb.), when prices at some of the larger hotels rise above the ones listed here. The budget lodging area lies along and around Aragón y León, a few blocks south of the Flecha Roja bus station and north of the zócalo. If the places below are booked, try the beautiful **Hotel Las Hortensias** (Hidalgo 22, tel. 73/18–52–65), with a pleasant courtyard and lumpy beds. A single here is $11.50 and a double is $15. If you're planning an extended stay, many of the city's language schools (*see* Schools, *above*) give students, and sometimes travelers, the option of living with a family.

➢ **UNDER $10** • **Casa de Huéspedes la China Poblana.** Hidden behind the restaurant of the same name, this hotel is clean and spacious, though the architecture leaves a bit to be desired. There are only eight rooms ($5.50 singles, $7 doubles, all with private bath) so reservations are essential. *Aragón y León 110, tel. 73/12–37–12. Luggage storage. Wheelchair access.*

Hotel Roma. The sunny courtyard with palm trees is more inviting than the clean, basic rooms with tiny bathrooms. Singles and doubles cost $8–$9, and quads are only $12. *Matamoros 17, tel. 73/18–87–78. 1 block east of Flech Roja station. 40 rooms, all with bath.*

➢ **UNDER $15** • **Hotel Colonial.** Smack in the middle of the budget lodging area, this hotel is a step above the competition. The large, clean rooms sport high ceilings, and some boast wrought-iron terraces. Others don't even have windows, so ask to see a few before paying. The young female staff is friendly and helpful, and silence is observed beginning at 10 PM. Singles cost $8–$9.50, doubles go for $10.50–$12, and triples are $14. *Aragón y León 104, tel. 73/18–64–14. 14 rooms, all with bath. Luggage storage. Wheelchair access.*

Hotel España. This hotel lives up to its name, with Spanish arches, patterned tiles, and palm trees. The first floor contains a Spanish restaurant, a reception area, and a small lounge. Clean rooms ($10 singles, $13.50 doubles) occupy the second and third floors and cluster around a courtyard with potted flowers. Although all rooms have TVs, the furniture is worn, some rooms reek of cigarette smoke, and the noise level can be bothersome in the rooms facing the street. *Morelos 200, at Rayón, tel. 73/18–67–44. 24 rooms, all with bath. Reservations advised.*

Hotel Iberia. The exceptional entranceway, covered with tiles and plants, gives way to plain, muggy rooms. However, there's hot water, a TV downstairs, and a location to be proud of. Singles run $11.75, doubles $13.50. *Rayón 9, tel. 73/12–60–40. 25 rooms, all with bath. Luggage storage. Wheelchair access.*

FOOD

Small, cheap restaurants abound in the budget lodging area and on the streets surrounding the zócalo. Most serve a mix of *antojitos* (appetizers) and tourist grub such as burgers and fries. While scrutinizing menus, look for the following Morelos specialties: *tamales de frijole* (bean tamales) from Axochiapan; *tamales de bagre* (catfish tamales) from Miacatlán; *mole verde*, also called *mole pipián* (the same recipe as Puebla's famous mole poblano but with green salsa instead of red), found in Laguna de Coatelco; *cecina de yecapixtla*, a dry, salty beef; and *tacos acorazados*, tortillas filled with rice, beans, or whatever your heart desires. For decent eats, try **Los Arcos** (Jardín de los Héroes 4, tel. 73/12–44–86), a popular patio restaurant with a sparkling fountain, shady plants, and a generous comida corrida ($2.75). Jumping at night, **La Universal** (Guerrero 2, tel. 73/18–67–32) serves stingier portions of traditional food to a crowd of gringos, but the $2 daiquiris may prompt you to forget its faults. The **Mercado Principal** (central market; off Guerrero, north of the zócalo) is filled with cheap eats, but has a reputation for being particularly unhygienic.

➢ **UNDER $5 • Gin Gen Comida China.** If you're looking for a break from tacos and tortas, this sharp, red-and-white restaurant won't disappoint. Mexican/American fare fills the breakfast menu and Chinese food is served after noon—the shrimp chop suey ($4) is mouthwatering. Mary, the outstanding cook, and her husband, whose paintings grace the walls, are both well-versed in many languages and create a lively environment. *Rayón, at Alarcón, tel. 73/18–60–46. Open Mon.–Sat. 8–8, Sun. until 6.*

Naturiza. Health-conscious locals of all ages gather here to fill up on generous portions of creative vegetarian cooking or to buy vitamins from the small counter in the back. The menu changes daily, but look for such delights as creamed carrot soup and cauliflower dumplings. Comidas corridas run $2.50, and the à la carte breakfasts, like granola and yogurt or omelets, are even cheaper. *Alvaro Obregón 327-1, btw Victoria and Ricardo Linares, tel. 73/12–46–26. Open Mon.–Sat. 8:30–7.*

Restaurant El Salto. In the village of San Antón, this off-the-beaten-track restaurant is filled with cuernavaquenses noisily eating and drinking. The menu includes a selection of fish, chicken, and game dishes, served in pottery made in the village. The most expensive dish is pigeon for two ($4); the garlic soup ($2), the cactus tamale ($3), and the bowl-size rum-and-tequila "Convento" ($2.50) are all recommended. *Bajada del Salto 31, San Antón, tel. 73/18–12–19. Take RUTA 4 combi from Artega, at Morelos. Open daily 10:30–8:30.*

La Tarterie. This restaurant serves a $2 comida corrida, espresso, and a large variety of desserts under outdoor umbrellas. A breakfast of fried eggs or not-too-tender steak with beans, tortillas, fresh-squeezed orange juice, and coffee is $3.50. Vegetarians can enjoy the $2 soups and salads. *Fray Bartolomé de las Casas 103, tel. 73/12–41–52. In Plazuela Zacate (a.k.a. Plaza 2 de Mayo de 1812). Open daily 9–8.*

➢ **UNDER $10 • Los Pasteles de Vienes.** Continental cuisine and European-style pastries are served here, while lace curtains and jazz music float on the breeze. The restaurant is a meeting place for couples and students, and its location—around the corner from the Teatro Ocampo—makes it a great spot to grab a cappuccino after the show. Recommended dishes include the veal cutlet in wine and mushroom sauce ($8), asparagus stuffed with ham in béarnaise sauce ($5), and spinach crepes ($4). *Lerdo de Tejada 302, at I. Comonfort, tel. 73/14–34–04. Open daily 8 AM–10 PM.*

WORTH SEEING

The zócalo is the heart of Cuernavaca; it's made up of the **Plaza de Armas,** where you can unwind beside the fountain, and the more lively **Jardín Juárez,** the oldest park in the city. The zócalo is also near a number of attractions easily visited in a day. Other sites, particularly Casa de Maximiliano, the Jungla Mágica, San Antón Falls, and Pirámide de Teopanzolco, are in outlying *colonias* (neighborhoods), so plan on taking combis. Most museums and historical sites are closed on Monday.

AYUNTAMIENTO DE CUERNAVACA Also known as the Palacio Municipal, the Ayuntamiento displays murals by Salvador Tarazona that depict Cuernavaca's history and scenes of the Tlahuica civilization. *Morelos 199, at Callejón Borda. Admission free. Open weekdays 8–8.*

For a glimpse of local life, visit Mercado Principal López Mateos, where mounds of chiles tower over women selling huitlacoche (a corn-fungus delicacy), and eloquent herbolarios (herb vendors) will guarantee a cure for whatever ails you.

BALNEARIO TEMIXCO This aquatic park offers 15 swimming pools, 10 wading pools, waterslides, sports fields, gardens, a full bar, and a history. Originally a 16th-century sugar plantation, it was used as a fort in the Mexican Revolution and as a prisoner-of-war camp during World War II. The 8-kilometer bus trip from downtown takes half an hour. Ask the driver to let you off at the gate. *Emiliano Zapata 11, Col. Temixco, tel. 73/25–03–55. Take TEMIXCO combi from Galeana. Admission: $4.50. Open daily 9–6.*

CASA DE MAXIMILIANO This adobe house (also called Casa del Olvido) was bought by Emperor Maximilian in 1866, and is known as the "House of Forgetfulness." One reason given for this name is that Maximilian came here to escape political and domestic troubles. Another is that he "forgot" to build a room for his wife Carlota—but made sure to include a small house in the garden for his lover, La India Bonita. Today the Casa features the **Museo de Medicina Tradicional,** which features exhibits about the medicinal and religious uses of Mexican plants and herbs since pre-Columbian times (*see box* Folk Medicine, *below*). Many of the plants described in the museum can be found in the adjoining botanical garden and some are available for purchase; ask in the musuem. *Matamoros 14, Col. Acapantzinga, tel. 73/12–59–55. Take RUTA 6 combi from Degollado, btw Guerrero and Clavijero. Admission free. Open daily 9–5.*

CATEDRAL DE LA ASUNCION In use between the early 16th and late 19th centuries, this cathedral encloses a convent and three *capillas* (chapels) within its high walls. The oldest

Folk Medicine

Morelos is infused with a rich history of herbal medicine practice that dates back to the Aztec people. At that time illnesses were categorized by four possible causes: infliction by the gods, negative energy, evil spells, and a loss of destiny. Today, traditional healers only distinguish two categories of sickness: natural (parasites, rheumatism) and supernatural (evil eye, spirits, fright). These groups are further subdivided into hot ailments (fever, nervousness, shock) and cold ailments (sterility, bronchitis).

When the Spaniards arrived in the 16th century, Mexican herbology enriched the less-sophisticated medicine of the Europeans. Two centuries later, the birth of botany initiated the empirical study of medicine, but herbal medicine retained its popularity and respect. Today, modern medicine is expensive and difficult to access from rural communities. This, combined with a strong faith in the healing properties of herbology, means that herbal medicine continues to play an important role in Morelos. Herbs are harvested in the state's 300 rural communities, curanderos (natural healers) flock to the mercados on weekends to offer advice and sell their concoctions, and several stores still sell natural antidotes for every ailment imaginable, from hangnails to herpes. To study the history of herbology and purchase healing plants, visit Casa de Maximiliano (see above) and the weekend mercado in Tepoztlán (see Near Cuernavaca, below) where you'll find a concentration of ancient healers.

structure in the complex, the **Capilla Abierta de San José,** was built by Hernán Cortés in 1522. Its design, with only a partial roof, was fashioned so the indigenous people, used to worshipping outside, would feel more at home, and would therefore be more likely to convert. The **Templo de la Asunción Gloriosa de la Virgen María** was completed in 1552. Inside, newly uncovered remnants of early 17th-century frescoes, supposedly painted here by a Japanese immigrant, depict the crucifixion of Christian missionaries in Japan. Near the entrance gate to the cathedral grounds, the smaller **Templo de la Tercera Orden de San Francisco,** took 13 years to build due to the elaborate gilded ornamentation. The newest structure is the **Capilla de Carmen,** which dates from the late 19th century and has beautiful *retablos* (altarpieces) on the walls. Sundays at 11 AM and 8 PM, you can witness a "mariachi mass" (*see box* Liberation Theology, *below*). *Hidalgo 17, at Morelos, tel. 73/12–12–90. 3 blocks west of zócalo. Admission free. Open Mon.–Sat. 9–2 and 4–8, all day Sun.*

JARDÍN BORDA The mansion, landscaped grounds, and botanical gardens here were built by Taxco silver millionaire Manuel de la Borda as a retreat for his father. In 1865 it became a symbol of imperial Mexico when the estate was turned into a summer retreat for Emperor Maximilian and his wife, Carlota. The original fruit trees and ornamental plants still flourish in 100 varieties, and the six refurbished front rooms of the mansion now house the **Centro de Arte Jardín Borda,** where you can view the work of local and international artists. The **bookstore,**

Liberation Theology

Liberation theology is an interpretation of the gospels emphasizing Christ's involvement in social justice; since the early 1960s it has been the point of intersection between religion and Latin American politics. Cuernavaca's bishop, Sergio Méndez Arceo, acted as the cornerstone of this movement, and played a prominent role in the Second Vatican Council (1962–65), which made a historic revision of Catholic doctrine. Arceo had a growing following among Latin America's Catholic leadership, and Cuernavaca became an international center for the reform-minded during the '60s and '70s. Ideas that Arceo had implemented nearly a decade earlier were adopted by the church, including administering mass in the vernacular (Spanish instead of Latin), and moving the figure of Jesus Christ so the priest no longer had to turn his back to the congregation to face it when leading prayer. Arceo also began using the music of the people to accompany religious services, and the "Mariachi Mass" is still held every Sunday in the cathedral.

Members of the church still uphold the ideals of liberation theology and continue to play a role in Latin American politics. Recently, Bishop Samuel Ruíz of Chiapas came into political prominence with his public support of indigenous peoples' demands for land and democracy in Chiapas. He has also worked as a facilitator in the negotiations between the Zapatista rebels and the Mexican government. Ray Plankey, a Catholic lay minister who had worked with Arceo, founded the Cuernavaca Center for International Dialogue on Development—a nonprofit educational organization. The CCIDD runs two-week programs and day trips to rural churches that give groups of North Americans an opportunity to experience firsthand the harsh economic reality of many Mexicans, and to challenge their religious and social visions. Room, board, and the program cost $40 a day. For more information, write to CCIDD at 9051-C Siempre Viva Rd., Suite MX, 921-63, San Diego, CA 92173, or contact the center directly in Cuernavaca: Leyva 39, Centro Cuernavaca, Morelos, CP 62000, México, tel. 73/12–65–64, fax 73/12–93–92.

open Tuesday–Sunday 11–3 and 6–10, sells classical music on CD, rare Frida Kahlo post-cards, and books (some in English) on topics ranging from Picasso's works to Mexican cooking. **Cine Morelos** (*see* Cinemas and Theatres, *below*) hosts international and cultural films here every Friday at 7:30 PM. *Morelos 103, at Hidalgo, tel. 73/12–92–37. Admission: 70¢, free Wed. Open Tues.–Sun. 10–5:30.*

JUNGLA MAGICA It's not Disneyland, but it's not the local fair either. This wonderland boasts waterslides, a haunted house, a small aquatic park, a natural lake, an aviary, a chilling serpentarium, and a planetarium. *Chapultepec 27, tel. 73/15–34–11. From cnr of Las Casas and Leyva, take RUTA 11 combi and ask driver to let you off at Jungla Mágica; walk 1 block downhill on Chapultepec. Admission: $3.50; rides and attractions an additional 10¢–60¢. Open Tues.–Sun. 9:30–6.*

PALACIO DE CORTÉS Built by the Tlahuica, this imposing building has been a potent symbol of power throughout Cuernavaca's history. At first it followed a simple plan, but as Cortés gained wealth, influence, titles, and a wife, the palace grew. It later passed into the hands of the crown and, during the War of Independence, was used as a prison for revolutionaries José María Morelos, Ignacio López Rayón, and Nicolás Bravo. During the Revolution of 1910, the palace was abandoned and later became the office of the municipal government. Today the palace houses the **Museo Cuauhnáhuac,** which traces the history of man and Morelos from pre-colonial settlers to the present. To the right of the palace is the **Jardín de Arte Luis Betanzos,** where indigenous artists sell everything from brightly painted wooden toys to beautiful silver work fairly cheap. *Juárez, at Hidalgo. Palacio/museo admission: $2; free with ISIC card and on Sun. Open Tues.–Sun. 10–5.*

PIRAMIDE DE TEOPANZOLCO This small, Tlahuican ceremonial center predates the Aztec presence in Cuernavaca, as its name (Place of the Old Temple) suggests. When the Aztec conquered the Tlahuica, they began building a new temple around the old one to prove their domination, but were interrupted by the Spanish conquest. The unfinished remains were rediscovered in 1910, and today you can scramble up the stairs of the 30-foot central pyramid. It's a 15-minute ride out here, and you'll probably have the place to yourself. *From east side of Mercado Principal, take RUTA 19 combi. Admission: $1.50. Open daily 10–4:30.*

SAN ANTON FALLS Although this 40-meter waterfall cascades into a brown, littered pool, the winding sidewalks around and under the falls make a trip here worth your while. Half the fun is strolling through the barrio of San Antón, where vendors sell Virgin Mary figurines and terra-cotta pots of colorful flowers. While here, stop for a meal at **Restaurant El Salto** (*see* Food, *above*), a half block away from the waterfall. *Bajada del Salto, Barrio de San Antón. From Arteaga and Morelos, take RUTA 4 combi, then walk downhill on Av. del Salto for 3 blocks; a sign on your right leads to the falls. Admission: 70¢. Open weekdays 10–6, weekends 8–6.*

AFTER DARK

Participate in the free art classes at Alfer Importaciones (Abasolo 18, at Galeana), held weekdays 10:30–2 and 4–7, and you'll learn to paint ceramics, create handicrafts with felt, work with macramé, and design Spanish-style cards.

There's a night scene all week long in Cuernavaca, but it especially perks up on weekends jammed with students, locals, and travelers. Those interested in cultural events should check the bulletin board at the **University Cultural Center** (Morelos Sur 136), as well as the booth on the corner of Morelos and Rayón.

BARS The cafés on the zócalo are the most pleasant places to drink beer. **Harry's Bar** (Gutemberg 5, tel. 73/12–76–39) where yuppie chilangos and cuernavaquenses hang out, is the first place any young resident will send you. All week long international students and locals guzzle drinks amid the blaring music and videotaped sports games. It's a meat market on weekends. The bar labeled "second best" by locals is **Sapo-Sabio** (Madero 503, Col. Mira, tel. 73/18–48–83), located 15 minutes out of town in the Francisco Madero area. It too plays U.S. and Mexican rock music Wednesday–Saturday 7 PM–5:30 AM.

CINEMAS AND THEATERS **Teatro Ocampo** (tel. 73/18–63–85), on the Jardín Juárez, is home to Cuernavaca's repertory company. Posters around town and on the pillars in front of the theater display upcoming events; tickets for live performances cost $4 ($2 students). **Cine Morelos** (Morelos, at Rayón, tel. 73/18–84–18) screens a variety of international films (with Spanish subtitles) and regularly hosts national and international music and dance performances. Events are posted on a banner at the corner of Morelos and Rayón. **Cinematográfica Las Plazas** (Gutemberg 101, tel. 73/14–07–93), in Las Plazas shopping center, shows mostly Hollywood films with Spanish subtitles.

DANCING Cuernavaca flaunts a number of flashy clubs with high cover charges. Two happening discos are **Baby Rock** (Nueva Italia 11-N, tel. 73/13–90–97), a classy Mexican chain and favorite among international language students, and **Barba-Zul** (Prado 10, Col. San Jerónimo, tel. 73/13–19–76), north of the centro. Both charge a $7 cover on Fridays and Saturdays, but are free for everyone on Wednesdays, and for women on Thurdays. The closest popular disco to the zócalo and the budget hotel zone is **Kaova** (Morelos Sur 302, tel. 73/15–43–88), a private club frequented by *juniors* (sons and daughters of the wealthy elite). Cover is $7 on Friday and Saturday, and free Wednesday, but come on Thursday when it's not only free, but has an open bar. Popular with locals, **Zumbale** (Chapultepec, tel. 73/22–53–43) plays salsa and merengue music Thursday–Saturday 9:30 PM–7 AM, and RUTA 17 and RUTA 20 buses from Degollado pass right by it. Only men pay the $7 cover. There's also a huge gay disco called **Shadé** (López Mateos, east side of Mercado Principal), where DJ's spin a variety of music until 5 AM Wednesday–Saturday. The bus ride here is long and meandering, so catch a $1 cab from the zócalo.

LIVE MUSIC Live music plays on Sunday and Thursday in **Jardín Juárez,** and just about every weekend at **Jardín Borda** (*see* Worth Seeing, *above*). For your own private concert, hire one of the mariachi bands that loiter on the northeast corner of **Plaza de Armas.** The **Catedral de la Asunción** occasionally sponsors choral performances, but if you'd prefer a club atmosphere, **Flamingo's Teatro Bar** (Herradura de Plata 102, tel. 73/17–15–54) hosts jazz on weekends with a $3.50 cover.

Near Cuernavaca

TEPOZTLÁN

The small town of Tepoztlán rests north of Cuernavaca, in a valley surrounded by rugged mountains eroded into eerie forms by wind and water. The Nahuatl Indians compose the largest indigenous group here, and their language and customs continue to prevail. Their rich heritage, both ceremonial and supernatural, is clearly evident; everyone from *curanderos* (healers) to Nahuatl authors infiltrates the mercado on weekends, dispensing their rich culture to those with an eager ear.

The Parque Nacional el Tepozteco—covering four states and almost all of Tepoztlán—offers exciting hiking and camping opportunities in a majestic landscape. Contact Campamento Meztitla (see Where to Sleep, below) for further info.

To trace the fascinating history and mysticism of this town and its people, begin with a hike to the **Tlahuica ruins,** gravely capped by the towering **Pirámide Tepozteco**; you'll almost feel the spirits pushing you along as you weave in and out of the sacred rooms. The pyramid was named in honor of Tepoztécatl, the god of pulque. According to legend, the gods Mayahuel and Patécatl discovered how to ferment maguey into pulque. They bore 400 children, one of which, Tepoztécatl, became a great leader and accidentally stumbled upon the curative and stimulative properties of pulque. The walls surrounding the pyramid are covered with bas-reliefs representing the 20 symbols of the days and depicting the gods of the carinal points and other mythological figures. You'll also notice drawings of important historical symbols, including the crown of a king and a bronze axe. The path leading to the Tlahuica ruins begins at the end of Avenida Tepozteco, a 15-minute walk past the plaza. Look for the formation said to look like a flying saucer among the scarred cliffs of the looming *cerro* (hill) as you make the rocky, 45-minute climb—1½ hours if it's wet and rainy. A small stand at the top sells water and soft drinks for about 75¢ each. *Admission: $1.50, free Sun. Open daily 10–4:30.*

Although the Tlahuica, related to the Nahuatl, were continually attacked by the Aztec, they were never fully conquered until Cortés arrived in 1521. At that time, Christianity was strictly imposed, and it's rumored that a Dominican friar tore down the Tepoztécatl statue that used to reside in the pyramid, sending its fragments to the nearby town of Oaxtepec to serve as the cement of the new convent. The **Ex-Convento de la Natividad** was thus constructed, with imposing walls more than 2 meters thick—all the better to defy any natural (or supernatural) storms. The convent is known for its syncretic *tequitqui* style, in which Christian and indigenous symbols mingle in faded frescoes. Notice the subtle image of Quetzalcoatl, god of fertility, painted into the intricate black and white border design running high along the antechamber walls. The convent's original bathrooms are another unusual preservation. Take a peek in the **Iglesia de la Asunción** next door and in the **Museo Arqueológico Colección Carlos Pellicer,** which exhibits pre-colonial artifacts and photos of the archaeological sites where these relics were recovered. *Next to mercado, 1 block east of Av. Tepozteco. Museum entrance on Calle de la Conchita, a small road behind the church, tel. 739/18–51–01. Museum admission: $1. Open Tues.–Sun. 10–6.*

On September 8th and 9th, the Fiesta de Tepozteco is celebrated, honoring Tepoztécatl, the god of pulque. The festival features a procession to the Tepoztlán pyramid. In a time-honored attempt to erase "pagan" practices, the convent holds its own festival at the same time.

COMING AND GOING Tepoztlán-bound buses (1 hr, 75¢) leave every half hour until 9 PM from Mercado Principal in Cuernavaca. To reach town from Tepoztlán's bus station (a 10-minute walk), follow the highway downhill; it will become Avenida Tepozteco, which leads straight to the pyramid. The last bus to Cuernavaca leaves at 8:30 PM.

WHERE TO SLEEP Budget lodging is scarce, but if you're willing to pay $18 ($25 with meals) for a smallish single and $32 ($46 with meals) for a double, **Casa Iccemanyan** (Calle del Olvido 26, tel. 739/5–08–99) has a beautiful swimming pool and an outdoor restaurant. A cheaper option is **Las Cabañas** (Cinco de Mayo 54, no phone), a tiny family-run hostel on the edge of town. Campers should visit **Campamento Meztitla** (Rte. 2, tel. 739/5–00–68) on the Tepoztlán–Yautepec highway, but it takes a taxi (15 min, $3.50) to get here. Camping costs $4 per person per night, and $2 to rent a six-person tent. Bathrooms, showers, and drinking water are provided. You can't camp at the ruins anymore—the uncompromising entrance gate is locked by guards every night. But you're free to scour the surrounding hillsides for a comfy spot.

On Sundays, market vendors sell yummy enchiladas and tortas. Look for the Tepoznieves stand selling tequila ice cream, a Tepoztlán specialty.

FOOD There are several good restaurants along Avenida Tepozteco. Try the chicken mole ($5) at **Los Colorines** (Tepozteco 13, tel. 739/5–01–98), popular with locals in town. For Mexican and Hindu cuisine, stop by the **Restaurante Vegetariano Govinda** at the **Proyecto Milenio** (Tepozteco 19, tel. 739/5–17–15). The "om" burgers are delicious. The Proyecto also houses the adjoining **Café la Arábica,** where you can sip coffee and peruse the book collection. You can also use the Proyecto's long-distance phone and fax services.

XOCHICALCO

Located 38 kilometers southeast of Cuernavaca, the ancient city of Xochicalco ("Place of the House of the Flowers") sits atop terraced hills overlooking a valley and a small city of the same name. These partially excavated ruins are the most fascinating in Morelos, displaying elements of Olmec and Mayan architecture; the Toltec, Mixtec, or Zapotec may also have inhabited this site at different points in time. Some believe that Xochicalco was a ceremonial center where scholars met to correct their calendars. In any case, when the Spaniards arrived in the early 16th century, it's believed that the people of the valley came from miles around to protect the ancient city by covering it with rocks and earth. The pre-Columbian ruins of both Xochicalco and Teopanzolco weren't rediscovered until the Mexican Revolution. During a battle in the early 1900s, Emiliano Zapata and his troops found that bullets ricocheted off the hill they were holding; they later discovered they had been bouncing off grass-covered walls.

Opened in April 1996, the **Museo de Sitio de Xochicalco,** 300 meters before the ruins, hosts a huge display of archaeological pieces excavated over the years. The six rooms contain intricate hieroglyphics and statues of the gods. In the second room, *Señor de Rojo* (sun god) has retained its orginal form and color, with the exception of its deteriorated face. The museum guides possess an extensive knowledge of the site and its history that should be taken advantage of; you're on your own at the site.

The center of Xochicalco is the **Plaza Ceremonial** (Plaza 1), located at the city's highest base elevation. Only priests were allowed here, in what is believed to be the main ceremonial enclosure, with people of the valley congregating to trade goods in a local bazaar on the surrounding grounds. The intricately carved **Pirámide de la Serpiente Emplumada** (Pyramid of the Feathered Serpent) depicts the alignment of the calendars of several Indian tribes. These are presided over by Quetzalcoatl, shown as a headdressed serpent with two mouths, two tongues, and a fan of feathers for a tail. His left hand discards an erroneous date (represented by a hieroglyph) while his right hand pulls in a correct one. The correct date has been identified as 13 Monkey, of the 260-day Mesoamerican calendar. You can climb the steep staircase of the **Temple of the Stelae,** also on the Plaza Ceremonial, to get a commanding view of the surrounding hills and the valley below.

Down the hill in the **main plaza** (Plaza 2) is the **Two Glyph Stelae Square,** arranged to chart the sun's path through the day. Below this is a ball court—one of many found in ruins throughout Mexico. It is believed that the game played here involved two teams of five men, each attempting to get a small, hard ball through the circular stone hoops on either end of the court.

The underground **observatory,** one of 32 interconnected tunnels below the pyramids, was used to trace the sun's path throughout the year; its movement is traced by the small circle of light on the cavern floor. At noon on the annual summer solstice (usually June 21), the sun's rays completely illuminate the chamber's interior. The event held great religious significance—for one moment each year the celestial, the terrestrial, and the subterranean were united.

The small snack bar at the ruins offers nothing substantial; take a picnic lunch or hitchhike toward the village of El Rodeo, about a kilometer east past the Crucero de Xochicalco (the intersection of Ruta 166 and the road to the ruins). The guards seem pretty vigilant about keeping campers away, so make sure you're on the last bus. *Admission: $2; free Sun. and with student ID. Ruins open Tues.–Sun. 10–5. Observatory open daily 10–4.*

COMING AND GOING **Autotransportes Chapultepec** is the only bus line that runs from the bus station in Cuernavaca all the way to the site. Their CUENTEPEC–ALPUYECA buses (50¢) leave from the Mercado Prinicpal every hour 5:30 AM–8 PM. Fewer buses take you back, however, passing the ruins at approximately 1, 3, 6, and 7 PM. If you have a car, take Highway 95 (Mexico-Acapulco) until you arrive at the fork in the road. Bear to your right and you'll see the ruins gleaming in the sunlight at the top of the hill. If you reach Alpuyeca or El Rodeo Lake, you've chosen the wrong road.

CUAUTLA

Warmer, drier, and less built-up than Cuernavaca, Cuautla is the second-largest city in Morelos. Located about 12 kilometers southeast of Cuernavaca, its dusty provinciality belies the fact that this is a favorite vacation spot for the many Mexicans drawn here by Cuautla's famed mineral baths. The tradition of the wealthy elite soaking in sulphur water reportedly dates back to *Moctezuma* (Montezuma), who apparently enjoyed the restorative powers of these springs. The city was built into a prosperous colonial spa by the Spanish in the 17th century, but today the palm-lined streets roar with traffic, and the natural hot springs are now more like unkempt public pools than therapeutic spas.

The few remaining historical attractions are clustered in the town center and are a source of local pride. Cuautla was a revolutionary stronghold during the War of Independence and the Mexican Revolution, and both rebel leader Emiliano Zapata and revolutionary priest José María Morelos are honored here. In 1812 Morelos and his 3,000 men held the city for 72 days against the attacking Royalist force of 20,000. It was only when starvation set in that they surrendered. The Battle of Cuautla is commemorated by a dominating statue of Morelos, who now waves a machete over the Plaza Galeana.

Across from this statue is the church that served as Morelos's headquarters, the **Iglesia de San Diego,** and the adjacent **Convento de San Diego.** This graceful convent was later converted into a railway station and today houses the **Casa de la Cultura.** The convent also contains Cuautla's helpful **tourist office** (Galeana, tel. 735/2–52–21; open weekdays 8–6, Sat. 8–5, Sun. 8–3) and the tiny **Museo José María Morelos** (open Tues.–Sun. 10–5), featuring historical items from the wars of Spanish conquest.

It's a five-minute walk south on Galeana from the convent to the zócalo. On its northeast corner is the **Palacio Municipal** (tel. 735/2–65–11); on the west side is the **Iglesia de Santo Domingo** (tel. 735/2–00–06), which served as a hospital during the War of Independence and was defended by four cannons, one on each corner. At the southeast corner of the zócalo sits **Casa de Morelos** (Callejón del Castigo 3, tel. 735/2–83–31), Morelos's home while defending Cuautla. This small building, with peeling red paint and a white doorway, now houses the free **Museo de la Independencia,** open Tuesday–Sunday 10–5.

A 15-minute walk south of the zócalo on Guerrero brings you to **Jardín Revolución del Sur** where Emiliano Zapata is buried. Zapata was assassinated at Chinameca, 31 kilometers away, and his image assumed renewed political meaning with the armed uprising of the Zapatista Army in Chiapas. Facing the Jardín is **Iglesia Señor del Pueblo,** named in Zapata's honor.

COMING AND GOING Although it's the second largest city in Morelos, Cuautla is fairly manageable on foot—but be prepared for frequent street-name changes and a scarcity of street signs. The city is shaped roughly like an L, with the centro at the crook and the Alameda a few blocks north of the zócalo, on Galeana. Most colectivos run on Zavala/Reforma and Alvaro Obregón, and cost about 15¢.

There are two neighboring bus stations in Cuautla. **Cristóbal Colón** (2 de Mayo 97, at Reforma, tel. 735/2–31–68) is located four blocks from the zócalo. It serves Mexico City (1½ hrs, $3.50) every 15 minutes and Oaxaca (7 hrs, $10) at 9:45 AM, 11:15 AM, and 11:30 AM. **Estrella Roja** (Costeño, at Vásquez, tel. 735/2–05–49) serves Cuernavaca (1 hr, 75¢) every 15 minutes, Mexico City (2 hrs, $3.25) every 20 minutes, and Puebla (3 hrs, $2.50) at 5 PM. To get from either station to the zócalo, walk 3–4 blocks west. From the Estrella Roja station in Cuernavaca, buses to Cuautla leave every 15 minutes between 6 AM and 10 PM.

WHERE TO SLEEP Cuautla's hotels aren't the cheapest in the region, but prices aren't ridiculous. **Hotel Central** (Fin del Rul 21, off Plaza Galeana, no phone) has very basic rooms grouped around a grassy courtyard. Some of the bathrooms here are very small and dark, so ask to see a few rooms before paying; singles are $5.50, doubles $11. The **Villa Juvenil Cuautla** (Unidad Deportiva Morelos, tel. 735/2–02–18) is the best deal in town. The parklike grounds are well groomed, and it's only $3.50 for a dorm bed and use of the sparkling-clean communal bathrooms. The hostel is 10 minutes from the Cristóbal Colón bus station: Walk west on 2 de Mayo, right on Niños Héroes, over the bridge, and enter the parking lot to your right. If you get lost, just keep asking where the Villa Juvenil is; everyone in town knows. For camping info see Outdoor Activities, *below.*

FOOD There's no lack of cheap dining establishments in Cuautla. On the northeast side of the zócalo, the cafetería **Colón** (tel. 735/2–23–17) sells cheap comida corrida until fairly late and offers a good view of the square. Also try **Mario** (Ramierez Ferrara 10, tel. 735/2–08–16) which serves traditional Mexican food, **Cafetería y Jugos Alameda** (Galeana 40, tel. 735/2–24–52), where you can slurp milkshakes and juices, or the popular burger joint **Las Tortugas** (Plaza Fuerte de Galeana 84, tel. 735/2–35–08). For a more formal dinner, try the restaurant in **Hotel Colonial** (José Perdiz 18, tel. 735/2–21–64), known for its $7 *cabrito colonial* (specially prepared kid—goat meat).

OUTDOOR ACTIVITIES Splashing around in one of Cuautla's many *balnearios* (spa and swimming areas) isn't all it's cracked up to be. The baths are more like pleasant municipal pools, but if you're dying to get wet, these are your best options. Beware: pools get crowded with schoolkids July–September, December, and the week before Easter. **Oaxtepec** (Carretera México–La Pera–Oaxtepec, tel. 735/6–01–01) is the showpiece of the resorts, with 25 pools, a cable car, lodging, and waterslides. Catch a blue OAXTEPEC combi (½ hr) from three blocks north of the zócalo and have $6 ready for admission. **El Rollo Las Olas** (Carretera Alpuyera–Jojutla–Tlaquiltenango, tel. 734/2–19–88) takes second place with two waterslides, 14 toboggans, and 15 pools. **Las Estacas** (Carretera México–La Pera–Ticumán, tel. 734/2–14–44), about 24 kilometers outside town, features a spring-fed river that floats guests through a patch of jungle. The resort also has a restaurant and camping facilities; admission is about $4. If resort prices are too steep, there are four other pool areas in Cuautla. **Los Limones** (tel. 735/2–70–02) is the smallest and best, with two clean pools and grassy campsites for $2.50. **Agua Linda** (next to Villa Juvenil Cuautla) and **El Almeal** (two blocks east of Los Limones, tel. 735/2–17–51) each have a few pools and lots of aqua-blue cement. Admission to either balneario is $2. **Agua Hedionda** (tel. 735/2–00–44) is a sulphur spring whose name means "stinking water." If you can stand the rotten-egg stench, the water circulating in the pools is fresh and rumored to possess curative properties. To reach the springs, catch the AGUAS HEDIONDAS combi either across from Plaza Galeana or just past the Niños Héroes bridge, in front of Unidad Deportiva. Oaxtepec is great for camping, but avoid Los Limones, Agua Hedionda, and El Almeal if you're looking to stay the night.

Taxco

Taxco is a city of twisting, cobblestone streets, red-tile colonial houses, silversmiths' shops, and, of course, busload upon busload of tourists, most of them hell-bent on bringing half of the town's silver supply home in their carry-on luggage. The town, so picturesque it hardly seems real, was built in a small cleft in the Sierra Madre mountains. As the city grows, it creeps higher into the mountains, and now many streets sport steep grades and sharp right-angle turns— unique and inviting, but unnavigable in a wheelchair. Anyone else will find this town of just 150,000 manageable, however, and may be pleasantly surprised by its concentrated atmosphere, compared to sprawling Puebla and Cuernavaca. Discover this for yourself any evening in **Plaza Borda,** the peaceful zócalo, where local families mingle and gossip among the wrought-iron benches and well-kept walkways.

Overlooking the zócalo is the **Catedral de Santa Prisca,** Taxco's incredibly ornate, pink-stone cathedral—a testament to the silver industry that sustains this town. Cortés's men set up the first mine in the Americas here in 1531, but it was only briefly profitable, and the aqueducts arching over the city's western entrance are the sole architectural remains of their stay. Following a 200-year lull, however, a more lucrative silver vein was found—this time by José de la Borda. According to local legend, the Frenchman accidentally discovered this vein when his horse stumbled on a rocky pathway. The cathedral, Borda's ostentatious gift to the city, is the source of the local aphorism: "If God gives to Borda, Borda gives to God." The Borda family also built a few of the mansions that surround the zócalo, but the restaurants and shops that now inhabit these buildings indirectly owe their existence to yet another foreign fortune hunter, U.S. college professor William Spratling. Spratling settled here in the 1930s, and his innovations in handwrought silver design inspired the tourist industry that thrives here today.

Taxco is famous for milagros—silver or tin pieces representing afflicted parts of the human anatomy, such as the eyes, feet, arms, or legs. As an appeal for healing, the figurines are pinned on the skirts of saints in churches.

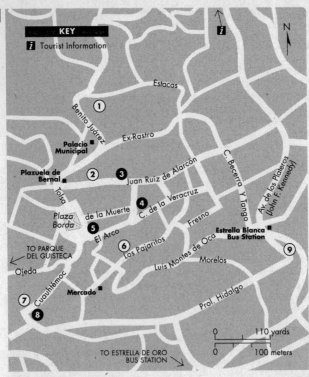

Sights ●

Casa Humboldt, **3**

Catedral de
Santa Prisca, **5**

Museo de
Arqueología, **4**

Plazuela de
San Juan, **8**

Lodging ○

Casa de Huéspedes
Arellano, **6**

Hotel
Casa Grande, **7**

Hotel Los Arcos, **2**

Hotel Posada
Santa Anita, **9**

Posada
San Javier, **1**

KEY

i Tourist Information

BASICS

CASAS DE CAMBIO Silver shops usually accept U.S. dollars, but you should change money at the banks along Cuauhtémoc. **Banco Confia** (Plaza Borda 2, tel. 762/2–01–92) exchanges money weekdays 8:30–3. **Monedas Continentales** (Plazuela de San Juan 5, tel 762/2–12–42), open weekdays 9–3 and 5–7, Saturdays 9–2, also changes traveler's checks and dollars. The ATM at **Banamex** (Plazuela del Convento 2, down Juárez from zócalo) accepts Plus, Cirrus, Visa, and MasterCard.

EMERGENCIES The number for **police** is 762/2–06–66; for the **Cruz Roja** (ambulance) call 762/2–32–32.

LAUNDRY Lavandería la Cascada (Delicias 4, tel. 762/2–17–21; open 24 hrs) is located in Bora Bora Pizza, half a block west of the zócalo. The minimum load is 4 kilos for $3.

MAIL The post office is next to the Estrella de Oro bus station. They'll hold your mail for up to 10 days at the following address: Lista de Correos, Taxco, Guerrero, CP 40200, México. Av. de Los Plateros 124, no phone. Open weekdays 8–7, Sat. 9–1.

MEDICAL AID There are many pharmacies near the zócalo and Plazuela de San Juan. A particularly well-stocked one is **Farmacia Guadalupana** (Hidalgo 8, tel. 762/2–03–95; open daily 8:30 AM–10 PM). For more urgent medical attention, the **Clínica de Especialidade** offers 24-hour emergency care. Av. de Los Plateros, near Hotel Posada de la Misión, tel. 762/2–11–11.

PHONES There are working pay phones on the zócalo and all over Taxco, where you can place collect or credit card calls. A more expensive option ($3–$5 for collect calls) is to make your call from **Farmacia de Cristo,** down the street from Plazuela de San Juan. Hidalgo 18, tel. 762/2–11–19. Open daily 8 AM–9 PM.

VISITOR INFORMATION Taxco's tourist office is run by a helpful, English-speaking staff. Although it's a 10-minute walk or combi ride from the zócalo, have your questions answered here, rather than by the dubious guides on the highway. *Av. de Los Plateros 1, tel. 762/2–07– 98. From Plaza Borda, ZOCALO combi to gas station. Open daily 9–7.*

COMING AND GOING

BY BUS Taxco has two bus stations. **Estrella Blanca,** a few blocks downhill from Plaza Borda, offers first- and second-class service (both with air-conditioning). Buses serve Mexico City (2½ hrs; $7 1st class, $4.50 2nd class) and Cuernavaca (2 hrs; $4 1st class, $3 2nd class). Only *ordinario* (second-class) buses go to Acapulco (5 hrs, $7.50) and Chilpancingo (3 hrs, $4.50). *Av. de Los Plateros 104, tel. 762/2–01–31.*

The first-class **Estrella de Oro** bus depot sends six direct buses a day to Mexico City: three *plus* (3 hrs, $3.25) and three *primera* (5 hrs, $2.75) pull out at 7 AM, noon, and 6 PM. Combis marked LOS ARCOS run between the two bus stations, while ZOCALO combis make the loop between the stations and the zócalo. You can also walk uphill 10–15 minutes, keeping the spires of Santa Prisca Cathedral in sight. A taxi to the zócalo will cost 75¢. *Av. de Los Plateros 126, tel. 762/2–06–48.*

BY CAR The new Highway 95 runs through Taxco, leading to various destinations. Driving south takes you to Chilpancingo (2 hrs, toll free) and to Acapulco (3 hrs, $18.95 toll). Northbound cars will hit Cuernavaca (1 hr, $7 toll) and Mexico City (2 hrs, $33 toll).

GETTING AROUND

Taxco is fairly accessible by foot, and most sights and budget hotels are clustered around **Plaza Borda,** also known as the zócalo. As you move outward, the twisted, steep streets become increasingly difficult to navigate. If you need to be rescued, hop on one of the many 15¢ combis roaming the area—that is, if you haven't already been run over by one. Driving on these narrow, crowded streets is stressful; better to walk or leave the hassle to combi drivers. Combis labeled LOS ARCOS travel the length of Avenida de Los Plateros (formerly named Avenida John F. Kennedy), which traverses the lower part of the city from north to south. Plaza Borda is uphill from Avenida de Los Plateros, easily identifiable by the pink spires on **Catedral de Santa Prisca.** The main west–east road is Benito Juárez, which most people still call by its old name, Las Grutas. Taxco's other hub is **Plazuela de San Juan,** 1½ blocks southwest of Plaza Borda, up Cuauhtémoc.

WHERE TO SLEEP

Your pack may feel heavy, but your wallet will certainly feel lighter after a night here—hotels aren't cheap. The less-expensive ones surround Plaza Borda and cluster on the hill between the plaza and Estrella Blanca. You won't find any real bargains, but the picturesque setting and great views may compensate for the cash drain. Reservations are a good idea on holidays and weekends, especially Semana Santa (the week preceding Easter) and during July, August, and December. If the places below are full, try the quiet **Posada San Javier** (Estacas 1, tel. 762/2–31–77), which features courtyards, bougainvillea, and a large pool. The spacious, clean rooms are $15– $20 for a single, $20–$23 for a double. Ángel Cervantes, the receptionist, is friendly, garrulous, and eager to offer information about Taxco shopping and day trips. Although camping may be tempting, no formal campsites are available, and roughing it in the surrounding forests is not a good idea.

➤ **UNDER $10 • Casa de Huéspedes Arellano.** Only the most determined budget travelers will be able to find this well-hidden hotel, although every Taxco resident knows where it is— just keep asking and you'll get there. Although the administration can be brusque, and the decor and standard of cleanliness leave a bit to be desired, it's the cheapest hotel in town and relatively quiet. Singles and doubles with communal bath go for $4.50 and $9.50 respectively. *Pajaritos 31, tel. 762/2–02–15. Down alley to right of cathedral, right through market, and 3 levels down. 13 rooms, 5 with bath. Laundry, luggage storage.*

➤ **UNDER $15** • **Hotel Casa Grande.** Probably the best deal for the price, this large, old, stone building is clean and well-kept. Rooms vary from plain with small grungy bathrooms, to nicely decorated with elaborately tiled bathrooms and terrace views of the town. Beware: Some beds are flea-ridden and the noise from the street video arcade next door can get annoying. Rooms are all the same price (singles $8, doubles $11) so ask to see several. *Plazuela de San Juan 7, tel. 762/2–11–08. 12 rooms, all with bath. Luggage storage.*

Hotel Posada Santa Anita. The good news about this hotel is that it's near the bus stations and is clean and nicely furnished; the bad news is that it's a 10-minute uphill hike to the zócalo. Rooms can be small, but those in the back are quiet and have a charming view of some of Taxco. Singles cost $8, doubles $14. *Av. de Los Plateros 106, tel. 762/2–07–52. 29 rooms, 23 with bath. Luggage storage. Wheelchair access.*

➤ **UNDER $20** • **Hotel Los Arcos.** This hotel was originally a gift for a viceroy of "New Spain," as Mexico was known during the colonial era. Some rooms have lofts, with beds overlooking the sitting area, and all open up to a cool patio of brick, stone, and tile. The hotel is quiet and gorgeous and the clientele mostly consists of middle-aged travelers. Singles are $12, doubles $17. *Juan Ruíz de Alarcón 12, tel. 762/2–18–36. 24 rooms, all with bath. Luggage storage. Reservations advised.*

FOOD

If you're not careful, Taxco's tourist-friendly restaurants will empty your wallet without filling your belly. Cheap meals can be had in the taquerías near the Estrella Blanca bus station and in restaurants on the side streets surrounding the zócalo. Purchase inexpensive fresh fruits and vegetables as well as baked bread from one of the many panaderías in the **market** (*see* Shopping, *below*), down the alley to the right of the cathedral. The specialty of the region is iguana; locals say it's an aphrodisiac, and that it tastes like chicken (surprise). Find out for yourself at **Casa Borda** (Plazuela de Bernal 1, ½ block from zócalo, no phone), open daily 9–9, where $4 buys a plate of fried iguana and rice.

➤ **UNDER $5** • **La Concha Nostra.** This second-story bar/restaurant overlooks Plazuela de San Juan and draws both locals and travelers for Italian and Mexican cuisine and MTV and sports broadcasts. Traditional breakfasts of juice, coffee, fruit, and eggs cost $2. The calzone with ham, olives, and mushrooms ($4.50) is mouthwatering. *Plazuela de San Juan 7, tel. and fax 762/2–11–08. Open daily 8 AM–midnight.*

Jugos y Tortas Restaurante Cruz. Whitewashed walls adorned with folk art and guitars add charm to this family-run restaurant, a favorite with locals wanting a quick lunch. Tacos are 75¢, the $1 tortas are some of the best in town, and a burger, fries, and soda go for $2. *El Arco 11, tel. 762/2–70–79. 2 blocks from zócalo. Open daily 9–6. Wheelchair access.*

Restaurant Sante Fé. Ask anyone in Taxco where they spend their precious pesos when taking the family to dinner, and they'll point you toward this colorful restaurant, around the corner from Plazuela de San Juan. The comida corrida features an entrée such as chile relleno or chicken in garlic sauce, with soup, beans, rice, tortillas, and dessert, all for $3.50. If you're not that hungry, try the $1 sandwiches or $2.50 enchiladas. *Hidalgo 2, tel. 762/2–11–70. 1 block east of Plazuela de San Juan. Open daily 7 AM–11 PM.*

➤ **UNDER $10** • **Pizza Pazza.** The pungent aroma of pizza and garlic bread wafts over the zócalo from this pleasant place. The view is awesome and so is the pizza. A large cheese pie for 2–3 people is only $5, $10 with everything on it. Or try the spaghetti ($3), *queso fundido* (cheese fondue; $2.50), or *pozole* (corn soup; $2). *Calle del Arco 1, next to cathedral, tel. 762/2–55–00. Open daily noon–midnight.*

WORTH SEEING

The city itself is the major attraction—which is why the Mexican government declared Taxco a national monument in 1928—but there aren't many individual sights aside from the endless procession of silver shops. If you're in good shape, simply wandering through Taxco's many cramped alleyways and stairs makes for a strenuous but pleasant urban hike.

The Catedral de Santa Prisca on Taxco's zócalo is considered one of the best examples of baroque architecture in Mexico.

CASA HUMBOLDT This 18th-century mansion is named after Alexander von Humboldt, a German explorer who stayed here in 1803 and later traveled throughout South America, making maps and conducting scientific surveys. The interior was recently reconstructed, and 16th-century artifacts found in the Ex-Convento and the Santa Prisca cathedral during renovations adorn the rooms. *Juan Ruíz de Alarcón 6, tel. 762/2–55–01. Admission: $1.50, 75¢ students. Open Mon.–Sat. 10–5.*

MONTE TAXCO RESORT A 10-minute ride on the *teleférico* (tram) takes you from the north side of Taxco to the luxurious resort at Monte Taxco, with its swimming pools, gardens, golf course, and spa. It costs $4 to use the pool and $3 to take a 20-minute horseback ride around the grounds. Enjoy the incredible view with a drink at the bar. Trams run every five minutes, 8 AM–7 PM and cost $2.50 round-trip. If it's after 7 PM, you can taxi to the zócalo (it's just less fun) for $2. *Monte Taxco, tel. 762/2–13–00. From zócalo, take ARCOS/ZOCALO combi and ask to be let off at the teleférico; walk up hill on south side of street.*

MUSEO DE ARQUEOLOGIA GUILLERMO SPRATLING A short walk from Catedral de Santa Prisca, this museum used to be professor William Spratling's house, and now consists of three galleries: two dedicated to pre-Columbian artwork and artifacts, the third to rotating exhibits of contemporary art. The museum is fairly small, its collection isn't extraordinary, and it costs $1.50, so it's only worth seeing on Sunday or if you have a student ID (in which case it's free). *Delgado 1, tel. 762/2–16–60. Open Tues.–Sun. 10–3.*

CHEAP THRILLS

Cheap thrills in Taxco are more or less limited to Sunday nights on the zócalo, and the eternal search for the most incredible views of town—said to be from the Monte Taxco Resort (*see* Worth Seeing, *above*) or **El Mirador,** a mountain view of the city so steep you'll feel like you're flying. Think twice about visiting El Mirador alone; there have been several robberies here. If you can't stand the thought of what you might be missing, catch a PANORAMICA combi at Plazuela de San Juan and ask the driver to drop you at the top. Combis run 8 AM–9 PM.

FESTIVALS Aside from the usual festivals (Semana Santa, Navidad, Día de los Muertos), Taxco celebrates two special events. **La Feria Nacional de La Plata** (Silver Festival), held during the first week of December, features the crowning of a Silver Queen and several silver exhibitions. **El Día del Jumil** (Day of the Jumil Bug), held the first weekend in November, honors an insect supposedly found nowhere else in the world but in Cerro de Huizteco, near Taxco. Traditional healers use the bugs for medicine, while others crush them into a tasty salsa. During the festival, families and groups of friends camp on the hill near town and sing and drink in between bug-hunting expeditions. All this merrymaking, however, is destroying what was once a pristine virgin forest. Nevertheless, the entire town of Taxco moves to the hill for the night. The cerro is 6 kilometers away, but it's not difficult to hitch a ride or catch a taxi or combi.

SHOPPING

Prices at the shops around Plaza Borda are outrageously high—the shopkeepers have figured out that many foreigners are rich and gullible. To see the prettiest silver work in Taxco, peek into **Los Castillos** (Plaza Bernal 10, tel. 762/2–06–52). If you want to actually buy some, stick to the vendors and small, crowded shops located below street level. To reach these stores, head down Cuauhtémoc from Plaza Borda and turn down the small alley at Banco Mexicano Somex. Also try the stores in the **El Pueblito** complex, down Hidalgo from Plazuela de San Juan and across from the park. Another place featuring jewelry is **Platería Guillermo Spratling,** located at the bottom of Los Arcos next to the chapel. Most shopkeepers have two price tiers: *Mayoreo* is the wholesale price given to those who buy at least $100 worth of silver, and *menudeo* is the price per gram for people buying less.

You're likely to see three types of merchandise in Taxco's silver shops: alpaca, a silver-colored metal also known as fool's silver; silver-coated alpaca; and solid sterling silver, identifiable by the .925 imprint. Authentic silver is priced by weight and intricacy of workmanship.

Taxco's extensive **mercado,** extending from the cathedral to **Avenida de Los Plateros,** is another good place to find less-expensive silver, as well as just about anything else. Haggling is common—two-thirds of the initial price is usually about the best you'll do. The market is held daily, but really heats up on weekends when merchants from nearby towns come to hawk their wares.

AFTER DARK

Most nights the zócalo is the hottest spot around—the place where Taxco youth flirt and local families gather for nightly gossip. Buy yourself a bag of popcorn from one of the street vendors and settle onto a park bench to watch the nighttime spectacle unfold. If you're lucky, you may see a small parade of adolescents dressed like wedding-cake decorations: This is a party for a girl's *quinceañera,* celebrating her 15th birthday and passage into womanhood.

The town's few drinking-and-dancing establishments close fairly early, and you can forget serious partying during the week. Your best bet is the bars and restaurants next to the zócalo. **Restaurant/Bar Paco** (Plaza Borda 12, tel. 762/2–00–64) has the best view around and $1 beers. At **Señor Costilla's** the same beer costs $1.50, and the imitation-Hard Rock Cafe atmosphere is somewhat obnoxious. At the other end of the ambience spectrum is **Bar Berta** (Plaza Borda 9, tel. 762/2–01–72), a tiny place with a men's-club atmosphere. For dancing anywhere close to the town center, **Freed's** (de la Muerte 4, no phone; $1 cover) open Friday and Saturday, is your only choice. A little out of town, the disco at the **Monte Taxco Resort** (*see* Worth Seeing, *above*) is hopping (especially during summer). Cover runs $4.

Near Taxco

LAS GRUTAS DE CACAHUAMILPA

The Cacahuamilpa caves, 30 kilometers north of Taxco, are an amazing expanse of subterranean chambers and crusty rock formations that extend 2 kilometers into the earth. The downward trek into this dimly lit world is occasionally steep and slippery, but otherwise fairly tame: The way is lit and marked by a smooth cement walkway. Guides conduct tours each hour in Spanish, but an English-speaking guide can be hunted up on request. The two-hour group tour is large, slow, and not particularly fascinating—basically, the guide points out forms resembling everything from the Virgin Mary to two lovers dancing. Just stick with it—you can't go exploring on your own. Be sure to wear good walking shoes. To reach the caves, take a bus from Taxco's Estrella Blanca station bound for Ixtapa and Toluca ($1.50). If you tell the driver where you're going, he'll drop you off at the crossroads, just a 300-meter walk from the caves. Large highway signs point you in the right direction, so follow the road downhill to the entrance. Buses for the return trip pass every half hour or so. You can also catch a LAS GRUTAS combi across the street from the bus station in Taxco, which will take you all the way to the caves. It costs the same as the bus, but can be a lot more crowded. Combis leave Taxco at 7, 10, 2, 3, and 5, and return at 8, 11, 2, 4, and 6:30. *Admission: $1.50. Open daily 10–5.*

VERACRUZ 11

By Rachael Courtier

Veracruz—a narrow, verdant crescent of land—is warmed and watered by humid, tropical breezes drifting across the Gulf of Mexico. Much of Veracruz's unique ambience derives from the diversity of its population; the prolonged interaction of African, Spanish, and indigenous peoples has produced a rich array of cultural traditions, including vibrant festivals celebrated all over the state.

Ever since that fateful Good Friday in 1519, when Hernán Cortés dropped anchor along this lush green coast, Veracruz has been a popular gateway between Mexico and the rest of the world. But even before the Spanish arrived, Veracruz was the site of several influential cultures. The most ancient of all Mesoamerican cultures—the enigmatic Olmec—raised the first centers of civilization here; the monumental basalt heads they carved provide mute testimony to their mighty culture, which ruled the coast as early as 1200 BC. Originators of a ball game whose indigenous name has been lost, and of the calendrical system adopted by the Maya, the Olmec are considered to be the "mother culture" of Mesoamerica. Little is known about the later city-states that flourished here, but the ruins at El Tajín, near Papantla de Olarte, indicate that a highly complex culture—perhaps the early Totonac—governed the northern area of the state between AD 600 and 900. When the Aztec came along and conquered this region, they left the area and its people ripe for rebellion: At Zempoala, the Totonac became the first allies of Cortés's conquering army. Soon after the Spanish came into power, they brought in boatloads of African slaves to fulfill their labor needs; by 1640, nearly 150,000 people of African descent were living here.

Today, Veracruz state is relatively wealthy due to tourism and a thriving oil industry. The region is still largely undiscovered by foreign tourists, which keeps the prices low and makes Veracruz attractive to Mexican vacationers seeking delicious seafood, Caribbean music, and a relaxed, open attitude. Along the coast, the calm beaches of Tuxpán offer a quiet place to relax, while the many marimba bands in Veracruz city can keep you dancing all night long. The hilly, tobacco-growing region of Los Tuxtlas lures visitors with its many lakes and waterfalls. Jalapa, the state capital, boasts a progressive university population, colorful markets, and many lively *peñas* (musical gatherings) that make it an excellent place to beat the coastal heat.

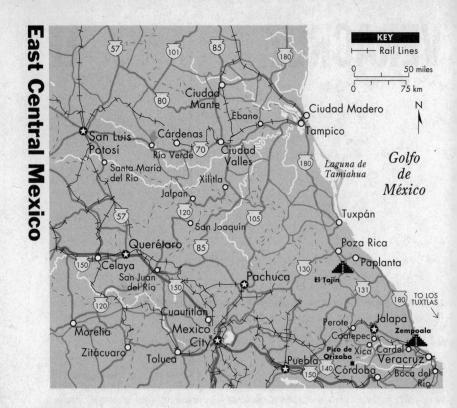

KEY
┼─┼ Rail Lines

0   50 miles
0   75 km

N

Golfo
de
México

Veracruz

The city of Veracruz is a raucous, humid port town. With its Caribbean flavor, lively music, and multiracial population, the city holds a special place in the hearts of many Mexican tourists, who come to admire the welcoming, ready-to-celebrate attitude of the *jarochos,* as the city's residents are known. The exuberance of the city's over one million inhabitants never falters, even when heavy flooding or strong *vendavales* (winds) sweep the unsuspecting streets. Veracruz city's diversity is rooted in its residents, some of whom are of Afro-mestizo origin. Multicultural influences are most evident in Veracruz city's famous cuisine and music; an African slave created the popular seafood dish known as *pescado a la veracruzana,* and Cuban immigrants brought over the slow, sensual rythms of *danzón.* In the white-tiled main square, salsa music, the Chiapan xylaphone music known as *marimba,* and

Veracruz is the birthplace of the song "La Bamba," and of Yuri, Mexico's answer to Madonna.

birds chattering as loud as monkeys in the palm trees overhead all compete for an aural space. Jarochos and tourists sit in outdoor cafés, soaking up the scenery and savoring the strong brews of coffee and potent cigars that the region is known for. Most tend not to frolic in the ocean, however. Since the day in 1519 when Cortés and his men landed here, Veracruz has been one of Mexico's most important ports, and more than five centuries of heavy traffic has taken its toll on the area's beaches.

The principal entry point for both people and goods headed to Mexico City, Veracruz city has been a bitterly contested prize in many of the country's conflicts. An array of forts and walls, originally built as protection against pirates, failed to save the city from a succession of foreign attacks. Pirates sacked the city a number of times, most viciously in 1683, when a Frenchman known as Lorenzillo held the town hostage for three days and carried off enormous quantities of loot. The French invaded again in 1838, and the United States seized the town twice, first

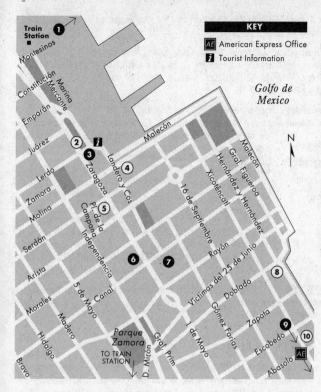

KEY

AE American Express Office

ⓘ Tourist Information

Golfo de Mexico

N

Sights ●

Acuario, **9**

Fuerte de San Juan de Ulúa, **1**

Instituto Veracruzano de la Cultura, **7**

Museo de la Ciudad, **6**

Plaza de Armas (zócalo), **3**

Lodging ○

Gran Hotel Balneario Royalty, **10**

Hotel Amparo, **5**

Hotel Santander, **4**

Hotel Sevilla, **2**

Hotel Villa Rica, **8**

in 1847 and again in 1914. The most dramatic of the fortifications—the castle at San Juan de Ulúa—is one of the city's most popular attractions.

BASICS

AMERICAN EXPRESS **Viajes Olymar** is a travel agency that also serves as the American Express representative in Veracruz. The agency provides the usual services for cardholders, including personal check cashing and holding mail sent to the following address: Ávila Camacho 2221, Veracruz, Veracruz, CP 91700, México. It also delivers MoneyGrams, sells traveler's checks, and exchanges money. *South of downtown, tel. 29/31–34–06. Open weekdays 9–1:30 and 4–6, Sat. 9–noon.*

CASAS DE CAMBIO Rates in town are similar wherever you go. **Bancomer** (Juárez, at Independencia, tel. 29/32–74–34) only changes money weekdays 9–2, and you'll have to arrive early to make it through the lines. For later hours, try **Casa de Cambio Puebla** (Juárez 112, tel. 29/31–24–50), open weekdays 9–5, or use the 24-hour ATM at **Banamex** (Independencia 1027, near Juárez, tel. 29/32–47–00).

CONSULATES **United States.** *Víctimas del 25 del Julio 384, btw Gómez Farías and 16 de Septiembre, tel. 29/31–58–21. Open weekdays 9–1.*

EMERGENCIES Call the **police** at 29/38–05–67 or 29/38–06–93; for an **ambulance,** dial 29/37–55–00 or 29/37–54–1. **Oficinas Para la Seguridad del Turista** (tel. 91/800–90–392) operates a 24-hour, toll-free hotline to provide legal and medical help for tourists in Veracruz. Services are available in English and in Spanish.

LAUNDRY The bad news at **Lavandería Automática del Parque** is that there are no self-service machines; the good news is that it's relatively cheap to have them do the job for you: 50¢

for every kilo of your dirtiest. *Collado 23, btw Juan de Dios and Begrete, tel. 29/31–06–75. Open weekdays 8–2 and 4–8, Sat. 8–3.*

MAIL The central **post office,** a magnificent building dating from the Porfirio Díaz era, will hold mail sent to you at the following address for up to 10 days: Lista de Correos, Administración No. 1, Veracruz, Veracruz, CP 91700, México. *María Mercante 210, tel. 29/32–20–38. Open weekdays 8–8, Sat. 9–1.*

MEDICAL AID **Benavides** (Independencia 1291, at Serdán, tel. 29/31–89–29) is a big, convenient drugstore downtown, but it closes nightly at 10. For 24-hour service, try **Farmacia de la Sociedad Española Beneficencia** (16 de Septiembre, btw Escobedo and Abasolo, tel. 29/32–05–59).

Veracruz's port-city swagger has earned its inhabitants the nickname "jarochos"—rude ones—due not only to the exuberant manner of expressing their feelings, but also to their purportedly uninhibited sexuality.

PHONES **Latadel** phone cards are the only way to go if you don't want to have the irritation of shoving coins into the phone every minute. Most kiosks sell them; look for the LATADEL sign out front. The zócalo is sprinkled with Ladatel phones, or try the ones inside Gran Café la Parroquia (*see* Food, *below*), which is quiet and air-conditioned. If you don't mind shelling out big bucks, you can also make long-distance calls ($3 per min) at **Caseta Lissy** (5 de Mayo 1085, btw Lerdo and Juárez, tel. 29/34–99–96; open daily 8 AM–9 PM).

VISITOR INFORMATION The bilingual staff at the **Subdelegación Federal de Turismo** has few helpful pamphlets but a lot of enthusiasm. *Palacio Municipal, on the zócalo, tel. 29/32–19–99. Open daily 9–9.*

COMING AND GOING

BY BUS The main bus terminal (Díaz Mirón 1698, tel. 29/37–57–44) sits 4 kilometers south of the zócalo. The main bus company is **Autobuses del Oriente** (ADO) (tel. 29/37–57–88), which serves Jalapa (3 hrs, $3) every 15–30 minutes between 5:30 AM and 11 PM; Mexico City (9 hrs, $14); and Reynosa (17 hrs; $36 1st class, $46 2nd class). First-class buses run to both San Andrés Tuxtla (2½ hrs, $4.75) and Santiago Tuxtla (2 hrs, $4.50) every 15–30 minutes 7 AM–midnight daily; buses head for Catemaco (3 hrs, $5) every couple hours 9:30–5:30. For those headed farther south, **Cristóbal Colón** (tel. 29/07–57–44) runs to Oaxaca city (6 hrs, $18) daily at 11 PM, and to Tuxtla Gutiérrez (11 hrs, $25) daily at 6 PM. **Cuenca** (tel. 29/35–54–05) also has service to Oaxaca city (9 hrs, $10) daily at 7 AM and 8 PM. The station is graced with luggage storage ($2.50 per day), public phones, and a *caseta de larga distancia.* **Autobuses Unidos** (**AU**) (tel. 29/37–57–32) and **Transportes Los Tuxtlas** (tel. 29/37–28–78) operate from the second-class station on the same block and offer frequent service to Jalapa (3½ hrs, $2) and San Andrés Tuxtla (3 hrs, $3.75). Any city bus marked DIAZ MIRON on Avenidas Zaragoza or 5 de Mayo near the zócalo will stop right by both terminals. A taxi from the zócalo to the terminal should cost no more than $2.

BY CAR Highway 140, a modern, well-maintained freeway, runs northwest to Jalapa. Highway 180 runs along the Gulf coast from Nuevo Laredo to Mérida, and Highway 150 heads southwest to Córdoba. You can rent a car at **Avis** (Collado 241, tel. 29/32–98–34), **National** (Díaz Mirón 1036, tel. 29/31–17–56), or **Budget** (Díaz Mirón 1123, tel. 29/31–21–39).

BY TRAIN The train station (tel. 29/32–32–72) inhabits a romantic 19th-century building, five long blocks from the zócalo. The **Jarocho** train departs nightly at 10 PM for Mexico City (10 hrs). Classes of service include: first class ($9), first class *especial* (with air-conditioning; $9), sleeper car ($25), and second class ($5). Another second-class train runs to Mexico City (12 hrs) daily at 8:20 AM for $5. Trains also depart daily for Jalapa (5 hrs, $4.50) at 7:30 AM and Orizaba (5 hrs, $3.50) at 8 AM. Tickets are sold at the *taquilla* (ticket booth) Monday–Saturday 6–11 and 2–9. If you're traveling first class during peak tourist season (July, August, and holidays), buy your tickets in advance—they're available up to a month before the departure date. To reach the station, follow María Mercante until it ends, then turn right.

BY PLANE The airport lies 15 kilometers southwest of Veracruz city. **Mexicana** (tel. 29/32–22–42) has three direct flights a day to Mexico City for $87 one-way. The airline also has flights to other major cities, including Cancún and Monterrey. To reach the airport, catch a cab ($7) or ride the minivan ($6) that runs between the office of **Transportación Terrestre Aeropuerto** (Hidalgo 826, btw Canal and Morales, tel. 29/32–32–50) and the airport.

GETTING AROUND

Downtown Veracruz centers around two plazas: the **Plaza de Armas,** also known as the zócalo, and **Parque Zamora,** with its decorative old trolley car. The two are connected by Avenida Independencia, the city's busiest shopping street. While this downtown area is compact and walkable, you'll need to take buses (50¢) to the outlying beaches and some of the secluded sights (such as Uluá). Most of the useful buses run along Molina and Zamora, just behind the cathedral. The *malecón* (boardwalk) parallels the seashore. Called Molina in the downtown area, the malecón becomes Boulevard Manuel Ávila Camacho, referred to by everyone as *el bulevard,* as it heads south. This winding street follows the southern coast of Veracruz, passing Playa de Hornos and Playa Mocambo before arriving in Boca del Río. Fortunately, most other streets adhere to a grid system.

WHERE TO SLEEP

More than 60 hotels are scattered throughout this relatively small city, so finding a place to stay should be simple. Because Veracruz city is a popular Mexican vacation spot, prices tend to be higher during July, August, and Carnaval (February/March). Lodging in the older, more urban center of town is cheap, but the quality is low, and the area is unsafe at night.

NEAR THE ZÓCALO Hotels near the zócalo tend to be less expensive than those near the beach, although luxuries like air-conditioning will bump up the price in either location. Downtown hotels are in the middle of the action, but the all-night noise might make you wish you'd taken a room in a less busy area.

Hotel Amparo. Big rooms, turquoise-blue walls, plenty of hot water, and enough little soaps to open a store make this hotel one of the best deals in town. The blaring TV in the lobby is *always* on, and the same old crowd of *cuates* (buddies) are slouched on the uncomfortable chairs in front of it day in and day out. The rooms on the main courtyard tend to be cleaner and cooler than interior rooms. Singles are a steal at $6, and doubles are only $7. *Serdán 482, btw Zaragoza and Independencia, tel. 29/32–27–38. 64 rooms, all with bath. Luggage storage.*

Hotel Santander. This place is perhaps the only hotel in town with any character. Colored tiles, high ceilings, breezy balconies, and bamboo bed frames make it a refreshing place to stay. Interior rooms, although hotter in the summer months, are surprisingly quiet. Singles with narrow beds are a manageable $8.50 and doubles run $13. *Landero y Cos 123, at Molina, tel. 29/32–45–29. 42 rooms, all with bath. Luggage storage.*

Hotel Sevilla. Everything in this small, otherwise nondescript hotel, right off the zócalo, is light blue—the walls, the tiles, and the sheets. Rooms tend to be noisy, especially those that open onto Zaragoza, but all have ceiling fans, TVs, and clean bathrooms with plenty of hot water. Singles are $8, doubles $10. *Morelos 359, btw Lerdo and Juárez, tel. 29/32–42–46. 30 rooms. Luggage storage.*

NEAR THE BEACH Hotels by the water may have breezier, slightly cooler rooms than those near the center of town, but don't count on it. If you're a light sleeper you may want to keep distance between you and the boardwalk, as the social scene here, although more mellow than in the city itself, often continues until 10 PM.

Gran Hotel Balneario Royalty. Known to locals as "El Royalty," this gigantic building is one of the largest budget hotels in the city. Many of the pastel-colored rooms have breezy balconies with nice views of the bay, and all have phones and TVs. Singles and doubles with ceiling fans cost $11.50 and $16, respectively; for air-conditioning, add an extra $7 to your tab. *Abasolo 34, at Ávila Camacho, tel. 29/32–39–88. 270 rooms, all with bath. Restaurant. MC, V.*

Hotel Villa Rica. The green-and-yellow lobby of this small hotel is welcoming, but the robust señora in charge is all business. The worn rooms are decent, if bare, but the bathrooms are slightly moldy. Still, it's a cheapie for the waterfront—$8.50 singles, $10 doubles. Some oceanside rooms have balconies, which cost $5 more in the high season, but these rooms tend to be the nosiest. The restaurant next door serves a filling breakfast of coffee, eggs, and toast for $1.50. *Ávila Camacho 165, tel. 29/32–48—54. 1 block south of Mar y Tierra hotel. 33 rooms, all with bath. Luggage storage.*

CAMPING **Isla de en Medio,** an island off the coast of Antón Lizardo (*see* Outdoor Activities, *below*), lies just south of Boca del Río. Most people come to the isla to snorkel along the coral reefs, but camping is another draw: Look for a cottage next to the lighthouse and ask for the keeper; he'll get you accommodated. Campsites are pretty rugged, so stock up on food and water in Antón Lizardo before kicking back and enjoying the lush scenery. At the Terminal de Autobuses, take an AU bus headed for Antón Lizardo; they run approximately every 20 minutes. At the beach, *lanchas* (flat-bottom boats) will take you to the island.

FOOD

Veracruz offers a mind-boggling array of culinary choices, from tempura to lasagna, but seafood is the star attraction. The **municipal fish market,** one block south of the zócalo, supplies scores of stands where vendors cook up all kinds of seafood until late into the night. The stretch of Serdán between Zaragoza and Madero also offers plenty of good cheap eats. Picnic supplies, such as fresh vegetables, fruits, nuts, and cheeses, are available at the **outdoor market** on Guerrero between Juan Soto and Serdán. Fresh bread and pastries at **Panadería País** (cnr of Molina and 5 de Mayo, tel. 29/32–12–13) are a yummy treat.

Keep your tastebuds tuned for "tortillas de plátano" (banana tortillas), "tamales de calabaza con camarones" (pumpkin and shrimp tamales), and "huachinango a la Veracruzana" (red snapper in tomato sauce), all specialties from the Afro-mestizo tradition.

El Galleón Antillano. Chairs and walls painted as green as a mermaid's tail, murals of Spanish galleons, and live *música criolla* (daily 2–7 PM) provide a refreshing escape from the afternoon humidity. Relax in this air-conditioned seascape as you dive into the comida corrida, featuring a fresh meat or seafood dish ($2.50), and enjoy a cold glass of *sangría* (sweetened red wine with fruit) ($1.75) *5 de Mayo 1039, tel. 29/32–57–97. Open daily 9:30 AM–8 PM.*

Gran Café La Parroquia. Veracruz's busiest and most venerable café is best known for its coffee, sandwiches, and eggs. When you want some *café con leche* (coffee with milk; $1), bang your glass with your spoon and a waiter armed with pitchers of hot milk and coffee will scurry over. The *tortilla parroquia* (chile-and-onion omelet cooked in chicken broth; $2) or the *frijoles con plátanos fritos* (black beans with fried plantains) makes a filling meal, as do the other egg dishes or crepes on the menu. *Gómez Farías 34, facing the malecón, tel. 29/82–25–84. Open daily 6 AM–1 AM.*

Mariscos El Veracruzano. Locals make the 10-minute trip here for the fresh seafood at low prices. Tucked away behind the Hotel Mocambo inside a bamboo cabana with ceiling fans, you almost expect Rita Hayworth to saunter off the beach and order a *piña colada* ($1.75) with her *jaiba al mojo de ajo* (garlic-sautéed crab; $4.25). *Fraccionmiento de Playa de Oro, tel. 29/22–22–10. From center, take BOCA DEL RIO bus and ask to be let off at "los balnearios del Hotel Mocambo." Open daily 11 AM–7 PM.*

WORTH SEEING

Most main attractions are either near the zócalo and easily accessible on foot or served by convenient public transportation. The malecón is lively day and night, with men selling boat rides, kids driving tiny toy cars, and scores of tacky souvenir shops. If you plan on cruising here at night (a popular weekend activity among young jarochos in the throes of puppy love), watch out for the street brawls that break out all too frequently.

ACUARIO The aquarium, located in a shopping plaza on Playa de Hornos (a quick bus ride from the center), is extremely popular with locals, who flock here on weekends. The main attraction is a round tank with 3,000 different species of marine life native to the Gulf of Mexico, including nurse sharks, manta rays, barracudas, and sea turtles. Shark movies of the make-you-never-want-to-set-foot-in-the-ocean-again variety are shown near the exit. If that doesn't do the trick, check out the enormous, actual-size outline of a shark caught off the coast drawn on the far wall. *Plaza Acuario, tel. 29/32–79–84. Take* VILLA DEL MAR *or* BOCA DEL RIO *bus from cnr of Molina and Zaragoza to huge VIP's plaza on Ávila Camacho. Admission: $2. Open Mon.–Thurs. 10–7, Fri.–Sun. 10–7:30.*

Jarochos know how to cool down with freshly made "nieves" (sherbet). Try the various tropical flavors at Nevería Molina (Zamora, at Landero y Cos): mamey, guanábana, and cacahuate are among the tastiest.

FUERTE DE SAN JUAN DE ULUA Built on the ruins of a Totonac temple, and now a miniature city in itself, the island fort of San Juan de Úlua is a maze of moats, ramparts, and drawbridges smack in the middle of the busy port area. Connected to the mainland by a causeway, this "island" was witness to some of the most momentous events in Mexican history. Cortés landed here in 1519, establishing Veracruz as a major gateway for Spanish settlement in Mexico. Fortification of the island began in 1535 and ground coral, sand, and oyster shells were used for the walls. A few centuries later, the fort served as a prison, housing such figures as Benito Juárez. Stand in the small prison hole known as *el infierno* (hell) to get an eerie sense of what it was like to be a prisoner. Among other gory details, cannibalism, pestilence, and insanity took place within its windowless, stifling walls. *Tel. 29/38–51–51. From zócalo, take* SAN JUAN DE ULUA *bus. Admission: $2, free Sun. and holidays. Open daily 9–4:30.*

INSTITUTO VERACRUZANO DE LA CULTURA The bright blue Veracruz Cultural Institute building was a hospital until atrocious conditions caused health authorities to close it down in 1975. The massive 18th-century structure, with its long, arched hallways and green, tree-filled garden, now hosts cultural events and rotating art exhibits. Grab a schedule of events at the reception desk. *Canal, at Zaragoza, tel. 29/31–66–45. Admission free. Open Mon.–Sat. 9–9, Sun. 10–2.*

MUSEO DE LA CIUDAD If you've just arrived in Veracruz, the city museum is a good place to start exploring. The region's history is narrated via artifacts and displays, and scale models of the city give you a sense of the lay of the land. Also exhibited are copies of pre-Columbian statues and contemporary indigenous art. *Zaragoza 397, near Morales. Admission: 50¢. Open Mon. 9–4, Tues.–Sat. 9–8, tel. 29/31–84–10.*

FESTIVALS

March/April: Carnaval. Since 1925, jarochos have been celebrating the eight days before Lent with the tradition of *Los Bacanales* (Bachanalia), hedonistic tributes paid to Bacchus, the Greek wine god. Merrymaking tends to be more satiric than esoteric in Veracruz: Festivities symbolically start out with the burning of an effigy, a doll named *Mal Humor* (bad humor), usually in the personage of a currently unpopular political figure (1996's Mal Humor was called "Devaluación," for the devaluation of the peso). People come from all over to dance in the streets to the rhythms of the *danzónes* and *huapangos,* and gorge themselves on food and drink. The party ends when the Carnaval King and Queen, dressed in black, burn another effigy—"Juan Carnaval."

December: Las Ramas and **El Viejo.** Navidad in Veracruz is far from puritanical, with the gala beginning 10 days before Christmas. Families go door to door, holding branches decorated with lanterns, singing *las ramas*: clever and funny songs designed to make the neighbor open the door, listen, and offer treats for a song well-performed. Similar to a poetry slam or rap contest, rama competitions take place in the zócalo December 20–25, where contestants vie for cash prizes with the best improvised rama. Midnight on December 31st sees the burning of an effigy named *El Viejo* (the old man). Symbolizing the old year, he is carried to his fiery end in the zócalo, while songs are sung in his honor.

AFTER DARK

To get away from the zócalo and soak in some of the grittier port atmosphere, try one of the traditional bars just south of the plaza, such as **Bella Época**, on Lagunilla, an alley cordoned off for pedestrians. Open nightly, the bar serves seafood, and drink prices are lower than what you'll find on the square. Bella Época's clientele is mostly male, so unaccompanied women can count on getting lots of attention here.

Every Tuesday and Friday night after 8 PM, the Plaza de Armas is the scene of open-air dances, with a dressed-up crowd and live marimba music. Sunday nights the dancing moves to Parque Zamora.

Discos and video bars are plentiful along the malecón, especially as you move south toward the beaches of Villa del Mar. Buses run down here until about 10:30 PM, but you'll have to catch a cab ($2) to get back. The hippest places are **Boca del Océano** (Ruíz Cortínez 8, at Ávila Camacho, tel. 29/37–63–27), a flashy, modern discotheque, and **Blue Ocean** (Ávila Camacho 9, tel. 29/22–03–66), a video bar with a light show. Both play a wide variety of music and are open Thursday–Saturday nights, when they're packed with a young, local crowd. Boca del Océano charges a cover ($8) on Saturdays only. The more relaxed Blue Ocean charges $5 at the door and has a small dance floor and some pool tables. To reach the bars, take any BOCA DEL RIO bus on Ávila Camacho.

Teatro de la Reforma (5 de Mayo, at Rayón, near Parque Zamora, tel. 29/31–79–99) showcases dance and music performances two to three times a week. Tickets, which run $3–$11.50, and schedules of performances can be found at the theater.

OUTDOOR ACTIVITIES

Boat tours of the bay leave from the malecón daily 7–7 whenever they're full. The $2, half-hour ride includes a talk (in Spanish) on Veracruz history. Longer trips to nearby **Isla Verde** (Green Island), **Isla de en Medio** (Middle Island), **Isla de los Sacrificios** (Island of Sacrifices), and **Isla de Pájaros** (Island of Birds) leave daily from the small dock near the Instituto Oceanográfico, on Ávila Camacho, and from the beach next to the Plaza Acuario. The draw to these islands is their relatively clean and quiet beaches. However, in an effort to preserve the islands and prevent damage caused by tourists, the Mexican coast guard randomly rotates the availability of the islands; the lancha guides will tell you which ones are accessible. Island-bound boats also leave whenever they're full, so it's best to come in a big group. The cost should be $5–$7 per person, but feel free to bargain; the old men near the Instituto tend to give better deals. Before you decide to spend the larger part of the day sunning on the islands, make sure your guide doesn't charge by the hour—it can get quite pricey.

Landlubbers can stop by **Bicicentros Lezama** (Juan de Dios Peza 180, near Parque Zamora, tel. 29/31–04–32) daily 9–9 to rent a bicycle ($1.50 per hr or $7 per day) or a motor scooter ($4 per hr).

BEACHES Veracruz's beaches are much less inviting than you might expect: Although some locals aren't deterred from swimming, most of the shores are dirty, and the water is fairly polluted. The coast at Isla Verde, Isla de en Medio, and Isla los Sacrificios are more isolated, but you're still swimming in the same water, so don't expect a noticeable improvement. For lounging, the **Playa Cancunito** on the Isla de Pájaros is the best choice. **Villa del Mar** is the beach closest to downtown, 2 kilometers south along the malecón, but also the most crowded. Locals frequent the beaches behind the Torremar Resort, 6 kilometers south of Villa del Mar, known as **Playas Curazau**. The long, uninterrupted stretches of white sand are good for soaking in the sun, and they're cleaner and less built up than at **Playa Mocambo**, 2 kilometers farther south. The water is still murky at both beaches, however. The **Hotel Playa Mocambo** (Ruíz Cortínes 4000, tel. 29/22–00–11) charges $4 to use their pools until 6 PM.

Better beaches lie farther from town. About 4 kilometers south of Playa Mocambo is **Boca del Río,** a small fishing community at the mouth of the Río Jamapa, which is quickly getting sucked into greater Veracruz. Though Boca's beach gets dirtier as you move closer to the center of town, it's uncrowded, and the water is relatively unpolluted. Don't expect a charming little seaside village, though: Boca is basically a suburb that happens to be by the water. Its beaches can be reached via any of the BOCA DEL RIO buses that run along the malecón, leaving from Calle Serdán, a block east of the zócalo. Playa Curazau and Playa Mocambo are en route.

If you want to find water conducive to good snorkeling and scuba diving, head 20 kilometers south of Veracruz city to the village of **Antón Lizardo.** Off its coast lie islands, low-lying coral reefs, and two shipwrecks (the *Valientes* and the *Ana Elena*). You can rent snorkel gear ($3 per hr) or scuba equipment ($18 per hr) at the local branch of **Tridente** (Pino Suárez, at Av. de la Playa, tel. 29/34–08–44), which also arranges boat rides to the islands. Three-hour boat trips are $10 per person (six-person minimum), and it's a good idea to call ahead and reserve at least a day in advance. **AU** serves the town frequently from the main station in Veracruz (20 min, $2). The last bus back to Veracruz leaves the station at Antón Lizardo around 8:30 PM.

Near Veracruz

ZEMPOALA RUINS

Thick cane fields press against the perimeter of the small ruins of Zempoala, while the irregular peaks of the Sierra Madre Oriental rise dramatically in the distance. Located just outside the small town of **José Cardel** (1 hr north of Veracruz), Zempoala's pyramids are not particularly exciting architecturally, but they do have a distinguished past. Once a sizeable Totonac town, Zempoala was the first settlement to rebel against Moctezuma's empire. Resentful over the excessive tributes the Totonac had to pay to the Aztec, the Totonac joined Cortés's army; they're still looked upon by some as the "Judas" of Mesoamerica. Originally plastered with white stucco and topped with small square shrines, the pyramids here gleamed so brightly that Cortés's first scouts reported that the city was made of silver (and we know what was on their minds). Time has now worn away the plaster, revealing surprisingly regular, rounded riverbed stones beneath.

The **Templo Mayor** lies directly in front of you as you enter the site. Its steep staircase ascends 13 levels to the faint remains of a three-room temple on top. To the right of the Templo Mayor sits a smaller pyramid, **Las Chimeneas** (The Chimneys), named after the remains of two round towers in front of it. Cortés may have lodged at the top of this temple; before this, the chimneys were probably used for storage. Behind Las Chimeneas, out in the cane fields, lies another small structure, called **Las Caritas** (Little Faces) for the many pottery heads that once decorated its walls. Today you'll only find graffiti scratched into the remaining traces of original paint. The **Gran Pirámide** and the **Temple of the Wind God,** resting under the jacaranda trees at the western edge of the site, do little to invoke any long-lost Totonac gods—but you may run into guides trying to sell you on their still-lingering powers.

All of the ruins lie close together, so walking around the site shouldn't take more than 20 minutes. At the entrance you'll find friendly guards happy to discuss the region (in Spanish) or sell you colorful, informative pamphlets (some in English) for 50¢. Just beyond the fences, you can't help but notice the poor, almost squalid, homes hugging Zempoala's grassy, once-majestic parameters. The site is open daily 9–6; admission is $2, $1 for students.

COMING AND GOING To reach Zempoala from Veracruz, take a **TRV** bus (tel. 29/37–57–32) from the second-class bus station to Cardel (45 min, $1). Buses leave every 10 minutes between 8 AM and 7 PM. In Cardel, turn left out of the **bus station** (tel. 296/2–01–69) and walk one block to the corner of Zapata and Avenida Cardel, on the zócalo. From here, white *micros* (minibuses) marked ZEMPOALA and *colectivos* (collective taxis) can take you to the ruins (15 min, 50¢) 6 AM–8 PM. The last bus returns to Veracruz from Cardel at 10:30 PM. To reach Zempoala from Jalapa, catch a TRV bus from the central bus station in Jalapa (1½ hrs, $2).

WHERE TO SLEEP You can't camp at the ruins, but if you want to stay overnight, **Hotel Garelli** (Flores Magnón, at Juárez, tel. 296/2–05–69) is basic and clean. Its jovial owner charges $4 per person. If you're dying for air-conditioning, try the frilly pink rooms at **Hotel Cardel** (Zapata, at Martínez, tel. 296/2–00–14); singles here are $13, doubles $17.

TLACOTALPAN

The town of Tlacotalpan looks much the same as it did 100 years ago, when one-time resident, President Porfirio Díaz, made its dock into an important trade center for Veracruz. Nevertheless, the Revolution came, Porfirio went, and Tlacotalpan didn't develop—a stroke of luck if you're an architecture buff or a weary traveler. This sleepy, riverside village's pristine colonial architecture and popsicle-colored houses really soothe the senses. Laze the day away on a riverboat ride or in the quiet zócalo, listening to the plaintive songs of the old-timers strumming their guitars.

Touring Tlacotalpan takes no time at all. The **Museo Salvador Ferrando** (Alegre 6, in Plaza Hidalgo, no phone; open weekdays 10–5) features furniture and crafts from Tlacotalpan's last century. A 15-minute walk to the western edge of town takes you to the **cemetery,** whose marble mausoleums and Italian angels have unfortunately suffered recent looting. The zócalo features the Moorish arquitecture of the **Iglesia de la Candelaria,** home to the Virgin of Candelaria for 200 years. On February 2, bedecked with hundreds of shimmering candles, she sails down the river with a full regatta for the **Festival de la Candelaria.** Two days before the event, the town peps up with masquerades and bulls running à la Pamplona through the streets.

BASICS Inverlat (Carranza, below Hotel Doña Lala) is the only bank in town and changes money weekdays 9–2. Unfortunately, it doesn't have an ATM. The **Oficina de Correos** (Pablo Díaz 3, off Plaza Zaragoza; open weekdays 8–3) offers the usual mail services. For telephone and fax services, visit **Servicios Multiples** (Alegre, at Iglesias, tel. 288/42–0–21; open daily 8 AM–10 PM), where a long-distance call is about $2.25 a minute. You can pick up a small pamphlet and map of the city at **Museo Salvador Ferrando** (*see above*) for $2.

COMING AND GOING Tlacotalpan is centered around two main squares, the Plaza Zaragoza and Hidalgo park (which lie right next to each other). Within one or two blocks of the squares lies the river, and most of the restaurants and sights. The only transport hub in Tlacotalpan is the **ADO** and **Cuenca** terminal (Beltrán 43, 1 block west of Plaza Zaragoza, tel. 288/4–21–25). Buses leave hourly 6:15 AM–10:15 PM for Veracruz and 7:35 AM–8:35 PM for San Andres Tuxtla. If you're coming by car, Highway 180 connects Tlacotalpan to Veracruz city.

WHERE TO SLEEP AND EAT Hotel Doña Lala (Carranza 11, tel. 288/4–25–80) provides a 19th-century feel with its dark wooden staircases and hallways. Rooms are clean, bright, and yellow, though a bit bare. Rooms for one person cost $11.50 ($15 with air-conditioning); two people bumps the price to $16.50 ($24.50 with air-conditioning). Just two storefronts down is the **Hotel Reforma** (Carranza 2, tel. 288/4–20–22). Rooms here are clean, but smaller and more modest than the big, airy lobby would have you think. Singles run $7 ($11.50 with air-conditioning), doubles $10 ($14 with air-conditioning). You can camp at the far north side of the river, known as **Cancha del Bosque**; just go into the Palacio Municipal, located on the zócalo, for permission. **Doña Leo** (Gutiérrez Zamora 1, at Carranza, tel. 288/4–24–58; open daily 7–5:30) dishes up big, economic breakfasts (75¢–$1.25) and a generous comida corrida ($1.50). **Café Rockola** (Plaza Zamora, no phone; open 6 PM–2 AM) is good for late-night sandwiches served by a young and restless staff who keep the tunes in the jukebox spinning. Just a block away from Plaza Zaragoza, a string of fresh seafood restaurants line the riverside, serving local specialties like robalo (regional fish cooked with garlic) and *mojarra,* a local freshwater fish cooked with lime and chiles, oranges, or garlic.

Los Tuxtlas

The small volcanic mountain range of Sierra de Los Tuxtlas meets the sea 140 kilometers south of Veracruz. Simply known as Los Tuxtlas, the area has lakes, waterfalls, rivers, mineral springs, and access to beaches making it a popular stopover for travelers heading east from Mexico City to the Yucatán. The region's three principal towns—Santiago Tuxtla, San Andrés Tuxtla, and Catemaco—rest in mountains more than 200 meters above sea level, lending them a coolness even in summer that is the envy of the perspiring masses on the coast.

Though much of Los Tuxtlas architecture is of the 1960s school (looming cement), all three towns are laid out in the colonial style, around a main plaza and a church, and retain a certain charm. This old-fashioned, small-town atmosphere (especially in Santiago and San Andrés) extends to the warm and friendly residents, who still treat foreigners with an air of novelty. The region was a center of Olmec culture, and Olmec artifacts and small ruins abound, especially around Santiago Tuxtla. Today, the economic life of Los Tuxtlas depends on cattle raising, cigar manufacturing, and tourism. The largest of the three towns is San Andrés, which is also the local transport hub. With plenty of hotels, it's a good base from which to explore the entire region. From Santiago, you can visit the ruins at Tres Zapotes; the town also has an informative museum where you can learn about the region's indigenous heritage. Lake Catemaco is popular among Mexicans as a summer and Christmas resort; it's also the place to go for a *consulta* (consulation) with a brujo or curandero, should you have any questions that require spiritual clarity or supernatural intervention.

The Tuxtlas gain an air of mystery not only from the cool, gray fog that slips over the mountains and lakes but also from the whisperings among townspeople about the "brujos" (witches), also called "curanderos" (healers), who read tarot cards, prescribe herbal remedies, and cast spells here.

BASICS

CASAS DE CAMBIO The only place in the Tuxtlas to change money is San Andrés, where **Bancomer** (Madero 20, tel. 294/2–00–41) changes cash and traveler's checks weekdays 9–1. **Banamex** (Madero 4, tel. 294/2–13–50) only changes traveler's checks weekdays 9–2:30, but it has a 24-hour ATM that accepts Plus, Cirrus, MasterCard, and Visa.

EMERGENCIES The **Cruz Roja** (González Boca Negra 242, tel. 294/2–05–00) in San Andrés provides emergency care for all three towns. You can reach the **police** in San Andrés at 294/2–02–34, in Santiago at 294/7–00–92, and in Catemaco at 294/3–00–55.

MEDICAL AID **Farmacia Garysa** (Madero 3, tel. 294/2–44–34) in San Andrés is open 24 hours, and you can get just about any prescription drug or remedy there.

PHONES AND MAIL The largest **post office** (tel. 294/2–01–89; open weekdays 8–8, Sat. 9–1) in the region is in San Andrés on the corner of 20 de Noviembre and La Frauga, a block down the hill from the main square. Mail will be held for you for up to 10 days at the following address: Lista de Correos, San Andrés Tuxtla, Veracruz, CP 95701, México. There are a few small **phone offices** in all three towns—just look for the blue-and-white signs marked LARGA DISTANCIA. One of the most convenient is in San Andrés at **Caseta "Pipisoles"** (Madero 6-B, tel. 294/2–25–88; open daily 8 AM–9 PM), just past the Banamex.

COMING AND GOING

The transport hub for Los Tuxtlas is San Andrés's **ADO** terminal (Juárez 762, tel. 294/2–04–46), a short six blocks from the zócalo. Buses for Veracruz city (2½ hrs, $4) leave hourly between 5 AM and 8 PM. Several night buses leave around midnight for Mexico City (9 hrs, $18), and there are also frequent departures for Villahermosa (5 hrs, $9) and Jalapa (8 hrs, $7).

Second-class buses based in San Andrés connect the three towns—it's a 15-minute ride to both Catemaco and Santiago from here. Buses for Santiago leave the **Terminal de los Rojos** station (Juárez, 1 block past ADO on Hwy. 180) in San Andrés every 10 minutes. You don't have to go to the station to get the bus for Catemaco—just wait on Highway 180 around the corner from the ADO terminal for one of Rojos's CATEMACO buses, which pass every 10–15 minutes. In Catemaco, the second-class company operates a small station two blocks from the main square. In Santiago, the bus stop is at the corner of Morelos and Ayuntamiento, three blocks from the plaza. All three towns are connected by Highway 180 (known locally as the Carretera de Golfo), which is narrow but well-paved. It heads southeast, hitting Santiago de las Tuxtlas, then San Andrés, and on to Catemaco.

San Andrés Tuxtla

San Andrés Tuxtla is the largest and most modern town in Los Tuxtlas with approximately 80,000 inhabitants. A graceful, red-domed cathedral presides over the central plaza, which is bordered by Madero (running east–west) and Calles Juárez and Rascón (running north–south), and surrounded by relaxed, open-air cafés. In the summer evenings, you can find the zócalo filled with groups of kids walking around in the warm rain, eating homemade *paletas*—traditional Mexican desserts like *flan* or *arroz con leche* (rice pudding) frozen on a stick. The pleasant atmosphere combined with the town's central location and cool evenings make it an ideal stopover for travelers feeling abused by too many hours on the bus. Those in need of more than just relaxation can try some of the curative teas and medicinal herbs at the **Farmacia Homeopática La Esperanza** (Juárez 264, at Hidalgo, tel. 294/2–08–79), two blocks from the zócalo on the way to the ADO station. If you're more interested in polluting your body than purifying it, there's always the **Fábrica de Puros Santa Clara** (5 de Febrero 10, tel. 294/2–12–00), a huge cigar factory where you can see experts making fine cigars ($60 for a box of 24). If you buy a box, they'll print your name or slogan on each cigar at no extra charge.

WHERE TO SLEEP On a quiet side street near the cathedral lies the spotless **Hotel Catedral** (Pino Suárez 3, tel. 294/2–02–37). A night here costs $4 for one person, $5 for two; most rooms have large comfortable beds, and all have clean bathrooms with decent plumbing.

The precolonial name for San Andrés—Zacoalcos—means "locked up place." Some say it referred to the confusing landscape of rugged hills and narrow valleys, which made it difficult for people to find a way to the town.

At **Hotel San Andrés** (Madero 6, tel. 294/2–06–04), all 31 rooms ($10–$11.50 singles, $13–$14 doubles) are graced with Diego Rivera prints and balconies. **Hotel de Los Pérez** (Rascón 2, tel. 294/2–07–77) is your best bet at the high end. All rooms ($14 singles, $18.50 doubles) come with phones, TVs, blissfully quiet air conditioners, and spotless bathrooms. The hotel also has a decent restaurant.

FOOD San Andrés is not renowned for its restaurants. If you want quality seafood or regional specialties, take a short trip to Catemaco. Otherwise, the cafés near the zócalo on Madero serve cappuccino and fixed-price breakfasts. In the afternoons, the restaurant at **Hotel del Parque**, right on the zócalo, serves a filling comida corrida for $3. The small, outdoor **Caperucita Roja** (Juárez 108, tel. 294/2–05–11) whips up sandwiches and tacos at rock-bottom prices. Or escape to **Restaurante Tortacos** (tel. 294/2–31–00), in the cool, quiet La Fuente shopping center (cnr of Juárez and Argudín); the *mole poblano* (chicken in mole sauce) and mojarra costs $2. This is also the place to satisfy late-night cravings—it's open daily 7:30 AM–3 AM. For picnic supplies, head to **El Fénix** (Constitución 125), a big supermarket open daily 8:30 AM–9 PM.

OUTDOOR ACTIVITIES In the wet, tropical hills of Los Tuxtlas, opportunities abound for day trips to local swimming holes, rivers, and beaches. Just 3 kilometers outside San Andrés, the **Laguna Encantada** (Enchanted Lagoon) fills a small volcanic crater; the lake gets its name from its strange propensity to rise in the dry season and fall during the rains. Some taxis might brave the rutted road to the lake (for a $5 fee). You can also walk (take Highway 180 until you see the sign for the lake, follow the trail and bear left when the trail forks, and continue uphill), although locals warn travelers not to go alone—thieves occasionally assault the unwary. More easily reached and more impressive is **Salto de Eyipantla,** 20 kilometers from town on Highway 180. A roaring, 40-meter-wide waterfall crashes 50 meters down into shallow, churning pools. It's a popular picnic spot with the locals. The falls are served by greenish micros marked SALTO that run every 5–10 minutes from the zócalo in San Andrés. Micros cost about 50¢, and it's a 20-minute ride to the falls.

Catemaco

On the western shore of Lake Catemaco, 12 kilometers southwest of San Andrés on Highway 180, the town of Catemaco is now almost entirely devoted to tourism, but has lost little of its bizarre personality. A small town populated by approximately 40,000 people of Spanish,

African, and indigenous descent, Catemaco is dotted with *consultorios* (consulting rooms), where brujos ply their trade. If you'd like to sample their services, the best way to avoid being scammed is to ask the locals to recommend someone—most residents have snuck off for a *limpia* (spiritual cleansing) once or twice themselves.

In stark contrast to the lush beauty of the lake, the countryside, and the unabashed tourism, the muddy foothills of Catemaco are home to rows of makeshift houses and shacks. Just two blocks downhill from the bus station and the zócalo, Catemaco's lakeside walkway, or malecón, is the town's center of activity. The malecón contains what little nightlife Las Tuxtlas has to offer, with the discoteque **Luna 90,** and the bar **El Pescado Loco.** It also bustles with seafood vendors, souvenir stands, small restaurants, and men hawking boat rides—all set against a gorgeous backdrop of lake and mountain. The fauna and wildlife are also spectacular. You can see *changos* (monkeys), parakeets, and white herons without leaving the shore, and taking a tour in a lancha to **Isla de los Changos** offers a peek at the peaceful monkeys with bright red behinds. Brought from Thailand by the University of Veracruz for research purposes, a recent sickness (perhaps due to their consumption of rotten food) has halved their population; the university asks that you do not feed them. On the way to visit the monkeys, you'll also pass by **Isla de Garzas,** a resting spot for herons, and **El Tegal,** a grotto where the Virgin made a local appearance. It's now a shrine lit with countless votive candles. The lancha tours also include a couple of other beaches, a swimming hole, a ride past floating aquatic flowers, and transportation to Nanciyaga (*see* Outdoor Activities, *below*). You can get off and walk around at most places, except for Isla de los Changos and Isla de Garzas. Lancha tours charge $21 for one–six people, so come in a large group and stay at each site as long as you want. Back on shore, cavorting on the lakeside beaches is free, but they're pretty unspectacular. **Playa Hermosa** is more mud than sand, but buses (20¢) go there frequently; you can catch them in the zócalo.

The town's other attractions include the gaudy church on the zócalo dedicated to Catemaco's patron saint, the Virgen del Carmen, who appeared in 1714 to Juan Catemaxca—a local fisherman for whom the town is named. Every year on May 30, locals descend upon the malecón,

Be Witched

Do you want to gain the undying love of someone who has spurned you? Is so, bring his/her photo and between $70 and $140, and a brujo will perform a "trabajo" (a spell-casting) for you. A cheaper option ($5–$30) is to purify your own soul with a "limpia," which cleanses your aura of the negativity that causes blockages in luck and love. A typical cleansing consists of you being placed in front of an altar that sparkles with Catholic icons and often a liberal dose of Christmas lights. The objects used in the ritual have a European-pagan tradition: The egg was a symbol of new life and fertility, while the basil plant was believed to be so powerful that smelling too much of it would cause a scorpion to grow in your brain. Both objects are doused with a secret "sacred" water and brushed all over your body while Catholic incantations are intoned a mile a minute by the brujo. The ritual culminates in the brujo blowing the water on you and then pouring it on your head— a lot like being baptized, only you're old enough to know what's going on. And does it work? Who knows, but there is a lingering feeling of euphoria and cleanliness . . . at least until the sacred water (whose main ingredient is Avon perfume) wears off. Call Nanciyaga (see Outdoor Activities, below) to make an appointment for your limpia ($5). In Catemaco, José Luis Martínez Miros (tel. 294/3–07–91) is reputed to be a genuine curandero, but his fees tend to be on the steep side: His limpias run $14–$28, depending on if you bargain with him or not. He also performs trabajos but at higher prices.

where lanchas await to take them out to the **Monumento a Juan Catemaxca** to leave offerings of fish, flowers, and fruit. If you're in town on the first Friday in March, don't miss the conference of brujos who gather on the misty hillside of **Cerro Mono Blanco** (Hill of the White Monkey), overlooking Lake Catemaco, to conjure up the spirits.

WHERE TO SLEEP You're allowed to camp by the lake (behind La Ceiba restaurant), but it's not very safe nor attractive. If you really want to plop down in the sand, you're better off taking a bus to the Gulf Coast (*see* Near Catemaco, *below*), although it's no longer perfectly safe there either. **Hotel Los Arcos** (Madero 7, at Mantilla, tel. 294/3–00–03) provides comfy rooms loaded with phones, TVs, private bathrooms, and balconies that overlook the lake. Rooms cost $14 ($21 with air-conditioning), and there's even a small pool in the courtyard. At **Posada Koniapan** (Revolución, at malecón, tel. 294/3–00–63), air-conditioned rooms on the ground floor cost $11.50, and upstairs rooms with ceiling fans cost $14, both of which have balconies facing the lake and can fit up to two people. The posada sits at a quiet end of the malecón, and a good-size pool beckons from the grassy front yard.

FOOD The malecón is lined with small restaurants overlooking the lake. Most serve a variety of seafood—mojarra is always a good choice and usually costs about $2 a plate. **Las 7 Brujas** (tel. 294/3–01–57) is a two-story bamboo hut with a great view of the lake, not to mention a yummy, $4 robalo al mojo. **La Ceiba** (tel. 294/3–00–51) is the most economical of the sit-down eateries on the malécon and serves an outstanding *ceviche de jaiba* (crab ceviche; $3). Those who want to try the regional specialty *ceviche de tegogolos* had better be adventurous in two ways: (1) not mind eating lake mollusks (snails), and (2) be able to withstand its reputed aphrodisiac qualities. There's always the **mercado** (market) just off the malecón, where *comedores* (sit-down food stands) sell hearty meals for less than $2, and a cocktail of shrimp, oysters, or octopus won't cost more than $2.50.

OUTDOOR ACTIVITIES For mud and mineral water baths, massages, sweatlodge rituals, and even guided tours of the rain forest, head to the self-proclaimed ecotourist paradise at **Nanciyaga** (tel. 294/3–01–99). A simple resort run by locals on the edge of Lake Catemaco, Nanciyaga is open daily 9:30–7; for the $1 admission fee you'll be treated to a guided tour of the forest, historical tibits on pre-Colonial traditions like the sweat lodge, and a mud facial (yes, all for $1). You can also rent cabañas here for $10 a night, which include a mud and mineral water bath. If you want the works, a full body massage costs $14 per hour and the *temascal* (sweat lodge) runs $8.50 (call ahead to make a reservation). Nanciyaga can be reached by bus (15 min, 50¢) from the zócalo in Catemaco, or by lancha from the malecón (10 min, $4–$6). If you're driving, take the Coyame highway that runs southwest from San Andrés to Nanciyaga. About a 15-minute drive past Nanciyaga is **Río Cuetzalapan,** a cold-water mountain stream popular for swimming and fishing.

NEAR CATEMACO

The Gulf Coast beaches, 1½ bumpy hours by bus out of Catemaco, are one of Los Tuxtlas's great secrets. Foreign tourists rarely venture down this far, unless they're staying at one of the few isolated hotels scattered among the tiny fishing villages. Buses marked SONTECOMOPAN leave Catemaco at the corner of Revolución and the malecón every 20 minutes ($1.50). The 25-minute ride down skinny Highway 180 takes you through some beautiful ranching country before stoping at **Sontecomopan,** a small town on the shore of a quiet lagoon. Near the lagoon lies **Poza Enano,** a fresh-water swimming hole frequented by locals. They say the reflections in the water make you look like an *enano* (dwarf). From Sontecomopan, lanchas ($3) will take you to the small, pleasant beach called **La Barra.** If you're still on a quest for the perfect beach, pickups ($1) from Sontecomopan run down the dirt road towards the Gulf Coast beaches. About 10 kilometers along this road is the stop for **Playa Jicacal** and **Playa Escondida,** two of the best beaches in the region. When you get off the bus, follow the marked trail downhill for about a kilometer to the sandy expanse of Playa Jicacal. Playa Escondida lies on the other side of the promontory at the far end of the beach (keep your eyes open in the water here: Locals claim the area is frequented by sharks). Pickups leave Playas Jicacal and Escondida for the return trip to Catemaco as late as 8 PM, but you'd be crazy to try hiking back up the hill after nightfall. On top of the promontory, the basic **Hotel Playa Escondida,** with double rooms for

$13 a night, is your best overnight option. You're allowed to camp, but the beach is narrow, and locals warn that it's unsafe.

The farthest beach, at the spot along the sand most resembling a town, is **Montepío,** the end of the line for the SONTECOMOPAN bus; the last bus to return to Sontecomopan leaves at 7 PM. If you want to spend the majority of your day on the beaches rather than on a bus, stay overnight. Some say it's perfectly safe to camp here; others disagree. If you'd rather be safe, the **Hotel San José** (tel. 294/2–10–10) charges $12 a room. You can usually find someone around town who will rent a horse for $2 an hour if you feel like galavanting about.

Santiago Tuxtla

With its winding streets, red-tile roofs, and small market, Santiago Tuxtla, northwest on Highway 180 from San Andrés, has managed to retain more of its colonial character than the other two Tuxtla towns. Most visitors come to see the older traces of Olmec civilization here, centered at the nearby ruins of **Tres Zapotes.** A huge stone Olmec head dominates the town's zócalo, and the **Museo Tuxteco** (open Mon.–Sat. 9–6, Sun. until 3; admission $1.50), also on the plaza, displays a collection of Olmec and early Huastec pieces, including clay sculptures, obsidian blades, and a skull showing evidence of ritual deformation. The museum's director, Dr. Fernando Bustamante, is an expert on local indigenous cultures and more than willing to answer (in Spanish) any question you may have. He is usually at the museum weekday mornings.

The ruins themselves lie 21 kilometers west of town. Tres Zapotes, now decidedly unspectacular, was once an important Olmec ceremonial center; the city was believed to have been occupied as early as AD 100. Little remains of the original site, except for **La Camila,** a burial mound that rises from the corn fields outside town. More than 15 meters tall, this large mound is rumored to be an important nexus of spiritualism and cosmic energy. It doesn't look like anything now except a pretty grassy knoll with cattle grazing around it. Unless you're planning on dabbling in metaphysics yourself, skip the muddy walk through the ruins and head for the **museum** in the village of Tres Zapotes. From where your ride dropped you off at the ruins, hang a left on the dirt road and walk for 1 kilometer until you come to a large grassy field, where you'll find the outdoor museum. Here you'll see **Stela C,** a slab of bas-relief carving, with the date 7.16.6.16.18 (the 3rd of September 32 BC) inscribed upon it in the bar-and-dot calendrical system. This stela is one of the earliest examples of the "Long Count" calender, suggesting that the Olmec were the originators of a system the Maya would later adopt and perfect.

COMING AND GOING The only way to make the bumpy, 25-minute trip from Santiago Tuxtla to the ruins is by colectivo (50¢) or by taxi ($5.75). Both leave from **Los Pozitos** bar (just over the bridge from Hidalgo) in Santiago Tuxtla. You may have to wait up over an hour to leave in a colectivo though; they only depart when they're full.

WHERE TO SLEEP **Casa de Huéspedes Morelos** (Obregón 15, at Morelos, tel. 294/7–04–74) is the cheaper of Santiago's two lodging options and feels like what it is: someone's cramped but comfy home. There's no air-conditioning, but each room has a fan, and the owner doesn't mind if you use her washboard and clothesline. Rooms cost $5 for a single and $8 for a double. The wheelchair-accessible **Hotel Castellanos** (5 de Mayo, at Comonfort, tel. 294/7–03–00), right off the main square, is a small glass-and-iron tower with balconies off every room. The grandiose rooms have TVs, rugs, air-conditioning, and spotless bathrooms. Be forewarned though: The place feel like an old castle—dusty, musty, and filled with bugs. The price is $15–$20 a night, $3 less if you forgo the air-conditioning.

FOOD If you need nourishment, head for the area near the bus terminal, which houses several inexpensive *fondas* (covered food stands), or the market near the zócalo, which sells fruit and bread. For a little more atmosphere (and better tasting food) try **Parrilla la Ribera** (Castellanos Quinto 43, tel. 294/7–06–73). The chicken tacos are a steal at $1 for an order of five, and the owner, Señor Gutiérrez, is super friendly. To get here, walk down Morelos to Victoria and go left over the bridge. **Restaurant Los Faisanes** (tel. 294/7–02–00), inside Hotel Castellanos, is spotless and attractive. The seafood is decent; a plate of the *robalo al ajillo* is $4, and a satisfying breakfast will run you $2.

Jalapa

Home to 400,000 *xalapeños,* **as the city's residents are** called, Jalapa is perched on the side of a mountain, between the coastal lowlands of Veracruz and the high central plateau. A little more than 1,400 meters above sea level, the city has an enviable climate that will come as a pleasant surprise to perspiration-soaked escapees from Veracruz city, which swelters on the coast some 100 kilometers to the southeast. The capital of the state of Veracruz and a university town, Jalapa is known as "The Athens of Veracruz" because of its thriving arts scene; it also boasts the finest anthropology museum outside Mexico City. This community of artists runs the gamut from smaller experimental dance and theater troupes to a symphony orchestra and a state theater that attracts big-name performers. Lucky for you, there is very little industry in Jalapa, although you'll find plenty of businesses and international restaurants supported by a substantial student and government-worker population. The university's presence makes for a diverse population as well, and you are as likely to see longhaired twentysomethings sipping strong coffee in cafés as you are wizened *campesinos* (rural dwellers) walking to work.

BASICS

AMERICAN EXPRESS The travel agency **Viajes Xalapa** functions as the local AmEx representative and provides all AmEx services, including exchanging traveler's checks and holding cardholders' mail at Carillo Puerto 24, Jalapa, Veracruz, CP 91000, México. *3 blocks east of Parque Juárez, tel. 28/17–87–44. Open weekdays 9–1:30 and 4–7, Sat. 9–1.*

CASAS DE CAMBIO Five blocks west of Parque Juárez, **Casa de Cambio Jalapa** (Zamora 36, tel. 28/18–68–60) offers excellent rates weekdays 9–2 and 4–6. You can also change money on weekday mornings at several banks near Parque Juárez. **Bancomer** (Lázaro Cárdenas, at Ferrocarril, tel. 28/14–43–22; open weekdays 8:30–2) only changes traveler's checks. **Banamex** (Xalapeños Ilustres 3, tel. 28/15–64–01) has similar rates, changes both cash and traveler's checks, and has an ATM that accepts Cirrus, Plus, Visa, and MasterCard.

EMERGENCIES To contact the **police** call 28/17–33–43, or call the **Cruz Roja** at 28/17–34–31 for an ambulance. In an emergency dial 06.

LAUNDRY **Easy Launder** has "easy" prices: For 50¢ a kilo, someone will wash, dry, and fold your clothes and return them to you the same day. *201-C Ávila Camacho, at Mártires 28 Agosto, no phone. 7 long city blocks east of Parque Juárez. Open Mon.–Sat. 9–8.*

MAIL Seven blocks west of Parque Juárez, the full-service **post office** (Diego Lenyo, at Zamora, tel. 28/11–03–40) is open weekdays 8–8, Saturday 9–1. They will hold mail sent to you at the following address for up to 10 days: Lista de Correos, Administración No. 1, Jalapa, Veracruz, CP 91000, México. Next door, the **Centro de Servicios Integrados de Telecommunicaciones** (Zamora 70, tel. 28/17–71–60; open weekdays 8–6, Sat. 9–noon) offers fax, telegram, and telex services.

MEDICAL AID Calle Enríquez is lined with pharmacies. For 24-hour service, the pharmacy in **Super Tiendas Ramón** (Revolución 171, at Sagayo, tel. 28/18–09–35) is your best option, as some of the staff speaks English.

PHONES **Ladatel** phones huddle in front of the Palacio del Gobierno (Enríquez, at Revolución). Alternately, the long-distance service inside the **Restaurant Mariscos** charges $1.50 per minute for international calls. *Zaragoza 70, tel. 28/17–84–36. Open daily 7 AM–11 PM.*

SCHOOLS The **Escuela Para Estudiantes Extranjeros,** of the Universidad Veracruzana, offers six-week summer and four-month semester programs for foreign students. The department can also tailor courses to your needs, and arrange homestays. Contact Maestra Berta Cecilia Murrieta Cervantes (who speaks English) by phone for more info or write to: Escuela Para Estudiantes Extranjeros, AP 440, Jalapa, Veracruz, CP 91000, México. *Juárez 55, 2nd floor, btw Lucío and Revolución, tel. 28/17–86–87, fax 28/17–64–13, eeeuv@dino.coacade.uv.mx.*

VISITOR INFORMATION The restaurant **La Sopa** (*see* Food, *below*) hands out a trilingual brochure (Spanish, English, French) with detailed info and a map of Jalapa. The friendly staff at the **tourist office** is not terribly well informed, and if you don't ask for the green *folleto* with a map of Jalapa, you'll just get an unreadable map and useless pamphlets. *Av. de las Améri-cas, 1st floor of Torre Ánimas building, tel. 28/12–72–84. From Parque Juárez, walk west on Hidalgo, ½ block past Baderas, then take a pesero marked* CENTRO TORRE ANIMAS *or* SEC. *Open weekdays 9–3 and 6–9, Sat. 9–1.*

COMING AND GOING

BY BUS Jalapa's modern **Central de Autobuses de Xalapa** (20 de Noviembre Ote. 571, tel. 28/18–92–29), commonly called CAXA, lies 2 kilometers east of the city center. It's served by the first-class **Autobuses del Oriente** (**ADO**) line (tel. 28/18–98–55 or 28/18–92–40), as well as the second-class **Autobuses Unidos** (**AU**) (tel. 28/18–70–77). ADO has frequent departures to Veracruz city (2 hrs, $3.50), Mexico City (5 hrs, $10.50), Catemaco (4½ hrs, $8.50), Papantla (4 hrs, $8), and Puebla (3 hrs, $6). AU has equally frequent service and slightly lower prices. The terminal has a 24-hour pharmacy, a long-distance phone office, and 24-hour luggage storage (25¢ per hr). To reach the center of town, walk down the wide stone stairs to the local bus stop and catch any bus marked CENTRO. To reach the terminal from downtown, catch a bus marked CAXA going east from Enríquez, between Clavijero and Revolución.

BY TRAIN The small **Estación Nueva Miguel Alemán** (tel. 28/15–17–64) is in the northern part of Jalapa. Two painfully slow second-class trains creep to Mexico City (7½ hrs, $3.50) and Veracruz (3½ hrs, $1.50) daily. A cab from here to downtown will cost less than $2.

GETTING AROUND

Walking up and down Jalapa's labyrinthine, cobblestoned streets can test the stamina of even the fittest, but there are plenty of beautiful parks to rest your bones in at every turn. The hilly streets make the town wheelchair-unfriendly, and the central streets' frequent name changes can get confusing. Orient yourself around **Parque Juárez,** the city's emotional, if not geographic, heart. Enríquez runs along the northern edge of the park, becoming Zamora as it heads east past the purple Banamex building, and Ávila Camacho as it heads west and passes the **Teatro del Estado** (state theater). Allende flanks the southern edge of the plaza, and Zaragoza mysteriously stems from the plaza's east side, while Revolución branches from its northeast corner.

The most important city buses originate in front of the **3 Hermanos** shoe store on Enríquez, two blocks east of Parque Juárez. Buses (25¢) and colectivos (30¢) run 5 AM–11 PM. Taxis, which roam all main streets, are also relatively cheap and extremely convenient. They don't have meters—just get in, name your destination, and don't pay more than $1.

WHERE TO SLEEP

Because of its triple function as the seat of state government, a university town, and the only big city in a poor, thickly settled rural area, Jalapa offers plenty of lodging choices. You'll find several clean, comfortable, and surprisingly cheap hotels right in the center of town.

➤ **UNDER $10** • **Hotel Limón.** Just one block north of the cathedral and set back from the busy traffic of Revolución under a pretty, tiled archway, the Limón is a great bargain. It features hand-painted tiles, brightly colored floors, and small, clean bathrooms with hot showers. The management charges solo travelers $6 and couples $7, regardless of room size, so you might as well take the biggest one available. *Revolución 8, tel. 28/17–22–04. 45 rooms, all with bath. Laundry, luggage storage.*

Hotel Plaza. Smack in the middle of the bustle on Enríquez, the rooms here are tidy and fan-cooled, and the bathrooms have hot water, soap, and clean towels. Some rooms are a bit gloomy, but all of them are spacious. The rooms on the street are more airy—and more noisy—than their interior counterparts. A single here costs $5.50, and doubles are $6.50. The reception desk is hidden at the top of a flight of stairs at the end of a long, yellow-tiled hallway next to Enrico's restaurant. *Enríquez 4, tel. 28/17–33–10. 36 rooms, all with bath. Luggage storage.*

➤ **UNDER $15** • **Hotel Posada del Virrey.** As if trying to live up to its conquistador-inspired name, this hotel has a Spanish coat of arms engraved into every available window. The tastefully decorated and immaculate rooms offer TVs, phones, and modern bathrooms; some have wrought-iron balconies. Singles cost $13.50, doubles $18. *Dr. Lucío 142, tel. 28/18–61–00. Laundry, luggage storage, restaurant, safe-deposit boxes.*

Hotel Principal. This aging but immaculate hotel is a short walk from Parque Juárez. Get an interior room or the traffic will set your teeth rattling. The rooms (singles $9, doubles $11) are big and comfy, with phones and ceilings high enough to accommodate a small herd of giraffes. The clean bathrooms are, oddly enough, configured to allow you to use the toilet and sink while showering. *Zaragoza 28, tel. 28/17–64–00. 3½ blocks east of Parque Juárez. 40 rooms, all with bath. Laundry, luggage storage. Wheelchair access.*

CAMPING Camping is available 20 minutes outside Jalapa, on the shores of the **Río de los Pescados.** The shores are safe, and you can stock up on food supplies at stores in the nearby town of Jalcomulco. If you're driving, take the Las Trancas exit from Jalapa toward Veracruz, which turns into the Coatepec/Huatusco highway. This will bring you to the town of Jalcomulco, where you can access the river. Or catch a southbound JALCOMULCO bus ($3) from 7 de Noviembre, between Úrsulo Galván and Allende; buses leave every 20–40 minutes.

FOOD

Good restaurants are cheap and plentiful. If you eat all your meals at the markets on Altamirano, you'll spend less than $5 for breakfast, lunch, and dinner combined. You might even develop a taste for *hormigas chichantanas* (dried ants), a local delicacy. More familiar food can be found down the hill from the markets in the grocery section of the super-store **Chedraui Centro** (Lucío 28, tel. 28/18–71–77), open daily 8 AM–9 PM, or in the health food stores and bakeries dotting Lucío. Restaurants here don't cost much more than the markets, especially if you hang out around **Callejón Diamante,** a skinny, cobblestone alleyway off Enríquez whose brightly painted restaurants serve cheap, flavorful meals to crowds of hungry students. You've found the Callejón when you've spotted the white-and-red second-story restaurant **La Fonda.** The cozy atmosphere includes a view of the cooks making fresh tortillas and preparing regional delicacies in big, clay pots. Try such specialties as the *hongos de la casa* (regional mushrooms cooked with garlic and purple chilis; $2.50) or the dessertlike *camote con piña* (yam and pineapple pudding; $1). Wash it all down with *tepache* (fermented pineapple juice). *Callejón Diamante 1, tel. 28/18–45–20. Open Mon.–Sat. 8–6.*

Café La Parroquia. At this bustling restaurant—*the* place for breakfast—anxious patrons tap their glasses with spoons to signal for another *lechero* (coffee and steamed milk). Tables are always filled with white-haired professor types, slouching school kids, and university students who all linger over baskets of sweetbreads. Breakfast or lunch here will only set you back $3. *Zaragoza 18, 2 blocks east of Parque Juárez tel. 28/17–44–36. Open Mon.–Sat. 7:30 AM–10:30 PM. Sun 8 AM–11 PM.*

Jalapa is home to the jalapeño pepper. With almost every bite of this city's spicy food, you'll be reminded of where you are.

El Macondo. This tidy, blue-walled restaurant attracts students from the nearby university, who come for the varied menu with a gourmet flair. Try the vegetarian pizza ($3), *espaguetti al aj* (garlic pasta; $1.75) or the *choriqueso macondo* (goat cheese, sausage, and chiles served with tortillas; $2). The comida corrida costs $1.25. *Morelos 13, at Alonso Guido, tel. 28/18–52–15. Open Mon.–Sat. 9–5 and 7–midnight.*

La Sopa. You won't find better food at cheaper prices anywhere in town. Refreshing *agua d fruta* (fruit juice) and terrific garbanzo-bean soup come with the $2 comida corrida, which i served daily 1–5. The place is usually packed, but once you get a table the service is promp and polite. La Sopa has live music Thursday–Saturday after 9 PM. *Antonio M. de Rivera (a.k.a Callejón Diamante) 3-A, tel. 28/17–80–69. Open Mon.–Sat. 1–11. Wheelchair access.*

WORTH SEEING

The terraced gardens of **Parque Juárez** should be your starting point for exploring Jalapa. It offers gorgeous views of Mexico's highest peak, the 5,610-meter Pico de Orizaba (or Citlaltépetl, as it was originally known), a favorite with mountain climbers. Next to the park sits the massive **Palacio del Gobierno** (Enríquez, at Revolución; open weekdays 6 AM–9 PM), where you may find machine-gun-toting guards protecting the government offices from either teachers seeking a 100% salary hike or the indigenous campesinos demanding improvements in education and medical aid. Directly across the street, the imposing **catedral**, featuring a veritable dollhouse of life-size saint statues, opens its doors daily 8–1 and 4–8.

CASA DE ARTESANIAS Jalapa's state-run handicrafts center is housed in a beautifully renovated colonial mansion that sits on a hill overlooking the lakes of the **Parque Paseo de los Lagos,** whose parameters are graced with morning exercisers and lovey-dovey couples. Inside the center is a studio with rotating exhibits and a shop selling locally produced crafts and clothing. Fruit wines ($3 a bottle) are also sold. *Paseo de los Lagos, tel. 28/17–08–04. From Parque Juárez, straight down the hill on Herrera, right on Domínguez, left on Dique. Open weekdays 9–8, Sat. 10–1.*

CENTRO DEL ARTE This small, free cultural center hosts exhibitions of everything from photography and sculpture to finger painting. A billboard on the wall by the entryway provides the scoop on current cultural events. *Xalapeños Ilustres, at Insurgentes, no phone. From Parque Juárez, walk east on Enrique until it forks; Xalapeños Ilustres will be the street to your left. Open Mon.–Sat. 11–8, Sun. 11–6.*

GALERIA UNIVERSITARIA RAMON ALVA DE LA CANAL This two-story university gallery, with its polished wood floors and clean, white walls, houses rotating exhibits of art and photography, almost all of which are produced by university students. *Zamora 27, tel. 28/17–75–79. From Parque Juárez, walk east on Enrique unti it becomes Zamora. Admission free. Open weekdays 9–2 and 5–8, Sat. 10–noon.*

JARDIN BOTANICO FRANCISCO JAVIER CLAVIJERO These well-kept botanical gardens about 2 kilometers outside town contain more than 1,500 varieties of flora from throughout the state of Veracruz. A small arboretum houses a slew of palm species, and a large pond showcases a vast array of aquatic plants. Hilly stone walkways and narrow steps guide you into the woods, where most plants sport placards that bear their Spanish and scientific names and explain any useful properties the plants possess. Buses marked COATEPEC BRIONES will bring you here from the stop in front of the **Teatro del Estado** (cnr of Ignacio de la Llave and Ávila Camacho) for 25¢. *Carretera Antigua a Coatepec Km. 2.5, no phone. Open Tues.–Sun. 10–5.*

MUSEO DE ANTROPOLOGIA DE JALAPA With more than 29,000 pieces on display, Jalapa's anthropology museum is second only to Mexico City's. The building's long central corridor opens out onto extensive gardens and displays stunning artifacts from the primary indigenous cultures of Veracruz: Olmec, Totonac, and Huastec. Highlights include massive stone Olmec heads, lively, grinning Remojadas figurines, graceful jade masks, and a burial mound complete with bones, ritually deformed skulls, and ceremonial statuettes. There is also an exhibit on the clothing and customs of contemporary Totonac and Huastec cultures. Guided tours by English-speaking students are available weekdays, but you have to call in advance and make an appointment. *Av. Jalapa, tel. 28/15–07–08. Take ALVARIO PANTEON or MERCADO TESORARIA bus from cnr of Revolución and Abasolo. Admission: $1.50, $1 students. Open daily 9–5.*

PARQUE ECOLOGICO MACUILTEPEC This park was once a pre-Columbian town called Mazcuilxochitlan (Place of the Flower God); because of its historical richness and the lush subalpine forest that covers the mountainside, the Veracruz state government declared the spot an ecological reserve. The paved trail that winds up the mountainside offers great views of Jalapa, and it's a favorite with joggers or people seeking to escape the city below. You can picnic at the parrillas (barbeque pits), or ascend to the top, where famous historical figures in Veracruz history are buried inside a pink, art nouveau pyramid. The park itself actually rests on an inactive volcano; at the entrance you can gaze into its crater, now covered in a patchwork rug of grass, swing sets, and soccer fields. *Miguel Alemán, no phone. Admission free. Open daily 10–5. Take* MIGUEL ALEMAN *bus from in front of Palacio Municipal.*

AFTER DARK

Jalapa sleeps Sunday through Wednesday nights and parties—usually to live music—Thursday through Saturday. While lots of clubs still think black lights and billowing clouds of dry ice are imperative for a good time, most local bands (especially those at salsa clubs) are worth the damage to your senses. **La Sopa** (*see* Food, *above*) is a popular student hangout, mostly due to the free folklore and jazz offered Thursday–Saturday nights from 9 to 11 PM. Two doors away, the popular salsa club **El Callejón** (Callejón Diamante 7, tel. 28/18–77–46) draws an enthusiastic crowd with live shows 10 PM–2 AM. More laid-back is the live samba and jazz at the restaurant/bar **La Casona del Beaterio** (Zaragoza 20, tel. 28/18–21–19); there's no cover, and you can linger over coffee and dessert as long as you like. **Juanote** (Xalapeños Ilustres 22, tel. 28/12–

The arts department of the university frequently opens dress rehearsals of upcoming presentations. Performances run the gamut from modern dance to Shakespeare, and take place on campus and in the Teatro del Estado. Check the city newspaper "El Diario de Jalapa," available at newsstands, for details on these and other events.

48–50) is an artsy restaurant with artwork scattered on its colorful walls. Juanote features local live music and theater and dance performances Monday–Saturday from 10 PM to 2 AM. Covers get more expensive as the weekend approaches, but usually run 75¢–$1.50. If you want to rock, head to the other side of Parque Juárez; about four blocks along Ávila Camacho you'll find **B42** (Ávila Camacho 42, tel. 28/12–08–93), a video bar and rock club packed with well-dressed students and young professionals. Local groups play here Fridays and Saturdays 11 PM–2 AM for a $3 cover. Even more upscale is **La 7a Estación** (20 de Noviembre, near CAXA), the biggest, fanciest disco in Jalapa. It features pop music, and is free before 10 PM; after that, it's $5.

Agora (SW cnr of Parque Juárez, downstairs, tel. 28/18–57–30) is a cultural center that shows classic and avant-garde films. Stop by after 6 PM to see what's planned; it's open daily 9–9, and admission is free. While you're here, you can also inquire about performance schedules for the **Orquestra Sinfónica de Jalapa,** which performs in the **Teatro del Estado** and often gives free concerts during its off-season (early June to mid-August).

Near Jalapa

COATEPEC

Just 8 kilometers southwest along the highway from Jalapa, the colonial city of Coatepec is a center for coffee and orchid cultivation. There is no "café society" here though; supposedly, all of the good coffee gets exported, leaving Coatepec to sell the lowest quality in their own stores.

In a small park north of the plaza on Hernández y Hernández sits a big cement structure called el hongo (the mushroom). Walk silently to the center, then speak softly, and see what happens.

However you can see the beautiful orchids in perpetual bloom at the **Invernadero María Cristina** (Miguel Rebolledo 4, tel. 28/16–03–79; open Mon.–Sat. 9–7, Sun. 10–2), near the main square. Fruit wines are sold (and free samples offered) at **Licores Finos Bautista Gálvez** (Hernández y Hernández 5, no phone). And if you ever wanted to see a 13-hectare eco-tourism wonderland, now's your chance. At **Agualegre** (Río la Marina, 5 blocks NW of plaza, no phone), you can enjoy the four swimming pools, water slide, restaurant, or trails for horseback riding or hiking, and then camp among the jagged green hills. Admission is $1.50, campsites are an additional $2, and an hour of horseback riding through the reserve costs $5. Longer trips to sites as far off as Xico (*see below*) can be arranged with advance notice.

COMING AND GOING To reach Coatepec from Jalapa, first catch a bus marked TERMINAL (10 min, 15¢) from the stop in front of the **3 Hermanos** shoe store on Enríquez; it'll deposit you at a collection of bus stands near the rusty, white TERMINAL EXCELSIOR sign. From here, blue buses marked COATEPEC 15 min, 30¢) leave every 5–10 minutes.

XICO

About 19 kilometers southwest from Jalapa, Xico (pronounced He-koe) is a tiny town at the base of the steep, coffee-growing Perote foothills; it's also one of the few places left on earth where donkeys are the major mode of transportation. Influenced by the heavy Spanish presence in the 16th century (Cortés passed through Xico on his way to the Aztec capital of Tenochtitlán), this very traditional town holds bullfights and *pamplonadas* (running of the bulls) each year as part of the **Feria de Santa María Magdalena** (July 22). However, Xico's year-round selling point is the roaring, 40-meter **Cascada de Texolo**, a long 3-kilometer walk outside town. A cobblestone path leads through banana plantations to the falls, but it's not easy to find. From the entrance to town on the main street (at the sign marked ENTRADA), go up the hill. When the path forks, bear left and follow the CASCADA TEXOLO sign down the unpaved road. At the next fork, take the high road. You can swim in the small pool at the bottom of the waterfall. Near the waterfall, there's also a restaurant that serves a $2 comida corrida; the owner moonlights as a taxi driver and will take you back to Xico ($3) if you're too beat to walk.

Be sure to leave Xico for Jalapa before nightfall, as there are no hotels here. The food is great, though, and almost all the restaurants near the plaza serve excellent dishes with *mole* (chile and chocolate sauce). Another local specialty is *verde*, a liqueur made with herbs.

Legend has it that a bishop used to perform exorcisms on the red fish that swam through Agua Bendita and Cajón de Pextla, two small "rios" (rivers) in Xico.

COMING AND GOING To reach Xico from Jalapa (40 min, $1), first catch a bus marked TERMINAL from the stop in front of the **3 Hermanos** shoe store on Enríquez; it'll deposit you at a collection of bus stands, near the rusty, white TERMINAL EXCELSIOR sign. From here, blue buses marked XICO leave every 5–10 minutes.

Papantla de Olarte

Papantla de Olarte sits amid tropical hills, 250 kilometers (420 mi) northwest of Veracruz. The town's character is distinctive, largely due to the mix of Spanish and indigenous traditions here. The Festival of Corpus Christi, held nine weeks after Easter, is perhaps the best example of this syncretism, celebrating both the Spanish-Catholic sacrament of the Eucharist and ancient Totonac harvest rituals. Festooned with enormous wreaths of flowers, vanilla leaves, and ears of corn, the **cathedral** is the focal point of the festivities, and Totonac dances are performed outside. During the rest of the year, Totonac men in flowing white pants lead their donkeys through crowded streets; palm trees shade the traditional, tiled zócalo; and a 25-meter pole next to the ornate cathedral is set up for a Totonac ritual in which four *voladores* (fliers) plummet toward the ground (*see box*, Voladores de Papantla, *below*). Papantla's main draw, however, is its proximity to the ruins of **El Tajín** (*see* Near Papantla, *below*). You'll find a small number of Mexican and foreign tourists using this town as a base for exploring the ruins, but the town is far from being a tourist trap.

BASICS

CASAS DE CAMBIO Papantla lacks a casa de cambio, but the **Banamex** (Enríquez 102, tel. 784/2-01-89), two blocks east of the zócalo, changes both cash and traveler's checks weekdays 9–2. It also has a 24-hour ATM that accepts Cirrus, Plus, Visa, and MasterCard.

EMERGENCIES **Police** (tel. 784/2-27-84); **Cruz Roja** (tel. 784/2-01-26).

MAIL The **post office** is down the hill from the zócalo; walk one block south on 20 de Noviembre, turn left on Serdán, right on Azueta, and then look for the CONSULTORIO MEDICO sign.

The post office is in the same building. Mail will be held for you for up to 10 days if sent to the following address: Lista de Correos, Azueta 198 Altos, Papantla, Veracruz, CP 93400, México *Tel. 784/2–00–73. Open weekdays 9–4, Sat. 9–1.*

MEDICAL AID Farmacia Médico is the biggest pharmacy in Papantla, and it's right on the zócalo. The staff doesn't speak English but is good at charades. *Gutiérrez Zamora 3, tel. 784/2–06–40. Open daily 7:30 AM–10 PM.*

PHONES The three **Ladatel** phones in town are down the hill in the **Teléfonos de México** caseta (5 de Mayo 201, tel. 784/2–05–35), which only offers long-distance services. **Farmacia Médico** (*see above*) also has a caseta de larga distancia, but they only do collect calls.

VISITOR INFORMATION The **tourist office** has an attentive staff who hands out free maps and loads of good advice. Margarita Pérez is especially helpful, speaks some English, and will gladly make arrangements to visit the vanilla plantation for you. *Palacio Municipal, in zócalo, tel. 784/2–01–77. Open weekdays 9–3 and 6–9, Sat. 9–1.*

COMING AND GOING

Situated just off the modern Highway 180, Papantla can be easily covered on foot. The zócalo, or **Parque Telléz,** is bordered by the cathedral to the south and Calle Enríquez to the north. The first-class **Autobuses del Oriente** (**ADO**) station (Juárez 207, tel. 784/2–02–18) is a five-minute walk downhill from the zócalo. Eight buses leave daily for Jalapa (4 hrs, $8), and five leave for both Veracruz city (4 hrs, $8) and Mexico City (5 hrs, $9.50). One bus also leaves at 7:30 PM daily for Villa Hermosa. The second-class **Transportes Papantla** station (20 de Noviembre, tel. 784/2–00–15) lies two blocks downhill from the zócalo behind the 15-10-15 superstore; buses serve the surrounding villages and a few major cities in Veracruz, such as Jalapa (6½ hrs, $7), Veracruz city (6½ hrs, $6.50), and Zempoala (3½ hrs, $5). Buses to Poza Rica (20 min, $1) run every five minutes between 4 AM and 11 PM. Once in Poza Rica, you can transfer to an ADO bus for a direct ride to farther destinations.

WHERE TO SLEEP

Hotels in Papantla are either cheap and lousy or expensive and passable, but almost all are within a block or two of the zócalo. If you have cash to burn, the **Hotel Premier** (Enríquez 103, tel. 784/2–00–80) sports large rooms ($18 singles, $24 doubles) with modern bathrooms and tiny balconies overlooking the square. Despite the lack of aesthetics at **Hotel Pulido** (Enrique 205, tel. 784/2–00–38), rooms are inexpensive: $7 singles, $8.50 doubles. Test the ceiling fans in a few rooms before you bed down; some are rickety and look like they're about to do a cartwheel off the ceiling. **Hotel Tajín** (Núñez y Domínguez 104, 1½ blocks west of cathedral, tel. 784/2–06–44) offers a lovely view of the city, the convenience of an in-house upscale restaurant, and laundry, making your stay in the clean rooms (with TVs, phones, and large bathrooms) worth it. Singles cost $10.50 ($15.50 with air-conditioning) and doubles run $13 ($17.50 with air-conditioning).

CAMPING Pipos (Lorenzo Collado, tel. 784/2–39–32) serves as the local **Unidad Deportiva.** It's $1.25 to camp here and use their facilities, which include a swimming pool. Camping is also available about 10 minutes away from El Tajín on the **Río Molino.** According to locals, it's safe, and the restaurant **El Mirador,** near the bridge, will satisfy your hunger pangs. Catch a 25¢ Transportes Papantla bus (*see* Coming and Going, *above*) marked EL CHOTE, and get off at El Chote; cross the street, and take a 50¢ SAN ANDRES or MARTINEZ DE LA TORRE bus and get off before you arrive at the bridge. Both buses run every 20 minutes until 7 PM. From El Tajín, walk to the highway, and take any bus going southeast; ask the driver to let you off at Río Molino.

FOOD

Papantla doesn't offer many culinary options, but you'll be hard-pressed to blow more than $5 on a meal here. As usual, the fondas in the market (btw Azueta and 20 de Noviembre) are your cheapest option. The restaurant at **Hotel Tajín** (*see* Where to Sleep, *above*) is one of the better places in town, serving generous breakfasts and $2–$3 comida corridas. You can stock up on tacky souvenirs while you wait for your meal at **Restaurante Plaza Pardo** (Enríquez 105, tel. 784/2–00–59), on the south side of the zócalo, which doubles as a gift shop but specializes in delicious chicken tacos ($2) and sweet *aguas de fruta* (fruit juices; $1). **Restaurant Enríquez** (Reforma 100, no phone) on the northeast corner of the zócalo, serves tasty seafood dishes ($3) and bite-size tacos (20¢).

Near Papantla de Olarte

EL TAJÍN

Just 15 minutes outside Papantla is El Tajín, the ruins of an extensive city that dates back to AD 100. Although the central structures have been excavated and restored, many more remain hidden under thick jungle growth. Archaeologists speculate that the entire city covered about 58 hectares (146 acres), and that smaller, related structures could be spread over several thousand acres.

Little is known about the people who built El Tajín. Early theories attributed the complex to either the Totonac or Huastec, the two most important cultures of the Veracruz area. Today, local Totonac people claim it as part of their heritage—"Tajín" is a Totonac word meaning "thunder"—although archaeologists remain unconvinced. Various clues reveal that whoever built El Tajín also had important ties to other Mesoamerican cultures. Archaelogical motifs that adorn the pyramids here, such as the repeated scroll pattern (symbolizing sea shells) and the step-and-fret design (symbolizing lightning), also show up at Teotihuacán and Xochicalco in the central highlands.

Guided tours of the site are not available, but the blue-shirted guards who wander the complex often know a great deal about the site. Near the entrance, the unremarkable **Plaza del Arroyo** is likely to have been the city's commercial center; pass by the four large pyramids of the plaza to reach El Tajín's ceremonial heart. Here, a squat statue of Mictlantecuhtli, a death god, guards the central stairway to a steep, blackened pyramid (structure 5). This pyramid is attached to the central **ball court** (shaped like a wide H), which is famous for the series of bas-relief (sunken-in, as opposed to auto-relief, which is raised) carvings that adorn its walls (*see box*, Play Ball!, *below*). At the north corners of the court, two panels depict pre- and post-game rituals; the death god watches both these scenes, floating eerily out of a jar.

Behind structure 5 stands the ornate **Pyramid of the Niches.** Also called the *edificio calandario* (calendar building), its seven levels are punctuated by 365 framed, square cubby holes—one for each day of the solar year. Now bleached white, this pyramid, like all buildings at El Tajín,

Voladores de Papantla

The ritual of the voladores was originally performed as a tribute to the gods of the sun and rain: The fliers, dressed in bright red trousers, black boots, and tassled red caps, dive backwards off a small platform at the top of a pole; tied at the ankle, they swing upside down in the air, each one twisting 13 full rotations (to mark the months of the lunar calendar). Between them, the four fliers circle the pole 52 times, once for each year of the cycle of the Totonac calendar. A fifth man, the "caporal," or prayer giver, sits atop the pole and plays a small flute while keeping rhythm on a drum as the fliers descend. Originally, the ceremony was held on the spring equinox, but Catholicism and tourism have changed all that. Now the voladores fly for the crowds every Saturday and Sunday at noon at Tajín, and give special performances during Corpus Christi.

The ritualized piercing of tongues and genitals was a sacred practice among the rulers and priests of Mesoamerican civilizations. Check out the excellent depiction of penis piercing at El Tajín in an intricate bas-relief carving on the southern wall of the central ball court.

was once painted in vivid reds and blues—surely an impressive contrast to the surrounding green hills. Past the steep rise to the north lies **El Tajín Chico,** which is thought to have been the secular or poorer part of the city. The most important structure here is the **Building of the Columns.** Carved with complex narrative scenes, three of these columns are now housed in the museum near the entrance. Several carved human figures on the column, such as 13 Rabbit, bear names taken from the 260-day Mayan ceremonial calendar, but the relationship between El Tajín and the Mayan empire remains unknown.

The ruins are open daily 9–5 and admission is $2, except on Sunday, when it's free. Don't worry about finding food—the entrance is lined with fondas that sell cheap eats and mountains of tacky souvenirs, and there's even a big cafeteria-style restaurant at the site. El Tajín is a good place to see the voladores (*see box, above*); their pole is right outside the entrance. Performances take place on weekends, beginning at noon and continuing hourly; they also perform during the week if enough people show up. Donations are the only wages the fliers receive.

COMING AND GOING The EL TAJIN/CHOTE buses ($1 round-trip) that run along 16 de Septiembre in Papantla will take you to the ruins; catch them at the bus stop behind the church. The last bus back from El Tajín to Papantla leaves at 5:45 PM.

Tuxpán

Tuxpán is a peaceful riverside town of approximately 128,000 residents that lies an hour and a half north of Papantla. The city's main attraction is **Playa Tuxpán,** also known as **Playa Norte** by locals, a 42-kilometer stretch of Gulf Coast beaches. Perhaps due to the town's lack of impressive sights and development, the area is still relatively undiscovered

Play Ball!

To the Totonac inhabitants in the ancient city of El Tajín, "playing ball" meant more than a sport or a diversion. The 16 ball courts found in the ruins here suggest that the game was played anywhere between 300–1200 BC. Blessed as sacred spaces by the city's temple, the courts were actually "I"-shaped, rectangular area in between the walls of the city's buildings. Although its original purpose may have been solely athletic, the game was slowly integrated into the spiritual life of the community, and its outcome was considered to be a divination of the gods. The game was played between two teams consisting of three players each. The object was to pass the ball through an "aro"—a ring-like fixture carved from stone, which was attached to the side of the city wall—using only the waist, hips, or forearms. It was common for teams from the lower class "El Tajín Chico" to play against their wealthier neighbors in "El Tajín Grande." Despite the socio-economic disparity, the outcome would make the winner spiritually superior. Although still subject to debate, researchers are now more inclined to believe that the captain of the winning team, NOT the losing team, was ritually sacrificed at the end of the game. Sacrifice to the gods was the highest honor an individual could receive in his community and was akin to becoming a demi-god oneself. Numerous bas-reliefs at El Tajín depict the post-game sacrifice, with the death god looking on.

by tourists; this lack of visitors, plus white sandy beaches, beautiful green river, and a tranquil setting, makes Tuxpán a prime destination for anyone seeking relative solitude. The surf isn't huge here, but there's enough action to warrant shelling out $2 to rent a surfboard for the day. You'll find them for hire at the seafood and beer stands in the pine grove behind the beach.

The indigenous Huastec, concentrated in Tuxpán and Tampico, earned the reputation of being great runners after being commissioned by the Aztec to routinely deliver fresh fish to the Aztec capital of Tenochtitlán—a 377-kilometer dash.

Tuxpán itself is a pleasant town, with winding streets lined with two-story buildings. Juárez, the main street, runs parallel to the river and is home to numerous diners, hotels, and shops. The **Parque Reforma** is the center of social activity in town, with more than a hundred tables set around a hub of cafés and fruit stands. On the western edge of the Parque is the free **Museo Arqueológico** (tel. 783/4–61–80; open weekdays 9–7, Sat. 9–2), a small museum featuring Huastecan pottery, crafts, and a couple of burial mounds. Lanchas shuttle passengers across the river to the **Casa de Fidel Castro** (Obregón, no phone), where Castro lived for a time while planning the overthrow of dictator Fulgencio Batista. Tuxpán was chosen as a launching pad by Castro because it offered a direct route to Cuba through the Gulf. Now a museum of sorts, the casa is open daily 9–5, and you can wander in at no charge. The interior is bare save some black-and-white photos of Fidel and former Mexican president Lázaro Cárdenas.

BASICS

CASAS DE CAMBIO **Bancomer** (Juárez, at Escuela Médico Militar, tel. 783/4–00–09) changes cash and traveler's checks weekdays 8:30–1:30. **Banamex** (Juárez, at Corregidora, tel. 783/4–08–40) has a 24-hour ATM that takes Cirrus, Plus, Visa, and MasterCard.

EMERGENCIES **Police** (tel. 783/4–02–52); **Cruz Roja** (tel. 783/4–01–58).

MEDICAL AID **Farmacia Benavides** is a gleaming, modern pharmacy whose sterile-looking shelves are amply stocked. *15 Juárez, tel. 783/4–51–93. Open 24 hrs.*

PHONES AND MAIL The full-service **post office** (Mina 16, btw Ocampo and Colón, tel. 783/4–00–88) is open weekdays 9–4 and Saturdays 9–1. Mail will be held for you for up to 10 days at the following address: Lista de Correos, Administración 1, Tuxpán, Veracruz, CP 92801, México. You can make both long-distance and local calls at the ADO station (*see* Coming and Going, *below*).

VISITOR INFORMATION The small **tourist office** is in the red municipal building across the street from the cathedral. The friendly staff only speaks Spanish, and maps are in chronic short supply. *Juárez 23, tel. 783/4–01–77. Open daily 9–8.*

COMING AND GOING

Highway 180 runs right through Tuxpán, making it a snap to get here from the north or south. Central Tuxpán is small and easily maneuvered on foot; Juárez, the main street, runs parallel to the river, one block inland. Boat rides across the river cost only pennies. Frequent PLAYA buses run east along Reforma, the street that borders the river's edge. The easiest place to flag down buses in the centro is along the river dock, at the corner of Rodríguez and Reforma.

Tuxpán doesn't have a central first-class bus terminal; instead, each line has its own depot. Bus tickets are a prized commodity during such holidays as Christmas, Semana Santa, and the entire month of July. To avoid getting stuck here, it's best to buy your ticket at least two days before you want to leave. The **Autobuses del Oriente (ADO)** station (Rodríguez 1, tel. 783/4–01–02), five minutes east of Parque Reforma on Juárez, is the most convenient, with nine buses a day to Mexico City (6 hrs, $10.50) and seven buses a day to Papantla (1½ hrs, $2.25). If you can't get a ticket at the ADO terminal, try **Omnibús de México** (Independencia 50, tel. 783/4–11–47), which has a depot 1 kilometer farther down the river, near the bridge. Their service is similar to ADO's. Take a bus marked PLAYA going east along the riverside, on Reforma, and get off at Reforma and Independencia, where the terminal is located. Second-class buses operate from the outdoor **Terminal ABC** (tel. 783/4–20–40) on Cuauhtémoc. Service is available to destinations such as Tampico (4½ hrs, $6.50), Nuevo Laredo (15 hrs, $27.50), Monterrey (12 hrs, $20.50), and Reynosa (12 hrs, $22.50).

WHERE TO SLEEP

Hotels tend to be expensive, but you'll find a few moderately priced establishments near the center. If the places below are full, try the bare but passable **Hotel del Parque** (Humboldt 11, on the zócalo, tel. 783/4–08–12), where both singles and doubles cost $7. If you have the funds, crash at **Hotel Florida** (Juárez 23, tel. 783/4–02–22), where all rooms have TVs, air-conditioning, and phones. Singles cost $17, doubles $21. **Hotel El Huasteco** (Morelos 41, tel. 783/4–18–59) lies just a block east of Parque Juárez, and all 40 rooms tend to fill up fast. The rooms are basic, but clean and air-conditioned. Singles cost $8.50, one-bed doubles run $9, and two beds are $11. Laundry and luggage storage is also available. At the wheelchair accessible **Hotel Posada San Ignacio** (Melchor Ocampo 29, 1 block north of the zócalo, tel. 783/4–29–05), potted plants fill the small central courtyard. Rooms in this pretty hotel ($7 for one bed, $10 for two) are spotless and all have fans. Sparkling-clean tile bathrooms have plenty of hot water.

CAMPING Although it's free and legal to pitch a tent on **Playa Tuxpán**, it's become increasingly less safe. If you want to risk it, hammocks are $1 per day, though you have to sweet-talk an overnight rental. It's also possible to camp on **Isla Lobos** (see Outdoor Activities, below), but you must first obtain a permit from the Coast Guard office (tel. 783/4–03–43), about 3 kilometers from the center, on the way to Playa Tuxpán. Permits can take up to four days to process, so plan ahead. More safe might be the **Unidad Deportiva** (Colonia Jardines, tel. 783/4–42–09). It's not close to the beach, but it has a pool, and camping is free. From the center of town, take the UV (Universidad Veracruzana) bus, which heads west along the river, and get off at the Coca-Cola factory.

FOOD

Restaurants congregate on Juárez in the center of town. There are also several good, cheap taco stands up the street from the ADO depot. The menu at **Antonio's** (Juárez 25, at Garizurieta, tel. 783/4–16–02; open daily 7 AM–11 PM) runs the gamut from prohibitively expensive to budget-friendly. The *desayuno americano* (American breakfast) includes eggs, toast, jam, juice, and tea for $3.50. A plate of chicken enchiladas will run you $4, cheese enchiladas $1.50. There's also a full bar here, and Friday and Saturday nights are graced with live music beginning at 9 PM. Hungry locals pour into **Cafetería el Mante** (Pipila 8, at Juárez, tel. 783/4–57–36; open daily 6 AM–midnight), especially for breakfast. The most popular dish is *bocoles rellenos* (fried dough filled with egg, meat, or cheese; 50¢).

FESTIVALS

Recent efforts to bolster tourism in Tuxpán include the **Carnaval de la Primavera.** Knowing it can't compete with other Carnavals—namely, Veracruz city's—Tuxpán's is celebrated during the last week of April. Extracted from the pre-Lent significance that Carnaval usually holds, it's simply a rowdy way to celebrate spring with dancing, drinking, and music. More authentic to the city is the **Día del Niño Perdido** (December 17), which commemorates the day young Jesus "got lost." At 8 PM, the electricity in Tuxpán is shut off, and the whole city is illuminated by thousands of votive candles in an effort to light Jesus's way back home. The event lasts a couple of hours, and groups of children walk through the street, calling for him. Tuxpán is the only city in the world that celebrates this.

OUTDOOR ACTIVITIES

Playa Tuxpán is the most accessible beach in the area, about 7 kilometers from downtown. The beaches in Tuxpán are lined with cheap *palapa* (thatched-hut) restaurants selling everything from crab burritos to ice-cold coconuts. The palapas closest to the bus stop charge the most. Further down the beach you can chow on dishes like *ensalada de camarones* (shrimp salad) for $3. For picnic supplies, visit the fresh fruit stands on the river dock (Reforma, at Rodríguez), where the lanchas are. The **Dauzan** bakery (Juárez 15, tel. 783/4–37–77; open daily 8 AM–10 PM) sells hot fresh rolls and pastries. For scuba diving or snorkeling, head to **Tamiaula,** a small village just north of Tuxpán, where you can hire a fishing boat for the 45-minute journey to the prime diving around **Isla Lobos** (Island of Wolves). In the shallow water offshore there are a few shipwrecks and colorful reefs that are home to a large variety of sea life, including pufferfish, parrotfish, damselfish, and barracuda. If you didn't bring your own equipment you can rent gear from **Aquasport** (tel. 783/7–02–59), just before Playa Tuxpán. Equipment is $32 a day. It's best to round up a group of people, since the lancha ride costs an additional $114, whether one person or five people go; if you manage to get six people together, you'll get the lancha for free. No scuba classes are offered, so nonexperts are stuck with snorkeling.

To reach Playa Tuxpán, pick up a PLAYA bus near the dock where the lanchas leave to cross the river, near Rodríguez and Reforma. The last bus back to town leaves the beach at about 8:30 PM. Hitch back to town if you miss it—hammocks can be rented for a night on the beach, but a number of assaults have recently taken place. Buses to Tamiaula (30 min, $1) leave from the Terminal ABC (*see* Coming and Going, *above*).

OAXACA

12

By Andrew Dean Nystrom

Oaxaca comes closer to the Mexico of dreams than any other state in the country. Here, customs dating back 10,000 years are alive and well, not just relegated to museums; artisans, farmers, fishermen, and oral historians still practice their traditional arts throughout the state; and the lifestyles of indigenous peoples such as the Zapotec, Mixtec, Huave, and Triqui have been somewhat preserved, protected by the Sierra Madre mountains cutting through the region. Today, more than 17 distinct Indian languages are spoken in Oaxaca, and cultures within this mountainous southern state vary as greatly as the landscape, which encompasses sunset-colored canyons, cacti-carpeted deserts, tropical jungles, scrubby coastland, and thriving cities.

Recently, unfavorable economic conditions, particularly in the Mixteca region and the Isthmus of Tehuantepec, have turned Oaxacans into a *pueblo peregrino* (nomadic people). In search of work at a decent wage, hundreds of thousands of *campesinos* (rural dwellers) have abandoned their families and migrated to Northern Mexico, Baja California del Norte, and even the San Joaquin Valley in Northern California, where they can earn as much in one hour as they can in a day in Oaxaca. Aside from the presence of beggars in Oaxaca de Juárez, however, these current economic hardships aren't normally seen by travelers to the state.

At the confluence of three river valleys sits Oaxaca de Juárez, the state's capital. Pre-Columbian sites such as Monte Albán and Mitla are easily accessible from here, as are many small towns filled with artisans and craftspeople. Farther from the city, the landscape changes drastically. To the south, the Sierra Madre mountains drop sharply to the sea, forming a long stretch of Pacific Coast beaches frequented by everyone from hippies to Mexican families. Puerto Escondido is *the* surfer mecca, while Puerto Ángel, a cliffside fishing village, is a peaceful place to snorkel and enjoy some stunning views. Although the Isthmus of Tehuantepec is often viewed as a dull, dusty gateway to Chiapas and Tabasco, this is partly because the region reacts to the modern world by clinging to its old traditions and customs. You may not be wowed by exquisite scenery in the isthmus, but the friendly people and the intricacies of Zapotec culture will make your stay, however brief, a pleasant one.

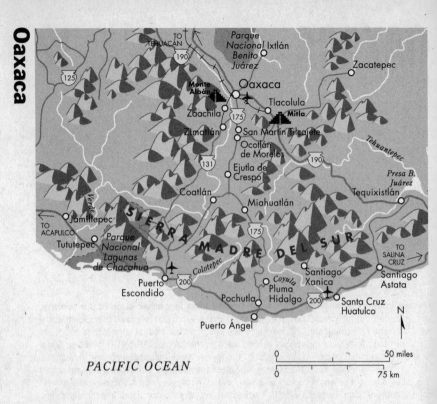

PACIFIC OCEAN

0 ——————— 50 miles
0 ——————— 75 km

Oaxaca de Juárez

Bustling with the traditions and cultures of the surrounding area, Oaxaca de Juárez's zócalo is a microcosm of the state's diversity: Triquis selling weaving made in the high mountain villages sit alongside colorfully clothed Tehuanas from the isthmus. To get an unadulterated feel for the region's cultural richness, grab a bike from Pedro Martínez (*see* Getting Around, *below*) and head to the *pueblos* (towns) near the capital; these offer unfiltered versions of indigenous culture at much lower prices.

Happily, the capital city is a logical base for this type of exploration. Budget travelers meet and reunite here, and cheap food and lodging provide comfort after intense day trips to places such as the ruins of Monte Albán or the village of Arrazola. And when you're tired of bumpy bike or bus rides, Oaxaca de Juárez's numerous cathedrals and museums provide a few days of relaxed sightseeing.

Many Oaxacans are politically active: Demonstrations in front of government buildings and around the centro (downtown) are common, whether they be for students' and indigenous rights or better pay for school-teachers.

The city also offers insight into how economics have affected indigenous culture. Tourism, catering to both domestic and foreign visitors, has brought an influx of tacky commercialism, creating an awkward contrast between rich and poor. If your Spanish is good, you'll be able to speak with locals eager to talk about these discrepancies and other current events. Even if your Spanish is shabby, don't despair; most sights in and around the city can be enjoyed by everyone.

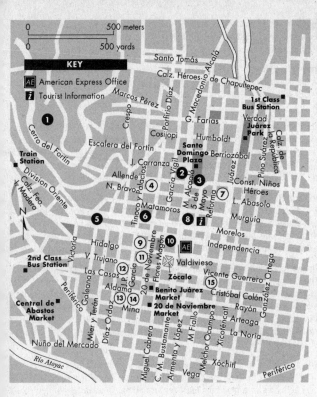

Sights ●
Basílica de la
Soledad, **5**
Catedral de
Oaxaca, **10**
Cerro del Fortín, **1**
Iglesia y
Ex-Convento de
Santo Domingo, **3**
Instituto de Artes
Gráficas, **2**
Museo de Arte
Contemporáneo, **8**
Museo Rufino
Tamayo, **6**

Lodging ○
Las Bugambillas, **7**
Las Golondrinas, **4**
Hostal
El Pasador, **15**
Hotel Central, **9**
Hotel Francia, **11**
Hotel El Palmar, **13**
Hotel Pasaje, **14**
Hotel Vallarta, **12**

BASICS

AMERICAN EXPRESS The AmEx office, inside the travel agency **Viajes Micsa** (NE cnr of zócalo), exchanges all traveler's checks at no commission. They also replace lost checks, deliver MoneyGrams, cash personal checks, hold mail, and replace AmEx cards. *Valdivieso 2, Oaxaca, Oaxaca, CP 68000, México, tel. 951/6–27–00, fax 951/6–74–75. Open weekdays 9–2 and 4–6, Sat. 9–1.*

CASAS DE CAMBIO Although exchange places stay open longer, the banks around the zócalo give slightly better rates for dollars and traveler's checks. Arrive as early as possible to avoid long lines—it's not unusual to see locals queuing up before the banks even open. **Banamex** (Hidalgo 821, 1 block east of zócalo, tel. 951/6–59–00) is open for exchange weekdays 9–1, and changes AmEx traveler's checks. **Bancomer** (García Vigil 202, tel. 951/6–76–43) exchanges AmEx, Thomas Cook, and Visa checks 9–1:30, and has an ATM that accepts Plus, Cirrus, Visa, and MasterCard. Several casas de cambio are located on Hidalgo, half a block northeast of the zócalo; they're open Monday–Saturday 8–8, Sunday 9–5.

CONSULATES **Canada and United Kingdom.** *Hidalgo 817-5, Oaxaca, Oaxaca, CP 68000, México, tel. 951/3–37–77. Open weekdays 11–3.*

United States. *Alcalá 201, Rooms 204 and 206, Oaxaca, Oaxaca, CP 68000, México, tel. 951/4–30–54. Open weekdays 9–3.*

EMERGENCIES For all emergencies, dial 06 (no coins necessary) from any phone. The **tourist police** (tel. 951/6–38–10) patrol the zócalo and are friendly and ready to answer your queries.

INTERNET SERVICES You can send and receive e-mail ($1.60 per message) and surf the net ($8 per hour) at **Makedonia** (20 de Noviembre 225, at V. Trujano, tel. 951/4–07–62, makedoni@antequera.antequera.com) daily 8 AM–10:30 PM.

LAUNDRY **Superlavandería Hidalgo** (J. P. García, at Hidalgo, tel. 951/4–11–81) charges $2.75 for up to 3½ kilos of laundry. They're open Monday–Saturday 9–6. **La Espuma** (Yagul 405, tel. 951/4–41–82) will pick up your filthy clothes in the morning and deliver them the same day for 75¢ a kilo.

MAIL The **post office** (just off zócalo, facing the cathedral, tel. 951/6–26–61; open weekdays 8–7, Sat. 9–1) will hold mail sent to you at the following address for up to 10 days: Lista de Correos, Administración 1, Oaxaca, Oaxaca, CP 68001, México. However, you can only pick up mail weekdays 8–2. Next door, **Telecomunicaciones de México** provides telegram, money order, and fax service. *Tel. 951/6–42–55. Open weekdays 9–6, Sat. 9–noon.*

MEDICAL AID The **Cruz Roja** (Armenta y López 700, tel. 951/6–78–28) offers free 24-hour medical service and emergency care. The **Sanatorio del Carmen** (Abasolo 215, tel. 951/6–26–12) has English-speaking doctors on call 24 hours a day. If you need a dentist or specialist, the tourist office at 5 de Mayo and Morelos can refer you to someone who speaks English. **La Farmacia Guadalupana** (Hidalgo 340, tel. 951/6–53–82) is open round the clock.

PHONES You can make local and international collect calls from the orange phones scattered around town. The blue phones on the zócalo accept major credit cards, but not international calling cards. If you need to use your calling card, head for the public phones in front of **Telmex** (Matamoros, at Valdivieso). **Computel**'s two locations provide the fastest and most expensive international calls, as well as fax service. *Trujano 204, tel. 951/4–73–19. Off zócalo, btw Cabrera and 20 de Noviembre. Other location: Independencia 601, tel. 951/4–80–84. Open daily 7 AM–10 PM.*

SCHOOLS Oaxaca de Juárez has a number of reputable language schools, most of which will arrange homestays. The **Instituto Cultural de Oaxaca** offers seven hours a day of intensive instruction and cultural activities in a gracious 19th-century home. Classes are limited to six students and cost $100 per week. Cultural workshops, a daily conversation hour, and homestays round out the comprehensive program. *Juárez 909, tel. 951/5–34–04, inscoax@antequera. antequera.com. Mailing address: A. P. 340, Oaxaca, Oaxaca, CP 68000, México.*

The **Centro de Idiomas** at the Universidad de Benito Juárez offers intensive Spanish programs to small groups in a more institutional setting. Classes cost $80 per week or $200 per month. You'll also have the opportunity to meet local students eager to practice their English. *Burgoa, btw Armenta y López and Bustamente, tel. 951/6–59–22. Mailing address: Centro de Idiomas, UABJO, A. P. 523, Oaxaca, Oaxaca, CP 68000, México.*

VISITOR INFORMATION Stop by the **Oficina de Turismo** (5 de Mayo, at Morelos, tel. 951/6–48–28; open daily 9–8), where the bilingual staff is more than happy to assist you and let you leave notes for fellow travelers. To find out what's going on in town, pick up a free copy of the English-language *Oaxaca Times* or *Oaxaca.* The Spanish *Guía Cultural,* which lists free films, art exhibits, and music and theater performances, is available here or at magazine stands on the zócalo for 75¢. **Sedetur** (Independencia, at García Vigil, no phone), open daily 9–8, provides free maps and bus schedules.

COMING AND GOING

BY BUS Oaxaca's crowded and noisy first-class bus terminal (Calzada Niños Héroes 1306) is 11 long blocks north of the zócalo—a 20-minute walk or a $1.25 taxi ride from downtown. **Cristóbal Colón** (tel. 951/5–12–14) offers frequent service to Mexico City's TAPO terminal (7 hrs, $13.50) and also serves San Cristóbal (2 per day, 12 hrs, $14). **Autobuses del Oriente (ADO)** (tel. 951/5–17–03) has frequent service to Puebla (4 hrs, $10), Veracruz city (9 hrs, $17), and Salina Cruz (5 hrs, $5.50).

The second-class station is west of the railroad tracks and across from the Central de Abastos market, on the corner of Trujano and the Periférico expressway. The many bus companies based here serve outlying towns, as well as Mexico City (6 hrs, $11), Tapachula (10 hrs, $15), and other major cities. **Estrella del Valle** (tel. 951/4–57–00) runs to Puerto Escondido (8 per day, 7½ hrs, $5), Santa Cruz Huatulco (8 hrs, $8), and Pochutla (7 hrs, $5.50). **Autobuses Unidos (AU)** also serves these coastal towns, with similar schedules and prices. The station isn't the safest place to crash overnight.

BY TRAIN Every night at 7 PM, the Oaxaqueño train departs from the station on Madero and Periférico and runs (slowly) to Mexico City via Tehuacán and Puebla. The station is a 15-minute walk from the center of town, but take a taxi at night. Tickets must be bought on the day of departure and cost $10 first-class and $5.50 second-class. Only ride in second-class if you are really broke, love farm animals, or enjoy having your luggage stolen. *Station open daily 6:30–11 and 3:30–7.*

BY PLANE The **Aeropuerto Nacional de Oaxaca-Zozocatlán** (tel. 951/6–23–32) is 8 kilometers south of town. At least two daily flights go to Mexico City (1 hr, $80 one-way). Tickets can be purchased at the airport or from agencies downtown—try **AVIACSA** (Porfirio Díaz 102 No. 2, tel. 951/3–18–01). For $3, **Transportes Terrestres Aeropuerto** (in front of cathedral, tel. 951/4–43–50) will shuttle you between the airport and downtown Monday–Saturday 9–8.

HITCHING Due to the current volatile state of the region, hitching is risky and not recommended. Also, gringo hitchers tend to be looked on as ne'er-do-wells. Unless you can score a ride with an expatriate, stick to the always cheap and plentiful buses.

GETTING AROUND

At the heart of walker-friendly Oaxaca de Juárez is the **zócalo,** bordered by the mammoth cathedral and the **Parque Alameda de León.** North of the zócalo is the posh part of town, where you can find (or avoid) luxury hotels with tourist-oriented discos. The **Periférico** runs around the southern rim of the city proper. Here you'll find the second-class bus station, the huge **Central de Abastos** market, and the red-light district. The hill that overlooks Oaxaca, **Cerro del Fortín** (Fort Hill), is a 20-minute walk northwest from the zócalo. Keep in mind that most streets change names as they cross Avenida Independencia going north–south and Bustamante/Alcalá going east–west.

Buses are hardly used—or necessary—in the downtown area. Taxis are best for getting to and from the bus and train stations after dark, when the southwest corner of town gets a bit dicey. Standard fares within downtown are $1–$3, but agree on a price before getting in. **Martínez Mountain Bikes** (J. P. García 509, tel. 951/4–31–44; open Mon.–Sat. 10–2 and 4–7) rents bikes for $10 a day. Knowledgable owner Pedro provides maps for routes of varying difficulty. The bikes are top quality and the advice excellent.

WHERE TO SLEEP

There are two main areas to crash in Oaxaca, one north and one south of the zócalo. You'll pay more to stay on the quiet, residential north side. The south side, near the markets and second-class bus station, caters to working-class Mexicans and shoestring travelers. The tourist office provides lists of local families with rooms to let; the rates ($5–$15 per night) often include laundry service and meals. Oaxaca's Spanish-language schools (*see* Schools, *above*) can also arrange homestays for their students. If you're desperate for a room, the tourist office is open late and will call around until you have a place to sleep.

Relatively new to Oaxaca are *recámaras con desayuno* (bed-and-breakfasts). At **Las Bugambillas,** all eight double rooms ($11 per person) have private baths and include a filling breakfast. Owner Mariana Arroyo administers Aztec *temazcals* (vapor baths) and massages that are to die for: Either one costs $25 per blissful hour. *Reforma 402, btw Abasalo and Constitución, tel. and fax 951/6–11–65. Luggage storage, restaurant. Reservations advised. Wheelchair access.*

SOUTH OF THE ZOCALO

➢ **UNDER $15** • **Hotel El Palmar.** The simple, clean rooms here are $6.50 per person, $7 with private bath. Rooms facing the street are brighter but noisier than those in the interior. Be sure to shower in the morning, because the hot water is shut off in the afternoons. *J. P. García 504, btw Aldama and Mina, tel. 951/6–43–35. 30 rooms, 8 with bath. Luggage storage. Wheelchair access.*

Hotel Pasaje. A courtyard with blooming tropical foliage, festive tiles, and a gregarious green parrot make the Pasaje a favorite among budget travelers. The clean, comfy rooms have desks and private baths with hot showers. Ask to try out the beds in your room first—some are more uncomfortable than others. Singles are $7, doubles $10.50. *Mina 302, tel. 951/6–42–13. ½ block west of 20 de Noviembre market, btw J. P. García and 20 de Noviembre. 18 rooms, all with bath. No check-in midnight–6 AM. Luggage storage. Reservations advised.*

Hotel Vallarta. The clean, freshly painted rooms here are plain but blessed with amenities: private bathrooms, purified water, towels, soap, and desks. A TV can be added for an extra $1.50. Doubles with one bed cost $11; with two beds it's $12.50. *Díaz Ordaz 309, tel. 951/6–49–67. 3 blocks SW of zócalo, btw Trujano and Las Casas. 30 rooms, all with bath. Luggage storage. Wheelchair access.*

NORTH OF THE ZOCALO

➢ **UNDER $10** • **Hotel Central.** The small, spartan rooms are always clean and usually noisy. Ground floor rooms that face the street might as well be inside the disco next door, but at $9 a double ($6 a single) with private bath, your wallet will be happy. *20 de Noviembre 104, tel. 951/6–59–71. 1 block west of zócalo, btw Hidalgo and Independencia. 26 rooms, all with bath. Luggage storage. Reservations advised. Wheelchair access.*

➢ **UNDER $20** • **Las Golondrinas.** "The Swallows" offers quiet, clean, tastefully decorated rooms and a number of patios overflowing with roses and tropical flowers. Sun-worshippers are welcome on the roof. Doubles cost $18.50, singles $14.50. A triple with a tiny living room is a great deal at $22.50. *Tinoco y Palacios 411, tel. 951/4–21–26. 5 blocks north of zócalo. 27 rooms, all with bath. Laundry, luggage storage. Reservations advised.*

Hotel Francia. The Francia is where writer D. H. Lawrence stayed during his 1925 visit to Oaxaca. Mexico's colonial past is recalled in the dramatic rooms of the old wing, with high ceilings and tiled floors. The past is lost in the new wing, where rooms have modern furniture and bigger bathrooms. Ask to see a few before you choose. Doubles $16, singles $14. *20 de Noviembre 212, tel. 951/6–48–11. 1 block west of zócalo, btw Hidalgo and Trujano. 45 rooms, all with bath. Luggage storage. Reservations advised. Wheelchair access. MC, V.*

HOSTELS **Hostal El Pasador.** This is the cheapest sleep in town, which means you'll be shacking up with other bargain-hunting globe-trotters in the South Pacific–style dorms ($4 per person, minimum two people). If you prefer, you can seclude yourself in one of the rooftop cabañas for the same price. There are plans to open up a vegetarian restaurant and jazz venue on the premises. *Fiallo 305, tel. 951/5–41–07. 2 blocks east and ½ block south of zócalo. Reception open daily 6 AM–11 PM. Bike rental, kitchen, laundry, luggage storage ($1.25).*

FOOD

Oaxacan cuisine is spicy, delicious, and famed throughout Mexico (*see box, below*). If you have a tolerant palate, the *comedores* (sit-down food stands) at the Central de Abastos, 20 de Noviembre, and Benito Juárez markets offer a gastronomical extravaganza of local specialties that won't break the bank. Go in the morning while the pots are still full and fresh. Restaurants on the south side of the zócalo are generally cheap and cater to a local crowd. More gringo-oriented fare can be had on Avenidas Morelos and Independencia, just north of the zócalo.

SOUTH OF THE ZOCALO

➢ **UNDER $5** • **Café Alex.** This popular restaurant near the second-class bus station offers a variety of Oaxacan specialties. Share the back patio with cages full of chattering parrots and parakeets as you sample the hearty chicken mole ($2.50). Breakfast specials are also a good deal, with juice and fruit salad with granola for less than $2. *Díaz Ordaz 218, at Trujano, tel. 951/4–07–15. Open Mon.–Sat. 7 AM–9 PM, Sun. 7–noon.*

Cafetería Tayu. This restaurant's tranquil patio is just steps away from the bustle of the 20 de Noviembre market. The simple but filling comida corrida includes a meat entrée, soup, *agua fresca* (fresh fruit drink), and a dessert for less than $2. Be prepared to share your table with Oaxacans who know a good value when they eat one. *20 de Noviembre 416, tel. 951/6–53–63. Open Mon.–Sat. 7–7.*

Pozole. Also known as Cafetería La Grantorte, this kitchen dishes out the best *pozole* (hominy soup) south of Mexico City. The chicken-based soup ($1.50) comes in three varieties: Michoacán (red broth, radishes, and chiles), Guerrero (green broth, pork rind, and avocado), and Jalisco (clear broth). *Independencia, at Alameda de León, no phone. Just west of cathedral; look for big* POZOLE *sign. Open daily 5 PM–11 PM.*

NORTH OF THE ZÓCALO

➤ **UNDER $5 • El Mesón.** The buffet-style lunches at this joint are a great way to sample the region's famed dishes, such as *mole oaxqueño* (Oaxacan mole). The all-you-can-eat lunch buffet is $2.50. *Hidalgo 805, at Valdivieso, no phone. Open daily 8 AM–10 PM.*

Flor de Loto-Plaza Gourmet. Decorated with work by local artists, this eatery offers a tantalizing array of vegetarian regional specialties, in addition to excellent soups and breads. The owner personally shops for the fresh fruit, vegetables, and meats every day. Breakfast specials cost $2, the comida corrida $2.50. *Morelos 509, tel. 951/4–39–44. Next to Museo Rufino Tamayo. Open Wed.–Mon. 8 AM–10 PM, Tues. 8–6. AE.*

Nutritortas Gigantes. This hole-in-the-wall serves a variety of sandwiches priced at under a buck. The ones with tangy chapulines (*see box, above*) are perfect for an after-dinner snack. *Nicolás Bravo 216, tel. 951/6–64–69. 4 blocks NW of zócalo. Open daily 9–9.*

Quickly. This is probably how you'll attack the $2 *chilaquiles* (tortilla strips doused with salsa and sour cream). Also worthwhile is the dubiously named but tasty *gringa* hamburger ($2.25), loaded with ham, bacon, cheese, and tomato. Tlayudas (*see box, above*), at $2.50 apiece, are popular with locals. *Alcalá 100-B, ½ block NW of zócalo, tel. 951/4–70–76. Open weekdays 8 AM–11 PM, weekends 2–11. MC, V.*

Eat This!

Modern Oaxacan food continues to be based on local ingredients and traditional recipes, elements of which predate the Spaniards' arrival. Oaxaca's three markets are the best places to sample any of the following regional specialties without paying tourist prices.

- *CHAPULINES: tangy fried grasshoppers prepared with chile and lime. They go down a bit easier if you pull off the legs first. According to local folklore, one taste will charm you into never leaving Oaxaca.*

- *JICUATOTE: a wiggly, sweet, white gelatin made with milk, cloves, cinnamon, and cornmeal. It's served in tubs and usually colored red on top.*

- *TEJATE: a beverage made from the flowers and roasted seeds of the cacao tree, corn, coconut milk, sugar, water, and spices. Look for huge bowls of white paste and watery, brown liquid.*

- *TLAYUDAS: huge, flat tortillas spread with refried beans and topped with Oaxacan string cheese, cilantro, fresh vegetables, and guacamole.*

Señor de la Salud. The "Lord of Health" lives up to its name, offering nutritious vegetarian and meat dishes in an open, clean setting. Try the veggie chilaquiles with beans, tortillas, juice, and coffee for $2.50. *Juárez 201-D, btw Morelos and Murgia, no phone. Open Mon.–Sat. 8–8.*

CAFÉS The tourist scene in Oaxaca revolves around the cafés on the zócalo. However, these wrought-iron tables crowded with gringos are far from the last word on the city's café culture (though they are the only place you'll be able to grab a cuppa java on a Sunday). The following are a couple of out-of-the-way spots recommended by Oaxacans.

Antojitos de los Olmos. It's easy to miss their tiny black sign on touristy Alcalá, but pass through the small doorway and you'll step into Antonia Olmos Guebarra's patio. She serves the best *atole* (a sweet, corn-based drink, similar to hot chocolate) in town to her festive crowd of loyal customers for only 35¢. Delicious tamales, tacos, and tostadas are cooked up before your eyes for less than $1. *Alcalá 301, tel. 951/6–44–10. Open Mon.–Sat. 7:30 PM–11 PM.*

Café Hipótesis. This cozy café features an eclectic selection of literature and live piano and guitar duets Thursday–Saturday at 9:30 PM. Pick an interesting book, sit back, and work on a *yarda* (a tall glass, literally a yard) of beer or sangría for $2. They also offer quesadillas, tostadas, and excellent sandwiches. *Morelos 511, no phone. Open Mon.–Sat. 1–1.*

Cafetería Morgan. Their bulletin board claims they serve "the best coffee for 4,000 miles," and though the quote is a few years old, it may well be true. Morgan's breakfasts ($1.50–$3) include a cup of their authentic Italian cappuccino. *Morelos 601-B, no phone. Open Mon.–Sat. 8–1 and 5:30–10.*

WORTH SEEING

Oaxaca de Juárez boasts a wealth of Roman Catholic churches, convents, and monasteries dating from the colonial period, only a few of which are mentioned below. Some have been converted into government offices and museums, but many remain active places of worship, where rituals have changed little in the past century. The life of the city is in the zócalo, markets, and busy southside streets, where buskers play the accordion and Zapotec vendors hawk their handmade crafts. It's possible to see most of Oaxaca's main sites in a day on foot; check the maps in *Oaxaca* or *Oaxaca Times* for suggested walking tours.

BASÍLICA DE LA SOLEDAD This 17th-century baroque church contains a black-draped figure of Nuestra Virgen de la Soledad (Our Lady of Solitude), to which believers ascribe healing powers. On December 18, the **Danza de la Pluma** (Feather Dance), a dramatization of the Conquest, is performed here as part of the festival in her honor. The church is particularly breathtaking at sunset, when it reflects a golden glow. Behind the church is the **Museo Religioso de la Soledad** (tel. 951/6–75–66), which displays a fascinating collection of trinkets dedicated to the Virgin. *Independencia 107, at Galeana. Museum admission: 35¢. Open daily 9–2.*

CATEDRAL DE OAXACA Construction of the cathedral began in 1553 but was interrupted by earthquakes, leaving the church unfinished for another 200 years. The beautifully carved baroque facade depicts the assumption of the Virgin Mary, and the centerpiece of the cathedral is a bronze altar imported from Italy. The cathedral also houses the Señor del Rayo, a giant gold-and-silver crucifix that, legend has it, miraculously survived a fire begun by a bolt of lightning. *On the zócalo, facing the Alameda. English mass held Sun. at 10 AM.*

CERRO DEL FORTÍN The hill dominating the city has been a site of festivals and celebrations since pre-Columbian times. A long flight of stairs leads up to the Cerro from Avenida Crespo, about 2 kilometers northwest of the zócalo. Crowning the Cerro is an open-air auditorium used for the festivities of **La Guelaguetza** (*see* Festivals, *below*), as well as a planetarium and observatory, which host cultural and educational events evenings and weekends. Check with the tourist office for details. The lookout point has an awesome view of the city and a huge bronze statue of Oaxaca native Benito Juárez, captioned by his famous phrase: "*El respecto al derecho ajeno es la paz*" ("Respect for the rights of others is peace"). *From zócalo, walk north 7 blocks along Díaz Ordaz to stairs.*

IGLESIA Y EX-CONVENTO DE SANTO DOMINGO Santo Domingo, built in the 16th century, is one of Oaxaca de Juárez's most ornate houses of worship. The rose-colored exterior is striking but pales in comparison to what is found inside. The ceiling of the entryway is decorated with an amazing tree sprouting depictions of church benefactors, and busts of saints and martyrs observe you from every corner and archway. The adjacent monastery, built in 1619, now houses the **Museo Regional de Oaxaca.** Exquisite Mixtec artifacts from the tombs of Monte Albán are artfully displayed here, including skulls encrusted with jade and turquoise, gold earrings and ornaments, and elaborately carved jaguar bones. *Alcalá, at Gurrión, 5 blocks NE of zócalo, tel. 951/6–29–91. Museum admission: $3, free Sun. Open Tues.–Fri. 10–5:30, weekends 10–5.*

INSTITUTO DE ARTES GRÁFICAS This often overlooked but splendid museum, library, and art gallery features a collection of books in Spanish on contemporary and classic art, with an emphasis on graphic art prints. The café in the rear of the building is a superb place to pass a rainy afternoon reading from the collection; books cannot be checked out. *Alcalá 507, near Santo Domingo, tel. 951/6–69–80. Donations encouraged. Open Wed.–Mon. 10:30–8.*

MUSEO DE ARTE CONTEMPORÁNEO DE OAXACA This excellent museum is dedicated to contemporary Oaxacan artists, both mestizo and indigenous, but occasionally features big-name European exhibits as well. Free art films are shown Friday–Sunday at 6 PM. *Alcalá 202, tel. 951/4–22–28. Admission: 75¢. Open Wed.–Mon. 10:30–8.*

MUSEO DE ARTE PREHISPÁNICO "RUFINO TAMAYO" Pre-Columbian artifacts from all over Mexico are displayed in this beautifully restored colonial mansion. The collection, which belonged to Rufino Tamayo, one of Mexico's premier artists, is arranged chronologically to give an idea of the artistic development that preceded the Conquest. *Morelos 503, tel. 951/6–47–50. Admission: $1.25. Open Mon. and Wed.–Sat. 10–2 and 4–7, Sun. 10–3.*

CHEAP THRILLS

The **Casa de la Cultura Oaxaqueña** (González Ortega 403, tel. 951/6–18–29) features free films, dance, theater, art, and musical events. You can stop by weekdays 9–9 or Saturday 9–2 to find out what's going on. The theater at **Centro Cultural Juan Rulfo** (Independencia 300, at Mier y Terán, tel. 951/6–34–56) has nightly musical performances as well as frequent cultural events, most of which are free. Wednesdays there is live music, usually *nueva canción* (Latin American folk music), and Fridays are devoted to women's issues. Another freebie is the beautiful murals by Arturo García Bustos depicting Oaxaca's pre-Columbian and revolutionary history, which are located in the **Palacio del Gobierno** (south side of zócalo). In case you get homesick for English reading material, the **Biblioteca Circulante de Oaxaca** (Alcalá 200, no phone) has an extensive selection of books in English and over 50 different magazines—everything from *The Economist* to *Spin*. *Guía Cultural* (*see* Visitor Information, *above*) has a comprehensive list of other libraries and archives in the city.

"La Guelaguetza" can be figuratively translated as "The Zapotec Contribution." The underlying theme of the festival is one of mutual charity and celebration of community. Similar festivities are performed by expatriate Oaxacan communities living as far away as Los Angeles and San Diego.

FESTIVALS

The most famous and stunning Oaxacan festival is **La Guelaguetza,** which is celebrated annually the first two Mondays following the Fiesta de la Virgen del Carmen (*see below*). The festivities, which take place atop the Cerro del Fortín (*see* Worth Seeing, *above*), summon thousands of Oaxacans and tourists to the capital to exchange gifts and perform folk dances representative of their regions. The preceding week is filled with music, parades, and cultural events. The best tickets cost upwards of $35 and are sold at tourist agencies throughout the city; a better idea is to arrive early (8 AM) on the day of the performances and secure a free seat in the upper two rings. You can also catch less-touristed versions of the festivities in nearby towns; check at the tourist office for more info.

A bizarre display of Oaxacan craftsmanship and creativity can be seen on the **Noche de los Rábanos** (Night of the Radishes), on December 23. Everything from nativity scenes to the resurrection of Christ is carved almost exclusively out of radishes. The following evening, Christmas Eve, features an impressive collection of floats that are paraded around the zócalo.

Other festivities in Oaxaca de Juárez include **La Virgen del Carmen** on July 16, when the Virgin's likeness is paraded around the Templo del Carmen Alto on García Vigil; the **Bendición de los Animales** on August 31, when family pets are brought to church to be blessed; **El Señor del Rayo** during the third week of October, when firework displays dominate the landscape; **La Virgen de la Soledad** on December 8–18, culminating in processions to the Basílica de la Soledad and in the *Danza de la Pluma* (*see* Worth Seeing, *above*); and the typical Mexican festivities of **El Día de los Muertos** (Day of the Dead, November 2) and **Semana Santa** (Holy Week, the week before Easter Sunday).

SHOPPING

Oaxacan artisans are famous for the quality and inventiveness of their work. If you only want to browse, explore the expensive boutiques along the Andador Turístico and the shops north of the zócalo. The **MARO** women artisans' collective (5 de Mayo 204, tel. 951/2–01–62) is open daily 9–8 and stocks an excellent selection of crafts and textiles at reasonable prices.

MARKETS The markets of Oaxaca present an adventure for all the senses. The **Central de Abastos** market, across from the second-class bus station, is a labyrinth of hanging bags, shoes, hammocks, exotic fruits, witchcraft stores, and gory meat stands. On Saturdays, you'll find regional crafts: Black-and-green ceramics, gold filigree jewelry, *alebrijes* (brightly painted wooden animals), *rebozos* (shawls), engraved knives, and *huipiles* (intricately embroidered tunics). The **Benito Juárez** market, bordered by 20 de Noviembre and Las Casas, offers a smaller selection of the same. It lies just one block southwest of the zócalo and is ringed by *artesanía* (crafts) vendors. The **20 de Noviembre** market, on Aldama across from the Benito Juárez market, contains mostly food and cheap *comedores* (sit-down food stands). Outside the city, the best market takes place in Tlacolula (*see* Near Oaxaca, *below*) on Sunday morning.

AFTER DARK

The heart of Oaxaca's nightlife is the zócalo. Families stroll the main square until about 11 PM, when the younger set heads to the discos to shake it until the wee hours. Those interested in meeting *gente del ambiente* should check out **Zorba**—ask around for the location of this gay bar.

BARS If you're not content simply having a beer on the zócalo, **La Casa del Mezcal** (Flores Magón 209, no phone) offers many different flavors and concentrations of tequila's sister drink in a Mexican saloon setting; the house closes its swinging wooden doors at 11 PM. **El Sol y La Luna** (M. Bravo 109, tel. 951/4–81–05), with its candlelit atmosphere and antique decor, is a tranquil place to bring your significant other. Their international menu includes small but succulent crepes for $3. The bar is open daily 7 PM–midnight, and live music fills the front room weekends after 9 PM. Cover is $2.

CINEMA A number of movie theaters often show subtitled or dubbed American movies. Right off the zócalo is **Plaza Alameda** (Independencia, at 20 de Noviembre, tel. 951/6–11–99), where admission is $1.50. The **Museo de Arte Contemporáneo** (*see* Worth Seeing, *above*) offers free films, usually with political or cultural themes, Friday–Sunday at 6 PM.

DANCING **Candela** (Ignacio Allende 211, tel. 951/6–79–3) heats up with live salsa and Caribbean rhythms Monday–Saturday 9:30 PM–1:30 AM. A shot of mezcal is less than $2, and gay couples, rhythmically impaired gringos, and single women feel at ease jumping about on the dance floor. Depending on the band, the cover charge runs $2–$5. If you prefer to swim through smoke and flashing lights to the sound of technopop, go to **Eclipse** (Porfirio Díaz 219, tel. 951/6–42–36). It's as packed with young people as it is with attitude, and is open Thursday–Saturday 10 PM–2:30 AM and Sunday 7 PM–midnight. There's a cover charge for men (about $5 Thurs.–Sat.); women pay the same on weekends but get in free Thursday nights. Sundays, everybody pays $2.

LIVE MUSIC Monday, Wednesday, Friday, and Saturday nights at 7 PM, the state band plays free marimba in the zócalo's gazebo. Tuesday and Thursday nights feature salsa and mariachi numbers. Itinerant mariachi bands roam the zócalo serenading anyone who'll buy a song. **Los Tres Patios** is the place to chill out and sip a mixed drink while listening to live jazz. The cover is usually about $1.50. *Cosijopi 208, btw Porfirio Díaz and García Vigil, no phone. Open Mon.–Sat. 7 PM–2 AM.*

Near Oaxaca

Within 50 kilometers of Oaxaca are a number of important pre-Columbian ruins—most notably Monte Albán and Mitla. Nearby are indigenous communities that maintain distinct languages, customs, and folklore, as well as ties to the sacred ruins. The Oaxaca valleys are also dotted with small towns whose inhabitants have lived for generations largely from a particular craft, such as pottery, carving, or weaving; these artisans have earned a national and, in some cases, international reputation. Visiting the ruins and the indigenous communities on their market days is an unobtrusive way to gain an appreciation of the culture of this region. As in all of Mexico, admission to the ruins described below is free on Sundays and holidays. Bring a flashlight for optimal tomb viewing.

MONTE ALBÁN

High on an artificially leveled plateau overlooking Oaxaca de Juárez lie the ruins of Monte Albán, the greatest ceremonial center in the Valles de Oaxaca. The Zapotecs began building Monte Albán as early as 500 BC, and at the height of its power the center had a population of over 40,000—more than any European city of that time. The evidence of Zapotec, Mixtec, and even Olmec and Aztec civilizations here have baffled archaeologists in their attempts to piece together Monte Albán's history. Even the indigenous name for the city remains a mystery—the center had been abandoned more than 500 years before the Spanish arrived and named it Monte Albán (White Mountain).

The site covers an area of more than 40 square kilometers, but the most impressive structures are in the **Gran Plaza.** At each end of the plaza are ceremonial platforms aligned along a north–south axis. The acoustics here are such that sound carries clearly from one platform to the other. Going clockwise from the monument to Dr. Alfonso Caso (the Mexican archaeologist who began excavations in 1930), you'll first find the **Juego de Pelota** (ball court). Its capital "I" shape and sloping side walls are distinctive to the region. In contrast to the contests played in the ball courts of the Yucatán, those in Monte Albán didn't end in sacrifice.

Next is an open-air structure known as **Edificio P,** where a tunnel runs from the inner stairway in one corner to the central altar. Zapotec priests may have used the tunnel to appear, as if magically, during ceremonies. Next door is **El Palacio,** apparently the residence of a high-status Zapotec. A tomb was found in the middle of the patio, which is circled by 13 chambers, some with sleeping ledges. Not much of the **Plataforma Sur** (South Platform), which looms above the plaza, has been excavated, so little is known about its construction.

Edificio L, more commonly known as the **Edificio de los Danzantes** (Building of the Dancers), is the oldest building at the site and is covered with carvings of human figures. Originally the figures were thought to represent swimmers, acrobats, or dancers; the current theory is that the building once served as a medical school and the carvings depict various medical conditions. Others say that the figures represent tortured captives—though the figure of a woman in childbirth seems to rebuff this claim. In **Sistema IV,** the next building over, archaeologists constructed a tunnel that lets you view an enormous *talud* (altar) of large stones. Some are carved with dancing figures, indicating that later inhabitants may have stripped older buildings and recycled the stones.

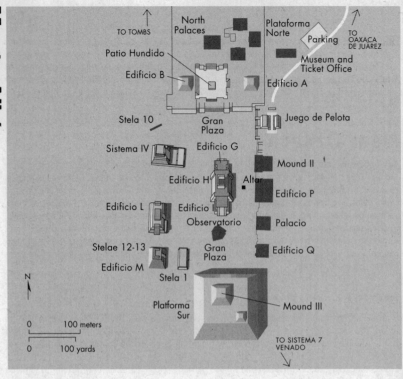

The massive **Plataforma Norte** (North Platform) completes the circle. A path behind the platform leads to the entrances of a number of tombs: **Tomb 104** contains some of the site's best-preserved carvings and murals, which are said to depict the day the deceased passed away and their most notable lifetime achievements. Others suggest that the paintings could be written formulas soliciting the benevolence of the gods.

The **Observatorio** and **Edificios I, H,** and **G** are in the middle of the plaza. The arrowhead-shaped structure close to Plataforma Sur is the observatory. Unlike the other buildings, it's aligned with the pathway of the sun, not along the cardinal points. Its dancing figures are often upside down or placed on an incline, suggesting that they may have been recycled from older buildings.

On the descent from the ruins to the visitor center are various paths leading to the remains of **Tombs 7, 72,** and **105.** These tombs were not built by the Zapotecs, who originally inhabited Monte Albán, but by their conquerors, the Mixtecs, who used the city as a necropolis. Tomb 7, behind the visitor's center to the left, divulged some of the richest art finds in the world, now on display in the Museo Regional de Oaxaca (*see* Worth Seeing, *above*).

COMING AND GOING Buses from **Hotel Mesón del Ángel** (Mina 518, tel. 951/6–53–27) in Oaxaca de Juárez run to Monte Albán (20 min, $2). Hourly departures begin at 8:30 AM; the last bus returns at 5:30 PM. The buses allow only two hours at the site, which is barely enough time, but you can opt to come back on a later bus for an extra surcharge—negotiate with your driver. If you'd rather go the cheap route, catch a bus to Colonia Monte Albán (the town) from the second-class bus station in Oaxaca de Juárez for 30¢. From the colonia, the 30-minute walk to the ruins is painfully steep but beautiful. Hitching or walking from Oaxaca de Juárez is also possible. The ruins are open daily 8–5, and admission is $2.50.

MITLA AND THE EASTERN VALLEY

While most visitors head in this direction just to see the ruins of Mitla, there are a number of worthwhile stops on the way, including less well-known archaeological sites, and little towns where traditional crafts are still produced. If you're planning to visit several towns, consider staying in one of the newly built **YU'U** (House of the Tourist) cabañas set up in Teotitlán del Valle, Tlacolula, Santa Ana del Valle, or Hierve el Agua. They offer comfortable dorm-style beds, kitchens, and super-clean bathrooms for under $10. Ask at the tourist office in Oaxaca de Juárez for details before you head out.

Mitla-bound buses (1 hr, 50¢) leave Oaxaca every 20 minutes from the second-class bus station and drop you off less than a mile away from the ruins. Return buses pass by on the main highway every half hour until 8 PM. If you want to be dropped off at the ruin's doorstep, a bus leaves every hour from **Hotel Mesón del Ángel** (Mina 518, tel. 951/6–53–27) and costs about $2.

THE ROAD TO MITLA All buses for Mitla (*see above*) pass the places listed below—just let the driver know where you'd like to get off, and sit close to him so he doesn't forget you. The highway is well marked, and the stops along the road are easily accessible. The first stop out of Oaxaca de Juárez on your way east is the 2,000-year-old **Tule tree** in tiny Santa María del Tule, supposedly the largest cypress in the world. Farther on, you'll come to the crossroads for the partially unearthed Zapotec ruins of **Dainzú**. From here, walk about 20 minutes to the site, whose main attraction is its many carved bas-reliefs, some depicting ball players in full costume. The ruins are open daily 8–6, and admission is $1.25.

After Dainzú, you can hop off the bus at the crossroads for **Teotitlán del Valle**. Teotitlán is a small village whose inhabitants specialize in woven serapes, some still colored with homemade dyes from dried insect carcasses and the ink of sea snails. Monday is market day. Farther down the road to Mitla is the **Chagoya Mezcal Factory** (open daily 9–5), where free tours teach visitors the traditional methods used to make this potent potable. Next the bus passes the crossroads for **Tlacolula**, known for its lively Sunday market, quite possibly the best in the area.

Somewhat more spectacular than Dainzú are the ruins at **Yagul**, about halfway between Tlacolula and Mitla. Yagul is believed to have been a residential area for Zapotec priests and aristocrats. It features a grand **Palacio de 6 Patios** (Palace of 6 Patios) and a completely restored **Juego de Pelota**. A scramble up the path to the right of the entrance will give you a panoramic view of the ruins, tomb, and fortifications. Yagul is open daily 9–6; admission is $1.25.

MITLA The name Mitla (Mictlán) is Nahuatl for "place of the dead" or "place of rest." Mitla's Zapotec name is *Lyobaa*. Here, 34 kilometers southeast of Oaxaca, the Zapotecs established a massive burial ground in 100 BC. The Mixtecs conquered the site in 1250 and it remained important up to the time of the Spanish invasion. According to popular myths, Quetzalcoatl came here in search of bones that would aid in the formation of man.

Of the five groups of square structures at Mitla, only two have been fully excavated and restored. The **Conjunto de Columnas** (Group of Columns) was part of an official's private home.

Hierve el Agua

After you've seen Mitla, consider trekking out to Hierve el Agua ("the water boils"), a group of spectacular, bubbling, turquoise mineral springs. After clambering around the cliffs or swimming, you can either camp out or stay in the newly built YU'U cabañas (see above). To get here, catch the 4:30 PM bus to Ayutla ($1.50 one-way) from the second-class bus station in Oaxaca. The bus will let you off at the crossroads to Hierve, from which you must walk a long, hot hour and a half. Otherwise, get a group together and hire a taxi from Mitla—be sure to set a round-trip fare (about $35) before leaving.

Inside the north structure is a room covered from stone floor to wooden ceiling with three distinct patterns of *greca* (mosaic) unique to Mitla, composed of thousands of bits of well-cut stone set in clay to form geometric patterns. These particular grecas represent air, earth, and water and at one time were coated with stucco and painted red. Some believe that this room was a library, and that the patterned greca hold coded knowledge. Also in this group you'll see what is popularly referred to as the **Columna de la Vida.** According to legend, you can tell how many years you've got left by embracing the column and calculating the space left between your outstretched hands. Presumably, the longer your arms, the sooner you can expect to die. The site is directly in front of the Iglesia San Pablo, about a mile uphill from where the second-class bus lets you off. *Admission: $1.25. Open daily 8–6.*

Downhill from the ruins, close to the center of Mitla village, the **Frissell Museum** exhibits beautiful pottery and other pieces recovered in Mitla and nearby sites. It's open Thursday–Tuesday 10–5; admission is $1.25. The adjacent restaurant, **La Sorpresa,** serves very good, healthy meals daily 9–4:30.

SOUTH OF OAXACA DE JUÁREZ

In the valley to the south of Oaxaca de Juárez you can meet the personalities behind the green-and-black pottery, embroidered blouses, and painted wooden beasties that fill the city's open markets. All the villages listed below are 20 minutes to one hour away via frequent second-class buses from Oaxaca de Juárez. Arrazola and Zaachila both lie on one road, and together make an enjoyable day trip. San Martín Tilcajete and Ocotlán de Morelos can also be visited in the same day. Special markets are held on Thursday in Zaachila and on Friday in Ocotlán de Morelos.

ARRAZOLA Five kilometers off the main road between Oaxaca de Juárez and Zaachila is the small village of Arrazola, internationally famous for its wood carvers, who create fantastic animals called *alebrijes* out of copal wood (also valued for its resin, which is used to make incense). These small wooden coyotes, elephants, and hybrid figurines fetch a pretty penny, especially if they bear the name of Don Manuel Jiménez, one of the town's best-known artisans and original creator of the brightly colored pieces. To get here, take a bus bound for Zaachila, get off at the Zaachila crossroads, and wait patiently for a colectivo to take you the 3 kilometers (2 mi) into Arrazola. Infrequent but direct colectivos to Arrazola (50¢) also leave from the corner of the Periférico and Parque del Amor in Oaxaca de Juárez. The whole trip takes about 30 minutes.

Many place names in southern Mexico and Guatemala are Nahua, some because they were once part of the expanding Aztec empire, others because the conquistadors traveled with Aztec guides who gave place names in their own language.

ZAACHILA Eighteen kilometers south of Oaxaca, Zaachila was once the Zapotec capital, long before the arrival of the Mixtecas. It's also the site of an archaeological find that was never looted, thanks to the townspeople's devotion to their ancestors' graves. When archaeologists discovered the tombs in Zaachila, residents insisted on being involved in the excavations. One tomb is empty, but all the artifacts it once held are now in museums. The other tomb has tiny grecas similar to those found in Mitla (*see above*) and depictions of two figures. One figure, wearing a long alligator mask, represents the god of death. The other carries a bag of copal resin, suggesting that it represents a priest. *Admission: $2. Open daily 8–5.*

More exciting than the ruins is Zaachila's Thursday market, which feels a bit like a country fair, with dozens of bulls, rabbits, chickens, sheep, and goats being hauled from one prospective buyer to another. Hourly buses to Zaachila (30 min, 50¢) depart from the second-class bus station in Oaxaca de Juárez.

SAN MARTÍN TILCAJETE In this tiny town, you'll be invited into private homes to see fantastically painted animals, the sale of which supports entire families. It's well worth the half-hour bus ride and 20-minute walk. It's best to buy here, where you can be sure the money goes straight to the artist. To reach this hospitable town, ask the driver of any bus headed to Ejutla de Crespo to drop you off at the road leading to San Martín, and walk or hitch the rest of the way.

OCOTLÁN DE MORELOS This wonderful little town is home to the famous Aguilar Sisters: Guillermina, Josefina, Irene, and Concepción, all of whom are skilled pottery painters. You can visit their adjoining homes and workshops on Continuación de Morelos, near the entrance to town. The best day to come is Friday, when Ocotlán holds its small market. It takes about an hour on the Ejutla del Crespo bus to get here, and the ride costs $1.

Oaxaca Coast

The Sierra Madre del Sur mountain range looms over almost 400 kilometers of scorching hot Oaxacan coastline, including many, many deserted beaches. Because much of this region is undeveloped, most visitors do their frolicking around three main tourist destinations: Puerto Escondido, Puerto Ángel, and the Bahías de Huatulco. Within the last decade, all three spots have seen an influx of tourists and and a flurry of construction, but the devaluation of the peso has brought much of the commercialization to a halt. Nonetheless, developers still like to predict that Huatulco will eclipse Cancún as the premier resort destination in Mexico by the year 2000.

Sporting opportunities abound here. In Puerto Escondido, surfers from around the world congregate to ride the Mexican Pipeline at Playa Zicatela. Snorkelers head out to the calmer waters at nearby Puerto Angelito and Carrizalillo, or to Estacahuite near Puerto Ángel. Scuba enthusiasts make their way to Roca Blanca off the shores of Cacoletepec. Most travelers, however, come here just to kick back and enjoy the sun and ocean breeze. Zipolite beach, near Puerto Ángel, is famous for the hippies who come to commune with nature and each other, and get sunburned (and otherwise baked) on the beach. Santa Cruz Huatulco is the Mexican government's latest target for development, which means you'll have to get your butt down there soon to enjoy the still-undisturbed campers' paradises.

Puerto Escondido

One of the few resorts left on the coast that doesn't serve as a port of call for cruise ships, Puerto Escondido is much less flashy and pretentious than most of Mexico's coastal hot spots. Still, Puerto Escondido does draw a number of tourists to its two separate but coexisting beaches: Zicatela, home of the famous Mexican Pipeline and the site of surfing contests in August and November; and the Playa Principal, where Mexican families on vacation hang out. High seasons for tourism are *Semana Santa* (Holy Week, the week before Easter), summer, and Christmas. If you decide to visit during any of these peak times, make reservations and be prepared for the *pachanga* (party) that ensues. Standing in marked contrast to this unabashed tourism is the "other" Escondido, which lies to the north away from the resort areas, on the other side of the Carretera Costera (Highway 200). This is where the locals live, and where you'll find the post and telegraph offices, the bus stations, and a more typical Mexican town atmosphere with cheap food, busy streets, and friendly people.

If you want a glimpse of what life in Puerto Escondido was like before all the fishermen became tour operators, visit the impromptu fish market on the west end of Playa Principal. Fish are sold daily from 6 AM until they're gone.

BASICS

➢ **CASAS DE CAMBIO** • The most centrally located casa de cambio is on Pérez Gasga, across from Farmacia Cortés; it's open weekdays 9–2 and 5–8. **Bancomer** (Pérez Gasga, across from Rincón del Pacífico, tel. 958/2–04–11) and **Banamex** (Pérez Gasga, at Andador Unión, tel. 958/2–03–52) change cash and traveler's checks weekdays 9 AM–1:30 PM. They also have 24-hour ATMs.

➢ **LAUNDRY** • **Lavamatica del Centro** (west end of Pérez Gasga, no phone; open daily 8–8) washes real cheap ($1 a kilo).

➢ **MEDICAL AID** • Emergency medical care is available 24 hours a day at the **Comisión Nacional de Emergencia** (Tlacochahuaya, at Fracc. Bacocho) and the **Centro de Salud** (Pérez Gasga 409, tel. 958/2–60–16), where the English-speaking Dr. Luis Flores is on staff. The free **Cruz Roja** (Marina Nacional, at Pérez Gazga, tel. 958/2–01–46) is open round the clock.

➢ **PHONES AND MAIL** • You can make collect and cash calls at the **caseta de larga distancia** (long-distance telephone office) on Pérez Gasga by the Andador Unión, a stairway connecting Pérez Gasga to the Carretera Costera. There are also public phones that accept credit cards in front of the pharmacy at the west end of Pérez Gasga. The **post office** (Calle 7 Nte., at Oaxaca, tel. 958/2–09–59) is a long, uphill walk on the inland side of the highway. They'll hold mail sent to you at the following address for up to 10 days: Oficina de Correos, Puerto Escondido, Oaxaca, CP 71980, México. You can send or receive telegrams, money orders, and faxes at the **telegraph office** (tel. 958/2–09–57) next door. Both are open weekdays 9–7, Saturday 9–noon.

➢ **VISITOR INFORMATION** • The main **tourist office** (Calle 5 Pte., at highway, tel. 958/2–01–75; open weekdays 9–2 and 5–8, Sat. 9–1) is at least a half-hour walk west from town, but they do provide maps, semi-useful hotel info, and an earful of warnings about theft. In the minuscule booth on Pérez Gasga, across from the Hotel Roca Mar, Gina provides friendly information on hotels, guided tours, and general directions daily until 1 PM.

COMING AND GOING The town is split in two by the **Carretera Costera** (coastal highway). Uphill to the north is the untouristed, residential part of town. The street that snakes south down the hill from the highway and then east along the coast is Pérez Gasga, popularly known as the **Andador Turístico** (tourist walkway). Running parallel to the main beach, **Playa Principal**, the Andador is where many of the town's hotels and restaurants are located. **Zicatela**, the town's most famous surfing spot, lies directly to the southeast.

➢ **BY BUS** • All the bus terminals are north of Highway 200, a good 15-minute walk from the beach. **Estrella del Valle-Oaxaca Pacífico** (cnr of Hidalgo and 16 de Septiembre) serves Oaxaca city (7 hrs, $7) at 9 AM and 9 PM; Pochutla (90 min, $1.50) every hour 5:30 AM–7:30 PM; and Acapulco (7 hrs, $8) at 6 AM, 8 AM, 8 PM, and 11 PM. **Cristobal Colón** (Hwy. 200, 2 blocks west of Estrella del Valle terminal) sends first-class buses to San Cristóbal (12 hrs) daily at 9 AM and 9:30 PM; book in advance. Their service to Oaxaca city and Mexico City, however, should be avoided: Buses go through Salina Cruz, often doubling the advertised duration of the journey. **Transportes Oaxaca-Istmo** and **Transportes Galeca/Estrella Blanca** (both on Hidalgo, at 5 de Mayo) offer frequent service to Pochutla, Oaxaca city, Salina Cruz, and Acapulco. You can also flag down a bus for Pochutla along the highway—there's one every 15–20 minutes.

➢ **BY PLANE** • The airport (info tel. 958/2–04–91) is at Kilometer 3 of the Carretera Costera, a 10-minute ride from town. **Mexicana** (tel. 958/2–04–22) flies daily to Mexico City (1 hr, $100), while **Aeromorelos** (tel. 958/2–07–34) and **Aerovega** (Peréz Gasga, at Marina Nacional, tel. 958/2–01–51) fly small planes to Oaxaca city (30 min, $45). **Transportes Aeropuerto y Turístico** (tel. 958/2–01–23) will take you in and out of town in a VW van for less than $2; look for their signs at the airport. You can also make arrangements with your hotel to be picked up by a **Transportes Terrestres** (tel. 958/2–01–15) van.

WHERE TO SLEEP During Semana Santa, summer, surfing championships, and around the Christmas and New Year holidays, prices for accommodations are often double the prices listed below. Whenever possible, make reservations during these peak times. During the low season look for ROOM FOR RENT/RENTAN CUARTOS signs.

➢ **ANDADOR TURISTICO** • **Cabañas Aldea Marinero.** Not to be confused with Bungalows Marinero across the way, this small cluster of hammocks and huts lies up a sandy lane just off Playa Marinero. The brick-floored cabañas ($4 per person) have cots, electric lights and outlets, and mosquito netting. The semi-clean bathrooms are communal. *Calle del Morro, at Playa Principal, no phone. 14 cabañas, none with bath. Bar and restaurant.*

Hotel Mayflower. This hotel boasts spotless rooms, all equipped with ceiling fans, private baths, hot water, and balconies with an ocean view. Singles are $13, doubles $16. Dorm-style accommodations ($3.50 per person) with kitchen access are the best value in town. The rooftop bar brings together a diverse crowd during the daily happy hour (5–10 PM). *Andador Libertad, just uphill from Pérez Gasga, tel. 958/2–03–67, fax 958/2–04–22. 12 rooms, all with bath. Bar, laundry, luggage storage, safe deposit box. Reservations advised.*

Hotel San Juan. The clean rooms here have fans and private baths with hot water for $8 a single, $11 a double. Ask for an interior room; those facing the outside catch lots of highway noise. *Felipe Merklin 503, tel. 958/2–03–36, fax 958/2–06–12. 26 rooms, all with bath. Luggage storage.*

➤ **ZICATELA** • **Bungalows/Cabañas Acuario.** The humble cabañas here are simply furnished, but some of the larger bungalows have full kitchens. The friendly, laid-back management can provide info on excursions and scuba lessons. They also operate a pharmacy and a phone/fax office in front of the hotel. A two-person cabaña is $13.50, a two-person bungalow (with kitchen) about $30. *Calle del Morro, tel. 958/2–03–57. 26 cabañas, all with bath.*

Rockaway Surfer Village. A wall encloses this well-kept, inexpensive, beachfront cabaña village, where guests drink beer on the porch of the surf shop. They also have a clean freshwater pool. Cabañas with ceiling fans, mosquito netting, and private bathrooms run $12 for two people. *Just west of Bruno's, tel. 958/2–06–68. 12 cabañas, all with bath. Bar and restaurant.*

➤ **CAMPING** • It's illegal to just plop down on the beach, but you can pitch a tent ($1.50 per person) at **Neptuno** (Pérez Gasga, tel. 958/2–03–27). Next door is the similar **Las Palmas,** where car camping costs $8 for two people. Simple (and most likely mosquito-infested) cabañas here run $5 per person.

FOOD The vast selection of lobster, fish, shrimp, squid, and cuttle fish makes seafood your best bet in Puerto Escondido. A smattering of cafés, comedores, and paleterías (Popsicle shops) along Pérez Gasga make for good snacking. Locals shop at **Mercado Benito Juárez** (near the post office), held daily 8–4.

➤ **ANDADOR TURISTICO** • **La Gota de Vida.** Homemade vegetarian food, including fresh tempeh and tofu, will make you forget you ever left Berkeley. Juice bar offerings run the gamut from chlorophylled to extra-acidic. Before you dig into the daily lunch special, try the veggie tamales or mushroom pâté ($1.50 each). *West end of Pérez Gasga, no phone. Open daily 8 AM–10 PM.*

La Patisserie. Also known as Carmen's Bread, this bakery lies up the sandy lane from Playa Marinero. Hungry beachcombers come to feed on superb breads (50¢) and sandwiches ($1.50). *Across from Cabañas Aldea Marinero, no phone. Open Mon.–Sat. 7–6, Sun. 7–noon.*

La Pergola Mexicana. An extensive selection of cheap, fresh seafood dishes, as well as traditional comidas corridas and breakfasts, keep this place packed with locals and tourists in the know. Most dishes cost about $2. *Pérez Gasga, near casa de cambio, no phone. Open daily 7 AM–11 PM.*

Restaurant Alicia. Mexican families, barefoot surfers, and Teva-wearing tourists come here to chow down on a wide variety of seafood specialties ($2–$3), including the infamous "cocty pus" (octopus). *Pérez Gasga, next door to casa de cambio, tel. 958/2–06–90. Open daily 8 AM–11 PM. Wheelchair access.*

➤ **ZICATELA** • **Bruno's.** Expat surfers who are into healthy food, mellow music, and slow service fill this place regularly. They've got a happening bar and a rotating menu featuring Thai, Japanese, and Indian dinners for about $5. *South end of Playa Zicatela, no phone. Open Tues.–Sun. 8 AM–11 PM.*

BEACHES The beaches around Puerto Escondido offer a variety of sporting opportunities. If you want to snorkel (best at Puerto Angelito and Carrizalillo), boogieboard (best at Playa Principal and Carrizalillo), or surf (best at Zicatela), you're better off renting your equipment in town for the entire day, rather than hourly on the beach. You can get surfing equipment, lessons, and advice (as well as scuba gear) at **Bungalows/Cabañas Acuario** (*see above*). **Mango Club** (Pérez Gasga 605-E, tel. 958/2–01–67) rents snorkel gear ($7 a day), inflatable rafts ($10 a day), and boogieboards ($10 a day). If you'd like to explore farther afield, they also rent motorcycles ($25 a day) and bicycles ($15 a day), but only with a deposit or a credit card. They're supposedly open daily 9–8, but often close down for a while in the afternoon.

➤ **PLAYA PRINCIPAL** • Running parallel to the Andador Turístico, the main beach is a favorite spot for strollers and sun worshipers. You can also go sailing ($10 per hr), rent horses ($8.50 per hr), or hire any one of the numerous *lanchas* (motorboats; $10 per hr) and go to Puerto Angelito, Carrizalillo, or out to sea to frolic with the sea turtles. The eastern section of the beach, called **Playa Marinero,** is separated from the rest by a lagoon. It's ideal for swimming, exploring tidepools, and learning to surf.

➤ **ZICATELA** • This famed and perilous surfing spot lies east of Playa Marinero. Along with Hawaii's North Shore and Australia's Barrier Reef, Zicatela is considered one of the top surfing beaches in the world; waves here roll in with impressive force. If you're not a surfer, you can also rent horses or dune buggies from vendors who set up tents on the sand. When you do venture into the water, be careful of the currents—they're notoriously deadly.

➤ **PUERTO ANGELITO** • It's about a 20-minute walk or a $2 taxi ride to this small inlet and the neighboring beach of **Manzanillo.** The calm water attracts families with young children, and it's a great area for swimming and snorkeling. Sure enough, young boys rent out the necessary gear for about $2.50 an hour. To get here, walk west along Pérez Gasga until it curves uphill toward the highway. Here you'll see the Camino a Puerto Angelito, which leads to a set of cement stairs down to the beach.

➤ **CARRIZALILLO** • Relatively free of the families that crowd Puerto Angelito, this U-shaped cove draws snorkelers and strong swimmers (the currents can be tricky). You can make the hour-long dusty trek on land by walking west along the Carretera Costera toward Bacocho; the sign pointing to Carrizalillo is visible from the carretera. Or take a motor-boat ride from Puerto Angelito or Playa Principal (see above), and have them pick you up two hours later. **Bacocho,** the most westerly beach, is good for swimming, but the resort development here may not sit well with all beach bums.

AFTER DARK During the summer, November surfing championships, and around Christmastime, the Andador Turístico itself is the party, with locals checking out the tourists, surfers mingling with sightseers, and everybody out to have a good time. The Andador is also lined with quite a few bars and clubs, which are absolutely dead in the low season and jam-packed when everyone's in town.

At the western end of the Andador, **Bananas** (Pérez Gasga, tel. 958/2–00–05; open daily 8 AM–12:30 AM) offers canned pop music to accompany Ping-Pong and Foosball. A more out-of-the-way spot for American music is **El Tubo,** down a flight of stairs on the beach side of Pérez Gasga (look for the sign with a surfer riding a tube), which rocks 11 PM–3 AM. Open nightly from 8 PM on, **Barfly** (Pérez Gasga, no phone) has an extensive drink menu and a rickety upstairs overlooking the Andador. Downstairs, surfers down beer after beer while watching reruns of old surfing championships. After 10 PM, **El Son y La Rumba** (Andador Mar y Sol, above Pérez Gasga, no phone) features dancing to live salsa, jazz, or reggae on a small dance floor. **Babalu** (Pérez Gasga, no phone) plays live Latin rhythms nightly starting at 10:30 PM. If you prefer an evening away from the bar scene, **Cine Club Ariel** screens imported flicks ($2) nightly at 7 and 9 PM in the Hotel Villa Del Mar (southern end of Zicatela, tel. 958/2–02–44).

NEAR PUERTO ESCONDIDO

Trying to organize the following trips on your own can be frustrating, because once you get where you're going, you still need to negotiate horse or boat rentals. This is one time when working with a guide will save you time, money, and hassles. Contact Ana Márquez, a native Mixteca who can arrange any of the following excursions, at her office in the **Sociedad Cooperativa Turística.** *Av. Marina Nacional, south of Pérez Gasga, tel. 958/2–16–78 or 958/2–13–97 at night. Office open daily 8–3.*

MANIALTEPEC This briny lagoon 18 kilometers northwest of Puerto Escondido is home to a remarkable variety of wildlife, including wild geese and herons. If you want to explore the lagoon, rent a boat (about $12 an hr) from the bar/restaurant **Isla del Gallo.** There aren't any hotels out here, just the beach and a lot of mosquitos, so plan your transportation carefully. A guided tour with Ana Márquez takes half a day and costs $16. If you prefer to go on your own, take an Acapulco-bound bus from Puerto Escondido and get off at any of the restaurants along the left-hand side of the road. A taxi ride here should cost no more than $3.

ZAPOTALITO AND PARQUE NACIONAL LAGUNAS DE CHACAHUA About 74 kilometers west of Puerto Escondido is a tropical park encompassing **Chacahua** lagoon, deserted beaches, and much wildlife. The town of **Zapotalito,** many of whose inhabitants are descended from African slaves, sits close to the entrance of the park. Your options here are numerous: You can enjoy the pristine beaches, lunch on the grilled fish and banana tortillas sold by kids at **Playa Chacahua,** or visit the *crocodrilario* (alligator hatchery) in Chacahua village. The hatchery workers can show you small bathtubs full of tiny, squirming alligators, their eyes still shut but their jaws already snapping. It takes about an hour to cross the lagoon to Chacahua in a hired boat. Closer to Zapotalito (about a 45-minute boat ride down the river) is **Playa Cerro Hermoso,** an isolated windswept beach where the ocean meets the lagoon. Here, you can hunt for rare black orchids or play in the gentle surf with Mexican families.

Chacahua is Mixtec for river shrimp; these are the tiny critters you'll see kids selling in bags in Puerto Escondido.

Ana Márquez's tours are well worth the $20 and include your transportation to, from, and within the park. If you prefer to hire a guide in Zapotalito, catch an early Acapulco-bound bus (1 hr, $1) and ask to get off at the road leading to the park. It's about a 10-kilometer (6-mi) hike or hitch to Zapotalito. Park admission is free, but boat rentals run $45–$60. To make it worth your while, go with a group and allow a full day for the excursion.

Puerto Ángel

Puerto Ángel, 11 kilometers off the main highway, is touted as an unspoiled beach paradise. In fact, the tranquil fishing village *has* managed to stave off much of the development and commercialization that has plagued Puerto Escondido. And now that Huatulco is hogging all the developers' attention, it looks as though the Navy will remain the most influential force in town. A rustic atmosphere prevails in Puerto Ángel: You can join the locals for a swim in the blue-green bay off the main beach, or arrange for a day of snorkeling or sightseeing by boat from one of the coves on either side of town.

Playa Panteón, in a sheltered cove just west of town (walk along the Andador just west of Puerto Ángel's *muelle,* or dock), is where local families splash around in gentle waves; here you can rent snorkel equipment ($5 per day) or arrange a boat trip. In the opposite direction (about a 20-minute walk east of town), you'll find **Estacahuite,** where you can rent snorkel gear on the beach and explore the offshore coral reef. After Estacahuite, the next beach is **La Mina,** an undeveloped, palm-shaded lounger's paradise. Puerto Ángel also serves as a comfortable base for trips up into the rarely visited towns of the green Sierra Madre del Sur mountains to the north.

BASICS In addition to the places listed below, you can change money, send a letter, or make a long-distance call in nearby Pochutla. **Hotel Soraya,** at the entrance to Puerto Ángel, will change your dollars at a lousy rate. There aren't any pay phones in town—**Ferretería Velasco** (in front of the naval base; open Mon.–Sat. 9–9) charges $1 to make an international collect call. The **post and telegraph offices** (open weekdays 9–3) lie along the main road, at the entrance to town. For medical care, both the **Centro de Salud** (no phone; take stairway up to Rincón Sabroso—it's past the church) and the naval base's emergency center at Playa Principal are open 24 hours. The **visitor information** booth (main road, in front of dock, no phone; open weekdays 9–2 and 5–7) can provide you with maps, hotel phone numbers, and directions.

COMING AND GOING There's no direct bus service to Puerto Ángel—to get here you need to take a bus to the nearby town of **Pochutla** and catch a colectivo, bus, or cab from there. The bus to and from Pochutla (30 min, 20¢) runs every half hour 6 AM–8 PM. Frequent colectivos run the same route for about 50¢; a private taxi shouldn't cost you more than $2.50.

GETTING AROUND Puerto Ángel is a tiny town, but finding places can be somewhat complicated since very few have street addresses. The highway from Pochutla turns into Avenida Principal at the entrance to town, and later turns into Boulevard Virgilio Uribe (though few make this distinction). The bus will drop you off or pick you up at *el árbol* (the tree), on the main street just before the naval base. Farther on, the road crosses a dry creek bed and then forks just after the supermarket—the high road leads to Zipolite, the low road to Playa Panteón.

WHERE TO SLEEP Most of Puerto Ángel's hotels are planted atop rocky hillsides, and reaching them often requires climbing a healthy number of stairs. The rewards for your efforts include unobstructed ocean breezes, in-house restaurants serving good food, and great views of the cove. One of the best of these hotels is **La Buena Vista** (tel. 958/4–31–04), where comfortable, fan-cooled double rooms go for $17.50–$23.50. You can also talk to Lourdes, La Buena Vista's cook, about the cheap double rooms with private bath that she rents out in her home. To reach the hotel, follow the main road across the bridge and continue uphill past Alex's; it's on the left. One of the cheapest sleeps in town is **Casa de Huéspedes El Capy** (Playa Panteón, tel. 958/4–30–02), where clean but cramped rooms run $6 a single, $9.50 a double.

Gundi y Tomás. This homey hilltop guesthouse provides hammocks ($2) and basic rooms with communal bath and no hot water. Singles are $5.25, doubles are $7. *Up the stairs just west of el árbol, no phone. 8 rooms and 6 hammocks, none with bath. Laundry, luggage storage. Café open daily 7 AM–9 PM.*

Pensión Puesto del Sol. This red-roofed pension is perched amid a profusion of hibiscus flowers and lemon and pomegranate trees. The rooms are simple and clean; the spotless bathrooms, both private and communal, have cold water round the clock. Harold, the German proprietor, will share his maps and bus schedules (and perhaps a beer) in the open-air lounge. The cheapest doubles are $8.50, $13 with bath. *Tel. 958/4–30–96. From el árbol, follow road toward Zipolite; it's up the hill just beyond supermarket. 13 rooms, 8 with bath. Breakfast, laundry, luggage storage.*

Posada Cañon de Vata. This posada is spread out over a tranquil valley just behind Playa Panteón. Rooms run $10–$23 a single, $15–30 a double, depending on whether or not you want a private bath or a stunning view. The owners, Suzanne and Mateo, are friendly and freely give advice on all of Puerto Ángel's offering. When it's not raining, outdoor yoga classes ($7 each) are conducted here by some serious swamis. The posada also offers holistic massages year round, and their small restaurant features vegetarian fare. *Playa Panteón, fax 958/4–30–48 for reservations. 20 rooms, 17 with bath. Luggage storage, restaurant. Closed May and June.*

FOOD The best food is served in the hotels listed above, and you needn't be a guest to partake of their cuisine. Gundi y Tomás offers healthy breakfasts, including granola with yogurt and fruit for $1.75, fruit smoothies for $1.25, and homemade whole-wheat bread. La Buena Vista has awesome veggie tamales ($3.50), chiles rellenos ($4), and Kahlua flan ($1.75). The panoramic view from the terrace restaurant only adds to the enjoyment of delicious, authentic oaxqueño cooking. The seafood palapas along Playa Principal are overpriced and to be avoided.

Restaurante Beto. Obscured by heavy foliage, this patio-style restaurant is the place to sip cheap beer (50¢) and enjoy their *atún al mojo de ajo* (tuna in garlic sauce) for $2. *No phone. Follow main road past naval base and turn right at fork; it's just past Puesto del Sol. Open Mon.–Sat. 4–11.*

NEAR PUERTO ÁNGEL

CHACALAPA This quiet town, set in a green valley, is just 12 kilometers from Pochutla. Here you'll find Tom Bachmaier, an artist who etches Oaxacan landscapes on small bamboo beads. Even if you're not interested in buying, stop by his meticulous home to admire his beautiful work and garden. Across the path is **Alberca El Paraíso** (closed Tues. and Wed.), a swimming pool filled with turquoise mineral water from a nearby natural spring. Octavio Ramos, who owns the pool and surrounding ranch, will happily guide you through the forest and show you how those weird tropical fruits you see in the markets grow. There's a $1 charge to use the pool for a day; if you're drawn in by the warmth of the Ramos family, you can enjoy free use of the pool and stay in one of the four cabañas ($7.50) with hot water, private baths, and ceiling fans. To get here, catch a microbus (25¢) across from the Freedom Language School in Pochutla or any Oaxaca city–bound bus (25¢) north to the entrance of Chacalapa. Ask for the *callejón* (alley) that leads to "La Alberca" and walk for about 2 kilometers.

ZIPOLITE A sweaty 30-minute walk west from Puerto Ángel brings you to Zipolite (Beach of the Dead) and another world. The feeling here is 1970s—Led Zep, Marley, scruffy gringos, and lots of dope. Recently, this beach has begun to receive day-trippers from Puertos Ángel and Escondido, giving it a more touristy feel than before. Most people either come for the novelty of the nude beach, the drug scene, or to see how long they can stretch their skinny budget. Nudity is common on the western end of the beach, and the southern section, known as **Playa del Amor,** has a pretty active gay scene. Be *extremely* cautious about swimming here: The name Beach of the Dead refers not, as some seem to think, to the Grateful Dead, but to the many lost to its currents every year.

San José del Pacífico, located off Route 75 about an hour from Pochutla, is a favorite destination for amateur mycologists: After being transformed into beach bums in Zipolite, they come in search of hallucinogenic mushrooms. As with anything that might get you in trouble with the Mexican police, caution is the watchword.

➢ **COMING AND GOING** • Buses (30 min, 50¢) run to Zipolite from Puerto Ángel and Pochutla approximately every half hour 6 AM–8 PM. If coming from Puerto Escondido, you can avoid Pochutla by jumping off the bus at the crossroads for San Antonio on Highway 200, where you can catch a direct bus to Manzunte or Zipolite (20 min, 25¢). It's hard to find taxis out of Zipolite after 9 PM. Taxis between Pochutla and Zipolite cost about $2.50.

➢ **WHERE TO SLEEP AND EAT** • Hammocks in a communal palapa on the beach fetch $1, double that amount if you want a little privacy. Extras you'll pay more for include fans, mosquito netting, and security boxes where available. Flush toilets are rare, and while showers or *regaderas* are abundant, in some places there's no water 10 AM–6 PM. Ask before you pay. Also keep in mind that theft is common, so leave the bulk of your stuff in Puerto Ángel.

Some people never stray from the sand, but the *posadas* (inns) up in the hills merit the diversion. One of the coolest is **Shambala,** also known as Gloria's, on the hillside at the western end of the beach. Sprawling over most of the cliff, the posada has meditation altars, a café, and a patio restaurant serving mostly vegetarian food. Spectacular views of a hidden bay are an extra bonus. Despite the owner's requests, drug use is all too common here. Your lodging options range from a beach cabaña ($7.50) to a hammock hook ($1) and no one is turned away for lack of space. Luggage storage and a safe-deposit box are provided. **Lo Cósmico,** just east of Shambala, offers clean, cool palapas slung with two hammocks for $6.50. Open-air terraces with hammocks are slightly cheaper.

Zipolite has no market, but the cheapest and best eats can be found right in your hotel. You can get a California-style granola breakfast in Shambala's restaurant, or try their tasty chicken mole or vegetarian turnovers (each about $2.50). For pizza, try **Gemini's** on the eastern end of the beach or **El 3 de Diciembre** (in front of La Puesta disco on main road; open daily 7 PM–3 AM), which serves an exquisite slice of pie ($1). A battalion of palapas catering to travelers loom on the beach, serving seafood and tortilla dishes at exorbitant prices.

West of Mazunte is Punta Cometa, a cactus-ridden set of cliffs with a fantastic view of the coast. It's a great place from which to appreciate the force of Oaxaca's coastal currents without being a casualty. Ask someone in Mazunte to point out the path.

MAZUNTE AND PUNTA COMETA Just outside of Zipolite, you'll notice a cluster of dilapidated, rusty buildings on the far end of the beach, once centers for processing 2,000 sea turtles daily for their meat and shells. Today, just past them in Mazunte, is a center for the turtles' protection. The **Centro Mexicano de la Tortuga** (tel. 958/4–00–58) offers educational tours in Spanish and English Tuesday–Saturday 10:30–4:30 and Sundays 11–2:30. You can watch eight of 10 species of sea turtles that inhabit Mexico's coastal waters swim in huge tanks and aquariums. Baby turtles are only kept on display a short time, after which they're released or used in conservation research. The $1.50 entrance fee (75¢ with student ID) goes toward conservation and education projects. The center is always looking for volunteers to help protect the sea turtle's coastal habitat, especially during June and July, when they come ashore to lay their eggs. Write to: A.P. No. 16, Puerto Ángel, Oaxaca, CP 70902 México, or fax 958/4–30–63 for more details. Buses come here from Zipolite (10 min, 25¢), Puerto Ángel (20 min, 40¢), and Pochutla (45 min, 75¢). You can stay in Mazunte with local families—ask around.

Bahías de Huatulco

The area often referred to simply as Huatulco consists of nine bays spread out over 20 miles of coast. At the heart of it all is Santa Cruz Huatulco, which as late as 1986 was a small fishing village of simple adobe huts on a pristine bay. That was before the Mexican government chose it as the site of a luxury tourist development meant to duplicate Cancún's success in attracting foreign sunseekers and their money. Due to the government's policy of "responsible ecodevelopment," the outlying bays and the forests that ring them remain relatively unspoiled.

Huatulco's bays, from west (closest to Puerto Ángel) to east, are: San Agustín, Chachacual, Cacaluta, Maguey, Órgano, Santa Cruz, Chahué, Tangolunda, and Conejos. Santa Cruz and Tangolunda are the most developed, while Órgano, which can usually only be reached by foot or water, is the most pristine. The rapidly growing town of **La Crucecita** (five minutes inland from Santa Cruz by bus) is where most of the people who work in Santa Cruz's boutiques and hotels live, shop, and eat, and is the budget traveler's base for the area.

BASICS All of the places listed below are in Santa Cruz unless we say otherwise. **Bancomer** and **Banamex,** next to each other at the end of Boulevard Santa Cruz, have ATMs and change traveler's checks 9 AM–1:30 PM. The **post and telegraph offices** offer fax service and are located in La Crucecita, south of the Plaza Principal, on Boulevard Chahué. Ladatel **public phones** are located on the south side of the Plaza Principal in La Crucecita. You can find maps and helpful English speakers at the **Asociación de Hoteles y Moteles** (Monte Albán, at Blvd. Santa Cruz, tel. 958/7–08–48; open Mon.–Sat. 9–2 and 4–7), at the **kiosk** just east of the plaza (open daily 9–2 and 4–7) and at the **Tourist Information Center** in Tangolunda (Benito Juárez, across from Hotel Fasol, tel. 958/1–03–88). For medical aid contact **IMSS** (next door to Telmex, tel. 958/7–11–82), the **Cruz Roja** (tel. 958/7–11–88), or the **Centro de Salud** (tel. 958/7–04–03).

COMING AND GOING Buses run between Pochutla and La Crucecita every 15 minutes (1 hr, $1). Direct Cristóbal Colón (tel. 958/7–02–61) buses to Oaxaca city (7 hrs, $9.50) leave La Crucecita (cnr of Yuca and Gardenia) at 5:30 PM and 10 PM; arrive a half hour before departure. Buses depart from the **Estrella Blanca** terminal (Gardenia, at Paloma Real) frequently for Salina Cruz (3 hrs, $3), Tehuantepec (4 hrs, $4) and even Chiapas. There are daily flights to Oaxaca city and Mexico City from the Santa María de Huatulco airport (tel. 958/1–90–04). **Transporte Terrestre** runs colectivos to and from the airport ($3.50), or you can arrange a taxi ride (tel. 958/7–08–88) for under $10.

GETTING AROUND The bays are extremely spread out, and though they're now accessible by paved roads, it's a bit of a haul to get from one to the other. The three central bays—Tangolunda, Chahué, and Santa Cruz—are serviced by blue *urbanos* (city buses; 20¢). They run from about 6 AM to 11 PM, but there are about half as many on the weekends as on the weekdays. Taxis between La Crucecita, Santa Cruz, and Tangolunda shouldn't cost more than $1.50 if you're an insistent bargainer.

Colectivos ($2) leave early in the morning along the Santa Cruz–Chahué road and from the crossroads for Santa María Huatulco to take workers out to Conejos, Maguey, and Cacaluta. To reach Santa Cruz from La Crucecita, catch one of the frequent buses ($1) that run past the Plaza Principal and along the main road. To reach Órgano, walk over the hill on the east end of Maguey; it should take about half an hour. To reach San Agustín and Chachacual, catch an bus toward Pochutla and get off at the crossroads for Santa María Huatulco. From here it's

$3.50 taxi ride or $1 colectivo (if you're lucky enough to get one) to the bay of your choice. Another option for all the bays is to show up at the Santa Cruz marina bright and early and try to hitch a ride with someone boating out to one of the beaches to work. If you luck out and someone's willing, expect to pay between $2 and $7.

Day-long bay cruises ($20), which include use of snorkeling gear, drinks, and a taxi ride to and from your hotel, visit several outlying beaches and are probably the best way for the budget traveler to see Huatulco in full. Boats depart every morning around 10 AM from the Santa Cruz and Tangolunda docks.

WHERE TO SLEEP AND EAT If you must be on the beach, camping is the way to go. It's officially allowed only on Chahué, but you'll find deserted beaches and forest galore if you venture farther afield. If you prefer not to camp, try **Posada Primavera** (Palo Verde, btw Bugambilias and Gardenia, tel. 958/7-11-67), in La Crucecita. Rooms are the cleanest and cheapest around: $15 a single and $20 a double, with fans and private baths. If Primavera is full, try **Posada Michelle** (cnr of Gardenia and Palma Real, tel. 958/7-05-35), where simple doubles with fan and private bath run $20. **Trailer Park Los Mangos** (right-hand side of road, btw La Crucecita and Santa Cruz, no phone) provides the cheapest official campsites near Bahía Chahué. Tent sites are $2 per person, with access to communal bathrooms and showers. Órgano is the most deserted bay; it has no palapas or tourist facilities, so you'll have to bring food, fresh water, and plenty of insect repellant if you're going to stay the night. Most of the other beaches have palapas, but these close by late afternoon, and the beaches are deserted in the evenings.

Comidas corridas and 35¢ tacos abound in La Crucecita; avoid the touristy restaurants around the plaza and you'll find no shortage of cheap eats. **La Crucecita** (Chacah, at Bugambilias, no phone; open daily 7 AM-10 PM) serves up comidas corridas ($2) and good breakfasts. Near the bus stations, **Pozolería Guerrero** (Gardenia, at Jarumbo, no phone) doles out overflowing bowls of pozole blanco (white hominy soup; $2.50), served with love and fresh oregano daily 8 AM-11 PM. In Santa Cruz, the comedores on Monte Albán at Andador Coyula serve comidas corridas ($2) to the local workers in Santa Cruz, 24 hours a day.

OUTDOOR ACTIVITIES Budget travelers aren't what the Mexican government had in mind when they built up Huatulco, but you can still have some fun without draining your pockets. Most people come here simply to lie on exquisitely groomed or exceptionally empty beaches. The most accessible, but least exciting beaches are La Entrega (near Santa Cruz) and Chahué, and no one seems to mind if you plop down on the fine sands in front of the resorts at Tangolunda. Snorkeling is best at Cacaluta and Chachacual: Snorkeling gear rents for $5 at most places around town and on the beaches. **Soc. Cooperativa Turística** (tel. 958/7-00-81) rents snorkeling gear ($5 a day) on the Tangolunda dock. There are also on- and off-road bike paths to several of the bays. To rent bikes ($20 a day), inquire at one of the travel agencies in Santa Cruz, next to Hotel Castillo on Avenida Santa Cruz.

The Isthmus of Tehuantepec

Stretching 215 kilometers from the Caribbean to the Pacific, the isthmus encompasses parts of both Oaxaca and Tabasco. Most tourists do not consider it a destination in itself, but a stop along the gringo trail between Oaxaca and Chiapas, a place to switch buses or refuel. From that vantage point the isthmus can seem particularly unattractive—dusty, hot, provincial, and boring, especially after the Oaxaca coast or the Chiapan highlands. If, however, you're interested in meeting friendly locals, you'll find the region rather hospitable. The large Zapotec population here has resisted being "Mexicanized" and instead identifies with the isthmus itself. You'll see this in the teaching of Zapotec poetry in the cultural centers, and in the distinctive local costumes, festivals, and foods.

The three main cities on the isthmus are Salina Cruz, Tehuantepec, and Juchitán. Despite the fact that they are all within 32 kilometers of one another, they have developed in very different

Calls in Zapotec announcing "geta tzuki" (small, dense breads) and "geta bingi" (shrimp-filled tortillas) for sale resound in the plazas and marketplaces of the isthmus towns.

ways. Salina Cruz has the most modern conveniences, Tehuantepec is the smallest, and Juchitán, recognized as the cultural center of the isthmus, is where the Zapotec influence is most prominent.

Salina Cruz

Salina Cruz is an industrial port city with not much in the way of distinguishing features other than its friendly people. It's a convenient base town from which to explore the rest of the isthmus, as well as a good stopover point between the Oaxaca coast and Chiapas, but that's about it. If you're desperate to hit the beach, catch the VENTOSA bus (20 min, 20¢), which runs every half hour from the corner of 5 de Mayo and Acapulco (SE cnr of zócalo) to **Bahía La Ventosa,** a clean, windswept stretch of coast 10 kilometers (6 mi) south of town. From where the bus drops you off, head northwest (left) toward the sandy strip of beach. On the rocky eastern end of the bay, at the edge of a windy cliff, stands a lighthouse Cortés utilized as he was conquering the Pacific. Back in town, there's not much to do except hang out and talk to oil workers.

BASICS Bancomer (NW cnr of plaza, at Camacho) has an ATM and exchanges currency weekdays 10–noon. For medical aid, both **IMSS** (on the Carretera Transístmica, on the outskirts of town, tel. 971/4–15–72) and the **Centro de Salud** (cnr of Camacho and Frontera, near the post office) are open 24 hours. For the best rates on international and domestic calls and fax service, head to **SONEX** (cnr of Camacho and Mazatlán, tel. 971/4–56–21, fax 971/4–57–10), open daily 8 AM–midnight. The **post office** (cnr of Camacho and Frontera, no phone) is open weekdays 8–6, Saturday 9–2.

COMING AND GOING Cristóbal Colón (5 de Mayo 412, tel. 971/4–02–59), two blocks from the plaza, serves Tapachula (3 per day, 10 hrs, $12), Tuxtla Gutiérrez (2 per day, 6 hrs, $6.50), and San Cristóbal (1 per day, 8 hrs, $10) in Chiapas, as well as Huatulco (2½ hrs, $3) and Puerto Escondido (6 hrs, $7) on the Oaxaca coast. There are several buses to Oaxaca city (5 hrs, $6) and three evening buses to Mexico City (12 hrs, $28). Frequent micros and second-class buses also depart daily from the railroad tracks for Puerto Escondido and Santa Cruz. Frequent local buses to Tehuantepec (30 min, 50¢) and Juchitán (1 hr, $1) leave from the same location.

WHERE TO SLEEP AND EAT Hotels in Salina Cruz cater to businessmen and tend to be expensive. **Hotel Fuentes** (Camacho 114, tel. 971/4–34–03) has clean rooms with color TVs; a double is $8, $12 with air-conditioning. A few doors down and a bit cheaper is **Hotel Posada del Jardín** (Camacho 108, tel. 971/4–01–62), with secure singles ($5.50) and doubles with industrial-strength fans ($8). You'll pay $1.50 more for noisier rooms with TV's. You'll find taco stands and women selling dried fish and seafood around the market on 5 de Mayo (NE cnr of zócalo). If you want to enjoy your seafood sitting down, **La Pasadita** (Camacho 603-A, no phone; open daily 7 AM–11:30 PM) serves the best shrimp cocktail around ($2.50). **Café Istmeño** (east side of plaza, tel. 971/4–17–40) serves great coffee and desserts daily 7 AM–midnight. Head next door for tasty tortas ($1). **Jugos Hawaii** (two locations on Camacho, north of plaza) offers a good selection of fruit drinks and munchies daily 8–8.

Tehuantepec

Tehuantepec, Nahuatl for "Jaguar Hill," feels the least modern and most inviting of the main isthmus towns. Start exploring at the **Casa de la Cultura** (Callejón Rey Cosijopi, off Guerrero) housed in a 16th-century convent. The Casa de la Cultura recently opened an anthropology museum and gallery, which host photo expositions and local contemporary art. Director Julí Contreras provides tourist info daily 11–2. Ask about their calender of events and local festivals. Julín can also tell you how to reach **Guiengola,** the site of a Zapotec fortress that was the locus of battles between the Zapotecs and Aztecs. The breezy mountain site offers good views of the surrounding area, although the isthmus landscape isn't that impressive. If you want a guide u the mountain, seek out the Boy Scouts, who tend to congregate at the Palacio Municipal Saturday 10–noon. Located 12 kilometers out of town, the site is prime for camping.

Locals often gather in the neighborhoods surrounding Tehuantepec for festivals, or *velas* (vigils), honoring patron saints. The Jasmine Vigil, held during the third week of May, features ostentatious displays of typical Tehuana dress, marimba music, and, best of all, women pelting the local men with fruit to assert their superiority as matriarchs.

BASICS Bancomer and Serfin, near the zócalo, have ATMs and change money weekdays 9–noon. Both the **Centro de Salud** (Guerrero, 3 blocks NE of plaza) and the **Cruz Roja** (cnr of Roberto E. Salazar and Soto, near Carretera Transístmica) offer emergency care. **El Paraíso** (5 de Mayo 1, tel. 971/5–02–12) provides long-distance and collect service 8 AM–10 PM. The **post office** (cnr of Hidalgo and 22 de Marzo) is open 8–6.

The Casa de la Cultura in Tehuantepec is looking for volunteers interested in helping curate cultural exhibitions and restore their building. Minimum commitment is one month. For more info, contact Julín Contreras at the Ex-Convento Dominico, Tehuantepec, Oaxaca, CP 70760, México, tel. 971/5–01–14, fax 971/ 5–08–35.

COMING AND GOING Long-distance buses operate out of the terminal at the north side of town, on the *Carretera Transístmica* (Transisthmus Highway). From here, **Cristóbal Colón** (tel. 971/8–57–52) serves Oaxaca city (8 per day, 5 hrs, $6), Tuxtla Gutiérrez (4 per day, 5 hrs, $6), and San Cristóbal (7½ hrs, $9.50). The latter bus comes from Oaxaca, and may be full. **Istmeños** buses to Juchitán (30 min, 35¢) and Salina Cruz (25 min, 30¢) depart every half hour from the highway, two blocks east of the plaza. During daylight hours, local buses (15¢) depart for the main bus terminal from the northwest corner of the plaza.

In Tehuantepec, don't miss your chance to ride on the motocarros—open-air three-wheel ATV taxis (20¢).

WHERE TO SLEEP The regal **Hotel Donaji** (Juárez 10, tel. 971/5–00–64), two blocks southeast of the plaza, is built around a peaceful, ivy-covered courtyard. A double with private bath costs $10; a few dollars more gets you air-conditioning. One block south of the plaza's west side is **Hotel Oasis** (Ocampo 8, tel. 971/5–00–08). Dilapidated doubles with private baths and ceiling fans are $10; singles are $6.50. For the cheapest beds, head west from the Oasis toward the railroad tracks to **Posada Hasdar** (Ocampo 10, tel. 971/5–02–07), where slightly rumpled rooms with private baths and ceiling fans are $4.

FOOD **El Portón** (Juana C. Romero 54, 1 block south of zócalo; open Mon.–Sat. 8–6, Sun. 8–1) sells fresh, simple regional food. Soups are 50¢ a bowl, and big plates of enchiladas, chiles rellenos, or tacos are a steal at $1.25. Two blocks southwest of the plaza is **Café Colonial** (Juana C. Romero 66, tel. 971/5–01–15; open daily 8 AM–10 PM), where a filling comida corrida with fish and fresh fruit goes for $2.25. Good comedores are clustered on the top floor of the market, on the plaza's west side.

Juchitán

Located 26 kilometers from Tehuantepec, the friendly town of Juchitán buzzes with Zapotec culture, but is seldom visited by gringos. The **Mercado 5 de Septiembre** (Gómez, east of zócalo) is an excellent place to find cheap food; it's also the place to observe Juchitán's matriarchal society, with boisterous women hawking the goods that give them economic power. Their excellent hammocks are a good buy. The **Casa de la Cultura** (cnr of Belsario Dominguez and 5 de Septiembre, tel. 971/1–13–51; open daily 9–2 and 4–7) is a free regional art center housed in the 16th-century **Iglesia San Vicente Ferrer**. The contemporary collection includes works by Rufino Tamayo. Come in the early afternoon, when Juchitán children attend catechism and sing church hymns. About 10 kilometers (6 mi) outside of town you'll find an estuary called **Mar Muerto** (Dead Sea), ideal for fishing and boating; you can try to get one of the fisherman here to take you out on his boat for a couple of dollars. To get here, take a bus labeled 7TH SEC (35¢) from behind the market in Juchitán. Don't confuse this Mar Muerto with the one farther away from town.

Like Tehuantepec, Juchitán likes to go crazy with dance, food, and libations, all in the name of a patron saint. Most of the 26 local festivals happen between April and September, the largest one being the **Vela de San Vincente Ferre**. The festival occurs in May and features bull-fights, parades, and women pelting helpless men with fruit—a distinguishing characteristic of festivals throughout the isthmus. To get exact info on where you can participate (or where you can avoid getting pulp in your hair), talk to the folk at the Casa de la Cultura (*see above*).

BASICS **Banamex** (5 de Septiembre, at Gómez) exchanges currency weekdays 10–noon. For medical attention, **IMSS** (eastern end of Gómez, past Constitución) is open 24 hours. The **Centro de Salud** (Libertad, near Gómez) offers emergency service daily 8–3. **Ladatel** phones are located all along 16 de Septiembre. The **post office** (cnr of 16 de Septiembre and Gómez, no phone) is open weekdays 8–5. Fax and long-distance phone service are also available in the bus terminal.

COMING AND GOING The main bus terminal (16 de Septiembre, 10 blocks north of zócalo, tel. 971/1–20–22) is open 24 hours and houses Cristóbal Colón, ADO, Sur, and AU buses, as well as the local Istmeño company. Many long distance buses come from other cities and arrive in the wee hours, making it next to impossible to find a spare seat; during peak periods, be prepared to take a bus to a nearby town, such as Arriaga. Otherwise, you can get almost anywhere in the country from this station.

Cristóbal Colón offers first-class service to Tapachula (6 hrs, $8.50), Tuxtla Gutiérrez (5 hrs, $7), and San Cristóbal (7 hrs, $9.50), departing at 1 AM or 2:30 PM. Hourly second-class Sur buses go to Oaxaca (5 hrs, $5), Pochutla (5 hrs, $5), and Huatulco (3½ hrs, $4). Istmeños buses depart every half hour to Tehuantepec (30 min, 35¢) and Salina Cruz (1 hr, 60¢) from outside the main terminal, near the highway.

WHERE TO SLEEP All hotels listed below have fans and private baths and are located on the plaza. **Hotel Juchitán** (16 de Septiembre 51, tel. 971/1–10–65) is closest to the bus station and offers clean doubles for $6.25; air-conditioning will cost you a couple more bucks. South of Hotel Juchitán is **Hotel Don Alex** (16 de Septiembre, btw Aldama and Hidalgo, tel. 971/1–10–64), which maintains clean, basic rooms: Singles are $5.50, plus $1.50 for each extra person. Nearest the plaza, **Casa de Huéspedes Echazarreta** (Juárez 23, south side of plaza, tel. 971/1–12–05) offers secure doubles for $6.50.

FOOD In Juchitán's market, women sell iguana eggs as well as live iguanas with their mouths sewn shut and legs tied behind their backs. The little leathery eggs are eaten by biting off the top of the shell and sucking out the yolky, slightly salty contents. The iguanas are also tasty, especially *entomado* (cooked in tomato sauce); look for this treat at the comedores in the market. Juchitán is also regionally famous for its seafood. The popular **Mariscos Sylvia Juchitán** (2 de Abril, btw Aldama and Hidalgo, tel. 971/1–22–35; open daily 8–7) serves an enormous *vuelve a la vida* (back to life) cocktail ($4), crammed with chunks of octopus, shrimp, conch, oysters, avocado, onion, and cilantro. **Restaurant Casa Grande** (Juárez 12, south of zócalo, tel. 971/1–34–60; open daily 8 AM–11 PM) has linen tablecloths and a cool courtyard; their *aguacate relleno de camarones* (avocado stuffed with shrimp) is almost a meal in itself ($2).

CHIAPAS AND TABASCO

13

By Andrew Dean Nystrom

The states of Chiapas and Tabasco share a narrow strip of land between the Gulf of Mexico, the Pacific Ocean, and Guatemala, encompassing mountains, swampy lowland, volcanoes, cloud forests, and thick jungle. This region, at the heart of the great Olmec and Classic Mayan empires, was hotly contested by many Mesoamerican civilizations. Despite the close geographical proximity and shared history of these two states, however, the present-day contrast between them couldn't be more striking. The oil boom of the 1970s left Tabasco with many air-conditioned buildings, massive cement expressways, and modern, flashy hotels—an urban setting in which indigenous people are a rare sight. The larger and more mountainous Chiapas, on the other hand, is rich in colonial history and indigenous culture, with Spanish being the *second* language of much of the population. Disparity can also be seen in the states' economic status: Although Chiapas provides Mexico with abundant agricultural goods and enough electricity to light up Mexico City, it remains the poorest state in the country.

It was partially in response to this type of regional inequity that, in January 1994, the Zapatista National Liberation Army (EZLN) invaded the historic Chiapan city of San Cristóbal de las Casas and effectively thrust some of Chiapas's chronic problems into the political limelight. Although many middle-class *mestizos* (people of mixed ancestry) who lost businesses during the uprising and the ensuing economic crisis bear some ill will, most *indígenas* (indigenous people) extend their thanks to the Zapatistas. Since peace talks began in 1995, Chiapas has received much more governmental attention and an influx of social services. However, army repression is on the rise, along with a campaign of low-intensity warfare designed to squelch dissention. Although the *diálogos* (dialogues) drag on, the state remains relatively safe for travel. The press's coverage of the situation has actually attracted more visitors, many of whom come to express solidarity with the Zapatistas and get a firsthand feel for the reality behind the conflict. Prepare for a passive but heavy military presence, check on current conditions before wandering around outlying areas, and make sure your documents are handy and in order at all times.

The natural wonders of Chiapas have received less fanfare than its politics but are mind-blowing to even the most worldly of travelers. The state contains a large tract of endangered rain forest and is home to vital indigenous cultures unlike any others in the country. The hilly terrain near San Cristóbal is the living fabric of Mayan culture, with a multitude of indigenous groups speaking several Mayan languages. San Cristóbal itself, just two hours from the hot and humid state capital of Tuxtla Gutiérrez, offers a cool climate, pine forests, and some of the country's best-preserved colonial architecture. The residual effects of the Zapatista occupation still linger here: On every other corner you'll find political graffiti and *indígenas* hawking Subcomandantes Marcos and Tacho dolls.

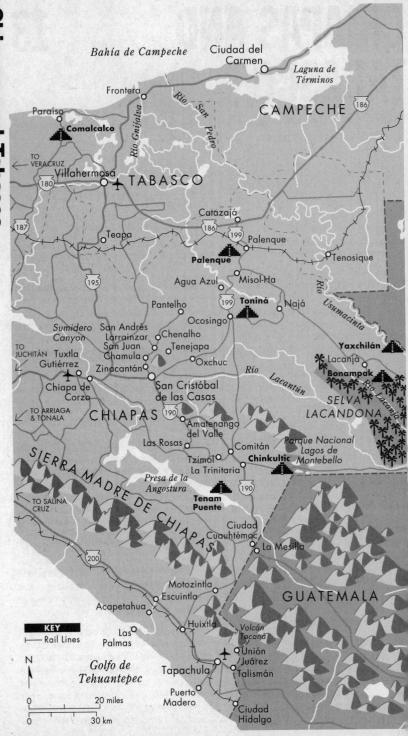

Bahía de Campeche

Ciudad del Carmen

Laguna de Términos

Frontera

CAMPECHE

186

Paraíso

Comalcalco

Río Gnijalva

Río San Pedro

TO VERACRUZ

180

Villahermosa

TABASCO

187

Catazajá

186

199

Palenque

Tenosique

Teapa

Palenque

195

Agua Azul

Misol-Ha

Río Usumacinta

Pantelho

199

Toniná

Najá

Ocosingo

Sumidero Canyon

San Andrés Larrainzar

Chenalho

Yaxchilán

San Juan Chamula

Tenejapa

Lacanjá

TO JUCHITÁN

Tuxtla Gutiérrez

Zinacantán

Oxchuc

Río Lacantún

Bonampak

Chiapa de Corzo

San Cristóbal de las Casas

SELVA LACANDONA

Río Lacanja

TO ARRIAGA & TONALA

CHIAPAS

190

Amatenango del Valle

Las Rosas

Comitán

Parque Nacional Lagos de Montebello

Tzimol

Chinkultic

La Trinitaria

SIERRA MADRE

Presa de la Angostura

190

TO SALINA CRUZ

Tenam Puente

DE CHIAPAS

Ciudad Cuauhtémoc

La Mesilla

200

GUATEMALA

Motozintla

Escuintla

Acapetahua

Huixtla

Volcán Tacaná

KEY

Rail Lines

Las Palmas

Unión Juárez

Talismán

N

Golfo de Tehuantepec

Tapachula

Puerto Madero

0   20 miles
0   30 km

Ciudad Hidalgo

The coffee- and cacao-growing region of southern coastal Chiapas is almost never visited by the package-tour crowd. The town of Tapachula has a Chinese-shantytown feel, and is a gateway to Guatemala. From here you can hit a few undeveloped beaches or head for the beautiful mountain town of Unión Juárez, perched below Volcán Tacaná amidst foothills dotted with coffee plantations. Farther inland are Comitán and the Parque Nacional Lagos de Montebello, home to more blue-green lakes than one person could ever swim in; surrounding the park are several Mayan archaeological sites still waiting to be discovered.

The eastern region of Chiapas is mostly rain forest, though more and more acreage is being lost to cattle ranching. Here you'll find the famous ruins of Palenque and Toniná, along with rivers and waterfalls offering luxurious escapes from the heat. In the southeast corner of Chiapas, the Lacandón rain forest hides the remote ruins of Yaxchilán and Bonampak. This ever-shrinking paradise is home to the Lacandón Indians, whose culture and religious rites are considered by many to be more closely related to the ancient Maya than those of any other living group. Conversion to Evangelical Protestantism and co-optation by well-meaning social service groups are just two of the struggles the Lacandón continue to face since contact with Western society.

In contrast to Chiapas, Tabasco offers relative isolation. The state's dense jungles, dotted with impressive Mayan ruins and intriguing caves, are rarely explored. Even the state's beaches are hidden paradises where you can feast on seafood and tropical fruit concoctions for less than most places in Mexico. However, Tabasco is by no means an untouched Eden: While the oil boom encouraged new businesses and funded the arts in the capital, parts of the gulf coastline were contaminated. Though Tabascans now enjoy a relatively high standard of living, the cost to the environment (not yet known) could be high. But most residents point proudly to the cultural vitality of Villahermosa and to the fact that oil money paid for projects like the draining of the basin containing La Venta, the largest Olmec archaeological find in Mesoamerica.

Tuxtla Gutiérrez

Tuxtla Gutiérrez isn't exactly easy on the eyes: As Graham Greene declared in 1939, "The new ugly capital of Chiapas is like an unnecessary postscript to Chiapas, which should be all wild mountain and old churches and swallowed ruins . . ." This busy administrative and university city with its long, well-lit commercial strip evokes images of Las Vegas. Unless you're desperate for a hot shower, want a dose of unadulterated mestizo culture, or are stuck waiting for a connection to Oaxaca, San Cristóbal, Tabasco, or the Yucatán, it's unlikely you'll want to spend more than a day or two here. However, in the midst of all the cement islands and super-expressways, you'll find a great zoo, botanical gardens, and cultural museums worth at least one day of exploration. A short trip outside the city takes you to the colonial town of Chiapa de Corzo, the departure point for boat rides through the spectacular Sumidero Canyon.

Tuxtla became the capital of Chiapas in 1892, after a bloody battle in the old capital of San Cristóbal de las Casas. Tensions arose because of Tuxtla's support of dictator Porfirio Díaz's land policy, which favored a few *ladino* (Spanish-descended) families over the indigenous *campesinos* (peasants). To this day, Chiapas's fertile land is concentrated in the hands of a tiny, powerful fraction of the population. Although land reform is still a hot issue in Chiapas, Tuxtla's status as the state capital means that any pro-reform graffiti is fastidiously sandblasted off government buildings as soon as it appears. However, occasional protests by the EZLN and its supporters still take place in the main plaza.

BASICS

AMERICAN EXPRESS AmEx operates through **Agencia de Viajes Marabusco.** Cardholders can cash personal checks, receive advances on AmEx cards, or have their mail held here; anyone can change money, receive a MoneyGram, or have lost traveler's checks replaced. *Av. Central, across from federal tourist office, tel. 961/2–69–98 or 961/2–84–49. Mailing address:*

Pl. Bonampak, Local 14, Sedetur, Tuxtla Gutiérrez, Chiapas, CP 29030, México. Open weekdays 9–2 and 4–7, Sat. 9–2.

CASAS DE CAMBIO **Bancomer** (Av. Central, at 2a Pte. Nte., tel. 961/2–82–51) and **Banamex** (1a Sur Pte. 141, tel. 961/2–87–44) both change traveler's checks weekdays 10–noon. You'll have to wait longer than at private exchange places but you'll get slightly better rates. Bancomer changes cash and offers cash advances on credit cards until it closes at 3 PM. If you're low on dough after hours or on weekends, **Cafetería Bonampak** (Blvd. Belisario Domínguez 180, tel. 961/3–20–50 ext. 127) will change cash or traveler's checks or give you a cash advance on your credit card daily 7 AM–midnight.

EMERGENCIES For an ambulance, call the **Cruz Roja** at 961/2–95–14. For any other emergency, call the **police** (tel. 961/2–05–36).

LAUNDRY **Lavandería La Burbuja** will wash and dry 3 kilos of clothes for $4. *1a Nte. Pte., at 3a Pte. Nte., tel. 961/1–05–95. Open weekdays 8–8, Sat. 8–2.*

MAIL The **post office** (NE cnr of Parque Central, tel. 961/2–04–16) will hold mail sent to you at the following address for up to 10 days: Lista de Correos, Tuxtla Gutiérrez, Chiapas, CP 29002, México. Next door, the **telegram office** (tel. 961/2–02–81) sends packages and faxes. Both are open weekdays 8–7, Saturday 9–1.

MEDICAL AID The **Centro de Salud** (9a Sur Ote., at 2a Ote. Sur, tel. 961/2–03–15) is open for walk-in appointments Monday–Saturday 7:30–noon. Free, round-the-clock medical attention is available at the **Cruz Roja** (5a Nte. Pte. 1480, tel. 961/2–95–14). The **farmacia** (tel. 961/3–88–18; open daily 8 AM–10 PM) on Avenida Central at Calle Central sells legal drugs.

PHONES Blue Ladatel phones (dial 09 for collect calls) can be found in front of the movie theaters near the plaza and on every other corner downtown. Cash calls can be made from *casetas de larga distancia* (long-distance telephone offices), as can collect calls, which generally cost $1–$2. There's a convenient caseta on 2a Norte Oriente, outside Hotel Plaza Chiapas (*see* Where to Sleep, *below*), that's open daily 9–8. Several others line 2a Oriente Norte, just east of the plaza.

VISITOR INFORMATION The central **local tourist office** is the place to pick up maps, restaurant and hotel guides, and information on everything from taxi fares to boat rides up the Sumidero Canyon. *2a Pte. Nte., at Av. Central, beneath Parque Central, tel. 961/3–76–90. Open weekdays 9–3 and 6–9, Sat. 9–1.*

The **federal tourist office** is staffed by helpful young people fresh out of college who speak decent English. While you're here, try to get your hands on *La Cartelera*, a monthly publication that lists cultural events taking place in Tuxtla and other Chiapan cities. Photocopied brochures with maps and practical information about other towns in Chiapas are also available *Blvd. Belisario Domínguez 950, tel. 961/3–48–37. Open weekdays 8 AM–9 PM.*

COMING AND GOING

BY BUS The first-class **ADO/Cristóbal Colón** station (2a Nte. Pte. 268, tel. 961/2–51–22 is two blocks west of the northwest corner of the plaza. Buses to San Cristóbal (2 hrs, $2.25) leave frequently 5 AM–9 PM. Every day after 1 PM, several regular first-class buses and two plush, bathroom-equipped "Servi-Plus" buses leave for Mexico City (12 hrs; $31.50, $35 for Servi-Plus), stopping in Puebla (10 hrs, $27) and Córdoba (9 hrs, $21). The red *juguería* (juice bar) across from the station will hold luggage all day until midnight for 40¢. Lock your bag and don't leave any money or valuables in them.

Autotransportes Tuxtla Gutiérrez (3a Sur Ote. 712, tel. 961/2–02–30), near the San Roque market, offers both first- and second-class service to Ocosingo (3½ hrs, $3.25), Palenque (6 hrs, $6), Tapachula (8 hrs, $8.25), San Cristóbal (2 hrs, $1.75; departing at 7:45 AM and 2:45 PM), and Villahermosa (8½ hrs, $6). Inquire at the window about service to other destinations in Chiapas. **Tuxtla-Chiapa** buses leave from the corner of 3a Oriente Sur and 3a Sur Oriente for Chiapa de Corzo (30 min, 40¢) every five to 10 minutes, daily 6 AM–8 PM.

BY PLANE **Aeropuerto Francisco Sarabia** (Carretera Panamericana, 10 km west of Tuxtla, tel. 961/5–10–11) is commonly known as "Terán." **Aerocaribe** (tel. 961/2–00–20) serves Mérida, Cancún, Villahermosa, and Oaxaca; a one-way flight to Mexico City costs about $100 during the higher seasons. **AVIACSA** (tel. 961/2–80–81) flies to the Yucatán, Oaxaca, Tapachula, Monterrey, and Mexico City. **Mexicana** (Av. Central Pte. 206, tel. 961/1–14–90) soars thrice daily to Mexico City (1 hr, $100). Taxis ($2.75) are the best means of transport to Terán from downtown, and your only option when going in the opposite direction.

GETTING AROUND

Although Tuxtla is a large, sprawling city, it's fairly easy to navigate. Two main thoroughfares (the north–south Calle Central and the east–west Avenida Central, a.k.a. Boulevard Ángel Albino Corzo) intersect at the main plaza and divide the city into quadrants. All the other streets are named and numbered according to their position relative to the main plaza. Avenidas are labeled with a number, then "Sur" or "Norte," then "Oriente" or "Poniente" (e.g., 2a Sur Oriente); Calles are labeled in the opposite manner (e.g., 2a Oriente Sur). To reach the American Express office, the federal tourist office, and the discos from the center you'll need to take an AV. CENTRAL colectivo down Avenida Central until it turns into Boulevard Belisario Domínguez on the western outskirts of town.

BY BUS **Colectivos** (30¢) run throughout the city 6 AM–9 PM. Destinations are plainly marked on the front windshields, and stops are indicated on the street by blue signs. Unlike those in many Mexican cities, the colectivos here only pick up passengers at marked stops. **Microbuses** (50¢) are bigger and run to Tuxtla's outlying sights, such as the zoo and botanical gardens. They can be hailed on most main streets and their destinations are also clearly marked.

BY CAR **Budget** (Blvd. Domínguez 2510, tel. 961/5–06–83), **Dollar** (5a Nte. Pte. 2260, tel. 961/2–89–32), and **Hertz** (Blvd. Domínguez 180, tel. 961/1–39–50) are the best budget rental agencies. The going day rate for a sedan is $36, which includes insurance, 200 free kilometers, and a full tank. The rate almost doubles if you're under 25; if you're young and desperate for private transportation, consider hiring a taxi for the day or getting some fellow travelers together for a group rental.

BY TAXI Taxis are necessary if you want to return from one of the discos late at night— thankfully they run 24 hours. The most you should pay within city limits is $1; agree on the price before getting in.

WHERE TO SLEEP

Most hotels in Tuxtla are modern and bland, but relatively clean and cheap rooms are easy to come by. Rather than ambience, look for a working fan and clean sheets. If you're too lazy to lug that backpack, **Hotel Santo Domingo,** across from the Cristóbal Colón bus station, is the cheapest dive you'll find: Noisy singles ($4) and doubles ($7.50) have private baths but no hot water.

Casa de Huéspedes Muñiz. The dusty upper rooms of this guest house have a view of the surrounding urban squalor, but for $3.50 a single and $4.75 a double ($2 each additional person) with private bath, one shouldn't expect to be insulated from reality. The water's not hot, but there are fans, and a nice family runs the place. *2a Sur Ote. 733, at 7a Ote. Sur, no phone. 12 rooms, 13 with bath. Laundry, luggage storage.*

Hotel Casablanca. The Casablanca features a pleasant courtyard filled with plants, and all its rooms have ceiling fans. The clean bathrooms are stocked with towels, soap, and toilet paper. With communal bath, singles are $6, doubles $8 (add $2 for a private bath). Hot water pours from the showers 24 hours a day. *2a Nte. Ote. 251, 1 block NE of plaza, tel. 961/1–03–05. 42 rooms, 37 with bath. Luggage storage.*

Hotel La Catedral. A maze of stairways and corridors leads to sparkling clean and quiet rooms. All have ceiling fans and private bathrooms with hot showers. Singles are $5.25, doubles $6, triples $7.25. *1a Nte. Ote. 367, at 3a Ote. Nte., tel. 961/3–08–24. 30 rooms, all with bath.* **429**

Hotel Plaza Chiapas. Clean rooms come complete with fans and cheery pink bathrooms with hot water and towels. Singles are $6.75, doubles $8, triples $10.75. Those seeking air-conditioning should head to the cheap eatery downstairs. *2a Nte. Ote. 299, at 2a Ote. Nte., tel. 961/ 3–83–65. 2 blocks NE of zócalo. 34 rooms, all with bath. Restaurant open daily 8 AM–10 PM.*

Hotel San Antonio. The 20 exceptionally clean rooms—all with fans and private bathrooms— are often full, but it's worth a try. Singles cost $5.50, doubles $6.75, triples $8. *2a Sur Ote. 540, tel. 961/2–27–13. Around eastern cnr of 2nd-class bus station.*

HOSTELS **INDEJECH Villa Juvenil/Chiapas.** Located in a youth sports center, this clean hostel provides single-sex dorm-style accommodations complete with clean sheets, pillowcases, and towels for $2.25 a night. Meals ($1.25) are available at the cafeteria whenever there are groups of people. It's an excellent deal, even with the cold showers and 11 PM curfew. *Ángel Albino Corzo 1800, at 18a Ote., tel. 961/3–34–05. From downtown, take a colectivo east along Av. Central for about 10 min.*

FOOD

Because people from all over the state come here on business, Tuxtla offers a chance to sample cuisine from almost anywhere in Chiapas. Most restaurants serve traditional favorites, including crumbly Chiapan cheese, tamales, and spicy tacos top-heavy with chiles. The city's prosperity has also bred a substantial middle class, which, like its counterparts worldwide, has time to worry about things like whether meat is good for them. The result: Gyms and health-food stores are scattered about town, and most restaurants have a selection of vegetarian dishes. Cheap tortas, tacos, and jugos are easy to come by near the bus stations, and the center swarms with eateries and cafés; look for the striped umbrellas off the plaza.

In the morning or early afternoon, look for people sitting around the plaza drinking out of gourd bowls. These are filled with pozol—a cold, corn-based drink with chewy cornmeal at the bottom.

➤ **UNDER $5** • **Las Pichanchas.** The menu here includes *tamales chiapanecos* (with mole sauce, olives, raisins, and meat wrapped in banana leaves; $2) and *milanesas de ternera* (breaded cuts of veal; $2). Live marimba music (2:30–5:30 PM and 8:30–11:30 PM) adds to the festive atmosphere, and a *danza folklórica* is put on around 9 PM every evening. *Av. Central 837, tel. 961/2–53–51. Open daily 8 AM–midnight. Wheelchair access. AE, MC, V.*

Restaurante Imperial. This central restaurant serves tasty and inexpensive local fare such as *entomatadas de pollo* (chicken in tomato sauce). The ample *menu del día* includes soup, a meat entrée, tortillas, a drink, and dessert for $2. *Calle Central, at 2a Nte. Ote., no phone Open daily 7–6:30.*

Restaurante Vegetariano Nah-Yaxal. Vegetarians are in for a treat here. Tasty *tortas* (sandwiches) made with soy beef on whole wheat, or chilaquiles with gluten are both $1.25, and the mammoth Energética Nah-Yaxal (fruit salad smothered in yogurt and granola) is $1.75. Cook books for sale include *The Power of Respiration* and *Sprouts: The Most Perfect and Complete Natural Food. 6a Pte. Nte. 124, tel. 961/3–33–16. Open Mon.–Sat. 7:30 AM–9 PM.*

Trattoria San Marco. Of all the eateries near the plaza, this place wins for variety. Specialties include spaghetti bolognesa ($2.75) and crepes ($2–$3). Come and enjoy a cappuccino for under $1 or a $1.25 beer alongside executives, teenagers, and a cadre of chess players *Behind cathedral, tel. 961/2–69–74. Open daily 7 AM–midnight.*

WORTH SEEING

Tuxtla's main attractions lie in three distinct areas: **Parque Madero,** in the northeast; **Parque Zoológico,** to the southeast; and the city center, which contains **Parque Central,** the sprawling **Plaza Cívica,** and the **cathedral,** which houses one of the world's first musical clocks. You' need to use public transportation to reach the zoo from the center, but the other two areas can be easily reached on foot. The **market,** just two blocks south of the zócalo, is a dimly lit maze of giant papayas, local cheeses, crispy *chicharrón* (pork rind), and costume jewelry.

PARQUE MADERO At the intersection of 5a Norte Oriente and 5a Oriente Norte, six blocks northeast of the plaza, the Parque Madero complex brings together a variety of indoor and out-door wonders, all within easy walking distance. The park's central landmark is the **Teatro Emilio Rabasa,** which hosts frequent free cultural events. Two tree-lined walkways extend from the theater: The western path, lined with bronze busts of famous Mexican leaders, winds its way to the museums and botanical garden; the eastern path cuts through the children's park. Imme-diately outside Parque Madero is **Teatro Bonampak,** an open-air theater for cultural events. Consult *La Cartelera* (*see* Visitor Information, *above*) for a list of special performances at both theaters.

➤ **CENTRO DE CONVIVENCIA INFANTIL** • You don't have to be a child to enjoy this kiddie park on the east walkway, which resembles a wanna-be Disneyland. There are boat rides (30¢), a miniature train, and putt-putt golf for your cavorting pleasure. *Admission free. Open Tues.–Sun. 9–6.*

➤ **MUSEO REGIONAL DE CHIAPAS** • This sleek, air-conditioned museum provides a look at Chiapas's past and present. Permanent exhibits—packed with Olmec, Mayan, and Aztec artifacts—trace the growth of early indigenous civilizations. Look for oddly shaped Olmec skulls: Cosmetic cranial deformation was performed on noble Olmec children. Across the courtyard and upstairs is an exhibition on the Spanish invasion: Contrasting with huge colonial paintings of the Virgin Mary and numerous Spanish artifacts are historical narratives and images of the enslavement and displacement of indigenous peoples. Exhibits are in Spanish only. *Admission free. Open Tues.–Sun. 9–4.*

➤ **MUSEO Y JARDIN BOTANICO** • Run by the Chia-pan Botanical Institute, this botanical museum displays native trees, flowers, and medicinal plants, providing a sense of the scope of preservation efforts being undertaken across the state. Across the path is the botanical garden. The wind-ing paths that crisscross the garden are filled with amorous teenagers strolling through canopies of bamboo, mango trees, and twisting vines. *Admission free. Museum open Tues.–Sun. 9–3; garden open Tues.–Sun. 9–6.*

The Chiapan rain forest is home to representatives of 40% of all species found in Mexico, yet it's rapidly disappearing as a result of the government's eagerness to sell the highly marketable wood.

PARQUE ZOOLÓGICO The Parque Zoológico, one of the best in Latin America, features a selection of the spectacular and diverse flora and fauna of Chiapas. Concrete paths climb through lush tropical canopies ringing with the songs of birds and insects. More than 100 species of native Chiapan creatures, many of them endangered, wander here in an approxima-tion of their natural surroundings. There's an environmental education center, an aviary, and even an insect zoo filled with giant roaches and huge, hairy spiders. The zoo affords rare glimpses of tapirs, black panthers, *guacamayas* (macaws), and the spectacularly plumed quet-zal. *SE of town, off Libramiento Sur. Take a CERRO HUECO or ZOOLOGICO bus, which leave every ½ hour from 1a Ote. Sur, btw 6a and 7a Sur Ote. Donations encouraged. Open Tues.–Sun. 9–5.*

AFTER DARK

Tuxtla's university students and restless teenagers fuel a lively, if uncouth scene. In addition to the movie theaters near the plaza, you'll find a wide variety of nightlife options. The music of street performers—which can be anything from a marimba ensemble or romantic balladeer to a military band—is common in the Parque Central, especially on Sundays. For authentic and free marimba, stroll by the *kiosko* in the appropriately named **Parque de la Marimba** (Av. Cen-tral, 7 blocks west of Parque Central) weekdays 7 PM–10 PM, rain or shine. When Kiss or any other monster metal band comes to town, there'll be plenty of flyers posted to let you know. *La Cartelera* (*see* Visitor Information, *above*) provides the rundown on more folkloric cultural events. The nameless **café** beneath Hotel Serano (Av. Central 230) serves great coffee to a sagey crowd of convivial codgers daily 8–1 and 4–8.

BARS The clientele at Tuxtla's bars and cafés tends to change as the evening passes. Early on, a college-age crowd congregates to find out where the real action will be taking place later that night. Next, middle-aged regulars come around to listen to live bands and/or watch *fútbol* (soccer) on TV. Check out **Obsession** (3a Ote. Nte. 142) and **Bar El Nucu** (Hotel María Eugenia, Av. Central 507) for throaty Mexican ballads 9 PM–3 AM.

DANCING Tuxtla's discos attract a young crowd and tend to host events like bikini and "best legs" contests. The cover is generally about $2–$4 (usually a little less for women for some odd reason), and Fridays tend to be the liveliest. Some weekend boogeying options include **Sheik** (Hotel Flamboyant, Blvd. Belisario Domínguez Km. 1081, tel. 961/5–08–88), **Colors** (Hotel Arecas, Blvd. Belisario Domínguez Km. 1080, tel. 961/5–11–21), and **Freeday** (Blvd. Los Laureles, at Blvd. Belisario Domínguez). All are too far from the zócalo to walk. You can take a colectivo down Avenida Central until 9 PM, but after that you'll need to take a taxi ($1). Closer to the center is **Úngalo** (Av. Central, 3 blocks east of zócalo), which is packed with teenyboppers rockin' to reggae and American pop on weekend nights. The cover here is $2.

Near Tuxtla Gutiérrez

CHIAPA DE CORZO

After the hustle and bustle of Tuxtla Gutiérrez, you might not guess that a quiet, friendly riverside town awaits you only 15 kilometers (9 mi) to the east. But Chiapa de Corzo is the type of place where you'll hear crowing roosters in the early morning and the clang of church bells intertwined with the putt-putt of cars. The town was once an important pre-Columbian colonial center because of its strategic location on the Río Grijalva, and today you'll find the ruins of a **pre-Classic Mayan site** on private property just outside of town, behind the Nestlé factory. To reach the ruins, follow the signs from the center and ask the owner's permission to enter the site during daylight hours. Chiapa de Corzo's sights are clustered around the large **main plaza**, with its colonial clock tower and 16th-century fountain representing Queen Isabella's crown (the latter in the Moorish-influenced *mudéjar* architectural style). The **Palacio Municipal**—just off the zócalo in the arched **Plaza de Ángel Albino Corzo**—has murals depicting scenes from local and national history, including portrayals of the Chiapa Indians, who threw themselves into the Sumidero Canyon to escape enslavement by the Spanish.

The fountain in Chiapa's plaza is connected to an abundant underground water source that helped townspeople to survive the epidemics that swept through much of Mexico in colonial times.

Nearly every Tuxtlan you meet will ask if you've taken the boat ride through the **Cañón del Sumidero** from Chiapa de Corzo. The locals' opinion of the place is exalted but justified: Gliding between the kilometer-high canyon walls is an experience not to be missed. The best way to enjoy the Cañón del Sumidero is to take the two-hour cruise along the Río Grijalva. The canyon is full of birds, crocodiles, and iguana, and your pilot will be more than eager to maneuver into caves and close to shore to point them out. In July and August, heavy rains create four waterfalls, the largest of which is the **Árbol de Navidad**, a conical plume of water that cascades down the green canyon wall in the shape of a giant Christmas tree. If you opt not to take the boat ride through the canyon, you can take a taxi from Tuxtla or Chiapa to any of four *miradores* (lookouts), which afford a bird's-eye view of Sumidero.

Those who would rather be in the water should head to **Cascada El Chorreadero,** a waterfall and swimming hole 7 kilometers east of Chiapa toward San Cristóbal. The site is most beautiful in the rainy season (June–September), when the waterfall is strongest. Go on a weekday if you want some solitude. To reach the falls, take any bus from Chiapa or Tuxtla toward San Cristóbal or pay $1.50 for a taxi. Return buses run along the highway all night long, though it's best to leave by dark.

COMING AND GOING Direct microbuses to Chiapa (30 min, 40¢) leave from 3a Oriente Sur and 3a Sur Oriente in Tuxtla every five to 10 minutes, 6 AM–8 PM. Chiapa's bus station is one block east of the zócalo on 21 de Octubre, but you can always jump on a bus as it passes the Parque Central. Several daily buses also depart for San Cristóbal (1 hr, $1) from here. To reach the zócalo from the station, follow the signs for the post office. Taxis between Tuxtla and Chiapa are also readily available and cost about $3.

Boat tours of the Sumidero Canyon originate from Chiapa's *embarcadero* (dock) and from the town of Cahuaré (about five minutes before Chiapa coming from Tuxtla). To reach Chiapa's embarcadero from the zócalo, head past the cathedral and down the hill on Calle 5 de Febrero for two blocks. Boats charge $55 for up to 10 people and $5.50 for each additional person. It's cheaper to hire *lanchas* (motorboats) in Cahuaré, but harder to form groups. Trips run daily, from early morning until around 4 PM. Come in the morning if you're alone and want to get in on a group deal.

WHERE TO SLEEP AND EAT Chiapa is an easy day trip from Tuxtla and even from San Cristóbal, so few visitors stay the night. **Hotel Los Ángeles** (Julián Grajales 2, southern end of zócalo, tel. 961/6–00–48) is the only budget lodging in town. The slightly grimy but spacious rooms cost $8 for singles and $10.75 for doubles, all with fans. In high season (December and January, Semana Santa, and late summer), it's best to call ahead and make reservations.

Central Chiapa has a number of food stands and small restaurants. For a little extra money and a lot more ambience, head down the hill to one of the restaurants at the embarcadero and try the local fare. You'll also get a view of the river and perhaps some live marimba music. **El Ausente** (embarcadero, no phone; open daily 8–6), a local favorite, serves a whopping plate of prawns fried in garlic with tortillas and condiments for $4. **Jardines de Chiapa** (Francisco I. Madero 395, 1 block from zócalo toward pier, tel. 968/6–01–98; open daily 9–8) serves tasty and unusual local specialties unavailable elsewhere, including *sopa fiestera,* a soup with shredded chicken, avocado, hard-boiled eggs, tomatoes, onions, cheese, and noodles ($1.50) and *chiplín con bolita* (balls of corn paste, tomato sauce, and cheese cooked with a local tarragonlike herb; $2.50). Dinners run $5–$10. Don't confuse this restaurant with another one of the same name on the zócalo. On a corner just outside the Museo de la Laca (*see* box, above), a local family sells some of the best pozol in Chiapas: Try both the *blanco* (consumed with chile and salt) and the chocolatey sweet cacao flavor. On weekdays the pozol is only served before noon, so come early.

FESTIVALS Every January, Chiapa de Corzo plays host to the lively **Fiesta de Enero.** The festival is kicked off on January 9 with a series of dances, including **La Chuntá,** in which men dress as women. On January 15, street dancers perform the **Parachico,** wearing wooden masks and mimicking Spanish conquistadores. The **Combate Naval,** a reproduction of a famous naval battle, takes place on January 21 on the river and is followed by a day or two of festivities.

Godly Gourds

Chiapa's master artisans are famous nationwide for the art of lacquerware, which involves a labor-intensive process in which a gourd is rubbed with fat, then with a natural colorant (such as charcoal or earth), and buffed. This process is repeated at least four times before the gourd is ready to be painted. The most common form of lacquerware is the jícara (bowl), used to serve food and drink such as pozol. The Popol Vuh (an ancient Maya codex) described the importance of the jícara in its creation myth: "The sky is no more than a immense blue jícara, the beloved firmament in the form of a cosmic bowl." The impressive and free Museo de la Laca (Lacquerware Museum; open Tues.–Sun. 10–4), on the top floor of the 16th-century Ex-Convento de Santo Domingo, behind the cathedral, has an extensive collection of bowls from all over the state.

San Cristóbal de las Casas

The capital of Chiapas until the 1890s, San Cristóbal still maintains an unmistakably colonial and mestizo-dominated feel. Crisp mornings see Chiapan highlanders in traditional dress flood the city's markets, main plazas, and church steps to sell homegrown produce and woven clothing. Long favored by European backpackers heading to and from Guatemala, the city has been receiving a more international crowd who are eager to show their solidarity with the Zapatistas. A large expatriate population means San Cristóbal is well equipped to cater to visitors with good coffee and a variety of healthy food. The city is the best base for exploring most of Chiapas. Here you can meet other travelers, find out which outlying areas are safe to visit, and discuss border-crossing strategies.

BASICS

BOOKSTORES Librería La Quimera (Real de Guadalupe 24-B, tel. 967/8–59–70; open Mon.–Sat. 9–2 and 4–8), run by a friendly Frenchman named Lucas, carries a wide selection of Spanish, English, French, and German literature. Books on Mayan culture and history are featured. **Soluna** (Real de Guadalupe 13-B, no phone) has a similar selection and is open weekdays 9:30–8:30. **La Pared** (Hidalgo 2, tel. 967/8–63–67) buys, sells, trades, and rents guidebooks, fiction, and nonfiction in several languages. They're open Monday–Saturday 10–2 and 4–8, Sunday 9–1 in high season; hours fluctuate in the off-season. They also provide the best fax and phone services in town.

CASAS DE CAMBIO Bancomer, Banamex, and Serfín, all clustered around the zócalo, exchange currency weekdays 9–11 AM. Banamex offers advances on both Visa and MasterCard but won't change traveler's checks. For after-hours or weekend currency exchange, go to **Casa de Cambio Lacantún** (Real de Guadalupe 12-A, tel. 967/8–30–63), half a block from the zócalo. It's open for exchanging cash and traveler's checks Monday–Saturday 9–2 and 4–8, Sunday 9–noon.

¡Viva Zapata!

On January 1, 1994, San Cristóbal de las Casas made front-page headlines abroad when the EZLN, made up mostly of Tzeltal and Tzotzil speakers, took over the main square and demanded national agrarian reform. The stated objective of the Zapatistas (the group's name honors Mexican revolutionary hero Emiliano Zapata) was to focus international attention on their demands for democratic reform, land redistribution, and improved education and health care for the region's desperately poor indigenous population. The occupation left the municipal palace in shambles and called into question the ruling elite's moral commitment to the poor, indigenous, and exploited.

Contrary to the impression created by the international press, the bulk of the initial armed conflicts took place around Ocosingo and the Lacandón jungle, not in San Cristóbal. Nevertheless, the EZLN's occupation continues to have an impact on Chiapas's second largest city. A statewide protest on April 10, 1996 drew 5,000 indígena farmers to San Cristóbal's zócalo, and the city remains a base for foreign volunteers of non-governmental organizations, who are helping to pick up the pieces in the face of stagnating peace talks and continued human rights violations.

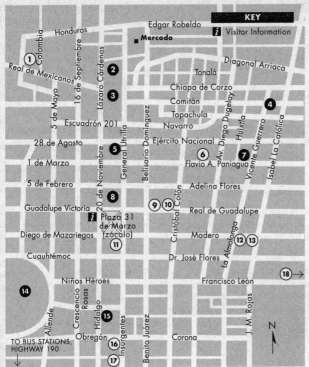

KEY

i Visitor Information

Sights ●

Casa de la
Cultura, **15**

Catedral, **8**

Ex-Convento de
Santo Domingo, **3**

Iglesia de
San Cristóbal de
las Casas, **14**

Museo Cultural
de los Altos, **2**

Museo del Ambar, **5**

Na-Bolom, **4**

Taller Leñateros, **7**

Lodging ○

Casa Margarita, **10**

Hotel Posada
San Cristóbal, **11**

Posada di Gladys, **1**

Posada
Insurgentes, **17**

Posada Jovel, **6**

Posada Lucella, **16**

Posada Quetzal, **12**

Posada
Santiago, **9**

Rancho San
Nicolás, **18**

Villa Betania, **13**

EMERGENCIES These days there are several different **police** units scattered around town, guarding against invisible insurgents. Call 967/8–05–54 in an emergency. For an ambulance, call the **Cruz Roja** at 967/8–07–72.

LAUNDRY Lavorama (Guadalupe Victoria 20-A, tel. 967/8–35–99; open Mon.–Sat. 9–7, Sun. 9–2) washes and irons your clothes in a couple of hours for $1 per kilo.

MAIL The post office will hold mail sent to you at the following address for up to 10 days: Lista de Correos, San Cristóbal de las Casas, Chiapas, CP 29200, México. *Cuauhtémoc 13, at Crescencio Rosas, tel. 967/8–07–65. Open weekdays 8–7, Sat. 9–1.*

MEDICAL AID The **Hospital Regional** (Insurgentes, at Santa Lucía, tel. 967/8–07–70) offers 24-hour emergency care. **Cruz Roja** (Prolongación Ignacio Allende 57, tel. 967/8–07–72) does the same, and it's free. **Farmacia Regina** (Diego de Mazariegos, at Crescencio Rosas, tel. 967/ 8–02–41) is open day and night; after 10 PM, knock on the metal door for service.

PHONES To use the public phones in front of the Palacio Municipal, buy your Ladatel Plus cards at the telephone office (cnr of Niños Héroes and Miguel Hidalgo) before 1:30 PM weekdays, or at **Casa de Cambio Lacantún** (*see above*). **El Puente** (*see* Schools, *below*) claims they will beat anyone's rate for long-distance and collect calls Monday–Saturday 7 AM–10:30 PM.

SCHOOLS The **Centro Bilingüe**, in **El Puente** cultural center, offers Spanish classes year-round for $140 per week (walk-in rate), including 15 hours of one-on-one instruction per week and room and board with a local family. Their cultural center hosts craft workshops, videos, and live music on a regular basis. A comfortable café, travel agency, and art gallery complete the package. Pre-registration from the states is subject to higher tuition and a nonrefundable $75 fee. *Real de Guadalupe 55, tel. 967/8–41–57, fax 967/8–37–23. In U.S., call 800/ 300–4983. Mailing address: Real de Guadalupe 55, San Cristóbal de las Casas, Chiapas, CP 29230, México.*

TOURS AND GUIDES Privately run tours to the ruins and the surrounding indigenous communities are cheaper than those arranged by travel agencies. See Moisés at **Casa Margarita** (Real de Guadalupe 34, tel. 967/8–09–57) for information about trips to Toniná, the Sumidero Canyon, Palenque, Agua Azul, and the Lacandón jungle. Prices may seem steep to budget travelers ($130 per person for a minimum of four people to see the Lacandón jungle, Yaxchilán, and Bonampak; around $20 for day trips to Palenque and other sites), but keep in mind that the cost includes a bilingual guide, transportation, and several meals. For a guided visit to nearby villages, meet Mercedes Hernández Gómez (*see* Near San Cristóbal, *below*) on the zócalo at 9 AM.

VISITOR INFORMATION The local **SEDETUR** tourist office (Miguel Hidalgo 2, west of Palacio Municipal, tel. 967/8–06–70) can answer questions in English and French Monday–Saturday 9–8, Sunday 9–2. They provide free maps and their bulletin board often has notices about cheap rooms for rent in private homes. **SECTUR** (Hidalgo, next to La Pared; open Mon.–Sat. 9–9, Sun. 9–2), the national tourist office, is better equipped to answer questions about the entire state of Chiapas.

VOLUNTEERING Na-Bolom (*see* Worth Seeing, *below*) receives volunteers who are willing to donate a minimum of three months to photo archival, reforestation, and cultural preservation projects. Room and board are provided for full-time volunteers. *Mailing address: c/o Ana Maria Visser, Vicente Guerrero 33, San Cristóbol de las Casas, Chiapas, CP 29220, México.*

Global Exchange offers several volunteer opportunities in and around San Cristóbal, including working in civilian peace camps, attending seven-day human rights delegations, and working in San Cristóbal's international peace center. Volunteers should be fluent in Spanish, knowledgeable about the current political situation, and able to support themselves in Mexico. Write to: *Global Exchange, Attn. Ted Lewis, 2017 Mission St. Suite 303, San Francisco, CA 94110. In the U.S., tel. 415/255–7296, fax 415/255–7498, globalexch@igc.org.*

COMING AND GOING

BY BUS From the first-class **Cristóbal Colón** bus terminal (Insurgentes, about 8 blocks south of zócalo, tel. 967/8–02–91), buses depart daily for Mexico City (4 per day, 21 hrs, $35), with luxury service ($45) at 4:30 PM. Buses also leave daily for Oaxaca city (4 per day, 12 hrs, $16); Ocosingo (4 per day, 3 hrs, $2); Palenque (7½ hrs, $4), with two buses at 9 AM and frequent buses in the evening; Tapachula (4 per day, 9 hrs, $8); Tuxtla Gutiérrez (2 hrs, $2) and Comitán (1½hrs, $1.25), hourly 6:30 AM–10 PM; Mérida (15 hrs, $20) at 5:30 PM and 7:30 PM; and even Cancún (21 hrs, $30) at 4:35 PM. It's wise to book ahead since buses fill up quickly.

Several second-class bus stations along the Carretera Internacional can get you almost anywhere in Chiapas cheaper than Colón. At **Transportes Tuxtla Gutiérrez** (Allende, ½ block up from Carretera Internacional, tel. 967/8–48–69), 10 buses per day serve Palenque (8 hrs, $3.50), with a stop in Ocosingo (3½ hrs, $2). There's hourly service to Tuxtla Gutiérrez (2 hrs, $1.25) and Comitán (2 hrs, $1) during the day.

Sketchy school buses and microbuses run by **Transportes Lacandonia** (Pino Suárez, at Carretera Internacional, tel. 967/8–14–55) leave for Ocosingo (3½ hrs, $1.75) and Palenque (8 hrs, $3.50) almost every hour 7 AM–6 PM. Buses also run to Villahermosa (9 hrs, $6) at 7 AM and to Mérida (18 hrs, $15) at 6 PM. To reach the station from the zócalo, walk eight blocks down Insurgentes to the Carretera Internacional, then head right two blocks. All prices and durations are subject to change, due to volatile gas prices and frequent roadblocks.

GETTING AROUND

Most sights are within easy walking distance of the center, and the farthest are only a 20- or 30-minute walk away. The hub of the town is the zócalo, otherwise called the **Plaza 31 de Marzo,** which is bordered on the north by the cathedral. Although they're clearly labeled, remember that all streets change names as they cross the zócalo.

BY BUS Crowded colectivos and cramped combis run until about 10 PM, charging 20¢ per ride. Major routes are north–south along Insurgentes/Utrilla from the Carretera Internacional to the market, and east–west along Real de Guadalupe/Guadalupe Victoria. To get a ride, flag down one of the always attentive drivers at any point on the road and pay him directly. To get off, shout "¡Se baja!" ("Someone's getting off!").

BY TAXI Taxis await passengers in front of the cathedral on the north side of the zócalo. Rates within the city and to and from the bus stations are standardized; without baggage the cost is $1, with baggage $1.50. Rates to surrounding sites and villages are negotiable.

BY BIKE Bicicrent (Blvd. Domínguez 5-B, no phone) will lead you to local villages, take you to remote mountain paths, or let you cruise on your own for $10 a day; they're open daily 9–8. **Bici-Tours Los Pinguinos** (5 de Mayo 10-B, tel. 967/8–02–02; open daily 9–2 and 3:30–6:30) rents bikes for $1.25 an hour or $10 a day; guided tours are $7 for a half day, $15 for a full day.

WHERE TO SLEEP

Loads of hotels—many with colonial flourishes—have sprung up here in the last two decades. Competition keeps prices low and cleanliness standards high. Several good *posadas* (inns) are located along Insurgentes, just north of the Cristóbol Colón terminal. Especially noteworthy are **Posada Insurgentes** (Insurgentes 73, no phone) and **Posada Lucella** (Insurgentes 55, tel. 967/8–09–56), with cheap ($4–$5 per person), warm rooms. The new **Posada Quetzal** (Madero 81, no phone) offers cheap and secure rooms ($2 per person, shared bath; $3.25 per person with private bath) next door to the popular but shady **Hospedaje Bed and Breakfast.** No matter where you stay, make sure the hot water is in working order; the morning air in San Cristóbal can be chilly. Look on bulletin boards at the tourist office and in bookstores for rooms for rent in people's homes: Clean and hospitable digs can be had for $2–$4 per person during busy tourist seasons, when hotels fill up quickly.

➢ **UNDER $10 • Casa Margarita.** At this formerly private mansion, rooms have high ceilings and triple-blanketed beds. Coed dorm beds cost $3, singles $5, doubles $7. Everyone shares the clean communal bathrooms, and the showers are hot until the water runs out. Here you can make contact with lost companions via the bulletin board and arrange horseback-riding trips and excursions (*see* Tours and Guides, *above*). *Real de Guadalupe 34, 3 blocks east of zócalo, tel. 967/8–09–57. 26 rooms, none with bath. Laundry, luggage storage, money exchange, travel agency. Reservations advised. Wheelchair access.*

Posada di Gladys. You'll feel like one of the family in this inn's cozy dorm-style rooms ($2.75 per person). Private doubles with shared bath and hot water are also available for $6.75. Camping and hammock spots ($2 per person) surround the sociable patio. Gladys serves breakfast in the morning and locks the front door at 11 PM. Ask about horse and bike rentals. *Real de Mexicanos 16, tel. 967/8–57–75. From Santo Domingo, walk 2 blocks west. 15 beds, none with bath. Laundry sink, luggage storage.*

Posada Jovel. Ideally located a few blocks from the hustle and bustle of the center, this posada's third-floor doubles with private bath ($8) offer breezy views and plenty of hot water. Avoid the tiny, cell-like second-floor singles with communal baths ($4.75). The friendly family serves a good breakfast and rents horses for touring. *Flavio A. Paniagua 28, btw Cristóbal Colón and Dugelay, tel. 967/8–17–34. 19 rooms, 6 with bath. Laundry, luggage storage.*

Posada Santiago. Next door to Casa Margarita, Santiago's small rooms are dark and comfortable. Clean singles ($6.50) and doubles ($9.50) all have private baths with hot water. The rooftop terrace and good café promote socializing. *Real de Guadalupe 32, tel. 967/8–00–24. 9 rooms, all with bath. Luggage storage. MC, V.*

Villa Betania. This hotel offers a homey refuge on the sedated east side of town. Spacious singles ($5.50) and doubles ($8) are spotless and have private baths with hot water. The Salazar family encourages you to use their kitchen and rooftop terrace, or you can watch TV with them in the living room. *Madero 87, tel. 967/8–44–67. 4½ long blocks east of zócalo. 7 rooms, all with bath. Kitchen, laundry sink, luggage storage. Reservations advised. Wheelchair access.*

➤ **UNDER $20** • **Hotel Posada San Cristóbal.** The huge rooms in this grand old building have high ceilings, white walls, dark plank floors, antique furniture, and tall, heavy French doors that block all light and sound. Newly remodeled bathrooms and balconies off every room are a plus. Singles are $15, doubles $19, triples $23, and quadruples $25. *Insurgentes 2, 2 blocks south of zócalo, tel. 967/8–38–42. 10 rooms, all with bath. Luggage storage.*

CAMPING **Rancho San Nicolás Camping and Trailer Park** (tel. 967/8–00–57), less than 2 kilometers east of town, is ideally situated at the end of Francisco León. Facilities include kitchens, electricity, and hot water for showers. Camping for two people costs $2.50; a cabin for two is about $5. If you don't mind going without amenities, you can bypass the park and camp for free a short way downriver. To get here, catch a RANCHO SAN NICOLAS combi (20¢) on Francisco León.

FOOD

The large expatriate presence has had a decisive influence on San Cristóbal's cuisine. In addition to Chiapan fare, many restaurants and cafés serve yogurt, whole-wheat bread, green salads, and pizza. Locals congregate around **Los Merenderos** (Insurgentes, near Iglesia de San Francisco), a group of cheap food stands, until the wee hours of the morn. Also look for red lamps hanging outside homes on weekends: They signal that toothsome tamales and atole (20¢) await within. Insurgentes 3 is a good place to try. If you have $5 to spend, the Sunday brunch at **Na-Bolom** (*see* Worth Seeing, *below*) is a must. The spread includes organic vegetable dishes and salads from their garden, as well as meat entrées, drinks, and dessert.

➤ **UNDER $5** • **Casa de Pan.** This bakery/restaurant is run by friendly baker extraordinaire Kippy Nigh. Fresh bread, the best bagels in Mexico, organic salads, and veggie empanadas with curry ($2) are served on the meditative patio. Popular breakfast plates ($2.50) include fresh fruit, tea, and bread. There's live music Thursday–Saturday (nightly during high season). *Navarro 10, at Domínguez, tel. 967/8–04–68. Open Mon.–Sat. 8 AM–10 PM.*

Comedor Familiar Normita II. Set yourself down in Norma's recently refurbished kitchen and enjoy the tasty enchiladas in red mole ($2) or the red Jalisco-style pozole ($2). A fireplace takes the bite out of the cold mountain air. *Benito Juárez 6, at José Flores, no phone. Open Mon.–Sat. 8 AM–10 PM.*

Madre Tierra. "Mother Earth" gives birth to homemade yogurt, whole-wheat bread, and big bowls of vegetable soup ($1.75), but the *platos del día* ($3.25), with your choice of chicken or vegetarian entrée, are the best deals. The white iron chairs on the patio make for a good place to enjoy a casual beer when it's not raining. There's live Latin music upstairs on weekends (no cover). *Insurgentes 19, 3 blocks south of zócalo, tel. 967/8–42–97. Open daily 8 AM–9:45 PM. Bakery open Mon.–Sat. 9–8, Sun. 9–2.*

Restaurant Las Estrellas. Tangy brown rice with veggies and salad will set you back $1 at this unpretentious but tourist-filled eatery. A heaping plate of spaghetti with meat sauce ($1.50) and the filling quiche ($1.25), followed by a goblet of creamy hot chocolate (75¢), primes you for a deep sleep. If you're still awake, the pies (70¢), especially the lemon chiffon, are wonderful. *Escuadrón 201 No. 6-B, in front of Santo Domingo, no phone. Open daily 9 AM–10 PM.*

➤ **UNDER $10** • **El Fogón de Jovel.** Traditional Chiapan fare is served in an open-air colonial patio setting. The *parrilla coleto* (Chiapan mixed grill; $6) presents the best of local meats with a salad; plenty of veggie selections and a tamale sampler ($2.50) round out the menu. A full bar of regional moonshine cocktails ($1) is backed by live marimba daily. *16 de Septiembre 11, tel. 967/8–25–57. Open daily 12:30–10. AE, MC, V.*

DESSERT/COFFEEHOUSES Espresso, cappuccino, tea, and pastries are always at hand in San Cristóbal. **Café Bar Los Amorosos** (Dr. José Felipe Flores 12-A, at Blvd. Domínguez, no phone; open daily 9 AM–midnight), in the Jaime Sabines cultural center, is the preferred haunt of local intellectuals and artists. The patio out back is an ideal spot to sample the bevy of cof-

`fee drinks (50¢–$1) and philosophize. Locals spend hours playing chess and reading newspapers at **Cafetería San Cristóbal** (Cuauhtémoc 2, at Insurgentes, no phone; open Mon.–Sat. 10–8). Coffee and espresso are 50¢; the excellent desserts are $1. The spacious, sun-lit parlor above the popular café/art gallery/handicrafts shop **La Galería** (Hidalgo 3, south of zócalo, tel. 967/8–15–47) lures locals and foreigners alike with their excellent pies and cakes (less than $2) and live music after 8:30 PM. The **Casa de las Imágenes** (Blvd. Domínguez 11, no phone) is a multipurpose space housing a café, art gallery, bookstore, and occasional foreign films. Stop by and see what's shakin'.

WORTH SEEING

San Cristóbal is a conglomeration of many neighborhoods, each with its own church and patron saint, but the center of town is the **Plaza 31 de Marzo**, or the zócalo. The **Hotel Santa Clara**, on the south side of the zócalo, was supposedly the house of conquistador Diego de Mazariegos and is adorned with stone sirens and the royal lions of Castille, Spain. On the north side of the zócalo is the **Catedral.** It was first constructed in 1528 as a run-of-the-mill church, but 10 years later the pontiff declared it a cathedral, and paintings, altars, and an ornate facade were added. San Cristóbal's daily **market** (8 blocks north of zócalo on Utrilla) is a huge conglomeration of vegetables, tropical fruits, medicinal herbs, poultry, and cassette stands blaring reproduced regional music and American pop from dusk to early afternoon. The produce comes from the small plots of land farmed by local Tzotzil and Tzeltal people.

Typically filled with political and human rights overtones, Sunday Spanish mass at the cathedral (held 6 AM, noon, and 7 PM) is given by Bishop Samuel Ruíz when he's not busy mediating peace talks between the Mexican government and the EZLN in San Andrés Larrainzar.

For a good view of the city, walk seven blocks east of the zócalo on Real de Guadalupe and continue up the stairs to the yellow-and-white **Iglesia de Guadalupe.** You can see even farther from the **Iglesia de San Cristóbal de las Casas,** at the opposite end of the city, west of Allende. A 15-minute climb to the top leads you to the vista point and a quirky cross made from discarded license plates.

CENTRO DE ESTUDIOS CIENTIFICOS NA-BOLOM This cultural center, museum, library, garden, home, and guest house is devoted to the study and preservation of the culture and rain forest environment of the Lacandón Indians. The center was established by the late Frans and Gertrude Blom, a Danish/Swiss couple who dedicated much of their lives to the study of and advocacy for the Lacandón people. The house has a comfortable library (open Mon.–Thurs. 8–3, Fri. 8–11:30 AM) housing 2,500 books on Chiapan culture, as well as travel guides, the Bloms' writings, and other books on Mexico. Frans's collection of religious art is on display in the chapel; an exhibit of Lacandón artifacts fills the museum; and Gertrude's black-and-white photos of Chiapan Indians decorate the halls of the house. The bookstore carries volumes of Gertrude's photography and Frans's map of the Lacandón jungle, supposedly the best available.

Hour-long tours ($2) take place twice a day and are followed by a film. Rooms ($25–$32) and meals ($3.50–$5) are some of the best in town. Make reservations in the morning for meals, and reserve way in advance for rooms. *Vicente Guerrero 33, at Comitán, tel. and fax 967/ 8–14–18 or 967/8–55–86. Tours Tues.–Sun. in English at 11:30 and 4:30, Spanish at 11:45 and 4:45. Café open ½ hour before tours.*

MUSEO CULTURAL DE LOS ALTOS DE CHIAPAS At this small museum focusing on local history and culture, all posted explanations are in Spanish, but you'll get the gist even if you can't read the signs. The upstairs exhibits focus on the *encomienda* system, by which the conquistadores were awarded the right to exact tribute from certain groups of Indians, and on the quantities of booty the Spanish sent back to Europe. Textiles from surrounding indigenous communities are displayed downstairs. *Next to Ex-Convento de Santo Domingo. Admission free. Open Tues.–Sun. 10–5.*

MUSEO DEL AMBAR DE LOS ALTOS DE CHIAPAS Amber, a dark yellow fossil tree resin, is displayed and sold at this tiny museum. Most of it comes from the Simojovel Valley and Totolapa, two of only a few areas in Mexico where amber is still mined. After excavation, the amber is tediously polished and set in earrings, necklaces, and other ornaments and sold at a moderate price—especially when you consider that some sediment and bugs trapped in amber have been carbon-dated to the Jurassic period. Be sure to check out the display of ants, beetles, butterflies, and mosquitos trapped in the resin, as well as the carvings of Mayan figures. *Utrilla 10, 2 blocks north of zócalo, tel. 967/8–35–07. Open Sun.–Fri. 9–7.*

TALLER LENATEROS This award-winning press has been producing handmade stationery, books, and silk screens—all out of 100% natural and recycled materials—for almost 20 years. The facility is open to the public for free hands-on tours in English and Spanish that guide visitors through the paper-making process. Check out their publication, *La Jícara*—a literary review featuring major Mexican writers and Mayan poets, printed with silkscreen and original block prints. *Flavio A. Paniagua 54, tel. 967/8–51–74. Open Mon.–Sat. 9–5. Donations encouraged.*

CHEAP THRILLS

The **Casa de Cultura** (Hidalgo, across from Iglesia del Carmen, no phone) sponsors a diverse range of events, including concerts, films, and lectures. If you want to shoot some pool, **billiards parlors** can be found on Madero, just east of the zócalo; unaccompanied women may feel uncomfortable at these places at night. A relaxing treat, particularly if your hotel doesn't have hot water, are the **Baños Mercedarios,** where you can choose between a private steam or dry-heat sauna followed by a shower. The whole ritual comes to less than $3. Soap, towels, razors, and refreshments cost about 50¢ each. *1 de Marzo 55, tel. 967/8–10–06. Open Mon.–Sat. 6 AM–7 PM, Sun. 6 AM–2 PM.*

FESTIVALS

With its many neighborhoods and their patron saints, San Cristóbal celebrates something almost every week. Relatively reserved during Semana Santa, Chiapans come out of their shells during the annual **Fería de la Primavera y la Paz,** which takes place the week after Easter Sunday. Bull- and cockfights, ballet and folkoric dance, parades, and choral music all take place amidst a carnival-like atmosphere at the fairgrounds south of town. Most events are free. On November 22, the **Fiesta de Santa Cecilia,** honoring the patron saint of musicians, is held. Other festivals include the **Fiesta de San Cristóbal** on July 25 and the **Fiesta de la Virgen de Guadalupe,** held December 12–14. Check with SEDETUR (*see* Visitor Information, *above*) for a comprehensive list of events, prices, and locations.

Sergio Castro's Private Museum

A longtime resident of Chiapas, Sergio Castro has dedicated most of his life to preserving local indigenous cultures, working particularly with the Tzotzil community of Chamula. Today he has a one-of-a-kind collection of indigenous textiles and a detailed photographic record of local community development projects. Sergio works 7–5 every day in local indigenous communities and entertains small groups at his house (Guadalupe Victoria 47, tel. 967/8–42–89) after 6 PM. You'll need to get some friends together and call in advance after 4 PM for an appointment, but the effort is well worth it—Sergio is one of the best resources in the area for Chiapan history and current events. The tour is free, but donations are strongly encouraged. Sergio speaks some French, English, and Italian as well as Spanish.

SHOPPING

Once upon a time, San Cristóbal was divided into sectors, each dedicated to one trade or skill. Those in the sector of La Merced, for example, were known for their candle work, and would sell or trade candles to the merchants in the central sector, who were skilled in making sweets and *embutidos* (jam-filled candies). The tradition still continues: The sector of San Antonio is well-known for its fireworks, La Cerrería for its carpentry, and San Ramón for its baked goods. Shops crowd Real de Guadalupe and Utrilla, selling quality woven and leather goods and amber jewelry. You can also buy Guatemalan goods in many of these shops, but they cost a lot more than they would across the border. The finest weaving is to be found in the cooperatives Sna Jolobil and J'pas Joloviletik (*see below*) and the government-run Casa de Las Artesanías de Chiapas (*see below*). Don't buy amber off the street—it could easily be plastic or glass.

CASA DE LAS ARTESANIAS DE CHIAPAS   This store/museum is run by a government program meant to encourage handicraft production while improving the quality of life in indigenous villages. The handicrafts for sale are quality controlled, and the excellent ethnographic museum is free. *Hidalgo, at Niños Héroes, tel. 967/8–11–80. Open Mon.–Sat. 9–2 and 5–8.*

SNA JOLOBIL AND J'PAS JOLOVILETIK   Housed in the 16th-century **Ex-Convento de Santo Domingo,** Sna Jolobil (Utrilla, at Comitán, tel. 967/8–26–46) functions as an outlet store for a weaver's cooperative made up of about 800 Tzotzil and Tzeltal women. The cooperative's aim is to preserve Mayan techniques of weaving on the back-strap loom, and to ensure that the artisans receive a fair price for their work. Local *huipiles* (embroidered tunics), wool vests, brocade shirts, and ribboned hats are displayed and sold here. Depending on the tourist flow, the store is open Monday–Saturday 9–2 and 4–7, Sunday 9–2. J'pas Joloviletik (Utrilla 43, tel. 967/8–28–48), another weaver's cooperative store across the street, is open Monday–Saturday 9–1 and 4–7, Sunday 9–1.

AFTER DARK

San Cristóbal holds tightly to Mexican colonial traditions: In the evenings, especially on Sundays, everyone congregates on the zócalo, strolling with cotton candy or popcorn from the numerous stands and soaking in the scene. Many restaurants feature live music around dinnertime (from 8 PM on), usually without a cover charge. The few spots that stay open past midnight cater strictly to tourists, with the exception of the teenybopper discos near the highway. For the best salsa and *nueva canción* (Latin American folk music), try **La Galería, Madre Tierra,** or **Casa de Pan** (*see* Food, *above*), where the music starts around 9 PM. For candlelit ambience decorated with images of Marilyn Monroe and Jim Morrison, try **Las Velas Bar** (Madero 14, no phone). Live music (salsa, rock, reggae) starts at around 11 PM; crowds suck down $1 beers until 3 AM. Cultural center **El Puente** (*see* Schools, *above*), run by California expatriate Bill English, shows free, smart international films Tuesday–Saturday at 8 PM.

OUTDOOR ACTIVITIES

Trails for hiking and mountain biking abound in the mountains surrounding San Cristóbal. For more detailed info on trails and bike rentals, head to the bike shops listed in Getting Around, *above.* You can also take horseback-riding excursions to Chamula or **Las Grutas de San Cristóbal,** dank, stalactite- and stalagmite-filled caves about 11 kilometers (6 mi) southeast of town; bring a flashlight. Two-hour horseback trips from Casa Margarita (*see* Where to Sleep, *above*) cost $20–$25 per person. Others leave from **Hotel Real del Valle** (Real de Guadalupe 14, tel. 967/8–06–80) and cost $25–$30 per person. Alternately, head out to the grutas by hopping on any Comitán-bound bus and telling the driver where to let you off. Many individuals post flyers in budget hotels about horse rentals, which are usually considerably cheaper than private tours; ask around.

The **Huitepec Ecological Reserve,** just 3 kilometers out of town, is alive with hundreds of birds, bright flowers, and 600 species of plants. There's a 4-kilometer loop trail that affords a quiet, 1½-hour hike up through the cloud forest on the side of the Muktevitz volcano. The reserve is run by **Pronatura** (Juarez 9, tel. 967/8–50–00), a conservation group in San Cristóbal that buys land and establishes parks to preserve wildlife for educational purposes and to promote sustainable farming alternatives. To reach the reserve, take a colectivo bound for Chamula or Zinacantán from the market and ask to be let off at Huitepec; or hire a taxi from town ($2). Sign up in advance for group tours (donations encouraged) at the Pronatura office. Admission to the park is free, and it's open Tuesday–Sunday 9–5.

Near San Cristóbal

Several indigenous communities, each 30 minutes to two hours from San Cristóbal, can easily be visited on day trips. Sundays—when Tzotzil and Tzeltal people from the surrounding highlands congregate in the markets to sell livestock, fruits, vegetables, and textiles—are the best days to go. Wonderful tours to Chamula and Zinacantán are led by Mercedes Hernández Gómez, who grew up in Zinacantán and speaks English. Look for Mercedes's umbrella daily (except major holidays) around the kiosk in the zócalo. The tour includes transportation and is well worth the $8.

If you look closely in Chamula, you'll notice mirrors behind the saints in the church and tiny mirrors sewn into some of the women's blouses. Chamulans believe that evil is reflected by mirrors—which is probably why people feel you've snatched their soul when you take a picture of them.

All villages listed below are accessible by infrequent bus service or VW colectivo, with the exception of Zinacantán and Chamula, which are served frequently. If you do choose to go on your own, dress conservatively, leave your camera at home, and stick to the main public areas—injudicious wandering will not be appreciated.

SAN JUAN CHAMULA Chamula's wood-and-mud houses and the surrounding cornfields spread out into a small valley. Residents are recognizable by their dark blue shawls and shirts, with ribboned braids for women and wool serapes and leather belts for men. The religion of the Chamula people is unique in that it's a hybrid of Mayan rituals and Catholicism: In their church you'll see patron "saints" not found in the Bible, and the cross they've erected is not the Catholic cross, but a broader Mayan style that you'll find in archaeological stelae around the region. Atypical of a Catholic church, the floor is devoid of pews and covered with pine needles. Shamans heal sick villagers here and conduct other ceremonies. Ever since Evangelical Protestant missionaries arrived in 1968, outsiders have been treated with detached suspicion. Heed posted warnings about photography when you enter the church (admission 70¢) and keep your distance from worshippers.

The best time to visit Chamula is during the Sunday morning market, when thousands descend from their *parajes* (parishes) to the ceremonial center to socialize, visit shamans, and take care of business. One of the most impressive Chiapan festivals is San Juan Chamula's **Carnaval,** one week before Ash Wednesday, when Chamulans dance atop fire to purify their souls. Colectivos to Chamula (20 min, 70¢) leave from the San Cristóbal market.

ZINACANTEÁN The men of Zinacantán wear elaborate, hot pink serapes; the women wear beautifully embroidered huipiles and colorful shawls with red borders. This quiet town's main industry is the cultivation and sale of chrysanthemums and gladiolas. Sunday morning brings a small market (come early for the freshest flowers) and religious services; if you're lucky you may also catch the town's elders—wearing ceremonial white shorts with high-backed Mayan sandals—as they exit the church playing handmade guitars, harps, and drums. The new **Ik'al Ojov museum** (Isabel la Católica, at 5 de Febrero, open daily 9–6) presents a collection of local clothing, historical photography, and musical instruments. To reach Zinacantán, take a VW colectivo (30 min, 70¢) from the San Cristóbal market. There is also a footpath between Zinacantán and Chamula, but it has been the site of several assaults and should be avoided.

Shamans in the Chiapan highlands use a variety of materials to heal the sick: Eggs and white chickens remove impurities, while Coke or Pepsi causes burping, a signal that evil spirits are leaving the body.

SAN ANDRES LARRAINZAR The Tzotzil village of San Andrés is about half an hour north of Chamula by bus. The people are friendly, and the Sunday market is interesting mainly for the brocade shirts sold here. San Andrés continues to make international headlines as the host of peace negotiations between the Zapatistas and the Mexican government. Be sure to make the 15-minute trek from the center of town to the **Iglesia de Guadalupe,** which offers a stunning view of the surrounding highlands. The town's major festivals include the Fiesta de Santiago Apóstol (July 24–26), the Fiesta de la Virgen de Guadalupe de Santa Lucía (December 12–13), and the Fiesta de San Andrés (November 30), featuring drunken dancing, music, and loads of pyrotechnics. Buses to San Andrés (45 min, $1) leave from San Cristóbal's market. There are no hotels, so leave early to catch a colectivo from the church back to San Cristóbal.

Historically, shamans worked with psychoactive substances such as peyote and mushrooms to produce trance states. Distilled alcohols, introduced by the Spaniards, replaced these drugs; a rise in alcoholism has been an unfortunate side effect.

CHENALHO The less-touristed town of Chenalhó lies about an hour's bus ride north of San Cristóbal through tiny settlements and dramatic mountain scenery. On Sundays, a market fans out from the Iglesia de San Pedro in the center of town. The major festival here (June 27–30) honors San Pedro and features a terrific procession of horses, children, women, and men in their traditional garb, chanting in Tzeltal as they carry a statue of their patron saint into the incense-fogged church. Buses (70¢) depart from San Cristóbal's market. If you don't plan to stay over, plan a morning visit, since colectivos become scarce in late afternoon.

The Father, Sun, and Holy Ghost

While pre-Hispanic religions are still practiced in various forms throughout Mexico, the beliefs of many modern indigenous people combine the symbols and deities of their ancestors with the Catholicism brought by the Spaniards and the Protestantism of more recent missionaries. The conventional exteriors of Catholic churches in the Indian pueblos of southern Mexico often give way to pine-strewn, candlelit interiors redolent of the fumes of copal, an incense sacred to the Maya. The sun god of the Mayan pantheon has been recast in the figure of Jesus Christ—who has taken on many of his attributes—and San Juan Bautista is worshipped with many of the ritual elements once reserved for Chaac, god of rain and lightning. The most famous example of this sort of syncretism is the cult of the Virgin of Guadalupe, the brown-skinned Mary who first appeared in 1531 in a vision to a converted indígena, Juan Diego, on the hill of Tepeyacac.

Even before the Spanish arrived in Mexico, however, the groundwork was laid for a union of Christian and native religions. The symbol of the cross, for example, was a potent one for ancient Mexico; it is said that just before he disappeared from the Earth, the feathered serpent god Quetzalcoatl planted a giant wooden cross on the beach at Huatulco that resisted all efforts to pull it down. The cross symbolized the ceiba tree that held up the Mesoamerican world, and life itself. Also, the stone covering the sarcophagus of Lord Escudo Pakal, 7th-century ruler of Palenque, depicts his descent into the underworld with a giant cross, representing life, emerging from his body. And the underground tombs of Mitla beneath the Columnas de Vida also form a cross. Today, pine branches (another symbol of life) are tied to crosses overlooking highland towns, a testament to the blending of Mesoamerican and European beliefs.

AMATENANGO DEL VALLE This Tzeltal town, about 39 kilometers (22 mi) south of San Cristóbal on the road to Comitán, is known for its pottery. Local red clay is mixed with black or white sand, and a ground rock called *bash* is added to help the pottery harden. The work is done entirely by hand, without the aid of a pottery wheel (incredible, given the uniformity of the pieces). The town may seem deserted at first, but soon a child will probably approach and ask you to look at her clay animals. People work out of their houses and are likely to invite you in to look at their wares if you show an interest. The major festivals here are celebrations of patron saints: Village patron San Francisco is honored April 28–30, San Pedro Mártir on October 4, and Santa Lucía on December 13. Any Comitán-bound bus (40 min, 70¢) will get you here.

Palenque

The ruined Classic Mayan city of Palenque is truly magical. As you watch the morning mist rise over the temples and listen to the unmistakable pitch of the howler monkeys reverberate through the jungle, it's hard not to be awestruck. The nearby modern-day town of Palenque isn't half as impressive, but it remains surprisingly friendly despite recent rapid growth. The Zapatista uprising shut down a number of businesses, but tourism has returned at unprecedented levels, which means you'll have to enjoy the ruins with hordes of package tourists who descend on Palenque's archaeological sites. Start your day early and plan a leisurely exploration of the ruins and rain forests: The dense and exotic jungle vistas from atop Palenque's temples are not to be missed.

BASICS

CASAS DE CAMBIO Queue up early and expect to wait up to two hours to exchange traveler's checks and receive Visa advances at either **Bancomer** (Juárez 25, tel. 934/5–01–98) or **Banamex** (Juárez 28, tel. 934/5–01–30), both a few blocks west of the Parque Central. Both are open weekdays 10–noon and have ATMs. **Viajes Yax-ha** (Juárez, at Aldama; open daily 8 AM–9 PM), along with most other travel agencies, changes cash and traveler's checks at lousy rates.

LAUNDRY If you leave your clothes early in the morning, **Lavandería Mundo Maya** will wash and dry a 3-kilo load for $2 by the end of the day. *Jiménez 2, 1 block south of Parque Central, no phone. Open Mon.–Sat. 7–7.*

MEDICAL AID The **Centro de Salud** (Prolongación Juárez, tel. 934/5–00–25), at the west end of town, is open weekdays 7 AM–8 PM and charges $2 for a general consultation. Next door the **Hospital Regional** (tel. 934/5–07–33) has expensive 24-hour emergency service. **Farmacia Lastra** (Juárez, at Allende, no phone) is the place for 24-hour self-medication.

PHONES AND MAIL The blue Ladatel **phones** around the Parque Central are plagued by vandalism, but if they're in working order, they're your best bet (dial 09 for an international collect call). The 24-hour **caseta de larga distancia** (Juárez, next to Hotel Misol-Ha, tel. 934 5–12–71) offers the best phone and fax service in town. A temporary **post office** in the Casa de Cultura has the usual services and will hold mail sent to you at the following address for up to 10 days: Lista de Correos, Palenque, Chiapas, CP 29960, México. *South side of Parque Central. Open weekdays 9–1 and 3–6, Sat. 9–1.*

TOURS AND GUIDES A number of travel agencies offer charter flights and other package deals to Bonampak, Yaxchilán, Tikal, and the Lacandón jungle. Two-day trips to Yaxchilán and Bonampak include transportation, meals, lodging, and guides for $55 per person. Day trips to Yaxchilán (van and boat) and Bonampak (van and a two-hour hike) cost about $40 and $30 per person, respectively. Most require a minimum of four people. Other options include jungle tours, horseback riding, and fishing trips. Most agencies are clustered around Avenida Juárez between Allende and Abasolo, and coordinate with each other in putting groups together. Travelers who have taken the trips advise you to establish a big group and haggle like mad.

STS (Jiménez 6, in Hotel Palenque, tel. 934/5–13–54) is run by young, enterprising students who are eager to please (and undercut the competition). Pick up a flyer from Francoise or Fernando for a free map of town and additional discounts on their already low prices. Other reputable agencies include **Viajes Misol-Ha** (Juárez 48, tel. 934/5–04–88), **Viajes Toniná** (Juárez 105, tel. 934/5–02–09), and **Viajes Yax-Ha** (Juárez 123, tel. 934/5–07–67). If you want to see the Chiapan countryside, ruins, and sites on your own, these agencies will rent you a VW bug for $36 per day with 300 free kilometers and insurance.

VISITOR INFORMATION There are two tourist offices in town: The smaller office (Juárez, in Mercado de Artesanías; open weekdays 8 AM–9 PM, Sat. 8–7) has an English-speaking staff, but tends to be short on maps. The main office (Jiménez, at 5 de Mayo, tel. 934/5–03–56; open weekdays 9–3 and 6–9), on the southeast end of the park, is somewhat disorganized but friendly. They hand out travel agencies' business cards and distribute maps of the city with a brief explanation of the Palenque ruins in Spanish.

COMING AND GOING

BY BUS All bus stations are downhill and within walking distance of the Parque Central on Avenida Juárez. First-class, air-conditioned **ADO** buses (5 de Mayo, at Juárez, tel. 934/5–00–00) serve Mexico City (14 hrs, $30) at 6 PM and Villahermosa (10 per day, 2 hrs, $4). The Mérida-bound bus (3 per day, 8 hrs, $13) stops in Campeche (6 hrs, $10). **Cristóbal Colón** (5 de Mayo, at Juárez, tel. 934/5–01–40) runs buses to Villahermosa (2 hrs, $4), as well as San Cristóbal (5 per day, 5½ hrs, $5) and Tuxtla Gutiérrez (4 per day, 7½ hrs, $7), stopping in Ocosingo (2 hrs, $2.50) on the way.

Roomy, second-class **Transportes Tuxtla Gutiérrez** (Júarez, at 20 de Noviembre, tel. 934/5–10–12) has six daily buses that leave from the end of Avenida Juárez and run to Tuxtla Gutiérrez (8 hrs, $6) and San Cristóbal (6 hrs, $4), stopping in Ocosingo (2½ hrs, $2). The station has day-long luggage storage with purchase of a ticket. If you want to try your luck getting to the Lacandón jungle without paying exorbitant package prices, check with **Autotransportes Río Chancala** (5 de Mayo 120, opposite Hotel Kashlan; open daily 6 AM–8 PM) about their early departures for Lacanjá and Bonampak (5 hrs, $5).

BY TRAIN Unless you've got lots of time and/or very little money, pick some other way to travel to and from Palenque; the train that passes through the station (10 km north of town) offers incredibly cheap and unbelievably slow third-class service to Campeche (7½ hrs, $3) and Mérida (11 hrs, $4.50). Check with the tourist office for timetables, which are usually unreliable due to delays.

GETTING AROUND

Easily covered on foot, Palenque centers around the Parque Central, which is only blocks from most hotels, restaurants, and bus stations. Most of what you'll need is on the main drag, Avenida Juárez. In typical Chiapan fashion, calles run north–south and avenidas run east–west. Taxis congregate on the east side of the park and charge $1.50 for getting to the train station and to the Mayabell campground (see below). They're a rip-off to the ruins or Agua Azul.

Microbuses and colectivos run by **Transportes Palenque** (20 de Noviembre, at Allende, 3 blocks east and 2 blocks south of park) and **Transportes Chambalu** (Allende, at Juárez, 3 blocks east and 1 block north of park) go to the ruins, Misol-Ha, and Agua Azul. Both offer service to the ruins (30¢) every 10 minutes, daily 6–6. Package plans to Misol-Ha and Agua Azul leave at 9 AM, 10 AM, and noon, spending 30 minutes at Misol-Ha and three to four hours at Agua Azul. The whole deal lasts about six hours and costs $6, which is a bargain since it includes admission. It costs almost $5 to reach these places on your own, and you can't count on front-porch delivery to the sites on local buses.

WHERE TO SLEEP

You can find fairly cheap dives as well as the purest air-conditioned luxury in Palenque, although most places fall in the middle to upper price range. If you want to sleep surrounded by jungle, camp out at Mayabell (*see below*) or rent a hammock in Agua Azul (*see Near Palenque, below*). In town, various posadas—offering simple fan-equipped rooms with toilet paper, clean towels, and luggage storage—are the cheapest accommodations. At **Posada Santo Domingo** (20 de Noviembre, at Allende, tel. 934/5–01–46), singles cost $5.50, doubles $6.75. For cheaper rooms with lumpier beds, try **Posada Charito** (20 de Noviembre 15-B, no phone). One final consideration is the time of year you're in town: Prices jump by about 15% in July, August, November, and December.

➤ **UNDER $10** • **Hotel Misol-Ha.** Straightforward lodging in the heart of the city, Misol-Ha is refreshingly quiet and clean. In the low season singles cost $5.50, doubles $6.75. All have fans, hot water, and access to sunny communal balconies. *Juárez 14, tel. 934/5–00–92. 28 rooms, all with bath. Luggage storage.*

Hotel Posada San Juan. On a dirt road off the tourist track, San Juan feels like it's in a cooler climate than the rest of Palenque. The pleasant, airy singles ($5.50), doubles ($7), and triples ($8) are a real deal. *Off Allende, near cnr of Emilo Rabasa, tel. 934/5–06–16. From park, walk down Juárez to Allende, then left 4 blocks. 18 rooms, all with bath. Luggage storage.*

➤ **UNDER $15** • **Hotel Lacroix.** This unique place has been an institution since 1956, when archaeologists began to frequent the ruins. Painted on the lobby walls are replicas of letters written by colleagues of late French archaeologist Señor Lacroix, who owned Palenque. The few rooms with fans and cold water baths tend to fill quickly. Singles cost $8, doubles $9.50, and triples $10.50. *Hidalgo 10, tel. 934/5–00–14. ½ block east of NE cnr of park. 8 rooms, all with bath. Luggage storage. Wheelchair access.*

HOSTELS Youth Hostel Posada Canek. Because it's the cheapest in town at $2.75 per person, and the place to meet fellow travelers, beds in the comfortable coed rooms fill up fast. Private doubles with clean shared baths are $6.50. Come in around the 10 AM checkout to get first dibs on a bed. *20 de Noviembre 43, across from Posada Charito, tel. 934/5–01–50. 8 rooms, all with bath; 10 dorm beds. Laundry, luggage storage.*

CAMPING Mayabell (tel. 934/5–05–97 for reservations) is known worldwide as a hip home-away-from-home for wandering minstrels, craftspeople, and shaman wanna-bes who come to camp in overgrown surroundings and get the score on the *hongos* (mushrooms). Avoid loose drug talk; locals have turned traveling *jipis* (hippies) over to the authorities. Pitching a tent runs $2 per person, stringing your own hammock costs about $1.50 per night, and renting a hammock is another $2 (plus a $13.50 deposit). Cabañas for two with private bath are $12 (plus a $13.50 deposit). The communal bathrooms lack hot water but are usually clean, and there's a full-service restaurant on the premises. The campground is on the road to the ruins, several kilometers out of town. Take a colectivo (35¢) headed for the ruins for about 10 minutes and tell the driver to let you off at Mayabell.

FOOD

Most restaurants along Avenida Juárez and around the park cater to tourists, many of whom are Mexican nationals. For a simple, cheap meal, try the snack stands on the upper side of the square, where you can find tortas, *licuados* (smoothies), and corn on the cob all for under $1. Buy cheap bread and cheese to take to the ruins at the small market four blocks south of the zócalo. For cheap beer (50¢) and tacos (35¢), head to **Chan-Bahlum** (Hidalgo, 2 blocks from park), where locals socialize daily 6 PM–1 AM.

➤ **UNDER $5** • **Restaurante El Rodeo.** The Rodeo serves a decent, ample *comida corrida* for $2.50 and soups for $1.25. Their eponymous burger comes with ham, cheese, bacon, and all the trimmings ($2.50). Upstairs from El Rodeo, **El Patio**'s terrace is perfect for sipping coffee or beer. The management also changes traveler's checks at the bank rate and is a good source of info on the surrounding area. *Juárez 10, tel. 934/5–02–03. Open daily 7 AM–11 PM.*

Restaurante Girasoles. "Sunflowers" is the best cheap tourist restaurant in town, with breakfast for only $1–$2. Its proximity to the bus stations is an added bonus. Although it doesn't appear on the menu, the gargantuan strawberry yogurt and granola-topped fruit salad ($2.25) won't leave you hungry. A hamburger piled high with bacon, cheese, and avocado comes with fries for just $2. *Juárez 189, tel. 934/5–03–83. Open daily 7 AM–11 PM.*

Restaurante Maya. Popular with Mexicans and international travelers alike, this place has served quality local food since 1958. The best deals are the sandwiches ($1.50–$2.50) and breakfast specials ($2–$3). Breakfasts include fruit, bread and jam, eggs, black beans, a stack of tortillas, and coffee. The pleasant atmosphere and view of the Parque Central invite you to sip cappuccino (70¢) and write postcards after dinner. There's also a full bar. *Independencia, at Hidalgo, tel. 934/5–00–42. Open daily 7 AM–11 PM. MC, V.*

Restaurante Mero-Lec. Live romantic music and starlight seating are extra perks here, but the real attraction is the good food at good prices. A shrimp cocktail or a hearty order of tacos is just $2.50. After dinner you can have a drink or play a game of Ping-Pong. *No phone. From traffic circle on highway to ruins, walk along dirt path (follow neon signs) to Centro Turístico la Cañada; it's on your right. Open daily 4 PM–midnight. Live music Wed.–Sat. 9:30 PM–midnight.*

Restaurante Yunyuén. This restaurant in Hotel Vaca Vieja serves generous *antojitos* (appetizers) for $1.50 and light meals of yogurt and fruit for just $2. A monstrous goblet of chocolate milk is $1. The entertaining bilingual menu advertises tantalizing "sparro gas" (asparagus). *5 de Mayo, at Chiapas, tel. 934/5–03–77. 3 blocks east of park. Open daily 7 AM–11 PM.*

WORTH SEEING

Palenque's ruins retain more of a lost-in-the-jungle feel than any of Mexico's other easily accessible sites. No one should miss scaling these ancient ruins for the view of the surrounding vegetation: It's hard to imagine that what you see is only a fraction of the ancient city—the rest lies buried in dense foliage. The city—probably founded in the 3rd century and abandoned for unknown reasons in the 9th—was at the height of its glory in the 7th century under the rule of Escudo Pakal. He is represented in numerous bas-reliefs and is most remembered for his tomb, one of the most important archaeological finds of the century.

Palenque's rulers did not often marry outside the dynasty, and the physical deformations that resulted were considered marks of divinity. Zak-Kuk, mother of Pakal, had a massive head and jaw. Pakal, who was clubfooted, may have married both his mother and his sister. His son, Chan-Bahlum, had six toes on each foot and six fingers on one hand.

You should allow about a day to see everything. Guidebooks to the ruins are not sold on the premises, but you can buy a pamphlet with a map and description of each major structure. The English version is $1.50, the Spanish 50¢. For more in-depth explanations, a private tour arranged by a local travel agency or at the entrance to the ruins costs $15–$20 per group. A cheaper and more flexible alternative is to simply blend in with another guided tour. The ruins are open daily 8–5, and the entrance fee is $2.25, free on Sunday. Colectivos shuttle frequently between the town and the ruins (*see* Getting Around, *above*).

MAYAN MUSEUM This museum features bits and pieces from the site's digs as well as a general overview of the religious, social, and political structures of the Maya. Most notable are the stone slabs covered with hieroglyphics and the carved sculptures of Maya faces, which illustrate the custom of cranial deformation for aesthetic ends. It's a good idea to hit the museum before getting bedraggled and sweaty at the ruins. Catch a colectivo (30¢) along the main drag in town to get here. *1 km before ruins on main highway. Admission: $2 (includes ruins). Open Tues.–Sun. 10–5.*

TEMPLE OF THE INSCRIPTIONS This structure wins the building-you're-most-likely-to-see-on-a-postcard contest. For the vertigo-free, the spectacular view from the top of the 26-meter pyramid provides a sense of the vast lands once under Palenque's domain. It's also the vantage point from which to see the surrounding buildings' roof combs—vertical extensions

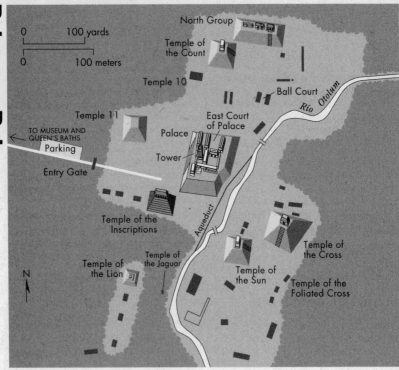

that are characteristic of southern Mayan architecture. If you'd prefer not to pass out before reaching the top, ascend from the back side.

From the top of the pyramid you can descend to Pakal's tomb, a chamber 1½ meters below ground. The six-toed Chan-Bahlum, Pakal's son, buried his father here in AD 683 and then had the entire 38-meter space above the tomb filled with debris. Mexican archaeologist Alberto Ruíz uncovered the tomb in 1952 after spending four years plowing through the rubble, thwarting Chan-Bahlum's efforts to deter grave-robbers and nosy academics. Ruíz found Pakal's body wrapped in red cloth and decorated with jade jewelry, an obsidian death mask, and other items to ensure his comfort in the next world. These are now exhibited in Mexico City's Museo Nacional de Antropología. At the site you can see the tomb's 5-ton lid, intricately carved with a likeness of Pakal as a young man descending through the gateway to the afterworld. The enormous crypt is comparable to the huge tombs found in Egypt. The tomb, open daily 10:30–4, is definitely worth the slimy, narrow, downward trek.

PALACE Next to the Temple of the Inscriptions, in the center of the site, is a cluster of buildings including steam baths, latrines, dwellings supposedly inhabited by priests, and rooms for religious ceremonies. From the center tower you can see walls covered with stucco friezes and masks in relief, many depicting Pakal and his dynasty.

THE THREE TEMPLES Across the river, to the east of the Temple of the Inscriptions, these three pyramids were constructed by Chan-Bahlum. The **Temple of the Cross** holds an image of a cross, representing the ceiba tree; the **Temple of the Foliated Cross,** which looks like a gingerbread house with giant keyholes for windows, has a stone slab whose hieroglyphs recount the Maya's stuggles for survival in the jungle. The **Temple of the Sun** houses a depiction of a shield, a symbol of the sun god. Modern Mayan culture is certainly far removed from the Classic period, but such symbols retain their significance. In contemporary indigenous villages, for example, crosses decorated with pine branches still mark sacred places of worship.

TEMPLE OF THE JAGUAR This tiny temple is hidden up a short trail to the left of the Temple of the Inscriptions—follow the dirt path into the jungle alongside the Otolum River. The temple features a slippery stairwell leading to an exposed chamber. The trail continues on to smaller ruins amid dense jungle, ending 8 kilometers (5 mi) uphill at a friendly village.

QUEEN'S BATHS Pakal's wife reportedly dipped her queenly body into the various small waterfalls and swimming holes that dot a 3-kilometer trail leading to the ruins from the museum. You can refresh your aching bones in these pools set against the rain forest, but good luck trying to sneak into the ruins along this path—the guards are wise to that trick. If you just want to cool off before entering the ruins legally, the guard will let you splash around the first pool for free. *From Mayan Museum, walk across street to path leading through dense vegetation; it's about 100 meters to first swimming hole.*

Near Palenque

MISOL-HA AND AGUA AZUL

Rivers snake through the Chiapan rain forest, forming crashing waterfalls and deep swimming holes. **Misol-Ha** and **Agua Azul** are two such places, and are popular tourist stops for Mexican families, especially during high seasons. Eighteen kilometers (10 mi) down Route 199 from Palenque, the single towering cascade at Misol-Ha thunders into a deep, cold, green pool. Here you can swim, sun on the rocks, or scramble and slide on the slippery boulders in the misty areas behind the falls, where a cave leads to a subterranean pool, more falls, and lots of bats.

Forty-six kilometers (27 mi) farther south toward Ocosingo is Agua Azul, which, during the rainy months (July–Sept.) isn't quite the vibrant blue depicted in postcard photos. Nevertheless, it's still a treat to float down the river or play on the rope swing. To get away from most of the families and souvenir vendors, walk up the trail that runs along the cascades from the main swimming area for 2 kilometers. Once there, you'll find calm, colorful pools that alternate with waterfalls in a steplike pattern. You can continue up the trail to a large waterfall or climb from one level to the next in the water. It's safe to climb in this spot but watch for areas clearly marked with skulls and crossbones and multilingual warnings.

COMING AND GOING Microbuses from **Transportes Chambalu** and **Transportes Palenque** (*see* Getting Around, in Palenque, *above*) run directly to both spots from Palenque, and the journey takes about two hours one-way. If you prefer to go at your own pace, all buses bound for Ocosingo or Yajalón from Palenque pass the *cruceros* (crossroads) for Misol-Ha and Agua Azul. The Misol-Ha crossroads is about 3 kilometers from the falls, and the ride will cost you 70¢. The 1½-hour ride to the crossroads for Agua Azul costs $1.25, and the bus lets you off about 5 kilometers from the river. The downhill walk is on a narrow, hot, paved road; watch out for microbuses swerving around corners. When you enter Agua Azul, you may be asked to pay an entrance fee of 70¢ ($3 if you come by car), depending on how attentive the guards are. To return to Palenque, hitch a ride or hook up with a colectivo for around $3.

WHERE TO SLEEP AND EAT At the base of the Misol-Ha waterfall are several family-style cabañas with all the modern amenities—refrigerators, stoves, ovens, and cooking utensils. Best of all is the private access to the spectacular falls and surrounding rain forest; for the moment, Misol-Ha remains relatively undiscovered. The simple double cabañas ($13.50 in low season, $15 high season) have private baths with hot water, mosquito screens, and color TVs. Get a group of four friends and rent the *familiar* (family-size) for $27 during low season, $30 during high season. Pitching a tent costs $14 year-round. There is a full-service restaurant at the site, but bring food if you plan to stay for a while.

Locals at Agua Azul hang cardboard signs outside their houses advertising hammocks and camping spots. You can hang your own hammock upriver at Agua Azul for $1–$2, or rent one for $1–$2 more from the locals; tent spots are also $1–$2. Another alternative is to head toward the uppermost falls, where the people who run the *comedores* (food stands) serve three cheap meals daily. If you eat with them, they may let you hang your hammock for free and offer you shelter if the rain sets in.

OCOSINGO AND TONINA RUINS

Located 20 kilometers (12 mi) south of Palenque, Ocosingo is an unassuming town. It was here, in January 1994, that the Zapatista rebels confronted the Mexican army in one of the bloodiest battles of the uprising. Peasants suspected of rebel activity were executed by the army in Ocosingo's central plaza—the images of the victims made front pages worldwide. These events have contributed to an attitude of suspicion in Ocosingo, but the little-known ruins of **Toniná**, just over 10 kilometers (6 mi) away, are still worth a visit. A Mayan city that reached its height in AD 500–1000, Toniná's ruins are tough to reach, but well worth the effort. Passageways wind through the imposing seven-tiered pyramid and descend into tombs complete with stone sarcophagi and still-discernible depictions of jaguars, skeletons, and the god of the underworld clutching the heads of decapitated ball players. A small museum displays a fair selection of Toniná statuary; many of these pieces were also decapitated, supposedly by the invading forces of a rival city. The site and museum are open daily 9–4; ask the caretaker to show you around. Admission to the pyramid and museum is $1.50 (free Sundays).

COMING AND GOING Frequent buses connect Ocosingo with San Cristóbal and Palenque. The **Cristóbal Colón** station (Carretera Ocosingo–Palenque Km. 2, tel. 967/3–04–31) is a 20-minute walk from the zócalo along 1a Avenida Oriente Norte. From here, first-class buses depart for Palenque (3 hrs, $3) and Tuxtla Gutiérrez (5 hrs, $4). **Transportes Tuxtla Gutiérrez**, located in the second-class bus station 3½ blocks up the hill on 1a Avenida Norte Poniente, has the most reliable service to Tuxtla (4 hrs, $3), San Cristóbal (2 hrs, $1.50), and Palenque (3 hrs, $2).

There is no public transportation to Toniná, so unless you have a car or want to take a tour from Palenque or San Cristóbal ($20–$25 with Casa Margarita), you'll need to go to the Ocosingo market around 9 AM and ask around until you get on a truck that passes the road leading to the ruins ($1 is a reasonable fee). Your best bet is finding someone headed to Guadalupe, a town just past the ruins, but make it clear where you're headed. Don't be fooled by the signs for Toniná—the first, which is about 2 kilometers from Ocosingo, is a good three-hour walk from the site. With luck, you'll be let off at the last crossroads, a 20-minute walk from the ruins. Be sure to head out early to hitch a ride for the return trip, as traffic is light and you may be in for a 3½-hour walk back to town. If it's late, you might be able to scam a ride home with the people who work at the site and museum. You'll be expected to pay $1 for the ride.

WHERE TO SLEEP AND EAT Ocosingo's few hotels are nothing to write home about, but it's a hell of a day trip from either San Cristóbal or Palenque if you don't stay here. For rooms with a cabaña-in-the-jungle feel, head to **Hotel Agua Azul** (1a Ote. Sur 127, tel. 967/3–03–02). The cheap, clean rooms here come with private baths and hot water; singles cost $5.50, doubles $8, triples $9.50, quadruples $10.50. Fans in every room of **Hotel Bodas de Plata** (1a Sur, at 1a Pte., just south of Palacio Municipal, tel. 967/3–00–16) cool things off during the midday heat, while the piping hot water warms you on chilly Ocosingo mornings. Singles are $6.75, doubles $8, triples $9.50. **Hotel Central** (Central 5, tel. 967/3–00–24) provides small, comfortable rooms furnished with tiny black-and-white cable TVs, fans, and bathrooms with plenty of hot water. The restaurant downstairs offers a vantage point for viewing the happenings on the zócalo. Singles cost $8, doubles $9.50, triples $13.50.

Ocosingo's morning **market** (located downhill on 2a Avenida Sur Oriente, on the left just before the dusty lot) offers cheap fruit, bread, fresh tortillas, and locally made cheese. Good, cheap tacos (30¢) are prepared in front of you at **El Buen Taquito** (tel. 967/3–02–51), on Avenida Central near the zócalo. Fill up on quesadillas made with local cheese (3 for $1) at **La Michoacana** (Central Ote. 3, on zócalo, tel. 967/3–02–51; open daily 8–8), or order *sincronizadas* (tortilla sandwiches; 70¢) with cheese, ham, onions, chiles, and avocados. The patio at **Restaurante La Montura** (under Hotel Central, tel. 967/3–05–50; open daily 7 AM–11 PM) is a great place to enjoy a platter of spicy chicken *chilaquiles* (tortilla strips doused with salsa and sour cream; $3), or filling fried plátanos with cream ($1).

THE LACANDÓN RAIN FOREST

The Lacandón rain forest is not as untouched as one might imagine, especially where humans have encroached, stripping it of its precious wood and razing the land for cattle ranches and farms. A road built smack-dab through the forest—connecting Palenque with Najá—has effectively done away with the natural and cultural isolation of the region. More roads are being built to connect Ocosingo with the heart of the jungle, ostensibly to bring package tours to unspoiled lagoon areas such as **Metzaboc** and **Mira Mar**. In reality, these projects give the military more access to what is the last Zapatista stronghold. The forest is still home, however, to the Lacandón Indians—considered to be the living indigenous group most similar to their Mayan ancestors—and contains two important Mayan archaeological sites: Bonampak and Yaxchilán. Most of the southern Lacandón live in Lacanjá, and until very recently, most of them worshipped at Yaxchilán (the northerners worshipped at Palenque). These days northerners worship at Yaxchilán, while most of the southerners have converted to Christianity. Though some Lacandón speak only Mayan languages, many—especially those living in Lacanjá—now speak Spanish. Crafts, including bows, arrows, and seed jewelry, are for sale in both towns.

NAJA AND LACANJA Most Lacandón people now live in or around these two main towns, and a number of them are quite rich, having sold off their land rights to timber interests. Neither town offers hotel lodging, but local families will often let visitors sling hammocks in their homes. It is advised to bring a letter of introduction from Na-Bolom (*see* Worth Seeing, in San Cristóbal, *above*), and to come with a purpose other than a vague interest in experiencing Lacandón life. In the past, exposure to outsiders has brought some tragic results to the Lacandón people, resulting in justifiable skepticism and suspicion on their part. Be respectful and bring your own provisions plus food gifts such as sugar and salt. Check with Na-Bolom for more info about events coordinated through the new **casas de cultura** in Najá and Lacanjá.

The Lacandón Maya

With the arrival of the Spanish in Chiapas, many diverse Mayan groups banded together and fled into the jungle; the Spaniards (wisely) didn't follow them into the treacherously unfamiliar territory. These Maya called themselves Hachack-Winick (the True People) and lived in isolation—scattered throughout the rain forest—until they were first contacted by anthropologists this century.

Currently, the physical existence of the Lacandón people is not in jeopardy, but they are becoming assimilated in greater numbers. Phillip Bayer, a Baptist missionary, spent 12 years trying to convert the people of Najá with meager results. When he heard the last two elders of Lacanjá had died, he rushed in and successfully converted virtually all of southern Lacandón to Christianity in just a couple of years. In Najá however, the 100-plus-year old patriarch, Chan K'in Viejo, has bestowed upon his many sons the task of preserving Lacandón social and cultural traditions.

To the many who have turned away from tradition, Chan K'in warns that to "cut the umbilical cord connected to one's traditions" means to "be denied the key to the heavens." Some predict that traditional Lacandón culture will fall apart when Chan K'in Viejo dies. Chan K'in has had three wives, one of whom has passed away; two still live with him. Together, their children (the youngest of which is said to have been conceived when Chan K'in was 102) are estimated to comprise 35% of the population of Najá.

The best road into the Lacandón jungle runs straight to Lacanjá, a four- to six-hour trip from Palenque. Najá is closer, but on a poorer road, and takes about seven hours to reach from Palenque, or six hours from Ocosingo (see Ocosingo and Toniná Ruins, above). Driving on your own is not advised due to the current political situation in the region. Buses depart daily for Najá from Ocosingo at 9 AM. From Palenque, **Transportes Chamcala** goes to Lacanjá via the San Javier military installation, daily at 10 AM and 2 PM. You should bring a tent or hammock, and locals will tell you where you can spend the night. Before venturing off into the jungle, it's a good idea to pick up a map, available in bookshops and at Na-Bolom. You may also check travel agencies in San Cristóbal and Palenque for tours.

BONAMPAK In the grand scheme of things, this small ceremonial center played only a minor role during the late Classic Maya period. What's notable about Bonampak, built between AD 400 and 700, are the colorful frescoes in three distinct rooms, complete with altars that seem to depict an epic. Room 1 supposedly illustrates preparation for a war; Room 2, the battle in action (Yaxchilán under the reign of Governor Chaan Muan is the supposed foe); and Room 3, the various bloodletting rituals associated with victory, and the passing of Bonampak to a young heir. The first white explorers to the region were on a 1946 National Fruit Company expedition looking to build a road through the rain forest. They stumbled upon this tiny palace, its murals strangely preserved in living color by a thin coating of limestone. Excavations took place soon after (National Fruit footed much of the bill), and several partially destroyed buildings and a plaza were uncovered. The colors in rooms 2 and 3 are rather faded, and some claim that seeing the reproductions in Mexico City's anthropology museum will save you a lot of time and unnecessary effort, but don't believe it: Seeing the remnants of a great civilization in its original context, plus the adventure of getting to the site, is worth the trip. Just don't expect comic-strip clarity on the walls. Admission to the site is $2, free on Sundays.

Most health workers at archaeological sites carry injections to counteract snakebites—the most venomous of them all comes from a slithery serpent known as the nahauyaca. Locals say that if you encounter one of these fanged, striped vipers more than a mere 15 minutes away from a life-saving injection, you might as well kiss your butt goodbye.

➤ **COMING AND GOING** • Transportation to the ruins is most easily set up through a travel agency (see Tours and Guides, in Palenque or in San Cristóbal, above); tours by a combination of driving and walking with a guide last two to three days. You can also get here by bus. From Palenque, make the six-hour trip on a frequent **Transportes Lagos de Montebello** bus to Lacanjá; from Lacanjá, walk the 13 kilometers (7 mi) to the ruins. Bring all you need to be self-sufficient for a few days, plus gifts of alcohol, smokes, and food for caretakers.

YAXCHILAN The Yaxchilán ruins lie on the shores of the Usumacinta River, 32 kilometers (19 mi) north of Bonampak, at the Guatemalan border. This ceremonial center, built between AD 500 and 800, was considerably more important than Bonampak and is still considered sacred by the present-day descendents of the Maya. Excavations continue, promising to reveal many more Mayan secrets. For several years, the Lacandón people were prevented from worshipping at Yaxchilán and Palenque because it was feared they would damage the temples. Today access has been restored, and inhabitants of the northern Lacandón once again perform their ceremonies here. They used to worship at Palenque, but according to Lacandón elder Chan K'in Viejo, "the spirits have left there now" to retreat to their last home in Yaxchilán.

The site was ingeniously landscaped around the twisting Usumacinta River, and therefore remains accessible only by boat. The highlight is the series of high temples, many with stela and glyphs. Carvings depict the two most important rulers: Jaguar Escudo (Shield Jaguar), in power in the 7th century, and Jaguar Pájaro (Bird Jaguar), who ruled a century later. You'll probably have to fork out a tidy sum for a visit here, so try to see everything you can—don't miss the series of temples dedicated to Jaguar Pájaro, set high on a hill, deeper in the jungle behind the eastern structure.

There's a large palapa for sleeping in Yaxchilán, but no facilities; bring a hammock and a mosquito net. You can bathe and fish in the river, and have your catch or any other food prepared by the woman who cooks for the guards. You'll pay a $2 fee to enter the ruins, except on Sundays. Spanish-language guided tours are free and mandatory.

➤ **COMING AND GOING** • Transportation is usually arranged by travel agencies. The trip typically involves a four-hour bus ride to the border town of Frontera Echeverría (called Corozal on the Guatemalan side) and a one-hour boat ride to Yaxchilán, where you can see the ruins and camp before heading on to Bonampak (*see above*). STS (*see* Tours and Guides, in Palenque, *above*) does the two-day trip for $55 a person. You can also try to arrange boat transportation with a local resident in Lacanjá for about $15, or from Frontera Echeverría for $40 each way (up to eight people).

Comitán and Lagos de Montebello

Though usually only used as a stopover for those traveling to and from Guatemala, Comitán has a pleasantly cool climate, some unusual little museums, and a pretty zócalo complete with ceiba trees, bougainvillea, flowers, and white benches. The real draw to this area, however, is the Parque Nacional Lagos de Montebello, comprised of over 2,000 acres of pine-forested hills dotted with lakes in brilliant shades of blue, green, and gray.

Comitán was originally a Tzeltal-speaking Mayan community called Balún-Canán, meaning "Place of the Nine Stars," and it remains a primary Tzeltal trading post. Its current name is derived from the name given by the Aztecs: Comitlán, which translates from Nahuatl as "Place of the Potters." You can see remnants of Mayan civilization dating back as far as AD 900 at the Chincultic and Tenam Puente ruins (*see* Near Comitán, *below*), near the Lagos de Montebello, and in the archaeology museum in the library adjoining the Casa de Cultura (*see* Worth Seeing, *below*).

Since 1981, thousands of Guatemalan refugees have called the area east of Comitán home. Though the indígenas who fled from the terror of the Scorched Earth counterinsurgency campaign have begun to resettle Guatemala's Ixcán jungle, camps still remain on the Mexican side of the border.

BASICS

CASAS DE CAMBIO Bancomer (1a Av. Ote. Sur 10, SE nr of zócalo, tel. 963/2–02–10) has an ATM and is open weekdays 9:30–11:30 AM for exchanging cash and traveler's checks and getting advances on Visa cards.

CONSULATES The **Guatemalan Consulate** (Calle 1a Sur Pte. 26, at 2a Av. Pte. Sur, tel. 963/2–26–69) is open weekdays 8–4:30, though they may open up shop for you on Saturdays if you pay an "overtime surcharge." For specific information on visas and border crossings, *see* Box, Going to Guatemala, in Near Comitán, *below*.

CROSSING THE BORDER The border crossing at **Ciudad Cuauhtémoc** doesn't quite live up to its billing as a city, but it's reported to be less dicey than those further south, near Tapachula. In any case, it affords good scenery and frequent transportation from La Mesilla, Guatemala to the heart of the Guatemalan *altiplano* (highlands). The border is open daily 8 AM–6 PM. For general border info, *see* box Going to Guatemala, in Near Tapachula, *below*.

If you're coming from Guatemala, pickup trucks (50¢) and taxis ($1) bridge the 3-kilometer gap between La Mesilla and Ciudad Cuauhtémoc. From Cuauhtémoc, sporadic buses make the trip to Comitán (1½ hrs, $2.25) from the Cristóbal Colón terminal across from the immigration office, or you can try your luck at hitching. If you reach the border too late, don't despair; there is a very civil hotel next door to the bus terminal and a restaurant across the street. For info on how to reach the border from Comitán, *see* Coming and Going, *below.*

LAUNDRY **Lavandería Takana** (Calle 1 Sur Pte., at 2a Av. Pte. Sur, next to Guatemalan Consulate; open Mon.–Sat. 9–2 and 4–8) washes and dries your clothes for $1 a kilo. If you can't get next-day service there, try **Lavandería Chulul** (2a Av. Pte. Sur, around cnr from Restaurant Alis), which has identical hours.

MAIL The post office provides the usual services and will hold mail sent to you at the following address for up to 10 days: Lista de Correos, Comitán, Chiapas, CP 30000, México. *Central Belisario Domínguez Sur 45, tel. 963/2–04–27. Open weekdays 8–7, Sat. 9–1.*

MEDICAL AID The **Centro de Salud** (Calle 7 Sur Ote. 3, tel. 963/2–36–49 or 963/2–01–64; open weekdays 8 AM–3 PM) is well prepared to treat cholera or *turista*. At the **Cruz Roja** (tel. 963/2–18–89), doctors are on call 24 hours and speak some English.

PHONES There are Ladatel phones on the west side and at the southeast corner of the zócalo. **Caseta Maguis** charges a 20¢ per minute commission on international collect calls, and a $1.25 fee if the party doesn't accept your call. *Calle 2 Sur Pte. 6, at Av. Central Belisario Domínguez, tel. 963/2–29–55, fax 963/2–43–52. Open Mon.–Sat. 8 AM–9 PM, Sun. 9–2 and 5–8.*

VISITOR INFORMATION The tourist office in the Palacio Municipal on the zócalo is stocked with an excellent selection of brochures, as well as good maps of the city and region. The staff is well versed in local history, geography, and transportation options, but doesn't speak English. *Tel. 963/2–40–47. Open Mon.–Sat. 9–2 and 4–8, Sun. 9–2.*

COMING AND GOING

The first- and second-class bus terminals are located on the highway (called Boulevard Belisario Domínguez or Carretera Internacional), west of the center. The walk from here with a loaded pack seems endless—it's better to cross the highway and catch a frequent CENTRO colectivo (20¢) to the plaza or take a taxi ($1). To get back to the terminals, hop on a CARRETERA INTERNACIONAL colectivo, which leaves from the east side of the zócalo daily 6 AM–9 PM.

The first-class **Cristóbal Colón** station (Blvd. Belisario Domínguez Sur 43, tel. 963/2–09–80 is on the highway about 12 blocks southwest of the center. Frequent buses to Tuxtla Gutiérrez (3½ hrs, $4.25), with stops in San Cristóbal (1½ hrs, $1.50), leave daily 6:30 AM–7 PM. Buses leave for the Guatemalan border town of Ciudad Cuauhtémoc (7 per day, 1½ hrs, $2.25 8 AM–11:30 PM and head out to Villahermosa (8½ hrs, $10) at 6:30 PM. Two buses leave daily at noon and 2 PM, making the 22-hour haul to Mexico City; it's $32 for regular first-class and $37.50 for the luxurious version, with extra-comfortable seats, TV, and beverage service.

Second-class **Transportes Tuxtla Gutiérrez** and **La Angostura** (tel. 963/2–10–44 for both buses leave from the station at Boulevard Belisario Domínguez Sur 27. The buses serve Tuxtla Gutiérrez (4 hrs, $3) and San Cristóbal (2 hrs, $1.25) 5 AM–7:30 PM. Buses for Ciudad Cuauhtémoc (2 hrs, $1.75), on the Guatemalan border, leave daily. Buses to Tzimol (30 min, 50¢) and La Mesilla (45 min, 70¢) leave about every half hour between 8 and 5, as do colectivo pickup trucks. To reach the station from the zócalo, head six blocks west on Calle Central Benito Juárez Poniente, turn left, and go 1½ blocks down the highway.

GETTING AROUND

Comitán is easy to navigate once you master the grid system. Calle Central Benito Juárez runs east–west, Avenida Central Belisario Domínguez (otherwise known as "el boulevard") north–south. The two divide the city into quadrants. All calles run east–west, all avenidas north–south. The Palacio Municipal (with its clock facade) sits on the north side of the zócalo and the Santo Domingo Church on the east side. The number in each street name indicates how far it is from either Avenida Central Belisario Domínguez or Calle Central Benito Juárez. For example, Calle 2 Sur Poniente runs east–west two blocks south of Calle Benito Juárez the southwestern quadrant of the city. As the street crosses Avenida Central Belisario Domínguez into the southeastern quadrant of the city, it's called Calle 2 Sur Oriente. Got it?

WHERE TO SLEEP

Many of Comitán's budget hotels are near the center of town. The climate here is cooler than in most other areas of Chiapas, so when it comes to choosing a room, hot water should be more of a consideration than fans or air-conditioning. If there's no room at the places listed below, first try **Posada Las Flores** (1a Av. Pte. Nte. 17, tel. 963/2–33–24) then **Posada San Miguel** (1a Av. Pte. Nte. 19, tel. 963/2–11–26) next door. Both have clean, wheelchair-accessible double rooms for $2 per person, but only San Miguel offers single rates. Head to Lagos de Montebello (*see* Near Comitán, *below*) to camp.

Hospedaje Montebello. An amiable young couple runs this rather noisy but clean and traveler-friendly place, which is usually full. The hot water is erratic in the private bathrooms, but the communal showers are reliable. Singles with communal bath are $3.25 per person, $4 with private bath. *Calle 1 Nte. Pte. 10, at 1a Av. Pte. Nte., tel. 963/2–35–72. 14 rooms, 8 with bath. Luggage storage. Reservations advised.*

Hotel Internacional. Just one block south of the center, this spacious hotel with perfumed, spotless rooms and plentiful hot water is a luxurious bargain for two or more. For better or worse, it's crawling with jovial Mexican businessmen. Singles are $12, doubles $14.75, triples $17.50; recently spruced-up rooms cost an extra $4. *Central Belisario Domínguez Sur 16, tel. 963/2–01–12. 28 rooms, all with bath. Luggage storage, restaurant. MC, V.*

Posada Continental. Squeaky clean singles with communal bathrooms (stocked with soap, towels, and toilet paper) go for $2. Doubles without bath are $4, and a double or single room with bath goes for $5.50. *1a Av. Pte. Sur 12, tel. 963/2–37–52. 13 rooms, 8 with bath. Luggage storage.*

FOOD

The affordable restaurants lining Comitán's zócalo serve international dishes and regional specialties, particularly soups and coffee made from locally grown beans. Try **Restaurant Nevelandia** (west side of zócalo, tel. 963/2–00–95; open daily 7 AM–midnight) for tacos and quesadillas (under $2) or breakfast specials of eggs, tortillas, beans, fruit, and coffee ($2.50). The **market,** in a huge, tan building one block east of the zócalo, is the place to find the cheapest eats, including Ocosingo cheese, fruits, and veggies. It is open daily until late afternoon.

Café Gloria. You can find both regional and non-regional treats in this family-owned restaurant, including locally grown coffee and tasty *sopes* (fried tortillas topped with beans, salsa, and meat or cheese) at three for $1. Other dishes are similarly priced, and all come with four kinds of homemade salsa. Little boys sometimes serve as waiters here, and they'll introduce each dish to you as if it's a person. *Av. Central Belisario Domínguez Nte. 22, tel. 963/2–16–22. Open daily 4:30 PM–11:30 PM.*

Restaurant Alis. Local immigration officials and their families come here for excellent typical Comitecan food. Their *platón chiapaneco* (plate of Chiapan meats; $4.75) includes *butifarras* (beef sausage) and *cecina* (dry, salted beef), and is enough for 2–3 people. Their five-course lunch specials are a tasty bargain for under $3. *Central Benito Juárez Pte. 21, tel. 963/2–12–62. Open daily 8:30 AM–9 PM.*

WORTH SEEING

Comitán has some fine examples of colonial architecture and well-curated museums. The 16th-century **Templo de Santo Domingo** on the zócalo displays elements of the Moorish-influenced *mudéjar* style. Just off the northeast corner of the zócalo stands the **Iglesia del Calvario,** whose columns and gables are probably Islamic-influenced via Andalucía, Spain.

CASA DE CULTURA The casa encompasses an archaeological museum, a multimedia performance space, an extensive library, and a café. The energetic young students who direct the programs and workshops (music, dance, theater, painting, poetry slams) are always eager to chat with visiting students about their ongoing projects. Stop by the café or box office to see what's cooking. The new archaeological museum displays Mayan artifacts from the sites near Comitán. Especially notable is the display of bones and ornately decorated pottery found in the caves of Cam-Cum and Los Andasolos. *Calle 1 Sur Ote., no phone. Next to Santo Domingo, east side of zócalo. Museum located behind Casa de Cultura. Admission free. Open Tues.–Sun. 10–5. Café open daily 7 AM–11 PM.*

MUSEO DE ARTE HERMILA DOMINGUEZ This museum, two blocks south of the center, features modern works by Mexican artists, including Rufino Tamayo. Many of the pieces deal with mystical themes, depicting mestizo and indigenous people and their connections to the earth, sky, and water. *Av. Central Belisario Domínguez Sur 53, no phone. Admission: 30¢. Open weekdays 10–1:45 and 4–6:45, Sat. 10–1:45.*

MUSEO DR. BELISARIO DOMINGUEZ Dr. Domínguez was a statesman and proponent of preventive medicine who represented Chiapas in the Senate under President Francisco Madero, just after the Mexican Revolution. After Madero was assassinated by U.S.-backed General Victoriano Huerta in 1913, Dr. Domínguez publicly denounced Huerta as a brutal tyrant. Predictably, Domínguez was then murdered. Once his home, this extensive, well-organized museum displays the doctor's pharmaceuticals, ominous-looking medical instruments, photographs, letters, and other personal belongings. *Av. Central Belisario Domínguez Sur 35, tel. 963/2–13–00. Admission: 15¢. Open Tues.–Sat. 10–6:45, Sun. 9–12:45.*

FESTIVALS

Comitán has many festivals, some barrio-specific and others citywide. The **Festival de San Caralampio,** featuring floats, flowers, music, and processions February 8–22, is one of the biggest religious events of the year. Caralampio was a pious Christian who was burned to death by non-believers in his native Greece. Years later, a rancher named Raymundo Solís, inspired by a book about Caralampio, commissioned a statue of him for his ranch. At the time, a cholera epidemic was devastating Comitán, and when no one on Don Solís's ranch was affected, townspeople attributed this to Caralampio's protection. Other festivals include **Semana Santa** (Holy Week; the week before Easter) and the **Feria de Agosto,** a 10-day festival of Comitecan agriculture, theater, and cuisine in honor of Santo Domingo that takes place in early August.

AFTER DARK

Since the Zapatista uprising in 1994, there has ceased to be a band on every block, but there are still plenty of places to hear live music at no charge. **Helen's Enrique** (Av. Central Belisario Domínguez Sur 19, across from zócalo, tel. 963/2–17–30) is a prime hangout. Cappuccino costs a dollar here, and Thursday–Saturday after 8 PM there's live Mexican pop. The bar in **Restaurant Nevelandia** (*see* Food, *above*), with nightly live *ranchera* and *banda* music, is a equally mellow scene. More alcohol-driven, smoky, and male-dominated is **El Rincón de la Guitarra** (Calle 1 Sur Ote. 13, no phone), which has live music of the Mamita-come-home-with-me-tonight ilk, every night 7 PM–3 AM. It also offers some dangerous drinks, like the Muppe (tequila with Squirt) or the Cucaracha (tequila, anise, and Kahlua) for $2.50 each, presumably to help you get Mamita to come home with you. A more relaxed spot is **Casa del Recuerdo** (1 Av. Ote. Nte. 6, tel. 963/2–05–44; open daily 11 AM–2 AM), housed within the elegant confines of Plaza Margarita.

Near Comitán

The main draw to the area surrounding Comitán is the lake country, but there are some other nice swimming spots, quiet towns, and Mayan ruins to visit nearby. Be prepared to revel in the attention that lone gringos get as the most interesting thing to come to town for a while. Th town of **Tzimol,** set in a green valley 8 kilometers (5 mi) southwest of Comitán, is where sugar has been cultivated with the same farming methods for hundreds of years. The town is known for its *panela* (cakes of hardened sugarcane juice used in Chiapan pastries). If you want to learn more about sugar processing, ask local plantation owners for an informal tour. A 15-minute bus ride past Tzimol brings you to **La Mesilla,** from which a 5-kilometer (3-mile) path leads to great swimming at an isolated waterfall called **El Chiflón.** Any La Mesilla local can direct you to the path once you get to town. **Transportes La Angostura** buses serve both towns (*see* Coming and Going, *above*). You'll want to catch the last bus back at 4:30 PM.

Twenty-five minutes northwest of Comitán is the pretty town of **Villa Las Rosas.** To get here from Comitán, take a direct **Transportes Cuxtepeque** (Blvd. Belisario Domínguez 12, at Calle 1 Nte. Pte., tel. 963/2-17-28) microbus (they leave every half hour) to the center of Las Rosas. If you decide to go to the freshwater spring **Manantial el Vertedor,** just outside of town, take another micro (60¢) from the center of Las Rosas to the Manantial bridge (ask the driver if he's going to "el puente al manantial" first). From the bridge it's a 1-kilometer (⅔-mile) hike down a dirt road; follow the muddy path behind the dam and you can take a cool dip in the clear pool. In May and June, you'll see tiny shrines dedicated to the rain god.

Eight kilometers (5 mi) south of Comitán is the Maya-Toltec site of **Tenam Puente.** Some feel that once the site is fully unearthed, it may prove to encompass an area larger than that of Palenque, and so far archaeologists and INAH workers have dug up several good-sized pyramids and three ball courts. Excavations are currently on hold due to a dispute between the archaeologists and the land owners, but the site is still open to visitors; weekdays 8-5 are the best time to visit. Donations are encouraged. To get here, catch any bus or colectivo marked LAGOS (35¢) and get off at the signs for Tenam Puente. To get back, walk to the highway and take any bus headed back to town (last bus passes around 6 PM). Licenciada María Trinidad Pulido, who is in charge of the archaeological museum at the Casa de Cultura (*see* Worth Seeing, *above*), is very knowledgeable about the site and can answer all your queries.

LAGOS DE MONTEBELLO

Set among pine trees, blackberry bushes, and maples, the 60-odd blue, gray, and green lakes of the **Parque Nacional Lagos de Montebello** provide a spectacular setting for wonderful hikes and swimming. The most popular lakes are those close to the road: Esmeralda, Ensueño, Agua Tinta, La Encantada, and Bosque Azul. A 45-minute walk on the unpaved road from the park gates leads to **Lago Montebello,** the larger **Laguna Tziscao,** and a dozen tiny lakes. A bus continues north past this junction and parks at Lago Bosque Azul. Two dirt paths lead into the forest from here. The one to the left takes you to a riverside picnic spot called **El Paso del Soldado.** The other takes you to **San José El Arco,** a natural limestone arch and series of *grutas* (caves). Bring a flashlight to explore the caves and offerings to leave for the gruta gods. Little boys will offer to guide you; their services are well worth a $1 donation.

At Bosque Azul, older boys will offer to take you to more isolated lakes on foot or horseback. Be sure to agree on a price before setting out ($1.25 an hour is acceptable) and wear a watch, since most guides aren't too concerned about getting you back in time for the last bus. The lakes Peinita and Bartolo, surrounded by white cliffs that offer spectacular views of the surrounding farmland and mountains, are best reached accompanied by a guide. You can pick up a useful map of the lakes at the tourist office in Comitán (*see* Visitor Information, *above*).

Just at the edges of the park are the Mayan ruins of **Chinkultic** ("terraced well"). This site has a number of stelae, a ball court, and pyramids from which you can admire the surrounding lakes. You can also swim in the deep *cenote* (spring-fed water hole) from which Chinkultic gets its name. The ruins are a half-hour hike from the main road that leads to the lakes, and buses between Comitán and the park pass the turnoff; ask the driver to let you off at Chinkultic. The ruins are open daily 8:30-4; admission is $1 Monday-Saturday, free Sundays and holidays.

COMING AND GOING Colectivos and combis from **Transportes Comitán-Montebello** (2a Av. Sur 17, btw 2a and 3a Calles Sur Pte., tel. 963/2-08-75) terminate at Lago Bosque Azul;

they leave every half hour, 5:45 AM–4:45 PM. The trip takes about an hour and costs $1.25. The last bus back to Comitán leaves Bosque Azul around 4 PM. Hitching is also possible.

WHERE TO SLEEP AND EAT You can easily stay in Comitán and make day trips to the lakes, but if you want to stay overnight, bring warm gear and expect a chilly evening. The restaurant at Lago Bosque Azul offers simple cabañas for $2 a night, and Doña Maria at **Posada Las Orquideas,** at the turnoff for the ruins, offers basic cabins ($2 per person) and cheap meals. Out here, however, camping is the way to go. It's free, and officially permitted at Bosque Azul and La Encantada, which are outfitted with palapas, fire pits, and restrooms. The village of Tziscao on the south end of the park has lodging ($3 per person) as well as camping sites ($1). Make sure to bring your own food.

Tapachula

The southernmost city of any size in Mexico, Tapachula lies at the center of the Soconusco mountain region, which extends from the Chiapan mountains to the coast and down into southwestern Guatemala. Significant numbers of European and Asian immigrants—many fleeing World War II and the Communist Revolution in China—were attracted to the area by its coffee- and cacao-driven prosperity, and modern-day Tapachula is still home to a diverse population. Guatemalans come here to shop, do business, find work on the plantations, or escape political persecution, while budget travelers are attracted by the city's amenities and proximity to the border. All this activity has rendered Tapachula a bustling, cosmopolitan town blessed with budget hotels and good cappuccino. The area also has much to offer outdoorsy types: The nearby beach towns of Puerto Madero and Las Palmas are pleasant places to cool off in the gentle ocean waves. The Izapa archaeological zone, where easy hikes through cacao fields lead you to infrequently visited ruins, also lies close to the city. A bit farther away, at the foot of the Tacaná volcano, the cool mountain town of Unión Juárez offers limitless camping, hiking, and swimming.

Tapachula, which means "place of sour prickly pears" in Nahuatl, was originally designated an administrative, tribute-paying region of the Aztec empire. The Aztecs demanded colored feathers, jade, jaguar pelts, and cacao from their southern subjects.

BASICS

CASAS DE CAMBIO BITAL (2a Av. Nte., at Calle 1 Pte., tel. 962/5–05–01) changes traveler's checks and cash weekdays 10–noon. **Serfin** (Calle 1 Pte., at 4a Av. Nte.) doesn't change money, but has a 24-hour ATM. The **Casa de Cambio** (4a Av. Nte., at Calle 3 Pte., tel. 962/6–51–22) is the only place in town to exchange Central American currencies, but it does so at poor rates, Monday–Saturday 7:30–7:30 and Sunday 7–1.

CONSULATES Get a visa ($5) for travel into Guatemala at the **Guatemalan Consulate.** Take a photocopy of your passport for faster service. *Calle 2 Ote. 33, at 7a Av. Sur, tel. 96/6–12–52. Open weekdays 8–4.*

CROSSING THE BORDER Two border crossings lie within easy reach of Tapachula and both are open 24 hours a day, 365 days a year, to accommodate the constant flow of migrant workers. The **Talismán/El Carmen** crossing, located 15 kilometers (9 mi) north of Tapachula, the most convenient for travelers, with frequent onward buses for Quetzaltenango and Guatemala City close at hand. **Ciudad Hidalgo/Tecún Umán** lies farther out of the way—some 40 kilometers (24 mi) south of Tapachula—and sees little tourist traffic. Avoid bathrooms at the border—they are prime sites for no-holds-barred stickups that can be rather embarrassing. For more general border advice, *see* box Going to Guatemala, in *Near Tapachula, below.*

Frequent VW colectivos ply the routes to the Talismán border, leaving every few minutes from outside Tapachula's Unión y Progreso terminal (Calle 5 Pte., btw Avs. 12 and 14 Nte.). The 45-minute trip costs 50¢. Paulino Navarro buses service Ciudad Hidalgo (45 min, $1) every 15 minutes. Taxis from Tapachula to Talismán and Hidalgo cost $1.50 and $3 respectively.

LAUNDRY Lava Ropa will wash and dry 3 kilos of clothing for $2. *Av. Central Nte. 33, btw Central Ote. and Calle 1 Ote., tel. 962/6-35-25. Open Mon.-Sat. 8-8.*

MAIL The post office is a seven-block trek from the center. They offer all the usual services and will hold mail sent to you at the following address for up to 10 days: Lista de Correos, Tapachula, Chiapas, CP 30700, México. *Calle 1 Ote. 32, at 7a Av. Nte., tel. 962/6-39-22. Open weekdays 8-7, Sat. 9-1.*

MEDICAL AID Farmacia 24 Horas (8a Av. Nte. 25, at Calle 7 Pte., tel. 962/6-24-80) offers chips and Coke as well as medication round the clock. For emergencies, call the **Cruz Roja** (tel. 962/6-19-49).

PHONES There are two blue Ladatel phones on the southwest corner of the zócalo and more in the quieter area a block south of the zócalo on Calle 1 Poniente, at 6a Avenida Norte. These phones are your best bet for an international collect call (dial 09 for an operator).

VISITOR INFORMATION Housed in the Casa de Cultura, the **SEDETUR** office has two wonderful employees, Magui and Amelinda, who are very proud of their region and will help you plan treks into the countryside or provide information on crossing into Guatemala. *Btw Palacio and Museo, west side of zócalo, tel. 962/5-54-09. Open weekdays 9-3 and 6-9.*

COMING AND GOING

BY BUS The first-class bus terminal (Calle 17 Ote., at 3a Av. Nte., tel. 962/6-28-81) is a good 12 blocks north of the center. To get here, either take a taxi (75¢) or a CRISTOBAL COLON or LOMA DE SAYULA combi (20¢) down Avenida Central Norte. **Cristóbal Colón** and **UNO** offer first-class direct service to San Cristóbal (10 hrs, $7.50), with six departures a day, and Oaxaca city (14 hrs, $20), with two departures a day. Four buses a day go to Salina Cruz (8 hrs, $10) and Mexico City (24 hrs, $35); the evening luxury service is worth the extra bucks.

If your next destination is San Cristóbal (10 hrs, $6) or Comitán (6 hrs, $3), second-class **Transportes Sur** (Calle 9a Pte. 63, btw 12a and 14a Avs. Nte.) offers the most frequent service, with about 10 departures per day to each city. **Autobuses General Paulino Navarro** (Calle 7 Pte., at Av. Central Nte., tel. 962/6-31-02), located four blocks northeast of the zócalo, offers two second-class buses a day to Tuxtla Gutiérrez (7 hrs, $8) and frequent service to nearby towns and border crossings. **Unión y Progreso** (Calle 5 Pte., btw 12a and 14a Avs. Nte., tel. 962/6-33-79) collectivos serve Talismán and Unión Juárez infrequently 5:30 AM-8 PM for 50¢. Frequent colectivos (75¢) also depart for Ciudad Hidalgo and Talismán from the bus stations and along 10a Avenida Norte, near the market.

BY TRAIN The train station (Av. Central Sur, at Calle 20 Pte., tel. 962/5-21-76) is a long taxi ride ($1.50) from the center. A train departs early in the morning for Juchitán, Mexico City, and Veracruz; check with the station for prices and times the day before departure. Service in this area is slow and uncomfortable—the trip to Mexico City takes three days. If for some odd reason this sounds like fun, head to the station early in the morning, buy your tickets in advance, and physically secure your seat as soon as possible.

BY PLANE Aeroméxico (tel. 962/6-20-50), **AVIACSA** (tel. 962/6-31-47), and **Taesa** (tel. 962/6-37-32) take off from the airport (Carretera 225 Km. 22, tel. 962/6-22-91) for Mexico City. Fares vacillate wildly, from $55 during low season to as much as $189. All planes depart daily at 7:30 AM, with an additional Taesa flight weekdays at 5 PM. Call or stop by the airport bus office (2 Av. Sur 40, tel. 962/5-12-87) in advance to make arrangements for a colectivo pickup at your doorstep ($3). Private taxis from the airport charge $7.

GETTING AROUND

The city's main sights and many budget establishments are clustered around the zócalo, at the intersections of Calles 3 and 5 Poniente and 4a and 6a Avenidas Norte. Most of the city is easily walkable, but taxis ($1) and colectivos (20¢), which run daily 5 AM-10 PM, crowd the streets and can move you around town cheaply. Two long boulevards—the north-south Avenida

Central Norte/Sur and the east–west Calle Central Oriente/Poniente—divide the city into quadrants. Even-numbered calles are south of Avenida Central Poniente/Oriente, and odd-numbered calles are north of it. Even-numbered avenidas are west of Calle Central Norte/Sur, and odd-numbered avenidas are east of it.

WHERE TO SLEEP

Many better-than-average budget hotels are concentrated around the city center. If you're broke, **Casa de Huéspedes Yuli** and **Hospedaje La Mexicana** (both on 8a Av. Nte., at Calle 11 Pte., no phones), a few blocks west of second-class bus stations, offer fairly clean, padlocked double rooms for less than $3 a night.

Hospedaje Colonial. Although it looks like a hole-in-the-wall from the street, this downtown hotel is overflowing with plants and character. According to the owners, "hanging herbs keep the bats away," and the beautiful gardens keep the guests happy. The front door is perpetually locked, and if you come in past 11:30 PM, the owners will give you hell. Beds are $4.75 per person. *4a Av. Nte. 31, tel. 962/6–20–52. 10 rooms, all with bath. Luggage storage.*

Hospedaje Las Américas. This hotel is just steps away from the market and second-class bus stations. The quiet, clean rooms open onto a tree-filled central courtyard and are a terrific deal at $4 a single and $5 a double. *10a Av. Nte. 47, tel. 962/6–27–57. 20 rooms, all with bath. Luggage storage.*

Hotel Cervantino. Four blocks from the center, this is an exceptionally clean hotel, and all rooms have fans and tables. The management is friendly and extremely helpful. Singles cost $5, doubles $7.50, and a room for four (two beds) is $9.50. *1a Av. Ote. 6, tel. 962/ 6–16–58. 21 rooms, all with bath. Luggage storage. Wheelchair access. MC, V.*

Hotel Puebla. You pay a premium for location at this four-story hotel right next to the Palacio Municipal. Spacious rooms have fans, hot water, and access to communal balconies overlooking the Parque Central. Singles are $8, doubles $9. *Calle 3 Pte. 40, behind Palacio Municipal, tel. 962/6–14–36. 40 rooms, all with bath. Luggage storage. Wheelchair access.*

FOOD

Perhaps because many of the migrant Guatemalan workers who toil on the plantations have no place to go for the night, Tapachula has a number of 24-hour restaurants. Most of them cluster around the zócalo. **La Parrilla** (8a Av. Nte. 20, west of zócalo, tel. 962/6–51–98; open daily 7 AM–midnight) offers cheap sandwiches and breakfasts, as well as filet mignon with a baked potato for $5. **La Flor de Michoacán** (6a Av. Nte., at Calle 7 Pte., no phone) is filled with Guatemalan workers watching TV and slowly sipping 70¢ licuados and nibbling 20¢ tacos into the wee hours.

El Mestizo. Savory one-dollar Chinese entrées beckon from the window of this cross-cultural comedor. *Pozole* (hominy soup; $1.25) and pancakes (80¢) are served up lickety-split. *Calle Pte. 32-A, btw 8 and 10 Avs. Nte., no phone. Open daily 7 AM–10 PM.*

Restaurant Longyin. You won't find any fortune cookies, but the *chop suey* ($3) and *chow mein* ($3) are served in heaping portions, with extra MSG, in a commodious open-air setting. The restaurant offers a unique opportunity to pepper your Chinese food with salsa picante. *2a A Nte. 36, tel. 962/6–24–67. Open daily 10–6.*

WORTH SEEING

The labyrinthine **Mercado Sebastián Escobar** (behind the cathedral) is a two-block indoor/outdoor market where tropical fruits, vegetables, live birds, and every trinket you can imagine are sold. The indoor part is open in the morning only, and the fruit selection is best before midday. Also worth a visit is the **Museo Regional del Soconusco**, inside the art deco **Palacio Municipal** (just west of zócalo, tel. 962/6–35–43). The museum displays bits of stelae and other artifacts from nearby ruins, as well as photos of excavation sites. Admission is $1.25 (free Su days) and it's open Tuesday–Sunday 10–5. Next door is the **Casa de Cultura** (admission free; open daily 9–9), offering music, art, and dance classes. Upstairs, regional displays of arts and crafts appear from time to time. Marimba, classical, and ambient music is often featured in the **Parque Central**'s gazebo at 6 PM. Check with the Casa de Cultura for a schedule of free events. The **Banana Safari** and **Chula Zoo** complex (Libramiento Sur Km. 1, tel. 962/ 6–39–36; open daily 9–5) offers a glimpse of wild animals on a former banana plantation. Admission is $3. To get here, take a taxi ($2) from the center.

If you're in town the first two weeks of March, you'll witness the **Feria Internacional,** Tapachula's big yearly bash in celebration of the agricultural, artistic, and commercial richness of the area. Another big event is the **Feria de San Agustín,** which celebrates the town's patron saint with songs, libations, and dance August 20–28.

Near Tapachula

There are a number of towns near Tapachula easily visited in a day. The seaside town of **Puerto Madero,** 27 kilometers (16 mi) southwest of Tapachula, is the closest place to breathe some sea air, although its little beach, **Playa San Benito,** is a bit dirty and should be avoided at night. The water is pleasant and warm though, and iguanas bake themselves on the boulders that line the beach. Fresh fish is available from beachfront palapas. Microbuses (20 min, $1) from Tapachula's General Paulino Navarro bus station (*see* Coming and Going, *above*) leave about every half hour until 5:30 PM. A better beach a bit farther away (a 45-minute ride up the coast) is the gloriously quiet, palm-fringed **Las Palmas.** To get here from Tapachula, take a bus to Acapetahua or Escuintla, where you can catch a colectivo to Las Palmas. If you're not camping and cooking, plan on catching a bus back by afternoon.

Also easily accessible is the seldom-visited **Izapa** archaeological zone, only 15 minutes away on the road to Talismán. The ruins are said to provide a link between Olmec and early Mayan cultures. Closest to Tapachula are groups A and B, about 20 minutes down a jungle path marked by a sign at the highway. Group A is sadly uncared for. Continue farther along the path and through the cacao fields to Group B, where you'll find a huge pyramid and some better-preserved stelae. The largest and most impressive ruins (Group F) are visible from the highway and are less than a kilometer farther along the path, on the lefthand side. This fully restored ceremonial center—complete with pyramids, a ball court, altars, and stelae—enjoyed its hey-day around 300–200 BC. To reach the sites, take one of the frequent Talismán-bound colec-tivos from either of Tapachula's second-class stations and ask the driver to let you off at Izapa. Buses (60¢) run 5:30 AM–8 PM. The sites are open during daylight hours and are officially free, but if you give a donation to the caretakers, they are likely to show you around.

UNIÓN JUÁREZ

If you're going to be in the area for any length of time, do not fail to visit Unión Juárez, 30 kilo-meters (18 mi) northeast of Tapachula. This coffee-growing town clinging to the base of the 4,110-meter **Volcán Tacaná** offers great swimming and hiking, plus good food and lodging. Its steep cobblestone roads wind through coffee plantations and cool, lushly forested valleys criss-crossed by rivers. Close to town, the **Cascadas de Muxbal** (Muxbal Waterfalls) have a deep pool for swimming and are situated in a narrow canyon hung with gargantuan ferns. There are also pools for bathing on the nearby **Río Mala.** If you're up for a short hike, two sublime vantage points each lie about an hour's trek out of town: **Pico de Loro** (Parrot's Beak) is a rock out-cropping that affords a beautiful view of Guatemala and the ocean. **La Ventana** (The Window), the other vista point, is on a hill overlooking a forested valley. Ask for directions and maps at the Palacio Municipal on the zócalo during business hours. If you're looking for something more challenging, the climb to the top of Tacaná is a day-long enterprise. You'll have to spend the night on the summit in some simple, free huts; bring a warm bedroll. Ask Don Humberto Ríos at **Restaurante La Montaña** or Roberto Moody at **Posada Aljoad** (*see* Where to Sleep and Eat, *below*) about guide service and accommodations up the volcano. Whatever you choose to do, head out early in the morning, since the fog and rain arrive like clockwork in the afternoon.

COMING AND GOING Direct buses between Tapachula and Unión Juárez are hard to come by. The simplest way to get here is to catch a minibus or combi from 12a Avenida Norte in Tapachula to the town of Cacahuatán (40 min, 70¢), where you can squeeze into one of the always-crowded VW buses that frequently make the trip to Unión Juárez (1 hr, $1).

WHERE TO SLEEP AND EAT Pay $12 a night for a double room or $22 for a private chalet at the A-frame **Hotel Colonial Campestre** (Hidalgo 1) and enjoy hot water, TVs, phones, and even a disco. Your other option is to join nature enthusiasts and groups of young hikers at the **Hotel Posada Aljoad** (Mariano Escobedo, right off zócalo), where doubles cost $8 and the hot water is temperamental. Neither hotel has a private line, but you can call 962/2–02–25 for lodging information. **La Montaña** and **Restaurante Carmelita**, both on Avenida Juárez in the zócalo, serve three tasty meals daily at shoestring prices. Don't leave without trying La Montaña's *plátanos fritos* (fried plantains) for less than $2.

Villahermosa

Villahermosa, as the capital of Tabasco, is largely the product of the region's rich oil reserves, which in the '70s brought prosperity and expansion to the city. Huge luxury hotels, active cultural centers and museums, and the massive Tabasco 2000 complex—with its decadent, post-mortem architecture—are among the additions. The result is a city that lacks the natural beauty of the verdant highlands and forests outside its boundaries, but that does have enough parks and pedestrian-only streets to give it a certain appeal.

Villahermosa was originally established farther north as the capital of Tabasco, but was relocated after British, French, and Dutch pirates repeatedly looted the area for cacao and *palo de tinta* (a tree used for making dyes) during the 16th and 17th centuries. The city was moved south, away from the river connecting it to the pirates' sea route, and was renamed San Juan Bautista. In the late 1700s, King Felipe II of Spain gave it its final name: Villahermosa. The region came back into prominence in the world market in the early 1900s, when exports of bananas and cacao began to flourish.

At its worst, Villahermosa is an excessive jumble of streamlined '70s cement architecture expressways reminiscent of Southern California, and huge multipurpose stores filled with imported modern amenities. At its best, Villahermosa is an oasis of culture, with museums, a beautiful archaeological park, and an ecological reserve that puts Sea World to shame. Many affordable hotels serve as a base for exploring the rest of the state, where non-touristed beaches and quiet towns await. At any rate, do be prepared for a brief bit of culture shock, especially if you've been tramping around the remote Chiapan highlands.

Going to Guatemala

To facilitate onward passage at the border, arrive early with your Mexican tourist card ready to be stamped at immigration. You should also have small denominations of both U.S. dollars and quetzals, as well as your passport, onhand to help wend your way through the excessive bureaucracy. Guatemalan tourist cards cost $5, regardless of nationality: Be insistent that you receive a 90-day stay, as 30-day stints are often handed out. Check with the consulates in Comitán and Tapachula (see above) for the latest requirements. You should rebuff shifty money-changers and their poor rates, but realize this may be your last opportunity to get rid of unwanted pesos. Border crossings in Chiapas are located at Ciudad Cuauhtémoc, Talismán, and Hidalgo—for specific information on hours and transportation, see Basics, in Comitán and Tapachula, above.

BASICS

AMERICAN EXPRESS The air-conditioned **Turismo Nieves** travel agency also runs a full-service American Express desk that will hold mail, replace lost cards, and cash personal checks for cardholders, as well as deliver MoneyGrams and exchange or replace traveler's checks for anyone. *Sarlat Incidencia 202, at Fidencia, tel. 93/14–18–88. From Zona Luz, walk 1 block north on Carranza past Parque Juárez and turn left. Mailing address: American Express, Turismo Nieves, Sarlat Incidencia 202, Villahermosa, Tabasco, CP 86000, México. Open weekdays 9–6, Sat. 9–noon.*

BOOKSTORES Books in English are hard to come by, but if you read Spanish, **Librería Bookworm de Cultura** (27 de Febrero 603, Plazuela la Aguila, tel. 93/12–24–24) has a large selection of novels and books on Tabasco's natural and cultural heritage. **Librería El Alba** (Madero 616, tel. 93/12–22–24) also has Spanish novels, textbooks, and crafts. Both are open Monday–Saturday 8–8.

CASAS DE CAMBIO At last count, there were nine banks squeezed in among the shops and budget hotels of the Zona Luz area. All major banks (**Banamex, Bancomer,** and **BITAL**) have ATM's and will change U.S. dollars and traveler's checks weekdays 10–5.

For longer hours, head to **Blahberl** (27 de Febrero 1537, tel. 93/13–34–19), open weekdays 8:30–6:30 and Saturday 8:30–4. They change Canadian dollars as well as cash from most major European countries. For a commission, you can also cash personal checks written in U.S. dollars. To get here, take a cathedral-bound bus down 27 de Febrero and ask to be let off at *"el reloj con tres caras"* ("the clock with three faces").

EMERGENCIES The **police** can be reached at 93/13–21–10 or 93/3–37–32. For emergencies, dial 06.

LAUNDRY **Acua Lavandería** (Reforma 502, tel. 93/14–37–65; open Mon.–Sat. 8–8), just out of the Zona Luz toward the river, will wash 1 kilo of clothes for about $1. Same-day service is 50¢ more. **La Burbuja** (Bastor Zozaya 621, at Joaquín Camelo, no phone) offers reliable next-day service at $1 per kilo, weekdays 8–8 and Saturday 8–4.

MAIL The most convenient post office is in the Zona Luz. They'll hold mail sent to you at the following address for up to 10 days: Lista de Correos, Villahermosa, Tabasco, CP 86001, México. *Sáenz 131, tel. 93/12–10–40. Open weekdays 8–7, Sat. 9–noon.*

MEDICAL AID Two of several places to get 24-hour emergency service are the **Cruz Roja** (Cesar Saudino, Col. Primera de Mayo, tel. 93/15–55–55) and **Rescate Civil** (cnr of Periférico and 16 de Septiembre, tel. 93/13–19–00). Pharmacies abound in the Zona Luz, but all close by 9 PM. **Farmacia Mariana** (27 de Febrero 626, tel. 93/14–23–66), a few blocks up from the Zona Luz, is open 24 hours a day.

PHONES You can't walk 10 paces in the Zona Luz without running into a Ladatel phone, from which you can make international calls with a Ladatel Plus card—sold at most *papelerías* (stationery stores) in the area. For collect calls, dial 09. If you want to make a cash call, head for the caseta in **Café Barra** (Lerdo de Tejada 608). It's open Monday–Saturday 7–1 and 3:30–10, and charges a small fee for unaccepted collect calls. There is also a 24-hour caseta across from the ADO station (*see* Coming and Going, *below*).

VISITOR INFORMATION The unorganized **SECTUR** federal tourist office offers the glossy *Mundo Maya* magazine, a blurry map of the city, and information on cultural events. The office is ensconced within an unmarked stone building. To get here, take the TABASCO 2000 or PALACIO MUNICIPAL bus from either the *malecón* (boardwalk) or Parque Juárez. *Paseo Tabasco 1504, Tabasco 2000 Complex, tel. 93/16–36–33. Open weekdays 9–3 and 6–9.*

COMING AND GOING

BY BUS The first-class bus station (Francisco Javier Mina 297, at Lino Merino) is big and efficient, with computers, reservation systems, and a couple of overpriced places to eat. **ADO**

(tel. 93/12–89–00), **Cristóbal Colón** (tel. 93/14–56–80), and **UNO** (tel. 93/14–20–54) all provide frequent service to the following destinations: Chetumal (9 hrs, $15), Mérida (10 hrs, $17), Mexico City (16 hrs, $27), Oaxaca city (16 hrs, $20), Palenque (2 hrs, $4), Tapachula (16 hrs, $20), Teapa (1½ hrs, $1.50), and Tuxtla Gutiérrez (6½ hrs, $7). Be sure to buy your ticket in advance, as lines are always long and seats sell out. Luggage storage ($1–$2 per day) is available at the station 24 hours. To reach the city center, walk a good 12 blocks southeast or take a bus marked PARQUE JUAREZ. Buses marked CENTRO will take you to the Palacio Municipal; those marked CENTRAL will take you to the Central Camionera (*see below*). A collective taxi to the center from outside the station costs 65¢.

The huge **Central Camionera** (Ruíz Cortínez, east of intersection with Javier Mina) is the city's second-class bus station. Buses range from clean and plush to fleabags on wheels, and serve a dizzying array of destinations more frequently and cheaply than the first-class buses. Ticketsellers from a zillion different bus companies will get you to Mexico City ($20), Puebla ($16), Jalapa ($14), Veracruz ($9), Palenque ($2), and Teapa ($1). To arrive here from the Zona Luz, take any bus marked CENTRAL along the malecón.

Buses to the coast and Comalcalco leave from the **Transportes Somellera** terminal (Ruíz Cortínez, at Llergo, tel. 93/14–41–18). There is service to Comalcalco (1½ hrs, $1.50) every half hour and to Paraíso (2 hrs, $2) every hour. The easiest way to get here is to take a bus to the Central Camionera, cross the bridge over the highway, and walk three long blocks down Ruíz Cortínez toward the Hotel Maya Tabasco. A block or so past the hotel you'll see the station on your left.

BY PLANE The airport (tel. 93/12–18–30) is served by **Aeroméxico** (tel. 93/14–16–75), **AVIACSA** (tel. 93/14–47–55), **Mexicana** (tel. 93/12–11–64), and **Aerolitoral** (tel. 93/14–36–14). There are daily flights to Acapulco, Cancún, Havana, Los Angeles, Mazatlán, and Mérida, as well as several daily flights to México City ($50–$100 one-way). No public transportation goes to the airport. Taxis charge $7 for private service or $4 for collective service to town, but you might be able to bargain. Luggage storage ($2) is available at the airport.

GETTING AROUND

Villahermosa can be difficult to navigate, even with the blurry map given out at the tourist office, but a few prominent landmarks, abundant city buses, and cheap taxis help somewhat. The center of town is bordered by three avenues, along which lie many of the major points of interest. The main highway is **Ruíz Cortínez,** a huge express way with fast and deadly traffic. The Central Camionera, the Transportes Somellera terminal, and the largest food market are all here. Cortínez turns south at the **Parque Museo L. Venta**—you'll see the rectangular *mirador* (viewing tower) jutting out where it intersects with **Paseo Tabasco,** another main avenue. This street runs from the **Tabasco 2000 complex** in the west—with its huge, black mushroom of a water tower—to the **malecón,** which runs along the bank of the Río Grijalva, in the east. CICOM (*see* Worth Seeing, *below*) is south of the center on **Carlos Pellicer,** which is the name the malecón takes on just past the roundabout where it hits Paseo Tabasco.

The bus system in Villahermosa can be confusing—so confusing, in fact, that you'll probably see more than one local anxiously asking the bus driver for reassurance about the route. You would be wise to follow suit.

Within this ring, the streets that will be most important to you are: Francisco Javier Mina, which heads north to Cortínez and the bus stations along the highway; Méndez, which runs from Llergo to the malecón and crosses Mina; and Madero, which runs eight long blocks from Cortínez to the malecón, parallel to Mina. Follow the one-way flow of traffic north on Madero and you'll pass the **Parque Benito Juárez,** at the northeast corner of the **Zona Luz.** The Zona Luz (or Zona Remodelada) is a recently remodeled pedestrian-only area bordered by Madero on the east, Zaragoza on the north, Castillo to the west, and 27 de Febrero to the south. This where you'll find the best budget lodging and restaurants.

BY BUS Destinations are usually marked on windshields, but routes are often very round-about. To reach the tourist office or La Venta, take either the TABASCO 2000 or PALACIO MUNICI-PAL bus from Madero, one block north of Parque Juárez. From the same stop, you can catch buses for CICOM (*see* Worth Seeing, *below*). For buses to the second-class bus station or market, take either the CENTRAL or MERCADO bus from the malecón to the highway. Fare is 20¢.

BY TAXI Because drivers pack their tiny Nissans with passengers, rides are cheap within the city (60¢–$1), but are a rip-off to the airport and Yumká, neither of which are served by public transit. In front of the first-class bus station and on Madero near Reforma, wait in line at a taxi stand and someone will find you the right car once you announce your destination. Taxis ($7) are unfortunately the only way to the airport. Call 93/15–83–33 for a pickup.

WHERE TO SLEEP

Villahermosa has a number of large hotels with standard rooms and competitive prices. Fans or air-conditioning are more important (and easier to come by) than hot water. Since many hotels have permanent residents, you may have to check a few before you find space, but most places will store your luggage for you while you look. The best time to search is noon–1, the usual checkout time. Budget hotels are clustered in the Zona Luz on Madero and side streets such as Lerdo de Tejada, where the quietest hotels overlook pedestrian walkways. **Hotel Tabasco** (Lerdo de Tejada 317, tel. 93/12–00–77) and the adjacent **Hotel Oviedo** (Lerdo de Tejada 303, tel. 93/12–14–55) are the cheapest digs in town that still maintain reasonable standards. At Oviedo, singles cost $5.25, doubles $6.75, and triples $8 (Hotel Tabasco's rooms are a dollar cheaper).

Hotel Madero. The conscientious proprietor has seen to it that this is one of the cleanest, most comfortable inexpensive hotels in the city. The rooms are decorated in various tranquil shades of blue, the bathrooms have hot water, and the staff is more than eager to help you find your way around town. Singles are $6.75, doubles $8, and triples $9.50. *Madero 301, tel. 93/12–05–16. 28 rooms, all with bath. Luggage storage.*

Hotel Oriente. On a busy section of Madero, under an arched awning, this modest, fairly clean (although somewhat dark) hotel is a decent value. Request the "penthouse" rooms (Nos. 43 and 44), with cross-ventilation from three sets of windows. Simple singles are $5.50, doubles $6.75, triples $9.50. Air-conditioning and TV run a few bucks more. *Madero 425, tel. 93/12–11–01. 22 rooms, all with bath. Luggage storage.*

Hotel Palma de Mallorca. The majesty of this hotel is fading fast, but rooms are large and airy. With fans, singles cost $6, doubles $9, triples $11 (add $1.25 for air-conditioning). The hot water in the shower eventually comes after some well-timed foreplay with a steady hand. *Madero 510, tel. 93/12–01–45. 36 rooms, all with bath. Luggage storage.*

Hotel San Miguel. This is one of the more popular budget places and is consistently full. The clean, basic rooms all have phones and private bath. Singles are $5, doubles $6.25, and triples $7.75, and for a few dollars more you'll get air-conditioning. *Lerdo de Tejada 315, tel. 93/12–15–00. 45 rooms, all with bath. Luggage storage.*

Hotel Santa Lucia. This centrally located hotel provides well-furnished, clean singles ($6.75), doubles ($8), and triples ($9.50) with hot water and real bathtubs. Some rooms are darker than others, but all go quickly. Make sure your fan works before settling in. *Madero, btw Lerdo de Tejada and Reforma, no phone. Next to Hotel Don Carlos. 30 rooms, all with bath.*

FOOD

Variety is not a problem in Villahermosa. The large, enclosed **Mercado Pino Suárez** (Bastar Ozaya, 2 blocks west of Río Grijalva) is open mornings and has a good selection of fruit and bread and a bunch of dirt-cheap taco stands. You can also cool off with a *paleta* (popsicle) or ladle of liquid heaven from the many *agua fresca* (juice drink) stands featuring icy vats of tamarind, lime, pineapple, horchata, and other thirst quenchers. **Mini-Leo** (Juárez 504) is a citywide chain with burgers, fries, tacos, quesadillas, and the like. Frozen-yogurt shops, bakeries, and supermarkets fill the Zona Luz. **Las 2 Naciones** (Juárez 533, tel. 93/12–12–22) has tempting pastries Monday–Saturday 7 AM–9 PM.

➤ **UNDER $5 • Aquarius.** You'll find vegetarian sandwiches, soups, and yogurt, as well as medicinal herb teas and vitamins at both Aquarius locations. A hot, filling sandwich with beans, cheese, avocado, alfalfa sprouts, and more is $1.25. For 65¢, serious health-food nuts can detoxify their systems with a beet, carrot, and celery juice concoction called *vampiro,* which leaves the mouth bright red. Wheat breads are also sold at the health-food store in front. *Zaragoza 513, in Zona Luz, tel. 93/12–05–79. Open Mon.–Sat. 8 AM–9 PM. Other location: Javier Mina 309, 2 blocks from ADO bus station, tel. 93/14–25–37. Open daily 8 AM–10 PM.*

La Noria. A welcome addition to the Villahermosa eating scene, this Lebanese enclave serves homemade *hummus* ($2.50) and *tabouli* ($2), as well as an authentic barrage of breads, brochettes, and beans. Owner Señora Amalin Yabor Elías has been weaning locals away from grease for five years, and the trend is finally starting to catch on. *6a Av. Méndez 1008, tel. 93/14–16–59. From 1st-class bus station, walk 2 blocks south on Mina, right on Méndez. Open weekdays 9–8, Sat. 9–6.*

El Torito Valenzuela. The specialty here is the tender, meaty tacos—your choice of pork, beef, and even brains—served on fresh, handmade tortillas with lots of cilantro and onion (35¢–65¢ each). The *queso fundido* (cheese fondue), quesadillas ($1), and the hearty breakfast specials are also excellent. Their comida corrida ($3) is more than one person should ever eat in one sitting: soup, tortillas, entrée, french fries, beans, rice, fried plantains, a drink, and dessert. *27 de Febrero, at Madero, tel. 93/14–18–89. Open daily 7 AM–midnight.*

➤ **UNDER $10 • Birbiri's.** This teal-and-pink restaurant is a bit pricey and out of the way, but locals swear by the seafood. Have the shrimp in garlic ($5) and linger after dinner, sipping a drink from the full bar and listening to the singer who performs in the evenings. *Madero 1032, tel. 93/12–32–41. Open Mon.–Sat. 10–8.*

WORTH SEEING

Villahermosa is rich with places to stroll: along the river's malecón, through Benito Juárez Park above the river at the end of Aldama, and around the Zona Luz. Sunday is the big day for families, who often head for nearby beaches. Festivals are also an important part of local life. **La Feria del Desarrollo** (Development Fair), held during late April and early May, celebrates the diversity of culture in Tabasco, with all 17 municipalities showcasing their typical dances, arts, and music. There's also a parade of decorated boats down the Río Grijalva, with fireworks and general revelry. The main action takes place in **Parque de la Choca,** past Tabasco 2000. In February, **Carnaval** is especially big here, with music, dance contests, and processions. Ash Wednesday is marked by citywide water-balloon fights.

In La Venta, check out the exaggerated, Easter Island-esque, cranially deformed heads with baby faces, which are said to be proof of either endocrine deficiencies or intimate contact with Phoenician slaves or space invaders.

MUSEUMS Most of Villahermosa's museums offer free guided tours in Spanish. The museums in the Zona Luz are cheap (or free), only a short walk from the budget lodgings and hold worthwhile evening events. All museums are closed Mondays.

➤ **PARQUE-MUSEO LA VENTA •** Villa's most touted attraction, this sprawling park displays all the major finds from the La Venta archaeological site, located on the border with Veracruz. The site was threatened by oil drilling in the late '50s, but saved by cultural patron and poet extraordinaire Carlos Pellicer Cámara. The jungly park has dirt paths that wind past 30 or so Olmec carvings, mosaics, and stelae. Provided there's a group of four or more, free guided tours in Spanish leave every half hour from the entrance; tours in English can be arranged with guides at the entrance for around $5. Buy your tickets before 4 PM and bring bug repellent for the 30 to 40-minute walk through the steamy jungle. *Ruíz Cortínez, tel. 93/15–22–28. From Parque*

Juárez, take a TABASCO 2000 bus, get off at cnr of Paseo Tabasco and Ruíz Cortínez, and walk NE along lakeshore to entrance. Admission: $2. Open daily 9–5. Wheelchair access.

➤ **MUSEO REGIONAL DE ANTROPOLOGIA CARLOS PELLICER CAMARA** • This museum in the CICOM cultural center (*see below*) emphasizes the Olmec's influence on the cultures that succeeded them, particularly the Maya to the south and the Huasteca to the north. There are a few well-worn Olmec heads, altars, and stelae, as well as a number of pieces from as far away as Nayarit, Chihuahua, and the Yucatán. *CICOM, Carlos Pellicer 511, tel. 93/12–32–00. Catch any CICOM bus along Madero. Admission: $1.25. Open daily 9–8.*

➤ **MUSEUMS IN THE ZONA LUZ** • Near the budget lodgings are three museums, each worth a quick peek. The small, free **Casa-Museo Carlos Pellicer** (Sáenz 203, tel. 93/12–01–57) has miscellanea that once belonged to this famous Tabascan poet, who funded the excavation of La Venta and helped save its treasures from destruction. Be sure to check out the definitive plaster cast of his face taken at his death. The **Museo de Cultura Popular** (Zaragoza 810, tel. 93/12–11–17) has mannequins dressed in local costumes, as well as a collection of Tabasco's famous carved gourds. In the back is a dusty "typical" hut and a small pond with *pejelargarto* (alligator gar), large, toothy freshwater fish popular in regional dishes around Nacajuca. Admission is free here, too. The largest of these museums is the **Museo de Historia de Tabasco** (Juárez, at 27 de Febrero, no phone), with displays chronicling the history of Tabasco from pre-Hispanic times through the modern industrial age. It houses mostly posters and illustrations, but there are also a few old books, colonial uniforms, and even an antique X-ray machine that once belonged to a Villahermosan doctor. The interior is covered with many beautiful tiles, hence its nickname *La Casa de los Azulejos* (House of Tiles). Admission is 65¢. All three museums are open Tuesday–Sunday 10–4.

CULTURAL CENTERS Villahermosa's numerous free cultural centers are a testimony to the fact that Tabasco's oil revenues were put to good use. Galleries, music, and dance performances are all available at the places below free of charge or damn near it.

➤ **CENTRO CULTURAL DE LA UNIVERSIDAD AUTONOMA DE TABASCO** • Just steps away from the Zona Luz, this cultural center sponsors a wide variety of events and has two galleries showcasing local artists. There are free films Wednesday nights, and "cultural Thursdays" feature music, dance, or performing arts. Every couple of Saturdays the center holds *paseos culturales* (cultural outings) to nearby towns and archaeological sites. Sign up in advance to be sure you'll get a spot. It usually costs $3–$5 for an all-day outing that includes transportation and a knowledgeable guide. *27 de Febrero 640, tel. 93/12–45–57. Open weekdays 8 AM–9 PM.*

➤ **CENTRO CULTURAL DE VILLAHERMOSA** • Across from the Zona Luz, this air-conditioned center has wonderful art exhibits from all over Mexico, foreign films, concerts, a shop dedicated to Tabasco's crafts, and a good café. All performances and exhibits are free. *Madero, at Zaragoza, tel. 93/14–55–52. Open Mon.–Sat. 10–9.*

➤ **CICOM** • The Center for the Investigation of Olmec and Maya Cultures lies along the malecón, just west of the Río Grijalva. Of main interest is the Museo Regional de Antropología Carlos Pellicer Cámara (*see above*). Near the museum is the **Teatro Esperanza Iris,** a modern, plush, red-curtained center for national and regional events. Major events, such as performances by the National Ballet, tend to be jam-packed and cost $3–$7, although frequent lesser-known attractions—such as local dance and folk-music performances—are often free and usually only half full. The **CEIBA** arts center offers classes in music, dance, theater, and graphic arts. They also have a small gallery and poetry readings.

CICOM also houses the mammoth **public library** (open Mon.–Sat. 9–8, Sun. 9–6), where you'll find an impressive collection of books in Spanish and English (look on the shelves upstairs and to the right for English titles). On Sundays, free movies are shown three times a day in the auditorium to the left of the main library entrance. On weekdays, videos are shown at 7 PM. The bookstore here is also worth checking out. *Carlos Pellicer, south of Paseo Tabasco. From Parque Juárez, take a CICOM bus. Open Tues.–Sun. 10–4.*

ART GALLERIES Calle Sáenz in the Zona Luz features two small art galleries. Located in an old house, the **Galería Tabasco** (Sáenz 122, tel. 93/121–43–66; open Tues.–Sat. 3–8) features exhibits by local artists. Styles range from your basic still-life oil paintings to surreal dreamscapes. Just up the street is **Galería El Jaguar Despertado** (Sáenz 117, tel. 93/14–12–44; open Tues.–Sat. 3–10), a combination café, art gallery, and bookshop. Admission to both galleries is free.

YUMKA: CENTRO DE INTERPRETACION Y CONVIVENCIA CON LA NATURALEZA

Yumká, the Mayan name for a magical dwarf who looks after the jungles, is a 617-hectare (250-acre) ecological park featuring tropical rain forest, savanna, and a lagoon, each with its corresponding flora and fauna. Yumká's brochures highlight the imported African animals that draw Tabascans into the park, but the main focus is actually the Tabascan rain forest and lagoon ecosystems. The two-hour guided quest takes you through the rain forest by foot, across the savanna by open-air tram, and over the lagoon by raft—all, of course, in the most environmentally friendly manner. Yumká was set aside as a nature reserve in 1984, but not developed as an eco-tourism project until 1992. The guides are professional biologists, gifted at instilling a deeper appreciation of (and, it is hoped, a desire to preserve) the natural beauty and diversity of Tabasco. Dr. Luis Palazuelos, who oversees the operation, can provide further details for those interested. *No phone. From Restaurant Turístico La Venta (outside of Parque La Venta on hwy.), take a* YUMKA *bus ($1) or a taxi ($6.50). Admission: $3.50. Open daily 9–5.*

AFTER DARK

For a modern and apparently cosmopolitan city, most of Villahermosa goes to bed early. Around dinnertime (7-ish) is the prime time to be out and about, as this is when street bands entertain crowds, dancers fill the plazas, and the septuagenarian set makes the rounds. **Café Casino** (Juárez 531, at Zaragos) and **Café Barra** (Lerdo de Tejada 608), both open Monday–Saturday 9–9, offer cappuccino, espresso, and the buzz of animated conversation. By 10 PM, however, the Zona Luz is a virtual ghost town. The cultural centers (*see* Worth Seeing, *above*) put on frequent events, but most students head to discos when they really want to let loose.

BARS For a variety of live Latin music, hit the bar in **Hotel Don Carlos** (Madero 518, tel. 93/12–24–99), just across from the Zona Luz. Bands start about 9:30 PM and keep swingin' until 1:30 in the morning. There's no cover, no minimum, and drink prices aren't too outrageous ($1.25 for a beer, $1.75 for a margarita). **Baccarat "Ladies Bar"** (Sánchez Marmol 410, across from Parque Juárez, tel. 93/14–17–50) is a small, upstairs place with soft lights, wood paneling, and velvet seats. Live, mellow jazz plays from 8 to 11 on weekend nights. Contrary to the name, most of the clientele seems to be single and male, but the atmosphere is relatively relaxing.

DANCING The young and trendy spend their weekend evenings at **Tequila Rock** (tel. 93/16–44–00), a modern, neon-lit extension of the Holiday Inn in Tabasco 2000. **Ku Rock House** (Prolongación de Saudino 548, tel. 93/15–94–31) hosts *Jueveves*: open-bar, no-cover Thursday night bonanzas popular with horny university students. Cover charges are stiff (usually $5–$10), but the action starts about 10 and lasts until 1 or 2 AM. **The Factory** on Méndez draws crowds when school is not in session.

Near Villahermosa

COMALCALCO

One of the easternmost Mayan sites, Comalcalco is best known for the fired brick with which all of its lasting edifices were constructed. Because the jungle in these parts had no rock, the Chontal Maya who lived here used a mixture of clay, sand, and ground conch shell to form their reddish bricks that were fired and used for 282 buildings covering an area of 10 square kilometers. The city was built in the 7th century, and its sloping roofs (suitable for heavy rains) and stucco figures show evidence of the influence of Palenque.

Comalcalco has two major groups of buildings and many unexcavated grassy mounds. **Temple I,** the main pyramid, is on the large plaza. A flight of red-painted steps leads you up to the **Great Acropolis** and **Temples IV–VII.** Temple VI features a huge stucco mask representing the sun god. From the hill of the acropolis, you can enjoy the cooling winds and a view of the emerald green mounds and thick jungle canopy interrupted by cacao plantations. Since the temples at the site lack description, visit the **museum** first for a chronological breakdown of the site. The ticket window closes at 4 PM. Don't forget the insect repellent. *Admission to site and museum: $1.25, free Sun. Open daily 10–5.*

COMING AND GOING Buses to Comalcalco leave every half hour from **Transportes Somellera** in Villahermosa (*see* Coming and Going, *above*). The last buses back to Villahermosa leave Comalcalco's main bus station, known as La Central/Comalcalco (Méndez 411, tel. 931/4–00–27), around 6 PM. From the Comalcalco station you can take a microbus (25¢) directly to the ruins or to the highway drop-off point for the ruins, a 1-kilometer walk away. Comalcalco has modest hotel and food offerings, but it's easier to commute from Villahermosa. Tabasco's coast is only 21 kilometers (12 mi) from the Comalcalco ruins; you can catch a bus (35¢) marked PARAISO at the intersection of the highway and the road from the ruins.

THE TABASCAN COAST

Although once pristine, Tabasco's coastline suffered a sort of black death during the '70s oil boom. Right now the effects aren't readily apparent in the beaches listed below; here, the most visible uncleanliness stems from humans too lazy to pick up their trash. Few foreign travelers pass through, and—other than on weekends and during Semana Santa (Holy Week)—the beaches are often empty. Apart from palapas with hammock hooks, there is generally not much lodging here, but most beaches are within day-trip distance of towns with hotels and restaurants, such as Villahermosa, Comalcalco, and Paraíso.

The beaches with the most facilities (showers, lockers, shaded restaurants, and palapas) are **Limón** and **El Bellote,** both within a short bus ride of the medium-size city of **Paraíso.** Both have long stretches of white sand and pleasant shallow water with small waves. Palm tree–lined **Limón** has family-size cabañas that go for $15 (double that in April), lots of palapas, and a few restaurants offering grilled chicken. A better place to eat is in El Bellote at **Restaurante/Bar Viña del Mar,** which offers a never-ending list of tasty Atlantic-coast seafood dishes for under $5. Sometimes a local Mexican jazz ensemble will accompany your dinner. Nearby, the staff at **La Posta** gives out information on boat rentals to beach spots along the Laguna Mecoacán ($5 for a boat ride) and places to hang your hammock for $2 a night. Limón has endless rows of coconut trees, giving you a better chance to hang your hammock for free.

Colectivos leave for the beaches fairly frequently from Paraíso's bus station. Second-class **Transportes La Somellera** buses run between Paraíso and Villahermosa (1½ hrs, $2), and microbuses leave from Comalcalco (15 min, 20¢), or take a taxi for $3 from Comalcalco.

TEAPA

Tabasco is not all oil fields and muggy wetlands. The air feels remarkably clean and fresh in the city of Teapa, just one hour's worth of banana fields south of Villahermosa. The pretty zócalo, shaded by enormous trees, houses a community library at one end, and the Río Teapa runs right through town, offering lazy swimming (the best spot is just off the main street as it approaches the zócalo on the way into town). Otherwise spend your time taking excursions out of town for a cooling swim, a healing sulfur bath, or some subterranean exploration.

The Puyacatengo river in **Tacotalpa,** a short bus ride away on the road between Teapa and Villahermosa, has rapids and is a popular place with locals. Camping is safe here if you're not alone; there are no real facilities though, so bring everything you'll need to be self-sufficient for a few days. A 6-kilometer bus ride toward the town of Pichucalco and a $1.50 entrance fee will buy you free camping and almost unlimited hedonism at **El Azufre Spa,** where the noxious sulfur springs are known for their healing properties. Once you've paid the entrance fee, you're free to store your stuff in the administration office, enjoying use of the pools, palapas, and picnic tables.

If you prefer something a bit more strenuous, you can roam around inside the **Grutas de Coconá,** a set of spectacular caves out in the country. A bus marked MULTIGRUTAS leaves for the caves every half hour or so from the zócalo. To walk here, go down Méndez to the Pemex station and turn right onto Carlos Madrazo—a green sign alerts you—and follow the road about 2 kilometers until it turns to countryside; you'll find the grutas shortly thereafter. Once here, pay the 50¢ fee and enter the still darkness, where you'll hear only the squeaking of tiny bats and the dripping of water. The caves may not be lighted, so bring a flashlight and see if you can make out the figures of King Kong and his family, a giant peanut, a cow's tongue, a headless chicken, and, of course, Jesus Christ in the rocks. Be careful about going late in the afternoon, as robberies have been known to occur. The caves are open daily 10–4.

COMING AND GOING **Autotransportes Villahermosa Teapa** (Méndez 218, tel. 932/2–00–07) has hourly buses to Villahermosa ($2 1st class, $1 2nd class) between 5 AM and 8 PM. The station can be hard to find—look for a small square with a giant tree in the middle, and lots of maroon taxis parked outside; it's about five blocks from the zócalo, where the island in the middle of the main road begins. Arrive early; buses fill quickly and tickets only go on sale 15 minutes before departure, so you'll need to queue up ahead of time.

Those headed farther afield can take advantage of the Córdoba–Mérida **train** that creeps through town daily. The station (Ignacio Zaragoza, end of main drag, tel. 932/2–01–65) is a 20-minute walk from the zócalo. If you're headed for Veracruz (18 hrs, $4.50) or Mexico City, you'll have to take the train to Córdoba (16 hrs, $6), which hypothetically leaves between 6 AM and 8 AM, and transfer there. The train leaves for Mérida (14 hrs, $6.50) daily sometime between 7 PM and 11 PM, passing Palenque (2 hrs, $1.50), Tenosique (4 hrs, $2), and Campeche (10 hrs, $4.25) on the way. The trains through the Yucatán are infamously slow and dangerous.

GETTING AROUND Teapa has one main street that stretches from the train station (about a kilometer from the center) to the zócalo. It begins as 21 de Marzo, changes to Carlos Ramos at the Pemex station, and changes again to Gregorio Méndez as it approaches the zócalo. Many of the city's side streets are pedestrian walkways, and the town is definitely manageable on foot. Buses and colectivos to the grutas and other attractions leave from the zócalo and from the lime-green clock on the outskirts of town.

WHERE TO SLEEP AND EAT In addition to the places listed below, you can camp around Teapa if you keep a low profile. No formal camping facilities exist, but the area along the river offers several spots to lay your weary head. The worst hazard you're likely to face is mosquitoes. The **Hotel Azufre** (for directions see El Azufre Spa, *above*) rents huge rooms with fans and bathrooms for $14 (1–4 person occupancy), and the price includes entrance to the spa. Plant-strewn hallways make up for small rooms at **Casa de Huéspedes Miye** (Méndez 211, 2 blocks from zócalo, tel. 932/2–04–20). Singles with communal baths are $4, doubles $5; rooms with private baths for one or two are $10. There's no hot water, but you probably won't need it anyway. Pastel rooms and a lobby filled with porcelain animals make the wheelchair-accessible **Hotel Jardín** (Plaza Independencia 123, tel. 932/2–00–27) unique. The airy rooms with bath (cold water) overlooking the patio are $4.50 for singles, $7.50 for doubles.

Restaurants in Teapa tend to be either greasy or expensive. It's better to stick to the 50¢ sandwiches from any of the many hole-in-the-wall joints like **Café y Antojitos Queta** (across from Casa de Huéspedes Miye; open daily 8–8), rather than endanger your digestive system exploring more ambitious fare. Another safe option is the **market** right across from the lime-green clock, open early morning to late afternoon.

THE YUCATÁN PENINSULA

14

By Marisa Plowden

At the heart of the ancient Mayan city of Chichén Itzá stands El Castillo, a soaring 27-meter pyramid honoring the god Kukulcan. Every year at the spring and autumn equinoxes, the sun casts a shadow on the temple that makes it appear as if the serpent god is slithering down the pyramid to the city's sacred well. In a way, this monument of astrological precision embodies everything that attracts visitors to the Yucatán: the ingenuity of the ancient Maya, whose ruined cities dot the peninsula, and an attraction to the sun that manifests itself today in the form of pale gringos immolating themselves on the beaches of Cozumel, Cancún, Playa del Carmen, and Isla Mujeres.

Encompassing the states of Yucatán, Campeche, Quintana Roo, the country of Belize, and part of Guatemala, the Yucatán Peninsula covers 113,000 square kilometers (70,000 sq mi). Much of the peninsula is vast, scrubby desert covering porous limestone ("one living rock," as an early Spanish priest put it), which is dotted with *cenotes* (spring-fed water holes), jungles, and telltale mounds hiding unexcavated ruins. The peninsula's eastern coastline has everything you could ask for—clear Caribbean waters, a tropical climate, unbroken stretches of beach, and stunning coral reefs. Although much of this land is being sold to foreign resort developers and government-owned tourism agencies (causing nearby families to rely more heavily on the tourist trade for their survival), so far only Cancún has been transformed into an obscene tourist complex. Isla Mujeres, Playa del Carmen, and Tulum, though tourist-oriented, offer a mellow respite to the budget traveler. Many other beautiful beaches along the Caribbean coast remain tranquil and undeveloped.

Kukulcan is the Mayan name for Quetzalcoatl, the feathered serpent god of the Toltec (and Aztec) pantheons. Evidence that Kukulcan took on added importance after Toltec incursions into the Yucatán is found in architecture of the post-Classic period, most prominently at Chichén Itzá.

Along with the beaches, visitors to the Yucatán are attracted by the Mayan ruins—ancient cities dating back as far as 2,000 BC. Although hundreds of Mayan sites dot the Yucatán, only a handful have been excavated. Chichén Itzá is the best known, although Uxmal, near Mérida, and Cobá, within easy reach of Caribbean beaches, are also pretty major. If you're prepared to forgo the most famous Mayan ruins in favor of less spectacular or unexcavated sites, you can wander through entire ruins with no company but the jungle and the occasional reptile.

Often overlooked in the sprint for the beaches and ruins, though, are the Yucatán's towns. Huge baroque churches, old mansions, and winding cobblestone streets give these towns a distinctly European look, albeit softened by age and tropical heat. The peninsula was one of the first areas of the New World to be settled by the Spanish, and the legacy of the colonists lives

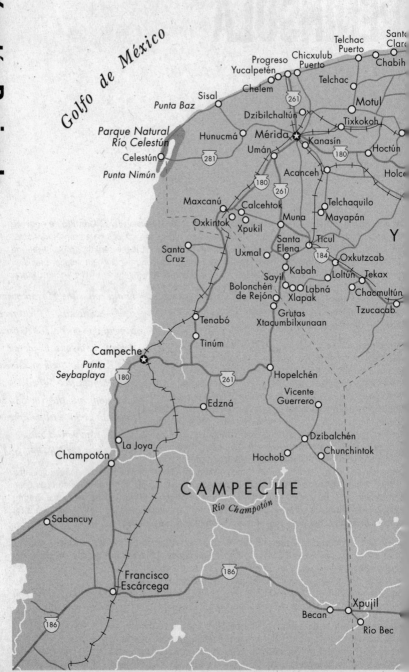

Golfo de México

Santa
Claro

Telchac
Puerto

Chabih

Progreso
Yucalpetén

Chicxulub
Puerto

Telchac

Chelem

Motul

261

Punta Baz

Sisal

Dzibilchaltún

Tixkokoh

Parque Natural
Río Celestún

Hunucmá

Mérida

Kanasín

Hoctún

Celestún

281

Umán

Acanceh

180

Holc

Punta Nimún

Maxcanú

Calcehtok

Telchaquilo

180

261

Muna

Mayapán

Oxkintok

Xpukil

Santa
Elena

Ticul

Y

Santa
Cruz

Uxmal

184

Oxkutzcab

Kabah

Loltún

Tekax

Sayil

Bolonchén
de Rejón

Labná

Chacmultún

Xlapak

Tzucacab

Grutas
Xtacumbilxunaan

Tenabó

Tinúm

Campeche

Hopelchén

Punta
Seybaplaya

180

Vicente
Guerrero

Edzná

261

La Joya

Dzibalchén

Chunchintok

Champotón

Hochob

CAMPECHE

Río Champotón

Sabancuy

Francisco
Escárcega

186

Xpujil

Becan

186

Río Bec

Natural
Felipe

San
Felipe

Parque Natural
Río Lagartos

Santa
Teresa

Sinaí

Cabo
Catoche

Isla
Contoy

Río
Lagartos

Holbox

Isla Holbox

295

El
Cuyo

Chiquilá

Isla
Mujeres

76

Sucilá

Yucatán

Punta Sam

Cancún

Puerto
Juárez

nkas

Tizimín

Kantunilkin

180

X-Can

Puerto Morelos

307

Pisté

Chichén
Itzá

Valladolid

Punta
Bete

anché

180

Dzitnup

Chemax

Playa del Carmen

Xcaret

San Miguel

á

Cobá

Paamul

Akumal

Palancar
Reef

Cozumel

Chemuyil

Xcacel

ÁN

Xel-Ha

Xcacel

Punta Sur

Tihosuco

Parque
Natural de
Quintana Roo

Tulum

Boca Paila

295

307

Punta Allen

a Rosa

Sian Ka'an
Biosphere
Reserve

Punta Pájaros

Caribbean Sea

Polyuc

184

Felipe Carrillo
Puerto

Tupak

NTANA ROO

Punta Herrero

293

Limónes

Punta El Placer

307

Puerto Bravo
Punta Río Indio

Laguna de
Bacalar

El Cocal

Majahual

Bacalar

Cenote
Azul

Bahía de
Chetumal

Cayo
Centro

Ucum

Chetumal

N

ás

Palmar

Bahía de
Corozal

Río Hondo

Xcalak

0   30 miles

0   40 km

BELIZE

on in towns such as Mérida and Campeche. Despite the best efforts of the early Spanish colonists, however, the Mayan people and their culture are very much alive in the Yucatán. Indeed, traveling here from elsewhere in Mexico is like entering another country. The people are visibly different: Most of the population is *mestizo* (people of mixed ancestry), and a fair amount are pure Maya, identifiable by their broad faces, dark skin, and short stature. Mayan, not Spanish, is the predominant language in many country towns and villages.

Christianity for many *yucatecos* (Yucatecans) is a mix of Catholicism and traditional animism, a belief that the sun, the earth, the plants, the animals, and the rain are gods. This melding of the ancient and the new is the result of a particularly bloody and cruel period of colonization. Since Hernán Cortés landed on the shores of the Yucatán in 1519, the Maya have battled for their land and their freedom. The Spanish burned religious texts, including astronomical works, and destroyed stone idols. Disease and forced labor decimated the Maya, but the Spanish never really succeeded in breaking their resistance. In the 1840s, after losing much of their lands, the Maya re-captured a good portion of the peninsula during the War of the Castes, but they failed to follow through and take the principal city, Mérida. The inevitable retaliation of the *hacendados* (landowners) resulted in the extermination of nearly half the Maya. Not until 1935, when the Chan Santa Cruz people signed an accord with the government, did the fighting cease.

Here, as in much of Mexico, poverty is the enemy, aggravated by the peninsula's thin, parched topsoil. Increasingly, Yucatecans are turning away from agriculture to more lucrative jobs; after oil, tourism is the second-largest industry here. As is the case with most tourist-driven economies however, the Yucatán's fragile environment has suffered unfortunate side effects. The destruction of delicate coral reefs to make room for new cruiseship piers has many residents and visitors questioning the relative costs and benefits of opening up paradise to so many people.

Cancún

Visiting Cancún is a lot like being seduced for the first time by the stereotypical Latin lover. If you're a Caribbean virgin, Cancún's warm, aquamarine waters caressing white-sand beaches will instantly enchant you. You'll think, "This is *it*. How could it be better than this?" Then you'll start listening to more experienced Yucatán travelers and you'll wise up. You'll realize that there's no soul behind Cancún's flashy exterior. That you don't have to max out your credit cards to experience hedonism. That it's not necessary to always share your fun with 18-year-olds enthusiastically dancing the *Macarena*. And with this coming of age you'll toss the easily accessible but culturally immature Cancún aside for hipper spots such as Playa del Carmen and Isla Mujeres; places that leave you with the same satisfied feeling, but where you can wake up in the morning with wallet and dignity intact.

The story of how Cancún became a tourist mecca is fairly well known. Looking for a new location for a money-making resort, the Mexican government asked a computer to come up with a site. Apparently a computer knows a good stretch of silicon when it sees one.

BASICS

AMERICAN EXPRESS The office has a travel agency, replaces lost cards and checks, cashes personal and traveler's checks, changes cash, and holds customers' mail for up to 30 days. *Tulum 208, American Express, Cancún, Quintana Roo, CP 77500, México, tel. 988/4–19–99. Btw Calles Agua and Viento. Open weekdays 9–6, Sat. 9–1.*

CASAS DE CAMBIO Cancún's many casas de cambio are open until 9 or 10 PM. Rates at banks are better, but the lines are long. **Banamex** (Tulum 19, tel. 988/4–54–11) and **Banco del Sureste** (Sunyaxchen 64, at Yaxchilán, tel. 988/4–51–61) change money weekdays 9–2. Both banks have an ATM that accepts Plus and Cirrus cards, and you can also get cash advances with a Visa or MasterCard.

CONSULATES Canada. *Plaza México 312, 2nd floor, tel. 988/4–37–16. Open weekday 10–2.*

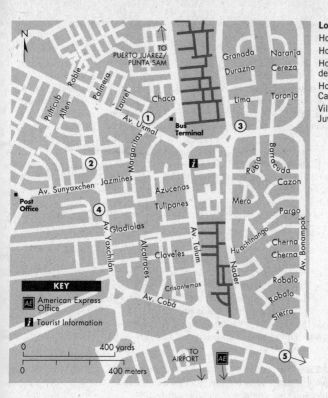

Lodging ○
Hotel Alux, **1**
Hotel Canto, **2**
Hotel El Rey
del Caribe, **3**
Hotel Villa Rossana
Cancún, **4**
Villa Deportiva
Juvenil Cancún, **5**

KEY
⒜Ｅ American Express
Office
𝑖 Tourist Information

0   400 yards
0   400 meters

United States. If you're unlucky enough to lose your passport or if you're involved in an accident or robbery, the U.S. consulate can help. *Plaza Caracol 2, Paseo Kukulcan, 3rd floor, tel. 988/3–22–86. Open weekdays 9–2 and 3–5:30.*

EMERGENCIES The **police** station (tel. 988/4–19–13) is downtown, next to the banks on Avenida Tulum. **Cruz Roja** (Labná 2, at Yaxchilán, tel. 988/4–16–16) has 24-hour ambulance service. For all other emergencies, dial 06.

LAUNDRY **Lavandería Lavamorena** does up to 3 kilos of your laundry for $2. *Grosella 105, at Xel-ha, Supermanzana 25, tel. 988/7–30–29. In front of post office. Open Mon.–Sat. 8 AM–9 PM.*

MEDICAL AID The **Hospital Americano** (Viento 15, at Tulum, tel. 988/4–61–33) is open 24 hours. **Farmacia París** (Yaxchilán 32, in Edificio Marruecos, tel. 988/4–30–05) is also open round the clock. The tourist information booklet *Cancún Tips* provides a list of English-speaking doctors.

PHONES AND MAIL You can place collect calls from **Computel** (Av. Tulum, near bus terminal, tel./fax 998/7–42–24) daily 7 AM–10 PM; the service charge for five minutes is $1. The **post office** will hold mail sent to you at the following address for up to 15 days: Administración 1, Lista de Correos, Cancún, Quintana Roo, CP 77501, México. *Sunyaxchen, Supermanzana 28, tel. 988/4–14–18. Open weekdays 8–7, Sat. 9–noon.*

VISITOR INFORMATION The **Secretaría Estatal de Turismo** (Av. Tulum, next door to Palacio Municipal, tel. 988/4–80–73) has a knowledgeable, English-speaking staff ready to shower you with brochures. The magenta building, marked by a FUNDACION LOLITA DE LA VEGA sign, is open daily 9–9. Your best printed resource is the ubiquitous *Cancún Tips*. The publication's frank and helpful staff (Tulum 29, near bus station, tel. 988/4–48–04), on duty weekdays 8–7, is a valuable source for the most up-to-date discounts offered by local sport and tour companies.

COMING AND GOING

BY BUS The bus station is downtown, on Uxmal near Avenida Tulum. Two major bus companies, the first-class **Autotransportes del Oriente (ADO)** and the second-class **Autotransportes del Sur (ATS)** (tel. 988/4–48–04), serve most points in Quintana Roo and the Yucatán, as well as other major cities in Mexico. Buses leave frequently for Mérida (4 hrs, $8.50 1st class), Valladolid (3 hrs, $3 2nd class), Chichén Itzá (3 hrs, $6 1st class; 4 hrs, $4 2nd class), and Chetumal (6 hrs, $8 2nd class), stopping at smaller towns en route. Buses for Playa del Carmen ($2) and Puerto Morelos ($1) depart every 15 minutes from the southeast side of the station. The bus stop for Puerto Juárez, where you can catch a ferry to Isla Mujeres, is on the east side of Avenida Tulum near the Monumento a la Historia. The budget hotels are within walking distance of the station; you can store luggage at the station for a ridiculous 75¢ per hour, but it probably won't be necessary. To reach the Zona Hotelera from the station, cross Avenida Tulum and catch a HOTELES bus.

BY CAR If you've got the money to rent a car, the drive from Cancún to Tulum is a pleasant one: There are no tolls, and Highway 307 is well maintained. The road to the ruins near Valladolid and Mérida, however, is another story. Many an unsuspecting driver has paid through the nose after taking the *carretera de cuota* (toll road) to Mérida, which costs $24 ($12 at X-Can and $12 at Pisté). The toll is charged in both directions. Highway 180, which is a *carretera libre* (free road), follows the same route as the toll road but passes through small towns. Sure, it's a little slower and bumpier, but the savings and scenery are worth it. To avoid the toll road, take the highway out of Cancún and keep going straight—a CUOTA sign on your right will try to lure you in, but don't bite.

➤ **RENTAL CARS** • You can rent cars at the airport, in hotels, and all along Avenida Tulum; try **Avis** (in the airport, tel. 988/3–08–03). VW bugs typically cost $35 a day, but look around for discounts and check for coupons in *Cancún Tips*.

BY PLANE Cancún's airport is the largest and busiest on the peninsula and is a frequent destination for many U.S. airlines. Domestic airlines include **Aeroméxico** (tel. 988/6–00–59) and **Mexicana** (tel. 988/6–01–20). The casas de cambio at the airport, humorously named $EXCHANGE, have awful rates. You're better off changing your money downtown. It's possible to crash in the airport; tourists clear out by nighttime and comfortable chairs can be found in the upstairs restaurant.

➤ **AIRPORT TRANSIT** • Unfortunately, no public buses serve the airport. A taxi into Cancún costs about $16 and a combi costs $7; you'll see the station wagons lined up outside as you leave the terminal. The alternative involves a hot, 1½-kilometer trek down the road all the taxis take out of the airport. When you get to the highway, cross the street and flag down a CANCUN bus from below the overpass. The $1, 20-minute ride takes you right to the bus station in the center of town. No combis return to the airport from downtown Cancún, so you can either take a taxi or hitch from the crossroads at the end of Avenida Tulum.

GETTING AROUND

Cancún is divided into two sections: the **Zona Hotelera** (Hotel Zone), home to monstrous resorts, and the **centro** (downtown). The centro is on the mainland at the base of the elbow-shaped sand bar that contains the Zona Hotelera. The centro is divided into dozens of numbered zones—some only one block long—called *supermanzanas*, and addresses are often designated as "S.M." followed by a number. Avenida Tulum is the main drag of Cancún's center, and it's lined with restaurants and shopping centers selling expensive Mexican crafts. Only one street, Paseo Kukulcan, runs through the Zona Hotelera. Buses marked HOTELES, CENTRO and HOTELES/DOWNTOWN run west from the centro down Avenida Tulum, then through the Zona Hotelera, returning along the same route. Buses (50¢) run every few minutes 5 AM–2 AM.

BY TAXI Taxis are as expensive as you'd expect in Cancún. Fare within downtown should be around $1.50, an outrageous $6 to the Zona Hotelera, and about $16 to the airport.

WHERE TO SLEEP

Unless you just won the lottery, your hotel room will be downtown, away from the water. If you want to stay near the beach, your only option is the youth hostel (*see below*). Camping on the beach is out of the question.

➤ **UNDER $20** • **Hotel Alux.** This painstakingly sterilized place has air-conditioning and hot showers. Singles are $13, doubles $16. *Uxmal 21, tel. 988/4–05–56. ½ block north of bus station. 32 rooms, all with bath. Laundry, luggage storage.*

Hotel Canto. This hotel offers air-conditioned rooms with large, clean bathrooms and all the *agua purificada* you can swallow. If you get lonely, hang out in the lobby and watch cartoons with the kids. Singles and doubles are $16, triples $18. *Yaxchilán 22, at Sunyaxchen, tel. 988/4–12–67. 23 rooms, all with bath. Luggage storage.*

Hotel Villa Rossana Cancún. This conveniently located hotel is cheap, and you're bound to meet some pretty interesting neighbors. The singles are huge, and some rooms have decks that look out above the city. Singles are $10, doubles $13. Air-conditioning will cost more ($20 for a single or double), but the ceiling fans should keep you cool during most of the year. *Yaxchilán 68, just north of Sunyaxchen, tel. 988/4–19–43. 10 rooms, all with bath. Luggage storage.*

➤ **UNDER $30** • **Hotel El Rey del Caribe.** If atmosphere is more important than proximity to the beach, this is the place: It's set in a junglelike garden with tropical plants, a pool, and a Jacuzzi. Rooms are spacious and comfortable, with kitchens and clean bathrooms. Singles and doubles cost $27, plus $3 for each additional person. *Uxmal, at Náder, tel. 988/4–20–28. 23 rooms, all with bath. Luggage storage. Reservations advised. Wheelchair access. MC, V.*

HOSTELS **Villa Deportiva Juvenil Cancún.** This is the cheapest place in town and the only budget lodging on the beach. Ping-Pong tables, a volleyball net, and a swimming pool provide recreation when you're tired of baking your bod on the sand. There are separate wings for men and women, and dorm rooms are equipped with bunks and lockers—some even have views of the sea. The hostel attracts the most travelers in the winter months (December–March): If you stay here during the rest of the year, you just might have your own room. The place stays fairly clean, though bathrooms lack toilet paper and hot water; during the rainy season, leaks cause ants and mice to seek refuge here. Beds cost $4 plus a $4 deposit for sheets and towels. The Villa also lets travelers camp on its grassy lawns and use the facilities for $2 per person. *Paseo Kukulcan Km. 3.2, tel. 988/3–13–37. 300 beds. Luggage storage, meal service during high season. Wheelchair access.*

FOOD

Food isn't cheap in Cancún, but if you're willing to stick to typical Mexican fare, it's affordable. In the Zona Hotelera, the budget pickings are extremely slim—guests at the youth hostel can choose between the meager fare offered there and **Deliquor**, a 24-hour minimarket 200 meters east of the hostel. Downtown, look for cheaper options on Avenidas Uxmal and Cobá and nearby streets. **Comercial Mexicana** (Av. Tulum, at Uxmal) serves ready-made food by weight, from spaghetti dishes ($2 per pound) to black beans and rice ($1 a pound). **Mercado 28** (Av. Xel-Ha, across from post office), a pseudocolonial shopping mall, has an array of loncherías serving cheap, homemade meals and antojitos. Fruit vendors also swamp the morning market, held daily behind the post office.

➤ **UNDER $5** • **Lalos & Denise.** This restaurant's attempt to integrate Mexican and Canadian culture is cheesy, but who comes to Cancún for culture? A plate with three red enchiladas, three chicken tacos, or three meat burritos costs $4, and they'll even throw in a free beer or Coke. *Tulum 26, north of Palacio Municipal, tel. 988/4–54–45. Open daily 7 AM–11 PM.*

Restaurant Tlaquepaque. Candy-colored tablecloths and high-backed bamboo chairs make you feel like you're sitting in a dollhouse. The owner is great company and a true connoisseur of Mexican cuisine—his delicious *ceviche* (steamed shrimp and raw fish with lemon juice, cilantro, and onion) is $4.25. Four tacos cost $3.25. *Yaxchilán 59, no phone. Next to Hotel Villa Rossana. Open daily 6–6.*

Rincón Yucateco. Low prices and a pleasant outdoor patio make this low-key restaurant a great place to grab some soup ($1.75) or *parmuchas* (crisp, bean-filled tortillas topped with sliced chicken; $1.75) before a long bus ride. *Uxmal 24, next to Hotel Alux, no phone. Open daily 7:30 AM–9 PM.*

➤ **UNDER $15** • **La Parrilla.** This colorful labyrinth of tables entices even the most timid passerby. Unfortunately it's not a secret; you'll find the dining room dotted with yuppie tourists sharing the *parrillada mexicana,* a combination of grilled beef, pork, chicken, and vegetables, served with tortillas, salad, beans, and rice ($11). Vegetarians will delight in the *nopalitos* ($1.75)—cactus- and onion-filled tacos topped with cheese and salsa. *Yaxchilán 51, tel. 988/7–61–41. Open daily noon–4 AM.*

OUTDOOR ACTIVITIES

BEACHES Beaches in Cancún usually face the Caribbean Sea or the calmer Bahía de Mujeres, but the ones on the Caribbean side have become very narrow since Hurricane Gilbert swept through. Warning flags indicate the water's danger lever: Green or blue means calm, yellow means caution, and red or black signifies danger. Many of the best beaches are backed by luxury hotels but all are public. If you're discreet, you can make easy use of hotel facilities such as hammocks, lounges, huge pools, bars (watch out—a Coke could set you back $3.50), and showers.

The best Caribbean beaches are **Playa Chac Mool** and those in front of the **Hyatt Cancún** and **Sheraton** hotels, all of which are near **Punta Cancún,** the northeast point of the Zona Hotelera. Calm **Playa Linda,** near the youth hostel, is just 10 minutes from town by bus, and **Playa Tortugas,** another mile farther along Paseo Kukulcan, boasts some of Cancún's clearest water. If you're bent on avoiding the crowds, head to **Playa Ballenas** (Km. 14, just north of Cancún Palace Hotel), where bigger waves and rocky outcroppings make for slightly hazardous swimming but beautiful views. If you want to take it all off, head for the **nude beaches** near Club Med, at the southern end of the Zona Hotelera. Buses don't make it all the way out here, so you'll need to take a taxi or hitchhike. To reach the beaches along the Zona Hotelera, hop one of the HOTELES buses (50¢) and tell the driver where you're going.

➤ **DEEP SEA FISHING** • Cancún is known as one of the best game-fishing spots in the world, with year-round barracuda, red snapper, bluefin, grouper, and mackerel. **Marina Aqua Tours** (Kukulcan Km. 6.25, tel. 988/3–04–00) arranges four- to six-hour tours ranging in price from $70 to $99. Beer, bait, and gear are all supplied.

➤ **SNORKELING** • Despite the incredible clarity of the water, snorkeling off the beaches around Cancún is not as rewarding or affordable as at some other Caribbean resorts—it's usually cheaper to snorkel from Isla Mujeres. Many marinas in town offer tours to **Los Chitales** (2 km north of Cancún) or **Punta Nizuc,** a tropical underwater grove at the island's southernmost tip. Snorkeling tours usually run $40 for 3½ hours (including lunch and beer), or you can rent your own gear (about $25 a day) and head to Punta Nizuc by bus—take the HOTELES bus to the Westin Regina resort, 2 kilometers from the best snorkeling spots.

➤ **STUPID GRINGO TRICKS** • Motorized or sailing-type water sports in Cancún are fun but overpriced, and you probably won't see any Mexicans doing them. Street vendors and hotels offer fairly consistent prices for parasailing ($35 for a 15-minute ride) and waverunners ($40 for a half-hour ride on a Jet Ski–like machine). If you plan on windsurfing (about $15 per hour), be aware that the current can get pretty strong beyond the shoreline. Lifeguards keep a good watch, but you might want to get their attention before heading out just to be sure. Windsurfer rentals and lessons can be arranged at **Marina Aqua World** (Paseo Kukulcan Km. 15, tel. 988/3–30–07).

AFTER DARK

The great advantage Cancún has over other Caribbean coastal towns is the abundance of nightlife, but it's generally what you'd expect: Bars offering every drink imaginable compete with huge discos bedecked with pseudo-Mayan motifs illuminated by flashing lights. Cover charges are a high $8, but many set aside one day a week (usually Monday) for free admission; also check *Cancún Tips* for special offers. Discos in Cancún are known for their discriminatory policies: Several places in the Zona Hotelera prohibit Mexicans from entering, lest they offend gringos by their presence or behavior. The places listed below do not follow this policy.

If you are in downtown Cancún on a Friday night, head to the park behind Calle Tulipanes. At around 8 PM, a special show called **Noche Caribeña** (Caribbean Night) features songs, dances, poetry readings, and raffles. On Sunday evenings at 7:30, cultural events such as a *baile de jarana,* a typical Yucatecan dance, are held in the **Parque Las Palapas,** between Avenidas Yaxchilán and Tulum. Both events are for locals, giving you a chance to escape the tourist crowd.

BARS The majority of bars in Cancún feature "shows"— usually female strip acts. If this doesn't appeal to you, ask about the nightly show before you enter. One lively bar without a striptease is **No Way, José** (Cobá 89, at Nader, tel. 988/4–22–80), which features popular events such as televised sporting events but also has nightly karaoke. For $7 you'll get unlimited drinks and a nasty hangover; otherwise, beers cost about $1.25. A diverse crowd parties at **Karamba** (Tulum 9, tel. 988/4–00–37), a gay bar with $1.50 beers and a small dance floor, as well as occasional events like "The Queens Tranvesti Show."

DANCING There are plenty of places to shake your thang in Cancún as long as you're willing to pay the price. Always packed is **La Boom** (Paseo Kukulcan Km. 3.5, a short distance from hostel, tel. 988/3–11–52), which boasts a smoky multilevel dance floor with artificial stars and extravagant light displays. In the same building, **Tequila Rock** encourages dancing on the bar after you've downed a few $4 margaritas. The city's salsa hub, **Batachá** (Hotel Miramar, Zona Hotelera, tel. 988/3–17–55) starts up at around 11 PM, when happy couples fill the bamboo hut and breezy patio.

Near Cancún

PUERTO MORELOS

South of Cancún is the tranquil fishing town of Puerto Morelos, a welcome change from the resort frenzy to the north. It's a fairly upscale place, benefiting from the overflow of tourists on country drives in rented 4x4s. There isn't much to do in town (locals affectionately call it Muerto Morelos) and the beaches in town aren't that great. If you want to absorb a few UV rays, walk a couple of kilometers south to more secluded, attractive shores. Morelos's main draw is an offshore reef where you can snorkel or dive. **Sub Aqua Explorers** (SW cnr of zócalo, tel. 987/1–00–78) rents snorkel equipment ($10 per day), offers diving trips ($55 for 2 tanks, $45 for 1 tank, $100 cavern dive), and fishing trips ($80 for 2 hrs). If you're staying overnight, consider **Posada Amor** (Javier Rojo Gómez, tel. 987/71–00–33), a quirky little hotel just south of the zócalo that offers doubles for $18; a private bath costs about $5 extra. For $15 you can stay in a rustic palapa complete with mosquito netting and feel like you're part of the Swiss Family Robinson. **Restaurant Las Palmeras** on Avenida Rafael Melgar serves typical seafood dishes for about $5–$6, Monday through Saturday 10:30–10.

COMING AND GOING ATS buses (30 min, $1) run daily from Cancún's bus station to Puerto Morelos every 20 minutes 8–8:30 en route to Playa del Carmen. Ask the driver to let you know when you arrive in Puerto Morelos. Seven buses return to Cancún, with the last bus returning around 5 PM. Return tickets are sold at *el crucero*: the junction of Highway 307 and the road leading east into town. A man sitting on a bench at the junction will sell you a ticket. If you're continuing on to Playa del Carmen, buy your ticket at the caseta on the opposite (west) side of the highway.

Isla Mujeres

At first sight, Isla Mujeres, just 10 kilometers (6 mi) east of Cancún, is a stereotypical resort: A handful of expensive restaurants and charmless hotels jostle for space with souvenir shops selling decadent piles of conch shells and pornographic pseudo-Mayan figurines. But Isla Mujeres has retained its sweet and simple essence, drawing budget travelers from all over the world. They come for quiet and peaceful white beaches perfect for reading, walking, and playing ball, and snorkeling and diving opportunities that include trips to the Cave of Sleeping Sharks, a natural phenomenon straight out of *National Geographic*. Still, the main reason to come to the island is to relax, read a couple books, make new friends, and avoid doing much of anything.

One of Isla Mujeres's most important events is the Regata del Sol al Sol, celebrated yearly in late April, when boats leave St. Petersburg, Florida, and arrive here amid much partying. The event is concluded with a basketball game between Mexican and American teams, which the Mexicans always win.

How the island got its alluring name is open to debate. One fanciful story says pirates stashed their women here while they went off for a good plunder. A more plausible explanation is that the island is named after Mayan female figurines found here by Francisco Hernández de Córdoba, the commander of a Spanish expedition, who "discovered" the island in 1517. The subsequent history of the island is common to the Caribbean: It was a hideaway for pirates and later became a fishing village. During the late '60s and '70s the island was a hammock haven for hippie castaways, but that's pretty much faded with the movement.

BASICS

CASAS DE CAMBIO **Banco del Atlántico,** on your right as you come off the ferry from Puerto Juárez, offers good exchange rates. *Rueda Medina 3, btw Morelos and Bravo, tel. 987/7–00–05. Money exchange weekdays 9–4:30.*

LAUNDRY **Tim Phó** does up to 4 kilos of laundry for $2.50, often in less than two hours. *Juárez, at Abasolo, tel. 987/7–05–29. 2 blocks from zócalo. Open Mon.–Sat. 7 AM–9 PM, Sun. 8–2.*

MEDICAL AID The **Centro de Salud** (Guerrero 5, tel. 987/7–01–17) offers 24-hour emergency service. **Dr. Antonio Salas** (Hidalgo, next to Farmacia Lily, tel. 987/7–04–77) speaks English and makes house calls round the clock. **Farmacia Lily** (Madero, at Hidalgo, tel. 987/7–01–64) is open Monday–Saturday 9–9:30, Sunday 9–3:30.

PHONES AND MAIL The **post office** will hold mail sent to you at the following address for up to 10 days: Lista de Correos, Isla Mujeres, Quintana Roo, CP 77400, México. *Guerrero, at Mateos, tel. 987/7–00–85. Open weekdays 9–6, Sat. 9–1.*

The long-distance **telephone office** located in Hotel María José (Rueda Medina 9-B, at Madero, near ferry terminal) is open daily 9–9. You can also find coin- and card-operated phones scattered about the town. Buy phone cards at **Yamili Crafts & Shirts** (Hidalgo 4, tel. 987/7–05–20) Monday–Saturday 9–9 and Sunday 9–3. You can place or receive a fax at **Telecomm** (Guerrero, next to post office, fax 987/7–01–13) weekdays 9–3.

VISITOR INFORMATION The staff at the **tourist office** (Hidalgo, at Mateos, 2nd floor of Plaza Isla Mujeres Altas, no phone) is knowledgeable but speaks little English. Make sure to pick up a copy of *Islander,* a monthly publication with good maps of the island and general tourist information. The office is open weekdays 8–4. For a free map and some friendly advice, you can also try the **tourist information booth** at the Puerto Juárez ferry dock, in downtown Isla Mujeres.

COMING AND GOING

You can reach Isla Mujeres from either Puerto Juárez or Punta Sam, both located north of Cancún. From Puerto Juárez, older ferries chug to Isla (40 min, 75¢), or you can take the quicker

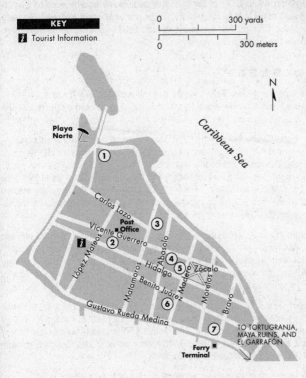

0 _____ 300 yards

0 _____ 300 meters

N

Lodging ○
Hotel Caribe
Maya, **5**
Hotel Carmelina, **4**
Hotel Casa Maya, **1**
Hotel Gomar, **7**
Hotel Osorio, **6**
Hotel Xul-Ha, **2**
Poc-Na, **3**

Playa
Norte

Caribbean Sea

Carlos Lazo

Post
Office

Vicente Guerrero

López Mateos

Abasolo

Matamoros

Hidalgo

Benito Juárez

Madero

Zócalo

Morelos

Bravo

Gustavo Rueda Medina

TO TORTUGRANJA,
MAYA RUINS, AND
EL GARRAFÓN

Ferry
Terminal

air-conditioned ferry (15 min, $2). Both types of ferries run daily 7–7:30. Puerto Juárez is 15 minutes from Cancún by bus (50¢)—catch one marked PUERTO JUAREZ from any of the bus stops on Avenida Tulum. A taxi will cost about $3.

Although it's farther from Isla Mujeres than Puerto Juárez, Punta Sam is the best departure point if you're bringing a car over. Ferries (45 min, $1) leave every two to three hours. The cost of transporting a car starts at about $6, depending on the car's size. To reach Punta Sam from Cancún, drive north up Avenida Tulum, turn right (east) on Avenida Portillo, and follow the signs to Punta Sam.

GETTING AROUND

The island of Isla Mujeres is only about 8 kilometers long and less than a kilometer wide, and most travelers stay in the town at the northern tip of the island. The majority of shops and restaurants are on the west side of town, and the zócalo is at the town's southernmost end, at Morelos and Benito Juárez.

BY BUS The only bus on the island (25¢) runs down the main street at the ferry docks, passing the designated bus stops just north of the taxi stands every half hour. From here the bus heads south to Playa Lancheros, then turns around and makes its way through the residential areas on the island's edge before heading back into town.

BY TAXI Because the island is small, taxis are a pleasant and affordable way to get around. For regulated rates, try the taxi stand near the dock for ferries from Puerto Juárez. A taxi from town to the Tortugranja (*see* Worth Seeing, *below*) costs $1.50.

BY MOPED AND BIKE Consider renting a bicycle or moped to see the "other" Isla Mujeres, consisting of locals' houses and unspoiled coastal views. Several places around town rent

481

mopeds for about $4.50 per hour, $20 per day (gas included); you'll usually need to leave a deposit or your ID. You can rent bicycles for only $3.50 per day at **Micha's Motorent** (Abasolo 13). **Sport Bike** (Juárez and Morelos, just below zócalo, tel. 987/2–00–36) rents bikes with locks overnight for $4.50; they're open daily 8–5.

WHERE TO SLEEP

Most hotels on Isla Mujeres are in town. Prices, which have skyrocketed over the last few years, rise even more during high season (Nov.–Apr., July, and Aug.); prices listed below reflect the low-season range.

➤ **UNDER $15** • **Hotel Caribe Maya.** This hotel near the main ferry terminal is comfortable, clean, and bugless, and the water gets so hot you can actually steam your clothes in it. The $10.50 fan-only rooms (singles and doubles) stay pretty cool, but air-conditioning is also available for a mere $3 extra. They also rent mopeds for $20 a day and offer trips to Isla Contoy (see Near Isla Mujeres, below) for $22.50. There's a 6% usage fee on credit cards. *Madero 9, tel. 987/1–04–23. From Rueda Medina, head east on Madero about 2 blocks. 25 rooms, all with bath. Luggage storage. Reservations advised Dec.–Apr. MC, V.*

Hotel Carmelina. Despite the occasional cucaracha, rooms are large and sunny and have fans and clean bathrooms. Ask for a top-floor room; they're bright, cheery, and overlook the rest of town. Singles cost $10, and doubles are $14 ($2.50 more with air-conditioning). They also rent bicycles for $3.50 per day. *Guerrero 4, tel. 987/7–00–06. From ferry, walk up Morelos and left on Guerrero. 18 rooms, all with bath. Laundry, luggage storage. Wheelchair access.*

Hotel Osorio. You'll spot Osorio by its bright red-and-green balconies overlooking the street. Beds are small, and the place is not exactly picturesque, but rooms are about as cheap as they get—$6.50 for a single or $10.50 for a double. The hotel also offers daily trips to Isla Contoy for $25. *Madero 10, at Juárez, tel. 987/7–02–56. 40 rooms, all with bath. Luggage storage. Reservations advised Dec. and Jan. Wheelchair access.*

Hotel Xul-Ha. If you can see past the ruinous appearance of this hotel's unoccupied portion, you'll appreciate the value of the available rooms. Bathrooms are pleasantly grunge-free, and large shower stalls with hot water provide a welcome end to a long day at the beach. Singles cost $8, doubles $10.50. *Hidalgo 23, tel. 987/7–00–75. From Rueda Medina, east on López Mateos 1 block, then left on Hidalgo. 11 rooms, all with bath. Luggage storage. Wheelchair access. MC, V.*

➤ **UNDER $25** • **Hotel Casa Maya.** Romantics will love the breezy beachside palapas and inviting patio hammocks of this small hotel. Common areas include a bright, cozy living room, kitchen facilities, and a shaded terrace. Doubles with a spotless shared bath (you share with one other room) cost $20 a night. A double with private bath goes for $25. Reservations are recommended during the high season. *Calle Zazil-Ha, tel. 987/7–00–45. At Playa Norte, near abandoned Zazil-Ha Hotel. 10 rooms, 7 with bath. Luggage storage, MC, V.*

Hotel Gomar. If cleanliness and convenience are your top priorities, stay here. Located directly across the street from the Puerto Juárez ferry, this hotel allows you to drop your bags and take a siesta immediately upon arrival. Doubles ($18) come with steamy hot water, cooling fan breezes, and ocean views from the balcony. *Medina 150, tel. 987/7–05–41. 16 rooms, all with bath. Luggage storage. Reservations advised Dec.–Apr. MC, V.*

HOSTELS **Poc-Na.** Budget travelers and adventure seekers from all over the world converge here for good company and comfy hammocks. Hang out on the rooftop or play your guitar under the large palapa that doubles as a dining room and living area. The dorm rooms ($2.50 per person) have bunks and hammock hooks, and you can use towels, sheets, and pillows for a $3 deposit. The hostel's restaurant serves pizza and huge pasta dishes that two people can share for $3. The food is, as one visitor put it, "brilliant." *Matamoros, tel. 987/7–00–90. From main ferry docks, north on Rueda Medina, east 4½ blocks on Matamoros toward east coast beach. Laundry, luggage storage, meal service. Wheelchair access.*

CAMPING Camping is not allowed here and police do patrol the beaches. However, if you're in a secluded enough spot, they aren't likely to notice. You can also camp at the beach by Poc-Na, but they'll charge you the regular $2.50 room fee.

FOOD

Inexpensive loncherías are scattered throughout town, including four on Avenida Guerrero between Matamoros and Mateos. Small sandwiches cost $1, a plate of tacos is $1.50, and main dishes, such as fish, cost about $3. Especially good is the tiny nameless lonchería on Guerrero between Matamoros and Abasolo. If you have your own stove or are staying at a hotel with cooking facilities, buy your food at the **market** on Guerrero at Mateos. **Panadería La Reina** (Madero, at Juárez) sells fresh pastries and great banana bread.

➢ **UNDER $5** • **Cafecito.** Sitting beside a stained-glass wave at a table decorated with seashells, you may think you've fallen into a tourist trap, but as you sip a cappuccino ($1.50) or nibble your crepes with ice cream, chocolate sauce, and bananas ($2.50), you probably won't care. Breakfast lovers take note: Belgian waffles smothered with whipped cream and strawberries fetch $2.25, and a variety of egg dishes go for $1.75. *Matamoros 42, at Juárez, tel. 987/7–04–38. Open Mon.–Wed. 8–noon and 6–10, Sun. 8–noon.*

Chen Huaye. With Silvio Rodríguez tapes in the stereo and pink flamingos on the wall, this is the path to enlightened eating. The name of the place means "always here," which describes where you might be after you discover *chaya* ($1), a green drink made from a tropical plant resembling spinach. Popeye never had it so good. The chicken tortas, at $1.25 a pop, make the wallet as happy as the soul. *Bravo 6, no phone. Near zócalo, btw Juárez and Hidalgo, behind basketball courts. Open Wed.–Mon. 9 AM–11 PM.*

El Nopalito. Start your day in a spiritual way at this small café hidden within a crafts store. Festively painted wood tables compliment the New Age flute music. The french toast ($2) is buried under a blizzard of powdered sugar and comes with honey and fresh marmalade. *Cnr Guerrero and Matamoros, no phone. Open Mon.–Sat. 8 AM–noon.*

La Peña. Perched atop a rock outcropping on the island's western shore, this restaurant serves smaller portions than most other places in town, but romantics can't resist sipping a margarita ($1.75; half-price 4–8 PM) as the salty breeze drifts in through the open windows. The tomato-based fish soup ($1.50) is incredibly fresh. For something more filling, try the *chicken mole* (chicken in red chile and chocolate sauce; $3). *Guerrero 5, in front of zócalo, tel. 987/7–03–09. Open Mon.–Sat. 8 AM–11 PM.*

Restaurant Portales. This small place has whitewashed walls, an outdoor grill, and live music. If you want to ignore Mom's perennial advice, plunge into their pool after taking advantage of the $5 all-you-can-eat lunch buffet. *Juárez 32, btw Mateos and Matamoros, tel. 987/7–05–06. Open daily 12:30–3:30.*

WORTH SEEING

MAYAN RUINS The island's Mayan ruins are just that—ruins—and visitors today see little. A small sandstone building at the southern tip of the island was once a temple to Ixchel, the Mayan goddess of fertility. Female figurines, believed to be votive offerings, were found here by Hernández de Córdoba and provide the most plausible explanation of the island's name. Despite the temple's disrepair, the striking effect of the waves breaking on the steep cliffs below is spectacular. Ask the lighthouse keeper if you can climb to the top floor for the beautiful view; if you're lucky, he may also have some ice-cold Cokes for sale. *From town, follow road as far south as possible and walk up dirt path. Or, take bus to Playa Lancheros and walk 2 km.*

TORTUGRANJA Among many ardent save-the-sea-turtle enterprises dotting the Quintana Roo coastline, this is probably the most elaborate. The turtle farm is government funded and features a small informational museum as well as multilingual guides who give detailed info on the life cycle and mating habits of the turtles. The best time to come is near the end of the egg-laying season (May–October), when newly hatched baby turtles can be found darting around the central building's shallow, raised tanks. It gets hot here, so bring water. You can also opt to take a dip off the dock out front—just make sure you jump in the non–turtle-inhabited side. Some snorkeling tours include a stop at the Tortugranja. *Tel. 987/7–05–95. Take the (only) bus, get dropped off at Mondaca, and walk north 20 min. Admission: $1. Open daily 9–5.*

OUTDOOR ACTIVITIES

BEACHES Northwest of town is **Playa Norte,** a wide, white-sand beach. It's the traditional topless beach, but until the Europeans arrive in July and August, mammary toasting is not all that common. A plethora of water sports are available at Playa Norte, including snorkeling, water cycling, sailing, and water skiing (*see* Snorkeling, *below*). You can use the bathrooms and showers on the beach near Hidalgo for $1.

The three modest beaches on the west coast of the island—**Playa Paraíso, Playa Lancheros,** and **Playa Indios**—don't have the fine white sand you'd expect from a Caribbean island. The shallow sea is rocky and full of seaweed, making it a less than ideal place to swim and snorkel. Still, Playa Paraíso sees its share of visitors, as it's a popular harbor for tourist boats from Cancún. The beach has quite a few restaurants, a number of small stands selling souvenirs, and clean bathrooms. Someone may ask you to pay an entrance fee, but the beaches are government-owned and the fee is a scam. From town, take a bus, bicycle, or moped south down the main road about 4 kilometers.

SCUBA DIVING Isla Mujeres offers some of the world's most exciting and unusual diving trips. Aside from the obvious attraction of the coral reefs, divers have a chance to explore the **Sleeping Shark Caves** (*see* box, *below*). Diving trips to the coral reefs around the island (such as the Chitales, Banderas, and Manchones reefs) cost $20–$65, depending on the amount of gear and tanks you use, and where you go. Trips to the Sleeping Shark Caves are usually about $15 more than other dives, and there's no refund if you don't see a shark. If you're not certified, you must take the $80, three-hour introductory course before diving with an instructor. **Bahía Dive Shop** (Rueda Medina, near ferry dock, tel. 987/7–05–00) offers trips to all of the locations listed above. Carlos Gutiérrez at **Mexico Divers** (Rueda Medina, near ferry dock, tel. 987/7–02–74) is helpful and has reasonable prices.

If you're really serious about getting into diving, consider taking a PADI certification course. The course usually lasts 4–5 days, costs around $350, and includes four tanks worth of diving: two in shallower waters and two deep-water dives. With a certificate, you can dive anywhere you want at cheaper rates; if you've only taken an introductory course, you'll have to retake the course every time you dive with a different company or in a different place. Carlos Gutiérrez (*see above*) is a good person to talk to if you're considering taking the plunge.

SNORKELING The island is fringed by coral reefs, and in many places you can just wade in and start snorkeling. Remember that coral is a living organism—walking on or just touching the coral can easily damage or kill it. **Marina Amigos del Mar** (Playa Norte, near Hidalgo, tel. 987/7–03–92) rents almost every type of water equipment. Snorkeling equipment is $5 a day, and hourly rates for aqua cycles ($8.50), sailboats ($7.50), Windsurfers ($7.50), and kayaks ($5) are reasonable. If you want to snorkel close to town, the best spot is on the northern corner of the island, across from the bridge connecting the town to a small peninsula and a luxury hotel.

A few years ago the **Parque Nacional El Garrafón,** at the southern tip of the island, was a paradise for snorkelers. There's still a lot to see here, but as a result of Hurricane Gilbert much of the coral has died, and many of the fish have found new homes. What remains are hundreds of day-trippers from Cancún, floating on the surface of the water like a fat, white, algae bloom. The tourist-geared park complex includes a diving center, shops, a restaurant and snack bar, bathrooms, showers, and lockers (too small for a backpack; $1.50). The dive shop rents snorkels, masks, and fins for about $4. You can easily bike to El Garrafón, or take the bus to Playa Lancheros and walk the rest of the way. *Admission: $1.75. Open daily 8–4.*

You can also take a 1½- to three-hour snorkeling trip to the huge coral reef of **Manchones.** Here brightly colored fish will surround you, and you may see some barracuda. What you won't see are the bevy of floating tourists fresh off the boat from Cancún. Another option is **El Farrito Reef** which is supposed to be the best snorkeling experience off Isla Mujeres. All agencies in town, as well as the one at El Garrafón, offer almost identical snorkeling trips to Manchones and El Farrito Reef for $20 per person. Both trips usually include a visit to a couple of small coral reefs, and all trips should include use of snorkeling gear. Poc-Na (see Where to Sleep, above) offers a particularly good trip; try asking them for a discount. If you want to rent snorkeling gear and hit the beach by yourself, La Isleña, (see Isla Contoy, below), rents the snorkel, mask, and fins for $4 per day.

AFTER DARK

For weekend shebangs, check the postings at Poc-Na (see Where to Sleep, above). For the best in thumping bass and piano tracks, head for **La Peña** (see Food, above), which transforms into a steamy (and touristy) disco after 11. There's a 75¢ cover, and beers are under $2. A sand-dusted crowd of younger Mexicans goes to **Las Palapas** (Hidalgo, at Playa Cocos) for merengue and disco dancing right on the beach. There's no cover and drinks are two-for-one 9 PM–midnight. **Buho's Bar** allows you to enjoy your margaritas in a swing or even a hammock (although the latter can get pretty messy) while watching the sunset during the two-for-one happy hour (5:30 PM–sunset). If you're looking for some company, a *mojito* (rum with mint, lime, and soda water; $2) can lead to a long, adventure-filled night at **Cuba Ron** (Guerrero, at Morelos), which closes at 11 or midnight and features live music on weekends. The **zócalo** is also a fun place to hang out at night, with music, games, fried plantain stands, and basketball under the lights.

Near Isla Mujeres

ISLA CONTOY

Isla Contoy, 45 minutes north of Isla Mujeres by boat, is a lush bird sanctuary where you can see brown pelicans, cormorants, frigate birds, herons, and flamingos. Snorkeling is also a pop-

Sleeping Shark Caves

It may sound like something from "Ripley's Believe It Or Not," but a series of underwater caverns off Isla Mujeres are a crash pad for a dangerous species of shark. The sharks are not actually sleeping but are in a state of relaxed nonaggression seen nowhere else. There are two explanations for why the sharks come to the caves. One theory is that the water inside the caves has a different makeup than the water outside. It contains more oxygen, more carbon dioxide, and less salt. The decrease in salinity causes the parasites that plague sharks to loosen their grip and allows the remora fish (the sharks' personal vacuum cleaner) to eat the parasites more easily.

Because of the deep state of relaxation of these sharks, another theory (our personal favorite) is that the sharks come to the caves to get high. Fresh water seeps up into the caves from the ground, and the combination of fresh and salt water may produce an effect akin to that of humans' smoking marijuana. Whatever they experience while "sleeping" in the caves must be well worth the extra effort: The sharks inside the caves must continuously pump water over their gills to breathe, which requires more energy than swimming does. If you dive in this area, be cautious: Many of the sharks are reef sharks, a species normally responsible for the largest number of attacks on humans. Dive with a reliable guide and be on your best diving behavior.

ular pastime here, although visibility off the thin strip of white-sand beach depends on the weather—if it's windy, don't expect to see much. You can only get to Isla Contoy with a tour, but luckily most travel agencies and several hotels in town offer day trips to the island. **Poc-Na** (*see* Where to Sleep, *above*) arranges day-long sailboat trips to the island for $18 a person ($20 for fewer than 10 people), including snorkeling and fishing equipment as well as food and drink. **La Isleña** (Morelos, at Juárez, tel. 987/7–05–78) arranges four-hour tours for $30 per person that include food, drink, and snorkeling equipment. They usually require a six-person minimum, but you may be able to talk them down to four. Tours consist of a boat ride, a stop on the beach to snorkel and eat lunch, and bird-watching on the island.

Playa del Carmen

Like **Cancún, Playa del Carmen is a tourist**-oriented beach town. Unlike Cancún, Playa is a place you'll find hard to leave. Musicians fill the almost magical *malecón* (boardwalk) and surrounding streets, providing harmony for the breaking waves and the sounds of people conversing in dozens of different languages. After a day in Playa, you'll begin to recognize people on the street. After a week here, you'll feel like you're at home. And if Playa's mellow sand-and-sea atmosphere begins to bore you, convenient day trips to Mayan ruins and isolated cenotes are plentiful.

Depending on when you go, you'll find two different types of visitors. The Playa of July, August, and December through April is a destination for package tourists, as travelers spill over from Cancún and Cozumel. The beaches are packed, gasoline from the boats pollutes the water in the harbor, and hotel prices skyrocket—even the roach motels are full. The rest of the year, Playa is relatively peaceful, with a group of hip, young travelers taking advantage of empty hotels offering great deals.

BASICS

CASAS DE CAMBIO The **money exchange center** (cnr of 5a Av. and Juárez) offers lousy rates, but it's open daily 8 AM–10 PM. **Banco del Atlántico** (Juárez, 1 block from bus station, tel. 987/3–02–70) changes cash and traveler's checks weekdays 8–1:30 and 5–7. Bring your empty wallet and your Visa to the ATM at **Bancomer** (Juárez, 4 blocks from 5a Av., tel. 987/3–04–08), where they keep the cash flowing.

LAUNDRY **Maya Laundry** washes clothes for $1 per kilo and underwear and socks for 15¢ pair. *Calle 2, at 5a Av., tel. 987/3–02–61. Open Mon.–Sat. 8–8.*

MEDICAL AID The **clinic** (tel. 987/3–03–14) on Avenida Juárez, three blocks up from 5 Avenida, is open 24 hours. **Farmacia La Salud** (cnr of Juárez and 30a Av., tel. 987/3–10–50 is open daily 8 AM–midnight to serve your late-night antacid needs.

PHONES AND MAIL The **post office** (Juárez, btw Calles 15 and 20) is open weekdays 8 7, Saturdays 9–1. They will hold mail sent to you at the following address for up to 10 day Lista de Correos, Playa del Carmen, Quintana Roo, CP 77710, México. Public, card-operated **phones** are located near the post office on Juárez and across from the bus station on 5 Avenida and Juárez. The **Computel** long-distance phone office (Juárez, ½ block NW of bus station, tel. 987/3–04–69) is open daily 7 AM–10 PM.

VISITOR INFORMATION Playa's information booth supplies free maps and copies of *De tination,* the monthly tourist magazine, which has useful tips, phone numbers, a map, an snippets of Quintana Roo history. They also sell Latadel cards. *Juárez, at 5a Av., no phone. B bus station and zócalo. Open daily 7 AM–11 PM.*

COMING AND GOING

The malecón, also known as 5a Avenida, is the social center of town. Playa del Carmen's ma street is Avenida Juárez, also known as Avenida Principal, and runs perpendicular to the beac

All other avenues run parallel to the beach and are numbered in multiples of five. Calles are numbered in multiples of two and run perpendicular to the beach.

BY BUS Three bus lines serve Playa del Carmen. **ADO** and **ATS,** both with first- and second-class service, operate out of the building on 5a Avenida and Juárez, which is conveniently located one block from the beach. One second-class bus travels hourly 6 AM–8 PM from Playa del Carmen to Tulum ($1.50), stopping in Xcaret (50¢), Akumal ($1), and Xel-Ha ($1.25), as well as other coastal destinations. Both companies also have five daily buses to Chetumal (4 hrs, $8.25 1st class; 5 hrs, $6.50 2nd class), Mérida (4 hrs, $11 1st class; 7 hrs, $8.25 2nd class), and three daily trips to Cancún (1 hr; $2 1st class, $1.50 2nd class). There's also direct service to Cancún every two hours and to Tulum (1 hr; $1.75 1st class, $1.50 2nd class) every 1–2 hours.

WHERE TO SLEEP

Playa del Carmen is affordable during the off-season, but in July, August, and December, rates tend to run $5–$10 higher than those listed here. Most budget hotels are on 5a Avenida close to the beach or on Juárez near the bus station.

➤ **UNDER $10 • La Ruina.** More like an international hippie commune than a hotel, this spot on the beach is the cheapest and by far the most fun place to stay in Playa, as long as you don't mind a little grit in your backpack. Hang your hammock in an open-air communal palapa and stash your stuff in a locker (palapa rental $3.50; locker and hammock rental 75¢), or rent a cabaña for two ($9, $2 each extra person). You can also pitch a tent in the grass for $3. The shared bathrooms are passable, and the women's shower farthest west usually has hot water—no one will hassle guys if they use it. *Calle 2, on beach, tel. 987/4–11–23. From bus station, 1 block left on 5a Av. and first right. 21 huts, 32 palapa spaces. Luggage storage.*

Posada Mayeli. Rooms here aren't anything spectacular, but it's a great place to be—the neighbors are friendly and you'll soon feel like one of the family. Plus, you're just seconds away from Playa's pulse: the malecón. Bare, fan-equipped singles and doubles cost $13. *Calle 2a Nte, at 5a Av., no phone. Behind Pez Vela restaurant. 6 rooms, all with bath. Luggage storage.*

➤ **UNDER $15 • Hotel Playa del Carmen.** The walls and floors here gleam with fresh paint, and dark-wood dressers and doorways have a nice, cooling effect. It's $13 for a single or double only three blocks from the beach. *Juárez, at 10a Av., 1½ blocks from bus station, tel. 987/3–02–94. 17 rooms, all with bath. Laundry, luggage storage. Wheelchair access.*

Posada Marinelly. Lonely travelers appreciate the incredibly friendly family that owns this place. The large rooms are bare, but the floors sparkle and the fan somehow manages to keep things pretty cool. The owners are happy to help you with the temperamental plumbing. Singles are $9.50, doubles $11. *Juárez, at 10a Av., tel. 987/3–01–40. Next to Hotel Playa del Carmen. 10 rooms, all with bath. Wheelchair access.*

➤ **UNDER $25 • Copa Cabañas.** Even if you don't like Barry Manilow, you'll love this place. Single ($15) and double ($20) cabañas come complete with attractive tilework, an outdoor patio and hammock, and sometimes even an ocean view. A Jacuzzi in the courtyard clinches the deal. *5a Av., at Calle 10, tel. 987/3–02–18. 10 cabañas, all with bath. Luggage storage.*

HOSTELS **Villa Deportiva Juvenil Playa del Carmen.** This hostel is way out in the boonies, about a kilometer from civilization and (more importantly) far from the beach. The only reason you should stay here is if La Ruina is full and you don't want to splurge on a hotel. The pink sex-segregated dorm rooms are bare and basic. For $4 you get a bunk and a locker without a lock. The bathrooms are clean but lack toilet paper, hot water, and shower walls. A $4 deposit is required, and guests receive a 10% discount with an HI card. *Calle 8, at 30a Av., no phone. From bus station, walk up Juárez 5 blocks, right on Av. 30a and continue NE 4 blocks to Muscle Beach Gym; hostel is just beyond gym, down a short dirt road running NW. 198 beds; 18 people per room. Luggage storage. Wheelchair access.*

CAMPING You can pitch your tent in the yard of La Ruina (*see above*) and have access to their facilities for $3 per tent. Camping on the beach is not recommended.

FOOD

An array of restaurants and loncherías makes it easy to eat cheaply in Playa del Carmen. Supermarkets and stores line 5a Avenida, but you'll find better deals on Juárez. **El Super del Ahorro** (Juárez, at 30a Av., tel. 987/3–03–06) offers the best selection of foods at reasonable prices and is open daily 6:30 AM–10:30 PM. Across the street, **Frutería Marsan** sells fruits and veggies Monday–Saturday 7 AM–9 PM, Sunday 7–2. **Panificadora del Carmen** (Juárez, at 10a Av.) sells cheap pastries daily 6 AM–10 PM. Most restaurants are also on 5a Avenida, and a few cheap taco stands dot Juárez and 10a Avenida.

La Cabaña del Lobo. Hang with the locals while you eat your huevos rancheros ($1.50) or ham and cheese sandwich ($1) in this clean, cool restaurant. *Juárez, btw 5a and 10a Avs., no phone. Open daily 8–8.*

Media Luna. This little vegetarian brunch spot is only discernible from the street by a black rusting sign with a white half-moon. Tropical combinations like crepes stuffed with banana, mango, granola, and fresh sweet cream ($2.75) will have you licking your fingers. Or try hot cheese and veggie sandwiches stuffed with juicy tomatoes on wheat bread ($2.75). Finish off the meal with a *café frío* (iced coffee with milk, cream, vanilla, cinnamon, and sugar; $1.25). *5a Av., 4½ blocks from Juárez, no phone. Open Mon.–Sat. 8:30 AM–11 PM.*

Pez Vela. This lively restaurant serves elaborate fish and meat dishes that are a little pricey, but the waiters will supply you with all the chips and salsa you can handle. Try the Veracruz-style squid, in a fresh tomato sauce flavored with onions, olives, and capers ($3.25) or the *ceviche* (chunks of raw fish marinated in lemon, onions, and herbs; $3). They also serve gargantuan-size nachos ($1.75) and cheap quesadillas ($2.25). Save your beer money for another place though: One measly Corona costs $1.75. *5a Av., at Calle 2, tel. 987/3–09–99. Open daily 7 AM–midnight.*

Sabor. A mellow, newspaper-reading crowd comes here to pick at the tasty pastries ($1) and indulge in a vast array of tropical fruit drinks ($1.50). Tofu enthusiasts shouldn't leave here without trying the odd-looking soy tacos ($2). *5a Av., next to Pez Vela, no phone. Open daily 8 AM–10 PM.*

OUTDOOR ACTIVITIES

Playa del Carmen is a beach town and little else. If you don't like sand and swimming, keep on going. The beaches here are spectacular—seaweed-free surf rolls onto shore, and the long stretches of white sand are perfect for barefoot walks or lounging with a book. The best section of beach in town is near La Ruina (*see* Where to Sleep, *above*), though during peak season (June–Nov.) litter and the lack of trees turn some people off. Walking south along the beach a couple of kilometers brings you to narrow, deserted stretches backed by thick vegetation. More than 1 kilometer north of Playa del Carmen is a series of protected lagoons with cleaner water and few visitors beyond the occasional fisherman.

> Playa del Carmen isn't known for its archaeological sites, but locals take pride in the ruins of Xaman-Ha, in the woods behind the Continental Plaza Hotel. If you arrive just before sunset, you can meditate in ribbons of light pouring through the building's small stone windows.

Hotel Maya Bric (5a Av. Nte., btw Calles 8 and 10, tel. 98 3–00–11; open daily 7–7) charges $4.50 a day for snorkeling equipment and throws in lots of free advice. To snorkel the beach, head around the point north of the Blue Parrot In to a small coral reef. It's also possible to organize snorkeling, diving, and fishing on charter boats, but these trips may break the bank: A small-boat fishing excursion can cost up to $150 for six people. Jaime at **Price Tours** (5a Av., ½ block from Juárez, tel. 987/3–09–25) can arrange big- and small-boat fishing. For snorkeling, try **Seaf**

Adventures Dive Shop (5a Av., at Juárez, tel. 987/3–09–01), open daily 8–1 and 5–10; a trip runs $30 per person, including lunch and drinks. Scuba-diving tours go to a number of reefs lying just offshore: **Playacar Divers** (in front of Plaza Marina Playacar, south of ferry dock, tel. 987/3–04–49) and **Tank-Ha Dive Center** (5a Av. Nte., btw Calles 8 and 10, tel. 987/3–03–02), next to Hotel Maya Bric, offer comparable prices and a professional dive staff. A two-tank dive is $55, and a snorkeling trip to the shallower reefs is $25 per person, with a minimum of two people.

AFTER DARK

After building sand castles and swaying in a hammock all day, you'll probably want to enjoy Playa's inexpensive nightlife. Almost every hour is happy hour at the **Blue Parrot** (6 blocks north of Juárez, on the beach), where couples nurse banana daiquiris ($2.50) and a live rock band plays nightly 8–11 PM. Pick your bar-side swing and take advantage of two-for-one drink specials, offered noon–3, 6–8 PM, and 11 PM–3 AM. After the Blue Parrot, move on to **Caribe Swing** (Calle 4, on the beach), where a local reggae band keeps the dance floor packed until 4 or 5 AM. To get away from the tourist scene, try **Calypso Bar** (5a Av, btw Calles 4 and 6), open nightly 8 PM–4 AM). After a couple rounds of two-for-one $2.50 margaritas, you'll salsa like you've never salsa'd before.

Near Playa del Carmen

THE COASTAL ROAD

The road (Highway 307) running between Playa del Carmen and Tulum passes some of the most spectacular beaches in the Caribbean, as well as a variety of lagoons that support a vast array of fish and wildlife. The PLAYA DEL CARMEN–TULUM bus runs hourly 6 AM–8 PM (see Coming and Going in Playa del Carmen, *above*) and will stop at or near any of the places listed below, with the exception of Punta Bete (see *below*), which is north of Playa del Carmen. From Tulum, you can take a bus running north along the highway every half hour until 9 PM. Either way, be sure to tell the driver where you want to get off. Hitching is also a possibility, particularly during the day.

PUNTA BETE Punta Bete, especially the southern end of it, is isolated and idyllic, with kilometers of pristine white sand, coconut palms, and gentle waves curling in from the sea. The only thing missing is naked dancers singing "Bali Hai." If you can't arrange that, try the snorkeling, which is excellent just 20–40 meters offshore. Schools of fantastically colored fish, octopus, and stingrays are within wading distance; slap on those fins on the southern end of the beach, as the northern part of Punta Bete is more rocky. Overnight visitors can hang their hammocks under a palapa roof for about $2 at either **Palapas Los Pinos** or **Palapas Playa Xcalacoco**. For an extra $2, you can rent a hammock. If you don't want to rock yourself to sleep in the open air next to crashing waves, rent a cabaña ($13–$20 depending on size) or camp ($3 per person) at Xcalacoco. Clean showers and a restaurant are footsteps away. Both Palapas Los Pinos and Xcalacoco rent snorkeling gear (about $5 a day) and offer snorkeling and fishing trips (about $20 per person per day).

> **COMING AND GOING** • If you've got the energy, the 1½-hour, 12-kilometer walk from Playa del Carmen to Punta Bete takes you along a gorgeous stretch of beach. Start early in the morning before the sun gets too high. You can lock your things up at La Ruina (see *Where to Sleep, above*) if you're just going for the day. Otherwise take an ADO or ATS bus (75¢) heading toward Cancún, tell the bus driver to let you off at Punta Bete, and walk 30 minutes down the bug-ridden, pot-holed, dirt road. To get back, wave down the same bus heading the opposite direction.

XCARET No more than 10 kilometers (6 mi) south of Playa del Carmen (40 km north of Tulum) lies Xcaret (ISH-carey), where the Maya used to come for purifying bathing rituals before canoeing to Cozumel. Although the site is still surrounded by lagoons, cenotes, and voluptuous jungle brush, it's about as authentically Mayan as Disneyland. The main attraction is a 530-meter underground river, which would make for beautiful snorkeling if it didn't get so packed. You can rent snorkeling equipment for $6; lockers are 30¢. The biggest drawback is the price—the entrance fee is an astounding $30 Monday–Saturday. "Bargain" Sunday will still cost you $25. Your only hope of a discount is through the park's publicist, **La Comercial-izadora de Xcaret** (tel. 988/3–06–54, fax 988/3–37–09), which sometimes gives deals to teachers or educational groups. The fee goes toward the park's upkeep and the preservation of endangered animal species and also allows you access to the light show, music, and dancing of "Xcaret at Night," which starts at 7 PM.

➤ **COMING AND GOING** • Your best bet is to get here early and make a day of it. Take a bus from anywhere along the highway—it passes about every half hour—and ask to be dropped off at Xcaret. From there, walk 20 minutes to the park's entrance, or wait for the free tourist-toting buggy. *Open daily 8:30 AM–10 PM.*

PAAMUL About 15 kilometers (9 mi) south of Xcaret is Paamul, the famous nesting site of giant turtles weighing upward of 200 pounds. Now an endangered species, the turtles emerge from the ocean on June and July nights to lay as many as 200 eggs each. They may like Paa-mul's beach, but you probably won't—it doesn't have the white sandy expanses found in tourist brochures. It is a great spot for beachcombing, though, since shells and dead coral wash ashore in abundance. Snorkeling over the reef, about 375 meters offshore, is excellent. **Scuba Mex** (next to Restaurant Arrecifes, tel. 987/4–17–29) rents snorkeling equipment for $6 a day. For $25 per person they'll take you out to the reef for three hours and give you a few drinks. Other-wise, just slip on your fins and swim on out. To reach Paamul, take any Tulum-bound bus and ask to be dropped off at Paamul; it's a five-minute walk down the road to the beach. To return flag down the bus on the opposite side of the highway. Note that more buses will stop for you earlier in the day. Around 4 or 5 in the afternoon you may have to resort to a taxi or hitchhiking

YAL-KU LAGOON Yal-Ku has everything that nearby Xel-Ha has, without the manicured environment and the price. Come in the morning before other tourists make it out here, and come soon—Xel-Ha's owner has plans to develop the lagoon into a tourist trap. In the mean-time, you'll have access to interesting underwater cavern formations, where schools of small yellow-nosed barracuda and parrotfish munch coral so loudly that you can actually hear them *Take a* PLAYA DEL CARMEN–TULUM *bus and ask to be dropped off at Hotel Club Akumal Caribe From inside hotel's gates, walk north 3 kilometers and follow signs to lagoon. Admission free Open daily 8–4:30.*

XCACEL About 14 kilometers (9 mi) south of Yal-Ku, Xcacel (pronounced ISH-ka-sel) pro-vides an excellent refuge from the pricey tourist stops along the highway. Many people come here to park their campers and hang out in the sand. The beach is free of rocks and seaweed and there usually aren't many people here. There's also a small, privately funded turtle farm where you can look as long as you don't touch. The impressive cenote, dark with salt- and freshwater animal life and untouched by divers, lies at the beach's southern end and is reached by a swampy jungle path rife with scurrying hermit crabs. Just south of the cenote is a giant coconut grove where some of the only remaining *palmeras reales* (royal palms) still stand. arrange diving and snorkeling trips in the nearby breathtaking underwater caves and cenote visit Buddy in the camper just west of the turtle farm, or call Tony and Nancy Derosa of **Aquat Divers** (tel. 987/4–12–71) in nearby Akumal. *Take a* PLAYA DEL CARMEN–TULUM *bus and ask be dropped off at Xcacel. Admission to beach $1.50; $2 extra to camp overnight.*

XEL-HA LAGOON Now a national park, Xel-Ha ("clear water" in Maya) is home to parrot fish, angelfish, manta rays, and giant barracudas. Underwater caverns filled with coral (and, one case, a Mayan altar) make for interesting snorkeling. Though tourists and their various oin ments have polluted the lagoon—resulting in the current prohibition of sunscreen lotions—t place remains irritatingly popular. If you're determined, come early in the morning, before t rush starts, and explore the entire lagoon; don't be afraid to stray from where the tourists a swimming. Admission is a whopping $10, and on the northeast side of the lake, you can re snorkeling equipment ($6), lockers ($1; $2 deposit), and towels ($1). *40 km (25 mi) south Playa del Carmen, 15 km (9 mi) north of Tulum; take a bus and ask driver to let you off at X Ha, or hitch along hwy.*

Cozumel

If you want to dive, come to Cozumel—it's as simple as that. Even jaded Jacques Cousteau raved about the coral reefs that ring this island, located 19 kilometers (12 mi) from Playa del Carmen. While Cozumel is not the paradise it once was (tourism has killed a lot of the coral), it's still the best site on the Yucatán Peninsula. Most famous of all the reefs is the Palancar Reef, where underwater visibility extends more than 65 meters. Divers can experience the whole gamut of underwater excitement at other reefs, too, including plunging walls, passages, caves, and even a phony airplane wreck left behind by a film crew. Most people also come to Cozumel prepared to drop a bundle on diving and accommodations, so it's not exactly a budget paradise. Consider staying in Playa del Carmen and taking the ferry to Cozumel.

During Mayan times, Cozumel was a sacred island covered with temples and shrines to Ixchel, the goddess of fertility. Mayan women from all over what is now Central America and southern Mexico were expected to make the pilgrimage here at least once in their lifetime to pray and leave offerings. Unfortunately, many temples were ransacked by Cortés in 1519, and the U.S. military destroyed others while constructing an airstrip during World War II. What does remain are vast tracts of thick jungle covering the entire northeast half of the island, as well as much of its interior. Even if you're only on Cozumel a couple of days, it's worth renting a scooter or bike and exploring the teeming jungles and swamplands, if only to escape the tourist scene.

BASICS

AMERICAN EXPRESS The AmEx representative here is **Fiesta Cozumel.** They cash and issue traveler's checks but don't give cash advances. *Calle 11 Sur 598, btw Pedro Joaquín and 25a Av. Sur, tel. 987/2−07−25. Follow Rafael Melgar south to Calle 11, take a left, and walk 5½ blocks. Open weekdays 8−1 and 4−8.*

CASAS DE CAMBIO Most banks are in downtown San Miguel. You can change cash or traveler's checks weekdays 9−2 and Saturday 10−1 at **Banco del Atlántico** (Calle 1 Sur 11, southern cnr of zócalo, tel. 987/2−01−42). The ATM at Banco del Atlántico accepts MasterCard, Cirrus, and Visa. American dollars are accepted all over the island.

CONSULATES Cozumel has no consulates, but citizens of all nations can get help from **Bryan Wilson** (Calle 13 Sur, at 15a Av. Sur, tel. 987/2−06−54), who works as an unofficial ombudsman and interpreter. On call 24 hours a day, he speaks perfect Spanish, is well acquainted with Mexican law, and can help you out of sticky situations. He can also recommend great restaurants. His services are free unless they result in considerable savings for you, in which case he'll take a commission.

EMERGENCIES Contact the **police** (Rafael Melgar, at Calle 13 Sur, tel. 987/2−00−92) or an **ambulance** (tel. 987/2−06−39).

LAUNDRY **Margarita Laundromat** charges $2.50 per load to wash, 50¢ per 10 minutes of drying, and sells detergent. *20a Av. Sur, at Calle 3 Sur, tel. 987/2−28−65. Open Mon.−Sat. 7 AM−9 PM, Sun. 9−5.*

MEDICAL AID For 24-hour medical assistance, contact **Dr. Gustavo Ambriz** or go to his clinic (Calle 5 Sur 21-B, 4 blocks south of ferry dock, tel. 987/2−16−71 or 987/2−14−30). He specializes in travel medicine and diving-related problems (he has a decompression tank). **Farmacia Dori** (Rosado Salas, at 15a Av. Sur, tel. 987/2−05−59) is open daily 7 AM−midnight.

PHONES AND MAIL The **post office** (Rafael Melgar, at Calle 7 Sur, tel. 987/2−01−06) is open weekdays 8−8, Saturdays 9−1. They will hold mail sent to you at the following address for up to 10 days: Lista de Correos, Cozumel, Quintana Roo, CP 77600, México. **Computel** (Calle 1 Sur 165, btw 5a and 10a Avs., tel. 987/2−40−87, fax 987/2−41−54) lets you make local and long-distance calls. It's open daily 7 AM−10 PM. Farmacia Dori (*see above*) sells Ladatel phone cards.

VISITOR INFORMATION *The Blue Guide* is a pocket-size publication with important phone numbers and a small map of the city, found at any hotel or at the ferry dock. Cozumel's **Oficina**

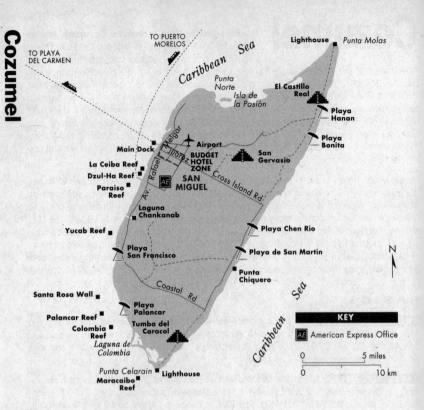

Cozumel

TO PLAYA
DEL CARMEN

TO PUERTO
MORELOS

Caribbean Sea

Lighthouse *Punta Molas*

Punta
Norte

Isla de
la Pasión

El Castillo
Real

Playa
Hanan

Playa
Bonita

Main Dock

Airport
BUDGET
HOTEL
ZONE

San
Gervasio

La Ceiba Reef

Dzul-Ha Reef

Paraíso
Reef

AE
SAN
MIGUEL

Cross Island Rd.

Laguna
Chankanab

Playa Chen Río

Yucab Reef

Playa
San Francisco

Playa de San Martín

Punta
Chiquero

Santa Rosa Wall

Coastal Rd.

Caribbean Sea

Playa
Palancar

Palancar Reef

Tumba del
Caracol

Colombia
Reef

*Laguna de
Colombia*

Punta Celarain Lighthouse
Maracaibo
Reef

N

KEY

AE American Express Office

0   5 miles

0   10 km

Estatal de Turismo is difficult to find and often closed, but they do have some interesting infor
mation on the island's wildlife and plants and can supply you with free maps of the island a
well as a self-guided tour of San Gervasio (*see* Worth Seeing, *below*). *Edificio Plaza del Sol, te
and fax 987/2–09–72. From tall clock on east side of zócalo, head east behind farmacia towar
Centro de Convenciones, then head north and look for tower on the left. Office is on west sid
of upper-level balcony. Open weekdays 8:30–3.*

COMING AND GOING

BY FERRY The **Cruzeros Maritimo** (tel. 987/2–15–08) ferry departs from Playa del Carme
for Cozumel (45 min; $3.25 one-way, $6.50 round-trip) every 2–3 hours daily 5:15 AM–8:4
PM. The ferry leaves from the pier just in front of Plaza Marina Playacar in Playa.

BY PLANE Cozumel has a small international **airport** (tel. 987/2–06–47), with flights
and from the States on **Continental** (tel. 987/2–08–47). Fares vary dramatically, but a rea
sonable low-season round-trip fare from Houston to Cozumel is about $420. **Mexicana** (te
987/2–29–45) and **Aero Cozumel** (tel. 987/2–34–56) offer service to cities all over Mexic
including Cancún, Mérida, and Mexico City. **Aero Banana** (tel. 987/2–50–40) flies to near
Isla Mujeres and Cancún. To reach town from the airport, walk two minutes out of the termin
to the *glorieta* (traffic circle) with the big sparrow and catch a $3.50 taxi. The CIRCUMNAVEG
CIÓN bus will take you right to the ferry terminal from the airport for a mere 25¢.

GETTING AROUND

Cozumel is the largest of Mexico's islands, 53 kilometers (33 mi) long and 14 kilometers
mi) wide. San Miguel de Cozumel, the small town on the western coast of the island, is the h
of activities. It's easy to get around San Miguel on foot, since the streets are laid out in a g

and run either parallel or perpendicular to the coast. Apart from the main avenues, all streets have numerical designations. The avenue running along the malecón is Rafael Melgar; parallel avenues are numbered in multiples of five (5a Avenida is followed by 10a Avenida and 15a Avenida). Avenida Benito Juárez, the main drag, begins at the ferry dock and cuts the town in two. The main plaza is directly adjacent to the ferry dock, between 5a Avenida and the malecón at Avenida Juárez. Streets and avenues north of Juárez receive the appellation Norte; those to the south, Sur. To further confuse the situation, streets north of Juárez have even numbers, and those to the south have odd numbers. If you have some sort of transportation, a road circles the rest of the island, making it easy to explore, and several other roads and trails cut through the flat jungle.

BY SCOOTER The most popular way to see the island is by scooter. The going rate is $20 for 24 hours, but bargaining is not out of the question. **Rentadora Leo** (5a Av. 199, at Rosado Salas, tel. 987/2–43–81) charges only $15 for same-day returns. Don't forget to wear a helmet, or you'll be fined $25.

BY BIKE The island is a bit too large to explore thoroughly on a bicycle, but if you do ride, take plenty of water. Taxis constantly circle the island, so bring enough money to take one back if you get stranded—if the driver is feeling benevolent, he'll let your bike come along for the ride. **Rentadora Águila** (685 Rafael Melgar, btw Calles 3 and 5 Sur, tel. 987/2–07–29 or 987/2–25–09) rents bikes for $5 a day and is open Monday–Saturday 8–8, Sunday 8–7.

BY BUS There are three bus routes in Cozumel, connecting downtown to the *colonias* (residential areas). The CIRCUMNAVEGACION bus (25¢) is most useful for visitors; it runs up Calle 11 from Rafael Melgar and turns north on 65 Avenida; after passing through the eastern colonias, it returns to town via Boulevard Aeropuerto. The bus runs every 20 minutes until about 7:30 PM.

BY TAXI Taxi rates are regulated, so you have the right to report any excessive charges to the local **Sitio de Taxis** (Calle 2 Nte., btw 5a and 10a Avs., tel. 987/2–00–41), and you may even get your money back. Within town, you shouldn't be charged more than $1; if you're going as far as Chankanab, you'll have to pay about $1.50 (rates rise slightly after midnight). If you take a taxi from the ferry dock, ask to see the driver's *tarjeta de tarifas* (rate card) to make sure you're getting a good price.

WHERE TO SLEEP

After Cancún, Cozumel is the most expensive place on the peninsula. Budget travelers should choose between staying in the hotels in San Miguel, most of which are within a few blocks of the central plaza, and camping. You can crash on **Playa del Sol** or **Playa Casita,** both a short walk south of town, or try the secluded places on the southern and eastern portions of the island. Try the 4-kilometer stretch of dirt road that follows the beach to **Punta Celarain.** Also, several spots along the paved road parallel to the eastern shore are sequestered by dunes or scrub. Authorities will warn you to be careful of thieves because the beaches are not patrolled, but there have been few incidents recently. If you plan to camp out on the beach during the sea turtle's egg-laying season (May–Oct.), you'll need to get permission from the **Zona Federal** Edificio Plaza del Sol, second floor, near Visitor Information Office, tel. 987/2–09–66). During any other time of year, permission isn't necessary.

UNDER $10 • Hotel Posada Edém. This is the cheapest downtown hotel, and it's conveniently located next to a taxi stand, bakery, and the main plaza. There are a few friendly bugs and rather gloomy rooms, but overall this place is clean and well-kept. You can even watch Mexican soap operas with the owner in the lobby. Singles and doubles are $8.50, and air-conditioning is an extra $5. You can also rent mopeds for $20 a day. *Calle 2 Nte. 12, btw 5a and 10a Avs. Nte., tel. 987/2–11–66. 14 rooms, all with bath. Luggage storage. MC, V.*

Posada del Zorro. Down-and-out scuba-diving junkies flock here when downtown prices rise. The walls are patched with blistering paint and the bathrooms are rust-tinted and bare, but at least there aren't any noticeable forms of animal life. Large rooms with two double beds are only $9.50 for one or two people; squeeze in as many friends as you want for an extra $2 each.

Juárez, at 30a Av., 6 blocks east of ferry dock, tel. 987/2–07–90. 6 rooms, all with bath. Luggage storage.

➤ **UNDER $20** • **Hotel Cozumel Inn.** The sunny balconies of this three-tiered hotel look out onto a plant-filled inner patio, where a large frog statue guards a small pool. Tiny but tidy bedrooms come equipped with shoebox-size bathrooms, and the patio rooms are perfectly positioned for the occasional afternoon breeze. Singles are $14, doubles $18, and triples $28 (add $5 for air-conditioning). *Calle 4 Nte. 3, at Rafael Melgar, tel. 987/2–03–14. 30 rooms, all with bath. Luggage storage.*

Hotel Kary. Spacious rooms, free agua purificada, and a midnight skinny dip in the refreshing courtyard pool will make you forget you're a budget traveler. Singles and doubles are $14.50 ($16 with air-conditioning), and triples with air conditioning cost $20. If you're a party of three, beware: Apparently your right to a third towel is not guaranteed, and you may have to tackle the maid to get one. *25a Av. Sur, at Rosado Salas, tel. 987/2–20–11. From ferry dock, 2 blocks south (right) and 5 blocks east. 17 rooms and 2 suites, all with bath. Luggage storage.*

➤ **UNDER $25** • **Hotel Marycarmen.** Just when you think it can't get any better than wood furniture, air-conditioning, and great bathrooms, you get plush bedding with satin ruffles. The small atrium is ideal for sunbathing, and the location is ideal. Singles and doubles cost $22, triples $30. *5a Av. Sur 4, btw Calle 1 Sur and Rosado Salas, tel. 987/2–05–81. From ferry dock, 1 block inland and 1½ blocks right. 27 rooms, all with bath. Luggage storage. Wheelchair access. MC, V.*

Hotel Pepita. Located on a somewhat run-down street, the photo-filled office of this lovely hotel is a welcome surprise, with complimentary coffee provided in the lobby. Rooms are small but sunny and surprisingly quiet, with refrigerators, air-conditioning, and colorful bedspreads. Doubles are $20, triples $25. *15a Av. Sur, at Calle 1 Sur, 3 blocks from main pier, tel. 987/2–00–98. 30 rooms, all with bath. Wheelchair access.*

FOOD

If you're willing to walk a little, you can eat quite cheaply in Cozumel. The **mercado** (Rosado Salas, at 25a Av.) sells fresh fruits and vegetables daily 7–5. Several **loncherías** in the market also offer breakfast deals and main dishes for less than $2. **Panaderia La Cozumeleña** bakes the world's greatest cream puff–churro hybrid (30¢). *Calle 3, at 10a Av., tel. 987/2–01–89. Open Mon.–Sat. 7 AM–10 PM, Sun. 7 AM–8 PM.*

➤ **UNDER $5** • **La Casa del Wafle.** A couple of surfers named Raul and Jeannie got together and formed this waffle joint to finance their aquatic habit. Delicacies include plain waffles ($3), waffles Benedict ($4), excellent pancakes ($2.50), and the Waffle Supreme, a obscenely sweet waffle with fruit, syrup, and whipped cream ($4). Bathing suit–clad tourists stop for a bite to eat and end up staying for the bottomless coffee. *Juárez, btw Avs. 20 and 25, no phone. Open daily 8–1 and 6–10. Other location: Bottom floor of Vista del Mar Hotel, Av Melgar, 4 blocks south of ferry dock, tel. 987/2–05–45. Open daily 6 AM–10 PM.*

Casa Denis. Breathe in the fresh air while you admire the adjacent Virgin Mary altar and slowly sip exotic avocado soup ($1.50). The book-size menu offers choices such as fresh fish kabobs ($4) and *enchiladas suizas* (enchiladas with cheese sauce; $2.50). Beer is less than $1. *Calle 1 Sur, btw 5a and 10a Avs., ½ block east of zócalo, tel. 987/2–00–67. Open Mon.–Sat. 7 AM–11 PM.*

Los Moros del Morito. The location is a little out of the way, but this restaurant is a hidden treasure. Popular with locals and foreign residents of Cozumel, the setting is festive and the portions are decadent. Fish and chicken shish kabobs cost $5.50 and enchiladas with rich mole sauce go for $2.75. *35a Av. Sur, btw. Calle 3 and Morelos, tel. 987/2–28–67. Open Wed.–Mon. 10 AM–11 PM.*

Restaurant Toñita. Strategically placed fans protrude from the walls and ceiling to keep flies off your food. The food is cheap and the menu changes daily. Great meals including soup, meat dish, veggies, rice, and tortillas will run you about $3. *Rosado Salas, btw 10a and 15a Avs., 2½ blocks east of zócalo, tel. 987/2–04–01. Open Mon.–Sat. 8–6.*

DESSERT/COFFEEHOUSES **Café Caribe.** A welcome relief for travelers in a serious Nescafé rut, this place has more character than the sports bars and Texas-style grills that prevail in San Miguel. It's a Euro-coffeehouse where quiet jazz and classical music play. Bring the last book you read and exchange it for one that someone else left behind. The pastry selection isn't all that inviting, but the iced cappuccino ($1.50) is excellent. *10a Av. Sur, btw Rosado Salas and Calle 3 Sur, tel. 987/2–36–21. Open Mon.–Sat. 8–1 and 6–9:30.*

WORTH SEEING

The wild and rocky eastern coast of Cozumel is well worth exploring: It's still mostly deserted despite the paved road that runs along the shoreline. You can swim in some places, especially **Punta Chiquero, Chen Río,** and the beach at **Punta Morena Hotel.** At other points, however, the strong undertow makes a leisurely dip dangerous. You can get a great view of the island from the top of the lighthouse on **Punta Celarain** (southern tip of island, at end of 4-km dirt road), which looks out over the pounding surf that hurls spray high over the rocks. If you clamber over the sand dunes, you'll find some empty, untouristed beaches where you can swim nude in relative privacy.

SAN GERVASIO RUINS The recently restored ruins of San Gervasio are situated in 10 acres of jungle in the middle of Cozumel. The site is said to have been used as a ceremonial center throughout several Mayan periods, and the remains of fertility shrines, residential units, and mural paintings are still visible today. Information for a self-guided tour is available at the Visitor Information Office (*see above*). To get here, take the cross-island road until you see the sign for San Gervasio, then turn right on the dirt road and head northeast to the ruins. **Turismo Aviomar** (5a Av., btw Calles 2 and 4 Nte., tel. 987/2–04–77 or 987/2–05–88) offers a two-hour tour of the ruins for $35. Tours leave weekdays at 9 and 11 AM—call ahead to check availability. You can also take a taxi to the ruins, but it'll cost $30 round-trip. Admission to San Gervasio is $2, free Sunday and holidays.

MUSEO DE LA ISLA DE COZUMEL This beautiful whitewashed museum is a necessary stop for anyone wanting to learn more about the island's spectacular array of exotic plants and animals. Clearly drawn, color-coded maps with English subtitles explain the island's geographic history and the development of the island's ecological riches. In addition to life-size nature scenes and an entire room dedicated to the origins and nature of coral, the museum also has a gallery delineating the history of the Maya, complete with replicas of important ruins and artifacts found on the island. The doorman is also a great source of information—if business is slow enough, he'll walk you through the museum himself. *Rafael Melgar, btw Calles 4 and 6 Nte., tel. 987/2–14–34. Admission: $2, free Sun. Open daily 9–5.*

OUTDOOR ACTIVITIES

Prime snorkeling and diving spots can be found all over Cozumel, though equipment rental and transport to the reefs may leave your wallet limper than usual. Most trips, however, are well worth the pesos: The wide variety of marine life combined with the astonishing visibility of Cozumel's clear Caribbean waters is beyond description—we won't even try.

SNORKELING Snorkeling is a cheap and relatively painless way to explore Cozumel's sea life. Particularly good is the snorkeling off the beach on the western coast, especially in the area between Hotel Sol Caribe and Playa Maya. Equipment rental costs about $6 at any of the five shops in town; a snorkeling trip to the shallow reefs is about $20. **Bel Mar Aquatics** (Hotel La Ceiba, 1 km south of ferry dock on Rafael Melgar, tel. 987/2–16–65), **Blue Bubble Divers** (5a Av. Sur and Calle 3 Sur, tel. 987/2–18–65, blubub@aol.com), and **Diving Adventures** (Calle 5 Sur, at Rafael Melgar, tel. 987/2–30–09) all offer snorkeling trips.

> **LA CEIBA REEF** • La Ceiba Reef, in front of La Ceiba Hotel, is a good place to snorkel or dive. A 120-meter trail has been marked out on the reef, starting at a fake airplane wreck (it

was sunk during the filming of a movie) and continuing past several interesting coral formations. *4 km south of San Miguel; walk or take a scooter or taxi ($3). Admission free.*

➤ **DZUL-HA** • Dzul-Ha Reef boasts two important features: free admission and few tourists. About 2 kilometers south of La Ceiba Reef (*see above*), Dzul-Ha doesn't plant airplane wrecks or religious icons to amuse snorkelers. What you will see are beautiful angel fish, amazing coral formations, and even starfish on the ocean floor. You can rent equipment for $6 at the Blue Bubble dive shop branch in front of the reef or just bring your own. *6 km south of town, across from Hotel Club de Sol; take a bike, scooter, or taxi ($4).*

➤ **LAGUNA CHANKANAB** • This national park 9 kilometers south of San Miguel is the most popular snorkeling spot in Cozumel. At the center of the park is a lagoon separated from the beach, fed by an underwater cave; a large botanical garden with replicas of Mayan dwellings surrounds the lagoon. Swimming is no longer allowed in the lagoon (paddling tourists were slowly killing it), but snorkeling in the clear waters of the adjacent bay is spectacular, as is diving at the offshore reef. Once underwater, you can see interesting coral heads, a myriad of tropical fish, and a large statue of Christ, sunk for the entertainment of divers. Chankanab is, unfortunately, a little too crowded: Head elsewhere if you want a solitary snorkel. Four dive shops on the premises rent snorkeling and diving equipment. To get here, take a taxi ($5) or rent a scooter or bike. *Admission: $5. Open daily 9–5:30.*

SCUBA DIVING Diving is the raison d'être of tourism in Cozumel. Dozens of dive shops offer instruction, as well as a wide range of boat trips to shallow and deep reefs; anybody, from beginner to expert, can find a suitable dive. Beginners hone their skills on the shallow **Yucab Reef,** close to shore and just south of Laguna Chankanab. Expert divers will want to head for

Endangered Reefs

The Yucatán may offer some of the most beautiful coral reefs in the world, but some of these areas have paid a high price for their popularity. Coral reefs are the undersea equivalent of rain forests: They're one of the most complex ecosystems on earth, and, like rain forests, they're severely threatened and underprotected. Once damaged, coral reefs repair themselves slowly, growing at a rate of just one centimeter every 10 years. They're endangered by divers, boat anchors, overfishing, severe storms and hurricanes, and pollution. One of Cozumel's most beautiful reefs, Paraíso, is now threatened by the construction of a new cruise ship pier. After a long fight by divers and environmentalists, financial interests won over ecology, and pier construction is well under way. Although the reef is large, and divers still have access to the majority of Paraíso, the construction foreshadows an uncertain future for one of Cozumel's most beautiful and fragile natural assets.

The following are a few tips for environmentally aware travelers: When diving in reef areas, do not break off a piece of coral for a keepsake of your trip to Mexico—it may be beautiful, but it is also home to thousands of tropical fish, plants, and crustacea, and is itself a living organism. Coral is often used to create souvenirs and jewelry. Do not purchase these items. Like the trade in elephant ivory and tortoise shells, each purchase you make supports exploitation and is detrimental to the coral's survival. Finally, if you're mooring a boat, be careful where you drop anchor—a 30-pound weight can do a lot of damage.

the more challenging (and thrilling) reefs, such as **Maracaibo, Santa Rosa Wall,** and **Colombia.** You must be certified to rent diving gear and take diving trips. At the more reputable agencies, the staff will test your diving ability before letting you attempt advanced dives. Good agencies are more expensive but safer: **Aqua Safari** (Rafael Melgar 429, btw Calles 5 and 7 Sur, tel. 987/2–01–01), **Cozumel Equalizers** (Rosado Salas 72, at 5a Av. Sur, tel. 987/2–35–11), and **Dive Paradise** (Rafael Melgar 601, tel. 987/2–10–07) are among the most reputable. Four-day certification courses cost about $300. Two-tank dives cost about $50 (usually with a six-diver minimum), and night dives are $30.

➤ **PALANCAR REEF** • The most famous of Cozumel's reefs, Palancar lies about 1½ kilometers from Playa Palancar on the island's southwestern shore. The reef stretches intermittently for about 5 kilometers and offers divers a range of underwater experiences. The best-known formation is the **Horseshoe,** a collection of coral heads that form a horseshoe curve right at the drop off. The visibility—some 85 meters in places—is extraordinary.

➤ **PARAISO REEF** • Just north of the Stouffer Presidente Hotel, near San Miguel, this reef lies 12–22 meters deep and has excellent star and brain coral formations. The northern part of Paraíso may be affected by the new pier construction (see box, *below*). The southern part is farther offshore but merits taking a boat to see the extensive marine life there. **Diving Adventures** (Calle 5 Sur, at Melgar, tel. 987/2–30–09, solymar@rce.com.mx) offers daily dive trips to Paraíso for $35.

AFTER DARK

Although Cozumel boasts the usual gringo-packed bars, Carlos 'n Charlie's and Hard Rock Café are not your only options for a memorable night. At **Joe's Reggae Bar** (10a Av. Sur, at Rosado Salas, tel. 987/2–32–75), high school students on their senior class trip are refreshingly absent. With no cover charge, bottomless popcorn baskets, live music, and quirky Fiji-meets-Rome decor, you won't mind that beers cost $1.75. Around the corner, **Raga** (Rosado Salas, btw 10a and 15a Avs., no phone) presents live pop music Monday–Wednesday 9:30 PM–midnight and Thursday–Saturday 10:30 PM–1 AM.

On Sunday nights, local bands gather in the main plaza to play everything from mambo and salsa to jarana, a fast-paced Yucatecan step dance that requires the tiptoeing dancer to sidestep an invisible bull to the rhythm of a yelping crowd.

Tulum

The setting of the ancient Maya city of Tulum is breathtaking. A backdrop of talcum-powder beaches, rocky cliffs, and clear Caribbean waters gives the crumbling gray ruins a unique aura. Tourists generally come here on organized day trips from Cancún to admire the ruins, take a few pictures, buy some souvenirs, and get back to their air-conditioned hotel rooms. Budget travelers, on the other hand, have made Tulum one of their favorite hangouts. The beaches south of the ruins attract a friendly, low-budget crowd in various stages of undress—mostly young Europeans who come here to let their hair grow, peel off their tie-dyed shirts, and make jewelry. The beaches at Tulum are secluded and relatively untouched compared with those at Playa del Carmen.

Tulum was built and rebuilt in various stages, beginning sometime between AD 700 and 1300 with the Putún-Maya. This tribe was also associated with Mayapán, the last site of prehistoric Mayan civilization. Originally named "Zama" (Mayan for "sunrise"), Tulum was intended as an observatory and ceremonial center. Burial platforms surround the leftover buildings and the tiny, windowed observatory hovers above the old city. Juan de Grijalva, who sighted the city in 1518 when his Spanish expedition sailed past the coast, compared Tulum, with its red, white, and blue buildings, with Seville. The city was still occupied by the Maya at the time of the Spanish conquest: One of the images in the Temple of the Paintings depicts Chaac riding a horse, an animal introduced by the Spanish.

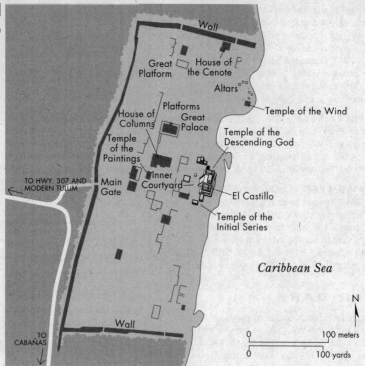

Wall
Great
Platform
House of
the Cenote
Altars
Temple of the Wind
House of
Columns
Platforms
Great
Palace
Temple of the
Descending God
Temple
of the
Paintings
TO HWY. 307 AND
MODERN TULUM
Main
Gate
Inner
Courtyard
El Castillo
Temple of the
Initial Series
Caribbean Sea
N
Wall
TO
CABAÑAS
0   100 meters
0   100 yards

COMING AND GOING

The ancient city of Tulum is 63 kilometers (39 mi) south of Playa del Carmen and 127 kilo-meters (79 mi) south of Cancún. The first-class **Premier** bus station (serving Mérida and Val ladolid) is downtown, across from the Maya Hotel; second-class buses can be caught opposite the first-class station. From Tulum there's frequent second-class service to Playa del Carmen (2 per hr, 45 min, $1.50), Cancún (2 per hr, 1½ hrs, $3), Chetumal (5 per day via Bacalone 3½ hrs, $6.50; last bus 6:30 PM), Cobá (4 per day, 45 min, $1), and Valladolid (1 per day, 2½ hrs, $4). One lone bus heads to Mérida (5 hrs, $8) at 1:30 PM. If you're broke, hitchhiking along the main highway is common and relatively easy.

GETTING AROUND

The crucero (turnoff) for the ruins and budget lodging is about 4 kilometers north of the moder town of Tulum. To reach the ruins, ask the driver to let you off at the crucero, then continue eas down the paved road for five minutes, toward the coast. There's also a $1 trolley bus runnin from the parking lot just south of the crucero to the entrance to the ruins. As you enter the ruins another paved road heads south along the coast to the cabañas and beaches. It's a five-minut taxi ride ($1.50) from the ruins and campgrounds to the modern town of Tulum, equipped wit one budget hotel, a handful of restaurants and fruit stands, and a few other basic services.

WHERE TO SLEEP

The cabañas that lie along the beach south of the ruins are the best (but most primitive) lodg ing option. If you plan to stay at the beach, arrive before 9 PM, when the managers head else where. The **Hotel Maya** (Av. Tulum 32, across from bus terminal, no phone) has singles fc $8.50 and doubles for $11.50. Rooms here are clean and, unlike the cabañas, have electri ity, but the only good reason to stay here is to catch the 6 AM bus to Cobá—the next one leaves at 11 AM and only gives you about three hours at the ruins.

➤ **UNDER $10** • **Cabañas El Mirador.** These cabañas are quieter than Santa Fe and Don Armando and attract fewer people. The two cabañas with beds ($9.50 each) go quickly. Cabañas with hammocks are $6.50 for two people, and hammock rental is $1.50. The showers are collective (though single-sex), so modesty will get you nothing except dirty. The friendly owners serve up a hearty plate of spaghetti at Restaurant El Mirador (*see below*), which overlooks the cabañas. *On the beach, 1 km from ruins, no phone. 20 cabañas. Laundry, luggage storage, meals.*

Camping Santa Fe. This place is very popular with budget travelers, especially earthy types who get a primal thrill from grungy huts and candlelight. On the plus side, the toilets flush and the showers are in individual stalls, though you may share your bathing experience with a cucaracha. Renting a hammock and mosquito net and hanging it in a communal hut costs $2.75 per person, while a small, bare hut filled with all of your friends costs $5.50 ($6.50 with a bed). With the latter option, you can rent mosquito netting (recomended late May–early July) and hammocks for $1.50 apiece. Camping on the grass costs $1.50 per person. You could store your belongings with the administration, though it's best to keep valuables at your side. *On beach, 1 km south of ruins, no phone. Take turn-off marked by Don Armando sign, pass Don Armando restaurant, and walk to office. 15 cabañas. Key deposit ($6.50), laundry, meals.*

➤ **UNDER $15** • **Cabañas Don Armando.** The owner is pleased to announce that there are "no hippies" at Don Armando. The well-constructed cabañas are comfortable but more expensive than the ones at Camping Santa Fe. The cabañas have beds on cement platforms, hammock hooks, sand floors, and windows. The bathrooms are clean and locked (you get a key). Light sleepers beware: The nearby disco plays the same loud, obnoxious music every night until about 2 AM. Cabañas cost $8.50 with one bed and one hammock, $10 with two beds, and $12 for a beachfront hut with one bed and one hammock. Camping costs $3 per person. *1 km south of ruins, tel. 984/5–05–96. 24 cabañas. Laundry, luggage storage, meals.*

Cabañas Los Gatos. After one night nestled in these palm-shaded cabañas, you may decide to stay indefinitely. A 20-minute walk south of the other cabañas, Los Gatos sits atop a rocky, rain-whipped shelf overlooking the vigorous surf. Cozy cabañas have small double beds swinging from sturdy knotted ropes, mosquito-net canopies, wood furniture, and elegant candleholders. Cabañas with one bed cost $10.50. Those with two beds (for 3 or 4 people) cost $17. *Take wheelchair-accessible road leading south by ruins 2 km. Or walk south along beach to rocky curve in the shore and climb around to your right. Wheelchair access.*

FOOD

The restaurants outside the ruins and at the crucero are nothing spectacular and ridiculously expensive. Instead, go downtown or eat at one of the cabaña sites. **Don Armando** and **Santa Fe** (*see* Where to Sleep, *above*) offer main dishes such as fish, chicken, eggs and beans for $2–$3 and beer for less than $1. The food is particularly good but pricey at **Restaurant El Mirador**, where chicken fajitas are $3, a huge plate of spaghetti with shrimp is $4.50, and a pile of hot cakes is $1.50. All three restaurants are open daily 8 AM–9 PM. If you come into town, eat at **Restaurant Maya** (in Hotel Maya; open daily 7 AM–11 PM), where chicken tacos with rice and veggies cost $2.75 and vegetable soup is $2. A more expensive option is the 24-hour **Restaurant Ambrosia** (next to bus terminal), which serves tasty *salbutes* (fried tortillas topped with chicken, lettuce, onion, and tomato; $2.50) and generously cheesed quesadillas ($3).

WORTH SEEING

The ruins of Tulum are open daily 8–5, and admission is $2.25, free Sunday and holidays. The admission price pays for maintenance and workers, but if you're determined not to pay, it's fairly easy to climb over the city wall where it runs along the road. Tagging along with the guided tours is equally manageable. Bring a bathing suit and a book and come early—when the onslaught of tour buses arrives at 10:30, head to the grassy south end of the ruins where the trees provide pleasant shady spots, or take a dip in the nearby surf.

Tulum wasn't constructed as a fortress of defense, but the structure's thick walls and watch-towers proved useful in times of war. Tulum's most prestigious inhabitants (priests, astrologers, and carpenters) were separated from outlying peasant farmers by a 7-meter wall. The city's castle and the nobles' homes surrounding it are evidence of three different building phases, each using the previous structure as a base from which to erect the building's next level. There are some reliefs carved into the stucco walls of the buildings, but frescoes were the most prevalent form of decoration in Tulum.

➤ **TEMPLE OF THE PAINTINGS** • This small yet well-preserved structure consists of two temples, one inside the other. Large stucco masks, probably representing the god Quetzalcoatl, stare from the corners of the outer facade. The mask on the southern corner, with one eye open and one shut, symbolizes the duality of the Maya belief system, which understood evil and darkness (the closed eye) not as the absence of good and light, but as equally important aspects of nature.

Inside the temple, the murals are divided into three sections, symbolizing the realms of the universe: the underworld, the mortal world, and the heavens. Archaeologists point to the depiction of Chaac riding a horselike animal as an indication that the murals were completed or reworked after the Spanish arrived. Unfortunately, the images are difficult to see from outside the roped-off entrance.

➤ **EL CASTILLO** • The most impressive structure at Tulum, El Castillo is not a castle as its name would suggest, but a small, two-chamber temple built atop a tall pyramid. A staircase on the western side leads to the temple, from which you get an extensive view of the sea, jungle, and surrounding ruins. At some point, the columns supporting the doorway were modified to look like feathered serpents, the symbol of Kukulcan—evidence of a strong Toltec influence in Tulum.

➤ **TEMPLE OF THE DESCENDING GOD** • Immediately north of El Castillo, this temple is a small, elevated structure that received its name from the beautiful relief above the doorway. The stucco carving depicts a deity diving headfirst from the sky. This deity is thought to represent Quetzalcoatl—it has wings and a strange pointed tail, and carries what seems to be a flower. Some say the figure is a honeybee, of central significance in Yucatecan Maya religion, medicine, and commerce.

➤ **TEMPLE OF THE WIND** • This small structure north of the Temple of the Descending God was acoustically designed to whistle when winds blew through at a velocity of 160 kilometers (99 mi) per hour or greater. The storm warning whistle can be heard 34 kilometers (21 mi) away.

OUTDOOR ACTIVITIES

Even if you're not a snorkeling fan, the many underground cenotes scattered throughout the Tulum/Cobá area are worth a look, and many are sufficiently remote to enjoy the experience in the buff—just make sure to slather sunscreen on your unmentionables. One of the most beautiful cenotes near Tulum is the **Gran Cenote,** first discovered after Hurricane Gilbert caved in its porous limestone roof, exposing the cenote's cavernous interior. To reach the Gran Cenote, take a taxi ($1.50) down the road opposite the crucero, 4 kilometers west of the ruins. Otherwise, make the half-hour walk or hitch a ride. The family that lives on the land surrounding the cenote usually charges about $2.50 at the entrance, but the price is negotiable.

Near the ruins is a small beach that's clean and free of seaweed. The beach continues south, but a wall divides it in two at the ruins. To reach the rest of the beach, enter through the campground at El Mirador (*see* Where to Sleep, *above*). Nude bathing is allowed at the beaches in front of the cabañas, and you can snorkel over a reef about 500 yards offshore. The water is not as clear as Playa del Carmen's, but the sea life is just as abundant. There is a small dive shop between Camping Santa Fe and Cabañas Don Armando, under a red-flagged palapa—if the owners aren't there, ask at the bar at Santa Fe. Snorkeling and scuba-diving trips are available; ask at the dive shop for details and prices.

Near Tulum

COBÁ

This site, covering more than 70 square kilometers (43 square mi), has been largely ignored by archaeologists and the Mexican government. Dense jungle envelops much of it, and visitors will feel like pioneers stumbling onto something unknown and exotic. Distances between the structures are all 1–2 kilometers, so be prepared to walk; bring water and *lots* of insect repellent.

Mayan Civilizations: Time Periods

The Maya first settled in the lowland areas of Guatemala, Mexico, and Belize and then moved north onto the Yucatán Peninsula. Hence, the height of the Classic period in the northern settlements occurred at about the same time the southern centers were being abandoned. The history of Mayan civilization is traditionally broken down into the following eras. These divisions are not absolute, and archaeologists often differ on the criteria used to designate them.

PRE-CLASSIC PERIOD (1500 BC–AD 300, also called the Formative Period): During this time, agriculture replaced the hunter/gatherer, nomadic lifestyle. Toward the end of this era, monumental buildings with corbeled arches and roof combs appeared, as did the first hieroglyphics and early calendric notation.

CLASSIC PERIOD (AD 300–900): During this period, the Maya developed a strong self-identity, and their architecture shows few traces of outside influence. Inspiration for the Maya's art, language, science, and architecture came from a unified way of thinking about the world. Temples and pyramids built with precise relation to one another illustrate the close tie between religion and aesthetics. Buildings were placed on super-structures atop stepped platforms and were often decorated with bas-reliefs and ornate frescoes. The population's growing dependence on agriculture inspired the creation of the highly accurate Maya calendar, which is based on planting cycles. Economy and trade flourished, and the Maya began to observe class distinctions and live extremely lavish lifestyles around great ceremonial centers. Toward the end of this period, more palaces were constructed on top of or in place of temples, evidence of the growth of secular authority and centralized political rule. Some examples of Classical period architecture are found at Uxmal and Sayil.

POST-CLASSIC PERIOD (900–1520): Maya civilization declined during this period, which is marked by increased military activity and the growth of conquest states. The Toltecs of Mexico invaded the Yucatán during this time, greatly influencing the Mayan architecture and lifestyle. The invasion ultimately led to a more warlike society, more elaborate temples and palaces, and a greater number of human sacrifices. Architectural techniques involved less detailed and careful craftsmanship. For example, carved-stone building facades were replaced at this time by carved stucco. Mayapán is an example of post-Classic architecture.

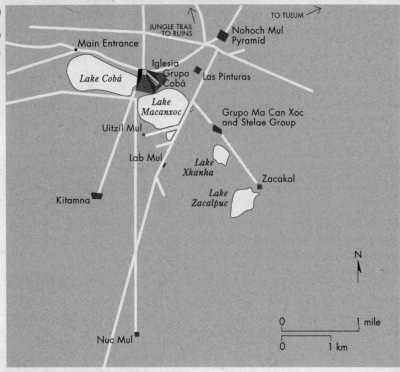

The jungle that surrounds the ruins is no less an attraction. If you're adventurous and not afraid of snakes, follow any of the paths into the undergrowth. Snorkeling or swimming in the many lakes is not allowed, as the lakes are home to several families of crocodiles.

Cobá is one of the oldest sites on the peninsula. It was built around several shallow lakes and marshes and was settled about 400 BC but didn't develop into a city until roughly AD 500. The city's inhabitants mysteriously died out 600 years before the arrival of the Spanish, and the ruins weren't discovered until the late 19th century. The remains of more than 30 roads, once paved with smoothed stones, indicate that Cobá was a large commercial center. The two huge pyramids that archaeologists have unearthed here bear more resemblance to the structures at Tikal, Guatemala, than to local architecture, suggesting royal ties with the wealthy Maya of the Petén jungle. More than 6,500 structures have yet to be excavated.

For optimum exploration, start at the group of temples closest to the main entrance, known as **Grupo Cobá.** The first of these temples is the enormous pyramid called the **Iglesia,** the second-largest on the peninsula (26 meters high). The vigorous climb to the top rewards you with a fantastic view of two lakes, the jungle surrounding the ruins, and Nohoch Mul (*see below*). In front of the pyramid is a small shrine where local Maya occasionally leave offerings to the gods.

Continue past Grupo Cobá and follow **Lake Macanxoc**'s eastern edge; after about 300 meters you'll pick up the trail to **Grupo Macanxoc** and the **Stelae Group.** More than 30 deteriorating but intricately carved stelae have been found at Cobá, depicting tyrannical rulers standing imperiously on the backs of captives, subjects, and slaves. After the Stelae Group, walk back up the way you came and bear right after the path to reach **Las Pinturas** (The Paintings). Because the structures in Cobá were originally rustic looking, the Maya covered them with stucco. They then adorned the stucco with paintings. Unfortunately, the pyramidal temple bears only scant remnants of frescoes on its walls, but it's still worth climbing up the pyramid's clunky steps and pok ing around its topmost level for a peek into the surrounding jungle. At the foot of the pyramid lie 13 square stone wells, thought to be altars or sites for offerings to the gods.

Finally, walk up from Las Pinturas to get back on the main trail and follow the signs to **Nohoch Mul,** the Yucatán's tallest Mayan structure. It's well worth the trek to see this pyramid, which soars 41 meters from the jungle floor. The climb is not for the weak of heart, but the view from the top is superb. Chances are you'll have the summit to yourself, a rarity in this region. The temple on top of the pyramid is thought to have been constructed long after the pyramid itself was finished, and it's said that the temple was used as a pen for jaguars at one point. The bones of birds and small animals were found inside. Note the carvings of diving gods on the front wall of the temple.

A stela is a large stone (usually in the shape of a surfboard) that acted as a kind of diary for the Maya. Dates, astronomical happenings, and special events were carved into the stelae, perhaps as a historical record meant to be discovered later on.

Cobá is open daily 8–5. Admission is $2, free on Sundays and holidays, but the adventurous can enter clandestinely. Remember, the admission price pays workers and goes toward the upkeep of the ruins, which may or may not matter to you. Here goes: About 20 meters from the bus terminal is an abandoned restaurant called Restaurant Isabel. Across from the restaurant, a dirt road passes by a white-and-blue water tower. Take the road straight through the village and follow it past the small pharmacy and a square thatched home with a red roof. There the road turns into a trail and enters the jungle. When you reach a fork in the trail, stay left. Stay on the main trail for about 15 minutes, and you'll hear the voices of tourists nearby. When you come to a wider, well-trod road, take a left and emerge victorious from the bush like Indiana Jones. The Nohoch Mul pyramid is 100 meters ahead.

COMING AND GOING Getting to Cobá is not too difficult. Four daily buses make the 45-minute trip from Tulum ($1), with the last bus leaving at 6 PM. Though buses rarely leave early, it's best to wait at the downtown Tulum bus stop ahead of time—drivers won't wait if the stop is empty. The last bus back to Tulum leaves at 4:30 PM, so take a morning bus from Tulum if you want to make Cobá a day trip. If you're desperate to get back to Tulum, take a taxi to the main highway (10 km, about $2) and flag down a Valladolid–Tulum bus.

WHERE TO SLEEP AND EAT Hotel El Bocadito (main road, no phone) has eight dusty rooms with beds on cement bases and private bathrooms; they charge $5.50 for a single or double. If you have your own hammock, most people will let you hang it in their houses—look for SE RENTAN CUARTOS signs or ask in the stores. If you're desperate you can camp, but slather yourself with bug repellent beforehand. Try the lakeshore south of the ruins near the Club Med or the patch of grass near the entrance to the ruins.

Eating in Cobá doesn't have to be expensive: **Restaurant El Bocadito,** (next to the hotel, no phone; open daily 6 AM–9 PM) serves main dishes for around $4 and will prepare a cooked vegetable dish for $2.50. Behind the basketball court, **Lonchería La Amistad** is an even cheaper option, with sandwiches for 75¢, salbutes for 50¢, and great licuados with fresh fruit for $1.

SIAN KA'AN BIOSPHERE RESERVE

This expanse of quiet bays, deserted beaches, mangrove swamps, and jungle is populated with birds, crocodiles, jaguars, and boars, as well as wild orchids. Within the reserve, **Isla Pájaros** and the coast are popular rest stops and habitats for more than 300 species of birds, including flamingos, herons, and egrets, as well as crocodiles. Small canals believed to have been built by the Maya are also of interest. Sian Ka'an is only affordable as a day trip—there are no facilities or infastructure for camping within the reserve, and you must get permission from the owners of beach front property in order to camp on the coast. Cabañas at the northern entrance of the reserve start at about $60, and lodging in the fly-fishing resort of **Boca Paila** is even deeper. Restaurants are few and far between, and those that exist are expensive, so bring your own food. During the tourist season (December–April, July, and August), taxis depart sporadically for Sian Ka'an from the intersection about 3 kilometers south of the Tulum ruins (just past Cabañas Los Gatos), or you can try calling **Victor Barrera,** a local cab driver (tel. 987/1–1–18) to arrange for a pick up. Drivers should fill up at the gas station in Tulum before making the trip out. **Amigos de Sian Ka'an** (tel. 988/4–95–83) runs tours to the reserve for $50 per person; the 6-hour tour leaves daily at 9 AM from Cabañas Ana y José in Tulum and includes a three-hour boat ride, a bilingual guide, refreshments, and snacks. If you can somehow get to Boca Paila on your own, the above tour costs $40. For more information on the reserve itself, contact Alfredo Arreyano (tel. 988/3–05–63) in Cancún at the **SEMARANAP** office.

Chetumal

Travelers come to Chetumal, at the southern tip of Quintana Roo, for two reasons: to use the city as a springboard for trips to Belize and Guatemala, and to take advantage of duty-free bargains on stereos, refrigerators, and every other kind of electronic gadget. Architecturally, this state capital has little to offer: Its modern block-style buildings are dull at best. Still, Chetumal isn't a total letdown. The **Museo de la Cultura Maya** offers an excellent overview of Mayan history and culture, and the beautiful lagoons on the city's outskirts make for worthwhile day trips. For a dose of mayhem, visit the **mercado nuevo** (new market), 10 blocks north of the city center, where regional fruit and vegetable vendors pour in to sell produce from their bikes and trucks at rock-bottom prices.

BASICS

CASAS DE CAMBIO **Bancomer** (tel. 983/2–53–00) and **Banamex** (tel. 983/2–11–22), both on Juárez at Obregón, change money weekdays 9–2 and have ATMs that accept Master-Card, Visa, and Cirrus cards. If you need Belizean dollars, try one of the casas de cambio on Héroes, such as **Centro Cambiario** (Héroes 67, at Zaragoza, tel. 983/2–38–38). You should wait to change the bulk of your money in Belize though, as you'll get a better rate.

CROSSING THE BORDER

➤ **TO BELIZE** • American and British Commonwealth citizens do not need visas to enter Belize, but they do need passports. For additional information, contact the **Belizean Consulate** (Obregón and Juárez, next to Bancomer, tel. 983/2–01–00), open weekdays 9–2 and 5–8, Saturday 9:30–2. For information on reaching the Mexico–Belize border, *see* Coming and Going, *below*.

➤ **TO GUATEMALA** • For information on visas and tourist cards, *see* box Going to Guatemala, in Chapter 10. You can also contact the **Guatemalan Consulate**. *Chapultepec 354 at Cecilio Chi, tel. 983/2–30–45. Open weekdays 9–5, but try knocking after hours.*

MEDICAL AID There are a number of clinics near the budget hotel area. The **Centro de Salud** (Juárez 147, at Aguilar, tel. 983/2–00–95) is open weekdays 8–2:30. The **Cruz Roja** (tel. 983/2–05–71) provides 24-hour emergency ambulance service. For minor medical needs, **Farmacia Canto** (Héroes, at Gandhi, tel. 983/2–04–83) is open Monday–Saturday AM–11 PM, Sunday 7–5.

PHONES AND MAIL The **post office** (Plutarco Elías, at Calle 5 de Mayo, 2 blocks east of Héroes, tel. 983/2–25–78) is open weekdays 8–7, Saturdays 9–1. The office will hold mail sent to you at the following address for up to 10 days: Lista de Correos, Chetumal, Quintana Roo, CP 77000, México. The **Ladatel** phone cards used here may be different from those used in Playa del Carmen and Cancún. If your card doesn't work, purchase a new one at **Super Las Arcadas** (*see* Food, *below*) or **Hotel Tulum** (*see* Where to Sleep, *below*).

VISITOR INFORMATION The **tourist booth** (Héroes, at Águilar, in front of mercado viejo, tel. 983/2–36–63) is open Monday–Saturday 8:30–1:30 and 6–9 for information and free maps. The **Secretaría de Turismo** (Palacio Municipal, on Bahía, 1 block west of Héroes, tel. 983/2–08–55) is open Monday–Saturday 8–2 and has a helpful English-speaking staff.

COMING AND GOING

BY BUS Chetumal's **Central de Autobuses** (Insurgentes, at Belice, about 15 blocks north of downtown) is a 75¢ taxi ride from downtown. The 24-hour station has a Computel office (open daily 7 AM–10 PM), a restaurant, and luggage storage (20¢ per hr). Frequent first- and second-class buses leave daily for Cancún (5 hrs, $9.50 1st class; 5½ hrs, $7.50 2nd class) and Playa del Carmen (2½ hrs, $8 1st class; 3 hrs, $6.50 2nd class). Four direct buses head to Tulum (3½ hrs, $6.50) every two hours 12:30–6:30 PM. The first-class bus to Campeche leaves at noon (6 hrs, $12), and second-class buses leave at 4:30 AM and 3:30 PM. Four first-class buses head to Mérida (6 hrs, $10 1st class; 8 hrs, $8.50 2nd class). One bus makes a direct trip to Palenque (8 hrs, $14.50) at 10:15 PM , and three buses a day leave for Mexico City (23 hrs, $40).

Batty's runs buses every half hour to Belize 11:30 AM–7:30 PM (4½ hrs, $4.50), which leave from the mercado nuevo (Segundo Circuito, at Calzada Veracruz, 10 blocks north of downtown). If you're heading to Belize, pay the bus fare in Belizean dollars—you'll get a better exchange rate. **Servicio San Juan** provides daily direct service from Chetumal's bus terminal to Flores, Guatemala at 2:30 PM ($28).

To reach Bacalar, Cenote Azul, or Laguna Milagros (see Near Chetumal, below), take one of the small buses that leave from the station at Hidalgo and Francisco Primo de Verdad. Buses for Xcalak ($5) leave at 7 AM from the corner of Avenida 16 de Septiembre and Gandhi. To reach Calderitas, take a combi from the station on Belice, between Colón and Gandhi.

BY PLANE The small airport 2 kilometers outside of Chetumal only handles destinations in Mexico, Guatemala, and Belize. Carriers serving the airport include **Aeroméxico** (tel. 983/2–15–76) and **Aerocaribe** (tel. 983/2–66–75). A one-way ticket from Chetumal to Guatemala City should cost about $90. Be forewarned that Aerocaribe only flies to Guatemala City three days a week. To reach downtown, either take a taxi ($2) or walk east on Revolución (the main street north of the airport), which becomes Águilar.

GETTING AROUND

It's easy to get around Chetumal on foot, and almost everything you need is in the downtown area. The most important street running north–south is Avenida Héroes, where the **mercado viejo** (old market), budget lodging, and tourist information booth are all located. The bus station is located about 15 blocks north of the center; the mercado nuevo, where buses depart for Belize, is five blocks south of the bus station. Taxis are cheap and abundant: Within the downtown area, you shouldn't pay more than 50¢; north of Insurgentes, you'll have to pay 75¢.

WHERE TO SLEEP

Plenty of budget hotels in Chetumal cater to shoppers who come for the city's cheap wares. The best place to seek lodging is the plaza around the intersection of Héroes and Águilar; you'll find the hotels squeezed between cheap loncherías (snack bars) and bookstores.

➤ **UNDER $10** • **Hotel Cristal.** This centrally located hotel has narrow, prison cell–style rooms. On the plus side, the bathrooms feature reliable hot water and fluorescent soap. Windowless, airless singles go for a mere $5.25, doubles $7.50 ($12 with air-conditioning), triples $14. Cristóbal Colón 207, btw Juárez and Belice, tel. 983/2–38–78. Wheelchair access.

Hotel Tulum. Singles in this hotel cost a mere $4, and doubles are only $5.25. Unfortunately, the cleaning lady often forgets to sweep up the cockroach cadavers in the large, bare rooms. The breezy but often noisy hallway leads to clotheslines and patios—relief for the claustrophobic. Héroes 164, btw Gandhi and Águilar, tel. 983/2–05–18. 17 rooms, all with bath. Luggage storage. Reservations advised in summer.

Hotel Ucum. The bright-red tubes and barrel-shaped tanks on the roof make you feel like you're going to sleep in a boot-making factory, but the dark-wood furniture and freshly painted rooms make for a down-home feel. Beds are small and rickety, but adequate, and bathrooms supply a healthy jet of piping-hot water. Singles are a cheap $4.50 and doubles are $6.50; either one will cost you $10 with air-conditioning. Gandhi 167, btw Héroes and 16 de Septiembre, tel. 983/2–07–11. 58 rooms, all with bath. Luggage storage.

➤ **UNDER $15** • **Hotel Real Azteca.** Shiny wooden carvings of Mayan gods and modern-looking hieroglyphics decorate this unabashedly tourist-friendly hotel. A circular stairway winds up to air-conditioned rooms equipped with TVs and black-and-white checkered bathrooms reeking of industrial-strength air-freshener. Bring your own agua purificada—they charge 50¢ a glass here. Singles are $9.25, doubles $11.25, and triples $13.25. *Belice 186, btw Águilar and Gandhi, tel. 983/2–06–66. 30 rooms, all with bath. Luggage storage.*

HOSTELS **Albergue Juvenil CND.** One of the best-run hostels on the peninsula, CND is clean and well staffed. Four-person, wood-shuttered rooms have a fan and lockers, and guests get a free chocolate bar with their sheets and towel (BYO soap). The 11 PM curfew is negotiable with the friendly manager. Beds are $4 and HI cardholders get a 10% discount. *Naval, at Veracruz, tel. 983/2–34–65. 1 block north of Obregón and 5 blocks east of Héroes. 66 beds. Key deposit ($2.50), luggage storage, meal service.*

CAMPING You can tent camp on the lawn of the youth hostel for $1 per person. A more scenic option is **Laguna Milagros** (*see* Near Chetumal, *below*), 12 kilometers west of town.

FOOD

In Chetumal you'll find Yucatecan food, sometimes with a Belizean influence, including lime soup and *tikinchic* (fried fish seasoned with sour orange). If you're trying to save money, pick up some fruit at **Frutería La Merced** (Héroes, at Cristóbal Colón). There's a convenient bakery, **Pan La Terminal,** at Héroes and Colón.

Restaurant/Super Las Arcades. Open-air seating and clean wood tables make this a preferred spot among tourists, but 24-hour service and consistently good food also attracts a group of local regulars. Mean appetites can be sated with the *cubana,* a bulging sandwich stuffed with ham, beef, cheese, and breaded chicken, slathered in salsa, and accompanied by potato chips ($1.75). Choose from an elaborate selection of egg, bean, and rice dishes ($2–$3) or try yogurt and granola for $1.25. *Héroes 74, at Zaragosa, no phone.*

Restaurant Ucum. This is probably the only color-coordinated place in Chetumal—too bad they chose mint green. Fortunately, there's more variety in their cuisine. Hearty breakfast dishes ($1.75) include eggs, rice, beans, salad, and tortillas. Also good is the $2 comida corrida. *Gandhi 167, btw 16 de Septiembre and Héroes, no phone. Open Mon.–Sat. 7:30 AM–9 PM.*

El Vaticano. Nestled in a corner across from the old market, this is a nice place to sit outside and sip a beer (5¢). They serve large plates of fresh fish for much less than in Cancún or Playa del Carmen, and excellent dishes with fried, grilled, or marinated conch in lemon and garlic are $3.75. Octopus goes for $3. *Belice, at Gandhi, no phone. Open Mon.–Sat. 10–6, Sun 10:30–3. Wheelchair access.*

Want to know your Mayan birthdate? Head to the Museo de la Cultura Maya, where you'll find gear-shaped wheels that correspond dates on the Roman calendar to dates on the 18-month Mayan calendar.

WORTH SEEING

If you plan to check out any of the peninsula's ruins or i you've already done so and are looking for a refresher or Mayan history and culture, it's worth your while to pay a visi to the **Museo de la Cultura Maya.** Inside you'll find interactive computers that offer a variety of information on Mayan histor as well as regional plants and animals. You can also wal along glass-encased replicas of the peninsula's ancient tem ples and hieroglyph-covered stelae. Virtual realists will get kick out of the subterranean models of Uxmal and Tulum, which you can peer down at throug brightly lit glass floor panels. A central gallery exhibits contemporary photography, sculpture and paintings. *Héroes, at Colón, just north of mercado viejo, tel. 983/2–38–68. Admission t permanent exhibit: $2; gallery free. Open Tues.–Sun. 9–7.*

Near Chetumal

Calderitas, a beach town 8 kilometers north of Chetumal, is the closest place to take a dip in the ocean. To get here, take one of the minibuses (10 min, 25¢) that run every half hour from the bus stop in back of the mercado viejo (Belice, btw Colón and Gandhi). Diving enthusiasts should head for **Banco Chinchorra,** a 42-kilometer coral reef littered with shipwrecks, about two hours offshore from **Xcalak** beach. Two buses leave daily for Xcalak (5 hrs, $4) at 6 AM and 3:30 PM from the bus terminal. If you need snorkeling and diving gear, you can rent it right on the beach or at **Costa de Cocos,** 1 kilometer before the bus stop in Xcalak. Chetumal's major water attractions, however, are inland: Laguna Milagros, Cenote Azul, and Laguna de Bacalar (*see below*) are all easily reached by combi ($1) from the corner of Hidalgo and Primo de Verdad in Chetumal. The last buses head back to Chetumal around 7 PM.

LAGUNA MILAGROS The area surrounding Laguna Milagros is unspectacular, but the warm water is inviting and peaceful. It's also a good place to pitch a tent free of charge: From the main road, walk straight about 100 meters to the water and on your left you'll see the patio and lawn of an abandonded restaurant just waiting for your hammock or tent. Otherwise, you can bed down on the southern shore of the lake (beware of falling coconuts). If you didn't bring food, you can choose between four restaurants at the lake, including **El Campesino** and **Las Brisas del Caribe,** which are open daily 8–5. The 12-kilometer trip here by minibus takes 15 minutes, and the lake is about 110 meters from the main road. Catch a bus back to Chetumal at one of the stops on the road.

CENOTE AZUL If you have time to visit only one place near Chetumal, it should be Cenote Azul. The largest cenote in the world, it's 89 meters deep, 220 meters across, and surrounded by thick jungle. Its name derives from the intensity of its blue waters, home to an array of beautiful fish. Unfortunately, strong underwater currents make diving dangerous, but careful floaters can see plenty from the water's surface (bring your own gear—there aren't any shops here). Located 30 kilometers north of Chetumal, the cenote is a popular watering hole, especially on weekends, so come early or late in the day to avoid crowds. From Chetumal, take any minibus toward Bacalar and ask the driver to let you off at Cenote Azul. To get back, stand on the roadside and flag down a passing bus or minibus.

LAGUNA DE BACALAR About 40 kilometers north of Chetumal, this is a favorite destination for day-tripping locals. Also known as Laguna de Siete Colores (Lagoon of Seven Colors), the lagoon changes color according to the light and the depth of the water; its warm, shimmering waters are safe and attract families on holidays and weekends. The lagoon is surrounded by private property and the neighboring town of Bacalar, accessible by bus from Chetumal. An hour-long boat ride around the lagoon and down the adjoining Río Depiratas costs about $30 for groups of up to eight people. Another option is to make the three-hour boat trip to Belize ($100 for up to 10 people). For more information concerning either trip, talk to the bartender at **Restaurant Ejidal.** A fish fillet or shrimp dish prepared to your taste costs $3–$4 here, and several other nearby restaurants offer comparable prices. Camping at Ejidal costs $2, including use of the toilet and shower facilities, but you'll have to move out at daybreak, since the restaurant/bar is open all day. To reach Ejidal, walk away from the central square toward the water, turn left on the road that runs along the water, and continue about 800 meters. While in Bacalar, take a look at the perfectly preserved **Fuerte San Felipe Bacalar,** just east of the park. The fort has an impressive view of the area, and the main room serves as the own museum. The nearby lawn is a great spot for a picnic. The fort is open Tuesday–Sunday 10–6; admission is 50¢.

Campeche

One of the few walled cities in the Amer-icas, Campeche charms its visitors with lofty churches, Moorish arches, and cannon-laden forts, which stand like disintergrating monuments to a long-forgotten era. It was through Campeche that Mexican gold and silver were shipped to Spain during the 16th and 17th centuries, making it the target of raids by Dutch and English pirates. A brutal pirate attack in 1663 resulted in the massacre of almost the entire population of Campeche, spurring the construction of its sturdy forts. Today, Campeche is all business, serving as a meeting place for executives from Mexico's oil industry and bustling with the daily transport of goods from nearby towns to be sold in the main market. Still, Campeche's colonial sights, along with its refusal to succumb to blatant tourism, makes the city a pleasant place to spend a day before exploring the ruins, caves, and small towns that lie between Campeche and Mérida.

A playful, ongoing rivalry exists between Campecheans (people from Campeche state) and Yucatecans (people from Yucatán state). Yucatecans claim Campecheans do everything backwards, citing examples like the speed bump on the road from Campeche to Mérida: First you hit the bump, then a sign warns about it. The Campecheans' retort is pretty weak; they just say Yucatecans have big heads.

BASICS

AMERICAN EXPRESS Anyone can replace lost traveler's checks at the AmEx office run by the **Viajes Programados** travel agency, but only cardholders can pick up mail sent to: Prolongación Calle 59, Edificio Belmar, Apartado Postal 82, Campeche, Campeche, CP 24000, México. No one gets to change money or cash personal checks here. *Behind Ramada Inn, tel. 981/1–10–10. Open weekdays 9–2 and 5–7, Sat. 9–1.*

CASAS DE CAMBIO Bancomer (16 de Septiembre 120, tel. 981/6–66–22) changes money weekdays 9–2. On weekends, your only option is the **Ramada Inn** (Ruíz Cortínez 51, tel. 981/6–22–33), where you can exchange money daily 5 PM–10:30 PM. The ATMs at **Bancomer** and **Banamex** (cnr of Calles 10 and 53, tel. 981/6–06–29) accept Visa, MaterCard, and Plus.

EMERGENCIES The **police** station (Calle 12, btw Calles 57 and 59, tel. 981/6–21–11) is open 24 hours a day. For **emergencies,** dial 06.

MEDICAL AID You can walk into the **IMSS** (López Mateos, at Baluartes, tel. 981/6–09–2C or 981/6–43–33) for 24-hour emergency service. For minor medical needs, try **Farmacia Canto** (Calle 10, at Calle 55, tel. 981/6–52–48), open Monday–Saturday 8–2 and 5–9, Sunday 9–1.

PHONES AND MAIL There are very few coin-operated phones in Campeche; try the main bus terminal on Gobernadores or the public library (Calle 12, btw Calles 61 and 63). Buy **Ladatel** cards at **Tel Mex** (Calle 10, btw Calles 61 and 63) weekdays 8–1:30. **Computel** (Calle 8 No. 255 fax 981/1–01–29; open daily 7 AM–10 PM) lets you place international collect calls. The **Oficina de Correos** is the joint post/telephone office, offering fax, telex, and mail services. They'll hold mail sent to you at the following address for up to 10 days: Lista de Correos, Oficina Urbana 1 Campeche, Campeche, CP 24000, México. *16 de Septiembre, at Calle 53, 2 blocks east of Parque Principal, tel. 981/6–21–34, fax 981/6–52–10. Open weekdays 8–8, Sat. 9–1.*

VISITOR INFORMATION For information about the city's churches, museums, and upcoming public events, ask the ticket man at the **Puerta de Tierra** (*see* Worth Seeing, *below*). The friendly and enthusiastic staff at the **state tourist office** gives out information on Campeche and nearby ruins. *Calle 12, btw Calles 53 and 55, tel. 981/6–60–68. Open weekdays 8–8.*

COMING AND GOING

BY BUS The main bus terminal is on Gobernadores, about a kilometer north from Parque Principal, just outside the city walls. Actually composed of two adjoining stations, the termin-

offers first- and second-class service. **Autobuses del Oriente (ADO)** (tel. 981/6–28–02), the principal first-class carrier, runs daily trips to Mérida (2½ hrs, $5), Mexico City (18 hrs, $38), and Veracruz (14 hrs, $25). You can store luggage here for 50¢ per day, and the station is open 24 hours. The dusty and dilapidated second-class bus station (tel. 981/6–23–32) is only open until 7 PM; from here you can catch frequent buses to Hopelchén (1½ hrs, $1.50), Bolonchén (2 hrs, $2.25), and Dzibalchén (2 hrs, $2.25). Five daily buses also leave for Iturbide (3 hrs, $2.50), Uxmal (2½ hrs, $3), Santa Elena (3 hrs, $3.25), and Mérida (4 hrs, $4.50). To reach town from the ADO terminal, turn left onto Gobernadores; the first fort you reach marks the beginning of the old town. Otherwise, catch a bus (35¢) across the street and ask to be left near the Parque Principal.

BY CAR Maya Rent-a-Car (Ruíz Cortínez, at Calle 59, tel. 981/6–22–33, fax 981/1–16–18; open Mon.–Sat. 9–2 and 5–8), in the Ramada Hotel, rents Volkswagen bugs for $38 a day, including insurance and unlimited mileage. You'll need to show your passport and license. The agency also provides maps and information on road conditions. The roads leading to the outlying ruins and caves are well maintained; there's the occasional dirt road, but your average VW bug can take you just about anywhere you want to go. If you can afford it, having a car will make exploring the region much easier.

GETTING AROUND

Virtually everything of interest lies inside the walls of the *villa vieja* (old city) and is easily accessible on foot. Even-numbered streets run parallel to the waterfront, and odd-numbered streets run perpendicular. **Avenida Ruíz Cortínez** (a.k.a. the *malecón*, or boardwalk) runs along the water and is the location of Campeche's more expensive hotels, such as the Ramada. The market and the bus terminal are located on the southeast side of Campeche on Avenida Circuito Baluartes Este and Avenida Gobernadores, respectively. Local buses (35¢) run daily 5 AM–11 PM, stopping at the mercado and at the **Palacio de Gobierno** (malecón, at Calle 61).

WHERE TO SLEEP

Hotels in Campeche host more businesspeople than tourists. If you arrive at the bus station in the wee hours, you're better off paying the cab fare (about $1.75) to any of the following hotels (all located in the old city) rather than staying in one of the noisy, overpriced holes near the station.

➤ **UNDER $10** • **Hotel Campeche.** This rambling colonial mansion was a single-family home during the colonial era, and the wide stairways and shoulder-height doorways are a holdover from this time. Slightly neglected rooms are equipped with sturdy beds, some with windows overlooking the park. Some rooms boast a small cross over the sink, but using the run-down, cold-water bathroom is far from a religious experience. Singles cost $5.25, doubles $6.50, and doubles with hot water $8. *Calle 59 No. 2, tel. 981/6–51–83. 42 rooms, all with bath. Luggage storage.*

Hotel Castelmar. A friendly family keeps the gigantic rooms in this airy, colonial-style hotel fairly clean. Some sport balconies with sea views, while others face onto a noisy street. The beds must have made good trampolines once, because they're uncomfortable now. Dingy bathrooms are separated from the rooms by curtains and don't afford much privacy. Singles and doubles cost $6. *Calle 61 No. 2, btw Calles 8 and 10, tel. 981/6–28–86. 18 rooms, all with bath. Luggage storage. Reservations advised July–Sept.*

Hotel Colonial. This beautifully tiled, chandelier-adorned hotel has a shady, rocking chair–equipped rooftop patio, as well as a pleasant, palm-fringed inner courtyard. At $8 a single, $9 for a double, the sparkling-clean rooms get snatched up pretty quickly, especially during July and August. Reservations are accepted until 7 PM. *Calle 14 No. 122, btw Calles 55 and 57, tel. 981/6–22–22. 30 rooms, all with bath. Luggage storage.*

➤ **UNDER $15** • **Posada San Angel.** You'll be impressed right away by the sunny lobby with huge plants, comfortable chairs, and a color TV. When you reach your spacious room decorated with brightly colored fish paintings, you'll think it can't get better than this. Then you'll see your own clean, private bathroom complete with shower curtain, toilet seat, *and* lid, and you'll probably just drop dead from luxury overload. Singles cost $10, doubles $12, triples $14 ($2.50 extra for air-conditioning). *Calle 10 No. 307, across from Catedral de la Concepción, tel. 981/6–77–18. 14 rooms, all with bath. Luggage storage.*

HOSTELS Villa Deportiva de Campeche. Like most hostels, this place is dirt cheap ($2.50 a night, plus $2.50 deposit). At first glance it appears to be perfectly clean and functional, but—surprise!—the only rooms with fans belong to the administrators, water subsides to a trickle during prime shower hours, and bug spray is a must. Don't bother with the meals here—you'll get much better food for the same price downtown. *Agustín Melgar, tel. 981/6–18–02. From ADO station, take DIRECTO/UNIVERSIDAD bus (25¢); ask driver to let you off close to CREA hostel. 76 beds. Curfew 11 PM. Meal service. Wheelchair access.*

FOOD

Campeche's seafood has a well-deserved reputation throughout Mexico. Local specialties include *pan de cazón* (finely shredded baby shark layered with tortillas, beans, fresh tomato purée, and avocado) and *camarón chiquito* (an ultra-small shrimp). Many of the city's better restaurants, as well as a handful of small sandwich shops, line Calle 8 across from the Parque Principal. If you're pinching pennies, go to the huge, frenzied market on Gobernadores just outside the city wall, open daily 5 AM–3 PM. Here you can buy luscious regional fruits such as *pitaya* (a pink fruit with black seeds that tastes like pineapple) and *mamey* (a red kiwilike fruit), as well as *panuchos* (fried tortillas topped with chicken and onions), tacos, and tamales for less than 25¢.

➤ **UNDER $5** • Marganzo. For occasional live music and truly fabulous regional dishes served by suave waiters in festive costumes, count your pesos and head for Marganzo. Seafood specialties run $4–$6, but the delicious shrimp or crab salads are only $3.75. Pan de cazón ($3), the regional specialty, is outstanding. *Calle 8 No. 268, btw Calles 57 and 59, tel. 981/1–38–99. Open daily 7 AM–10 PM.*

La Perla. Whirring fans and the constant buzz of the TV keep locals pinned to their tables after a filling meal of shrimp or conch with rice ($1.50). Also good is the fish *filete* (filet) stuffed with shrimp and shellfish ($2.75). You can get any number of alcoholic beverages, including beer and tequila (50¢ each). *Calle 10, btw Calles 57 and 59, in same building as Lonchería Colón, tel. 981/6–40–92. Open Mon.–Sat. 7 AM–11 PM, Sun. 10–6.*

Restaurant La Parroquia. Despite the warehouselike atmosphere, La Parroquia is a friendly place to eat, featuring a huge menu, daily specials, and low prices. The bankrupt sate themselves with a rice and fried plantain combo for only 75¢, or indulge in a generously stuffed *torta de camarón* (french bread crammed with chunky shrimp salad) for $2.50. A fluffy pile of pancakes with hot honey and syrup (75¢) can be ordered round the clock. Also try *jamaica,* a sweet juice made from the iced pulp of boiled hibiscus (50¢). *Calle 5 No. 8, 1 block west of Parque Principal, tel. 981/6–80–86. Open daily 24 hrs.*

Restaurante Portales. Campechean couples and families come here to enjoy a *sandwich claveteado* (a sweet honey-flavored ham sandwich; $1), *panuchos* (Yucatecan tacos; 50¢), and the best *horchata* (a rice drink flavored with cinnamon; 50¢) in town. Orange-and-white checkered tablecloths and a cobblestone courtyard provide a lively atmosphere, and the nearby vendor serves up coconut ice cream (40¢) for dessert. *Calle 10 No. 86, at Plaza San Francisco tel. 981/1–14–91. From Parque Principal, walk 8 blocks NE on Calle 10. Or take a taxi ($1 to Plaza San Francisco. Open daily 7 PM–1 AM.*

WORTH SEEING

A walk through Campeche is like a trip through the military and commercial history of the Spanish colonies. Forts that protected the city from marauding pirates still stand, as do centuries-old churches and homes. Recently restored museums have attracted newly found arti facts from the nearby ruins of Edzná and Calaknul. Most of the interesting colonial buildings in Campeche are within the old city, and all are easily accessible on foot.

CIRCUITO DE BALUARTES Five years after much of the city was wiped out by pirates in 1663, the first stones of a new defense system were laid. The fortifications consisted of a 10-foot-thick wall running around the city, protected by seven *baluartes* (watchtowers). Even ships had to pass through the four gates that controlled access to the city. The construction took more than 35 years but effectively ended Campeche's role as the Yucatán's 98-pound weakling. Today, it's possible to follow the Circuito de Baluartes around the various watchtowers, many of which are now government buildings.

Aside from admiring the forts and watchtowers themselves, visitors can enjoy the museums, exhibits, and even gardens found inside. Of particular interest is the **Baluarte de Santiago** in the northern corner of the city, which was demolished at the end of the last century and reconstructed in the 1950s. Today it houses a beautiful **Jardín Botánico,** where you can admire a wide variety of regional flora, such as tiny orchids from the Campechean jungle. *Calle 8, at Calle 49, tel. 981/6–68–29. Admission: $1. Open weekdays 8–3 and 6–8.*

Another relic of the old city wall is the **Baluarte de San Carlos** (Calle 8, at Calle 65), on Campeche's east side. Completed in 1676, the baluarte is now the site of the **Museo de la Ciudad,** which hosts a collection of photos, maps, and models illustrating Campeche's history. The real attraction, however, is the fort itself: Standing in the turrets, you can imagine yourself fending off pirates and other vermin. Admission is free, and the museum is open Tuesday–Saturday 8–8, Sunday 8–6. Farther along Calle 8 stands the **Baluarte de la Soledad** (Calle 8, btw Calles 55 and 57, tel. 981/6–91–11), now a three-room museum featuring some 30 Mayan stelae (carved stone slabs), mostly from the ruins of Cayal, Acannuíl, and Xcalumkin. Admission to the stelae museum is 50¢, and it's open Tuesday–Saturday 8–8, Sunday 8–6.

The most impressive of the city's forts is the **Fuerte de San Miguel.** Located at the city's highest point, San Miguel is surrounded by a moat, and the cannon-ringed rooftop offers an extensive view of Campeche's shoreline ports. San Miguel now hosts the **Museo Regional de Campeche,** a consolidation of Campeche's most important historical pieces. Pre-Conquest artifacts, such as the skull of a child whose head was flattened with boards (thought to be a mark of beauty) and detailed statuettes from the Classic period, are found on the first floor of the fort. Low-relief stelae and jade-work complete the collection. Spanish artifacts include a full-size cabriolet and the usual assortment of swords, guns, and armor. *Take LERMA bus from in front of Hotel Baluartes or the market (about 10 min). Fort admission: $2.25; 50¢ Sun. Open Tues.–Sat. 8–8, Sun. 8–6.*

CHURCHES Facing the **zócalo,** the beautiful **Catedral de la Concepción** dates from the 18th century. Inside, note the illustrations of the Stations of the Cross, each placed under a fan so that worshippers can keep cool while they reflect on Christ's burden. As you approach the altar, look for the small but brilliant stained-glass windows under the cupola at the front of the church. Other beautiful churches in the old city include the **Iglesia de San Francisquito** (Calle 12, btw Calles 59 and 61), which dates from the 18th century, and the **Iglesia de Jesús El Nazareno** (Calle 55, at Calle 12), which features dramatic, elaborate icons on ostentatious altars. Farther away from Campeche's center is **Iglesia San Francisco** (Plaza San Francisco, at Calle 10, 8 blocks NE of zócalo), where the first mass in Latin America was held. The churches are open weekdays 9–noon, Saturday 5–7 PM, and all day Sunday.

AFTER DARK

On weekends the malecón is the happening place to be—it's perfectly safe to cruise the well-lit walk until around midnight, when people head indoors. Lovers can take advantage of the free *música romántica* in the Parque Principal on Sunday nights, usually starting around 8 PM. The light show at **Puerta de Tierra** (Gobernadores, toward old city from main bus station) rehashes Campeche's history of pirate invasions in Spanish and shaky English and French. The spectacle is performed by local musicians and dancers at 8 PM on Fridays and costs $1.50

(75¢ students). You can talk to the man working at Puerta de Tierra or someone in the tourist office (*see above*) for more information.

BARS AND DISCOS Commonly acknowledged as the hippest disco in town, **Atlantis** (Ruíz Cortínez 51, in Ramada Inn, tel. 981/6–46–11) is decorated like a ship, with netting, railings, portholes, and a fish video screen. Promotions vary by night, whether it be two-for-one drinks or free margaritas for women. Usually only men get slapped with the $4–$5 cover. Atlantis is open Thursday through Saturday 10 PM–3 AM. For a more diverse crowd of locals, try **Dragon** disco (Resurgimiento 87, in front of Hotel Alhambra on the malecón, tel. 981/6–42–89), which is open Friday and Saturday nights year-round and Thursdays in December, July, and August. Friday nights feature salsa and merengue music 10 PM–4 AM. Saturdays, the club is host to a mix of Latin and American music until 5 AM. Cover hovers around $4 (when it's charged at all). **Mazehual** (Gobernadores 551, across from Pemex station, tel. 981/1–11–74), a vast, palapa-covered beer hall, features a variety of music, including live funked-out '50s tunes sung by satin-bedecked soloists striding around in sparkling 10-inch heels. There's no cover and beers are only $1, but the place is only open daily 2–10:30 PM.

Near Campeche

EDZNÁ

Slightly less accessible than the more popular archaeological sites, Edzná is a virtual jungle gym of hills, tunnels, and tumbling stairways. Evidence suggests that this large site 60 kilometers (37 mi) southeast of Campeche may have been settled as early as 600 BC, but the city thrived during the late Classic period, from AD 600 to 900. The beauty here lies in the overall building scheme rather than in ornamentation. Later styles of architecture (as seen at Uxmal, for example) may be more elaborate, but according to some they signal the decline of the Mayan unity and autonomy that produced grand achievements in science and art. Edzná's Classic style is characterized by superb stelae (stone slabs); many of these are still on the premises, although they have been moved to a roped-in, palapa-covered gallery outside the ruins.

Edzná's main attraction is the **Temple of Five Stories,** an example of early Puuc architecture situated on the Plaza Central. To reach the temple, climb the stairway of the **Gran Acrópolis** (the long structure on your left as you enter the ruins). The temple on the top story is capped with a 7-meter roof comb, once decorated with a mask of Chaac the rain god, which seemed to change expression as the sun rose and fell. The mask is believed to be the origin of the name Edzná, meaning "House of the Expressions." Edzná can also be translated as "House of Echoes," probably referring to the amazing acoustics among the principal buildings—standing in the doorway at the top of the pyramid, you can hear the voice of someone at the far end of the Gran Acrópolis. Several other excellently restored buildings cluster around the Gran Acrópolis, including the **House of the Moon,** the **Temazcal** (sweat house), and three additional structures. On the first day of the Mayan year the sun reaches its zenith over Edzná, leading to speculation that the amazingly accurate Maya calendar was devised here. Vicious mosquitoes breed in surrounding swamps and stagnant water holes, so bring repellent. *Admission: $2, free Sun. and holidays. Open daily 8–5.*

Every year on May 1, schoolchildren from Campeche come to Edzná to sing, dance, and perform traditional Mayan ceremonies to celebrate the beginning of the agricultural season.

COMING AND GOING Servicios Turísticos Picazh (Calle 16 No. 348, btw Calles 57 and 59, tel. 981/6–44–26) in Campeche has organized tours departing from the Puerta de Tierra (Calle 59, at Gobernadores) at 9 AM and 2 PM. They can also pick you up at your hotel. The cost is $8 per person for a minimum of two people: An extra $5 per person pays your admission and gets you a guided tour of the site. A cheaper but riskier option is to take a PICH bus (1 hr, $1.50) from **Terminal Joaquín Pacheco** (Alameda, at Salvador, SW of market) and ask the driver to let you off at the Edzná ruins. From there you'll only have to walk about 300 meters to the site. The risk involved comes with the uncertainty of the bus schedule: One bus leaves daily around 6:30 AM and another at around 10:30 AM, but other departure times vary. Be sure to ask the driver what time you should wait at the entrance to the ruins for a return bus to Campeche; a bus usually passes by Edzná at around 2 PM. If you're in a car, take Highway 180 toward Mérida, then change to Highway 188, following signs to Edzná. Hitching to and from the ruins is your last, least certain, and possibly most miserable option.

CHENES RUINS/
X'TACUMBILXUNAAN

Any comprehensive tour of Mayan archaeology in the region should include the Chenes ruins. The remote ruins at **Hochob** and **El Tabasqueño**, outside the town of Dzibalchén, are rarely visited, in part because reaching them is tough, even if you have a car. Those who persevere will discover that their solitude is interrupted only by the occasional animal. Hochob displays one of the purest styles of Chenes architecture, which is characterized by elaborate decoration. Naturally ornate and more accessible than the ruins are the **Grutas X'tacumbilxunaan** (pronounced shta-koom-bil-sho-NON), lying just off Highway 261. **Servicios Turísticos Picazh** (Calle 16 No. 348, Campeche, tel. 981/6–44–26) arranges pricey trips there, but with a little fortitude you can get there on your own. The easily-accessible ruins of **Dzibilnocac**, only a kilometer outside of Iturbide, are the best bet for those short on time.

VISITOR INFORMATION **José William Chan** (tel. 982/2–01–06) is *the* source for information on visiting the Chenes Ruins. He can also tell you just about everything you need to know about Mayan culture or other sights in the area. He rents bikes ($3.25 per day) and is more than happy to show you the way to Hochob or El Tabasqueño. José and his two sons offer guide services that cost $8–$10, depending on the number of people and your financial means. If you want to visit the ruins by car, José can usually rent you one for about $13 (for your own use) or $20 (for him to accompany you). If you brought your own car, you can just pick him up along the way. José lives about 800 meters from the plaza in Dzibalchén, on the road heading out of town toward Iturbide. Follow his signs reading TOURIST INFORMATION, or ask anyone in town where Maestro William lives.

COMING AND GOING It's virtually impossible to make the bus odyssey to any of the Chenes ruins and return to Campeche in one day. It's best to stay the night in **Hopelchén,** 53 kilometers (33 mi) east of Campeche, en route to Mérida, and leave early in the morning for the ruins. Starting at 8 AM, six buses leave Campeche daily for Hopelchén (1½ hrs, $1.50). The

The Mennonites of Hopelchén

Hopelchén is home to a community of tall, blue-eyed people who look like they just stepped off the set of "Little House on the Prairie." Their typical garb of overalls and straw hats for men and cotton dresses and head scarves for women perpetuates the illusion of being in the frontier-era American Midwest. The Mennonites are actually descendants of 16th-century Swiss Anabaptists and have preserved their unique German dialect in the depths of the Yucatán. They left Zacatecas in search of available land to pursue their agricultural interests (cheese is their main product), winding up in Holpechén in 1985. Separation from the outside world, conformity to scripture, and an aversion to modern technology keep the Mennonites firmly rooted in the time of their ancestors. Orthodox "horse-and-buggy" Mennonites shun all contact with the modern world, but the Mennonite sect in Hopelchén is less strict. You'll often see Mennonite men accepting car rides and conversing in Spanish with the locals; Mennonite women rarely communicate with anyone except other Mennonites.

ATS station in Hopelchén is across from the park, two doors down from the hotel, marked by a disconcerting BURGER CHEN sign. From Hopelchén, six direct buses run daily 8–8 to Dzibalchén (45 min, 75¢), which serves as the crossroads for Hochob and El Tabasqueño. Buses leaving Hopelchén at 9:30 AM, 2:30 PM, and 5:15 PM also stop at Dzibalchén before continuing on to Iturbide (1 hr, $1). The last bus back to Holpechén leaves Iturbide at 3:30 PM; the final bus from Dzibalchén leaves at 5:30 PM. Five buses depart Hopelchén for Mérida daily 7:30 AM–6:30 PM (2½ hrs, $3). Campeche-bound buses also leave frequently.

WHERE TO SLEEP AND EAT   If you're left high and dry at any of the ruins, you can pitch a tent or string a hammock—although the mosquitoes will drive you stark raving mad. The only hotel in the area is **Los Arcos** (Calle 20, at Calle 23, tel. 981/2–01–23) in Hopelchén, which offers huge, sunny rooms and clean bathrooms with hot water ($5.25 singles, $6.50 doubles, $7.75 triples). If you miss the last bus out of Dzibalchén at 5:30 PM, José William Chan (*see above*) and his family will probably let you crash in a hammock in their back room. In Holpechén, several open-air *loncherías* (snack bars) line the avenue between the church and Los Arcos, where you can eat like a king (two fat tamales and a Coke) for less than $1. The restaurant at Hotel Los Arcos serves chicken (Kentucky-style) and fries ($1.50) along with cold beers (75¢). **Casa Alpuche** (tel. 982/2–00–07), the mini-supermarket across from the park, supplies a reasonable selection of foods and is open daily 7:30–2 and 5:30–9.

WORTH SEEING

➤ **DZIBILNOCAC** • Among the scattered dirt mounds hidden in the thick vegetation are two buildings which, until a few years ago, were unrecognizable. Recently, however, the western pyramid has been excavated and reconstructed and now stands in almost perfect condition. Masks of Chaac cover the uppermost temple, and the curled pattern of his nose is repeated in relief on all sides. A neighboring structure, as yet unrestored, houses the remains of beautiful red-and-green frescoes. Admission to the ruins is free, and the site is open daily 8–5. To reach Dzibilnocac (pronounced Tsee-bil-no-KAK), walk 1 kilometer west of Iturbide on the dirt road leading out of town. Don't be intimidated if you encounter a large bull chained near the entrance to the ruins: He's as harmless as an iguana.

➤ **HOCHOB** • Reaching this site deep within the rain forest is not easy, but Hochob's appeal lies in its splendid isolation. There is little to suggest that you aren't the true discoverer of a long-lost civilization, a sensation that is heightened if you camp overnight. Only the central plaza has been excavated, but countless other buildings lie unexplored under the thick vegetation. The main building is the **Temple of Chaac,** a rectangular building 40 meters long and 7 meters high. Look carefully at the facade to see a giant image of the god: The motifs on the lintel above the entrance to the temple are his eyes, and the open door represents his mouth.

Getting to Hochob is difficult, even if you have your own car. There is no public transport, so your only option is to drive, bike, or walk the 13 kilometers (8 mi) from Dzibalchén. Take the

Chaac: More Than Just a Funny Nose

Water, the source of all life, was sacred in the Mayan religion. Water was essential not just for human consumption but also for growing corn (the staple food of the Maya). Thus Chaac, the god of rain, rivers, cenotes, lakes, and oceans, was possibly the most revered god in the Mayan religion; his image can be seen everywhere throughout the ruins on the peninsula, especially in areas such as Chenes and Puuc, which are drier than other regions. Chaac often assumes the form of a snake but can also be identified by a long nose that can point upward or downward. The ceremony of Ch'a Chak, a dusk to-dawn ritual of Catholic prayers and Mayan offerings and divination, is performed by the Maya to this day to appeal to Chaac for rain.

road toward Campeche north for 1 kilometer, then turn left onto a dirt road leading to the tiny village of Chencoh. The 8 or so kilometers to Chencoh are clay, sand, and rock—not ideal for traversing on a bike. The trek is even worse if it's raining—bicycles (and cars) will slowly grind to a stop after 25 pounds of instant pottery has glommed onto the tires. Hitching is nearly impossible unless you're naturally a very lucky person.

Avoid visiting Hochob on a bicycle during the rainy season (June–August); gallons of water pour down, and rattlesnakes come out of their holes to avoid drowning. Also don't go alone—if you fall down one of the many hidden chultunes (underground cisterns), you'll be food for the worms.

➤ **EL TABASQUENO** • If your Indiana Jones ambitions haven't been satisfied by Hochob, El Tabasqueño, a.k.a. Xtabas, may be just the place for you. Seven kilometers from Dzibalchén and 2 kilometers off the road, El Tabasqueño is completely hidden in the forest. The trek through the jungle to reach the site is probably the most interesting part of the trip. The site has only one building, a temple featuring masks of Chaac and the face of Itzamná, the spiritual guide of the Maya. Decorations also include the double-headed serpent, the symbol of Kukulcan. The only way to reach El Tabasqueño is through the paid services of José William Chan (*see* Hochob, *above*); there is no sign indicating where to begin your hike and no discernible path leading to the ruins. In the rainy season, you may be especially glad to have José trailblazing through the jungle with his machete. He charges $8–$10 to accompany you on this trip.

➤ **GRUTAS X'TACUMBILXUNAAN** • Two kilometers from the town of Bolonchén and 34 kilometers north of Hopelchén are the Grutas X'tacumbilxunaan (Caves of the Hidden Girl). Legend has it that the Maya lost a young girl here when they arrived searching for water. The colorful caves are unbelievable, especially if you see them before heading on to the Loltún Caves in the Puuc Region, which spoil you for anything else. Seven underground wells, each of a different color, lie deep beneath the main caverns and are accessible only to those with climbing equipment, lanterns, and a sense of adventure. The surreal two-day excursion is rarely attempted. If you want to see the wells, you'll need to negotiate the price for a trip with a guide with the necessary equipment—you can find them hanging around during open hours. If you just want to see the main caves, bring a flashlight in case the electricity fails. Plan to spend about an hour at the caves. You may also camp for free at the site, but be prepared to share your flesh with thirsty mosquitoes. An attendant charges $1 to visit the site daily 8–5.

X'tacumbilxunaan lies on Highway 261 between Hopelchén and Bolonchén. Take the Mérida-bound bus from Hopelchén (30 min, 75¢) and ask the driver to drop you at the grutas. The turn-off point for the caves is well marked, and the entrance is close to the road. On the way back, catch the same bus; the last one passes the caves at about 7:30 PM.

The Puuc Region

The Puuc Hills, a low-lying mountain range covering about 156 square kilometers (97 sq mi), contain six major archaeological sites and some of the most distinctive Mayan architecture on the peninsula. You'll want to dedicate at least three days to the region: one to see the main site at Uxmal; another for the surrounding Mayan ruins of Kabah, Sayil, Labná, and Xlapac; and a third to explore the spectacular caves at Loltún.

Considered the most beautiful of all Mayan building styles, Puuc architecture is characterized by finely shaped limestone veneers applied to lime-base concrete. The lower facades of Puuc buildings are typically smooth and plain, contrasting with elaborate upper facades decorated with intricate mosaics. Among the most common motifs are X-shape lattices, geometric designs, serpents, and masks. It is a highly complex architectural style that draws on the simple idea of the *choza*, or one-room thatched hut, common in the region. Stylized representations of the choza appear on the greatest works, such as the archway at Labná. Later Puuc architecture, with its profusion of mosaics, serpents, and masks, displays a Toltec influence that is somewhat top-heavy with decoration.

BASICS

VISITOR INFORMATION If you want to buy a guidebook to the Puuc Hills (a good idea since there are no guides at the smaller sites), get it before you leave Mérida or Campeche, or you'll pay through the nose. One thorough, reasonably priced guide is Jeff Karl Kowalski's *Guide to Uxmal and the Puuc Region* (Dante, 1990). The book ($5) can be purchased at any Dante bookstore in Mérida (*see* Basics, in Mérida, *below*). Otherwise, Uxmal has a large tourist center, which runs half-hour documentaries on the archaeological, cultural, and environmental riches of the Yucatán. A small museum in Uxmal also displays a few archaeological remains with descriptions printed in Spanish. Apart from small tourist shops selling crafts and soft drinks, smaller sites have no amenities, not even bathrooms.

WHEN TO GO The best time to visit the Puuc Region is between February and May. In these months, there are few tourists, little rain, and the heat is bearable. Admission fees to the archaeological sites (used for maintenance and employee salaries) can quickly destroy your budget: Try and schedule your visit to Loltún and the Puuc towns around a Sunday or holiday, when admission is free.

COMING AND GOING The Puuc route snakes its way from Campeche to Mérida, and many travelers take in the sights on their way between the two towns. The main attractions, Uxmal and Kabah, are about 25 kilometers (15.5 mi) apart along Highway 261. To reach Uxmal from Campeche, take one of the buses (5 per day, 2½ hrs, $3) that leave from the second-class station at Gobernadores. From Mérida's main second-class station (Calle 70, btw Calles 69 and 71), six second-class buses make the 1½-hour trip ($1.50) to Uxmal daily; or take the daily direct bus ($6 round-trip) that leaves Mérida at 8 AM and returns from Uxmal at 2 PM. To return to Mérida or continue on to Kabah from Uxmal, flag down a bus along Highway 261—north to Mérida or south to Kabah. The problem is getting them to stop: Some of the bus drivers consider passengers an unnecessary nuisance and won't stop even if you wave your arms madly. I you're coming by car from Mérida, take Avenida Internacional south to Umán and then hop on Highway 261—the journey to Uxmal is about 97 kilometers (60 mi).

All of the other sites in the Puuc region—Labná, Xlapak, Sayil, and the Loltún Caves—lie along the 48-kilometer (30-mile) back road that runs from Highway 261 to the town of Oxkutzcab and Highway 184. If you have the money, it's a good idea to spend $20 on a rental car in Campeche or Mérida and spend as much time as you want at each site. Try to leave by mid

Some Helpful Phrases in Mayan

Mayan	English
B'ish a ka' ba?	What is your name?
Im ka' ba. . .	My name is. . .
Baax a kajal?	Where are you from?
In kajale'. . .	I live in. . . .
Bis a wool?	How are you?
Jach kimac in wool	I'm content.
Takin jahnal	I'm hungry.
Takin ukik a sis bah	I want something cold to drink.

morning though—the ruins all close by 5 PM. Exploring the lesser-known Puuc ruins by bus can be frustrating. The **Ruta Puuc ATS** bus ($4.50) leaves Mérida's second-class station daily at 8 AM and deposits you unceremoniously for about 25 minutes at each site, giving you just enough time to scan the plaques, climb a few rubbled steps, and poke your nose into a crevice or two. You get an added hour and a half at Uxmal before returning to Mérida between 4 or 5 PM. The bus stops at the plaza in the town of Santa Elena both coming and going.

A less reliable option is to hitch around the sites—a foolish undertaking in the dark. During the day, the road is not regularly traveled, but you can usually get a ride. Just be patient and bring lots of water; it could take a couple hours. The best places to pick up rides with tourists are in Kabah or Loltún (*see* Oxkutzcab and the Loltún Caves, *below*).

WHERE TO SLEEP Many people visit the Puuc region as a day trip from Mérida, since lodging options here are severely limited. But if you want to explore the area in depth, it doesn't make sense to keep commuting back and forth; staying in the small towns of **Santa Elena, Ticul,** or **Oxkutzcab** (*see below*) is a more convenient option. You can also camp for $4 a night at Loltún (*see* Oxkutzcab and the Loltún Caves, *below*) as long as you have no problems sleeping next to a gaping black hole in the ground.

For more comfortable camping, check out the **Sacbé Campgrounds,** about 1½ kilometers outside of Santa Elena; the town is 15 kilometers (9.3 mi) west of Ticul along Highway 261, halfway between Uxmal (to the north) and four other major archaeological sites (to the south). The campground is clean and pleasant, and you can sling a hammock or pitch a tent for $2. They have three bungalows as well for less than $8.50 for a single or a double. The cheerful owners also cook a reasonably priced breakfast or dinner for guests. They know the local bus schedules and offer insider info about free activities, shortcuts to sites, and local wildlife. ¼ m south of road to Santa Elena. From Mérida or Campeche, take any bus that travels down Hwy. 261 and ask driver to let you off at "campo deportivo." From Ticul, take a combi (tarp-covered truck) to Santa Elena and walk north 1½ km on hwy.

TICUL

The small town of Ticul, 86 kilometers (53 mi) south of Mérida, is a convenient base from which to explore the region. The town itself has little to offer, but those with a shoe fetish will have a fine old time in this shoe manufacturing center: Piles of high heels can be seen poking out of plastic milk crates strapped to the bicycles of local shoemakers on their way to the market (Calle 23, btw Calles 28 and 30). Prices for shoes here run about $5–$10, depending on size, but you'll have to sniff around for quality. Though expensive (upwards of $75), the local hand-embroidered shoes are at least worth a look. **Camita España** makes her own and is hired out on special occasions by women around town. You can visit her at her home (Calle 32, btw Calles 25 and 27, Colonia San Román) or you can drop by her store, **La Camita** (cnr of Calles 28 and 23, near the market). To see the cobblers in action, pay a visit to **Abigail y Aurora** (Calle 30, btw Calles 17 and 19, tel. 997/2–04–45), where an extensive two-level factory supplies everything from patent-leather party shoes to fat-buckled leather sandals.

BASICS Banco Atlántico (Calle 23, tel. 997/2–02–48), diagonally across from the plaza, changes money weekdays 9–1:30. Medical aid is available 24 hours at the **Centro de Salud** (Calle 27, btw Calles 30 and 32, tel. 997/2–00–86).

COMING AND GOING Combis leave Mérida for Ticul ($1.75) from the Parque San Juan whenever they are full. Buses also make the 80-minute trip from the second-class bus station in Mérida every hour 6 AM–7 PM for about the same price. To reach Ticul from Campeche or Hopelchén, you'll have to take a Mérida-bound bus along Highway 261 and change at Santa Elena (2 hrs, $3), where combis await incoming buses to take passengers on to Ticul 8:30 AM–6 PM.

To reach Uxmal and Kabah from Ticul, take a combi (20 min, 50¢) to Santa Elena from the plaza or from the combi station (Calle 30 No. 214, at Calle 25); from Santa Elena catch the Campeche-bound bus to Kabah (50¢) or the Mérida-bound bus to Uxmal ($1). To reach Loltún, your best bet is to take a combi (20 min, 50¢) to Oxkutzcab. They idle near the plaza in Ticul at Calle 25, between Calles 26 and 28.

WHERE TO SLEEP AND EAT The little old man who runs **Hotel San Miguel** (Calle 28 No. 213, btw Calles 21 and 23, tel. 997/2–03–82) speaks Mayan, but his Spanish is rough. The clean singles ($3.25) and doubles ($4.25) have hot water and fans. The woman who works at **Hotel Sierra Sosa** (Calle 26 No. 199, btw Calles 21 and 23, tel. 997/2–00–08) in the afternoons speaks excellent English. The simple rooms have comfortable beds, fans, and hot water, but street noise can be annoying in the front rooms, so request a room in the back. Singles are $5.25, doubles $6 ($10 with air-conditioning). They have laundry facilities and will hold your luggage.

Probably the most interesting feature of Ticul is the extent to which Mayan is spoken—you are likely to hear it as often as Spanish. One important discrepancy between the two languages is that in Spanish, malo means bad, while in Mayan, malo means good.

Unlike the Puuc sites, Ticul has plenty of cheap eateries. For breakfast, head to the market (*see above*), open daily 6 AM–noon, for fruit or food from one of the many *fondas* (covered food stands). For lunch or a snack, **Lonchería Mary** (Calle 23, btw Calles 26 and 28) serves licuados for 50¢ and tamales for 10¢ daily 8:30 AM–10 PM. **Restaurant Los Almendros** (Calle 23, btw Calles 26 and 28, tel. 997/2–00–21), open daily 9–9, has excellent Yucatecan dishes ($3–$4). If you need a break from Mexican food, head for **Cafetería y Pizzería La Góndola** (cnr of Calles 23 and 26, tel. 997/2–01–12), open daily 7–1 and 6–midnight. Come for the spaghetti ($3) or stay in your hotel room and have pizza delivered to you for $3–$4.

Snake Charmers in Ticul

A 72-year-old snake expert, Don Toribio Na'a Tzul lives with his knowledgeable wife, Juana María Yam in Ticul (Calle 31 No.181, at Calle 24), where they have been curing snake bites and making medicines from snake venom and meat for years. The couple prescribes powdered rattlesnake meat as a cure for people in the beginning stages of cancer, and rattlesnake oil to alleviate the symptoms of rheumatism. For 10 pesos (a little more than a dollar) you can even buy a powdered snake potion that will make the person you love pursue you endlessly for the rest of his or her life—just put a little snake powder in the person's taco, wait eight days, then repeat the dose. Warning: The effects of the potion are supposedly irreversible! Don Toribio and Juana María speak limited Spanish, but if you bring a Mayan-speaking interpreter, you can hear hundreds of stories about the Yucatán's snakes, including the boa roja, a snake that cries like a baby, and the chicotera, which laughs like a woman.

If you're unfortunate enough to be bitten by a snake, seek medical attention as soon as possible. In the meantime, Don Toribio suggests eating a whole lime (peel and all) to calm yourself. If you suck the venom out of your skin, make sure not to swallow it. Also try to slow the circulation from the bitten area to the rest of your body by squeezing the area above the bite. It's a good idea to try and eat something, as food absorbs the venom.

UXMAL AND THE PUUC ROUTE

Although the carefully kept lawns and plaid-clad tourists at Uxmal (pronounced oosh-MAHL) provide an unfortunate reality check, the beauty and scale of the buildings are such that you will soon forget the manicured surroundings. The *Chilam Balam,* a chronicle of the Maya of this region, says that Uxmal was founded in the mid-6th century. Uxmal means "built three times," but the structures were apparently reconstructed at least five times. No one knows exactly who used these buildings, but one theory suggests that the Xives (pronounced SHEE-base), a people from the central Mexican plain, occupied Uxmal briefly in the 10th century. Some evidence of this remains in inscriptions, but their paucity suggests that the Xives's stay was relatively short. Whatever the case, the city was abandoned soon afterward.

The satellite Puuc towns of Kabah, Sayil, Labná, and Xlapak (pronounced shla-PAK) are not as large or as historically impressive as Uxmal, but their remote setting in the Puuc Hills adds to their appeal. Many of the temples and pyramids remain hidden by the low vegetation, and tropical birds flit among the ruins. If you're on a Puuc ruins road trip, it's worth your while to check these sites out, but if you're pressed for time, just go to Uxmal.

UXMAL The archaeological ruins are open daily 8–5. Admission is $4, except on Sunday, when it's free. Mayan history and culture is the focus of the nightly light-and-sound shows (Spanish $3.25, 8 PM; English $4.50, 9 PM).

The magnificent **Pyramid of the Magician** (*see* box, *below*) is the first thing you'll see when you enter the archaeological site. The first stage of the pyramid's construction dates to the 6th century, and five temples were added during the next 400 years. The pyramid has an unusual oval base and stands 39 meters tall; to reach the fifth temple, you'll have to climb 150 narrow steps at a 60° angle. If vertigo hasn't done you in, climb down the west side to the temple just below it, with an entrance framed by the mouth of a huge mask of Chaac. Most impressive is the careful stone-by-stone construction and the way the shape of the pyramid seems to change when viewed from different perspectives.

Behind the pyramid is the Nun's Quadrangle, an imposing complex of four long, narrow buildings around a central courtyard. The complex received its name from the Spanish, who thought the layout and the 74 small rooms inside resembled a European convent. Its real purpose remains unclear: Red handprints covering one wall have led to speculation that the building was associated with Itzamná, the god of sun and sky. However, images of Chaac, the rain god with the distinctive hooked nose, are also prevalent. Many walls are decorated with geometric patterns and animal carvings, including images of a two-headed serpent. Facing the Nun's Quadrangle is a four-building complex called the **Cemetery Group.** Now badly decayed, the structures were once decorated with carved skulls and bones.

Head southwest from the Nun's Quadrangle to reach the **juego de pelota** (ball court). The badly deteriorated complex used to have stone bleachers from which spectators watched players knock balls through stone rings using only their hips, elbows, and knees. Close to the ball court is the **House of the Turtles,** a simple structure typical of Puuc architecture. The upper half of the building, which consists of a series of rooms, is most interesting: A series of columns supports a cornice sculpted with small turtles; use your imagination, as they look more like muffins. The Maya believed that turtles would appeal to Chaac on behalf of drought-stricken humans.

Set on a large raised platform, the **Governor's Palace** is one of the finest examples of pre-Columbian architecture in Mesoamerica. Its 107-meter length is divided by three corbeled arches, creating narrow passageways or sanctuaries. The friezes along the uppermost section of the palace are as intricate as any in Maya architecture, with carvings of geometric patterns overlaid with plumed serpents and Chaac masks. These mosaics supposedly required more than 20,000 individually cut stones.

Southeast of the Governor's Palace is a badly deteriorated pyramid with a rectangular base and the remains of a temple on its top. Now covered by vegetation, the whole complex is known as the **Pyramid of the Old Woman,** referring to a Mayan legend that claims the Pyramid of the Magician was built by an old witch and her dwarf son, who was hatched from an egg. Continu-

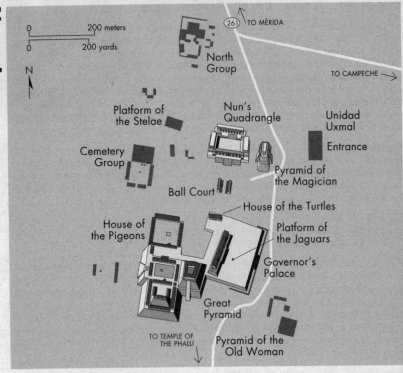

ing south from the Pyramid of the Old Woman, you'll reach the small **Temple of the Phalli** Suspended from the cornices, the phalli were used to channel rain into storage containers Most phalli have been destroyed or stolen (you know how it is—everyone wants a bigger one) but you can see one lone phallus in the museum at the tourist center.

Southwest of the Governor's Palace are the remains of the **Great Pyramid.** The structure is in poor condition and cannot compare with the Pyramid of the Magician, but the view from the 33-meter mound is rewarding and the climb up the reconstructed stairway is relatively easy Inside the temple at the top is a shrine to Chaac. Small bowls are carved into parts of the mask presumably to hold water or a small offering. Behind the Great Pyramid is the **House of the Pigeons,** a long building topped by eight triangular belfries perforated with what appear to be pigeonholes, hence the name of the building. No one has a clue as to what the place was actually used for. About half a kilometer south from the House of the Pigeons is a small building half-covered by dirt and vegetation. The geometric carvings on its facade look like a centipede giving the building the name *Chimez* (centipede in Mayan).

➤ **WHERE TO SLEEP** • Of the Puuc sites, only Uxmal has accommodations, most of which are expensive hotels. If you insist on staying in the area, head for **Rancho Uxmal,** a hot 6 kilometers north of the ruins. Singles here are $13.25 and doubles are $20. However, you can pitch a tent or hang a hammock on the palapa-covered cement platforms (and still have use of bathrooms, hot showers, and an enticing swimming pool) for only $2 per person, $1.7 extra per rented hammock. *Hwy 261, no phone. From Uxmal, walk, hitch, or flag down Mérida-bound bus and ask to be let off at Rancho Uxmal. 20 rooms, all with bath. Laundry luggage storage, restaurant.*

KABAH About 25 kilometers (15.5 mi) south of Uxmal, Kabah is among the most impressive sites in the Puuc region and dates from AD 850–900. Highway 261 splits Kabah in two: The most interesting structures uncovered so far lie on the eastern side of the road, while the rui on the western side remain partly hidden beneath dense vegetation. You should devote at least an hour to seeing the main sights here, if possible.

The **Codz Pop** is the principal structure at Kabah. The fantastic western facade is decorated with nearly 300 masks of Chaac, to whom the building was dedicated. The name Codz Pop means "coiled mat," possibly a reference to the noses, which curl like rolled-up mats. The noses may have been used as supports for lanterns, in which case the wall would have been brilliantly lit and visible for miles. Some archaeologists have suggested that the building had a legal or military function. Behind the Codz Pop are two structures built in the plainer, more traditional Puuc style: **El Palacio,** a palace that featured over 30 chambers, half of which still remain; and the **Temple of the Columns,** which boasts well-preserved columns at the back of the building.

On the other side of the road are several more magnificent structures, still largely unexcavated. Over hundreds of years, the roots of jungle vines and trees have transformed the **Great Pyramid,** once the most important temple in Kabah, into a mound of rubble. Traces of a stairway appear on its southern side. Nearby, the **Arch of Triumph** marks the end of a *sacbé,* a raised road leading from Kabah to Uxmal; the link to Uxmal demonstrates that Kabah was a politically important center. Southwest of the arch is the newly excavated **Templo de las Manos Rojas** (Temple of the Red Hands), which features small red hands similar to those seen in Uxmal imprinted in the northern wall of the first chamber. The handprints have been interpreted as either the signatures of the ancient architects or the marks of Itzamná, the spiritual guide of the Maya. *Admission: $1.25, free Sun. and holidays. Open daily 8–5.*

SAYIL Meaning "the place of the ants" in Mayan, Sayil, 10 kilometers south of Kabah, is best known for its magnificent palace. Built in AD 730, the palace is 65 meters long, with more than 50 rooms sprawling over three levels. The second level is decorated with columns similar to those found in Greek temples. The sculpted frieze above these columns features masks of Chaac, as well as images of the Descending God, an upside-down figure diving from the sky to the earth in order to grant the wishes of the Maya. Also visible is the Blue Lizard, a snakelike figure. South of the palace is the badly decayed **El Mirador,** which features a rooster-comb roof and a *juego de pelota* (ball court). Don't leave Sayil without getting a good look at the city from a distance—the best view is from the hill across the road from the entrance. *Admission: $1.25, free Sun. and holidays. Open daily 8–5.*

On the southeasternmost edge of Sayil's ancient city center stands a lone stela representing the importance of fertility to Maya culture. The carved male figure appears, at first glance, to have three legs— this is not the case.

XLAPAK About 6 kilometers east of Sayil is Xlapak, the smallest and least impressive site on the Puuc Route, with only one partially restored palace. Unless you're on the Ruta Puuc ATS bus, there's no real reason to stop here. The smooth-wall structure is typical of Puuc style, featuring geometric designs and masks of Chaac. *Admission: $1, free Sun. and holidays. Open daily 8–5.*

LABNA Probably the oldest of the Puuc cities, Labná (4 kilometers from Xlapak) is thought to have been built during the early Classic period (about AD 500). Labná means "the old house" in Mayan, but it probably received this name after the city was abandoned. Only a few structures have been uncovered at Labná, but they are exquisite. The best-preserved structure is the **arch,** whose stones stand without the aid of any mortar; once part of a larger building, the arch now stands alone, except for two surviving rooms—richly decorated with geometric patterns, mosaics, and small columns—that lead off the corbeled passageway. The **palace,** probably built some time in the 9th century, is the other major structure at Labná. The largest complex in the Puuc Hills, it sits on a huge platform more than 150 yards long. Despite its size, the palace isn't nearly as inspiring as the palace at Sayil. However, the decoration on its facade is noteworthy. Another impressive structure at Labná is **El Mirador,** a pyramid with a temple on top. The pyramid is little more than rubble today, but the temple has survived better. *Admission: $1.25, free Sun. and holidays. Open daily 8–5.*

OXKUTZCAB AND THE LOLTÚN CAVES

Sixteen kilometers southeast of Ticul, the small town of Oxkutzcab (pronounced osh-kootz-KAAB) is seldom explored by tourists—most of whom come only to get a bus or taxi to the nearby caves at Loltún. Ticul works better as a base town, but if you decide to spend the night in Oxkutzcab, try **Hospedaje Trujeque** (Calle 48 No. 102-A, btw Calles 51 and 53, tel. 997/5–05–68), which has pleasant rooms with private bathrooms and hot water for $5.25 (singles) and $6.50 (doubles). The huge daily **market** (Calle 51, btw Calles 48 and 50) draws people from throughout the region who come to buy produce at some of the lowest prices in Mexico.

The Grutas de Loltún are the largest and most spectacular caves on the peninsula and definitely deserve your time. About 19 kilometers (12 mi) east of Labná and 10 kilometers (6 mi) west of Oxkutzcab, Loltún consists of a maze of underground labyrinths filled with enormous stalagmites and stalactites. Archaeologists have had a field day here, unearthing evidence about the Maya and their ancestors, who inhabited these caves for more than two millennia. Religious ceremonies were held in the **Catedral,** a vast chamber crowded with stalagmites and stalactites. Some formations in the center of the chamber resemble an altar. In another cavern you can see the soot from cooking fires and the remains of *metates* (stones used for grinding corn). The caves also contain several carvings of figures and hieroglyphs, some of which date back to 2000 BC, as well as black-ink paintings. Over thousands of years, dripping water has carved the rocks into bizarre shapes, and tour guides find no end of amusing resemblances, including the Virgin of Guadalupe, a dolphin's head, a camel, a jaguar, and an eagle. Especially interesting are two semihollow rock formations extending from the ceiling to the floor. If you tap them the right way, they produce musical tones. According to legend, only virgins can produce this sound, so think twice before you strike.

You cannot enter the caves without a guide. Daily guided tours leave every 1½ hours 9:30–3. If you arrive after 3, you won't be allowed to enter. Guides expect a tip—a dollar or two each is about right. The floor of the dark caves is slippery and uneven, so bring a sturdy pair of shoes. As you leave the caves, pause near the ticket office to admire the austere stone monument to a phallus-worshipping cult, which looks a little out of place in the middle of the driveway. *Admission: $3, $1.75 Sun.*

COMING AND GOING Combis leave from the Parque San Juan in Mérida (Calle 62, btw Calles 69 and 67) for Oxkutzcab whenever they're full; ADO buses leave from Mérida's bus terminal (Calle 71, btw Calles 68 and 70) about every three hours, 9 AM–8:30 PM. Both combis and buses take 1½ hours and cost $3. From anywhere besides Mérida, you'll have to go to Ticul first and catch a combi (20 min, 50¢) from Calle 25 (btw Calles 26 and 28) to Oxkutzcab. The last bus leaves Ticul at 7 PM. To reach Loltún from Oxkutzcab, you'll have to wait until one of the trucks carrying workers to the fields fills up—wait in front of the market. The trip costs one 50¢ and takes about 20 minutes. If you don't want to wait around, you can hire one of the many taxis or combis to take you to the grutas for about $4.

There are three ways to return from Loltún: Wait (and hope) for the truck to come back; wait for a combi outside the entrance of the main parking lot; or hitch. Hitching is pretty easy (especially if you've made friends during the cave tour) and isn't dangerous during the day. From Oxkutzcab, combis leave for Ticul from Calle 52 (btw Calles 51 and 53) or from the northwest corner of the park (the last leaves at 7 PM). Buses leave for Mérida from Oxkutzcab every half hour until 9 PM.

Mérida
Mérida is the largest and most elegant city on the Yucatán Peninsula, perfect for a romantic Yucatecan rendezvous. But even if you can't muster up a date, you'll appreciate Mérida's sophisticated beauty. From aging, tranquil neighborhoods to frenzied commercial districts, each sector of the city has a distinct ambience: The Paseo de Montejo, a broad street harboring restored mansions, sidewalk cafés, and ritzy hotels. In the Parque Central, students, tourists, and locals hang out near the cathedral and the Palacio de Gobierno—monuments to the 500-year struggle between European and Mayan culture. In fact, the city itself is built on the site of the Mayan settlement of T'hó, whose temples and columns

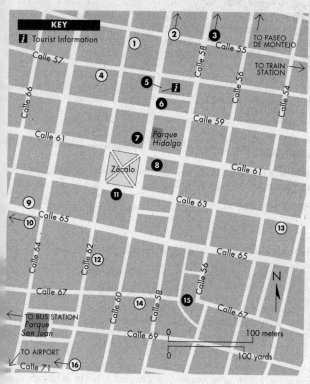

Sights ●

Casa de
Montejo, **11**

Catedral, **8**

Iglesia de la
Tercera Orden, **6**

Mercado
Municipal, **15**

Museo Regional
de Antropología, **3**

Palacio de
Gobierno, **7**

Teatro Peón
Contreras, **5**

Lodging ○

Hotel Alamo, **16**

Hotel América, **14**

Hotel Casa
Bowen, **10**

Hotel Dolores
Alba, **13**

Hotel Galería
Trinidad, **2**

Hotel La Gran
Posada, **9**

Hotel Montejo, **4**

Hotel Trinidad, **1**

La Paz, **12**

reminded the Spanish of the Roman ruins at Mérida, Spain. The colonists forced the Maya to dismantle their temples and used the masonry to create new buildings, churches, and mansions. Like its buildings, Mérida's residents are the result of a merger of indigenous and European cultures: Mayan aesthetics and tradition flavor the opulence and formality of Spanish colonial culture.

Mérida is a wonderful place to dawdle and a good base from which to explore the Gulf Coast and the ruins of the Puuc Hills. If you only have one day to spend in Mérida, try to make it a Sunday, when the central streets are closed off and the whole city turns out for festivities like Zacatecan folk dancing and an especially grand market. The best time to visit is generally during the dry season, November–April.

ASICS

AMERICAN EXPRESS AmEx sells traveler's checks and offers emergency check cashing as well as lost-card and lost-check services. They hold clients' mail for a month. *Paseo de Montejo 494, Mérida, Yucatán, CP 97000, México, tel. 99/24–43–26. Btw Calles 43 and 45. Open weekdays 9–2 and 4–5, Sat. 9–noon.*

AUTO PARTS/SERVICE The **Ángeles Verdes** (Green Angels), a government-funded road service agency with a small office in Mérida, answers questions about service, tolls, and other car-related matters. *Calle 14 No. 102, btw Calles 73 and 75, tel. 99/83–11–84. Open daily 8–8.*

BOOKSTORES All the Mérida branches of **Librería Dante** offer a limited selection of English titles. One branch is located in the **Teatro Peón Contreras** (Calle 60, at Calle 57, tel. 9/24–95–22) and is open weekdays 8 AM–9:30 PM, Saturday 8–2 and 5–9, and Sunday 9–2 and 4–8.

CASAS DE CAMBIO Most banks are on Calle 65, between Calles 60 and 62, and change money weekdays 9–12:30. **Profesionales en Cambio** (Calle 61 No. 500, btw. Calles 60 and 62, tel. 99/24–06–31) is open daily 8 AM–9 PM. Exchange rates at the banks are slightly better than at the *casas de cambio*. The **Banamex** ATM at the corner of Calles 56 and 59 accepts Visa, MasterCard, Cirrus, and Plus cards.

CONSULATES For information about Belize, visit the **United Kingdom/Belize Vice-Consulate.** *Calle 53 No. 498, btw Calles 56 and 58, tel. 99/28–61–52. Open weekdays 9–1 and 4–5.*

United States. *Paseo de Montejo 453, at Colón, tel. 99/25–50–11. Open weekdays 7:30–4.*

EMERGENCIES The **police** station (tel. 99/25–25–55) is on Calle 72, between Calles 39 and 41. For emergencies, dial 06.

LAUNDRY La Lavamática La Fé charges $2 to wash and dry 3 kilos of clothing. *Calle 61 No. 518, btw Calles 62 and 64, tel. 99/24–45–31. Open weekdays 8–7, Sat. 8–4.*

MAIL The **post office** will hold mail sent to you at the following address for up to 10 days: Lista de Correos, Administración Urbana 1, Mérida, Yucatán, CP 97000, México. *Calle 65, at Calle 56, tel. 99/28–54–04. Open weekdays 7–7, Sat. 9–1.*

MEDICAL AID Farmacia Noemi Virginia (Calle 67 No. 550-D, btw Calles 66 and 68, tel. 99/24–52–90) is open round the clock. For medical attention, visit **Clínica Yucatán** (Calle 66 No. 528, at Calle 65, tel. 99/24–93–91), open 24 hours daily. The **Cruz Roja** (Calle 68, btw Calles 65 and 67, tel. 99/28–53–91, or 99/24–98–13 for emergencies) offers 24-hour ambulance service.

To ensure your stay in Mérida is fun *and* safe, **Hospital O'Horan**'s Medicina Preventiva division gives out free condoms Monday–Saturday 9–5. *Av. de Los Itzaes 59, tel. 99/24–41–11 Take CENTENARIO bus from north side of zócalo.*

PHONES You can find **public telephones** on the zócalo, at the Palacio Municipal, and in parks around the city. Dial 09 for international collect calls. You can only call direct from *casetas* (booths); the **Caseta de Larga Distancia** (Calle 60, at Calle 61, tel. and fax 99/24–19–07) charges $2.75 a minute for calls to the United States.

SCHOOLS The **Academia de Cultura e Idiomas** offers beginning through advanced Spanish courses, including classes geared toward scientists, businesspeople, and anthropologists. Four-week programs entail four hours of class per day and cost $280 for the first two weeks, $100 for each additional week. The school arranges affordable homestays for students. *Calle 13 No. 23, tel. and fax 99/44–31–48. Take SAN ANTONIO bus from cnr of Calles 56 and 59. Mailing address: AP 78-4, Mérida, Yucatán, CP 97100, México.*

TOURS AND GUIDES Shop around for tours to the Mayan ruins near Mérida—prices for day trips fluctuate widely. Trips to Uxmal and Chichén Itzá should cost about $25. Reliable travel agencies include **Ceiba Tours** (Calle 60 No. 495, tel. 99/24–44–77; open weekdays 8–7, Sat 8–2) and **Eco-Turismo Yucatán** (Calle 3 No. 235, btw Calles 32 and 34, tel. 99/20–27–72).

VISITOR INFORMATION The **tourist information center** at Teatro Peón Contreras has knowledgeable staff that speaks English fairly well. They also have copies of *Yucatán Today* with general info and some maps. Information booths at the airport and the bus station stock similar material. *Calle 60, btw Calles 57 and 59, tel. 99/24–92–90. Open daily 8–8.*

COMING AND GOING

BY BUS Mérida is home to several exhaust-filled transport hubs, the biggest and most confusing of which is **Unión de Camioneros del Yucatán** (Calle 70, btw Calles 69 and 71). From here, **ADO** (tel. 99/24–86–10) has first-class service to Cancún (3½ hrs, $9) and Villahermosa (9 hrs, $17), as well as frequent first-class service to Campeche (2½ hrs, $5). Other destinations include Chetumal (4 per day, 6 hrs, $10), Palenque (2 per day, 9 hrs, $15), and San Cristóbal de las Casas (1 per day, 14 hrs, $20). **ATS** (Calle 69, btw Calles 68 and 70, tel. 9

23–22–87) sends second-class buses every three hours 6 AM–7 PM to Uxmal (1½ hrs, $1.50), Hopelchén (3 hrs, $2.75), and Maxcanú (1 hr, 75¢).

Buses to smaller regional towns leave from various points around the city. Buses to Dzibilchaltún (hourly, 1 hr, 50¢) or Umán (every ½ hr, 45 min, 50¢) leave from the corner of **Parque San Juan** (Calle 64, btw Calles 69 and 71). To reach Hunucmá (1 hr, 75¢), Sisal (1½ hrs, $1), or Celestún (2 hrs, $1.50), go to the station on Calle 71, btw Calles 64 and 66, around the corner from Parque San Juan. Frequent buses to Mayapán (1½ hrs, $1), and Dzilam de Bravo (2 hrs, $1.50) leave from the station at Calle 50, between Calles 65 and 67. Buses for Progreso (1 hr, 75 ¢) leave every 20 minutes 6 AM–9 PM from the station on Calle 62, between Calles 65 and 67.

BY CAR Avoid the evil toll road ($6 to Valladolid, another $10 to Cancún) by veering to the right at Kilometer 67 of Highway 180 out of Mérida. The *carretera de cuota* (toll road) and the *carretera libre* (free road) go through the same places, but you can't get off the toll road (which, admittedly, is a hell of a lot faster) until Valladolid. If you're going the other direction, you're in luck—there are no tolls between Campeche and Mérida.

BY PLANE Mérida's airport is 7 kilometers west of the city's central square. **Aeroméxico** (Paseo Montejo 460, tel. 99/27–90–00) has pricey one-way fares to Cancún ($49) and Mexico City ($114). **Aerocaribe** (Paseo Montejo 500-B, at Calle 47, tel. 99/28–67–90) flies to Oaxaca ($135 one-way) and Villahermosa ($74 one-way) It's fairly easy and cheap to get to town: Just take Autobus 79 (AVIACION) to the corner of Calles 67 and 60 downtown. The half-hour trip costs about 25¢. An airport taxi (usually a VW combi) to your hotel costs $5 for up to four people.

GETTING AROUND

Despite its size, Mérida is easy to figure out, with most of the interesting buildings and budget hotels clustered near the zócalo. Streets are numbered, not named, with odd-numbered streets running east–west and even-numbered streets running north–south. The zócalo is bordered by Calles 60, 61, 62, and 63.

BY CAR Most rental agencies are on Calle 60, between Calles 55 and 59. At about $21 a day, including insurance and unlimited mileage, the cheapest place is **México Rent-a-Car** (Calle 60 No. 495, btw Calles 57 and 59, tel. 99/27–49–16; open Mon.–Sat. 8–1 and 5–8, Sun. 8–1). Despite the suspiciously low price, the VW bugs seem to be in good condition. The other cars look pretty sketch. **National InterRent** (Calle 60, btw Calles 55 and 57, tel. 99/28–63–08; open daily 7 AM–10 PM) charges about $26 a day with unlimited mileage and insurance, and you must be 21 or older with a credit card.

BY BUS You won't need to use the bus to see the sights in Mérida's center, but if you want to go beyond the area around the zócalo, bus travel is a cheap option. City buses (25¢) run daily 5 AM to midnight; some buses stop earlier though, so be sure to ask the driver. Buses leave from Calle 59 between Calles 56 and 58, and from Calle 56 between Calles 59 and 67, around the market area. Destinations are marked on the windshields.

BY TAXI Avoid the regular taxis, which are very expensive. Instead, look for *colectivos,* or shared taxis (50¢), which have fixed routes throughout the city. Tell the driver where you want to go before you get in, and he'll tell you if it's on his way. Colectivos leave from the zócalo, the market area, and Parque San Juan at Calles 67 and 62.

WHERE TO SLEEP

Mérida's best budget hotels are conveniently located near the zócalo. If you must stay near the bus station, try **Hotel Alamo** (Calle 68 No. 549, at Calle 71, tel. 99/28–62–90), which rents boxes with breathing-holes and private bath for $4 (nicer doubles $5), or the more comfortable **Hotel Casa Bowen** (*see below*). Real penny-pinchers can hang a hammock in giant, bare rooms for $2 at **La Gran Posada** (Calle 65, btw Calles 64 and 66). For $2.50 you can sleep in a single bed here with a shoebox-size shared bathroom—but bring the mosquito netting and be prepared for a cold shower.

> **UNDER $10** • **Hotel América.** The simple rooms here have private bathrooms (most with hot water), but the beds are a bit uncomfortable. A couple of blocks from the zócalo, the hotel is popular with families, but the owner is not used to chatting it up with solo backpackers. Singles cost $9.50, doubles $10. *Calle 67 No. 500, btw Calles 58 and 60, tel. 99/28–58–79. 43 rooms, all with bath (30 with hot water). Luggage storage, meal service. Wheelchair access.*

Hotel Casa Bowen. The wood and wicker furniture, wrought-iron railings, and open-air lending library in the lobby make you look forward to coming home to this hotel. Big windows let light into the rooms, and ceiling fans keep things cool. Singles cost $7.25, doubles $8.75. Suites ($10) have their own kitchens, equipped with a stove and fridge. *Calle 66 No. 521-B, btw Calles 65 and 67, tel. 99/28–61–09. 28 rooms, all with bath. Laundry, luggage storage.*

Hotel Galería Trinidad. This funky hotel is decorated with everything from weathered sculptures to avant-garde Mexican paintings to blow-up plastic Mickey Mouses. After admiring the lobby and hallways, though, you'll probably be disappointed by the relatively bland rooms. The swimming pool is refreshing but is sometimes neglected and tends to flood when it rains. Rooms start at $8 for doubles with a shared bath and $10.50 for a single with a private bath. Air-conditioning is an extra $2.50. *Calle 51, at Calle 60, tel. 99/23–24–63. 30 rooms, 27 with bath. Luggage storage. Wheelchair access.*

Hotel Montejo. A gorgeous courtyard, stout columns, and colonial-style arches are what you'd expect in a hotel of this caliber in Mérida. Elegant singles cost $8, doubles $8.75. Air-conditioned rooms are worth shelling out a mere $1.25 more. *Calle 57 No. 507, btw Calles 62 and 64, tel. 99/28–03–99. 22 rooms, all with bath. Luggage storage, restaurant.*

Hotel Trinidad. Oddly carved wood columns, tons of plants, and a hodgepodge of paintings give this place a homey, atticlike feel. The communal bathrooms aren't luxurious, but they're kept relatively clean. Guests can enjoy coffee and toast with eggs or cereal (not included with lodging) on the hotel's central patio. Singles are $6, $7.50 buys one bed with a private bath, and doubles with private bath start at $8.25. *Calle 62 btw Calles 55 and 57, tel. 99/23–20–33. Laundry (75¢ per piece), luggage storage.*

La Paz. This plaster-dusted, sunlit hotel has a large patio, pastel-colored rooms, and a narrow whitewashed balcony. Somewhat stuffy, fan-cooled rooms with private bathrooms are about as cheap as they come ($5.25 singles, $6 doubles). Rooms have beds and hammock hooks. Following the Mexican custom of odd juxtaposition, La Paz is identifiable by a HOTEL MILO sign at the entranceway. *Calle 62, btw Calles 65 and 67, tel. 99/23 94–46. 15 rooms, all with bath. Wheelchair access.*

You haven't really experienced the Yucatán until you've sampled one of the region's staple dishes. Poc chuc (grilled pork marinated in orange juice) and pollo pibil (marinated chicken baked in banana leaves) are among the favorite regional meat dishes. Non-meat dishes include papadzule (hard-boiled eggs wrapped in a tortilla with pumpkin sauce).

> **UNDER $20** • **Hotel Dolores Alba.** When you emerge from your cozy room with a clean bath, lively paintings, and red tiled floor, pull up a chaise lounge and daydream by the pool. Rocking chairs fill the common areas, along with a guitar and chess set. Singles cost $14.50, doubles $17.25, and triples go for $20. Air-conditioning is an extra $2.50. *Calle 6 No. 464, btw Calles 52 and 54, tel. 99/28–56–50. 5 rooms, all with bath. Laundry, luggage storage, meal service. Wheelchair access.*

FOOD

Eating is one of the highlights of a trip to Mérida: Yucatecan food is delicious, and nowhere is it better prepared than here. Unfortunately, eating out can be downright expensive. However, many small loncherías and street stands around town sell *antojitos* (appetizers), *tortas* and *panuchos* and *salbutes* (both variations on the taco)—all for under $1. The second floor of the **mercado municipal** (Calles 65 and 67, btw Calles 54 and 56) has more than 20 simpl loncherías offering full lunches for under $3; on the north side of the market are dozens of cheap *cocktelerías,* selling amazingly fresh ceviches and full-sized shrimp and conch cocktail cups for $2–$3. The municipal market is also a wonderful place to buy fresh fruits and vegetables brought daily from the villages.

➤ **UNDER $5** • **Amaro.** Lilting music and flickering candles make this shaded courtyard kitchen almost embarrassingly romantic. Specialties include vegetarian delights, such as cream of zucchini soup ($1.50) and eggplant curry with cheese (or soy) and rice ($3). For something more filling, try the delicious grilled green peppers stuffed with a savory mixture of tofu, onion, and cheese ($3.50). Finish it all off with a rice and almond or *chaya* (Mayan spinach) shake ($1). *Calle 59 No. 507, btw Calles 60 and 62, tel. 99/28–24–51. Open daily 9 AM–11 PM.*

Café y Restaurante El Louvre. There's nothing French about Mérida's answer to the American coffee shop. Stout waiters with little black bow ties and white shirts patrol the brown-tiled restaurant yelling orders to the cook, who stands behind a glass counter hacking at a pot roast. If you're still up before sunrise, try the pancakes ($1.50) or eggs ($1–$2). The hot lime soup with bits of chicken and fried tortilla ($1) is amazing. Huge daily specials are only $2.25. *Calle 61, at Calle 62, on the zócalo, tel. 99/24–50–73. Open daily 24 hrs.*

Cafetería Pop. This "concept" café is brilliantly decorated with orange and lavender pop art designs. Vigorously air-conditioned and often crowded, Pop is always a good place for conversation if you don't mind cigarette smoke. A standard breakfast (eggs, beans, fruit, coffee, and meat) is $2.25. Chicken mole is $2.50, and the club sandwich $2. Iced coffee goes for 75¢. *Calle 57 No. 501, btw Calles 60 and 62, tel. 99/28–61–63. Across from the university. Open daily 7 AM–11 PM.*

Restaurante Nicte-Há. Raucous groups of men wearing *guayaberas* (big-collared, button-down cotton blouses) flock here to enjoy delicious Yucatecan specialties at amazingly cheap prices. The *combinación yucateca* is a must—for only $3.75 you get a panucho, papadzule, pollo pibil, tamale, and a Yucatecan sausage. Vegetarians can feast on rice and banana soup ($1) or *frijoles kabax* (savory whole-bean soup; 75¢). *Calle 61, btw Calles 60 and 62, tel. 99/23–07–34. Open daily 7 AM–11:30 PM.*

El Trapiche Restaurant y Juguería. Papayas, watermelon, and glistening mameys are piled along the back wall of the bar, within easy reach of deft smoothie makers. Fresh juices and smoothies cost about 75¢. Sandwiches are tasty and cheap—try the veggie sub with mushrooms, onion, peppers, and tomatoes ($1). Garlic lovers won't be able to get enough of the 50¢ *pan con ajo* (toasted french bread smothered with grilled garlic and melted cheese). *Calle 62 No. 13, btw Calles 59 and 61, tel. 99/28–12–31. Open daily 7:30 AM–10:30 PM.*

➤ **UNDER $10** • **Restaurant Express.** The food here is quite good and servings are abundant, but plan to spend $4–$5 for typical Yucatecan dishes. The specialty is pollo pibil ($4.75), or try the *chilaquiles* (tortilla strips and chicken doused with salsa and sour cream) for $3.25. Save room for dessert: *pasta de guayaba* ($1), a square of luscious guava paste wrapped in a cool blanket of creamy cheese. *Calle 60, at Calle 59, tel. 99/28–16–91. Open daily 7 AM–11 PM.*

WORTH SEEING

Since Mérida was founded, wealthy residents have invested an enormous amount of money and pride in their city, and the government continues to dole out the dough to keep the city's colonial heritage in good shape. Museums, galleries, and stores are stocked with antiques and artwork from ancient, colonial, and contemporary times, and every week new listings of dance, theater, and music performances appear. For info on upcoming events, ask at the tourist office or check the local newspaper, *Por Esto* (25¢). The tourist office also has a list of weekly events *Yucatán Today,* a free magazine.

The sites listed below are only part of what makes Mérida interesting. Take the time to walk around the zócalo area and you will find old mansions, churches, and theaters. Some restora-

If you're near the Banamex branch on Calle 63, between Calles 60 and 62, check out the bas-relief on the facade, which depicts Francisco de Montejo (destroyer of the Mayan city of T'hó and founder of Mérida), his wife and daughter, and a number of Spanish soldiers standing on the heads of the vanquished Maya.

tion jobs are better than others, but even if you walk into a run-down hotel, you're likely to see beautiful stained glass, decaying hardwood furniture, oil paintings dating back one or two hundred years, columns, marble and ceramic tiles, and beautiful courtyards.

CHURCHES The splendid twin-spire **cathedral** (Calle 60, at Calle 61; open daily 7–noon and 5–8) stands austerely at the front of the zócalo. It looks more like a fort than anything else and is a subtle reminder of how difficult the Spanish found it to convert the Maya to Christianity. Built in 1561 entirely of stone (much of which came from razed Mayan buildings), the cathedral was indeed designed for defense—gunnery slits, not windows, stare out onto the square. The interior is rather bleak, having been ransacked during the Mexican Revolution and never restored. However, the pillagers did not touch **El Cristo de las Ampollas,** which translates as "Christ of the Blisters." Legend has it that a local peasant once claimed he saw a tree burning all night, but that the tree was not consumed by the flames. A statue of Christ was carved from the tree and placed in a church in a nearby town. Later, the church burned down, but the statue survived, albeit covered in blisters.

The **Iglesia de la Tercera Orden** (Church of the Third Order), across from Parque Hidalgo at Calles 60 and 59, was built by Jesuit monks in the 17th century. The stones of the facade come from the great pyramid of T'hó; if you look carefully, especially on the Calle 59 side, you can still distinguish Mayan designs on them. *Open daily 7–11 and 5–8.*

MERCADO MUNICIPAL Mérida's gargantuan municipal market, occupying the area between Calles 65 and 67 and Calles 54 and 56, is considered by many travelers to be the best on the peninsula. If you're hunting for a hammock, hold out for the fine ones sold here (*see* Shopping, *below*). You'll also find a huge selection of embroidered shirts and dresses, ceramics, silver, and some crazy-looking, wood-eating insects called *maquech,* which have jewels and gold chains glued to their hard, shell-like backs. There's even a saint-repair shop, **La Reina de Tepeyac** (bottom floor of market, across the aisle from Edmundo Pinzon Lara Artesanías y Ropa Típica), in case your traveling icon has been damaged. *Market open daily 6–5.*

MUSEO REGIONAL DE ANTROPOLOGIA This museum, about a kilometer from the zócalo, is worth visiting despite the $2 admission fee. Exhibits consist mainly of Mayan artifacts, including figurines of the Mayan messenger between the gods and man, Chac Mool, and artifacts retrieved from the sacred cenotes at Dzibilchaltún and Chichén Itzá. There are also reconstructions of burial chambers, as well as deformed skulls: The Maya flattened their children's skulls with boards for cosmetic reasons. *Paseo de Montejo, at Calle 43. Admission: $2, free Sun. and holidays. Open Tues.–Sat. 8–8, Sun. 8–2. From zócalo, take northbound* PASEO DE MONTEJO *bus or walk 9 blocks.*

PALACIO DE GOBIERNO Built in 1892 on the northern side of the zócalo, the Governor's Palace is a beautiful example of neoclassical architecture, with Doric columns topped by arches. Inside, murals by Fernando Castro Pacheco, a Yucatecan painter, depict the tumultuous history of the Yucatán, including the Caste War (*see box, below*), in which the Maya fought against Mexicans of European descent. *Calle 61, btw Calles 60 and 62. Admission free. Open daily 8 AM–9:30 PM.*

TEATRO PEON CONTRERAS Right in front of the Iglesia de la Tercera Orden, this theater is another city landmark. The current building dates from 1877 but has undergone several transformations, the most drastic in 1905, when Italian artists gave it a neoclassical design. The theater hosts classical music recitals and ballets on Tuesdays at 9 PM; check *Por Esto* for current shows. For ballet, plays, and concerts, same-night seats go on sale at 9 AM. Ballet tickets vary in price, sometimes starting as low as $2; you can sometimes get two-for-one tickets with an ISIC card. *Calle 60, at Calle 57. Ticket office open Mon.–Sat. 9–9, Sun. 9–1:30.*

SHOPPING

Mérida is the best place on the Yucatán Peninsula to buy a hammock, but the experience can be like looking for a used car. Salesmen are aggressive and will tell you anything, so visit at least two shops and don't be afraid to bargain. Street vendors near the zócalo and the bus station offer the best bargains, but it's wiser to cruise the shops along Calle 58 near the market (btw Calles 63 and 69) to see what's out there. The best places to go are **El Hamaguero** (Calle 58, btw Calles 69 and 71, tel. 99/23–21–17), which makes and sells their own hammocks, and **Artesanías Uxmal** (Calle 58, btw Calles 63 and 65, tel. 99/23–36–33). In both of these places, be ready to bargain and have some prices in mind before walking in.

Hammocks come in several sizes—single, double, matrimonial, large matrimonial, and family. Judge the size for yourself by comparing the weights of different hammocks—don't trust a salesman's claims. The larger hammocks are probably your best bet, since they allow you to sleep diagonally, which is better for your back. Prices vary, but the smallest ones should be no more than $9 for the cotton-nylon type, $11 for nylon only. Matrimonial hammocks cost about $15 for cotton-nylon, $20 for nylon. Cotton and nylon-cotton hammocks are the most comfortable, however pure nylon hammocks last longer, and the colors don't fade. Whether you buy a cotton or a nylon hammock, the end-strings should be nylon for greater strength. Also, several long, straight strings should run along each side of the hammock for stability. Ask the salesman to hang the hammock for you, and see how closely it's woven.

AFTER DARK

The bar and disco scene in Mérida isn't that exciting—residents are content just strolling around the zócalo. Things liven up a bit on the weekends, when the city goes all out, staging huge cultural events and folkloric shows that are often free. For more information on upcoming shebangs, visit the tourist information center (*see above*) or the **Oficina de la Cultura del Ayuntamiento** (Calle 62 btw Calles 61 and 63, tel. 99/24–69–00), inside the Palacio Municipal.

The Caste War

When Mexico earned its independence from Spain in 1821, the Maya had no reason to celebrate. The land they had lost under Spanish rule was not returned to them by the new government, and they still suffered the condemnation of their religion. In 1847, a Maya rebellion began in Valladolid. Not only did the Maya win control of the town, but within a year, they conquered all of the Yucatán except Mérida and Campeche. Europeans in the capital appealed for help from Spain, France, and the United States, but none was forthcoming. The outnumbered Europeans made plans to evacuate. Just as the Maya prepared for a final, decisive assault, the winged ant (symbolic of coming rains) made an early appearance. The Maya took the insects' arrival as an omen, packed up their weapons, and returned to the fields to plant the sacred corn, without which they could not survive.

Help for the Spanish settlers then arrived with a vengeance from Mexico City, Cuba, and the United States. The Maya were mercilessly slaughtered, their population dropping from 500,000 to 300,000. Survivors escaped into the jungles of Quintana Roo and held out against the Mexican government until 1974, when the region officially accepted statehood with Mexico. For this reason, Yucatecans are less willing to blend in with the rest of Mexico and adamantly maintain their unique customs and traditions.

BARS Music by Gloria Gaynor and Madonna characterize **Kabukis** (Calle 84, btw Calles 61 and 65, across from zoo; open Thurs.–Sat. until 3 AM), which is frequented by a predominantly gay crowd. A mellow bar during the early evening, Kabukis turns into a sizzling disco after 10 PM, and transvestites strut their stuff nightly at 12:30 AM. Cover is $2.75 Thursday and $5.25 Friday and Saturday; two drinks are always included in the charge. Waiters in giant sombreros carry drinks (beers $1.50, piña coladas, $2) to patrons at intimate wrought-iron patio tables at **Panchos** (Calle 59 No. 509, btw Calles 60 and 62, tel. 99/23–09–42), open daily 6 PM–2 AM). It's hardly a secret, but the lack of cover and the lively bands that take the stage keep it a favorite among locals. If you want to hang with the under-25 crowd downtown, try **Pancho Villa's** (Calle 60, btw Calles 55 and 57, tel. 99/24–22–89), popular with locals and tourists who don't want to go all the way out to the popular discos. Pancho Villas is open nightly from 6 PM until 3 or 4 AM and serves $1.25 beers and $1.50 margaritas. The music is mostly Latin rock and pop music, but the dance floor is rarely packed.

DANCING The dance scene downtown is nonexistent. The really slick discos, popular among the upper-class youth, line Prolongación Montejo. The bus situation is sketchy at night though, and a taxi from Mérida costs about $4. Serious dancers should go to **Kalia** (Calle 22 No. 282, btw Calles 37 and 39, tel. 99/44–42–35; open Wed.–Sat. until 3 AM), where an 18- to 40-year-old crowd works up a healthy sweat on a multiplatformed stage lit by a huge video screen. The cover charge is $4.75 for men, $3.50 for women. Downtown, a somewhat older crowd dances to salsa at **Estelares** (Calle 60 No. 484, btw Calles 55 and 57, tel. 99/28–28–58; open Thurs.–Sat. 9 PM–3 AM). Cover is $1.50. The **Sala de Fiesta Montejo** (Calle 62, at Calle 65, in front of bus station, tel. 99/24–90–36) is a parking lot during the week, but on weekend nights between 8 and 3, it's where working-class Mexicans come to dance to live tropical music and drink $1 beers. Cover is $5 for men and free for women, who should think twice about coming here alone.

Near Mérida

Yucatán state is home to some of the most exciting sites in Mexico, from beautiful caves and impressive ruins to deserted fishing villages. In your rush to visit these places, don't overlook the inhabitants though: Scattered around Mérida are numerous *pueblos* (villages) that provide a window on the real Yucatán. Most Yucatecan towns flaunt quaint colonial churches, the largest and most elaborate of which can be seem at **Umán**, 18 kilometers (11 mi) southwest of Mérida, and **Hunucmá**, 29 kilometers (18 mi) west of Mérida. For info on how to reach these two towns, *see* Coming and Going, *above*.

CALCEHTOK AND OXKINTOK

The spectacular caves at Calcehtok (Mayan for "Bleeding of the Deer's Throat") are unknown to all but the most ambitious travelers because they aren't easily accessible. Although they are only 70 kilometers (43 mi) southwest of Mérida and about 15 kilometers (9.3 mi) from Maxcanú you'll have to wait an eternity for transport to the village of Calcehtok and then hike 3 kilometers on a dirt road to the caves. Just when you think the heat and the monochromatic vegetation will drive you mad, you reach the caves. After the first immense chamber, where sunlight illuminates tropical plants and singing, swooping birds, it's pure obscurity and silence, except for the sound of water dripping from stalactites and the occasional chirping of a bat or two. A lantern reveals formations in the multicolored rock and the remnants of ancient visitors. Don't explore these endless, narrow caves on your own unless you're an expert. Adjacent to the bus stop in Calchetok village, in the adobe house marked by a CAVE TOURS sign, you'll find **Roger Cu** and his sons, who have been leading tours of the caves for three generations (Roger's grandfather actually discovered the caves). A complete tour lasts up to six hours, but you can ask to return at any point during the tour (2–3 hours may be plenty to get a good feeling for what's there). Roger doesn't charge a set fee, but $5 an hour is about right, more if you have a large group. Ropes and ladders, mud, bees, and lots of bat guano are involved in a cave trip—it's not for the weak of heart or the less than agile. A flashlight of your own is also helpful.

On the road back to the village of Calcehtok is the turnoff for the badly preserved and seldom visited ruins of **Oxkintok.** The enormous site, about 2 kilometers square, was probably the largest of all Puuc cities and was populated during the late Classic period. The central area features three large pyramids, as well as the pitiful remains of small pyramid temples, palacelike buildings, a ball court, and a variety of houses. Of particular interest are the three carved anthropomorphs (stylized human figures) that stand in their original places in front of a slightly better preserved temple. Ringing the central area like suburbs are three other sets of ruins, each connected by a system of *sacbés* (roads). Despite the relative isolation of the site, an informally dressed state official at the ruins will emerge from his VW to charge you the $1.50 entrance fee (free Sundays and holidays). Oxkihtox is open daily 8–5.

COMING AND GOING Getting to Calcehtok and Oxkintok by public transport is tiring and time-consuming. From the main bus station in Mérida, take a Maxcanú-bound bus; they make the one-hour trip every hour or so. The detour for Calcehtok is a few hundred yards before Maxcanú—just tell the driver you want to get off at the *grutas* (caves) or *ruinas* (ruins). From here, either hitchhike or catch a minitruck taxi to the village. From Calcehtok, it's 5 kilometers to Oxkintok and 3 kilometers to the caves. You may be able to arrange transport in the village; otherwise you'll have to walk or hitch. If you're visiting the caves, pick up Roger in the village. If you're driving from Mérida, take Highway 180 toward Campeche and turn off at the detour for Calcehtok.

WHERE TO SLEEP AND EAT In between the village of Calcehtok and the turnoff to the Oxkihtok ruins you'll find paradise; that is, **Paraíso Oxkihtok Cabañas y Restaurantes** (tel. 992/8–21–87). The clean cabins ($7) here have printed curtains and private bath. At the restaurant, order some beers (50¢) or Cokes (25¢) and you'll get all the salbutes and *empanadas* (fried tortillas filled with mashed potatoes) you can eat.

MAYAPÁN

A day trip to Mayapán, about 52 kilometers southeast of Mérida, is a must for every amateur archaeologist. The ruins, dismissed by many as cheap imitations of Chichén Itzá, are nevertheless impressive. Even more astounding is the fact that so few tourists come this way. Mayapán was built during the post-Classic period and inhabited by the Cocam, a tribe of Mexican origin. The Cocam, along with the Xiú of Uxmal and the Itzá of Chichén Itzá, formed a powerful alliance that lasted from about AD 1000 to 1200, when Mayapán broke off and established its hegemony over the already weakened Mayan empire. The city's dominance lasted only a couple of centuries, however—a coup d'état by a noble family ousted the rulers, leading to the city's demise some time before 1450.

The buildings of Mayapán have not fared as well as those of Chichén Itzá, partly due to the poorer quality of the construction. The most interesting building is the **Great Pyramid,** similar to El Castillo at Chichén but without the temple chamber at the summit. The **Temple of Chaac,** next to the pyramid, is a long, low building decorated with carved masks of the rain god. This is also an excellent place to check out colorful birds like the chachalaca, which can be heard from its perch in the surrounding flora. The site's rock-rimmed cenote sustains a bonanza of floral life, including banana trees and a dark-leafed avocado tree. *Admission: $1.25, free Sun. and holidays. Open daily 8–5.*

COMING AND GOING From the station at Calles 50 and 67 in Mérida, hourly buses (1½ hrs, $1 round-trip) travel down Road 18 to Telchaquillo and the Mayapán turnoff. Ask the driver to drop you off at *las ruinas.* Buses from Mayapán back to Mérida are pretty frequent until 5:30 PM; after that it's a long wait for the last bus (8 PM) back. There are no hotels anywhere in the area, so you'll probably have to return to Mérida for the night.

DZIBILCHALTÚN

Dzibilchaltún (pronounced tsee-bil-chal-TOON) is one of the most visited archaeological sites in the region, perhaps because of its proximity to Mérida. As popular as it is, Dzibilchaltún will not impress most visitors. Most of its archaeological riches lie underground, and the two remaining buildings cannot compare with the grandeur of Uxmal and the Puuc Hills or even Mayapán. Still, Dzibilchaltún's location, within a natural park just 20 kilometers (12 mi) north of Mérida, makes it an accessible half-day trip. The site was first inhabited in about 2000 BC, reaching its apogee during the Classic period, from AD 600 to 900, when it became a major ceremonial and residential center. In the late 1500s it was turned into an open chapel and, about 200 years later, a cattle ranch. Remains of all three epochs litter the city "center," giving one the strange feeling of being plopped into a cemetery of forgotten artifacts. At the southern end of a well-maintained 20-meter-wide sacbé is the **Temple of the Seven Dolls,** noteworthy for its structural elegance and for the fact that it is the only known Mayan temple with windows. The temple received its name from the seven clay dolls found under the floor.

Near the ruins is the **Cenote Xlacah,** a natural, fresh-water pool that supplied the population of Dzibilchaltún with drinking water; it now provides visitors with a refreshing dip. It was also used for religious ceremonies, judging from the bones of sacrificial victims found inside. The small **museum** at the entrance to the ruins displays pottery samples found in the cenote, as well as the original seven dolls from the temple. Outside the museum is a modest stela garden with artifacts from several Mayan sites—especially interesting are the *jugadores de pelota* (ball players), with their heavily ornamented sumo-wrestler-like belts. *Admission to ruins and museum: $2.25, free Sun. and holidays. Open daily 8–5; museum closes at 4.*

COMING AND GOING   Buses to Dzibilchaltún (45 min, 50¢) leave Mérida from the station at Parque San Juan every hour. Otherwise, you can catch a bus or combi heading north along Highway 261 to Progreso. These drop you at the turnoff to the ruins, which lie about 6 kilometers down a side road. Hitching is fairly easy, especially during late morning. To return to Mérida or Progreso, flag down a passing bus or combi at the end of the driveway to the ruins (a five-minute walk); they run every 1–2 hours, cost 65¢, and the last one leaves for Mérida at 7 PM. Otherwise, flag down a bus to either Mérida or Progreso from the highway.

THE GULF COAST

If you're in Mérida and you'd like to spend a day or two at the beach, try the Gulf Coast. If you want an aesthetically pleasing beach and you have more time, hop on the next bus to the Caribbean. The Gulf Coast has a look all its own, quite different from the azure perfection of the Caribbean coast. The coast road between Progreso and Dzilam de Bravo passes by savannas and *aguadas* (shallow silted puddles) to one side, and grassy dunes, palm trees, and the dark sea on the other. Birds fly in patterns overhead or float in the waters, seemingly oblivious to the awesome summer storms that occasionally pass through. Modern beach houses here belong to wealthy residents of Mérida, who use them only in July and August. During the rest of the year, you can share miles of white beaches and the sea with a few fishermen. In most of these villages accommodations are limited or nonexistent, but don't despair: If you look respectable enough, it's easy to convince a local family to rent you hammock hooks.

PROGRESO   The largest town on the Gulf Coast is one of those curious hybrids that is increasingly common in Mexico. On the one hand, Progreso is a growing tourist resort, catering mainly to residents of Mérida who make the 32-kilometer (20-mile) pilgrimage to its beaches during the latter half of summer. On the other hand, Progreso maintains a small-town atmosphere, and most locals live their lives independent of the tourists. During the low season (September–June), Progreso is the ideal destination for those looking to enjoy mostly deserted beaches but not yet ready to abandon the comforts of city life. During July and August everything is crowded, so be prepared to have difficulty finding a room (at higher prices), to wait for tables, and to share the beach with countless others. Progreso's beaches are nice enough, although you can walk for hundreds of meters before the water becomes deep enough to cover your belly button, and seaweed can be a nuisance. The town itself is charmless, with cold cement architecture.

➤ **COMING AND GOING** • In Mérida, Progreso buses (1 hr, 50¢) leave every 20 minutes between 6 AM and 9 PM from the station on Calle 62 between Calles 65 and 67. Buses back to Mérida leave the Progreso bus station (Calle 29, btw Calles 80 and 82) every 15 minutes between 5 AM and 9:30 PM; combis (50¢) leave for Mérida every 10 minutes until 9:30

PM from Calle 31, between Calles 78 and 80. Buses for Dzilman de Bravo ($1.25) leave Progreso (Calle 82, btw Calles 29 and 31) at 7 AM and 2 PM.

> **WHERE TO SLEEP** • During the low season, you should have no problem getting a room in one of Progreso's several hotels. Prices fluctuate but never get dirt cheap. Each of the large, sandy rooms at **Playa Linda** (Av. Malecón, at Calle 76, tel. 993/5–14–23) has two double beds and hammock hooks, as well as a small pseudokitchen with a table, chairs, and a burner; those on the second floor have balconies. Rooms cost $16 and can fit up to six people. **Hotel Progreso** (Calle 78, at Calle 29, tel. 993/5–00–39) offers immaculate rooms and the nicest bathrooms in the Yucatán. It's five short blocks from the beach, but the added comfort is worth the walk. Singles are $8, doubles $9.25 ($12 and $13.25 with air-conditioning, respectively). If you're eager to camp, you're not alone; during July and August, the beach in front of the *malecón* (boardwalk) is covered with noisy, beer-toting "campers" doing everything but sleeping. Unfortunately, the less crowded parts of the beach (east or west of the malecón) are not policed and can be dangerous—nighttime robberies are not uncommon.

> **FOOD** • Progreso is a port town surrounded by fishing villages, so it's no surprise that seafood is a staple at the town's restaurants. If cheap food is what you're looking for, head for the **market** (cnr of Calles 27 and 80; open daily 6–6), where you can buy fresh fruits and vegetables or eat in one of the many fondas or loncherías. For fresh bread and drinks, try the supermarkets and bakeries on Calle 27. **Sol y Mar** (Av. Malecón, at Calle 80, tel. 993/5–29–79; open daily 11–8) is a great place to hang out with a beer (80¢) while you munch on free nachos and *botanas* (seafood chip dips). Shrimp dishes, prepared in various styles, are $4–$5. Ceviche costs $2.75.

CELESTÚN On the tip of a narrow strip of land that separates the estuaries of Río Esperanza from the Gulf of Mexico, Celestún is one of the most-visited places around Mérida, and with good reason. Set in the middle of the **Parque Natural Río Celestún,** the town flaunts beaches and large colonies of exotic birds. Star billing goes to the flamingos, thousands of which stand quietly in the waters of the estuary in pink formations. Although it's illegal to approach them closely enough to make them fly, they might give you a show anyway if you wait long enough. To see the flamingos up close, you'll need to rent a boat. Tours leaving from the beach are ridiculously expensive; your best bet is to walk about 1½ kilometers southeast from the zócalo, where you can hire a boat at the dock under the bridge that spans the river. The boat tour lasts about 1½ hours and includes a visit to the flamingos' hangout, an *ojo de agua* (freshwater spring), and the *Isla de los Pájaros* (Bird Island). The boat guides often clap their hands and make a lot of ruckus for your flying flamingo–viewing enjoyment—if you'd prefer to leave the poor birds in peace, let the guide know. The tour costs about $25 and can be divided among up to six people.

The beaches at Celestún are speckled with glittering white shells, and the warm, clear waters make for beautiful swimming, but afternoon winds can kick up clouds of sand. If you can arrange to stay here for the night, be sure not to miss the magnificent sunset over Celestún's calm, misty blue waters. Buses for Celestún leave Mérida almost every hour from the bus station (Calle 71, btw Calles 64 and 66) and cost about $1.50. From Celestún, first-class buses return to Mérida about every two hours, the last one leaving Celestún at 8:30 PM.

> **WHERE TO SLEEP AND EAT** • The few budget accommodations on the beach fill up during July and August and on weekends. **Hotel María del Carmen** (Calle 12, at Calle 15, tel. 993/6–20–51) offers clean new rooms (singles $12, doubles $17.25), all with nice ocean views and some with great sundecks. **Hotel San Julio** (Calle 12 No. 93-A, no phone), also on the beach, has comparable rooms at $6.75 for singles, $8 for doubles, and $9.50 for two beds. Camping is free along the beach, but stay within the town limits or you may have trouble with homeless locals. Free camping on the beach in front of Hotel María del Carmen is allowed. There are plenty of restaurants on the main street between the zócalo and the beach, and on the beach itself. Most serve only seafood, but **Restaurant La Playita** (Calle 12, btw Calles 7 and 9, no phone; open daily 8–8) always has one non-seafood dish for about $2. Fish fillets are about $3.25 and shrimp dishes run $4–$5.

DZILAM DE BRAVO Seventy-five kilometers northeast of Mérida is Dzilám de Bravo, a birdwatcher's paradise. (Unfortunately, sand flies make the beach a sunbather's nightmare.) A thin strip of land just offshore serves as a resting place for birds nesting in the nearby savannas. This "island" is just a five-minute boat ride from shore, and you can get a fisherman to bring you out here for a few dollars. If you're feeling rich or traveling with a fairly large group, consider a day trip to the **Bocas de Dzilám,** a group of freshwater springs flowing from the sea floor about 40 kilometers away; the region around the springs is an avian extravaganza, with colonies of pelicans, albatross, and seagulls. The one-day excursion, including stops at various beaches and islets, costs about $60–$70 for up to six people. To arrange a trip, ask around for Javier "Chacate" Nadal (Calle 11, 2 blocks east of park, tel. 991/5–02–55 ext. 164). Dzilám's sole decent hotel is **Hotel y Restaurant Los Flamencos** (Calle 11 No. 120, btw Calles 22 and 24, no phone), which offers clean, basic rooms, some with great sea views. You can fit up to four people in one room for $6.75, but unfortunately the bathrooms are tiny and lack hot water. The other option is to stay at **Cabañas Totolandia,** on the beach 2 kilometers west of town (toward Progreso). A cabaña with private bath costs $6.75 a night (up to four people). The palapa-cum-restaurant here is only open July and August. **Restaurante El Pescador** (Calle 11, across from the park, no phone; open daily 9:30–6) serves fried fish with salad and tostadas ($2.25) and breaded shrimp ($4.50).

➤ **COMING AND GOING** • From Mérida, take one of the nine daily buses (2 hrs, $1.50) from the Autobuses del Noroeste station (Calle 50, btw Calles 65 and 67). To return to Mérida, catch the bus outside the store at the southern end of the park—the last bus leaves around 5 PM). Two buses also depart from Progreso (2 hrs, $1.25) at 7 AM and 2 PM, traveling along the coastal road to Dzilám. From the park, you can catch a COSTERA bus back to Progreso and Telchac at 9 AM and 4 PM.

IZAMAL

Tourism boosters often point to Izamal, 70 kilometers (43 mi) east of Mérida, as *the* colonial city in the Yucatán. The well-kept buildings around the main plaza do indeed recall the peninsula's colonial past, but most actually weren't built until the 19th century. There isn't really any reason to spend a great deal of time in Izamal, but it breaks up the long bus trip between Mérida and Valladolid or Cancún. Particularly impressive is the **Convento de San Antonio de Padua,** a magnificent example of colonial architecture. Built in 1533 by Franciscan monks, the convent is the largest of its kind in the Yucatán and looms above the surrounding buildings. The bright yellow convent complex is built on the ancient ruins of the Mayan temple Popol-Chac and contains a church, a chapel, a sacristy, and an 80-square-meter grassy atrium surrounded by arched galleries. *Admission free. Open daily 6 AM–8 PM. Mass held daily at 6:30 AM and 7:30 PM.*

Two blocks north of the main plaza are the remains of the **Pyramid of Kinichkakmo,** whose summit is the highest point for miles around. The large pyramid and four other scarcely discernible structures are all that remain of the ancient Maya city of Itzamal, founded in AD 500 and named after the great Maya sun god Itzamná. The site has deteriorated but remains interesting both for its proximity to the colonial city and the fact that it is of pure Maya design, free of Toltec or Aztec influence. *From main plaza, follow Calle 28 north past the park to where it runs into Calle 27. Admission free. Open daily 8–5.*

COMING AND GOING Buses for Izamal (15 per day, 2 hrs, $1.50) leave Mérida from the station on Calle 50 (btw Calles 65 and 67). You can also catch a bus here from Valladolid (2 per day, 2 hrs, $2). The best way to see Izamal is en route from one city to another, since you can see everything in an hour or two and be on the next bus out of town. To do so, take an early bus to Izamal and ask permission to store your luggage at the station, or ask any local policeman if he will store your luggage at the police station. To reach Chichén Itzá from Izamal, take a bus from in front of Restaurant Wayné Né (Calle 33, at Calle 30) to Kantunil (45 min, $1). Buses for Kantunil leave about every two hours, with the last bus leaving at 5 PM. Wait in Kantunil for the next bus to Valladolid, and tell the driver to let you off in Chichén Itzá (45 min, 75¢).

WHERE TO SLEEP AND EAT Izamal is ill-prepared for visitors: Rooms in the two hotels here are small, dark, and bug-infested. The nicer of the two, **Hotel Canto** (Calle 31 No. 303 across from Plaza 5 de Mayo, no phone) has a pleasant courtyard and rooms (singles and doubles $4, triples and quads $5.50) that look like jail cells. If you're determined to enjoy the lux uries of hot water, air-conditioning, and spotless bedcovers, try finding **Naifa,** who rents six *apartamentos* (two-room flats) for $10 each. Naifa can usually be reached at her liquor store (Calle 28, across from movie theater, tel. 995/4–00–59) until 7 PM; afterward, try her at home (Calle 29 No. 300, btw Calles 28 and 30). Restaurants and loncherías are plentiful around the zócalo, and the market in front of the convent is also a good place to forage for cheap nourishment. **Restaurant Wayné Né** (Calle 33, at Calle 30, no phone; open Wed.–Sun. 9–9) serves pollo pibil ($2.50) and enchiladas de mole for $2. Fresh juices are 40¢–55¢. If you just want a snack, sit on the patio under the golden arches of **Restaurante Los Portales** (Calle 30, next to the market, no phone; open daily 7 AM–10 PM) and nibble on crunchy chicken tacos with slices of fresh avocado (20¢ each) or arroz con pollo for $1.50.

Chichén Itzá

Chichén Itzá is probably the most complex and interesting archaeological site on the peninsula, and also the most crowded. Located only 120 kilometers (74 mi) east of Mérida and 157 kilometers (97 mi) southwest of Cancún, Chichén can be hurriedly explored on a day trip from either town. A better idea, though, is to stay in the nearby village of Pisté, or even in Valladolid, and save yourself the two- or three-hour bus ride to the ruins. Another advantage of staying nearby is that you can avoid the crowds. Around midday literally scores of tour buses arrive, and the mass of humanity completely changes the feel of the place. It's much better to arrive early in the morning, when relatively few people are around and the sun isn't as intense.

Chichén Itzá is Mayan for "opening of the wells," a reference to the area's cenotes, around which the Maya first settled. Humans built this site into a major metropolis around AD 520, centuries before Mayan tribes emigrated from northern Guatemala. The new occupants modified many of the existing buildings, creating an eclectic architecture. For this reason, visiting Chichén is like being at several sites at one time, and trying to make sense of everything can be exhausting. Those who have been to Uxmal (and other Puuc and Chenes ruins) will notice similarities between the buildings there and the ones clustered around the observatory here—both include *choza* (thatched-roof hut) motifs, Chaac masks, and elaborate latticework on the upper facades. Added features—such as columns and carvings of serpents, jaguars, and eagles—are typical of a later Toltec-Maya style. The buildings surrounding **El Castillo,** the great pyramid of Kukulcan, were constructed from scratch by the Toltec-Maya and have a more definitive style, with exquisite stone carvings glorifying human sacrifice, and images of the messenger god Chac Mool, whose semirecumbent figure waits everywhere, ready to receive offerings from the high priests.

Visitors to Chichén Itzá and other popular ruins are often grossly misinformed by overly creative guides who try to titillate rather than inform. To avoid this problem, explain that you're interested in facts and theories about the ruins, not in graphically related stories. At Chichén, Eddy Garrido and Victor Olalde are two reliable guides who speak Spanish, English, and French.

COMING AND GOING

First- and second-class buses leave Mérida (2½ hrs, $2.50), Cancún (3 hrs, $4), and Valladolid (40 min, $1) on the hour for Chichén Itzá; there are also three daily buses from Playa del Carmen (5½ hrs, $6). Hourly second-class service returning to Valladolid and Cancún ends at 8 PM (9 PM to Mérida). Most buses stop at the ruins, the bus station (about 700 meters from the zócalo) in the nearby village of Pisté, and in downtown Pisté. If you have luggage in the storage compartment, you'll have to get off at the bus station. Most restaurants, hotels, and handicraft stores line Calle 15, the road leading from Pisté's zócalo to the ruins. You can walk between the two easily (it's only 2½ kilometers), or take a taxi for about $1.

WHERE TO SLEEP

Accommodations and food near Chichén Itzá are geared toward wealthy tourists; budget travelers will do much better in the small village of Pisté, a few kilometers to the west. Pisté is a

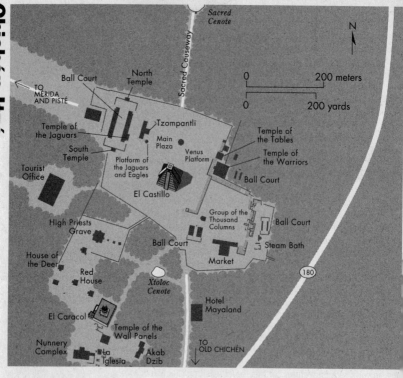

characterless town, but it's cheap. Campers can pitch a tent at the **Stardust Hotel RV Park** (Calle 15, next to bus station, tel. 985/1-01-22) for $3.25 per person or string a hammock on a tree in the park for the same price. If you're with a group of three or four people, a cheaper option is to get a room at the **Posada Novelo** annex of the Stardust Hotel, where $10 will get you two double beds and a clean bathroom with hot water. The annex has nine rooms, all with private bath. Either way, you get access to the hotel pool. During the fall and spring equinoxes (Sept. 20, 21 and Mar. 20, 21), be prepared to settle for any amount of square footage you can get; even the most rundown fleabags are packed, and sleeping next to a stranger on the floor of a private kitchen is not a rarity.

Posada Chac Mool. The cold cement platform beds and rough stucco walls of these rooms are softened a little by red tile floors and built-in shelves. Rooms include hammock hooks and a very clean bathroom with hot water. Singles cost $12, doubles $14. *Calle 15, no phone. A short walk toward town from Pisté bus station. 9 rooms, all with bath. Kitchen, laundry, luggage storage. Wheelchair access.*

Posada Olalde. Located down a side street from Pisté's main strip, this family-owned hotel offers quiet, cozy rooms with wood furniture and a little bit of charm. The bathrooms are immaculate, and you even get hot water. Singles cost $10.50, doubles $16, triples $18.50. *Calle 6 No. 49, no phone. From bus station, walk toward town, left at El Carrousel restaurant, continue down dirt road 150 meters. 6 rooms, all with bath. Kitchen, laundry sink, luggage storage. Wheelchair access.*

FOOD

Eating in Pisté is affordable as long as you avoid tourist-oriented restaurants. For drinks and snacks, head to the small stores along Calle 15, just east of Pisté's zócalo. **El Alba** and **La Lid**

(Calle 15, west of El Caroussel Restaurant; open daily 6:30 AM–10:30 PM) are convenience stores where you can buy fresh bread. The **market,** open each morning, is just east of downtown Pisté. In front of the plaza are three loncherías, where you can get tortas for 50¢, salbutes and panuchos for 25¢ each, and main dishes for $2.

Restaurant El Parador Maya. At this small, family-owned restaurant, Mama serves up daily specials, while neighbors drop in for cervezas (75¢). Poc chuc and pollo pibil cost $3.75; an order of salbutes or a quesadilla is only $1.25. This is also a good place for breakfast—try the veggie-packed huevos rancheros ($2). El Parador is only open when there are customers—just knock if the door isn't open between 7 AM and 11 PM, or inquire across the street at Posada Maya. *Calle 15, 2 blocks east of zócalo, no phone.*

Restaurant Los Pájaros. This restaurant seems to be popular among baby lizards waiting out the rain under the festive thatch roof. Sandwiches and veggie soup are both $1.25. If you're up for something more substantial, try the delicious poc chuc for $2.75. Beers are $1. *Calle 15, 2 doors west and across street from El Carrousel, no phone. Open daily 8:30 AM–10 PM.*

Restaurant Sayil. This tiny restaurant is about as close as you'll get to sitting in someone's kitchen. Flowered tablecloths cover three long tables overlooked by a small ceramic Virgin Mary. A dejected-looking chalkboard displays a limited menu, but they'll usually make a vegetarian dish to order. Main dishes (poc chuc, pollo pibil, beef filete) go for $1.75; for the same price you get an endless pile of rice, beans, and tortillas. *Calle 15 No. 57, west of bus station, no phone. Open daily 7 AM–10 PM.*

WORTH SEEING

Exploring Chichén Itzá can take a whole day—two if you're moving at a leisurely pace. The ruins can be divided geographically into three groups: **North Group** (El Castillo and surrounding ruins), **South Group,** and **Chichén Viejo.** If you want to visit the less-frequented ruins far into Chichén Viejo, speak with a tour guide or try to get a park caretaker employed by the federal government to take you for free (or a small tip). The caretakers are identifiable by shirts or caps bearing the letters INAH and their walkie-talkies. Guided tours of the main ruins in Spanish, French, German, or English are available: Make sure your guide is certified. Tours last about two hours and cost $26 for up to six people. Around noon, it's not too hard to tag along with one of the many tour groups. Every night an overwrought sound and light show is put on between the ball court and the Castillo, offering an entertaining, easy-to-swallow overview of the ancient city's history and the fall of the Mayan empire. The show in Spanish at 8 PM costs $3.50; the English one at 9 PM costs $4.75. Chichén has bathrooms, as well as an expensive refreshment stand serving cold drinks and snacks, but bring plenty of water—it's a large site. *Admission: $4, free Sun. and holidays. Parking: $3.50. Open daily 8–5.*

NORTH GROUP The first building you see when you enter Chichén is the awe-inspiring **El Castillo.** Ninety-one steps up is a temple to Kukulcan, the feathered serpent deity. By the base of one balustrade is the carved head of a giant serpent; at the spring and fall equinoxes, the afternoon light hitting the balustrade forms a shadow that resembles the slithering form of Kukulcan descending the pyramid toward the Sacred Cenote. This kind of symbolism abounds in El Castillo—the four stairways face the cardinal directions and the steps total 365, the number of days in the year. Fifty-two panels on the sides stand for the 52 years in the secular Maya calendar, and the 18 terraces symbolize the 18 months in the Maya year.

The **Temple of the Jaguars,** appended to the eastern side of the ball court, stands northwest of El Castillo. The columns that support the lower enclosure are thought to depict the cosmogony, or creation of the world and all of its beings—from plants, fish, and fowl to serpents and men—springing from the

Although not as well known as the male gods, there are some female deities in the Mayan religion. Ix Chel (pronounced Eesh-chel) is the goddess of fertility and childbirth. Midwives are human representations of Ix Chel. On the dark side, there is Ix Tap, the goddess of suicide, who is depicted with a noose wrapped around her neck.

head of a god. Inside the enclosure, a detailed mural of a village scene depicts soldiers and townspeople.

The **Ball Court** is similar to others found at ancient centers in Mexico, but this one is bigger and more elaborate. The long, rectangular stadium features two stone circles embedded high in the walls, into which players tried to shoot a large, rubbery ball using their hips, elbows, and knees. On either side of the ball court are two small temples decorated with images of warriors and Kukulcan. From the north temple you can clearly hear the voice of anyone in the south temple—the sound travels along the walls of the court.

Tzompantli means "place of the skulls" in Toltec, and the T-shape platform is indeed decorated with the carved images of hundreds of human skulls. Tribes from the west used to display the fleshless skulls of defeated captains stacked one on top of the other on stakes, and some think that the Maya-Toltecs used this platform for similar purposes.

Immediately southeast of the Tzompantli is **The Platform of Jaguars and Eagles,** a small rectangular structure with a staircase on each side. Supposedly both the eagles and jaguars carved here represent the kings or captains of certain tribes. Scroll-like designs coming out of their mouths suggest that they may be discussing the plight of the sacrificial victims whose hearts they clutch.

Many sacrifices took place at the **Sacred Cenote,** a well about 1 kilometer from the main ceremonial area. The cenote was considered to be the dwelling place of Chaac, the rain god. It was once believed that young virgins were hurled into these waters as a plea for rain, but diving archaeologists have since discovered skeletons belonging to individuals of all ages. The slippery walls were impossible to climb, and most sacrificial victims could not swim well enough to survive until noon, when the survivors were supposedly fished out to relate the stories of what they had learned from the spirits in the water. Thousands of gold and jade artifacts, highly precious to the Maya, have also been found in the murky depths of the cenote, which undoubtedly holds more treasures. First explored by Edward Thompson in 1903, the Sacred Cenote was excavated twice in the course of the next 60 years, both times resulting in the salvaging of scores of valuable pieces of jewelry and artifacts. During the second diving, a special chemical was used to make the water clearer, enabling divers to dredge up more than twice what had been previously found, but in the process the chemical also killed off most of the cenote's marine life.

Carved warriors adorning the rectangular columns in front of the **Temple of the Warriors** stand in perfect file guarding the staircase. The upper facade of the temple features gruesome masks of Chaac, as well as an eagle with a serpent head projecting itself fearsomely out of the stone surface. A closer look reveals the head of a human being emerging from the serpent's mouth. Just southwest of the temple, you'll notice the **Group of a Thousand Columns,** a large plaza surrounded by intricately carved columns that probably supported arches and a roof. Nobody knows the plaza's original purpose.

There is no evidence to suggest that the **Market,** just south of the Group of a Thousand Columns, was actually used for selling, but some have speculated that the columns supported a palapa-style roof under which vendors sold their merchandise. In Chichén's **steam bath,** right next to the market, you can still see the stone benches on which bathers waited their turn. A tiny doorway leads to a room containing two benches and a hearth where stones were heated then sprinkled with water to produce steam. Steam baths were popular for health and purification all over pre-Columbian Mesoamerica.

SOUTH GROUP Following the road southwest of El Castillo you'll reach the **High Priest's Grave,** with its succession of underground chambers. As is typical with Mayan sites, most of which are randomly named, no priest was found buried here. Most likely, Edward Thompson (the first explorer of the area) said this was a High Priest's grave so he could get funding to excavate. Farther along the road past the High Priest's Grave is the small **House of the Deer,** a Puuc-style building from the late Classic period. The house owes its name to the mural of a deer that once decorated a wall. Next door is a similar building known as the **Red House,** after the remnants of red paint inside. The building is pure Puuc style, and hieroglyphs on its frieze date to AD 870.

El Caracol, also called The Observatory, is the second most famous building in Chichén Itzá, after El Castillo. It was enlarged and renovated several times, making it a truly weird hybrid of shape and style. Astronomers probably used this building to observe the motion of the sun and stars in order to plan festivals, ceremonies, planting cycles, and other important events. A spiral staircase (hence the name, which is Spanish for "snail" or a "conch") leads to a small observation chamber. Square windows or slits are oriented toward key astronomical points. Southeast of the Caracol is **Akab-Dzib,** a 9th-century building. Akab-Dzib means "obscure writing" in Mayan, and if you look at the lintel of the southern doorway you'll notice a carving of a priest sitting on a throne surrounded by hieroglyphics.

La Iglesia stands behind the less interesting **Temple of the Wall Panels,** just southeast of El Caracol. It is a beautiful example of Puuc architecture, adorned with masks of Chaac and other geometrical motifs. In between the masks are animal gods—a bee, snail, turtle, and armadillo—which represent the four Bacabes, the beings that hold up the heavens. Next door to La Iglesia is the **Nunnery Complex,** a strange cluster of buildings named by Spaniards who thought it resembled a European convent (it was probably a palace). Chenes designs adorn the east building, whose doorway is the gaping mouth of Chaac. The form of the central building, with its classic corbeled arches, seems to suffer a bit from several additions.

CHICHÉN VIEJO Two kilometers down a path from the Nunnery Complex is group of poorly preserved ruins known as the **date group.** Here, two Atlantes (godlike figures who supposedly balance the weight of the world above their large heads) stand atop a black block carved with Mayan dates and hieroglyphs dating back to AD 879. If you're tired of dodging video cameras and potbellied tourists in order to get a glimpse of the ruins, try heading down the path to a barely excavated group of ruins about a kilometer from Chichén's more popular sites. Among the rubble lies what is thought to be a ceremonial center. The **Temple of the Phallic Symbols,** displaying early Maya triangular arches and the only examples of Toltec-influenced columns, was supposedly the place where virgins came to "know" a man's body. Indeed, numerous phallic reliefs jut out from the temple's walls. About 20 minutes farther into the jungle is another group of ruins, most badly decayed, with the exception of the **Temple of the Three Lintels,** a beautiful Puuc-style building similar to the buildings at Uxmal. The three-roomed building was supposedly used by healers, who brought the ailing here to be cured. Unless you're a real bushwhacker, it is *not* recommended that you go any farther than the date group on your own. Instead, strike up a deal with an official guide. Groups of four or five may end up paying $10–$15 each for the excursion. If you ask nicely, you can probably get a Park Custodian (*see* Worth Seeing, *above*) to take you on a quick jaunt to the depths of Old Chichén. Try to go in the morning, as the afternoon often brings rain, animals, and *lots* of mosquitos.

Near Chichén Itzá

BALANKANCHÉ CAVES

A mere 6 kilometers from Chichén Itzá are the immense Balankanché caves, thought to have been a Mayan ceremonial center in the 10th and 11th centuries. In 1959 a local tour guide tumbled upon the stalactite-filled caves and discovered a number of ceramic and carved artifacts inside. The images engraved on some of the artifacts are thought to represent Tlaloc, the Toltec god of rain. Although the cave's length and size are impressive, and the bulbous, petrified stalactites are fascinating to observe at eye-level, a visit to the caves is only recommended if you're not heading on to the more impressive caves of Loltún. The caves are open daily 9–; tours accompanied by audio-cassettes, which tell an indiscernible story in Spanish, English and French, supposedly leave every hour but are canceled unless at least two participants show up. You might as well give up trying to listen to the tape—the small museum by the entrance to the caves is much more informative. To reach Balankanché, take any second-class bus between Chichén Itzá and Valladolid, and ask the driver to drop you "*en las grutas.*" From the road it's a couple hundred yards to the caves. On the way back, flag down a bus on the road. Admission, including the mandatory audio tour, is $3 ($1.50 on Sunday).

Valladolid

Much slower-paced than Mérida or Cancún, Valladolid (which lies smack-dab between the two) is also less frequented by crowds of picture-snapping tourists. Behind this calm exterior lies a history of conflict, dating back to Valladolid's origins as the Maya ceremonial site of Zací. In 1543 the indomitable Maya drove off Spanish conquistador Francisco de Montejo, but Montejo's son, Montejo the Younger, succeeded where his father failed. He laid out Valladolid in the classic Spanish colonial style and built six churches. The Maya, who had been banned from the city, constantly raided Valladolid, sending many a Mexican fleeing back to Mérida.

Each year beginning January 22 and ending February 3, Valladolid celebrates La Fiesta de la Candelaria in honor of the Virgin of the Candelaria, the city's patron saint. This religious and cultural celebration features parades, masses, corridas (bullfights), food, and artesanía.

This colonial past provides a slightly dilapidated architectural framework for what is today a well-traversed commercial center, with people coming from miles around to sell their wares at the local market (Calles 37 and 34). Aside from the breathtaking nearby Cenote Dzitnup, there isn't much to see in Valladolid, but the town is a convenient base from which to explore Chichén Itzá. It also breaks up the six-hour bus ride from Mérida to Cancún.

BASICS

CASAS DE CAMBIO Bancomer (Calle 40, facing the zócalo, tel. 985/6–21–50) is open for currency exchange weekdays 9–2. The ATM accepts Visa.

EMERGENCIES You can call the **police** (Calle 41 No. 156-A, btw Calles 20 and 22, tel. 985/6–21–00) or an **ambulance** (tel. 985/6–24–13) round the clock.

MEDICAL AID For 24-hour medical needs, try **Farmacia El Descuento** (cnr of Calles 39 and 42, across from zócalo, no phone) or **Clínica Santa Anita** (Calle 40 No. 221, at Calle 47, tel. 985/6–28–11).

PHONES AND MAIL The **post office** (Calle 40, facing the zócalo, tel. 985/6–26–23) is open weekdays 8–3. They'll hold mail sent to you at the following address for up to 10 days: Lista de Correos, Valladolid, Yucatán, CP 97780, México. Card- and coin-operated phones are located just outside the bus terminal and near the zócalo. For privacy and air-conditioning, try the **Computel,** next door to Hotel San Clemente (Calle 42, at Calle 41, tel. and fax 985/6–39–77), open daily 7 AM–10 PM.

VISITOR INFORMATION A sporadically attended *módulo de turismo* (tourist info booth) is located just inside the doors of the *ayuntamiento* (city hall; SE cnr of zócalo), open Monday–Saturday 9–2 and 5–7. The English spoken here is shaky, but you can get free maps and copies of *Yucatán Today.* For more info on local fiestas, tours, and historical sites, call Emma Montes at **Hotel Mesón del Marqués** (tel. 985/6–20–73).

COMING AND GOING

Valladolid's geography is user friendly, and everything is within walking distance. Like many other Yucatecan cities, the streets here are numbered, with even-numbered calles running north–south, and odd-numbered calles running east–west. The zócalo is bordered by Calles 39, 40, 41, and 42.

Valladolid is a major crossroads for buses headed almost anywhere on the peninsula. Small and clean, the terminal is open 24 hours but is located six long blocks from downtown and can get fairly lonely at night. **Autobuses del Norte** and **Autobuses del Centro del Estado de Yucatán** share the same terminal (Calle 37, at Calle 54, tel. 985/6–34–49). All buses listed below are second class. Buses run to Cancún (3 hrs, $3.25) hourly 7 AM–8 PM and to Mérida (3 hrs, $3.25) hourly 6 AM–8 PM. There is also service to Cobá (2½ hrs, $2.50), Tulum (3 hrs, $3.50), Playa del Carmen (5 hrs, $4.75), and Tizimín (hourly, 1 hr, $1). Two buses leave for Izamal (1½ hrs, $2), and all of the Mérida-bound buses stop there, too. To reach Isla Holbox (*see* Near Cancún, *above*), take the 3 AM bus to the ferry port at Chiquilá (2½ hrs, $3.25).

WHERE TO SLEEP

The few budget hotels in Valladolid are conveniently located between the bus station and the zócalo. Nearest to the bus station, **Hotel Maya** (Calle 41 No. 231, btw Calles 48 and 50, tel. 985/6–20–69) is clean and quiet and has an inner patio blossoming with exotic flowers and palms. Singles and doubles with private bath and hot water go for $6, $11 with air-conditioning. **Hotel Lily** (Calle 44 No. 192, btw Calles 37 and 39, tel. 985/6–21–63) has singles with rather grimy shared baths for a mere $3.25, doubles $4.75 (private baths are $2 extra). Hot water here is sporadic and cockroaches are frequent, but the vigorous fan will send your clothes flying. **Hotel Zací** (Calle 44 No. 191, btw Calles 37 and 39, tel. 985/6–21–67) borders on deluxe. Hot water streams out of the showers (complete with shower curtain), and the hotel pool is big and clean enough to swim laps in. Singles are $9.50, doubles $12. Rooms with air-conditioning are $2 more, and all have cable TV.

FOOD

Valladolid's restaurants don't offer the variety that Mérida does, but you can still sample Yucatecan food at reasonable prices. The local hangout is **El Bazar** (Calle 39, at Calle 40, NE cnr of zócalo; open daily 8 AM–midnight), a plaza shared by many small *comedores* (sit-down food stands). Great comidas corridas with soup, a meat dish, tortillas, and a drink will run you about $3.25. Tacos and panuchos are readily available for about 40¢ each. **Restaurant del Parque** (Calle 42, at Calle 41, tel. 985/6–23–65) is open daily 7 AM–11 PM. Try the *pollo a la yucateca* (chicken baked in a tasty red sauce served with potatoes, rice, and beans) or the mushroom cream soup ($1.25). At **El Jacal de los Dzeles** (Calle 40 No. 211, btw Calles 41 and 43; open daily 11:30–9), small groups of tired-looking men sit around drinking beer (50¢) and eating large plates of beef filetes ($2.50). A heaping pile of beans, rice, and tortillas goes for $1.50. If you're just looking to soothe your sweet tooth, try the corn ice cream (65¢ a cone) at **Paletería La Flor de Michoacán** (Calle 41, btw Calles 42 and 44, no phone; open daily 11:30 AM–9 PM).

WORTH SEEING

CHURCHES Valladolid's churches are more impressive from the exterior, since interiors were looted during the Caste War. Nonetheless, for anyone interested in colonial architecture or exploring old buildings, the complex containing **Iglesia de San Bernardino de Siena** and the **Convento de Sisal** (Calle 41-A, at Calle 49) are definitely worth a visit. Currently the local priest's residence, the buildings are flanked on one side by an overgrown garden containing a grill-covered cenote. To enter the garden, you must ask permission from the priest or his secretary. Their office is across the driveway from the garden. *From zócalo, walk west on Calle 41 until intersection of Calles 41 and 46; from here, take diagonal road (Calle 41-A) SW 4 blocks. Admission free. Church open Tues.–Sun. 8–noon and 5–8.*

CENOTES Within walking distance of anywhere in town, the **Cenote Zací** (Calle 36, btw Calles 37 and 39; open for swimming daily 8–6) is well worth a visit on a hot afternoon. Though it glows an eerie green, the water is cool and fresh. Admission (50¢) includes access to the cenote and a museum (complete with historical photographs of Valladolid) and a peek at a few cooped-up animals in a haphazardly organized zoo. Much more beautiful, though not as convenient as Cenote Zací, **Cenote Dzitnup** will enlighten you as to why the Maya regarded these pools as sacred. If you haven't been paralyzed by awe, have a swim with the small catfish in the brilliant blue water. If you arrive early, enjoy the magic of having the place to yourself. Don't let the rain dissuade you from coming—it's underground. Admission is 75¢, and it's open daily 7–5 (there are also changing rooms and a shower). There's no place to rent snorkeling gear in Dzitnup or Valladolid, but don't worry—the most breathtaking scenery is above the water. To reach Cenote Dzitnup from Valladolid, take a combi from Hotel María

Guadalupe (Calle 44, btw Calles 39 and 41), which will let you off right at the cenote. You shouldn't pay more than 65¢ per person for the ride. Ask the driver when he is taking passengers back to Valladolid. You can also take a westbound bus on the highway, ask to be let off at the crossroads for the cenote, and walk 2 kilometers. Yet another option is to rent a bicycle for 50¢ an hour from Antonio "Negro" Águilar, whose shop (Calle 44, btw Calles 39 and 41) is open 6 AM–7 PM daily. The cenote is only about 6 kilometers from Valladolid.

Near Valladolid

RÍO LAGARTOS

The creatures that gave "Alligator River" its name have long since been sacrificed to fashion—flamingos steal the show here now. The people of this small fishing village, 103 kilometers (64 mi) north of Valladolid, are especially friendly and appreciate the peace and tranquility of their home. You won't find much in the way of nightlife here, but Río Lagartos outdoes itself during the **festival of Apostle Santiago** (July 20–26), with folk dances, bullfights, and processions. On the first of June, all the boats parade in the lagoon in celebration of **Día de Marina.**

Río Lagartos is a bird-watcher's heaven. Pelicans stand by the side of the road like old men, looking as if they'd strike up a conversation at any moment. You're also likely to see snowy egrets, red egrets, snowy white ibis, and great white herons, among other winged creatures. Flamingos supposedly inhabit the area throughout the year, but May through August is the time to catch them en masse. March and April, they're busy laying eggs, and nesting sites are a three- to four-hour boat ride away. Laws prohibit approaching the nesting areas too closely, for fear the birds will suddenly take flight and disturb the eggs. Arrangements for a boat trip to the flamingos' favorite hangout can be made with any of the motorboat owners along the malecón (usually about $32 for the three-hour trip). If you're traveling alone or in a pair, talk to Diego at *Restaurant Isla Contoy* (*see below*), who might be able to hook you up with some other visitors to cut costs. You can also take a shortened ride to see the flamingos (which doesn't include the mangroves, salt flats, or their nesting sites) with an added stop at the beach for about $15 (this can be split among a group). If you're only interested in swimming, paddle around in the gulf off the Río Lagartos Peninsula, or get a boat to take you across to the beach for about $5. **Chiquilá,** a natural *ojo de agua dulce* (freshwater pool) is 1 kilometer east of town (walk along the eastern shore from the malecón).

COMING AND GOING The 2½-hour excursion from Valladolid could be staged as a day trip if you live by a rigid itinerary. Otherwise, plan to spend at least one night. Buses leave Valladolid hourly for Tizimín (1 hr, $1) until 5 PM; combis to Tizimín ($1.25) leave Valladolid from in front of the liquor store (Calle 40, at Calle 37). From Tizimín, you'll have to transfer to a second-class bus to Río Lagartos (8 per day, 1 hr, $1), which leaves roughly every two hours between 5:15 AM and 7 PM. The last bus back to Tizimín leaves at 5:30 PM.

WHERE TO SLEEP AND EAT The only formal lodging in town, **Cabañas Los Dos Hermanos** (Calle 19, 50 meters from bus station, tel. 985/3–26–68 ext. 192) rents four cabins, all with private bath (cold water only), a large bed, and hammock hooks. The two less expensive cabins cost $9.25. The other two cabins, complete with mosquito netting and cable TV, cost $11. More than four people in the cabin might jack the price up to $13.50. If the cabins are full, you can ask around to see if someone in town has an extra room, or you can ask to hang a hammock at Restaurant Isla Contoy. If you're a beach lover, don't bother with the hotels—camp on the vast and unpeopled beaches along the gulf. Bring all the supplies you'll need, including antimosquito paraphernalia. Bargain with a fisherman to take you across the lagoon to the gulf—you should be able to get him down to $4 or $5.

Restaurant Los Negritos (2 blocks from bus station, no phone) serves fried manta ray in tomato sauce for $3.75, as well as a tasty fish soup for $2. They also serve egg breakfasts ($1.75). The kitchen is open daily 9–7; at 10 on Saturday nights Los Negritos becomes a disco. **Restaurant Isla Contoy** (Calle 19, no phone; open daily 7:30 AM–10 PM) is owned by a friendly family. Generous ceviches go for $2, and their fish fillets ($3.50) make a plentiful meal.

Spanish Glossary

In Spanish, what you see is what you get: Every letter is pronounced and the accent usually falls on the second-to-last syllable, unless there is an accent mark. Of course, there are exceptions to both rules. And, to confound matters, you'd be hard pressed to find a Mexican who actually pronounces everything clearly. Still, if you learn a few rules, you should be able to pronounce almost any Spanish word; figuring out what it means may take a little more effort. The following letters are pronounced as follows:

a like the **a** in ah
i like the **ee** in beet
u like the **oo** in loot
ñ like the **ni** in senior

e like the **e** in deck
o like the **o** in cold
y like the **ea** in eat
ll like the **y** in kayak

The **h** is silent in Spanish, and the Spanish **j** is pronounced like the **h** in horse. **G** before **a, o, u,** or a consonant is hard (like in gate); when before **e** or **i**, it's soft, sounding just slightly harder than the **h** in hay. However, when **g** is paired with **u** (**gu**), the **u** sounds like the English **w**. For all practical purposes, **b** and **v** sound the same—roughly like a **b** in English. **C** before **a, o,** and **u** is hard like the English **k**; before **e** and **i** it's soft like the English **s**.

English	Spanish
Basics	
Yes/no	Sí/no
Hello/goodbye	Hola/adiós
Good morning	Buenos días
Good afternoon	Buenas tardes
Good night	Buenas noches
How are you?	¿Cómo está?
I'm fine, thanks	Estoy bien, gracias
Pardon me	Perdóneme
Excuse me	Con permiso
What's your name?	¿Cómo se llama?
My name is. . .	Me llamo. . .
I'm from the United States	Soy estadounidense
I'm Australian	Soy australiano(a)
I'm Canadian	Soy canadiense
I'm English	Soy inglés(a)
I'm Scottish	Soy escocés(a)
Kiss me, I'm Irish	Bésame, soy irlandés
Do you speak English?	¿Habla inglés?
I don't speak Spanish	No hablo español
I don't understand	No entiendo
How do you say. . .	¿Cómo se dice. . . ?
More slowly, please	Más despacio, por favor
Could you please repeat that?	¿Podría repetir, por favor?
I don't know	No sé
Please	Por favor
Thank you	Gracias
You're welcome	De nada
Where is (are). . . ?	¿Dónde está(n). . . ?
Are there. . . ?	¿Hay. . . ?

Bathroom	Baño, sanitario
Backpack	Mochila
Post office	Oficina de correos
Long-distance telephone office	Caseta de larga distancia
Collect call	Llamada al cobrar
Laundromat	Lavandería
Bank/money exchange place	Banco/casa de cambio
Open	Abierto(a)
Closed	Cerrado(a)
Yesterday	Ayer
Today	Hoy
Tomorrow	Mañana
This morning	Esta mañana
This evening	Esta tarde
Tonight	Esta noche
What time is it?	¿Qué hora es?
Entrance	Entrada
Exit	Salida
Floor/story	Piso
Neighborhood	Colonia/barrio
How much is this/it?	¿Cuánto es?
Cheap	Barato
Expensive	Caro

Emergencies and Medical Aid

Help!	¡Socorro!
Leave me alone!	¡Déjame en paz!
Call the police	Llame la policía
Call a doctor	Llame un médico
Hospital	Hospital
I'm sick	Estoy enfermo(a)
I need a doctor	Necesito un médico
I have a headache	Me duele la cabeza
I have a stomachache	Me duele el estómago
Fever	Fiebre
Prescription	Receta
Medicine	Remedio
Aspirin	Aspirina
Condom	Preservativo
AIDS	SIDA

Coming and Going

Right	Derecha
Left	Izquierda
Straight	Derecho/recto
On foot	A pie
Hitchhike	Hacer dedo
Ride	Aventón
Ticket window	Taquilla
A ticket for. . .	Un boleto para. . .
One-way	Ida
Round-trip	Ida y vuelta
First/second class	Primera/segunda clase
Where are you going?	¿A dónde va?
How many kilometers?	¿Cuántos kilometros?
How long is the trip?	¿Cuánto tiempo dura el viaje?

I'm going to. . .	Me voy a. . .
I want to get off at. . .	Quiero bajar en. . .
Map	Mapa
Arrival	Llegada
Departure	Salida
Airport	Aeropuerto
Train station	Estación de ferrocarril
Bus	Autobús/camión
Bus station	Terminal de autobuses
Bus stop	Parada
Car	Carro
I'd like to rent a car	Me gustaría alquilar un carro
Insurance	Seguros
Gas	Gasolina
Tire	Llanta
Stoplight	Semáforo
Motorcycle	Motocicleta
Highway	Carretera
The road to. . .	El camino a. . .
Bridge	Puente
Metro stop	Estación de Metro
Fare	Tarifa
To cross	Cruzar
Bicycle	Bicicleta

Where to Sleep

Guest house	Casa de huéspedes
Key	Llave
Manager	Gerente
Room	Habitación/cuarto
For two people	Para dos personas
With/without	Con/sin
Shower	Ducha
Hot/cold water	Agua caliente/fría
Fan	Ventilador
Air-conditioning	Aire acondicionado
Double bed	Cama matrimonial
Sheets	Sábanas
Toilet paper	Papel de baño/papel higiénico
Included	Incluido
Camping	Campground
Hammock	Hamaca
I would like to make a reservation	Me gustaría hacer una reservación
Is there a private bathroom?	¿Hay un baño privado?
Can I leave my bags here?	¿Puedo dejar mi equipaje aquí?

Food

Food	Comida
Bakery	Panadería
Supermarket	Supermercado
Groceries	Abarrotes
I'm hungry/thirsty	Tengo hambre/sed
I'm a vegetarian	Soy vegetariano(a)
I'm diabetic	Soy diabético(a)
Waiter/waitress	Mesero(a)
Breakfast	Desayuno

Lunch	Almuerzo
Dinner	Cena
Daily special	Menú del día
Preprepared lunch special	Comida corrida
Bill/check	Cuenta
(Wheat) bread	Pan (integral)
Toast	Pan tostado
(Purified) water	Agua (purificada)
Ice	Hielo
Cocktail	Trago
Tea/coffee	Té/café
Soda	Refresco
Milk	Leche
Juice	Jugo
Vegetables	Verduras
Fruit	Fruta
Apple	Manzana
Orange	Naranja
Pineapple	Piña
Lemon/Lime	Limón/Lima
Coconut	Coco
Strawberry	Fresa
Potato	Papa
French fries	Papas fritas
Rice	Arroz
Egg	Huevo
Salt/Pepper	Sal/Pimienta
Sugar	Azúcar
Meat	Carne
Steak	Bistec
Chicken	Pollo
Pork	Puerco
Fish	Pescado
Shellfish	Mariscos
Fork	Tenedor
Spoon	Cuchara
Knife	Cuchillo
Napkin	Servilleta
Ice cream	Helado

Numbers

One	Uno/una
Two	Dos
Three	Tres
Four	Cuatro
Five	Cinco
Six	Seis
Seven	Siete
Eight	Ocho
Nine	Nueve
Ten	Diez
Eleven	Once
Twelve	Doce
Thirteen	Trece
Fourteen	Catorce
Fifteen	Quince
Sixteen	Dieciséis/diez y seis

Seventeen	Diecisiete/diez y siete
Eighteen	Dieciocho
Nineteen	Diecinueve/diez y nueve
Twenty	Veinte
Thirty	Treinta
Forty	Cuarenta
Fifty	Cincuenta
Sixty	Sesenta
Seventy	Setenta
Eighty	Ochenta
Ninety	Noventa
One hundred	Cien
One thousand	Mil

Days and Months

day	día
month	mes
Sunday	Domingo
Monday	Lunes
Tuesday	Martes
Wednesday	Miércoles
Thursday	Jueves
Friday	Viernes
Saturday	Sábado
January	Enero
February	Febrero
March	Marzo
April	Abril
May	Mayo
June	Junio
July	Julio
August	Agosto
September	Septiembre
October	Octubre
November	Noviembre
December	Diciembre

Index

TELL US WHAT YOU THINK

We're always trying to improve our books and would really appreciate any feedback on how to make them more useful. Thanks for taking a few minutes to fill out this survey. We'd also like to know about your latest find, a new scam, a budget deal, whatever . . . Please print your name and address clearly and send the completed survey to: The Berkeley Guides, 515 Eshelman Hall, U.C. Berkeley, CA 94720.

1. Your name _____

2. Your address _____

_____ Zip _____

3. You are: Female   Male

4. Your age: under 17   17–22   23–30   31–40   41–55   over 55

5. If you're a student: Name of school _____ City & state _____

6. If you're employed: Occupation _____

7. Your yearly income: under $20,000 $21,000–$30,000 $31,000–$45,000
                              $46,000–$60,000 $61,000–$100,000   over $100,000

8. Which of the following do you own? (Circle all that apply.)

   Computer   CD-ROM Drive   Modem

9. What speed (bps) is your modem?

   2400   4800   9600   14.4   19.2   28.8

10. Which on-line service(s) do you subscribe to apart from commercial services like AOL?

_____

11. Do you have access to the World Wide Web? If so, is it through a university or a private service provider? _____

12. If you have a CD-ROM drive or plan to have one, would you purchase a Berkeley Guide CD-ROM? _____

13. Which Berkeley Guide(s) did you buy? _____

14. Where did you buy the book and when?   City _____ Month/Year _____

15. Why did you choose The Berkeley Guides? (Circle all that apply.)

   Budget focus   Design

   Outdoor emphasis   Attitude

   Off-the-beaten-track emphasis   Writing style

   Resources for gays and   Organization
     lesbians
                                         More maps
   Resources for people with
     disabilities   Accuracy

   Resources for women   Price

   Other _____

16. How did you hear about The Berkeley Guides? (Circle all that apply.)

Recommended by friend/acquaintance   Bookstore display   TV

Article in magazine/newspaper (which one?) _____

Ad in magazine/newspaper (which one?) _____

Radio program (which one?) _____

Other _____

17. Which other guides, if any, have you used before? (Circle all that apply.)

Fodor's   Let's Go   Rough Guides

Frommer's   Birnbaum   Lonely Planet

Other _____

18. When did you travel with this book?   Month/Year _____

19. Where did you travel? _____

20. What was the purpose of your trip?

Vacation   Business   Volunteer

Study abroad   Work

21. About how much did you spend per day during your trip?

$0–$20 $31–$45 $61–$75   over $100

$21–$30 $46–$60 $76–$100

22. After you arrived, how did you get around? (Circle all that apply.)

Rental car   Personal car   Plane   Bus

Train   Hiking   Bike   Hitching

23. Which features/sections did you use most? (Circle all that apply.)

Book Basics	City/region Basics	Coming and Going
Hitching	Getting Around	Where to Sleep
Camping	Roughing It	Food
Worth Seeing	Cheap Thrills	Festivals
Shopping	After Dark	Outdoor Activities

24. The information was (circle one):   V = very accurate   U = usually accurat

S = sometimes accurate   R = rarely accurate

Introductions	V U S R		Worth Seeing	V U S R
Basics	V U S R		After Dark	V U S R
Coming and Going	V U S R		Outdoor Activities	V U S R
Where to Sleep	V U S R		Maps	V U S R
Food	V U S R			

25. I would _____ would not _____ buy another Berkeley Guide.